The 1998-99   Official PFA

FOOTBALLERS
FACTFILE

Edited by
Barry J Hugman

Photographs by
Colorsport

Queen Anne Press

First published in 1998

© Barry J Hugman

Barry J Hugman has asserted his right under
the Copyright, Designs and Patent Act, 1988
to be identified as the author of this work

First published in Great Britain in 1998 by
Queen Anne Press
a division of Lennard Associates Limited
Mackerye End, Harpenden
Hertfordshire AL5 5DR

A CIP catalogue record for this book
is available from the British Library

ISBN 1 85291 588 9

Typeset and designed by
Typecast (Artwork & Design)
8 Mudford Road
Yeovil, Somerset BA21 4AA

Printed and bound in Great Britain by
Butler & Tanner, London and Frome

Acknowledgements

Now into its fourth year, the Factfile continues to expand and reach out, not only as a media tool, and invaluable to those in the game, but as a part-work which, in due course, will cover the season-by-season record of every player's complete career and should be of interest to all who follow this great game of ours. There is no doubt that the World Cup has whetted the appetite and, with the Premiership providing many of the leading players in the world right now, there is no reason why our top clubs cannot take on the best and win. More importantly, the British-born youngsters coming through the ranks also continue to improve their skills and must be given every chance to progress.

The party political over, I would once again like to express my thanks to **Gordon Taylor**, the chief executive, and all those at the PFA, including **Brendon Batson** and **Garry Nelson**, who are genuinely supporting and helping to establish the Factfile. Their help is much appreciated.

Also, I am exceedingly grateful to all those at the Football League, such as **Sheila Andrew**, **Debbie Birch**, and **Jonathan Hargreaves**, and **Mike Foster**, **Adrian Cook**, and **Mike Kelleher** at the Premiership, for their help in establishing good, solid, and reliable information, especially regarding player appearance stats. That gratitude also extends to **Sandy Bryson** of the Scottish FA.

On the international front, I was lucky to have the help and co-operation of **David Barber** (English FA), **Brendan McKenna** (FA of Ireland), **Ceri Stennett** (official FA of Wales statistician), and **Marshall Gillespie** (editor of the Northern Ireland Football Yearbook). Having co-ordinated this exercise, **Roy Grant** also gave his time to numerous other tasks, including keeping note of all the goalscorers throughout the season. And, as in previous years, I was happy to call upon **Mick Featherstone**, who helped collate heights, weights, birthplaces, birthdates, and double checked the statistical input. Others who gave of their time were **Dick Barton**, **Alan Platt**, **Jenny Hugman**, and many Football League and Premiership staff members up and down the country.

For the fourth year, **Jonathan Ticehurst**, managing director of Windsor Insurance Brokers' Sports Division, has thrown his weight behind the Factfile, both financially and vocally. His and Windsor's support, as with the British Boxing Board of Control Yearbook, is greatly appreciated.

For details provided on players, I have listed below, in alphabetical order, the names of the "team", without whose help this book would not have been possible to produce. Once again, I thank every one of them for all the hard work they put in.

Audrey Adams (Watford): Producer and statistician for BBC Radio Sport and a Watford supporter since the days of Cliff Holton, Audrey is also the club statistician for the Ultimate Football Guide.

Steve Adamson (Scarborough): Married with three children, Steve is a 40-year-old postman who has supported Boro since the age of 11, when they were struggling in the Northern Premier League. Actively involved in local football, he is currently writing the official club history, due to be published in November by Yore Publications.

Denise Allibone (Aston Villa): In her own words, Denise is a mad, crazy Villa supporter, who follows them up and down the country without fail. Her only previous football work was to help me with the club's profiles required for the Premier League: The Players publication.

Geoff Allman (Walsall): A university lecturer by trade, he saw his first ever game in February 1944, Walsall versus Wolves. Has written for Walsall's programme for the last 30 seasons and, at one time or another, has provided articles for more than half of the clubs currently in the Premiership and Football League. Geoff is also a Methodist local preacher and press officer.

Stuart Basson (Chesterfield): Stuart has contributed the biographies of Chesterfield players since the inception of the Footballers' Factfile. A member of the AFS for more than ten years, his Definitive Chesterfield FC went into a second edition, and his Chesterfield FC Who's Who, Lucky Whites & Spireites will be published by Yore Publications this coming November.

Ian Bates (Bradford): Has followed City since 1951 and refereed in amateur football up until 1995-96. A member of the AFS, this is the first publication that Ian has been involved in.

David Batters (York City): A supporter since 1948, he is the club historian, a contributor to the programme and author of York City: The Complete Record 1922-1990. Also commentates on matches at York Hospital.

Harry Berry (Blackburn Rovers): Author of the club centenary history, A Century of Soccer and other books on Rovers, and co-author of the Preston North End history, along with several books on athletics.

Simon Bowden (Barnet): As sports editor of the Barnet Advertiser, he has followed the club home and away for the past five seasons.

Eddie Brennan (Sunderland): A regular at Roker since 1976 (aged nine) and currently the club statistician for the Ultimate Football Guide.

Stuart Brennan (Stockport County): As sports editor of the Stockport Express newspaper from 1989 to 1994, he covered the club's fortunes both home and away and was a programme contributor. Also County's statistician for the Ultimate Football Guide.

Jonathan Brewer (Plymouth Argyle): Currently the Argyle statistician for the Ultimate Football Guide, Jonathan also writes articles for the Pasty News, a publication run by the London branch of the supporters' club.

Jim Brown (Coventry City): The club's official statistician and contributor to the programme, he also pens a column for the local newspaper answering readers' queries.

Trevor Bugg (Hull City): A supporter of the Tigers for 29 years, Trevor is a major contributor to Hull City's much respected matchday programme.

Graham Caton (Bournemouth): Into his fourth year with the Factfile, Graham is a committed Cherries' supporter who has always enjoyed collating facts and figures relating to the club.

Wallace Chadwick (Burnley): A supporter for over 30 years, he has seen all the extremes in the period from the great days of the '60s, including the championship of all four divisions and a narrow escape from relegation to the Conference. Wallace is a regular contributor to the Clarets' programme.

Dennis Chapman (Manchester City): Now retired, Dennis has followed City since 1937-38. Has worked on several publications, including the FA Carling Premier League: The Players and the Ultimate Football Guide. Possesses possibly the largest collection of City programmes, the earliest being 1902-03.

Paul Clayton (Charlton Athletic): Writes in the club's matchday programme and various other publications connected with Athletic. A Charlton season ticket-holder, despite living in Wiltshire, and a member of the AFS, Paul also compiles the statistics for the Ultimate Football Guide.

Grant Coleby (Exeter City): A member of both Exeter City's Supporters' Club and the Association of Football Statisticians, Grant has been the official contributor to the Factfile since its inception.

Eddie Collins (Nottingham Forest): A Forest supporter since 1956, and a member of the Associated Football Statisticians, this is the first publication he has been involved in.

David Copping (Barnsley): The writer of the past meetings column in the Barnsley programme for the last eight seasons, he also commentated live hospital broadcasts from Oakwell between 1978 and 1991 and has since narrated for the club videos.

Frank Coumbe (Brentford): Frank has not missed a competitive Brentford home game for over 20 years. And, on a publications front, he has been the Bees' statistician for the Ultimate Football Guide for 14 years and was a contributor to A-Z of Bees: A Brentford Encyclopedia, last season.

Ken Craig (Colchester United): Ken, who continues to produce the monthly newsletter, U's from 'ome, for all United fans living away from home, has just celebrated 25 years of supporting the club. He is now looking forward to the next 25 years!

Peter Cullen (Bury): A life-long Bury supporter, Peter is 38 years old and now works full time at his beloved club as the ticket office manager and programme editor. He is also the club's official historian and a collector of all things connected with the Shakers.

John Curtis (Scunthorpe United): John, a life-long Scunthorpe fan, has seen all the team's games, home and away, for the past six seasons. And, as a sports journalist with the Scunthorpe Evening Telegraph, he has edited the award-winning matchday programme for the past four years.

Carol Dalziel (Tranmere Rovers): A Tranmere supporter for 30 years, Carol operates the club's electronic scoreboard on match days, and contributes regularly to the programme. She also acts as the supporters' liaison officer.

Gareth Davies (Wrexham): Assists in the much acclaimed club programme, the editor of which, **Geraint Parry**, also helped on heights and weights, etc, for this publication. Gareth has written and published the Coast of Soccer Memories, the centenary history of the North Wales Coast FA (1995), and co-authored with Ian Garland the Who's Who of Welsh International Soccer Players (1991). Also heavily involved in Wrexham, A Complete Record 1872-1992, written by Peter Jones. Currently researching Wrexham FC's Who's Who at the moment, he still finds time to compile the club section for the Ultimate Football Guide.

David Downs (Reading): A former schoolteacher who took early retirement in order to concentrate on his writing and television

appearances, and compiled *Reading FC: A Pictorial History*, which was published in November 1997. Still coaches at the club's Centre of Excellence, where he has also been appointed education officer.

Ray Driscoll *(Chelsea):* A life-long Blues' fan, born and bred two miles away from Stamford Bridge – he still has to pinch himself to make sure that he has not dreamed the last two seasons at Chelsea, although he was saddened by the departure of Ruud Gullit. Is a contributor to many football books, and also wrote articles for the *Euro '96* programmes.

Phil Duffell *(Swindon Town):* One of the club's off-the-field signings, having joined last season as the public relations/media manager, Phil was formerly chief soccer writer on the *Swindon Evening Advertiser*, and sports reporter/football commentator for HTV West in Bristol.

Mark Evans *(Leeds United):* Has supported United for the last 30 years and describes his association with the club as one of the loves of his life. The Leeds' statistician for the *Ultimate Football Guide* for nearly nine years, he was also involved in my two editions of the *FA Carling Premiership: The Players*.

Keith Evemy *(Fulham):* Long-standing supporter who was unfortunately away on military service when the club won its only post-war honour, the second division championship in 1948-49. Highly regarded at Craven Cottage, he contributes to the matchday programme and is never far from the ground.

Colin Faiers *(Cambridge United):* A 38-year-old chartered accountant, Colin, a fan for over 28 years, is the recognised club statistician and currently writes the historical features for the programme.

Harold Finch *(Crewe Alexandra):* The club's historian and a supporter for over 60 years, Harold has been the programme editor for more than 40 of them. A one-club man, he has travelled extensively to watch them play.

Mick Ford and **Richard Lindsey** *(Millwall):* Mick has been a life-long supporter of Millwall from childhood, through army service, and now back in civilian life 45 years later. Brought up in the New Den area, but now living in Worcester, he goes to all the home games and most of the away fixtures, and has a formidable collection of memorabilia which he adds to when attending many programme fairs right across the country. And, as a full dance licence holder, he likes to cast an eye over the team performance. Meanwhile, his Factfile partner, Richard, the author of *Millwall: The Complete Record*, continues to help estaablish the Millwall FC Museum at the New Den.

Paul Gilligan *(Doncaster Rovers):* A keen follower of Rovers for over 30 years, Paul has written three books on the club and is a regular contributor in the matchday programme. Also the official club photographer.

Dave Goody *(Southend United):* United historian, statistician and collector, he co-authored *Southend United: The Official History of the Blues* and is a regular contributor to the programme.

Frank Grande *(Northampton Town):* Author of *The Cobblers, A History of Northampton Town FC* and a *Who's Who* on the club, he has just written a fourth book titled *The Centenery History of Northampton Town*. Has contributed a regular column to the club programme for the past 18 seasons.

Roy Grant *(Oxford United):* Formerly assistant secretary at Oxford United, as well as being the club programme editor and statistician, he also handled the clubline telephone service. In the past, a contributor to the *Official Football League Yearbook*, he currently contributes to the *Ultimate Football Guide and Factfile*.

Michael Green *(Bolton Wanderers):* Despite being a fanatical Newcastle United supporter, Michael covers Bolton for the Factfile and his excellent efforts are much appreciated. Having a yearning to get involved in the area of freelance journalism, preferably concerning football or popular entertainment (music, films etc), he hopes to go full time sooner or later.

Don Hales *(Leyton Orient and Luton Town):* A staff writer and an events director at *Winning Business*, a sales management magazine, Don has contributed to *World Soccer, Team Talk*, and the *Ultimate Football Guide*, as well as compiling the obituary column for the AFS. In putting together the Orient and Luton information, he was assisted by **Paul Morant**, an O's fan of over 20 years standing, and his son, Daniel, currently at Warwick University.

Roger Harris *(Brighton & Hove Albion):* A life-long enthusiast of Brighton, and football in general, Roger co-authored *Seagulls: The Story of Brighton and Hove Albion FC* and is a life member of the Association of Football Statisticians.

Roger Harrison *(Blackpool):* Life-long supporter who has seen the Pool play every other league side both home and away. Joint programme editor and club statistician, Roger also contributes to other publications, including the *Ultimate Football Guide*.

Richard and **Janey Hayhoe** *(Tottenham Hotspur):* Despite Janey expecting their first child, due at this moment of writing, they were still

able to run their eye over most of Spurs' matches on behalf of the *Factfile* last season. And, despite Spurs' difficulties, they remain optimistic that the side will turn things around before too long.

Ron Hockings *(International football):* Has now published five books involving the history of Chelsea, European and South American Cups. *The Nations of Europe*, currently available in two volumes, includes every line-up for all the European countries' matches up until 1993, with volume three envisaged being ready shortly and has recently completed *90 Years of the "Blues"*, the statistical history of Chelsea. Provided all the international appearances for non-British teams in this year's *Factfile*.

Mike Jay *(Bristol Rovers):* Apart from helping out on other publications, notably the *Ultimate Football Guide*, Mike has had two books of his own published on Bristol Rovers, namely *The Complete Record (1883-1987)* and *Pirates in Profile, A Who's Who of the Players 1920-1995*.

Colin Jones *(Swansea City):* A fan since the early 1960s and a contributor to the club programme during the last six years. Played non-league football, before being involved in training and coaching.

Gordon Lawton *(Oldham Athletic):* Employed as the public relations officer at the club and Athletic's official photographer. Other publications contributed to, include *Carling Premiership: The Players, Rothmans Yearbook, Ultimate Football Guide* and *News of the World* annual.

Geoffrey Lea *(Wigan Athletic):* The club statistician for the *Ultimate Football Guide*, Geoffrey has been following the Latics for over 20 years and is a major contributor to the matchday programme that won the 'Third Division Programme of the Year" award in 1993-94. Also assists with the match commentary on the Clubcall.

John Lovis *(Torquay United):* A supporter since 1955, and a regular contributor to the club programme, he is also United's statistician for the *Ultimate Football Guide*.

Steve McGhee *(Derby County):* A collector of Derby memorabilia and a fan since 1969. Earlier involved in a bi-monthly historical magazine on County, he currently compiles the club section for the *Ultimate Football Guide*.

Peter Macey *(Portsmouth):* Currently undertaking the final year of a BSc in computer science at the University of Wolverhampton, Peter is a member of the AFS, as well as contributing to the Ultimate Football Guide.

John Maguire *(Manchester United):* A member of the AFS, John has been working on several sports-related topics during the past year. Is also a qualified FA coach.

John Martin *(Chester City):* Club statistician for both the *Rothmans Yearbook* and *Ultimate Football Guide*, he also contributes for various other publications. Was also City's programme editor for ten years up until 1993-94, winning the 'Third Division Programme of the Year" award that same season.

Wade Martin *(Stoke City):* For many years a major contributor to the club programme, as well as writing *A Potters Tale* and the *Master Potters'* series of books.

Tony Matthews *(West Bromwich Albion):* Official statistician and curator of Albion, his publications include, *the complete records of Aston Villa, Birmingham City, WBA, Wolves, Walsall and Stoke City*. Has also compiled *Who 's Whos* on the first four clubs listed above, plus Manchester United, and currently contributes to several programmes.

Ian Mills, Richard and **Sarah Taylor** *(Notts County):* Ian supplied the County stats, Richard the words, and Sarah the typing. Having seen his first game at Gay Meadow in 1959-60, Ian, who runs the matchday programme sales, has been hooked ever since, missing just one game since 1970. The Taylors, both recent additions to the *Factfile* "team", follow a similar family tradition. Richard (father) began watching County in the mid 1950s and needs to visit just five more league grounds to join the 92 Club, while Sarah (daughter) has been an avid fan for over ten years.

Ian Nannestad *(Lincoln City):* A past contributor to the Imps' programme and co-author of the *Who's Who of Lincoln City, 1892-1994* publication.

John Northcutt *(West Ham United):* Has supported the Hammers since 1959 and is the co-author of West Ham books, *The Complete Record* and the *Illustrated History*. A regular contributor to the club programme and the club adviser to the *Ultimate Football Guide*.

Brian Pead *(Liverpool):* Author of three editions of *Liverpool, A Complete Record, Liverpool: Champion of Champions (1990)* and *Ee Aye Addio - We've Won the Cup (1993)*, Brian was the statistician for the *Rush for Glory* video and has contributed to many publications, including the *Footballer* magazine and the *Ultimate Football Guide*.   **Steve Peart** and **Dave Finch** *(Wycombe Wanderers):* A former programme editor of the club and a supporter for over 20 years, Steve put together the player profiles, while the club statistics were supplied by Dave, the official Wycombe statistician.

Steve Phillips *(Rochdale):* A Dale fan of over 30 years standing, he is the club's official statistician and author of *The Survivors: The Story of Rochdale AFC*.

Terry Phillips *(Cardiff City):* Chief soccer writer for the *South Wales Echo* since 1994, and a sports journalist for 28 years – *Kent Evening Post* (1970-1977), *Derby Evening Telegraph* (1977-1986), *Gloucester Citizen* (1986-1994) – Terry has previously covered clubs at all levels, including Brian Clough's Nottingham Forest, Derby County, Gillingham, and Gloucester City.

Kevan Platt *(Norwich City):* Kevin has supported the Canaries for over 30 years and has been employed by the club in various full-time capacities since 1980, witnessing at first hand the enormous swings in fortune during that period. Currently City's programme editor and press officer, he also co-edits the official handbook, and is a keen statistician, keeping detailed records of all the club's representative sides. And, despite his official role, he remains a fan, and can still be witnessed leaping to his feet in celebration when surrounded by the gathered media within the press box.

David Prentice *(Everton):* Everton correspondent for the *Liverpool Echo* since 1993 and author of a club history five years earlier, when he was reporting both Everton and Liverpool for the *Daily Post*, he completed his Mersey set when reporting on Tranmere Rovers for three years from 1990.

Chris Pugsley *(Macclesfield Town):* Currently Macclesfield's official statistician, he was the supporters' club shop manager from 1990-1993, and was the supporters' vice chairman during 1992-93. Resigned from the committee to work with the parent club as first team kit man from October 1993, and edited the matchday programme from 1995-1997. Has missed very few games, home or away, since Town joined the Conference in 1987.

Mike Purkiss *(Crystal Palace):* Having supported Palace since 1950 and produced stats on them since 1960, Mike is the author of the *Complete History of Crystal Palace, 1905-1989*, the club statistician for the *Ultimate Football Guide*, and contributed to *Premier League: The Players*.

Mike Renshaw *(Sheffield Wednesday):* Has followed Wednesday for over 40 years and is a great supporter of European soccer. Currently produces the club section for the *Ultimate Football Guide*.

Jack Retter *(Mansfield Town):* First saw the team play over 60 years ago and is the club's official historian. Author of *Who's Who – The Stags*, and a regular contributor to the club's matchday programme, his *Mansfield Town – The First 100 Years* (with Paul Taylor) was published recently to mark the club's centenary. A member of the AFS, he contributes to a number of publications, and is president of the Staggs' supporters club.

Robert Ringsell *(Wimbledon):* A life-long Dons' supporter, and from a family who have seen the side through thick and thin, Robert enjoyed one of the club's most impressive seasons. Is currently working for WH Smith and hoping for a career in retail management.

Mick Robinson *(Peterborough United):* Another life-long fan, for a number of years Mick has contributed to the club programme and was the joint editor of the *Official Peterborough History*. Also the club statistician for the *Ultimate Football Guide*.

Phil Sherwin *(Port Vale):* As Vale's statistician, Phil works on a number of other publications and has contributed to the club programme for 17 years. A fan since 1968, he follows them home and away.

Andy Shute *(Queens Park Rangers):* Life-long QPR supporter and compiler of the QPR and Tottenham details for the *Ultimate Football Guide*.

Derrick Slasor *(Middlesbrough):* First saw the Boro play in December 1946 and, as Managing Director of Trapezium Transport Services, is well known in the area for sponsoring various club activities.

Mike Slater *(Wolverhampton Wanderers):* Mike has attended almost 1,000 Wolves' matches and, in 1988, wrote and published a book on their history called *Molineux Memories*. From 1989 to 1995 he compiled the annual *Brain of Wolves' Quiz*, prior to producing a booklet containing all the club's competitive results.

Gordon Small *(Hartlepool United):* Having supported United since October 1965, experiencing two promotions, two relegations, six re-elections, and several close calls, the 1997-98 season was relatively unstressful. Is the statistician for the *Ultimate Football Guide* and hopes to have the *Definitive Hartlepool United FC* produced by AFS in 1998-99.

Dave Smith *(Leicester City):* A regular columnist in the programme, co-author of *Fossils & Foxes* and the *Foxes Alphabet*, he assists with several other club handbooks.

Gerry Somerton *(Rotherham United):* Workwise, the deputy sports editor of the *Rotherham Advertiser*, and part-time sports reporter for *Hallam FM*, the local commercial radio station, Gerry is also the author of *Now we are United*, the official history of Rotherham United, and co-editor of the matchday programme. Last season he completed 51 years of watching the club.

Paul Stead *(Huddersfield Town):* A life-long supporter of Town, and brother to Richard, Paul is a regular spectator at the McAlpine Stadium. Apart from the *Factfile*, he also contributes to the *Ultimate Football Guide*.

David Steele *(Carlisle United):* A regular contributor to the club programme for several years now, his current interest is in tracking down ex-United players.

Richard Stocken *(Shrewsbury Town):* A supporter of 40 years and a collector of club programmes and memorabilia, Richard is an annual contributor to the *Ultimate Football Guide* and other publications.

Bill Swan *(Newcastle United):* A supporter since the early 1950s, and a long-term shareholder in the club, along with his wife and three children, he is also a member of the AFS, and a keen collector of programmes and memorabilia relating to United. He assisted in the production of the club's volume in the *Complete Record* series, and this is his third year as a contributor to the *Factfile*. His 12-year-old son, Richard, provided much of the "anorak" information in the player biographies.

Alan Tait *(Scottish clubs):* A regular contributor to Tony Brown's ultimate *Scottish League* book, and a compiler of statistics appertaining to that country, Alan is currently working on a project, probably still several years down the road, that will give line-ups for all Scottish League matches since 1890.

Colin Tattum *(Birmingham City):* Colin has reported the fortunes of Birmingham City and west midland's clubs for the *Birmingham Evening Mail* and *Sports Argus* newspapers for almost a decade. A native of the second city, he also covers the national side.

Chris Thompson *(Arsenal):* Born in Greenwich the week before Charlton won the FA Cup, Chris has held season tickets for both the Valley and Highbury. Publications worked on, include *FA Carling Premiership: The Players* and, currently, the *Ultimate Football Guide*.

Andrew Treherne *(Sheffield United):* Contributor to the *Ultimate Football Guide, The Premier League: The Players* and *Sheffield United: The first Hundred Years*. Also a member of the AFS.

Les Triggs *(Grimsby Town):* Became involved with the statistical side of the club when asked to assist with Town's centenary exhibition in 1978. A retired librarian, Les, who first saw the Mariners in a wartime league match, is the co-author of the Grimsby Town volume in the *Complete Record* series and has been club statistician to the *Ultimate Football Guide* since its inception.

Roger Triggs *(Gillingham):* Has written three books on the club, *Gillingham FC - A Chronology 1893-1984, Priestfield Profiles 1950-1988* and the centenary publication, *Home of the Shouting Men*, which he co-authored with Andy Bradley. Also a feature writer in the programme since 1975.

Frank Tweddle *(Darlington):* The club's official historian and statistician, Frank is the author of *Darlington's Centenary History* and the programme editor since 1975. Also a contributor for various other publications, including the *Ultimate Football Guide*.

Paul Voller *(Ipswich Town):* A Town supporter since 1963-64, Paul works at the ground on matchdays and is a member of the supporters' management committee. Other publications worked on include the *FA Carling Premier League: The Players* and the *Ultimate Football Guide*.

Tony Woodburn and **Martin Atherton** *(Preston North End):* Tony started watching the club in the late 1960s and is a life member of the AFS, the Ninety-Two club and the Scottish 38 club. Martin, a fan for over 30 years, lives within a long throw-in of Deepdale and has been able to watch the development of the ground from his front doorstep.

David Woods *(Bristol City):* Has supported Bristol City since 1958, becoming a shareholder in the old company in the early '70s and in the new organisation in the dark days of 1982. However, as a life member of the AFS, David's main interest is in the early days of the game through to the end of the First World War. Author of the *Bristol Babe*, as well as *Bristol City: The Complete Record* (with Andrew Crabtree), his latest work, in association with Lee Edwards, *Bristol City Football Club: The First 100 Years*, is currently on sale. A regular contributor to the City programme, he has also written for *Bristol Rovers*, the Footballer magazine, and is the City statistician for the *Ultimate Football Guide*.

Dick Wright *(Southampton):* Although supporting Saints for over 20 years, Dick was pleased to have had a season of relative comfort in 1997-98, especially after a touch and go 1996-97. Meanwhile, despite never working on a football publication previously, his input for the *Factfile* is now into its third year. He is the president of Goldsworth Park Rangers, Woking, which he helped found 15 years ago, and was extremely pleased to see Duncan Spedding progress to the Southampton first team, having been a member of a youth league representative squad that Dick managed a few years ago.

Finally, on the production side of the book, my thanks go to Jean Bastin, of Typecast (Artwork & Design), for her patience and diligent work on the typesetting and design, which again went far beyond the call of normal duty and was much appreciated. She was ably supported by Nina Whatmore (Orchard Design).

If you get carried off...

The rewards of a sporting life can be high – but so are the risks involved. One bad tackle can end a career that is already short by conventional standards. Which is why all the F.A. Premier and Football League clubs have Windsor Sports Insurance behind them to protect their players.

Why Windsor?

Because professional sport needs professional advice and the best advice comes from Windsor Sports Insurance – insurance consultants to The Football League, The F.A. Premier League and The Football Association.

Windsor is one of the world's largest specialist sports, leisure and entertainment brokers covering players, clubs, leagues and national sports associations throughout the UK, Europe and world-wide.

Beyond Personal Accident Insurance, we provide cover for Stadium Risks, Legal Liabilities, Event Cancellation, Prize Performance and Incentive Indemnities and other insurance-protected sponsorship enhancements and marketing initiatives.

A separate Group company also provides consultancy on Group Pensions, Pension Scheme Administration and Personal Financial Planning.

So whatever the sport, whatever the risk, we are here to help you carry on.

...we're here to help you carry on.

For further information call The Sports Division on:-

Tel: +44(0) 171 407 7144
Fax: +44(0) 171 378 7961

WINDSOR
Sports Insurance Brokers

Professionals Dealing With Professionals

Windsor Sports Insurance are Insurance Brokers and Consultants to:
THE FOOTBALL LEAGUE – THE F.A. PREMIER LEAGUE – THE FOOTBALL ASSOCIATION – PROFESSIONAL RUGBY UNION & LEAGUE CLUBS
THE CRICKETERS ASSOCIATION – THE BRITISH BOXING BOARD OF CONTROL – THE BRITISH OLYMPIC ASSOCIATION – FORMULA ONE GRAND PRIX DRIVERS' ASSOCIATION

Windsor Sports Insurance, Lyon House, 160/166 Borough High Street, London SE1 1JR.   A member of Windsor Insurance Brokers Ltd

Forewords

Once again I am extremely pleased to give the PFA's full endorsement and recommendation to Footballers' Factfile. I consider it the finest work of its kind, and one that presents a comprehensive coverage on statistics and profiles for every one of the 2,000 plus members of the PFA who played in first team football throughout the Premier League and Football League in England and Wales during 1997-98.

The publication has been sponsored by Windsor Insurance Brokers, the key figures in our industry with regard to the protection of players against injury, and written by Barry Hugman, whose record in this field is unsurpassed. Barry has a team of over 90 people who provide him with the invaluable aspects of local information that gives this book such credibility and makes it a must for every enthusiast, administrator, and commentator on our great game. It will occupy the most prominent position on my desk.

Gordon Taylor,
Chief Executive, The Professional Footballers' Association.

The Footballers' Factfile goes from strength to strength as the years go by. Barry Hugman and his research team are to be congratulated, yet again, on this season's publication, which I see on the desk or in the bookcase of almost everybody connected with the game today.

The Windsor Insurance Group continues its close association with professional football that was first established over 25 years ago. Together, with the Professional Footballers' Association, we manage the Players' Permanent Disablement Fund, by which every registered player in the English leagues receives an insurance benefit if his career is ended through injury or sickness. The level of benefit is continually reviewed and was increased significantly at the beginning of 1997-98.

Our close links with the Professional Footballers' Association, and the clubs, leagues, and national associations, give us a unique position from which we can offer advice on insurance-related matters to all in football. And, we are more than happy to continue to support and again lend our name as sponsors to this excellent publication.

Jonathan Ticehurst,
Managing Director of the Sports Division, Windsor Insurance Brokers Limited.

Editorial Introduction

Following on from last year's edition, the Factfile portrays the statistical career record of every FA Carling Premiership and Nationwide League player who made an appearance in 1997-98, whether it be in league football, the Football League (Coca-Cola) Cup, FA Cup (Sponsored by Littlewoods Pools), Charity Shield, European Cup, European Cup Winners' Cup, UEFA Cup, Auto Windscreen's Shield, or in the Play Offs. Not included are Inter-Toto Cup matches. It goes beyond mere statistics, however, with a write up on all of the 2,300 plus players involved, and also records faithfully last season's playing records separately by club.

The work falls into two sections, both inter-relating. Firstly, the main core, PFA Footballers' Factfile: A-Z (pages 9 to 336), and secondly, FA Carling Premiership and Nationwide League Clubs: Summary of Appearances and Goals for 1997-98 (pages 337 to 351). Below is an explanation on how to follow the PFA Footballers' Factfile.

As the title suggests, all players are listed in alphabetical order and are shown by Surnames first, followed by full Christian names, with the one the player is commonly known by shown in **bold.** Any abbreviation or pseudonym is bracketed.

Birthplace/date: You will note that several players who would be predominately classified as British, were born in places like Germany and India, for example. My book, Football League Players' Records, due to be published later this year, which covers every man who has played league football since the war, has, in the past, used the family domicile as a more realistic "birthplace". But, for our purposes here, I have reverted to that which has been officially recorded.

Height and Weight: Listed in feet and inches, and stones and pounds, respectively. It must be remembered that a player's weight can frequently change and, on that basis, the recorded data should be used as a guide only, especially as they would have been weighed several times during the season.

Club Honours: Those shown, cover careers from the Conference and FA Trophy upwards. For abbreviations, read:- European Honours: EC (European Cup), ESC (European Super Cup), ECWC (European Cup Winners' Cup). English Honours: FAC (FA Cup), FLC (Football League Cup), CS (Charity Shield), FMC (Full Members Cup, which takes in the Simod and Zenith Data sponsorships), AMC (Associated Members Cup - Freight Rover, Sherpa Van, Leyland DAF, Autoglass and Auto Windscreen), AIC (Anglo-Italian Cup), GMVC (GM Vauxhall Conference), FAT (FA Trophy), FAYC (FA Youth Cup). Scottish Honours: SPD (Scottish Premier Division), S Div 1/2 (Scottish Leagues), SC (Scottish Cup), SLC (Scottish League Cup). Welsh Honours: WC (Welsh Cup). Please note that medals awarded to P/FL, FLC, and AMC winners relate to players who have appeared in 25%, or over, of matches, while FAC, EC, and ECWC winners medals are for all-named finalists, including unused subs. For our purposes, however, Charity Shield winners' medals refer to men who either played or came on as a sub. Honours applicable to players coming in from abroad are not shown, but the position will be reviewed in future editions.

International Honours: For abbreviations, read:- E (England), NI (Northern Ireland), S (Scotland), W (Wales) and Ei (Republic of Ireland). Under 21 through to full internationals give total appearances (inclusive of subs), while schoolboy (U16s and U18s) and youth representatives are just listed. Not included are U20 matches. The cut off date used for appearances was 12 July.

Player Descriptions: Gives position and playing strengths and, in keeping the work topical, a few words on how their season went in 1997-98. This takes into account, in a positive fashion, key performances, along with value to the team, injuries, honours, and other points of interest, etc. To allow for play off and international input to be included, and the publication date to be maintained, the cut-off date used was 12 July. Transfers, however, are shown as stop press if they took place after 18 May, the cut-off date used by the Football and Premier Leagues to produce the close season retained and free transfer lists. The decision was taken on the grounds that the May/June Registration and Transfer booklets would not be available until after going to press. An * shown at the end of text determines that the player in question is over the age of 24 and out of contract on 30 June 1998, but his club has made him an offer of re-engagement,

Career Records: Full appearances, plus substitutes and goals, are given for all Carling Premiership and Nationwide League games and, if a player who is in the book has played in any of the senior Scottish Leagues, his appearances with the club in question will also be recorded. Other information given, includes the origination of players (clubs in the non- leagues, junior football, or from abroad), registered signing dates (if a player signs permanently following a loan spell, for our purposes, we have shown the initial date as being the point of temporary transfer. Also, loan transfers are only recorded if an appearance is made), transfer fees (these are the figures that have been reported in newspapers and magazines and should only be used as a guide to a player's valuation), and a breakdown of matches by P/FL (Premiership and Football League), PL (Premier League), FL (Football League), FLC (Football League Cup), FAC (FA Cup), and Others. Other matches will take in the Welsh Cup, play offs, Anglo-Italian Cup, Auto Windscreen Shield, Charity Shield, and any major European competition. All of these matches are lumped together for reasons of saving space. Scottish appearances for players on loan to P/FL clubs in 1996-97 are shown at the point of transfer and do not include games following their return to Scotland.

Career statistics are depicted as
Appearances + Substitutes/Goals

Whether you wish to analyse someone for your fantasy football team selection or would like to know more about a little-known player appearing in the lower reaches of the game, the *PFA Footballers' Factfile* should provide you with the answer.

Barry J. Hugman, Editor, PFA Footballers' Factfile

ABBEY Nathanael
Born: Islington, 11 July 1978
Height: 6'1" Weight: 12.0
Made his debut for Luton in the Coca Cola Cup against Colchester as an 18-year old during a goalkeeping crisis last season and, although he played well, conceding only one goal and seeing his team through to the next round, manager, Lennie Lawrence, signed replacements and allowed Nathan to continue his development in the reserves. Later, in February, he enjoyed an impressive spell on loan at Woking.
Luton T (From trainee on 2/5/96) FLC 1

ABLETT Gary Ian
Born: Liverpool, 19 November 1965
Height: 6'1" Weight: 12.7
Club Honours: Div 1 '88, '90; CS '88, '95; FAC '89; '95
International Honours: E: B-1; U21-1
Playing to a high standard week in and week out, his calm defending and sensible play making him a fixture alongside Steve Bruce, Gary was Birmingham's "Mr Consistency" in 1997-98. Although occasionally left out to make way for the pacier Michael Johnson, and missing the final five games, the vice captain was always a steadying influence when in the side, frequently playing the ball to feet rather than clearing his lines, his left foot as immaculate as ever. Rarely gives the ball away and is able to play in a number of defensive positions.
Liverpool (From apprentice on 19/11/83) FL 103+6/1 FLC 10+1 FAC 16+2 Others 9
Derby Co (Loaned on 25/1/85) FL 3+3 Others 2
Hull C (Loaned on 10/9/86) FL 5
Everton (£750,000 on 14/1/92) F/PL 128/5 FLC 12 FAC 12/1 Others 4
Sheffield U (Loaned on 1/3/96) FL 12
Birmingham C (£390,000 on 21/6/96) FL 73+5/1 FLC 9 FAC 6/1

ABOU Samassi
Born: Ivory Coast, 4 August 1973
Height: 6'0" Weight: 12.8
Signed from French League side, Cannes, last November, the French striker quickly became a cult hero at West Ham with his range of dazzling skills. Having made his Premiership debut at Chelsea, he opened his scoring account in a brilliant game against Barnsley in January, when he set up two goals and scored twice himself in the 6-0 rout. A further two goals against Leicester on the final day of the season brought the "Abooooo" chant ringing around the ground from a crowd who love him.
West Ham U (£300,000 from Cannes on 3/11/97) PL 12+7/5 FLC 1+1/1 FAC 3+2

ABRAHAMS Paul
Born: Colchester, 31 October 1973
Height: 5'10" Weight: 11.3
Paul started last season full of running at Colchester, and was quickly among the goals, playing as a central striker alongside Mark Sale. However, he was soon switched to play wider in order to accommodate the return of Tony Adcock, and continued to maintain his goalscoring ratio until long-term injury struck. "Abes" never really got back a regular starting place, although he picked up another three goals as a substitute during the promotion run-in.
Colchester U (From trainee on 11/8/92) FL 30+25/8 FLC 2+3 FAC 4/2 Others 3/2
Brentford (£30,000 on 9/3/95) FL 26+9/8 FLC 1+2 Others 1
Colchester U (Loaned on 29/12/95) FL 8/2 Others 1
Colchester U (£20,000 on 23/10/96) FL 43+11/14 FLC 2 FAC 2+1 Others 6+1/2

ADAMS Kieran Charles
Born: St Ives, 20 October 1977
Height: 5'11" Weight: 11.6
Kieran found it difficult to break into the first team squad at Barnet in 1997-98 since an influx of players arrived during the summer of 1997. A skilful, ball-playing midfielder, he scored a great header against Macclesfield last December to underline his, as yet, unfulfilled talent.
Barnet (From trainee on 3/7/96) FL 8+11/1 FLC 0+1

ADAMS Michael (Micky) Richard
Born: Sheffield, 8 November 1961
Height: 5'8" Weight: 11.11
International Honours E: Yth
In his day, a tenacious left back or left-sided midfielder who played at the highest level, Micky managed both Fulham and Swansea in 1997-98 before taking over the reins at Brentford in November. Made one appearance for the Bees, as a substitute at Luton in the Auto Windscreen Shield, prior to announcing his retirement to concentrate on his managerial duties.
Gillingham (From apprentice on 1/11/79) FL 85+7/5 FLC 5 FAC 6
Coventry C (£75,000 on 19/7/83) FL 85+5/9 FLC 9/1 FAC 7 Others 2
Leeds U (£110,000 on 23/1/87) FL 72+1/2 FLC 4 FAC 6/1 Others 6
Southampton (£250,000 on 14/3/89) F/PL 141+3/7 FLC 16 FAC 8 Others 6
Stoke C (Free on 24/3/94) FL 10/3
Fulham (Free on 14/7/94) FL 25+4/8 FLC 4 FAC 2/4 Others 3/1
Swansea C (Free on 21/10/97)
Brentford (Free on 26/11/97) Others 0+1

ADAMS Neil James
Born: Stoke, 23 November 1965
Height: 5'8" Weight: 10.12
Club Honours: Div 1 '87, Div 2 '91
International Honours: E: U21-1
Following on from his highly successful campaign in 1996-97, Neil struggled to make such a consistent impact at Norwich last season. Starting in his familiar right-

wing role, before the club's plight saw him switched to central midfield in early December, he then sustained a broken foot at Huddersfield that month, an injury that sidelined him until towards the end of March when he returned to first team duty at Middlesbrough. With pace and enthusiasm, he puts defenders under pressure as he looks to cross early, and as City's regular penalty taker, two of his five goals came from the spot.
Stoke C (Signed on 1/7/85) FL 31+1/4 FLC 3 FAC 1 Others 3
Everton (£150,000 on 7/7/86) FL 17+3 FLC 4+1/1 Others 5+1
Oldham Ath (Loaned on 11/1/89) FL 9
Oldham Ath (£100,000 on 21/6/89) F/PL 93+36/23 FLC 13+2/1 FAC 10+2/2 Others 1+1
Norwich C (£250,000 on 17/2/94) P/FL 149+15/22 FLC 14+1/4 FAC 6/1

ADAMS Tony Alexander
Born: Romford, 10 October 1966
Height: 6'3" Weight: 13.11
Club Honours: Div 1 '89, '91; PL '98; FLC '87, '93; FAC '93, '98; ECWC '94
International Honours: E: 55; B-4; U21-5; Yth
Despite being troubled by a long-term ankle injury that forced him on to the sidelines and extensive treatment in the south of France last December, Arsenal's captain came back strongly to flourish under the managership of Arsene Wenger. The central defender appeared to be better than ever, displaying skills that he was never noted for, and an enthusiasm for the job at hand. There was no doubt that he had seen it all slipping away from him, but he came back into the side at the end of January and, from then on, the Gunners did not lose a game until the Premiership title was safely wrapped up. At the same time, he led the team to the final of the FA Cup, which they won with an emphatic 2-0 victory over Newcastle, and went close in the Coca Cola Cup before losing 4-3 on aggregate to Chelsea after taking a 2-1 lead into the second leg at Stamford Bridge. Back in harness with England, having missed several games in the run up to the World Cup Finals to be held in France during the summer, and the proud possessor of championship and FA Cup winners' medals, after leading the Gunners to the double, his great comeback ran him close to his team mate, Dennis Bergkamp, who pipped him for the Football Writers' Player of the Year award. Strength and courage have always been high on his agenda, and he remains an exceptional player in both six-yard boxes. *Stop Press:* Played in all four of England's World Cup games and was an integral part of a magnificent defence that somehow kept the Argentinians at bay for most of the second half, and all of extra time, before going down 4-3 on penalties.
Arsenal (From apprentice on 30/1/84) F/PL 417+4/30 FLC 58+1/5 FAC 40+1/5 Others 31/3

ADAMSON Christopher (Chris)
Born: Ashington, 4 November 1978
Height: 5'11" Weight: 11.0
Having promised much at both reserve and intermediate level, the first-year professional goalkeeper made a nervous start for West Bromwich Albion at Stockport when standing in for the absent Alan Miller last April. Not terribly tall for a 'keeper, but with good hands and agile, the youngster appeared twice more, excelling in a 1-0 defeat at Huddersfield, before giving way to Paul Crichton.
West Bromwich A (From trainee on 2/7/97) FL 3

ADCOCK Anthony (Tony) Charles
Born: Bethnal Green, 27 February 1963
Height: 6'0" Weight: 11.9
For probably the first time in his Colchester career, Tony was not the club's top goalscorer in 1997-98! Now rapidly approaching the veteran stage, "Rooster" had a strange season when he found himself in and out of the team, before being sidelined through injury for the closing stages and play-off drama. Only four league goals away from a club record of 130 set by Martyn King between December 1956 and September 1964, and with a well-deserved testimonial year underway, he was released during the summer.
Colchester U (From apprentice on 31/3/81) FL 192+18/98 FLC 16+1/5 FAC 12+2/3 Others 9/6
Manchester C (£75,000 on 1/6/87) FL 12+3/5 FLC 2+1/1 FAC 2 Others 2/3
Northampton T (£85,000 on 25/1/88) FL 72/30 FLC 6/3 FAC 1 Others 4/1
Bradford C (£190,000 on 6/10/89) FL 33+5/6 FLC 1 FAC 0+1 Others 2
Northampton T (£75,000 on 11/1/91) FL 34+1/10 FLC 1 FAC 1/1 Others 2/1
Peterborough U (£35,000 on 30/12/91) FL 107+4/35 FLC 8+1/3 FAC 5/1 Others 3+2
Luton T (£20,000 on 4/8/94) FL 0+2 FAC 0+1
Colchester U (Free on 3/8/95) FL 86+16/28 FLC 5+3/2 FAC 4+2 Others 10+1/6

ADEBOLA Bamberdele (Dele)
Born: Lagos, Nigeria, 23 June 1975
Height: 6'3" Weight: 12.8
Having made great strides over the past couple of years, and becoming Crewe's leading scorer in 1996-97, despite several clubs expressing an interest in him during the 1997 close season he remained at Gresty Road. Although not being so prolific in 1997-98, Dele still managed to pop in the odd goal before moving in February to Birmingham, where he was an instant hit, scoring five times in seven starts. With pace and an eye for goal to go with his obvious physical attributes, he was too hot to handle for many defences, while his partnership with Peter Ndlovu steered City towards the play offs. Recommended to Nigeria by John Fashanu, he actually earned a call up from Northern Ireland, but had to withdraw from the squad because of injury.
Crewe Alex (From trainee on 21/6/93) FL 98+26/39 FLC 4+3/2 FAC 8+2/3 Others 10+1/2
Birmingham C (£1,000,000 on 6/2/98) FL 16+1/7

AGNEW Paul
Born: Lisburn, 15 August 1965
Height: 5'9" Weight: 10.12

International Honours: NI: U23-1; Yth; Sch
Freed by West Bromwich Albion during the summer of 1997, Paul was signed by Swansea's Jan Molby on an initial non-contract basis last September, but was released at the start of November after making just seven league appearances, following a change of management at the Vetch Field. At his best, the left back was strong in the tackle and an exciting link with the forwards.
Grimsby T (£4,000 from Cliftonville on 15/2/84) FL 219+23/3 FLC 17+1 FAC 23+1 Others 12+2
West Bromwich A (£65,000 on 23/2/95) FL 38+1/1 FLC 1 FAC 0+1
Swansea C (Free on 12/9/97) FL 7

AGNEW Stephen (Steve) Mark
Born: Shipley, 9 November 1965
Height: 5'10" Weight: 11.9
Club Honours: Div 1 '96
This unfortunate Sunderland midfielder's season in 1997-98 was ruined by injury. Following a hernia operation during the 1997 summer break, Steve was then hit by an achilles tendon problem early on, having appeared just four times, which ended his campaign. There is no doubt that his passing ability, and eye for goal have been important to the club in the past but, having been released during the summer and now entering the latter part of his career, he is more than capable. At his best, is a striker of great diagonal passes who can play both short and long, and always dangerous at free kicks.
Barnsley (From apprentice on 10/11/83) FL 186+8/29 FLC 13/3 FAC 20/4 Others 6+1
Blackburn Rov (£700,000 on 25/6/91) FL 2 FLC 2
Portsmouth (Loaned on 21/11/92) FL 3+2 Others 2
Leicester C (£250,000 on 9/2/93) F/PL 52+4/4 FLC 4+1 FAC 2 Others 2
Sunderland (£250,000 on 11/1/95) P/FL 56+7/9 FLC 4 FAC 2+1/1

AGOGO Manuel (Junior)
Born: Accra, Ghana, 1 August 1979
Height: 5'10" Weight: 11.7
Known as "Junior" Agogo, Manuel made just one appearance for Sheffield Wednesday last season, his Premiership debut, at Newcastle in the opening game, and is definitely one for the future. A mobile front player, he has pace, mobility, and just needs to keep working on his game to become a regular squad member in 1998-99. Has certainly done well at youth and reserve level to date.
Sheffield Wed (Signed from Willesden Constontaine on 8/10/96) PL 0+1

AINSWORTH Gareth
Born: Blackburn, 10 May 1973
Height: 5'10" Weight: 12.5
Beginning 1997-98 with Lincoln, and having scored a hat trick against Scarborough, the all-action right winger moved to Port Vale in early September and soon became the fans' favourite by scoring on his home debut against Bury, with his push it and chase style being exciting to watch. Never knows when to give up and, while still having a lot to learn, he has a bright future in the game, attracting more

than one Premiership scout to Vale Park. Scored five goals, all in games which the Vale picked up points, so if he can improve on that the team will really do well. Was a runaway winner of the supporters' Player of the Year award.
Preston NE (Signed from Northwich Vic, via Blackburn Rov YTS, on 21/1/92) FL 2+3 Others 1/1
Cambridge U (Free on 17/8/92) FL 1+3/1 FLC 0+1
Preston NE (Free on 23/12/92) FL 76+6/12 FLC 3+2 FAC 3+1 Others 8+1/1
Lincoln C (£25,000 on 31/10/95) FL 83/37 FLC 8/3 FAC 2 Others 4/1
Port Vale (£500,000 on 12/9/97) FL 38+2/5 FAC 2

Gareth Ainsworth

AISTON Samuel (Sam) James
Born: Newcastle, 21 November 1976
Height: 6'1" Weight: 12.10
Club Honours: Div 1 '96
International Honours: E: Sch
A promising and skilful left winger whose progress at Sunderland was cruelly cut short in 1997-98 by injury. Sam damaged his cruciate knee ligaments in a reserve team game in November, and needed two operations before the end of the season. Still only 20, with time on his side to establish himself in the first team, he has tremendous pace that can often leave full backs standing, while his ball-playing skills have seen him draw favourable comparisons with a young Chris Waddle. Those who should know are still predicting a great future for him.
Sunderland (Free from Newcastle U juniors on 14/7/95) P/FL 5+14 FLC 0+1 FAC 0+2
Chester C (Loaned on 21/2/97) FL 14 FLC 1 Others 2

AKINBIYI Adeola (Ade) Peter
Born: Hackney, 10 October 1974
Height: 6'1" Weight: 12.9
A speedy forward with an eye for goal, Ade was Gillingham's top scorer during 1997-98, netting in five successive matches at one stage. It was no great surprise that many

Premiership clubs watched him during the season, and it will only be a matter of time before he moves back into the top flight if he continues his improvement. Has great feet and balance. *Stop Press:* Transferred to Bristol City on 22 May for the sum of £1.2 million.

Norwich C (From trainee on 5/2/93) P/FL 22+27/3 FLC 2+4/2 FAC 1+2 Others 0+1
Hereford U (Loaned on 21/1/94) FL 3+1/2
Brighton & Hove A (Loaned on 24/11/94) FL 7/4
Gillingham (£250,000 on 13/1/97) FL 63/28 FLC 2 FAC 2/1 Others 0+1

ALBERT Philippe
Born: Bouillon, Belgium, 10 August 1967
Height: 6'3" Weight: 13.7
International Honours: Belgium: 41

An elegant central defender, Philippe continued to bring an element of European class to Newcastle in 1997-98, having the ideal physique for a centre back, and making good use of this in producing commanding performances at the heart of the defence. Yet, he has a deft touch on the ball for such a big man, and often uses his fine distribution skills to incisively turn defence into attack. Although the desire of Kenny Dalglish to tighten up the defence constrained his attacking ambitions last season he still enjoyed joining his forward colleagues whenever he could, and his powerful left foot was a weapon which continued to spell danger for opponents. His commitment to his club is such that, after being a regular in the Belgian national team for some time, he withdrew from the squad for the World Cup play off with the Republic of Ireland, declaring that he was retiring from international football to concentrate on his Newcastle career. His reward was that, despite the fierce competition for places in United's defence, he was a regular in the side for most of the season because of his consistently high standards.

Newcastle U (£2,650,000 from Anderlecht, via Charleroi and Mechelen, on 10/8/94) PL 84+6/8 FLC 11+1/2 FAC 7+1/1 Others 19+2/1

ALCIDE Colin James
Born: Huddersfield, 14 April 1972
Height: 6'2" Weight: 13.10

An extremely powerful Lincoln striker who formed a very effective partnership with Lee Thorpe in the second half of last season, having overcome early injury problems, Colin reached his highest goals total to date for the Imps, with 13 to his credit.

Lincoln C (£15,000 from Emley on 5/12/95) FL 85+13/26 FLC 5+2/2 FAC 1+2/1 Others 2+1

ALDERSON Richard
Born: Durham, 27 January 1975
Height: 5'10" Weight: 11.7

A former Newcastle United junior, Richard was signed by York City last December from Spennymoor United. Currently studying for a university degree, the part timer made a couple of substitute appearances for the Minstermen on the right wing before being released during the summer.

York C (Signed from Spennymoor U on 10/12/97) FL 0+1 Others 0+1

Colin Alcide

ALDRIDGE John William
Born: Liverpool, 18 September 1958
Height: 5'11" Weight: 12.3
Club Honours: WC '80; Div 2 '85, Div 1 '88; FLC '86; CS '88; FAC '89
International Honours: Ei: 69

At the end of 1997-98, a season in which the Tranmere player/manager picked himself only sparingly, John decided to "hang up his boots" as a first team player and concentrate fully on club management, although he is retaining his registration in case of reserve team emergencies. Still showing all the old killer instincts up front, he scored twice against Wolves in the final game of the campaign and, in an emotional farewell appearance, he was desperately unlucky not to grab a hat trick. He also became the club's oldest player to appear in a league match in this fixture, beating the record previously held by George Payne.

11

Newport Co (£3,500 from South Liverpool on 2/5/79) FL 159+11/69 FLC 11/5 FAC 12+1/7 Others 4/2
Oxford U (£78,000 on 21/3/84) FL 111+3/72 FLC 17/14 FAC 5/2 Others 5/2
Liverpool (£750,000 on 27/1/87) FL 69+14/50 FLC 7+1/3 FAC 12/8 Others 1/2 (£1,000,000 to Real Sociedad on 1/9/89)
Tranmere Rov (£250,000 on 11/7/91) FL 221+21/138 FLC 25/22 FAC 8+1/4 Others 18/10

John Aldridge

ALDRIDGE Martin James
Born: Northampton, 6 December 1974
Height: 5'11" Weight: 12.2
Martin had an injury and suspension in the middle of last season, and finished it on loan at Southend United, after apparently not featuring in new manager, Malcolm Shotton's plans at Oxford. 1997-98 started well enough, as he came off the bench in the opening game to score with his first touch against Huddersfield, but his best spell came between mid-September and mid-October, when his other three goals came. Sniffs out the scoring positions like his namesake, John, and also has a useful long throw. Was released during the summer.
Northampton T (From trainee on 27/8/93) FL 50+20/17 FLC 1+2 FAC 1+1/1 Others 5+2/4
Oxford U (Free on 22/12/95) FL 46+26/19 FLC 8+4/3 FAC 2+2
Southend U (Loaned on 23/2/98) FL 7+4/1

ALEXANDER Graham
Born: Coventry, 10 October 1971
Height: 5'10" Weight: 12.7
Enjoying his best ever campaign at Luton in 1997-98, despite the disappointing form of the team, his positive play on the right side of midfield was an important factor in the club's eventual scramble to safety. Scored his highest total of goals in a season with his powerful shooting from almost any range and also converted Town's only penalty. Would probably have enjoyed even better form had he not been frequently asked to play at full back to cover for injuries.
Scunthorpe U (From trainee on 20/3/90) FL 149+10/18 FLC 11+1/2 FAC 12/1 Others 13+3/3
Luton T (£100,000 on 8/7/95) FL 118+3/11 FLC 10 FAC 4+1 Others 6+2

ALEXANDERSSON Niclas
Born: Halmstad, Sweden, 29 December 1971
Height: 5'10" Weight: 11.8
International Honours: Sweden: 29
This young, busy, right-sided midfield player made a very favourable impression at Sheffield Wednesday in 1997-98. Signed from IFK Gothenburg in December, he adapted very well to the English game, having taken the advice of fellow Swede and ex-Owl, Roland Nilsson, to go to Hillsborough. Unfortunate to miss the last three months of the season, due to a bad leg injury he picked up at home against Wimbledon, hopefully, he will be back as good as new for the start of 1998-99. A Swedish international, prior to IFK Gothenburg, Niclas was at Halmstads.
Sheffield Wed (£750,000 from Gothenburg on 9/12/97) PL 5+1 FAC 2/1

Niclas Alexandersson

ALJOFREE Hasney
Born: Manchester, 11 July 1978
Height: 6'0" Weight: 12.1
International Honours: E: Yth
Now in his second term as a professional, Hasney, an England youth international who has come through the Bolton ranks, made his long-awaited league debut in the 2-1 win over Blackburn in April, delivering a confident and assured display in the left-back position against the likes of Steve Sutton, Kevin Gallacher, and Damien Duff! He had previously produced some outstanding performances for the reserve team and, with a cool head on his shoulders, he should be a name for the future, especially if last season's developments are to be built upon.
Bolton W (From trainee on 2/7/96) PL 2

ALLAN Derek Thomas
Born: Irvine, 24 December 1974
Height: 6'0" Weight: 12.1
International Honours: S: Yth
Though troubled with a series of injuries in 1997-98, Derek remained a reliable member of Brighton and Hove Albion's back line. Missed the opening of the season through injury, and a torn thigh muscle sustained in the 1-0 defeat at Football League newcomers, Macclesfield Town, on 27 January, followed by a frustrating hamstring problem, meant that he was also absent for the last three months of the Seagulls' tortuous campaign.
Ayr U (Trainee) SL 5
Southampton (£75,000 on 16/3/93) PL 0+1
Brighton & Hove A (Free on 28/3/96) FL 56+2/1 FLC 2 FAC 1 Others 2

ALLARDYCE Craig Samuel
Born: Bolton, 9 June 1975
Height: 6'3" Weight: 13.7
The son of Sam, the Notts County manager, Craig was skippering Chorley's Unibond League side when Chesterfield signed him on non-contract terms last March, as centre-half cover. Despite only making a two-minute appearance as a substitute, he may be given further chances to impress in the 1998 pre-season period.
Preston NE (From trainee on 16/7/93) FL 0+1 (Free to Macclesfield T on 16/4/94)
Blackpool (Free from Northwich Vic on 20/9/94) FL 0+1 (Freed on 23/11/96)
Chesterfield (Free from Chorley on 26/3/98) FL 0+1

ALLEN Bradley James
Born: Romford, 13 September 1971
Height: 5'8" Weight: 11.0
International Honours: E: U21-8; Yth
1997-98 was a disappointing season for Bradley, who found his opportunities at Charlton limited due to the abundance of strikers in the squad. Although a consistent scorer in the Football Combination side, he only made a handful of first team appearances, scoring in consecutive games against Crewe and Nottingham Forest in November. Is a hard-working player who is comfortable on the ball, and shows good awareness in front of goal.
Queens Park R (From juniors on 30/9/88) F/PL 56+25/27 FLC 5+2/5 FAC 3+2 Others 1
Charlton Ath (£400,000 on 28/3/96) FL 30+10/9 FLC 3/2 FAC 0+2 Others 1+1

ALLEN Christopher (Chris) Anthony
Born: Oxford, 18 November 1972
Height: 5'11" Weight: 12.2
International Honours: E: U21-2
1997-98 was not the best of seasons for this left-sided Nottingham Forest wingman, who can also be effective through the middle where his pace takes him clear of defenders. In a season where Forest regained Premiership status at the first time of asking, Chris made just three appearances for the club, all of them coming in the opening five games, before being loaned out to Luton in November. At Kenilworth Road, he enjoyed a sustained run of 14 games in the side without ever convincing the fans that he

could win matches, but his ability to motor down the left flank and deliver good crosses provided the width that had been lacking up until then. Then it was back to the City Ground and reserve team football.

Oxford U (From trainee on 14/5/91) FL 110+40/12 FLC 11+2/4 FAC 5+5/1 Others 5+3
Nottingham F (Loaned on 24/2/96) PL 1+2/1
Nottingham F (£300,000 on 3/7/96) F/PL 17+8 FLC 2/1 FAC 1/1
Luton T (Loaned on 28/11/97) FL 14/1

ALLEN Graham
Born: Bolton, 8 April 1977
Height: 6'1" Weight: 12.8
International Honours: E: Yth

A rugged and uncompromising Everton right back, Graham started just two Premiership matches in 1997-98. Despite impressing Howard Kendall with an excellent pre-season performance against Ajax, he had to wait until January for his full debut, but celebrated with a 3-1 win over Chelsea, while the second appearance, three months later, lasted only until half time as Sheffield Wednesday won at Goodison Park. After interest from Wigan Athletic, Graham committed himself to a new Goodison contract at the end of the season and will be looking forward to furthering his football education in 1998-99.

Everton (From trainee on 10/12/94) PL 2+4

ALLEN Martin James
Born: Reading, 14 August 1965
Height: 5'10" Weight: 12.6
International Honours: E: U21-2; Yth

Earlier, at the end of September, when unable to get into the squad, and in a bid to get him match fit, he was loaned out to Southend where he played five times before returning to Fratton Park. Nicknamed "Mad Dog", this battling midfielder, with good skills, and shooting ability, comes from the famous Allen footballing dynasty, his dad, Dennis, played for Charlton, Reading, and Bournemouth; Uncle Les was at Chelsea, Spurs, and QPR; while his cousins, Clive, Bradley, and Paul are from the modern game. Due to persistent knee problems, Martin spent most of last season on the sidelines at Portsmouth until the arrival of Alan Ball as manager brought him back into first team contention, mainly as a substitute, or when Michalis Vlachos was injured.

Queens Park R (From apprentice on 27/5/83) FL 128+8/16 FLC 15+3/1 FAC 9/1 Others 2/1
West Ham U (£675,000 on 24/8/89) F/PL 163+27/26 FLC 15+3/5 FAC 14/4 Others 10
Portsmouth (Loaned on 11/9/95) FL 15/3
Portsmouth (£500,000 on 22/2/96) FL 19+11/1 FAC 0+1
Southend U (Loaned on 26/9/97) FL 5 FLC 1

ALLEN Paul Kevin
Born: Aveley, 28 August 1962
Height: 5'7" Weight: 11.4
Club Honours: FAC '80, '91; Div 2 '96
International Honours: E: U21-3; Yth (UEFAYC '80)

Having signed for Millwall from Bristol City, immediately prior to the start of 1997-98, the much travelled 35-year old ended the campaign a few games short of 600

Football League appearances for his various clubs, which included West Ham, Spurs, Southampton, Swindon, and the aforementioned Bristol City. A right-sided player, he was mainly used as a stop gap, in defence or midfield, showing a great deal of skill, and proving a great asset in giving nothing less than 110 per cent. Given a free transfer in the summer, he is still an excellent motivator, a hard tackler, and, above all, a great team man.

West Ham U (From apprentice on 29/8/79) FL 149+3/6 FLC 20+4/2 FAC 15+3/3 Others 2+1
Tottenham H (£400,000 on 19/6/85) F/PL 276+16/23 FLC 42+2/4 FAC 26+1/1 Others 12+2
Southampton (£550,000 on 16/9/93) PL 40+3/1 FLC 4 FAC 2
Luton T (Loaned on 9/12/94) FL 4
Stoke C (Loaned on 20/1/95) FL 17/1 Others 2
Swindon T (Free on 11/10/95) FL 30+7/1 FLC 2 FAC 5/1 Others 1
Bristol C (Free on 16/1/97) FL 13+1 Others 3
Millwall (Free on 1/8/97) FL 21+7 FLC 3 FAC 1 Others 1+1

ALLEN Rory William
Born: Beckenham, 17 October 1977
Height: 5'11" Weight: 11.2
International Honours: E: U21-3

A natural striker who found first team football hard to come by at Tottenham last season, although reliable and enthusiastic when called upon, he made his first appearance against Liverpool in November, looking sharp and lively, both on and off the ball, with a confidence connected with the more established strikers. Despite a further three consecutive Premiership appearances, Rory could not establish himself above the more experienced strikers, such as Chris Armstrong and Les Ferdinand, and was loaned to Luton on transfer deadline day, scoring six goals in eight games for the Hatters. Almost certainly the main reason for Town avoiding the drop, the club had gambled on him due to him being short of match practice through injury, but his unnerving accuracy in front of goal, coupled to an outstanding workrate and the ability to harass defenders, justified the decision. Following this, there is no doubt that he has the potential to establish himself at a higher level. His ability was recognised at U21 level when playing in all three of England's matches in the end of season Toulon tournament.

Tottenham H (From trainee on 28/3/96) PL 10+6/2 FLC 2+1/2 FAC 1
Luton T (Loaned on 26/3/98) FL 8/6

ALLISON Wayne Anthony
Born: Huddersfield, 16 October 1968
Height: 6'1" Weight: 13.5
Club Honours: Div 2 '96

An ever present with Swindon in 1997-98, with three goals in 18 appearances, the Huddersfield-born striker finally came home, when signing in November and becoming the missing link in the front line duo. A typically big, strong figure who holds the ball up well and creates the space and chances for others, Wayne was quickly dubbed the battering ram of the front line, as the other strikers at the club, especially Marcus Stewart, benefited from his unsel-

fish workrate. Always ready to help in defence, and capable of scoring the odd goals himself, he soon went to the top of the goal assist list, prior to missing the final two games of the campaign due to a knee injury.

Halifax T (From trainee on 6/7/87) FL 74+10/23 FLC 3/2 FAC 4+1/2 Others 8+1/3
Watford (£250,000 on 26/7/89) FL 6+1
Bristol C (£300,000 on 9/8/90) FL 149+46/48 FLC 4+5/2 FAC 12+1/5 Others 6+2/2
Swindon T (£475,000 on 22/7/95) FL 98+3/31 FLC 9/3 FAC 7/2 Others 3
Huddersfield T (£800,000 on 11/11/97) FL 27/6 FAC 2

ALLON Joseph (Joe) Ball
Born: Gateshead, 12 November 1966
Height: 5'11" Weight: 13.6
Club Honours: FAYC '85
International Honours: E: Yth

Hartlepool's proven goalscorer began 1997-98 carrying a knee injury but, although this seemed no real problem at the time, as he showed good form scoring two goals in the first home game against Colchester shortly afterwards, he was forced to have surgery on his knee cap, and any hopes of an early return were soon dashed. Eventually he did resume training, and did play some games for the reserves, but in January he was forced to announce his retirement.

Newcastle U (From trainee on 16/11/84) FL 9/2 FLC 1
Swansea C (Free on 6/8/87) FL 27+7/11 FLC 2 FAC 2 Others 2/1
Hartlepool U (Free on 29/11/88) FL 112/48 FLC 5/2 FAC 6+1/5 Others 7/2
Chelsea (£250,000 on 14/8/91) FL 3+11/2 FLC 0+2 Others 1+1/1
Port Vale (Loaned on 27/2/92) FL 2+4
Brentford (£275,000 on 19/11/92) FL 38+7/19 FLC 2 FAC 2/2 Others 7/7
Southend U (Loaned on 16/9/93) FL 2+1
Port Vale (Signed on 24/3/94) FL 13+10/9 FLC 0+1 FAC 2/1
Lincoln C (£42,500 on 17/7/95) FL 3+1 FLC 1
Hartlepool U (£42,500 on 13/10/95) FL 52+4/19 FLC 3/2 FAC 1 Others 3/1

ALLOTT Mark Stephen
Born: Manchester, 3 October 1977
Height: 5'11" Weight: 12.0

1997-98 was the season that Mark established himself at Oldham, his ability to hold the ball up, along with his pace, auguring well for the future. A centre forward who scores a lot of goals for the reserves, he has yet to produce fireworks at first team level, but the two he scored for Athletic last season were both vital point savers. Highly thought of at Boundary Park, he could go a long way in the game.

Oldham Ath (From trainee on 14/10/95) FL 10+17/3 FLC 0+1 FAC 2+2

ALOISI John
Born: Australia, 5 February 1976
Height: 6'0" Weight: 12.13
International Honours: Australia: 13

Born of Italian parents, John started out with Adelaide City before moving to Europe, first with Standard Liege, and then Antwerp, both Belgian sides, prior to signing for the Italian Series "A" side, Cremonese, from whence Portsmouth captured him during the 1997 close season. As the most successful of

Pompey's Australians, John made an immediate impact, scoring on his debut at Manchester City, after being signed as a replacement for Lee Bradbury, who had been sold to City. At first, he had an effective partnership with Mathias Svensson, but a run of bad results meant that he played alongside a number of partners. Despite this, John still ended the campaign as the leading goalscorer with 12 to his credit.

Portsmouth (£300,000 from Cremonese on 8/8/97) FL 33+5/12 FLC 2 FAC 1

John Aloisi

ALSFORD Julian
Born: Poole, 24 December 1972
Height: 6'2" Weight: 13.7

A stylish central defender, Julian was an ever present for Chester City in 1997-98, before moving north of the border to join Dundee just before the transfer deadline. He made a great contribution to City's league campaign prior to leaving, and chipped in with four goals, one of them being an effective winner at home to Darlington.

Watford (From trainee on 30/4/91) FL 9+4/1 FLC 1 Others 2
Chester C (Free on 11/8/94) FL 136+5/6 FLC 8+1 FAC 8 Others 8

ALSOP Julian Mark
Born: Nuneaton, 28 May 1973
Height: 6'4" Weight: 13.0

As a tall target man, Julian found it difficult to hold down a place in Bristol Rovers' starting line-up in 1997-98, but remained a regular squad member who could always be relied upon to add physical presence in order to sharpen up any dull game. A committed player, his aerial strength was always a problem for defenders, and he certainly showed signs of an improved first touch and awareness in bringing other players into the game. After a loan spell at third division Swansea City, where he scored twice in five games, he returned to Rovers before both clubs agreed a transfer which involved goalkeeper, Lee Jones, moving from the Welsh club, and Julian returning to the Vetch Field.

Bristol Rov (£15,000 from Halesowen on 14/2/97) FL 20+13/4 FLC 2/1 FAC 1/1 Others 2
Swansea C (Loaned on 20/1/98) FL 5/2
Swansea C (£30,000 on 12/3/98) FL 7/1

ALVES Paulo Lourenco
Born: Portugal, 10 December 1969
Height: 5'11" Weight: 13.7
International Honours: Portugal: 13

A 28-year-old Portuguese centre forward, who joined West Ham in November on loan from Sporting Lisbon, he made his debut against Aston Villa and looked quite useful when coming on as a substitute, especially when producing a superb save from the 'keeper, Michael Oakes. However, unable to establish himself in the first team, after three more appearances from the bench he returned to Portugal in January.

West Ham U (Loaned from Sporting Lisbon on 21/11/97) PL 0+4

AMPADU Patrick Kwame
Born: Bradford, 20 December 1970
Height: 5'10" Weight: 11.10
Club Honours: AMC '94
International Honours: Ei: U21-4; Yth

Despite starting last season for Swansea as first choice, the midfielder struggled to hold down a regular place in the starting line-up during the rest of the campaign. Sidelined during the final third of the season with a hamstring injury and then a broken toe, both Leyton Orient and Cardiff attempted to sign him in March, but to no avail. Is not only an exciting player when going forward, but has sound defensive qualities also. Was somewhat surprisingly released during the summer.

Arsenal (From trainee on 19/11/88) FL 0+2
Plymouth Arg (Loaned on 31/10/90) FL 6/1 Others 1
West Bromwich A (£50,000 on 24/6/91) FL 27+22/4 FLC 6+1 FAC 1 Others 5/1
Swansea C (£15,000 on 16/2/94) FL 128+19/12 FLC 8+1/1 FAC 5+1/1 Others 16/1

ANDERSON Ijah Massai
Born: Hackney, 30 December 1975
Height: 5'8" Weight: 10.6

An attacking Brentford left back with good ball control and crossing ability, who positions himself well in defence, Ijah performed to his usual high standard, while ever present in Brentford's first 21 games of last season. Unfortunately, for both player and club, a freak training ground accident saw him break his leg, an injury that put him out of action for the rest of the campaign.

Southend U (Free from Tottenham H juniors on 2/8/94)
Brentford (Free on 31/7/95) FL 88/3 FLC 10/1 FAC 3+2 Others 4+1

ANDERSSON Anders Per
Born: Tomelia, Sweden, 15 March 1974
Height: 5'9" Weight: 11.5
International Honours: Sweden: 8

Signed from Malmo during the 1997 close season, Anders, a Swedish international, made his debut for Blackburn on the opening day of 1997-98 as a 90th-minute substitute in a 1-0 home win over Derby. Hardly what you might call an auspicious beginning, the midfielder eventually made four starts, and even scored in the 6-0 drubbing of Preston in the Coca Cola Cup, but, all-in-all, he seemed to lack the physical requirements of the Premiership and found it

difficult to adjust. Interestingly, he was discovered by Roy Hodgson when playing as a lad in Sweden.

Blackburn Rov (£500,000 from Malmo on 11/7/97) PL 1+3 FLC 3/1 FAC 0+1

ANDERSSON Andreas Claes
Born: Stockholm, Sweden, 10 April 1974
Height: 6'1" Weight: 12.1
International Honours: Sweden: 18

Andreas is a tall, strong striker, whose parents both played football to a good standard, and he built up a high reputation as a goalscorer in his native Sweden, including scoring twice on his international debut. This led to a big money transfer to Italy in the summer of 1997, but the competition for places at Milan was very hot and he spent most of his time on the bench, starting only a single Serie "A" match. A long-time target for Kenny Dalglish, he joined Newcastle at the end of January, and his pace, control, and movement enabled him to form an effective partnership with Alan Shearer, although he found goals hard to come by in the Premiership. Opening his account with the first goal in the crucial Easter Monday victory over Barnsley, he followed that up with another in the 1-1 draw at Manchester United, as the club fought tooth and nail to avoid the drop.

Newcastle U (£3,600,000 from AC Milan on 29/1/98) PL 10+2/2 FAC 2+1

ANDERTON Darren Robert
Born: Southampton, 3 March 1972
Height: 6'1" Weight: 12.5
International Honours: E: 22; B-1; U21-12; Yth

1997-98 was yet another season of torment for this talented Spurs' midfielder, suffering recurring groin and hamstring injuries which kept him out of much of the campaign. In his rare appearances, Darren looked lean and eager to get on the ball, but much of his confidence to take players on seemed to have taken a dent due to the injuries suffered. This giving claim that he was not fully fit when asked to play, but eager to do whatever he could to help Tottenham avoid relegation. Playing in the final games of the term, he looked to have regained much of the strength and pace that had made him a regular feature in the England line-up and, more importantly, he looked to have his quick reflexes and stamina back at their peak, and seemed to be fully fit. Glenn Hoddle, watching his comeback closely, especially in a "B" international against Russia at the end of April, gave him a massive boost by showing confidence in his return to full fitness by awarding him a place in the 22-strong squad for France. For Darren, the opportunity represented a chance to put a fairytale end to what has been a nightmare of a season for him. *Stop Press:* With many feeling that he did not warrant World Cup selection, due to his injury problems and lack of match practice, Darren quickly warmed to the task, appearing in all five matches, to prove that Glenn Hoddle was right and the doubters wrong. The great first goal in the 2-0 win over Colombia was the icing on the cake,

but what was probably more important was his workrate, especially in the Argentine game.

Portsmouth (From trainee on 5/2/90) FL 53+9/7 FLC 3+2/1 FAC 7+1/5 Others 2
Tottenham H (£1,750,000 on 3/6/92) PL 131+16/22 FLC 13/4 FAC 13+1/2

ANDRADE Jose Manuel Gomes
Born: Gaboverde, Portugal, 1 June 1970
Height: 5'11" Weight: 11.7

Last season saw Jose sign up for a second spell at Stoke, having been on loan from Academico del Coimbra in 1995. Tall, but slightly built, his return was popular with the fans and his transfer to the club was at no cost under the Bosman ruling. Although he was a member of the first team squad and made 14 appearances in all, he really lacked the presence in the box needed to make the grade at this level and being transfer listed in January, was quickly released back to Portugal.

Stoke C (Loaned from Academico del Coimbra on 23/3/95) FL 2+2/1
Stoke C (Free on 8/8/97) FL 4+8/1 FLC 2

ANDREWS Benjamin (Ben) Phillip
Born: Burton, 18 November 1980
Height: 6'0" Weight: 12.10

A Brighton and Hove Albion YTS trainee, the 17-year-old defender was given a one-year contract by manager, Brian Horton, at the end of March and made his first team debut at left back the following Saturday. Although having a fine match in the 0-0 draw at Cardiff, Ben had the misfortune to be sent off for a second bookable offence four minutes from time. Unflappable on the ball, good in the air, and able to perform a variety of defensive roles, the youngster looks set for a fine future.

Brighton & Hove A (Trainee) FL 2+1

ANDREWS Wayne Michael Hill
Born: Paddington, 25 November 1977
Height: 5'10" Weight: 11.6

A promising young Watford striker with great pace, Wayne was unlucky enough to suffer a broken ankle during a reserve match last October, having made only four substitute appearances in the first team. As a result, he missed all but the last few weeks of the season, and was unable to consolidate on the good impression he had made previously.

Watford (From trainee on 5/7/96) FL 16+12/4 FLC 3+2/1 FAC 0+2 Others 2/1

ANELKA Nicolas
Born: Versailles, France, 24 March 1979
Height: 6'0" Weight: 12.3
Club Honours: PL '98; FAC '98

It is hard to believe that Nicolas is only 19 years old, such was his late-season maturity at Arsenal in 1997-98, especially after the manager, Arsene Wenger, had earlier appeared to have doubts about him succeeding in England. However, after Christmas he was a revelation when coming in for Ian Wright and scoring nine goals. One of them, at Blackburn, had to be seen to be believed, as he dummied round the 'keeper, Alan Fettis, to score the fourth in a

4-1 win. There were others more vital though, such as the first in a 3-2 home win over Manchester United, and the second in a 2-2 draw at Coventry, while his strike at West Ham in the FA Cup quarter final after the Gunners were down to ten men, following Dennis Bergkamp's dismissal in the 32nd minute, took the club to penalties which they won. A forward with great touch and pace, and the ability to wrong foot the opposing defence, the man they call the "French Maradona" is surely set to become a big star. Having scored the second goal in the FA Cup final win over Newcastle at Wembley, he could boast of winning both championship and FA Cup medals in the same season, as Arsenal "did" the double for the second time in their history.

Arsenal (£500,000+ from Paris St Germain on 6/3/97) PL 16+14/6 FLC 3 FAC 8+1/3 Others 1+1

ANGEL Mark
Born: Newcastle, 23 August 1975
Height: 5'9" Weight: 11.10

Although a badly-torn thigh muscle kept Oxford's Mark out of action for much of the closing stages of last season, the tricky, wide player, with a good shot, did not feature as much as he would have hoped, making 16 substitute appearances, much of it down to the super form of Joey Beauchamp. However, one of his starts, in a wing-back berth, saw him score with a cracking 25-yard shot at his old club Sunderland, but that was to be his only goal, and he will be looking for better in 1998-99.

Sunderland (From Walker Central on 31/12/93)
Oxford U (Free on 9/8/95) FL 40+33/4 FLC 4+4 FAC 4+2 Others 2+1/1

ANGELL Brett Ashley Mark
Born: Marlborough, 20 August 1968
Height: 6'2" Weight: 13.11

Brett topped Stockport's goalscoring charts for the second season running in 1997-98, as he made a smooth transition from second to first division football. The big centre forward used all his experience, aerial ability, and goal-poaching instincts to maintain his form and continued to be a regular fixture in the side.

Portsmouth (From trainee on 1/8/86)
Derby Co (£40,000 from Cheltenham T on 19/2/88)
Stockport Co (£33,000 on 20/10/88) FL 60+10/28 FLC 3 FAC 3/1 Others 8/4
Southend U (£100,000 on 2/8/90) FL 109+6/47 FLC 7+1/4 FAC 3/2 Others 9+1/10
Everton (£500,000 on 17/1/94) PL 16+4/1 FLC 0+1
Sunderland (£600,000 on 23/3/95) FL 10 FLC 1/1
Sheffield U (Loaned on 30/1/96) FL 6/2
West Bromwich A (Loaned on 28/3/96) FL 0+3
Stockport Co (£120,000 on 19/8/96) FL 75+4/33 FLC 12+2/6 FAC 5/3 Others 4+1/1

ANSAH Andrew (Andy)
Born: Lewisham, 19 March 1969
Height: 5'10" Weight: 11.1

A much-travelled front runner, Andy joined Brighton and Hove Albion on a non-contract basis last November, but struggled to make the team initially, before being selected in a substitute role on numerous occasions. Eventually getting a run in the side during the managerial changeover period in

February and March, he had a particularly good game against Chester at Gillingham, when he clinically finished off an excellent three-man move that enabled the new manager, Brian Horton, to begin his tenure with a precious win. The 3-2 victory ended a ten-match win-less run by the Seagulls.

Brentford (Free from Dorking on 21/3/89) FL 3+5/2 FLC 0+1
Southend U (Free on 29/3/90) FL 141+16/33 FLC 7+2 FAC 4 Others 7+3/5
Brentford (Loaned on 4/11/94) FL 2+1/1 Others 2/1
Brentford (Loaned on 15/11/95) FL 6/1 Others 1
Peterborough U (Free on 15/3/96) FL 0+2/1
Gillingham (Free on 28/3/96) FL 0+2
Leyton Orient (Free on 19/12/96) FL 0+2 (Free to Hayes on 1/2/97)
Brighton & Hove A (Free from Heybridge Swifts on 7/11/97) FL 7+7/3 FAC 0+1 Others 1

ANTHONY Graham John
Born: South Shields, 9 August 1975
Height: 5'9" Weight: 10.8

A left-sided midfielder who started last season on trial at Plymouth, having been released by Swindon during the previous summer, Graham started the opening seven games before being surprisingly allowed to leave, and eventually finding his feet at Carlisle in a midfield berth where he adopted the role of playmaker. A skilful passer of the ball, his workrate and determination to be involved in the game are positive qualities that should stand him in good stead in the club's coming third division campaign. Scored his first ever league goal in a 3-1 home win over Oldham, when beating the 'keeper from the edge of the box.

Sheffield U (From trainee on 7/7/93) FL 0+3 FLC 1 Others 2
Scarborough (Loaned on 1/3/96) FL 2
Swindon T (Free on 26/3/97) FL 3
Plymouth Arg (Free on 7/8/97) FL 5 FLC 2
Carlisle U (Free on 26/11/97) FL 25/2 Others 3/1

Graham Anthony

ANTHROBUS Stephen (Steve) Anthony
Born: Lewisham, 10 November 1968
Height: 6'2" Weight: 13.0

After scoring his first goal for Crewe last September, the second in a 3-2 win at Portsmouth, Steve went on to impress all at Gresty Road with his leadership of the line, his fine close control and aerial presence being at the fore. Another string to his bow is his ability to play in the centre of the defence if required, but, with the club valuing his contribution up front highly, he has yet to appear there for Alex.

Millwall (From juniors on 4/8/86) FL 19+2/4 FLC 3 Others 1
Wimbledon (£150,000 on 16/2/90) F/PL 27+1 FLC 1 FAC 2
Peterborough U (Loaned on 21/1/94) FL 2
Chester C (Loaned on 26/8/94) FL 7
Shrewsbury T (£25,000 on 8/8/95) FL 60+12/16 FLC 4+1 FAC 5+3/1 Others 7+2/1
Crewe Alex (£75,000 on 24/3/97) FL 37+3/6 FLC 1

APPLEBY Matthew (Matty) Wilfred
Born: Middlesbrough, 16 April 1972
Height: 5'8" Weight: 11.5

With Barnsley being relegated from the Premiership, Matty experienced a frustrating season in 1997-98. A valuable squad member, who played in a number of positions on his limited opportunities – full back, central defender and midfield marker – he showed that he had a capacity to perform wherever and whenever needed. An astute reader of the game, and a good tackler and passer of the ball, he certainly did not look out of place, having some excellent games along the way.

Newcastle U (From trainee on 4/5/90) F/PL 18+2 FLC 2+1 FAC 2 Others 2+2
Darlington (Loaned on 25/11/93) FL 10/1 Others 1
Darlington (Free on 15/6/94) FL 77+2/7 FLC 2 FAC 4 Others 8/3
Barnsley (£200,000 on 19/7/96) F/PL 48+2 FLC 5+1 FAC 2+1

APPLEBY Richard (Richie) Dean
Born: Middlesbrough, 18 September 1975
Height: 5'9" Weight: 11.4
International Honours: E: Yth

Despite his over enthusiastic approach, which resulted in him being sent off in two consecutive matches in November and then receiving a further red card in his first game back from suspension, Richie was one of Swansea's most creative players last season, displaying good ball control and an ability to supply telling crosses from the flanks. Used as a wing back or further forward, his appearances could have been halted due to a groin problem that was picked up during the second half of the campaign, initially thought to be hernia related.

Newcastle U From trainee on 12/8/93) Others 2
Ipswich T (Free on 12/12/95) FL 0+3 Others 1
Swansea C (Free on 16/8/96) FL 41+5/4 FLC 3+1 FAC 1/1 Others 1

APPLETON Michael Antony
Born: Salford, 4 December 1975
Height: 5'9" Weight: 12.4

As Preston's record signing on the eve of last season, Michael took some time to adjust to the demands of second division

football. His situation was not helped by being asked to play out of position on both flanks, but when played in his favoured central midfield role by new manager, David Moyes, following a period on the bench, he really blossomed. An aggressive ball-winner, he makes quick incisive runs in support of both attack and defence, and distributes the ball confidently, as well as contributing his share of goals.

Manchester U (From trainee on 1/7/94) FLC 1+1
Lincoln C (Loaned on 15/9/95) FL 4 Others 1
Grimsby T (Loaned on 17/1/97) FL 10/3
Preston NE (Signed on 8/8/97) FL 31+7/2 FLC 2+1 FAC 4/1 Others 2/1

ARCHDEACON Owen Duncan
Born: Greenock, 4 March 1966
Height: 5'8" Weight: 11.0
Club Honours: SPD '86; AMC '97
International Honours: S: U21-1; Yth

As the Carlisle club captain, Owen was ever present at left back in 1997-98 until he returned to Scotland, and Morton FC in November. A neat and stylish performer, he converted three penalties, all away from home, in his limited time during the campaign, and his dead-ball expertise from corners and free kicks was especially missed during the second half of the season.

Glasgow Celtic (From Gourock U on 20/8/82) SL 38+38/7 SLC 1+4/1 SC 3+1 Others 1+3
Barnsley (£80,000 on 7/7/89) FL 222+11/23 FLC 15+1/2 FAC 14+1/2 Others 9+1/4
Carlisle U (Free on 12/7/96) FL 64/11 FLC 8/1 FAC 5/2 Others 6/4

ARDLEY Neal Christopher
Born: Epsom, 1 September 1972
Height: 5'11" Weight: 11.9
International Honours: E: U21-10

Neal carried on last season from where he left off in 1996-97, in adding an extra dimension to the Wimbledon team with his superb crossing from the right flank to the front men. A naturally right-sided winger, the former England U21 international is full of graft and pace, qualities that are well recognised by the Dons' manager, Joe Kinnear, which explains why he is a regular member of the first team squad. Missed six games through injury earlier in the season, and once back he was absent just one more time, scoring three goals, two of them winners – a penalty at home to Leeds in the Premiership, and a strike from the edge of the box at Huddersfield that took the Dons into the fifth round of the FA Cup. Is also a strong tackler who is never easily beaten.

Wimbledon (From trainee on 29/7/91) F/PL 123+16/10 FLC 13+3/2 FAC 18+2/1

ARENDSE Andre
Born: Capetown, South Africa, 27 June 1967
Height: 6'4" Weight: 11.5
International Honours: South Africa: 26

Andre signed for Fulham during the summer of 1997 when he was South Africa's number one 'keeper and was playing in the side which qualified for the World Cup Finals. Due to a delay in obtaining his work permit, and the excellent form of Mark Walton, he was unable to force his way into the side

until mid-September. He then shared the job with Walton until the arrival of Maik Taylor from Southampton, following which he only played one first team game, a 1-0 win over Bristol Rovers. Selected for South Africa's final 22 bound for the World Cup Finals in France during the summer, without being called upon, he is a tall, imposing figure, and a very good shot-stopper.

Fulham (Signed from Capetown Spurs on 7/8/97) FL 6 FLC 2 FAC 1

ARMSTRONG Alun
Born: Gateshead, 22 February 1975
Height: 6'1" Weight: 11.13
Club Honours: Div 1 '98

The blond striker had his best season yet for Stockport in 1997-98, before leaving to join Middlesbrough in February, in order to bolster their ultimately successful promoting bid. His pace, strength, and workrate had never been in doubt, but his improved strike rate at County proved to the Boro that he was their man, quickly establishing himself as a firm favourite with the Holgate Enders, through his sharp-shooting and powerful running, and winning acclaim for two brilliant goals in the 4-1 victory over Oxford, which helped to seal promotion. It was revealed later that he had played through the agony of a severely injured back. Is regarded as "the one who got away" after being rejected by Kevin Keegan at Newcastle.

Newcastle U (From trainee on 1/10/93)
Stockport Co (£50,000 on 23/6/94) FL 151+8/48 FLC 22/8 FAC 10+1/5 Others 7
Middlesbrough (£1,500,000 on 16/2/98) FL 7+4/7

Alun Armstrong

ARMSTRONG Christopher (Chris) Peter
Born: Newcastle, 19 June 1971
Height: 6'0" Weight: 13.3
Club Honours: Div 1 '94
International Honours: E: B-1

An athletic, versatile Tottenham striker, who has terrific ability in the air, Chris suffered another stop-start season in 1997-98, due to injury. Started on the bench and lacking

fitness, he made his first contribution by securing a draw away to Bolton in late September, followed by two classic drives that ended in goals against Carlisle United (Coca Cola Cup) and in the 3-2 home victory over Sheffield Wednesday. Whilst most at home when in the 18-yard box challenging for the ball, he has immense power in his shot and has the ability to delay the lift of the ball, as shown in the 3-0 victory over Blackburn Rovers, when firing in from 25 yards. With a liking to run at a defence from either flank, and a real danger in dead-ball situations, he will be looking forward to an injury-free campaign in 1998-99, and the opportunity to rediscover the form that had in previous seasons put him on the verge of an England call up.

Wrexham (Free from Llay Welfare on 3/3/89) FL 40+20/13 FLC 2+1 FAC 0+1 Others 5+1/3
Millwall (£50,000 on 16/8/91) FL 11+17/5 FLC 3+1/2 FAC 0+1 Others 0+1
Crystal Palace (£1,000,000 on 1/9/92) F/PL 118/45 FLC 8/6 FAC 8/5 Others 2/1
Tottenham H (£4,500,000 on 30/6/95) PL 61+6/25 FLC 8/5 FAC 6+1/4

ARMSTRONG Steven **Craig**
Born: South Shields, 23 May 1975
Height: 5'11" Weight: 12.10

Having been loaned out for six different spells with four different clubs since the end of 1994, and being a professional at Nottingham Forest since the 1992 close season without a first team game to his credit, Craig finally broke his duck when making 23 appearances for Forest in 1997-98. He also scored his first goal, direct from a corner kick, the ball going in off the 'keeper at Walsall in the Coca Cola Cup. More of a forward than a defender previously, Dave Bassett recognised his defensive qualities, using him at left back and at centre half, and his impressive form saw him represent the Nationwide U21 side against its Italian counterparts at Charlton in March. Won a first division championship medal as Forest went back to the Premiership at the first attempt.

Nottingham F (From trainee on 2/6/92) FL 4+14 FLC 2+2/1 FAC 1
Burnley (Loaned on 29/12/94) FL 4
Bristol Rov (Loaned on 8/1/96) FL 4
Bristol Rov (Loaned on 28/3/96) FL 9+1
Gillingham (Loaned on 18/10/96) FL 10 FLC 2 Others 1
Watford (Loaned on 24/1/97) FL 3
Watford (Loaned on 14/3/97) FL 12

ARMSTRONG Gordon **Ian**
Born: Newcastle, 15 July 1967
Height: 6'0" Weight: 12.11
Club Honours: Div 3 '88

In his second season at Gigg Lane, Gordon was a regular in Bury's first division side of 1997-98, initially filling in at the problem left-back spot but latterly switching to a sweeper's role and looking extremely comfortable in that position. Once, a regular goalscorer from midfield, he also scored two goals for the Shakers, strangely in their first and last league fixtures of the campaign.

Sunderland (From apprentice on 10/7/85) FL 331+18/50 FLC 25+4/3 FAC 19/4 Others 18+1/4
Bristol C (Loaned on 24/8/95) FL 6

Northampton T (Loaned on 5/1/96) FL 4/1 Others 1
Bury (Free on 16/7/96) FL 49+20/4 FLC 5/1 FAC 2+1 Others 1+1

ARMSTRONG Paul George
Born: Dublin, 5 October 1978
Height: 5'10" Weight: 10.3
International Honours: Ei: U21-1

A product of the Cherry Orchard club of Dublin, and a former trainee, Paul was a regular member of Brighton and Hove Albion's first team squad throughout last season. Employed mainly in a substitute role, the 19-year-old midfielder was troubled with a recurring back injury but, after being drafted into the Republic of Ireland U21 squad for the match with the Czech Republic in March, he was rewarded with a new contract by manager Brian Horton.

Brighton & Hove A (From trainee on 10/7/97) FL 12+8 Others 1

ARNOTT Andrew (Andy) John
Born: Chatham, 18 October 1973
Height: 6'1" Weight: 12.0

Signed by Fulham from Leyton Orient on a free transfer in the 1997 summer recess, Andy put in good performances in defence, midfield, and up front in the Capital League side, but had virtually no chance to make an impression in the first team, appearing from the bench just three times. Is a danger at set pieces and cool under pressure.

Gillingham (From trainee on 13/5/91) FL 50+23/12 FLC 2+3 FAC 10+2/1 Others 3+2
Leyton Orient (£15,000 on 25/1/96) FL 47+3/6 FLC 2 FAC 2 Others 1
Fulham (£23,000 on 17/6/97) FL 0+1 Others 0+2

ARPHEXAD Pegguy Michel
Born: Guadeloupe, 18 May 1973
Height: 6'2" Weight: 13.5

Signed as a free agent from Racing Club, Lens in August 1997, to replace the departed Kevin Poole, Pegguy acted as cover for Kasey Keller whenever the American was away on international duty and proved a more than able deputy. Outstanding in his Leicester debut at Stamford Bridge last October, where it took a 25-yard screamer into the top corner to finally beat him, he never let the team down and might have been a contender for the French World Cup squad with more exposure.

Leicester C (Free from Racing Club on 20/8/97) PL 6

ASABA Carl
Born: London, 28 January 1973
Height: 6'2" Weight: 13.0

Signed by Reading manager, Terry Bullivant, for a club record fee just before the start of last season, the tall, former Brentford striker struggled to justify the amount spent, when notching a total of 12 goals from 42 appearances. Despite failing to win over the fans, who expected a lot more aggression from the powerfully-built player, his potential was shown, however, in the home game against Sunderland, when scored two well-taken goals in a 4-0 win, the club's best performance of 1997-98.

Unfortunate to miss the latter part of the campaign with an achilles injury, Carl will be looking to come back with a bang in 1998-99.

Brentford (Free from Dulwich Hamlet on 9/8/94) FL 49+5/25 FLC 5 FAC 4 Others 7/2
Colchester U (Loaned on 16/2/95) FL 9+3/2
Reading (£800,000 on 7/8/97) FL 31+1/8 FLC 7/3 FAC 3/1

Carl Asaba

ASANOVIC Aljosa
Born: Croatia, 14 December 1965
Height: 6'0" Weight: 12.6
International Honours: Croatia: 44

A Croatian international midfielder who occupied a left-sided position throughout most of 1996-97, and whose main strengths lie in incisive passing and in dictating the pace of the game, his tendency to slow things down, however, did not really fit in with the way in which Jim Smith saw the tactical side of the game heading last season. Thus Aljosa struggled to make the first team squad, despite his ability at organising set-piece moves. The more technical style of Italy's Serie "A" looked a more likely home for his talents and in December he moved to Napoli for £350,000 and, despite their ultimate relegation, he managed to secure a place in the Croatian squad for France '98.

Derby Co (£950,000 from Hadjuk Split on 11/7/96) PL 37+1/7 FLC 2 FAC 3

ASHBEE Ian
Born: Birmingham, 6 September 1976
Height: 6'1" Weight: 13.7
International Honours: E: Yth

Featured at Cambridge in 1997-98 as a wing back, and also operated as a centre half, but when manager, Roy McFarland, changed to a 4-3-3 system he moved into midfield. Despite missing the early part of the campaign through injury, he gave the midfield extra strength and aggression, and showed his shooting power with an unstoppable 20 yarder into the top-right-hand corner against Mansfield in February.

Derby Co (From trainee on 9/11/94) FL 1
Cambridge U (Free on 13/12/96) FL 43+2/1 FAC 4 Others 1

ASHBY Barry John
Born: Park Royal, 21 November 1970
Height: 6'2" Weight: 13.8
Club Honours: FAYC '89

An excellent buy from Brentford during the summer of 1997, after an unsteady start for Gillingham, Barry settled into his central defensive position well and proved to be just the man the club needed. Steady and reliable, and good in the air, he was one of the players that made the run to the play-off position possible.

Watford (From trainee on 1/12/88) FL 101+13/3 FLC 6 FAC 4 Others 2+1
Brentford (Signed on 22/3/94) FL 119+2/4 FLC 11 FAC 9/1 Others 11+1
Gillingham (£140,000 on 8/8/97) FL 43 FLC 1 FAC 2 Others 1

ASHCROFT Lee
Born: Preston, 7 September 1972
Height: 5'10" Weight: 11.10
International Honours: E: U21-1

Described as "a scorer of great goals, rather than a great goalscorer", Lee nevertheless ended last season as Preston's leading scorer. Able to play on either flank, as an out-and-out striker, or just behind the front two, he recorded his first hat trick for the club against Fulham in November and his value to the side was graphically illustrated

Lee Ashcroft

during the following 12 matches, 11 of which he missed, when the team nose-dived down the table. Having rejected a putative move to neighbours Wigan in March, he celebrated by scoring his 50th career goal in his 150th FL game for North End against Wigan at the end of deadline week.

Preston NE (From trainee on 16/7/91) FL 78+13/13 FLC 3 FAC 5 Others 6+2/1
West Bromwich A (£250,000 on 1/8/93) FL 66+24/17 FLC 2+3 FAC 3+1/1 Others 8+3
Notts Co (Loaned on 28/3/96) FL 4+2
Preston NE (£150,000 on 5/9/96) FL 63+1/22 FLC 4 FAC 5/5 Others 2+1

ASHTON Jonathan (Jon) Frank
Born: Plymouth, 4 August 1979
Height: 5'11" Weight: 11.4

A young first-year professional who was limited to just seven minutes of first team experience for Plymouth in 1997-98, when coming on as a sub in round one of the Coca Cola Cup, Jon then went back to the reserves to continue his development. Tall, athletic, and very quick, he is a dominant centre back who wants to win the ball. He also wants to succeed in the game, working hard all day to that end, and has a great attitude.

Plymouth Arg (From trainee on 29/7/97) FLC 0+1

ASKEY John Colin
Born: Stoke, 4 November 1964
Height: 6'0" Weight: 12.2
Club Honours: GMVC '95, '97; FAT '96
International Honours: E: SP-1

As the longest serving player at Macclesfield, John proved equally at home as a striker or as a midfielder, cum winger in 1997-98, despite missing six weeks through strained knee ligaments. "Gentleman" John showed himself to be tenacious in the tackle, held the ball up, turned his man well to hammer the ball goalwards, and looked at ease in Town's first season in the Football League.*

Macclesfield T (Free from Milton U during 1987-88) FL 37+2/6 FLC 2 Others 1

ASPIN Neil
Born: Gateshead, 12 April 1965
Height: 6'0" Weight: 13.10
Club Honours: AMC '93

The Port Vale captain had another excellent season at centre half in 1997-98, but two bad injuries knocked over 20 games from his campaign. Fearsome in the challenge, a measure of his worth was proved by his departure at Oxford with a knee injury that began a run of six successive defeats, coupled to his return which saw the team achieve a goalless draw at Arsenal in the FA Cup! A dislocated shoulder sustained against Norwich in February ended his season early.

Leeds U (From apprentice on 6/10/82) FL 203+4/5 FLC 9/1 FAC 17 Others 11
Port Vale (£200,000 on 28/7/89) FL 315+3/3 FLC 19 FAC 23 Others 18

ASPINALL Warren
Born: Wigan, 13 September 1967
Height: 5'9" Weight: 12.8
Club Honours: AMC '85, '97
International Honours: E: Yth

A bustling midfielder who joined Brentford from Carlisle last November, Warren was quick to form a busy midfield trio with Charlie Oatway and Glenn Cockerill, and also chipped in with an occasional goal. Deputised as captain when Jamie Bates was absent and showed good skills and passing ability to go with endeavour.

Wigan Ath (From apprentice on 31/8/85) FL 21+12/10 FLC 1 FAC 2+3/2 Others 1+5/2
Everton (£150,000 on 4/2/86) FL 0+7 FLC 0+1 Others 0+2
Wigan Ath (Loaned on 6/2/86) FL 18/12 Others 2/2
Aston Villa (£300,000 on 19/2/87) FL 40+4/4 FLC 4/2 FAC 1+1
Portsmouth (£315,000 on 26/8/88) FL 97+35/21 FLC 8+3/3 FAC 4+5/2 Others 6+1/2
Bournemouth (Loaned on 27/8/93) FL 4+2/1
Swansea C (Loaned on 14/10/93) FL 5 Others 1
Bournemouth (£20,000 on 31/12/93) FL 26+1/8 FLC 4 FAC 1 Others 1
Carlisle U (Free on 8/3/95) FL 99+8/12 FLC 8/3 FAC 6 Others 10+1/1
Brentford (£50,000 on 21/11/97) FL 24/3 Others 1

ASPRILLA Hinestroza **Faustino (Tino)** Hernan
Born: Tulua, Colombia, 10 November 1969
Height: 5'9" Weight: 11.9
International Honours: Colombia: 39

The first Colombian to play in English football, Tino proved to be a maverick entertainer who captivated the Newcastle public with his delightful skills and his unpredictability, his deceptive pace providing the basis for many attacks, and his tight control and balance making him a real threat in the box. Expected by many to be one of the early 1997-98 departures, he took the opportunity afforded by Alan Shearer's injury and Les Ferdinand's transfer to demonstrate that he is one of the few South Americans to adjust successfully to English football, scoring twice against Wednesday in the opening fixture, one of which being the Premiership's first goal of the season after 98 seconds. Always at his best in big games, he scored twice in the pre-season friendly against Juventus, but really made his mark with a scintillating display in the home Champions League match against Barcelona, with a hat-trick, including two stunning headers. Unfortunately, he incurred a stomach injury in the tie in Kiev in October and needed an operation, which put him on the sidelines for over two months, and although returning to the side in December he lacked sharpness. He subsequently returned to Parma in January for £6.5 million, stating that he believed his international career would be better served by playing in Serie "A". Was a member of Colombia's final 22 that took part in the World Cup Finals in France during the summer.

Newcastle U (£7,500,000 from Parma, via Cueuta Deportivo and Atletico Nacional de Medellin, on 10/2/96) PL 36+12/8 FLC 2 FAC 1 Others 11+1/9

ATHERTON Peter
Born: Orrell, 6 April 1970
Height: 5'11" Weight: 13.12
International Honours: E: U21-1; Sch

1997-98 was another good, battling season for this hard-working Sheffield Wednesday defensive player. Really at ease in his midfield holding role which, coupled with his captaincy of the team, make him a key ingredient in the playing system, he tried to help out in attacking situations last season, adding his heading skills at set pieces. However, it was his solid tackling and fine reading of the game that made him invaluable to the team. Although other players supply the craft and the flair, Peter can also create when on song, having been an excellent servant to the club since he joined from Coventry four seasons ago.

Wigan Ath (From trainee on 12/2/88) FL 145+4/1 FLC 8 FAC 7 Others 12+1
Coventry C (£300,000 on 23/8/91) F/PL 113+1 FLC 4 FAC 2
Sheffield Wed (£800,000 on 1/6/94) PL 141/6 FLC 11 FAC 11

ATKIN Paul Anthony
Born: Nottingham, 3 September 1969
Height: 6'0" Weight: 12.11
International Honours: E: Yth; Sch

An experienced central defender who joined Scarborough from local rivals York City during the 1997 close season, and did a good job as back-up to both Gary Bennett and

Jason Rockett. Strong and dependable, he contributed to Boro's push for promotion, but was then released on a free transfer at the end of the campaign.

Notts Co (From trainee on 6/7/87)
Bury (Signed on 22/3/89) FL 14+7/1 Others 2+1
York C (Free on 1/7/91) FL 131+22/3 FLC 5+4 FAC 6 Others 10+1
Leyton Orient (Loaned on 21/3/97) FL 5
Scarborough (Free on 5/8/97) FL 26+8/1 FLC 1+1 FAC 1 Others 2+1

ATKINS Mark Nigel
Born: Doncaster, 14 August 1968
Height: 6'0" Weight: 13.2
Club Honours: PL '95
International Honours: E: Sch

Mark continued to be a versatile member of the Wolves' staff in 1997-98, playing in midfield on the opening day when he made a nice pass inside the defender to create a goal. When Keith Curle missed eight matches early on, he was captain for most of them, despite having to play an unfamiliar centre-back role and not being 100 per-cent fit. A spell at full back and two outings on the left side, while missing only one of the first 19 fixtures before being briefly dropped, was followed by a 12-game stint during which he showed his best form in midfield, prior to slipping out of contention and coming back for the final three games.

Scunthorpe U (From juniors on 9/7/86) FL 45+5/2 FLC 3+1 FAC 5 Others 6+1
Blackburn Rov (£45,000 on 16/6/88) F/PL 224+33/35 FLC 20+2/4 FAC 11+3 Others 17+2/1
Wolverhampton W (£1,000,000 on 21/9/95) FL 100+11/8 FLC 12/2 FAC 9+1 Others 2/1

ATKINSON Brian
Born: Darlington, 19 January 1971
Height: 5'10" Weight: 12.5
International Honours: E: U21-6

In his second full season with Darlington, Brian was again marred by a succession of niggling injuries in 1997-98 and played in only two thirds of the games, as he had in 1996-97. Still an aggressive, ball-winning midfielder, he scored three goals, including a crucial penalty at Solihull Borough in the FA Cup replay.

Sunderland (From trainee on 21/7/89) FL 119+22/4 FLC 8+2 FAC 13/2 Others 2+3
Carlisle U (Loaned on 19/1/96) FL 2 Others 1
Darlington (Free on 10/8/96) FL 54+8/5 FLC 5 FAC 4+1/1 Others 2/1

ATKINSON Graeme
Born: Hull, 11 November 1971
Height: 5'8" Weight: 11.3
Club Honours: Div 3 '96

The left-sided utility player failed to make the most of his limited first team opportunities at Preston in 1997-98, despite performing well in the reserves at left back, or in wide midfield, and was loaned to Rochdale before signing for Brighton in March. Graeme had been Brian Horton's first acquisition on his appointment as manager and he proved a valuable addition to the staff, when making an impressive debut, thumping a 20 yarder against a post in the goalless draw with Hartlepool United at Gillingham. Was released during the summer.

Hull C (From trainee on 6/5/90) FL 129+20/23 FLC 6+3/2 FAC 4+1/1 Others 9
Preston NE (Signed on 7/10/94) FL 63+16/6 FLC 5/1 FAC 2+1 Others 5/2
Rochdale (Loaned on 12/12/98) FL 5+1
Brighton & Hove A (Free on 5/3/98) FL 9

ATKINSON Patrick (Paddy) Darren
Born: Singapore, 22 May 1970
Height: 5'9" Weight: 11.6

Paddy made only a handful of senior appearances for York City in 1997-98, having started the campaign as first-choice left back. After losing his place, owing to a tactical switch, from then on the consistency of Wayne Hall, and later, on loan Neil Thompson, kept him mostly on the sidelines before he was released during the summer.

Hartlepool U (Free from Sheffield U juniors on 23/8/87) FL 9+12/3 FLC 0+1 FAC 2 Others 1+1 (Free to Gateshead during 1990 close season)
York C (Free from Workington, via Newcastle Blue Star and Barrow on 17/11/95) FL 36+5 FAC 3+1 Others 4+1

AUNGER Geoffrey (Geoff) Edward
Born: Red Deer, Canada, 4 February 1968
Height: 5'8" Weight: 11.10
International Honours: Canada: 40

A Canadian international midfielder, Geoff was on trial at Stockport when an injury crisis forced him into the squad for the league game at Nottingham Forest last December. Although managing 20 anonymous minutes as a substitute, his signature was not pursued and he returned to play in the North American leagues.

Luton T (Free from Vancouver 86ers on 6/9/93) FL 5/1 (Free to Sudbury T on 12/7/94)
Chester C (Free on 16/12/94) FL 1+4 (Freed in January 1995)
Stockport Co (Free from Seattle Sounders on 19/12/97) FL 0+1

AUSTIN Kevin Levi
Born: Hackney, 12 February 1973
Height: 6'0" Weight: 14.0

A Lincoln central defender whose performances earned him tremendous respect in the third division during 1997-98. Good in the air, and surprisingly fast on the ground for his size, he was an ever present, apart from missing the Coca Cola Cup tie at Burnley.

Leyton Orient (Free from Saffron Walden on 19/8/93) FL 101+8/3 FAC 6 Others 7
Lincoln C (£30,000 on 31/7/96) FL 90 FLC 7 FAC 4 Others 2

AWFORD Andrew (Andy) Terence
Born: Worcester, 14 July 1972
Height: 5'10" Weight: 12.0
International Honours: E: U21-9; Yth; Sch

Andy started last season unable to hold down a first team place at Portsmouth, but soon regained it to become one of the more consistent performers during the campaign, and it was noticeable that his performances dramatically improved on the arrival of Alan Ball as manager. His passing and reading of the game was one of the reasons for an improved defensive record, while his ability to coax the youngsters was paramount. Captained the team in the absence of Adrian Whitbread.

Portsmouth (From trainee on 24/7/89) FL 228+14/1 FLC 23+1 FAC 16 Others 12

'Savings made easy with the World's No.1'

Last season the Nationwide Football League saw some spectacular saves.

It pays to decide...

Contact your local Nationwide Building Society branch at
Nationwide House, Pipers Way, Swindon, SN38 1NW
Telephone: (01793) 513513
http://www.nationwide.co.uk

The World's No.1 Building Society

B

BAARDSEN Espen
Born: San Rafael, USA, 7 December 1977
Height: 6'5" Weight: 13.13
Having made his first appearance of last season as a substitute in the FAC third round home tie against Fulham, Espen became quickly acquainted to the Premiership with a baptism of fire at Old Trafford. Although Spurs were defeated 2-0, the towering youngster pulled off a string of line saves which saved the club from a heavy defeat, and being particularly agile for a 'keeper of such height he soon won the White Hart Lane crowd over, and proved himself a worthy understudy to Ian Walker. Mature in his ability to read the game, and organise the defence, he is sure to create a great deal of interest in the near future, both at club and international level. *Stop Press:* Selected as Norway's third-choice goalkeeper in France during the summer, Espen, who broke a finger playing for the "B" side against Scotland towards the end of the season, failed to make an appearance as the side went out in the second round.
Tottenham H (Free from San Francisco All Blacks on 16/7/96) PL 10+1 FAC 2+1

BABAYARO Celestine
Born: Nigeria, 29 August 1978
Height: 5'8" Weight: 10.4
Club Honours: FLC '98
International Honours: Nigeria: 10
Quiz question: Which Olympic gold medallist played Premiership football last season? Answer: Celestine Babayaro of Chelsea. Famous for his celebratory somersaults when his team scores, "Baba" is a perfect example of the term "teenage prodigy". After starring in Nigeria's victorious U17 World Youth tournament in 1993, the 15-year old was snapped up by the Belgian giants, Anderlecht. Signed by Chelsea during the summer of 1997, he had a particularly unfortunate first year in English football, picking up a leg injury in a pre-season friendly which kept him sidelined until October, then making 13 first team appearances over the next two months before breaking a bone in his foot against Tottenham in early December, which ended his campaign. A vital member of Nigeria's World Cup team, he is a talented, left-sided player who can perform either at full back or in midfield and, when fit, will provide Chelsea with a strong partnership on the left flank with Graeme le Saux, another attack-minded player. *Stop Press:* Played in three of Nigeria's four World Cup games in France during the summer, before Denmark brought the Africans' run in the tournament to an end.
Chelsea (£2,250,000 from Anderlecht on 20/6/97) PL 8 FLC 1+1 Others 2+1

BABB Philip (Phil) Andrew
Born: Lambeth, 30 November 1970
Height: 6'0" Weight: 12.3

Club Honours: FLC '95
International Honours: Ei: 25; B-1
Still a major player, despite sometimes appearing out of position for Liverpool in 1997-98, Phil remains a defender of the highest order, only enforced absences forcing him out of action. And, while there are those who think that his role is purely a destructive one, it is positively constructive because, when winning the ball, he is more often than not able to find the front runners with pin-point accuracy and thus set the side up for a dangerous attack. Continuing to play for the Republic, in October it was reported that he had agreed a new two-and-a-half-year contract with the club worth a staggering £1 million a year.
Millwall (From trainee on 25/4/89)
Bradford C (Free on 10/8/90) FL 73+7/14 FLC 5+1 FAC 3 Others 3+1
Coventry C (£500,000 on 21/7/92) PL 70+7/3 FLC 5/1 FAC 2
Liverpool (£3,600,000 on 1/9/94) PL 100+3/1 FLC 16 FAC 11 Others 9+1

BADDELEY Lee Matthew
Born: Cardiff, 12 July 1974
Height: 6'1" Weight: 12.7
International Honours: W: U21-2; Yth
Lee had a frustrating season for Exeter in 1997-98, being in and out of the first team. However, when he played he equipped himself well in the centre of the defence, using his strength and height to great advantage, and will be looking for an extended run in 1998-99.
Cardiff C (From trainee on 13/8/91) FL 112+21/1 FLC 4+2 FAC 8 Others 24
Exeter C (Free on 6/2/97) FL 37+6/1 FAC 1 Other 0+1

BAIANO Francesco
Born: Napoli, Italy, 24 February 1968
Height: 5'7" Weight: 10.7
International Honours: Italy: 2
Signed from Serie "A" side, Fiorentina, during the 1997 close season, the diminutive Italian international, who was bought as a quality link-man between midfield and attack, quickly settled into a role where he had the ability to create chances both for himself and others. Undoubtedly a major success in his first campaign, he ended up as the club's second-top scorer with 13 goals, despite spending time out with injury early on. Having started his scoring off with four in three consecutive early games, and although the rate slowed in the last third, he can look back with some satisfaction, especially at a brace at Leicester, against one of the Premiership's toughest defences.
Derby Co (£1,500,000 from Fiorentina on 8/8/97) PL 30+3/12 FLC 1 FAC 2/1

BAILEY Dennis Lincoln
Born: Lambeth, 13 November 1965
Height: 5'10" Weight: 11.6
Having scored just one goal in 13 outings for Gillingham last season, Dennis was released and signed for Lincoln on a non-contract basis on transfer deadline day. A squad player, used as a striker or in midfield, his most important contribution was to score the last-minute equaliser which earned City a point at Darlington.

Fulham (Free from Barking on 8/11/86)
Crystal Palace (£10,000 from Farnborough T on 2/12/87) FL 0+5/1
Bristol Rov (Loaned on 27/2/89) FL 17/9 Others 1+1/1
Birmingham C (£80,000 on 3/8/89) FL 65+10/23 FLC 6/2 FAC 6 Others 3+3
Bristol Rov (Loaned on 28/3/91) FL 6/1
Queens Park R (£175,000 on 2/7/91) FL 32+7/10 FLC 5/3 FAC 1+1 Others 1
Charlton Ath (Loaned on 29/10/93) FL 0+4 Others 2
Watford (Loaned on 24/3/94) FL 2+6/4
Brentford (Loaned on 26/1/95) FL 6/3
Gillingham (£25,000 on 15/8/95) FL 63+25/11 FLC 7+2/1 FAC 4+1/1 Others 1
Lincoln C (Free on 26/3/98) FL 1+4/1

BAILEY John Andrew
Born: Lambeth, 6 May 1969
Height: 5'8" Weight: 10.8
John had an excellent season in 1997-98, playing on the right-hand side of Bournemouth's midfield, the pinnacle being his goal at Wembley in the Auto Windscreens Shield final. A wholly committed player who will run at defenders and deliver numerous crosses during a game, he will also undertake his defensive duties with relish, giving 100 per-cent effort for 90 minutes.
Bournemouth (£40,000 from Enfield on 5/7/95) FL 106+10/6 FLC 6+1 FAC 5+1 Others 8+1/1

BAILEY Mark
Born: Stoke, 12 August 1976
Height: 5'9" Weight: 10.12
Mark followed up his debut the previous term by gaining a place in the Rochdale side right from the off in 1997-98. Appearing mostly on the right of midfield, though he can also play at full back, his hard-running style made him a virtual ever present in the squad, except for spells out through injury or suspension.
Stoke C (From trainee on 12/7/94)
Rochdale (Free on 10/10/96) FL 37+11 FLC 2 FAC 1 Others 3

BAIRD Andrew Crawford
Born: East Kilbride, 18 January 1979
Height: 5'10" Weight: 12.6
Andrew, a young striker, impressed in his handful of reserve appearances in 1997-98 and made his senior debut with a substitute appearance in the final home game against Chesterfield. He then appeared briefly in the final game, at Walsall, and, seen as a very bright prospect, he was rewarded with a contract.
Wycombe W (From trainee on 18/3/98) FL 0+2

BAIRD Ian James
Born: Rotherham, 1 April 1964
Height: 6'1" Weight: 12.12
Club Honours: Div 2 '90
International Honours: E: Sch
Brighton and Hove Albion's popular skipper missed the opening month of last season through suspension and injury, but returned to the side for a nine-match spell before undergoing an operation to cure a cartilage problem in his right knee. Unfortunately, the surgery proved unsuccessful and the robust striker was forced into retirement from the

full-time game in December. On leaving the Albion, Ian joined Salisbury City as player/coach, but soon departed for Hong Kong to assist the Instant Dict club.

Southampton (From apprentice on 5/4/82) FL 20+2/5 FLC 1+1
Cardiff C (Loaned on 1/11/80) FL 12/6
Newcastle U (Loaned on 1/12/84) FL 4+1/1
Leeds U (£75,000 on 10/3/85) FL 84+1/33 FLC 4 FAC 5/4 Others 7
Portsmouth (£285,000 on 12/8/87) FL 20/1 FLC 1 FAC 1
Leeds U (£120,000 on 4/3/88) FL 76+1/17 FLC 5/1 FAC 3/2 Others 6
Middlesborough (£500,000 on 29/1/90) FL 60+3/19 FLC 5+1 FAC 3/1 Others 4/1
Heart of Midlothian (£400,000 on 31/7/91) SL 64/15 SLC 5/2 SC 7/1 Others 3/1
Bristol C (£295,000 on 6/7/93) FL 45+12/11 FLC 3 FAC 2/1 Others 2
Plymouth Arg (Free on 29/9/95) FL 24+3/6 FAC 1+1/1
Brighton & Hove A (£35,000 on 31/7/96) FL 43+1/14 FLC 2 FAC 1+1 Others 1

BAKER Joseph (Joe) Philip
Born: London, 19 April 1977
Height: 5'8" Weight: 10.4

Joe proved to be a real crowd favourite at Leyton Orient in 1997-98, and something of a super sub who normally entered the field of play in the second half when defences were tiring, in an effort to change the course of the game. A good young right winger, who will be looking for a regular place in the first team this coming term, he added goalscoring to his armoury with a handful of strikes, including a superb 25-yard free kick at Bolton.

Leyton Orient (Free from Charlton Ath juniors on 24/5/95) FL 23+48/3 FLC 1+3/2 FAC 0+3 Others 1+3

BAKER David Paul
Born: Newcastle, 5 January 1963
Height: 6'1" Weight: 13.2

Hartlepool's big, powerful striker provided the necessary experience up front in the first half of last season and was a regular goalscorer. Unfortunately, a seemingly minor injury at Scunthorpe was subsequently found to be a broken leg, and although he planned an early return, there were complications with an infection causing him much pain. Thus, he was forced to concentrate on his other role as first team coach, and it was only at the end of the campaign that he was able to make a comeback in the reserve team.*

Southampton (£4,000 from Bishop Auckland on 1/7/84)
Carlisle U (Free on 2/7/85) FL 66+5/11 FLC 4/1 FAC 3 Others 2+1
Hartlepool U (Free on 31/7/87) FL 192+5/67 FLC 12/4 FAC 16/6 Others 16/5
Motherwell (£77,500 on 1/8/92) SL 5+4/1 SLC 1
Gillingham (£40,000 on 7/1/93) FL 58+4/16 FAC 5/1 Others 2
York C (£15,000 on 1/10/94) FL 36+12/18 FLC 2+2/2 FAC 3 Others 5+1/1
Torquay U (£25,000 on 19/1/96) FL 30/8 FLC 2/3
Scunthorpe U (£15,000 on 4/10/96) FL 21/9 FAC 3/5 Others 2
Hartlepool U (Signed on 27/3/97) FL 22/7 FLC 2/1

BAKER Steven Richard
Born: Pontefract, 8 September 1978
Height: 5'10" Weight: 11.11
International Honours: Ei: U21-2

This hard-tackling young Middlesbrough defender was pressed into first team action in 1997-98 through injuries to established players and suffered the wrath of officialdom for enthusiastic challenges on more than one occasion. However, highly regarded on Teeside, he will benefit from his experience and emerge as a very formidable talent, having also been recognised at U21 level by the Republic of Ireland.

Middlesbrough (From trainee on 24/7/97) FL 5+1 FLC 2+2 FAC 0+1

BALDRY Simon
Born: Huddersfield, 12 February 1976
Height: 5'11" Weight: 11.6

Simon made the breakthrough at the beginning of last season, making valuable contributions on either wing for Huddersfield, his pace, good passing skills, and accurate crossing taking the eye. Although this good form was prematurely cut short due to injury, he got back to full fitness and, following impressive reserve displays, was recalled to the first team in the penultimate home game against West Bromwich Albion, scoring the winning goal which assured Town's first division safety.

Huddersfield T (From trainee on 14/7/94) FL 31+22/3 FLC 3+2 Others 1+2/1

BALL Kevin Anthony
Born: Hastings, 12 November 1964
Height: 5'10" Weight: 12.6
Club Honours: Div 1 '96

Sunderland's inspirational captain missed two months of the promotion campaign, following an injury sustained at Stoke last October, but returned to play an important part in the run in. A tremendous tackler, and leader, Kevin notched a vital goal at Wolves in February, which pushed the club into the top three in division one for the first time in the season. Another truly important goal for both him and the Rokerites came in the first leg of the play-off semi final at Sheffield United, a terrific left-foot volley giving the team something to build upon.

Portsmouth (Free from Coventry C juniors on 6/10/82) FL 96+9/4 FLC 8+1 FAC 8 Others 6
Sunderland (£350,000 on 16/7/90) P/FL 281+5/19 FLC 19+2/3 FAC 15 Others 7/2

BALL Michael John
Born: Liverpool, 2 October 1979
Height: 5'10" Weight 11.2
International Honours: E: Yth

An unqualified success in 1997-98, Michael established himself as a first team regular at Everton, despite still qualifying for the club's successful youth team. Sharp tackling, quick, good in the air, and possessing composure well in advance of his 18 years, he showed that he was equally at home in central defence or at left back. Making his first appearance of the season against the champions elect, Arsenal, he celebrated with a goal in a 2-2 draw, and his following play was so good that the

manager, Howard Kendall, cited his emergence as the reason behind his decision to sell the England left back, Andy Hinchcliffe. After two midfield appearances over Christmas, he reverted to left-wing back against Newcastle on 4 January, and made 18 consecutive appearances there until the end of the season. Already an England U18 international, the youngster seems a certainty for U21 honours this coming season, while his former team mate, Hinchcliffe, has already tipped him for a full international call up if he maintains his current progress.

Everton (From trainee on 17/10/96) PL 23+7/1 FLC 1+1 FAC 1

Michael Ball

BALMER Stuart Murray
Born: Falkirk, 20 September 1969
Height: 6'0" Weight: 12.11
International Honours: S: Yth; Sch

A strong, right-footed Charlton central defender, who can also play at full back, Stuart is excellent in the air, a good distributor of the ball, and often scores important goals from corners and set pieces. Found his first team opportunities limited in 1997-98 due to injury and the consistent form of Richard Rufus and Phil Chapple, and later on Eddie Youds, but can always be relied upon to perform well when called into the side.

Glasgow Celtic (From juniors in 1987)
Charlton Ath (£120,000 on 24/8/90) FL 201+26/8 FLC 15 FAC 9+1 Others 11+1

BANGER Nicholas (Nicky) Lee
Born: Southampton, 25 February 1971
Height: 5'10" Weight: 11.6

Signed from Oldham during the 1997 close season, Nicky started 1997-98 alongside Nigel Jemson and the two worked well together, despite the tricky striker having to wait until the start of October for his first league goal for Oxford, a cracker at West

Bromwich. Unfortunately, a back injury sidelined him for a long spell around the turn of the year and, on his return, he had to battle with United's promising youngsters to regain his place. Never a prolific marksman, just four goals in the campaign, but a difficult player to mark around the edge of the box.

Southampton (From trainee on 25/4/89) F/PL 18+37/8 FLC 2+2/3 FAC 0+2 Others 1
Oldham Ath (£250,000 on 4/10/94) FL 44+20/10 FLC 6/1 FAC 2+1 Others 0+1
Oxford U (Free on 24/7/97) FL 18+10/3 FLC 4+1/1

BANKOLE Ademola
Born: Abeokuta, Nigeria, 9 September 1969
Height: 6'3" Weight: 13.0
Known as "George", and very popular with fans and players alike, as in 1996-97, the tall goalkeeper stood in for Jason Kearton in 1997-98, this time in four matches. Very unorthodox, but agile, he even saved a penalty in the 2-1 victory over Sheffield United and was hoping that his display was good enough for him to claim a Nigerian international spot. Certainly fit enough, his manager, Dario Gradi, says of him: "He has a superb physique and is awesome at times in training, and when he is not on the training pitch he is peddling away on the exercise bike". *Stop Press:* Signed by Queens Park Rangers for £50,000 on 18 May.

Doncaster Rov (Free from Nigerian football on 30/11/95)
Leyton Orient (Free on 27/12/95)
Crewe Alex (Free on 25/9/96) FL 6 FLC 1

BANKS Steven (Steve)
Born: Hillingdon, 9 February 1972
Height: 6'0" Weight: 13.2
Steve was ever present for Blackpool last season until a sending off at York City in March resulted in a one-match ban. Despite the goals against column not doing him justice during 1997-98, he made many important saves and was often the reason the Seasiders were able to eke out the odd result from a game that was slipping away from them.

West Ham U (From trainee on 24/3/90) Others 1
Gillingham (Free on 25/3/93) FL 67 FAC 7 Others 2
Blackpool (£60,000 on 18/8/95) FL 115 FLC 9 FAC 7 Others 10

BARACLOUGH Ian Robert
Born: Leicester, 4 December 1970
Height: 6'1" Weight: 12.2
Club Honours: Div 3 '98
International Honours: E: Yth
Ian was one of the players who benefited most from the new management regime at Notts County in 1997-98 as he established himself in the first team as a midfielder, cum centre back, following his displacement from the left-back slot. His good form soon attracted attention from clubs higher up the league, and he became a Queens Park Rangers player when signed by Ray Harford in March, making his Rangers' debut at Stoke City two days later. An enthusiastic player, who likes to get forward whenever possible, and a dead-ball specialist, this

wholehearted utility man aims to become a crowd favourite in 1998-99.

Leicester C (From trainee on 15/12/88) FAC 1 Others 0+1
Wigan Ath (Loaned on 22/3/90) FL 8+1/2
Grimsby T (Loaned on 21/12/90) FL 1+3
Grimsby T (Free on 13/8/91) FL 1
Lincoln C (Free on 21/8/92) FL 68+5/10 FLC 7/1 FAC 4 Others 7
Mansfield T (Free on 6/6/94) FL 47/5 FLC 7 FAC 4 Others 4
Notts Co (Signed on 13/10/95) FL 107+4/10 FLC 5+1/1 FAC 8 Others 2
Queens Park R (£50,000 on 19/3/98) FL 8

BARCLAY Dominic Alexander
Born: Bristol, 5 September 1976
Height: 5'10" Weight: 11.9
After making a goalscoring debut at the conclusion of the 1993-94 campaign, this talented Bristol City player has failed to make the impact expected in the intervening four years. Although a regular scorer for the reserves, he was again unable to find the net on his occasional first team appearances in 1997-98, and this coming season will be crucial for him with his current contract coming to an end.

Bristol C (From trainee on 3/7/95) FL 2+10 FLC 0+1 FAC 0+1

BARDSLEY David John
Born: Manchester, 11 September 1964
Height: 5'10" Weight: 11.7
International Honours: E: 2; Yth
After missing 20 months of first team football due to injuries, David made his comeback for Queens Park Rangers in the home game versus Sheffield United at the end of last February and went on to play in 12 of the final 13 matches, adding much-needed experience to a side attempting to avoid relegation. Released during the summer, at his peak, he was an attacking right back with an excellent right foot, who was brilliant at striking long balls behind the opposing full backs. Also very effective when getting forward to cross great early balls in the danger areas.

Blackpool (From apprentice on 5/11/82) FL 45 FLC 2/1 FAC 2
Watford (£150,000 on 23/11/83) FL 97+3/7 FLC 6/1 FAC 13+1/1 Others 2
Oxford U (£265,000 on 18/9/87) FL 74/7 FLC 12 FAC 5 Others 3
Queens Park R (£500,000 on 15/9/89) F/PL 252+1/4 FLC 20/1 FAC 19 Others 3/1

BARKER Richard Ian
Born: Sheffield, 30 May 1975
Height: 6'0" Weight: 13.5
International Honours: E: Yth; Sch
Signed on extended loan from Linfield last December in an effort to add some muscle to Brighton and Hove Albion's lightweight attack, the sturdy Yorkshireman quickly struck up a good understanding with another loan player, Paul Emblen, and played in ten successive matches, but failed to score a goal in a struggling side. When Emblen returned to Charlton Athletic at the beginning of February, Richard fell out of favour, before returning to the side and bagging his first two goals for the Seagulls in the final two fixtures.

Sheffield Wed (From trainee on 27/7/93 - Free to Linfield on 22/8/96)
Doncaster Rov (Loaned on 29/9/95) FL 5+1 Others 0+1
Brighton & Hove A (Loaned on 19/12/97) FL 15+2/2 Others 1

BARKER Simon
Born: Farnworth, 4 November 1964
Height: 5'9" Weight: 11.7
Club Honours: FMC '87
International Honours: E: U21-4
An attacking midfielder with an excellent footballing brain, 1997-98 was his testimonial season at Queens Park Rangers and though he was in and out of the side as the manager(s) varied their midfield options, he still gave 100 per-cent effort just as you would expect from a man of his calibre. Released during the summer, following a benefit game against the World Cup qualifiers, Jamaica, Simon may have lost some pace over the years but is still capable of opening up the tightest of defences. Scored three times last season, two of them coming from the penalty spot.

Blackburn Rov (From apprentice on 6/11/82) FL 180+2/35 FLC 11/4 FAC 12 Others 8/2
Queens Park R (£400,000 on 20/7/88) F/PL 291+24/33 FLC 29+2/5 FAC 22+1/3 Others 7

BARLOW Andrew (Andy) John
Born: Oldham, 24 November 1965
Height: 5'9" Weight: 11.1
Club Honours: Div 2 '91
Arriving from Blackpool on a free transfer during the 1997 close season, Andy quickly showed his former Premier League class in the left-back spot for Rochdale at the start of 1997-98, his overlapping runs being a feature of his play. However, niggling injuries, and loss of form of the whole team, in mid-term led to the number three shirt being shared with the much younger Dave Bayliss, before becoming the regular choice at the end of the campaign.

Oldham Ath (From juniors on 31/7/84) F/PL 245+16/5 FLC 22 FAC 19 Others 6
Bradford C (Loaned on 1/11/93) FL 2
Blackpool (Free on 13/9/95) FL 77+3/2 FLC 4+2 FAC 4 Others 6
Rochdale (Free on 7/7/97) FL 35+3 FLC 1 FAC 1

BARLOW Martin David
Born: Barnstaple, 25 June 1971
Height: 5'7" Weight: 10.3
A central midfielder who performed admirably for Plymouth throughout last season, Martin had a spell captaining the side in the absence of Mick Heathcote and led by example. Only 27 years old, but entering his testimonial year with Plymouth, his neat passing skills controlled most of the forward momentum for the side.*

Plymouth Arg (From trainee on 1/7/89) FL 231+31/19 FLC 7+1/2 FAC 12 Others 16+1

BARLOW Stuart
Born: Liverpool, 16 July 1968
Height: 5'10" Weight: 11.0
Having impressed as Oldham's leading scorer in 1997-98, it was a surprise when he was transferred to Wigan on transfer deadline day, especially as he was by far and away the Latics' leading front man.

However, Wigan did not complain as he scored his first goal for his new club in a 3-2 home win over first division bound Watford in April, and went on to pick up a couple more before the end of the campaign. With a good turn of pace, and the ability to hold the ball up well for others, he only once finished on a losing side.

Everton (Free from Sherwood Park on 6/6/90) F/PL 24+47/10 FLC 3+5/1 FAC 4+3/2 Others 0+2
Rotherham U (Loaned on 10/1/92) Others 0+1
Oldham Ath (£450,000 on 20/11/95) FL 78+15/31 FLC 5+1 FAC 6+1/1 Others 1
Wigan Ath (£45,000 on 26/3/98) FL 9/3

BARMBY Nicholas (Nick) Jonathan
Born: Hull, 11 February 1974
Height: 5'7" Weight: 11.3
International Honours: E: 10; B-2; U21-4; Yth; Sch

A supremely talented playmaker, Nick started last season out of favour with Everton manager, Howard Kendall, before showing how much he had won him over when he was made captain for three games in March. During an outstanding spell of form in January and February, there were suggestions that he would even reclaim his place in the England squad in time for the World Cup Finals, but after being called up for a "B" international against Chile, however, he sustained a groin injury which proved crucial. Although selected as an over-age player in an U21 international against Switzerland in March, and then again for a "B" international against Russia, it was too late to sway Glenn Hoddle. Suffered the misfortune of seeing a penalty saved during the club's crucial last match relegation decider against Coventry, but fortunately for him the miss made no difference as the Blues stayed up – just.

Tottenham H (From trainee on 9/4/91) PL 81+6/20 FLC 7+1/2 FAC 12+1/5
Middlesbrough (£5,250,000 on 8/8/95) PL 42/8 FLC 4/1 FAC 3/1
Everton (£5,750,000 on 2/11/96) PL 48+7/6 FLC 1+1/3 FAC 3/1

BARNARD Darren Sean
Born: Rintein, Germany, 30 November 1971
Height: 5'10" Weight: 12.0
International Honours: E: Sch. W: 1

Signed from Bristol City at the start of 1997-98, Darren made giant strides forward during the season with Barnsley, gaining confidence as the team developed, and making the left-wing back position his own. A good crosser of the ball, he possesses a fierce shot in open play, or from dead ball situations, and his improvement was seen further afield than Oakwell, when winning his first full international cap for Wales. He also scored four goals, including the winner, a delightful curling free kick that knocked Bolton out of the FA Cup, and two in succession, one of them being the equaliser in a 2-2 draw against Everton.

Chelsea (£50,000 from Wokingham T on 25/7/90) F/PL 18+11/2 FLC 1+1 FAC 1+1
Reading (Loaned on 18/11/94) FL 3+1
Bristol C (£175,000 on 6/10/95) FL 77+1/15 FLC 4/1 FAC 6 Others 6/1
Barnsley (£750,000 on 8/8/97) PL 33+2/2 FLC 3 FAC 5/2

BARNARD Mark
Born: Sheffield, 27 November 1975
Height: 5'11" Weight: 11.10

In his third year with Darlington in 1997-98, Mark lost his regular left-back spot to the Austrian, Franz Resch, and hardly appeared in the team at all during the last third, apart from when coming off the bench. A player who makes powerful surges down the flank, he failed to score for the second successive season, after getting three in his first.

Rotherham U (From trainee on 13/7/94. Free to Worksop T during 1995 close season)
Darlington (Free on 27/9/95) FL 102+8/3 FLC 7 FAC 5+1 Others 5

BARNES John Charles Bryan
Born: Jamaica, 7 November 1963
Height: 5'11" Weight: 12.7
Club Honours: FAYC '82; Div 1 '88, '90; FAC '89; CS '88, '89, FLC '95
International Honours: E: 79; U21-3

When John was given a free transfer by Liverpool in the summer of 1997, numerous Premiership clubs showed interest, recognising that his talent meant he still had much to offer at the top level. He chose to join his former colleague, Kenny Dalglish, on a two-year contract and, by so doing, provided the Newcastle squad with some welcome creative ability. Quickly establishing himself as a regular in the side, alternating between a midfield role and a striking one, netting regularly in the latter to become the club's leading scorer, and demonstrating his class, his cool head, and his thoughtful approach in the former, his experience was an asset, and he captained the side when Robert Lee and David Batty were absent. His strike at home to Bolton in January was his 200th league and cup goal in senior club football, and he also played a crucial part in setting Newcastle on the Wembley trail by crossing for another Liverpool colleague, Ian Rush, to score against old Merseyside adversaries, Everton, in the FA Cup third round, and by providing the cross from which Alan Shearer scored the winner in the semi final. Although losing his starting place on the arrival of Gary Speed, he remained a key member of the squad, often turning out to play a vital role as the club desperately tried to avoid the drop into the first division. As a point of interest, his subs' appearance at Wembley against Arsenal enabled him to achieve the rare feat of playing in FA Cup finals with three different teams.

Watford (Free from Sudbury Court on 14/7/81) FL 232+1/65 FLC 21/7 FAC 31/11 Others 7
Liverpool (£900,000 on 19/6/87) F/PL 310+4/84 FLC 26/3 FAC 51/16 Others 16/5
Newcastle U (Free on 14/8/97) PL 22+4/6 FLC 3 FAC 3+2 Others 5/1

BARNES Paul Lance
Born: Leicester, 16 November 1967
Height: 5'11" Weight: 12.9

Although breaking Burnley's scoring duck in the seventh game of last season, at York, he never recaptured his goal touch of the previous campaign and struggled before being exchanged for Huddersfield's Andy Payton in January. As a proven goalscorer,

and a fully qualified FA coach, Paul, who was originally a target for the Terriers three years ago, quickly settled into first team affairs after a short spell on the substitutes' bench, and contributed well to a new look, three-pronged attack. A skilful player, who holds the ball up well and possesses a good touch, he opened his account with a marvellous volley at his old club, Stoke City, before his season was cut short by an innocuous challenge in the home game against Crewe. The fans were delighted to see him back for the final two matches.

Notts Co (From apprentice on 16/11/85) FL 36+17/14 FAC 0+1 Others 4+6/5
Stoke C (£30,000 on 23/3/90) FL 10+14/3 FLC 0+2 Others 3+1/2
Chesterfield (Loaned on 8/11/90) FL 1 FAC 1/1
York C (£50,000 on 15/7/92) FL 147+1/76 FLC 10/5 FAC 5 Others 16/4
Birmingham C (£350,000 on 4/3/96) FL 15/7
Burnley (£350,000+ on 6/9/96) FL 63+2/30 FLC 5 FAC 5/1
Huddersfield T (Signed on 16/1/98) FL 11+4/1

BARNES Philip Kenneth
Born: Sheffield, 2 March 1979
Height: 6'1" Weight: 11.1

Having turned professional for Rotherham during the 1997 close season, within a month the young 'keeper had been transferred to Blackpool, but due to Steve Banks' excellent form he was only called upon once, a 3-1 defeat at Plymouth. Not to be faulted, Philip remains one for the future, possessing excellent shot-stopping ability and good hands.

Rotherham U (From trainee on 25/6/97) FL 2
Blackpool (£100,000 on 22/7/97) FL 1

BARNES Steven (Steve) Leslie
Born: Harrow, 5 January 1976
Height: 5'4" Weight: 10.5

The diminutive left winger was brought to the South Coast by Brighton manager, Steve Gritt, on a month loan period from Birmingham last January, to take over the role performed by the departed Paul McDonald. A two-footed player, with the ability to cross a fine ball, he impressed enough to have his loan spell extended to two months, but a subsequent further extension was refused and he returned to St Andrews at the end of March.

Birmingham C (£75,000 from Welling U on 9/10/95) FL 0+3 FLC 0+1 Others 0+1
Brighton & Hove A (Loaned on 23/1/98) FL 12

BARNESS Anthony
Born: Lewisham, 25 March 1973
Height: 5'10" Weight: 12.6

Having started last season as Charlton's first-choice left back, before losing his place to Mark Bowen in October, Anthony is a predominately right-footed defender who is equally comfortable in either full-back berth. Cool under pressure, with a liking to get forward, he scored the winning goal against Stoke City at the Britannia Stadium. Can also play in midfield.

Charlton Ath (From trainee on 6/3/91) FL 21+6/1 FLC 2 FAC 3 Others 1+1/1
Chelsea (£350,000 on 8/9/92) PL 12+2 FLC 2 Others 2+1
Middlesbrough (Loaned on 12/8/93) Others 1

Southend U (Loaned on 2/2/96) FL 5
Charlton Ath (£165,000 on 8/8/96) FL 66+8/3
FLC 5 FAC 2+1 Others 1+1

BARNETT David (Dave) Kwame
Born: Birmingham, 16 April 1967
Height: 6'1" Weight: 13.0
Club Honours: AMC '95; Div 2 '95
Previously with Birmingham, the big, strong central defender joined Port Vale on loan from Dunfermline last March and soon made his presence felt as a solid, if unspectacular defender. Improving with each game during the run-in that saw the team avoid relegation on the final day, he scored one goal, a header at Ipswich Town, before expressing a desire for a permanent move during the summer as he wished to return to his midland roots.
Colchester U (Signed from Windsor & Eton on 25/8/88) FL 19+1 FLC 2 FAC 3+2 Others 3 (Freed in June 1988)
West Bromwich A (Free from Edmonton Oilers on 13/10/89)
Walsall (Free on 17/7/90) FL 4+1 FLC 2 (Free to Kidderminster Harriers on 1/10/90)
Barnet (£10,000 on 29/2/92) FL 58+1/3 FLC 5 FAC 3 Others 5
Birmingham C (£150,000 on 20/12/93) FL 45+1 FLC 1 FAC 5 Others 8
Dunfermline (Free on 18/7/97) SL 21/1 SLC 3 SC 2
Port Vale (Loaned on 20/3/98) FL 8+1/1

BARNETT Jason Vincent
Born: Shrewsbury, 21 April 1976
Height: 5'9" Weight: 11.6
An enthusiastic Lincoln City right-wing back who was an ever present in 1997-98 until mid-December, when he developed a groin injury, he later underwent a hernia operation before returning to full fitness at the start of April. Was obviously delighted to be a leading light in a side that gained promotion to the second division, the club having been in the lower reaches since 1992.
Wolverhampton W (From trainee on 4/7/94)
Lincoln C (£5,000 on 26/10/95) FL 93+8/2 FLC 5 FAC 6 Others 5

BARNWELL-EDINBORO Jamie
Born: Hull, 26 December 1975
Height: 5'10" Weight: 11.6
1997-98 was a disappointing season for the striker as he struggled to break into the Cambridge first team, with his longest run being five games in March, just prior to being released. However, when the chances came he took them well, scoring two excellent goals against both Cardiff City and Colchester United.
Coventry C (From trainee on 1/7/94) PL 0+1
Swansea C (Loaned on 15/12/95) FL 2+2
Wigan Ath (Loaned on 2/2/96) FL 2+8/1
Cambridge U (Signed on 29/3/96) FL 52+10/12 FLC 2 FAC 2+1/1 Others 0+2

BARR William (Billy) Joseph
Born: Halifax, 21 January 1969
Height: 5'11" Weight: 10.8
Billy made a hesitant start to his Carlisle career in 1997-98, but his form soon improved and he looked equally at home in defence or midfield. A solid tackler, he took over the captaincy from Owen Archdeacon, when the latter returned to Scotland, and impressed with his determined attitude that at times deserved a better fate. Is expected to remain at Brunton Park for the 1998-99 campaign.
Halifax T (From trainee on 6/7/87) FL 178+18/13 FLC 8+1/2 FAC 11+1/2 Others 14+3
Crewe Alex (Free on 17/6/94) FL 73+12/6 FLC 2 FAC 4 Others 8+1
Carlisle U (Free on 18/7/97) FL 39/3 FLC 4 FAC 1 Others 2

Billy Barr

BARRAS Anthony (Tony)
Born: Billingham, 29 March 1971
Height: 6'0" Weight: 13.0
1997-98 was another good season for York City's captain, who was a virtual ever present until injury caused him to miss the last few games. Again a commanding figure at the heart of the defence, he took over the role of penalty taker which helped him to finish second top scorer with seven goals. Still highly thought of, City turned down a sizeable fee for his services from Wigan early in the New Year.
Hartlepool U (From trainee on 6/7/89) FL 9+3 FLC 2 FAC 1 Others 1
Stockport Co (Free on 23/7/90) FL 94+5/5 FLC 2 FAC 7 Others 19+1
Rotherham U (Loaned on 25/2/94) FL 5/1
York C (Signed on 18/7/94) FL 143+4/11 FLC 16/2 FAC 9/1 Others 7+1/1

BARRASS Matthew (Matt) Robert
Born: Bury, 28 February 1980
Height: 5'11" Weight: 12.0
Still a trainee, Matt was given his first team debut for Bury as a late substitute in the Coca Cola Cup tie at Sunderland last September, but soon afterwards suffered a particularly bad knee injury in a reserve game, which brought his season to a premature end. Having earlier shown impressive form in the reserve side, much is expected of this highly talented young defender.
Bury (Trainee) FLC 0+1

BARRETT Earl Delisser
Born: Rochdale, 28 April 1967
Height: 5'10" Weight: 11.7
Club Honours: Div 2 '91; FLC '94; CS '95
International Honours: E: 3; B-4; U21-4
A virtual ever present at Everton the season before, Earl found his place under constant threat in 1997-98 from a succession of right backs introduced by Howard Kendall, and was in and out of the side before Christmas, until being allowed to join Sheffield United on loan in January. He did well at Bramall Lane, making five appearances at full back and centre back, and was all set to sign for the club on a permanent basis until Sheffield Wednesday rushed through a deal for him at the end of February. Settled down well in place of the injured Ian Nolan, producing several sterling displays, while showing that he was still an excellent tackler, with few peers at man-to-man marking, and still had outstanding pace for a backline player, despite a knee injury which had given cause for concern at Goodison.
Manchester C (From trainee on 26/4/85) FL 2+1 FLC 1
Chester C (Loaned on 1/3/86) FL 12
Oldham Ath (£35,000 on 24/11/87) FL 181+2/7 FLC 20/1 FAC 14/1 Others 4
Aston Villa (£1,700,000 on 25/2/92) F/PL 118+1/1 FLC 15/1 FAC 9 Others 7
Everton (£1,700,000 on 30/1/95) PL 73+1 FLC 4 FAC 2 Others 3
Sheffield U (Loaned on 16/1/98) FL 5
Sheffield Wed (Free on 25/2/98) PL 10

BARRETT Scott
Born: Ilkeston, 2 April 1963
Height: 6'0" Weight: 14.4
Club Honours: GMVC '92; FAT '92
As Cambridge United's established first-choice goalkeeper, now in his third season with the club, Scott missed only a handful of games during 1997-98, taking him to a total of 119 league appearances. An old head behind a young defence, he was ever reliable and adapted well to changes in the

Tony Barras

Michael Barron

playing formation and, as in previous years, made some great saves, and will be difficult to move from the number-one spot in 1998-99.

Wolverhampton W (Signed from Ilkeston T on 27/9/84) FL 30 FLC 1 FAC 1 Others 3
Stoke C (£10,000 on 24/7/87) FL 51 FLC 2 FAC 3 Others 4
Colchester U (Loaned on 10/1/90) FL 13
Stockport Co (Loaned on 22/3/90) FL 10 Others 2
Gillingham (Free on 14/8/92) FL 51 FLC 7 FAC 4 Others 4
Cambridge U (Free on 2/8/95) FL 119 FLC 6 FAC 7 Others 3

BARRICK Dean
Born: Hemsworth, 30 September 1969
Height: 5'9" Weight: 12.0
Club Honours: Div 3 '96
The left-sided defender continued to be a regular first team squad member at Preston during 1997-98, featuring in the majority of matches, either as a starter or sub, and made his 300th career Football League appearance and 100th League appearance for the club in consecutive matches in February. Finally broke his duck for Preston in August, with a long-range shot at Chesterfield, after two years of trying, immediately following this up with the only goal of the match against Blackburn in the second leg of the Coca Cola Cup tie. Coincidentally, his last senior goal had been against Preston for his former club, Cambridge. Was released during the summer.

Sheffield Wed (From trainee on 7/5/88) FL 11/2
Rotherham U (£50,000 on 14/2/91) FL 96+3/7 FLC 6 FAC 8 Others 5/1
Cambridge U (£50,000 on 11/8/93) FL 90+1/3 FLC 7/1 FAC 7/1 Others 6
Preston NE (Signed on 11/9/95) FL 98+11/1 FLC 7+1/1 FAC 5 Others 6

BARRON Michael James
Born: Chester le Street, 22 December 1974
Height: 5'11" Weight: 11.9
Released by Middlesbrough, the promising young central defender, or midfielder, was signed by Hartlepool in the 1997 close season, being well known to supporters from a successful loan spell in 1996-97. After winning a first team place in 1997-98, he was unfortunate to suffer a bad leg injury, but made a speedy recovery, and was soon winning praise for his cool and calculated performances. His game continued to improve as the campaign progressed, culminating in him being chosen as the Supporters' Player of the Year.

Middlesbrough (From trainee on 2/2/93) P/FL 2+1 FLC 1 Others 3+3
Hartlepool U (Loaned on 6/9/96) FL 16
Hartlepool U (Free on 8/7/97) FL 32+1 FLC 1 FAC 1 Others 2

BARROW Lee Alexander
Born: Belper, 1 May 1973
Height: 5'11" Weight: 13.0
Virtually an ever present the previous season, Lee lost his number three shirt at Torquay in 1997-98 to the newcomer from Colchester, Paul Gibbs, and after just three subs' appearances was allowed to join non-league Barry Town in September. A pacy defender with good powers of anticipation, he had played in close on 200 games for United after arriving from Scarborough in February 1993.

Notts Co (From trainee on 9/7/91)
Scarborough (Free on 3/8/92) FL 11 FLC 2 Others 1
Torquay U (Free on 18/2/93) FL 154+10/5 FLC 11+1/2 FAC 10/1 Others 6

BARROWCLIFF Paul Joseph
Born: Hillingdon, 15 June 1969
Height: 5'7" Weight: 11.3
Made a late entry into league football when joining Brentford from non-league Stevenage in the 1997 close season, but soon showed himself to be a busy and tidy left-footed midfielder. Involved at the start of the campaign, until having a month on loan with his old club, on his return, the new manager, Micky Adams, selected him for ten consecutive games, before he went back to the reserves and was released during the summer.

Brentford (£60,000 from Stevenage Borough on 6/8/97) FL 5+6 FLC 3 FAC 2

BARRY Gareth
Born: Hastings, 23 February 1981
Height: 6'0" Weight: 12.6
An outstanding young Aston Villa central defender, Gareth graduated from the YTS ranks to turn professional last February, after starting out at the club as a midfielder. Having made his premiership bow in the penultimate game of 1997-98, at Sheffield Wednesday, when coming on for Ian Taylor, he then made his full debut in the final game, at home to Arsenal, and celebrated a 1-0 win over the new champions with his team mates. This boy is most definitely a comer.

Aston Villa (From trainee on 27/2/98) PL 1+1

BART-WILLIAMS Christopher (Chris) Gerald
Born: Freetown, Sierra Leone, 16 June 1974
Height: 5'11" Weight: 11.6
Club Honours: Div 1 '98
International Honours: E: B-1; U21-16; Yth
Despite normally being a central midfielder, Dave Bassett moved Chris to the wide left in 1997-98 and he showed impressive form as Nottingham Forest went back to the Premiership at the first time of asking, winning a first division championship medal along the way. As a player with much stamina and commitment, he could probably play almost anywhere, on one occasion partnering Kevin Campbell up front, and he scored the only goal of the penultimate game against Reading, which virtually ensured promotion. Occasionally giving way to Ian Woan, it will be interesting to see where he plays in 1998-99.

Leyton Orient (From trainee on 18/7/91) FL 34+2/2 FLC 4 Others 2
Sheffield Wed (£275,000 on 21/11/91) F/PL 95+29/16 FLC 14+2/4 FAC 9+3/2 Others 1+3/2
Nottingham F (£2,500,000 on 1/7/95) F/PL 79+3/5 FLC 8 FAC 9 Others 7+1

BARTON Warren Dean
Born: Stoke Newington, 19 March 1969
Height: 6'0" Weight: 12.0
International Honours: E: 3; B-3
Although bought originally as a defender, Warren's pace, energy, and aggressive tackling fit him well for a midfield holding role, and he performed well for Newcastle in this position for much of last season. This also provided an outlet for his attacking instincts, for he enjoys raiding down the flanks and crossing dangerous balls into the

box for his strikers. His flexibility also proved an asset, as he moved back to replace Steve Watson at right back, when the latter suffered a broken foot, and was one of the more consistent players during the vital late stages of the campaign. Although not known for his goals, he drew much satisfaction from scoring against both his former club, Wimbledon, and the club he supported as a boy, Arsenal, the latter being the first Premiership goal the Gunners had conceded for almost nine games.

Maidstone U (£10,000 from Leytonstone on 28/7/89) FL 41+1 FLC 0+2 FAC 3/1 Others 7
Wimbledon (£300,000 on 7/6/90) F/PL 178+2/10 FLC 16/1 FAC 11 Others 2
Newcastle U (£4,500,000 on 5/6/95) PL 61+11/4 FLC 8/1 FAC 7+2 Others 9+2

Warren Barton

BARTRAM Vincent (Vince) Lee
Born: Birmingham, 7 August 1968
Height: 6'2" Weight: 13.4
Unable to get a game at Arsenal in 1997-98, way down the pecking order behind David Seaman, Alex Manninger, and John Lukic, this sound and competent goalkeeper was loaned out to Huddersfield in October. Although making a shaky start, being on the receiving end of 11 goals in his first four starts, he settled down to show a good pair of hands in the next eight games before returning to Highbury. Still not making any progress, Vince joined Gillingham in March, appearing in their final nine matches, and nearly helped them into the play offs. Confident of his own ability, he was commanding in the air and dealt competently with every ball that came his way. Signed until June 1998, his contract was not renewed.

Wolverhampton W (From juniors on 17/8/85) FL 5 FLC 2 FAC 3
Blackpool (Loaned on 27/10/89) FL 9 Others 2
Bournemouth (£65,000 on 24/7/91) FL 132 FLC 10 FAC 14 Others 6

Arsenal (£400,000 on 10/8/94) PL 11 FLC 0+1
Huddersfield T (Loaned on 17/10/97) FL 12
Gillingham (Free on 20/3/98) FL 9

BARWOOD Daniel (Danny) David
Born: Caerphilly, 25 February 1981
Height: 5'9" Weight: 11.0
International Honours: W: Yth
The son of a former Welsh Rugby League player, Danny made his league debut for Swansea whilst still a first-year YTS, when coming on as a substitute against Hull City last January. He then went on to score his first goal in his first full league appearance as City beat Chester 2-0 in March, before going on to join the Welsh U18 side due to play in a competition involving Italy, Switzerland, Norway, and the USA. Currently plays as a left winger.
Swansea C (Trainee) FL 1+2/1

BASFORD Luke William
Born: Croydon, 6 January 1980
Height: 5'6" Weight: 8.5
A live wire, confident, attacking left-full back, and still a trainee, Luke made an immediate impression last December when giving a Man of the Match performance on his league debut for Bristol Rovers against Grimsby Town. The match itself turned out to be the club's heaviest home defeat for five years, but it did not stop the youngster from making further first team appearances. Was very unfortunate to have been sent off at Gillingham in January for two bookable offences and became the youngest player to be dismissed in Rovers' history, at 18 years, 25 days old.
Bristol Rov (Trainee) FL 5+2 Others 3

BASHAM Michael (Mike)
Born: Barking, 27 September 1973
Height: 6'2" Weight: 13.2
Club Honours: AMC '94
International Honours: E: Yth; Sch
Signed from Peterborough immediately prior to the start of 1997-98, Mike took time to establish himself in the Barnet first team, but became a regular at centre half after Christmas. Cool and calm, he scored his only goal of the season at Doncaster. Is a hard tackler who wins the ball and distributes well.
West Ham U (From trainee on 3/7/92)
Colchester U (Loaned on 18/11/93) FL 1
Swansea C (Free on 24/3/94) FL 27+2/1 FAC 6 Others 8+2
Peterborough U (Free on 18/12/95) FL 17+2/1 FLC 1 FAC 0+1
Barnet (Free on 5/8/97) FL 19+1/1 Others 3

BASHAM Steven (Steve)
Born: Southampton, 2 December 1977
Height: 5'11" Weight: 11.3
After making his Southampton debut in 1996-97, Steve may have been expected to play more senior games last season, but the form of Egil Ostenstad, David Hirst, and Kevin Davies meant a perhaps disappointing nine appearances as substitute. A regular in the reserves, having scored six goals during the campaign, this promising young striker will be looking for a breakthrough next season. An old-fashioned centre

forward, who holds the ball up well and possesses a good shot from either foot, he was loaned to Wrexham in February and, despite not getting on the scoresheet, created quite a good impression when finding good positions. A willing front runner, he will continue to improve with experience.
Southampton (From trainee on 24/5/96) PL 1+14
Wrexham (Loaned on 6/2/98) FL 4+1

BASS David
Born: Frimley, 29 November 1974
Height: 5'11" Weight: 12.7
Freed by Reading, David joined Rotherham during the 1997 close season and played in midfield in the early part of 1997-98, where he proved to be a hard worker. Unfortunately, he lost his place and a subsequent hamstring operation left him on the sidelines.
Reading (From trainee on 14/7/93) FL 7+4
Rotherham U (Free on 7/7/97) FL 13+5 FLC 1 FAC 0+1

BASS Jonathan (Jon) David
Born: Weston super Mare, 1 January 1976
Height: 6'0" Weight: 12.2
International Honours: E: Sch
The sort of player who never lets the side down, Jon played with great determination and intelligence to make the right-back position his own at Birmingham in 1997-98 after the enforced absence of Darren Wassall left the side in need of continuity. With the added responsibility, his positioning and distribution improved notably as he forged a hard-working partnership with newcomer, Jon McCarthy, down the right-hand side of the pitch. Is also steady and cool under pressure.
Birmingham C (From juniors on 27/6/94) FL 46+2 FLC 5+1 FAC 4
Carlisle U (Loaned on 11/10/96) FL 3

Jamie Bates

BATES James (Jamie) Alan
Born: Croydon, 24 February 1968
Height: 6'2" Weight: 14.0
Club Honours: Div 3 '92
Tall, strong, and commanding at centre half for Brentford again in 1997-98, Jamie has now completed 12 seasons with the Bees. The club captain was a regular throughout the campaign, but found it difficult as a succession of defensive partners were selected to play alongside him when the formation changed from a flat back four to a three-man central defensive formation. Scored against Plymouth in January with a powerful header.
Brentford (From trainee on 1/6/87) FL 372+20/17 FLC 33+3/2 FAC 17+1/1 Others 42/1

BATTERSBY Anthony (Tony)
Born: Doncaster, 30 August 1975
Height: 6'0" Weight: 12.7
Having had his loan transfer firmed up during the 1997 close season, and then steering clear of injury, Bury's powerful striker took some time before finding his form – and his scoring touch – finally ending 1997-98 as the Shakers' joint-top league scorer with just six goals. Although his effort and endeavour were never in doubt, a lack of confidence led to a downturn in form and he spent the closing two months of the season on the substitutes' bench.
Sheffield U (From trainee on 5/7/93) FL 3+7/1 FLC 1+1 Others 2+1/1
Southend U (Loaned on 23/3/95) FL 6+2/1
Notts Co (£200,000 on 8/1/96) FL 20+19/8 FLC 1 FAC 0+3 Others 4
Bury (£125,000 on 3/3/97) FL 37+11/8 FLC 3+1/1 FAC 2

BATTY David
Born: Leeds, 2 December 1968
Height: 5'8" Weight: 12.0
Club Honours: Div 2 '90, Div 1 '92; CS '92
International Honours: E: 35; B-5; U21-7
David is a real "Yorkshire Terrier" of a player, whose combative instincts and bite in the tackle continued to provide an excellent shield in front of Newcastle's back division in 1997-98. His wholehearted approach to the game, and his consistent high level of performance have not only made him popular with the club's supporters, but also with Glenn Hoddle, who has made him a regular fixture in the England squad. Sent off at Villa for two bookable offences, giving him the doubtful honour of being the Premiership's first dismissal of the season, he was also shown the red card at Derby and Blackburn. However, there is much more skill to his game than he is often given credit for, his workrate being very high, while he is always available whenever a colleague has the ball, and his distribution over both short and long distance is crisp and rarely wasteful. Much of his good work goes unnoticed, as it is concerned with hustling opponents into mistakes and nullifying their effect in midfield. A rare goalscorer, his counter late in the FA Cup tie with Barnsley was his first in any cup competition in senior football,

and was struck sweetly with his left foot! Captained United early in the season when Robert Lee was absent, and was again selected for the Premiership team at the PFA annual awards dinner. *Stop Press:* Played in all four of England's World Cup games in France during the summer and did well, especially when coming on for the last 23 minutes of extra time against Argentine, but will be better remembered – with great sympathy – for missing the final penalty in the shoot-out.
Leeds U (From trainee on 3/8/87) F/PL 201+10/4 FLC 17 FAC 12 Others 17
Blackburn Rov (£2,750,000 on 26/10/93) PL 53+1/1 FLC 6 FAC 5 Others 6
Newcastle U (£3,750,000 on 2/3/96) PL 75/3 FLC 4 FAC 9/1 Others 15

BAYES Ashley John
Born: Lincoln, 19 April 1972
Height: 6'1" Weight: 13.5
International Honours: E: Yth
In 1997-98, Ashley again showed what a good shot-stopper he was, his reflexes being second to none when he was on top of his game. Consistent and enthusiastic, he missed only one league game for Exeter and remains a great favourite of the fans.*
Brentford (From trainee on 5/7/90) FL 4 FLC 5 FAC 2 Others 1
Torquay U (Free on 13/8/93) FL 97 FLC 7 FAC 9 Others 6
Exeter C (Free on 31/7/96) FL 86 FLC 4 FAC 4 Others 2

BAYLISS David (Dave) Anthony
Born: Liverpool, 8 June 1976
Height: 5'11" Weight: 12.4
Despite an excellent performance at left back against Stoke in the Coca Cola Cup, Dave was mostly used as a stand-in for the regular defenders, appearing all along the Rochdale back line in 1997-98. Though always in the squad when available, he was often on the bench and was unable to claim a regular spot in the starting line-up, until having a late run at centre back.
Rochdale (From trainee on 10/6/95) FL 71+11/2 FLC 4 FAC 2+1 Others 5

BAZELEY Darren Shaun
Born: Northampton, 5 October 1972
Height: 5'10" Weight 11.2
Club Honours: Div 2 '98
International Honours: E: U21-1
Versatile and very athletic, with good pace and control, and normally deployed as right-wing back, Darren suffered a knee injury on Watford's pre-1997-98 season tour which proved troublesome and eventually required surgery. As a result, he missed most of the campaign, though when he did return in March it was as if Watford had signed a new player, such was his dash and enthusiasm. Played some of his matches on his return as a striker and scored a great goal at Blackpool. His 16 league games saw him win a second division championship medal, as the Hornets went back to division one after a two-year break.
Watford (From trainee on 6/5/91) FL 151+49/19 FLC 12+4/2 FAC 11+1/3 Others 6+1/1

BEADLE Peter Clifford
Born: Lambeth, 13 May 1972
Height: 6'1" Weight: 13.7
Peter adapted to a new role at Bristol Rovers in 1997-98, switching from a striker to an attacking midfielder, and looking comfortable at creating goalscoring opportunities with his penetrating and powerful runs. Bagging two impressive hat tricks against Bournemouth and Wigan Athletic, the latter taking him just 11 minutes to complete, "Beads" matured into a consistent player and was handed the captain's armband earlier in the season in the absence of Andy Tillson. Scored a vital penalty, his 18th of the campaign, in the first leg of the play-off semi final against Northampton Town, which Rovers won 3-1.
Gillingham (From trainee on 5/5/90) FL 42+25/14 FLC 2+4/2 FAC 1+1 Others 1
Tottenham H (£300,000 on 4/6/92)
Bournemouth (Loaned on 25/3/93) FL 9/2
Southend U (Loaned on 4/3/94) FL 8/1
Watford (Signed on 12/9/94) FL 12+11/1 FLC 1
Bristol Rov (£50,000 on 17/11/95) FL 98+11/39 FLC 2+1 FAC 5/2 Others 7+1/1

BEAGRIE Peter Sydney
Born: Middlesbrough, 28 November 1965
Height: 5'8" Weight: 12.0
International Honours: E: B-2; U21-2
Signed from Manchester City during the 1997 close season, Peter continued to show up as a very skilful and tricky winger, who, at times, mesmerised the opposition defences, while sending the Bradford fans ecstatic. His famous somersault after scoring was sorely missed, although not for the want of trying, and it was a real surprise when he moved to Everton on loan on transfer deadline day. However, he made only four starts for the Toffees and it remains to be seen where his future lies in 1998-99.
Middlesbrough (From juniors on 10/9/83) FL 24+9/2 FLC 1 Others 1+1
Sheffield U (£35,000 on 16/8/86) FL 81+3/11 FLC 5 FAC 5 Others 4
Stoke C (£210,000 on 29/6/88) FL 54/7 FLC 4 FAC 3/1
Everton (£750,000 on 2/11/89) F/PL 88+26/11 FLC 7+2/3 FAC 7+2 Others 5+1/1
Sunderland (Loaned on 26/9/91) FL 5/1
Manchester C (£1,100,000 on 24/3/94) F/PL 46+6/3 FLC 8/1 FAC 4+1/1
Bradford C (£50,000 on 2/7/97) FL 31+3 FLC 2 FAC 1
Everton (Loaned on 26/3/98) PL 4+2

BEALL Matthew (Billy) John
Born: Enfield, 4 December 1977
Height: 5'7" Weight: 10.6
In his second season as a professional at Cambridge, Billy continued to improve and was an integral part of the midfield in 1997-98. Hard working and industrious, he can run all day between both penalty areas, passes the ball well, and is still young, with time on his side, to develop into an all-round midfielder.
Cambridge U (From trainee on 28/3/96) FL 73+8/7 FLC 2 FAC 6/2 Others 1+1

Billy Beall

BEARD Mark
Born: Roehampton, 8 October 1974
Height: 5'10" Weight: 11.3
A defender who only rarely featured in the Sheffield United first team squad during last season after being made available for transfer at the start of it, he was released at the end of it, having spent two months on loan at Southend United, and turning down possible moves to Brentford, and later on, Notts County, after initially agreeing to the move. Able to play in midfield, he is both tenacious, willing, and a strong tackler.
Millwall (From trainee on 18/3/93) FL 32+13/2 FLC 3+1 FAC 4/1
Sheffield U (£117,000 on 18/8/95) FL 22+16 FLC 2+1 FAC 2+2
Southend U (Loaned on 24/10/97) FL 6+2 Others 1

BEARDSLEY Peter Andrew
Born: Newcastle, 18 January 1961
Height: 5'8" Weight: 11.7
Club Honours: Div 1 '88, '90; FAC '89; CS '88, '89
International Honours: E: 59; B-2
Signed from Newcastle early in 1997-98, the former international striker left his beloved "Toon Army" for the promise of first team football at Bolton, but it did not turn out as planned. Regularly finding himself on the subs' bench, it became apparent that he would not be a first-choice member of the team and was allowed to go out on loan, first to Manchester City (December), and then Fulham (March). Made just six appearances at City before Joe Royle decided not to extend his loan period, but at Fulham it was different as he became the missing piece of the jigsaw in the club's march to the play offs and, at the same time, joined up with his former manager, Kevin

Keegan. Showing the energy of a man ten years younger, his probing runs and passes contributed to several good wins, and his perfectly placed pass in the home play off against Grimsby kept hopes alive. Unfortunately, he pulled a hamstring which put him out of the return leg and saw his season end at that point. Peter could still do the business for any number of teams in 1998-99.
Carlisle U (Free from Wallsend BC on 9/8/79) FL 93+11/22 FLC 6+1 FAC 15/7 (£275,000 to Vancouver Whitecaps on 1/4/82)
Manchester U (£300,000 on 9/9/82) FLC 1 (Free to Vancouver Whitecaps on 1/3/83)
Newcastle U (£150,000 on 23/9/83) FL 146+1/61 FLC 10 FAC 6 Others 1
Liverpool (£1,900,000 on 24/7/87) FL 120+11/46 FLC 13+1/1 FAC 22+3/11 Others 5/1
Everton (£1,000,000 on 5/8/91) F/LP 81/25 FLC 8/5 FAC 4/1 Others 2/1
Newcastle U (£1,400,000 on 16/7/93) PL 126+3/47 FLC 11/4 FAC 11/3 Others 11/4
Bolton W (£450,000 on 20/8/97) PL 14+3/2 FLC 3 FAC 0+1
Manchester C (Loaned on 17/2/98) FL 5+1
Fulham (Loaned on 26/3/98) FL 8/1 Others 1/1

BEARDSMORE Russell Peter
Born: Wigan, 28 September 1968
Height: 5'7" Weight 10.4
Club Honours: ESC '91
International Honours: E: U21-5
Russell had a mixed season at Bournemouth in 1997-98, starting and finishing well, but unfortunately missing a good part of the middle of it through injury. The games he did play in saw him involved in the centre of midfield, taking up a holding role to great effect, and always quick to support the front players.
Manchester U (From apprentice on 2/10/86) FL 30+26/4 FLC 3+1 FAC 4+4 Others 2+5
Blackburn Rov (Loaned on 19/12/91) FL 1+1
Bournemouth (Free on 29/6/93) FL 167+11/4 FLC 14/1 FAC 9/1 Others 8+1/1

BEASANT David (Dave) John
Born: Willesden, 20 March 1959
Height: 6'4" Weight: 14.3
Club Honours: Div 4 '83, Div 2 '89; Div 1 '98; FAC '88; FMC '90
International Honours: E: 2; B-7
Loaned to Nottingham Forest by Southampton a week of so into the 1997-98 season, when Forest had Mark Crossley, Alan Fettis, and Marco Pascolo all injured, the giant goalkeeper performed so well, keeping three clean sheets in his first three games, that he was signed on a free transfer and given an 18-month contract. Big, strong, and brave, always talking to his defence, Dave was one of the first goalies to run the ball out of the area to get the ball further afield. Overall, the former England man kept 21 clean sheets in 44 league and cup matches, and his experience was a major factor in the club achieving promotion at the first time of asking. Also sets up attacks with excellent throws.
Wimbledon (£1,000 from Edgware T on 7/8/79) FL 340 FLC 21 FAC 27 Others 3
Newcastle U (£800,000 on 13/6/88) FL 20 FLC 2 FAC 2 Others 1
Chelsea (£725,000 on 14/1/89) F/PL 133 FLC 11 FAC 5 Others 8

Grimsby T (Loaned on 24/10/92) FL 6
Wolverhampton W (Loaned on 12/1/93) FL 4 FAC 1
Southampton (£300,000 on 4/11/93) PL 86+2 FLC 8 FAC 9
Nottingham F (Free on 22/8/97) FL 41 FLC 2 FAC 1

BEATTIE James Scott
Born: Lancaster, 27 February 1978
Height: 6'1" Weight: 12.0
Having made his debut for Blackburn in 1996-97, the former youth team star, who was averaging a goal a game for the reserves last season, started at Preston in the Coca Cola Cup before going back to the reserves and later making four more first team appearances from the bench. Too early to make a judgement but, unable to get the same amount of freedom for shooting opportunities as accustomed to, he will be working on that aspect of his game during the summer recess.
Blackburn Rov (From trainee on 7/3/95) PL 1+3 FLC 2 FAC 0+1

BEAUCHAMP Joseph (Joey) Daniel
Born: Oxford, 13 March 1971
Height: 5'10" Weight: 12.5
In 1997-98, the left-footed winger had his best season so far for his hometown club of Oxford, scoring 19 goals, and missing just one game, and often producing the skills that make him one of the club's major assets. He scored some tremendous goals from long range, with the best probably being the free kick which beat Stoke's Neville Southall from 30 yards, closely followed by his brace at champions elect, Nottingham Forest, in a 3-1 win. Pacy and tricky, and often playing on the right wing, it would not surprise United fans if Joey had another chance to play in the Premiership in the near future, but it would need a big fee to force the club to sell.
Oxford U (From trainee on 16/5/89) FL 117+7/20 FLC 6+1/2 FAC 8/3 Others 5+1
Swansea C (Loaned on 30/10/91) FL 5/2 Others 1
West Ham U (£1,000,000 on 22/6/94)
Swindon T (£850,000 on 18/8/94) FL 39+6/3 FLC 7+2/1 FAC 2 Others 4
Oxford U (£300,000 on 4/10/95) FL 105+16/22 FLC 14/6 FAC 4+2/1 Others 0+2

BEAUMONT Christopher (Chris) Paul
Born: Sheffield, 5 December 1965
Height: 5'11" Weight: 11.7
Chris fulfilled a "play anywhere" role for Chesterfield last season. Anyone labelled with a "utility" tag runs a risk of not being considered unless others are injured, but this imaginative midfielder embraced this role with his customary commitment, and took on board regular substitutions with good grace, always putting the team first.*
Rochdale (Free from Denaby U on 21/7/88) FL 31+3/7 FLC 0+1/1 FAC 2/1 Others 2
Stockport Co (£8,000 on 21/7/89) FL 238+20/39 FLC 14+3/3 FAC 15/2 Others 34+2/7
Chesterfield (£30,000 on 22/7/96) FL 61+11/2 FLC 5+1 FAC 6+2/1 Others 1

BECK Mikkel
Born: Aarhus, Denmark, 12 May 1973
Height: 6'2" Weight: 12.9
International Honours: Denmark: 14

A hard-working Middlesbrough striker who simultaneously enthralled and frustrated his fans through inexplicable form changes in 1997-98. Going forward in full flight he is an exciting prospect, exuding the ever-present promise of a spectacular goal. To his credit, he probably brought the best out of the "Turbulent Italian", Fabrizio Ravanelli, in the palmy days of their strike force partnership. Was a contender for a place in the Danish national squad for World Cup '98 but, ultimately, missed out on selection.
Middlesbrough (Free from Fortuna Cologne on 13/9/96) F/PL 53+11/19 FLC 12+2/5 FAC 5+2/2

BECKHAM David Robert
Born: Leytonstone, 2 May 1975
Height: 6'0" Weight: 11.12
Club Honours: FAYC '92; PL '96, '97; FAC '96; CS '96, '97
International Honours: E: 18; U21-9; Yth
An excellent Manchester United midfielder with a wonderful range of passing and shooting skills, David was straining at the leash at the start of last season, when Alex Ferguson gave him enough time to recover from his exertions for England at the end of the previous campaign. Quick to prove that you cannot hold a good player down for long, he scored United's winner as a substitute against Southampton, in their second Premiership game of the season, and added a further strike against Everton, two games later. Although the Old Trafford faithful had to wait until November before he found the net again, scoring two against Wimbledon at Selhurst Park, his next contributions were among his finest of the campaign. Always a danger at set plays, he scored an absolute "cracker" against Liverpool at Anfield in the Premiership, then helped to put Chelsea out of the FA Cup at Stamford Bridge in January. Although every aspect of his life continues to dominate the headlines – notably his engagement to "Posh Spice," Victoria Adams – his form continues to earn rave notice, both on the domestic and international scene, and it came as no surprise when he was named as one of Glenn Hoddle's England squad for the World Cup Finals during the summer. Was also recognised by his fellow professionals when selected for the award-winning PFA Premiership side. *Stop Press:* Thought by many to be a player who would grace the World Cup stage, he failed to make an appearance in the first match, came on for Paul Ince against Romania, started and scored a wonderful free kick in the 2-0 win over Colombia, before being sent off against Argentine and effectively limiting England's chances of victory. One of England's greatest creative talents, he must be encouraged to walk away from provocation.
Manchester U (From trainee on 29/1/93) PL 95+15/24 FLC 5+1 FAC 9+2/4 Others 22+1/4
Preston NE (Loaned on 28/2/95) FL 4+1/2

BEDEAU Anthony (Tony) Charles Osmond
Born: Hammersmith, 24 March 1979
Height: 5'10" Weight: 11.0
As a first year professional, having come

through the ranks at Torquay, he established himself as a valuable member of the first team squad in 1997-98, scoring a number of important goals. Good in possession and pacy, Tony was used mainly as an out-and-out striker.
Torquay U (From trainee on 28/7/97) FL 18+28/6 FLC 1+1 FAC 1+2 Others 0+4

BEECH Christopher (Chris)
Born: Congleton, 5 November 1975
Height: 5'10" Weight: 11.12
International Honours: E: Yth; Sch
Signed from Manchester City prior to 1997-98 getting underway, without appearing at Maine Road, Chris remained ever present through Cardiff City's third division campaign, but was surprisingly given a free transfer at the end of the season. A speedy left-wing back, he was among 11 players freed by City, and part of the reason for his departure was the club's terrible record of having finished in the bottom four twice in the last three seasons. Despite the manager, Frank Burrows, recognising his ability and willingness to learn, he was one of the unlucky ones.
Manchester C (From trainee on 12/11/92)
Cardiff C (Free on 7/8/97) FL 46/1 FLC 2 FAC 6

BEECH Christopher (Chris) Stephen
Born: Blackpool, 16 September 1974
Height: 5'11" Weight: 11.12
A hard-working Hartlepool midfielder, Chris had a comparatively quiet season in 1997-98, while team-mates, Jon Cullen and Jan Ove Pedersen received most of the praise. With the departure of these two players, he again came to prominence playing a more attacking role, coming forward to score some important goals, and showing the kind of form that had made him a firm favourite the previous campaign.
Blackpool (From trainee on 9/7/93) FL 53+29/4 FLC 4+4 FAC 1 Others 3+3/2
Hartlepool U (Free on 18/7/96) FL 76+2/14 FLC 3/1 FAC 3/1 Others 3/1

BEENEY Mark Raymond
Born: Tunbridge Wells, 30 December 1967
Height: 6'4" Weight: 14.7
Club Honours: GMVC '89
International Honours: E: SP-1
A strong, reliable goalkeeper who has spent nearly all of his Leeds' career as an understudy to John Lukic and, more recently, Nigel Martyn. In 1997-98, Mark again had to be content in playing the odd game – the home fixture with Sheffield Wednesday, while Martyn was suspended. A good shot-stopper, he is still an excellent man to have in the wings, his ability to come for crosses and command his box, being paramount to United's requirements. Is also a tremendous kicker of the ball, especially from his hands.
Gillingham (From juniors on 17/8/85) FL 2 FLC 1
Maidstone U (Free on 31/1/87) FL 50 FLC 3 FAC 11 Others 6
Aldershot (Loaned on 22/3/90) FL 7
Brighton & Hove A (£30,000 on 28/3/91) FL 68+1 FLC 6 FAC 7 Others 6
Leeds U (£350,000 on 22/4/93) PL 35 FLC 3 FAC 4+1

BEESLEY Paul
Born: Liverpool, 21 July 1965
Height: 6'1" Weight: 12.6
Having spent the 1997 summer months recuperating from an ankle injury, the strong, uncompromising central defender came back for Manchester City's opening game of 1997-98, only to go down with a knee injury. After playing his way back to full fitness in the reserves, he was recalled at the end of September, but, following the game at Ipswich, he appeared to be out of contention for a first team place and eventually went out on loan to Port Vale immediately prior to Christmas. Returning to Maine road after five games for Vale, he was informed that he was up for transfer, even though used as a sub for three games during February, before taking on board another loan spell, this time at West Bromwich in March. Paul settled in well at Albion, playing alongside a variety of fellow centre halves until suffering another knee injury late on in the campaign.
Wigan Ath (Free from Marine on 22/9/84) FL 153+2/3 FLC 13 FAC 6 Others 11
Leyton Orient (£175,000 on 20/10/89) FL 32/1 FAC 1 Others 2/1
Sheffield U (£300,000 on 10/7/90) F/PL 162+6/7 FLC 12+1 FAC 9+2/1 Others 3/1
Leeds U (£250,000 on 2/8/95) PL 19+3 FLC 5+1 FAC 5 Others 2+2
Manchester C (£500,000 on 7/2/97) FL 10+3
Port Vale (Loaned on 24/12/97) FL 5
West Bromwich A (Loaned on 12/3/98) FL 8

BEESTON Carl Frederick
Born: Stoke, 30 June 1967
Height: 5'10" Weight: 12.12
Club Honours: Div 2 '93
International Honours: E: U21-1
Carl joined Southend United for a trial period at the start of the 1997-98 season, after being released by Stoke City, and immediately made a place of his own in midfield. His battling qualities were allied to neat passing skills, and it was a disappointment when the club's offer of a contract was rejected, allowing him to return to his native midlands to join Hednesford Town in September 1997 after only nine appearances.
Stoke C (From apprentice on 1/7/85) FL 224+12/13 FLC 12/1 FAC 7+1/1 Others 15/2
Hereford U (Loaned on 23/1/97) FL 9/2
Southend U (Free on 7/8/97) FL 5+1 FLC 3

BEETON Alan Matthew
Born: Watford, 4 October 1978
Height: 5'11" Weight: 11.0
A left-footed Wycombe defender who came from the club's 1996-97 youth team, Alan made his senior debut on the opening day of last season at Wigan, coming on as substitute, and quickly establishing himself at left-wing back. Strong in the tackle, and comfortable going forward, he picked up a knee injury in mid-season, but re-established himself in the final weeks, where his outstanding form earned him some Man of the Match awards.
Wycombe W (From trainee on 1/7/97) FL 15+5 FAC 1+1

BELL Michael (Mickey)
Born: Newcastle, 15 November 1971
Height: 5'10" Weight: 11.4
A 1997 close season signing for Bristol City from Wycombe Wanderers, Mickey smoothly filled the left-back spot vacated by Darren Barnard's departure to Barnsley, scoring many crucial goals, though his prowess from the penalty spot and free kicks have been in marked contrast to that of his predecessor, who obtained many goals from general play. Extremely popular at Ashton Gate, he has already endeared himself to City supporters with his left-sided upfield surges.
Northampton T (From trainee on 1/7/90) FL 133+20/10 FLC 7+1 FAC 5/1 Others 9+2/1
Wycombe W (£45,000 on 21/10/94) FL 117+1/5 FLC 5 FAC 9/2 Others 3+1
Bristol C (£150,000 on 2/7/97) FL 44/10 FLC 4 FAC 2 Others 2

BELLAMY Craig Douglas
Born: Cardiff, 13 July 1979
Height: 5'9" Weight: 10.12
International Honours: W: 3 U21-7; Yth; Sch
Having started 1997-98 well when making his full Norwich debut in the second game of the season, Craig eventually topped the club's scoring charts with 13 goals, despite playing much of the time in midfield. His form was such, that it prompted Crystal Palace to offer £1 million for his services in December and saw the youngster signing a new contract with the Canaries shortly after. A player who enjoys taking defenders on, and who possesses good passing skills, in adding to his Welsh international experience of youth and U21 caps, on winning his first full cap, against Jamaica at Ninian Park last March, he became his country's third youngest debutant behind John Charles and Ryan Giggs.
Norwich C (From trainee on 20/1/97) FL 30+9/13 FLC 1 FAC 1

BENALI Francis (Franny) Vincent
Born: Southampton, 30 December 1968
Height: 5'10" Weight: 11.0
International Honours: E: Sch
As usual, it was another mixed season for the battling Southampton defender in 1997-98. After more than 11 years at the club and 300 first team games, Franny finally scored his first senior goal in the 2-1 home win against Leicester in December, a glorious header. Having originally been left out with the new signing, Lee Todd, being preferred, he became a near ever present in Saints' rise to mid-table safety, although he again fell foul of referees and was dismissed twice, resulting in him being suspended for the start of this coming term. Is a very determined left back, who is aggressive in the tackle, and has a lovely left foot which he uses to deliver excellent early crosses.
Southampton (From apprentice on 5/1/87) F/PL 225+28/1 FLC 19+7 FAC 20 Others 3+1

BENJAMIN Trevor Junior
Born: Kettering, 8 February 1979
Height: 6'2" Weight: 13.2
The second half of last season saw this exciting young striker make his mark on the Cambridge first team. Appearances had been limited in the first part, but coming off the bench in the Cup tie against Plymouth he transformed both the team and the game, scoring as United turned a 2-0 deficit into a 3-2 win. Big and aggressive, a cross between Frank Bruno and John Fashanu, his pace and strength caused chaos in opposing defences, and four goals in three games towards the end of the campaign showed that he has the makings of an excellent striker.
Cambridge U (From trainee on 21/2/97) FL 17+20/5 FLC 0+3 FAC 2+1/1

BENNETT Frank (Frankie)
Born: Birmingham, 3 January 1969
Height: 5'7" Weight: 12.1
After recovering from a right-knee injury, and starting to establish himself as a first team regular at Bristol Rovers in 1997-98, the speedy forward, who scored a spectacular goal against Carlisle, had to have more surgery on his left knee which kept him out for a further period of three months. Became involved again with the first team squad after Christmas, and added a superb volleyed goal against Chesterfield, after being switched to play in a wide-right midfield role, but primarily used as substitute. Following an injury to Jamie Cureton, he was given the opportunity in the play-off matches against Northampton Town, but the Rovers' supporters have yet to see the best of a fully fit and injury-free Frankie Bennett.
Southampton (£7,500 from Halesowen T on 24/2/93) PL 5+14/1 FLC 1+2 FAC 0+1
Shrewsbury T (Loaned on 25/10/96) FL 2+2/3
Bristol Rov (£15,000 on 22/11/96) FL 14+16/3 FLC 1+1 FAC 0+2 Others 3/2

BENNETT Gary Ernest
Born: Manchester, 4 December 1961
Height: 6'1" Weight: 13.0
Club Honours: Div 3 '88
An elegant and immensely skilful Scarborough player, he is an outstanding central defender, but can also operate in midfield or as an emergency striker and enjoyed a wonderful season in 1997-98, scoring some vital goals, and leading Boro to the promotion play offs. Voted the club's Player of the Year and, for the second year in succession, was named the Sunday Sun North-East Player of the Year.
Manchester C (Free from Ashton U on 8/9/79)
Cardiff C (Free on 16/9/81) FL 85+2/11 FLC 6/1 FAC 3
Sunderland (£65,000 on 26/7/84) FL 362+7/23 FLC 34+1/1 FAC 17+1 Others 21/1
Carlisle U (Free on 16/11/95) FL 26/5 Others 5/1
Scarborough (Free on 2/8/96) FL 86+2/18 FLC 6/3 FAC 4 Others 3

BENNETT Gary Michael
Born: Liverpool, 20 September 1962
Height: 5'11" Weight: 12.0
Club Honours: AMC '85; WC '95
A very popular striker who re-joined Chester City at the start of last season from local rivals, Wrexham, following a six-year absence from City, and having seen service with Preston, Tranmere, and, of course, Wrexham. Started the campaign well, hitting the back of the net 11 times up to November, but, unfortunately, the goals dried up and, despite giving 100 per cent every game, he did not add to that tally before 1997-98 ended. Able to play on the wide right, Gary can create as well as finish.
Wigan Ath (Free from Kirby T on 9/10/84) FL 10+10/3 FAC 1 Others 3+1/1
Chester C (Free on 22/8/85) FL 109+17/36 FLC 6+4/1 FAC 8+1/5 Others 10/5
Southend U (Signed on 11/11/88) FL 36+6/6 FLC 4/4 FAC 1 Others 2+1
Chester C (£20,000 on 1/3/90) FL 71+9/15 FLC 8/2 FAC 5/1 Others 4+1/1
Wrexham (Free on 12/8/92) FL 120+1/77 FLC 17/9 FAC 7/3 Others 9/9
Tranmere Rov (£300,000 on 13/7/95) FL 26+3/9 FLC 4
Preston NE (£200,000 on 27/3/96) FL 15+9/4 Others 1/1
Wrexham (£100,000 on 28/2/97) FL 15/5 FAC 0+1
Chester C (£50,000 on 25/7/97) FL 37+4/11 FLC 2 FAC 2

Gary Bennett (Chester City)

BENNETT Ian Michael
Born: Worksop, 10 October 1971
Height: 6'0" Weight: 12.10
Club Honours: Div 2 '95; AMC '95
The goalkeeper clocked up his 200th appearance for Birmingham, at Crewe, last January, and was able to boast of keeping 97 clean sheets since first coming into the side in 1993-94. An agile shot-stopper, Ian played to a consistently high level throughout last season, missing just the final game due to a broken hand, and improving both his ability to handle crosses into the area and to deal with dead-ball situations. Possessing lightning reflexes, there is no doubt that his success in keeping clean sheets, 21 in league games during 1997-98 being a high percentage, instils confidence within the defence and should be the benchmark for an assault on the Premiership this coming term.

31

Newcastle U (Free from Queens Park R juniors on 20/3/89)
Peterborough U (Free on 22/3/91) FL 72 FLC 10 FAC 3 Others 4
Birmingham C (£325,000 on 17/12/93) FL 177 FLC 21 FAC 13 Others 11

Ian Bennett

BENNETT Michael (Micky) Richard
Born: Camberwell, 27 July 1969
Height: 5'11" Weight: 11.11
Capable of playing at right back or on the wide right of midfield, where he gets forward well in order to deliver excellent crosses, Micky came back into the Football League with Leyton Orient last December on non-contract terms after a spell with non-league, Cambridge City. Only used a couple of times in the first team, but a good squad member, he rejoined Cambridge City on loan on transfer deadline day.
Charlton Ath (From apprentice on 27/4/87) FL 24+11/2 FLC 4 FAC 1 Others 6+1
Wimbledon (£250,000 on 9/1/90) FL 12+6/2 FLC 1+1 FAC 0+1 Others 1+1
Brentford (£60,000 on 14/7/92) FL 40+6/4 FLC 4+1 FAC 1 Others 6+1
Charlton Ath (Free on 24/3/94) FL 19+5/1 FAC 1
Millwall (Free on 16/5/95) FL 1+1
Cardiff C (Free on 14/8/96) FL 5+9/1 FLC 2 FAC 1+1 Others 0+1 (Free to Cambridge C in December 1996)
Leyton Orient (Free on 8/12/97) FL 1+1 Others 1

BENNETT Thomas (Tom) McNeill
Born: Falkirk, 12 December 1969
Height: 5'11" Weight: 11.8
A dynamic midfielder, Tom, whose name had been mentioned in terms of Scotland "B" international terms, was enjoying his best season for Stockport when it came to a horrific end with a double compound leg fracture at Birmingham last January. There were initial fears that his career was over, but he now expects to be back in a blue shirt before the end of 1998.

Aston Villa (From apprentice on 16/12/87)
Wolverhampton W (Free on 5/7/88) FL 103+12/2 FLC 7 FAC 5+2 Others 3+1
Stockport Co (£75,000 on 23/6/95) FL 94/5 FLC 20/2 FAC 9 Others 6+1

BENNETT Troy
Born: Barnsley, 25 December 1975
Height: 5'9" Weight: 11.13
International Honours: E: Yth
Having had his loan transfer from Barnsley made permanent during the 1997 close season, Troy proved to be a creative midfielder with a strong left foot, and a valuable squad member as Scarborough pushed for promotion in 1997-98, slotting into the team when required, and never letting them down. An accurate passer, who also battles when the need arises, he was released at the end of the campaign when Scarborough lost in the play-off semi finals and the manager looked to rebuild his squad.
Barnsley (From trainee on 23/12/93) FL 2
Scarborough (Free on 27/3/97) FL 28+11/3 FLC 1+1 Others 2+1

BENSTEAD Graham Mark
Born: Aldershot, 20 August 1963
Height: 6'2" Weight: 12.12
Club Honours: Div 3 '92
International Honours: E: Yth
Graham returned to Brentford in the 1997 close season, primarily as a goalkeeping coach, following four years playing in the non leagues. At his best, a brilliant shot stopper who played in Brentford's 1991-92 championship side, he made one appearance in 1997-98, at York, when Kevin Dearden was injured, and was clearly past his best. Was released in January and joined Basingstoke.
Queens Park R (From apprentice on 8/7/81) FAC 1
Norwich C (£10,000 on 28/3/85) FL 16 FLC 3
Colchester U (Loaned on 14/8/87) FL 18 Others 1
Sheffield U (£35,000 on 22/3/88) FL 47 FLC 5 FAC 8 Others 2
Brentford (£60,000 on 30/7/90) FL 112 FLC 10 FAC 5 Others 15 (Free to Kettering on 22/11/93)
Brentford (Free from Rushden & Diamonds on 25/7/97) FL 1

BENT Junior Antony
Born: Huddersfield, 1 March 1970
Height: 5'6" Weight: 10.9
Despite strenuous efforts being made to keep this fast and exciting winger at Bristol City, Junior wanted the move in the hope of getting on the team sheet more often, and joined Blackpool at the end of last August after scoring the extra-time winner against arch-rivals, Bristol Rovers, in the first round of the Coca Cola Cup. Quickly appreciated at Bloomfield Road, for his electrifying runs down the flank, he scored important goals, especially winners at Oldham, which dented the Latics' home record, and Burnley.
Huddersfield T (From trainee on 9/12/87) FL 25+11/6 FLC 1 FAC 3+1/1 Others 4
Burnley (Loaned on 30/11/89) FL 7+2/3
Bristol C (£30,000 on 22/3/90) FL 142+41/20 FLC 10+3/1 FAC 12+3/2 Others 7+3
Stoke C (Loaned on 26/3/92) FL 1
Shrewsbury T (Loaned on 24/10/96) FL 6
Blackpool (Signed on 29/8/97) FL 25+11/3 FAC 2 Others 3

BENT Marcus Nathan
Born: Hammersmith, 19 May 1978
Height: 6'2" Weight: 12.4
International Honours: E: U21-2
A tall exciting winger, cum striker, who was a regular for Brentford under Eddie May last season, scoring five goals and creating several others, Marcus was an integral part of an entertaining forward front four that also included Ryan Denys, Robert Taylor, and Kevin Rapley. However, when Micky Adams took over as manager, he was relegated to the subs' bench before being transferred to Crystal Palace in January, in what was seen as a surprise move at the time. The youngster did well, scoring five times in 16 appearances, six of them coming from the bench, and replaced Michele Padovano at the end of a campaign that saw the club relegated from the Premiership. Was selected for the England U21 squad in Toulon and played twice.
Brentford (From trainee on 21/7/95) FL 56+14/8 FLC 7/1 FAC 8/3 Others 5+1/1
Crystal Palace (£150,000+ on 8/1/98) PL 10+6/5

BERESFORD David
Born: Middleton, 11 November 1976
Height: 5'8" Weight: 11.4
International Honours: E: Yth; Sch
The speedy Huddersfield winger started 1997-98 in the right-wing position, but, unfortunately, any chance of a lengthy spell in the side was cut short so that he could have a hernia operation in November, his third in 12 months. Sensationally, however, he returned to the side in April, playing his part in a creditable draw against Bury, before injury struck again, and although not as serious as previous, the young man's season was all over bar the shouting. Always looks to create chances for others with his excellent crossing ability.
Oldham Ath (From trainee on 22/7/94) P/FL 32+32/2 FLC 3+3 FAC 0+1 Others 3
Swansea C (Loaned on 11/8/95) FL 4+2
Huddersfield T (£350,000 on 27/3/97) FL 11+3/1 FLC 1

BERESFORD John
Born: Sheffield, 4 September 1966
Height: 5'6" Weight: 10.12
Club Honours: Div 1 '93
International Honours: E: B-2; Yth; Sch
A compact left back who is ever eager to use his pace to supplement the attack, although never forgetting that his role is primarily defensive, John was thought to be on his way out at Newcastle at the start of 1997-98, following the signings of Stuart Pearce and Alessandro Pistone, but won and retained a place in the side as an attacking left-wing back. A rare goalscorer, with only two in five years at United, by October he was the club's leading scorer with six, and when he left for Southampton in February only John Barnes had surpassed his total. Despite being predominantly recognised as a left back at Newcastle, he was used in a wide midfield role by Saints to great effect and proved invaluable to them as they rose well away from relegation danger, linking well with Francis Benali down the left-hand side.

With the skills and pace of a winger, he is a great provider of pin-point crosses for the forwards.

Manchester C (From apprentice on 16/9/83)
Barnsley (Free on 4/8/86) FL 79+9/5 FLC 5+2/2 FAC 5/1
Portsmouth (£300,000 on 23/3/89) FL 102+5/8 FLC 12/2 FAC 11 Others 2
Newcastle U (£650,000 on 2/7/92) F/PL 176+3/3 FLC 17 FAC 17+1/1 Others 17+1/4
Southampton (£1,500,000 on 6/2/98) PL 10

BERESFORD Marlon
Born: Lincoln, 2 September 1969
Height: 6'1" Weight: 13.6
Ever present in the 1997-98 Burnley side until his March transfer to Middlesbrough, having been a solid last line of defence at Turf Moor, the £500,000 transfer fee represented good business acumen for the Clarets in getting that kind of money for a player who could have left for nothing under the Bosman ruling at the end of the season. Joining Boro in mid-season, when they were slipping rapidly down from the comfort of a near-certain promotion spot, his presence certainly "stopped the rot" and he kept three consecutive clean sheets in the club's search for stability. A very agile, no nonsense goalie, who settled to the job in hand without fuss, and with commendable endeavour, he won recognition as being a very formidable shot-stopper in any company.

Sheffield Wed (From trainee on 23/9/87)
Bury (Loaned on 25/8/89) FL 1
Northampton T (Loaned on 27/9/90) FL 13 Others 2
Crewe Alex (Loaned on 28/2/91) FL 3
Northampton T (Loaned on 15/8/91) FL 15
Burnley (£95,000 on 28/8/92) FL 240 FLC 18 FAC 20 Others 16
Middlesbrough (£500,000 on 10/3/98) FL 3

BERG Henning
Born: Eidsvell, Norway, 1 September 1969
Height: 6'0" Weight: 12.7
Club Honours: PL '95
International Honours: Norway: 54
A solid central defender, whose timing and judgement is always impeccable, Henning finally rekindled his love affair with Manchester United when he moved to Old Trafford from Blackburn in the summer of 1997 for £5m – a new record for a defender. Having made his first appearance as a substitute against Southampton in August, he was an ever present during the early part of the season, but missed several games through injury, notably in October, December, and January. Having celebrated his first goal of the campaign against Kosice in the Champions' League in September, he opened his Premiership account with a fine strike against Everton at Old Trafford in December, and his outstanding partnership with Gary Pallister has been compared to the glory days of Pallister and Steve Bruce, which is a fine tribute to a player who originally came to United as a hopeful 17-year-old trialist in 1988. *Stop Press:* Played in all four World Cup games for Norway in France during the summer, as the side reached the second round before going out of the competition when beaten 1-0 by Italy.

Blackburn Rov (£400,000 from Lillestrom on 26/1/93) PL154+5/4 FLC 16 FAC 10 Others 9
Manchester U (£5,000,000 on 12/8/97) PL 23+4/1 FAC 2 Others 5+2/1

BERGER Patrik
Born: Prague, Czechoslovakia, 10 November 1973
Height: 6'1" Weight: 12.6
International Honours: Czechoslovakia: 26
A central midfield playmaker who inspired Czechoslovakia to the Euro '96 final, and was thought to be the missing piece of the jigsaw when signing for Liverpool in the 1996 close season, Patrik has yet to set Anfield on fire, appearing usually on the wings, or in a floating role behind the front runners. Selected 28 times in 1997-98, 19 of his appearances being from the bench, the Czech needs a far better run of starts to show the knowledgeable Anfield crowd what he is really all about. Scored just three times during the campaign, all three coming in the 4-2 Anfield defeat of Chelsea.

Liverpool (£3,250,000 from Borussia Dortmund on 15/8/96) PL 19+26/9 FLC 5+1/2 FAC 1+2 Others 7+1/2

BERGKAMP Dennis
Born: Amsterdam, Holland, 18 May 1969
Height: 6'0" Weight: 12.5
Club Honours: PL '98
International Honours: Holland: 64
In what was probably the best spell of his career, 1997-98 more than made up for his two poor seasons in Italy with Inter Milan, and culminated in Dennis receiving both the PFA and Football Writers' Player of the Year awards. He was also elected by his fellow professionals to the award-winning Premiership team. Scoring 22 goals for Arsenal from 40 starts was excellent, but there is more to his games than just scoring. In possessing a great first touch and vision, having an excellent range of passing skills, and capable of flicking on long balls, either from his head or feet, almost all of Arsenal's attacking moves came through him in one way or another. Also, it was no coincidence that the Gunners' late autumn dip in form came when the Dutchman was serving a three-match ban. After getting the scoring side of his game underway with two in a 3-1 win at Southampton, he then notched a hat trick in a 3-3 draw at Leicester, stating that the third goal – having taken the ball down the left-hand side of the area before turning inside and curling it into the far top corner of the net – was the greatest of his life. Many of his goals were long-range strikes, the two against Barnsley, home and away, being typical. In terms of club football, last season was a massive success for Arsenal and ended with the Premiership and FA Cup trophies being on display at Highbury, the second time that the club had done the double. Although collecting a championship winning medal, unfortunately, after breaking down in training, Dennis was forced to miss the FA Cup final, having already missed the semi, after scoring three of the goals that took the side to Wembley. On the international front, with seven goals in six qualifying games for his country, he was probably the foremost reason for Holland reaching the World Cup Finals in France during the summer, and before departing for the tournament was expected to be one of the stars. *Stop Press:* Ever present in six games for Holland in the summer, scoring a wonderful winner in a 2-1 victory over Argentine, he and his team mates will have considered themselves very unfortunate to have lost on penalties in the World Cup semi-final match against Brazil. That was followed by yet another disappointment – a 2-0 defeat by Croatia that decided third place in the tournament.

Arsenal (£7,500,000 from Inter Milan, via Ajax, on 3/7/95) PL 89+1/39 FLC 13/8 FAC 10/4 Others 2/1

BERGSSON Gudni
Born: Iceland, 21 July 1965
Height: 6'1" Weight: 12.3
Club Honours: Div 1 '97
International Honours: Iceland: 76
Bolton's "Mr Dependable", Gudni was as reliable as ever in his defensive duties for the Wanderers last season. A solid performer, without ever doing anything flashy, he must be one of the biggest bargains in the club's illustrious history, performing with a consistency which belies his 31 years of age. Won his 75th international cap for Iceland in July of 1997, and will certainly retain his place in the Trotters' defence this coming season.

Tottenham H (£100,000 from Valur on 15/12/88) F/PL 51+20/2 FLC 4+2 Others 5+1
Bolton W (£115,000 on 21/3/95) P/FL 106+4/9 FLC 12+1 FAC 3 Others 3

Gudni Bergsson

BERKLEY Austin James
Born: Dartford, 28 January 1973
Height: 5'11" Weight: 11.6
This highly regarded left-sided Shrewsbury

midfielder, cum winger had a tremendous second half to 1997-98 and added a higher workrate to his game, together with a great improvement in his tackling. Very tricky on the ball, and a provider of good crosses from the byeline, his greater involvement was rewarded with a best-ever season goal tally.*

Gillingham (From trainee on 13/5/91) FL 0+3 Others 0+3
Swindon T (Free on 16/5/92) FL 0+1 FLC 0+1 Others 3+1/1
Shrewsbury T (Free on 29/7/95) FL 84+14/4 FLC 4+2 FAC 5+1 Others 10/1

Austin Berkley

BERKOVIC Eyal

Born: Haifa, Israel, 2 April 1972
Height: 5'7" Weight: 10.2
International Honours: Israel: 45

Transferred from Southampton during the summer of 1997, for a fee agreed at arbitration, the impish midfield maestro had an excellent season in 1997-98 at West Ham. Having great ball control and vision, he was the main playmaker, and on many occasions his final through ball set up goalscoring chances for John Hartson and company. Although not a proven goalscorer, he did, however, score seven league goals, which he took in his usual cool and calm manner. There is no doubt that Eyal is an outstanding player who was inspirational behind West Ham's best ever Premiership campaign and, as a regular in the Israeli national side, it is a pity his talents were not on show in the 1998 World Cup Finals in France during the summer.

Southampton (Leased from Maccabi Tel Aviv on 11/10/96) PL 26+2/4 FLC 5+1/2 FAC 1
West Ham U (£1,700,000 on 30/7/97) PL 34+1/7 FLC 5 FAC 6/2

Eyal Berkovic

BERNAL Andrew (Andy)

Born: Canberra, Australia, 16 May 1966
Height: 5'10" Weight: 12.5
International Honours: Australia: 18

One of the more consistent Reading players during a difficult season in 1997-98, Andy continued to show the physical commitment and bravery which has characterised his time at the club. While spending a major part of the campaign trying to shore up a rather diffident midfield, he also showed that he could play with composure anywhere along the back four and, despite adding two more sendings-off to his three in 1996-97, he remained greatly respected by the fans for his obvious enthusiasm.

Ipswich T (Free from Sporting Gijon on 24/9/87) FL 4+5 Others 0+2
Reading (£30,000 from Sydney Olympic on 26/7/94) FL 142/2 FLC 14+1 FAC 9 Others 3

BERRY Trevor John

Born: Haslemere, 1 August 1974
Height: 5'7" Weight: 10.8
Club Honours: AMC '96
International Honours: E: Yth

At the start of last season he was fancied to reach double figures for Rotherham as a right winger, but his brace against Doncaster in April only took his league total to three. A skilful winger on his day, he was often used in the wing-back role, although he grabbed the limelight thanks to a wonder goal in a televised FA Cup replay at Burnley.

Aston Villa (£50,000 from Bournemouth juniors on 3/4/92)
Rotherham U (£20,000 on 8/9/95) FL 92+16/14 FLC 3+1 FAC 4+1/2 Others 8/1

BERTI Nicola

Born: Parma, 14 April 1967
Height: 6'1" Weight: 12.2
International Honours: Italy: 38

An extremely experienced central midfielder who joined Tottenham on loan from Inter Milan last January, on the eve of the club's trip to Manchester United, having spent much of the season on the bench Nicola had to work hard in training to regain full match fitness. Once achieved, he was instrumental in Spurs' Premiership survival, with his strength and stamina holding the centre of the midfield together. Covering a great deal of ground throughout 90 minutes, and able to create space in the middle of the field in which to deliver accurate service to the wings, he also proved to be strong in the tackle, tenacious when defending, and very pacy when attacking. His keenness to get into opponents' penalty areas being rewarded with valuable goals, most notably at Blackburn Rovers in February, where an all-round good performance was topped by Nicola attacking a goalmouth ball flanked by three defenders and still managing to get on the scoresheet in a 3-0 win.

Tottenham H (Loaned from Inter Milan on 9/1/98) PL 17/3 FAC 2

Nicola Berti

BESWETHERICK Jonathan (Jon) Barry
Born: Liverpool, 15 January 1978
Height: 5'11" Weight: 11.4
A young left-sided Plymouth full back, who was in his first year as a professional, Jon was limited to two substitute appearances throughout last season but, when called upon, proved an able deputy to the regular left back, Paul Williams. On the bench for another 14 games, but not required, there should be more opportunities in 1998-99.
Plymouth Arg (From trainee on 27/7/96) FL 0+2

BETTNEY Christopher (Chris) John
Born: Chesterfield, 27 October 1977
Height: 5'10" Weight: 10.10
Signed on loan from Sheffield United last September, Chris made such an impression that Hull City persuaded the Blades to extend the deal until the end of the season, something that created a loophole in the new ruling. With Notts County wanting to sign him, the Tigers could not sell him (he was not their player) and neither could United. A tricky forward, often used in a central role, "Trigger" was seen at his most effective on the right wing, with his ability to regularly deliver a quality cross, and could prosper with more devilment in front of goal.
Sheffield U (From trainee on 15/5/96) FL 0+1
Hull C (Loaned on 26/9/97) FL 28+2/1 FLC 2 Others 1

BETTS Robert
Born: Doncaster, 21 December 1981
Height: 5'9" Weight: 10.0
Still a trainee, Robert made the giant step from schoolboy soccer to the tumult of Doncaster's relegation battle last April. Having passed the test with flying colours, Rovers would have been looking to sign the talented 16-year-old striker on contract during the course of the summer.
Doncaster Rov (Juniors) FL 2+1

Simon Betts

BETTS Simon Richard
Born: Middlesbrough, 3 March 1973
Height: 5'7" Weight: 11.4
Simon's injury problems continued into last season, and he did not appear for Colchester until November, ironically against Lincoln City, almost a year to the day since he was first injured – at Lincoln. Within days he had scored the winning FA Cup penalty against Brentford, and three weeks later had his vital penalty saved at Hereford in the next round. Finally, won a regular place at left back in February and kept it for the remaining months, including Wembley, making up for missing out last year in the AWS final. Was released during the summer.
Ipswich T (From trainee on 2/7/91)
Wrexham (Free on 13/8/92)
Scarborough (Free on 3/11/92)
Colchester U (Free on 11/12/92) FL 160+3/9 FLC 7 FAC 8+2 Others 13/2

BIBBO Salvatore (Sal)
Born: Basingstoke, 24 August 1974
Height: 6'2" Weight: 14.0
Regarded as Reading's third-choice goalkeeper throughout last season, he had a run of three games in early February, during which he conceded eight goals, despite a brave performance in the FA Cup tie at Sheffield United. But his commitment was never in doubt, and he spent much time and energy in coaching the club's schoolboy goalkeepers at the Centre of Excellence, before being given a free transfer during the summer.
Sheffield U (Free from Crawley T on 18/8/93) Others 2
Chesterfield (Loaned on 10/2/95) FL 0+1
Reading (Free on 15/8/96) FL 7 FAC 2

BIGNOT Marcus
Born: Birmingham, 22 August 1974
Height: 5'10" Weight: 10.8
International Honours: E: SP
Previously an apprentice with Birmingham City, on being released he went into non-league football with Telford United, and then on to Kidderminster Harriers before signing for Crewe last September. Having impressed with the England semi-pro side, he stepped straight into the right-back spot and stayed, proving to be a revelation. Competes for every ball and has terrific enthusiasm.
Crewe Alex (£150,000+ from Kidderminster Hrs on 1/9/97) FL 42 FAC 1

BILIC Slaven
Born: Croatia, 11 September 1968
Height: 6'2" Weight: 13.8
International Honours: Croatia: 42
A classy, ball-playing centre half, Slaven was Britain's most expensive defender when he switched from West Ham to Everton for £4.5m in May 1997. Unfortunately, for club and player, the move turned sour as the Croat suffered suspension after suspension in the worst season for red and yellow cards of his career. He was dismissed three times, all for tackles from behind, and picked up eight yellow cards, his last caution coming in January. A topsy-turvy campaign saw him

captain Everton against Newcastle in February, named as Croatia's Footballer of the Year and Sports Personality of the Year, but ended 1997-98 on the substitutes' bench. Despite the difficulties, he continued to express his desire to remain at Goddison and help turn the club's fortunes around.
Stop Press: Playing in all of Croatia's World Cup games that took them to the semi-final stage of the competition before being defeated by France, Slaven was vilified by many as overdoing a push by Laurent Blanc that got the Frenchman sent off and out of the final. Came back strongly as an integral part of the side that beat Holland 2-1 to win the third place.
West Ham U (£1,300,000 from Karlsruhe on 4/2/96) PL 48/2 FLC 5/1 FAC 1
Everton (£4,500,000 on 16/7/97) PL 22+2 FLC 3

BILLIO Patrizio
Born: Treviso, Italy, 19 April 1974
Height: 5'11" Weight: 10.5
Arriving at Crystal Palace last March, on trial through Monza, who had released him, Patrizio became the fourth Italian to find his way to Selhurst Park during 1997-98. Signed by Attilio Lombardo on non-contract forms, and a central midfielder with a good range of passing skills, he was not really up to the dog-fight at the bottom of the Premiership and, consequently, made just three appearances, two of them from the bench, before going home. Was replaced by Bruce Dyer after 55 minutes of his only Palace start, at home to Leicester City on 11 April.
Crystal Palace (Free from Monza on 16/3/98) PL 1+2

BILLY Christopher (Chris) Anthony
Born: Huddersfield, 2 January 1973
Height: 5'11" Weight: 11.8
Plymouth's Player of the Season in 1996-97 again displayed excellent skills as an attacking right-wing back in 1997-98, showing excellent pace and always willing to take on defenders. He also added a sound defensive side to his game, which made him a valuable asset that was well sought throughout the Football League. Absent just six times, Chris missed the all-important final game of the season through injury.*
Huddersfield T (From trainee on 1/7/91) FL 76+18/4 FLC 8+2 FAC 5 Others 15+2/2
Plymouth Arg (Signed on 10/8/95) FL 107+11/8 FLC 5 FAC 8/1 Others 5+1

BIMSON Stuart James
Born: Liverpool, 29 September 1969
Height: 5'11" Weight: 11.12
A left-sided Lincoln player, equally at home in midfield or defence, his appearances were restricted to the subs' bench in the first half of last season, but made the starting line-up on an occasional basis after Christmas. Is a strong tackler who likes to get forward, when at the back.
Bury (£12,500 from Macclesfield T on 6/2/95) FL 36 FLC 5 Others 3
Lincoln C (Free on 29/11/96) FL 20+7/1 FAC 0+1 Others 1+1

BIRCH Paul
Born: Birmingham, 20 November 1962
Height: 5'6" Weight: 11.0
Club Honours: FAYC '80; ESC '82

Although sidelined through various injuries at times last season, the veteran showed what a quality player he was when performing consistently well, and orchestrating things for Exeter in the centre of the pitch. A hard-working, bustling midfielder, Paul still entertains the idea of going into management at the end of his career.
Aston Villa (From apprentice on 15/7/80) FL 153+20/16 FLC 21+4/5 FAC 9+5/3 Others 5+2/1
Wolverhampton W (£400,000 on 1/2/91) FL 128+14/15 FLC 11+1/3 FAC 2+1 Others 8+1/1
Preston NE (Loaned on 7/3/96) FL 11/2
Doncaster Rov (Free on 20/7/96) FL 26+1/2 FLC 2 FAC 1 Others 1
Exeter C (Free on 27/3/97) FL 33+2/5 FLC 1 FAC 2

BIRCHAM Marc Stephen John
Born: Wembley, 11 May 1978
Height: 5'10" Weight: 10.12

A product of the Millwall youth side, who was voted the Young Player of the Year in 1996-97, Marc was sidelined for much of last season through injury. Quite at home in defence or midfield, with a liking to get forward, for a youngster he has great strength and endurance and is a good team player. At one stage, early in 1997-98, he was the reserve's leading scorer with five goals.
Millwall (From trainee on 22/5/96) FL 9+1 FAC 0+1 Others 2

BIRD Anthony (Tony)
Born: Cardiff, 1 September 1974
Height: 5'10" Weight: 10.7
International Honours: W: U21-8; Yth

Following a two week trial prior to the start of last season, the former Cardiff striker returned to league action after a fee had been agreed between Swansea and Barry Town, where he had top scored with 42 goals in 1996-97. Although achieving a reasonable tally, at one stage of 1997-98 Tony was on target to become the first City player to score more than 20 league goals in a season since Bob Latchford in 1982-83, and will be looking to better that in 1998-99.
Cardiff C (From trainee on 4/8/93) FL 44+31/13 FLC 8/2 FAC 4+1/1 Others 12+4/3 (Free to Barry T in January 1996)
Swansea C (£40,000 on 8/8/97) FL 35+6/14 FLC 2 FAC 1 Others 1

BISHOP Charles (Charlie) Darren
Born: Nottingham, 16 February 1968
Height: 6'0" Weight: 13.7
Club Honours: Div 3 '97

Having come back from a serious ankle ligament injury in 1996-97, the central defender played just eight times for Wigan in 1997-98 before being transferred to Northampton in December. Unfortunately, from the moment he appeared in the Cobblers' line-up, his season was blighted by both injury and suspension, and he was unable to put together a proper run of games. At his best, Charlie is noted for his strong heading ability and sound defensive qualities.

Watford (Free from Stoke C juniors on 17/4/86)
Bury (Free on 10/8/87) FL 104+10/6 FLC 5 FAC 4/1 Others 12+1
Barnsley (£50,000 on 24/7/91) FL 124+6/1 FLC 11+1 FAC 9 Others 5
Preston NE (Loaned on 12/1/96) FL 4
Burnley (Loaned on 28/3/96) FL 9
Wigan Ath (£20,000 on 28/6/96) FL 27+1 FLC 1 Others 2
Northampton T (£20,000 on 12/12/97) FL 7 FAC 1 Others 1

BISHOP Ian William
Born: Liverpool, 29 May 1965
Height: 5'9" Weight: 10.12
International Honours: E: B-1

Unable to hold down a regular place at West Ham in 1997-98, playing just four times, Ian returned to Manchester City on transfer deadline day, having earlier in his career left Maine Road bound for Upton Park in 1989. Signing a two-and-a-half year contract, Joe Royle brought him back as a steadying influence in midfield, but, caught up in the midst of the club's relegation struggle, he needed more time to settle and that was what he did not have. Although providing a couple of polished performances, spraying passes to all areas of the pitch, he was subbed in other games and will need time to acclimatise himself to the demands of second division football this coming term before the best is seen of him.
Everton (From apprentice on 24/5/83) FL 0+1
Crewe Alex (Loaned on 22/3/84) FL 4
Carlisle U (£15,000 on 11/10/84) FL 131+1/14 FLC 8/1 FAC 5/1 Others 4
Bournemouth (£35,000 on 14/7/88) FL 42/2 FLC 4 FAC 5 Others 1
Manchester C (£465,000 on 2/8/89) FL 18+1/2 FLC 4/1 Others 1
West Ham U (£500,000 on 28/12/89) F/PL 240+14/12 FLC 21+1/1 FAC 22+1/3 Others 4+1/1
Manchester C (Free on 26/3/98) FL 4+2

Stig-Inge Bjornebye

BJORNEBYE Stig-Inge
Born: Norway, 11 December 1969
Height: 5'10" Weight: 11.9
Club Honours: FLC '95
International Honours: Norway: 64

Continuing where he left off in 1996-97, when having a fine season in 1997-98, injuries apart, this hard-working Liverpool wing back, who can play on either flank, and who combines excellent tackling ability to getting up the line, where his crosses continued to be an asset when the side was going forward, rounded it off when selected for Norway in World Cup '98 in France during the summer. He was even used further forward for the Reds on occasion, in order for the club to take advantage of super crosses that were whipped in with some power and occasionally deceived goalkeepers and defenders alike and, on similar lines, often took corners and free kicks. *Stop Press:* Played in all four World Cup games for Norway, prior to the side being knocked out of the competition by Italy.
Liverpool (£600,000 from Rosenborg on 18/12/92) PL 112+4/2 FLC 14 FAC 9+2 Others 12/2

BLACK Anthony (Tony) Paul
Born: Barrow, 15 July 1969
Height: 5'9" Weight: 11.1

An old-fashioned Wigan right winger, Tony made just one substitute appearance in the opening match of last season, having been out of action during 1996-97. Sadly, he never fully recovered from a broken fibula sustained in March 1996 and announced his retirement from the game in November on medical advice.
Wigan Ath (£12,500 from Bamber Bridge on 22/3/95) FL 17+14/2 FLC 0+1 FAC 2/2 Others 0+1

BLACK Kingsley Terence
Born: Luton, 22 June 1968
Height: 5'9" Weight: 11.12
Club Honours: FLC '88; FMC '92; AMC '98
International Honours: E: Sch. NI: 30; B-2; U21-1

Following the departure of Kenny Swain as the Grimsby manager, and the transfer of John Oster to Everton, Kingsley managed to re-establish himself as a regular member of the senior squad in 1997-98, proving he had lost none of his ability. The arrival of David Smith from West Bromwich meant the former Northern Ireland international left winger often had to vie with the latter for a place in the second half of the season, but, whether from the start, or coming off the bench, he made a full contribution to what must be considered a successful season for the Mariners. Is an excellent crosser of the ball with good skills, especially when running at defenders. Won an AWS winner's medal following Town's victory over Bournemouth at Wembley, having scored the winner.*
Luton T (From juniors on 7/7/86) FL 123+4/26 FLC 16+2/1 FAC 5+1/2 Others 3+2/1
Nottingham F (£1,500,000 on 2/9/91) F/PL 80+18/14 FLC 19+1/5 FAC 4 Others 4+2/1
Sheffield U (Loaned on 2/3/95) FL 8+3/2
Millwall (Loaned on 29/9/95) FL 1+2/1 FLC 0+1
Grimsby T (£25,000 on 16/7/96) FL 43+20/2 FLC 7 FAC 5 Others 2+5/1

BLACK Michael James
Born: Chigwell, 6 October 1976
Height: 5'8" Weight: 11.8
International Honours: E: Sch

Loaned from Arsenal to Millwall last October, in order to further his experience, Michael made his Football League debut at the New Den against Blackpool, before opening his goalscoring account in his next match, against Oldham, also on home territory. It was no ordinary goal. With the scores level, he collected the ball in his own half, beat two or three players, before slipping the ball under the 'keeper to score the winner, and one for the scrapbook. Playing on the wide right, among his attributes is his ability to take defenders on to deliver quality crosses into the danger area. Returned to Highbury after 14 games to continue his learning curve in the reserves.
Arsenal (From trainee on 1/7/95)
Millwall (Loaned on 3/10/97) FL 13/2 Others 1

BLACKMORE Clayton Graham
Born: Neath, 23 September 1964
Height: 5'8" Weight: 11.12
Club Honours: FAC '90; ECWC '91; ESC '91; PL '93; Div 1 '95
International Honours: W: 39; U21-3; Yth; Sch

Now in the twilight of his illustrious career, Clayton still harbours an ambition to return to first team duty in the Premiership. He still trains long and hard in the belief that there are two or three good seasons left for him at the highest level, a belief that literally shines from his eyes with a boyish enthusiasm. His far too infrequent appearances for Middlesbrough in 1997-98 still gave the fans plenty to shout about, and the experienced midfielder proved he was still a force to be reckoned with, when displaying his consummate skill and boundless energy on the pitch.
Manchester U (From apprentice on 28/9/82) F/PL 150+36/19 FLC 23+2/3 FAC 15+6/1 Others 19/4
Middlesbrough (on 11/7/94) P/FL 45+8/4 FLC 3+2 FAC 4+1 Others 1
Bristol C (Loaned on 1/11/96) FL 5/1

BLACKWELL Dean Robert
Born: Camden, 5 December 1969
Height: 6'1" Weight: 12.7
International Honours: E: U21-6

This agile Wimbledon central defender came on in leaps and bounds in 1997-98 and dealt with the leading Premiership strikers extremely well. Tough-tackling, good in the air when attacking the ball, and with plenty of pace, he missed just three league games and proved his value to the club in some style. A former England U21 international, Dean has spent a number of seasons in the background since joining the club straight from school, but now seems set to remain at the heart of the defence for many years.
Wimbledon (From trainee on 7/7/88) F/PL 132+22/1 FLC 11 FAC 20+1 Others 1
Plymouth Arg (Loaned on 15/3/90) FL 5+2

BLAKE Mark Antony
Born: Nottingham, 16 December 1970
Height: 5'11" Weight: 12.9

International Honours: E: U21-9; Yth; Sch

Mark had an in-and-out season for Walsall in 1997-98, his best moments being his superb chip shot to give his side the lead at Barnet within minutes of coming on as substitute in December, and his shock match winner at Watford in March. He was released soon after the arrival of the new manager, Ray Graydon, in May, but has some good football left in him as a versatile midfielder or defender.
Aston Villa (From trainee on 1/7/89) FL 26+5/2 FLC 1+1 FAC 2 Others 2
Wolverhampton W (Loaned on 17/1/91) FL 2
Portsmouth (£400,000 on 5/8/93) FL 15 Others 4+1
Leicester C (£360,000 on 24/3/94) F/PL 42+7/4 FLC 4 Others 3
Walsall (Free on 23/8/96) FL 51+10/5 FLC 2 FAC 0+4 Others 2+2/1

BLAKE Mark Christopher
Born: Portsmouth, 17 December 1967
Height: 6'1" Weight: 12.8
International Honours: E: Yth

Mark was again reliability itself at Fulham in 1997-98, despite his first team appearances for the club being restricted after the arrival of Chris Coleman and Alan Neilson. Being a good pro though, he battled away in the reserves and when Neilson was injured, stepped into the breach. Has always been a good marker, with excellent heading ability, but his association with Ray Wilkins improved his distribution, although he was still ready to clear the ball into "Row 2" if the situation required it.
Southampton (From apprentice on 23/12/85) FL 18/2 FLC 2 FAC 3 Others 1+2
Colchester U (Loaned on 5/9/89) FL 4/1
Shrewsbury T (£100,000 on 22/3/90) FL 142/3 FLC 12 FAC 9 Others 12
Fulham (Free on 16/9/94) FL 133+7/17 FLC 10/1 FAC 9/2 Others 6+2

Mark Blake (Fulham)

BLAKE Nathan Alexander
Born: Cardiff, 27 January 1972
Height: 5'11" Weight: 13.12
Club Honours: WC '92, '93; Div 3 '93, Div 1 '97
International Honours: W: 7; B-1; U21-5; Yth

Last season was a much happier time for Nathan than his previous stint in the Premier League, where he scored only one goal in 14 full games, his goalscoring exploits establishing him as one of the most feared strikers in the British game. Now considered as the main centre forward at the Reebok, following John McGinlay's departure in November, he is a strong, robust player, who, at times, literally bundles players off the ball in his powerful attempts to score goals. Is also back in the Welsh squad after a much publicised bust up with Bobby Gould, and his current form suggests that he will be one of their main strikers for many years to come, while his club partnership with Dean Holdsworth looked increasingly more promising with every game played, and will certainly be one to watch this year. However, do not mention the name of Chelsea to him. Rejected by the Blues as a youngster, he was a member of the Sheffield United (1993-94) and Bolton (1997-98) sides that were relegated on the final day of the season after losing at Stamford Bridge.
Cardiff C (Free from Chelsea juniors on 20/8/90) FL 113+18/35 FLC 6+2 FAC 10/4 Others 13+2/1
Sheffield U (£300,000 on 17/2/94) P/FL 55+14/34 FLC 3+1/1 FAC 1 Others 1
Bolton W (£1,500,000 on 23/12/95) F/PL 91+4/32 FLC 8/5 FAC 6/2

Nathan Blake

BLAKE Noel Lloyd George
Born: Jamaica, 12 January 1962
Height: 6'1" Weight: 14.2

As Exeter's assistant manager, Noel played in most games in 1997-98 and was rested only when the team played a different formation. Among the dependable central defender's main attributes were an ability to organise the defence, while his aerial

strength at both defending and attacking set-pieces helped City through a difficult mid-season period, when collecting points was proving difficult.

Aston Villa (Signed from Sutton Coldfield T on 1/8/79) FL 4
Shrewsbury T (Loaned on 1/3/82) FL 6
Birmingham C (£55,000 on 15/9/82) FL 76/5 FLC 12 FAC 8
Portsmouth (£150,000 on 24/4/84) FL 144/10 FLC 14/1 FAC 10/2 Others 5/1
Leeds U (Free on 4/7/88) FL 51/4 FLC 4+1 FAC 2 Others 4
Stoke C (£175,000 on 9/2/90) FL 74+1/3 FLC 6 FAC 3+1 Others 4+1
Bradford C (Loaned on 27/2/92) FL 6
Bradford C (Free on 20/7/92) FL 38+1/3 FLC 2+1 FAC 5/1 Others 4
Dundee (Free on 10/12/93) SL 52+2/2 SLC 2 SC 5 Others 3
Exeter C (Free on 18/8/95) FL 126+2/8 FLC 6 FAC 5 Others 3

BLAKE Robert (Robbie) James
Born: Middlesbrough, 4 March 1976
Height: 5'9" Weight: 12.0

A hard-working Bradford front runner, who also helped out in midfield, Robbie found it tough going last season, being mainly confined to the role of substitute until Christmas, before coming back into the side to score five goals in ten games. Has a great attitude to the game in general, which was reflected in him signing a new contract that took him to the end of 2000-01, and filled in admirably when playing alongside a number of different partners during the enforced absence of John McGinlay. Takes the eye with darting runs around the box.

Darlington (From trainee on 1/7/94) FL 54+14/21 FLC 4+2/1 FAC 3+1 Others 3+1/1
Bradford C (£300,000 on 27/3/97) FL 26+13/7 FLC 0+2 FAC 1

BLAMEY Nathan
Born: Plymouth, 10 June 1977
Height: 5'11" Weight: 11.5

A right-sided full back in his second season at Shrewsbury, Nathan made a very promising start early in 1997-98, but injury curtailed his progress and he was not able to break back into the team. Scoring his first league goal in September against eventual champions, Notts County, he is equally at home defending as in going forward with the ball.

Southampton (From trainee on 1/7/95)
Shrewsbury T (Free on 14/2/97) FL 15/1 FLC 1

BLANEY Steven (Steve) David
Born: Orsett, 24 March 1977
Height: 6'0" Weight: 13.0
International Honours: E: Sch. W: U21-3

Freed by West Ham, having been at Upton Park as a professional since the 1995 close season without getting a first team opportunity, Steve, a full back who enjoys going forward, joined Brentford on transfer deadline day last March. A good passer of the ball, he made a few appearances before the end of the campaign, after making his Football League debut as a sub at Wrexham, prior to being released during the summer.

West Ham U (From trainee on 1/7/95)
Brentford (Free on 26/3/98) FL 4+1

BLATHERWICK Steven (Steve) Scott
Born: Nottingham, 20 September 1973
Height: 6'1" Weight: 14.6

Signed from Nottingham Forest during the summer of 1997, the powerful central defender looked the pick of Chris Waddle's new players, with some dominant performances in the early-season spell when Burnley were conceding few goals. Unfortunately, injury ruled him out in September, and a combination of the intense competition for his position and a failure to recover his previous form, saw him struggle to regain his first team place after that.

Nottingham F (Free from Notts Co juniors on 2/8/92) FL 10 FLC 2 FAC 1 Others 2
Wycombe W (Loaned on 18/2/94) FL 2 Others 1
Hereford U (Loaned on 11/9/95) FL 10/1 Others 2
Reading (Loaned on 27/3/97) FL 6+1
Burnley (£150,000 on 18/7/97) FL 13+8 FLC 3 FAC 1+1 Others 3

BLONDEAU Patrick
Born: Marseille, France, 27 January 1968
Height: 5'9" Weight: 11.5
International Honours: France: 2

When he signed for Sheffield Wednesday from French club, Monaco, in the summer of 1997, he seemed the perfect solution for the troublesome right-back role, not adequately filled at Hillsborough since Roland Nilsson left several seasons ago. However, after just six matches, including a sending off against Derby, he was dropped from the team, his lack of awareness and general "out of sorts" displays leaving everyone at Hillsborough disappointed. Despite having come with a great reputation, his departure midway through 1997-98, to Bordeaux, was not seen as being the end of the world, especially as he had obviously not been able to settle.

Sheffield Wed (£1,800,000 from Monaco on 10/7/97) PL 5+1

BLOOMER Matthew Brian
Born: Grimsby, 3 November 1978
Height: 6'0" Weight: 11.8

Grimsby Town central defender. As a junior professional and third generation of the well-known local footballing family to appear for the Mariners, Matthew proved to be a highly promising member of the reserve squad in 1997-98, and made a brief senior appearance as substitute in the Auto Windscreen Shield.

Grimsby T (From juniors on 3/7/97) Others 0+1

BOATENG George
Born: Ghana, 5 September 1975
Height: 5'9" Weight: 11.7

With George's contract at Feyenoord expiring at the end of last season, Coventry bought him in December and he had an immediate impact, despite being sent off in his second game at Upton Park. After that, he did not appear on the losing side for the next 14 games and his influence on the team was enormous. He gave Paul Ince the shock of his life in the Christmas game at Highfield Road and his performance in the cup victory at Villa Park was awesome, his run and pass setting up the winning goal. A fiery tackler with enormous energy, and the

ability to spray passes about, and get up in support of his attack, he would be arguably the buy of the season. Injured at Easter against Aston Villa and only returned for the last two games, he scored his first goal, against Blackburn, and was Man of the Match again. Is captain of the Dutch U21 side.

Coventry C (£250,000 from Feyenoord on 19/12/97) PL 14/1 FAC 5

BODIN Paul John
Born: Cardiff, 13 September 1964
Height: 6'0" Weight: 13.1
Club Honours: Div 2 '96
International Honours: W: 23; U21-1; Yth

The Welsh international full back played a few times for Reading in 1997-98, always replacing injured players, and joined Wycombe on loan in September. At Adams Park, Paul made five appearances as a left-wing back, putting in some solid defensive performances, and it was only the disparity of wages that stopped the move being permanent. Back at Wanderers, he was involved in a bizarre incident in the 0-0 draw against Wolves, when being sent off in a case of mistaken identity and, becoming disillusioned with his prospects at the club after that, he took the opportunity to become player/manager at Bath City, one of his former clubs, in May.

Newport Co (Free from Chelsea juniors on 28/1/82)
Cardiff C (Free on 1/8/82) FL 68+7/4 FLC 11 FAC 4 (Free to Bath C during 1985 close season)
Newport Co (£15,000 on 27/1/88) FL 6/1
Swindon T (£30,000 on 7/3/88) FL 87+6/9 FLC 12 FAC 6 Others 8/1
Crystal Palace (£550,000 on 20/3/91) FL 8+1 FLC 1
Newcastle U (Loaned on 5/12/91) FL 6
Swindon T (£225,000 on 10/1/92) F/PL 140+6/28 FLC 14 FAC 10/1 Others 8/1
Reading (Free on 11/7/96) FL 40+1/1 FLC 1 FAC 3
Wycombe W (Loaned on 18/9/97) FL 5

BODLEY Michael (Mick) John
Born: Hayes, 14 September 1967
Height: 6'1" Weight: 13.2
Club Honours: GMVC '91

A ball-playing Peterborough central defender, whose season was interrupted by injury in 1997-98, Mick is a wholehearted player who looks for a constructive forward pass rather than a hefty clearance. Always good for the odd goal, being a danger at set pieces with his aerial ability, he picked up one in a 3-1 win at Scunthorpe.

Chelsea (From apprentice on 17/9/85) FL 6/1 FLC 1 Others 1
Northampton T (£50,000 on 12/1/89) FL 20 Others 2
Barnet (£15,000 on 1/10/89) FL 69/3 FLC 2 FAC 10 Others 9
Southend U (Free on 15/7/93) FL 66+1/2 FLC 3 FAC 2 Others 7
Gillingham (Loaned on 23/11/94) FL 6+1 Others 1
Birmingham C (Loaned on 23/1/95) FL 3
Peterborough U (£75,000 on 27/7/96) FL 62/1 FLC 7 FAC 7 Others 6

BOERE Jeroen Willem
Born: Arnhem, Holland, 18 November 1967
Height: 6'3" Weight: 13.5

Jeroen's performances for Southend United during the 1997-98 season showed much greater commitment than in the previous campaign, and his rapport with the fans improved greatly. His undoubted skill in the air and on the ground brought him, and the team, many goals, but his playing time was again punctuated by injury.

West Ham U (£250,000 from Go Ahead Eagles on 22/9/93) PL 15+10/6 FLC 1+1/1 FAC 2
Portsmouth (Loaned on 24/3/94) FL 4+1
West Bromwich A (Loaned on 8/9/94) FL 5
Crystal Palace (£375,000 on 7/9/95) FL 0+8/1
Southend U (£150,000 on 1/3/96) FL 61+12/25 FLC 4+1 FAC 1+2 Others 1

BOERTIEN Paul
Born: Haltwhistle, 20 January 1979
Height: 5'10" Weight: 11.2

A first-year professional and one of the latest products to emerge from the junior ranks at Brunton Park, Paul made a promising start to his Carlisle career in 1997-98, with some impressive displays at full back. A knee cap injury sustained in December unfortunately ended his season, but he will be hoping for better luck and a longer run in the team this coming term.

Carlisle U (From trainee on 13/5/97) FL 8+1 FLC 0+2 FAC 1 Others 1

BOGIE Ian
Born: Newcastle, 6 December 1967
Height: 5'8" Weight: 12.0
International Honours: E: Sch

Had a very good 1997-98 season in the Port Vale midfield, in which he was more of a regular than he had been in the previous three years, showing the ability to put his foot on the ball, while his passing skills prompted many a Vale attack. Scored just the one goal, an impressive 20-yard shot at Bury, but missed the chance of a reunion against former room-mate, Paul Gascoigne, when the Middlesbrough ace was injured for the Vale Park clash.

Newcastle U (From apprentice on 18/12/85) FL 7+7 FLC 0+1 FAC 1+2 Others 3/1
Preston NE (Signed on 9/2/89) FL 67+12/12 FLC 3+1 FAC 3 Others 4+1
Millwall (£145,000 on 16/8/91) FL 44+7/1 FLC 1 FAC 2 Others 3
Leyton Orient (Signed on 14/10/93) FL 62+3/5 FLC 2 FAC 2 Others 8+1
Port Vale (£50,000 on 23/3/95) FL 94+16/7 FLC 7/1 FAC 7+2/2 Others 8

BOHINEN Lars
Born: Vadso, Norway, 8 September 1969
Height: 6'0" Weight: 12.2
International Honours: Norway: 48

Having started last season at Blackburn, where no-one doubted that he was the most creative player on the staff, he was never given the role that he was best suited to, that of playing behind the front two, and his appearances were sporadic. With that in mind, the Norwegian international moved to Derby on transfer deadline day with the intent of adding his craft to midfield, his game being based more on reading the play ahead of him, rather than involving the more defensive aspects of the role. Naturally right footed, and currently out of favour with the Norwegian management due to a dispute over tactics, Lars will be a very useful member of the County squad once his style of play can be fully adapted to Jim Smith's particular tactics.

Nottingham F (£450,000 from Young Boys of Berne on 5/11/93) F/PL 59+5/7 FLC 7+1/2 FAC 2/1 Others 1
Blackburn Rov (£700,000 on 14/10/95) PL 40+18/7 FLC 3+2/1 FAC 2+1/1
Derby Co (£1,450,000 on 27/3/98) PL 9/1

BOLAND William (Willie) John
Born: Ennis, Ireland, 6 August 1975
Height: 5'9" Weight: 11.2
International Honours: Ei: B-1; U21-11; Yth; Sch

Having failed to breakthrough on a regular basis in 1996-97, the Irish midfielder was a regular on the Coventry bench in 1997-98 and started six games, although never on the winning side in a league game. A product of the club's youth scheme, Willie is a skilful midfielder who rarely wastes the ball and, although chances were limited by the arrival of George Boateng and Trond Soltvedt, he is sure to come again. Added two more Republic of Ireland U21 appearances to his record and also played for the "B" team that met Northern Ireland in February.

Coventry C (From juniors on 4/11/92) PL 43+20 FLC 5+1 FAC 0+1

BOLI Roger Zokou
Born: Ivory Coast, 29 June 1965
Height: 5'7" Weight: 11.0

The quicksilver striker made a sensational start for Walsall in 1997-98 with five goals in his first six games, including a hat trick in a 3-1 home win over Southend, after being signed from Lens at the beginning of the campaign. His ability to turn on the ball brought him numerous goals "out of nothing" as scouts flocked to Bescot and, although his goals rather dried up in the second half of the season, he still totalled 24, including one in the FA Cup defeat at Old Trafford, to finish up second to Barry Hayles in the second division scoring charts. Selected for the award-winning PFA second division team by his fellow professionals, Roger sought a transfer and one wonders where he might be at the start of 1998-99. Is a former French U21 international.

Walsall (Free from Lens on 8/8/97) FL 41/12 FLC 6/2 FAC 4/4 Others 6/6

Roger Boli

BOLLAND Paul Graham
Born: Bradford, 23 December 1979
Height: 6'0" Weight: 11.0

Paul is yet another promising youngster to come through the Bradford City ranks, first

Ian Bogie

as a YTS, and then as a professional last March. Still a trainee when making his Football League debut at Stockport in early January, despite having just two minutes in which to acclimatise, the management could see that the young midfielder was up for it, something that was recognised six games later when he started at Middlesbrough. A midfielder who gives 100 per-cent effort, he was not overawed by the occasion and gave a good account of himself. Is most certainly one for the future.

Bradford C (From trainee on 20/3/98) FL 2+8

BONALAIR Thierry
Born: Paris, France, 14 June 1966
Height: 5'9" Weight: 10.8
Club Honours: Div 1 '98

Signed on a free transfer from the Swiss club, Neuchatel Xamax during the 1997 close season, Thierry started Nottingham Forest's opening game of 1997-98, playing on the wide left of midfield, before moving over to the right and then alternating between the two until going down at the start of the New Year with an achilles problem. Came back into the team in March at right back, when Des Lyttle was suspended, and played the last 11 games, making the position his own. Obviously a fair utility player, it will be interesting to see how he performs in the Premiership.

Nottingham F (Free from Neuchatel Xamax on 17/7/97) FL 24+7/2 FLC 1 FAC 1

BONETTI Ivano
Born: Brescia, Italy, 1 August 1964
Height: 5'10" Weight: 11.0
International Honours: Italy: 1

Having been released by Tranmere during the 1997 close season, Ivano went back to Italy and joined up with Bologna but, unable to secure a regular place, and wanting to try his luck in England again, he trialled at Crystal Palace on non-contract terms last October. Obviously into the final stages of a successful career which had earlier seen him capped for his country, there were just two first team appearances as a sub before he returned to Italy to play for Genoa at the end of the month. At his best, an attacking, ball-playing, left-sided midfielder who is capable of producing great crosses for the front men.

Grimsby T (Signed from Torino, via Brescia, Atalanta and Sampdoria, on 29/9/95) FL 19/3 FLC 1 FAC 2/1
Tranmere Rov (Free on 9/8/96) FL 9+4/1 FLC 2/1 (Free to Bologna during 1997 close season)
Crystal Palace (Free on 17/10/97) PL 0+2

BONNER Mark
Born: Ormskirk, 7 June 1974
Height: 5'10" Weight: 11.0

Working hard from the middle of the park, the Blackpool midfielder continued to display his liking for getting forward, and scored some important goals in 1997-98, especially the fourth in a 4-3 win at Wrexham after the Seasiders had been 3-0 down at one stage. Is also a very skilful and thoughtful player.*

Blackpool (From trainee on 18/6/92) FL 156+22/14 FLC 15+3 FAC 11 Others 10+3/1

BOOTH Andrew (Andy) David
Born: Huddersfield, 6 December 1973
Height: 6'0" Weight: 12.6
International Honours: E: U21-3

Hampered in the early part of last season by a cartilage injury, Andy came back after the operation and in his first match back, against Bolton, scored a hat trick in a 5-0 win. Although never quite hitting that sort of form again, despite scoring an important equaliser at Leicester and the winner at Leeds, he led the line well, proving to be a wholehearted player, who was good in the air, and good for the team. Could now do with a long injury-free run, to not only see the very best of him, but to see how far he could go in the game.

Huddersfield T (From trainee on 1/7/92) FL 109+14/54 FLC 6+1/3 FAC 8/3 Others 12+1/4
Sheffield Wed (£2,700,000 on 8/7/96) PL 53+5/17 FLC 2 FAC 6/3

BOOTY Martyn James
Born: Kirby Muxloe, 30 May 1971
Height: 5'8" Weight: 11.2

Martyn was one of the more reliable of the vast number of defenders that Reading used during its relegation season of 1997-98, even though he missed several games through injury. Performing at right back throughout, his best moment came when his low, scudding volley found the back of the Cheltenham Town net to give his team a 2-1 victory in the FA Cup third round replay. Is a good passer of the ball.

Coventry C (From trainee on 30/5/89) FL 4+1 FLC 2 FAC 2
Crewe Alex (Free on 7/10/93) FL 95+1/5 FLC 6 FAC 8/1 Others 13
Reading (£75,000 on 18/1/96) FL 55+1/1 FLC 6+1 FAC 7/1

BORBOKIS Vassilios
Born: Greece, 10 February 1969
Height: 5'11" Weight: 12.0
International Honours: Greece

Signed from AEK Athens, during the 1997 summer recess, the Greek international defender performed brilliantly at wing back throughout last season for Sheffield United, although occasionally found wanting when asked to play as an orthodox full back. Experienced a traumatic week back home in Greece to spoil his ever present record, when called upon to complete two days of national service. Fortunately, this was postponed until the end of the campaign! Scored some amazing goals, including two in his first two games, and a classic free kick against Sunderland in the play-off semi final, following which he was called into the Greek international squad. Was linked with a big-money move to the Premier League at the time of going to press.

Sheffield U (£900,000 from AEK Athens on 9/7/97) FL 36/2 FLC 5/2 FAC 6 Others 1/1

BORG John Carmel Adam
Born: Salford, 22 February 1980
Height: 5'9" Weight: 10.4

Given his first team debut in Doncaster's midfield at Rochdale last March, John was yet another of the Rovers' youngsters promoted to the league side after a number

of senior players had left the club prior to the transfer deadline. Still a trainee, the experience should have done him good.

Doncaster Rov (Trainee) FL 1

BORROWS Brian
Born: Liverpool, 20 December 1960
Height: 5'10" Weight: 11.12
International Honours: E: B-1

Initially taken on loan from Coventry City last September, he was soon snapped up on a free transfer to add some much needed experience to the Swindon rearguard. A model of consistency, and an example to other players approaching the later years of their careers, he missed just two matches through injury, including the disastrous FA Cup defeat at the hands of non-league, Stevenage. Comfortable on the ball, with a good range of passing skills, both long and short, Brian won manager Steve McMahon's vote as Town's Player of the Season after giving a series of outstanding performances.

Everton (From juniors on 23/4/80) FL 27 FLC 2
Bolton W (£10,000 on 24/3/83) FL 95 FLC 7 FAC 4 Others 4
Coventry C (£80,000 on 6/6/85) F/PL 396+13/11 FLC 42/1 FAC 26/1 Others 10+1
Bristol C (Loaned on 17/9/93) FL 6
Swindon T (Free on 5/9/97) FL 40

BOS Gijsbert
Born: Spakenburg, Holland, 22 February 1973
Height: 6'4" Weight: 13.7

Signed as a player for the future, having arrived in the 1997 close season from Lincoln, he was thrust into Rotherham's first team earlier than anticipated. Although netting four goals up to the end of September, Gijsbert failed to live up to expectations, never really taking full advantage of his height, and was loaned to Walsall on transfer deadline day.

Lincoln C (£10,000 from Ijsselmeervogels on 19/3/96) FL 28+6/6 FLC 6/3 FAC 1/1 Others 1
Rotherham U (£20,000 on 4/8/97) FL 6+10/4 FLC 1+1

Jovo Bosancic

BOSANCIC Jovo
Born: Novi Sad, Yugoslavia, 7 August 1970
Height: 5'11" Weight: 12.4
Jovo was another Barnsley player who took time to settle into the rigours of the Premiership in 1997-98. However, once that had been achieved he showed that he could more than hold his own. A good passer of the ball, he also had the ability to drift past opponents and create space for the forwards, while proving himself a good foil for the skipper, Neil Redfearn, in midfield. He only scored twice during the campaign, both in successive games, and one of them a stunning 20-yard drive for the equaliser at home to Blackburn. Was released during the summer.
Barnsley (Free from Iniao Madeira on 2/8/96) F/PL 30+12/3 FLC 3+1 FAC 5+1

BOSNICH Mark John
Born: Sydney, Australia, 13 January 1972
Height: 6'2" Weight: 13.7
Club Honours: FLC '94, '96
International Honours: Australia: 19
1997-98 was another season of fine form and consistency for the Aston Villa goalkeeper, despite missing the opening two games due to a hamstring injury picked up during a "friendly", along with another game later on, and five more when called up for international duty with Australia. His form with his country was also excellent and some high-class performances saw him named the Oceanic Player of the Year. There is no doubt that he is still in the top bracket as a brave shot-stopper who is not afraid to come for crosses, and is active between the posts at all times, his good left-footed kicking being a bonus. Kept 15 clean sheets from his 42 appearances, and defended the net resolutely as Villa gradually climbed the table.
Manchester U (Free from Sydney Croatia on 5/6/89) FL 3
Aston Villa (Free on 28/2/92) F/PL 164 FLC 20+1 FAC 17 Others 9

Mark Bosnich

BOULD Stephen (Steve) Andrew
Born: Stoke, 16 November 1962
Height: 6'4" Weight: 14.2
Club Honours: Div 1 '89, '91; PL '98; ECWC '94; FAC '98
International Honours: E: 2; B-1
Steve was yet another player to be given a new lease of life under the Arsene Wenger regime at Arsenal last season, when appearing in the centre of the defence, either as a starter or from the bench on 34 occasions. Indeed, Steve has credited his manager for extending his career by at least another two years. In vying with Martin Keown for a place alongside Tony Adams, he showed great vision in setting up the latter's goal with a superb chip in the 4-0 title clincher against Everton, having earlier stood in for the then injured captain at the beginning of the New Year. An unsung hero, but not with the fans who know better, he is reliable, good in the air at both ends of the park, is always likely to pop up with the odd goal at set pieces, apart from in 1997-98 that is, and is never afraid to come out of defence with the ball in looking to make the right pass. Although not playing against Newcastle in the FA Cup final, he sat on the bench to collect a medal following the 2-0 Gunners' victory, having earlier won his third championship medal.
Stoke C (From apprentice on 15/11/80) FL 179+4/6 FLC 13/1 FAC 10 Others 5
Torquay U (Loaned on 19/10/82) FL 9 FAC 2
Arsenal (£390,000 on 13/6/88) F/PL 257+11/5 FLC 33/1 FAC 24+1 Others 16+4/2

BOUND Matthew Terence
Born: Melksham, 9 November 1972
Height: 6'2" Weight: 14.6
Dominant in the air and a tough tackler on the ground, having been unable to establish himself at Stockport Matthew signed for Swansea last November and immediately added height and strength to a defence that had been noted for its ability to give away soft goals earlier in the season. Used primarily in a three-centre-back formation, he was also a danger at dead-ball situations with his strong left-footed free kicks.
Southampton (From trainee on 3/5/91) F/PL 2+3
Hull C (Loaned on 27/8/93) FL 7/1
Stockport Co (£100,000 on 27/10/94) FL 44/5 FLC 1 FAC 3/1 Others 3/1
Lincoln C (Loaned on 11/9/95) FL 3+1 Others 1
Swansea C (£55,000 on 21/11/97) FL 28 Others 1/1

BOWEN Jason Peter
Born: Merthyr Tydfil, 24 August 1972
Height: 5'6" Weight: 11.0
Club Honours: AMC '94
International Honours: W: 2; B-1; U21-5; Yth; Sch
Out of favour at Birmingham last season, Jason was loaned out to Southampton early in September, making just three appearances before going back to St Andrews. Still on the sidelines, the former Welsh international was eventually transferred to Reading in December, but failed to make any real impression down the right-hand side and was not selected again following the arrival of a new manager in the shape of Tommy

Burns. Despite being unfortunate with injuries, his pace and strong running is more than a match for all but the very best and this he proved to the Royals' faithful when tearing the Swindon defence to shreds in a 2-0 away victory.
Swansea C (From trainee on 1/7/90) FL 93+31/26 FLC 6+1/2 FAC 9+2/1 Others 15+3/8
Birmingham C (£350,000 on 24/7/95) FL 35+13/7 FLC 4+6/2 FAC 1+4 Others 2/2
Southampton (Loaned on 2/9/97) PL 1+2
Reading (£200,000 on 24/12/97) FL 11+3/1 FLC 0+1 FAC 5

BOWEN Mark Rosslyn
Born: Neath, 7 December 1963
Height: 5'8" Weight: 11.11
International Honours: W: 41; U21-3; Yth; Sch
This vastly experienced defender was signed by Charlton from Japanese club, Shimizu S-Pulse, last September, and made his debut at Carrow Road when he came on as substitute against his old club. Although he favours his right foot, Mark played all his games at left back for Charlton, and became first choice in that position. Very calm under pressure, and a good passer of the ball, he likes to join in attack, although yet to score for the Addicks.*
Tottenham H (From apprentice on 1/12/81) FL 14+3/2 FAC 3 Others 0+1
Norwich C (£97,000 on 23/7/87) F/PL 315+5/24 FLC 34/1 FAC 28/1 Others 17/1
West Ham U (Free on 10/7/96) PL 15+2/1 FLC 3 (Free to Shimizu SP on 17/3/97)
Charlton Ath (Free on 16/9/97) FL 34+2 FAC 3 Others 3

BOWER Mark James
Born: Bradford, 23 January 1980
Height: 5'10" Weight: 11.4
Having progressed well through the juniors as a central defender at Bradford, he was rewarded with a professional contract last March and made his Football League debut at Norwich a few days later, when coming off the bench for the last 35 minutes to fill in at left back. A youngster for whom a big future is predicted, despite the unaccustomed role he obviously impressed and, with Wayne Jacobs unavailable, his first start was in that position.
Bradford C (From trainee on 28/3/98) FL 1+2

BOWLING Ian
Born: Sheffield, 27 July 1965
Height: 6'3" Weight: 14.8
Mansfield's Player of the Year for the previous two seasons, Ian suffered an elbow injury last October, which kept him sidelined for a time, before he came back strongly in the New Year to perform as well as ever, keeping four clean sheets in his first five games. Was released during the summer.
Lincoln C (£2,000 from Gainsborough Trinity on 23/10/88) FL 59 FLC 3 FAC 2 Others 4
Hartlepool U (Loaned on 17/8/89) FL 1
Bradford C (Loaned on 25/3/93) FL 7
Bradford C (£27,500 on 28/7/93) FL 29 FLC 2 FAC 2+1 Others 1
Mansfield T (Free on 11/8/95) FL 123 FLC 6 FAC 6 Others 4

BOWMAN Robert (Rob)
Born: Durham City, 21 November 1975
Height: 6'1" Weight: 12.4
International Honours: E: Yth

A 1997 close season signing from Rotherham, Rob made a handful of appearances at full back for Carlisle in 1997-98, but could not command a regular place. Often looking more comfortable coming forward, his only goal, a long-range strike against Wrexham, was voted Goal of the Season by the United fans.
Leeds U (From trainee on 20/11/92) PL 4+3 FLC 0+1 Others 1
Rotherham U (Free on 21/2/97) FL 13
Carlisle U (Free on 14/8/97) FL 6+1/1 Others 1

BOWRY Robert (Bobby)
Born: Croydon, 19 May 1971
Height: 5'9" Weight: 10.8
Club Honours: Div 1 '94

Bobby was an integral part of Millwall's side in 1997-98, being the mainstay in midfield, and despite being the butt of a minority of supporters, it did not deter him from frequently earning Man of the Match awards for his good performances. He certainly showed his dedication to the cause when he turned down international honours with St Kitts in favour of continuing to help the club stave off relegation worries, and has now made 100 Football League starts since his arrival in 1995. Is strong, has great vision, and can pass with either foot.
Queens Park R (Signed on 8/8/90)
Crystal Palace (Free from Carshalton on 4/4/92) F/PL 36+14/1 FLC 10 FAC 1
Millwall (£220,000 on 5/7/95) FL 100+9/5 FLC 7 FAC 5

Bobby Bowry

BOWYER Lee David
Born: London, 3 January 1977
Height: 5'9" Weight: 9.11
International Honours: E: U21-9; Yth

Lee began last season in the Leeds' first team, after being one of the most consistent performers the previous difficult term, but was dropped after the first three games and was then in and out of the side for most of 1997-98. To his credit, he kept going and hit a rich vein of form in March, having produced excellent performances in the victories against Tottenham, Blackburn, and at Derby, scoring well-taken goals in the latter two games. He also notched the brilliant winner in the 4-3 comeback victory over Derby at Elland Road. Although linked by the media with a move away from the club, after being dropped, he fought back and appeared to benefit from having more experienced players around him. A player with endless stamina, he provides an essential service to the team as a gritty box-to-box midfielder and should have a big future at Elland Road.
Charlton Ath (From trainee on 13/4/94) FL 46/8 FLC 6+1/5 FAC 3/1 Others 2
Leeds U (£2,600,000 on 5/7/96) PL 53+4/7 FLC 2+1/1 FAC 7/2

BOXALL Daniel (Danny) James
Born: Croydon, 24 August 1977
Height: 5'8" Weight: 10.5
International Honours: Ei: U21-2

Unable to get a break at Crystal Palace in 1997-98, apart from a Coca Cola Cup appearance against Hull in September, and recovering from a cruciate knee ligament injury, Danny spent two spells on loan at Oldham during the season – the first coming in November and December, the second at the end of February, right through to the penultimate game – before going back to Selhurst to sit on the bench in Palace's final match. The first spell saw him playing in both full-back slots, while the second saw him perform mainly in the centre of defence. Good enough for the Republic of Ireland U21 squad, playing twice, he remains a talented, versatile youngster who could still come good with Palace, either as an attacking player or in defence.
Crystal Palace (From trainee on 19/4/95) F/PL 5+3 FLC 1+1
Oldham Ath (Loaned on 21/11/97) FL 5 Others 1
Oldham Ath (Loaned on 27/2/98) FL 12

BOYAK Steven
Born: Edinburgh, 4 September 1976
Height: 5'10" Weight: 10.7
International Honours: S: U21-1

Joining third division Hull City on loan from Rangers last February, Steven made a scoring debut in the Yorkshire derby at Scarborough, but injuries and suspensions meant that manager, Mark Hateley, had to initially use his former Ibrox colleague in an advanced position, despite him looking even more impressive just behind the front two. Has excellent vision and passing ability and, like fellow Tiger, Brian McGinty, he is a product of Rangers' Boys Club.
Glasgow Rangers (From juniors on 1/7/93) SL 0+1
Hull C (Loaned on 27/2/98) FL 12/3

BRABIN Gary
Born: Liverpool, 9 December 1970
Height: 5'11" Weight: 14.8
International Honours: E: SP-4

The hard-working midfield man was unfortunate to miss a good many games for Blackpool through injury last season, but when he did appear he was always in the thick of things, and scored the winner against Bristol Rovers in the penultimate game. A hard tackler, and a player who gives his all for the cause, when not required for first team duty Gary played a great part in helping the reserve side, scoring several goals.
Stockport Co (From trainee on 14/12/89) FL 1+1 Others 1+1
Doncaster Rov (£45,000 from Runcorn on 26/7/94) FL 58+1/11 FLC 2 FAC 2 Others 4
Bury (£125,000 on 29/3/96) FL 5
Blackpool (£200,000 on 30/7/96) FL 45+11/5 FLC 5 FAC 2 Others 2+2

BRACE Deryn Paul John
Born: Haverfordwest, 15 March 1975
Height: 5'8" Weight: 10.12
Club Honours: WC '95
International Honours: W: U21-8; Yth

Wrexham first team appearances were a rarity for Deryn in 1997-98, due to persistent injuries and illness which seemingly have dogged his career. Had begun the season well, appearing for the Welsh U21 side against Turkey and holding down the left-back position with his usual combative style, although it can be said that the latter description seems to be an "achilles heel", with his fine competitive spirit often resulting in him sustaining injuries because of his superb commitment towards the side. But, having said that, it is his "never-say-die" spirit that endears him to the Racecourse faithful. Can play in either full-back slot and enjoys supporting his team mates in attack.
Norwich C (From trainee on 6/7/93)
Wrexham (Free on 28/4/94) FL 61+4/2 FLC 5 FAC 5 Others 6

BRACEWELL Paul William
Born: Heswall, 19 July 1962
Height: 5'9" Weight: 12.5
Club Honours: CS '84, '85; ECWC '85; Div 1 '85, '93, '96
International Honours: E: 3; U21-13 (UEFAC '84)

With just three games under his belt at Sunderland in 1997-98, the veteran midfielder became the first signing by the Kevin Keegan/Ray Wilkins regime at Fulham last October. An excellent passer of the ball, Paul anchored the midfield in their failed attempt to win promotion via the play offs. At the time of writing, it appears that he might be first team coach in the club's bid to go up in 1998-99. Along with Chris Coleman, Paul was delighted to be voted into the PFA award-winning second division team by his fellow professionals.
Stoke C (From apprentice on 6/2/80) FL 123+6/5 FLC 6 FAC 6/1
Sunderland (£250,000 on 1/7/83) FL 38/4 FLC 4 FAC 2
Everton (£425,000 on 25/5/84) FL 95/7 FLC 11/2 FAC 19+2 Others 17+2/1

Sunderland (£250,000 on 23/8/89) FL 112+1/2 FLC 9 FAC 10 Others 6
Newcastle U (£250,000 on 16/6/92) F/PL 64+9/3 FLC 3+1/1 FAC 6+2 Others 2
Sunderland (£100,000 on 23/5/95) P/FL 76+1 FLC 8 FAC 3
Fulham (£75,000 on 10/10/97) FL 36 FAC 3 Others 2

BRADBURY Lee Michael
Born: Isle of Wight, 3 July 1975
Height: 6'1" Weight: 13.10
International Honours: E: U21-3

Signed from Portsmouth prior to 1997-98 getting underway, for what was a new record fee for Manchester City, Lee made his debut for his new club on the opening day of the new season against Pompey, showing neat touches and looking sharp up front. Unfortunately, as the sole striker, he did not score for nine games, until netting at Norwich and, even more unfortunately, having represented the England U21 side against Moldova, and then Italy, on his return from the latter he complained of a back pain which, diagnosed as a fine break, put him out of action for five months. Although coming back in January and playing on a regular basis, the goals were still not forthcoming and the bustling young forward will be looking to put things right in 1998-99.
Portsmouth (Free from Cowes on 14/8/95) FL 41+13/15 FLC 1+2 FAC 4/2
Exeter C (Loaned on 1/12/95) FL 14/5
Manchester C (£3,000,000 + on 1/8/97) FL 23+4/7 FLC 2

Russell Bradley

BRADLEY Russell
Born: Birmingham, 28 March 1966
Height: 6'2" Weight: 13.0
Club Honours: WC '90

Released by Scunthorpe during the previous summer, 1997-98 turned into a great season for Hartlepool's left-sided central defender,

who had been signed from the Irons after playing on loan in 1996-97. He was immediately appointed captain and throughout the campaign was a tower of strength, always commanding respect from his team mates. A strong player, good in the air, and good at bringing the ball forward, in mid-term he was rewarded with a one-year extension to his contract and has stated he will be happy to end his playing career with the Pool.
Nottingham F (Signed from Dudley T on 20/5/88)
Hereford U (Loaned on 13/11/88) FL 12/1 FAC 1 Others 3
Hereford U (£15,000 on 26/7/89) FL 75+2/3 FLC 7 Others 5+1
Halifax T (£45,000 on 6/9/91) FL 54+2/3 FLC 2 FAC 3 Others 4
Scunthorpe U (Free on 30/6/93) FL 116+3/5 FLC 6 FAC 11 Others 9
Hartlepool U (Loaned on 14/2/97) FL 12/1
Hartlepool U (Free on 8/7/97) FL 43/1 FLC 2 Others 2

BRADSHAW Carl
Born: Sheffield, 2 October 1968
Height: 5'11" Weight: 11.11
International Honours: E: Yth

Unable to hold down a regular place at Norwich in 1997-98, Carl was recruited by ·Wigan Athletic after being released from his contract in October, following a well documented off-field offence. A revelation in the Wigan Athletic defence, with his hard but fair defensive approach and forcing right-flank runs from full back, saw Carl collect the Player of the Year award. Proved his versatility when called to keep goal in the away victory at Wycombe and scored his first goal for the club from the penalty spot in a 2-0 win at Brentford in April.
Sheffield Wed (From apprentice on 23/8/86) FL 16+16/4 FLC 2+2 FAC 6+1/3 Others 1
Barnsley (Loaned on 23/8/86) FL 6/1
Manchester C (£50,000 on 30/9/88) FL 1+4 FAC 0+1 Others 0+1
Sheffield U (£50,000 on 7/9/89) F/PL 122+25/8 FLC 10+1/2 FAC 12+1/3 Others 4
Norwich C (£500,000 on 28/7/94) P/FL 55+10/2 FLC 6+1/1 FAC 2
Wigan Ath (Free on 6/10/97) FL 27+1/1 FAC 1

BRADSHAW Darren Shaun
Born: Sheffield, 19 March 1967
Height: 5'11" Weight: 11.4
International Honours: E: Yth

Having started last season in Blackpool's first team, making nine appearances in the opening 14 fixtures, Darren was released at the end of October in order to join non-league Rushden & Diamonds. At his best, he is a player who is calm and controlled on the ball, and able to operate either in midfield or defence.
Chesterfield (On trial from Matlock T on 12/8/87) FL 18 FLC 2
York C (Free from Matlock T on 14/11/87) FL 58+1/3 FLC 2 FAC 2 Others 3
Newcastle U (£10,000 on 16/8/89) FL 32+6 FLC 3 FAC 2+1 Others 3
Peterborough U (Free on 13/8/92) FL 70+3/1 FLC 7/1 FAC 4 Others 2
Plymouth Arg (Loaned on 18/8/94) FL 5+1/1 FLC 1
Blackpool (£35,000 on 20/10/94) FL 61+6/1 FLC 5 FAC 4 Others 6

BRADY Garry
Born: Glasgow, 7 September 1976
Height: 5'10" Weight: 11.0
International Honours: S: Yth

A natural midfielder who joined Tottenham in 1992 from Celtic at the tender age of 16, Garry was handed his first team debut in the FA Cup third round home tie against Fulham last January, followed by an appearance the following week at Old Trafford when coming on as a sub for Stephen Clemence in the Premiership clash with Manchester United. Impressing with his confidence to get forward and commitment in the challenge, the young Scot made consecutive appearances in the following seven games and looked sharp and intelligent both on and off the ball. Is a definite prospect for the future.*Stop Press:* Due to a contract mix-up, Garry signed for Newcastle on a free transfer on 7 July.
Tottenham H (From trainee on 9/9/93) PL 0+9 FAC 1+1

BRAITHWAITE Leon Jerome
Born: Hackney, 17 December 1972
Height: 5'11" Weight: 12.0

Unfortunately, Exeter's Leon did not make the progress he wished for in 1997-98 and was transferred to non-league Welling early in the season, after making just one league start and a handful of substitute appearances. A forward with natural pace, he is the brother of the sprint champion, Darren.
Exeter C (Free from Bishops Stortford on 3/11/95) FL 40+26/9 FLC 3 FAC 0+3 Others 1+1

BRAMMER David (Dave)
Born: Bromborough, 28 February 1975
Height: 5'10" Weight: 12.0

Last season saw Dave give the Wrexham fans some indication of what he is really capable of, proving himself to be a strong-running central midfielder who is not afraid to try his luck at goal, and possessing a powerful shot. At home with either foot, he could well feature strongly in a higher grade of football with his fine passing of the ball, although one gets the impression there is a need to acquire a steadier consistency. Scored a superb individual goal when intercepting a pass on the half-way line and finishing his run in fine style in the home game against Wycombe Wanderers during March.
Wrexham (From trainee on 2/7/93) FL 87+16/10 FLC 5+1 FAC 3+2 Others 7+2

BRANAGAN Keith Graham
Born: Fulham, 10 July 1966
Height: 6'0" Weight: 13.2
Club Honours: Div 1 '97
International Honours: Ei: 1; B-1

One of the most consistent and competent goalkeepers in the league, Keith yet again had an outstanding season for Bolton in 1997-98. As a member of three Wanderers' promotion winning sides, he has become a dependable fixture in their goalmouth and his considerable abilities instil much confidence in his defenders and fans alike. Produced a number of world-class performances that saved the Trotters a number of

Keith Branagan

club in the 4-0 home win over Bury in April.
Middlesbrough (£1,000,000 from Inter Milan on 17/2/98) FL 11/9 FLC 2/1

BRANCH Graham
Born: Liverpool, 12 February 1972
Height: 6'2" Weight: 12.2

This enigmatic player, a cousin of Everton's Michael, continued to either frustrate, amaze, or thrill Tranmere followers during 1997-98. Confidence plays a large part in Graham's game, and he seemed unable to transfer his frequent brilliance on the training pitch to first team games with any run of consistency. Unable to claim a regular place in the line-up, he was loaned out to Wigan, only to be recalled following a hamstring injury after three games, and eventually released in the early close season. A tall, pacy forward, with a venomous shot, and not afraid to run at opposing defenders, played in a position in which his talents can best be exploited he should be an asset to any team.
Tranmere Rov (Free from Heswall on 2/7/91) FL 55+47/10 FLC 4+8/1 FAC 1+2 Others 2+1
Bury (Loaned on 20/11/92) FL 3+1/1 Others 1
Wigan Ath (Loaned on 24/12/97) FL 2+1

BRANCH Paul Michael
Born: Liverpool, 18 October 1978
Height: 5'10" Weight: 11.7
International Honours: E: U21-2; Yth; Sch

A lightning-fast young striker, Michael started last season as one of Everton's bright young things, but ended it kicking his heels in frustration on the sidelines – the legacy of a broken leg. Already capped at England U21 level, the youngster started on the substitutes' bench at Everton before finally being granted his long-awaited first start of the campaign, at Derby County. Unfortunately, it lasted just nine minutes before he limped off with a serious hamstring injury. Recovering from that setback to make two substitute appearances for the first team, before limping out of a reserve team match against Leeds, he was diagnosed as having broken a bone in his leg and was forced to sit out the rest of 1997-98. Still promising, and highly rated at Goodison, hopefully, his best years are still ahead of him.
Everton (From trainee on 24/10/95) PL 15+19/3 FLC 0+1 FAC 1

points last season, most notably an astonishing save from Matt Elliott in the game against Leicester at the Reebok in March, which drew comparisons with the famous Gordon Banks save from Pele in the 1970 World Cup!
Cambridge U (From juniors on 4/8/83) FL 110 FLC 12 FAC 6 Others 6
Millwall (£100,000 on 25/3/88) FL 46 FLC 1 FAC 5 Others 1
Brentford (Loaned on 24/11/89) FL 2 Others 1
Gillingham (Loaned on 1/10/91) FL 1
Bolton W (Free on 3/7/92) P/FL 200 FLC 29 FAC 10 Others 6

BRANCA Marco
Born: Italy, 6 January 1965
Height: 6'0" Weight: 11.7

Charlie Wayman and Mickey Burns will not mean a thing to Marco, nor should they! Their names emerge from the dusty cupboards of yesteryear and are relevant only because the Italian surpassed their goalscoring records with his amazing run of ten goals in his first 12 games for Middlesbrough last season, after being signed from Inter Milan in February. Taking post-war games into account, only his fellow countryman, Fabrizio Ravanelli, can beat that tally, but the "White Feather" cannot match Marco's popularity, while his transfer fee far surpassed that of the latest Italian to visit the Riverside. Regardless of that, the fans are delighted that this down-to-earth striker is delivering goals, due to his opportunism and all-round powerful performances. Scored his first hat trick for the

BRANNAN Gerard (Ged) Daniel
Born: Prescot, 15 January 1972
Height: 6'0" Weight: 12.3

An ever present for Manchester City up until the New Year last season, having played in 39 successive matches, the then manager, Frank Clark, changed the system and Ged was out. A solid player on either side of midfield, probing and supplying the front men, he had earlier scored his first goal of 1997-98 in a splendid 3-2 win at Nottingham Forest, and had followed it up with another, a spectacular swivelled lob from 25 yards. Despite suffering a hairline leg fracture in training in early February, he took up training just four weeks later and was back in the first team at Port Vale two weeks after that. Can also play at full back.

Tranmere Rov (From trainee on 3/7/90) FL 227+11/20 FLC 26+1/4 FAC 10+1 Others 26+1/1
Manchester C (£750,000 on 12/3/97) FL 38+5/4 FLC 2 FAC 1

BRANSTON Guy Peter Bromley
Born: Leicester, 9 January 1979
Height: 6'0" Weight: 13.4
A strong young centre half taken on three-month's loan from Leicester City to cover Colchester's injury problems in defence over the latter half of the season, having previously been on loan to Rushden & Diamonds, Guy was an instant hit with U's supporters and, on his arrival, the previously leaky defence suddenly produced five consecutive clean sheets, during which he also scored the winner against Peterborough – not bad for a raw beginner! This new defensive solidity provided the launch pad for the run which was to take the U's up, but, unfortunately, for Guy, his loan period expired after the first play-off game at Barnet (in which he was sent off) so he missed out on Wembley glory. Incidentally, Crosse & Blackwell, the makers of Branston Pickle, got to hear about his exploits and promptly sponsored him because they liked the way he tackled the job with "relish".
Leicester C (From trainee on 3/7/97)
Colchester U (Loaned on 9/2/98) FL 12/1 Others 1

BRASS Christopher (Chris) Paul
Born: Easington, 24 July 1975
Height: 5'10" Weight: 12.6
Burnley's Player of the Season at centre-back in 1996-97, Chris found himself back in his old right-back slot under new boss, Chris Waddle, in 1997-98. Although he seldom shone, as in the previous campaign, he was still one of the few successes of a disappointing season, combining defensive solidity with a willingness to push forward, and also scored his first senior goal in the 7-2 win against York in January.
Burnley (From trainee on 8/7/93) FL 83+10/1 FLC 5+1 FAC 5+1 Others 7+1
Torquay U (Loaned on 14/10/94) FL 7 FAC 2 Others 1

BRAYSON Paul
Born: Newcastle, 16 September 1977
Height: 5'4" Weight: 10.10
International Honours: E: Yth
Small and compact, with the quick reflexes and sharp mind of a natural goalscorer, Paul still found it almost impossible to break into the Newcastle side in 1997-98, making a single subs' appearance against Hull in the Coca Cola Cup before Tommy Burns took him to Reading on transfer deadline day last March. Unfortunately, there was little time to settle, with the club fighting an uphill battle to avoid relegation, and he managed just one goal from mainly subs' appearances. Was distraught when hitting first the goalkeeper and then a post from close range in the penultimate game against Nottingham Forest, when a conversion would have offered the Royals a slim chance of staying in the first division at that moment in time.
Newcastle U (From trainee on 1/8/95) FLC 1+1
Swansea C (Loaned on 30/1/97) FL 11/5
Reading (£100,000 on 26/3/98) FL 2+4/1

BRAZIER Matthew Ronald
Born: Leytonstone, 2 July 1976
Height: 5'8" Weight: 11.6
Having appeared, one way or another in Queens Park Rangers opening three games last season, injury then ruled him out of contention until November. Started a further seven games before becoming the third left-sided midfielder, cum defender to be signed by Fulham from Rangers, following in Robbie Herrera and Rufus Brevett's footsteps, and made the perfect start for his new club with a goal on his full debut against Preston. At his best when going forward, Matthew lost his place when Brevett recovered from injury, but remained a valuable member of the squad.
Queens Park R (From trainee on 1/7/94) P/FL 36+13/2 FLC 3+2/1 FAC 3
Fulham (£65,000 on 20/3/98) FL 3+4/1

BREACKER Timothy (Tim) Sean
Born: Bicester, 2 July 1965
Height: 6'0" Weight: 13.0
Club Honours: FLC '88
International Honours: E: U21-2
Tim started last season well at West Ham and his foraging runs down the right flank brought goals for John Hartson and Eyal Berkovic. With a liking to go forward, thus bringing an extra option to the Hammer's play, unfortunately, injuries again played their part, and a groin strain sustained against Arsenal in March brought his campaign to an early end.
Luton T (From apprentice on 15/5/83) FL 204+6/3 FLC 22+2 FAC 21 Others 7
West Ham U (£600,000 on 12/10/90) F/PL 227+10/8 FLC 20 FAC 26+1 Others 7

BREBNER Grant Iain
Born: Edinburgh, 6 December 1977
Height: 5'10" Weight: 11.5
International Honours: S: U21-8
A Scottish U21 international, despite being unable to get a break at Manchester United, having been on the club's books as a professional since March 1995, Grant was loaned to Cambridge last January and made six appearances in midfield. Showing his class, he moved into first team football well, scoring on his league debut against Scarborough at the Abbey, and there was disappointment when he returned to Old Trafford in February. Was later loaned to Hibernian.
Manchester U (Free from Hutchinson Vale BC on 17/3/95)
Cambridge U (Loaned on 9/1/98) FL 6/1
Hibernian (Loaned on 26/2/98) SL 9/1

BRECKIN Ian
Born: Rotherham, 24 February 1975
Height: 6'0" Weight: 12.9
Club Honours: AMC '96
After an uncertain start for Chesterfield, Ian grew in confidence and assurance as last season progressed. A tall and commanding central defender, his ability to read the game is good for one so young and offers much promise for the future. Voted the Players' Player of the Year, he is the nephew of the former Rotherham player, John Breckin.

Rotherham U (From trainee on 1/11/93) FL 130+2/6 FLC 6 FAC 5 Others 11
Chesterfield (£100,000 on 25/7/97) FL 40+3/1 FLC 3 FAC 3/1

BREEN Gary Patrick
Born: Hendon, 12 December 1973
Height: 6'2" Weight: 12.0
International Honours: Ei: 15; U21-9
A skilful right-footed Coventry central defender who likes to bring the ball out of defence, and is also very good in the air, Gary started last season as a right back and was very uncomfortable in that role. He then returned to centre half in October when Paul Williams was suspended and made the place his own with some composed displays. An outstanding disciplinary record was blemished at Villa Park when he was sent off and suspended for three games over Christmas, but he returned for the cup win at Anfield and played a major part in City's unbeaten run. Totally dominating in the cup replay at Bramall Lane, he was recalled to the Eire squad in the spring in recognition of his excellent progress. Scored his first goal for City in the home win over Spurs.
Maidstone U (Free from Charlton Ath juniors on 6/3/91) FL 19
Gillingham (Free on 2/7/92) FL 45+6 FLC 4 FAC 5 Others 1
Peterborough U (£70,000 on 5/8/94) FL 68+1/1 FLC 6 FAC 6 Others 6/1
Birmingham C (£400,000 on 9/2/96) FL 37+3/2 FLC 4 FAC 1
Coventry C (£2,400,000 on 1/2/97) PL 38+1/1 FLC 3+1 FAC 5

BRENNAN James (Jim) Gerald
Born: Toronto, Canada, 8 May 1977
Height: 5'9" Weight: 12.5
A left back, or to use the modern jargon - left-wing back, Jim has proved himself to be a good solid performer during his four years with Bristol City, and provided reliable cover for Mickey Bell whenever he was called upon in 1997-98. As you would expect of someone who plays at wing back, he gets forward well when there are attacking options, and has fair recovery rate.
Bristol C (Free from Sora Lazio on 25/10/94) FL 11+3 FAC 1

BRESLAN Geoffrey (Geoff) Francis
Born: Torbay, 4 June 1980
Height: 5'8" Weight: 11.0
Still a trainee, and a first-year one at that, the young Exeter midfielder made his Football League debut at home to Macclesfield, when coming on for the last 33 minutes of the final game of 1997-98. Is highly thought of at St James' Park.
Exeter C (Trainee) FL 0+1

BREVETT Rufus Emanuel
Born: Derby, 24 September 1969
Height: 5'8" Weight: 11.0
Missing just six games between the start of 1997-98 and the end of January for Queens Park Rangers, and having a good season, Rufus was a shock signing for Fulham, when it was known that Robbie Herrera would be sidelined for a considerable time. Showed good defensive attributes in the left-back role, and was also a potent force with

marauding runs down the flank in his 13 games for the Cottagers, his only blip being a short absence due to injury.
Doncaster Rov (From trainee on 8/7/88) FL 106+3/3 FLC 5 FAC 4 Others 10+1
Queens Park R (£250,000 on 15/2/91) F/PL 141+11/1 FLC 9+1 FAC 8
Fulham (£375,000 on 28/1/98) FL 11 Others 2

BRIDGES Michael
Born: North Shields, 5 August 1978
Height: 6'1" Weight: 10.11
Club Honours: Div 1 '96
International Honours: E: U21-1; Yth
The highly-rated young Sunderland striker, who made such an impact in the club's 1996 promotion campaign, must have thought that this would be the season that he established himself in the first team. However, a damaged groin in December, coupled with the success of the Niall Quinn/Kevin Phillips partnership up front, meant Michael's opportunities were limited. Nevertheless, his undoubted goalscoring ability will surely lead to regular first team football in the not too distant future. Has pace and skill to spare, and the ability to hold the ball up for others to arrive.
Sunderland (From trainee on 9/11/95) P/FL 18+31/8 FLC 3+1/1 FAC 2

BRIEN Anthony (Tony) James
Born: Dublin, 10 February 1969
Height: 6'0" Weight: 13.2
International Honours: Ei: Yth
After appearing in much of the first half of the Hull City 1997-98 season, "TB" announced his retirement due to injury on 12 January at the age of 28, having struggled with an arthritic hip for several months. Despite requiring a replacement in a few years time, without the constant wear and tear of day-to-day training, Tony will be allowed to continue in non-League football and joined Stalybridge Celtic, whilst training for a commercial pilot's license.
Leicester C (From apprentice on 13/2/87) FL 12+4/1 FLC 1 FAC 1 Others 3
Chesterfield (£90,000 on 16/12/88) FL 201+3/8 FLC 14 FAC 7 Others 14
Rotherham U (Signed on 8/10/93) FL 41+2/2 FLC 2 FAC 4 Others 6
West Bromwich A (Free on 13/7/95) FL 2 FLC 1 Others 1
Mansfield T (Loaned on 16/2/96) FL 4
Chester C (Loaned on 22/3/96) FL 8
Hull C (Free on 12/7/96) FL 43+4/1 FLC 7 FAC 3 Others 2

BRIGHT Mark Abraham
Born: Stoke, 6 June 1962
Height: 6'1" Weight: 13.4
Club Honours: FMC '91
An experienced Charlton striker who missed most of the early part of last season due to an injury that required a hernia operation, Mark played fairly regularly after the turn of the year, competing with Steve Jones for the striker's slot alongside Clive Mendonca. Netted some valuable goals for the Addicks, mostly with his head, including the equaliser in the 1-1 draw with Sunderland, and the winner against Huddersfield, being at his most dangerous when running on to crosses from the wingmen.*

Port Vale (Free from Leek T on 15/10/81) FL 18+11/10 FLC 1+1 FAC 0+1/1 Others 2
Leicester C (£33,000 on 19/7/84) FL 26+16/6 FLC 3+1 FAC 1
Crystal Palace (£75,000 on 13/11/86) F/PL 224+3/92 FLC 22/11 FAC 13+1/2 Others 23/9
Sheffield Wed (£1,375,000 on 11/9/92) PL 112+16/48 FLC 20+1/11 FAC 13/7 (Free to Sion on 27/1/97)
Millwall (Loaned on 13/12/96) FL 3/1 Others 1
Charlton Ath (Free on 4/4/97) FL 17+5/9 FLC 0+2 FAC 2+1 Others 3

BRIGHTWELL David John
Born: Lutterworth, 7 January 1971
Height: 6'2" Weight: 13.5
Released by Bradford during the summer of 1997, the central defender joined Northampton in time for the beginning of last season, and immediately commanded a first team place, before losing out towards the latter part of the campaign as competition for defensive roles hotted up. Has a laid back style, but is good in the air, and has a strong kick that has often converted defending into attacking.*
Manchester C (From juniors on 11/4/88) F/PL 35+8/1 FLC 2+1 FAC 5+2/1
Chester C (Loaned on 22/3/91) FL 6
Lincoln C (Loaned on 11/8/95) FL 5 FLC 2
Stoke C (Loaned on 11/9/95) FL 0+1 Others 1
Bradford C (£30,000 on 22/12/95) FL 23+1 FAC 1 Others 2
Blackpool (Loaned on 12/12/96) FL 1+1
Northampton T (Free on 29/7/97) FL 34+1/1 FLC 2 FAC 5 Others 2+1

BRIGHTWELL Ian Robert
Born: Lutterworth, 9 April 1968
Height: 5'10" Weight: 12.5
International Honours: E: U21-4; Yth
Ian takes his testimonial this coming season, despite being released during the summer, having delayed it for two years so that Paul Lake could take his due to early retirement. Currently the longest serving player at Manchester City, the brother of David, now at Northampton, and the son of the famous Olympians, Robbie Brightwell and Ann Packer, started 1997-98 well, but four yellow cards, coupled with a hamstring injury, put him out of contention for the next nine league games. Came back to perform consistently well, even taking over the armband for a short while, before picking up a number of injuries in the latter stages of the campaign. Is sound and reliable whether at full back or in midfield. *Stop Press:* Signed for Coventry on 19 June.
Manchester C (From juniors on 7/5/86) F/PL 285+36/18 FLC 29+2 FAC 19+4/1 Others 4+3

BRISCOE Lee Stephen
Born: Pontefract, 30 September 1975
Height: 5'11" Weight: 10.9
International Honours: E: U21-5
1997-98 was yet another season where Lee was unable to make the expected breakthrough as a first team regular on the left-hand side of Sheffield Wednesday's defence or midfield, the presence of Dejan Stefanovic, Mark Pembridge, and Andy Hinchcliffe, combining to halt his opportunities, and he was loaned out to Manchester City in February. With the new City manager, Joe Royle, requiring a natural

left-sided defender, he fitted the bill perfectly, giving the side more balance when acting as an overlapping winger, and scoring his first goal, at Huddersfield, in an excellent performance on a rain soaked surface. Returned to Hillsborough, much to Royle's disappointment, hoping for a good run and looks to 1998-99 with prospects in view.
Sheffield Wed (From trainee on 22/5/94) PL 36+10 FLC 2+1
Manchester C (Loaned on 20/2/98) FL 5/1

BRISSETT Jason Curtis
Born: Wanstead, 7 September 1974
Height: 5'10" Weight: 12.7
Jason found it difficult to sustain a first team place at Bournemouth last season, playing up front and on the left-hand side of midfield. Quick, and not afraid to run at defenders, who often found it difficult to contain him when he was playing well, he will be looking not only to claim a permanent place, but for a more consistent time of it in 1998-99.
Peterborough U (Free from Arsenal juniors on 14/6/93) FL 27+8 FLC 5+1/1 FAC 2+1/1 Others 3+1/1
Bournemouth (Free on 23/12/94) FL 96+28/8 FLC 5+2 FAC 4 Others 6+2/2

BRODIE Stephen (Steve) Eric
Born: Sunderland, 14 January 1973
Height: 5'6" Weight: 10.6
A pacy and hard-working Scarborough striker, Steve improved as last season progressed and scored some vital goals, including the winner against Barnet and a brace against Exeter. A good team player, who always gives 100 per-cent commitment, he was the runner up in the league scoring status with ten goals, as Boro qualified for the play offs.
Sunderland (From trainee on 1/7/91) FL 1+11
Doncaster Rov (Signed on 31/8/95) FL 5/1
Scarborough (Free on 20/12/96) FL 66+2/15 FLC 2 FAC 1 Others 2+1

BROLIN Tomas
Born: Sweden, 29 November 1969
Height: 5'8" Weight: 12.2
International Honours: Sweden: 52
Freed by Leeds, having failed to settle at Elland Road following a £4.5 million transfer in November 1995, and after spending much of the last 18 months on trial with a number of clubs in Europe, Tomas came on trial to Crystal Palace last January and found himself thrust into Premiership action, against Everton at Selhurst Park, a few days later. Obviously not match fit, Steve Coppell explained afterwards that the Swedish international had done the club a favour by playing. The Palace manager said: "He was not even being paid for his services, just his hotel bill. When I asked him to play he fell about laughing, saying he was not fit enough, but I explained that a wise head can save miles in legs." A creative, hard-running midfielder who can score goals, apart from hitting the woodwork and occasionally delivering quality long-range passes, he failed to score in 16 outings as Palace revisited the first division for the third time since the

Premiership came into being. Signed on a short-term contract, the chunky little Swede was released during the summer.

Leeds U (£4,500,000 from Parma on 25//11/95) PL 17+2/4 FLC 2+2 FAC 1+1
Crystal Palace (Free on 8/1/98) PL 13 FAC 3

BROOKER Paul
Born: Hammersmith, 25 November 1976
Height: 5'8" Weight: 10.0
This exciting right-sided Fulham midfielder, cum striker, who had promised so much the previous season, was rarely in contention in 1997-98 and had a disappointing campaign. The fact that Kevin Keegan put him on the bench for the play-off decider at Grimsby, and brought him on when Fulham were desperately in need of a goal might bode well for his prospects in 1998-99. "Bozzie", as he is known to all at the Cottage, is still only 21 and if he can fine tune his dribbling ability, and vital final pass, or shot, he has a great deal to offer.
Fulham (From trainee on 1/7/95) FL 13+42/4 FLC 1+2/1 FAC 1+3/1 Others 3+2

BROOKES Darren Paul
Born: Sheffield, 7 July 1973
Height: 6'3" Weight: 12.2
Signed from non-league Worksop during the 1997 close season, Darren started his first campaign in professional football up against Pierre Van Hooijdonk, when Doncaster let in eight goals against Nottingham Forest in a Coca Cola Cup game. Eventually lost his place at the heart of the Rovers' defence through injury early on, but then found himself "frozen out" of the first team following a difference of opinion with the hierarchy at Belle Vue.
Doncaster Rov (Free from Worksop on 31/7/97) FL 9+2 FLC 2 FAC 1 Others 0+1

BROOMES Marlon Charles
Born: Birmingham, 28 November 1977
Height: 6'0" Weight: 12.12
International Honours: E: U21-2; Yth; Sch
One of the most likely products of Blackburn's youth scheme to make a name for himself before too long, having been loaned out to Swindon in 1996-97, Marlon was finally presented with first team opportunities at Ewood, making his debut against Preston in the Coca Cola Cup last September, and impressing. While there is no doubting his potential, if he can add a bit more aggression to his cultured approach, the England U21 central defender could be on the verge of a breakthrough in 1998-99. Watch this space.
Blackburn Rov (From trainee on 28/11/94) PL 2+2 FLC 1
Swindon T (Loaned on 22/1/97) FL 12/1

BROUGHTON Drewe Oliver
Born: Hitchin, 25 October 1978
Height: 6'3" Weight: 12.0
Started in the opening line-up for Wigan Athletic in their first away match of last season at Bournemouth, while on loan from Norwich. A scorer for the youth and reserve team at Carrow Road, the willowy framed, tall centre forward returned to his club after

his spell at Springfield Park, only to find that Adrian Coote had moved ahead of him in the strikers' pecking order. Following just one subs' appearance for City in early November, at home to Bury, he was sidelined by a hernia operation and will look back with disappointment when assessing his progress in 1997-98.
Norwich C (From trainee on 6/5/97) FL 3+6/1
Wigan Ath (Loaned on 15/8/97) FL 1+3

BROWN Andrew Stewart
Born: Edinburgh, 11 October 1976
Height: 6'3" Weight: 13.10
Although the former Leeds' junior was impressive in Hull City's pre-season friendlies, Andrew soon slipped out of the first team frame when the real action got underway, making just three subs' appearances. With playing prospects looking sparse, the lanky forward agreed to a return to his native Scotland in September, and joined second division, Clydebank.
Leeds U (Signed from St Johnstone juniors on 1/4/95)
Hull C (Free on 13/5/96) FL 7+22/1 FLC 0+2 FAC 2

BROWN David Alistair
Born: Bolton, 2 October 1978
Height: 5'9" Weight: 12.6
A prolific scorer in Manchester United's "A" and "B" teams, he agreed a loan move to Hull City on transfer deadline day, last March, and, in relishing the chance of first team football, the powerfully-built striker showed his true colours with a two-goal salvo in the vital win against Hartlepool. David first shot to prominence when he was at the centre of a poaching row, after United "took" him from Oldham, where he had been a schoolboy. Fined £20,000 by the FA, and forced to pay £75,000 compensation to Athletic after signing him in July 1995, if the young forward goes on to play for England, United will have to splash out a further £525,000. Holds the ball up well and is very alert around the six-yard box.
Manchester U (From trainee on 27/10/95)
Hull C (Loaned on 26/3/98) FL 7/2

BROWN Grant Ashley
Born: Sunderland, 19 November 1969
Height: 6'0" Weight: 11.12
A solid Lincoln central defender who missed the first six months of last season as a result of back and hernia problems, when he returned in mid-February he showed he had lost none of his ability and proved an important part of the Imps' defence in the run in to the end of the campaign. Is City's longest-serving player, having completed nine seasons at Sincil Bank.*
Leicester C (From trainee on 1/7/88) FL 14 FLC 2
Lincoln C (£60,000 on 20/8/89) FL 303/12 FLC 18/1 FAC 11 Others 17/2

BROWN Gregory (Greg) Jonathan
Born: Manchester, 31 July 1978
Height: 5'10" Weight: 11.6
Released by Chester in the 1997 close season, and taken on by Football League first timers, Macclesfield, as a non-contract

player, this local lad made a promising start as a stand-in for an injured full back in midterm. A useful squad player, having been on the bench numerous times, but remaining unused, Greg would have had regular football had Town got a reserve team.
Chester C (From trainee on 20/6/96) FL 1+3 FAC 0+1 Others 0+1
Macclesfield T (Free on 19/12/97) FL 2

BROWN Kenneth (Kenny) James
Born: Upminster, 11 July 1967
Height: 5'9" Weight: 11.6
Signed from Birmingham during the 1997 close season, Kenny, the son of a former West Ham and England centre half, quickly settled down at Millwall, being mainly used in the right-back position, or occasionally as a sweeper, where his reading of a game was outstanding. An accomplished defender, who has seen service with many clubs, he likes getting forward and has a good shot on him. Very experienced and is a most useful role model for any youngster playing alongside him.
Norwich C (From juniors on 10/7/85) FL 24+1 Others 3
Plymouth Arg (Free on 10/8/88) FL 126/4 FLC 9 FAC 6 Others 3
West Ham U (£175,000 on 2/8/91) F/PL 55+8/5 FLC 2+1 FAC 7+2/1 Others 2+2
Huddersfield T (Loaned on 7/9/95) FL 5
Reading (Loaned on 27/10/95) FL 12/1 FLC 3
Southend U (Loaned on 1/3/96) FL 6
Crystal Palace (Loaned on 28/3/96) FL 5+1/2 Others 3/1
Reading (Loaned on 9/9/96) FL 5
Birmingham C (£75,000 on 27/12/96) FL 11 FAC 1
Millwall (£40,000+ on 31/7/97) FL 45 FLC 4 FAC 1 Others 2

BROWN Linton James
Born: Hull, 12 April 1968
Height: 5'10" Weight: 12.7
Unable to commit himself to satisfy the demands of either Jan Molby or Alan Cork at Swansea last season, Linton was made available for transfer, having had a spell on loan at Scarborough in August, where he scored on his debut in a 3-3 draw against Lincoln. However, with no takers, the striker eventually made his first league appearance of 1997-98 in January, when coming off the bench against his old club, Hull City, before leaving for non-league Emley on transfer deadline day after his contract had been paid up.
Halifax T (Free from Guisley on 18/12/92) FL 3
Hull C (Free on 8/1/93) FL 111+10/23 FLC 6 FAC 4+1/1 Others 4
Swansea C (£60,000 on 22/3/96) FL 16+11/3 FLC 1+1 FAC 1 Others 1+2
Scarborough (Loaned on 29/8/97) FL 4/1

BROWN Michael (Mickey) Antony
Born: Birmingham, 8 February 1968
Height: 5'9" Weight: 11.12
Club Honours: Div 3 '94
In this third spell at Shrewsbury, this speedy right winger can leave defenders standing in order to deliver devastating crosses from the touchline. Never renowned as a goalscorer, he has always disappointed in his goals tally, but he did bag a couple in 1997-98 and would have enjoyed that, but, unfortunately,

on the playing front, his season was interrupted with injury on more than one occasion.

Shrewsbury T (From apprentice on 11/2/86) FL 174+16/9 FLC 17/2 FAC 10/1 Others 11
Bolton W (£100,000 on 15/8/91) FL 27+6/3 FLC 0+1 FAC 3 Others 2
Shrewsbury T (£25,000 on 23/12/92) FL 66+1/11 FLC 8/1 FAC 3 Others 2
Preston NE (£75,000 on 30/11/94) FL 11+5/1 FLC 0+1 Others 1
Rochdale (Loaned on 13/9/96) FL 5
Shrewsbury T (£20,000 on 12/12/96) FL 41+8/3 FLC 1+1 Others 4

BROWN Michael Robert
Born: Hartlepool, 25 January 1977
Height: 5'8" Weight: 11.8
International Honours: E: U21-4

A hard-tackling and committed Manchester City midfielder, having been plagued with an ankle injury Michael came back into the side last October, in Paul Lake's testimonial match, and treated the game as though his whole career depended on it. Virtually an ever present from the beginning of December, he produced several eye-catching, and vigorous performances, and even scored his first City goal in the home FA Cup tie against Bradford, his good form being rewarded with selection for the Football League U21 side that played the Italians. The only downside to his game appears to be the amount of bookings he picks up, but he is a winner and Manchester City certainly need a few of them if they are going to climb back to the first division at the first time of asking.

Manchester C (From trainee on 13/9/94) F/PL 41+17 FLC 1+3 FAC 8/1
Hartlepool U (Loaned on 27/3/97) FL 6/1

BROWN Simon James
Born: Chelmsford, 3 December 1976
Height: 6'2" Weight: 15.0

A young goalkeeper signed on loan from Tottenham Hotspur last December, following injuries to both Barry Richardson and John Vaughan, Simon made his Football League debut in Lincoln's 5-1 defeat at Peterborough before being recalled to White Hart lane shortly afterwards as cover after Ian Walker had been injured.

Tottenham H (From trainee on 1/7/95)
Lincoln C (Loaned on 19/12/97) FL 1

BROWN Steven (Steve) Byron
Born: Brighton, 13 May 1972
Height: 6'1" Weight: 14.3

Tall and versatile, the right-sided Charlton defender held down the right-back spot for most of last season before a sceptic shin and the signing of Danny Mills cost him his place. Equally comfortable at centre half, Steve can also play in midfield, and once again was called upon as an emergency goalkeeper, for the third time in successive campaigns, when he played for the whole second half against Manchester City at Maine Road. Possesses a hard shot, is very good in the air, and likes to get forward to deliver telling crosses into the box.

Charlton Ath (From trainee on 3/7/90) FL 126+16/5 FLC 7 FAC 13/1 Others 3+2

BROWN Steven (Steve) Ferold
Born: Northampton, 6 July 1966
Height: 6'1" Weight: 11.8

1997-98 was another excellent season at Wycombe for this skilful, left footed midfielder. Starting in the problem left-wing back position, he was soon switched to central midfield, from where his combative tackling and long legs helped to steal the ball away from many an opponent. Extremely versatile, he even produced a remarkable display as a stand-in goalkeeper at Chesterfield, and his disciplinary record improved greatly, before being released during the summer.

Northampton T (From juniors on 11/8/83) FL 14+1/3 (Free to Irthlingborough T in December 1985)
Northampton T (Free on 21/7/89) FL 145+13/19 FLC 10/1 FAC 12/2 Others 10+1/1
Wycombe W (£60,000 on 9/2/94) FL 152+9/11 FLC 10+2 FAC 8+1 Others 5+2

BROWN Steven (Steve) Robert
Born: Southend, 6 December 1973
Height: 6'0" Weight: 12.7

A hard-running and enthusiastic Lincoln striker whose ability to hustle defenders caused plenty of problems for the opposition in 1997-98, Steve was used very effectively as a second-half substitute, his three goals coming in this way. A hamstring injury kept him out for the last two months of the season, but he had already played his part in the successful run to promotion, prior to being released during the summer.

Southend U (From trainee on 10/7/92) FL 10/2 FAC 0+1 Others 1
Scunthorpe U (Free on 5/7/93)
Colchester U (Free on 27/8/93) FL 56+6/17 FLC 2 FAC 5/1 Others 4/1
Gillingham (Signed on 22/3/95) FL 8+1/2
Lincoln C (£20,000 on 6/10/95) FL 47+25/8 FLC 0+3 FAC 3+1 Others 3+1/1

BROWN Wayne Larry
Born: Southampton, 14 January 1977
Height: 6'1" Weight: 11.12

Since the departure of Ronnie Sinclair at the end of last season, Wayne is the number one choice goalkeeper for Chester City's 1998-99 campaign. Broke into the first team last November, making a total of 11 appearances before giving way to Sinclair, but came back in April to play in the last five games. Is a very agile 'keeper and looks set to have a good future.

Bristol C (From trainee on 3/7/95) FL 1 (Free to Weston super Mare during 1996 close season)
Chester C (Free on 30/9/96) FL 15 FAC 2 Others 1

BROWN Wayne Lawrence
Born: Barking, 20 August 1977
Height: 6'0" Weight: 12.6

Having been a pro at Ipswich since May 1996, the young central defender finally progressed through the youth and reserve sides to make his first team debut at Middlesbrough last January, alongside Tony Mowbray and Adam Tanner in a three-man central defence. Strong in the air, he had earlier made two appearances for Colchester on loan, as cover for David Greene, and, as

in his one and only game for Town, acquitted himself well.

Ipswich T (From trainee on 16/5/96) FL 1
Colchester U (Loaned on 16/10/97) FL 0+2

BROWN Wesley (Wes) Michael
Born: Manchester, 16 March 1979
Height: 6'1" Weight: 12.2
International Honours: E: Yth

A solid Manchester United central defender, who is dominant in the air, Wes made his Premiership debut against Leeds last May, having earned rave reviews in the reserves. His performance that afternoon, suggests a promising future for yet another of "Fergie's Fledglings," and he followed it up with his full debut at Barnsley.

Manchester U (From trainee on 13/11/96) PL 1+1

BROWNING Marcus Trevor
Born: Bristol, 22 April 1971
Height: 6'0" Weight: 12.10
International Honours: W: 5

Almost the forgotten man of the McAlpine in 1997-98, Marcus spent five months sidelined by a troublesome back related hamstring injury, before coming into the heart of Huddersfield's midfield and producing some solid displays of running and tackling. As if jinxed, injury struck again after only six consecutive appearances, this time a groin problem keeping him on the sidelines. Throughout a tough campaign, the Welsh international's ball-winning capabilities were sadly missed.

Bristol Rov (From trainee on 1/7/89) FL 152+22/13 FLC 7+3 FAC 8/1 Others 13+5/3
Hereford U (Loaned on 18/9/92) FL 7/5
Huddersfield T (£500,000 on 17/2/97) FL 23+4 FLC 1

BRUCE Paul Mark
Born: London, 18 February 1978
Height: 5'11" Weight: 12.0

Having come through the ranks at Queens Park Rangers, Paul made his debut last January as a substitute against Tranmere Rovers and, following two further appearances from the bench and a goal in the 5-0 home win over Middlesbrough, he was awarded his full league debut at Birmingham City in early March. Is an attack minded, left-sided player who can play in midfield or further forward, as demanded.

Queens Park R (From trainee on 15/7/96) FL 1+4/1 FAC 0+1

BRUCE Stephen (Steve) Roger
Born: Corbridge, 31 December 1960
Height: 6'0" Weight: 13.0
Club Honours: Div 2 '86, PL '93, '94, '96; FLC '85, '92; FAC '90, '94; CS '93, '94; ECWC '91; ESC '91;
International Honours: E: B-1; Yth

An inspiration in the heart of Birmingham's defence in 1997-98, Steve's reading of the game and leadership was again top class and there appears to be no reason why he should not continue in that vein. Although his legs may be slowing up, his football brain is as sharp as ever and, in a testament to his competitive spirit, he was annoyed at being

rested on a handful of occasions. Voted Player of the Year by a landslide margin, whenever he was not in the team, it showed. As reliable as ever in the air, and still a danger at corners and set pieces, he scored two goals, one of them an 80th-minute equaliser in the 1-1 home draw against Ipswich. Still a strong tackler and one of the hardest men to get round. *Stop Press:* Took his first steps in management when joining Sheffield United on 2 July as player/manager.

Gillingham (From apprentice on 27/10/78) FL 203+2/29 FLC 15/6 FAC 14/1
Norwich C (£125,000 on 24/8/84) FL 141/14 FLC 20/5 FAC 9/1 Others 10
Manchester U (£800,000 on 18/12/87) F/PL 309/36 FLC 32+2/6 FAC 41/3 Others 32+2/7
Birmingham C (Free on 17/6/96) FL 70+2/2 FLC 6 FAC 6/1

BRUMWELL Phillip (Phil)
Born: Darlington, 8 August 1975
Height: 5'8" Weight: 11.0

A versatile player, Phil played in the majority of defensive and midfield positions during his third season at Darlington in 1997-98. Both tenacious and a strong tackler, the local boy can always be relied upon to give his all for the club.

Sunderland (From trainee on 30/6/94)
Darlington (Free on 11/8/95) FL 73+28/1 FLC 5+1 FAC 5+3/2 Others 3+3

Phil Brumwell

BRUNO Pasquale
Born: Lecce, Italy, 19 June 1962
Height: 6'0" Weight: 11.7

An experienced Italian centre half, Pasquale was recruited from Heart of Midlothian on a short-term contract by Wigan Athletic last February, having once been a serie "A" winner with Juventus. Made only one appearance for the club, before walking away after failing to gain assurances that he would be selected in his preferred sweeper role.

Hearts (Signed from Fiorentina on 17/11/95) SL 33+2/1 SLC 4 SC 4 Others 2
Wigan Ath (Free on 6/2/98) FL 1

BRYAN Derek Kirk
Born: London, 11 November 1974
Height: 5'10" Weight: 11.5

A fast and exciting Brentford striker who came to Griffin Park from non-league Hampton early in 1997-98, Derek had his season continually interrupted by injuries, most notably by a ruptured thigh muscle and an ankle. Because of these problems, he was only in the starting line-up on two occasions, but scored each time, at Bristol City and against Bournemouth, and, strangely, each goal was timed at 44 minutes! Great things are hoped from him in 1998-99.

Brentford (£50,000 from Hampton on 28/8/97) FL 2+9/2 FAC 0+1

BRYAN Marvin Lee
Born: Paddington, 2 August 1975
Height: 6'0" Weight: 12.2

In missing just four games for Blackpool in 1997-98, and those through injury, Marvin yet again proved to be a dominant feature at Bloomfield Road as an attacking right back who could get forward to set up attacks, or use his speed to defend well. Having started life as a winger, his speed and strength are an added bonus when coming from the back, while his goal in the 3-0 home win over Millwall, a 25-yard rocket, was, surprisingly, his only strike throughout the campaign.

Queens Park R (From trainee on 17/8/92)
Doncaster Rov (Loaned on 8/12/94) FL 5/1
Blackpool (£20,000 on 10/8/95) FL 121+2/3 FLC 8+2 FAC 5 Others 11

BRYANT Matthew (Matt)
Born: Bristol, 21 September 1970
Height: 6'1" Weight: 13.2

After the previous season when he was a regular, Matt struggled to gain a first team place at Gillingham in 1997-98 and, when he did appear, he was used in the unaccustomed position of either full back or sweeper. Is a wholehearted defender with commitment to spare.

Bristol C (From trainee on 1/7/89) FL 201+2/7 FLC 9+1 FAC 11 Others 9
Walsall (Loaned on 24/8/90) FL 13 FLC 4
Gillingham (£65,000 on 8/8/96) FL 63+11 FLC 8 FAC 3 Others 1

BRYDON Lee
Born: Stockton, 15 November 1974
Height: 5'11" Weight: 11.0

This former Liverpool trainee made only spasmodic appearances for Darlington throughout last season in defence and was released after two years at Feethams, during which time he never registered a goal for the Quakers. Able to play anywhere in defence, he is fast in recovery, and composed on the ball.

Liverpool (From trainee on 24/6/92)
Darlington (Free on 14/8/96) FL 28+12 FLC 1+1 FAC 1+2 Others 1

BRYSON James Ian Cook
Born: Kilmarnock, 26 November 1962
Height: 5'11" Weight: 12.12
Club Honours: Div 3 '96

A pre-season signing for Rochdale, having been freed by Preston, the experienced midfielder was an early victim of the club's injury jinx in 1997-98, being ruled out for the first dozen games. On his delayed appearance in the first team, Ian helped Dale to two successive victories, but was then injured again and his season continued to be interrupted with an even longer lay-off in the New Year.

Kilmarnock (Signed from Hurlford on 22/10/81) SL 194+21/40 SLC 12+7/1 SC 14+2/3
Sheffield U (£40,000 on 24/8/88) F/PL 138+17/36 FLC 11+2/1 FAC 18+4/4 Others 7/3
Barnsley (£20,000 on 12/8/93) FL 16/3 FLC 2/1 Others 2
Preston NE (£42,500 on 29/11/93) FL 141+10/19 FLC 6+1/1 FAC 7+2 Others 12/1
Rochdale (Free on 21/7/97) FL 12+3/1 FAC 1 Others 2

BUCKLE Paul John
Born: Hatfield, 16 December 1970
Height: 5'8" Weight: 11.2
Club Honours: Div 3 '92

A dynamic and popular midfield dynamo, "Bucks" missed the previous season's Wembley visit through suspension, and so all Colchester followers were delighted when he was a part of their play-off triumph this time around in 1997-98. Paul's all-action style was a feature of United's midfield again, and he popped up with his share of goals too, including a penalty to win the opening game against Darlington, when he struck a bet that he would score the spot kick with the Quaker's goalkeeper!*

Brentford (From trainee on 1/7/89) FL 42+15/1 FLC 5+1 FAC 3+1 Others 6+5
Torquay U (Free on 3/2/94) FL 57+2/9 FLC 8 FAC 3 Others 1
Exeter C (Free on 13/10/95) FL 22/2 FAC 1 Others 2
Northampton T (Free on 30/8/96)
Wycombe W (Free on 18/10/96)
Colchester U (Free on 28/11/96) FL 57+5/5 FLC 2 FAC 1 Others 9/3

BULL Garry William
Born: West Bromwich, 12 June 1966
Height: 5'10" Weight: 12.2
Club Honours: GMVC '91

For the second successive campaign, Gary found goals hard to come by and only managed to notch a couple for York. These were at Port Vale in an early season Coca Cola Cup win, and in a home game against Millwall in January. Once again, however, he often shone with his skill, ball control, and overall ability, before being released during the summer.

Southampton (Signed from Paget R on 15/10/86)
Cambridge U (Signed on 29/3/88) FL 13+6/4
FLC 0+1 Others 0+2
Barnet (£2,000 on 1/3/89) FL 83/37 FLC 4/4 FAC
11/3 Others 8/2
Nottingham F (Free on 21/7/93) F/PL 4+8/1 FLC
2 FAC 0+3
Birmingham C (Loaned on 12/9/94) FL 10/6
Others 2/1
Brighton & Hove A (Loaned on 17/8/95) FL 10/2
Others 1/2
Birmingham C (Free on 29/12/95) FL 3+3 FLC
0+1 FAC 0+2 Others 1/1
York C (Free on 4/3/96) FL 66+17/11 FLC 7+2/2
FAC 5+1

BULL Stephen (Steve) George
Born: Tipton, 28 March 1965
Height: 5'11" Weight: 12.11
Club Honours: Div 4 '88, Div 3 '89; AMC
'88
International Honours: E: 13; B-5; U21-5
Remaining a determined striker in 1997-98,
Steve's goals usually came from his right
foot or his head. His testimonial against
Santos had been scheduled for May 1997
and, although delayed until August due to
Wolves' involvement in the play offs, it still
attracted over 20,000 fans to Molineux.
While not scoring in the first five matches,
he then had a spell of eight goals in 11,
highlighted by one against Port Vale when
he took a pass well, lost his marker, beat
three men, and scored from outside the area.
Sent off for reacting to an awful foul on a
team mate against Swindon, Steve was
given a reprieve as the referee later admitted
his error. Despite a lean period, six games
without a goal, he was ever present before a
patella knee tendon problem required
surgery to remove a protruding bone.
Finally returned as a 74th-minute sub at
home to Bradford, stooping down to head a
late winner, his 300th goal for Wolves,
having been stuck on 299 for over four
months. In struggling to find the net from
then on, his 12th season was destined to be
the first one in which he had scored less than
15 goals for the club.
West Bromwich A (Free from Tipton T on
24/8/85) FL 2+2/2 FLC 2/1 Others 1+2
Wolverhampton W (£35,000 on 21/11/86) FL
450+9/246 FLC 30+1/15 FAC 18+2/7 Others
33+1/32

BULLIMORE Wayne Alan
Born: Sutton in Ashfield, 12 September 1970
Height: 5'9" Weight: 12.1
International Honours: E: Yth
The left-sided midfielder failed to get a
regular first team place at Peterborough in
1997-98, although showing signs of the skill
he possesses. It was unfortunate that when
given his chance, the physical side of the
game, plus the fact that he still travels down
from the Bradford area, seemed to work
against him. Never really a goalscorer, there
was only one last season, he remains
dangerous from free kicks around the box,
however. Was released during the summer.
Manchester U (From trainee on 16/9/88)
Barnsley (Free on 9/3/91) FL 27+8/1 FLC 2+1
FAC 1+1
Stockport Co (Free on 11/10/93)

Scunthorpe U (Free on 19/11/93) FL 62+5/11
FLC 2+2/1 FAC 7/1 Others 5/1
Bradford C (£40,000 on 15/12/95) FL 1+1
Doncaster Rov (Loaned on 20/9/96) FL 4
Peterborough U (Free on 26/3/97) FL 10+11/1
FLC 0+3 FAC 0+1 Others 1

BULLOCK Darren John
Born: Worcester, 12 February 1969
Height: 5'9" Weight: 12.10
Darren's season in 1997-98 began amid
uncertainty as Swindon agreed a transfer
with Stockport, only for the player to reject
the move on personal terms and, despite
being one of the club's biggest recent
signings, he was not a regular in the starting
line-up. When called upon, however, he
provided a powerful presence in the
midfield and could always be relied upon for
100 per-cent commitment to the cause, but
continued to fall foul of referees and served
several suspensions, including one after
being red carded against Birmingham. A
dogged and ferocious tackler on one hand,
and a player who likes to get forward on the
other, Darren has still not added to the goal
he scored on his Town debut.
Huddersfield T (£55,000 from Nuneaton
Borough on 19/11/93) FL 127+1/16 FLC 11/1
FAC 8/2 Others 9/1
Swindon T (£400,000 on 24/2/97) FL 38+6/1

BULLOCK Martin John
Born: Derby, 5 March 1975
Height: 5'5" Weight: 10.7
International Honours: E: U21-1
This will o' the wisp Barnsley attacker
showed on numerous occasions in 1997-98
why he was selected for the England U21s.
At his most dangerous when running at
defenders, and causing them terrible
problems with his skilful dribbling, he also
improved his passing skills and created a
number of goalscoring situations with an
astute pass. He was certainly not out of
place in the Premiership, and is certain to be
one of the players that the club look to in
their efforts to rejoin the "Big Boys" at the
first attempt.
Barnsley (£15,000 from Eastwood T on 4/9/93)
F/PL 72+59/1 FLC 4+3 FAC 4+6/1 Others 1

BURGESS Daryl
Born: Birmingham, 24 January 1971
Height: 5'11" Weight: 12.4
With a good recovery rate and tackle to
match, allied to strength in the air, Daryl has
turned out for West Bromwich Albion at
right back, centre back, and as a sweeper,
having been one of the most consistent
members of the team in recent years,
especially in forming partnerships at the
heart of the defence with both Paul Raven
and Shaun Murphy. Troubled by injury, he
missed the start of 1997-98 before getting
his place in the side back, but then another
leg injury suffered later in the year saw him
ruled out of action until the end of February.
Now in his tenth season as a professional,
and still totally committed to his only senior
club, there is still plenty left in the tank.
West Bromwich A (From trainee on 1/7/89) FL
278+5/9 FLC 16+2/3 FAC 8 Others 14

BURNETT Wayne
Born: Lambeth, 4 September 1971
Height: 5'11" Weight: 12.6
Club Honours: AMC '98
International Honours: E: Yth
Started the first part of last season as a
regular playmaker in midfield for
Huddersfield, scoring a scorcher in the Coca
Cola Cup second leg tie against Bradford
City, before drifting out of the side as his
form dipped, and subsequently going on
loan to Grimsby in January. Some creative
play and the ability to get among the goals,
lobbing the Fulham 'keeper for a late-home
equaliser, served to make the move
permanent, and he soon became a vital cog
in a side aiming to make an immediate
return to first division football. He did just
that, his "Golden Goal" taking Town to
victory over Bournemouth in the Auto
Windscreen Shield final – the first leg of a
Wembley double that ended with the
Mariners defeating Northampton in the
play-off final.
Leyton Orient (From trainee on 13/11/89) FL
34+6 FLC 3+1/1 FAC 3+1 Others 4
Blackburn Rov (£90,000 on 19/8/92)
Plymouth Arg (Signed on 9/8/93) FL 61+9/3 FLC
3 FAC 8 Others 4+1
Bolton W (£100,000 on 12/10/95) F/PL 0+2
Huddersfield T (Signed on 6/9/96) FL 44+6 FLC
6+1/1 FAC 1+1
Grimsby T (£100,000 on 9/1/98) FL 20+1/1
Others 8/3

BURNS Liam
Born: Belfast, 30 October 1978
Height: 5'11" Weight: 12.5
International Honours: NI: U21-3; Yth
Having come through the ranks at Port Vale
as a trainee, the Northern Ireland U21
international marked his first season as a pro
with just the one senior appearance in the
Port Vale defence in 1997-98. A regular
central defender in the reserves, his big
chance came at Sunderland when he entered
the fray as a half-time substitute in the
unaccustomed position of left-wing back.
He did pretty well, and the experience of
making his debut in front of over 40,000
screaming fans will do him no harm for the
future.
Port Vale (From trainee on 2/7/97) FL 0+1

BURROWS David
Born: Dudley, 25 October 1968
Height: 5'10" Weight: 11.8
Club Honours: CS '89; Div 1 '90; FAC '92
International Honours: E: B-3; U21-7
A left-sided or central Coventry defender,
who had a good season in 1997-98, he was
close to joining Ron Atkinson at
Hillsborough in November, and but for
Mark Pembridge not wanting to join City he
probably would have gone. His tough
tackling, good positional play, and strength
in the air, came to the fore in Coventry's
excellent run after Christmas, a run which
saw the club move up the table away from
the danger zone. Although he does not get
up in support of his attack quite as often as
he used to at Anfield, when he does overlap
his crossing is excellent.

West Bromwich A (From apprentice on 8/11/86)
FL 37+9/1 FLC 3+1 FAC 2 Others 1
Liverpool (£550,000 on 20/10/88) F/PL 135+11/3
FLC 16 FAC 16+1 Others 14
West Ham U (Signed on 17/9/93) PL 29/1 FLC
3/1 FAC 3
Everton (Signed on 6/9/94) PL 19 FLC 2 FAC 2
Coventry C (£1,100,000 on 2/3/95) PL 72+1 FLC
6 FAC 6

David Burrows

BURTON Deon John
Born: Ashford, 25 October 1976
Height: 5'8" Weight: 11.9
International Honours: Jamaica: 16
Signed from Portsmouth during the 1997
summer recess, the outgoing striker had
more of a squad role at Derby in 1997-98
and struggled to displace the regular
strikers, but showed what the future may
hold with two well-taken goals in April
against Bolton. Like Darryl Powell, a
Jamaican international, you might be right
in thinking that Deon was somewhat
preoccupied with the World Cup throughout
the campaign, as the Reggae Boyz aimed to
reach France '98 and succeeded. Has
explosive pace. *Stop Press:* With the great
experience now over, Jamaica being put out
in the opening series, he can now
concentrate on getting among the goals at
County in 1998-99.
Portsmouth (From trainee on 15/2/94) FL
42+20/10 FLC 3+2/2 FAC 0+2/1
Cardiff C (Loaned on 24/12/96) FL 5/2 Others 1
Derby Co (£1,000,000+ on 9/8/97) PL 12+17/3
FLC 1 FAC 2

BURTON-GODWIN Osagyefo (Sagi) Lenin
Ernesto
Born: Birmingham, 25 November 1977
Height: 6'2" Weight: 13.6

A promising young Crystal Palace right
back, and a product of the YTS ranks, Sagi
finally got his chance of first team football
after two years as a professional when
making his Premiership debut at Derby last
December. Although there were two further
appearances from the bench, with the full-
back pairing of Marc Edworthy and Dean
Gordon in good form, despite it being a
difficult season for the club that ultimately
ended in relegation, he went back to the
reserves. Highly thought of, there should be
further opportunities for this defender who
is more than useful in aerial skirmishes.
Crystal Palace (From trainee on 26/1/96) PL 1+1
FAC 0+1

BUSHELL Stephen (Steve) Paul
Born: Manchester, 28 December 1972
Height: 5'9" Weight: 11.6
A virtual ever present for York City in 1997-
98, Steve showed consistent form in
midfield and was voted Clubman of the Year
by the supporters. In netting four goals
during the season, including a dramatic late
winner in an exciting 4-3 victory over
Carlisle United, the popular hard-working
and tigerish player now tops 200 games for
the club.*
York C (From trainee on 25/2/91) FL 156+18/10
FLC 8+1/2 FAC 5 Others 11+2/1

BUTLER Philip Anthony (Tony)
Born: Stockport, 28 September 1972
Height: 6'2" Weight: 12.0
The big, strong Blackpool defender proved
to be an important member of the team in
1997-98, taking over when David Linighan
was out injured, and forming partnerships
with any number of players, often bringing
them safely through a crisis. There are not
many centre forwards who get the better of
him, especially in the air, where he remains
dominant.
Gillingham (From trainee on 13/5/91) FL 142+6/5
FLC 12 FAC 12+1 Others 5+1/1
Blackpool (£225,000 on 30/7/96) FL 78+1 FLC 5
FAC 3 Others 4/1

BUTLER Lee Simon
Born: Sheffield, 30 May 1966
Height: 6'2" Weight: 14.4
Club Honours: Div 3 '97
After starting last season as Wigan
Athletic's number one goalkeeper, Lee
found it hard to regain his first team place
because of the excellent form of Roy
Carroll. Completed his 200th Football
League appearance in the 1-1 home draw
against Luton Town and continued to show
himself to be an excellent and agile shot-
stopper, who is still a good man to be able to
fall back on.
Lincoln C (Free from Haworth Colliery on
16/6/86) FL 30 FLC 1 FAC 1
Aston Villa (£100,000 on 21/8/87) FL 8 Others 2
Hull C (Loaned on 18/3/91) FL 4
Barnsley (£165,000 on 22/7/91) FL 118+2 FLC 5
FAC 9 Others 4
Scunthorpe U (Loaned on 5/2/96) FL 2
Wigan Ath (Free on 5/7/96) FL 63 FLC 3 FAC 2
Others 2

BUTLER Martin Neil
Born: Wordsley, 15 September 1974
Height: 5'11" Weight: 11.9
As a rarity in the current Cambridge team, a
player who was signed for a transfer fee –
Roy McFarland paid Walsall £22,500 for
this lively striker during the 1997 close
season – he repaid the manager with some
good performances in 1997-98, scoring ten
league goals. Out of action for some 14
games, Martin returned to the side in April
and, with Trevor Benjamin, formed a
partnership that began to terrify defences in
the latter part of the campaign.
Walsall (From trainee on 24/5/93) FL 43+31/8
FLC 2+1 FAC 2+5/2 Others 2+2/2
Cambridge U (£22,500 on 8/8/97) FL 28+3/10
FLC 2/1 FAC 2+2/2 Others 1

BUTLER Paul John
Born: Manchester, 2 November 1972
Height: 6'2" Weight: 13.0
Club Honours: Div 2 '97
The strapping centre half, missed just three
games during Bury's first division campaign
in 1997-98 – and they were due to suspension. A revelation in a tough campaign, he
turned in particularly consistent displays
week in, week out, and looked completely at
ease at a higher level of football as his
reputation continued to grow. After being
voted runner up in the Player of the Year
poll and included in Mick McCarthy's
Republic of Ireland squad, Paul can look
back with some satisfaction, especially in
efforts to help the club avoid the drop. *Stop
Press:* Having failed to entice David
Holdsworth to Sunderland, Peter Reid
purchased Paul on 6 July for £900,000.
Rochdale (From trainee on 5/7/91) FL 151+7/10
FLC 8+1 FAC 6+2 Others 12+1
Bury (£100,000 on 22/7/96) FL 83+1/4 FLC 8
FAC 2 Others 3/1

BUTLER Peter James
Born: Halifax, 27 August 1966
Height: 5'9" Weight: 11.1
Into his second full season at West
Bromwich Albion in 1997-98, Peter missed
a few games before Christmas but after the
turn of the year he was one of the club's
most consistent performers, tackling well
and generally giving a good account of
himself in anchoring the midfield, before
falling victim to a hernia operation. Apart
from his ability to win the ball he also has
good distribution skills and, despite having
to carry the odd injury, is a player you can
still rely upon.
Huddersfield T (From apprentice on 21/8/84) FL
0+5
Cambridge U (Loaned on 24/1/86) FL 14/1
Others 1
Bury (Free on 8/7/86) FL 9+2 FLC 2/1 FAC 1
Cambridge U (Free on 10/12/86) FL 55/9 FLC 4
FAC 2 Others 2
Southend U (£75,000 on 12/2/88) FL 135+7/9
FLC 12/1 FAC 2 Others 11/2
Huddersfield T (Loaned on 24/3/92) FL 7
West Ham U (£125,000 on 12/8/92) F/PL 70/3
FLC 4 FAC 3 Others 1
Notts Co (£350,000 on 4/10/94) FL 20 FLC 2
FAC 2 Others 3

Grimsby T (Loaned on 30/1/96) FL 3
West Bromwich A (£175,000 on 28/3/96) FL 52+8 FLC 2+1 FAC 1+2

BUTLER Stephen (Steve)
Born: Birmingham, 27 January 1962
Height: 6'2" Weight: 12.12
Club Honours: GMVC '89
International Honours: E: SP-3

Now 36, the years are catching up on Steve! Despite still having the control and ability to turn defenders, he found it difficult to play two games a week for Gillingham in 1997-98, and was often used as substitute when he could change the course of a game. There was no better proof of this than when the former Army man lashed in a 20 yarder against Carlisle to bring Gills a third consecutive win during February.*
Brentford (Free from Windsor & Eton on 19/12/84) FL 18+3/3 Others 2
Maidstone U (Free on 1/8/86) FL 76/41 FLC 4/3 FAC 18/7 Others 10/4
Watford (£150,000 on 28/3/91) FL 40+22/9 FLC 4+3 FAC 1 Others 2+1
Bournemouth (Loaned on 18/12/92) FL 1
Cambridge U (£75,000 on 23/12/92) FL 107+2/51 FLC 4+1 FAC 6/5 Others 3
Gillingham (£100,000 on 15/12/95) FL 73+28/20 FLC 6+1/1 FAC 5/1 Others 1

BUTT Nicholas (Nicky)
Born: Manchester, 21 January 1975
Height: 5'10" Weight: 11.3
Club Honours: FAYC '92; CS '96, '97; PL '96, '97; FAC '96
International Honours: E: 6; U21-7; Yth (UEFA Yth '93); Sch

A gritty midfielder with neat skills and a hardened edge, Nicky had the added responsibility of holding Manchester United's midfield together following the injury to Roy Keane at Leeds last September. And, although he was missing from the side himself that day, he was soon back in the thick of the action as the Reds continued their quest for domestic and European honours. Unfortunately, he suffered a recurrence of the double-vision problem against Southampton in January, which had affected him the season before, but came back without any ill-effects. Never a prolific scorer from midfield, he did manage to score three important goals during the campaign, the first against Spurs in August, and a brace in United's 5-2 win against Wimbledon at Selhurst Park in November. Blighted by several injury problems during the latter stages of the campaign, he was not named among Glenn Hoddle's final 22 for France '98, despite having made four appearances for England during the season, but was recognised by his fellow professionals when being selected for the PFA award-winning Premiership side.
Manchester U (From trainee on 29/1/93) PL 97+18/11 FLC 3 FAC 11+2/1 Others 24+2/1

BUTTERFIELD Daniel (Danny) Paul
Born: Boston, 21 November 1979
Height: 5'11" Weight: 11.3
Club Honours: AMC '98
International Honours: E: Yth

Grimsby right-wing back. Yet another graduate of John Cockerill's fruitful youth scheme, this skilful young player is forecast to follow Gary Croft and John Oster to the highest level. A solid defender who is fast and tenacious when going forward, Danny was in no way overawed by his elevation to the senior squad in 1997-98 and turned in some excellent performances, being rewarded by a call up to Howard Wilkinson's England U18 squad against Israel.
Grimsby T (From trainee on 7/8/97) FL 4+3 FLC 1 FAC 0+1 Others 1+1/1

BUTTERS Guy
Born: Hillingdon, 30 October 1969
Height: 6'3" Weight: 13.0
International Honours: E: U21-3

Strong in the tackle and good in the air, and always a danger at set pieces, Guy was Gillingham's most consistent player last season, but had the bad misfortune to break his leg at Millwall in March, which brought his campaign to an end. The club's usual penalty taker, the central defender ended 1997-98 with seven goals to his credit.
Tottenham H (From trainee on 5/8/88) FL 34+1/1 FLC 2+1 FAC 1
Southend U (Loaned on 13/1/90) FL 16/3 Others 2
Portsmouth (£375,000 on 28/9/90) FL 148+6/6 FLC 15+1/1 FAC 7 Others 7+2
Oxford U (Loaned on 4/11/94) FL 3/1 Others 1
Gillingham (£225,000 on 18/10/96) FL 61/7 FLC 2 FAC 5

BUXTON Nicholas (Nicky) Garreth
Born: Doncaster, 6 September 1976
Height: 6'1" Weight: 13.2

Nicky, an impressive young 'keeper, joined Scarborough from non-leaguers Goole Town early last season, making his debut as substitute for the injured Kevin Martin in the FA Cup tie at Scunthorpe. Three full league appearances followed, and he also figured in the reserve team which clinched the Pontins League third division championship.
Bury (Free from Doncaster Rov juniors on 20/8/96 - Freed during 1997 close season)
Scarborough (Free from Goole T on 23/10/97) FL 3 FAC 0+1

BYFIELD Darren
Born: Birmingham, 29 September 1976
Height: 5'11" Weight: 11.11

A pacy young Aston Villa striker who has consistently found the net at youth and reserve team level since first arriving at the club as a trainee, and having been a professional since February 1994, Darren finally got his big break last Boxing Day, when named as a sub for the visit of Spurs. Although not called upon, two days later he made his full Premiership debut in a 1-1 draw at Leeds and did well, going on to make a further seven appearances from the bench before the campaign came to a halt. Showing the capability of handling hard work and commitment, you will hear a lot more of this youngster.
Aston Villa (From trainee on 14/2/94) PL 1+6 FAC 0+1

BYRNE Christopher (Chris) Thomas
Born: Liverpool, 9 February 1975
Height: 5'9" Weight: 10.4

Despite being snapped up by Sunderland in November after his impressive displays in Macclesfield's promotion season, the skilful, waifish midfielder was home-sick in the north-east and Stockport picked him up for £200,000. Although the County boss, Gary Megson, saw him as "one for the future", injuries meant that Chris was soon established as a regular, and popular first teamer.
Sunderland (Signed from Macclesfield T on 11/6/97) FL 4+4 FLC 1+1
Stockport Co (£200,000 on 21/11/97) FL 21+5/7 FAC 1+1

BYRNE Paul Peter
Born: Dublin, 30 June 1972
Height: 5'11" Weight: 13.0
International Honours: Ei: U21-1; Yth; Sch

Never able to find the consistency of his first season at Southend, Paul was eventually released by the club in October 1977 to return to his native Ireland, where he joined Glenavon in the Smirnoff Irish League. A skilful, jinking winger with good close control, his reported off-field problems seemed to finally get to him, thus ending his career with the Blues.
Oxford U (From trainee on 4/7/89) FL 4+2 (Free to Bangor in September 1991)
Glasgow Celtic (Signed on 26/5/93) SL 24+4/4 SLC 1+1 SC 1 Others 2
Brighton & Hove A (Loaned on 10/3/95) FL 8/1
Southend U (£50,000 on 25/8/95) FL 70+13/6 FLC 6/2 FAC 2 Others 4

BYWATER Stephen Michael
Born: Manchester, 7 June 1981
Height: 6'3" Weight: 12.10
International Honours: E: Yth

Rochdale's 16-year-old England starlet was handed the first team goalkeeper's jersey for the pre-1997-98 season friendlies at literally an hour's notice, when Ian Gray moved to Stockport. He was then named as a substitute for several league games and made his senior bow at Carlisle in the AWS, where he was rather let down by his more experienced colleagues as Dale went down 6-1. After being expected to sign for Lancashire neighbours, Blackburn Rovers, Stephen went on trial to West Ham and, despite being sent off for a professional foul when playing for their reserves, he impressed the Hammers so much that they agreed to pay £300,000 immediately and up to another £2m in the future, dependent on his progress into the Premier League and the England side, the deal to be finalised on his 17th birthday in June. Remarkably, Stephen is a fourth generation goalkeeper, his father, grandfather (who also played for Rochdale), and great-grandfather all being professional players.
Rochdale (Trainee) Others 1

CADAMARTERI Daniel (Danny) Leon
Born: Bradford, 12 October 1979
Height: 5'7" Weight:11.12
International Honours: E: Yth

A strong and pacy Everton forward, Danny burst onto the Premiership scene last season with trademark dreadlocks and a flurry of goals, following his one-game experience of 1996-97. Handed an unexpected first team chance, following an injury to Michael Branch, he scored on his full debut against Barnsley, and followed up with further strikes against Arsenal – who included his childhood hero Ian Wright – Scunthorpe, Sheffield Wednesday, and a spectacular solo effort in the Merseyside derby against Liverpool. It was always to be expected that the youngster would not maintain such an explosive start and towards the end of the campaign he went back into the reserve team to continue to learn his trade. With his dreadlocks shaved off for charity, he scored with his head in the first leg of the FA Youth Cup final against Blackburn Rovers, netted his first goal for England U18s, and signed a long-term contract tying him to the Goodison club.

Everton (From trainee on 15/10/96) PL 15+12/4 FLC 1+2/1 FAC 1

Danny Cadamarteri

CADETTE Nathan Daniel
Born: Cardiff, 6 January 1980
Height: 5'10" Weight: 11.1
International Honours: W: Yth

A talented Cardiff City midfield player who increasingly caught the eye during 1997-98 in the reserve and youth teams, Nathan made a handful of first team appearances as a substitute, after appearing in the FAW Invitation cup tie against Merthyr Tydfil during December, when he went on for Scott Partridge. Rewarded with a full senior contract at the end of the season, he is cool and composed, with a good attitude, and ability to work on. Is one to watch out for.
Cardiff C (Trainee) FL 0+4

CAHILL Timothy (Tim)
Born: Sydney, Australia, 6 December 1979
Height: 5'10" Weight: 10.11

A product of the Australian Football Academy, Tim joined Millwall during the 1997 close season from Sydney United. An 18-year-old midfielder, with great control and vision, who can use either foot, he gave several impressive performances with the youth team until being sidelined for several months following a hernia operation. Came back for the last third of the campaign with more excellent reports, leading to a Football League debut in the final game at home to Bournemouth, where he earned himself the Man of the Match award. Watch out for him being on hand to sneak a goal or two.
Millwall (Signed from Sydney U on 31/7/97) FL 1

CAIG Antony (Tony)
Born: Whitehaven, 11 April 1974
Height: 6'1" Weight: 13.4
Club Honours: Div 3 '95; AMC '97

For the second year in succession, Tony was ever present in the Carlisle goal – a record that speaks for itself. A fine shot-stopper, who now has a greater command of his area, he took over as the team captain near the end of last season after Billy Barr was injured and, with his form continuing to attract the attention of scouts from higher divisions, it was no surprise he was voted Player of the Season.
Carlisle U (From trainee on 10/7/92) FL 186 FLC 14 FAC 12 Others 27

CALDERWOOD Colin
Born: Glasgow, 20 January 1965
Height: 6'0" Weight: 12.12
Club Honours: Div 4 '86
International Honours: S: 29; Sch

This gritty Tottenham central defender, who was played out of position in midfield for prolonged periods of 1997-98, had another consistent season, being good in the air, and scoring vital goals from set pieces during the campaign, most notably in the 1-0 defeat of Derby County in August. Never looking particularly at home in midfield, it was no surprise that Colin's best performances were when he played in his more familiar defensive role, in which he continued to impress for his native Scotland. Good stamina, and maintenance of his personal fitness, saw him secure his place in Craig

Colin Calderwood

Brown's Scotland squad, giving him the opportunity to take on the best strikers in the world, most notably the young messiah, Ronaldo, in the curtain raiser to the World Cup Finals. *Stop Press:* Played in Scotland's first two round one games before being injured and sitting out their third and final game, a 3-0 defeat at the hands of Morocco.

Mansfield T (Signed on 19/3/82) FL 97+3/1 FLC 4 FAC 6/1 Others 7
Swindon T (£30,000 on 1/7/85) FL 328+2/20 FLC 35 FAC 17/1 Others 32
Tottenham H (£1,250,000 on 22/7/93) PL 141+10/7 FLC 14+1 FAC 15+1/1

CALVO-GARCIA Alexander

Born: Ordizia, Spain, 1 January 1972
Height: 5'10" Weight: 11.0

Alex's first full season in English football in 1997-98 saw him establish himself as a regular member of the Scunthorpe midfield. With good ball skills and technique, his main strength was his goalscoring from midfield, reaching double figures before the end of February, and being particularly dangerous at getting on the end of set-piece flick-ons. Certainly, he looked to be relishing his midfield role, after switching back from centre forward, and has become a firm favourite with the United supporters.*

Scunthorpe U (Free from Eibar on 4/10/96) FL 46+11/7 FLC 4/3 FAC 6/1 Others 3/1

CAMPBELL Andrew (Andy) Paul

Born: Stockton, 18 April 1979
Height: 5'11" Weight: 11.7
International Honours: E: Yth

A bright, young Middlesbrough prospect, Andy started 1997-98 in the reserves before being called up for league action at Bradford, and eventually scoring his first goals for the club at home against Sunderland and Queens Park Rangers in the Coca Cola Cup and FA Cup, respectively. A regular scorer at youth and reserve levels, who takes chances in his stride and is quite unflappable in front of goal, the youngster will be looking to take those performances into the Premiership this coming term, where great things are predicted for him by those who should know.

Middlesbrough (From trainee on 4/7/96) F/PL 6+6 FLC 3+1/1 FAC 2/1

CAMPBELL Jamie

Born: Birmingham, 21 October 1972
Height: 6'1" Weight: 12.11

A versatile left-sided defender, Jamie settled in well at Cambridge following a summer free transfer from Barnet, showing himself to be a good defender in the middle three when wing backs were used, and also being able to play as an orthodox full back, getting forward to score two goals last season. The only ever present in the team, he can look back on a job well done.

Luton T (From trainee on 1/7/91) FL 10+26/1 FLC 1+1 FAC 1+3 Others 1+2
Mansfield T (Loaned on 25/11/94) FL 3/1 FAC 2
Cambridge U (Loaned on 10/3/95) FL 12
Barnet (Free on 11/7/95) FL 50+17/5 FLC 3+3/1 FAC 4+2/1 Others 1
Cambridge U (Free on 8/8/97) FL 46+2 FLC 2 FAC 4 Others 1

CAMPBELL Kevin Joseph

Born: Lambeth, 4 February 1970
Height: 6'1" Weight: 13.8
Club Honours: FAYC '88; FLC '93; FAC '93; ECWC '94; Div 1 '98
International Honours: E: B-1; U21-4

There was no doubting that Kevin had his best season to date in Nottingham Forest's colours in 1997-98, his deadly partnership with Pierre van Hooijdonk being a vital element in the club's first division championship win and return to Premiership status. It had long been thought that the former Arsenal striker had a lot more to give and this was his answer to his critics. With strength and pace, two good feet, and more than useful in the air, his 23 league goals was his highest aggregate yet, and included three braces and a hat trick in a 4-1 win at Crewe. Most certainly, it was a fitter and more leaner Kevin Campbell that the fans saw during the campaign, and it will be interesting to see how he handles the Premiership this coming term.

Arsenal (From trainee on 11/2/88) F/PL 124+42/46 FLC 14+10/6 FAC 13+6/2 Others 15+4/5
Leyton Orient (Loaned on 16/1/89) FL 16/9
Leicester C (Loaned on 8/11/89) FL 11/5 Others 1/1
Nottingham F (£3,000,000 on 1/7/95) F/PL 79+1/32 FLC 2 FAC 11/3 Others 3

CAMPBELL Neil Andrew

Born: Middlesbrough, 26 January 1977
Height: 6'2" Weight: 13.7

Having made a couple of early appearances for York in 1997-98, the powerfully-built striker, who has good pace and is at his best when running at defenders, moved to Scarborough on a free transfer. Showed flashes of outstanding form, which at one stage attracted the attention of scouts from West Ham, and scored eight goals, while working well with Steve Brodie. His younger brother, Andrew, is on the books of Middlesbrough.

York C (From trainee on 21/6/95) FL 6+6/1 FLC 1 FAC 0+2 Others 2
Scarborough (Free on 5/9/97) FL 20+14/7 FAC 0+1 Others 3/1

CAMPBELL Paul Andrew

Born: Middlesbrough, 29 January 1980
Height: 6'1" Weight: 11.0

Still a trainee when called up for first team duty for Darlington last March, coming off the bench during the Shrewsbury fixture at Feethams, the promising youngster had pointed the way as the leading scorer for the youth team in the Northern Intermediate League. Obviously highly thought of, he scored on his full debut against Barnet in early April and will be hoping for more of the same in 1998-99.

Darlington (Trainee) FL 4+2/1

CAMPBELL Stuart Pearson

Born: Corby, 9 December 1977
Height: 5'10" Weight: 10.8
Club Honours: FLC '97
International Honours: S: U21-4

A right-sided Leicester midfielder, Stuart started last season in the first team, but was

more frequently used from the bench as the campaign unfolded. However, he showed plenty of promise, as evidenced by his call up to the Scottish U21 squad, an honour that he defended by claiming to be "more Scottish than teammate, Matt Elliott", having qualified through his parents. Highly thought of at City, he will be pushing for a regular place in the starting line-up this coming term.

Leicester C (From trainee on 4/7/96) PL 10+11 FLC 1+2 FAC 2

CAMPBELL Sulzeer (Sol) Jeremiah

Born: Newham, 18 September 1974
Height: 6'2" Weight: 14.1
International Honours: E: 20; B-1; U21-11; Yth (UEFA Yth '93)

A rock-solid central defender, whose versatility stretches to midfield and attack when called upon, Sol had another consistent season at the heart of Tottenham's defence in 1997-98 with a level of personal fitness second to none. As attackers became stronger, he took it all in his stride with the confidence of knowing that his strength and pace, complimented by his agility, was enough to make even the hardest attackers think twice about entering the 50/50 challenge with him. Taking on the captain's armband, his understanding of the game grew with every match, and despite his youth, was able to gain the respect of the more mature and experienced campaigners. Being announced as the England Player of 1997 was the highlight of a year that was indifferent at club level and although there were reported bids in excess of £10 million, he quashed all rumours of a move by signing a new deal with Spurs, which extends his current contract for the next four years. Named number two in Glenn Hoddle's final 22, France '98 could provide the stage for Sol to establish himself as one of the world's great defenders. *Stop Press:* Ever present in all four of England's World Cup games in the summer, he created an excellent impression with last-ditch tackles, forays into the opposition's half, and, especially with his back-to-the-wall defending against Argentine.

Tottenham H (From trainee on 23/9/92) PL 159+9/2 FLC 17/2 FAC 14+2/1

CANHAM Scott Walter

Born: Newham, 5 November 1974
Height: 5'9" Weight: 11.7

As Brentford's central midfield playmaker, who specialises with dead-ball kicks, Scott was in and out of the Bees' side throughout 1997-98, his best performances being against Wrexham and Oldham late in the campaign, when deputising for the suspended Warren Aspinall. His exquisite through ball that set up Andy Scott for a vital goal against Oldham showed him at his best. Was somewhat surprisingly released during the summer.

West Ham U (From trainee on 2/7/93)
Torquay U (Loaned on 3/11/95) FL 3
Brentford (Loaned on 19/1/96) FL 14
Brentford (£25,000 + on 29/8/96) FL 23+11/1 FLC 4+2 FAC 1+1 Others 1+2

CARBON Matthew (Matt) Phillip
Born: Nottingham, 8 June 1975
Height: 6'2" Weight: 14.0
International Honours: E: U21-4

The talented, ball-playing central defender never quite managed to fully press his case for a regular place in the Derby team in 1997-98, even playing as an emergency striker on the opening day, and after playing at the back at Leeds when the Rams threw away a three goal lead to lose 3-1 he moved to West Bromwich Albion in January. In becoming Albion's most expensive defensive signing ever, Matt quickly established himself, despite having six different partners during his 16 games, and proved to be a cool, competent player with good aerial ability. Scored in a 2-0 win at Swindon, a result that moved the club back into the play-off positions, and looked good in doing so.

Lincoln C (From trainee on 13/4/93) FL 66+3/10 FLC 4/1 FAC 3 Others 4+3
Derby Co (£385,000 on 8/3/96) P/FL 11+9 FLC 1 FAC 0+1
West Bromwich A (£800,000 on 26/1/98) FL 16/1

CARBONE Benito
Born: Italy, 14 August 1971
Height: 5'6" Weight: 10.8

This very skilful Italian import enjoyed quite a good season at Sheffield Wednesday in 1997-98, his first full one. Playing as a striker, linkman, or wide on the right, he tried to impress the new boss, Ron Atkinson, but was still not guaranteed a permanent place in the team, there being doubts about his ability to link with Andy Booth and Paolo Di Canio. Starting the campaign well enough, scoring Wednesday's opening goal, he went on to bag winners against Leicester and Southampton, and picked up braces against Blackburn and Everton, but still has a tendency to drift out of games. At his best, though, he can be spectacular, and that is the side of his game that the Owls want to see more of.

Sheffield Wed (£3,000,000 from Inter Milan on 18/10/96) PL 52+6/15 FLC 1 FAC 4

CARDEN Paul
Born: Liverpool, 29 March 1979
Height: 5'8" Weight: 11.10

Having signed pro forms for Blackpool during the 1997 close season, the former trainee striker, in finding opportunities scarce at Bloomfield Road, moved to Rochdale on trial in February and impressed in a couple of reserve outings before being thrust into the senior side's midfield at Lincoln, in place of the suspended Andy Farrell. However, his debut lasted just 28 minutes before manager, Graham Barrow, decided to bring on an extra defender instead, although he went on to figure in the squad for most of the late season games.

Blackpool (From trainee on 7/7/97) FL 0+1 FAC 0+1 Others 1
Rochdale (Free on 3/3/98) FL 3+4

CAREY Brian Patrick
Born: Cork, 31 May 1968
Height: 6'3" Weight: 14.4
International Honours: Ei: 3; U21-1

As the "kingpin" of the side in the last campaign, and fully justifying many punters' choice of Wrexham's Player of the Season, his superb organising of the back division, and assured displays at the heart of the defence, were a major factor in the club's push for the play-off positions. One of Wrexham's best ever signings, and a credit to the club, one of his biggest assets is being able to use his height to great advantage in either penalty area.

Manchester U (£100,000 from Cork C on 2/9/89)
Wrexham (Loaned on 17/1/91) FL 3
Wrexham (Loaned on 24/12/91) FL 13/1 FAC 3 Others 3
Leicester C (£250,000 on 16/7/93) F/PL 51+7/1 FLC 3 FAC 0+1 Others 4
Wrexham (£100,000 on 19/7/96) FL 81/1 FLC 4 FAC 12 Others 2

CAREY Louis Anthony
Born: Bristol, 22 January 1977
Height: 5'10" Weight: 11.10
International Honours: S: U21-1

1997-98 was a great season for Louis, who appears to have found his best position for Bristol City in a sweeper's role alongside Shaun Taylor, whose tremendous presence allowed the youngster's natural talent to flower. His form was such that, in consequence of family links, he was rewarded with an appearance for the Scottish U21 side in a friendly against Denmark, but turned down the opportunity of a second cap as he did not wish to compromise future England possibilities by aligning himself to Scotland's cause at this early stage of his career.

Bristol C (From trainee on 3/7/95) FL 99+4 FLC 4+1 FAC 8 Others 3+2

CAREY Shaun Peter
Born: Kettering, 13 May 1976
Height: 5'9" Weight: 10.10
International Honours: Ei: U21-2

Unfortunately, a succession of injuries hampered his progress during the first half of last season, before he was thrust into first team action at Norwich in mid-February for the longest spell of senior football in his career, eight successive starts, and responded well to the confidence shown in him. A player with vision and good passing skills, who operated in the holding position just in front of the defence, apart from injury he was always a recognised squad player, and came back strongly in the final two games.

Norwich C (From trainee on 1/7/94) FL 25+12 FLC 2+2 FAC 1+1

CARLISLE Clarke James
Born: Preston, 14 October 1979
Height: 6'1" Weight: 12.7

Having come through the YTS ranks at Blackpool, and a first-year professional, young Clarke made his debut at Wrexham on 2 September 1997, and five days later scored a last-minute winner against Carlisle, would you believe! An outstanding prospect, the central defender even scored again – the equaliser in a 1-1 draw at Chesterfield on the last day of the season. Despite both goals coming from corners, he seems to know where the goal is.

Blackpool (From trainee on 13/8/97) FL 8+3/2 Others 1

CARPENTER Richard
Born: Sheerness, 30 September 1972
Height: 6'0" Weight: 13.0

Despite being the leading scorer in Fulham's midfield with four goals in 1997-98, Richard lost his place when Paul Trollope was signed in December, and never made the starting line-up again. A strong tackler, with an eye for goal, he will undoubtedly force his way back into first team action, hopefully at the Cottage.

Gillingham (From trainee on 13/5/91) FL 107+15/4 FLC 2+1 FAC 9+1 Others 7/1
Fulham (£15,000 on 26/9/96) FL 49+9/7 FLC 4/1 FAC 2/1 Others 2

CARR Darren John
Born: Bristol, 4 September 1968
Height: 6'2" Weight: 13.7

Darren had his opportunities at Chesterfield limited by injury last season. Having attended Lilleshall in January to recuperate, he returned to first team action in March, but suffered the misfortune of being harshly sent off on his first game back. His patience was well rewarded, however, for his play on his return to the centre of the Spireites' defence was just as dominant and redoubtable as it ever has been.*

Bristol Rov (From trainee on 20/8/86) FL 26+4 FLC 2+2 FAC 3 Others 2
Newport Co (£3,000 on 30/10/87) FL 9
Sheffield U (£8,000 on 10/3/88) FL 12+1/1 FLC 1 FAC 3+1 Others 1
Crewe Alex (£35,000 on 18/9/90) FL 96+8/5 FLC 8 FAC 12/2 Others 10
Chesterfield (£30,000 on 21/7/93) FL 84+2/4 FLC 9 FAC 6+3 Others 8

CARR Franz Alexander
Born: Preston, 24 September 1966
Height: 5'7" Weight: 11.12
Club Honours: FMC '89; FLC '90
International Honours: E: U21-9; Yth

Unable to further his career at Aston Villa, having failed to get on the team sheet for some while, the highly experienced winger was released to join Bolton last October, but made just five appearances from the bench before being on his way to West Bromwich Albion in February. Signed on a short-term contract to cover the right-hand side of midfield in the absence of Sean Flynn and Ian Hamilton, he showed only fleeting glimpses of his once-famed ability in the four matches played and, obviously not the Franz Carr of old, it is difficult to know where he goes from here.

Blackburn Rov (From apprentice on 30/7/84)
Nottingham F (£100,000 on 2/8/84) FL 122+9/17 FLC 16+2/5 FAC 4 Others 5+2/1
Sheffield Wed (Loaned on 22/12/89) FL 9+3 FAC 2
West Ham U (Loaned on 11/3/91) FL 1+2
Newcastle U (£250,000 on 13/6/91) FL 20+5/3 FLC 2+2 Others 3+1
Sheffield U (£120,000 on 12/1/93) P/FL 18/4 FAC 4 Others 1/1
Leicester C (£100,000 on 8/9/94) PL 12+1/1
Aston Villa (£250,000 on 10/2/95) PL 1+2 FAC 1/1 (Free to Reggiana on 23/10/96)
Bolton W (Free on 31/10/97) PL 0+5
West Bromwich A (Free on 12/2/98) FL 1+3

CARR Stephen
Born: Dublin, 29 August 1976
Height: 5'9" Weight: 12.2
International Honours: Ei: U21-12; Yth; Sch

A hard-working wing back who increased in stature at Tottenham in 1997-98 to establish himself as a regular first choice in the defence, Stephen likes to push forward and is confident on the ball. The ability and confidence to take players on also makes him valuable, coupled with a grit like commitment in the challenge when in defence. Although yet to be one step ahead of the more experienced attackers, his graduation into the Republic of Ireland first team squad will see this enthusiastic youngster benefit from the experience of the likes of Dennis Irwin and Roy Keane, and he is sure to continue to grow in confidence in 1998-99.
Tottenham H (From trainee on 1/9/93) PL 62+3 FLC 6 FAC 4

CARR-LAWTON Colin
Born: South Shields, 5 September 1978
Height: 5'11" Weight:11.7

One of several young strikers on the verge of first team recognition at Burnley in 1997-98, Colin made his league debut as a sub at Grimsby in November, but failed to make any further progress against the more experienced forwards at the club. Will be hoping for better fortune this coming season.
Burnley (From trainee on 21/1/97) FL 0+1 Others 0+1

Jamie Carragher

CARRAGHER James (Jamie) Lee
Born: Bootle, 28 January 1978
Height: 6'0" Weight: 12.0
Club Honours: FAYC '96
International Honours: E: B-2; U21-11; Yth
Having made his first team start in

Liverpool's midfield in 1996-97, and looking promising, Jamie began to prove himself a more than useful central defender in 1997-98, especially as the season progressed. Many at Anfield feel that he could become a top-quality centre back in a flat back four, and the former Liverpool and England defensive legend, Phil Thompson, has stated that he thinks the club has unearthed a real gem in this youngster. Strong and powerful, and a good passer of the ball, those are the qualities needed to succeed as a defender at Anfield and Jamie fits the bill. Was selected for both of the England "B" matches, against Chile and Russia, during the campaign, as well as playing in seven of the eight available U21 fixtures.
Liverpool (From trainee on 9/10/96) PL 18+4/1 FLC 2+1 Others 1

CARRAGHER Matthew (Matty)
Born: Liverpool, 14 January 1976
Height: 5'9" Weight: 10.7
Club Honours: Div 3 '97

Having been released by Wigan during the 1997 close season, Matty shared the full-back duties for Port Vale with Andy Hill in 1997-98, and generally did well in his first taste of football at first division level. Very good when going forward, he settled down to be a steady defender with a bright future in front of him, winning the club's Young Player of the Year award. Unfortunately, his only goal of the campaign came at the wrong end of the field in front of over 40,000 at Sunderland.
Wigan Ath (From trainee on 25/11/93) FL 102+17 FLC 6+1/1 FAC 10+1/2 Others 7+1
Port Vale (Free on 3/7/97) FL 26

CARROLL David (Dave) Francis
Born: Paisley, 20 September 1966
Height: 6'0" Weight: 12.0
Club Honours: FAT '91, '93; GMVC '93
International Honours: E: Sch

After ten years as a Wycombe player, Dave was rewarded with an enjoyable testimonial match against Leicester City and his old boss, Martin O'Neill. Briefly dropped at the start of last season, a rare event in his career, he soon established himself in his favoured central right-midfield position and got through his usual prodigious amount of work. Possessing excellent close control, his elegant runs at defences caused numerous problems, the only disappointment being his goal tally, just one, compared to ten in 1996-97. Was released during the summer.
Wycombe W (£6,000 from Ruislip Manor in 1988 close season) FL 205+5/31 FLC 16 FAC 22/4 Others 12/3

CARROLL Roy Eric
Born: Enniskillen, 30 September 1977
Height: 6'2" Weight: 12.9
International Honours: NI: 1; U21-2; Yth

Despite being Wigan Athletic's record signing, Roy did not start last season as the club's first-choice goalkeeper, that honour belonging to Lee Butler, but took his chance at the end of November, displaying a presence and maturity way beyond his years, with a series of eye-catching performances. Destined to play at the highest level, his form earned him a recall to the Northern Ireland U21 side that played Scotland and the Republic during 1997-98, and saw him become the runner-up for the club's Player of the Year award.
Hull C (From trainee on 7/9/95) FL 46 FLC 2 FAC 1 Others 1
Wigan Ath (£350,000 on 16/4/97) FL 29 FLC 1 FAC 2 Others 2

Roy Carroll

CARRUTHERS Martin George
Born: Nottingham, 7 August 1972
Height: 5'11" Weight: 11.9

An extremely hard-working and skilful Peterborough front runner, Martin was on the bench for the opening fixture last season, before equalling the club record when scoring in the next six league games. Strangely, having scored 15 goals by Christmas, he only managed another three by the end of the campaign as the team struggled to find its early form, but it was not through lack of trying though.

Aston Villa (From trainee on 4/7/90) F/PL 2+2 FAC 0+1 Others 0+1
Hull C (Loaned on 31/10/92) FL 13/6 Others 3
Stoke C (£100,000 on 5/7/93) FL 60+31/13 FLC 7+3/1 FAC 3+1 Others 10+4/6
Peterborough U (Signed on 18/11/96) FL 50+3/19 FLC 3+1/1 FAC 6/4 Others 5

CARSLEY Lee Kevin
Born: Birmingham, 28 February 1974
Height: 5'10" Weight: 11.11
International Honours: Ei: 6; U21-1

A tough and tenacious Derby midfield player, with a marked similarity to David Batty, his continued progress earned him a regular place in the central area of the Rams' line-up in 1997-98, where he tended to stay back and cover the area in front of the central defenders. Having moved from the Republic of Ireland U21 side to earn a place in the full international squad, for whom he will hope to be a permanent fixture for years to come, Lee has now made over 100 league appearances for County since his debut in 1994. Occasionally captained the team.

Derby Co (From trainee on 6/7/92) P/FL 102+14/4 FLC 8+2 FAC 7 Others 3

Lee Carsley

CARSS Anthony John
Born: Alnwick, 31 March 1976
Height: 5'10" Weight: 12.0

A left-sided forward who joined Cardiff City on a free transfer from Darlington during the 1997 close season, Anthony has undoubted ability, but was unable to reproduce his training-ground talent consistently in the first team in 1997-98, despite appearing in most of the games, and was given a free transfer the day after playing in the last match of the season – the FAW Invitation Cup final against Wrexham in May. His main forte is his ability to produce excellent crosses from the left, either when clear of the defender or earlier.

Blackburn Rov (Free from Bradford C juniors on 29/8/94)
Darlington (Free on 11/8/95) FL 33+24/2 FLC 5/1 FAC 2+1 Others 4
Cardiff C (Free on 28/7/97) FL 36+6/1 FLC 2 FAC 5+1 Others 1

CARTER James (Jimmy) William Charles
Born: Hammersmith, 9 November 1965
Height: 5'10" Weight: 11.1
Club Honours: Div 2 '88

For the most part of last season, Jimmy spent his time in the reserves at Portsmouth, unable to play his way into manager, Terry Fenwick's thoughts, and it took the arrival of Alan Ball as the new manager to give him his chance in the team. He played in the first six games of Ball's reign before giving way to Andy Thomson, as the team continued to under perform. Although a tricky, pacy right winger, who on his day is as good as anyone, with the ability to knock the ball past defenders to get in excellent crosses, he was released during the summer.

Crystal Palace (From apprentice on 15/11/83)
Queens Park R (Free on 30/9/85)

Millwall (£15,000 on 12/3/87) FL 99+11/10 FLC 6+1 FAC 6+1/2 Others 5+1
Liverpool (£800,000 on 10/1/91) FL 2+3 FAC 2 Others 0+1
Arsenal (£500,000 on 8/10/91) F/PL 18+7/2 FLC 1 FAC 2+1
Oxford U (Loaned on 23/3/94) FL 5
Oxford U (Loaned on 23/12/94) FL 3+1
Portsmouth (Free on 6/7/95) FL 60+12/5 FLC 5+1/1 FAC 0+2

CARTER Mark Colin
Born: Liverpool, 17 December 1960
Height: 5'9" Weight: 12.6
Club Honours: Div 2 '97
International Honours: E: SP-11

The veteran striker initially teamed up with Robbie Painter as one of Rochdale's front men, before being relegated to the bench when Dale signed Graham Lancashire. With things not going his way at Spotland, "Spike" went on loan to Gateshead for a couple of months in mid-season and, though returning to the Dale squad, the nearest he got to further senior appearances was as an unused substitute.

Barnet (£40,000 from Runcorn on 20/2/91) FL 62+20/30 FLC 5/2 FAC 4+1/6 Others 7+2/8
Bury (£6,000 on 10/9/93) FL 113+21/62 FLC 10+1/4 FAC 5 Others 12+1/2
Rochdale (Free on 17/7/97) FL 7+4/2 FLC 1+1

CARTER Timothy (Tim) Douglas
Born: Bristol, 5 October 1967
Height: 6'2" Weight: 12.8
International Honours: E: Yth

Started the first nine games of last season in Millwall's goal, until sustaining an injury that saw him play just once more before Christmas and five times in January. A good shot-stopper, who shows much awareness, especially in one-on-one situations, hopefully, fully recovered, he will find another club in time for 1998-99, having been released during the summer. Commands his box well and starts up many attacks with excellent distribution.

Bristol Rov (From apprentice on 8/10/85) FL 47 FLC 2 FAC 2 Others 2
Newport Co (Loaned on 14/12/87) FL 1
Sunderland (£50,000 on 24/12/87) FL 37 FLC 9 Others 4
Carlisle U (Loaned on 18/3/88) FL 4
Bristol C (Loaned on 15/9/88) FL 3
Birmingham C (Loaned on 21/11/91) FL 2 FLC 1
Hartlepool U (Free on 1/8/92) FL 18 FLC 4 FAC 1 Others 2
Millwall (Free on 6/1/94) FL 4 FLC 0+1
Blackpool (Free on 4/8/95)
Oxford U (Free on 18/8/95) FL 12 FLC 4 Others 1
Millwall (Free on 6/12/95) FL 62 FLC 5 FAC 3 Others 1

CARTWRIGHT Lee
Born: Rawtenstall, 19 September 1972
Height: 5'8" Weight: 11.0
Club Honours: Div 3 '96

Now in his seventh season at Preston, making him the club's longest-serving professional, Lee had a mixed 1997-98 on the right flank, and consequently found himself in and out of the side, although he remained a regular in the squad. Scored his first ever double in the away win at Wigan, but also picked up a niggling injury which did not help in his attempts to find some

consistent form. Quick, and a good crosser, he remains a favourite with the fans, however.

Preston NE (From trainee on 30/7/91) FL 198+34/16 FLC 10+1/2 FAC 12+2/1 Others 14+4/1

CARTWRIGHT Mark Neville
Born: Chester, 13 January 1973
Height: 6'2" Weight: 13.6

1997-98 was yet another frustrating season for Mark, due to the now familiar "limited opportunities" in the Wrexham first team. Once again he did a good job when Welsh international goalkeeper, Andy Marriott, was injured, but he needs more regular work at a higher level than the Pontins' League if he is to progress further. Interested in a move to Bournemouth before the transfer deadline, the clubs could not agree a fee and, for the time being, he remains at the Racecourse.

Stockport Co (Free from York C juniors on 17/8/91 - Released during 1992 close season)
Wrexham (Signed from USA soccer scholarship on 5/3/94) FL 7 FAC 1

CASEY Ryan Peter
Born: Coventry, 3 January 1979
Height: 6'1" Weight:11.2
International Honours: Ei: Yth

A strong-running Swansea left winger, who displays good ball skills and has the ability to pass defenders with ease, having scored on his debut for the Ireland U18 side against Northern Ireland last October, Ryan unfortunately returned with a twisted ankle that kept him out of action for a few weeks. However, he was soon back in the swing of things and remains an excellent prospect.

Swansea C (From trainee on 7/5/97) FL 5+11 Others 1

CASKEY Darren Mark
Born: Basildon, 21 August 1974
Height: 5'8" Weight: 11.9
International Honours: E: Yth (UEFAYC '93); Sch

In making a delayed start to last season after recovering from a broken left leg, Darren at last began to show the form and consistency the Reading fans had been expecting since his move from Spurs. At his best, his passing from midfield could destroy opposing defences, as he hits the ball accurately over more than 40 metres, while his defending skills improved too, and he was a regular choice both before and after the arrival of the incoming manager, Tommy Burns.

Tottenham H (From trainee on 6/3/92) PL 20+12/4 FLC 3+1/1 FAC 6+1
Watford (Loaned on 27/10/95) FL 6/1
Reading (£700,000 on 28/2/96) FL 60+13/2 FLC 2+1 FAC 2+1/1

CASPER Christopher (Chris) Martin
Born: Burnley, 28 April 1975
Height: 6'0" Weight: 11.11
Club Honours: FAYC '92
International Honours: E: U21-1; Yth (EUFAC '93)

Steve McMahon turned to the Manchester United youngster for defensive cover after

Swindon's club captain, Mark Seagraves, was ruled out through injury last September. Town had kept tabs on Chris, following his impressive display for United against them in a Coca Cola Cup tie the previous year, and his loan spell started well with a clean sheet on his debut at home to Nottingham Forest, followed by a winning goal from the elegant central defender against Tranmere. Unfortunately, two bookable offences brought a red card at Wolves and a one-match ban which brought his stay at the County Ground to a premature end. The son of Frank, a former Burnley star, is a good passer of the ball, who likes to come from the back to set up attacks, and is an excellent reader of the game.

Manchester U (From trainee on 3/2/93) PL 0+2 FLC 3 FAC 1 Others 0+1
Bournemouth (Loaned on 11/1/96) FL 16/1
Swindon T (Loaned on 5/9/97) FL 8+1/1

CASTLE Stephen (Steve) Charles
Born: Barking, 17 May 1966
Height: 5'11" Weight: 12.10

Signed from Birmingham during the 1997 close season, Steve proved to be a tireless midfielder, whose non-stop competitive workrate quickly won over the Peterborough fans in 1997-98. Unfortunate to suffer with injuries throughout the campaign, it did not stop him talking on the pitch and helping the youngsters who found their way into the side. Is never one to shirk the responsibility of having to defend when up against it.

Leyton Orient (From apprentice on 18/5/84) FL 232+11/55 FLC 15+1/5 FAC 23+1/6 Others 18+2
Plymouth Arg (£195,000 on 30/6/92) FL 98+3/35 FLC 5/1 FAC 8/2 Others 6/1
Birmingham C (£225,000 on 21/7/95) FL 16+7/1 FLC 11 FAC 1 Others 3/1
Gillingham (Loaned on 15/2/96) FL 5+1/1
Leyton Orient (Loaned on 3/2/97) FL 4/1
Peterborough (Free on 14/5/97) FL 34+3/3 FLC 4 FAC 2+1/2 Others 2+1/1

CASTLEDINE Stewart Mark
Born: Wandsworth, 22 January 1973
Height: 6'1" Weight: 12.13

An aggressive Wimbledon striker, Stewart made 12 appearances for the club last season, a slight increase on his 1996-97 total, and scored in both legs of the Coca Cola Cup games against Millwall. The "Top Man" model who is very popular with the fans, not just the females either, uses his height to great effect, an asset which has made him a force to be reckoned with in the reserves, and something he would like to transcend at senior level. Can also be used in midfield where his terrific stamina sees him never giving the opposition a moments peace.

Wimbledon (From trainee on 2/7/91) F/PL 17+10/4 FLC 4/3 FAC 2+3
Wycombe W (Loaned on 25/8/95) FL 7/3

CAVACO Luis Miguel Pasaro
Born: Portugal, 1 March 1972
Height: 5'9" Weight: 11.5

The Portuguese striker is a huge favourite at Edgeley Park, and his return after an 11-month fightback from a badly-broken leg was greeted with huge cheers from the

Stockport faithful. He returned to first team action in March, but it quickly became apparent that this was premature and he was forced to return to reserve football so that he could continue his rehabilitation, prior to being released in the summer.

Stockport Co (Free from Estoril on 27/8/96) FL 19+10/5 FLC 7+1/2 FAC 3 Others 3+2/1

CAWLEY Peter (Pete)
Born: Walton on Thames, 15 September 1965
Height: 6'4" Weight: 15.7

An inspirational centre half, now in the closing stages of a glittering Colchester career, Pete missed out on the second half of last season as the injuries which had plagued him throughout the campaign eventually forced him out of the team, finally limping off in the 1-0 home win over Torquay in January. Two operations have since failed to restore him to full fitness, and he was released during the summer.

Wimbledon (Signed from Chertsey T on 26/1/87) FL 1 Others 1
Bristol Rov (Loaned on 26/2/87) FL 9+1
Fulham (Loaned on 14/12/88) FL 3+2
Bristol Rov (Free on 17/7/89) FL 1+2
Southend U (Free on 6/7/90) FL 6+1/1 FLC 1 FAC 1 Others 1
Exeter C (Free on 22/11/90) FL 7
Barnet (Free on 8/11/91) FL 3 Others 1
Colchester U (Free on 9/10/92) FL 178+2/8 FLC 8 FAC 12 Others 13+1/1

CHALK Martyn Peter Glyn
Born: Swindon, 30 August 1969
Height: 5'6" Weight: 10.0

A busy little winger who, on his day, can be a "tricky" problem for any defender, Martyn is a right-sided flank player who competed with Craig Skinner for the number seven shirt at Wrexham in 1997-98. Could do with adding to his goal tally more often, but always makes himself available, and is always looking to get crosses on target. Is an avid collector of antiques in his spare time.

Derby Co (£10,000 from Louth U on 23/1/90) FL 4+3/1 FAC 3/1 Others 0+1
Stockport Co (£40,000 on 30/6/94) FL 29+14/6 FLC 7+1/2 FAC 2+3 Others 2+2
Wrexham (Signed on 19/2/96) FL 68+20/6 FLC 2+1 FAC 7+2 Others 1

CHALLINOR David (Dave) Paul
Born: Chester, 2 October 1975
Height: 6'1" Weight: 13.0
International Honours: E: Yth; Sch

In his first season as a Tranmere first team player in 1997-98, Dave was feted mainly for being the possessor of possibly the longest throw in the Football League, but he has since begun to demonstrate that this ability is only one aspect of his rapidly-maturing game. A number of impressive displays, strangely, many of them away from Prenton Park, gained him a first team slot on merit, and justified his decision to turn down a university place in favour of life in the Football League. Fast, and gifted, with good heading ability, he should consolidate his position even further during the coming season.

Tranmere Rov (Signed from Bromborough Pool on 18/7/94) FL 32+5/1 FLC 2 FAC 3

CHAMBERLAIN Alec Francis Roy
Born: March, 20 June 1964
Height: 6'2" Weight: 13.9
Club Honours: Div 1 '96; Div 2 '98

A goalkeeper who has made over 500 appearances for five different clubs, and having spent a year understudying Kevin Miller, he made the Watford first team spot his own in 1997-98 when playing in every league match in the club's second division championship campaign. Calm, competent, and completely unflappable, he is capable of pulling off spectacular saves when required, as he did against Gillingham and Carlisle to name but two instances. Quiet and thoughtful off the field, Alec was deservedly selected for the PFA second division team and then voted Watford's Player of the Year to cap a marvellous season.

Ipswich T (Free from Ramsey T on 27/7/81)
Colchester U (Free on 3/8/82) FL 188 FLC 11 FAC 10 Others 12
Everton (£80,000 on 28/7/87)
Tranmere Rov (Loaned on 1/11/87) FL 15
Luton T (£150,000 on 27/7/88) FL 138 FLC 7 FAC 7 Others 2
Sunderland (Free on 8/7/93) FL 89+1 FLC 9 FAC 8 Others 1
Watford (£40,000 on 10/7/96) FL 50 FLC 3 FAC 5

CHAMBERS Leroy Dean
Born: Sheffield, 25 October 1972
Height: 5'11" Weight: 12.0

Signed from Boston United, having been their top scorer in 1996-97, with 23 goals, and 12 in the first half of this season, Leroy made a tremendous impact in his first few games for Football League first-timers, Macclesfield, scoring three goals in two games. A tricky striker, who is fast on the ball, holds up play well, and twists defenders, unfortunately the strike rate dried up until he scored from a super header against Shrewsbury in mid-March.

Sheffield Wed (From trainee on 13/6/91)
Chester C Free on 11/8/95) FL 29+4/1 FLC 2 Others 1 (Free to Boston U during 1996 close season)
Macclesfield T (£6,000 on 18/12/97) FL 17+4/4 Others 1

CHANDLER Dean Andrew Robert
Born: Ilford, 6 May 1976
Height: 6'2" Weight: 11.10

The tall central defender who signed for Lincoln in the summer of 1997, following his release by Charlton Athletic, was unable to break through into the first team because of the form of Kevin Austin, his only opportunity coming in the Coca Cola Cup clash at Burnley when he had the misfortune to concede an early penalty. Otherwise confined to the reserves, apart from a two-month spell on loan at Yeovil Town, he was released during the summer.

Charlton Ath (From trainee on 13/4/94) FL 1+1/1
Torquay U (Loaned on 27/3/97) FL 4
Lincoln C (Free on 4/8/97) FLC 1

CHANNING Justin Andrew
Born: Reading, 19 November 1968
Height: 5'11" Weight: 11.7
International Honours: E: Yth

Despite starting last season as Leyton Orient's first-choice right-wing back before losing his place through injury and coming back for intermittent spells, his longest being between November and January, Justin never let the side down, especially in distributing the ball. With his contract at an end, he was released at the end of the campaign.

Queens Park R (From apprentice on 27/8/86) F/PL 42+13/5 FLC 4+1 FAC 2 Others 5
Bristol Rov (£250,000 on 24/10/92) FL 121+9/10 FLC 5 FAC 4+1 Others 11+1
Leyton Orient (Free on 25/7/96) FL 69+5/5 FLC 3+1 FAC 4/1 Others 3

CHAPMAN Benjamin (Ben)
Born: Scunthorpe, 2 March 1979
Height: 5'4" Weight: 11.0

Grimsby left back. As a hard-tackling first-year professional, Ben's impressive performances for the reserve squad in 1997-98 were rewarded by a brief appearance as a sub in the Auto Windscreen Shield. With that experience under his belt there is every chance that he will be challenging for a first team place this coming term.

Grimsby T (From trainee on 11/7/97) Others 0+1

CHAPMAN Ian Russell
Born: Brighton, 31 May 1970
Height: 5'9" Weight: 12.5

1997-98 was a season of disaster for Ian, after he picked up a bad knee injury at Wycombe in a reserve-team match in October which basically ended his campaign, his only appearance being at Birmingham in the first round of the Coca Cola Cup. Released during the summer, he is a hard-working, natural left footer, who can play either in defence or midfield as required.

Brighton & Hove A (From trainee on 5/6/87) FL 265+16/14 FLC 18+2 FAC 12+2/2 Others 12+4
Gillingham (Free on 1/8/96) FL 20+3/1 FLC 6 FAC 1+2 Others 1

Phil Chapple

CHAPPLE Philip (Phil) Richard
Born: Norwich, 26 November 1966
Height: 6'2" Weight: 13.1
Club Honours: Div 3 '91

A right-sided Charlton central defender who is excellent in the air and a strong tackler, despite not being the quickest of players, he always gives 100 per cent, and is often likely to grab a goal from set pieces and corners. Created a solid partnership with Richard Rufus in the centre of the defence in 1997-98, but missed the promotion run-in due to an ankle injury, and was released during the summer.

Norwich C (From apprentice on 10/7/85)
Cambridge U (Signed on 29/3/88) FL 183+4/19 FLC 11/2 FAC 23/1 Others 17
Charlton Ath (£100,000 on 13/8/93) FL 128+14/15 FLC 11 FAC 9 Others 5

CHAPPLE Shaun Ronald
Born: Swansea, 14 February 1973
Height: 5'11" Weight: 12.3
International Honours: W: B-1; U21-10; Sch

One of the longest serving members of the Swansea squad at the beginning of last season, Shaun, despite starting as first choice in midfield, was allowed to join non-league Merthyr on a free transfer at the end of October. A good passer of the ball, he also scored some vital goals during his time at Vetch Field.

Swansea C (From trainee on 15/7/91) FL 72+35/9 FLC 4+2/1 FAC 8+2 Others 9+3/1

CHARLERY Kenneth (Kenny) Leroy
Born: Stepney, 28 November 1964
Height: 6'1" Weight: 13.3

Another signing for Barnet just before 1997-98 got underway, having been at Peterborough previously, this much-travelled centre forward added his experience to the Bees' hunt for honours. Expert at leading the line, he found himself relegated to the subs' bench because of the form of Scott McGleish and Sean Devine. Can play deeper if required.

Maidstone U (£35,000 from Fisher on 1/3/89) FL 41+18/11 FLC 1+3/1 FAC 0+3 Others 5+4
Peterborough U (£20,000 on 28/3/91) FL 45+6/19 FLC 10/5 FAC 3/1 Others 11/7
Watford (£350,000 on 16/10/92) FL 45+3/13 FLC 3 FAC 1 Others 0+1
Peterborough U (£150,000 on 16/12/93) FL 70/24 FLC 2 FAC 2+1/3 Others 2/1
Birmingham C (£350,000 on 4/7/95) FL 8+9/4 FLC 3+1/2 Others 2+1
Southend U (Loaned on 12/1/96) FL 2+1
Peterborough U (Signed on 9/2/96) FL 55+1/12 FLC 4/1 FAC 6/6 Others 6/1
Stockport Co (£85,000 on 25/3/97) FL 8+2
Barnet (£80,000 on 7/8/97) FL 18+14/6 FLC 4 FAC 1 Others 2+1

CHARLES Gary Andrew
Born: Newham, 13 April 1970
Height: 5'9" Weight: 11.8
Club Honours: FMC '92; FLC '96
International Honours: E: 2; U21-4

Having been out of action since the end of 1995-96, after suffering an horrendous ankle injury at home to West Ham, Gary finally got himself back to full fitness and returned to the side at the start of last season. Playing

in the Premiership was a struggle to start with and, by his own admission, the run of three games, against Newcastle, Spurs, and Leeds, was too much after being out of the game for so long. After concentrating on getting in as many reserve games as he could, he came back to the side in late October when Fernando Nelson was switched to a midfield role, and was a regular member of the squad from thereon, despite making just 16 starts in all. Primarily a right back, with both balance and pace, who likes to get forward to join up with the attack, he scored his second goal for Villa, at Everton, when he dashed into the penalty area to drive home an Alan Wright cross in a 4-1 win.

Nottingham F (From trainee on 7/11/87) F/PL 54+2/1 FLC 9 FAC 8+2/1 Others 4+2
Leicester C (Loaned on 16/3/89) FL 5+3
Derby Co (£750,000 on 29/7/93) FL 61/3 FLC 5+1 FAC 1 Others 9
Aston Villa (Signed on 6/1/95) PL 62+6/2 FLC 8+1 FAC 5+1 Others 2+3

CHARLES Lee
Born: Hillingdon, 20 August 1971
Height: 5'11" Weight: 12.4

Unable to get a look in at Queens Park Rangers, Lee had a spell on loan at Cambridge last February, where much was expected from this young forward. Unfortunately, his spell at United coincided with personal problems and, after scoring one goal in seven appearances, he was allowed to return to Loftus Road, prior to being released during the summer. Confident, pacy, and with good first touch, there was no doubting his enthusiasm when running at defenders.

Queens Park R (£67,500 from Chertsey on 4/8/95) P/FL 6+10/1 FLC 0+1
Barnet (Loaned on 22/9/95) FL 2+3 Others 0+1
Cambridge U (Loaned on 20/2/98) FL 7/1

CHARLTON Simon Thomas
Born: Huddersfield, 25 October 1971
Height: 5'8" Weight: 11.10
International Honours: E: Yth

Injured at the end of 1996-97, and unable to get his place back at Southampton, Simon was rescued from reserve team football when signing for Birmingham last December. The footballing left back quickly became regarded as a bargain buy, being solid in the tackle and providing City with more quality when going forward, which was exactly what the manager, Trevor Francis, had been searching for. Chirpy and confident, he likes nothing better than getting forward to deliver good early crosses to the front men and possesses an excellent long throw.

Huddersfield T (From trainee on 1/7/89) FL 121+3/1 FLC 9/1 FAC 10 Others 14
Southampton (£250,000 on 8/6/93) PL 104+10/2 FLC 9+4/1 FAC 8+1
Birmingham C (£250,000 on 5/12/97) FL 23+1 FAC 1

CHARNOCK Philip (Phil) Anthony
Born: Southport, 14 February 1975
Height: 5'11" Weight: 11.2

A hard-working Crewe midfielder whose appearances are always marked with maximum effort, Phil unfortunately had to miss ten games in 1997-98 after breaking a wrist when hit by the ball at West Bromwich Albion in January. Once back in action, however, he soon got down to business, even finding time to add to his earlier goal at Gresty Road against Huddersfield with a couple more at Sunderland and Ipswich. Can also play at full back.

Liverpool (From trainee on 16/3/93) FLC 1 Others 0+1
Blackpool (Loaned on 9/2/96) FL 0+4
Crewe Alex (Signed on 30/9/96) FL 57+8/4 FLC 2 FAC 3 Others 6

CHARVET Laurent Jean
Born: Beziers, France, 8 May 1973
Height: 5'10" Weight: 12.3
Club Honours: ECWC '98

This talented addition to the Chelsea squad joined the Blues last January from the French club, Cannes, in a loan deal until the end of the season. A versatile right-sided player, who can perform either as wing back or in midfield, he has a keen eye for goal – top-scoring for Cannes before his move. Fast, aggressive, and good in the air, Laurent's first taste of English football came with his appearance as substitute at Highbury in the Coca Cola Cup semi final, when he acquitted himself confidently in the white-hot atmosphere. He also figured in a second semi-final – the European Cup Winners Cup – surely some sort of record by a loan signing! He scored his first goals with fiercely struck shots at Upton Park and Elland Road.

Chelsea (Loaned from Cannes on 22/1/98) PL 7+4/2 FLC 0+1 Others 0+1

CHENERY Benjamin (Ben) Roger
Born: Ipswich, 28 January 1977
Height: 6'1" Weight: 12.5

Signed on a free transfer from Luton Town in the summer of 1997, Ben occupied Cambridge's right-back position for the first 11 games of 1997-98, before suffering a serious head injury that kept him out for six weeks, and saw the team struggle without him. Returned in mid-November to reclaim his place, virtually making the number two shirt his permanent property, he also scored two goals, one in the live Sky game against Lincoln City in February.

Luton T (From trainee on 3/3/95) FL 2 FAC 1
Cambridge U (Free on 3/7/97) FL 36/2 FLC 2 FAC 4

CHETTLE Stephen (Steve)
Born: Nottingham, 27 September 1968
Height: 6'1" Weight: 13.3
Club Honours: FMC '89, '92; FLC '90; Div 1 '98
International Honours: E: U21-12

Started last season at Nottingham Forest as the club captain when Colin Cooper was unavailable through injury and formed a good understanding in the heart of the defence with the Norwegian newcomer, Jon Olav Hjelde, missing just one league game as Forest won the first division champion-ship and returned to the Premiership at the first attempt. Comfortable in possession, and a player who makes great interceptions,

to come out looking for attacking options and to pass the ball to feet, Steve is the kind of cultured defender that Forest fans have come to accept and expect. Also scored his first goal for two years, and an important one at that, the winner at Portsmouth in February. Is due a well-earned testimonial in 1998-99.

Nottingham F (From apprentice on 28/8/86) F/PL 356+14/8 FLC 42+3/1 FAC 35+1 Others 21+2/2

CHRISTIE Iyseden
Born: Coventry, 14 November 1976
Height: 6'0" Weight: 12.6

Signed from Coventry during the 1997 close season, having spent a loan period at Field Mill during the previous term, Iyseden started last season for Mansfield with a bang, scoring a hat trick in a 4-2 Coca Cola Cup win over Stockport at home on 12 August, and the goals flowed. However, he struck a lean spell from November onwards and, relegated to the subs' bench, scored only three more times to the end of the campaign. A striker with a future, his time will yet come.

Coventry C (From trainee on 22/5/95) PL 0+1 FLC 0+1
Bournemouth (Loaned on 18/11/96) FL 3+1
Mansfield T (Loaned on 7/2/97) FL 8
Mansfield T (Free on 16/6/97) FL 26+13/10 FLC 2/4 FAC 0+2 Others 0+1

CLAPHAM James (Jamie) Richard
Born: Lincoln, 7 December 1975
Height: 5'9" Weight: 10.11

After failing to add to his solitary Tottenham subs' appearance of 1996-97, Jamie joined Ipswich on loan last January to provide left-sided cover at a time when injuries and suspensions left the club weak in this area. Made his debut in a 0-0 home draw with Queens Park Rangers and, apart from FA Cup games, when he was ineligible, played in every game thereafter, with his loan period being extended to a second month before Town signed him permanently in March. Whilst initially concentrating on his defensive responsibilities, he grew in confidence with every game he played and developed more in an attacking role, while becoming something of a lucky charm for the club, in that he was only on the losing side once. Establishing a good rapport with Bobby Petta down the left flank, his left foot was responsible for some excellent "assists", notably in the home game with Sunderland, when his pin-point cross was volleyed home by Alex Mathie.

Tottenham H (From trainee on 1/7/94) PL 0+1
Leyton Orient (Loaned on 29/1/97) FL 6
Bristol Rov (Loaned on 27/3/97) FL 4+1
Ipswich T (£300,000 on 9/1/98) FL 22 Others 1

CLARE Daryl Adam
Born: Jersey, 1 August 1978
Height: 5'9" Weight: 11.0
Club Honours: AMC '98
International Honours: Ei: U21-1

Right-sided Grimsby midfielder, cum striker. Following his debut during 1995-96, Daryl surprisingly failed to make the senior squad under Kenny Swain and had to wait over a year to establish himself as a first

team player. Injuries to both Lee Nogan and Jack Lester gave him his chance, and some impressive displays, intelligent use of the ball, strength and speed in the box, and the occasional goal, helped to establish him at senior level in 1997-98. On the verge of international recognition at U21 level, having trained with the England squad, he was omitted from the Eire squad only because of the Mariners' heavy league and AWS programme, both of which ultimately proved successful. Eventually made an impressive U21 international debut for the Republic in a win over Scotland, before being named as the Mariners' Young Player of the Year.

Grimsby T (From trainee on 9/12/95) FL 8+15/3 FLC 0+1 FAC 1+4 Others 4+2

CLARIDGE Stephen (Steve) Edward
Born: Portsmouth, 10 April 1966
Height: 5'11" Weight: 12.10
Club Honours: Div 3 '91, Div 2 '95; AMC '95; FLC '97

A bustling, right-footed striker, who is ever popular with the fans, Steve's aversion to hot climates caused him to miss out on the pre-season preparation, costing him a place in the Leicester line-up at the start of last season, and setting the seeds of discontent. His heart was never really in it thereafter and, with the goals also drying up, a move looked the obvious solution. An extended loan spell at Portsmouth early in the New Year saw him quickly forming an effective partnership with John Aloisi, and scoring two goals in ten games before returning to Filbert Street when Pompey's financial straits precluded a permanent move. Following that, he became a surprise signing for Wolves on transfer deadline day, the club requiring someone with the ability to hold the ball up. When purchasing him, it seemed as though Wolves had the FA Cup semi final in mind but, apart from his fighting spirit, he made little impact and will be looking for better results in 1998-99.

Bournemouth (Signed from Fareham on 30/11/84) FL 3+4/1 Others 1 (£10,000 to Weymouth in October 1985)
Crystal Palace (Signed on 11/10/88)
Aldershot (£14,000 on 13/10/88) FL 58+4/19 FLC 2+1 FAC 6/1 Others 5/2
Cambridge U (£75,000 on 8/2/90) FL 56+23/28 FLC 2+4/2 FAC 1 Others 6+3/1
Luton T (£160,000 on 17/7/92) FL 15+1/2 FLC 2/3 Others 2/1
Cambridge U (£195,000 on 20/11/92) FL 53/18 FLC 4/3 FAC 4 Others 3
Birmingham C (£350,000 on 7/1/94) FL 86+2/35 FLC 14+1/2 FAC 7 Others 9+1/5
Leicester C (£1,200,000 on 1/3/96) P/FL 53+10/17 FLC 8/2 FAC 4/1 Others 3+1/1
Portsmouth (Loaned on 23/1/98) FL 10/2
Wolverhampton W (£400,000 on 26/3/98) FL 4+1 FAC 1

CLARK Dean Wayne
Born: Hillingdon, 31 March 1980
Height: 5'10" Weight: 12.6

A young Brentford midfielder from the YTS ranks who was given his chance as a substitute on a few occasions in 1997-98, he first appeared at Luton in an AWS tie in January, before being given his league debut

at the end of the month against Plymouth. Is highly thought of by Bees' manager, Micky Adams.

Brentford (From trainee on 1/10/97) FL 0+4 Others 0+1

CLARK Ian David
Born: Stockton, 23 October 1974
Height: 5'11" Weight: 11.7

Left out in the cold at Doncaster in 1997-98, apart from two appearances, this hard-working utility player was signed by Hartlepool as a trialist to rescue him from his disappointing spell at Belle Vue. Determined to do well, he overcame some initial problems to prove himself a good opportunist goalscorer and, towards the end of the season, required to play as a defender he gave several impressive displays to suggest that his best position may yet be as an attacking left back.

Doncaster Rov (Free from Stockton on 11/8/95) FL 23+22/3 FLC 1+2 FAC 1+1 Others 4/1
Hartlepool U (Free on 24/10/97) FL 19+5/7 FAC 0+1 Others 1

CLARK Lee Robert
Born: Wallsend, 27 October 1972
Height: 5'8" Weight: 11.7
Club Honours: Div 1 '93
International Honours: E: U21-11; Yth; Sch

A midfield general who became Sunderland's record signing in the summer of 1997 when he arrived from Newcastle, Lee immediately won over the fans with typical displays full of 100 per-cent effort and accurate passing. "Clarkie" was also awarded the team captaincy in the absence of Kevin Ball and scored 13 goals in the promotion push, including braces at Stoke in October, and at home to Tranmere in November, as well as creating many others for his team mates. Capped a superb first year at the club, as an ever present, by being named in the PFA division one select XI.

Newcastle U (From trainee on 9/12/89) F/PL 153+42/23 FLC 17 FAC 14+2/3 Others 7+5/1
Sunderland (£2,750,000 on 25/6/97) FL 46/13 FLC 1 FAC 2 Others 3

CLARK Martin Alan
Born: Accrington, 12 September 1970
Height: 5'9" Weight: 10.12

Signed from non-league Southport during the 1997 close season, Martin gave up his job as a postman to turn full time and went straight into the Rotherham team, where his pace served him well in the heart of the defence. Although probably best used as a sweeper, the newcomer played many of his games at right back in his first term as a professional.

Rotherham U (Free from Southport on 25/6/97) FL 28 FLC 2 FAC 3

CLARK Simon
Born: Boston, 12 March 1967
Height: 6'1" Weight: 12.12

A 1997 close season signing from Peterborough, Simon arrived at Leyton Orient as a big, strong left-sided central defender who is excellent in the air and a good tackler. Those attributes always spell

danger at set pieces and he scored some important goals, including a hat trick of headers against Doncaster, as well as producing flick ons for others.

Peterborough U (Free from Stevenage Borough on 25/3/94) FL 102+5/3 FLC 5 FAC 12 Others 7+1/1
Leyton Orient (£20,000 on 16/6/97) FL 39/5 FLC 3 FAC 2 Others 1

CLARK William (Billy) Raymond
Born: Christchurch, 19 May 1967
Height: 6'0" Weight: 12.4

Unable to get a game at Bristol Rovers in 1997-98, Billy signed for Exeter in November, from which point on he was an ever present, and showed what a good signing he was by putting in many consistent performances. His strengths include his tackling abilities, vision, when looking to pass, and his role at flicking on set pieces.

Bournemouth (From apprentice on 25/9/84) FL 4
Bristol Rov (Signed on 16/10/87) FL 235+13/14 FLC 11+1 FAC 8+1 Others 19+2/1
Exeter C (Free on 30/20/97) FL 31/3 FAC 2/1 Others 1

CLARKE Adrian James
Born: Cambridge, 28 September 1974
Height: 5'10" Weight: 11.0
Club Honours: FAYC '94
International Honours: E: Yth; Sch

After firming up his transfer from Arsenal during the 1997 summer recess, Adrian was one of the few highlights of another poor season for Southend United in 1997-98, as he developed his game to include tough tackling and defensive covering, as well as his natural wing play. Unfortunately, he seemed to suffer from a lack of confidence at times and had a tendency to drift out of games, when his natural ability could have seen him take more control. However, he has the ability to go far.

Arsenal (From trainee on 6/7/93) PL 4+3 FAC 1+1
Rotherham U (Loaned on 2/12/96) FL 1+1 Others 1
Southend U (Free on 27/3/97) FL 49+3/5 FLC 4 FAC 2 Others 1

CLARKE Andrew (Andy) Weston
Born: Islington, 22 July 1967
Height: 5'10" Weight: 11.7
Club Honours: GMVC '91
International Honours: E: SP-2

Signed from non-league Barnet in 1991, Andy continued to add life to the Wimbledon side in 1997-98, when coming off the bench for 18 substitute appearances (there were just three starts) in order to attack tiring defences, and always received a big cheer when doing so. There is no doubt that the Selhurst faithful fully appreciate his total commitment and endeavour when wearing the club's colours, despite him not finding the net as readily as he and they would like, but a more popular player you could not find. The scorer of just one goal during the past campaign, but still an option in Joe Kinnear's plans, he is charismatic, hard working, and "crazy" through and through.

Wimbledon (£250,000 from Barnet on 21/2/91) F/PL 74+96/17 FLC 13+12/4 FAC 9+8/2

CLARKE Darrell James
Born: Mansfield, 16 December 1977
Height: 5'10" Weight: 12.0

After an outstanding previous campaign, Darrell failed to continue his previous promise with Mansfield in 1997-98 and had a somewhat inconsistent season. However, he is still only 20 years of age, and there is plenty of time for the midfielder, cum forward to mature. Having scored the second goal of 1997-98 for Town, in a 2-0 home win against Hull, he netted the winner at Swansea, before producing a dramatic late equaliser at Scarborough and a goal that saved the game for the Stags at Leyton Orient.

Mansfield T (From trainee on 3/7/96) FL 44+13/6 FLC 1 FAC 1+1 Others 0+2

CLARKE Matthew (Matt) John
Born: Sheffield, 3 November 1973
Height: 6'4" Weight: 13.8

Apart from three games in 1997-98, this competent goalkeeper was still unable to oust Kevin Pressman from between Sheffield Wednesday's posts. The three games in question saw him come off the subs' bench after 22 minutes of the home match against Coventry, when Pressman was injured, to keep a clean sheet, prior to making his first start for the Owls against Derby. Unfortunate to be on the receiving end of a 5-2 home blitz, he then performed well in a 2-2 draw at Aston Villa, before once again going back to the role of deputy. However, he certainly has the attributes to be a fine 'keeper, with height, strength, agility and, hopefully, time on his side to make the big-time breakthrough.

Rotherham U (From trainee on 28/7/92) FL 123+1 FLC 4 FAC 3 Others 11
Sheffield Wed (£325,000 + on 10/7/96) PL 2+2

CLARKE Stephen (Steve)
Born: Saltcoats, 29 August 1963
Height: 5'10" Weight: 12.5
Club Honours: Div 2 '89; FAC '97; FLC '98; ECWC '98
International Honours: S: 6; B-3; U21-8; Yth

As Chelsea's club captain and longest serving player, Steve is currently playing under his seventh different manager in his ten-year career at The Bridge and when he made his 400th first team appearance last January, he became only the eighth player in the club's 92-year history to achieve this milestone. It was a momentous 12 months for the defender, playing in three winning finals, but his crowning moment came in the 4-1 home victory over Liverpool on 25 April when he scored Chelsea's second goal – his first for the club since a header against QPR on 18 April 1992 – six years and one week earlier! Steve has been a model professional in his time at Chelsea and, as he nears the veteran stage, would appear to have all the attributes that make a successful coach.

St Mirren (Free from Beith Juniors on 9/7/81) SL 151/6 SLC 21 SC 19/1 Others 6
Chelsea (£422,000 on 19/1/87) F/PL 321+9/7 FLC 24+2/1 FAC 34+2/1 Others 28+1/1

CLARKE Timothy (Tim) Joseph
Born: Stourbridge, 19 September 1968
Height: 6'3" Weight: 14.7
Club Honours: AMC '96

Scunthorpe's regular first-choice goalkeeper throughout last season, Tim started off superbly with his large presence dominating the penalty area and being good on crosses. Unfortunately, he was kicked unconscious against Hull in September and it took him a long time to get back to the standard he was at before, his form eventually leading to him being dropped for a game in January. Immediately got his place back though and began to return to his best before missing the run-in with a groin injury.*

Coventry C (£25,000 from Halesowen T on 22/10/90)
Huddersfield T (£15,000 on 22/7/91) FL 70 FLC 7 FAC 6 Others 8 (Free to Halesowen on 19/8/93)
Rochdale (Loaned on 12/2/93) FL 2
Shrewsbury T (Free from Altrincham on 21/10/93) FL 30+1 FLC 3 Others 1 (Free to Witton A during 1996 close season)
York C (Free on 7/9/96) FL 17 FLC 1 FAC 4 Others 1
Scunthorpe U (Signed on 21/2/97) FL 56 FLC 3 FAC 4 Others 3

CLARKSON Ian Stewart
Born: Solihull, 4 December 1970
Weight: 5'11" Weight: 12.0
Club Honours: AMC '91

As Northampton's right-wing back, Ian likes to get forward and support the attack, despite being called upon to play in midfield several times last season. Made with such little piece of history when he scored his first goal, versus Chesterfield in April, after some 400 first team appearances during his career. Is also a sound tackler.

Birmingham C (From trainee on 15/12/88) FL 125+11 FLC 12 FAC 5+1 Others 17+1
Stoke C (£40,000 on 13/9/93) FL 72+3 FLC 6 FAC 5 Others 8+2
Northampton T (Free on 2/8/96) FL 87/1 FLC 6 FAC 6 Others 10/1

CLARKSON Philip (Phil) Ian
Born: Garstang, 13 November 1968
Height: 5'10" Weight: 12.5

As Blackpool's top scorer in 1997-98, Phil certainly showed his strength in opponents' penalty areas and, at one stage, had scored six goals in six matches, including two in a 4-3 FA Cup victory over Blyth Spartans. Not the tallest of players, but one with excellent aerial ability, and able to perform in midfield or up front, where he thrives off the target man, his final goals of the campaign came at Preston where he both opened and finished the scoring in a 3-3 thriller.

Crewe Alex (£22,500 from Fleetwood T on 15/10/91) FL 76+22/27 FLC 6+2/1 FAC 3+2/2 Others 7+4/1
Scunthorpe U (Loaned on 30/10/95) FL 4/1
Scunthorpe U (Free on 13/2/96) FL 45+3/18 FLC 2/1 FAC 3/2 Others 1
Blackpool (£80,000 on 6/2/97) FL 59+3/18 FLC 3 FAC 2/2 Others 3/1

CLAYTON Gary
Born: Sheffield, 2 February 1963
Height: 5'10" Weight: 12.8
International Honours: E: SP-1

Signed from Plymouth early in 1997-98,

Gary proved to be an inspirational and competitive midfield player, who became a natural successor at Torquay to the departing Charlie Oatway. Equally at ease in a number of positions, including central defence, he scored brilliant goals from free kicks in the cup at Watford, and at home to Peterborough.*

Doncaster Rov (Signed from Burton A on 23/8/86) FL 34+1/5 FLC 2 FAC 3 Others 2
Cambridge U (£10,000 on 2/7/87) FL 166+13/17 FLC 17+1/3 FAC 9 Others 7/2
Peterborough U (Signed on 25/1/91) FL 4
Huddersfield T (£20,000 on 18/2/94) FL 15+4/1 FAC 0+1 Others 4/2
Plymouth Arg (Signed on 10/8/95) FL 32+6/2 FLC 2 FAC 2 Others 1
Torquay U (Free on 21/8/97) FL 41/2 FLC 3 FAC 3/1 Others 4

CLEAVER Christopher (Chris) William
Born: Hitchin, 24 March 1979
Height: 5'10" Weight: 11.3

Unable to get an extended run in the Peterborough team in 1997-98, due to more experienced players being used, although he figured in half of the squads, he started just four games. A non-stop, wholehearted trier, Chris scored two goals, both at home, the first in a 3-1 win against Rochdale and the equaliser in a 1-1 draw with Exeter. With a bit more edge, he could score on a regular basis.

Peterborough U (From trainee on 22/3/97) FL 10+17/3 FLC 0+2 FAC 0+1 Others 1+2

CLEGG Michael Jaime
Born: Ashton under Lyne, 3 July 1977
Height: 5'8" Weight: 11.8
Club Honours: FAYC '95
International Honours: E: U21-2

A very able full-back, who is good in the tackle and excellent on the overlap, Michael was hopeful of forging a regular place in the Manchester United side in 1997-98, after showing such excellent promise the season before. Opportunities, however, remained thin on the ground, owing to the outstanding form of Gary Neville and Denis Irwin. Having made only two full appearances during the course of the season, in the FA Cup against Barnsley, he was given his European debut against Monaco in March, when replacing the injured Paul Scholes. Despite facing an uphill battle in vying for a regular place alongside the likes of the Neville brothers and Denis Irwin, he continues to make excellent progress. Was selected at England U21 level to play in the end of season Toulon tournament and appeared in two of the three games on offer, versus France and South Africa.

Manchester U (From trainee on 1/7/95) PL 4+3 FLC 1 FAC 3+1 Others 0+1

CLEMENCE Stephen Neal
Born: Liverpool, 31 March 1978
Height: 5'11" Weight: 11.7
International Honours: E: Yth; Sch

In being handed his first team debut for Tottenham in the curtain raiser at home to Manchester United last August, this youthful attacking midfielder was given an opportunity to demonstrate the skill and

ability which had already made him a regular in the England youth set up. Despite his years, Stephen is extremely mature in the positions he gets himself into, and the space that he creates when applying his pace in going forward. In that, his role is similar to that of Allan Nielsen, and it was an injury to the latter which brought the youngster the opportunity of a prolonged spell in the first team, during which he impressed a great deal and slotted into the role without being overawed by the responsibility. An accurate passer of the ball, his workrate over 90 minutes is reminiscent of David Howells, while his confidence to shoot at goal is apparent, and was rewarded with his first goal in the FA Cup third round clash with Fulham in January. The son of the former England goalkeeper, Ray, he will undoubtedly continue to feature as a long-term prospect at White Hart Lane in 1998-99.

Tottenham H (From trainee on 3/4/95) PL 12+5 FLC 2 FAC 2/1

CLITHEROE Lee John
Born: Chorley, 18 November 1978
Height: 5'10" Weight: 10.4

A first-year professional at Oldham in 1997-98, Lee burst on the first team scene at the back end of the season when coming off the bench to make his Football League debut against Wycombe at Boundary Park. He played twice more, including a start, and impressed as a natural attacking right winger who is extremely quick, skilful, and a great crosser of the ball. Make a note of the name!

Oldham Ath (From trainee on 1/7/97) FL 1+2

CLODE Mark James
Born: Plymouth, 24 February 1973
Height: 5'10" Weight: 10.10
Club Honours: AMC '94

After recovering from the broken ankle suffered in 1996-97, Mark made his first league appearance of 1997-98 at Cardiff in November, before having to return to hospital for surgery on a chronic shin problem early in the New Year. An exciting young left back, who is at his best when going forward to link up with his team mates, his comeback to the first team was further delayed when having an operation to remove an appendix in March.

Plymouth Arg (From trainee on 30/3/91)
Swansea C (Free on 23/7/93) FL 107+10/3 FLC 7+2 FAC 6 Others 9+2

CLOUGH Nigel Howard
Born: Sunderland, 19 March 1966
Height: 5'10" Weight: 12.3
Club Honours: FLC '89, '90; FMC '89, '92
International Honours: E: 14; B-3; U21-15

On loan from Manchester City last September, Nigel's brief spell with Sheffield Wednesday was not successful either for player or club and, after just two starts, the son of Brian returned to Maine Road. Despite keeping himself fit and in good condition, there were to be no further opportunities at City during the season and he languished on the sidelines. At his best, a striker with subtle touches and penetrating passes, who could create as many goals as

he scored, his brilliant attitude to the game surely warrants another chance, possibly in the managerial side of the game.

Nottingham F (Free from Heanor T on 15/9/84) F/PL 307+4/101 FLC 46/22 FAC 28/6 Others 11+3/1
Liverpool (£2,275,000 on 7/6/93) PL 29+10/7 FLC 3/2 FAC 2
Manchester C (£1,500,000 on 24/1/96) P/FL 33+5/4 FLC 2 FAC 3/1
Nottingham F (Loaned on 21/12/96) PL 10+3/1
Sheffield Wed (Loaned on 12/9/97) PL 1 FLC 1

COATES Jonathan Simon
Born: Swansea, 27 June 1975
Height: 5'8" Weight: 10.4
International Honours: W: U21-5; Yth

The talented left-sided Swansea midfielder was switched to good effect from midfield to a left-wing-back role in 1997-98, where he continued to make good progress. With eight goals to his credit during the campaign, almost double the amount of his career total at that point, his strong shooting ability saw him score one of the goals of the season at Leyton Orient in February. Capable of playing at higher level, he was included in the Welsh "B" squad picked to play its Scottish counterparts in March, but was forced to withdraw due to injury, having earlier played for the U21 side in Turkey.

Swansea C (From trainee on 8/7/93) FL 87+24/11 FLC 4+1/1 FAC 4 Others 7+1

Jonathan Coates

COCKERILL Glenn
Born: Grimsby, 25 August 1959
Height: 5'10" Weight: 12.4

Before following manager, Micky Adams, to Brentford last November, Glenn played a few games for Fulham in 1997-98 and showed that, despite his advancing years, his skill in midfield as both a ball winner and distributor had not waned. Having moved to Griffin Park as the assistant player/manager,

he made 25 appearances and never looked out of place, often being the best of the Bees on the park.

Lincoln C (Free from Louth U on 1/11/76) FL 65+6/10 FLC 2 FAC 2
Swindon T (£11,000 on 6/12/79) FL 23+3/1 FLC 3
Lincoln C (£40,000 on 12/8/81) FL 114+1/25 FLC 16/1 FAC 7 Others 1
Sheffield U (£125,000 on 23/3/84) FL 62/10 FLC 6/1 FAC 1
Southampton (£225,000 on 17/10/85) F/PL 272+15/32 FLC 35+2/5 FAC 20+2/2 Others 12
Leyton Orient (Free on 10/12/93) FL 89+1/7 FLC 4/1 FAC 3 Others 10
Fulham (Free on 5/7/96) FL 32+8/1 FLC 5+1 FAC 1
Brentford (Free on 6/11/97) FL 23 FAC 2

COLDICOTT Stacy
Born: Redditch, 29 April 1974
Height: 5'8" Weight: 11.2

A determined, aggressive and totally committed West Bromwich Albion midfielder, Stacy again had to compete for a place in the side in 1997-98, never really establishing himself, but always ready to do the business when called upon. Able to play in midfield or at right back, where he is good on the overlap, he continued to be well thought of at the Hawthorns by fans and management alike.

West Bromwich A (From trainee on 4/3/92) FL 64+40/3 FLC 8+1 FAC 2+2/1 Others 7+3
Cardiff C (Loaned on 30/8/96) FL 6

COLE Andrew (Andy) Alexander
Born: Nottingham, 15 October 1971
Height: 5'11" Weight: 11.12
Club Honours: Div 1 '93; PL '96, '97; FAC '96; CS '97
International Honours: E: 2; B-1; U21-8; Yth, Sch

A quick and elusive striker, with lightening speed and good skills to match, his future at Manchester United was still the main topic of conversation when 1997-98 began. Having had a minor operation to remove an abscess after playing in the Charity Shield against Chelsea, he made his first appearance of the campaign as a substitute at Everton in August, before celebrating his first goal against Coventry in United's next Premiership game, and then catching fire during October and November when he netted 11 goals, including hat tricks against Barnsley and Feyenoord. Sharing the Carling Player of the Month award with Southampton's Kevin Davies in October, he was also elevated to the England squad by Glenn Hoddle, though groin and back problems prevented him from making his bow against Chile at Wembley in February. Despite Alex Ferguson continuing to show an interest in the Chilean striker, Jose Marcello Salas, Andy continued to match his phenomenal workrate with a regular supply of goals and, having signed a new five-year contract in October, he ended the campaign among the Premiership's leading scorers.

Arsenal (From trainee on 18/10/89) FL 0+1 Others 0+1
Fulham (Loaned on 5/9/91) FL 13/3 Others 2/1

Andy Cole

Bristol C (£500,000 on 12/3/92) FL 41/20 FLC 3/4 FAC 1 Others 4/1
Newcastle U (£1,750,000 on 12/3/93) F/PL 69+1/55 FLC 7/8 FAC 4/1 Others 3/4
Manchester U (£6,000,000 on 12/1/95) PL 90+15/45 FLC 2 FAC 12+1/7 Others 10+4/6

COLEMAN Christopher (Chris)
Born: Swansea, 10 June 1970
Height: 6'2" Weight: 14.6
Club Honours: WC '89, '91; Div 1 '94
International Honours: W: 19; U21-3; Yth; Sch

Having recovered from serious ligament damage suffered at Coventry in 1996-97, Chris came back for Blackburn in the Coca Cola Cup but, not being in the new manager, Roy Hodgson's plans, was transferred to Fulham last December. Undoubtedly the best defender the club have had since Tony Gale left for West Ham, he was very rarely beaten on the ground, or in the air, and if encouraged to go forward more often would score many more goals, as he did in his Crystal Palace days. Voted by his fellow professionals into the PFA award-winning second division team, it was no surprise that he was again a regular in the Welsh team.
Swansea C (From from Manchester C juniors on 1/9/87) FL 159+1/2 FLC 8 FAC 13/1 Others 15
Crystal Palace (£275,000 on 19/7/91) F/PL 143+11/13 FLC 24+2/2 FAC 8/1 Others 2
Blackburn Rov (£2,800,000 on 16/12/95) PL 27+1 FLC 2 FAC 2
Fulham (£2,100,000 on 1/12/97) FL 26/1 FAC 1 Others 3

COLEMAN Simon
Born: Worksop, 13 June 1968
Height: 6'0" Weight: 10.8

After finding his first team chances limited at Bolton last season, making no appearances, Simon was loaned to Wolves in September. With their four main central

defenders out injured, they were desperate, but having had his own fitness problems his stay at Milineux was not the best. However, after playing his way back into condition with Wanderers, he joined Southend in February and soon showed the skills that had seen him perform in higher divisions. A centre back who is equally at home on the ground or in the air, he formed a strong partnership with first, on-loan Richard Jobson, and then, Keith Dublin. Is a player who keeps it simple and has the skill to move forward and cause the opposition problems, especially at set pieces.
Mansfield T (From juniors on 29/7/85) FL 96/7 FLC 9 FAC 7 Others 7/1
Middlesbrough (£600,000 on 26/9/89) FL 51+4/2 FAC 5 Others 10/1
Derby Co (£300,000 on 15/8/91) FL 62+8/2 FLC 5+1 FAC 5 Others 12
Sheffield Wed (£250,000 on 20/1/94) PL 11+5/1 FLC 3 FAC 2
Bolton W (£350,000 on 5/10/94) P/FL 34/5 FLC 4 FAC 2
Wolverhampton W (Loaned on 2/9/97) FL 3+1
Southend U (Free on 20/2/98) FL 14

COLGAN Nicholas (Nick) Vincent
Born: Drogheda, Eire, 19 September 1973
Height: 6'1" Weight: 13.6
International Honours: Ei: B-1; U21-9; Yth; Sch

Unable to figure at Chelsea, with Dmitri Kharine, Ed de Goey, and Kevin Hitchcock in front of him in the pecking order, the tall, laid-back goalie was loaned to Brentford last October in order to get some match practice and kept two clean sheets in five games before returning to the Bridge. He was next called upon in February, by Reading, who had lost Steve Mautone and Nicky Hammond to injury. Arriving understandably rusty, he conceded an embarrassing goal at Crewe, when a clearance bounced off

an opponent into the net, but showed considerable courage in his fifth and final game for the club, when completing the match after suffering a nasty leg injury. Back at Stamford Bridge, and despite having kept a clean sheet for the Republic of Ireland "B" team, he was released during the summer.
Chelsea (From trainee on 1/10/92) PL 1
Brentford (Loaned on 16/10/97) FL 5
Reading (Loaned on 27/2/98) FL 5

COLKIN Lee
Born: Nuneaton, 15 July 1974
Height: 5'11" Weight: 12.4
A left-sided Northampton defender, and the club's longest serving player, Lee was unable to break into the first team in 1997-98, and had a trial with St Mirren before going on loan to Leyton Orient three weeks into the season. An aggressive and wholehearted left-wing back, who proved to be a good crosser when attacking opposing defences, he was unlucky not to gain a regular place with the O's and returned to Town. Well known as the dressing room joker, he joined non-league Hednesford on transfer deadline day.
Northampton T (From trainee on 31/8/92) FL 74+25/3 FLC 6+3/1 FAC 2+2 Others 4+3
Leyton Orient (Loaned on 29/8/97) FL 5+6 FLC 0+1

COLLETT Andrew (Andy) Alfred
Born: Stockton, 28 October 1973
Height: 6'0" Weight: 12.10
The Bristol Rovers' goalkeeper had a mixed season in 1997-98, as he struggled to reach the consistent performance levels of the previous campaign. As Rovers' regular 'keeper up until January, following a 3-1 defeat at Carlisle, Andy came under intense pressure from reserve 'keeper, Shane Higgs, who replaced him for a short spell. In the last two months of the campaign, with the new signing, Lee Jones, holding the number one jersey, he turned down a proposed loan move to Norwich on transfer deadline day, preferring to remain at Rovers in an effort to regain his first team place.
Middlesbrough (From trainee on 6/3/92) PL 2 Others 3
Bristol Rov (£10,000 on 18/10/94) FL 104 FLC 4 FAC 7 Others 8

COLLINS James Ian
Born: Liverpool, 28 May 1978
Height: 5'8" Weight: 10.0
A product of Crewe's youth side, and a second-year professional, James had been patiently finding his feet with the reserves prior to being given the opportunity to sit on the first team bench in 1997-98. From there, the young midfielder made his debut as a sub in a 3-3 Coca Cola Cup game at Bury, and came off the bench a week or so later in a league game, before being loaned out to non-league Northwich Victoria in December. Interestingly, the Bury game gave him the club record as the sub who has spent the longest time on the field – 106 minutes – having come on after just 14 minutes, and playing the next 76, plus extra time.
Crewe Alex (From trainee on 4/7/96) FL 0+1 FLC 0+1

COLLINS Lee

Born: Bellshill, 3 February 1974
Height: 5'8" Weight: 10.8

Lee was probably Swindon's most improved player in 1997-98, after being banned for seven games and told to clean up his act or his County Ground career would be over. Successfully channelling his aggression and energies into developing as a player when he returned to the side before Christmas, he was still as tough in the tackle, but less likely to dive in. Scored his first goal for the club to net an important away win at Port Vale in February, and was rewarded with a new two-year contract the following month. His season ended just a few matches early, when he was ordered to rest an injured shoulder.

Albion Rov (Signed from Pollock on 25/11/93) SL 43+2/1 SLC 2 SC 2 Others 2
Swindon T (£15,000 on 15/11/95) FL 27+8/1 FAC 3 Others 1

COLLINS Samuel (Sam) Jason

Born: Pontefract, 5 June 1977
Height: 6'2" Weight: 13.7

A promising Huddersfield centre back who made his debut in 1996-97, following some impressive performances in the reserves, Sam got off to a good start last season before suffering knee ligament damage, which kept him out of action for a while. Part way through the campaign, he turned down a loan move to Conference side, Halifax Town, determined to break into the first team, and finally grasped the chance, giving some very solid defensive displays, especially in the two fixtures against Tranmere Rovers and Reading, which launched his recent contributions. Is equally sound in the air and on the ground.

Huddersfield T (From trainee on 6/7/94) FL 12+2 FLC 2+1

COLLINS Simon

Born: Pontefract, 16 December 1973
Height: 5'11" Weight: 13.0

One of the unsung heroes of the 1997-98 campaign, Simon is a very versatile player who started his Plymouth career as a centre forward. However, last season saw him used as a right back and central defender, and he looked very much at home in the centre of defence, where he turned in some excellent displays. A wholehearted tackler, and a good distributor, he unfortunately missed a month of the campaign after damaging his leg in the Coca Cola Cup first round tie with Oxford United.

Huddersfield T (From trainee on 1/7/92) FL 31+21/3 FLC 6+3/2 FAC 1+4 Others 1+3
Plymouth Arg (£60,000 on 6/3/97) FL 41+3/3 FLC 1 Others 1

COLLINS Wayne Anthony

Born: Manchester, 4 March 1969
Height: 6'0" Weight: 12.0

A versatile player, Wayne weighed in with more than his fair share of goals for Sheffield Wednesday in 1997-98, before being surprisingly sold to Fulham in January. A hard-working midfielder, he suffered a little at the Cottage when being switched from central midfield to both wings in an endeavour to get the balance of the team right. He did, however, score a superb 20 yarder in the 2-1 win over Preston and should add many more in the coming season. Possesses lots of grit, no little skill, and is capable of playing in a number of different positions as his new club well knew before signing him.

Crewe Alex (£10,000 from Winsford U on 29/7/93) FL 102+15/14 FLC 5/1 FAC 8+1 Others 14+1/2
Sheffield Wed (£600,000 on 1/8/96) PL 16+15/6 FLC 2 FAC 1
Fulham (£400,000+ on 23/1/98) FL 10+3/1 Others 3

COLLYMORE Stanley (Stan) Victor

Born: Cannock, 22 January 1971
Height: 6'3" Weight: 14.10
International Honours: E: 3

On becoming Aston Villa's record signing, and thus fulfilling a childhood dream, after arriving from Liverpool during the 1997 summer recess, Stan would have been a regular feature in the Villa line-up in 1997-98 had it not been for injury and suspension. Missed a handful of games during October and November, due to an operation to ease a breathing problem, followed by a three-match suspension after being sent off at Bolton, before he began to be plagued by ankle and groin injuries in the latter part of the campaign. With pace and strength to succeed at the highest level, he has yet to realise his potential, especially in front of the demanding fans at Villa Park. His more memorable performances, however, came against Liverpool at home, and when he came off the bench to score a superb goal against Atletico Madrid. Although not being in the final England 22 for the World Cup Finals in France '98, he came on as a sub against Moldova and was an unused sub against Italy. Was the subject of much newspaper print in the summer, due to an unsavoury, well-documented version of events that took place in France, and it remains to be seen what effect it will have on his career.

Wolverhampton W (From trainee on 13/7/89)
Crystal Palace (£100,000 from Stafford R on 4/1/91) FL 4+16/1 FLC 2+3/1
Southend U (£100,000 on 20/11/92) FL 30/15 FAC 3/3
Nottingham F (£2,000,000 on 5/7/93) F/PL 64+1/41 FLC 9/2 FAC 2/1 Others 2/1
Liverpool (£8,500,000 on 3/7/95) PL 55+6/26 FLC 2+2 FAC 9/7 Others 5+2/2
Aston Villa (£7,000,000 on 16/5/97) PL 23+2/6 FLC 1 FAC 4/1 Others 6+1/1

Stan Collymore

65

CONLON Barry John
Born: Drogheda, 1 October 1978
Height: 6'3" Weight: 13.7
International Honours: Ei: U21-1
Released by Queens Park Rangers at the end of his YTS period during the summer of 1997, Barry signed up for Manchester City at the start of 1997-98 as a strong-running, left-footed forward with a deft touch and neat control. Given an early opportunity, he made his Football League debut when coming off the bench during a 6-0 drubbing of Swindon in September, and slotted in well as the replacement for Georgi Kinkladze, before making a full appearance at Maine Road against Port Vale. He then gained a Republic of Ireland U21 cap against Romania in October, before slipping out of the City squad and going on a long-term loan to Plymouth in February. Also proving to be good in the air, he saw out the season at Home Park, forming a good partnership with Carlo Corazzin, and scoring twice in 13 games.
Manchester C (Free from Queens Park R juniors on 14/8/97) FL 1+6
Plymouth Arg (Loaned on 26/2/98) FL 13/2

CONLON Paul Robert
Born: Sunderland, 5 January 1978
Height: 5'9" Weight: 11.7
Previously seen as a future prospect when at Hartlepool, this diminutive striker joined Doncaster during the summer of 1997, having been released by Sunderland without a game under his belt. Although he started in grand style by scoring on the opening day of last season, after coming on as a substitute, he never became a first team regular and was eventually released in January.
Hartlepool U (Trainee) FL 11+4/4
Sunderland (Free on 19/7/96)
Doncaster Rov (Free on 7/8/97) FL 4+10/1

Sean Connelly

CONNELLY Sean Patrick
Born: Sheffield, 26 June 1970
Height: 5'10" Weight: 11.10
Stockport's "Mr Consistency" continued to inspire transfer speculation in 1997-98 after a series of sterling displays at right back or as a right-wing back. A determined attacker, and resolute defender, as well as being the club's assistant physio, Sean was a major factor in Stockport's successful first-ever season in the first division.
Stockport Co (Free from Hallam on 12/8/91) FL 206+5/2 FLC 24/1 FAC 12+1 Others 15+1

CONNOLLY Karl Andrew
Born: Prescot, 9 February 1970
Height: 5'10" Weight: 11.2
Club Honours: WC '95
Whether Karl is more effective up front or on the left flank is often a talking point among the Wrexham fans. A Connolly firing on all cylinders is a joy to behold, but the most recent term was by no means his best ever, due to niggling injuries and loss of form. With his skilful and penetrating play he is the jewel of the side, but, unfortunately, his darting, mazy runs and ability to sniff out chances were missing from the disappointing run in to the play offs, having scored the opening goal in 1997-98. Among his better performances was a hat trick at Luton in the league and a brace at Wimbledon in the FA Cup.
Wrexham (Free from Napoli, in local Sunday League, on 8/5/91) FL 259+14/68 FLC 18/3 FAC 28/10 Others 26+1/5

CONNOR Paul
Born: Bishop Auckland, 12 January 1979
Height: 6'1" Weight: 11.5
Having been on loan at Gateshead at the start of 1997-98, the highly-rated young Middlesbrough forward joined Hartlepool in February, also on loan, to gain experience, and was thrown in at the deep end when making his debut against arch-rivals, Darlington. He showed some good touches, but in a one-month spell was unable to open his goalscoring account, being unlucky to be playing in a Hartlepool side which was going through a bad period. His time will come though.
Middlesbrough (From trainee on 4/7/96)
Hartlepool U (Loaned on 6/2/98) FL 4+1

CONROY Michael (Mick) Kevin
Born: Glasgow, 31 December 1965
Height: 6'0" Weight: 13.3
Club Honours: Div 4 '92
"Super Mick" as he had been christened by the Fulham fans as a result of the 21 league goals which had been a major factor in the club's promotion in 1996-97 was always under pressure in 1997-98 because of the close season signing of Paul Moody. It soon became obvious that they were too alike and would not hit it off as a partnership, but Mike only played four games under the Kevin Keegan/Ray Wilkins regime before receiving an injury which kept him out for several months. Made a few reserve team appearances before being transferred to Blackpool just prior to the deadline and,

despite his problems, still scored four goals in 14 games for Fulham, with his physical presence contributing to several others. Although failing to score for his new club in six appearances, 1998-99 should rectify that.
Clydebank (Free from Coventry C juniors on 15/5/84) SL 92+22/38 SLC 4+1 SC 5+2
St Mirren (Signed on 12/12/87) SL 9+1/1 SC 0+1
Reading (£50,000 on 28/9/88) FL 65+15/7 FLC 3+2 FAC 8+2/1 Others 2+2
Burnley (£35,000 on 16/7/91) FL 76+1/30 FLC 4/1 FAC 9+1/4 Others 7+1/4
Preston NE (£85,000 on 20/8/93) FL 50+7/22 FLC 2+1 FAC 7/2 Others 2+3
Fulham (£75,000 on 9/8/95) FL 88+6/32 FLC 11/6 FAC 5+1/3 Others 4/1
Blackpool (£50,000 on 26/3/98) FL 5+1

CONWAY Paul James
Born: Wandsworth, 17 April 1970
Height: 6'1" Weight: 12.10
Club Honours: Div 3 '95; AMC '97
International Honours: USA: U21
A talented central midfielder, who was snapped up by Northampton on a free transfer from Carlisle during the summer of 1997, he failed to hold a first team place before going on loan to Scarborough in December, where he rediscovered his goalscoring form. However, despite an offer from the Boro to join them he decided to try his luck in the States, and was released from his Cobbler's contract. Is the son of former Fulham and Republic of Ireland international, Jimmy.
Carlisle U (Signed on 29/10/93) FL 75+14/22 FLC 5+1 FAC 8+1/3 Others 14+3/4
Northampton T (Free on 2/6/97) FL 2+1 FLC 1
Scarborough (Loaned on 11/12/97) FL 13/2

COOK Aaron
Born: Caerphilly, 6 December 1979
Height: 6'1" Weight: 11.4
Still a trainee, Aaron started last season at Portsmouth hoping to earn himself a professional contract and to become a contender for the reserve team, but an injury crisis and number of suspensions meant the youngster made his full debut at home to Stockport County in February. Aaron played at left back with some confidence, and will be hoping to establish himself in the first team squad this coming term.
Portsmouth (Trainee) FL 1

COOK Andrew (Andy) Charles
Born: Romsey, 10 August 1969
Height: 5'9" Weight: 12.0
1997-98 was a disappointing season for Andy. Having started the campaign at Portsmouth, he made just one appearance, at Stockport, and unable to get himself into the plans of manager, Terry Fenwick, he was transferred to Millwall in January. Brought in to give much-needed balance on the left-hand side, and at home either in defence or midfield, after just two games, in which he showed a lot of promise, he was laid low by injury. Returned, however, to play a few reserve games, before appearing in the final fixture and having to be replaced in the 80th minute. Looks for better luck in 1998-99.
Southampton (From apprentice on 6/7/87) FL 11+5/1 FLC 4 FAC 1 Others 1

Exeter C (£50,000 on 13/9/91) FL 70/1 FLC 2 FAC 7/1 Others 6/1
Swansea C (£125,000 on 23/7/93) FL 54+8 FLC 2 FAC 3 Others 9+1/2
Portsmouth (£35,000 on 20/12/96) FL 7+2
Millwall (£50,000 on 8/1/98) FL 3

COOK James (Jamie) Steven
Born: Oxford, 2 August 1979
Height: 5'10" Weight: 12.0
Jamie, a first-year professional, made his Oxford debut early last season against Nottingham Forest, giving an accomplished display, and really benefited under new manager, Malcolm Shotton, who gave him a good number of starts. A winger who plays mainly on the left, and likes to run at players, he is well liked by the fans for his hard work and effort, and should develop into a useful player. Managed a couple of goals, his first coming at Maine Road, to clinch a win.
Oxford U (From trainee on 1/7/97) FL 9+11/2 FAC 0+1

Paul Cook

COOK Paul Anthony
Born: Liverpool, 22 February 1967
Height: 5'11" Weight: 11.0
Stockport broke their club transfer record to bring the left-sided midfielder to Edgeley Park from Tranmere last October, and the wily campaigner soon paid back a big chunk with spectacular goals against former club, Wolves, Swindon, and Manchester City. An ankle injury saw him miss six weeks of the season, and he later fractured his skull in a fall at home, only to make an unexpected comeback in the closing stages of the season.
Wigan Ath (Signed from Marine on 20/7/84) FL 77+6/14 FLC 4 FAC 6+1 Others 5+1/1
Norwich C (£73,000 on 23/5/88) FL 3+3 Others 1+1
Wolverhampton W (£250,000 on 1/11/89) FL 191+2/19 FLC 7/1 FAC 5+2 Others 6+1/1

Coventry C (£600,000 on 18/8/94) PL 35+2/3 FLC 3 FAC 3
Tranmere Rov (£250,000 on 29/2/96) FL 54+6/4 FLC 8 FAC 1
Stockport Co (£250,000 on 24/10/97) FL 25/3 FAC 1

COOKE Andrew (Andy) Roy
Born: Shrewsbury, 20 January 1974
Height: 6'0" Weight: 12.8
Suspended at the start of last season, Andy finally regained a regular place up front after the recall of loan man, Gerry Creaney, when hitting a rich vein of scoring form in Burnley's good run through January and February. A big crowd favourite for his non-stop running and effort, and a fine finisher, he is a constant target of other clubs. Scored a hat trick in the 7-2 home win over York in January.
Burnley (Signed from Newtown on 1/5/95) FL 55+33/33 FLC 3+2/2 FAC 3+3/1 Others 8+2/2

Andy Cooke

COOPER Colin Terence
Born: Sedgefield, 28 February 1967
Height: 5'10" Weight: 11.9
Club Honours: Div 1 '98
International Honours: E: 2; U21-8
Appointed Nottingham Forest's club captain when Stuart Pearce moved to Newcastle during the 1997 close season, he was unable to wear the armband immediately as he suffered a badly gashed shin in a summer friendly, and did not make the side until late September. However, when he did get back, he had to settle for a central midfield spot due to the form of Steve Chettle and Jon Olav Hjelde in the centre of the defence, before finally making the centre-back position his own again when the latter was injured. A good captain and leader, the club surprisingly accepted a £2.5 million offer for him from West Ham early in the campaign, but Colin refused to move and

how glad the fans were that he did, his performances being one of the main reasons that promotion to the Premiership was attained. Recognised by his fellow professionals when elected to the PFA award-winning first division team, he is good in the air at both ends of the park, and a tough tackler to boot.
Middlesbrough (From juniors on 17/7/84) FL 183+5/6 FLC 18 FAC 13 Others 19+1/2
Millwall (£300,000 on 25/7/91) FL 77/6 FLC 6 FAC 2 Others 2
Nottingham F (£1,700,000 on 21/6/93) F/PL 179+1/20 FLC 14/2 FAC 12/1 Others 7

Colin Cooper

COOPER Kevin Lee
Born: Derby, 8 February 1975
Height: 5'7" Weight: 10.7
An impressive pre-season trial game for Stockport earned the little winger a permanent move from Derby, after spending the last three months of 1996-97 season on loan at Edgeley Park. Usually the first player to be sacrificed when manager, Gary Megson, wanted a more defensive line-up, his darting runs and occasional stunning goals still made him a crowd favourite and a handy man to have in the squad.
Derby Co (From trainee on 2/7/93) FL 0+2 FLC 0+2 Others 0+1
Stockport Co (£150,000 on 24/3/97) FL 41+9/11 FLC 3+1/1 FAC 2 Others 1

COOPER Mark Nicholas
Born: Wakefield, 18 December 1968
Height: 5'9" Weight: 12.3
Club Honours: Div 4 '90
Surplus to Hartlepool's requirements in 1997-98, Mark was loaned to Macclesfield in September, immediately fitting into their midfield, where he created many opportunities for the strikers with long pin-point crosses, and scored two all-important goals. However, unable to agree personal terms he returned to the Pool before signing for Leyton Orient on Christmas Eve and making

his debut in the Auto Windscreen Shield game at Bournemouth. This was followed by a brief league appearance at Cardiff as a second-half substitute, prior to joining Rushden & Diamonds on a permanent contract in January.

Bristol C (From trainee on 10/9/87)
Exeter C (Free on 3/10/89) FL 46+4/12 FLC 4+1 FAC 3+1/1 Others 5
Southend U (Loaned on 22/3/90) FL 4+1
Birmingham C (Signed on 5/9/91) FL 30+9/4 FAC 2 Others 3/1
Fulham (£40,000 on 21/11/92) FL 10+4 FLC 2 Others 3
Huddersfield T (Loaned on 25/3/93) FL 10/4
Wycombe W (Free on 10/1/94) FL 0+2/1
Exeter C (Free on 11/2/94) FL 78+10/20 FLC 3 FAC 2 Others 4/1
Hartlepool U (Free on 26/7/96) FL 33/9 FLC 2 FAC 1 Others 1
Macclesfield T (Loaned on 26/9/97) FL 8/2
Leyton Orient (Free on 24/12/97) FL 0+1 Others 1

COOTE Adrian

Born: Great Yarmouth, 13 September 1978
Height: 6'1" Weight: 11.11
International Honours: NI: U21-2

Adrian made giant strides for Norwich in 1997-98, having finished the previous campaign as top scorer for the reserve and youth teams. Still decidedly raw, he came

Carlo Corazzin

off the bench at Carrow Road against Port Vale in September to make his Football League debut, before scoring his first senior goal seven days later, the winner at Manchester City, which, incidentally, was the first time City had won at Maine Road in 35 years. A competitive and pacy, direct forward who attacks the ball well in the air, he marked his Northern Ireland U21 debut with the winning goal. Can also perform on the wide left.

Norwich C (From trainee on 3/7/97) FL 11+12/2

CORAZZIN Giancarlo (Carlo) Michele

Born: Canada, 25 December 1971
Height: 5'10" Weight: 12.7
International Honours: Canada: 32

Carlo returned to his natural role as central striker at Plymouth in 1997-98 and performed admirably. Always willing to chase a lost cause and put defenders under pressure, his neat footwork and passing ability created numerous chances for himself and his colleagues, and he finished the season as top goalscorer with 17 league goals. Also earned a share of the Player of the Year award.*

Cambridge U (£20,000 from Vancouver 86ers on 10/12/93) FL 104+1/39 FLC 4/2 FAC 5 Others 3/2
Plymouth Arg (£150,000 on 28/3/96) FL 61+13/23 FLC 1+1 FAC 0+2/1 Others 2+1

CORBETT James (Jim) John

Born: Hackney, 6 July 1980
Height: 5'9" Weight: 10.12

The find of the 1997-98 season as far as Gillingham were concerned, Jim was selling matchday programmes at the club before coming in as a trainee. Quick over ten yards, and having the ability to take on players with superb dribbling techniques, he joined the full-professional ranks in January when other clubs started taking an interest, and scored the all-important second goal when the Gills won 2-0 at top-of-the-table, Bristol City. Can play equally well either in midfield or up front. *Stop Press:* In signing for Blackburn on 21 May, the Premiership club paid Gillingham an initial £525,000 which, appearance related, is expected to eventually reach £1 million.

Gillingham (From trainee on 13/1/98) FL 8+8/2 FLC 0+1 Others 0+1

CORDEN Simon Wayne

Born: Leek, 1 November 1975
Height: 5'9" Weight: 11.3

Appearing regularly on the Port Vale left wing in 1997-98 for the first time in his career, Wayne, who is predominately right footed, proved a headache for opposing right backs, and if he shows a bit more confidence he certainly has the ability to make a name for himself. Scored the first senior goal of his career, against Arsenal in the FA Cup, and followed that up with a 30 yarder at Sheffield United.

Port Vale (From trainee on 20/9/94) FL 26+22/1 FLC 3 FAC 2/1

CORICA Stephen (Steve) Christopher

Born: Cairns, Australia, 24 March 1973
Height: 5'8" Weight: 10.10
International Honours: Australia: 14

A right-sided Wolves' midfield player, Steve had suffered a cruciate knee ligament injury in April 1997 and had played little football prior to returning as an 88th-minute sub at Stockport last October. Two days later, while turning out for the reserves, sadly the same joint went again, thus ruling him out for the rest of 1997-98.

Leicester C (£325,000 from Marconi on 11/8/95) FL 16/2 FAC 2
Wolverhampton W (£700,000 on 16/2/96) FL 50+4/2 FLC 2 FAC 1

CORNFORTH John Michael

Born: Whitley Bay, 7 October 1967
Height: 6'1" Weight: 12.11
Club Honours: Div 3 '88; AMC '94
International Honours: W: 2

1997-98 was a very mixed season for this two-footed Wycombe midfield playmaker. A first choice from the start, his long-range shooting quickly earned him three goals, but he was dropped in October when a further transfer payment was due to Birmingham after one more game. A proposed move to Swansea then broke down before the manager brought him back for the FA Cup game against Basingstoke, and he scored two with a penalty and a free kick from 20 yards. An excellent passer of the ball, and always dangerous on the edge of the box, he

joined Peterborough on loan in February but returned after four games and was involved in the final weeks of the campaign.
Sunderland (From apprentice on 11/10/85) FL 21+11/2 FLC 0+1 Others 1+3
Doncaster Rov (Loaned on 6/11/86) FL 6+1/3 Others 2
Shrewsbury T (Loaned on 23/11/89) FL 3 Others 2
Lincoln C (Loaned on 11/1/90) FL 9/1
Swansea C (£50,000 on 2/8/91) FL 147+2/16 FLC 14 FAC 11/1 Others 19/1
Birmingham C (£350,000 on 26/3/96) FL 8
Wycombe W (£50,000 on 5/12/96) FL 26+8/5 FLC 2 FAC 2/2 Others 0+1
Peterborough U (Loaned on 13/2/98) FL 3+1

CORT Carl Edward Richard
Born: Southwark, 1 November 1977
Height: 6'4" Weight: 12.7
A Wimbledon product through and through, Carl is a young striker who is very quick, very keen, and will be very dangerous once he has tempered experience to his raw aggression. Made his first appearance of last season up at Newcastle and scored the first goal in a 3-1 win with an unstoppable header, and went on to collect five more, all of them coming in the space of his opening 11 games. Looking confident and skilful, the youngster continued to give defenders all kinds of problems, but needs a longer run of games to build on. Holds the ball up well for one so young, and is definitely one for the future.
Wimbledon (From trainee on 7/6/96) PL 16+7/4 FLC 1+1/2 FAC 4+1
Lincoln C (Loaned on 3/2/97) FL 5+1/1

COTTEE Anthony (Tony) Richard
Born: West Ham, 11 July 1965
Height: 5'8" Weight: 11.5
International Honours: E: 7; U21-8; Yth
Having been rescued from a nightmare spell with Selangor in Malaysia by Leicester's Martin O'Neill in August 1997, the pint-sized livewire striker spent much of last season on the bench, from where he was finally able to fulfil one ambition, by playing in a European competition at last. Scored his first goal for the club in the FA Cup tie against Northampton, then made the headlines with the winner at Old Trafford later that month. He followed that up with a brief run in the starting line-up as cover for the injured Ian Marshall, and coming off the bench to a rousing reception in the final game of the campaign at West Ham, and scoring a brace on his old stamping ground. Earlier in 1997-98, a spell on loan at Birmingham saw him score the one goal in five appearances.
West Ham U (From apprentice on 1/9/82) FL 203+9/92 FLC 19/14 FAC 24/11 Others 1/1
Everton (£2,300,000 on 2/8/88) F/PL 161+23/72 FLC 19+4/11 FAC 15+6/4 Others 11+2/12
West Ham U (Signed on 7/9/94) PL 63+4/23 FLC 8/4 FAC 5/1 (Signed by Selangor on 3/3/97)
Leicester C (£500,000 on 14/8/97) PL 7+12/4 FLC 1 FAC 0+2/1 Others 0+1
Birmingham C (Loaned on 14/11/97) FL 4+1/1

COULBAULT Regis (Reggie) Arnaud Vincent
Born: Brignoles, France, 12 August 1972
Height: 5'9" Weight: 11.3
Signed from the French club, Toulon, last October, Reggie soon became a favourite of

Carl Cort

the Southend United fans with his battling midfield qualities suiting the needs of a club who struggled all season. In only his third full game, he showed that he also possessed a good shot, scoring a screamer at home to Oldham, and his presence in the team helped to soften the blow of Mike Marsh's retirement, before he left during the summer.
Southend U (Free from Toulon on 10/10/97) FL 30+4/4 FAC 2 Others 1

COUSINS Jason Michael
Born: Hayes, 14 October 1970
Height: 5'11" Weight: 12.4
Club Honours: GMVC '93; FAT '93
After a cartilage operation in the summer of 1997, this right-sided Wycombe defender re-established himself as a right-wing back last September. He was dropped in December when the on-loan David Kerslake was preferred, asking to be put on the transfer list, but he came back a regular, however, in the final two months of the season, where he was excellent in central defence, especially in the air. His total commitment and fierce tackling continued to endear him to the fans.
Brentford (From trainee on 13/7/89) FL 20+1 Others 2+2
Wycombe W (Free on 1/7/91) FL 167+7/3 FLC 12/1 FAC 19 Others 14

COUZENS Andrew (Andy)
Born: Shipley, 4 June 1975
Height: 5'10" Weight: 11.11
Club Honours: FAYC '93
International Honours: E: U21-3
Great things were expected of this former England U21 player who joined Carlisle from Leeds during the 1997 close season. However, despite 18 league starts, plus nine more as a substitute, he struggled to make a

major impact at the club in 1997-98. Capable of performing in either defence or midfield, his lack of a settled role may have made life more difficult, but he will be hoping to put the last year behind him as the new campaign in division three begins.
Leeds U (From trainee on 5/3/93) PL 17+11/1 FLC 4+1/1 Others 0+2
Carlisle U (£100,000 on 21/7/97) FL 18+9/2 FLC 3/1 Others 0+3

COWANS Gordon Sidney
Born: Cornforth, 27 October 1958
Height: 5'7" Weight: 10.6
Club Honours: FLC '77; Div 1 '81; EC '82; ESC '82
International Honours: E: 10; B-2; U21-5; Yth
Released by Stockport during the 1997 close season, and then employed by Burnley, primarily as reserve team coach, the veteran former England man had a brief spell of first team action, including an outstanding display against Walsall, which showed he had lost none of his old class and guile. At his best, Gordon was a classy midfielder with great vision and passing ability.
Aston Villa (From apprentice on 1/9/76) FL 276+10/42 FLC 23+4/5 FAC 19+1/3 Others 23+1/2 (£500,000 to Bari on 1/7/85)
Aston Villa (£250,000 on 13/7/88) FL 114+3/7 FLC 15 FAC 9 Others 11+1
Blackburn Rov (£200,000 on 28/11/91) F/PL 49+1/2 FLC 4 FAC 5/1 Others 3
Aston Villa (Free on 5/7/93) PL 9+2 FLC 2 Others 4
Derby Co (£80,000 on 3/2/94) FL 36 FLC 3 Others 5+1/1
Wolverhampton W (£20,000 on 19/12/94) FL 31+6 FLC 2 FAC 5/1 Others 2
Sheffield U (Free on 29/12/95) FL 18+2 FAC 3
Bradford C (Free on 17/7/96) FL 23+1 FLC 2
Stockport Co (Free on 24/3/97) FL 6+1 Others 0+1
Burnley (Free on 1/8/97) FL 5+1 FLC 1 FAC 2

COWE Steven (Steve) Mark
Born: Gloucester, 29 September 1974
Height: 5'7" Weight: 10.10
The pint-sized Swindon striker often found himself at the back of the queue for places up front in 1997-98, and was most commonly used as a substitute, his longest run of consecutive starts being just three in February and March. Managed just two goals – the first, a superb solo effort that netted all three points in the home fixture against Bradford, merely highlighted his undoubted quality and skill, but his lack of physical presence seems to be restricting his chances at present.
Aston Villa (From trainee on 7/7/93)
Swindon T (£100,000 on 22/3/96) FL 40+26/9 FLC 3+2 FAC 1

COX Ian Gary
Born: Croydon, 25 March 1971
Height: 6'0" Weight: 12.2
As first team captain and a crucial member of Bournemouth's back four during 1997-98, as an ever present, Ian again produced some outstanding performances at centre back, in his second season playing in that position, following his conversion from an attacking midfielder. Is strong in the air, has excellent control, and is comfortable carrying the ball forward.
Crystal Palace (£35,000 from Carshalton on 8/3/94) F/PL 2+13 FAC 1+2/1
Bournemouth (Free on 28/3/96) FL 98/11 FLC 4 FAC 4 Others 7

COX Neil James
Born: Scunthorpe, 8 October 1971
Height: 6'0" Weight: 13.7
Club Honours: FLC '94; Div 1 '95
International Honours: E: U21-6
A bargain signing from Middlesbrough in May of 1997, Neil played only two games for Bolton before sustaining a leg injury which kept him out for four months, prior to his return as a substitute against Barnsley on Boxing Day. He then produced some excellent performances at right back in the wing-back formation favoured by Colin Todd in the latter stages of the season, a formation which also brought out the best in Jimmy Phillips in the left-back position. Now on song, his rich vein of form coincided with a change of fortune for the Trotters, and he scored his first goal in the marvellous away victory at his old club, Aston Villa, at the end of April.
Scunthorpe U (From trainee on 20/3/90) FL 17/1 FAC 4 Others 4+1
Aston Villa (£400,000 on 12/2/91) F/PL 26+16/3 FLC 5+2 FAC 4+2/1 Others 2
Middlesbrough (£1,000,000 on 19/7/94) P/FL 103+3/3 FLC 14+1 FAC 5/1 Others 2
Bolton W (£1,200,000 on 27/5/97) PL 20+1/1 FAC 0+1

COYNE Daniel (Danny)
Born: Prestatyn, 27 August 1973
Height: 5'11" Weight: 13.0
International Honours: W: 1; U21-9; Yth; Sch
Danny began 1997-98 for Tranmere as first choice between the posts, ahead of Eric Nixon, but was plagued by a number of different and persistent injuries, and his

appearance against Port Vale at Prenton Park in November turned out to be his swansong for the campaign. The highlight of a season, which he will surely prefer to forget, was a brilliant penalty save against Huddersfield that secured a precious Rovers' victory. Off the field, he continued to be a fine ambassador for the club and will start 1998-99 determined to regain his place.
Tranmere Rov (From trainee on 8/5/92) FL 93+1 FLC 13 FAC 1 Others 2

CRADDOCK Jody Darryl
Born: Bromsgrove, 25 July 1975
Height: 6'1" Weight: 12.4
Jody joined Sunderland during the 1997 summer recess from Cambridge United, initially as cover for the team's central defensive positions. However, following Andy Melville's injury at Reading in November, he took his chance and forged a tremendous partnership with Darren Williams at the heart of Sunderland's defence, which helped to launch the club on the promotion trail and only came to a halt at the final stage of the play offs. The 22-year old is strong in the air, tackles well, is an excellent reader of the game, and looks to be one of the club's all-time bargain buys.
Cambridge U (Free from Christchurch on 13/8/93) FL 142+3/4 FLC 3/1 FAC 6 Others 5
Sunderland (£300,000+ on 4/8/97) FL 31+1 FLC 3 FAC 2 Others 3

CRAMB Colin
Born: Lanark, 23 June 1974
Height: 6'0" Weight: 13.0
Club Honours: B&Q '93
A 1997 close season signing from Doncaster Rovers, Colin's wholehearted attitude soon made him popular with the Bristol City fans. Whilst his shooting was often instinctive, he obtained many crucial strikes, none more so than at Wycombe, when a spectacular 30-yard goal in the first half and a matchwinner after the break that owed everything to his never-give-up approach, summed up his immense value to City's promotion winning side.
Hamilton Academical (From juniors on 1/6/93) SL 29+19/10 SC 0+1 Others 1+3
Southampton (£75,000 on 8/6/93) PL 0+1
Falkirk (Signed on 30/8/94) SL 6+2/1 SLC 0+1
Heart of Midlothian (Signed on 1/3/95) SL 3+3/1
Doncaster Rov (£25,000 on 15/12/95) FL 60+2/25 FLC 2/1 FAC 1/1 Others 1/1
Bristol C (£250,000 on 10/7/97) FL 34+6/9 FLC 2 FAC 1/1 Others 1+1

CRAVEN Dean
Born: Shrewsbury, 17 February 1979
Height: 5'7" Weight: 10.10
Dean started last season as a first-year professional with West Bromwich, but, unable to get close to a first team opportunity, was allowed to move to neighbouring Shrewsbury Town on transfer deadline day on a month-to-month contract. A right-sided midfielder, who looked quite pacy, he made his Football League debut on the final day of the season, a 2-0 defeat at home to Scunthorpe not being the most auspicious of occasions for a youngster playing in his first game.
West Bromwich A (From trainee on 1/7/97)
Shrewsbury T (Free on 26/3/98) FL 1

CRAWFORD James (Jimmy)
Born: Chicago, USA, 1 May 1973
Height: 5'11" Weight: 11.6
Club Honours: S Div 1 '93; SLC '94
International Honours: Ei: U21-2
Having failed to get on the Newcastle team sheet in 1997-98, Jimmy was signed by the new manager, Tommy Burns, on transfer deadline day, last March, along with Paul Brayson, and made his debut as substitute at Ipswich two days later. He hardly had time to settle into the team, wearing five different shirts in his six appearances, but showed potential both as an orthodox midfield player, or as a more advanced wing back, his best performance coming in the Royals' final win of the season, a 2-0 home victory against Stoke City. Will be one of the players that the club will be looking at to bring them a swift return to the first division.
Newcastle U (£75,000 from Bohemians on 23/3/95) PL 0+2 FLC 0+1
Rotherham U (Loaned on 27/9/96) FL 11
Dundee U (Loaned on 20/2/98) SL 0+1
Reading (£50,000 on 26/3/98) FL 5+1

CREANEY Gerard (Gerry) Thomas
Born: Coatbridge, 13 April 1970
Height: 5'11" Weight: 13.6
International Honours: S: B-1; U21-11
Not in contention for first team football at Manchester City for the beginning of 1997-98, Gerry turned out for the Central League side a few times before going on loan to Burnley for a two-month spell, playing nine games and scoring eight goals. During that period, the classy Scottish striker almost single-handedly cured the Clarets' inability to hit the net in the early part of the season, but they were unable to afford him on a permanent basis and he returned to Maine Road. Recalled by Frank Clark, due to a spate of injuries, he was subbed at half time at Sheffield United and later went on loan to Chesterfield, where he failed to get on the scoresheet in four games. Released during the summer, he could be a good acquisition for the right club.
Glasgow Celtic (From juniors on 15/5/87) SL 85+28/36 SLC 9+1/7 SC 9/8 Others 6+3/3
Portsmouth (£500,000 on 25/1/94) FL 60/32 FLC 7/3 FAC 2/1
Manchester C (£2,000,000 on 8/9/95) P/FL 8+13/4 FAC 0+4/1
Oldham Ath (Loaned on 28/3/96) FL 8+1/2
Ipswich T (Loaned on 25/10/96) FL 6/1
Burnley (Loaned on 19/9/97) FL 9+1/8 FLC 1
Chesterfield (Loaned on 2/1/98) 3+1

CRESSWELL Richard Paul Wesley
Born: Bridlington, 20 September 1977
Height: 6'0" Weight: 11.8
In the second half of the 1997-98 season, Richard established himself in York's attack and began to fulfil the promise he had shown a couple of years ago. He netted crucial goals in the closing weeks of the campaign, including the winner in vital away victories at Bristol Rovers and Wrexham, and also an equaliser at home to Blackpool.
York C (From trainee on 15/11/95) FL 36+23/5 FLC 1+3 FAC 1+2 Others 3
Mansfield T (Loaned on 27/3/97) FL 5/1

CRICHTON Paul Andrew
Born: Pontefract, 3 October 1968
Height: 6'1" Weight: 12.2

After taking over in West Bromwich's goal from Nigel Spinks in 1996-97 and doing quite well before losing his place to Alan Miller, with Mark Bosnich unavailable at the start of 1997-98 Paul went on loan to Aston Villa as cover for Michael Oakes, returning to the Hawthorns having only sat on the bench. A good shot-stopper, with anticipation and reflexes to match, he came back into the Albion side right at the end of the campaign and excelled in a 4-2 win at Sheffield United.

Nottingham F (From juniors on 23/5/86)
Notts Co (Loaned on 19/9/86) FL 5
Darlington (Loaned on 30/1/87) FL 5
Peterborough U (Loaned on 27/3/87) FL 4
Darlington (Loaned on 28/9/87) FL 3 FLC 1 Others 1
Swindon T (Loaned on 24/12/87) FL 4
Rotherham U (Loaned on 9/3/88) FL 6
Torquay U (Loaned on 25/8/88) FL 13 FLC 2
Peterborough U (Signed on 3/11/88) FL 47 FAC 5 Others 3
Doncaster Rov (Free on 25/8/90) FL 77 FLC 5 FAC 3 Others 5
Grimsby T (Free on 9/7/93) FL 133 FLC 7 FAC 8 Others 2
West Bromwich A (£250,000 on 9/9/96) FL 32 FAC 1

CRITTENDEN Nicholas (Nick) John
Born: Ascot, 11 November 1978
Height: 5'8" Weight: 10.7

A very promising young Chelsea midfield player who made his first team debut in the fourth round Coca Cola Cup tie at home to Southampton last November. In driving rain he gave an assured performance alongside his player/manager, Ruud Gullit, who described him as "the best player on the pitch". Nick made two further appearances as substitute – both in the Premiership – before the season's end and is clearly one for the future.

Chelsea (From trainee on 9/7/97) PL 0+2 FLC 1

CROCI Laurent
Born: Montbeliard, France, 8 December 1964
Height: 5'11" Weight: 12.6

A veteran of over 400 games in the French League, the ex-Bordeaux midfielder made one appearance for Carlisle as a non-contract player in the live televised game against Preston last October, having arrived at Brunton Park just two days earlier. He showed some nice touches, but no permanent deal ensued and he returned to France. (Il a disparu et il est retourné tout de suite en France!)

Carlisle U (Free from Bordeaux on 15/10/97) FL 1

CROFT Gary
Born: Burton on Trent, 17 February 1974
Height: 5'9" Weight: 11.8
International Honours: E: U21-4

After marking time since his arrival from Grimsby, Gary was given the opportunity to replace Graeme le Saux in 1997-98 and initially was promising. An enthusiastic raider, his assets were his ability to cover large areas of the left-hand side of the field.

A superbly struck winning goal against Chelsea was the height of his season, but he never really recovered from gifting Derby a goal and his place in the side was often assigned to the left winger, Jason Wilcox. Unfortunately, a back injury frequently impeded his progress and having fallen behind both Wilcox and Callum Davidson, he will be hoping to be fully fit and in contention for a place come 1998-99.

Grimsby T (From trainee on 7/7/92) FL 139+10/3 FLC 7 FAC 8+2/1 Others 3
Blackburn Rov (£1,700,000 on 29/3/96) PL 23+5/1 FLC 5 FAC 2

CROOKS Lee Robert
Born: Wakefield, 14 January 1978
Height: 5'11" Weight: 12.1
International Honours: E: Yth

Still on the fringe of first team duty at Manchester City in 1997-98, his starts were curtailed by a foot injury that caused problems well into the season. However, he eventually came back in January to play three league games on the trot before coming off the bench on a couple of occasions and playing out the remainder of the campaign in the Central League. Selected for the Football League U21 side that played its Italian counterparts at Charlton, Lee is a wide midfielder who can play further back if required, his strength taking him into good crossing positions.

Manchester C (From trainee on 14/1/95) FL 11+9 FLC 0+1 FAC 2

CROSBY Andrew (Andy) Keith
Born: Rotherham, 3 March 1973
Height: 6'2" Weight: 13.7

After five years at Darlington in the heart of defence, and as captain for the majority of that time, Andy exercised his right over freedom of contract at the end of last season to move on. Strong and commanding in the air, and firm in the tackle, he has been a tremendous servant of the club and led them out at Wembley for the 1996 play-off final.

Doncaster Rov (Free from Leeds U juniors on 4/7/91) FL 41+10 FLC 1+1 FAC 2 Others 4+1/1
Darlington (Free on 10/12/93) FL 179+2/3 FLC 10 FAC 11/1 Others 9

CROSS Jonathan (Jon) Neil
Born: Wallasey, 2 March 1975
Height: 5'10" Weight: 11.7

As in 1996-97, Jon failed to impose himself at Wrexham in 1997-98 and made just two appearances at left back early on in the campaign before returning from a transfer deadline day loan spell at Tranmere without making an appearance, and being released during the summer. Still felt to be a talented player who can play all over the pitch - at the back, in midfield, or up front - he probably needs a run of games in a set position to bring the best out of him and, to that end, he will be looking for a side prior to 1998-99 getting underway. At his best, he is fast, strong on the ball, and carries a powerful shot.

Wrexham (From trainee on 15/11/92) FL 92+27/12 FLC 4+3/1 FAC 4+1/1 Others 9+6/1
Hereford U (Loaned on 2/12/96) FL 5/1 Others 1

CROSSLEY Mark Geoffrey
Born: Barnsley, 16 June 1969
Height: 6'0" Weight: 16.0
International Honours: E: U21-3. W: 1; B-1

Injured at the start of 1997-98, the big goalkeeper subsequently lost his place at Nottingham Forest to Dave Beasant, who was brought in from Southampton as emergency cover, as both Alan Fettis and Marco Pascalo were also sidelined. Having had no further opportunities at the City Ground, he was loaned to Millwall in February as both of their main 'keepers, Tim Carter and Nigel Spink, were out injured, and his experience was invaluable to a defence that had just conceded three goals. Apart from showing himself to be a great shot-stopper, he also dominated the area to a great extent and, at the same time, set up attacking moves with excellent distribution from both hands and feet. Returned to Forest after 13 games, but continued to wait in the wings, despite being called up to represent the Welsh "B" side against Scotland in March.

Nottingham F (From trainee on 2/7/87) F/PL 270+1 FLC 34 FAC 32 Others 18
Millwall (Loaned on 20/2/98) FL 13

CROWE Dean Anthony
Born: Stockport, 6 June 1979
Height: 5'5" Weight: 11.3

His reserve team performances had ear-marked Dean for an early breakthrough into the first team squad at Stoke in 1996-97 and so it proved. Indeed, whilst injuries to key players presented him with his chance, he took it with open arms and kept that spot on merit. Sharp in and around the box, blessed with an eye for the target, not afraid to shoot, with good mobility, and very competitive, he was City's main catch of the season from their youth ranks and was duly rewarded with a new contract in February.

Stoke C (From trainee on 5/9/96) FL 10+6/4 FLC 1+1

Dean Crowe

CROWE Glen Michael
Born: Dublin, 25 December 1977
Height: 5'10" Weight: 13.1
International Honours: Ei: U21-2; Yth

The left-footed striker was determined to make his mark at Molineux in 1997-98, doing well in pre-season but having to wait until the second half of the seventh match for a chance. To gain further experience he went out on loan to Cardiff and scored on his October debut, before re-appearing in March for another Wolves' first team run out, again as sub. Continued to add to his Republic of Ireland U21 caps with an appearance against the Czech Republic in March.
Wolverhampton W (From trainee on 3/7/96) FL 6+4/1
Exeter C (Loaned on 21/2/97) FL 10/5
Cardiff C (Loaned on 24/10/97) FL 7+1/1 Others 1

CROWE Jason William
Born: Sidcup, 30 September 1978
Height: 5'9" Weight: 10.9
International Honours: E: Yth

A young second-year Arsenal professional who has come up through the club's junior ranks, Jason made his first team debut last season when coming off the bench at Highbury in the 90th minute of the third round Coca Cola Cup game against Birmingham, which ultimately ended in a 4-1 win for the Gunners. In doing so, he created something of a record when being dismissed before the final whistle. Possibly seen as the long-term replacement for Nigel Winterburn, he is a strong, resolute tackler, who has plenty of pace and looks as if he could make a wing back. Also appeared in the fifth round FA Cup replay at Crystal Palace, when coming on for the last eight minutes.
Arsenal (From trainee on 13/5/96) FLC 0+1 FAC 0+1

CRUYFF Jordi
Born: Holland, 9 February 1974
Height: 6'0" Weight: 11.0
Club Honours: PL '97; CS '96, '97
International Honours: Holland: 9

A versatile front-line player, with excellent skills and a terrific shot in either foot, Jordi had a frustrating start to last season when he sustained ankle ligament damage against Leicester in Manchester United's third Premiership game of the campaign. Having then played against Ipswich in the Coca Cola Cup in October, he suffered a hairline fracture of his right leg against Derby at Pride Park in the Reds' next Premiership game. However, despite his injury woes, he was determined to show Alex Ferguson that he had the right credentials to make a success of his career at Old Trafford, something which he said was of greater importance than playing for Holland in the World Cup Finals during the summer.
Manchester U (£1,400,000 from Barcelona on 12/8/96) PL 14+7/3 FLC 2 FAC 0+1 Others 3+2

CUERVO Philippe
Born: Calais, France, 13 August 1969
Height: 5'11" Weight: 12.6

The skilful Frenchman became an instant crowd favourite from the moment he arrived at Swindon on a brief trial during the summer of 1997. He also won over manager, Steve McMahon, and was given a three-year contract after being released by St Etienne. Began 1997-98 in great form and was instrumental in the club's flying start to the campaign, playing in a number of positions, including right-wing back, and as a conventional right-sided midfielder, although seemingly more effective when deployed just behind the two strikers. Unfortunately out of action from late September to January with a mysterious hip injury, which was eventually cured by a specialist in France, Philippe, whose English is improving all the time, looks awkward with his long, rangy stride, but is deceptively skilful.
Swindon T (Free from St Etienne on 8/8/97) FL 14+9 FLC 2

CULLEN David **Jonathan (Jon)**
Born: Durham, 10 January 1973
Height: 6'0" Weight: 12.0

As a big central defender who looked impressive in Hartlepool's pre-season games, Jon was determined to do well and in the early weeks of 1997-98 emerged as a useful forward, his strong running causing problems for opposing defences. In scoring several memorable goals, probably the best being a great 45-yard chip at Swansea, it was inevitable that he would attract the attention of the bigger boys and, in January, he was transferred to Sheffield United, a club who had watched him carefully over a couple of months. Signed as one for the future, despite being 25, he made just two appearances from the bench for United, while continuing his football education in the reserves. Interestingly, he remained Hartlepool's top scorer with 12 to his name and was selected by his fellow professionals for the PFA award-winning third division team.
Doncaster Rov (From trainee on 16/9/91) FL 8+1 FLC 2+1/1 FAC 0+1 Others 1 (Free to Spennymoor in September 1993)
Hartlepool U (Free from Morpeth on 27/3/97) FL 33+1/12 FLC 2 FAC 1 Others 2
Sheffield U (£250,000 on 26/1/98) FL 0+2

CULLIP Daniel (Danny)
Born: Bracknell, 17 September 1976
Height: 6'1" Weight: 12.7

Despite starting the first 14 games for Fulham last season, the strong, aggressive centre back obviously did not figure in Kevin Keagan's long-term plans, and was transferred to Brentford in February. It was the second time Micky Adams had signed Danny, and he helped stop the Bees' defence leaking so many goals when teaming up with the experienced Graeme Hogg and Jamie Bates in a three-man central defence. Is clearly a player with a bright future.

Oxford U (From trainee on 6/7/95)
Fulham (Free on 5/7/96) FL 41+9/2 FLC 8 FAC 2 Others 1
Brentford (£75,000 on 17/2/98) FL 13

Danny Cullip

CULVERHOUSE Ian Brett
Born: Bishops Stortford, 22 September 1964
Height: 5'10" Weight: 11.2
Club Honours: Div 2 '86, '96
International Honours: E: Yth

Ian, a classy defender who has often been employed as a sweeper in Swindon's five-man defence, missed the start of last season with a long-term ankle injury, his first appearance coming in mid-October. A good all-rounder who reads the game well and intercepts well, he kept his place until he was one of several players axed in the wake of a heavy defeat at Stockport. Was transfer listed in March, and became a free agent under the Bosman ruling in the summer.
Tottenham H (From apprentice on 24/9/82) FL 1+1
Norwich C (£50,000 on 8/10/85) F/PL 295+1/1 FLC 23 FAC 28 Others 22/1
Swindon T (£250,000 on 9/12/94) FL 95+2 FLC 9 FAC 10 Others 1

CUNDY Jason Victor
Born: Wimbledon, 12 November 1969
Height: 6'1" Weight: 13.13
International Honours: E: U21-3

With the troubles of the previous season behind him, Jason had an outstanding 1997-98 at the heart of the Ipswich defence, particularly away from home. As one of the few players to maintain their form during the difficult first half when, because of injuries, he never had a chance to establish a partnership in central defence, he was unfortunate to concede some own goals in

this period, the most galling being the one which turned out to be the winning goal in the local derby at Norwich, when Tony Mowbray's clearance rebounded off him into the net. Very quick, he was also on hand to make several last-ditch tackles which prevented the opposition from scoring. In the home game with Port Vale, for instance, he flung himself across goal to block a goal-bound shot at a time when Ipswich were leading 1-0, a game they went on to win 5-1. Scored three times during the regular term, all of them headers, including a last-minute winner at WBA, and captained the side at the climax of the campaign in the absence of Mowbray and Geraint Williams.

Chelsea (From trainee on 1/8/88) FL 40+1/1 FLC 6 FAC 6 Others 4
Tottenham H (£750,000 on 26/3/92) F/PL 23+3/1 FLC 2
Crystal Palace (Loaned on 14/12/95) FL 4
Bristol C (Loaned on 23/8/96) FL 6/1
Ipswich T (£200,000 on 29/10/96) FL 53+1/5 FLC 8 FAC 4 Others 2

CUNNINGHAM Daniel **Harvey**
Born: Manchester, 11 September 1968
Height: 5'9" Weight: 11.0
Doncaster's Harvey missed a large portion of last season through a series of disciplinary indiscretions, all of which concealed the fact that, as a one-touch player, he was a particularly useful passer of the ball, and a fine asset to the side when on top form. His reputation as a midfield "hardman" also masked other talents.

Doncaster Rov (Free from Droylesden on 14/2/97) FL 43+1/1 FLC 1+1 Others 1

CUNNINGHAM Kenneth (Kenny) **Edward**
Born: Dublin, 28 June 1971
Height: 6'0" Weight: 11.8
International Honours: Ei: 16; B-2; U21-4; Yth
A versatile Wimbledon defender who linked up with his old Millwall boss, Mick McCarthy, in the Republic of Ireland squad in 1997-98, Kenny can play effectively as a full back, centre back, or wing back, with a talent to go forward to supply pin-point crosses to the strike force. Missed very few games during the campaign, and again proved a reliable man to have in the side, being a key member of a defensive network that works hard as a unit and always watches out for one another. Is comfortable on the ball.

Millwall (Signed from Tolka Rov on 18/9/89) FL 132+4/1 FLC 10 FAC 1 Others 5+1/1
Wimbledon (Signed on 9/11/94) PL 128+1 FLC 12 FAC 22

CUNNINGTON Shaun **Gary**
Born: Bourne, 4 January 1966
Height: 5'10" Weight: 11.12
Club Honours: WC '86
A tough-tackling, ball-winning midfielder with a wealth of experience, a number of injury problems frustrated Shaun after his move to Notts County in March 1997 and he

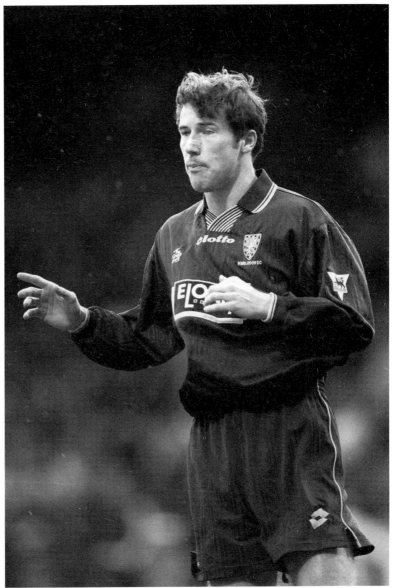

Kenny Cunningham

was released at the end of his contract during the summer. At his best in a wide-right position, where he can weigh in with his share of goals, he was unfortunate not to have played enough games in 1997-98 to warrant a third division championship medal, as County romped to the title.

Wrexham (From juniors on 11/1/84) FL 196+3/12 FLC 13 FAC 9/1 Others 21/2
Grimsby T (£55,000 on 19/2/88) FL 182/13 FLC 11 FAC 11/3 Others 9
Sunderland (£650,000 on 17/7/92) FL 52+6/8 FLC 3 FAC 2/1 Others 2
West Bromwich A (£220,000 on 11/8/95) FL 8+5 FLC 1+2 Others 2
Notts Co (£25,000 on 14/3/97) FL 9+8 FLC 1+2 Others 1

CURCIC Sasa
Born: Belgrade, Yugoslavia, 14 February 1972
Height: 5'9" Weight: 11.2
International Honours: Yugoslavia: 13
Although becoming Aston Villa's record signing when arriving from Bolton at the beginning of 1996-97, Sasa eventually fell out of favour with Brian Little, something which led to him submitting a transfer request in February 1997. Still unable to hold down a regular place at Villa Park in 1997-98, and with fears that a work permit might be a problem, the Yugoslav midfielder got married, got his work permit authorised, and joined Crystal Palace on transfer

deadline day. He soon found his feet at Selhurst Park, playing in the final eight games of the season and performing well, despite relegation reality An attacking player with great vision, passing skills, and the liking for long-range shooting, he had an excellent game against Derby, almost running the show single-handedly, scoring, and making two goals in a 3-1 win, the club's first home success of the campaign, and endearing himself to the fans. With Terry Venables at the helm in 1998-99, Sasa should well be able to express himself more fully.

Bolton W (£1,500,000 from Partizan Belgrade on 28/10/95) PL 28/4 FLC 3/1 FAC 2/2
Aston Villa (£4,000,000 on 23/8/96) PL 20+9 FLC 1+1 FAC 2/1 Others 0+1
Crystal Palace (£1,000,000 on 26/3/98) PL 6+2/1

CURETON Jamie
Born: Bristol, 28 August 1975
Height: 5'8" Weight: 10.7
International Honours: E: Yth

The locally-born Jamie, playing in a wide role on Bristol Rovers' right wing, did not enjoy a regular place early last season, and certainly his goalscoring suffered as did his confidence. However, once he had scored at Bournemouth from the penalty spot his confidence grew and his performances improved. Unfortunately, after scoring his 14th goal and Rovers' vital opening goal in the tense last match against Brentford, which propelled Rovers into the second division play offs, he sustained a broken left leg and took no further part in the club's quest for promotion. Is now acknowledged by the fans as a better all rounder who, besides his goal contribution, works hard to link up the attack, and has matured into a much more consistent player.

Norwich C (From trainee on 5/2/93) P/FL 13+16/6 FLC 0+1 FAC 0+2
Bournemouth (Loaned on 8/9/95) FL 0+5 Others 0+1
Bristol Rov (£250,000 on 20/9/96) FL 72+9/24 FLC 2 FAC 3 Others 3/1

CURLE Keith
Born: Bristol, 14 November 1963
Height: 6'1" Weight: 12.12
Club Honours: AMC '86; FMC '88
International Honours: E: 3; B-4

A right-footed central defender, Keith was captain of Wolverhampton Wanderers as well as having an outstanding 1997-98. Starting the season superbly, and forgiven for a nightmare mistake in the derby at West Bromwich, he had a niggling achilles problem and was advised to rest, missing eight matches. Back for the next 37, he again showed a penchant for venturing forward, scoring with a neat glancing header against Swindon. With organisational skills very much in evidence in the four FA Cup-ties against Premier League clubs, during which he proved he could still perform at that level, many feel he is the best signing Mark McGhee has made since coming to Molineux in 1995.

Bristol Rov (From apprentice on 20/11/81) FL 21+11/4 FLC 3 FAC 1

Torquay U (£5,000 on 4/11/83) FL 16/5 FAC 1/1 Others 1
Bristol C (£10,000 on 3/3/84) FL 113+8/1 FLC 7+1 FAC 5 Others 14+1
Reading (£150,000 on 23/10/87) FL 40 FLC 8 Others 5
Wimbledon (£500,000 on 21/10/88) FL 91+2/3 FLC 7 FAC 5 Others 6/1
Manchester C (£2,500,000 on 14/8/91) F/PL 171/11 FLC 18/2 FAC 14 Others 1
Wolverhampton W (£650,000 on 2/8/96) FL 60+1/3 FLC 2 FAC 7/1 Others 2

CURRAN Christopher (Chris)
Born: Birmingham, 17 September 1971
Height: 5'11" Weight: 12.4

Having joined Exeter from Plymouth in the 1997 close season, Chris was an ever present in the team until a cruciate knee ligament injury, following the game against Colchester in September, brought his campaign to a premature end after only nine league appearances. A speedy, hard-working central defender, who contests every ball, he will be looking to have better luck in 1998-99.

Torquay U (From trainee on 13/7/90) FL 144+8/4 FLC 15 FAC 8 Others 10/1
Plymouth Arg (£40,000 on 22/12/95) FL 26+4 FLC 1+1 FAC 1 Others 4
Exeter C (£20,000 on 31/7/97) FL 9 FLC 2

CURRIE Darren Paul
Born: Hampstead, 29 November 1974
Height: 5'10" Weight: 12.7

A left winger, cum midfielder, and a firm favourite with the Shrewsbury crowd with his runs at the opposition and devastating shooting ability. Equally at home on the wing or in midfield, he was the penalty taker for part of last season until it became clear in mid-term that he was no longer part of the club's plans. Following a heel-kicking spell, Darren joined Plymouth on a free on deadline day, and went straight into the side, firstly as a sub, and then on the flank from where he supplied the pass that brought about a welcome point at Millwall.

West Ham U (From trainee on 2/7/93)
Shrewsbury T (Loaned on 5/9/94) FL 10+2/2
Shrewsbury T (Loaned on 3/2/95) FL 5
Leyton Orient (Loaned on 16/11/95) FL 9+1
Shrewsbury T (£70,000 on 7/2/96) FL 46+20/8 FLC 2+1/1 FAC 3
Plymouth Arg (Free on 26/3/98) FL 5+2

CURTIS John Charles
Born: Nuneaton, 3 September 1978
Height: 5'10" Weight: 11.9
Club Honours: FAYC '95
International Honours: E: B-1; U21-6; Yth; Sch

As Manchester United's Young Player of the Year for 1997, the solid full back, with good tackling and recovery skills, had already made a highly promising start to his professional career when selected for the England U21 squad, even before he had made his full debut for his club. Thrust into the limelight by Alex Ferguson for United's Coca Cola Cup tie against Ipswich last October, he earned a glowing reference from his manager who said: "It was good for John Curtis. He had an excellent game and is

obviously a player with a good future." Having made his Premiership debut against Barnsley at Old Trafford at the end of October, his next big headline was his sending-off offence whilst playing for Young England against Greece in November. Apart from this minor transgression, the future looks extremely bright for the former England youth team captain.

Manchester U (From trainee on 3/10/95) PL 3+5 FLC 1

CURTIS Thomas (Tom) David
Born: Exeter, 1 March 1973
Height: 5'8" Weight: 11.7

All the tigerish, determined aspects of Tom's play were well to the fore again last term, but the all-action Chesterfield midfielder added more to his game, getting forward down the right on occasions and supplying good crosses for the front men. Has come on a lot since turning fully pro, and continues to develop at an encouraging rate.

Derby Co (From juniors on 1/7/91)
Chesterfield (Free on 12/8/93) FL 194+4/9 FLC 15+1 FAC 17/1 Others 10+1

CUSACK Nicholas (Nicky) John
Born: Maltby, 24 December 1965
Height: 6'0" Weight: 12.8

Having missed only one league match in Fulham's 1996-97 promotion run, playing sometimes in midfield, but more often in the back three, Nicky picked up an injury in pre-season and only made four appearances in 1997-98 before following Alan Cork to Swansea City in October. As the Swans most consistent player, it turned out to be a good move and, although primarily used as a central defender, he also played occasionally in central defence and as a striker.

Leicester C (Signed from Alvechurch on 18/6/87) FL 5+11/1 FAC 0+1 Others 1+1
Peterborough U (£40,000 on 29/7/88) FL 44/10 FLC 4/1 FAC 4/1 Others 2
Motherwell (£100,000 on 2/8/89) SL 68+9/17 SLC 5/4 SC 3+1/2 Others 1+1/1
Darlington (£95,000 on 24/1/92) FL 21/6
Oxford U (£95,000 on 16/7/92) FL 48+13/10 FLC 3/2 FAC 4+2/1 Others 2+1
Wycombe W (Loaned on 24/3/94) FL 2+2/1
Fulham (Free on 4/11/94) FL 109+7/14 FLC 6+4/1 FAC 7+1/1 Others 5+2/3
Swansea C (£50,000 on 30/10/97) FL 32 FAC 1 Others 1

CYRUS Andrew (Andy)
Born: Lambeth, 30 September 1976
Height: 5'8" Weight: 10.7

After joining Exeter on a free transfer from Crystal Palace during the 1997 close season, Andy was in and out of the side in 1997-98 and, although looking for an extended run this coming term, when he could put his strengths of pace and passing, and crossing ability down the left-hand side to full use, he was released during the summer. Recognised mainly as a wing back, his recovery rate helps to get tackles in.

Crystal Palace (From trainee on 22/8/95) FL 1
Exeter C (Free on 30/7/97) FL 17+4 FLC 2 FAC 1+1

DABIZAS Nikolaos (Nicos)

Born: Amyndaeo, Greece, 3 August 1973
Height: 6'2" Weight: 12.7
International Honours: Greece: 23

Nicos joined Newcastle shortly before the transfer deadline last March and went straight into the first team as a centre back, immediately impressing as an excellent buy. A regular in the Greece team, he helped his former club, Olympiakos, to last season's championship and then starred for them in this season's Champions League. Although not particularly tall for a central defender, he is very good in the air, in both his own and the opponents' penalty areas, and his willingness to attack the ball added bite to United's defence. He is also comfortable on the ball and this, with his coolness, enables him to play in midfield if desired. Has settled well and looks at home in the Premiership.

Newcastle U (£1,300,000 from Olympiakos on 13/3/98) PL 10+1/1 FAC 2

DAHLIN Martin

Born: Udevalla, Sweden, 16 April 1968
Height: 6'0" Weight: 13.2
International Honours: Sweden: 60

Thought to be an excellent signing for Blackburn, the Swedish international star striker arrived from Roma during the 1997 close season and was expected to form a deadly partnership with Chris Sutton in 1997-98. In the event, however, it did not quite work out like that. With a fitness programme in front of him, Martin never quite made it, being used as a sub for the opening four games, and then failing to establish himself, before missing 16 games due to an old back problem and hamstring trouble. Occasionally, he produced flashes of goalscoring genius of the highest order, but has yet to be fully attuned to the demands of the Premiership.

Blackburn Rov (£2,500,000 from Roma on 23/7/97) PL 11+10/4 FLC 2/2 FAC 0+1

DAILLY Christian Eduard

Born: Dundee, 23 October 1973
Height: 6'0" Weight: 12.10
International Honours: S: 13; B-1; U21-34; Yth; Sch

Signed in the previous season from Dundee United, for whom he moved from a central attacking position through midfield and eventually into central defence, his calm and unpressured style earned him an immediate position at the centre of Derby's defence in 1997-98, although his versatility also allows him to play up front or at left back. A full Scottish international who was looking forward to playing an important part in Scotland's World Cup squad in France during the summer, he is totally committed wherever you ask him to play and is a real asset. *Stop Press:* Started every first round

game for Scotland in France during the summer, the side being eliminated after finishing bottom of Group A.

Dundee U (From juniors on 2/8/90) SL 110+33/18 SLC 9/1 SC 10+2 Others 8+1/1
Derby Co (£1,000,000 on 12/8/96) PL 61+5/4 FLC 6 FAC 4+1

DALE Carl

Born: Colwyn Bay, 29 April 1966
Height: 5'9" Weight: 12.0
Club Honours: WC '92, '93; Div 3 '93

Dogged by injuries, the pity was that after suffering so many two seasons ago Carl entered 1997-98 looking sharp and eager, and was outstanding at Leyton Orient in the opening match, scoring the winning goal before being carried off with an ankle injury, which kept him out for months. Even as the campaign ended, he was recovering from a shoulder operation, following an injury sustained at Peterborough in April. Although a natural goalscorer, the City manager, Frank Burrows, eventually gave him a free transfer, insisting though, that the player would be paid even after his contract had run out and it would continue until he was fully fit. "Cardiff City have handled this well," said Carl after hearing the shock news that he would be leaving after seven years with the club, "They looked after me." His main regrets were failing to beat the club's goalscoring record of 31 in a season – he managed 30 and missed four games through injury – and finishing around 20 goals behind the record total, having netted more than 100 times for the Bluebirds.

Chester C (£12,000 from Bangor C on 19/5/88) FL 106+10/41 FLC 7+1 FAC 9/5 Others 6/2
Cardiff C (£100,000 on 19/8/91) FL 188+25/71 FLC 10+1/5 FAC 14/6 Others 21+1/20

DALEY Anthony (Tony) Mark

Born: Birmingham, 18 October 1967
Height: 5'8" Weight: 11.7
Club Honours: FLC '94
International Honours: E: 7; B-1; Yth

A right-footed winger, Tony has been plagued by knee problems during his four seasons at Wolves, missing 1996-97 altogether. It was last January before he was seen in action, coming on as sub at home to Norwich, and he must have been heartened by the reception given. There were more cheers when the ball seemed to be going out yet he got a good cross in, and he came on as sub in the next two matches before tearing a thigh muscle during shooting practice, and dropping out of the picture again, with it taking longer to heal than expected. Was released during the summer.

Aston Villa (From apprentice on 31/5/85) F/PL 189+44/31 FLC 22+2/4 FAC 15+1/2 Others 15+2/1
Wolverhampton W (£1,250,000 on 6/6/94) FL 16+5/3 FLC 4/1 FAC 0+2

DALGLISH Paul

Born: Glasgow, 18 February 1977
Height: 5'9" Weight: 10.0

A free transfer signing from Liverpool to Newcastle at the start of last season, Paul, the son of Kenny, joined Bury in December on loan until the end of 1997-98. Still

somewhat lightweight, the striker nevertheless impressed at Gigg Lane with his speed and ball skills, despite being used mainly as a substitute. Started just two games, a league game at Charlton, when he was superb in a left-sided role, and an FA Cup tie at Sheffield United, when he received a broken nose for his troubles. It is a tough world out there and he will be all the better for the experience.

Glasgow Celtic (From juniors on 20/7/95)
Liverpool (Free on 14/8/96)
Newcastle U (Free on 21/11/97)
Bury (Loaned on 21/11/97) FL 1+11 FAC 1

DALTON Paul

Born: Middlesbrough, 25 April 1967
Height: 5'11" Weight: 12.7

No doubt about it, Paul was the most revitalised player at the McAlpine in 1997-98 and the main reason why Huddersfield climbed away from the relegation zone. Previously in and out of the side, the new management team gave him a free role and he promptly rewarded their faith by scoring 11 goals in just 15 games. Probably the most important of the goals was his first, as it gave Town their first win in the league at the 15th attempt and was featured on Question of Sport as a "What Happened Next?" Due to a hernia operation, he missed the back end of the season, but much will be expected of this exciting winger in 1998-99, now he has put pen to paper on a two-year contract. Although predominantly left-footed, with the ability to get inside the full back, it was on the right that he finally became a star.

Manchester U (£35,000 from Brandon U on 3/5/88)
Hartlepool U (£20,000 on 4/3/89) FL 140+11/37 FLC 10/2 FAC 7/1 Others 9/3
Plymouth Arg (£275,000 on 11/6/92) FL 93+5/25 FLC 5/2 FAC 7/5 Others 6
Huddersfield T (Signed on 11/8/95) FL 72+17/22 FLC 6+2/1 FAC 5+1

DARBY Duane Anthony

Born: Birmingham, 17 October 1973
Height: 5'11" Weight: 12.6

An appendix operation last September kept the Hull City 1996-97 Player of the Year out for two months and he subsequently struggled to recapture the form of the previous campaign. A fractured cheekbone suffered in the Humber derby clash with Scunthorpe in February provided another setback, yet the forceful front runner still comfortably finished as the club's leading marksman, scoring a hat trick in the 7-4 home win over Swansea in August. A player who strongly favours his right foot, Duane has turned down a new contract and was set to leave Hull in the summer.*

Torquay U (From trainee on 3/7/92) FL 60+48/26 FLC 4+3/1 FAC 1+4 Others 5+3/2
Doncaster Rov (£60,000 on 19/7/95) FL 8+9/4 FLC 2 FAC 0+1 Others 1+1
Hull C (Signed on 27/3/96) FL 75+3/27 FLC 5/1 FAC 4/6 Others 4/2

DARBY Julian Timothy

Born: Bolton, 3 October 1967
Height: 6'0" Weight: 11.4
Club Honours: AMC '89
International Honours: E: Sch

An experienced midfielder, cum defender, Julian was signed from West Bromwich Albion during the 1997 close season as part of the Kevin Kilbane transfer, but, unable to establish a regular first team place, and fading from the picture after Christmas, he went on loan to Rotherham. Set to join earlier, he suffered an ankle injury before the forms could be completed, but finally arrived at Millmoor just before the deadline. However, he failed to make the desired impact in midfield and lost his place after three games.

Bolton W (From trainee on 22/7/86) FL 258+12/36 FLC 25/8 FAC 19/3 Others 31+1/5
Coventry C (£150,000 on 28/10/93) PL 52+3/5 FLC 3/1 FAC 2+2
West Bromwich A (£200,000 on 24/11/95) FL 32+7/1 FAC 1 Others 4
Preston NE (£150,000 on 13/6/97) FL 6+6 FLC 1+1 FAC 2+1 Others 0+1
Rotherham U (Loaned on 26/3/98) FL 3

DARRAS Frederic Guy Albert
Born: Calais, France, 19 August 1974
Height: 5'11" Weight: 11.5

A utility player who started last season as first-choice right back in a Swindon defence which was looking steady, Frederic was dropped following the calamitous 6-0 defeat at Manchester City and never held down a regular slot again. One of eight players transfer listed, as manager, Steve McMahon, threatened a wholesale clearout in the Spring, he returned to his homeland, joining French third division side, Red Star Paris, on a free in January.

Swindon T (Free from Bastia on 9/8/96) FL 42+7 FLC 6

D'AURIA David Alan
Born: Swansea, 26 March 1970
Height: 5'9" Weight: 11.11
Club Honours: WC '94
International Honours: W: Yth

The Scunthorpe skipper last season, David was a regular in the side with his hard-working displays in midfield. A good tackler, he also liked to get forward and reached double figures for league goals for the first time. Eight of his ten goals were vital, either winning matches or earning a point at the very least, and coupled with his ability to make chances for his team mates, should make his name the first on the team sheet in 1998-99.*

Swansea C (From trainee on 2/8/88) FL 27+18/6 FLC 2+2 FAC 1 Others 4 (Free transfer to Merthyr Tydfil during 1991 close season)
Scarborough (Signed from Barry T on 22/8/94) FL 49+3/8 FLC 3+2/1 FAC 4+1 Others 2
Scunthorpe U (£40,000 on 6/12/95) FL 103+4/18 FLC 6 FAC 7/1 Others 4+1

DAVENPORT Peter
Born: Birkenhead, 24 March 1961
Height: 5'11" Weight: 12.10
Club Honours: FMC '90; GMVC '97
International Honours: E: 1; B-1

Having joined Macclesfield from Southport in January 1997, after failing to get the manager's job, Peter was appointed player/coach at the start of last season, making just limited appearances but, when playing, worked hard on the left wing. With one to

go, the former England international was still hoping for a chance of scoring his 100th goal in the Football League, something he achieved in the final game of 1997-98.*

Nottingham F (Free from Camel Laird on 5/1/82) FL 114+4/54 FLC 10/1 FAC 7+1/1 Others 10+1/2
Manchester U (£750,000 on 12/3/86) FL 73+19/22 FLC 8+2/4 FAC 2+2
Middlesbrough (£750,000 on 31/11/88) FL 53+6/7 FLC 2 FAC 4 Others 7+1/1
Sunderland (£350,000 on 19/7/90) FL 72+27/15 FLC 5+2/1 FAC 9+1/2 Others 14+1
Airdrie (Free during 1993 close season) SL 35+3/9 SLC 3/1 SC 3+2
St Johnstone (Free on 16/8/94) SL 12+10/4 SLC 3 SC 0+1 Others 2/1
Stockport Co (Free on 23/3/95) FL 3+3/1 (Free to Southport on 24/8/95)
Macclesfield T (Free on 21/1/97) FL 2+2/1

Peter Davenport

DAVEY Simon
Born: Swansea, 1 October 1970
Height: 5'10" Weight: 12.2
Club Honours: Div 3 '95, '96

Only coming back into the first team picture at Preston in 1997-98 under new manager, David Moyes, after a spell on loan at Darlington, Simon added some much needed bite to midfield and gradually built a good partnership with Michael Appleton. Continued to supply his customary quota of goals, including a spectacular flying header at Bournemouth, and a fierce volley at Bristol Rovers, he remains an energetic "box-to-box" player.

Swansea C (From trainee on 3/7/89) FL 37+12/4 FLC 1 FAC 1+2/1 Others 2+3
Carlisle U (Free on 5/8/92) FL 105/18 FLC 10/1 FAC 7/2 Others 15/2
Preston NE (£125,000 on 22/2/95) FL 97+9/21 FLC 4/1 FAC 2+1 Others 9
Darlington (Loaned on 11/9/97) FL 10+1

DAVIDSON Callum Iain
Born: Stirling, 25 June 1976
Height: 5'10" Weight: 12.2
International Honours: S: U21-2

Signed from St Johnstone last February, the young Scot arrived at Blackburn with

hamstring trouble, developed a septic toe, and, when given a debut against Arsenal at Ewood after eight weeks, promptly pulled a muscle within an hour and was lost for the rest of the season. Having showed plenty of promise in his brief appearance, Callum is expected to be a leading contender for the left-back slot in 1998-99, although he will have to meet the challenge from other hopefuls, notably Gary Croft.

St Johnstone (From juniors on 8/6/94) SL 38+5/4 SLC 1 Others 3
Blackburn Rov (£1,750,000 on 12/2/98) PL 1

DAVIDSON Ross James
Born: Chertsey, 13 November 1973
Height: 5'9" Weight: 12.4

Ross had last season interrupted by injuries on several occasions, but still managed to make 24 league appearances as Chester City's right back. A strong-tackling player, he is a favourite with the crowd, mainly because he has a liking to get forward to join up with the attack. Was successful twice from the penalty spot in successive away games against Cardiff and Mansfield, both of them being powerful strikes.

Sheffield U (Signed from Walton & Hersham on 5/6/93) FL 2 Others 2
Chester C (Free on 26/1/96) FL 83/5 FLC 3 FAC 2+1 Others 4

DAVIES Gareth Melville
Born: Hereford, 11 December 1973
Height: 6'1" Weight: 11.12
International Honours: W: U21-8

By far Terry Bullivant's best signing, Gareth seemed a real bargain when he arrived from Crystal Palace last December, having made a lone subs' appearance in 1997-98 after a long spell out injured. A model of consistency at centre back, able to win the ball in the air and on the ground, as well as setting up counter attacks and featuring prominently in the club's FA Cup run to round five, curiously, however, he failed to impress the new manager, Tommy Burns, and ended the season by playing in the reserves. He was then told that he would be allowed to leave if he could find another club during the summer.

Hereford U (From trainee on 10/4/92) FL 91+4/1 FLC 5+2 FAC 4 Others 5
Crystal Palace (£120,000 on 1/7/95) F/PL 22+5/2 FAC 2 Others 1
Cardiff C (Loaned on 21/2/97) FL 6/2
Reading (£100,000 on 12/12/97) FL 17+1 FLC 1 FAC 3

DAVIES Glen
Born: Brighton, 20 July 1976
Height: 6'1" Weight: 13.8

An extremely capable central defender, who was more often than not the odd one out in what was Hartlepool's strongest position, he had several short first team runs in 1997-98, but in mid-season was out for several weeks when troubled by a groin injury. A good squad member, he always gave his best, and can consider himself most unlucky to have been given a free transfer during the summer.

Burnley (From trainee on 18/7/94)
Hartlepool U (Free on 19/6/96) FL 48+4/1 FLC 3/1 FAC 1 Others 1

DAVIES Kevin Cyril
Born: Sheffield, 26 March 1977
Height: 6'0" Weight: 12.10
International Honours: E: U21-1; Yth

A strong and skilful, thrusting forward, Kevin was the last signing for Southampton made by former manager, Graeme Souness, who bought the gifted young man from Chesterfield during the 1997 close season, after he had starred in their cup run in 1996-97. Getting off to a brilliant start, Kevin had scored 12 goals before an injury all but finished his campaign in January, the injury coming during a tremendous run of form by Saints when he limped off early in the home victory against Manchester United, having scored what proved to be the winning goal. He made only two further appearances, as a substitute, and had to withdraw from the England U21 squad for the Toulon Tournament. Loves taking defenders on, mainly from wide positions, but is equally effective when going through the middle, scoring one of the goals of the season when picking the ball up on the half-way line at Everton and going through four challenges before finishing off with a 15-yard shot in a 2-0 win. *Stop Press:* Signed for Blackburn on 1 June, for a fee thought to be in the region of £7.25 million.
Chesterfield (From trainee on 18/4/94) FL 113+16/22 FLC 7+2/1 FAC 10/6 Others 9+2/1
Southampton (£750,000 on 14/5/97) PL 20+5/9 FLC 3+1/3 FAC 1

DAVIES Lawrence
Born: Abergavenny, 3 September 1977
Height: 6'1" Weight: 11.8
International Honours: W: Yth

Picked up by Bradford City on a free after being released by Leeds during the 1997 close season, Lawrence was loaned out to Darlington last December and, following an appearance at Preston in the Auto Windscreens Shield, he played twice more before returning to Valley Parade. A hard-running, hard-working centre forward who showed a willingness to come back to help the defence out, he next made his debut for City at Norwich in April, but, unfortunately injured, had to be substituted after 35 minutes. City have forecast a bright future for this youngster.
Leeds U (From trainee on 19/8/96)
Bradford C (Free on 11/7/97) FL 1+3
Darlington (Loaned on 1/12/97) FL 2 Others 1

DAVIES Simon
Born: Haverfordwest, 23 October 1979
Height: 5'9" Weight: 11.4
International Honours: W: Yth

A bright young Peterborough midfielder who starred in the club's junior side that ultimately reached the semi-final stage of the FA Youth Cup in 1997-98, Simon came off the bench to make his first team debut at Hull last January and, in four starts and two subs' appearances, showed some nice touches and vision. Is yet another home-grown talent to emerge from the Barry Fry academy.
Peterborough U (From trainee on 21/7/97) FL 4+2 Others 1

DAVIES Simon Ithel
Born: Winsford, 23 April 1974
Height: 6'0" Weight: 11.11
Club Honours: FAYC '92
International Honours: W: 1

A left-sided midfielder, signed from Manchester United in the 1997 close season, Simon had a poor start to his career at Luton. Possessing good skills on the ball, he often appeared to find it difficult to react to the pace of the game and, after an initial run in the side, he was dropped and subsequently used mainly as a substitute. Towards the end of the campaign, however, he demonstrated that on his day he can show urgency and directness, and is young enough to come good.
Manchester U (From trainee on 6/7/92) PL 4+7 FLC 4+2 Others 2+1/1
Exeter C (Loaned on 17/12/93) FL 5+1/1 FAC 1
Huddersfield T (Loaned on 29/10/96) FL 3
Luton T (£150,000 on 5/8/97) FL 8+12/1 FLC 3+1 FAC 0+1 Others 3

DAVIS Craig
Born: Rotherham, 12 October 1977
Height: 6'4" Weight: 11.6

Signed from non-league Gateshead last November, and a former Rotherham player, Craig became the fifth goalkeeper to play for Doncaster in the league in 1997-98, when he appeared at Hull City. Although he rather undeservedly lost his place to Tony Parks, he was back between the posts as the Rovers' league tenure drew to its painful close, proving himself to be an excellent shot-stopper, with all the physical attributes to become highly competent.
Rotherham U (From trainee on 26/6/96) FAC 1 (Free to Gateshead on 1/6/97)
Doncaster Rov (Free on 27/11/97) FL 15 Others 1

DAVIS Kelvin Geoffrey
Born: Bedford, 29 September 1976
Height: 6'1" Weight: 14.0
International Honours: E: U21-3; Yth

After several years as a promising youngster, Kelvin finally established a regular place in the Luton team in 1997-98 and lived up to the potential of his teens. Always an outstanding re-active shot-stopper, he grew in confidence when recalled from a loan spell at Hartlepool and improved his general authority in the area. Originally playing in the place of the injured Ian Feuer, the giant American who had kept him out of the team for so long, he proved himself the better 'keeper and Feuer was eventually allowed to move on. Keeping a clean sheet on his return against Fulham, and going on to provide many breathtaking saves, he could be the Hatters' number one for years to come.
Luton T (From trainee on 1/7/94) FL 48 Others 6
Torquay U (Loaned on 16/9/94) FL 2 FLC 1 Others 1
Hartlepool U (Loaned on 8/8/97) FL 2 FLC 1

DAVIS Solomon (Sol) Sebastian
Born: Cheltenham, 4 September 1979
Height: 5'8" Weight: 11.0

This teenage defender broke into the Swindon side towards the end of last season, winning praise for a series of mature displays, having been first introduced as a

sub against QPR at the County Ground in November. Naturally left sided, Sol is equally at home at full back, or wing back, and can also play on the left side of midfield. Tenacious in the tackle, and able to deliver a telling cross, he was rewarded with a two-year deal in the summer – his first professional contract.
Swindon T (Trainee) FL 5+1

DAVIS Stephen (Steve) Mark
Born: Hexham, 30 October 1968
Height: 6'2" Weight: 14.7
Club Honours: Div 4 '92

Once again, Steve emerged as one of Luton's most consistent players in 1997-98, putting together performances that were rewarded by him winning the Players' Player of the Year award, and the highest number of Man of the Match awards. Solid as ever in the centre of defence, despite having to play alongside several different partners, as dictated by injury and form, good in the air, and extremely sure footed, such was his importance that he was picked even when not fully fit. Although in a struggling side he was not able to score as many goals as in the previous season, he nevertheless netted on half a dozen occasions and was always a danger when able to move forward.
Southampton (From trainee on 6/7/87) FL 5+1
Burnley (Loaned on 21/11/89) FL 7+2
Notts Co (Loaned on 28/3/91) FL 0+2
Burnley (£60,000 on 17/8/91) FL 162/22 FLC 10/2 FAC 18/1 Others 13
Luton T (£750,000 on 13/7/95) FL 117+1/15 FLC 12/1 FAC 3 Others 10/1

DAVIS Steven (Steve) Peter
Born: Birmingham, 26 July 1965
Height: 6'0" Weight: 12.12
International Honours: E: Yth

Loaned to York last September, the central defender scored on his debut against Burnley, but only played one other game before picking up a bad injury and returning to Oakwell. On recovering, Steve followed manager, Malcolm Shotton, from Barnsley to Oxford, initially on loan, and then full time, helping to steady the defence following the sale of Darren Purse to Birmingham, and missing just one game in the last three months of the season, while chipping in with a couple of goals. One of them came at Loftus Road, the scene of his broken leg the previous season. He remained a useful player at corners, often going close after defenders had been distracted by big Kevin Francis, and good in the air and tackle, he is set to be a regular for sometime yet.
Crewe Alex (Free from Stoke C juniors on 17/8/83) FL 140+5/1 FLC 10 FAC 3 Others 7+1
Burnley (£15,000 on 3/10/87) FL 147/11 FLC 7 FAC 9 Others 19/1
Barnsley (£180,000 on 26/7/91) FL 103+4/10 FLC 9 FAC 3
York C (Loaned on 12/9/97) FL 2/1
Oxford U (£75,000 on 16/2/98) FL 15/2

DAVISON Aidan John
Born: Sedgefield, 11 May 1968
Height: 6'1" Weight: 13.12
Club Honours: AMC '98
International Honours: NI: 3; B-1

Surprisingly released by Bradford City during the 1997 close season, following his vital role in maintaining their first division status at the Mariners' expense, Aidan joined Grimsby on a free transfer. Immediately establishing himself as the automatic first team goalkeeper behind a solid defence that gave little away during the charge to regain first division status, his sterling performances were rewarded with a third Northern Ireland cap against Germany. Solid, if unspectacular, you can rely upon him to do the job with the minimum of fuss, and he was delighted to be a member of the side that won the second division play-off final and the Auto Windscreen Shield.

Notts Co (Signed from Billingham Synthonia on 25/3/88) FL 1
Bury (£6,000 on 7/10/89)
Millwall (Free on 14/8/91) FL 34 FLC 3 FAC 3 Others 2
Bolton W (£25,000 on 26/7/93) P/FL 35+2 FAC 8 Others 4
Hull C (Loaned on 29/11/96) FL 9 Others 1
Bradford C (Free on 14/3/97) FL 10
Grimsby T (Free on 16/7/97) FL 42 FLC 5 FAC 6 Others 10

Nick Daws

DAWS Nicholas (Nick) John
Born: Manchester, 15 March 1970
Height: 5'11" Weight: 13.2
Club Honours: Div 2 '97

As Bury's longest serving player, and so often an unsung hero, Nick has made the gradual transition from non-league to division one over the past five years, and showed remarkable consistency once again for the Shakers last season. A midfield player whose non-stop running is his trademark, he played in all 52 league and cup games for the club in 1997-98 – his second ever-present campaign, and he was a runaway choice as the fans' Player of the Season.

Bury (£10,000 from Altrincham on 13/8/92) FL 223+13/9 FLC 16+3/2 FAC 12 Others 13+2/1

DAY Christopher (Chris) Nicholas
Born: Whipps Cross, 28 July 1975
Height: 6'2" Weight: 13.6
International Honours: E: U21-6, Yth

Having joined Watford from Crystal Palace in July 1997 as part of the deal that took Kevin Miller in the opposite direction, the consistency of Alec Chamberlain confined the young goalie to the reserve team for most of the 1997-98 season, and he was unfortunate to concede a controversial own goal on his first team debut against Sheffield United in the Coca Cola Cup. A former England U21 international, Chris seems sure to figure in the Hornets' future.

Tottenham H (From trainee on 16/4/93)
Crystal Palace (£225,000+ on 9/8/96) FL 24 FLC 2 FAC 2
Watford (£225,000 on 18/7/97) FLC 1 Others 1

DEAN Michael James
Born: Weymouth, 9 March 1978
Height: 5'10" Weight: 11.12

Michael spent most of 1997-98 on the fringes of the Bournemouth first team, making just four starts and five substitute appearances. A central midfielder who is a good passer of the ball, and who always looks comfortable in that position, having taken a couple of seasons trying to establish himself at Dean Court he will be looking to claim a regular place in the coming season.

Bournemouth (From trainee on 4/7/96)) FL 17+8 FAC 1 Others 1

DEANE Brian Christopher
Born: Leeds, 7 February 1968
Height: 6'3" Weight: 12.7
International Honours: E: 3; B-3

Hailed as the conquering hero when surprisingly returning from Leeds during the summer of 1997, Brian performed as if he had never been away from Sheffield United. He even managed to score after 31 seconds of his first match back, albeit only a friendly against Blackburn Rovers. Many powerful front-running performances assisted the run at the top of the table and he won the Nationwide League's quickest goal award for September for his 17-second strike at Oxford United. However, he had only been signed on the understanding that he could leave if an offer came in from a European club (he had allegedly been on the way to Holland when persuaded to sign for United) and the lure of Benfica proved greater than that of the Football League. Despite moving on in January he still finished the campaign as United's leading scorer with 13 goals in all competitions.

Doncaster Rov (From juniors on 14/12/85) FL 59+7/12 FLC 3 FAC 2+1/1 Others 2+2
Sheffield U (£30,000 on 19/7/88) F/PL 197/82 FLC 16/11 FAC 23+1/11 Others 2/2
Leeds U (£2,900,000 on 14/7/93) PL 131+7/32 FLC 8+3/2 FAC 13+3/4 Others 3
Sheffield U (£1,500,000 on 29/7/97) FL 24/11 FLC 4/2 FAC 1

DEARDEN Kevin Charles
Born: Luton, 8 March 1970
Height: 5'11" Weight: 13.12

For the experienced Brentford goalkeeper, who is a good shot stopper, 1997-98 was not one of his better seasons as the Bees struggled at the wrong end of the second division table. Missed six games in October/November, due to a knee injury, and a further five in January/February when it flared up again, but was coming back to his best form towards the end of the campaign, especially at Wrexham where he almost single handedly won the team a point with some great saves.

Tottenham H (From trainee on 5/8/88) PL 0+1 FLC 1
Cambridge U (Loaned on 9/3/89) FL 15
Hartlepool U (Loaned on 31/8/89) FL 10
Swindon T (Loaned on 23/3/90) FL 1
Peterborough U (Loaned on 24/8/90) FL 7
Hull C (Loaned on 10/1/91) FL 3
Rochdale (Loaned on 16/8/91) FL 2
Birmingham C (Loaned on 19/3/92) FL 12
Brentford (Free on 30/9/93) FL 198 FLC 16 FAC 12 Others 17

DEBENHAM Robert Karl
Born: Doncaster, 28 November 1979
Height: 5'8" Weight: 10.4

Yet another member of the Doncaster youth side, and still a trainee, Robert was given his league debut against Lincoln City last March, and impressed several good judges of the game with his ability to cope. This young full back will be a better player with further league experience behind him, and looks a good prospect for the future.

Doncaster Rov (Trainee) FL 4+2

DE GOEY Eduard (Ed) Franciscus
Born: Gouda, Holland, 20 December 1966
Height: 6'5" Weight: 12.0
Club Honours: FLC '98; ECWC '98
International Honours: Holland: 31

When the Dutch international goalkeeper joined Chelsea in June 1997 he took a long-standing record away from the legendary Mickey Droy by becoming Chelsea's tallest-ever player. Having joined Feyenoord from local rivals, Sparta Rotterdam, in 1990, and establishing himself as Holland's first-choice 'keeper, winning 29 caps before being usurped by Ajax's Edwin van der Sar, the towering Ed became the third player to join the Blues from Feyenoord in the last eight years. He proved his class in his first competitive match for Chelsea by saving three spot kicks in an Umbro Cup penalty shoot-out against Newcastle, which saw Chelsea reach the final against Everton, which they ultimately won. The big 'keeper was an automatic choice, playing in 34 of the first 36 league and cup matches before Luca Vialli took over and introduced his goalkeeping rotational policy, which saw Dmitri Kharine playing in the Premiership and Ed playing in cup matches. He was outstanding in Chelsea's cup triumphs, saving two penalties against Ipswich in the Coca Cola Cup quarter-final shoot-out, and playing superbly in the semi final away game at Highbury to keep Arsenal's lead down to 2-1, which The Blues overturned in

the home leg. During the Cup Winners' Cup campaign, he played superbly in away legs at Real Betis and Vicenza to keep Chelsea's hopes alive, and in the semi-final leg at the Bridge, he produced a magnificent, last-minute fingertip save to prevent the Italian side going through to the final. In the final itself, when Stuttgart were pressing hard in the first half, he saved brilliantly, low down to his right from Bulgarian star, Balakov, to keep his second clean sheet in a major final within six weeks. *Stop Press:* Selected for Holland's World Cup 22 that reached the semi-final stage of the competition, he was not called upon due to the excellent form of Edwin van der Saar.

Chelsea (£2,250,000 from Feyenoord on 10/7/97) PL 28 FLC 4 FAC 1 Others 10

DELAP Rory John
Born: Sutton Coldfield, 6 July 1976
Height: 6'0" Weight: 12.10
Club Honour: AMC '97
International Honours: Ei: 3; B-1; U21-4
An ankle injury incurred in August, while on duty with the Eire U21 squad, kept Rory out of the Carlisle side virtually until last Christmas, but his all-round performances had already attracted a number of Premiership clubs and he signed for Derby in February, having consistently impressed Jim Smith with his ability to switch roles effectively between right-wing back and attack. A Republic of Ireland squad member, who represented the "B" team and won the first of three full caps shortly after his move, he possesses great pace with a swerving shot, and looks especially effective out wide. Managed to force his way into the County side for the last three months of the season and, with the benefit of training on the more defensive aspects of his game, he will be difficult to drop from the team.

Carlisle U (From trainee on 18/7/94) FL 40+25/7 FLC 4+1 FAC 0+3 Others 12+2
Derby Co (£500,000+ on 6/2/98) PL 10+3

DELLAS Traianos
Born: Thessaloniki, Greece, 31 January 1976
Height: 6'4" Weight: 15.0
Signed from Thessalonika at the start of last season as a centre back, the giant Greek U21 captain proved to be a revelation in Sheffield United's midfield after a shaky debut at the back. Used mostly as a substitute, he put in some cultured performances and looks to have a promising future, either in defence or midfield. Skippered the Greek U21 side to victory over England and scored the first goal with a thumping free kick.

Sheffield U (£300,000 from Aris Salonika on 26/8/97) FL 5+4 FAC 0+2 Others 0+1

DEMPSEY Mark Anthony
Born: Dublin, 10 December 1972
Height: 5'7" Weight: 12.12
International Honours: Ei: U21-5; Yth
Shrewsbury left winger, turned midfielder, turned full back. Looks very comfortable in the latter role and uses the position to break

forward on attacking runs, but his appearances were limited to early last season, before he spent some time on loan at Dover. Was released during the summer.

Gillingham (From trainee on 9/8/90) FL 27+21/2 FLC 0+1 FAC 5 Others 6
Leyton Orient (Free on 4/7/94) FL 43/1 FLC 2 FAC 1+1 Others 5/1
Shrewsbury T (£25,000 on 4/7/95) FL 62+18/3 FLC 3+3 FAC 5+3/2 Others 7+1/1

DENNIS Kevin Jason
Born: Islington, 14 December 1976
Height: 5'10" Weight: 12.0
For the orthodox Brentford outside left with a sweet left foot and good crossing ability, 1997-98 turned out to be a bad season as he made just a few substitute appearances, due to both injury and non-selection. However, there is no doubting that Kevin clearly possesses the skill to make an impression at Football League level, and he is bound to be back.

Brentford (Free from Arsenal juniors on 23/7/96) FL 9+8 Others 3+1

DENYS Ryan Hayden
Born: Brentford, 16 August 1978
Height: 5'6" Weight: 11.2
As a first-year professional in 1997-98, the exciting, diminutive Brentford outside right quickly showed that he possessed loads of skill and that he was an excellent crosser of the ball. Made his debut in the first game of the season, as a sub at Millwall, and three days later opened his scoring account against Shrewsbury in the Coca Cola Cup. Such was his promise that the Bees' new manager, Eddie May, made him a fixture in the side, and he celebrated by scoring his first league goal against Walsall. However, when May was dismissed, the new manager, Micky Adams, dispensed with wingers and Ryan only made an occasional appearance thereafter, spending a month on loan at Yeovil in January.

Brentford (From trainee on 1/7/97) FL 12+7/1 FLC 4/1 Others 1

DERRY Shaun Peter
Born: Nottingham, 6 December 1977
Height: 5'10" Weight: 10.13
Club Honours: Div 3 '98
Having played mainly at full back the previous season, Shaun returned to his favoured central midfield position at Notts County in 1997-98 and developed very quickly as a playmaker with brilliant passing skills. Described by his manager as the best player in the division, he quickly attracted the attention of a number of clubs prior to signing for Sheffield United in January, after an initial bid had been rejected. Coming immediately into the side, he looked a cultured player before proving his versatility by playing in goal for 45 minutes at Portsmouth, following the dismissal of Simon Tracey, and keeping a clean sheet. He also later appeared at full back. An exponent of the long throw, being able to hit the penalty spot with ease, his good form was rewarded with a subs' appearance for the

Nationwide U21 side that played against their Italian counterparts at Charlton in March.

Notts Co (From trainee on 13/4/96) FL 76+3/4 FLC 4+1 FAC 6+1/1 Others 3
Sheffield U (£700,000 on 26/1/98) FL 8+4

DE SOUZA Miquel Juan
Born: Newham, 11 February 1970
Height: 5'11" Weight: 13.8
Injured early on last season, he failed to break back into the Peterborough side on a regular basis, due to the fine form of others, and when he did get an occasional game he was unable to grasp the opportunity. A central striker with speed that allows him to get in behind defenders, especially when going wide, and hard to knock off the ball, Miquel scored four times in all, two of them in back-to-back games against Swansea and Walsall.

Charlton Ath (Signed from Clapton on 4/7/89)
Bristol C (Free on 1/8/90)
Birmingham C (£25,000 from Dagenham & Redbridge, via Yeovil T, Dorchester T and Bashley, on 1/2/94) FL 5+10 FLC 2 Others 1
Bury (Loaned on 25/11/94) FL 2+1
Wycombe W (£80,000 on 27/1/95) FL 73+10/29 FLC 8/2 FAC 6/2 Others 3
Peterborough U (£50,000 on 26/3/97) FL 16+16/5 FLC 1+1 Others 1/1

DEVINE Sean Thomas
Born: Lewisham, 6 September 1972
Height: 6'0" Weight: 13.6
International Honours: Ei: B-1
As the main man at Barnet, and the top scorer for the club since his arrival from Cyprus, after a slow start in 1997-98, Sean formed a potent partnership with Scott McGleish and went on to notch 18 goals. Very fast and lethal in and around the penalty area, he was rewarded for a good season when selected for the Eire "B" squad.

Millwall (From trainee on 4/5/91 - Free to Bromley in August 1992)
Barnet (£10,000 from Famagusta on 5/10/95) FL 102+4/46 FLC 8/3 FAC 5/5 Others 5

DE VITO Claudio Gaeatano
Born: Peterborough, 21 July 1978
Height: 5'9" Weight: 11.2
A non-contract player at Northampton, having earlier been a trainee at the club, Claudio moved to Barnet immediately prior to the transfer deadline last March and made his Football League debut when coming off the bench at Underhill against Mansfield a few weeks later. Recommended to the club as a strong-running, old-fashioned centre forward, he should be in line for further games in 1998-99.

Northampton T (From trainee on 5/7/96)
Barnet (Free on 26/3/98) FL 0+1

DEVLIN Mark Andrew
Born: Irvine, 18 January 1973
Height: 5'10" Weight: 11.12
International Honours: S: Yth
Unable to further his opportunities at Stoke in 1997-98, Mark joined Exeter permanently after a successful loan spell, and was virtually ever present from that moment on, knitting into the midfield well. Despite

showing his versatility by moving to defence from his preferred midfield position when required, he was released during the summer.

Stoke C (From trainee on 6/4/91) FL 39+16/2 FLC 4+1 Others 3+2
Exeter C (Free on 10/10/97) FL 31+2/2 Others 1

DEVLIN Paul John
Born: Birmingham, 14 April 1972
Height: 5'9" Weight: 11.5
Club Honours: AIC '95

Started last season as a regular at Birmingham, scoring eight times, before falling out of favour with the manager, Trevor Francis, after being constantly substituted. Then, put up for sale after an agreement could not be reached on a new four-year deal, he signed for Sheffield United on transfer deadline day, but mainly sat on the bench until injuries gave him his full debut. Capable of playing on the wide right, or down the middle, his only United goal was the equaliser at Tranmere in the 90th minute, a goal which virtually assured the club of a place in the play offs at the end of a long, hard campaign that had seen them in contention throughout.

Notts Co (£40,000 from Stafford R on 22/2/92) FL 132+9/25 FLC 11+1/1 FAC 8/1 Others 17+2/4
Birmingham C (Signed on 29/2/96) FL 61+15/28 FLC 8+1/4 FAC 3+1/2
Sheffield U (£200,000+ on 13/3/98) FL 4+6/1 Others 2

DE VOS Jason Richard
Born: Canada, 2 January 1974
Height: 6'4" Weight: 13.7
International Honours: Canada: 4

Jason became the first Darlington player ever to represent his country when he played for Canada against Iran in Toronto in August 1997. He then went on to play in World Cup qualifying games against the United States and Costa Rica. Outstanding in the heart of Darlington's defence in 1997-98, he headed three goals from set pieces, before a foot injury ruled him out in mid-February until just before the end of the season.

Darlington (Free from Montreal Impact on 29/11/96) FL 31+1/3 FLC 1 FAC 4 Others 1

DEWHURST Robert (Rob) Matthew
Born: Keighley, 10 September 1971
Height: 6'3" Weight: 14.0

Rob lost his Hull City place after suffering a hamstring injury last September, followed by an ankle injury in October, and did not regain his Tigers' stripes until December. From then on the big centre half returned to his most dominant form, until finally having to give way to a hernia problem in March. Now approaching 200 career appearances, the former Blackburn back joined most of the City squad on the transfer list during the summer, despite having more than a year of his contract still to run.

Blackburn Rov (From trainee on 15/10/90) FL 13 FLC 2 Others 1
Darlington (Loaned on 20/12/91) FL 11/1 Others 1
Huddersfield T (Loaned on 2/10/92) FL 7
Hull C (Free on 5/11/93) FL 128+2/13 FLC 8 FAC 7 Others 7

DE ZEEUW Adrianus (Arjan) Johannes
Born: Holland, 16 April 1970
Height: 6'1" Weight: 13.11

Good in the air and strong in the tackle, Arjan was a regular in the Barnsley team in 1997-98. He learnt much in the early part of the season, and was a key player as the Tykes became more resilient, but his untimely groin injury, suffered at Old Trafford in the cup tie, meant that the team lost him for a considerable length of time as the campaign reached its crucial stage. An excellent clubman, he played through the pain barrier towards the end, as the club went in search of the points that would keep them in the Premiership, a task that ultimately proved unsuccessful.*

Barnsley (£250,000 from Telstar on 3/11/95) F/PL 100/3 FLC 6 FAC 9

DIAZ Isidro (Izzy)
Born: Valencia, Spain, 15 May 1972
Height: 5'7" Weight: 9.6
Club Honours: Div 3 '97

A pacy, right-sided winger with the ability to take on defenders at speed, Izzy left Wigan at the start of 1997-98 to spend a trial period with Wolves. However, having had to wait until the eighth match, at Oxford, before getting a game, he was pulled off at half time and eventually released. He then re-signed for Wigan on a short-term contract in December, but sadly broke a bone in his foot in his "second debut" game and that was it for the season, prior to being freed in the summer.

Wigan Ath (Free from Balaguer on 25/7/95) FL 57+19/16 FLC 2+1 FAC 4+1/2 Others 3
Wolverhampton W (Free on 8/8/97) FL 1
Wigan Ath (Free on 18/12/97) FL 1+1

DIBBLE Andrew (Andy) Gerald
Born: Cwmbran, 8 May 1965
Height: 6'2" Weight: 14.8
International Honours: W: 3; U21-3; Yth; Sch

Released by Glasgow Rangers during the 1997 summer recess, the journeyman 'keeper spent a month with Sheffield United before making a nostalgic return to Luton, having been the hero of their 1988 Football League Cup triumph. With Ian Feuer injured and Kelvin Davis cup-tied, Andy played in three games, and, although he could not be blamed for a 5-2 defeat at Wrexham, his monthly contract was not renewed and he eventually found his way to Middlesbrough in January. It was his second spell at Boro, only this time it did not go so well, and his two appearances saw him on the end of a nine goal deficit, prior to being released during the summer. Despite that, he will always remain a popular figure wherever he plays.

Cardiff C (From apprentice on 27/8/82) FL 62 FLC 4 FAC 4
Luton T (£125,000 on 16/7/84) FL 30 FLC 4 FAC 1 Others 1
Sunderland (Loaned on 21/2/86) FL 12
Huddersfield T (Loaned on 26/3/87) FL 5
Manchester C (£240,000 on 1/7/88) F/PL 113+3 FLC 14 FAC 8+1 Others 2 (Transferred to Glasgow R on 11/3/97) SL 7

Aberdeen (Loaned on 20/10/90) SL 5
Middlesbrough (Loaned on 20/2/91) FL 19 Others 2
Bolton W (Loaned on 6/9/91) FL 13 Others 1
West Bromwich A (Loaned on 27/2/92) FL 9
Sheffield U (Free on 8/8/97)
Luton T (Free on 15/9/97) FL 1 FLC 2
Middlesbrough (Free on 30/1/98) FL 2

DI CANIO Paolo
Born: Rome, Italy, 9 July 1968
Height: 5'9" Weight: 11.9

This exciting Italian striker quickly became a cult hero with the fans at Sheffield Wednesday after being signed from Glasgow in the 1997 close season, making the side a lot more adventurous and scoring goals as well. And, although he played in his own particularly individual way, he was more of a team player than given credit for. Paolo finished 1997-98 as the club's leading scorer with 14 goals to his credit, having got his campaign underway with the equaliser at Wimbledon in his third game. With winners against Grimsby in the Coca Cola Cup, and against Southampton, Barnsley, and Spurs in the Premiership, as well as a lightning 50-second strike at Hillsborough, versus Newcastle, it was hardly surprising that he was so well received by all and sundry at Wednesday.

Glasgow Celtic (Signed from AC Milan on 3/7/96) SL 25+1/12 SLC 2 SC 6/3 Others 2+1
Sheffield Wed (£3,000,000 on 8/8/97) PL 34+1/12 FLC 2/2 FAC 3

Paolo Di Canio

DICHIO Daniele (Danny) Salvatore Ernest
Born: Hammersmith, 19 October 1974
Height: 6'3" Weight: 12.3
International Honours: E: U21-1; Sch

Out of contract at Queens Park Rangers during the 1997 close season, Danny signed for the Italian club, Sampdoria, but following a move to Lecce in September and a frustrating seven months abroad, the tall striker was delighted to join Sunderland in January, primarily as cover for Niall Quinn. Excellent in the air, with nice touches, and a player who brings his team mates into the game, his appearances were made mainly from the substitutes' bench, although this coming season may well see him challenging for a regular first team slot.

Queens Park R (From trainee on 17/5/93) P/FL 56+19/20 FLC 6/2 FAC 3+3 (Free to Sampdoria during 1997 close season)
Barnet (Loaned on 24/3/94) FL 9/2
Sunderland (£750,000 from Lecce on 28/1/98) FL 2+11 Others 1+2

DICKINSON Patrick James
Born: Vancouver, Canada, 6 May 1978
Height: 5'10" Weight: 10.8
International Honours: Canada: Yth

After being given a three-match run in Hull City's right-wing berth last August, Patrick was surprisingly consigned to the second string for the remainder of the campaign, but remained commendably enthusiastic throughout a difficult time. Although preferring his right, the Canadian midfielder is comfortable on either side and will be looking for a way back this coming season.

Hull C (From trainee on 11/7/97) FL 2+2 FLC 1

DICKOV Paul
Born: Livingston, 1 November 1972
Height: 5'6" Weight: 11.9
Club Honours: ECWC '94
International Honours: S: U21-4; Yth; Sch

Having adjusted to life at Manchester City in 1996-97 under four different managers, Paul pushed hard to become a regular in 1997-98, his energy and workrate culminating in him scoring nine goals. One of the few successes of the club's disappointing season, the little Scot had a settled run from September to January, scoring twice in the home game against Swindon and then showing his spirit with a brave dive into the 'keeper's path to score the winner at West Bromwich. He could probably have had a hat trick in the Swindon game, but elected to square the ball across an open goal for Lee Bradbury to tap in. Towards the end of the campaign, struggling with an injury, coupled to suspension, he was mainly used as a striker.

Arsenal (From trainee on 28/12/90) PL 6+15/3 FLC 2+2/3
Luton T (Loaned on 8/10/93) FL 8+7/1
Brighton & Hove A (Loaned on 23/3/94) FL 8/5
Manchester C (£1,000,000 on 23/8/96) FL 46+13/14 FLC 2+1 FAC 2+1

DIGBY Fraser Charles
Born: Sheffield, 23 April 1967
Height: 6'1" Weight: 13.10
Club Honours: Div 2 '96
International Honours: E: U21-5; Yth; Sch

As Swindon Town's longest serving player, this fine goalkeeper started 1997-98 with a sell-out testimonial against Manchester United – a testament to his popularity with the fans – and ended it by being voted the club's Player of the Year for the second time in a row, and the third time in his County Ground career. A consistent performer who missed just nine games all season through illness and injury, a rare sending off against QPR for handball outside his area was later struck off on appeal. Very agile, and a great shot-stopper, who uses good early throws to set up attacking moves, after refusing a new contract towards the end of the season, he was told he could leave on a free transfer under the Bosman ruling.

Manchester U (From apprentice on 25/4/85)
Swindon T (£32,000 on 25/9/86) F/PL 417 FLC 33 FAC 21 Others 33+1

DI LELLA Gustavo Martin
Born: Buenos Aires, Argentine, 6 October 1973
Height: 5'8" Weight: 10.7

This exciting Argentinian forward, cum midfielder, first came to prominence last November when scoring a tremendous 25-yard goal for non-league Blyth Spartans against Blackpool in the FA Cup, having beaten three defenders. With the goal being highlighted on Match of the Day, Darlington moved to sign him up on non-contract forms a couple of weeks later, but after just five subs' appearances he was released and returned to Blyth. He then came back into the league with Hartlepool on John Burridge's recommendation in mid-March and, in his second subs' outing, scored two late goals to earn a draw at home to Cambridge. There is no doubting his ability, but it will be interesting to see whether he can fully adapt to the demands of the third division.

Darlington (Free from Blyth Spartans on 2/12/97) FL 0+5 (Free to Blyth Spartans on 3/2/98)
Hartlepool U (Free on 20/3/98) FL 1+4/2

DILLON Paul William
Born: Limerick, 22 October 1978
Height: 5'9" Weight: 10.11
International Honours: Ei: U21-1; Yth

Although injury ruled him out of contention for a Rotherham first team place until the New Year, when he forced his way into the team again, Paul demonstrated what a gutsy character he was with some determined displays in a left-sided defensive role. Definitely a star of the future, with a quick turn of speed, and a good tackler, he was selected for the Republic of Ireland U21 team.

Rotherham U (From trainee on 7/3/97) FL 25+4/1

DI MATTEO Roberto
Born: Switzerland, 29 May 1970
Height: 5'10" Weight: 12.5
Club Honours: FAC '97; FLC '98; ECWC '98
International Honours: Italy: 34

For the second year running, Roberto broke the hearts of Middlesbrough fans by scoring against them in a Wembley cup final – only this time, in 1997-98, it took him 106

minutes longer! An influential figure behind the rise of Chelsea over the last two years, and an automatic choice for Cesare Maldini's Assurri, the fact that he was also an automatic choice for Chelsea in the squad rotation days of Ruud Gullit and Gianluca Vialli speaks volumes for his worth to the Blues. A hard-working linkman with plenty of skill on the ball, and a keen eye for goal, he scored one of the goals of the season against Arsenal in the Coca Cola Cup semi final at the Bridge – almost a carbon copy of the FA Cup final goal against Middlesbrough – when he picked the ball up just inside the opposition's half, surged forward, and smashed a right-footed screamer into the roof of the net from 30 yards. He scored other super goals against Tottenham Hotspur and Real Betis to show his all-round quality. Expected to be an integral part of Italy's assault on the World Cup in France, he signed an extended contract with Chelsea until 2002. And as a confirmed Anglophile, he loves London's lifestyle and turned restaurateur when, in partnership with two friends, he opened up close to Stamford Bridge. *Stop Press:* Started the first two games for Italy in the World Cup, but was not called upon again prior to the side going out on penalties to France in the quarter-final stage.

Chelsea (£4,900,000 from Lazio, via FC Aarac, FC Zurich and Schaffhausen, on 17/7/96) PL 61+3/11 FLC 7/3 FAC 8/2 Others 9/3

DINNING Anthony (Tony)
Born: Wallsend, 12 April 1975
Height: 6'0" Weight: 12.11

Widely regarded as Stockport's most improved player in 1997-98, Tony was well on his way to establishing himself as a first team regular when he broke his leg at Sunderland in March. Filled a number of roles with steely efficiency, from right back to midfield and central defence, and scored five goals in the process. There was no doubting his importance to the side and, hopefully, he will be back on song before too long.

Newcastle U (From trainee on 1/10/93)
Stockport Co (Free on 23/6/94) FL 75+25/8 FLC 7+5/1 FAC 1+7 Others 6+1/2

DIUK Wayne John
Born: Nottingham, 26 May 1980
Height: 5'11" Weight: 11.0

Still a trainee, and still young enough to be eligible for youth football in 1997-98, Wayne continued to develop his skills in reserve football at Notts County, and began to press for a senior place. A fast, attacking right-sided midfield player, and wing back, he is definitely one for the future.

Notts Co (Trainee) FL 0+2 FLC 0+1 Others 0+1

DIXON Benjamin (Ben) Marcus
Born: Lincoln, 16 September 1974
Height: 6'1" Weight: 11.0

Again playing very few games for Blackpool in his second season at Bloomfield Road, Ben had a spell at left back during last November and December, before making way following the arrival of

John Hills from Everton. A useful player to have available when you want added height, and able to play in midfield as well as further forward if required, he was released during the summer.

Lincoln C (From trainee on 4/11/92) FL 33+10 FLC 2 FAC 0+1 Others 2+1
Blackpool (£20,000 on 12/7/96) FL 9+9 FLC 2 FAC 3 Others 3

DIXON Lee Michael
Born: Manchester, 17 March 1964
Height: 5'9" Weight: 11.8
Club Honours: Div 1 '89, '91; PL '98; FAC '93, '98; ECWC '94
International Honours: E: 21; B-4

Despite his age, Lee has lost none of his verve or enthusiasm. Indeed, such was his consistency in 1997-98 that the manager, Arsene Wenger, extended his contract, while his 40 games played saw him win championship and FA Cup winners' medals

as the Gunners stormed to the double for the second time in their history. Now in his testimonial year, and the very epitome of the Arsenal spirit, as witnessed by his salute to the fans after the club's victories over Manchester United and Wimbledon, he never hides when up against it, always ready to be counted, and has a great attitude to the game. A natural winner, the right back is still one of the best attacking full backs in the country when getting forward to deliver telling crosses, and remains cool under pressure. Has also developed an excellent understanding with Ray Parlour.

Burnley (From juniors on 21/7/82) FL 4 FLC 1
Chester C (Free on 16/2/84) FL 56+1/1 FLC 2 FAC 1 Others 3
Bury (Free on 15/7/85) FL 45/5 FLC 4 FAC 8/1 Others 1
Stoke C (£40,000 on 18/7/86) FL 71/5 FLC 6 FAC 7 Others 4
Arsenal (£400,000 on 29/1/88) F/PL 346+6/20 FLC 45 FAC 36/1 Others 31

Lee Dixon

DOBBIN James (Jim)
Born: Dunfermline, 17 September 1963
Height: 5'10" Weight: 11.0
International Honours: S: Yth

Released by Rotherham during the 1997 close season, Jim showed much of his old skill on his return to Doncaster, but was often fighting the battle on his own as the club's fight for league survival progressed. His departure to Scarborough, where he played one game before moving on to Grimsby a week later, in the last weeks of the campaign, was, in many ways, the final nail in the Rovers' coffin, and the midfield was much the poorer for his absence. Was freed by Town during the summer.

Glasgow Celtic (Free from Whitburn BC on 9/10/80) SL 1+1 SLC 4/1
Motherwell (Loaned on 1/2/84) SL 1+1
Doncaster Rov (£25,000 on 19/3/84) FL 56+8/13 FLC 5/1 FAC 2 Others 3
Barnsley (£35,000 on 19/9/86) FL 116+13/12 FLC 3+1 FAC 11 Others 4/1
Grimsby T (£55,000 on 15/7/91) FL 154+10/21 FLC 13/3 FAC 7+1/1 Others 5/1
Rotherham U (Free on 2/8/96) FL 17+2 FLC 0+1 FAC 1 Others 1
Doncaster Rov (Free on 22/8/97) FL 28+3 FAC 1 Others 1
Scarborough (Free on 20/3/98) FL 1
Grimsby T (Free on 26/3/98) FL 1+1

DOBIE Robert Scott
Born: Workington, 10 October 1978
Height: 6'1" Weight: 11.12

A locally-born player, who scored on his debut near the end of the 1996-97 season, Scott featured in half of Carlisle's league games last term, although the majority of these appearances were as a substitute, and his solitary goal came in the defeat at Oldham. Time though is on his side, and this tall, well-built striker will be hoping for better things in 1998-99.

Carlisle U (From trainee on 10/5/97) FL 9+16/2 FLC 0+4 FAC 0+1 Others 1+1

DOBSON Anthony (Tony) John
Born: Coventry, 5 February 1969
Height: 6'1" Weight: 12.6
Club Honours: FAYC '87
International Honours: E: U21-4

A free transfer signing from Portsmouth immediately prior to the start of 1997-98, Tony initially went to West Bromwich Albion on a non-contract basis before being upgraded to a full professional. Very strong and capable, and a defender who is able to occupy all five outfield positions in front of his 'keeper, although preferring a left-sided berth, he failed to hold down a regular place during the campaign but was a valuable member of the squad.

Coventry C (From apprentice on 7/7/86) FL 51+3/1 FLC 5+3 Others 0+1
Blackburn Rov (£300,000 on 17/1/91) F/PL 36+5 FLC 5 FAC 2 Others 1
Portsmouth (£150,000 on 22/9/93) FL 48+5/2 FLC 6 FAC 1+2 Others 4/1
Oxford U (Loaned on 15/12/94) FL 5
Peterborough U (Loaned on 29/1/96) FL 4
West Bromwich A (Free on 8/8/97) FL 6+5 FLC 0+2 FAC 2

DOBSON Ryan Adam
Born: Wellington, 24 September 1978
Height: 5'6" Weight: 10.10
A product of Chester City's youth policy, and a first year professional, Ryan made half a dozen appearances, deputising at right back last season, but, unfortunately, was not offered a contract and was released on a free during the summer.
Chester C (From trainee on 2/7/97) FL 6

DOBSON Warren Edward
Born: North Shields, 5 November 1978
Height: 6'1" Weight: 13.7
Released by Queens Park Rangers during the 1997 close season, having reached the end of his YT scheme, he was on trial at Scarborough when signed by Hartlepool to solve an urgent goalkeeping problem just one week into 1997-98. Although he acquitted himself well, he was allowed to leave the club, working as a barman, but three months later he was back to play in an FA Cup tie against Macclesfield Town and, shortly after, he was signed on a contract to the end of the campaign. Unfortunately, he did not get any further first team chances and was released in the summer.
Hartlepool U (Free from Queens Park R juniors on 22/8/97) FL 1 FLC 1 FAC 1

DODD Jason Robert
Born: Bath, 2 November 1970
Height: 5'10" Weight: 12.3
International Honours: E: U21-8
1997-98 was yet another splendid season for the Southampton captain and right back as he missed just three games throughout. A very experienced player, who is equally comfortable when defending or attacking, Jason is not a prolific scorer, but got his customary "one a season" screamer against West Ham in October. His ability to win the ball cleanly, without clattering his opponent, is a great asset, as is his distribution and crossing, and it is perhaps surprising that he has not been recognised at senior international level to date.
Southampton (£50,000 from Bath C on 15/3/89) F/PL 215+16/7 FLC 28+1 FAC 22/1 Others 5

DOHERTY Gary Michael Thomas
Born: Carndonagh, 31 January 1980
Height: 6'2" Weight: 13.1
International Honours: E: Yth
A tall, teenage striker, Gary had an impressive full debut for Luton in a 3-0 home win against Plymouth Argyle last October, heading on his 'keeper's clearance for Tony Thorpe to score, having signed professional forms during the 1997 close season. Brave in the air, he played for the Republic of Ireland's U18s, helped Luton's youth side to a second consecutive South East Counties title, and was joint Young Player of the Year. Very much a prospect for the future, he might have got more opportunities for the Hatters if the team had not been struggling.
Luton T (From trainee on 2/7/97) FL 1+9 FAC 0+1

DOHERTY Thomas (Tommy) Edward
Born: Bristol, 17 March 1979
Height: 5'8" Weight: 9.13
The introduction of this youngster into Bristol City's midfield last season transformed the Club's fortunes, as he added much bite and aggression to a department that was extremely deficient in these commodities. Looks to be City's best home produced young player for many years and reminds many of Gerry Gow, who performed so magnificently for the club throughout the 1970s. Unfortunately, a bout of influenza reduced his effectiveness somewhat towards the end of the campaign, though he was rewarded with selection for the England U19 squad.
Bristol C (From trainee on 8/7/97) FL 22+8/2 FLC 1 FAC 1+1

DOMINGUEZ Jose Manuel Martins
Born: Lisbon, Portugal, 16 February 1974
Height: 5'3" Weight: 10.0
Club Honours: Div 2 '95
International Honours: Portugal: 3
Having earlier spent time at Birmingham City in 1993-94 and 1994-95, this pacy Sporting Lisbon winger jumped at the opportunity to come back to England at the start of 1997-98, making his debut for Tottenham at home against Derby County. Jose impressed from the outset with his enthusiasm to win the ball and to raid down the wing, leaving even the most experienced defenders in his wake. An accomplished striker in his past, the diminutive Portuguese star bagged two goals in succession in the home 3-2 victory over Sheffield Wednesday and the away 3-2 defeat at Southampton. Despite his size, he has great strength on the ball and is very skilful at keeping it close to his feet and delivering quality crosses in his role as a utility player. Many opponents found it difficult to match his pace, which often made him the target of some hefty challenges throughout the campaign and eventually took their toll in December, as he became another casualty on Spurs' long injury list. Hoping to return to full fitness in 1998-99, Jose will find appearances a challenge with the reintroduction of Darren Anderton, Andy Sinton, and Allan Nielsen, to name a few, but still has a tremendous amount to offer the side as a squad player.
Birmingham C (£180,000 from Benfica on 9/3/94) FL 15+10/3 FLC 1+2 FAC 2+1 Others 2+2/1 (£1,800,000 to Sporting Lisbon on 1/8/95)
Tottenham H (£1,600,000 on 12/8/97) PL 8+10/2 FLC 2+1 FAC 1

DONALDSON O'Neill McKay
Born: Birmingham, 24 November 1969
Height: 6'0" Weight: 12.4
A pacy, enthusiastic striker who again, in 1997-98, was unable to secure a fair run at Sheffield Wednesday, he moved to Stoke on a free in March after partaking a loan spell at Oxford, where he scored in successive games against Ipswich and Stockport. On going straight into a side that was on a losing run, O'Neill proved to be a bubbly,

committed personality, but unfortunately suffered a leg injury in the home win over Queens Park Rangers – his second game for the club – which disrupted his chances and ended with him being released during the summer.
Shrewsbury T (Free from Hinckley T on 13/11/91) FL 15+13/4 Others 1
Doncaster Rov (Free on 10/8/94) FL 7+2/2 FLC 2 Others 0+1
Mansfield T (Loaned on 23/12/94) FL 4/6 FAC 1/1
Sheffield Wed (£50,000 on 9/1/95) PL 4+10/3
Oxford U (Loaned on 30/1/98) FL 6/2
Stoke C (Free on 13/3/98) FL 2

DONCEL-VARCARCEL Antonio
Born: Lugo, Spain, 31 January 1967
Height: 6'0" Weight: 12.1
Hull City's Spanish centre back began last season on a bad note, being sent off in a defeat at Peterborough in August and paying a heavy price for his dismissal as he struggled to regain regular selection until March. The right-footed defender, who is also studying at Hull University, returned with some typically cultured displays, but his year almost ended as it started when he saw the red card again against Brighton in City's penultimate game of 1997-98.
Hull C (Free from Ferrol on 8/8/96) FL 30+8/2 FLC 5 FAC 1+1 Others 1

DONNELLY Mark Paul
Born: Leeds, 22 December 1979
Height: 6'0" Weight: 12.0
Having made his league debut in 1996-97, and still a trainee, Mark was given another taste of first team football when a number of the Rovers' juniors were fielded against Lincoln City last March, following an exodus of senior players. Is a hard-working midfielder seeking to find his way in the game, and aims to do it.
Doncaster Rov (Trainee) FL 8+3/1

DONOVAN Kevin
Born: Halifax, 17 December 1971
Height: 5'8" Weight: 11.2
Club Honours: AMC '98
In following returning boss, Alan Buckley, from West Bromwich during the 1997 close season, Kevin quickly established himself with the Grimsby fans as an ever present in 1997-98. A battling midfielder, his penetrating runs down the right flank, and accurate cross balls, were the cause of much consternation amongst opposing defences, while his quick reactions and accuracy in front of goal made him the club's leading scorer for the season. Having already been to Wembley, when picking up an AWS medal from the victory over Bournemouth, it was his goal that beat Northampton in the second division play-off final. Was selected for the award-winning PFA second division side by his fellow professionals, before picking up the Mariners' Player of the Year award.
Huddersfield T (From trainee on 11/10/89) FL 11+9/1 FLC 1+1 FAC 1/2 Others 4

Kevin Donovan (right)

Halifax T (Loaned on 13/2/92) FL 6
West Bromwich A (£70,000 on 1/10/92) FL 139+6/11 FLC 9+2/6 FAC 7+1/3 Others 15+1/4
Grimsby T (£300,000 on 29/7/97) FL 46/16 FLC 6/1 FAC 6/1 Others 9/3

DONOWA Brian Louis (Louie)
Born: Ipswich, 24 September 1964
Height: 5'9" Weight: 12.2
Club Honours: FAYC '83; FLC '85; Div 2 '95; AMC '95
International Honours: E: U21-3
Signed on a free transfer from Birmingham at the start of 1997-98, Louie was released after seven games in the early part of the season, having failed either to get on the scoresheet or set Bescot alight. A great crowd pleaser on his day, as a pacy left winger who could leave defenders in his tracks, Walsall fans did not see the best of him.
Norwich C (From apprentice on 28/9/82) FL 56+6/11 FLC 13+2/3 FAC 1+2/1 (£400,000 to Real Deportivo on 1/2/86)
Stoke C (Loaned on 23/12/85) FL 4/1 FAC 0+1
Ipswich T (Free from Willem 11 on 14/8/89) FL 17+6/1 FLC 0+2 FAC 2 Others 2+1/1
Bristol C (£55,000 on 10/8/90) FL 11+13/3 FLC 1 FAC 0+1
Birmingham C (£60,000 on 30/8/91) FL 78+38/18 FLC 16+6 FAC 8/1 Others 9+3/2
Burnley (Loaned on 15/1/93) FL 4 Others 2
Shrewsbury T (Loaned on 27/1/94) FL 4
Walsall (Loaned on 14/10/96) FL 6/1
Peterborough U (Free on 13/12/96) FL 16+6/1 Others 4+1/2
Walsall (Free on 7/8/97) FL 5+1 FLC 1

DOOLAN John
Born: Liverpool, 7 May 1974
Height: 6'1" Weight: 13.0
After being linked with several other clubs during 1997-98, John joined Barnet in January, having made 28 appearances for Mansfield during the campaign to date. Playing no mean part in the Bees reaching the play offs, this tough midfielder is not only a destroyer, but is a good, neat passer in his own right.
Everton (From trainee on 1/6/92)
Mansfield T (Free on 2/9/94) FL 128+3/10 FLC 8/1 FAC 7/2 Others 4+1/1
Barnet (£60,000 on 13/1/98) FL 17

DORNER Mario
Born: Baden, Austria, 21 March 1970
Height: 5'10" Weight: 12.0
An Austrian forward who arrived at Darlington from Motherwell, along with fellow-countryman, Franz Resch, last October, his hard running and excellent close control soon made him popular with the Feetham's crowd. In ending the season as second top scorer with 11 goals, he especially impressed with winners against Leyton Orient, Macclesfield, and Brighton, and will be looking for more of the same in 1998-99. Also, very strong, and holds the ball up well.
Motherwell (Free from VFB Modling on 1/7/97) SL 2 SLC 0+2
Darlington (Free on 17/10/97) FL 25+2/10 FAC 3/1

DOUGLAS Stuart Anthony
Born: Enfield, 9 April 1978
Height: 5'9" Weight: 11.5
A lively, fast, and aggressive Luton striker, Stuart seems to be best used when introduced as a substitute, where his injection of pace catches out the tiring legs of the opposition defences. This was particularly illustrated in the televised home game against Southend last season, when he came

on and scored the only goal. Although harassing and pressurising defences, and chasing lost causes adds excitement and urgency to the game, with the effect of lifting his team mates, he is often less impressive when included in the starting line-up and needs to prove himself to be a 90-minute player if he is to build upon the reputation of his teenage years.
Luton T (From trainee on 2/5/96) FL 10+24/2 FLC 3+2/1 FAC 1 Others 0+1

DOWELL Wayne Anthony
Born: Durham, 28 December 1973
Height: 5'10" Weight: 12.6
A left back, Wayne signed for Doncaster during the 1997 close season, after being released by Rochdale, and showed up well in the summer friendlies. However, taken off after just half an hour of the opening game of 1997-98 at Shrewsbury, he was subsequently released during the following week.
Burnley (From trainee on 27/3/93) FL 6 FLC 1 FAC 2
Carlisle U (Loaned on 29/3/96) FL 2+5
Rochdale (Free on 25/7/96) FL 6+1
Doncaster Rov (Free on 4/8/97) FL 1

DOWIE Iain
Born: Hatfield, 9 January 1965
Height: 6'1" Weight: 13.11
International Honours: NI: 49; U23-1; U21-1
The big-hearted Northern Ireland international forward brought the curtain down on his eventful career at West Ham when he joined Queens Park Rangers last January, having been unable to score since October 1996, despite always giving 100 per-cent effort, and being a handful to any defender. Signed, along with Keith Rowland, in a deal that saw Trevor Sinclair going in the opposite direction, Iain scored his first goal in over a year in a 1-1 draw at West Bromwich, before injury kept him out of the last few games of the campaign. A good target man, and an excellent header of the ball, particularly at the far post, the youngsters at Loftus Road are sure to benefit from his invaluable experience.
Luton T (£30,000 from Hendon on 14/12/88) FL 53+13/16 FLC 3+1 FAC 1+2 Others 5/4
Fulham (Loaned on 13/9/89) FL 5/1
West Ham U (£480,000 on 22/3/91) FL 12/4
Southampton (£500,000 on 3/9/91) F/PL 115+7/30 FLC 8+3/1 FAC 6/1 Others 4
Crystal Palace (£400,000 on 13/1/95) P/FL 19/6 FAC 6/4
West Ham U (£500,000 on 8/9/95) PL 58+10/8 FLC 10+1/2 FAC 3+1/1
Queens Park R (Signed on 30/1/98) FL 9+2/1

DOYLE Maurice
Born: Ellesmere Port, 17 October 1969
Height: 5'8" Weight: 10.7
Maurice is one of those players that can perform anywhere you ask him to, although his ideal spot is in midfield where his tenacity is just what the Millwall faithful want from their players. Despite only starting 11 times in 1997-98, his level of fitness was unquestionable with his non-stop running throughout the game. Good in the air for such a small man, he reads the game well, tackles strongly, and gave the

team that extra motivation when most needed. Was released during the summer.

Crewe Alex (From trainee on 11/7/88) FL 6+2/2
Queens Park R (£120,000 on 21/4/89) PL 6
Crewe Alex (Loaned on 17/1/91) FL 6+1/2 FAC 2
Millwall (Signed on 16/5/95) FL 42+24/1 FLC 3 FAC 1 Others 2+2

DOZZELL Jason Alvin Winans
Born: Ipswich, 9 December 1967
Height: 6'1" Weight: 13.8
Club Honours: Div 2 '92
International Honours: E: U21-9; Yth

Released by Tottenham last September, Jason, who still lives in Ipswich, asked if he could train at Portman Road while he looked for a new club. However, the club's early season injury crisis led to him being offered a weekly contract and he returned to action in a Town shirt against Manchester City. He then went on to play in nine of the next ten games, scoring twice, including one of the goals which beat Oxford in the Coca Cola Cup to set up the home tie with Chelsea. The Oxford game proved to be his last appearance, as the club cancelled his contract two days later, but a month on he was back in league football, this time with second division Northampton, where he became an integral part of a side that reached the play-off final. As an experienced midfielder, with an excellent touch on the ball, most of his goals were scored by simply being in the right place at the right time, while his excellent aerial ability and lays off continued to bring others into play.

Ipswich T (From apprentice on 20/12/84) F/PL 312+20/52 FLC 29+1/3 FAC 22/12 Others 22/4
Tottenham H (£1,900,000 on 1/8/93) PL 68+16/13 FLC 8+2 FAC 4+1/1
Ipswich T (Free on 2/10/97) FL 8/1 FLC 2/1
Northampton T (Free on 19/12/97) FL 18+3/4 FAC 1 Others 3

DRAPER Mark Andrew
Born: Long Eaton, 11 November 1970
Height: 5'10" Weight: 12.4
Club Honours: FLC '96
International Honours: E: U21-3

As in 1996-97, Mark was a regular in the Aston Villa midfield in 1997-98, and again he was the lynchpin between defence and attack as he continued his improvement to put together a good run of performances. Apart from an ankle injury, sustained in the FA Cup tie against Coventry, he basically remained injury free and, despite being the only recognised midfielder in the side on many occasions, still found time to get forward to score the odd goal. Although possessing the ability to rifle shots in from the edge of the box, his three goals last season were all from close range, and included a brace at Tottenham on Boxing Day. A key player for Villa, he probably needs better support if the side are going to challenge for the Premiership this coming term.

Notts Co (From trainee on 12/12/88) FL 206+16/40 FLC 14+1/2 FAC 10/2 Others 21+2/5
Leicester C (£1,250,000 on 22/7/94) PL 39/5 FLC 2 FAC 2
Aston Villa (£3,250,000 on 5/7/95) PL 95+1/5 FLC 10+1/1 FAC 9/2 Others 9

Jason Dozzell

DREYER John Brian
Born: Alnwick, 11 June 1963
Height: 6'1" Weight: 13.2

A regular in Bradford's central defence at the beginning of 1997-98, although just as comfortable anywhere down the left-hand side, whether it be at full back or in midfield, John was unfortunate to suffer serious foot ligament damage in December, an injury that put him out of action for the rest of the campaign. Badly missed for his experience, 100 per-cent effort, and ability at set pieces, he is raring to go in 1998-99 and can hardly wait.*

Oxford U (Signed from Wallingford on 8/1/85) FL 57+3/2 FLC 10+1 FAC 2 Others 3
Torquay U (Loaned on 13/12/85) FL 5
Fulham (Loaned on 27/3/88) FL 12/2
Luton T (£140,000 on 27/6/88) FL 212+2/13 FLC 13+1/1 FAC 14 Others 8/1
Stoke C (Free on 15/7/94) FL32+17/3 FLC 5 FAC 1 Others 4+1/1
Bolton W (Loaned on 23/3/95) FL 1+1 Others 1+1
Bradford C (£25,000 on 6/11/96) FL 42+3/1 FLC 4 FAC 3/3

DRUCE Mark Andrew
Born: Oxford, 3 March 1974
Height: 5'11" Weight: 12.8

Having created quite an impression when first joining Rotherham on loan in 1996-97, he made only a handful of first team appearances last season, despite scoring several good goals for the reserves. Although a skilful striker with pace, he rarely displayed his full potential and could not hold down a regular place, before being released during the summer.

Oxford U (From trainee on 3/12/91) FL 18+34/4 FLC 1+3 Others 2+1
Rotherham U (£50,000 on 26/9/96) FL 21+13/4 FLC 2 FAC 1/1 Others 0+1

DRURY Adam James
Born: Cambridge, 29 August 1978
Height: 5'10" Weight: 11.8

The young Peterborough defender who, although not in the side at the start of 1997-98, made the left-back slot his own before suffering a dislocated shoulder which cut short his season. A confident youngster, who makes time on the ball, and one who is certain to eventually play at a higher level, Adam was voted Player of the Year by both the club and the supporters.

Peterborough U (From trainee on 3/7/96) FL 29+8/1 FLC 2 FAC 1 Others 4

DRYDEN Richard Andrew
Born: Stroud, 14 June 1969
Height: 6'0" Weight: 13.12
Club Honours: Div 4 '90

A Southampton defender who completed his second season at Premiership level in 1997-98, having been written off by some commentators was restricted to 14 first team appearances by the form of Claus Lundekvam and Ken Monkou, and injury. However, nonetheless, he performed with great composure and strength when called upon and the Saints are fortunate to have such a player to draft in whenever needed. Always reliable, the left-sided central defender is an added bonus at free kicks and corners, where his knock-ons create opportunities for others.

Bristol Rov (From trainee on 14/7/87) FL 12+1 FLC 2+1 FAC 0+2 Others 2
Exeter C (Loaned on 22/9/88) FL 6
Exeter C (Signed on 8/3/89) FL 86/13 FLC 7/2 FAC 2 Others 4
Notts Co (£250,000 on 9/8/91) FL 30+1/1 FLC 1+1 FAC 2+1 Others 2
Plymouth Arg (Loaned on 18/11/92) FL 5 Others 1
Birmingham C (£165,000 on 19/3/93) FL 48 FLC 5 FAC 1
Bristol C (£140,000 on 16/12/94) FL 32+5/2 FLC 4 FAC 1+1 Others 2
Southampton (£150,000 on 6/8/96) PL 39+3/1 FLC 7/3

DRYSDALE Jason
Born: Bristol, 17 November 1970
Height: 5'10" Weight: 13.0
Club Honours: FAYC '89; Div 2 '96
International Honours: E: Yth

A regular in the Swindon side at the start of last season, before injury sidelined him in early October, he was unable to force his way back into Steve McMahon's plans, making just two more starts for the club.

The left back's unhappy stay at the County Ground finally ended when his contract was cancelled in March and he left to join Northampton, who were flying high in the second division. However, with places few and far between, apart from one game, Jason has not yet really had a chance to adhere himself to Town's fans. Is the son of Brian, who played for Lincoln, Hartlepool, Bristol City, and Oxford, between 1960 and 1978.

Watford (From trainee on 8/9/88) FL 135+10/11 FLC 8+1/2 FAC 2 Others 4
Newcastle U (£425,000 on 2/8/94)
Swindon T (£340,000 on 23/3/95) FL 35+7 FLC 4 FAC 2+4 Others 2
Northampton T (Free on 26/3/98) FL 1

DUBERRY Michael Wayne
Born: Enfield, 14 October 1975
Height: 6'1" Weight: 13.6
Club Honours: FLC '98; ECWC '98
International Honours: E: U21-5

Unfortunately, Michael had another injury-interrupted season in 1997-98, after a ruptured achilles tendon sustained in January 1997 put an end to his previous campaign, thus denying him the chance of an FA Cup Winners' medal. The muscular central defender made his comeback in the third match, but could only put a run of five consecutive matches together before picking up a serious ankle injury against Arsenal in September. Thankfully, for all Blues' fans, he re-appeared in December, his return coinciding with a solid run by Chelsea as they remained unbeaten for six matches and challenged Manchester United at the top of the Premiership. His strength in the tackle, pace and power in the air, were vital factors in Chelsea's twin cup triumphs and his two medals were some consolation for missing the 1997 FA Cup final. After England's qualification for France '98, despite having made just two England U21 appearances during the season, the powerful "Doobs" was being touted as a surprise outsider for the World Cup squad and, although he just missed out, surely his turn will come in the future. With fellow London youngsters, Sol Campbell and Rio Ferdinand also showing outstanding potential, these three could form a strong defensive trio for England in the future.

Chelsea (From trainee on 7/6/93) PL 59+2/1 FLC 5 FAC 10/2 Others 6
Bournemouth (Loaned on 29/9/95) FL 7 Others 1

DUBLIN Dion
Born: Leicester, 22 April 1969
Height: 6'2" Weight: 12.4
Club Honours: Div 3 '91
International Honours: E: 3

1997-98 was an outstanding season for the big, jovial Coventry centre forward as he won his first England cap against Chile at Wembley in February, and lined himself up for Glenn Hoddle's France '98 squad, whether playing at centre forward or centre half. Nominated for the PFA player of the year, he was City's top scorer for the fourth year running and broke Cyrille Regis' record for the most goals scored by a Coventry City player in their top-flight

history and became the first City player for over 20 years to score 20 goals in a season. The only blemish was his sending off at Blackburn, for the second year running, when the referee felt he had lead with his elbow in a challenge with Colin Hendry. Despite video evidence showing he had not made contact, the suspension stood. This, however, seemed to motivate him to higher things and, whether playing centre forward or centre half, he always looked dangerous, scoring penalties in four successive home league games, and in the home cup tie with Sheffield United, ending with seven in all. His hat trick on the opening day against Chelsea brought the house down, and Dion was made skipper when Gary McAllister was injured, being an inspiration to the side in leading by example. Although his contract is up at the end of next season, and he rejected a new deal at Coventry in February, City fans hope and pray that the club up their offer and persuade him to stay.

Norwich C (From Oakham U on 24/3/88)
Cambridge U (Free on 2/8/88) FL 133+23/52 FLC 8+2/5 FAC 21/11 Others 14+1/5
Manchester U (£1,000,000 on 7/8/92) PL 4+8/2 FLC 1+1/1 FAC 1+1 Others 0+1
Coventry C (£2,000,000 on 9/9/94) PL 134+1/58 FLC 9+2/3 FAC 13/7

DUBLIN Keith Barry
Born: High Wycombe, 29 January 1966
Height: 6'0" Weight: 12.10
International Honours: E: Yth

Keith managed what was probably his best season for Southend United in 1997-98, with consistent defensive performances, whether at full back or centre half, being enhanced with some important goals, including two in the amazing 4-4 home draw with York City. Never one to give less than 100 per cent, he took over the captaincy from Andy Harris towards the end of the campaign, and led the team with full commitment.

Chelsea (From apprentice on 28/1/84) FL 50+1 FLC 6 FAC 5 Others 5+1
Brighton & Hove A (£3,500 on 14/8/87) FL 132/5 FLC 5 FAC 7/1 Others 7
Watford (£275,000 on 17/7/90) FL 165+3/2 FLC 12 FAC 4 Others 6
Southend U (Signed on 21/7/94) FL 169+1/9 FLC 9 FAC 5 Others 2

DUCROS Andrew (Andy) John
Born: Evesham, 16 September 1977
Height: 5'4" Weight: 9.8
International Honours: E: Yth; Sch

1997-98 was a disappointing season for the slight, young Coventry striker who was looking to substantially increase his appearances at the club, having promised much previously. In the event, he started only one game, against Crystal Palace at home, when City had an injury crisis, and was a sub on three other occasions, but suffered the embarrassment of being subbed himself against Leeds. Although well down the pecking order, Andy is still an exciting prospect, with an eye for goal and speed to match, and could come good if given a run of games.

Coventry C (From trainee on 16/9/94) PL 2+6 FLC 0+1

DUDLEY Craig Bryan
Born: Newark, 12 September 1979
Height: 5'10" Weight: 11.2
Club Honours: Div 3 '98
International Honours: E: Yth

A promising youngster who developed through the Notts County youth ranks where he was a prolific scorer and became a regular member of the England youth squad, Craig did not quite manage to establish and retain a first team place at County in 1997-98, and spent a short spell on loan at Shrewsbury in January to help broaden his experience. Made three starts at Town and, while unable to improve his strike rate, he showed enough natural speed on and off the ball and some fine lay-offs to indicate that he has a good future. Was delighted to receive a third division championship medal as his reward for 17 league appearances.
Notts Co (From trainee on 2/4/97) FL 11+16/3 FLC 1+1/1 FAC 1+2
Shrewsbury T (Loaned on 8/1/98) FL 3+1

DUERDEN Ian Christopher
Born: Burnley, 27 March 1978
Height: 5'9" Weight: 12.6
Another of Burnley's young strikers struggling for first team recognition in 1997-98, Ian made his debut at home to Bristol Rovers in September, but, thereafter, continued his progress in the reserves and on loan at Conference side, Telford. A first-year professional, and former trainee, the 20-year old was released during the summer.
Burnley (From trainee on 11/7/96) FL 1

DUFF Damien Anthony
Born: Ballyboden, 2 March 1979
Height: 5'10" Weight: 9.7
International Honours: Ei: 2; B-1; Yth; Sch
The youth team product was thrust into the Blackburn first team in 1997-98, and, while used sparingly, he showed himself to be fast, with great control, and a player who could comprehensively beat opponents. His ability to get to the by-line and pull the ball back thrilled the crowd, and when forced to play in the middle against West Ham he scored two fine goals. While promising to be the most exciting player within the club, there was no doubting his potential and, by the end of the season, he had moved on from the Republic of Ireland "B" side to make two full appearances, against Czechoslovakia and Mexico.
Blackburn Rov (Signed from Lourdes Celtic on 5/3/96) PL 18+9/4 FLC 2+1 FAC 3+1/1

DUGUID Karl Anthony
Born: Hitchin, 21 March 1978
Height: 5'11" Weight: 11.7
A young forward, or attacking Colchester midfielder, Karl successfully put the previous year's penalty disappointment at Wembley behind him and continued his progress last season. Appeared mainly as a substitute, contributing three goals and, most memorably, a last-minute effort to beat Hull City in a 4-3 thriller on Easter Monday. He also made his second appearance at

Wembley in May – quite a record for such a young player, who has only just turned 20.
Colchester U (From trainee on 16/7/96) FL 23+34/7 FLC 0+2 FAC 3+2 Others 1+5

DUNCAN Andrew (Andy)
Born: Hexham, 20 October 1977
Height: 5'11" Weight: 13.0
International Honours: E: Sch
A Manchester United professional since the summer of 1996, Andy was given his first taste of league football when signed on loan by Cambridge last January. Quickly developing from a wing back to a strong centre back, who read the game very well, he proved to be a sound footballer with a competitive attitude, and joined United on a permanent basis in April.
Manchester U (From trainee on 10/7/96)
Cambridge U (Signed on 9/1/98) FL 18+1

DUNGEY James Andrew
Born: Plymouth, 7 February 1978
Height: 5'10" Weight: 12.0
International Honours: E: Yth; Sch
Unable to get a game at Plymouth in 1997-98, the young goalkeeper arrived at Exeter in December, but found himself in a similar situation as Ashley Bayes deputy, playing just once. An agile, and sound shot-stopper, James will be looking for more experience in the first team this coming season.
Plymouth Arg (From trainee on 3/10/95) FL 9+1 Others 4
Exeter C (Free on 10/12/97) FL 1

DUNN Iain George
Born: Goole, 1 April 1970
Height: 5'10" Weight: 12.0
International Honours: E: Sch
Ian's second spell at Chesterfield, which began in February 1997, developed into something of a parody of his first. The clever midfielder's first team starts last season were limited as he spent most of his time on the bench, even finding himself substituted twice, having first come on as a sub! At his best, he fits in well behind the forwards, while bringing a range of options to the left-hand side.
York C (From juniors on 7/7/88) FL 46+31/11 FLC 3+1 FAC 3+1 Others 1+3
Chesterfield (Free on 14/8/91) FL 8+5/1
Scarborough (Free on 27/8/92)
Peterborough U (Free on 29/9/92) Others 0+1
Scarborough (Free on 9/10/92)
Huddersfield T (Free from Goole T on 4/12/92) FL 62+58/14 FLC 6+4/3 FAC 7+3/3 Others 11+7/9
Scunthorpe U (Loaned on 20/9/96) FL 3
Chesterfield (£30,000 on 28/2/97) FL 10+8 FAC 0+2 Others 1

DUNNE Joseph (Joe) John
Born: Dublin, 25 May 1973
Height: 5'9" Weight: 11.6
International Honours: Ei: U21-1; Yth; Sch
Joe scored a stunning 25-yard special in the opening pre-1997-98 season friendly, but five minutes later broke his ankle and was out of action for several months. He returned in November and played regularly, until going on the transfer list at his own

request after being dropped in January. However, after regaining and retaining a regular place at the start of March, he scored two absolutely vital goals in the promotion run-in, with the winner at Lincoln, and a late equaliser against Hull City at Layer Road. Was released during the summer.
Gillingham (From trainee on 9/8/90) FL 108+7/1 FLC 7 FAC 5+1 Others 4+2
Colchester U (Free on 27/3/96) FL 47+18/3 FLC 3/1 FAC 4+1 Others 6+1

DUNNE Richard Patrick
Born: Dublin, 21 September 1979
Height: 6'2" Weight: 15.0
International Honours: Ei: B-1; Yth; Sch
In 1997-98, the big, Irish centre half was a mainstay of Everton's FA Youth Cup winning team, in addition to furthering his Premiership ambitions with three first team appearances. A tall, powerful 18-year old, he played at Tottenham just days after helping the youth team to a semi-final victory over Leeds United. Deceptively quick, and sharp in the tackle, as well as commanding in the air, Richard has all the attributes to build an outstanding career and, after winning a Republic of Ireland "B" cap in February, he travelled with a full international squad during the summer.
Everton (From trainee on 8/10/96) PL 8+2 FAC 2

DURKAN Kieran John
Born: Chester, 1 December 1973
Height: 5'11" Weight: 11.5
Club Honours: WC '95
International Honours: Ei: U21-3
Although scoring Stockport's historic first-ever first division goal in an opening day defeat at Bradford last season, the winger faded from the first team scene, and then suffered a broken ankle in the reserves. Two brief appearances followed in 1998, but the former Eire U21 player moved to Macclesfield in transfer deadline week, having been sought after by Sammy McIroy for several months. An excellent crosser of the ball, the Town fans were greatly disappointed when Kieran came off with a pulled hamstring only 18 minutes into his debut at Hull.
Wrexham (From trainee on 16/7/92) FL 43+7/3 FLC 3+1 FAC 4+2/2 Others 15/1
Stockport Co (£95,000 on 16/2/96) FL 52+12/4 FLC 10+1 FAC 4/3 Others 4+2
Macclesfield T (£15,000 on 25/3/98) FL 2+2

DURNIN John Paul
Born: Bootle, 18 August 1965
Height: 5'10" Weight: 11.10
Although unable to make a first team place his own at Portsmouth during last season, he was still one of Pompey's more consistent performers when given the opportunity, either in the starting line-up, or on the substitutes' bench. However, when given the chance, he formed effective partnerships with whoever was picked alongside him and finished the campaign as the club's second highest goalscorer, half of his goals coming in the last six games, including two on the last day of the season at Bradford which

Lee Duxbury

West Bromwich A (Loaned on 20/10/88) FL 5/2
Oxford U (£225,000 on 10/2/89) FL 140+21/44
FLC 7/1 FAC 7/1 Others 4+1/1
Portsmouth (£200,000 on 15/7/93) FL 100+53/24
FLC 10+1/2 FAC 5+2 Others 4+2

DUXBURY Lee Edward
Born: Keighley, 7 October 1969
Height: 5'10" Weight: 11.13
Captain of the Oldham side, Lee missed very few games in 1997-98, but those he did were due to suspension rather than injury. Strong in the tackle, and an excellent passer from the centre of midfield, he proved yet again to be an inspirational figure at the heart of everything that was positive for Latics. He also scored four goals to add more weight to his importance at Boundary Park.
Bradford C (From trainee on 4/7/88) FL 204+5/25 FLC 18+1/3 FAC 11 Others 13
Rochdale (Loaned on 18/1/90) FL 9+1 FAC 1
Huddersfield T (£250,000 on 23/12/94) FL 29/2 FLC 1 Others 3
Bradford C (£135,000 on 15/11/95) FL 63/7 FLC 2 FAC 5 Others 3
Oldham Ath (£350,000 on 7/3/97) FL 48+2/5 FLC 2 FAC 4 Others 1

DYCHE Sean Mark
Born: Kettering, 28 June 1971
Height: 6'0" Weight: 13.2
Despite being one of Chesterfield's famous FA Cup run stars of 1996-97, Sean decided to move on when transferring to Bristol City during the 1997 close season, but, unfortunately, an injury jinx kept him out of most of City's promotion campaign. On the occasions that he started, between the end of September and early November, he demonstrated why City paid £350,000 (£275,000 + £75,000 on promotion) for his services, as his tough tackling and leadership skills clearly demonstrated his motivational qualities.
Nottingham F (From trainee on 20/5/89)
Chesterfield (Free on 1/2/90) FL 219+12/8 FLC 9 FAC 13/1 Others 16
Bristol C (£350,000 on 11/7/97) FL 10+1 FLC 1

DYER Alexander (Alex) Constantine
Born: Forest Gate, 14 November 1965
Height: 5'11" Weight: 12.0
A much-travelled striker, Alex joined Huddersfield from the Portuguese second division side, FA Maia, at the start of 1997-98, and was employed to add experience to the front line. Started well by scoring the winner against West Ham United in the Coca Cola Cup, but dropped out of first team reckoning and left to join the rampant and successful Notts County squad early in March, and quickly became "Mr Versatile". Playing at full back, wing back, and centre back, on either side of the field, although obviously more comfortable on the left side, he remained cool and calm under pressure and proved to be a valuable asset in the run-in.*
Blackpool (Free from Watford juniors on

were instrumental in the club staying in the first division. Predominately, a midfielder who looks good when going forward, he can play in a number of positions, from right back through to the forward line, and never gives less than 100 per cent.*
Liverpool (Free from Waterloo Dock on 29/3/86) FLC 1+1

20/10/83) FL 101+7/19 FLC 8+1/1 FAC 4+1 Others 7/1
Hull C (£37,000 on 13/2/87) FL 59+1/14 FLC 2 FAC 4/1
Crystal Palace (£250,000 on 11/11/88) FL 16+1/2 FLC 3+1 FAC 1+1 Others 3+1/3
Charlton Ath (£100,000 on 30/11/90) FL 60+18/13 FLC 2+1 FAC 1/1 Others 3+1
Oxford U (Free on 26/7/93) FL 62+14/6 FLC 4/1 FAC 5/1 Others 5
Lincoln C (Free on 21/8/95) FL 1 FLC 1
Barnet (Free on 1/9/95) FL 30+5/2 Others 1 (Freed on 9/5/96)
Huddersfield T (Signed from FA Maia on 13/8/97) FL 8+4/1 FLC 3/1
Notts Co (Free on 2/3/98) FL 10

DYER Bruce Antonio
Born: Ilford, 13 April 1975
Height: 6'0" Weight: 11.3
International Honours: E: U21-11

The England U21 international found scoring for Crystal Palace a different proposition in the Premiership in 1997-98 than he had done in the first division the previous season, especially when he was up front as a lone striker with no real service coming his way. However, he was a hero in the FA Cup fourth round 3-0 home win over Leicester, scoring all three goals, and could have had more, several times having the City defence at this mercy. His manager, Steve Coppell, said of him afterwards: "Sometimes he is blinkered and sometimes his touch can let him down, but he has resilience and the desire to learn. He is like a sponge, he just soaks everything up and comes back for more. He wants to improve." A powerful front runner, who can play both wide or through the middle, he will certainly be a thorn in the sides of first division defences this coming term.
Watford (From trainee on 19/4/93) FL 29+2/6 FLC 4/2 FAC 1 Others 2/1
Crystal Palace (£1,100,000 on 10/3/94) F/PL 90+39/35 FLC 7+4/1 FAC 7+3/6 Others 3+2

DYER Keiron Courtney
Born: Ipswich, 29 December 1978
Height: 5'7" Weight: 9.7
International Honours: E: B-2; U21-6; Yth

An Ipswich local lad, Kieron began to blossom last season, earning rave reviews from opposition managers, after unexpectedly starting in the first team and playing in the majority of games, initially at right-wing back, before filling several other positions in the team. Interestingly, the club's surge up the table in the second half of the campaign coincided with George Burley's decision to pair Kieron and Matt Holland together in central midfield. Having made his England U21 debut against Moldova, at Wycombe in September, and scoring the only goal in Italy, where his performance led Sky viewers to vote him Man of the Match, he was promoted to the England "B" team, making his debut against Chile, before being substituted early in the second half because of injury. He was also selected for a further "B" cap against Russia in April. The impact he made in 1997-98

can be summed up by the fact that he was named in the PFA first division select.
Ipswich T (From trainee on 3/1/97) FL 43+11/4 FLC 7/1 FAC 3 Others 3+1

DYSON Jonathan (Jon) Paul
Born: Mirfield, 18 December 1971
Height: 6'1" Weight: 12.9
The versatile Huddersfield defender certainly had a campaign to remember in 1997-98 and a new contract came his way as a reward for some solid and consistent displays, while he was awarded six Man of

the Match awards out of the first ten games. He also scored his first goal for three years, against Wolverhampton Wanderers, in the very last minute of the game, and rarely put a foot out of place in a difficult season. In total contrast to the previous term, when Jon struggled to hold a first team place down and even went on the transfer list, now when fully fit and free from suspension he is the first name on the team sheet. Voted Huddersfield's Player of the Year, he is also the clubs PFA representative.
Huddersfield T (From juniors on 29//12/90) FL 125+16/3 FLC 14+2 FAC 7 Others 7+4

Bruce Dyer

EADEN Nicholas (Nicky) Jeremy
Born: Sheffield, 12 December 1972
Height: 5'9" Weight: 11.9

Another of Barnsley's first team regulars in 1997-98, Nicky missed only a handful of games, due to an ankle injury and a virus. However, more was seen of him in a defensive capacity during the season, as the team were put more onto the back foot, but when on the attack his first-time crossing was second to none at Oakwell. He can certainly look back with some pride at his part in trying to keep the Tykes in the Premiership.
Barnsley (From juniors on 4/6/91) F/PL 205+6/8 FLC 12+1 FAC 14 Others 2

EADIE Darren Malcolm
Born: Chippenham, 10 June 1975
Height: 5'8" Weight: 11.6
International Honours: E: U21-7; Yth

A serious neck injury sustained against Stockport late last October completely disrupted Darren's season, which, in turn, threw Mike Walker's plans for Norwich into disarray. Having already won further England U21 honours earlier in the campaign, he was one of the men that the manager was hoping could lead the charge, but it was not to be as City faltered. Back in January, he quickly got off the mark with the opening goal in a 2-1 home win against Sunderland, a 40-yard chip after the 'keepers clearance had landed at his feet. A pacy left winger who runs at opponents and often hurdles over them, he was named in the England "B" squad to play Chile in February, before being forced to pull out following a hamstring injury.
Norwich C (From trainee on 5/2/93) P/FL 120+13/31 FLC 18+1/2 FAC 6+1/1 Others 1+1

EARLE Robert (Robbie) Gerald
Born: Newcastle under Lyme, 27 January 1965
Height: 5'9" Weight: 10.10
International Honours: Jamaica: 9

This popular attacking midfielder had a somewhat of a disturbed season at Wimbledon in 1997-98, injuries and international duties with Jamaica ruling him out of quite a few games, and he missed the final five due to a broken toe. An exciting player to watch, who always provides 100 per-cent commitment and dedication to the Dons' cause, Robbie has great energy, is excellent in the air, and times his runs into the box with great precision to score valuable goals. There were just three of them last season, all coming in games that were won, including the winner at Selhurst Park against Southampton. *Stop Press:* Selected for Jamaica's World Cup squad in France, he opened his country's scoring account with a superb headed goal in a 3-1 defeat at the hands of Croatia, before the side went out of the competition at the end of the first round.

Port Vale (From juniors on 5/7/82) FL 284+10/77 FLC 21+2/4 FAC 20+1/4 Others 18+1/5
Wimbledon (£775,000 on 19/7/91) F/PL 222+2/51 FLC 21/5 FAC 31/7 Others 1/1

EARNSHAW Robert
Born: Zambia, 6 April 1981
Height: 5'8" Weight: 10.10

A young, speedy Cardiff City striker who started to break through in 1997-98, while still a trainee, he scored 47 goals for the youth team and helped them win the Midland Bank Welsh Youth Cup, scoring a hat trick in the final against Llanelli. All his goals being followed by a somersault. Although selected for Welsh junior teams, he has said he wants to play for his native Zambia, adding: "They probably don't know about me yet, but I'd love to play for Zambia one day." His mother was a Zambian women's international, while his uncle played for a top Belgian club. Is rated very highly by his manager, Frank Burrows.
Cardiff C (Trainee) FL 0+5 Others 0+1

EASTON Clint Jude
Born: Barking, 1 October 1977
Height: 5'11" Weight: 10.8
Club Honours: Div 2 '98
International Honours: E: Yth

A left-sided midfield player in his second senior season with Watford, Clint made the most of his limited first team opportunities in 1997-98. Earlier, as a good passer of the ball and potential playmaker, with increased confidence and awareness, he represented England in the U19 World Championships held in Malaysia in June 1997. Although only making 12 appearances, they were enough to win him a second division championship medal as Watford regained their first division spot after a two-year break.
Watford (From trainee on 5/7/96) FL 25+4/1 FLC 0+1 FAC 3+1 Others 3

EASTWOOD Phillip John
Born: Blackburn, 6 April 1978
Height: 5'10" Weight: 12.2
The suspension of Andy Cooke resulted in this young striker making his first team debut in Burnley's opening game of last season at Watford, but his subsequent progress was mainly made in the reserves and on loan at Telford. Is yet another youngster at Turf Moor who will be looking for a step up in 1998-99.
Burnley (From trainee on 5/7/96) FL 1+2

EBDON Marcus
Born: Pontypool, 17 October 1970
Height: 5'10" Weight: 12.4
International Honours: W: U21-2; Yth

Marcus was the foundation on which Chesterfield endeavoured to build a more adventurous, passing side to their game in 1997-98. Astute, with good vision, he brings team mates into the game well, and is a useful man at set pieces with his curling kicks and long throw, and there is also a harder, determined side to his game that emerges when the need arises.
Everton (From trainee on 16/8/89)

Peterborough U (Free on 15/7/91) FL 136+11/15 FLC 14+2 FAC 12+3/1 Others 11+1
Chesterfield (£100,000 on 21/3/97) FL 40+5/3 FLC 2 FAC 3 Others 1

ECKHARDT Jeffrey (Jeff) Edward
Born: Sheffield, 7 October 1965
Height: 6'0" Weight: 11.7
Eckhardt Jeffrey Edward

Jeff was yet another Cardiff City player troubled by injuries last season. A consistent and gutsy performer, who can play in virtually any position, when City lost both their top strikers, Carl Dale and Kevin Nugent, with long-term injuries and struggled to find a replacement, many followers argued that he could be the answer. Having missed the first four matches of the campaign through suspension, he then netted some crucial goals, including the winner as a substitute against Rochdale. Those goals, netted when he was pushed into attack, added to the argument that he was the man for a stand-in striker role. That aside, he is a good tackler who gives everything in every match, adding steel in defence, midfield, or attack.
Sheffield U (From juniors on 23/8/84) FL 73+1/2 FLC 7 FAC 2 Others 5
Fulham (£50,000 on 20/11/87) FL 245+4/25 FLC 13 FAC 5+1 Others 5/3
Stockport Co (£50,000 on 21/7/94) FL 56+6/7 FLC 6+2/1 FAC 5/4 Others 2
Cardiff C (£30,000 on 22/8/96) FL 53+3/8 FLC 1 FAC 4+1 Others 4/1

EDEY Cecil (Cec)
Born: Manchester, 12 March 1965
Height: 6'1" Weight: 12.1
Club Honours: GMVC '97; FAT '96

A veteran of non-league football, Cec declined to go full time with Macclesfield on their entry to the Football League in 1997-98, but kept himself fit and proved to be a versatile cover player, stepping into any position in the back four when injury or suspensions occurred. Has played for a whole string of non-league clubs, including Lancaster City, Chorley, Morecambe, and Winsford.
Macclesfield T (£3,000 from Witton A on 13/10/95) FL 9+4 Others 1

EDGHILL Richard Arlon
Born: Oldham, 23 September 1974
Height: 5'9" Weight: 11.5
International Honours: E: B-1; U21-3

His return to the Manchester City first team, after a 21-month lay off with a career threatening knee injury, coincided with the club's first win in 1997-98, a 3-1 victory at Nottingham Forest, seven games into the season. Having given a positive performance, followed nine days later with the Man of the Match award at Bury, he played 28 consecutive league and cup games, forgetting the two-match ban over the New Year, before his run of appearances came to an end when an injury sustained against Ipswich saw him leave the field immediately following half time. Playing in both full-back slots, and in midfield, his speed crucial to both getting down the line to cross and recovering, he came back for the final nine games.
Manchester C (From trainee on 15/7/92) PL 85 FLC 10 FAC 2

EDINBURGH Justin Charles
Born: Brentwood, 18 December 1969
Height: 5'10" Weight: 11.6
Club Honours: FAC '91

An experienced left back, Justin started last season well for Spurs, regaining his regular place only to suffer injury later in the campaign, which kept him out of action for much of the winter. Confident on the ball, and a player who likes to get forward down the left flank, being is a competent crosser of the ball, he maintains a high level of personal fitness, and his enthusiasm is evident in every game, regardless of whether he plays the full 90 minutes, or is brought on as a substitute to bolster the defence late in a game. His keenness to play first team football every week has made him the subject of interest from managers wishing to add experience to their squads.
Southend U (From trainee on 5/8/88) FL 36+1 FLC 2+1 FAC 2 Others 4+1/1
Tottenham H (£150,000 on 30/7/90) F/PL 169+20/1 FLC 19+4 FAC 22 Others 3

[EDINHO] Amaral Neto Edon Do
Born: Brazil, 21 February 1967
Height: 5'9" Weight: 12.9

Adapting well to the demands of English football, Edinho ended 1997-98 as Bradford's joint top scorer, an honour he shared with Robert Steiner, after setting the ball rolling with the first of the season in a 2-1 win over Stockport. A typical Brazilian, with all the flamboyant skill and unpredictability to match, it is not surprising that the centre forward is the fans' favourite, and his celebrations when scoring are so wild that he sets them alight at the same time. As you would expect, many of his goals were critical, there being equalisers or effective equalisers against a number of sides, including Huddersfield, Portsmouth, and Swindon, and winners against Crewe and Manchester City, while a brace at home to Reading included an exquisite lob over the 'keeper. Big and strong, he mixes bustle and skill in one package.
Bradford C (£250,000 from VSC Guimaraes on 6/2/97) FL 49+7/15 FLC 2/1 FAC 1

EDMONDSON Darren Stephen
Born: Coniston, 4 November 1971
Height: 6'0" Weight: 12.11
Club Honours: Div 3 '95; AMC '97

Having missed the early part of last season due to injury, Darren then lost his Huddersfield first team place with a change of management, before battling his way back and rightly earning it back with some assured performances in the reserves. A positive defender, with a canny knack of getting into forward positions, he suffered towards the back end of 1997-98 due to suspension and a nasty facial injury, incurred during the home game against Manchester City.
Carlisle U (From trainee on 17/7/90) FL 205+9/8 FLC 15/1 FAC 15/3 Others 22/3
Huddersfield T (£200,000 + on 3/3/97) FL 25+4 FLC 2 FAC 0+1

EDWARDS Andrew (Andy) David
Born: Epping, 17 September 1971
Height: 6'3" Weight: 12.10

The strong Peterborough central defender and club captain was an ever present last season, always looking to play the ball out of defence to feet, rather than clear his lines, and always available to help the youngsters around him. A great favourite at London Road, he even got himself on the scoresheet a couple of times, his first goals for the club, and will undoubtedly be the mainstay of the team that hopes to climb out of the third division in 1998-99.
Southend U (From trainee on 14/12/89) FL 141+6/5 FLC 5 FAC 4 Others 9/2
Birmingham C (£400,000 on 6/7/95) FL 37+3/1 FLC 12/1 FAC 2 Others 5/1
Peterborough U (Signed on 29/11/96) FL 71/2 FLC 4 FAC 7 Others 9

EDWARDS Christian (Chris) Nicholas Howells
Born: Caerphilly, 23 November 1975
Height: 6'2" Weight: 11.9
International Honours: W: 1; B-1; U21-7

Unhappy with third division football, the central defender was placed on the Swansea City transfer list and spent a ten-day trial period with Nottingham Forest last January, making an appearance for their reserves. Included in the Welsh squad due to play Scotland in a "B" international, having already played for the U21 side, following the game he was transferred to Forest on transfer deadline day but, bought as a player for the future, was not called upon as the side went back to the Premiership at the first time of asking. Tall and commanding, he shines in aerial battles and can be used effectively at set pieces.
Swansea C (From trainee on 20/7/94) FL 113+2/4 FLC 5 FAC 4 Others 9+1
Nottingham F (£175,000+ on 26/3/98)

EDWARDS Michael
Born: Hessle, 25 April 1980
Height: 6'1" Weight: 12.0

The Hull City youth team captain earned a shock call up for the Christmas derby at Rotherham last season, when replacing the suspended left back, Gregor Rioch, but he settled in to first team football so well that he retained his place, usually in the centre defence, for much of the remainder of the campaign. Mainly right sided, Michael displays an excellent temperament, has already attracted the attention of higher clubs, and is sure to be rewarded with a pro contract at the end of his YTS. Was voted Young Player of the Year by the club's supporters.
Hull C (Trainee) FL 20+1 Others 1

EDWARDS Neil Ryan
Born: Aberdare, 5 December 1970
Height: 5'9" Weight: 11.10
International Honours: W: U21-1; Yth; Sch

The Stockport goalkeeper had been on Rochdale manager, Graham Barrow's wanted list at the start of last season, but it was not until November that he finally got his man. Not very big for a 'keeper, but a great shot-stopper, Neil kept a clean sheet on his debut and was instrumental in preventing several heavy defeats when Dale suffered a drastic loss of form in mid-season.
Leeds U (From trainee on 10/3/89) Others 1

Stockport Co (£5,000 on 3/9/91) FL 163+1 FLC 11 FAC 11 Others 31
Rochdale (£25,000 on 3/11/97) FL 27 FAC 1 Others 1

EDWARDS Paul
Born: Liverpool, 22 February 1965
Height: 6'2" Weight: 13.2
Club Honours: Div 3 '94

Having just completed his sixth year at Shrewsbury, Paul maintained his regular spot, apart from a spell in early 1997-98. A very confident 'keeper, bravery and reflex saves are a strong feature of his game, last season saw an improvement both in his aerial ability and his distribution. Is a good servant of the club and well regarded.*
Crewe Alex (Free from Leek T on 24/2/89) FL 29 FLC 4 FAC 3 Others 4
Shrewsbury T (Free on 6/8/92) FL 203 FLC 13 FAC 15+1 Others 16

Paul Edwards (Shrewsbury Town)

EDWARDS Paul
Born: Manchester, 1 January 1980
Height: 5'11" Weight: 10.12

Signed from non-league Ashton United on non-contract terms last February, Paul made the most of his Doncaster appearances at full back, despite being raw and untried. Although Rovers were ultimately relegated, his league experience will give him something to work on as his career progresses.
Doncaster Rov (Free from Ashton U on 2/2/98) FL 5+4

EDWARDS Robert (Rob)
Born: Manchester, 23 February 1970
Height: 5'9" Weight: 12.4

Signed by Huddersfield originally as a striker, Rob has also filled in as a winger, but for most of the 1997-98 campaign, he was used as a left back, to which his displays were highly commendable. The downside to that switch of position was that he scored

fewer goals then normal, just one to be precise, but it came against his boyhood heroes, Manchester City – a sweet left-foot volley after an incredible 16-pass move. Unfortunately, his season was cut short with two games to go in order for him to have a double hernia operation, but he signed off with high praise from the manager and was put forward as a contender for Player of the Season.

Crewe Alex (From trainee on 11/7/88) FL 110+45/44 FLC 8/5 FAC 13+5/5 Others 9+8/4
Huddersfield T (£150,000 on 8/3/96) FL 63+21/11 FLC 6+1/1 FAC 2+1/1

EDWARDS Robert (Rob) William
Born: Kendal, 1 July 1973
Height: 6'0" Weight: 12.2
International Honours: W: 4; B-2; U21-17; Yth

At long last Rob made his full Welsh debut when he came on as a substitute in a 6-4 defeat by Turkey in Istanbul on 20 August 1997. He then played from the start when Wales went down 3-2 against Belgium in Brussels two months later, before injuries robbed him of other appearances. Unfortunately, these injury problems had their effect on his performances in Bristol City's midfield in 1997-98 and, while his left foot was as effective as ever, he often appeared to be suffering in many games. A ball winner with good distribution, he will be hoping to come back strongly in 1998-99 for both club and country.

Carlisle U (From trainee on 10/4/90) FL 48/5 FLC 4 FAC 1 Others 2+1
Bristol C (£135,000 on 27/3/91) FL 169+24/5 FLC 15+1/1 FAC 13+2 Others 12+1/2

EDWORTHY Marc
Born: Barnstaple, 24 December 1972
Height: 5'8" Weight: 11.10

Despite Crystal Palace losing their Premiership status at the end of 1997-98, it was a highly successful season for Marc, who missed only the occasional game, replaced Andy Roberts as skipper, and scooped the Player of the Year award. According to Match Magazine, he was Palace's Man of the Match in both the Newcastle league matches, the away game in March ending in a shock 2-1 win, but ultimately coming too late to save the team from relegation from the Premiership. A versatile player who can play in the centre of defence, at full back, or in midfield, he has plenty of pace with which to get down the line and deliver accurate crosses for the front men, and can even play as a sweeper if needed.

Plymouth Arg (From trainee on 30/3/91) FL 52+17/1 FLC 5+2 FAC 5+2 Others 2+2
Crystal Palace (£350,000 on 9/6/95) F/PL 119+4 FLC 8/1 FAC 8 Others 6

EHIOGU Ugochuku (Ugo)
Born: Hackney, 3 November 1972
Height: 6'2" Weight: 14.2
Club Honours: FLC '96
International Honours: E: 1; B-1; U21-15

By his own admission, Ugo had his worst ever start to a season, in 1997-98, an achilles injury suffered almost immediately after

Villa reported back for training following the summer recess, leaving him with an uphill battle in terms of attaining match fitness for the opening games. Despite being involved in every fixture, in struggling for form, the central defender was subsequently left on the bench in mid-October, before coming back in determined fashion to remain ever present. A solid defender with pace, who reads the game well, and is dominant in aerial battles, you can rely upon him to snuff out key players if the manager uses him in a man-marking role. Always a threat at set pieces, he scored twice during the campaign, both from corners.

West Bromwich A (From trainee on 13/7/89) FL 0+2
Aston Villa (£40,000 on 12/7/91) F/PL 168+11/9 FLC 15+1/1 FAC 14+2/1 Others 13/1

EKOKU Efangwu (Efan) Goziem
Born: Manchester, 8 June 1967
Height: 6'1" Weight: 12.0
International Honours: Nigeria: 5

During a season in which he was plagued by injury, this pacy, long-striding striker, known to all and sundry at Wimbledon as "Chief", was unable to put together enough outings in 1997-98 to enhance his fine partnership with Marcus Gayle that had been fostered in 1996-97. Although the Nigerian international scored one of the Dons' goals of the season in the 3-1 defeat of Newcastle at St James' Park in September, and one at Leeds, normally a bad ground for any kind of positive result, in the final game, there were only two more in the bank during a campaign when the Dons went perilously close to relegation. At his best when running at defences, and difficult to shake off with his natural aggression, he combines well with team mates, has quick feet, and is always looking to get on the scoresheet. Would have been disappointed not to be involved in World Cup '96 for Nigeria.

Bournemouth (£100,000 from Sutton U on 11/5/90) FL 43+19/21 FLC 0+2 FAC 5+2/2 Others 3+1/2
Norwich C (£500,000 on 26/3/93) PL 26+11/15 FLC 3/1 FAC 1+1 Others 3/1
Wimbledon (£900,000 on 14/10/94) PL 91+10/31 FLC 7+1/1 FAC 16+1/3

ELLINGTON Lee Simon
Born: Bradford, 3 July 1980
Height: 5'10" Weight: 11.0

Lee scored his first senior goals for Hull City when coming off the Boothferry bench to grab a match winning brace against Exeter City last November, and also starred in the club's progress to the fourth round of the FA Youth Cup – their best effort since 1991. The youngster's eye for goal, and good turn of pace, saw him offered a professional contract at the end of another encouraging season.

Hull C (Trainee) FL 4+5/2 FLC 0+1 FAC 0+1 Others 0+2

ELLIOTT Andrew (Andy)
Born: Newcastle, 2 May 1974
Height: 5'9" Weight: 11.10

As a hard-working Hartlepool right winger,

who is a good crosser of the ball, Andy made a few substitute appearances early in 1997-98, while playing as a part timer, and also working as a driver. Later, he quit his job to become a full-time professional, but, unfortunately, his gamble did not really pay off and, although he played well for the reserves, he failed to win a regular first team place and was released in the summer.

Hartlepool U (Free from Spennymoor on 10/2/97) FL 2+6 FAC 0+1

ELLIOTT Anthony (Tony) Robert
Born: Nuneaton, 30 November 1969
Height: 6'0" Weight: 13.7
Club Honours: WC '90
International Honours: E: Yth; Sch

Proved to be a quality goalkeeper for Cardiff City, but a back injury kept him out of the last, crucial matches in 1996-97 and the opening games of 1997-98 and, on coming back, he found himself second choice after the club had signed Jon Hallworth, a high pedigree 'keeper, from Oldham Athletic. That left Cardiff City with two goalkeepers of real quality for the third division and Tony eventually left for Scarborough in February, and made an immediate impression, when breaking the club record by going 353 minutes without conceding a goal. His safe handling and agility inspired confidence in the defence, and he became a great crowd favourite as the team chased promotion.

Birmingham C (From apprentice on 3/12/86) FLC 1
Hereford U (Free on 22/12/88) FL 75 FLC 5 FAC 6 Others 9
Huddersfield T (Free on 29/7/92) FL 15 FLC 2 FAC 3 Others 3
Carlisle U (Free on 28/6/93) FL 21+1 FAC 1 Others 5
Cardiff C (Free on 4/7/96) FL 38+1 FLC 2 FAC 2 Others 1
Scarborough (Free on 12/2/98) FL 15 Others 2

ELLIOTT Matthew (Matt) Stephen
Born: Wandsworth, 1 November 1968
Height: 6'3" Weight: 14.10
International Honours: S: 3

A right-footed Leicester central defender who is commanding in the air, Matt acted as team captain in 1997-98 when Steve Walsh was out injured. He also scored a number of important goals throughout the campaign, appearing in the area at set pieces, or as an emergency striker late in the game if City were battling to salvage something. Marshalled the defence excellently, particularly during the early weeks when the team made an unexpectedly good start, and even took responsibility from the penalty spot to clinch victory at Highfield Road. Possessing a rasping drive, as well as a bullet-like header, he also turned provider on a couple of occasions with deft right-wing crosses and it was no real surprise when international honours came his way. Called up for Scotland, through his grandmothers nationality, a selection that saw him eventually form a formidable partnership with Colin Hendry, and appear in three games, he was selected in the final 22 bound for the World Cup Finals in France during

the summer. *Stop Press:* Despite being on the bench throughout Scotland's three games in Group A, he did not come on to the field of play and could only watch as the side were eliminated at the earliest stage.

Charlton Ath (£5,000 from Epsom & Ewell on 9/5/88) FLC 1
Torquay U (£10,000 on 23/3/89) FL 123+1/15 FLC 9/2 FAC 9/2 Others 16/1
Scunthorpe U (£50,000 on 26/3/92) FL 61/8 FLC 6 FAC 2 Others 8
Oxford U (£150,000 on 5/11/93) FL 148/21 FLC 16/1 FAC 11/2 Others 6
Leicester C (£1,600,000 on 18/1/97) PL 53/11 FLC 1 FAC 4 Others 2

ELLIOTT Robert (Robbie) James
Born: Newcastle, 25 December 1973
Height: 5'10" Weight: 11.6
International Honours: E: U21-2; Yth

Signed from Newcastle for a then record fee of £2.5 million last July, he played only four games for Bolton before breaking his leg in the first home fixture of the season, against Everton, and being promptly ruled out for the rest of the campaign, much to the dismay of the fans and the management team alike. A left-sided defender, who is also comfortable on the left side of midfield, much was expected of Robbie until his untimely injury, his form prior to his transfer having suggested that international honours would not be too long in coming. Hoping to be back in time for the start of 1998-99, Wanderers' fans will be praying that the Geordie will reproduce the kind of quality football they know he is capable of.

Newcastle U (From trainee on 3/4/91) F/PL 71+8/9 FLC 5 FAC 7+3 Others 5+1
Bolton W (£2,500,000+ on 2/7/97) PL 4

ELLIOTT Steven William
Born: Derby, 29 October 1978
Height: 6'1" Weight: 14.0
International Honours: E: U21-3

A first-year professional at Derby, the young central defender was, perhaps to his own surprise, given a league debut at Newcastle last December, following on from two appearances against Southend in the Coca Cola Cup. His debut was praised as one of the best he had ever seen by manager, Jim Smith, and after being a regular in the reserves, and a great prospect for the future, he was voted County's Young Player of the Year. Also played in all three games for the England U21 side in the end of season Toulon tournament.

Derby Co (From trainee on 26/3/97) PL 3 FLC 2 FAC 0+1

ELLIOTT Stuart Thomas
Born: Hendon, 27 August 1977
Height: 5'8" Weight: 11.5

Unable to get much joy at St James' Park, Stuart arrived at Swindon on loan from Newcastle in February and made an instant impression, scoring for the reserves. The midfielder was promptly promoted to the first team of the home game against Manchester City, but could do little to prevent a 3-1 defeat. He was scheduled to stay with Town to the end of the season, but an injury meant he returned early to the north east with just one more appearance as

a substitute to his name. Is one for the future though.

Newcastle U (From trainee on 28/8/95)
Hull C (Loaned on 28/2/97) FL 3
Swindon T (Loaned on 20/2/98) FL 1+1

ELLIS Anthony (Tony) Joseph
Born: Salford, 20 October 1964
Height: 5'11" Weight: 11.0

Despite missing the opening four games of last season, Tony came into the Blackpool side to play the next 23, scoring ten goals, including a hat trick at Wrexham, before leaving for Bury in a deal that saw Ian Hughes move in the opposite direction. Arriving in December, he was seen as the experienced striker who was going to help pep up a side struggling to score goals, but his introduction did not reap immediate rewards though, and it was not until his tenth game that he finally scored. However, his ability to hold the ball up, along with his hard-working approach, made him a popular figure and he eventually ended the season as Bury's joint top league scorer with six goals.

Oldham Ath (Free from Horwich RMI on 22/8/86) FL 5+3 FLC 1 Others 1
Preston NE (£23,000 on 16/10/87) FL 80+6/27 FLC 3 FAC 5 Others 11+1/5
Stoke C (£250,000 on 20/12/89) FL 66+11/19 FLC 5+1/1 FAC 1+4 Others 3+2
Preston NE (£140,000 on 14/8/92) FL 70+2/48 FLC 4/2 FAC 6/3 Others 6/3
Blackpool (£165,000 on 25/7/94) FL 140+6/55 FLC 10+1/6 FAC 7/1 Others 8/3
Bury (£75,000 on 12/12/97) FL 21+1/6

ELLISON Anthony **Lee**
Born: Bishop Auckland, 13 January 1973
Height: 5'11" Weight: 12.3
Club Honours: Div 4 '91

After five years away from Darlington, Lee was surprisingly re-signed on a month-by-month basis from near neighbours, Bishop Auckland, on transfer deadline day last March. He then proceeded to show that he had not lost his eye for goal, when scoring on his home debut to complete a fairytale recall. After notching two more in the remaining six games, Lee was hoping to be signed up permanently.*

Darlington (From trainee on 8/11/90) FL 54+18/17 FLC 2+1 FAC 4+2/2 Others 3+1/1
Hartlepool U (Loaned on 25/3/93) FL 3+1/1
Leicester C (Free on 12/8/94)
Crewe Alex (Free on 23/8/95) FL 3+1/2 FLC 1 Others 0+1 (Free to Halifax during 1996 close season)
Hereford U (Free on 11/10/96) FL 0+1 (Freed on 23/10/96)
Darlington (Signed from Bishop Auckland on 26/3/98) FL 4+4/3

EMBERSON Carl Wayne
Born: Epsom, 13 July 1973
Height: 6'2" Weight: 14.7

Carl was ever present in goal for Colchester in 1997-98 and continued to progress, although a dip in form in mid-season would have seen him dropped had Tamer Fernandes not picked up an injury. "Embo" responded to the challenge and hit imperious form, conceding only two goals in the following nine games, and crowned his campaign when named as Man of the Match in the play-off final at Wembley. As a point

of interest, he made his 150th FL appearance for the club on 3 April, becoming only the fifth 'keeper to reach that total; the other four being Mike Walker, Percy Ames, Alec Chamberlain, and George Wright.*

Millwall (From trainee on 4/5/91) Others 1
Colchester U (Loaned on 17/12/92) FL 13
Colchester U (£25,000 on 6/7/94) FL 141+1 FLC 7 FAC 7 Others 15

EMBLEN Neil Robert
Born: Bromley, 19 June 1971
Height: 6'1" Weight: 13.11

Originally bought as a central defender, Neil had often played in Wolves' midfield, but never really established a best position. Left out on the opening day of last season, amidst rumours that he was to be transferred, he duly made a move to Crystal Palace that saw him become the club's most expensive sale. However, it did not quite work out like that as Palace still owed Wolves a lot of the money in March, letting him return instead. Making his second Wolves' debut, against Portsmouth, he was unfortunately ineligible for the FA Cup semi-final game against Arsenal.

Millwall (£175,000 from Sittingbourne on 8/11/93) FL 12 Others 1
Wolverhampton W (£600,000 on 14/7/94) FL 80+8/9 FLC 2+2/1 FAC 7+2 Others 2+1
Crystal Palace (£2,000,000 on 21/8/97) PL 8+5 FAC 1+1/2
Wolverhampton W (£900,000 on 26/3/98) FL 6+1

EMBLEN Paul David
Born: Bromley, 3 April 1976
Height: 5'11" Weight: 12.5

Signed from Tonbridge at the end of 1996-97, Paul made his debut for Charlton as a substitute in the home game against Stockport County last September, but did not feature again until March, when he played in the last few games, coming off the bench to set up goals for Mark Kinsella and Clive Mendonca. In between, he spent three months on loan at Brighton, where the young striker impressed with his enthusiastic displays in a struggling side. The highlight of his stay at Albion was undoubtedly his second-half hat trick in the Boxing Day fixture with Colchester at Gillingham, which enabled the Seagulls to claw their way back from a three goal deficit to claim an unlikely 4-4 draw.

Charlton Ath (£7,500 + from Tonbridge on 16/5/97) FL 0+4
Brighton & Hove A (Loaned on 4/11/97) FL 15/4

EMERSON Moises Costa
Born: Rio de Janeiro, Brazil, 12 April 1972
Height: 6'0" Weight: 14.5

"Emmo" must rank alongside Wilf Mannion, Brian Clough, Alan Peacock, and Juninho as one of the most exciting players ever to grace a pitch in the name of Middlesbrough. He of the powerful running, thrilling flair, and the crazy hair-do, electrified the fans who were dismayed because his domestic "problems" were the main cause of his AWOL deprivation, but his talent knew no limits and his powerful dead-ball kicking had to be witnessed to be believed. He left the Boro under a cloud last

January to sign for Tenerife, and, as far as the fans were concerned, quite simply they gave their all for him and felt they got little in return because of his "walkabouts" and the international publicity they attracted.

Middlesbrough (£4,000,000 from Porto on 26/7/96) F/PL 53/8 FLC 12/2 FAC 5/1

ENES Roberto (Robbie) Manuel
Born: Australia, 22 August 1975
Height: 5'10" Weight: 12.7
International Honours: Australia: 7

An Australian international, Robbie started out in the game, playing for Preston, Melbourne Zebras, and Sydney United, before trying unsuccessfully to break into German football. He finally arrived at Portsmouth last October after the UK had earlier refused him a work permit until a change of citizenship to Portuguese, for which he qualified through his father, was approved. Although immensely talented, he found it difficult adapting to English football, making just a handful of appearances in midfield, and struggled to become a regular member of the first team squad, before having his contract terminated by mutual consent during the summer.

Portsmouth (£175,000 from Sydney U on 17/10/97) FL 1+4

ERANIO Stefano
Born: Genoa, Italy, 29 December 1966
Height: 5'11" Weight: 11.6
International Honours: Italy: 20
Signed from AC Milan in May 1997 on a free transfer under the Bosman ruling, the former Italian international proved to be an energetic and lively right-wing back, or midfielder, who formed a particular understanding with his Italian compatriot, Francesco Baiano, at Derby in 1997-98. In displaying all the expected ball control from someone with his background in the game, he would have played more had it not been for a hamstring injury that kept him out of action on and off, but if fully fit in 1998-99, watch him go.

Derby Co (Free from AC Milan on 15/7/97) PL 23/5 FLC 1 FAC 1

ESDAILLE Darren
Born: Manchester, 4 November 1974
Height: 5'8" Weight: 10.7

Darren flitted in and out of the Doncaster first team during the course of last season, generally featuring in either midfield or defence, but never appearing to have a clear cut role, and his play suffered accordingly. Is the brother of David, who also appeared regularly in the Rovers league side.

Doncaster Rov (Free from Hyde U on 27/1/97) FL 37+3/1 FLC 1

ESDAILLE David
Born: Manchester, 22 July 1963
Height: 5'8" Weight: 10.8

Making a re-entry into league football when signing for Doncaster from non-league Hyde during the 1997 close season, having earlier in his career played for Wrexham and Bury, the elder brother of Darren saw his first campaign at Belle Vue divided into two parts. Temporarily released in October, he was back in the Rovers' midfield by January, where he was a regular feature until the closing weeks of the season.

Wrexham (Free from Winsford U on 13/8/92) FL 4 FLC 0+1 FAC 1
Bury (Free on 31/12/92) FL 1+5 (Freed during 1993 close season)
Doncaster Rov (Free from Hyde U on 8/8/97) FL 10+3 FLC 2

ETHERINGTON Matthew
Born: Truro, 14 August 1981
Height: 5'10" Weight: 10.1

Still only 17, and a star of Peterborough's junior side that reached the semi-final stages of the FA Youth Cup in 1997-98, the speedy left-sided midfielder followed up his first team debut in 1996-97 with appearances in the final two games of last season. Still a trainee, and still the club's youngest ever first teamer, United have allegedly turned down offers in excess of £500,000 for this star in the making.

Peterborough U (Trainee) FL 3

EUELL Jason Joseph
Born: Lambeth, 6 February 1977
Height: 6'0" Weight: 12.7
International Honours: E: U21-2

Having shown much promise for Wimbledon during 1996-97, it was expected that the young striker would make further progress but, unfortunately, it turned out to be an injury plagued season for him. Blessed with lightning pace, and not afraid to take

Stefano Eranio

defenders on, both the club and the fans have high hopes of this super-charged youngster. He started well enough, scoring in a 1-1 draw at home to Sheffield Wednesday in his first outing but, following eight more appearances, he spent 16 games on the sidelines after dislocating his shoulder. Came back in subdued fashion before scoring in two successive home games, a 1-1 draw in the FA Cup against Wolves, and a 2-1 win over Aston Villa in the Premiership, and has a big future ahead of him. According to newspaper reports, Jason turned down offers to play for both Jamaica and Barbados this last year, and was rewarded with two England U21 appearances in the end of season Toulon tournament.

Wimbledon (From trainee on 1/6/95) PL 22+13/8 FLC 4/3 FAC 3+5/1

EUSTACE Scott Douglas
Born: Leicester, 13 June 1975
Height: 6'0" Weight: 14.2
Scott had a lean spell mid-last season for Mansfield, having started in 23 of the first 24 games and, following injury, had some difficulty in getting back into the squad. However, when the young central defender was available he never let the side down and, after missing 14 starts, he was back in time for the final match of the campaign.

Leicester C (From trainee on 9/7/93) FL 0+1
Mansfield T (Free on 9/6/95) FL 90+8/6 FLC 3 FAC 5/1 Others 3+1

EVANS Michael (Micky) James
Born: Plymouth, 1 January 1973
Height: 6'1" Weight: 13.4
International Honours: Ei: 1
Signed by West Bromwich Albion from Southampton last October, having appeared in the first 13 games until losing his place following the return of David Hirst, the strong running centre forward suffered a double fracture of the cheek bone while training with the Republic of Ireland squad, prior to making his debut for his new club. He had earlier won his first full cap against Romania. Eventually getting back into shape, he broke into the side at the end of November, but then found himself continually playing second fiddle to Andy Hunt, Lee Hughes, and Bob Taylor, scoring only one goal, before injury forced him out of contention for the final three months. Recognised as a scorer of spectacular goals, Micky is a player with pace who can be also used on the wide right.

Plymouth Arg (From trainee on 30/3/91) FL 130+33/38 FLC 8+1 FAC 10+2/3 Others 10/2
Southampton (£500,000 on 4/3/97) PL 14+8/4 FLC 2+1/1
West Bromwich A (£750,000 on 27/10/97) FL 2+8/1 FAC 1+1

EVANS Paul Simon
Born: Oswestry, 1 September 1974
Height: 5'7" Weight: 12.0
Club Honours: Div 3 '94
International Honours: W: U21-4; Yth
A terrier-like midfielder, Paul is always in the action and played in most of

Shrewsbury's games last season, injury apart. Looking to step up the divisions, he spent much of the campaign on the transfer list, but the manager, Jake King, regarded him so well that he was happy to see him retain the captaincy. Has and uses a lethal shot, scores some spectacular goals, and is the team's penalty taker.

Shrewsbury T (From trainee on 2/7/93) FL 146+20/20 FLC 10+2/1 FAC 11+1/2 Others 11/4

EVANS Thomas (Tom) Raymond
Born: Doncaster, 31 December 1976
Height: 6'0" Weight: 12.0
Joined Scunthorpe from Crystal Palace at the start of 1997-98 as reserve goalkeeper, and immediately impressed with his form in the second string. Was man of the match on his debut, in the Coca Cola Cup game at Everton, but still let in five goals and had to wait three months for another chance. It came in the league match at home to Swansea in January, but he suffered a bad knee ligament injury which was feared would keep him out for the season. However, he returned to keep goal in the closing five games, proving himself to be an excellent shot-stopper in one-on-one situations, and was offered a new contract.

Sheffield U (From trainee on 3/7/95)
Crystal Palace (Free on 14/6/96)
Scunthorpe U (Free on 22/8/97) FL 5 FLC 1

EVANS Duncan Wayne
Born: Abermule, 25 August 1971
Height: 5'10" Weight: 12.5
Wayne had another splendidly consistent season for Walsall on the right flank of the defence in 1997-98, missing only three games and netting a most popular match winner against Gillingham at the end of March, his first league goal in what was his 165th game. Also capable of playing on the left-hand side, he is a strong tackler who never gives anything less than 100 per-cent effort.

Walsall (Free from Welshpool on 13/8/93) FL 167+5/1 FLC 14+1/1 FAC 14+1 Others 11

EVERS Sean Anthony
Born: Hitchin, 10 October 1977
Height: 5'9" Weight: 9.11
An effervescent 20-year old who continues to develop at Luton, along with a clutch of other promising youngsters, Sean is a fast midfielder who takes the opportunity to shoot when it presents itself and three goals in 1997-98, his first in league football, was a good return at this stage of his career. A busy player, able to move the ball quickly from defence to attack, he can sometimes be knocked off the ball and will need to develop extra strength. He was rewarded for his displays at Kenilworth Road last season by a call up to the Republic of Ireland's U21 squad.

Luton T (From trainee on 16/5/96) FL 16+9/3 FLC 2 Others 5

EYDELIE Jean-Jacques
Born: France, 3 February 1966
Height: 5'8" Weight: 12.0

Signed on a three-month loan from Sion last March, this experienced midfielder made an impressive debut for Walsall in the 2-1 win at leaders Watford on the same day, and had played a total of 12 games by the end of the season, specialising in the telling through ball. Since he came initially on loan, his future at Bescot is uncertain at the time of writing.*

Walsall (Loaned from Sion on 3/3/98) FL 10+1 Others 1

EYRE John Robert
Born: Hull, 9 October 1974
Height: 6'0" Weight: 12.7
A regular in the Scunthorpe side throughout last season, unfortunately it was another frustrating campaign for him. When at his best he is a match for any defence, with terrific skill, pace, and the ability to run at the opposition, but was unable to repeat that kind of performance week in and week out. Still reached double figures for the season though, and showed himself to be a consistent penalty taker, occasionally being switched from his striker's role to right-wing back.

Oldham Ath (From trainee on 16/7/93) P/FL 4+6/1 FLC 0+2
Scunthorpe U (Loaned on 15/12/94) FL 9/8
Scunthorpe U (£40,000 on 4/7/95) FL 110+13/28 FLC 7/2 FAC 10/1 Others 5+1/3

EYRE Richard Paul
Born: Poynton, 15 September 1976
Height: 5'11" Weight: 11.6
A professional for three years, the right winger earned his call-up to the Port Vale first team squad against Ipswich last December, where he came on in the 90th minute to replace the injured Allen Tankard, and barely had time to run around in the fog before the referee blew for time. Hopefully, there will be more opportunities in the offing this coming term.

Port Vale (From trainee on 29/6/95) FL 0+1

EYRES David
Born: Liverpool, 26 February 1964
Height: 5'10" Weight: 11.8
Preston struggled early last season on the left side of midfield, following the summer sale of Kevin Kilbane, until the surprise arrival of David from Burnley in October. In joining the growing contingent of ex-Clarets at the club, and an experienced player who passed 350 league matches in March, he brought both attacking and defensive options to the first team, although perhaps lacking the overall consistency he would have liked. An excellent crosser of the ball, always prepared to take on his man, he also possesses a powerful shot, and his contribution of goals was vital to a low-scoring team. Interestingly, earlier in the season he had missed a penalty when playing against Preston for Burnley.

Blackpool (£10,000 from Rhyl on 15/8/89) FL 147+11/38 FLC 11+1/2 Others 13+2/4
Burnley (£90,000 on 29/7/93) FL 171+4/37 FLC 17/7 FAC 14/8 Others 9/3
Preston NE (£80,000 on 29/10/97) FL 26+2/4 FAC 4/2 Others 3/2

FACEY Delroy Michael
Born: Huddersfield, 22 April 1980
Height: 5'11" Weight: 12.10
Having made his Football League debut for Huddersfield in 1996-97, and with much expected of him, the homegrown product was thrust into action in the early part of last season, making his only start at home to Ipswich before going back to the reserves, apart from making a couple of subs' appearances. A big, strong, bustling striker, who is good in the air, despite his lack of experience, the management team at Town rate the youngster highly.
Huddersfield T (From trainee on 13/5/97) FL 2+4

FAIRCLOUGH Courtney (Chris) Huw
Born: Nottingham, 12 April 1964
Height: 5'11" Weight: 11.7
Club Honours: Div 2 '90, Div 1 '92, '97; CS '92
International Honours: E: B-1; U21-7
The 1997 Bolton Player of the Year did not have the best of times last season, being yet another defender at the club who missed a sizeable amount of the campaign due to injury. Although returning to action after a lengthy lay off, for the game against Derby in December, he found it hard to pin down a place in the starting line-up, facing stiff competition from Andy Todd and Mark Fish, before looking as solid as ever in the games in which he did participate. There is no doubt that his experience in the game proved invaluable at times to Bolton and, while he may have lost a yard of two of pace over the years, his enthusiasm and awareness of the game ensured that he was still a force to be reckoned with at the heart of the Wanderers' defence, before being released during the summer.
Nottingham F (From apprentice on 12/10/81) FL 102+5/1 FLC 9+1/1 FAC 6 Others 9+2
Tottenham H (£387,000 on 3/7/87) FL 60/5 FLC 7 FAC 3
Leeds U (£500,000 on 23/3/89) FL 187+6/21 FLC 17+2/2 FAC 14+1 Others 14
Bolton W (£500,000 on 4/7/95) F/PL 89+1/8 FLC 11 FAC 5

FARRELL Andrew (Andy) James
Born: Colchester, 7 October 1965
Height: 5'11" Weight: 12.3
Club Honours: Div 4 '92
As Rochdale's ubiquitous utility man, Andy was the regular centre-back partner for Keith Hill in the injury absence of Alan Johnson and John Pender in 1997-98, before figuring in various midfield roles, at left back, and even wearing the number nine shirt for a spell. Having passed 600 senior games during the season, he would have been an ever present but for regularly falling foul of referees and being suspended on three separate occasions. Is a solid and reliable, if unspectacular performer.*
Colchester U (From apprentice on 21/9/83) FL

98+7/5 FLC 9 FAC 8 Others 6
Burnley (£13,000 on 7/8/87) FL 237+20/19 FLC 17+4/1 FAC 19+2 Others 27+3/3
Wigan Ath (£20,000 on 22/9/94) FL 51+3/1 FLC 3 FAC 4+1 Others 5/1
Rochdale (Free on 3/7/96) FL 77+3/6 FLC 4 FAC 3 Others 2

FARRELL David (Dave) William
Born: Birmingham, 11 November 1971
Height: 5'10" Weight: 11.9
Signed from Wycombe during the summer of 1997, Dave played most of last season on Peterborough's right flank, but was just as comfortable on the left, being a pacy player with two good feet and fine control. Watched by a number of clubs throughout the campaign, he scored six times, including winners at Rochdale and Gillingham, and at London Road against Chester, and was one of three United players selected for the PFA award-winning third division team.
Aston Villa (£45,000 from Redditch U on 6/1/92) F/PL 2+1 FLC 2
Scunthorpe U (Loaned on 25/1/93) FL 4+1/1 Others 2
Wycombe W (£100,000 on 14/9/95) FL 44+16/6 FLC 6 FAC 3+2 Others 2
Peterborough U (Free on 21/7/97) FL 40+2/6 FLC 4/1 FAC 3 Others 4/1

FARRELL Sean Paul
Born: Watford, 28 February 1969
Height: 6'0" Weight: 13.7
Club Honours: Div 3 '98
Sean overcame an annoying early season injury in 1997-98 to establish himself as the regular first-choice target man at Notts County. In forming an uncanny understanding with his partner, Gary Jones, to create a formidable strike force in which he registered his share of goals, he again proved to be a hard working and selfless player with total commitment to the team cause. Four times during a campaign that saw County ultimately win the third division title, he struck a brace, but, more importantly, his goals brought about a result of some kind on at least seven occasions.
Luton T (From apprentice on 5/3/87) FL 14+11/1 FAC 2+1/1 Others 1+2/2
Colchester U (Loaned on 1/3/88) FL 4+5/1
Northampton T (Loaned on 13/9/91) FL 4/1
Fulham (£100,000 on 19/12/91) FL 93+1/31 FLC 5+1/3 FAC 2/3 Others 8/1
Peterborough U (£120,000 on 5/8/94) FL 49+17/20 FLC 4+2/1 FAC 4+1/3 Others 3+1/1
Notts Co (£80,000 on 14/10/96) FL 42+7/16 FLC 1 FAC 5/1 Others 1

FARRELLY Gareth
Born: Dublin, 28 August 1975
Height: 6'0" Weight: 12.7
International Honours: Ei: 5; B-1; U21-11; Yth; Sch
A 1997 close season signing from Aston Villa, Gareth ended 1997-98 on a spectacular high, scoring the goal which secured Everton's Premiership safety in the last match, against Coventry. A naturally left-sided midfielder, that goal was scored with his right, as was his only other previous strike with the Blues, in the Coca Cola Cup at Scunthorpe. Hindered by a knee injury earlier in the season, the Irishman found it difficult to make an impact in a side

constantly struggling against relegation, but, still young enough to develop in the Premiership, he captained both the Republic of Ireland's U21 and "B" teams during the period. He also made two further appearances as a full international. Has great ability, and is a natural passer of the ball who is always looking to pick out team mates.
Aston Villa (From trainee on 21/1/92) PL 2+6 FLC 0+1
Rotherham U (Loaned on 21/3/95) FL 9+1/2
Everton (£700,000+ on 9/7/97) PL 18+8/1 FLC 1/1 FAC 1

FEAR Peter Stanley
Born: Sutton, 10 September 1973
Height: 5'10" Weight: 11.7
International Honours: E: U21-3
A more than useful Wimbledon utility player who can perform to a high standard in a number of positions, notably in defence and midfield. Surprisingly, it was a stop-go-start type of season for Peter in 1997-98. After making his initial start against Millwall in the Coca Cola Cup in October, he did not re-appear for 18 games, then had a run of four, before returning for the final four games, where he came to life in the 6-2 home defeat at the hands of Spurs, when taking a leaf out of Jurgen Klinsmann's book, scoring twice and showing terrific sharpness in front of goal. Solid and composed at the back, never shirking a tackle, further forward he creates chances for others.
Wimbledon (From trainee on 2/7/92) PL 51+20/4 FLC 8+2/1 FAC 4

FEATHERSTONE James Lee
Born: Wharfdale, 12 November 1979
Height: 6'2" Weight: 12.12
A tall, strong striker who joined Scunthorpe in March after being given a free transfer by Premiership outfit Blackburn and winning a year's contract following a successful trial. Immediately impressed with his mobility up front in reserve and youth matches and made his league debut, when coming on as a second-half substitute in the last home match of the season against Exeter.
Scunthorpe U (Free from Blackburn Rov juniors on 26/3/98) FL 0+1

FENN Neale Michael Charles
Born: Edmonton, 18 January 1977
Height: 5'10" Weight: 12.6
International Honours: Ei: B-1; U21-4; Yth
Followed up his five games for Tottenham in 1996-97 with another five last season, only this time he opened up his scoring account with the first goal in Spurs' Coca Cola Cup campaign, a 3-2 home win over Carlisle. Very good with his back to the goal, the young central striker makes rather than takes chances, as he twists and turns defenders, either to lay the ball off or to get in shots, and shows plenty of nice touches and vision. Loaned out to Leyton Orient in January to further his experience, he was unlucky not to score during his short stay, but sustained an injury and returned to White Hart Lane. The next stop was

Norwich, where he signed the loan paper-work just ten minutes before the transfer deadline, playing in the last seven matches and scoring in the 5-0 win at Reading. His was not an insignificant part in helping City retain their first division status. Continued to add to his Republic of Ireland appearances during the season and was also selected for the "B" international against Northern Ireland in February.

Tottenham H (From trainee on 1/7/95) PL 0+8 FAC 2/1
Leyton Orient (Loaned on 30/1/98) FL 3
Norwich C (Loaned on 26/3/98) FL 6+1/1

FENSOME Andrew (Andy) Brian
Born: Northampton, 18 February 1969
Height: 5'8" Weight: 11.10
Club Honours: Div 3 '91, '96

The regular choice at right back for Rochdale for the second season running, Andy put in some steady performances in 1997-98, despite Dale's up-and-down form, missing only a handful of games. At the same time, he managed to stay both free of injury and – remarkably for a third division defender in the current climate – out of referee's notebooks. Released during the summer, he is a recognised long-throw specialist.

Norwich C (From apprentice on 16/2/87)
Cambridge U (Free from Bury T on 21/11/89) FL 122+4/1 FLC 11 FAC 17+2 Others 9+1
Preston NE (Signed on 8/10/93) FL 93/1 FLC 3/1 FAC 9 Others 11
Rochdale (Free on 3/7/96) FL 80+2 FLC 4 FAC 3 Others 3

Graham Fenton

FENTON Graham Anthony
Born: Wallsend, 22 May 1974
Height: 5'10" Weight: 12.10
Club Honours: FLC '94, '96
International Honours: E: U21-1

A right-sided striker, or occasional mid-

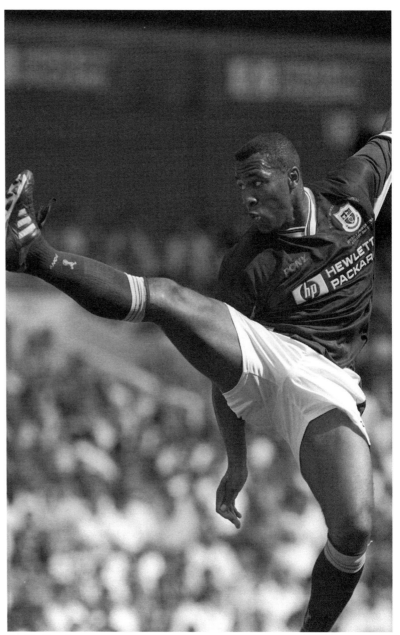

Les Ferdinand

fielder, Graham joined Leicester from Blackburn in August 1997 and made an instant impact when coming off the bench to score the winner at Anfield on his debut. Proved deadly from ten yards at Barnsley after the 'keeper had parried his effort from the penalty spot, but was generally used as a substitute throughout the campaign, though he managed a brief run in the team in December when Ian Marshall was injured. Is a hard worker, who will be keen to force his way into the first-choice reckoning this coming season, and a player who will keep others on their toes.

Aston Villa (From trainee on 13/2/92) PL 16+16/3 FLC 2+5
West Bromwich A (Loaned on 10/1/94) FL 7/3
Blackburn Rov (£1,500,000 on 7/11/95) PL 9+18/7 FLC 0+2 FAC 0+1
Leicester C (£1,100,000 on 8/8/97) PL 9+14/3 FLC 1 FAC 0+1 Others 0+2

FERDINAND Leslie (Les)
Born: Acton, 8 December 1966
Height: 5'11" Weight: 13.5
International Honours: E: 17; B-1

A strong, powerful striker who was signed by Tottenham's Gerry Francis from Newcastle at the second attempt during the 1997 close season, amidst rumours of financial pressures at St James', and with the desire to play first team football every week, Les became the second player to join the club from the Magpies last season, following David Ginola to London. Goals early into the campaign, most notably in the 2-1 defeat at West Ham and the 3-2 home victory over Aston Villa, saw him at his best, and with his strength in the air, and a powerful shot his trademark, the early signs were that he would really be making his mark at Tottenham, before injury struck just as it seemed that he had settled quickly into the side. Picking up a knock in the away tie at Leicester in September was the first in a series of injuries which were to plague him throughout the remainder of the campaign, much attributed to his physical style of play. His best performance came in early May, when linking up with Jurgen Klinsmann, in the relegation battle away to Wimbledon. In this one appearance, Les demonstrated his predatory instinct when poking in the opener, and his intelligence in the supporting role when making two of Klinsmann's four goals that day. Having won full caps against Moldova, Saudi Arabia, Morocco, and Belgium, and making a "B" team appearance against Russia, during 1997-98, Spurs' fans were delighted to see Les make the final 22 for France, feeling sure that he would add much needed experience to Glenn Hoddle's England side. *Stop Press:* On the bench for all four of England's World Cup games during the summer, he was not called upon and could only watch as the side cruelly went out to Argentina in the second round.

Queens Park R (£15,000 from Hayes on 12/3//87) F/PL 152+11/80 FLC 11+2/7 FAC 6+1/3 Others 1
Brentford (Loaned on 24/3/88) FL 3
Newcastle U (£6,000,000 on 7/6/95) PL 67+1/41 FLC 6/3 FAC 4+1/2 Others 5/4
Tottenham H (£6,000,000 on 5/8/97) PL 19+2/5 FLC 1 FAC 2

FERDINAND Rio Gavin
Born: Peckham, 7 November 1978
Height: 6'2" Weight: 12.1
International Honours: E: 3; U21-4; Yth

West Ham's Rio has superb natural talent and always looks good on the ball, and as the teenage central defender established himself in the West Ham team in 1997-98, he looked to be a fixture for many years to come. He was also called into the England squad and made his international debut in November against Cameroon, adding to that with appearances against Switzerland and Belgium, while continuing to play for the England U21 side. Although unfairly compared to Bobby Moore, he has the potential to become one of England's greatest, being selected for the 22 who travelled to France for the World Cup during the summer. A huge favourite with the fans at Upton Park, it was no surprise when he was awarded the Hammer of the Year trophy. *Stop Press:* Although not called upon during England's four World Cup

matches in France '98, the experience would have been priceless.
West Ham U (From trainee on 27/11/95) PL 46+5/2 FLC 5+1 FAC 7
Bournemouth (Loaned on 8/11/96) FL 10 Others 1

FERGUSON Darren
Born: Glasgow, 9 February 1972
Height: 5'9" Weight: 11.10
Club Honours: PL '93
International Honours: S: U21-5; Yth

A neat Wolves' midfielder, who is capable of producing telling through balls when on his game, he began last season brightly but seemed to deteriorate during the 90 minutes at West Bromwich and a poor spell ensued. Having started the first 23 matches, Darren was inspirational as Wolves beat Middlesbrough 1-0, and full of running in the next match at Crewe, but after five bookings he was suspended for two matches in December and found it difficult to re-establish himself. Despite a hernia operation in February, there is no reason to believe that Alex Ferguson's son will not come back better than ever.
Manchester U (From trainee on 11/7/90) F/PL 20+7 FLC 2+1
Wolverhampton W (£250,000 on 13/1/94) FL 92+21/4 FLC 13/2 FAC 9+2/3 Others 6

FERGUSON Duncan
Born: Stirling, 27 December 1971
Height: 6'4" Weight: 14.6
Club Honours: SL '94; SLC '94; FAC '95
International Honours: S: 7; B; U21-7; Yth; Sch

Already an idolised figure at Everton, Duncan's hero worship reached almost "Messianic" proportions during his most successful individual season at Goodison Park in 1997-98. A tall, aggressive centre forward in the old-fashioned mould, he finished as top scorer at the club for the first time, after Howard Kendall had pulled off a master-stroke of psychology by installing

him as captain. Following two goals in 16 appearances, before claiming the skipper's armband, he scored a hat trick of headers against Bolton in the first match as captain, and went on to score another six, including another goal against arch-rivals Liverpool at Anfield – down at the Kop End to boot. And, during the closing weeks of the campaign, he played on with a knee injury, which eventually required surgery, in order to aid Everton's ultimately successful battle against relegation. A private figure, who still refuses to conduct media interviews, the big Scot informed the Scottish FA that he no longer wished to be considered for selection for the international side. Instead, during the World Cup he was due to get married.
Dundee U (Signed from Carse Thistle on 1/2/90) SL 75+2/27 SLC 2+1/2 SC 6/4
Glasgow R (£4,000,000 on 20/7/93) SL 8+6/2 SLC 2+2/3 SC 0+3 Others 1
Everton (£4,400,000 on 4/10/94) PL 97+6/34 FLC 4 FAC 8+1/4

FESTA Gianluca
Born: Cagliari, Italy, 15 March 1969
Height: 6'0" Weight: 13.6

Having made an impressive start for Middlesbrough in 1996-97, this hard-tackling defender alternated between full back and central defence in 1997-98 and continued to put in wholehearted displays in helping the club back to the Premiership at the first attempt. Still enjoyed going forward on occasion, scoring Boro's opening goal of the season, against Charlton, one of two late efforts (Fabrizio Ravanelli scored the second) that helped overhaul a 1-0 deficit at the Cellnet, Gianluca's ability in the air can also be used effectively as an added weapon at set pieces. Always an adventure seeker, the Italian has the flair to stir up the emotions of the fans.
Middlesbrough (£2,700,000 from Inter Milan on 18/1/97) F/PL 51/3 FLC 11 FAC 7/1

Duncan Ferguson (centre)

FETTIS Alan William
Born: Belfast, 1 February 1971
Height: 6'1" Weight:12.10
International Honours: NI: 22; B-3; Yth; Sch

Signed from Nottingham Forest last September, after he had slipped to fourth choice, he joined Blackburn because of the early injury to Michael Watt. Given his debut, he went 193 minutes before he conceded a goal, which ranked him fourth on the club's all-time list of debutant goalkeepers, but when given an extended run because of the absence of Tim Flowers and John Filan it appeared that every shot on target went into the net. However, in continuing to play for Northern Ireland in 1997-98, making four appearances, he showed himself to be an excellent shot-stopper with great reflexes. Also played in the "B" international against the Republic in February and kept a clean sheet in a 1-0 win.
Hull C (£50,000 from Ards on 14/8/91) FL 131+4/2 FLC 7+1 FAC 5 Others 7
West Bromwich A (Loaned on 20/11/95) FL 3
Nottingham F (£250,000 on 13/1/96) PL 4 FLC 1 FAC 0+1
Blackburn Rov (£300,000 on 12/9/97) PL 7+1 FAC 1

FEUER Anthony Ian
Born: Las Vegas, USA, 20 May 1971
Height: 6'7" Weight: 15.6

After consistently producing stunning form since his 1995 transfer from West Ham, Ian endured a miserable season at Luton in 1997-98, which resulted in his leaving for the US Pro League in March. Having conceded just one goal in the first three games, despite playing with a damaged shoulder for most of the third game, whilst he was out of the side with injury, young Kelvin Davis returned from loan at Hartlepool and performed well. Although given a few games back in the first team after recovering, he appeared more hesitant, lacked his previous outstanding form, and was soon dropped, failing to get back in. His hopes for selection for the American World Cup squad seemed to be receding, although he was called up to face Paraguay, as deputy to Juergen Sommer, in March, while not a demonstrative person, he clearly felt that his record during the two previous terms deserved better treatment from Luton. However, in recognising the realities of the situation – especially with the Town in relegation trouble – the American moved back to the States, with the club losing over £400,000 on the deal.
West Ham U (£70,000 from Los Angeles Salsa on 23/3/94)
Peterborough U (Loaned on 20/2/95) FL 16
Luton T (£580,000 on 11/9/95) FL 97 FLC 7 FAC 5 Others 5

FEWINGS Paul John
Born: Hull, 18 February 1978
Height: 6'0" Weight: 12.6

One of four Hull City players transfer listed last August, "Fewy" impressed in the unfamiliar left-wing-back role, having made his name as a striker, but was replaced when the Tigers switched to a 4-4-2 system in December. Unfortunately, in losing over half a stone in weight when struck down by a mystery virus on the back of a hamstring injury, Paul struggled to regain his first team place and made only one more start.
Hull C (From trainee on 4/8/95) FL 32+25/2 FLC 4+3/1 FAC 2+1 Others 0+2/1

FICKLING Ashley
Born: Sheffield, 15 November 1972
Height: 5'10" Weight: 11.6
International Honours: E: Sch

Not called upon during Grimsby's promotion campaign last season, with Tony Gallimore and Kevin Jobling sharing the left-hand side ahead of him in the pecking order, he was loaned out to Darlington on transfer deadline day. Having been loaned to the Quakers twice before, in 1992 and 1993 when with Sheffield United, it was a welcome return for Ashley and he played out the remainder of the season in a left-wing-back role before being released by the Mariners during the summer. Hard tackling, and enthusiastic, and a passer of the ball, he is a versatile player who can also be used with confidence in central defence.
Sheffield U (From juniors on 26/7/91) FLC 2+1 Others 3
Darlington (Loaned on 26/11/92) FL 14 Others 1
Darlington (Loaned on 12/8/93) FL 1 FLC 1
Grimsby T (Free on 23/3/95) FL 26+13/2 FLC 2+1 FAC 2+1
Darlington (Loaned on 26/3/98) FL 8

FILAN John Richard
Born: Sydney, Australia, 8 February 1970
Height: 5'11" Weight: 13.2
International Honours: Australia: 2

Acquired for a small fee from Coventry during the 1997 close season, John was a revelation when filling in for Tim Flowers as the Blackburn custodian, going 234 minutes before conceding his first goal, which ranked him third in the club's all-time list of debutant goalkeepers. Unfortunately, two games later he received a horrendous injury when challenged by Sheffield Wednesday's Wayne Collins. A broken forearm, muscle and ligament damage, and a cut down to the bone was expected to keep him out for the rest of the season but the club was so desperate that he was rushed back into action. Very calm, certain in his decision making, and with good judgement, he may be placed to take over from Flowers at the club and possibly become Mark Bosnich's understudy with the national team. It was no coincidence that when he returned, the side, which had been leaking goals, kept clean sheets in two successive games.
Cambridge U (£40,000 from Budapest St George on 12/3/93) FL 68 FLC 6 FAC 3 Others 3
Coventry C (£300,000 on 2/3/95) PL 15+1 FLC 2
Blackburn Rov (£700,000 on 10/7/97) PL 7

FINLEY Gary
Born: Liverpool, 14 November 1970
Height: 6'3" Weight: 12.0

Signed on a non-contract basis from non-league Netherfield last August, the central defender made his first team debut for Doncaster against Nottingham Forest in the League Cup. Although doing well against Pierre Van Hooijdonk and company, Gary failed to secure a regular place in the Rovers' defence and was released in October.
Doncaster Rov (Free from Netherfield on 26/8/97) FL 6+1 FLC 1

FINNAN Stephen (Steve) John
Born: Limerick, 20 April 1976
Height: 5'10" Weight: 12.0
Club Honours: Div 3 '98
International Honours: Ei: B-1; U21-8

Steve returned to his best form at Notts County during the 1997 close season, when he was required to fill a variety of roles, including right-wing back, midfield, or his favoured right-wing position. His crosses and set pieces always spelt danger, while his pace and skill disturbed the most reliable of defenders. Selected for the Republic's "B" side in 1997-98, as well as appearing three times for the U21s, he added a third division championship medal to his collection of honours, as County romped away with the third division title.
Birmingham C (£100,000 from Welling U on 12/6/95) FL 9+6/1 FLC 2+2 Others 2+1
Notts Co (Loaned on 5/3/96) FL 14+3/2 Others 3/1
Notts Co (£300,000 on 31/10/96) FL 59+8/5 FLC 4 FAC 7/1 Others 1

FINNEY Stephen (Steve) Kenneth
Born: Hexham, 31 October 1973
Height: 5'10" Weight: 12.8
Club Honours: Div 2 '96

A player who will always be a crowd favourite at Swindon, following his goal-scoring exploits in the 1996 second division championship success, but, rather like 1996-97, he found scoring goals regularly at this level in 1997-98 a much tougher proposition. Forced out of the first team by the arrival of new boy, Chris Hay, from Celtic, he was loaned out to Cambridge in September to boost his confidence and fitness, and scored twice in seven appearances before returning in November, following the sale of Wayne Allison, and responding with a three-goal blast in as many games. He was hoping to re-establish himself as a regular when the arrival of another new striker, Iffy Onuora, prompted him to ask for a transfer and he was released in the summer.
Preston NE (From trainee on 2/5/92) FL 1+5/1 FAC 0+1 Others 1+1
Manchester C (Free on 12/2/93)
Swindon T (Free on 15/6/95) FL 47+26/18 FLC 6+1/1 FAC 2+5/2 Others 2+1/1
Cambridge U (Loaned on 10/10/97) FL 4+3/2

FINNIGAN John Francis
Born: Wakefield, 29 March 1976
Height: 5'8" Weight: 10.11

Brought in on loan from Nottingham Forest on transfer deadline day, John went on to produce some tremendous performances in Lincoln's final matches of last season. As a central midfield player, and dead-ball specialist, he is definitely one to watch for in the future and may get a breakthrough in the Premiership this coming term.
Nottingham F (From trainee on 10/5/93)
Lincoln C (Loaned on 26/3/98) FL 6

FISH Mark Anthony
Born: Capetown, South Africa, 14 March 1974
Height: 6'2" Weight: 12.7
International Honours: South Africa: 40
Signed from Lazio last August, Mark was, at that time, the joint record signing for Bolton and, as an international for South Africa, he was quite a coup for the club as both Manchester United and West Ham had been interested in signing him a season earlier. A speedy centre back, who enjoys making probing runs up field, the South African quickly established himself as first-choice centre half for the club, becoming an instant hit with the fans at the same time. Sorely missed when international duties involving the African Nations Cup beckoned in mid-season, he returned stronger than ever, scoring his long-awaited first goal for the club against Leeds in April, which was quickly followed up with a powerful header against Crystal Palace. *Stop Press:* Played in all three of South Africa's Group C World Cup games in France during the summer, before the side were eliminated at the end of the first round.
Bolton W (£2,500,000 from Lazio on 16/9/97) PL 22/2 FLC 1 FAC 1

FISHER Neil John
Born: St Helens, 7 November 1970
Height: 5'10" Weight: 11.0
Surprisingly released by Chester City during the summer after three years at the club, the stylish midfielder showed his versatility last season when he made a number of appearances at left back. Skilful and creative, and with a liking to get forward, he scored a contender for Goal of the Season with a thunderous shot against Colchester at the Deva.
Bolton W (From trainee on 12/7/89) FL 17+7/1 FLC 4 FAC 1
Chester C (Free on 5/6/95) FL 91+17/4 FLC 8 FAC 6 Others 3

FITZGERALD Scott Brian
Born: Westminster, 13 August 1969
Height: 6'0" Weight: 12.12
International Honours: Ei: B-1; U21-4
Signed from Wimbledon during the 1997 close season, following a loan period early in 1996-97, Scott started the first four games in the heart of Millwall's defence before going down from a whole range of illnesses and injuries, which saw him playing just here and there for quite some time. A Pierce Brosnan look-alike, he got back to something like his best towards the end of the campaign, reading the game well to make it look as though he was taking it easy. Is a good passer, likes to get forward, and tends to win aerial battles.
Wimbledon (From trainee on 13/7/89) F/PL 95+11/1 FLC 13 FAC 5 Others 1
Sheffield U (Loaned on 23/11/95) FL 6
Millwall (Loaned on 11/10/96) FL 7
Millwall (£50,000+ on 28/7/97) FL 16+2 FLC 1 Others 2

FITZHENRY Neil
Born: Wigan, 24 September 1978
Height: 6'0" Weight: 12.3
A first-year professional, Neil is recognised as an old-style centre back who is strong in the air and made his Wigan Athletic debut as a substitute in the opening away match of last season at Bournemouth. A local-born player, his first start came in the Auto Windscreens Shield tie against Rotherham United, before a cartilage operation sadly forced him to miss the rest of the campaign.
Wigan Ath (From trainee on 4/7/97) FL 1+2 Others 1

FITZPATRICK Trevor Joseph James
Born: Frimley, 19 February 1980
Height: 6'1" Weight: 12.10
Thrust into the first team due to injuries, 17-year-old Trevor made his debut for Southend United last January, and showed strong running and neat touches up front. A YTS trainee, his future looks good, and he is sure to add to his tally of three appearances this coming season.
Southend U (Trainee) FL 1+2

FJORTOFT Jan-Aage
Born: Aalesund, Norway, 10 January 1967
Height: 6'3" Weight: 14.2
International Honours: Norway: 73
Although the big striker's scoring rate was again first class at Sheffield United in 1997-98, Jan-Aage was frustrated by his failure to hold down a regular place in a team where workrate was paramount. Having managed 12 goals in 18 starts, which included a hat trick in a 5-1 home win over Stockport, before his desire for first team football was granted with a move to Barnsley in mid-January, despite a last-ditch attempt to halt the transfer when Brian Deane left the club, the Norwegian international moved on, being bought primarily to bolster the goal output from forwards who were having a difficult time of it in the Premiership. Although his efforts ultimately failed to save the club from relegation, he endeared himself to the fans with a number of match-winning strikes, while his close control and an eye for an opening caused even the most experienced defenders a problem. A natural goalscorer and crowd pleaser, when given sight of goal, he always looked likely to produce an effort that would give the fans something to cheer about.
Swindon T (£500,000 from Rapid Vienna on 29/7/93) P/FL 62+10/28 FLC 9/9 FAC 3+1/2 Others 1+1
Middlesbrough (£1,300,000 on 31/3/95) P/FL 37+4/10 FLC 7/2 FAC 0+2/1
Sheffield U (£700,000 on 31/1/97) FL 30+4/19 FLC 2+1/1 FAC 1+1/2 Others 3/1
Barnsley (£800,000 on 16/1/98) PL 12+3/6

FLACK Steven (Steve) Richard
Born: Cambridge, 29 May 1971
Height: 6'2" Weight: 14.4
Exeter's Steve was a revelation in 1997-98, when shrugging off injury problems that had hindered him during the previous season, and developing a good understanding with Darren Rowbotham. Using his height and strength to maximum advantage, without getting into the referee's book, the upshot was that he scored more goals than ever before, and proved to be much more than just a target man. Also, as you would expect from someone of his size, he is good in the air.
Cardiff C (£10,000 from Cambridge C on 13/11/95) FL 6+5/1
Exeter C (£10,000 on 13/9/96) FL 57+11/18 FLC 2 FAC 3/1 Others 2+1

FLAHAVAN Aaron Adam
Born: Southampton, 15 December 1975
Height: 6'1" Weight: 11.12
Apart from the opening game, Aaron started 1997-98 as the first-choice Portsmouth goalkeeper in front of veteran, Alan Knight, before being unfairly made the scapegoat for a number of sub-standard team performances and dropped in mid-October. However, when Knight lost form after 20 games, he came back into the team and performed with great confidence, keeping clean sheets in his first four games. Over the course of the season, despite the poor position of the club, he produced several great performances which kept the team in many games, especially during the run in when Pompey eventually maintained their first division in status by the skin of their teeth, his reflex saves and command of the penalty area being paramount.
Portsmouth (From trainee on 15/2/94) FL 50 FLC 6

FLASH Richard Garfield
Born: Birmingham, 8 April 1976
Height: 5'9" Weight: 11.10
Unable to get a game at Watford, the left-sided midfield player was loaned to Lincoln last September in order to provide width and pace to the Imps' attack, but flitted in and out of games and returned to Vicarage Road after four weeks. Was released during the summer.
Manchester U (From trainee on 1/7/94)
Wolverhampton W (Free on 22/9/95)
Watford (Free on 25/7/96) FL 0+1
Lincoln C (Loaned on 2/10/97) FL 2+3

FLECK Robert William
Born: Glasgow, 11 August 1965
Height: 5'8" Weight: 11.9
Club Honours: SPD '87; SLC '87, '88
International Honours: S: 4; U21-6; Yth
Robert continued to be an excellent influence on Norwich's blossoming young stars in 1997-98, but despite being the creator of many goals he was unable to find the net on a regular basis himself. Shortly after it was announced that he was not to be offered a contract for 1998-99, a decision that was totally unpopular with the fans, who presented him with their Player of the Season trophy at the end of the campaign, he signed for Reading and made a handful of appearances as the club put up a desperate attempt to retain its first division status. Although he failed to score, he very nearly became the last Royal to net in a league game at Elm Park when his volley shuddered against the bar in the final match against Norwich, of all teams.
Glasgow R (Free from Possil YM on 14/7/83) SL 61+24/29 SLC 3+5/2 SC 1+1 Others 3+4/3
Partick Thistle (Loaned in November 1983) SL 1+1/1

Norwich C (£580,000 on 17/12/87) FL 130+13/40 FLC 13/11 FAC 16+2/11 Others 7/4
Chelsea (£2,100,000 on 13/8/92) PL 35+5/3 FLC 7/1 FAC 1
Bolton W (Loaned on 17/12/93) FL 6+1/1 Others 1
Bristol C (Loaned on 12/1/95) FL 10/1
Norwich C (£650,000 on 29/8/95) FL 93+11/16 FLC 9+2/2 FAC 3
Reading (£60,000 on 26/3/98) FL 3+2

FLEMING Craig
Born: Halifax, 6 October 1971
Height: 6'0" Weight: 12.10
Signed from Oldham during the 1997 close season, Craig's 1997-98 campaign with Norwich was unfortunately interrupted by a series of niggling injuries, a badly bruised cheek and a twisted ankle to name but two. However, he eventually settled in well to give a string of highly consistent central defensive displays. Excellent in a man-marking role, where his speed and tackling capability make him a difficult opponent, he also takes up good positions for team mates to find him and is a more than capable right back. Scored in the 5-0 home win over Huddersfield.
Halifax T (From trainee on 21/3/90) FL 56+1 FLC 4 FAC 3 Others 3+2
Oldham Ath (£80,000 on 15/8/91) F/PL 158+6/1 FLC 12+1 FAC 11 Others 4
Norwich C (£600,000 on 30/6/97) FL 20+2/1 FLC 1 FAC 1

Craig Fleming

FLEMING Curtis
Born: Manchester, 8 October 1968
Height: 5'11" Weight: 12.8
Club Honours: Div 1 '95
International Honours: Ei: 10; U23-2; U21-5; Yth
By his own standards, Curtis will have endured a disappointing season for Middlesbrough last term. Niggling injuries kept him sidelined for longer than he would have liked, but he did manage 33 appearances and was able to demonstrate his great

defensive skills, and ability to retrieve the ball from the most penetrating attacking threats to his 'keeper. With a liking for going forward in attack, he scored his now customary annual goal in the match at Oxford. Continued to play for the Republic and is a great favourite of the Boro faithful.
Middlesbrough (£50,000 from St Patricks on 16/8/91) F/PL 172+15/2 FLC 17+2/1 FAC 12+1 Others 7+1

FLEMING Terence (Terry) Maurice
Born: Marston Green, 5 January 1973
Height: 5'9" Weight: 10.9
An all-action Lincoln midfield man, he had a superb season in 1997-98 as the Imps made it back to the second division after a gap of six years. Sharp in the tackle, but also a creative player, and City's long throw specialist, Terry occasionally filled in as a wing back.*
Coventry C (From trainee on 2/7/91) F/PL 8+5 FLC 0+1
Northampton T (Free on 3/8/93) FL 26+5/1 FLC 2 FAC 0+1 Others 0+1
Preston NE (Free on 18/7/94) FL 25+7/2 FLC 4 FAC 0+1 Others 3+2
Lincoln C (Signed on 7/12/95) FL 94+5/3 FLC 7+1/1 FAC 5/2 Others 1

FLETCHER Carl Neil
Born: Surrey Heath, 7 April 1980
Height: 5'10" Weight: 11.7
Still a Bournemouth trainee, Carl was thought to be promising enough to be given an early first team opportunity, and he duly came off the bench for the final 11 minutes at Grimsby last February to make his Football League debut. Able to play in defence or midfield, there were no further call ups, but he is undoubtedly a youngster of some promise who will be looking to make further inroads in 1998-99.
Bournemouth (Trainee) FL 0+1

Steve Fletcher

FLETCHER Steven (Steve) Mark
Born: Hartlepool, 26 July 1972
Height: 6'2" Weight: 14.9
In finishing 1997-98 as Bournemouth's joint top scorer with 13 goals, his best seasonal total since joining the club, Steve proved to be extremely sound in the air and good at holding the ball up while waiting for others to join him in attack. Much of the improvement in his goal tally is down to an injury-free campaign and he will be looking forward to leading the club's attack again in 1998-99, and continuing his goalscoring exploits.
Hartlepool U (From trainee on 23/8/90) FL 19+13/4 FLC 0+2/1 FAC 1+2 Others 2+2/1
Bournemouth (£30,000 on 28/7/92) FL 175+16/36 FLC 15/2 FAC 8/1 Others 9

FLITCROFT David (Dave) John
Born: Bolton, 14 January 1974
Height: 5'11" Weight: 13.5
After struggling with injuries during 1996-97, Dave missed just two games through suspension last season and played an important part in Chester City's midfield with some battling performances. The brother of Blackburn's Garry, he scored City's first goal of the campaign against Lincoln City and went on to notch four more.
Preston NE (From trainee on 2/5/92) FL 4+4/2 FLC 0+1 Others 0+1
Lincoln C (Loaned on 17/9/93) FL 2 FLC 0+1
Chester C (Free on 9/12/93) FL 104+21/12 FLC 6+1 FAC 6 Others 7/1

FLITCROFT Garry William
Born: Bolton, 6 November 1972
Height: 6'0" Weight: 12.9
International Honours: E: U21-10; Yth; Sch
Garry was Blackburn's midfield floater in 1997-98, filling in for any position, or when the side chose to go with three midfielders rather than two wingers. Energy and mobility are the facets of his game, but, like Billy McKinlay, his high-action style earned him bookings and contributed to an in-and-out selection throughout the campaign. The brother of Chester's David is a prodigious workhorse, who can tackle with the best of them and close down attackers, while on the other side of the coin he is both skilful and comfortable on the ball.
Manchester C (From trainee on 2/7/91) PL 109+6/13 FLC 11+1 FAC 14/2
Bury (Loaned on 5/3/92) FL 12
Blackburn Rov (£3,200,000 on 26/3/96) PL 58+6/3 FLC 3+1/1 FAC 3+1

FLO Tore Andre
Born: Norway, 15 June 1973
Height: 6'4" Weight: 12.1
Club Honours: FLC '98; ECWC '98
International Honours: Norway: 28
Everton's loss became Chelsea's gain when the Goodison board refused to sanction ex-manager, Joe Royle's £2.6 million bid for Norway's star striker before his contract expired with SK Brann Bergen. Tore Andre would have become a free agent, but Chelsea paid a bargain £300,000 prior to the start of 1997-98 for the last three months of his contract, so that he was eligible for the

Tore Andre Flo

Blues' Cup Winners' Cup campaign. Shortly before joining Chelsea, he scored twice in Norway's shock 4-2 victory over world champions, Brazil, and it took him less than five minutes to notch his first goal in English football when, in the opening match at Highfield Road, he came off the bench to put the Blues ahead. During the first half of the campaign, the Norwegian had to settle for fleeting appearances in the first team as Ruud Gullit alternated his central strikers – sharing the front-running role with Mark Hughes and Luca Vialli – scoring with a classic far-post header at Villa Park to clinch the points and following this up with a superb solo effort against Southampton in the Coca Cola Cup. After starring in Chelsea's 4-0 demolition of Derby County, Hughes was surprisingly rested for the London derby at White Hart Lane and Tore Andre stood in to devastating effect, scoring a stunning hat trick in Chelsea's record 6-1 away victory over Spurs – their heaviest home defeat for 62 years, and in doing so became the second Blues' player to score a hat trick in successive Premiership matches. After Vialli's shock managerial appointment, he left himself out of the Cup Winners' Cup quarter-final away leg against Real Betis and Tore Andre effectively wrapped up the tie with two tremendous goals. He gained his first medal in English football when coming on as substitute against Middlesbrough in the Coca Cola Cup final, started in the European Cup Winners' Cup final against VFB Stuttgart, and managed 15 goals in all competitions to become a firm favourite with the Chelsea crowd. A tall, rangy centre forward, with a very similar physique to his famous elder brother, ex-Sheffield United striker, Jostein – England's nemesis from the 1994 World Cup qualifiers – Tore Andre

kept up the family tradition as he top-scored in Norway's successful World Cup qualifying campaign. Norway's second successive qualification gave the classy centre-forward the perfect stage to demonstrate his rapidly maturing skills, and an opportunity to be compared with the world's top strikers. *Stop Press:* He did just that when scoring against Brazil again, before Norway went out of the competition after losing in the second round to Italy.
Chelsea (£300,000 from Brann Bergen on 4/8/97) PL 16+18/11 FLC 3+1/2 FAC 1 Others 3+2/2

FLOWERS Timothy (Tim) David
Born: Kenilworth, 3 February 1967
Height: 6'2" Weight: 14.0
Club Honours: PL '95
International Honours: E: 10; U21-3; Yth
The goalkeeper started 1997-98 late because of a hernia operation and almost ended it early because of a shoulder operation, being recalled for the final game of the season. In between, he recovered his position as David Seaman's deputy for the national side, a reward for his confidence engendering performances before Christmas. After that he was more fallible, with his shoulder inhibiting his play, and he ended the campaign with his manager questioning whether he or John Filan was the club's first choice. At his best, a positive influence on the team, and an excellent shot-stopper who can inspire others, the season ended on a high with his selection among 22 other hopefuls for England's World Cup squad bound for France. *Stop Press:* Like Nigel Martyn, Tim was not called up for World Cup action in France '98 – David Seaman being an ever present between the sticks for England – before the side crashed out of the World Cup via the penalty shoot-out.
Wolverhampton W (From apprentice on 28/8/84) FL 63 FLC 5 FAC 2 Others 2
Southampton (£70,000 on 13/6/86) F/PL 192 FLC 26 FAC 8
Swindon T (Loaned on 23/3/87) FL 2
Swindon T (Loaned on 13/11/87) FL 5
Blackburn Rov (£2,400,000 on 4/11/93) PL 165+1 FLC 13 FAC 13 Others 10

FLYNN Michael (Mike) Anthony
Born: Oldham, 23 February 1969
Height: 6'0" Weight: 11.0
Stockport's big-hearted skipper, and defensive stalwart of some five years, Mike led his side into the brave new world of the first division in 1997-98 with typical grit and resolve. Although a broken foot ruled him out for two months, he returned to help County towards their goal of league safety – and set himself up in business, dealing in security and plant hire.
Oldham Ath (From apprentice on 7/2/87) FL 37+3/1 FLC 1+1/1 FAC 1 Others 2
Norwich C (£100,000 on 22/12/88)
Preston NE (£125,000 on 4/12/89) FL 134+2/7 FLC 6 FAC 6+1/1 Others 13
Stockport Co (£125,000 on 25/3/93) FL 224+1/12 FLC 24/2 FAC 14/1 Others 19

FLYNN Sean Michael
Born: Birmingham, 13 March 1968
Height: 5'8" Weight: 11.8

Signed from Derby immediately prior to the start of last season Sean quickly settled in as a regular at West Bromwich Albion and, although unfortunate to suffer a leg injury in the home game against Ipswich which ruled him out for several weeks, he came back strongly. A hard-working, right-sided midfielder, who can also occupy the right-back position, he is positive in his play, has a terrific engine, packs a fine shot, and should prove to be an asset for Albion.
Coventry C (£20,000 from Halesowen T on 3/12/91) F/PL 90+7/9 FLC 5/1 FAC 3
Derby Co (£250,000 on 11/8/95) F/PL 39+20/3 FLC 3 FAC 3
Stoke C (Loaned on 27/3/97) FL 5
West Bromwich A (£260,000 on 8/8/97) FL 30+5/2 FLC 4 FAC 0+1

FOLAN Anthony (Tony) Stephen
Born: Lewisham, 18 September 1978
Height: 6'0" Weight: 11.0
International Honours: Ei: U21-2
Having come through the ranks as a YTS and waiting in the wings as a third-year professional, Tony made his first team debut for Crystal Palace in the final match of 1997-98, a 1-0 home win over Sheffield Wednesday, when coming on for the last 15 minutes and impressing. A wide, left-sided midfielder, with a fair range of passing skills, he has good pace, something he relies upon, apart from trickery, to get down the flank in order to deliver crosses to the front men. Played for the Republic of Ireland at U21 level during the season.
Crystal Palace (From trainee on 22/9/95) PL 0+1

FOLEY Dominic Joseph
Born: Cork, 7 July 1976
Height: 6'1" Weight: 12.8
International Honours: Ei: U21-8
This rangy Wolves' forward had to wait until the tenth match of 1997-98 for an appearance as a sub at Fulham, which lasted eight minutes. However, he soon had a run of five games, during which he was sub four times and actually started the match with Tranmere, replacing the absent Robbie Keane, playing behind the front two where he had excelled for the reserves. The clever touches and powerful shooting that he is capable of were rarely seen during this period, and he was not selected after October, before being loaned to Watford in February, where he soon notched a spectacular goal for them. Continued to add to his Republic of Ireland U21 caps with two further appearances last season.
Wolverhampton W (£35,000 from St James' Gate on 31/8/95) FL 2+13/1 FLC 0+3 FAC 0+1 Others 0+2
Watford (Loaned on 24/2/98) FL 2+6/1

FOLLAND Robert (Rob) William
Born: Swansea, 16 September 1979
Height: 5'8" Weight: 11.3
International Honours: W: Yth
Still a trainee, Rob made his debut for Oxford in 1997-98 as a midfield substitute in a home game with Ipswich, and followed that a few months later with another brief appearance at Forest, where he had a hand in the third goal. On the small side, but a useful

player, he could soon be knocking on the Wales U21 door, having been on the bench already.
Oxford U (Trainee) FL 0+2

FORAN Mark James
Born: Aldershot, 30 October 1973
Height: 6'4" Weight: 14.3
Not part of Barry Fry's plans at Peterborough in 1997-98, having played just six times, the big central defender was transferred to Crewe in December, mainly as a stand-in for defensive duties. Commanding in the air, and an asset at both ends of the pitch, he opened his scoring account with his new club with what was effectively the winner in a 3-2 win at Port Vale, and looks to figure more regularly in 1998-99.
Millwall (From trainee on 3/11/90)
Sheffield U (£25,000 on 28/8/93) FL 10+1/1 FLC 1 Others 0+1
Rotherham U (Loaned on 26/8/94) FL 3
Wycombe W (Loaned on 11/8/95) FL 5 FLC 2
Peterborough U (£40,000 on 8/2/96) FL 22+3/1 FAC 1 Others 2
Lincoln C (Loaned on 22/1/97) FL 1+1
Oldham Ath (Loaned on 3/3/97) FL 0+1
Crewe Alex (£25,000+ on 12/12/97) FL 10+2/1

FORBES Adrian Emmanuel
Born: Ealing, 23 January 1979
Height: 5'8" Weight: 11.10
International Honours: E: Yth
Adrian maintained the rate of progress in 1997-98 that brought him through Norwich's ranks the previous season and by the end of the campaign was almost regarded as a senior player in his own right, despite his tender years. Predominantly a right winger, although he can be used effectively on the left flank, where he can cut inside to use his favoured right foot for a crack at goal, he broke his goalscoring duck with a brace in City's 2-1 win at Birmingham in November. A player who is exceptionally quick, has good feet, and works hard in tracking back, an ankle injury forced him to pull out of the Nationwide U21 squad due to face its Italian counterparts at Charlton in March.
Norwich C (From trainee on 21/1/97) FL 31+12/4 FAC 1

FORBES Steven (Steve) Dudley
Born: Stoke Newington, 24 December 1975
Height: 6'2" Weight: 12.6
Steve built on his 1996-97 exceptional last-day debut for Colchester with an impressive pre-1997-98 season, following which he soon won a regular place in the starting line-up. Scored the clinching goal in United's win at Leyton Orient, also scored in the FA Cup at Hereford, and put in impressive performances in the play offs, when he was involved in the vital penalty awards against Barnet and at Wembley. Steve's smooth-running midfield style should allow him to improve even further in a higher division this coming term.
Millwall (£45,000 from Sittingbourne on 11/7/94) FL 0+5 FLC 0+1 FAC 0+1
Colchester U (Signed on 14/3/97) FL 26+10/2 FLC 1+1 FAC 2/1 Others 3+1

FORD Jonathan (Jon) Steven
Born: Birmingham, 12 April 1968
Height: 6'1" Weight: 13.4
Club Honours: AMC '94
Started last season as captain and centre half at Barnet, but lost his place to Michael Basham in the three-man central defensive set up. A strong and determined player, who can also play at left back where he enjoys getting forward, Jon can be a valuable asset at set pieces.
Swansea C (£5,000 from Cradley T on 19/8/91) FL 145+15/7 FLC 12+1 FAC 8+5/2 Others 15+5
Bradford C (£21,000 on 26/7/95) FL 18+1 FLC 4 FAC 2 Others 1
Gillingham (£15,000 on 16/8/96) FL 2+2 FLC 3 FAC 0+1 Others 1
Barnet (£25,000 on 21/2/97) FL 32/1 FLC 4 FAC 1

FORD Mark
Born: Pontefract, 10 October 1975
Height: 5'8" Weight: 10.8
Club Honours: FAYC '93
International Honours: E: U21-2; Yth
As the most expensive of Chris Waddle's summer signings in 1997, having transferred from Leeds, Mark failed to live up to his billing as the gritty midfielder Burnley badly needed, except on a few occasions. Often useful as a breaker up of opposition attacks, and occasionally as instigator of forward moves himself, he has still to justify the fee paid for him, while over enthusiasm, rather than malice, seemed responsible for his frequent bookings which brought two suspensions. However, the former England U21 star relishes a challenge and 1998-99 could be his season.
Leeds U (From trainee on 5/3/93) PL 27+2/1 FLC 7 FAC 5 Others 0+1
Burnley (£250,000 on 18/7/97) FL 32+4/1 FLC 2 FAC 0+1 Others 4+1

FORD Michael (Mike) Paul
Born: Bristol, 9 February 1966
Height: 6'0" Weight: 12.6
Club Honours: WC '88
Oxford's club captain had a wretched season in 1997-98, having had back, knee, and hamstring injuries, which meant that he was limited to just 26 starts, before being released in the summer. As usual, Mike played the part of an attacking full back, being ideally suited to the wing-back role that United started the campaign with, but when the team switched again to a back four he continued at left back, although his last few games were in the centre back role. A popular player, there were just a couple of goals, including one in the passionate derby game at Swindon.
Leicester C (From apprentice on 11/2/84)
Cardiff C (Free from Devizes T on 19/9/84) FL 144+1/13 FLC 6 FAC 9 Others 7
Oxford U (£150,000 on 10/6/88) FL 273+16/18 FLC 27+1/2 FAC 12+1/1 Others 8/1

FORD Robert (Bobby) John
Born: Bristol, 22 September 1974
Height: 5'9" Weight: 11.0
A creative midfielder, as always, Bobby was very consistent, showing good ball skills as well as an ability in dead-ball situations,

while managing a couple of goals for Oxford in 1997-98. Not surprisingly, United fans were up in arms when their hero was sold to Sheffield United in November for a "song", in an effort to ease the club's financial worries at that time. As they best knew, he turned out to be an excellent signing, and showed a coolness and battling quality in midfield that had been missing at Bramall Lane since Mark Patterson had left. Ironically, his only strike for the Blades came against his former club in a home victory, with what must have been his first-ever headed goal.
Oxford U (From trainee on 6/10/92) FL 104+12/7 FLC 14+2/1 FAC 10/2 Others 7/1
Sheffield U (£400,000 on 28/11/97) FL 20+3/1 FAC 8 Others 2

FORD Tony
Born: Grimsby, 14 May 1959
Height: 5'10" Weight: 13.0
Club Honours: Div 3 '80; FLGC '82
International Honours: E: B-2
The evergreen Tony, now Mansfield's assistant manager, had a memorable season in 1997-98, culminating in his 900th overall and 800th Football League appearance. Despite his age, still very much a class act, whether appearing in the centre of defence as a stand in for Scott Eustace, or as a wing back, he also found time to score a few useful goals, including a brace in a 3-2 win against Exeter, before being released in the summer.
Grimsby T (From apprentice on 1/5/77) FL 321+34/54 FLC 31+3/4 FAC 15+4/2 Others 2
Sunderland (Loaned on 27/3/86) FL 8+1/1
Stoke C (£35,000 on 8/7/86) FL 112/13 FLC 8 FAC 9 Others 6/1
West Bromwich A (£145,000 on 24/3/89) FL 114/14 FLC 7 FAC 4/1 Others 2+1
Grimsby T (£50,000 on 21/11/91) FL 59+9/3 FLC 1 FAC 3
Bradford C (Loaned on 16/9/93) FL 5 FLC 2
Scunthorpe U (on 2/8/94) FL 73+3/9 FLC 4/1 FAC 7/1 Others 4 (Free to Barrow on 22/8/96)
Mansfield T (Free on 25/10/96) FL 58+3/5 FLC 2/1 FAC 2/1 Others 3

FORINTON Howard Lee
Born: Boston, 18 September 1975
Height: 5'11" Weight: 11.4
A 1997 summer signing, having scored 38 goals during 1996-97, 15 of them for Oxford City prior to arriving at Yeovil, Howard eventually made his Football League debut for Birmingham when coming off the bench at St Andrews against West Bromwich Albion, after netting four times in six reserve games. Unfortunately, the stocky striker did not even touch the ball in the seven minutes he was on, mainly due to stoppages, and was himself substituted by a defender following Michael Johnson's dramatic 88th-minute goal which ultimately turned out to be the winner.
Birmingham C (Signed from Yeovil on 14/7/97) FL 0+1

FORREST Craig Lorne
Born: Vancouver, Canada, 20 September 1967
Height: 6'5" Weight: 14.4
Club Honours: Div 2 '92
International Honours: Canada: 45

Signed by West Ham from Ipswich during the 1997 close season, the experienced Canadian goalkeeper came into the side in October and was a steadying influence behind a young defence. In his 20 appearances, he only conceded 20 goals and proved to be an excellent shot-stopper after becoming the hero of the hour, when saving a penalty at Blackburn which took the Hammers to the FA Cup quarter final. Unlucky to lose his place in March, due to injury, no doubt will be back in contention for the number one jersey in 1998-99.

Ipswich T (From apprentice on 31/8/85) F/PL 263 FLC 16 FAC 11 Others 14
Colchester U (Loaned on 1/3/88) FL 11
Chelsea (Loaned on 26/3/97) PL 2+1
West Ham U (£500,000 on 23/7/97) PL 13 FLC 3 FAC 4

FORRESTER Jamie Mark
Born: Bradford, 1 November 1974
Height: 5'6" Weight: 10.4
Club Honours: FAYC '93
International Honours: E: Yth (UEFAYC '93); Sch

Started 1997-98 in tremendous form, with goals in the opening three games after a summer hernia operation, and remained Scunthorpe's top scorer throughout the campaign. Although only small, he has brilliant skills on the ground and loves running at opposition defenders, scoring a number of brilliant goals, including an equaliser to spare his team's blushes against Ilkeston Town in the FA Cup. Unfortunately, Jamie had a disappointing closing two months.

Leeds U (£60,000 from Auxerre on 20/10/92) PL 7+2 FAC 1+1/2
Southend U (Loaned on 1/9/94) FL 3+2
Grimsby T (Loaned on 10/3/95) FL 7+2/1
Grimsby T (Signed on 17/10/95) FL 27+14/6 FLC 0+2 FAC 3+1/3
Scunthorpe U (Signed on 21/3/97) FL 53+2/17 FLC 4/1 FAC 4/2 Others 3

FORSTER Nicholas (Nicky) Michael
Born: Caterham, 8 September 1973
Height: 5'10" Weight: 11.5
International Honours: E: U21-4

Having suffered serious damage to his knee ligaments towards the end of 1996-97, Nicky made an earlier than expected return to Birmingham's strike force in 1997-98 when coming into the side at Charlton in October. Obviously taking time to settle down, he played in a handful of matches before getting on the scoresheet in a 2-1 win over Manchester City, and then scoring an effective equaliser in a 1-1 draw at Swindon in his next game. Scoring once more over Christmas, certainly helped in City's upturn in fortunes, but after Dele Adebola's signing and Peter Ndlovu's return to form he was used sparingly from then on. At his best, blessed with considerable pace and good feet, he turns half chances into chances.

Gillingham (Signed from Horley T on 22/5/92) FL 54+13/24 FLC 3+2 FAC 6/2
Brentford (£100,000 on 17/6/94) FL 108+1/39 FLC 11/3 FAC 8/1 Others 7+1/4
Birmingham C (£700,000 on 31/1/97) FL 16+19/6 FAC 3

FORSYTH Michael (Mike) Eric
Born: Liverpool, 20 March 1966
Height: 5'11" Weight: 12.2
Club Honours: Div 2 '87
International Honours: E: B-1; U21-1; Yth

A reliable left-footed central defender for Wycombe Wanderers, Mike was ever present in 1997-98, until a hamstring injury in January, but regained fitness for a few games at the end of the season. Goes about defending in a quietly efficient way, showing excellent positional sense, and was sorely missed when absent from the team.

West Bromwich A (From apprentice on 16/11/83) FL 28+1 FLC 1 FAC 2 Others 1
Derby Co (£25,000 on 28/3/86) FL 323+2/8 FLC 36/1 FAC 15+1 Others 29/1
Notts Co (£200,000 on 23/2/95) FL 7
Hereford U (Loaned on 27/9/96) FL 12
Wycombe W (£50,000 on 6/12/96) FL 47+1/2 FLC 2 FAC 2 Others 2

FORSYTH Richard Michael
Born: Dudley, 3 October 1970
Height: 5'11" Weight: 13.0
International Honours: E: SP-2

Richard has much to look back on with pride, despite Stoke suffering a disappointing 1997-98 season. No one ever doubted his commitment to the shirt he wore, and he again chipped in with valuable goals from his midfield position wide on the left. Strangely, he seems to reserve his very best performances for the games against Wolverhampton Wanderers (the team his family supports) and the goal he scored in the 3-0 win at the Britannia Stadium was many supporters pick as their "goal of the season".

Birmingham C (£50,000 from Kidderminster Hrs on 13/7/95) FL 12+14/2 FLC 7+2 FAC 2 Others 3+1
Stoke C (£200,000 on 25/7/96) FL 77/15 FLC 7/1 FAC 2

FORTUNE-WEST Leopold (Leo) Paul Osborne
Born: Stratford, 9 April 1971
Height: 6'3" Weight: 13.10

Although on the verge of a regular first team place at Gillingham in 1997-98, Leo had to be content with sitting on the substitutes' bench for most of the campaign. As an aggressive, skilful front man, the highlight of his season came when he scored the winning goal against Plymouth in October from fully 30 yards.*

Gillingham (£5,000 from Stevenage Borough on 12/7/95) FL 48+19/18 FLC 3+1/2 FAC 3+1/2
Leyton Orient (Loaned on 27/3/97) FL 1+4

FOSTER Colin John
Born: Chislehurst, 16 July 1964
Height: 6'4" Weight: 14.1

Having played for Cambridge on loan from Watford in 1996-97, the move was firmed up early in 1997-98 and the experienced central defender showed his class in a three-man central defence during the first part of the season. Unfortunately, injury and a switch to a back four, ended his campaign and he was released in the summer.

Leyton Orient (From apprentice on 4/2/82) FL 173+1/10 FLC 12 FAC 19/5 Others 5/1
Nottingham F (Signed on 4/3/87) FL 68+4/5 FLC 8/1 FAC 5 Others 2

West Ham U (Signed on 22/9/89) F/PL 88+5/5 FLC 5 FAC 9/2 Others 2+2
Notts Co (Loaned on 10/1/94) FL 9 Others 2
Watford (£100,000 on 23/3/94) FL 66/7 FLC 6/1 FAC 6
Cambridge U (Free on 26/3/97) FL 33/1 FLC 2 FAC 4

FOSTER Craig Andrew
Born: Australia, 15 April 1969
Height: 5'11" Weight: 13.0
International Honours: Australia: 18

Prior to signing for Portsmouth last September, Craig spent three seasons with Adelaide City, had a spell in Hong Kong, and was at Marconi when the call to play for the Australian national coach, Terry Venables, in England came. As one of the last Australian internationals to sign for Pompey, Craig initially showed some good touches when he played for the first team, scoring both goals as the club held Aston Villa to a 2-2 draw at Fratton Park in the FA Cup, but his return of four goals was poor for a player of such talent and he was left out of the team on Alan Ball's arrival as manager. After almost moving to Sunderland just before the transfer deadline day, the classy midfielder had his contract terminated by mutual consent as the campaign ended.

Portsmouth (£320,000 from Marconi on 19/9/97) FL 13+3/2 FAC 2/2

FOSTER John Colin
Born: Manchester, 19 September 1973
Height: 5'11" Weight: 13.2
International Honours: E: Sch

Unable to make his mark at Manchester City, John was signed by Carlisle just before the transfer deadline last March, and played in the final seven games of the term. Fitting comfortably into the back four, and producing several promising displays, demonstrating particular ability in his tackling and interceptions, the centre back also showed a good range of passing skills. Can play in a number of defensive positions if required.*

Manchester C (From trainee on 15/7/92) P/FL 17+2 FLC 2+1 FAC 2+1
Carlisle U (Free on 26/3/98) FL 7

FOSTER Martin
Born: Sheffield, 29 October 1977
Height: 5'5" Weight: 10.10

Unable to get an opportunity at Leeds in 1997-98, Martin was loaned out to Blackpool last December in order to further his limited experience, and made his Football League debut in a 3-1 defeat at Brentford. Not really able to get going, and obviously finding the game passing him by, the young midfielder was replaced after 65 minutes and shortly afterwards returned to Elland Road.

Leeds U (From trainee on 30/6/96)
Blackpool (Loaned on 4/12/97) FL 1

FOSTER Stephen (Steve)
Born: Mansfield, 3 December 1974
Height: 6'1" Weight: 12.0

Runner up in the Supporters' Player of the Year award, the central defender proved to

105

be one of Bristol Rovers' most consistent players in 1997-98, after being recruited from non-league football, having won an FA Trophy medal at Wembley for Woking. Initially used as a left-full back, he suffered an ankle ligament injury in his second match at Bristol City in the Coca Cola Cup tie, but, on coming back and playing in his favoured centre-back position, he excelled with many Man of the Match performances. A good positional player, Steve was also an imposing presence in opponents' penalty areas for corners.

Bristol Rov (£150,000 from Woking on 23/5/97) FL 32+2 FLC 1 FAC 3 Others 4

FOTIADIS Andrew
Born: Hitchin, 6 September 1977
Height: 5'11" Weight: 11.7
International Honours: E: Sch

After the promise of the previous campaign, Andrew was unable to build upon his excellent start and, plagued by illness and injury, he scored just one goal in half a dozen starts in 1997-98, while making nearly twice as many substitute appearances. This was not a good return for a striker with an all-action style, and full of pace and aggression, and it remains to be seen whether he will accept Town's offer of re-engagement, although the fans would dearly like to see the local boy come good.

Luton T (Free from juniors on 26/7/96) FL 14+18/4 FLC 0+2 FAC 1 Others 1+2

FOWLER Jason Kenneth
Born: Bristol, 20 August 1974
Height: 6'3" Weight: 11.12

An attacking Cardiff midfield player, Jason is capable of producing top-quality displays and scored a magnificent winner in City's home FA Cup third round tie against Oldham. There were several more examples of his magnificent goals and he won the City Supporters' Club Goal of the Season award. Both the then City manager, Kenny Hibbitt, and, later, his new boss, Frank Burrows, both felt that he was a diamond, and the former went on record to say: "Jason has the talent to play at a far higher level, including the first division or even the Premiership, if only he can add a little more strength, power and stamina to his game, plus that consistency. His contract ran out at the end of 1997-98, but he was immediately offered new terms as Burrows sought to build him into his plans.

Bristol C (From trainee on 8/7/93) FL 16+9 FLC 1+2 Others 1+1
Cardiff C (Signed on 19/6/96) FL 75/10 FLC 4/1 FAC 5+1/1 Others 3/1

FOWLER Robert (Robbie) Bernard
Born: Liverpool, 9 April 1975
Height: 5'11" Weight: 11.10
Club Honours: FLC '95
International Honours: E: 7; B-1; U21-8; Yth (UEFAYC '93)

Before picking up a knee injury in the game against Liverpool's arch enemies, Everton, at Anfield towards the end of last February, Robbie had been in devastating form, scoring with regularity on the scale of his

mentor, Ian Rush. The injury saw him unavailable for selection for the rest of the campaign and, according to the physio, Mark Leather, the striker's comeback target would be January 1999. As in previous seasons, many of his goals were vital to the cause, his ability to be in the right place at the right time offering him more goalscoring opportunities than the vast majority of other strikers in the game, and his ability to produce a positive finish to a good percentage of them placing him in the top bracket. Comfortable in possession, with great technique, much guile, and the ability to hold the ball up or go it alone, the fans can hardly wait for his return, especially in partnership with the mercurial Michael Owen. Played just once for England in 1997-98, against Cameroon, but is bound to get further chances once fully fit.

Liverpool (From trainee on 23/4/92) FL 156+4/92 FLC 25/20 FAC 17/9 Others 13+1/8

FOX Ruel Adrian
Born: Ipswich, 14 January 1968
Height: 5'6" Weight: 10.10
International Honours: E: B-2

Although somewhat out of favour under Gerry Francis, this pacy Tottenham winger, with the ability to make the ball look like it is attached to his feet, had a tremendous revival in 1997-98, starting with a goal in the home 3-2 victory over Aston Villa, and being rarely out of the first team from then on, displaying the form that had brought him to White Hart Lane. Always looking so confident on the ball, Ruel loves to take opponents on and is tremendously agile. As well as being quick and industrious down the wing, and an accurate crosser of the ball, he loves to get in a position to shoot at goal himself when he is not frustrating defenders. The best demonstration of his all-round skill saw him scoring in the 3-0 defeat of high-flying Blackburn Rovers in February. Beating a tight midfield, he jetted down the right flank and cut into the 18-yard box to fire a venomous shot past the helpless Tim Flowers into the far corner. Spurs' fans will be hoping that he maintains his form for the coming season.

Norwich C (From apprentice on 20/1/86) F/PL 148+24/22 FLC 13+3/3 FAC 11+4 Others 12+4
Newcastle U (£2,250,000 on 2/2/94) PL 56+2/12 FLC 3/1 FAC 5 Others 4/1
Tottenham H (£4,200,000 on 6/10/95) PL 77+6/10 FLC 6+1/1 FAC 8

FOYLE Martin John
Born: Salisbury, 2 May 1963
Height: 5'10" Weight: 12.0
Club Honours: AMC '93

An experienced striker who plays his heart out for Port Vale whenever selected, once again he made a lot of his appearances from the substitutes bench, but managed to get on the scoresheet on eight occasions in 1997-98, to take him into fourth place in the club's all-time goalscoring list. Was linked to a move to nearby Crewe earlier in the season, but, thankfully, stayed to help the ultimately successful fight against relegation, in which he scored the first goal of the final match at Huddersfield.*

Southampton (From apprentice on 13/8/80) FL 6+6/1 FLC 0+2/2
Aldershot (£10,000 on 3/8/84) FL 98/35 FLC 10/5 FAC 8/5 Others 6
Oxford U (£140,000 on 26/3/87) FL 120+6/36 FLC 16/4 FAC 5/3 Others 3+1/1
Port Vale (£375,000 on 25/6/91) FL 181+58/67 FLC 17+3/7 FAC 13+4/9 Others 13+3/9

FRAIL Stephen
Born: Glasgow, 10 August 1969
Height: 5'9" Weight: 10.9

Signed from Hearts last January, a knee injury prevented the solid Scotsman from making more than a handful of first team appearances for Tranmere during the second part of the season. However, he is eagerly awaiting a fresh start this August, and the Prenton Park faithful will be relishing seeing him fulfil his potential when fully match fit, the move to Rovers, for this boyhood Celtic fan, achieving his long-held ambition to play south of the border. Can operate in a number of positions, but prefers right back or the wing-back role.

Dundee (Free from Possilpark YM on 10/8/85) SL 91+8/1 SLC 2 SC 7 Others 3
Heart of Midlothian (Signed on 31/3/94) SL 45+9/4 SLC 5+1 SC 4+1 Others 1
Tranmere Rov (£90,000 on 30/1/98) FL 4+2

FRAIN John William
Born: Birmingham, 8 October 1968
Height: 5'9" Weight: 11.9
Club Honours: AMC '91

As a left-sided wing back or midfielder, John became part of the Northampton folklore when he scored the winning goal in the 1997 play-off final against Swansea. Last season saw him spending a lot of his time in midfield, as Town aimed for promotion to the first division, where his reputation as a free-kick specialist remained intact, a feature of his play that was highlighted, especially when he created two late goals to save a home game against Preston at the end of the campaign.

Birmingham C (From apprentice on 10/10/86) FL 265+9/23 FLC 28/1 FAC 12 Others 22/2
Northampton T (Free on 24/1/97) FL 58/1 FLC 2 FAC 5 Others 12/2

FRANCIS Damien Jerome
Born: London, 27 February 1979
Height: 6'1" Weight: 10.7

A young Wimbledon striker of whom the club holds high hopes for, Damien was given a run out in 1997-98, mainly due to injuries forcing others on to the sidelines. Made his Premiership debut when coming off the bench for the last 15 minutes in a 5-0 defeat at Arsenal in mid-April and, despite the scoreline, looked quite useful as a lone forward. He then came on after 36 minutes at home to Tottenham, and again was used in the same fashion as the side went down 6-2. Despite all of that, he maintained his confidence and commitment, and made himself noticed as a bustling type of player who was capable of holding the ball up and not concerned to challenge defenders. Joe Kinnear sees this lad as a future star.

Wimbledon (From trainee on 6/3/97) PL 0+2

Kevin Francis

FRANCIS Kevin Michael
Born: Birmingham, 6 December 1967
Height: 6'7" Weight: 15.8
Club Honours: Div 2 '95; AMC '95
International Honours: St Kitts & Nevis

Having failed to agree a new two-year contract, and having mainly been used as a substitute by Birmingham in 1997-98, Kevin joined Oxford in February as part of the deal which took Darren Purse in the other direction. It did not take United fans long to take to the big striker, as he scored the winner on his debut over former manager, Denis Smith's West Bromwich side and, as expected, won everything in the air, in proving to be an excellent target for Joey Beauchamp's crosses. Scored five times in his first eight games, ending up with seven, and, at the same time, won international honours for St Kitts & Nevis, despite it being his first visit to the Caribbean Islands. It was great to see that, following United's last game of the season against Birmingham, Kevin was cheered off the pitch by both sets of fans.

Derby Co (Free from Mile Oak Rov on 2/2/89) FL 0+10 FLC 1+2 FAC 1+2/1 Others 0+1
Stockport Co (£45,000 on 21/2/91) FL 147+5/88 FLC 12/5 FAC 9/6 Others 25/18
Birmingham C (£800,000 on 20/1/95) FL 32+41/13 FLC 6+5/5 FAC 3+3/2 Others 4/1
Oxford U (£100,000+ on 17/2/98) FL 15/7

FRANCIS Stephen (Steve) Stuart
Born: Billericay, 29 May 1964
Height: 6'0" Weight: 14.0
Club Honours: FMC '86, '88
International Honours: E: Yth

Now in his fifth season with Huddersfield, the popular goalkeeper, has amassed over 200 senior appearances for the Terriers since his move from Reading. Still a classy shot-stopper, Steve opened and closed his 1997-98 campaign contributions with Man of the Match awards, before being found in the unusual position of being displaced by Derek O'Connor, Vince Bartram, and then Steve Harper.

Chelsea (From apprentice on 28/4/82) FL 71 FLC 6 FAC 10 Others 1
Reading (£20,000 on 27/2/87) FL 216 FLC 15 FAC 15 Others 13
Huddersfield T (£150,000 on 1//8/93) FL 183 FLC 20 FAC 9 Others 12

FRANDSEN Per
Born: Copenhagen, Denmark, 6 February 1970
Height: 6'1" Weight: 12.6
Club Honours: Div 1 '97
International Honours: Denmark: 13

An energetic and powerful central midfielder who often caught the eye when bursting through from midfield into shooting positions, Per's consistently good form in 1997-98 won him the Bolton player's Player of the Year award. Very much at home in the Premiership, he formed a formidable partnership with Alan Thompson at the heart of the Wanderers' midfield, from where his frightening shooting power brought him goals in the vital late-season wins against Sheffield Wednesday and Leicester. And, as the club's only ever-present player, the Dane proved himself to be a vital component of the never-say-die team spirit, his performances earning him valuable international call ups for Denmark, especially with the World Cup looming. *Stop Press:* Appeared twice for Denmark in World Cup during the summer, but failed to make the side for the Brazil game which ended the Danish run of success.

Bolton W (£1,250,000 from F.C. Copenhagen on 7/8/96) F/PL 78+1/7 FLC 8+1/1 FAC 3+1

FRASER Stuart Thomas
Born: Edinburgh, 9 January 1980
Height: 5'9" Weight: 10.4

A left back who starred in Luton's successful junior team, Stuart signed his first professional contract towards the end of last season and made his league debut in the final match, a 3-2 home win over Carlisle. Will obviously be looking to add to that experience this coming term.

Luton T (From trainee on 2/4/98) FL 1

FREEDMAN Douglas (Dougie) Alan
Born: Glasgow, 21 January 1974
Height: 5'9" Weight: 11.2
International Honours: S: B-1; U21-8; Sch

This talented striker was part of the deal that saw Jamie Smith move to Crystal Palace last October, and within 12 minutes of his Wolves' debut against Swindon he had scored a beauty. Good at turning defenders, he quickly developed an understanding with Robbie Keane, and it was a pity that Steve Bull's injury stopped a promising attacking trio. The hat trick against Norwich in January began with a real classic. Having taken the ball down with his chest, turning brilliantly to leave the defender, he then scored with the outside of his right foot from fully 25 yards. Despite not having a great physical presence, and seeming to be losing form a bit, especially during the FA Cup replay with Wimbledon, he raced past a defender and powered home a splendid winning goal. Although experiencing a brief outing for Scotland "B", and being Wolves' top scorer with 12 goals, he lost his place in the team and was surprisingly omitted from the squad for the FA Cup semi final.

Queens Park R (From trainee on 15/5/92)
Barnet (Free on 26/7/94) FL 47/27 FLC 6/5 FAC 2 Others 2
Crystal Palace (£800,000 on 8/9/95) F/PL 72+18/31 FLC 3+2/1 FAC 2+1 Others 3+2/2
Wolverhampton W (£800,000 on 17/10/97) FL 25+4/10 FAC 5+1/2

Dougie Freedman

FREEMAN Darren Barry Andduet
Born: Brighton, 22 August 1973
Height: 5'11" Weight: 13.0

To go from being the Third Division Player of the Year for 1996-97 to just seven league appearances as a sub and a free transfer in May was the depressing story of Darren's season at Fulham in 1997-98. An injury sustained in the summer sidelined him until mid-October, when he came on to pep up a dismal display by Fulham at Bournemouth. However, he was not 100 per cent fit and sustained a further setback which kept him out until January. With all the striking reinforcements at the club, he only made the occasional substitute appearance, despite scoring twice in his reserve team comeback at Gillingham. His pace and exciting style will certainly benefit another league club before long.

Gillingham (Free from Horsham on 31/1/95) FL 4+8 FAC 0+1 Others 2/1
Fulham (£15,000 + on 4/7/96) FL 32+14/9 FLC 2 Others 3/1

FREESTONE Christopher (Chris) Mark
Born: Nottingham, 4 September 1971
Height: 5'11" Weight: 11.7
Club Honours: AMC '97

An out-and-out striker, Chris quickly became a great favourite at Northampton when he came first on loan from Middlesbrough last December, a deal that was later firmed up. Speedy, clever, and a player who always gives of his best, he scored some important goals, including two against Plymouth in his debut for Town, and all three in the 3-1 win at Plymouth.

Middlesbrough (£10,000 from Arnold T on 2/12/94) P/FL 2+7/1 FLC 1+1/1 FAC 0+2
Carlisle U (Loaned on 3/3/97) FL 3+2/2 Others 2
Northampton T (£75,000 on 8/12/97) FL 23+2/11 FAC 1 Others 5+1/2

FREESTONE Roger
Born: Newport, 19 August 1968
Height: 6'3" Weight: 14.6
Club Honours: Div 2 '89; AMC '94
International Honours: W: U21-1; Yth; Sch

A reliable Swansea goalkeeeper who remains an excellent shot-stopper and possesses a safe pair of hands, Roger signed a four-year contract in the summer of 1997 before starting his seventh season at the Vetch. Recognised for his ability to keep a clean sheet, there were 13 of them last season, it would be difficult to imagine the side without him.

Newport Co (From trainee on 2/4/86 FL 13 Others 1
Chelsea (£95,000 on 10/3/87) FL 42 FLC 2 FAC 3 Others 6
Swansea C (Loaned on 29/9/89) FL 14 Others 1
Hereford U (Loaned on 9/3/90) FL 8
Swansea C (£45,000 on 5/9/91) FL 311+1/3 FLC 18 FAC 19 Others 33

FRENCH Jonathan (Jon) Charles
Born: Bristol, 25 September 1976
Height: 5'10" Weight: 10.10

A local-born midfielder or striker, and confident on the ball, Jon was included in the Bristol Rovers' squad for the first two months of last season, starting just one match at Northampton Town, and having two brief subs' appearances, one of which was an FA Cup tie with Gillingham. Without a reserve team in a competitive league, his progress to win back his place was limited, and during the course of 1997-98 he had trials at Woking, Plymouth Argyle, and Hull City, before being released by Rovers during the summer.

Bristol Rov (From trainee on 15/7/95) FL 8+9/1 FLC 0+1 FAC 0+3 Others 2+1/1

FRIEDEL Bradley (Brad) Howard
Born: USA, 18 May 1971
Height: 6'3" Weight: 14.7
International Honours: USA: 58

Brought over by Liverpool from America just before last Christmas, after waiting several weeks for a work permit to be granted, the Reds' manager, Roy Evans, had a tough decision to make – should he draft Brad into the side straight away or should he

give him time to settle, especially with David James having kept seven clean sheets in his last ten games. In the event, the American international 'keeper eventually came into the side when James hit a bad run, and played the last 11 games of the campaign. A big man, who commands his area with a huge competitive spirit, he did not have an easy time of it when he arrived between the posts, due to several changes in personnel in the back four, but survived with flying colours. Is registered with the club until June 2001. *Stop Press:* Played once for the USA in France '98, a 1-0 defeat at the hands of Yugoslavia, before the side was eliminated from the World Cup at the Group F stage of the competition.

Liverpool (£1,000,000 from Columbus Crew on 23/12/97) PL 11

FROGGATT Stephen (Steve) Junior
Born: Lincoln, 9 March 1973
Height: 5'10" Weight: 11.11
International Honours: E: U21-2

This speedy left-footed Wolves' player seemed to be used anywhere on that side last season, as an attacker, a defender, or in a more central role. In the second match he swerved the ball into the Queens Park Rangers' net from 22 yards and looked in good form, but was then hit by the injury jinx again when he tweaked a hamstring at Fulham, which kept him out for eight matches. Similarly, he was really looking the part in January until on the receiving end of a tackle by an Albion player which led to a nine-game absence. On his return, however, he continued to look one of Wolves' better players before his season petered out.

Aston Villa (From trainee on 26/1/91) F/PL 30+5/2 FLC 1+1 FAC 5+2/1
Wolverhampton W (£1,000,000 on 11/7/94) FL 91+7/7 FLC 8/2 FAC 3 Others 2

FRY Christopher (Chris) David
Born: Cardiff, 23 October 1969
Height: 5'10" Weight: 10.7
International Honours: W: Yth

Signed from Colchester during the 1997 close season, Chris was one of Exeter's more consistent performers in the defence when he played in 1997-98. Good at joining the attack, and an accurate passer, despite sometimes finding himself out of favour, he will be looking for a longer run out next time round.

Cardiff C (From trainee on 3/8/88) FL 22+33/1 FLC 1+2 FAC 0+2 Others 0+2
Hereford U (Free on 2/8/91) FL 76+14/10 FLC 6+2 FAC 8+2/1 Others 6+1
Colchester U (Signed on 24/10/93) FL 102+28/16 FLC 3+3/1 FAC 3+1 Others 12+2/1
Exeter C (Free on 29/7/97) FL 16+12/1 FLC 0+2 FAC 1 Others 1

FUGLESTAD Erik
Born: Stavanger, Norway, 13 August 1974
Height: 5'9" Weight: 11.4

Having arrived at Norwich from Viking Stavanger early last November, Erik only

had to wait a fortnight to make his senior debut, against Middlesbrough at Carrow Road. Quickly impressing the fans with his excellent technique and crossing skills from the wing-back position, and the speed with which he adapted to the demands of English football, he also impressed the Norwegian selectors, who called him up for their World Cup mini camp for English-based players held at Blackburn in February. Playing on both sides of the pitch, although favouring the left, he scored the winner in the 2-1 home victory over Sheffield United, his first goal in England.

Norwich C (Free from Viking Stavanger on 8/11/97) FL 23+1/2 FAC 1

FULLARTON James (Jamie)
Born: Glasgow, 20 July 1974
Height: 5'10" Weight: 10.6
International Honours: S: U21-17

A free transfer signing for Crystal Palace under the Bosman ruling immediately prior to 1997-98 getting underway, the former Scottish U21 international had been playing for Bastia, in France, during the past year and was delighted to be offered the opportunity of playing in the Premiership. On the bench for four of the five opening games, coming on in three of them, he made his full debut in a 3-0 home defeat at the hands of Chelsea, before getting on the scoresheet two games later when cracking in the equaliser at Coventry for his only goal of the campaign. A busy, tough-tackling ball winner, Jamie is signed up with Palace until June 2000.

St Mirren (Free from Motherwell BC on 13/6/91) SL 94+9/3 SLC 2 SC 4 Others 4+1 (Transferred to Bastia during 1996 close season)
Crystal Palace (Free on 7/8/97) PL 19+6/1 FLC 2 FAC 3

FURLONG Paul Anthony
Born: Wood Green, 1 October 1968
Height: 6'0" Weight: 13.8
Club Honours: FAT '88
International Honours: E: SP-5

In becoming the first Birmingham player to score two league hat tricks since Keith Bertschin in 1979-80, within 17 days of each other last January, Paul at last fully justified his transfer fee as his dominant front-line displays saw him end up as the club's leading scorer, with 19 goals in all competitions. Had not suspension and injury problems forced him to miss 23 matches, taking the same ratio into account he would have scored well over the 30 mark. Big, powerful, and full of running, even to the point of chasing lost causes, his commitment to the team is vital if they are to challenge for promotion in 1998-99.

Coventry C (£130,000 from Enfield on 31/7/91) FL 27+10/4 FLC 4/1 FAC 1+1 Others 1
Watford (£250,000 on 24/7/92) FL 79/37 FLC 7/4 FAC 2 Others 4
Chelsea (£2,300,000 on 26/5/94) PL 44+20/13 FLC 3+1 FAC 5+4/1 Others 7/3
Birmingham C (£1,500,000 on 17/7/96) FL 61+7/25 FLC 8/3 FAC 4/3

GABBIADINI Marco
Born: Nottingham, 20 January 1968
Height: 5'10" Weight: 13.4
Club Honours: Div 3 '88
International Honours: E: B-1; FL-1; U21-2

The Stoke management team of Chic Bates and Alan Durban spent a fair bit of time during the summer of 1997 helping to rescue Marco from his nightmare in Greek football at Panionis, a situation exacerbated by the fact he was not receiving wages. However, just as he was achieving match fitness, City ended Bates' spell as their manager and his replacement, Chris Kamara, did not fancy firming up the move to that of a full transfer. Offered a one-month trial, within days, Marco was off to his old club, York City, after an absence of 11 years, and gave an outstanding display on his debut against Watford, before scoring in a win at Brentford. Unfortunately, having been injured he never really recovered full fitness, scoring no more goals, and was released at the end of the campaign.

York C (From apprentice on 5/9/85) FL 42+18/14 FLC 4+3/1 Others 4/3
Sunderland (£80,000 on 23/9/87) FL 155+2/74 FLC 14/5 FAC 5 Others 9/4
Crystal Palace (£1,800,000 on 1/10/91) FL 15/5 FLC 6/1 FAC 1 Others 3/1
Derby Co (£1,000,000 on 31/1/92) F/PL 163+25/50 FLC 13/7 FAC 8+1/3 Others 16+1/8 (Free to Panionios during 1997 close season)
Birmingham C (Loaned on 14/10/96) FL 0+2
Oxford U (Loaned on 31/1/97) FL 5/1
Stoke C (Free on 24/12/97) FL 2+6 FAC 1/1
York C (Free on 20/2/98) FL 5+2/1

GADSBY Matthew John
Born: Sutton Coldfield, 6 September 1979
Height: 6'1" Weight: 11.12

Having signed professional forms for Walsall last February, after 18 months as a YTS, and following some impressive displays in the reserves throughout the season, in which he showed constructive ability and an eye for goal, this young midfielder made his debut in the final Nationwide League game of 1997-98, substituting for Adrian Viveash during the last nine minutes of a 1-0 home defeat against Wycombe. Is certainly one to watch out for in 1998-99.

Walsall (From trainee on 12/2/98) FL 0+1

GAGE Kevin William
Born: Chiswick, 21 April 1964
Height: 5'10" Weight: 12.11
Club Honours: Div 4 '83
International Honours: E: Yth

Kevin teamed up with former Wimbledon colleague, Glyn Hodges, at Hull City after signing from Preston last September, appearing to be the perfect candidate for the vital right-wing-back berth, and results were comparatively good while he was in the team. Unfortunately, he was troubled by an on-going calf problem that eventually sidelined him from early December, but, not before he had shown the Boothferry Park faithful the art of coupling solid defending with thoughtful use of the ball in the attacking third.

Wimbledon (From apprentice on 4/1/82) FL 135+33/15 FLC 7+2/1 FAC 8+3/1 Others 0+1
Aston Villa (£100,000 on 17/7/87) FL 113+2/8 FLC 13/3 FAC 9/1 Others 8
Sheffield U (£150,000 on 15/11/91) F/PL 107+5/7 FLC 6 FAC 10+2 Others 1
Preston NE (Free on 28/3/96) FL 20+3 FAC 1
Hull C (Free on 26/9/97) FL 8+2 FAC 1 Others 1

GALE Shaun Michael
Born: Reading, 8 October 1969
Height: 6'1" Weight: 11.10

Another 1997-98 close season signing for Exeter, the composed Shaun came from Barnet and immediately settled down to become a fans' favourite, his undoubted ability in the Grecians' defence shining through. A recognised corner kick specialist, and an accurate passer, with a liking to get upfield whenever possible to get his crosses in, he also contributed to several goals.

Portsmouth (From trainee on 12/7/88) FL 2+1 Others 0+1
Barnet (Free on 13/7/94) FL 109+5/5 FLC 10 FAC 6 Others 3
Exeter C (£10,000 on 23/6/97) FL 42+1/4 FLC 2 FAC 2 Others 1

GALL Benny
Born: Copenhagen, Denmark, 14 March 1971
Height: 6'1" Weight: 13.11

In his second season as the Shrewsbury goalkeeper, Benny played 13 times in 1997-98 before losing his place to suspension and never regaining it. Following that, he decided to return to Denmark in mid-term to take up other employment and play part time. A little eccentric but aren't all goalkeepers? His strength was in the air and in distributing the ball.

Shrewsbury T (Free from Dordrecht De Grashaarp on 16/8/96) FL 34 FLC 2 FAC 2 Others 2

GALLACHER Kevin William
Born: Clydebank, 23 November 1966
Height: 5'8" Weight: 11.0
International Honours: S: 39; B-2; U21-7; Yth

Kevin had his best-ever season with Blackburn in 1997-98, netting 20 goals in all competitions, including 16 in the Premiership. Among his outstanding strikes was a hat trick against Aston Villa, and a magnificent long-range effort at Highbury, but his most vital one was the toe poke that brought all three points against Chelsea at the end of April, a result that moved the club into the European placings for this coming term. Was extremely lively throughout the season, his quick turns and feints causing consternation among defenders and, despite being somewhat erratic in front of goal on occasion, Kevin achieved virtual cult status as a goalscorer in Scotland's World Cup campaign. Moved to the wide right at Rovers in September, when Stuart Ripley was injured, he frequently dropped back into midfield later on when substitutions were made. He was also the centre of controversy when sent off at West Ham in the FA cup for use of an elbow, a charge he denied vehemently and which, when offered up on TV, appeared unproven and totally out of character with the player. Stop Press: Played in all three of Scotland's Group A World Cup games during the summer as a regular starter and, along with all the fans and players alike, would have been bitterly disappointed to have been eliminated at the end of the first round, especially after drawing with Norway.

Dundee U (Signed from Duntocher BC on 2/9/83) SL 118+13/27 SLC 13/5 SC 20+3/5 Others 15+6/3
Coventry C (£900,000 on 29/1/90) F/PL 99+1/28 FLC 11/7 FAC 4 Others 2
Blackburn Rov (£1,500,000 on 22/3/93) PL 116+7/41 FLC 7+1/2 FAC 12/4 Others 1+1

GALLEN Kevin Andrew
Born: Chiswick, 21 September 1975
Height: 5'11" Weight: 12.10
International Honours: E: U21-4; Yth (EUFAC '93); Sch

Yet again this talented young forward had a season disrupted by injury, this time in 1997-98, as a knee injury (sustained in 1996-97), a stomach injury, and a virus limited his appearances to 31. Although obviously limiting his ability to score, there were four goals, including two against Middlesbrough, one in the FA Cup, the other in the league, and two vital headers that earned points against Oxford and Bradford, as Rangers battled to avoid relegation. Having made an excellent start to his career, it is a shame to see him struggling as, on his day, he is an intuitive marksman who causes all kinds of problems in and around the box. Is also an excellent runner off the ball.

Queens Park R (From trainee on 22/9/92) P/FL 78+18/24 FLC 4+2/2 FAC 4+2/2

GALLIMORE Anthony (Tony) Mark
Born: Crewe, 21 February 1972
Height: 5'11" Weight: 12.12
Club Honours: Div 3 '95; AMC '98

After initially failing to impress the new Grimsby boss, Alan Buckley, and at one time going on the transfer list, Tony battled to regain his left-back position with some sterling performances in 1997-98, that eventually made him automatic choice on the left side of defence. His solid defending and forward runs played a key part in the Mariners efforts to regain first division status and he was also a member of the side that won the Auto Windscreen Shield when beating Bournemouth at Wembley.

Stoke C (From trainee on 11/7/90) FL 6+5
Carlisle U (Loaned on 3/10/91) FL 8
Carlisle U (Loaned on 26/2/92) FL 8
Carlisle U (£15,000 on 25/3/93) FL 124/9 FLC 8/1 FAC 8 Others 24/1
Grimsby T (£125,000 on 28/3/96) FL 80+7/4 FLC 7 FAC 7 Others 10

GALLOWAY Michael (Mick) Anthony
Born: Nottingham, 13 October 1974
Height: 5'11" Weight: 11.5

Having been on loan at Gillingham during the latter part of 1996-97, Mick's transfer from Notts County was finally firmed up

just before the 1997-98 campaign got underway. A left-sided midfielder, who gained a regular place in the side after Christmas, again he proved himself to be good when going forward, and an accurate passer of the ball. Can also get amongst the goals.

Notts Co (From trainee on 15/6/93) FL 17+4 FLC 2 FAC 0+1 Others 4
Gillingham (£10,000+ on 27/3/97) FL 38+10/2 FLC 2 FAC 1+1

GANNON James (Jim) Paul
Born: Southwark, 7 September 1968
Height: 6'2" Weight: 13.0

In 1997-98, Stockport's longest-serving player resisted the temptation of semi-retirement to Ireland, and a job in accountancy, to bolster the ranks for the club's first-ever division campaign, playing a vital role as a defensive "shield" in front of two central defenders, before a broken leg sustained in training cut short his season in March. With undiminished ability in the air, he is still a good man to have at either end of the park, especially for set pieces.

Sheffield U (Signed from Dundalk on 27/4/89)
Halifax T (Loaned on 22/2/90) FL 2
Stockport Co (£40,000 on 7/3/90) FL 302+14/52 FLC 31+2/3 FAC 17/1 Others 37+2/8
Notts Co (Loaned on 14/1/94) FL 2

GARDE Remi
Born: L'Arbresle, France, 3 April 1966
Height: 5'9" Weight: 11.7
Club Honours: PL '98
International Honours: France: 5

Having made just enough appearances for Arsenal to win a championship medal, as the Gunners stormed to the Premiership and FA Cup double in 1997-98, Remi decided to retire from the game and take up a coaching position at Marseilles in the summer. Another one of Arsene Wenger's sound acquisitions from his homeland, when called up for the first team, Remi was normally to be seen assisting in defensive duties or on the right-hand side of midfield, where his immaculate passing and assured tackling often took the eye. At the time of going to press, however, both his manager and team mates were asking the former French international to reconsider his decision.

Arsenal (Free from Strasbourg on 14/8/96) PL 13+8 FAC 1

GARDINER Mark Christopher
Born: Cirencester, 25 December 1966
Height: 5'10" Weight: 11.7
Club Honours: FAT '96; GMVC '97
International Honours: E: SP-1

Having already experienced life in the Football League, and following a two-year spell as a semi-pro with Macclesfield, Mark proved to be versatile in midfield and at left back in 1997-98. However, finding the rigours of the return to full-time football difficult, and sustaining several niggling injuries (calf, knee and groin) in the first half of the season, he made the decision to return to non-league football with Northwich Victoria in December.

Swindon T (From apprentice on 1/10/84) FL 7+3/1 FAC 0+2/1

Torquay U (Free on 6/2/87) FL 37+12/4 FLC 3+1 FAC 1+1/1 Others 1+1
Crewe Alex (Free on 22/8/88) FL 179+14/35 FLC 13+3/3 FAC 18+1/5 Others 17+3/1 (Freed during 1995 close season)
Chester C (Loaned on 3/3/95) FL 2+1
Macclesfield T (Free from Frederikstad on 21/10/95) FL 7/2 FAC 1

GARDNER James (Jimmy)
Born: Dunfermline, 27 September 1967
Height: 5'11" Weight: 11.8

Signed from Cardiff in the summer of 1997, Jimmy was an ever present on the wing for Exeter in 1997-98 until he found himself out of favour. Good at picking the ball up from deep, and accurate in his finding of other players from the flank, the Scot will be looking for more opportunities this coming season. Is a fine crosser of the ball who can play on either flank.

Queens Park (Free from Ayresome North AFC on 1/4/87) SL 1+2
Motherwell (Signed on 1/7/88) SL 8+8 SC 0+1
St Mirren (Signed on 7/9/93) SL 31+10/1 SLC 1 SC 0+2 Others 2
Scarborough (Free on 25/8/95) FL 5+1/1
Cardiff C (Free on 28/9/95) FL 51+12/5 FLC 0+1 FAC 3 Others 4+1
Exeter C (Free on 29/7/97) FL 19+4/1 FLC 2 FAC 1 Others 1

GARNER Darren John
Born: Plymouth, 10 December 1971
Height: 5'9" Weight: 12.7
Club Honours: AMC '96

His all-action midfield play made him one of Rotherham's best players throughout 1997-98, after he had settled his early season differences. It was pleasing to see him get forward more often and he netted some superb goals as he bagged his best ever haul. Unfortunately, he picked up several bookings, which saw him miss games through suspension.

Plymouth Arg (From trainee on 15/3/89) FL 22+5/1 FLC 2+1 FAC 1 (Free to Dorchester T on 19/8/94)
Rotherham U (£20,000 on 26/6/95) FL 98+3/6 FLC 6 FAC 5/3 Others 6/1

GARNETT Shaun Maurice
Born: Wallasey, 22 November 1969
Height: 6'2" Weight: 13.4
Club Honours: AMC '90

As forceful as ever in the air, and with an adroit turn of pace, Shaun cut an important figure at the heart of Oldham's defence in 1997-98, despite having several different partners. After being left out due to lack of form, around the Christmas period, he stormed back to pick up the next three Player of the Month awards to show his real value to the side. Totally committed, he is a player you can rely on to produce everything and more to the cause.

Tranmere Rov (From trainee on 15/6/88) FL 110+2/5 FLC 13/1 FAC 4 Others 15+2
Chester C (Loaned on 1/10/92) FL 9
Preston NE (Loaned on 11/12/92) FL 10/2 Others 1
Wigan Ath (Loaned on 26/2/93) FL 13/1
Swansea C (£200,000 on 11/3/96) FL 15 FLC 2
Oldham Ath (£150,000 on 19/9/96) FL 54+3/4 FLC 2 FAC 3 Others 1

GARVEY Stephen (Steve) Hugh
Born: Stalybridge, 22 November 1973
Height: 5'9" Weight: 11.1

Yet another player who has come through the Crewe Alexandra academy, Steve was not a regular performer in 1997-98, having had a number of injuries, although he was always capable of forcing his way back into the side when fully fit. Able to play wide on either flank, where he attacks the full back, Steve scored Crewe's final goal of the season, before being released during the summer. Spent a month on loan at Chesterfield in October, making just three appearances before returning to Gresty Road.

Crewe Alex (From trainee on 25/10/91) FL 68+40/8 FLC 6+7/2 FAC 3+4/2 Others 8+3/1
Chesterfield (Loaned on 17/10/97) FL 2+1

Paul Gascoigne

GASCOIGNE Paul John
Born: Gateshead, 27 May 1967
Height: 5'10" Weight: 11.7
Club Honours: FAYC '85; FAC '91
International Honours: E: 57; B-4; U21-13; Yth

One of the most gifted midfielders ever produced in these Isles, Paul signed for Middlesbrough from Glasgow Rangers on transfer deadline day last March, and became the first player to make his debut in a Wembley cup final, when he came off the bench for the last 27 minutes of normal time in a 2-0 defeat at the hands of Chelsea. Although his skill is beyond doubt, from his formative days at Newcastle through to his triumphant days at Spurs, Lazio, and Rangers, "Gazza" has never been able to escape the searching spotlight of fame and notoriety. On his day, a brilliant talent, going forward, spraying passes to his colleagues, and unleashing powerful and spectacular shots at goal, his behaviour off the field has to be balanced against his prowess on it and his charisma in the dressing room, where he continually bolsters the morale of team

mates. There was no doubt that much of his positive side paved the way for Boro's late surge to gain automatic promotion to the Premiership, but, unfortunately, due to a well documented scenario, he was not among Glenn Hoddle's England team that went for World Cup glory in France '98. Hopefully, he can put his stamp on his first taste of the Premiership in 1998-99.

Newcastle U (From apprentice on 13/5/85) FL 83+9/21 FLC 8/1 FAC 4/3 Others 2+1
Tottenham H (£2,000,000 on 18/7/88) FL 91+1/19 FLC 14+1/8 FAC 6/6 (£5,500,000 To Lazio on 1/5/92)
Glasgow R (£4,300,000 on 10/7/95) SL 64+10/30 SLC 7/4 SC 7+1/3 Others 14/2
Middlesbrough (£3,450,000 on 27/3/98) FL 7 FLC 0+1

GAUGHAN Steven (Steve) Edward
Born: Doncaster, 14 April 1970
Height: 6'0" Weight: 13.6

Unable to hold down a regular place at Chesterfield in 1997-98, and following just three appearances during the campaign, it was a case of the prodigal returning when he re-signed for Darlington in November after spending 15 months at Saltergate. Tenacious and powerful, he quickly showed he had lost none of his hard running, and his distribution seemed to have improved as he soon re-established himself in the heart of the Quakers' midfield.

Doncaster Rov (Free from Hatfield Main Colliery on 21/1/88) FL 42+25/3 FLC 2+2 FAC 4+1 Others 5+1
Sunderland (Free on 1/7/90)
Darlington (£10,000 on 21/1/92) FL 159+12/15 FLC 8 FAC 6/1 Others 10+1
Chesterfield (£30,000 on 16/8/96) FL 16+4 FLC 1+1/1 FAC 0+1 Others 1
Darlington (Signed on 21/11/97) FL 23+1/1 FAC 2 Others 1

GAVIN Mark Wilson
Born: Bailleston, 10 December 1963
Height: 5'9" Weight: 11.1

Freed by Scunthorpe last September, Mark was signed as a trialist by Hartlepool, having been much travelled since his first spell with the club in 1984-85. The experienced midfielder made a number of substitute appearances, but did not make a big enough impression to persuade manager, Mick Tait, that he was any better than the existing players on his staff, and left a few weeks later.

Leeds U (From apprentice on 24/12/81) FL 20+10/3 FLC 4+1/1 FAC 0+1
Hartlepool U (Loaned on 29/3/85) FL 7/1
Carlisle U (Free on 4/7/85) FL 12+1/1 FLC 2/1 Others 1
Bolton W (Free on 27/3/86) FL 48+1/3 FLC 1 FAC 5/1 Others 10/1
Rochdale (£20,000 on 14/8/87) FL 23/6 FLC 3 FAC 1 Others 2
Heart of Midlothian (£30,000 on 3/2/88) SL 5+4
Bristol C (£30,000 on 4/10/88) FL 62+7/6 FLC 8 FAC 13/1 Others 6/1
Watford (Signed on 9/8/90) FL 8+5
Bristol C (£60,000 on 6/12/91) FL 34+7/2 FLC 0+1 FAC 4 Others 4
Exeter C (Signed on 11/2/94) FL 73+4/4 FLC 3 FAC 3 Others 5
Scunthorpe U (Free on 23/8/96) FL 10+1 FLC 1 Others 1+1
Hartlepool U (Free on 25/9/97) FL 0+3

GAYLE Brian Wilbert
Born: Kingston, 6 March 1965
Height: 6'1" Weight: 13.12

Freed by Bristol Rovers last December, Brian joined Shrewsbury to add some solidity to central defence, following the departure of Dave Walton. A short-term contract was definitely advantageous to Town, as his organising ability became very apparent after an uncertain start, and he looked very comfortable teaming up with a very inexperienced defence. As a result, the goals against began to dry up.*

Wimbledon (From apprentice on 31/10/84) FL 76+7/3 FLC 7/1 FAC 8/1 Others 2
Manchester C (£325,000 on 6/7/88) FL 55/3 FLC 8 FAC 2 Others 1
Ipswich T (£330,000 on 19/1/90) FL 58/4 FLC 3 FAC 0+1
Sheffield U (£750,000 on 17/9/91) F/PL 115+2/9 FLC 9 FAC 11/1 Others 1/1
Exeter C (Free on 14/8/96) FL 10 FLC 1
Rotherham U (Free on 10/10/96) FL 19+1 FAC 1 Others 1
Bristol Rov (Free on 27/3/97) FL 23 FLC 2
Shrewsbury T (Free on 9/12/97) FL 23

GAYLE John
Born: Bromsgrove, 30 July 1964
Height: 6'2" Weight: 15.4
Club Honours: AMC '91

John is a giant of a striker, whose presence for Northampton unsettles defences with his aerial power and general bustling style of play, making it hard for defenders to hold him. Although injuries and suspension limited his appearances for the latter part of last season, his all-round efforts could not be questioned, prior to him being released during the summer.

Wimbledon (£30,000 from Burton A on 1/3/89) FL 17+3/2 FLC 3
Birmingham C (£175,000 on 21/11/90) FL 39+5/10 FAC 2 Others 8+1/4
Walsall (Loaned on 20/8/93) FL 4/1
Coventry C (£100,000 on 13/9/93) PL 3 FLC 1+2
Burnley (£70,000 on 17/8/94) FL 7+7/3 FLC 1+1/1 FAC 1+1/1
Stoke C (£70,000 on 23/1/95) FL 14+12/4 FLC 2 FAC 0+1 Others 3+1
Gillingham (Loaned on 14/3/96) FL 9/3
Northampton T (£25,000 on 10/2/97) FL 35+13/7 FLC 1+1/2 FAC 4 Others 9+1/4

GAYLE Marcus Anthony
Born: Hammersmith, 27 September 1970
Height: 6'1" Weight: 12.9
Club Honours: Div 3 '92
International Honours: E: Yth. Jamaica: 5

This pacy and skilled Wimbledon forward, as in the case of several other Dons, had mixed fortunes in 1997-98. Having become one of the most feared of front men alongside Dean Holdsworth in 1996-97, with the latter moving on last October, many players carrying injuries, and the club struggling at the wrong end of the table, things were very different this time round. Called up by Jamaica was an honour, and going to the World Cup Finals in France, along with Robbie Earle, as one of the 22 selected was an even greater honour, but I guess he may have swopped some of that for better results at Selhurst Park last season. Still, he remained a threat for opposing defences, scoring a vital goal in a 1-0 win at

Leicester, and is bound to go better this coming term. *Stop Press:* Called up for the final game of Jamaica's World Cup, a 2-1 win over Japan, he will have relished the experience.

Brentford (From trainee on 6/7/89) FL 118+38/22 FLC 6+3 FAC 6+2/2 Others 14+6/2
Wimbledon (£250,000 on 24/3/94) PL 108+25/17 FLC 13+1/5 FAC 15+3/3

GAYLE Mark Samuel Roye
Born: Bromsgrove, 21 October 1969
Height: 6'2" Weight: 12.3

With Jason Kearton and Ademola Bankole in front of him in the battle for the goalkeeper's place at Crewe in 1997-98, Mark was loaned out to Chesterfield in October as a stand in for the injured Billy Mercer, keeping two clean sheets in his five games played, and being on the losing side just once. tall and commanding, and an excellent shot-stopper, he had earlier been loaned to non-league Hereford (September), and later spent a period on loan at Luton (March) without being called upon, before being released during the summer.

Leicester C (From trainee on 1/7/88)
Blackpool (Free on 15/8/89) FLC 1 (Free to Worcester C in July 1990)
Walsall (£15,000 on 8/5/91) FL 74+1 FLC 8 FAC 1 Others 8
Crewe Alex (£35,000 on 21/12/93) FL 82+1 FLC 6 FAC 5 Others 9
Chesterfield (Loaned on 20/10/97) FL 5

GEMMILL Scot
Born: Paisley, 2 January 1971
Height: 5'11" Weight: 11.6
Club Honours: FMC '92; Div 1 '98
International Honours: S: 13; B-2; U21-4

The son of the former Scottish international, Archie, of Derby County and Nottingham Forest fame, Scot has emulated his dad at international level, but has yet to get close to him on the club front. However, time will tell. Missing just two games last season as Nottingham Forest's midfield catch-and-carry man, who links defence and attack, he continued to show himself to be a good all-rounder with plenty of stamina and vision and is at his best when playing one-twos around the opponents' penalty box. There was no doubting his importance and he was delighted to be an integral part of the team that went back to the Premiership at the first time of asking. *Stop Press:* A member of Scotland's World Cup final 22, having played twice for the side in 1997-98, Scot was not called upon and could only watch on as the team went out at the end of the first round, despite drawing with Norway.

Nottingham F (From trainee on 5/1/90) F/PL 210+15/21 FLC 27+2/3 FAC 18+2/1 Others 13+1/4

GENTILE Marco
Born: Den Haag, Holland, 24 August 1968
Height: 6'1" Weight: 12.0

Signed for Burnley by Adrian Heath during the 1997 close season, shortly before the latter's departure for Everton, Marco joined the Clarets on a free from MVV Maastricht. However, with a change of management he proved surplus to Chris Waddle's requirements and returned to Europe in October

after only one appearance at centre half in a meaningless Coca Cola Cup second leg at Stoke.

Burnley (Free from MVV Maastricht on 10/7/97) FLC 1

GEORGE Daniel (Danny) Stephen
Born: Lincoln, 22 October 1978
Height: 6'1" Weight: 12.0

Danny became a fixture in Doncaster's overworked defence, following his move from Nottingham Forest last January, proving to have a wise head on young shoulders. Already a popular figure with the Rovers' supporters, and definitely a player to watch in the future, if he exercises the "get out clause" on his contract he will be sorely missed.

Nottingham F (From trainee on 31/10/95)
Doncaster Rov (Free on 16/1/98) FL 16+2/1

GEORGE Liam Brendan
Born: Luton, 2 February 1979
Height: 5'9" Weight: 11.3
International Honours: Ei: Yth

A tricky teenage striker, and another product of Luton's successful youth policy, Liam got a few chances in the Town's first team in 1997-98 and did well without suggesting that he is ready at this level just yet. However, as a regular scorer for the youth and reserve teams, and having played for the Irish U18 side, he will surely be given further opportunities in the coming season.

Luton T (From trainee on 20/1/97) FL 1 FLC 0+2 Others 0+1

GERMAINE Gary
Born: Birmingham, 2 August 1976
Height: 6'2" Weight: 14.0
International Honours: S: U21-1

Unable to get past Alan Miller in the West Bromwich Albion goal, with Paul Crichton and Chris Adamson ahead of him in the queue, the former Scottish U21 international goalkeeper was loaned out to Shrewsbury last January, having little opportunity to impress in a 1-0 defeat at Doncaster before returning to Albion and being released in the summer. Once highly thought of, he needs regular football.

West Bromwich A (From trainee on 5/7/94)
Scunthorpe U (Loaned on 8/3/96) FL 11
Shrewsbury T (Loaned on 2/1/98) FL 1

GERRARD Paul William
Born: Heywood, 22 January 1973
Height: 6'2" Weight: 13.1
International Honours: E: U21-18

A tall goalkeeper, with excellent shot-stopping reflexes, Paul finally got his wish to replace the legendary Neville Southall at Goodison in 1997-98, only to slip back again in the pecking order when the Blues signed Thomas Myhre. In making his first and last appearances of the season, in the Coca Cola Cup, he celebrated a clean sheet and an outstanding display at Scunthorpe, but at Coventry City a month later, however, he conceded four and lost his place. Towards the end of the season he expressed a desire to move away from Goodison to further his career.

Oldham Ath (From trainee on 2/11/91) P/FL 118+1 FLC 7 FAC 7 Others 2+1
Everton (£1,000,000 + on 1/7/96) PL 8+1 FLC 2

GHAZGHAZI Sufyan
Born: Honiton, 24 August 1977
Height: 5'8" Weight: 11.7
International Honours: E: Yth; Sch

A young forward who broke into Exeter's team in 1996-97, Sufyan had his chances of first team action in 1997-98 hampered by the form of Steve Flack and Darren Rowbotham, and made only one league start before being released during the summer. However, he is still young and time is most definitely on his side.

Exeter C (From trainee on 31/7/96) FL 2+13 FLC 0+1 FAC 1+1 Others 1

GIALLANZA Gaetano
Born: Dornach, Switzerland, 6 June 1974
Height: 6'0" Weight: 11.7

A Swiss-born striker who joined Bolton on loan from French club, FC Nantes, in March, Gaetano possesses a fine goal-scoring record overseas, and is eligible to play for Switzerland or Italy. Obviously, many Bolton fans were anticipating great things from him, after making his Trotters' debut in the home game against Leeds, when coming on as a substitute with ten minutes left on the clock and scoring what looked to be a perfectly legitimate goal in the dying seconds to give Wanderers a share of the points, only to have it disallowed. However, not figuring too highly in Colin Todd's plans, there were to be just two more appearances from the bench before he departed.

Bolton W (Loaned from Nantes on 25/3/98) PL 0+3

GIBB Alistair (Ally) Stuart
Born: Salisbury, 17 February 1976
Height: 5'9" Weight: 11.7

A right-sided Northampton winger, who has also played at wing back, Ally spent a lot of time on the substitutes' bench last season, but always gave the opposing full back a run for his money when in action. Fast and accurate, his crosses have accounted for many goals since he joined the club.

Norwich C (From trainee on 1/7/94)
Northampton T (Loaned on 22/9/95) FL 9/1
Northampton T (£30,000 on 5/2/96) FL 15+52/3 FLC 3+3 FAC 2+3 Others 4+3

GIBBENS Kevin
Born: Southampton, 4 November 1979
Height: 5'10" Weight: 12.13

Having impressed in the reserves during 1997-98, and having turned professional last January after coming through the YTS ranks, Kevin was introduced in Southampton's 4-2 win at West Ham in April, before having a further outing against Derby in the penultimate match of the season. A promising midfielder, the Saints have hopes of him.

Southampton (From trainee on 16/1/98) PL 2

GIBBS Nigel James
Born: St Albans, 20 November 1965
Height: 5'7" Weight: 11.11

Club Honours: FAYC '82; Div 2 '98
International Honours: E: U21-5; Yth

That modern rarity, a one-club man, Nigel has played more than 450 matches for Watford and now stands fourth in the all-time club appearances list behind Luther Blissett, Gary Porter, and Duncan Welbourne. After many years playing at right back, in 1997-98 he accepted the challenge of adapting to a wing-back role and worked successfully to improve his crossing. His new spirit of adventure resulting in a spectacular goal at Oldham – his first away goal for ten years – and he gave a fine performance against Sheffield Wednesday in the FA Cup. After 14 years at Vicarage Road, Nigel was able to celebrate a promotion for the first time, and nobody deserved it more.*

Watford (From apprentice on 23/11/83) FL 362+12/5 FLC 22/2 FAC 39+1 Others 16

GIBBS Paul Derek
Born: Gorleston, 26 October 1972
Height: 5'10" Weight: 11.10

Freed by Colchester during the 1997 close season, this left-wing back soon became a folk hero to the Torquay faithful. Ten goals from this position speak for themselves, with long-range shots, flying headers, tap ins, and penalties all contributing to a magnificent campaign, blighted only by a couple of suspensions.*

Colchester U (Signed from Diss T on 6/3/95) FL 39+14/3 FAC 1+1 Others 8+1
Torquay U (Free on 26/7/97) FL 40+1/7 FLC 4/1 FAC 3/1 Others 3/1

GIBSON Paul Richard
Born: Sheffield, 1 November 1976
Height: 6'3" Weight: 13.0

After two seasons in the wings as a professional at Manchester United, Paul was loaned out to Mansfield, who had a goalkeeping crisis following an injury to Ian Bowling last October. Despite keeping a clean sheet on his debut at Swansea, the youngster found things difficult at times but manfully stuck to his task, showing himself to be one for the future, until being carried off against Rochdale early in the New Year and returning to Old Trafford to continue his football apprenticeship.

Manchester U (From trainee on 1/7/95)
Mansfield T (Loaned on 20/10/97) FL 13

GIGGS Ryan Joseph
Born: Cardiff, 29 November 1973
Height: 5'11" Weight: 10.9
Club Honours: ESC '91; FAYC '92; FLC '92; PL '93, '94, '96, '97; CS '93, '94, '96, '97; FAC '94, '96
International Honours: W: 21; U21-1; Yth. E: Sch

A highly skilled Manchester United left winger, who packs a tremendous left-footed shot, Ryan produced some sparkling moments during the course of last season, but also suffered from his fair share of injuries. An absentee for most of September, when he played only one full Premiership game, he made a goalscoring return at the start of October with a cracking goal against

Ryan Giggs

summer. At his best, his close-dribbling skills trouble opponents, while his crossing ability provides chances for others.

Lincoln C (From apprentice on 29/6/81) FL 15+15/1 FLC 5 FAC 3
Scunthorpe U (Free on 18/8/82) FL 1 FLC 1 (Free to Boston U in September 1982)
Northampton T (Signed on 30/6/86) FL 120/21 FLC 10/2 FAC 6/3 Others 9/1
Grimsby T (£55,000 on 23/3/89) FL 259/41 FLC 18/4 FAC 11/2 Others 9
West Bromwich A (£50,000 on 8/8/95) FL 46+16/6 FLC 6 FAC 1 Others 7
York C (Loaned on 7/3/97) FL 9/1
Grimsby T (Loaned on 15/8/97) FL 5 FLC 1

GILCHRIST Philip (Phil) Alexander
Born: Stockton on Tees, 25 August 1973
Height: 5'11" Weight: 13.12

Phil enjoyed another consistently reliable season for Oxford in 1997-98, despite having to play alongside a number of central defensive partners, and missing a spell early on with a back injury. Sound in the air, he has tremendous pace, tackles well, and has a long throw, which is often used, especially now with the Kevin Francis aerial threat. Weighed in with a couple of vital goals, both headers, the second turned out to be the winner in the derby game with Swindon.

Nottingham F (From trainee on 5/12/90)
Middlesbrough (Free on 10/1/92)
Hartlepool U (Free on 27/11/92) FL 77+5 FLC 4+1 FAC 4 Others 5
Oxford U (£100,000 on 17/2/95) FL 133+4/8 FLC 14 FAC 7 Others 3

GILES Martin William
Born: Shrewsbury, 1 January 1979
Height: 5'10" Weight: 10.13

Although released at the end of last season, Martin made a number of appearances in 1997-98 at left back for Chester City, having signed professional forms during the previous summer. Can also play in midfield, which is his favoured position.

Chester C (From trainee on 2/7/97) FL 8+2 FAC 0+1

GILKES Michael Earl
Born: Hackney, 20 July 1965
Height: 5'8" Weight: 10.10
Club Honours: FMC '88; Div 3 '86, Div 2 '94

The Wolves' left-winger was wanted in a deeper role by Mark McGhee last season, but first he had to recover from a cruciate knee operation after an injury in April 1997. Returning at left back against Ipswich in November, he then surprisingly twice played at right back, but looked uneasy in that position and was booked for a tackle at Maine Road, before limping off with hamstring damage which was to prematurely end his season.

Reading (Free from Leicester C juniors on 10/7/84) FL 348+45/43 FLC 25+7/6 FAC 31+2/1 Others 26+2/2
Chelsea (Loaned on 28/1/92) FL 0+1 Others 0+1
Southampton (Loaned on 4/3/92) FL 4+2
Wolverhampton W (£155,000 on 27/3/97) FL 8/1

GILL Jeremy (Jerry) Morley
Born: Clevedon, 8 September 1970
Height: 5'7" Weight: 11.0
International Honours: E: SP-1

A late starter to the Football League, Jerry

Juventus in the Champion's League. Having rounded off that month with two against Barnsley in United's 7-0 win at Old Trafford, he also scored the winner against Aston Villa in December, and then netted two against Spurs at Old Trafford in January. With further strikes in consecutive games against Aston Villa and Derby in the Premiership in February, he sustained a niggling hamstring injury which kept him out of United's vital European Cup tie against Monaco in March. Although recovering to play in the vital Premiership game against Liverpool on Good Friday, he suffered more hamstring problems. However, on the top of his form, there is no finer sight in football than Ryan tearing down the left flank in search of goals and with more luck on his side, he should be raring to go at the start of the 1998-99 campaign. Possibly the first name on the team sheet, he continues to be a regular in the Welsh international side and was again recognised by his fellow professionals when selected for the PFA award-winning Premiership side. Scored his 50th League goal against Leeds at Old Trafford in May.

Manchester U (From trainee on 1/12/90) F/PL 217+19/50 FLC 16+4/6 FAC 29+2/5 Others 26+2/5

GILBERT David (Dave) James
Born: Lincoln, 22 June 1963
Height: 5'4" Weight: 10.8
Club Honours: Div 4 '87

Yet another left-sided player at West Bromwich Albion who had difficulty getting onto the team sheet in 1997-98, Dave was loaned out to Grimsby, taking over from Kingsley Black, and played in six successive games in August and September before going back to the Hawthorns. Reserve team football was the order of the day from then on, apart from five subs' appearances towards the end of the campaign, and he was released during the

experienced a number of clubs, including Backwell United, Trowbridge Town, Weston super Mare, Bath, and Yeovil, before transferring from the latter to Birmingham during the 1997 close season, at the age of 26. After an impressive non-league career, which saw him capped for the England semi-professional side, the former plasterer settled into City's reserve midfield before being called up to the first team for the Swindon game in April and producing an assured performance. Passes the ball well, is quiet, and plays with the minimum of fuss.

Birmingham C (£30,000 from Yeovil on 14/7/97) FL 3

GILL Matthew James
Born: Norwich, 8 November 1980
Height: 5'11" Weight: 12.2

A busy midfielder who came through the YTS ranks to turn professional last March, having been a member of the Peterborough side that reached the semi-final stage of the FA Youth Cup, Matthew was given a run out in the final two games of 1997-98. Is yet another of Barry Fry's youngsters who looks like he has what it takes.

Peterborough U (From trainee on 2/3/98) FL 2

Keith Gillespie

GILLESPIE Keith Robert
Born: Bangor, 18 February 1975
Height: 5'10" Weight: 11.3
Club Honours: FAYC '92
International Honours: NI: 21; U21-1; Yth; Sch

The Newcastle winger seems to have benefited from the guidance of Kenny Dalglish, achieving greater consistency in his performances, which was rewarded with a regular place in the side in 1997-98. Able to play on either flank, he seems most at

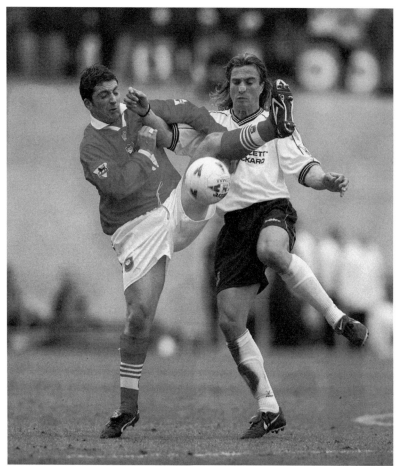

David Ginola (right)

home on the right, using his searing pace to provide a vital cutting edge to the attack, but his trademark close control and balance is such that he is able to deliver telling crosses on the run. This was best demonstrated in the home game against Barcelona, when he destroyed the left side of the Catalans' defence, enabling Tino Asprilla to complete a memorable hat trick. He was also influential in the FA Cup semi final, when he seemed to have a licence to roam, rather than being constrained to the touchline, and he clearly relished the freedom this provided. Although not a regular scorer, Keith notched two in the away game at Barnsley to secure an important point. Unfortunately, when coming on as a substitute in the game at Tottenham he suffered a bad ankle injury almost immediately, thus ending his season and, crucially, causing him to miss the FA Cup final. Continued to be a key member of the Northern Ireland team last season.

Manchester U (From trainee on 3/2/93) PL 3+6/1 FLC 3 FAC 1+1/1
Wigan Ath (Loaned on 3/9/93) FL 8/4 Others 2
Newcastle U (£1,000,000 on 12/1/95) PL 89+17/11 FLC 7/1 FAC 9+1/2 Others 11+5

GINOLA David
Born: Gassin, France, 25 January 1967
Height: 6'0" Weight: 11.10
International Honours: France:17

Naturally a winger, David enjoyed a tremendous season at Tottenham in 1997-98, following his transfer from Newcastle during the close season, it being arguably the best he has had in English football. Despite the early criticisms of him being a "luxury" player, the Frenchman won over even his most vociferous critics with a workrate, both in defence as well as attack, which was second to none. Being given the opportunity to have a free role in the Spurs' line-up, suited him immensely, and gave him the chance to express himself as only he could. In pointing out his strengths, his first touch when receiving the ball is faultless, his speed, dropping his shoulder and turning to beat his markers is instinctive, and his ferocious right-foot shots have become his trade mark, while his creativity and vision add depth and width to the midfield, his tenacity developing from what was once a weakness to a positive strength. In poise and stature, David is similar to former Tottenham favourite, Glenn Hoddle, at his

peak, whilst still retaining a style that would be hard to replicate. It would be impossible to pick out one performance when there were so many where his contribution was the difference between winning and drawing a game, most notably when relegation was a real threat. With the maturity in his all-round performance improving in every game he plays, he has the ability to fulfil all the expectations of him this coming season at White Hart Lane.

Newcastle U (£2,500,000 from Paris St Germain, via Toulon, Racing Paris and Brest, on 6/7/95) PL 54+4/6 FLC 6 FAC 4 Others 7+1/1
Tottenham H (£2,000,000 on 18/7/97) PL 34/6 FLC 3/2 FAC 3/1

GINTY Rory Vincent
Born: Galway, 23 January 1977
Height: 5'9" Weight: 11.0
A Crystal Palace professional since November 1994, having earlier come through the ranks as a trainee, Rory finally made his first team debut at Liverpool last December when he came off the bench in a 3-0 defeat. Able to play down the left or right-hand side as an out-and-out winger, or as a wing back, where he gets the ball across to the front men, he had a further five opportunities to impress before going back to the reserves and being released during the summer.

Crystal Palace (From trainee on 14/11/94) PL 2+3 FAC 0+1

GISLASON Valur Fannar
Born: Reykjavic, Iceland, 8 September 1977
Height: 6'1" Weight: 11.12
Unable to get a game at Arsenal, having been signed from France in July 1996, the well-built Icelandic midfielder came to Brighton on a month's loan in October, but struggled to shine as Albion failed to win any of his seven consecutive matches. After returning to Highbury, he was transferred to the Norwegian club, Stromsgodset, in February for an undisclosed fee.

Arsenal (Free from Fram on 16/7/96)
Brighton & Hove A (Loaned on 7/10/97) FL 7

GITTENS Jonathan (Jon) Antoni
Born: Birmingham, 22 January 1964
Height: 6'0" Weight: 12.10
Jon emerged from a period in the wilderness to deservedly win the Torquay Player of the Year award in 1997-98, his cool and authoritative defending, along with some decisive goals marking him out as the club's best defender. Unluckily conceded the decisive penalty in the play-off final at Wembley when it appeared to be "ball to hand", he was released during the summer.

Southampton (£10,000 from Paget R on 16/10/85) FL 18 FLC 4 FAC 1
Swindon T (£40,000 on 22/7/87) FL 124+2/6 FLC 15+1 FAC 9 Others 13+1/1
Southampton (£400,000 on 28/3/91) FL 16+3 FLC 4 Others 1
Middlesbrough (Loaned on 19/2/92) FL 9+3/1
Middlesbrough (£200,000 on 27/7/92) PL 13 FLC 0+1 FAC 1
Portsmouth (Free on 9/8/93) FL 81+2/2 FLC 10 FAC 3 Others 3/1
Torquay U (Free on 5/8/96) FL 78/9 FLC 6 FAC 4 Others 5/2

GIUMMARRA William (Willie) Giorgio
Born: Ontario, Canada, 26 August 1971
Height: 6'1" Weight: 12.7
Following in the footsteps of Jason de Vos, Willie trialled at Darlington early into last season, but was unable to impress the club into giving him a long-term contract. For the record, the Canadian left-sided midfielder made just three substitute appearances for the Quakers in September, before returning home midway through the winter.

Darlington (Free from Montreal Impact on 29/8/97) FL 0+4

GIVEN Seamus (Shay) John
Born: Lifford, 20 April 1976
Height: 6'1" Weight: 13.4
Club Honours: Div 1 '96
International Honours: Ei: 17; U21-5; Yth
Frustrated at being the understudy to Tim Flowers at Blackburn, Shay rejoined his former manager, Kenny Dalglish, at Newcastle during the 1997 close season, in order to secure first team football and to enhance his international prospects with the Republic of Ireland. He certainly did that, representing his country in eight of the nine available matches. Although considered small for a top-class 'keeper, he is athletic and agile, very quick on his feet, handles crosses well, and is a quality shot-stopper. Facing competition for the first team spot from Shaka Hislop and Pavel Srnicek, he was given the nod at the start of the campaign, and quickly demonstrated why he was so highly rated, establishing himself, and spreading confidence throughout his defence. Injured on international duty in November, he was replaced by Hislop and was unable to regain his place until February, although whilst on the bench he attracted interest from Sunderland, one of his earlier loan clubs with whom he had been outstanding. However, on returning to the side in February, when Hislop was dropped over his delay in signing a new contract, his consistency was rewarded with a regular place thereafter, and he played his part in helping the club reach Wembley with two excellent saves at critical points in the FA Cup semi final.

Blackburn Rov (Free from Glasgow Celtic juniors on 8/8/94) PL 2 FLC 0+1
Swindon T (Loaned on 4/8/95) FL 5
Sunderland (Loaned on 19/1/96) FL 17
Newcastle U (£1,500,000 on 14/7/97) PL 24 FAC 4 Others 6

GLASGOW Byron Fitzgerald
Born: Clapham, 18 February 1979
Height: 5'7" Weight: 10.12
Although he had been upgraded from YTS status to a three-year full professional contract during the previous season, Byron failed to make a significant impact at Reading in 1997-98, making just two first team appearances as a substitute, and one start in the 0-0 draw away to Port Vale. He holds one Royals' record which will never be beaten, however. In the club's final competitive match at Elm Park, a Capital League fixture against Rushden & Diamonds Reserves, played on 8 May, he scored Reading's goal in a 2-1 defeat, thereby becoming the last player to score a goal on this ground.

Reading (From trainee on 24/8/96) FL 3+4 FAC 0+1

GLASS James (Jimmy) Robert
Born: Epsom, 1 August 1973
Height: 6'1" Weight: 13.4
The first choice goalkeeper at Bournemouth who was ever present in the 1997-98 season, Jimmy again proved to be an excellent shot stopper and produced some memorable displays, none better than in the FA Cup third round tie against Bristol City. Is not afraid to come off his line and showed great agility in his performances. Was released during the summer. *Stop Press:* Signed for Swindon on 1 June.

Crystal Palace (From trainee on 4/7/91)
Portsmouth (Loaned on 10/2/95) FL 3
Bournemouth (Free on 8/3/96) FL 94 FLC 4 FAC 4 Others 7

GLEGHORN Nigel William
Born: Seaham, 12 August 1962
Height: 6'0" Weight: 13.7
Club Honours: AMC '91; Div 2 '93
An experienced, solid midfield general, Nigel was one of several Burnley players transfer listed by Chris Waddle early last season and made only one further appearance for the club prior to being signed by Brentford on three months loan in November. After scoring for the Bees in a 1-1 draw against their bitter rivals, Fulham, he later returned to Turf Moor, only to be loaned out to Northampton, and subsequently playing against the Clarets. A specialist in free kicks and corners, who enjoys the passing game, he is equally effective on the left-hand side or centre of midfield. Was released during the summer.

Ipswich T (Free from Seaham RS on 30/8/85) FL 54+12/11 FLC 3+2 FAC 3+1 Others 7+2/2
Manchester C (£47,500 on 4/8/88) FL 27+7/7 FLC 2+1/2 FAC 0+1/1 Others 1/1
Birmingham C (£175,000 on 9/9/89) FL 142/33 FLC 13/5 FAC 7/3 Others 14/2
Stoke C (£100,000 on 24/10/92) FL 162+4/26 FLC 10/2 FAC 10 Others 22/3
Burnley (Free on 15/7/96) FL 33+1/4 FLC 4 FAC 4/1 Others 2
Brentford (Loaned on 17/11/97) FL 11/1 Others 1
Northampton T (Loaned on 13/2/98) FL 3+5/1

GLOVER Dean Victor
Born: West Bromwich, 29 December 1963
Height: 5'11" Weight: 11.13
Club Honours: AMC '93
After only expecting to be a squad player in the Port Vale defence in 1997-98, injuries to others meant that he played the majority of the campaign in the team, and very well he did too. Using his experience to the fore, Dean took his number of league appearances to over 350, the fourth highest ever for the club, scoring with a cracking 30 yarder at Swindon Town, and ending the season with a well-deserved testimonial against Aston Villa to commemorate his tenth year with the Vale, before being released during the summer.

Aston Villa (From apprentice on 30/12/81) FL 25+3 FLC 7/1 FAC 3 Others 1
Sheffield U (Loaned on 17/10/86) FL 5

115

Middlesbrough (Signed on 17/6/87) FL 44+6/5 FLC 4 FAC 5 Others 7/2
Port Vale (£200,000 on 3/2/89) FL 354+9/15 FLC 26/1 FAC 19/1 Others 22/3

GLOVER Edward Lee
Born: Kettering, 24 April 1970
Height: 5'11" Weight: 12.1
Club Honours: FMC '92
International Honours: S: U21-3; Yth

Appointed Rotherham's team captain at the start of last season, Lee went on to show what a clever player he is, with his ability to hold the ball up, and hit some excellent strikes as he found his scoring touch again. His absence through injury in the latter half of the campaign probably cost the club promotion as no one was able to deliver as he had done. Hit four goals in a nine-goal thriller against Hull City.

Nottingham F (From apprentice on 2/5/87) F/PL 61+15/9 FLC 6+5/2 FAC 8+2/1 Others 4+1/1
Leicester C (Loaned on 14/9/89) FL 3+2/1
Barnsley (Loaned on 18/1/90) FL 8 FAC 4
Luton T (Loaned on 2/9/91) FL 1
Port Vale (£200,000 on 2/8/94) FL 38+14/7 FLC 5+1/4 FAC 0+2 Others 3+2/2
Rotherham U (£150,000 on 15/8/96) FL 52+7/18 FLC 3 FAC 5/1 Others 0+1
Huddersfield T (Loaned on 3/3/97) FL 11

Lee Glover

GOATER Leonard Shaun
Born: Hamilton, Bermuda, 25 February 1970
Height: 6'1" Weight: 12.0
Club Honours: AMC '96
International Honours: Bermuda: 8

Shaun continued his goalscoring exploits from the previous campaign to put Bristol City well on the way to clinching promotion before his deadline day move to Manchester City last March. At his best in the first half of last season, when he obtained 14 of his total of 18 goals in all competitions, his presence was sorely missed in City's run-in to promotion when the opportunity for the second division championship was lost, and allowed the local rivals, Bristol Rovers, to overtake them as the division's highest scorers. Shaun moved to Manchester City, saying he wanted to play a higher grade of football with a bigger team, and it was therefore ironic that the end of 1997-98 saw the paths of the two clubs cross upon the relegation of the Maine Road outfit to the second division, an outcome that cost Bristol City the extra £100,000 that was promised had Manchester City survived. Deservedly selected as a member of the PFA second division side, he is not only a recognised goalscorer, but his height enables him to win many balls for his team mates. Scored two hat tricks during the season, both for Bristol City – at home to Wigan, and at Brentford.

Manchester U (From juniors on 8/5/89)
Rotherham U (Free on 25/10/89) FL 169+40/70 FLC 13+4/4 FAC 12+3/7 Others 15+5/5
Notts Co (Loaned on 12/11/93) FL 1
Bristol C (£175,000 on 17/7/96) FL 67+8/40 FLC 7/2 FAC 5 Others 5+1/1
Manchester C (£400,000 on 26/3/98) FL 7/3

GODDARD-CRAWLEY Richard Lewis
Born: Burnt Oak, 31 March 1978
Height: 6'4" Weight: 14.2

Goddard-Crawley Richard Lewis

The tall, strong centre half made just two appearances for Brentford last season in the Coca Cola Cup, at Shrewsbury and Southampton, both as a sub, before spending a month on loan at Woking in October, prior to joining them permanently for £7,500 in March.

Brentford (Free from Arsenal juniors on 23/7/96) FL 0+1 FLC 0+2

GOMM Richard Alan
Born: Torbay, 24 May 1979
Height: 5'7" Weight: 10.7

While still a trainee, Richard made a brief substitute appearance in Torquay's midfield at Northampton in the AWS last season before being released during the club's summer clearout. A strong attacking type who goes forward looking for shooting opportunities, Richard could still figure in the Football League at some stage.

Torquay U (Trainee) Others 0+1

GOODEN Ty Michael
Born: Canvey Island, 23 October 1972
Height: 5'8" Weight: 12.6
Club Honours: Div 2 '96

The one-time Arsenal apprentice enjoyed his best and most consistent season for Swindon Town in 1997-98, often being employed as a left-wing back, but better used as an attacking midfielder with licence to run at the opposition. An excellent crosser of the ball, and often relied upon for inswinging corners with his trusty left boot, his early season form led to speculation about a possible move to Nottingham Forest, which was quashed when he signed a long-term contract to stay at Town. His only goals came against Bury and Oxford, something he will be looking to improve on next term, before his campaign was curtailed by an ankle injury which required summer surgery.

Swindon T (Free from Wycombe W on 17/9/93) P/FL 74+24/8 FLC 4+1/1 FAC 4+1 Others 3+1

GOODHIND Warren Ernest
Born: Johannesburg, South Africa, 16 August 1977
Height: 5'11" Weight: 11.2

One of the most improved players in the Barnet squad in 1997-98, the midfielder scored the goal which almost put Barnet into the play-off finals and has the potential to shine this coming season. A tough tackler who can also play at the back if needed, Warren gets the ball and uses it positively.

Barnet (From trainee on 3/7/96) FL 23+15/1 FLC 3+1 Others 3/1

GOODMAN Donald (Don) Ralph
Born: Leeds, 9 May 1966
Height: 5'10" Weight: 13.2
Club Honours: Div 3 '85

Although able to play up front for Wolves in 1997-98, Don often lined up on the right side where he worked equally hard, continuing to prove a good header of the ball and showing his bravery in the first seven matches, when battling on despite an ankle injury. Briefly out of the team, on his return he ran through to score his first goal of the campaign. However, his departure seemed imminent as he missed nine matches amidst controversy over his fitness, before coming back to score two against Queens Park Rangers and showing good form in the mid-season period. Although a kick caused a recurrence of his earlier problems, once again he made a storybook return, chipping in the winner in the FA Cup quarter final at Leeds. He was then unlucky to be taken off when looking Wolves' most likely scorer in the ensuing semi-final games against Arsenal, before being released in the summer.

Bradford C (Free from Collingham on 10/7/84) FL 65+5/14 FLC 5+1/2 FAC 2+3/4 Others 4+1/2
West Bromwich A (£50,000 on 27/3/87) FL 140+18/60 FLC 11/1 FAC 7/1 Others 5/1
Sunderland (£900,000 on 6/12/91) FL 112+4/40 FLC 9/1 FAC 2/1 Others 4/2
Wolverhampton W (£1,100,000 on 6/12/94) FL 115+10/33 FLC 8+1/4 FAC 16+1/2 Others 3

GOODRIDGE Gregory (Greg) Ronald St Clair
Born: Barbados, 10 July 1971
Height: 5'6" Weight: 10.0
International Honours: Barbados: 5

One of the stars of Bristol City's promotion in 1997-98, this electrifying winger added the required workrate to his game to enable him to hold down a place in the side for most of the campaign. Undoubtedly the most skilful player on City's books, his increased consistency has raised his status to a place among the very best of those who have turned out for the Robins over the years. Also scored some important goals.

Torquay U (Free from Lambada on 24/3/94) FL 32+6/4 FLC 4/1 FAC 2+1 Others 3+1/1
Queens Park R (£350,000 on 9/8/95) PL 0+7/1 FLC 0+1 FAC 0+1
Bristol C (£50,000 on 19/8/96) FL 47+12/12 FLC 4+1/1 FAC 5+1/1 Others 0+4

GOODWIN Shaun
Born: Rotherham, 14 June 1969
Height: 5'8" Weight: 11.4
Club Honours: Div 4 '89; AMC '96

The big disappointment for Rotherham fans in 1997-98 was that an on-form Shaun would surely have helped the club to promotion. But, as in the previous few years, he was more often out of action than playing, and he had his contract paid up several weeks before the end of the campaign. At his best, his ability to run at defenders spelt danger for the opposition, especially away from home.

Rotherham U (From trainee on 1/7/87) FL 258+22/39 FLC 19+8/1 FAC 17+3/3 Others 22+2/4

GORDON Dean Dwight
Born: Croydon, 10 February 1973
Height: 6'0" Weight: 13.4
Club Honours: Div 1 '94
International Honours: E: U21-13

An extremely athletic Crystal Palace left back who can perform equally well on the left wing, or in the centre of the defence, Dean missed just one game last season, when suspended after being sent off against Arsenal. Strong in the tackle, and adept at hitting long balls behind the defence, he can also score the odd goal here and there. There were two in 1997-98, both of them coming against Bolton; the first in a 2-2 home draw, and the second, a 25-yard drive at the Reebok in a 5-2 defeat. Despite playing well, it was a disappointing time for him as the campaign ended with Palace firmly rooted to the bottom of the Premiership and once again facing the prospect of life in the first division. *Stop Press:* Signed for Middlesbrough on 6 July, a fee of £900,000 changing hands.

Crystal Palace (From trainee on 4/7/91) F/PL 181+20/20 FLC 16+3/2 FAC 14+1/1 Others 5+1

GORDON Kenyatta **Gavin**
Born: Manchester, 24 June 1979
Height: 6'1" Weight: 12.0

The teenage striker who was signed from Hull City last November, went straight into the Lincoln first team and showed plenty of promise with his speed and power causing problems for defences. Later on, however, he marked time on the subs' bench after Colin Alcide resumed his striking partnership with Lee Thorpe.

Hull C (From trainee on 3/7/96) FL 22+16/9 FLC 1+4/1 Others 1+1
Lincoln C (£30,000 on 7/11/97) FL 9+4/3 FAC 4 Others 1

GORE Ian George
Born: Prescot, 10 January 1968
Height: 5'11" Weight: 12.4

Captain courageous for much of the 1997-98 campaign, Ian was another of Doncaster's more experienced players "paid off" as the team continued their descent into the Vauxhall Conference. His committed play at the heart of the Rovers' defence was not truly reflected in the eventual total of more than a hundred league goals conceded, and his departure was a key factor in the club's eventual league demise.

Birmingham C (From trainee on 1/5/86)

Blackpool (Free from Southport on 21/1/88) FL 196+4 FLC 15+1 FAC 11 Others 20+2
Torquay U (Free on 11/8/95) FL 25/2 FLC 4 FAC 1/1 Others 2
Doncaster Rov (£5,000 on 22/3/96) FL 65+1/1 FLC 4 FAC 2 Others 2

GOUCK Andrew (Andy) Scott
Born: Blackpool, 8 June 1972
Height: 5'10" Weight: 12.12

A regular ball winner in Rochdale's midfield for most of 1997-98, Andy, like the team as a whole, suffered a loss of confidence in mid-season. However, coming back strongly to put in some good performances when going forward from midfield and netting three goals in successive wins over Brighton and Cambridge in February, he virtually doubled his tally for the club in the space of a few days. Was relelased during the summer.

Blackpool (From trainee on 4/7/90) FL 121+27/12 FLC 9+3 FAC 4+1 Others 11+1/3
Rochdale (Free on 25/7/96) FL 58+8/8 FLC 2 FAC 2 Others 1+1

GRAHAM Mark Roland
Born: Newry, 24 October 1974
Height: 5'7" Weight: 10.12
International Honours: NI: B-4; Yth; Sch

A skilful Queens Park Rangers' left winger, despite having made a breakthrough in 1996-97, Mark made just one appearance last season when coming off the bench against Wolves in the Coca Cola Cup, and then went back to the reserves, where he remained out of contention for the duration. Can cause defenders all kinds of problems when running at them. Continued to add to his Northern Ireland "B" caps with an appearance against the Republic in February.

Queens Park R (From trainee on 26/5/93) FL 16+2 FLC 2+1 FAC 2

Richard Graham

GRAHAM Richard Ean
Born: Dewsbury, 28 November 1974
Height: 6'2" Weight: 12.10

1997-98 was another outstanding season for the youngster in the centre of Oldham's defence and a good many scouts continued to track him. A footballing defender, although excellent in the air, Richard loves the ball to feet and there is nothing he enjoys better than coming out in possession to make forward runs that unsettle the opposition. Fast and athletic, and a danger at set pieces, he also scores goals, five of them hitting the back of the net during the campaign, two of them in the 2-1 home win over Luton.

Oldham Ath (From trainee on 16/7/93) P/FL 114+8/9 FLC 9 FAC 9/1 Others 3

GRAINGER Martin Robert
Born: Enfield, 23 August 1972
Height: 5'11" Weight: 12.0

Both aggressive and enthusiastic, Martin had his best season to date at Birmingham in 1997-98. After losing his place at left back to Simon Charlton, he adapted to a wide left-midfield role, which not only saw him improve his attacking strengths but again saw him score a couple of goals, including the first in a 2-0 home win over Sheffield United. As a player who never lets the team down in terms of effort and commitment, and an obvious crowd pleaser, his ability to cause the opposition problems with his throw ins and free kicks are an added bonus.

Colchester U (From trainee on 28/7/92) FL 37+9/7 FLC 3 FAC 3+2 Others 3/1
Brentford (£60,000 on 21/10/93) FL 100+1/12 FLC 6/1 FAC 9/1 Others 8/2
Birmingham C (£400,000 on 25/3/96) FL 56+8/5 FLC 4+1 FAC 5

GRANT Anthony (Tony) James
Born: Liverpool, 14 November 1974
Height: 5'10" Weight: 10.2
Club Honours: CS '95

An elegant, cultured Everton midfielder, with the ability to deliver damaging and incisive passes through any defence, Tony's season was once again wrecked by injury. After starting 1997-98 with a succession of ankle, calf, and then shin problems, he finally enjoyed a run of games during January and February, before yet another injury, this time to his knee, ended his campaign. Up until then, he had shown flashes of his undoubted class, chipping a sublime goal at Barnsley, and carving open the Chelsea defence with one pass for a Gary Speed goal at Goodison. During his enforced absence, there was no doubting that the Blues missed his passing skills sorely.

Everton (From trainee on 8/7/93) PL 30+13/2 FLC 4 FAC 1+3 Others 2+2/1
Swindon T (Loaned on 18/1/96) FL 3/1

GRANT Gareth Michael
Born: Leeds, 6 September 1980
Height: 5'9" Weight: 10.4

Gareth, a young Bradford City striker in his first year as a YTS, became the club's youngest ever player, along with Andy Patterson, when signing professional forms

at the end of last April. A few days earlier, having scored a hat trick in a 3-0 Northern Intermediate League Cup win over Leeds, he made his Football League debut when coming off the bench at the Pulse Stadium against Queens Park Rangers, and followed that up with appearances in the remaining two games of the season. Is both fast and tricky, and definitely one to watch out for.

Bradford C (From trainee on 28/4/98) FL 1+2

GRANT Kim Tyrone

Born: Ghana, 25 September 1972
Height: 5'10" Weight: 10.12
International Honours: Ghana: 5

Signed from Wimbledon during the 1997 close season, Kim scored four times in his first four outings for Millwall in 1997-98, before finding it hard to remain in such consistent mode. Despite that, he remained the club's second leading scorer with ten under his belt, while proving to be a hard worker who never gave up the cause, and held the ball up well, enabling him to spin away from defenders with a great turn of pace. Equally good with either foot, if he can stay clear of niggling injuries he should score a lot more goals.

Charlton Ath (From trainee on 6/3/91) FL 74+49/18 FLC 3+9/1 FAC 8+5/5 Others 5+2/1
Luton T (£250,000 on 15/3/96) FL 18+17/5 FLC 4/2 FAC 0+2 Others 2+1/1
Millwall (Signed on 29/8/97) FL 31+8/8 FLC 3/1 FAC 0+1 Others 2/1

GRANT Peter

Born: Glasgow, 30 August 1965
Height: 5'10" Weight: 11.9
International Honours: S: 2; B-2; U21-10; Yth; Sch

Signed from Glasgow Celtic at the start of last season, the former Scottish international impressed everyone at Norwich with his thoroughly professional approach to the game, making his debut against Crewe at Carrow Road just 24 hours after arriving at the club. Playing in central midfield, his boundless enthusiasm and consistency was a feature of his play, as he closed down the opposition with his speed to the ball and terrier-like tactics. A more than useful acquisition, an added bonus was his three goals.

Glasgow Celtic (From juniors on 27/7/82) SL 338+27/16 SLC 40+3/3 SC 34+4/1 Others 27/1
Norwich C (£200,000 on 22/8/97) FL 33+2/3 FLC 0+1 FAC 1

GRANT Stephen Hubert

Born: Birr, 14 April 1977
Height: 5'10" Weight: 11.7
International Honours: Ei: U21-2

The sale of Alun Armstrong to Middlesbrough last February gave the 20-year-old Irishman another first team chance for Stockport after he made a brief and unremarkable appearance as a substitute at Stoke in September. Second time around, he took his opportunity well, coming off the bench to score the winner in the return fixture with Stoke to earn himself a run in the starting line-up, his good form seeing him rewarded with two Republic of Ireland U21 appearances. Rejected by Sunderland as an 18-year-old,

Stephen had returned to Ireland with Shamrock Rovers before being given another chance in English football, following his summer move to County.

Sunderland (Free from Athlone T on 10/8/95 - Free to Shamrock Rov on 17/10/96)
Stockport Co (£30,000 on 3/9/97) FL 9+7/3

GRANVILLE Daniel (Danny) Patrick

Born: Islington, 19 January 1975
Height: 5'11" Weight: 12.5
Club Honours: FLC '98, ECWC '98
International Honours: E: U21-4

An illustration of Danny's meteoric rise came when he gave an outstanding performance in Chelsea's first round European Cup Winners' Cup tie against Slovan Bratislava last season – 12 months to the day after playing for Cambridge United against Scarborough in a division three fixture. Deputising for the suspended Graeme le Saux, he scored a superb solo effort to clinch a 2-0 victory for the Blues over the resilient Slovakians and, in so doing, became Chelsea's 11th different goalscorer in their first six matches. Although spending the remainder of the campaign understudying Le Saux, when the England wing back was forced to miss the European Cup Winners' Cup final, Danny stepped in against VFB Stuttgart, in Stockholm, and gave a performance which won him rave reviews on a night where he won his first major medal. *Stop Press:* Third choice at Stamford Bridge, despite making two further appearances for the England U21 side during 1997-98, Danny joined Leeds for £1.6 million on 19 June.

Cambridge U (From trainee on 19/5/93) FL 89+10/7 FLC 3+2 FAC 2+2 Others 4+2
Chelsea (£300,000 + on 21/3/97) PL 12+6 FLC 3 Others 4+1/1

GRAVES Wayne Alan

Born: Scunthorpe, 18 September 1980
Height: 5'8" Weight: 10.7

A first-year trainee with Scunthorpe United, Wayne forced his way into the first team picture towards the end of last season after some superb performances in the reserves. A real utility player who can play at full back, wing back, or in midfield, with a good touch, and tremendous pace, he still has another year as a YTS, but can be expected to get further first team opportunities in 1998-99.

Scunthorpe U (Trainee) FL 0+3

GRAY Alan Muir

Born: Carlisle, 2 May 1974
Height: 6'0" Weight: 12.2

Having played a couple of games for Doncaster in 1996-97, before moving on to non-league Bishop Auckland in mid-season, Alan came back into the Football League with Darlington at the start of 1997-98, making eight appearances as a hard-tackling right back, prior to moving on early in the New Year. Recruited by Carlisle, the town of his birth, his only first team action came in a substitute appearance in the defeat at Plymouth and he was released at the end of the campaign.

Doncaster Rov (Signed from Richmond University on 1/8/96) FL 1 Others 1 (Free to Bishop Auckland on 28/12/96)
Darlington (Free on 4/8/97) FL 6 FLC 2
Carlisle U (Free on 2/2/98) FL 0+1

GRAY Andrew (Andy) Arthur

Born: Lambeth, 22 February 1964
Height: 5'11" Weight: 13.3
Club Honours: FMC '91
International Honours: E: U21-2

An enigmatic utility player who burst onto the scene at Bury last August, following a free transfer from Falkirk, Andy appeared in midfield and, as a sweeper, his experience shining through, and his array of close skills being a joy to watch. Unfortunately, following a succession of bookings, and a dismissal at Ipswich in November, he earned a six-match ban and his form upon returning almost two months later was a pale shadow of his early season sparkle, which subsequently led to him signing for Millwall in January. The change was as good as a rest, and on his debut he was a major factor in a 3-2 win at York. Then, with his experience invaluable in the middle of the park, once again injury and illness sidelined him at a critical time for the club. Hopefully, he will be fit and raring to go in 1998-99, when the push for promotion will be paramount.

Crystal Palace (£2,000 from Dulwich Hamlet on 8/11/84) FL 91+7/27 FLC 9+1/2 FAC 3 Others 0+1
Aston Villa (£150,000 on 25/11/87) FL 34+3/4 FLC 3/1 FAC 3+1/1 Others 0+2
Queens Park R (£425,000 on 2/2/89) FL 11/2
Crystal Palace (£500,000 on 18/8/89) FL 87+3/12 FLC 15/4 FAC 11/2 Others 14/4
Tottenham H (£900,000 on 27/2/92) F/PL 23+10/2 (Free to Marbella on 15/8/94)
Swindon T (Loaned on 23/12/92) FL 3
Falkirk (Free on 22/12/95) SL 29+5/1 SC 8 Others 1
Bury (Free on 22/7/97) FL 21/1 FLC 3/1 FAC 2/2
Millwall (Signed on 21/1/98) FL 12/1

GRAY Andrew (Andy) David

Born: Harrogate, 15 November 1977
Height: 6'1" Weight: 12.8
International Honours: S: Yth

A tricky right winger with a good pedigree, Andy joined Bury on loan from Leeds United last December and remained at Gigg Lane for two months. Tall and awkward, he appeared in six league games for the Shakers and, although preferring a wide role, he ironically scored his first and only league goal of his career after appearing as a substitute at Reading and playing as a central attacker. The son of Frank and the nephew of Eddie, former Leeds' stars, is skilful and has great crossing ability. He also has a good attitude.

Leeds U (From trainee on 1/7/95) PL 13+9 FLC 3+1 FAC 0+2
Bury (Loaned on 11/12/97) FL 4+2/1

GRAY Ian James

Born: Manchester, 25 February 1975
Height: 6'2" Weight: 13.0

Having impressed with Rochdale in 1996-97, attracting the scouts with good handling and agility, the young goalkeeper moved to Stockport last summer, but after just three

starts he was replaced by the more experienced Eric Nixon and spent the rest of the season in the reserves. Only 23 years of age, he is bound to come again.

Oldham Ath (From trainee on 16/7/93)
Rochdale (Loaned on 18/11/94) FL 12 Others 3
Rochdale (£20,000 on 17/7/95) FL 66 FLC 4 FAC 5 Others 4
Stockport Co (£200,000+ on 30/7/97) FL 3 FLC 2

GRAY Kevin John
Born: Sheffield, 7 January 1972
Height: 6'0" Weight: 14.0

After being in and out of the side since joining Huddersfield, Kevin was in danger of becoming the forgotten man at Town in 1997-98, but, establishing himself again in early October, he became the first name on the team sheet and was so highly rated that he signed a new contract until June 2000. Having marked his 100th appearance for the club by scoring an own goal against Middlesbrough, in distinct contrast he captained the side in his 300th career appearance against Crewe Alexandra. Certainly, all the hard work in training and the reserves for this no-nonsense defender paid off and long may it continue. Kevin's only goal of the season was in a Man of the Match performance against Queens Park Rangers, only his second strike in Town colours, before his run was unfortunately cut short by two games, due to a broken foot. Ended the campaign as the Players' Player of the Year.

Mansfield T (From trainee on 1/7/90) FL 129+12/3 FLC 8/1 FAC 6+1 Others 12+2/2
Huddersfield T (Signed on 18/7/94) FL 113+4/2 FLC 7 FAC 6 Others 3

GRAY Martin David
Born: Stockton on Tees, 17 August 1971
Height: 5'9" Weight: 11.4

A knee injury kept Martin out of the Oxford side for most of the first half of last season, but after regaining his place he was a regular again and continued to cover every blade of grass, winning balls that perhaps were not his. Always involved in the action, he was unlucky to be sent off in the FA Cup tie at Leeds, when United were enjoying their best spell and, while perhaps not the most creative player in the side, he did, however, pop up with a couple of goals, both first-time strikes from the edge of the area.

Sunderland (From trainee on 1/2/90) FL 46+18/1 FLC 6+2 FAC 0+3 Others 3+1
Aldershot (Loaned on 9/1/91) FL 3+2 Others 1
Fulham (Loaned on 20/10/95) FL 6 Others 1
Oxford U (£100,000 on 28/3/96) FL 75+6/4 FLC 8 FAC 2

GRAY Michael
Born: Sunderland, 3 August 1974
Height: 5'7" Weight: 10.10
Club Honours: Div 1 '96

In Sunderland's 1996 promotion season, Michael won rave reviews as an attacking midfielder. This time around, in 1997-98, he was one of the campaign's top performers at left back, at times being the oldest member of the back four at 23. His pace and ability to beat a man helped him to strike up an excellent partnership with Allan Johnston down Sunderland's left flank and, as a player of undoubted Premiership class, he has also been touted as a future England international. Certainly, he has the strength of character to overcome the disappointment of his penalty miss in the play-off final at Wembley.

Sunderland (From trainee on 1/7/92) P/FL 170+19/12 FLC 11+3 FAC 7+1/1 Others 2

GRAY Philip (Phil)
Born: Belfast, 2 October 1968
Height: 5'10" Weight: 12.5
International Honours: NI: 20; U23-1; Yth; Sch

A former Luton favourite, Phil was re-signed by the club from Fortuna Sittard last September and, as an aggressive, experienced, and, at times, unorthodox striker, a lot was expected from him. However, he was only able to display his form in patches, as knee and back injuries constantly kept him out of the side or impaired his performance whilst playing, but he impressed with a goal in his first game and scored another fine effort against York in April. Injury cost him a place in the Northern Ireland squad against Portugal in October and the hope in 1998-99 is that he can shake free from his troubles, recover his scoring form at club level, and return to international status.

Tottenham H (From apprentice on 21/8/86) FL 4+5 FAC 0+1
Barnsley (Loaned on 17/1/90) FL 3 FAC 1
Fulham (Loaned on 8/11/90) FL 3 Others 2/1
Luton T (£275,000 on 16/8/91) FL 54+5/22 FLC 4/3 FAC 2/1 Others 2
Sunderland (£800,000 on 19/7/93) FL 108+7/34 FLC 9/4 FAC 8/3 Others 2 (Free to Nancy during 1996 close season)
Luton T (£400,000 from Fortuna Sittard on 19/9/97) FL 14+3/2 FLC 1 Others 0+1

GRAY Stuart
Born: Hallogate, 18 December 1973
Height: 5'11" Weight: 11.2
International Honours: S: U21-7

Signed by Tommy Burns from Glasgow Celtic, Stuart was yet another transfer deadline day arrival who went straight into the Reading team for the final seven games of last season. His defensive qualities at full back were quickly apparent, though his interceptions and distribution were not enough to shore up a leaky defence which kept a clean sheet in only one of those matches. He may be lacking in pace slightly, but he more than compensates for that with his astute reading of the game.

Glasgow Celtic (Free from Giffnock North AFC on 7/7/92) SL 19+9/1 SC 1 Others 2+1
Reading (£100,000 on 27/3/98) FL 7

GRAYSON Simon Nicholas
Born: Ripon, 16 December 1969
Height: 6'0" Weight: 12.10
Club Honours: FLC '97

An extremely versatile player, Simon moved to Aston Villa during the 1997 close season, having been Leicester's Player of the Year in 1996-97, after carrying off a Coca Cola Cup winners' medal and generally being outstanding in a right-sided wing-back role. And, while not carrying on in the same vein at Villa Park, he did enough to show that he will become an asset, missing just seven games after making his debut at home to Blackburn, consistently featuring favourably, either in defence or in midfield, and generally settling in well with his new team mates. Thoroughly reliable, his only disappointment would have been the lack of goals.

Leeds U (From trainee on 13/6/88) FL 2 Others 1+1
Leicester C (£50,000 on 13/3/92) F/PL 175+13/4 FLC 16+2/2 FAC 9 Others 13+1
Aston Villa (£1,350,000 on 1/7/97) PL 28+5 FLC 0+1 FAC 4/2 Others 4+2

GREAVES Mark Andrew
Born: Hull, 22 January 1975
Height: 6'1" Weight: 13.0

Having established a place in Mark Hateley's Hull City team, "Greavsie's" progress was curtailed last December by a back strain, the highlight of his first team run being his late goal at Cambridge United which secured City's only away win of the season. However, in finding it difficult to regain his place, he became one of 19 players released by his hometown club, but has already shown the aptitude to extend his career.

Hull C (Free from Brigg T on 17/6/96) FL 40+15/4 FLC 2 FAC 2 Others 1

GREEN Francis James
Born: Nottingham, 25 August 1980
Height: 5'9" Weight: 11.6

A young forward signed from non-league Ilkeston last March, Francis made his Football League debut a day after arriving at Peterborough, when coming off the bench after 62 minutes at Darlington. Opened his scoring account in a 2-1 defeat at Torquay, and looked to have bags of potential as a tireless runner with no little skill.

Peterborough U (£25,000+ from Ilkeston T on 2/3/98) FL 2+2/1

GREEN Richard Edward
Born: Wolverhampton, 22 November 1967
Height: 6'1" Weight: 13.7

A highly-rated Gillingham central defender, who is good in the air and strong in the tackle, Richard struggled to gain a regular first team place at Priestfield in 1997-98, due to the good form of Guy Butters and Barry Ashby, and was only included when injuries or suspensions took its toll. Is a player who does good work in opposing penalty areas where his flick-ons can spell danger.

Shrewsbury T (From trainee on 19/7/86) FL 120+5/5 FLC 11/1 FAC 5 Others 5/1
Swindon T (Free on 25/10/90)
Gillingham (Free on 6/3/92) FL 206+10/16 FLC 12+1 FAC 16+1/1 Others 6+1

GREEN Scott Paul
Born: Walsall, 15 January 1970
Height: 5'10" Weight: 12.5
Club Honours: Div 1 '97

Signed from Bolton during the summer of 1997, the highly versatile Scott held down the Wigan Athletic right-back position for

the majority of last season. A scorer on his debut in a 5-2 victory against Wycombe Wanderers, his experience as a forward held him in good stead and he went on to complete his 200th Football League start during 1997-98. Confident on the ball, possessing a good engine, and enjoying the overlap, he can also play in midfield if required.

Derby Co (From trainee on 20/7/88)
Bolton W (£50,000 on 17/3/90) P/FL 166+54/25 FLC 19+4/1 FAC 20+3/4 Others 16+4/1
Wigan Ath (£300,000 on 30/6/97) FL 37+1/1 FLC 2 FAC 3 Others 2

GREENACRE Christopher (Chris) Mark

Born: Halifax, 23 December 1977
Height: 5'11" Weight: 12.8

Unable to hold down a regular place at Manchester City, although pleased to have got his first team career underway in 1996-97, the busy young striker was loaned to Cardiff at the start of last season for two months of added experience and appeared regularly, scoring two goals. On his return to Maine Road, having begun with a subs' appearance at Queens Park Rangers, he played his first full game for City at home to Crewe, scoring the only goal of the game, but, before too long, he was out of contention again and, following a spell in the reserves, was loaned to Blackpool in March.

Manchester C (From trainee on 1/7/95) FL 2+5/1 FAC 0+1
Cardiff C (Loaned on 22/8/97) FL 11/2
Blackpool (Loaned on 5/3/98) FL 2+2

GREENALL Colin Anthony

Born: Billinge, 30 December 1963
Height: 5'11" Weight: 12.12
Club Honours: Div 3 '97
International Honours: E: Yth

The club captain, and a vastly dependable figure at the heart of the Wigan Athletic defence with a wealth of experience, he completed his 100th game for the club and his 600th Football League game during last season. Consistent and competent, Colin was also a danger at set pieces, scoring four league goals in total. Not offered a playing contract at the end of the campaign, he will hope to use the respect gained from his team mates in a new coaching capacity within the club. Scored the winning goal in the home victory over Fulham, in what was Kevin Keegan's first game in charge for the opposition.

Blackpool (From apprentice on 17/1/81) FL 179+4/9 FLC 12/2 FAC 9 Others 2
Gillingham (£40,000 on 10/9/86) FL 62/4 FLC 3/1 FAC 6/1 Others 9/2
Oxford U (£285,000 on 15/2/88) FL 67/2 FLC 4 FAC 1 Others 1
Bury (Loaned on 4/1/90) FL 3 Other 1
Bury (£125,000 on 16/7/90) FL 66+2/5 FLC 3 FAC 1 Others 8/1
Preston NE (£50,000 on 27/3/92) FL 29/1
Chester (Free on 13/8/93) FL 42/1 FLC 2 FAC 4/1 Others 2
Lincoln C (Free on 27/7/94) FL 43/3 FLC 6 FAC 3/1 Others 2
Wigan Ath (£45,000 on 19/9/95) FL 122/8 FLC 3+1/1 FAC 7 Others 6+1

GREENE David Michael

Born: Luton, 26 October 1973
Height: 6'3" Weight: 14.4
International Honours: Ei: U21-14

A tall centre half, whose presence was vital in the Colchester rearguard in 1997-98, David scored four goals in five games early in the season, but his form and confidence dipped a little in mid-term. However, he seemed to blossom once again alongside loanee, Guy Branston, as United's defence suddenly clicked, and was rumoured to have attracted attention from bigger clubs. "Greeney" then hit tremendous form as the campaign approached its climax, and he contributed the aggregate equaliser against Barnet in the play-off semi final, before putting in a towering display at Wembley.

Luton T (From juniors on 3/9/91) FL 18+1 FLC 2 FAC 1 Others 0+1
Colchester U (Loaned on 23/11/95) FL 14/1 Others 2
Brentford (Loaned on 1/3/96) FL 11
Colchester U (£30,000 on 21/6/96) FL 82/6 FLC 6 FAC 5 Others 9/2

GREENING Jonathan

Born: Scarborough, 2 January 1979
Height: 5'11" Weight: 11.7
International Honours: E: Yth

Manchester United swooped to sign York's talented young forward last March for an initial fee believed to have been in the region of £500,000, rising to £2 million. Nurtured carefully by the Minstermen, he only made six-full starts during the 1997-98 season, but twice, when coming on as substitute, netted outstanding goals at home to Gillingham and away at Chesterfield.

York C (From trainee on 23/12/96) FL 5+20/2 FLC 0+1 Others 1
Manchester U (£500,000+ on 25/3/98)

GREGAN Sean Matthew

Born: Guisborough, 29 March 1974
Height: 6'2" Weight: 14.7

Originally bought by Preston as a centre half in 1997-98, Sean figured more often than not in central midfield, where his combative all-action style endeared him to the fans, if not the referees. Never afraid to try a shot, his goals were generally spectacular long-range efforts, as Grimsby, Gillingham, and Doncaster fans can testify. Decisive in the tackle, a strong header of the ball, and keen to get forward, he has the potential to go far in the game if he can channel his natural aggression, which led to him reaching double figures in bookings, despite being appointed captain in December.

Darlington (From trainee on 20/1/91) FL 129+7/4 FLC 8 FAC 7 Others 10+1/1
Preston NE (£350,000 on 29/11/96) FL 54+2/3 FLC 3 FAC 4/1 Others 4

GREGG Matthew Stephen

Born: Cheltenham, 30 November 1978
Height: 5'11" Weight: 12.0

This first year pro Torquay goalkeeper had an excellent start to last season, keeping clean sheets in two of the opening three games, before losing his place to Ken Veysey. Even then, he never let the side down and played at Wembley where he was

only beaten by a dubious penalty. Agile and attentive, he continues to gain in experience.

Torquay U (From trainee on 4/7/97) FL 21 FLC 4 FAC 1 Others 1

GREGORY David Spencer

Born: Sudbury, 23 January 1970
Height: 5'10" Weight: 12.8

A true utility player, "Greggers" completed a marvellous season for Colchester in 1997-98, in which he played at right back, left back, centre half, and in midfield, not to mention finishing as United's leading goalscorer! His hitherto-unsuspected goal-grabbing expertise first came to note in the FA Cup, when he produced a late equaliser at Brentford, and then opened the scoring against Hereford at Layer Road. Vital league goals followed in the Spring, but the real glory came with three goals in the play offs – a penalty equaliser, the winner against Barnet, and the all-important penalty at Wembley to take United up. As a point of interest, on 13 February, he scored United's 3,000th Football League goal. What a season!*

Ipswich T (From trainee on 31/3/87) F/PL 16+16/2 FLC 3+2 FAC 1 Others 3+2/4
Hereford U (Loaned on 9/1/95) FL 2 Others 1
Peterborough U (Free on 4/7/95) FL 0+3 FLC 1 FAC 1 Others 2
Colchester U (Free on 8/12/95) FL 81+11/6 FLC 3+1 FAC 5/2 Others 11/1

GREGORY Neil Richard

Born: Ndola, Zambia, 7 October 1972
Height: 5'11" Weight: 11.10

David's younger brother, Neil went to Colchester initially on three month's loan early last January and was quickly among the goals, although he was probably never completely match fit. Returned to Ipswich while protracted transfer negotiations took place, and also carrying a knee injury, until United broke the club's transfer record to make the move permanent just before the deadline. He then scored in each of the last two league games to cement the play-off place, and the U's look forward to much more of the same in division two this coming season. Earlier, in November, Neil had a spell on loan at Peterborough, where he scored within five minutes of his debut, before being allowed to return to Portman Road, unsigned. By the way, when playing alongside David at Wembley, they became the first brothers to appear in a play-off final.

Ipswich T (From trainee on 21/2/92) P/FL 18+27/9 FLC 2+3 FAC 0+1 Others 4+3/2
Chesterfield (Loaned on 3/2/94) FL 2+1/1
Scunthorpe U (Loaned on 6/3/95) FL 10/7
Torquay U (Loaned on 22/11/96) FL 5
Peterborough U (Loaned on 27/11/97) FL 2+1/1 Others 1
Colchester U (£50,000 on 2/1/98) FL 12+3/7 Others 3/2

GRIDELET Philip (Phil) Raymond

Born: Hendon, 30 April 1967
Height: 5'11" Weight: 13.0
International Honours: E: SP-5

1997-98 was another difficult season at Southend United for Phil, and his refusal to commit himself to a contract at the start of

the campaign made him unpopular with the fans, and this seemed to stick with him. A tigerish, tough-tackling midfielder, he again suffered from a lack of goals, although he did manage to seal the Blues' win in the FA Cup at Woking with a good header.*

Barnsley (£175,000 from Barnet on 21/1/90) FL 3+3 FAC 1 Others 1
Rotherham U (Loaned on 5/3/93) FL 9
Southend U (Free on 25/9/93) FL149+27/10 FLC 4 FAC 4/1 Others 7/1

Phil Gridelet

GRIEVES Daniel Leonard
Born: Watford, 21 September 1978
Height: 5'9" Weight: 10.7

A young midfield player with good passing skills who has Watford in his blood, as a great-grandson of the former Watford goalkeeper, Reg "Skilly" Williams, Daniel made his Hornets' first team debut against Fulham in the Auto Windscreens Shield, and looks set to be around for a fair while yet.

Watford (From trainee on 13/2/97) Others 1

GRIFFIN Andrew (Andy)
Born: Billinge, 7 March 1979
Height: 5'9" Weight: 10.10
International Honours: E: Yth

Although only 18, Andy, who is seriously quick when going forward, and able to tackle and recover, established himself at left back in the Stoke first team, where his high-quality performances attracted the attention of the Premiership managers. With City strapped for cash, following the building of a new stadium, a transfer soon became inevitable and last January Kenny Dalglish won the race to take him to Newcastle as part of his rebuilding, soon integrating him into the squad with occasional first team appearances. A player who enjoys getting forward to join the attack, in order to exploit his shooting abilities, although right footed, he is quite at

home on the left flank, and looks likely to be a big star of the future. Is a regular in the England youth team.

Stoke C (From trainee on 5/9/96) FL 52+5/2 FLC 4+1 FAC 2
Newcastle U (£1,500,000+ on 30/1/98) PL 4

GRIFFITHS Carl Brian
Born: Welshpool, 16 July 1971
Height: 5'11" Weight: 12.6
International Honours: W: B-1; U21-2; Yth

A real Leyton Orient favourite, Carl seems to have the knack of scoring vital goals, being the club's top scorer in 1997-98, and is good with both feet, and head, and in holding the ball up while waiting for others to support him. Returned to Bobby Gould's thinking last March and it can only be a matter of time before he plays for the full Welsh national side. Scored a hat trick against Doncaster in the 8-0 victory.

Shrewsbury T (From trainee on 26/9/88) FL 110+33/54 FLC 7+4/3 FAC 6/2 Others 7+3/3
Manchester C (£500,000 on 29/10/93) PL 11+7/4 FLC 0+1 FAC 2
Portsmouth (£200,000 on 17/8/95) FL 2+12/2 FLC 0+1
Peterborough U (£225,000 on 28/3/96) FL 6+10/2 FLC 0+2/1 FAC 1+1/1 Others 0+1
Leyton Orient (Loaned on 31/10/96) FL 5/3
Leyton Orient (£100,000 on 7/3/97) FL 39+2/21 FLC 4/3 FAC 2/1 Others 2

GRIFFITHS Gareth John
Born: Winsford, 10 April 1970
Height: 6'4" Weight: 14.0

A tall, imposing central defender, Gareth struggled with injury for virtually the whole of 1997-98 and made just three appearances in the Port Vale defence. Ironically, on loan at Shrewsbury in November, his presence helped the team to three wins and two draws in his six games before returning to Vale Park. Hampered by another knee injury after just two games in a Vale shirt, immediately before Christmas, he returned a month later at Sunderland, but had to come off at half time with Vale 3-0 down, that being the end of his campaign at first team level.*

Port Vale (Signed from Rhyl on 8/2/93) FL 90+4/4 FLC 8 FAC 7/1 Others 7
Shrewsbury T (Loaned on 31/10/97) FL 6

GRIMANDI Gilles
Born: Gap, France, 11 November 1970
Height: 6'0" Weight: 12.7
Club Honours: PL '98; FAC '98

Yet another player signed by Arsenal from Monaco, Arsene Wenger's former club, during the 1997 close season, although not making the same impression as Manu Petit, Gilles turned out to be a more than useful buy when called upon, and became a recognised squad member. Although able to play at centre back, where he had performed in France alongside his friend, Petit, he was more impressive when standing in for Lee Dixon as a right back. And, in a campaign where the Gunners needed to be in a position to call up quality players as they came with a late run to win both the Premiership and the FA Cup, the Frenchman was up for it, winning medals for both competitions, despite not being called upon at Wembley. Showed good positional sense

and neat, but simple passing skills, he scored his only goal in the 1-0 home win over Crystal Palace.

Arsenal (£1,500,000 from Monaco on 25/6/97) PL 16+6/1 FLC 4 FAC 3+2

GROBBELAAR Bruce David
Born: Durban, South Africa, 6 October 1957
Height: 6'1" Weight: 14.2
Club Honours: Div 1 '82, '83, '84, '86, '88, '90; FLC '82, '83, '84, '90; FAC '86, '89, '92; CS '82, '88, '89; EC '84
International Honours: Zimbabwe: 20

Having been freed by Plymouth during the 1997 close season, this well-known, quirky, and popular goalkeeper trialled at both Oxford and Sheffield Wednesday without getting a game, before arriving at Oldham last December. Remaining in the wings at Boundary Park, he was finally called up for the last four games of the campaign when Gary Kelly was injured and, while entertaining the crowd with his usual antics, kept three clean sheets. Despite all of his problems during the last couple of years, Bruce is still well worth the admission money alone, especially when he performs more like a sweeper.

Crewe Alex (On trial from Vancouver Whitecaps on 18/12/79) FL 24/1
Liverpool (£250,000 from Vancouver Whitecaps on 12/3/81) F/PL 440 FLC 70 FAC 62 Others 56
Stoke C (Loaned on 17/3/93) FL 4
Southampton (Free on 11/8/94) PL 32 FLC 3 FAC 5
Plymouth Arg (Free on 12/8/96) FL 36 FLC 2 FAC 3
Oxford U (Free on 17/9/97)
Sheffield Wed (Free on 23/9/97)
Oldham Ath (Free on 18/12/97) FL 4

GROVES Paul
Born: Derby, 28 February 1966
Height: 5'11" Weight: 11.5
Club Honours: AMC '98

Paul was never really accepted by the crowd after following ex-Grimsby boss, Alan Buckley, to West Bromwich during the 1996 close season and, following Buckley's sacking and subsequent return to Blundell Park, he also made the return trip. Quickly establishing himself as automatic choice for his old midfield spot in 1997-98, once again being an ever present, he was a key player in the Mariner's marathon season which took in 68 games. A right-footed ball winner, who makes telling forward runs, and also provides excellent service to the front men, he was delighted to be part of the side that won the Auto Windscreen Shield and went back to the first division at the first attempt, via the play offs. Along with Kevin Donovan, Paul was selected for the award-winning PFA second division team.

Leicester C (£12,000 from Burton A on 18/4/88) FL 7+9/1 FLC 1/1 FAC 0+1 Others 0+1
Lincoln C (Loaned on 20/8/89) FL 8/1 FLC 2
Blackpool (£60,000 on 25/1/90) FL 106+1/21 FLC 6/1 FAC 9/4 Others 13/3
Grimsby T (£150,000 on 12/8/92) FL 183+1/38 FLC 10+1/2 FAC 12/2 Others 4/1
West Bromwich A (£600,000 on 8/7/96) FL 27+2/4 FLC 2/1 FAC 1
Grimsby T (£250,000 on 21/7/97) FL 46/7 FLC 6/2 FAC 6/1 Others 10/2

GUINAN Stephen (Steve)
Born: Birmingham, 24 December 1975
Height: 6'1" Weight: 13.7

The big, strong Nottingham Forest striker again failed to force his way into the side on a permanent basis, having to make do with three games in 1997-98, but at least he broke his scoring duck at the club, when netting the first in the 2-1 home victory over Doncaster in the Coca Cola Cup. Then it was back to the reserves, and with Pierre van Hooijdonk and Kevin Campbell going so well, he had a spell on loan at Crewe in March, making three appearances before returning to the City Ground after being injured.

Nottingham F (From trainee on 7/1/93) F/PL 2+4 FLC 1/1
Darlington (Loaned on 14/12/95) FL 3/1
Burnley (Loaned on 27/3/97) FL 0+6
Crewe Alex (Loaned on 19/3/98) FL 3

GULLIT Ruud
Born: Surinam, 1 September 1962
Height: 6'3" Weight: 13.12
Club Honours: FLC '98
International Honours: Holland: 64

On Thursday, 12 February 1998 came the seismic shock that Chelsea fans had long dreaded – Ruud Gullit was to leave after failing to agree terms for a new contract. The news could not have come at a worse time for the club as they stood second in the Premiership, were involved in a Coca Cola Cup semi final against Arsenal, and a Cup Winners' Cup quarter final against Real Betis. Rarely can one individual have such a drastic impact on the playing affairs of a leading English club in such a short period of time as Ruud had at Chelsea. Capturing the FA Cup in his first season as player/manager in such an exciting fashion was just the prelude to a three-pronged assault on the major honours in his second season. Along with his unsung first lieutenant, Graham Rix, Ruud cleverly juggled his large, multi-talented squad to telling effect, keeping his players fresh for the fixture pile up that success inevitably brings. The faces may have changed but the exciting free-wheeling style remained the same, with wing backs and central defenders encouraged to get forward. Incredibly, up to the turn of the year, the Blues had scored 63 goals in 27 matches, with 15 different players getting on the scoresheet. On the playing side, however, the mercurial Dutchman made just three starts, all in the Coca Cola Cup, and a handful of substitute appearances. Although he was at Chelsea for less than three years, his achievements, both as player and manager, firmly established him as a legend in the Pantheon of Chelsea heroes, having played a leading role in putting the club at the forefront of domestic and European football. He will never be forgotten by the Chelsea faithful.

Chelsea (Free from Sampdoria, via Haarlem, PSV Eindhoven and AC Milan, on 1/7/95) PL 37+12/4 FLC 6+1 FAC 7+1/3

GUNN Bryan James
Born: Thurso, 22 December 1963
Height: 6'2" Weight: 13.13

Steve Guppy

International Honours: S: 6; B-4; U21-9; Yth; Sch

Having finally made way for the extremely promising Andy Marshall in the Norwich goal towards the end of 1996-97, Bryan made just four appearances last January before signing for the Scottish Premier League side, Hibernian, on a short-term contract, after the initial request for a three-month loan deal fell foul of the SFA's regulations. Despite performing heroically at Easter Road, his ability to come for crosses giving renewed confidence to an ailing defence, Hibs will be playing their football in the Scottish first division this coming season. With a view to management, and with Mike Walker resigning the post, Bryan has submitted an application for the vacant Norwich post. *Stop Press:* With nothing doing on the home front, Bryan signed a two-year deal with Hibernian on 8 July.

Aberdeen (Signed from Invergordon BC on 14/8/80) SL 15 SLC 4 SC 1 Others 1
Norwich C (£150,000 on 23/10/86) F/PL 390 FLC 38 FAC 27 Others 22

GUNNLAUGSSON Arnar Bergmann
Born: Iceland, 6 March 1973
Height: 6'0" Weight: 11.10
International Honours: Iceland: 23

An Icelandic international centre forward, Arnar joined Bolton in July 1997 from IA of Akranes, having previously been a member of the 1993 Feyenoord Dutch championship winning team. Despite being a pacy striker, he found his first team chances limited in 1997-98, making only two full starts and a number of substitute appearances, but his devastating turn of pace, and a willingness to chase every ball, proved a handful for opposing sides when he did play. Although yet to register his first league goal for the club, it will surely only be a matter of time before that is rectified.

Bolton W (£100,000 from IA Akranes on 7/8/97) PL 2+13 FLC 0+3/1 FAC 1

GUPPY Stephen (Steve)
Born: Winchester, 29 March 1969
Height: 5'11" Weight: 11.4
Club Honours: FAT '91, '93; GMVC '93
International Honours: E: B-1; U21-1; SP-1

The left-sided Leicester midfielder adapted well to the wing-back position during last season, winning a call up to the England "B" team and also, as an over-age player to the U21 line-up. One of the best crossers of the ball in the Premiership, he scored with a blistering drive in the home win over Tottenham and with a rare collectors item, a header against Sheffield Wednesday. A key member of Martin O'Neill's formation, whose transfer fee was finally settled after all the various conditions were met, he has already surprised a good many people with his confident displays and will, hopefully, continue to do so.

Wycombe W (Signed in 1989-90) FL 41/8 FLC 4 FAC 8/2 Others 10
Newcastle U (£150,000 on 2/8/94) FLC 0+1
Port Vale (£225,000 on 25/11/94) FL 102+3/12 FLC 7 FAC 8 Others 7+1/1
Leicester C (£950,000 on 28/2/97) PL 49+1/2 FLC 1 FAC 2 Others 2

GURNEY Andrew (Andy) Robert
Born: Bristol, 25 January 1974
Height: 5'10" Weight: 11.6

This right-wing back was snapped up by Torquay's Kevin Hodges after being released by Bristol Rovers during the 1997 close season and, like his left-sided counterpart, Paul Gibbs, Andy proved to be a revelation when scoring ten goals, many of them quite spectacular efforts. Also able to play on either flank and in midfield, his powerful shooting ability makes him a constant danger when within range.*

Bristol Rov (From trainee on 10/7/92) FL 100+8/9 FLC 7/1 FAC 5 Others 15
Torquay U (Free on 10/7/97) FL 44/9 FLC 4 FAC 3/1 Others 3

HAALAND Alf-Inge (Alfie) Rasdal
Born: Stavanger, Norway, 23 November 1972
Height: 5'10" Weight: 12.12
International Honours: Norway: 27
An extremely versatile player, Alf-Inge transferred to Leeds in the 1997 close season for a tribunal-fixed fee way short of Nottingham Forest's valuation, after United had earlier a £2 million bid turned down on transfer deadline day in 1996-97. After picking up a minor knock, he settled into a withdrawn central midfield position and, as the campaign progressed, he made this position his own. Has a wonderful "engine" and seems to cover every blade of grass during the 90 minutes. He is also a good man marker. For example, when West Ham's Eyal Berkovic was substituted in the 3-1 victory at Elland Road, having been played out of the game by Alfie, the Norwegian immediately went to the other end and scored the all-important second goal with a header from a corner. He went on to score his share of goals for the side, including a superb brace versus Blackburn in March, his second being a 35-yard drive to beat Alan Fettis in the Rovers' goal. An excellent acquisition, although this experienced Norwegian international was expected to take part in his second World Cup during the summer, he was not among the final 22 selected.
Nottingham F (Signed from Bryne on 25/1/94) F/PL 66+9/7 FLC 2+5 FAC 5+1 Others 2+3
Leeds U (£1,600,000 on 17/7/97) PL 26+6/7 FLC 3 FAC 2

Alfie Haaland

HACKETT Warren James
Born: Plaistow, 16 December 1971
Height: 6'0" Weight: 12.5
Club Honours: FAYC '90
International Honours: St Lucia
Continuing where he left off in 1996-97, despite missing the first six games for Mansfield in 1997-98, Warren came into the side in a midfield role before sustaining a niggling injury in mid-term. Came back strongly in February, just in time to win his first caps for St Lucia, and continued to show his class, whether it was in a defensive situation or an attacking one.
Leyton Orient (Free from Tottenham H juniors on 3/7/90) FL 74+2/3 FLC 4 FAC 8/2 Others 7
Doncaster Rov (Free on 26/7/94) FL 46/2 FLC 4 FAC 1 Others 4
Mansfield T (£50,000 on 20/10/95) FL 90+1/5 FLC 2 FAC 5 Others 1

HADDOW Paul Andrew
Born: Blackpool, 11 October 1978
Height: 5'8" Weight: 10.10
A professional signing from the YTS ranks at Blackpool during the 1997 close season, and having already made a first team debut in the Auto Windscreen Shield in 1996-97, Paul was given a taste of Football League action in 1997-98, when coming off the bench for the second half at Wycombe in January. However, that was to be his only opportunity and he went back to the reserves to further his experience, prior to being released during the summer.
Blackpool (From trainee on 7/7/97) FL 0+1 Others 1

HADLEY Stewart
Born: Dudley, 30 December 1973
Height: 6'0" Weight: 13.2
In coming back strongly for Mansfield at the end of 1996-97, it was felt that the hard-running striker would be refreshed in time for 1997-98 and be raring to go. Unfortunately, it turned out otherwise. Bedevilled with a long-term injury, and only managing two subs' appearances, Stewart was released in mid-season and will no doubt be looking back on his bad fortune.
Derby Co (Free from Halesowen T on 6/7/92)
Mansfield T (Signed on 9/2/94) FL 100+24/31 FLC 6+2 FAC 7/1 Others 5+1/3

HAILS Julian
Born: Lincoln, 20 November 1967
Height: 5'10" Weight: 11.1
The one major success story for Southend United during the 1997-98 season, Julian's game came on in leaps and bounds, and once he got into the right-back position in September he made it his own. Although possessing a small frame, his tackling was as strong as anyone's at the club, while his willingness to get forward to beat opponents won him countless sponsors' Man of the Match awards at Roots Hall. Extremely comfortable on the ball, Southend might have avoided relegation with more like him available for selection.*
Fulham (Signed from Hemel Hempstead on 29/8/90) FL 99+10/12 FLC 5+1 FAC 2 Others 9/1
Southend U (Free on 2/12/94) FL 132+17/6 FLC 5+2 FAC 3+1 Others 3

Julian Hails

HALL Gareth David
Born: Croydon, 12 March 1969
Height: 5'8" Weight: 12.0
Club Honours: Div 2 '89; Div 1 '96; FMC 90
International Honours: E: Sch. W: 9; U21-1
A Welsh international, Gareth made only one full league appearance for Sunderland last season and put in an excellent performance in a 1-0 win at Wolves. However, finding his way blocked as regards a regular slot by Darren Holloway and Chris Makin, he was loaned out to Brentford in October, making six appearances, firstly in a central midfield role, and then at right back. A player who is always willing to link up with the attack, and given a free transfer during the summer, there should be any number of clubs interested in acquiring his services. *Stop Press:* Signed for Swindon on 13 May.
Chelsea (From apprentice on 25/4/86) F/PL 120+18/4 FLC 12+1 FAC 6 Others 10+4/1
Sunderland (£300,000 on 20/12/95) P/FL 41+7 FLC 3 FAC 2
Brentford (Loaned on 3/10/97) FL 6

HALL Marcus Thomas
Born: Coventry, 24 March 1976
Height: 6'1" Weight: 12.2
International Honours: E: B-1; U21-8
After a season when so much was expected of him at Coventry, he benefited from a less pressurised situation in 1997-98 and developed as a player. With David Burrows fit, Marcus played most of his games on the left side of midfield, before losing his place there to Noel Whelan after Christmas. Rarely letting the side down, even when asked to play in central midfield against Palace, he was selected for England U21s again, and was in the team knocked out of the European Championships by Greece, when he scored at both ends. He later stepped up to the England "B" side, where he played in a three-man defence against Chile. Broke his scoring duck for City in the

123

Coca Cola Cup against Everton with a superb right-foot shot, and followed it up with the fourth goal in the hammering of Spurs.

Coventry C (From trainee on 1/7/94) PL 56+12/1 FLC 9+1/1 FAC 7+2

HALL Paul Anthony
Born: Manchester, 3 July 1972
Height: 5'9" Weight: 11.0
International Honours: Jamaica: 21

For the most part of last season Paul, along with Fitzroy Simpson, was out of the country helping Jamaica to qualify for the World Cup and, although playing in half of Portsmouth's games, his performances sometimes lacked a cutting edge, while his return of five goals was poor compared to previous seasons. Mainly a right-sided wide player who can attack the full back with speed and control to give himself the option of going inside for a crack at goal, or crossing for his team mates, Paul will be hoping that he can produce more consistent form in 1998-99, despite the distraction of international football. *Stop Press:* Played in all three of Jamaica's Group H World Cup games in France during the summer, the side losing heavily to Croatia and Argentina, but beating Japan, before going out of the competition.

Torquay U (From trainee on 9/7/90) FL 77+16/1 FLC 7 FAC 4+1/2 Others 5+1/1
Portsmouth (£70,000 on 25/3/93) FL 148+40/37 FLC 10+3/1 FAC 7+1/2 Others 6+2/2

HALL Wayne
Born: Rotherham, 25 October 1968
Height: 5'9" Weight: 10.6

For York's experienced left back, with over 350 appearances for the club to his credit, 1997-98 was his ninth season at Bootham Crescent and perhaps his best. As a player who can be used further up the flank if required, he showed consistent and outstanding form throughout the campaign, despite missing a few games in the closing weeks owing to injury.*

York C (Free from Hatfield Main Colliery on 15/3/89) FL 288+16/8 FLC 21+1 FAC 11+1/1 Others 20/1

HALLE Gunnar
Born: Oslo, Norway, 11 August 1965
Height: 5'11" Weight: 11.2
Club Honours: Div 2 '91
International Honours: Norway: 60

An experienced Norwegian international, who was George Graham's first signing for Leeds, Gunnar is an athletic player whose versatility means he can fill a number of positions, and he produced a very high consistency of performance throughout last season. Played in all the defensive positions and was even pushed on into a midfield role, where he scored his first goal for the club in the 5-0 victory at Derby County. Strong in the tackle, his distribution is of the highest standard, he also reads the game very intelligently. *Stop Press:* Was selected as one of Norway's named 22 players for the World Cup Finals in France '98 and played in the 1-1 draw against Scotland.

Oldham Ath (£280,000 from Lillestrom on 15/2/91) F/PL 185+3/17 FLC 16/2 FAC 8/2 Others 4
Leeds U (£400,000 on 13/12/96) PL 51+2/2 FLC 2+1 FAC 6

HALLIDAY Stephen William
Born: Sunderland, 3 May 1976
Height: 5'10" Weight: 12.12

1997-98 was a disappointing season for Hartlepool's fast-running, dangerous winger. Beginning it in dispute with the club, he remained on a week-to-week contract, and perhaps, inevitably, his form tended to fluctuate. At his best, he was again the player well worth the £375,000 set by a transfer tribunal in 1996, but there were other spells when he struggled with injury and could not find his best form. Often used from the bench, he now holds the overall club record for substitute appearances.

Hartlepool U (From trainee on 5/7/94) FL 111+29/25 FLC 8+3 FAC 4+1/1 Others 5+1

HALLWORTH Jonathan (Jon) Geoffrey
Born: Stockport, 26 October 1965
Height: 6'2" Weight: 14.3
Club Honours: Div 2 '91

Brought in by Cardiff City on a free transfer from Oldham during the 1997 close season, Jon signed a three-year contract, having been persuaded to join the club because of their ambitious approach to earning promotion. For his own part, he was outstanding throughout and won every Player of the Year award available at Ninian Park, the fans firmly believing him to be the best goalkeeper in division three and could not understand how he was not named in the PFA divisional team. Indeed, his own team mates rated him far and above other 'keepers and team captain, David Penney, said: "Jon was our best player. He was consistently outstanding and could be comfortably playing in higher divisions." A crucial part of City's promotion bid in 1998-99, a feature of his game is his booming kicks downfield, from penalty area to penalty area, which can be a major threat to the opposition.

Ipswich T (From apprentice on 26/5/83) FL 45 FLC 4 FAC 1 Others 6
Bristol Rov (Loaned on 1/1/85) FL 2 Others 1
Oldham Ath (£75,000 on 3/2/89) F/PL 171+3 FLC 20 FAC 20 Others 3
Cardiff C (Free on 6/8/97) FL 43 FLC 2 FAC 5

HAMILTON Derrick (Des) Vivian
Born: Bradford, 15 August 1976
Height: 5'11" Weight: 13.0
International Honours: E: U21-1

Having only arrived at Newcastle late the previous season, Des' selection for the England U21 side led to an expectation that he would challenge seriously for a first team place in 1997-98. However, he injured his right ankle in the pre-season friendly against Juventus, which proved a set back to his hopes, but being strong, aggressive, and hard working, his versatility will undoubtedly prove an asset to the club, as he is able to operate equally well at full back, wing back, or in midfield. Although his opportunities were restricted, he did score on his first team debut against Hull in the Coca Cola Cup.

Bradford C (From trainee on 1/6/94) FL 67+21/5 FLC 6/1 FAC 6 Others 4+1/2
Newcastle U (£1,500,000 + on 27/3/97) PL 7+5 FLC 1+1/1 FAC 1 Others 2

HAMILTON Ian Richard
Born: Stevenage, 14 December 1967
Height: 5'9" Weight: 11.3

Having had a fine season at West Bromwich in 1996-97, despite his form dropping slightly in 1997-98 he continued to give maximum effort, his prompting play and probing exploits from midfield always in evidence. As the club captain, it was therefore something of a surprise when he became a transfer deadline day signing for Sheffield United, especially as he was beginning to get back to his best. Not given much time to settle, with few games left and the play-off places very much in every Blade's mind, he was asked to play in a number of positions in order to cover for injuries and suspension, and did well. After playing in both play-off semi-final legs, and breaking his duck when scoring in the defeat at Crewe, he is sure to be awaiting 1998-99 with renewed anticipation.

Southampton (From apprentice on 24/12/85)
Cambridge U (Signed on 29/3/88) FL 23+1/1 FLC 1 FAC 2 Others 2
Scunthorpe U (Signed on 23/12/88) FL 139+6/18 FLC 6 FAC 6+1 Others 14+1/3
West Bromwich A (£160,000 on 19/6/92) FL 229+11/23 FLC 13+2/1 FAC 10+1/1 Others 14+2/3
Sheffield U (Signed on 26/3/98) FL 8/1 Others 2

HAMMOND Andrew (Andy) Bendall
Born: Rotherham, 21 November 1978
Height: 5'10" Weight: 11.0

While still a trainee, Andy made his first team debut in Doncaster's FA Cup first round tie at Preston, when he came on as a late substitute and scored the second goal in their 2-3 defeat. Somewhat surprisingly, the young striker was released in December, whereupon he moved to non-league Stalybridge Celtic.

Doncaster Rov (Trainee) FL 1 FAC 0+1/1

HAMMOND Nicholas (Nicky) David
Born: Hornchurch, 7 September 1967
Height: 6'0" Weight: 11.13

The most consistent of the five goalkeepers used by Reading during last season, his technique and commitment to the club was greatly appreciated by the fans, who voted him as runner up to skipper, Phil Parkinson, as their Player of the Season. Having come into the team as a last-minute replacement for Steve Mautone, who was injured during the warm-up at Port Vale, he stayed in the side for a run of 21 games, the high point being three penalty kick saves during the FA Cup fourth round replay shoot-out against Cardiff City, this despite a stomach injury received early in the game. Nicky also coaches the club's young 'keepers at the Centre of Excellence.

Arsenal (From apprentice on 12/7/85)
Bristol Rov (Loaned on 23/8/86) FL 3
Swindon T (Free on 1/7/87) F/PL 65+2 FLC 11 FAC 10 Others 6
Plymouth Arg (£40,000 on 14/8/95) FL 4 FLC 2 Others 1
Reading (£40,000 on 13/2/96) FL 24 FLC 2 FAC 5

HAMPSHIRE Steven (Steve) Gary
Born: Edinburgh, 17 October 1979
Height: 5'10" Weight: 10.10
Yet another promising graduate from the Chelsea youth scheme to make a breakthrough into the first team in 1997-98, young Steve came on as a 62nd-minute substitute for Mark Hughes in the Coca Cola Cup third round tie against Blackburn Rovers. A very promising player, who can play either in midfield or as a striker, he has been a consistent goalscorer in reserve and youth team football, and the club has forecast a bright future for him.
Chelsea (From trainee on 9/7/97) FLC 0+1

HANDYSIDE Peter David
Born: Dumfries, 31 July 1974
Height: 6'1" Weight: 13.8
Club Honours: AMC '98
International Honours: S: U21-7
Having missed most of 1996-97 due to injury, Peter at last returned to full fitness in 1997-98 and enjoyed what was undoubtedly his best season yet for Grimsby. Even more masterful at the centre of a very solid defence, he developed confidently when going forward, and in his ability to initiate attacks with his distribution from the back. Crowned a great campaign as a member of the side that went back to the first division, via the play offs, and won the Auto Windscreen Shield following a 2-1 win over Bournemouth at Wembley.
Grimsby T (From trainee on 21/11/92) FL 134+6/1 FLC 13 FAC 10 Others 13+1

HANMER Gareth Craig
Born: Shrewsbury, 12 October 1973
Height: 5'6" Weight: 10.3
Signed in the summer of 1997 from West Bromwich Albion, this local lad was a revelation. Having played just a couple of games for Shrewsbury early on, he became ever present from the end of September, making the right-full back position his own. Assured, good in the tackle, fast in the attack, and a good crosser, with more games under his belt he looks to be an excellent investment.
West Bromwich A (£20,000 from Newtown on 18/6/96)
Shrewsbury T (£10,000 on 25/7/97) FL 39/1 FLC 1 FAC 2 Others 1

HANSON David (Dave) Paul
Born: Huddersfield, 19 November 1968
Height: 6'0" Weight: 13.7
Started last season as the reserve centre forward at Leyton Orient, and made a few appearances as substitute before joining Dover at the end of September. Big and strong, with the ability to play with his back to the opposition's goal, he returned to Brisbane Road and made a few sporadic appearances prior to signing for non-league, Halifax, on a free transfer in January.
Bury (Free from Farsley Celtic on 19/7/93) FL 1 FLC 2 (Free to Halifax T on 18/8/94)
Leyton Orient (£50,000 from Hednesford T on 4/10/95) FL 26+22/5 FLC 1+1 FAC 1+1 Others 2+2
Chesterfield (Loaned on 10/3/97) FL 3/1

HAPGOOD Leon Duane
Born: Torbay, 7 August 1979
Height: 5'6" Weight: 10.0
Following up his first team opportunity of the previous season, Torquay's second year YTS scored on his first appearance of 1997-98 and proved to be an able deputy to the senior players when called upon. A busy midfielder who covers every blade of grass, Leon has already accepted a senior contract for 1998-99.
Torquay U (Trainee) FL 15+8/3 FLC 1+1 FAC 3 Others 0+1

HARDY Philip (Phil)
Born: Chester, 9 April 1973
Height: 5'8" Weight: 11.8
Club Honours: WC '95
International Honours: Ei: U21-9
Still only 25, Phil lived up to his surname in 1997-98 and returned to the Wrexham first team with a vengeance, following a disappointing 1996-97. After an early injury to Deryn Brace, he made the left-back position his own and was an ever present for the majority of the campaign, proving to be a reliable defender who never gave his opponents much room to manoeuvre. The U21 international was unlucky not to gain his first senior Republic of Ireland cap last season, unfortunately having to withdraw through injury.
Wrexham (From trainee on 24/11/90) FL 264+1 FLC 16 FAC 27 Others 33

HARE Matthew (Matty)
Born: Barnstaple, 26 December 1976
Height: 6'1" Weight: 13.0
Although recognised at Exeter for his man-marking ability, 1997-98 was a frustrating season for Matty, as he again found first team action hard to come by. Loaned to the Irish club, Sligo Rovers, in order to obtain experience, the young defender was released during the summer. Is also a long-throw specialist.
Exeter C (From trainee on 4/8/95) FL 31+14/1 FLC 0+2 FAC 2+1 Others 4

HAREWOOD Marlon Anderson
Born: Hampstead, 25 August 1979
Height: 6'1" Weight: 11.0
A product of Nottingham Forest's youth scheme, the young striker made his Football League debut at West Bromwich in the final game of last season, with the club already promoted to the Premiership and Kevin Campbell unavailable due to injury. Big and strong, and a player out of the Emile Heskey mould, Marlon certainly looked to be one for the future and will be looking for further opportunities this coming term.
Nottingham F (From trainee on 9/9/96) FL 1

HARKIN Maurice (Mo) Presley
Born: Derry, 16 August 1979
Height: 5'10" Weight: 11.11
International Honours: NI: Yth
A two-footed attacking midfielder who is the most exciting prospect to emerge from the Wycombe Wanderers youth team, Mo figured in 40 games last season, 23 of them as a substitute, as he was used in spells to

nurture his precocious talent. Was the star of the show in his first start of the campaign, at Fulham in the Coca Cola Cup, scoring with a 20-yard effort, and with the ability to pick the ball up from deep and run past several players, he was especially dangerous on the edge of the box, where he invariably got in hard shots on target.
Wycombe W (From trainee on 14/2/97) FL 13+26/2 FLC 1+1/1 FAC 1+2 Others 2/1

HARKNESS Steven (Steve)
Born: Carlisle, 27 August 1971
Height: 5'10" Weight: 11.2
International Honours: E: Yth
Steve has proved himself to be a real asset to Liverpool, having played in many positions and always giving 100 per-cent effort. His real strength is his fierce tackling and competitive spirit, but he is more than just a destroyer, his accurate passing enabling the Reds to move swiftly from defence to attack. 1997-98 was his best season yet, and was especially rewarding after recovering from a badly broken leg sustained at Coventry in 1995-96. In doing the simple things well, he is a player you can rely upon.
Carlisle U (From trainee on 23/3/89) FL 12+1
Liverpool (£75,000 on 17/7/89) F/PL 86+10/2 FLC 11+3/1 FAC 4 Others 12+2
Huddersfield T (Loaned on 24/9/93) FL 5 Others 1
Southend U (Loaned on 3/2/95) FL 6

HARLE Michael (Mike) James
Born: Lewisham, 31 October 1972
Height: 6'0" Weight: 12.6
Released by Millwall during the 1997 close season, Mike joined Barnet in time for 1997-98 and proved to be a solid, dependable full back who could also be employed in a wing-back role. More comfortable defending than attacking the opposition, he still found time to score a couple of goals during a campaign that saw the club reach the play offs.
Gillingham (Trainee) FL 1+1
Millwall (£100,000 from Sittingbourne on 8/11/93) FL 12+9/1 FLC 1+1 FAC 1 Others 1
Bury (Loaned on 8/12/95) FL 0+1
Barnet (Free on 16/7/97) FL 42+1/2 FLC 4 FAC 1 Others 2

HARLEY Jonathan (Jon)
Born: Maidstone, 26 September 1979
Height: 5'9" Weight: 10.3
International Honours: E: Yth
As Chelsea's youth team captain, 18-year-old Jon made his first team debut at Pride Park against Derby County last April and made the only goal of the game with a superb far-post cross which was powerfully headed home by Mark Hughes. A left-sided midfield player, and graduate of the FA School at Lilleshall, he is just one of a promising batch of youngsters who appear to have a great future ahead of them at Stamford Bridge.
Chelsea (From trainee on 20/3/97) PL 0+3

HARPER Lee Charles Phillip
Born: Chelsea, 30 October 1971
Height: 6'1" Weight: 13.11
Fourth choice goalkeeper at Arsenal behind David Seaman, John Lukic, and Vince

Bartram, following the arrival of the young Austrian, Alex Manninger, during the 1997 close season, there was no doubt that Lee's future was best served away from Highbury and he moved across London to Queens Park Rangers prior to 1997-98 getting underway. After making his debut on the opening day, he went a further 17 games before losing his place to Tony Roberts when the management duo of Stewart Houston and Bruce Rioch parted company with Rangers, but regained it early on in Ray Harford's reign, appearing in the remaining 20 fixtures. A shot-stopper who is big enough to command his box with assurance, he will continue to improve with further experience.

Arsenal (£150,000 from Sittingbourne on 16/6/94) PL 1
Queens Park R (£125,000+ on 11/7/97) FL 36 FLC 2 FAC 1

HARPER Stephen (Steve) Alan
Born: Easington, 14 March 1975
Height: 6'2" Weight: 13.0

A tall and commanding Newcastle goal-keeper who is good on crosses and has a useful pair of hands, in order to further his experience and to keep him match fit, Steve spent 1997-98 on loan at first with Hartlepool, and then Huddersfield. Started at the Pool and, in an impressive three-month spell, his form ensured that his fee was well out of range of the third division club when Mick Tait enquired about taking him on a permanent basis. Next loaned to Huddersfield, he played in the last two matches of 1997, and then right through to the end of the season, 26 games in all. In conceding just five goals, and keeping five clean sheets in his first ten appearances, 11 in all, his reputation was made, and he returned to St James' Park having become a huge favourite of the fans he was leaving behind.

Newcastle U (Free from Seaham Red Star on 5/7/93)
Bradford C (Loaned on 18/9/95) FL 1
Hartlepool U (Loaned on 29/8/97) FL 15
Huddersfield T (Loaned on 18/12/97) FL 24 FAC 2

HARPER Steven (Steve) James
Born: Newcastle under Lyme, 3 February 1969
Height: 5'10" Weight: 11.12
Club Honours: Div 4 '92

Continuing where he left off in 1996-97 for Mansfield, Steve revelled in his wing-back role and had a very successful 1997-98 campaign, ending the season as the only ever-present member of the team. A player who delights the crowd with his tricky runs and crosses, he was also good value for his five goals, a hat trick in the 4-0 win over Darlington being the highlight.

Port Vale (From trainee 29/6/87) FL 16+12/2 FLC 1+2 Others 1+1
Preston NE (Signed on 23/3/89) FL 57+20/10 FLC 1+1 FAC 1+2 Others 6+1/1
Burnley (Free on 23/7/91) FL 64+5/8 FLC 1+2 FAC 10/3 Others 8
Doncaster Rov (Free on 7/8/93) FL 56+9/11 FLC 2+1/1 FAC 3 Others 4
Mansfield T (£20,000 on 8/9/95) FL 112+3/12 FLC 4 FAC 6/1 Others 5

HARRIES Paul Graham
Born: Sydney, Australia, 19 November 1977
Height: 6'0" Weight: 13.7

A striker, Paul was one of a number of Australians signed by Terry Venables and Terry Fenwick for Portsmouth at the start of the 1997-98 season and, like most of the other Aussies, he found it difficult to adjust to English football and made only one appearance, as a substitute away at Stockport at the beginning of October. Loaned to non-league Basingstoke Town in January, he returned to Fratton Park prior to having his contract terminated by mutual consent during the summer.

Portsmouth (Free from NSW Soccer Academy on 8/9/97) FL 0+1

HARRINGTON Justin David
Born: Truro, 18 September 1975
Height: 5'9" Weight: 10.9

Having started out at Norwich before moving on to Leicester, prior to 1996-97 getting underway, Justin failed to make a first team appearance for either of the above clubs and it took a free transfer to Bournemouth during the 1997 close season for him to break his duck. A midfielder who can play in the centre or on either flank, he made his Football League debut as a sub at home to Wigan in the third match, but failed to make his mark in ten further appearances and was released during the past summer.

Norwich C (From trainee on 1/7/94)
Leicester C (Free on 14/8/96)
Bournemouth (Free on 4/7/97) FL 4+4 FLC 0+1 FAC 1+1

HARRIOTT Marvin Lee
Born: Dulwich, 20 April 1974
Height: 5'8" Weight: 11.6
International Honours: E: Yth; Sch

At his best as a full back with a useful turn of speed, having returned from Germany, Marvin was appearing in non-league soccer for Gloucester City and playing midweek cup matches for Cardiff during his trial period, but was never really able to shine and he soon drifted away from Ninian Park. As a youngster, Marvin had played in the same England schools team as Ryan Giggs, and while the latter went right to the top, he has struggled to break through.

Oldham Ath (Free from West Ham U juniors on 3/4/92)
Barnsley (Free on 26/4/93)
Leyton Orient (Loaned on 1/10/93) FL 8 FAC 1
Bristol C (Free on 9/12/93) FL 36 FLC 1 (Free to Fortuna Cologne on 27/7/95)
Cardiff C (Free from Gloucester C on 28/11/97) Others 1

HARRIS Andrew (Andy) David Douglas
Born: Springs, South Africa, 26 February 1977
Height: 5'10" Weight: 11.11

Andy made a brilliant start to 1997-98 at Southend United, which brought England U21 manager, Peter Taylor, to Roots Hall to watch him, but an injury suffered in February, and a general lack of form in a struggling side saw the youngster on the sidelines at the end of the season. A fully-

committed defender, with strong aerial skills, he took over the captaincy of the Blues when Mike Marsh retired, and is sure to feature in the first team in 1998-99.

Liverpool (From trainee on 23/3/94)
Southend U (Free on 10/7/96) FL 69+2 FLC 5 FAC 3

HARRIS James (Jamie) Christopher
Born: Swansea, 28 June 1979
Height: 6'2" Weight: 13.7

Signed from the local Swansea League side, Mumbles Rangers, in the 1997 close season, after impressing during a trial period, Jamie came off the bench to make his Football League debut at Barnet last September, and followed it up with six more subs' appearances during the following weeks. With the option of a new contract for 1998-99, the young striker was loaned out to League of Wales side, Haverfordwest, in March, scoring twice in his first two games, before having to undergo a knee operation at the end of the campaign.

Swansea C (Signed from Mumbles R on 22/7/97) FL 0+6 FLC 0+1

HARRIS Jason Andre Sebastian
Born: Sutton, 24 November 1976
Height: 6'1" Weight: 11.7

Signed on loan from Crystal Palace last August, the left-sided midfield man failed to impress and his only first team experience at Lincoln came when he was used as a substitute for the final 27 minutes of the home defeat at the hands of Mansfield. Transferred to Leyton Orient in September, he showed himself to be an exciting forward with tremendous pace, who, despite being unable to hold down a regular place, is reckoned to be one for the future.

Crystal Palace (From trainee on 3/7/95) FL 0+2 FLC 0+2
Bristol Rov (Loaned on 22/11/96) FL 5+1/2 Others 1/1
Lincoln C (Loaned on 11/8/97) FL 0+1
Leyton Orient (£20,000 on 23/9/97) FL 21+14/6 FLC 1 FAC 2 Others 1+1

HARRIS Mark Andrew
Born: Reading, 15 July 1963
Height: 6'3" Weight: 13.6
Club Honours: AMC '94

Brought in on a free transfer from Gillingham immediately prior to the start of 1997-98, to act as cover for Scott Young and Jeff Eckhardt who were to be first choice at the heart of Cardiff's defence, with the latter suspended for the start, and then suffering a series of injuries which kept him out, Mark stepped in and played most of the first team matches during a season of struggle. Brought in as a stopper centre half, who did his job well throughout, being a whole-hearted player who always gave of his best, he scored one goal in somewhat surprising fashion when he struck a magnificent volley against the eventual third division champions, Notts County, away. Can reflect on the job he did for Cardiff City with some satisfaction, but, at the age of 34, he was given a free transfer during the summer.

Crystal Palace (£25,000 from Wokingham T on 29/2/88) FL 0+2

Burnley (Loaned on 7/8/89) FL 4 FLC 2
Swansea C (£22,500 on 22/9/89) FL 228/14 FLC 16/1 FAC 18/1 Others 26/2
Gillingham (£50,000 on 11/8/95) FL 63+2/3 FLC 8 FAC 5+1 Others 0+1
Cardiff C (Free on 6/8/97) FL 38/1 FLC 2 FAC 6

HARRIS Neil
Born: Orsett, 12 July 1977
Height: 5'11" Weight: 12.9

Spotted in non-league football as a regular goalscorer for Chelmsford last season, Neil signed for Millwall on transfer deadline day and made his Football League debut at the New Den in early April against Bristol Rovers, appearing twice more before the campaign ended. Looking to be a sound investment for the future, he has good pace, can shoot with either foot, holds the ball up well, and is good in the air.
Millwall (£30,000 from Chelmsford on 26/3/98) FL 2+1

HARRISON Craig
Born: Gateshead, 10 November 1977
Height: 6'0" Weight: 11.13

An aspiring young Middlesbrough defender, Craig made his first team debut for his club in a 2-0 Coca Cola Cup win at Barnet last September, before making the league team at the Riverside against Port Vale a month later. Contesting the left-back slot with Vladimir Kinder throughout the campaign, the youngster was both competitive and gutsy in Boro's ongoing promotion battles and looked not to be far short of holding down a regular place. Fierce and strong in the tackle, and well capable of clearing his lines with precision passes from either foot, he was voted the Supporters' Young Player of the Year.
Middlesbrough (From trainee on 4/7/96) FL 16+4 FLC 3+1 FAC 2

HARRISON Gerald (Gerry) Randall
Born: Lambeth, 15 April 1972
Height: 5'10" Weight: 12.12
International Honours: E: Sch

Transfer listed and out of favour at the start of last season, Gerry regained his place in the Burnley side in late September and was more or less a fixture from then on. Most of his time was spent in his best position, in central defence, where he was often the rock on which opposing attacks floundered. He was also frequently menacing in his determined forays upfield, and is a player the Clarets will badly miss if he moves on.*
Watford (From trainee on 18/12/89) FL 6+3 Others 1
Bristol C (Free on 23/7/91) FL 25+13/1 FLC 2+2 FAC 1 Others 4+1
Cardiff C (Loaned on 24/1/92) FL 10/1
Hereford U (Loaned on 19/11/93) FL 6 FAC 1 Others 1
Huddersfield T (Free on 24/3/94)
Burnley (Free on 5/8/94) FL 116+8/33 FLC 5+1 FAC 6+2 Others 7+1

HARRISON Lee David
Born: Billericay, 12 September 1971
Height: 6'2" Weight: 12.7

Ever present at Barnet last season, Lee is a superb shot stopper and kept the team in many a game. Worked hard to improve his

Lee Harrison

kicking and has proved to be another great Ray Clemence find. Not only athletic and agile for a big man, but good in command of his area, also.
Charlton Ath (From trainee on 3/7/90)
Fulham (Loaned on 18/11/91) Others 1
Gillingham (Loaned on 24/3/92) FL 2
Fulham (Free on 18/12/92) FL 11+1 FAC 1 Others 6
Barnet (Free on 15/7/96) FL 67 FLC 4 FAC 1 Others 4

HARRISON Thomas (Tommy) Edward
Born: Edinburgh, 22 January 1974
Height: 5'10" Weight: 12.7
International Honours: S: Yth; Sch

Released by York City towards the end of 1996-97, Carlisle moved to sign him on a short-term contract early last season, and the ex-Hearts man gave some solid, hard-working performances in midfield during his spell at the club. However, no permanent deal ensued and his last game for the club was in early December.
Heart of Midlothian (Free from Salveson BC on 25/4/90) SL 5+5/1 SLC 0+2
Dunfermline (Loaned on 1/1/95) SL 1+1
Clyde (Signed on 4/8/95) SL 24+10/4 SLC 1 SC 3+1/1 Others 1
York C (Free on 31/1/97) FL 0+1 Others 0+1
Carlisle U (Free on 29/8/97) FL 6+4 FLC 2

HARSLEY Paul
Born: Scunthorpe, 29 May 1978
Height: 5'8" Weight: 11.5

Chose to rejoin his hometown club, Scunthorpe, ahead of staying at Grimsby in the summer of 1997, and immediately looked a good prospect in the reserves. A tough-tackling midfielder, he broke into the first team squad in February and made a starting place his own by the end of the season, getting better every game and opening his goalscoring account in the final home game against Exeter. He can expect to be a regular this term after signing a new contract in the summer.
Grimsby T (From trainee on 16/7/96)
Scunthorpe U (Free on 7/7/97) FL 11+4/1

HARTE Ian Patrick
Born: Drogheda, 31 August 1977
Height: 5'10" Weight: 11.8
International Honours: Ei: 18; U21-3

George Graham turned down a near £2 million offer from Tottenham for this versatile left-sided player in the 1997 close season, before Ian had the distinction of making more international appearances for the Republic of Ireland than for United's first team. It was not until the end of February that he broke into the side at left-wing back, mainly due to the injury to Dave Robertson, but given his chance, Ian produced consistent performances in the 5-0 victory at Derby, and then at West Ham. Equally adept in a variety of roles on the left-hand side of the field, he is good in the tackle and an excellent crosser of the ball.

Leeds U (From trainee on 15/12/95) PL 24+6/2 FLC 2+2/1 FAC 2+2

HARTFIELD Charles (Charlie) Joseph
Born: Lambeth, 4 September 1971
Height: 6'0" Weight: 13.8
International Honours: E: Yth
Released by Sheffield United during the 1997 summer, and following trials at Brentford, Southend, and Fulham, Charlie signed for Swansea last November on a month-by-month basis. A strong-tackling midfielder, with good shooting ability, although not noted as a goalscorer, he scored in consecutive games in February, one of them being a cheeky strike from a quickly-taken free kick at Notts County.

Arsenal (From trainee on 20/9/89)
Sheffield U (Free on 6/8/91) F/PL 45+11/1 FLC 2+1 FAC 4+1 Others 1
Fulham (Loaned on 5/2/97) FL 1+1
Swansea C (Free on 28/11/97) FL 22/2 Others 1

HARTSON John
Born: Swansea, 5 April 1975
Height: 6'1" Weight: 14.6
International Honours: W: 15; U21-9; Yth
The Welsh international striker scored 24 goals in 1997-98, his first full season with West Ham, and yet again proved to be big, strong, and good in the air, while coming close to being the complete centre forward. The only downside, however, was that he missed the last few games of the campaign after being sent off against Derby. Scored his first hat trick in club football, in the Coca Cola Cup against Huddersfield, and followed this up with two goals against Bolton, Blackburn, and Aston Villa. Still only 23, John could emerge as one of the goalscoring greats, certainly as far as the Hammers are concerned.

Luton T (From trainee on 19/12/92) FL 32+22/11 FLC 0+1 FAC 3+3/2 Others 2
Arsenal (£2,500,000 on 13/1/95) PL 43+10/14 FLC 2+4/1 FAC 2+1/1 Others 8+1/1
West Ham U (£3,200,000 + on 14/2/97) PL 43/20 FLC 5/6 FAC 5/3

HARVEY Richard George
Born: Letchworth, 17 April 1969
Height: 5'10" Weight: 11.10
International Honours: E: Yth; Sch
The career of this injury plagued left back has been on hold for some time at Luton and he was released during the past summer. At the start of last season he almost joined Stevenage, who eventually pulled out on medical grounds, but, despite that, his

wholehearted commitment, strong-tackling ability, excellent crosses, and powerful shooting, were all displayed when possible, although severely rationed by injury.

Luton T (From apprentice on 10/1/87) FL 134+27/4 FLC 10+1/1 FAC 7+2 Others 10
Blackpool (Loaned on 30/10/92) FL 4+1

HASSELBAINK Jerrel (Jimmy Floyd)
Born: Surinam, 27 March 1972
Height: 5'11" Weight: 13.4
International Honours: Holland: 4
Leeds' major problem in 1996-97 was in scoring goals, and it did not take long for this exotically named player to earn a cult status, following his signing from Boavista during the 1997 summer. Jimmy was in sparkling form in pre-season and began 1997-98 with an excellent strike against Arsenal on the opening day, before going 12 games without finding the target. At that stage, it appeared that he was struggling with the physical aspects of the Premiership and, having been suspended after being sent off at Bristol City in the Coca Cola Cup, he was then a substitute on his return. It was from the bench, however, that he came on to score the winner in the 4-3 victory over Derby County, and from then on he was a different player, scoring goals and showing fine form in using his tremendous speed and strength. Getting better with every game, after missing a penalty against Wolves in the FA Cup, his response was superb performances in the victories over Blackburn, Derby, and Chelsea. The Player of the Year, and top scorer with 22 goals, now he has settled, 1998-99 promises to be even better for this fine, skilful striker. *Stop Press:* Selected as one of Holland's 22-strong squad for the World Cup Finals during the summer, he appeared in a couple of first round games before the side left the competition at the semi-final stage.

Leeds U (£2,000,000 from Boavista on 18/7/97) PL 30+3/16 FLC 3/2 FAC 4/4

HASSELL Robert (Bobby) John Francis
Born: Derby, 4 June 1980
Height: 5'10" Weight: 12.6
Still a trainee, this youthful centre back was thrown in at the deep end by Mansfield early on last season, and was quite outstanding for one so young and relatively inexperienced. Definitely one to watch for in the future, Town may well have unearthed a future star in Bobby.

Mansfield T (Trainee) FL 8+1

HATELEY Mark Wayne
Born: Derby, 7 November 1961
Height: 6'3" Weight: 13.0
Club Honours: SPD '91, '92, '93, '94, '95; SC '92, '93; SLC '90, '92, '93
International Honours: E: 32; U21-10; Yth
Selected as the man to bring the glory days back to Boothferry Park as David Lloyd completed his takeover at Hull City, the Rangers' legend had to be content to fulfil more of the managerial side of his player/manager title as he was sidelined for much of the 1997-98 campaign, needing an operation on a career-threatening achilles tendon injury. Thankfully, Mark was able to make a comeback shortly before the season closed, but City had sorely missed the attacking skills of the classic English centre forward, particularly as their regular number nine, Duane Darby, also suffered from injuries. Having to contend with numerous behind the scene problems, and the fall out from the previous regime, Mark could not have wished for a tougher baptism, yet there was plenty of evidence to suggest that 1998-99 will be a much happier experience.

Coventry C (From apprentice on 1/12/78) FL 86+6/25 FLC 8/3 FAC 10+1/6
Portsmouth (£220,000 on 6/6/83) (£1,000,000 to AC Milan on 28/6/84) FL 38/22 FLC 4/2 FAC 2/1
Glasgow R (Signed from AS Monaco on 19/7/90) SL 158+7/85 SLC 15+3/11 SC 16/10 Others 17/7

Jimmy Floyd Hasselbaink

Queens Park R (£1,500,000 on 3/11/95) P/FL 18+9/3 FLC 0+1 FAC 3+2/2
Leeds U (Loaned on 19/8/96) PL 5+1
Glasgow R (£300,000 on 14/3/97) SL 4
Hull C (Free on 8/8/97) FL 4+5 FLC 4+1

HATHAWAY Ian Ashley
Born: Wordsley, 22 August 1968
Height: 5'7" Weight: 11.4
A left winger brought in from Torquay during the 1997 close season, to replace the departed Chris Fry as Colchester's main supply line to the forwards, Ian started 1997-98 by making the opening goal against Darlington and then scoring a terrific volley at Luton in the Coca Cola Cup. However, he soon lost his place, when Paul Abrahams moved to a wider role, and made only sporadic appearances thereafter.
Mansfield T (£8,000 from Bedworth U on 8/2/89) FL 21+23/2 FLC 1+1 FAC 1 Others 3+1/1
Rotherham U (Signed on 22/3/91) FL 5+8/1 Others 0+1
Torquay U (Free on 30/7/93) FL 114+26/14 FLC 9+1/1 FAC 9+1/2 Others 4+3/1
Colchester U (Free on 3/7/97) FL 5+7 FLC 2/1 FAC 1+1

HAWES Steven (Steve) Robert
Born: High Wycombe, 17 July 1978
Height: 5'8" Weight: 11.10
A fringe player at Sheffield United, Steve had two spells at Doncaster during 1997-98. His first, an extended loan period, saw him play frequently in the Rovers' midfield, where he proved to be a hard working, if inexperienced player, while his return to Belle Vue in February on a free transfer, lasted only a week before he was released.
Sheffield U (From trainee on 2/3/96) FL 1+3
Doncaster Rov (Loaned on 18/9/97) FL 7+1
Doncaster Rov (Free on 20/2/98) FL 1+2

HAWORTH Simon Owen
Born: Cardiff, 30 March 1977
Height: 6'3" Weight: 13.8
International Honours: W: 5; B-1; U21-6; Yth
A striker purchased from Cardiff in the summer of 1997, he made his first Coventry start against Everton in the Coca Cola Cup, due to Dion Dublin's suspension, and played well, scoring a good goal. Subsequent performances were not as impressive, and he played in the bad defeat at Barnsley before making a number of substitute appearances, including the FA Cup replay at Bramall Lane, where he missed in the penalty shoot-out. Having been a regular for the reserves, where he played well and scored a number of goals, he was called into the Welsh squad and played in four internationals that took in a game in Brazil, while also representing his country at U21 and "B" level.
Cardiff C (From trainee on 7/8/95) FL 27+10/9 FLC 4 FAC 0+1 Others 4/1
Coventry C (£500,000 on 4/6/97) PL 4+6 FLC 2/1 FAC 0+1

HAWTHORNE Mark
Born: Sunderland, 21 August 1979
Height: 5'10" Weight: 11.7
This young defender was unfortunate enough to have made his league debut for Doncaster in their 8-0 defeat at Leyton Orient last December, and did not appear in the first team again until April. However, a series of useful displays from then on suggested that his confidence was still intact, and he looks a good prospect for the future.
Doncaster Rov (From trainee on 16/12/96) FL 7+1

HAY Christopher (Chris) Drummond
Born: Glasgow, 28 August 1974
Height: 5'11" Weight: 11.7
Signed from Celtic immediately prior to the start of 1997-98, the Scottish striker began the season in a blaze of glory, with a rush of goals – 13 in his first 18 games, including a hat trick in a 4-2 home win over Port Vale, led to speculation that he might receive a full international call up. However, a three-match ban for accumulating five bookings – mostly for petty offences in November, and the sale of Wayne Allison, put pressure on him and he managed just one more goal, albeit a spectacular last-minute point saver at Bradford. Dropped at Bury in February, the shy striker then admitted he was feeling homesick and faces a fight for his place in the side this coming term, following the arrival of new frontmen, George Ndah and Iffy Onuora.
Glasgow Celtic (Free from Giffnock North AFC on 27/5/93) SL 9+16/4 SC 0+3 Others 0+2/1
Swindon T (£330,000 on 6/8/97) FL 30+6/14 FLC 1 FAC 1

Chris Hay

HAYDON Nicholas (Nicky)
Born: Barking, 18 August 1978
Height: 5'10" Weight: 11.6
Another homegrown product at Layer Road, Nicky built on his last-day debut from the previous season by forcing his way into the Colchester side, starting 11 times throughout 1997-98, playing both in defence and at wing back. Unfortunate to score a spectacular own-goal at Darlington in January, he lost his place following the re-shuffle of the team in February, which started the promotion run, but is still one for the future.
Colchester U (From trainee on 10/8/95) FL 9+9/1 FAC 1+1 Others 1

HAYES Adrian (Adi) Michael
Born: Norwich, 22 May 1978
Height: 6'1" Weight: 12.10
A talented young left-sided Cambridge midfielder who made just a handful of appearances in 1997-98, Adi failed to establish himself in the senior ranks and was given a free transfer at the end of the season. Constructive, skilful in possession, and fairly fluent in a wing-back role if required, he is young enough to come again.
Cambridge U (From trainee on 9/7/96) FL 25+9 FLC 0+1 FAC 2 Others 2

HAYFIELD Matthew (Matt) Anthony
Born: Bristol, 8 August 1975
Height: 5'11" Weight: 12.2
Returning from a loan spell with Conference club, Yeovil Town, last November, Matt, a strong ball winner, immediately established himself in Bristol Rovers' midfield. Also played at right back at Luton in a 4-2 victory, but it was his substitute appearances that livened up many matches, as his all-action performances ensured his presence in the squad for virtually all the second half of 1997-98. Came off the bench in Rovers last exciting league match of the season, against Brentford, which saw them reach the play offs, and was very unfortunate not to score with a powerful shot against the post. Has yet to open his goal account at first team level.
Bristol Rov (From trainee on 13/7/94) FL 24+17 FAC 4+1 Others 3+3

Barry Hayles

HAYLES Barrington (Barry) Edward
Born: Lambeth, London, 17 May 1972
Height: 5'9" Weight: 13.0

A very talented and exciting striker, Barry made a major contribution for Bristol Rovers after joining them from Conference club, Stevenage Borough, during the 1997 close season. Scored on his league debut against Plymouth Argyle, and continued to score consistently throughout the campaign, including the vital match winner against Brentford on the last day, which ensured Rovers were in the play offs. That superb headed goal was his 25th of the campaign and cost the club an extra £50,000 for Stevenage, as well as confirming him as the second division's top goalscorer. His pace and close control was always a major problem for opposing defenders, as Rovers became the divisions top scorers, and in missing just one match all season against arch rivals, Bristol City, he was selected as the supporters' Player of the Year.

Bristol Rov (£250,000 from Stevenage Borough on 4/6/97) FL 45/23 FLC 2 FAC 5/2 Others 3+2/2

HAYTER James Edward
Born: Sandown, IoW, 9 April 1979
Height: 5'9" Weight: 10.7

A young striker who has graduated through the ranks at Bournemouth, making his first team debut while still a trainee, James was given further opportunities in 1997-98 after signing professional forms during the summer. Very quick, and exciting to watch, many at the club feel that he could be on the verge of great things, and he certainly showed up well in his six appearances from the bench. Is a regular scorer for the reserves.

Bournemouth (From trainee on 7/7/97) FL 0+7 Others 0+1

HAYWARD Andrew (Andy) William
Born: Barnsley, 21 June 1970
Height: 6'0" Weight: 11.2
Club Honours: AMC '96

Although he only made a handful of starts for Rotherham in 1997-98, as he was unable to reproduce his goalscoring form for the reserves in the first team, on a couple of occasions he came up with vital last-minute goals when playing in a right-sided striker's role. A versatile forward who will play anywhere, even in midfield if required, he was surprisingly released during the summer.

Rotherham U (Free from Frickley Ath on 10/8/94) FL 93+27/15 FLC 4+2/3 FAC 3+2 Others 6+4/2

HAYWARD Steven (Steve) Lee
Born: Pelsall, 8 September 1971
Height: 5'11" Weight: 12.5
Club Honours: AMC '97
International Honours: E: Yth

As Carlisle's influential skipper in 1996-97, Steve was Micky Adams' first major capture for Fulham in the 1997 close season. His passing and vision in central midfield was the cornerstone of the side until the arrival of Paul Bracewell, and he was then switched to a wing role to which he was not really suited. With eight experienced midfielders on the books, Steve missed out on the final eight league matches, but would have been encouraged that Kevin Keegan selected him for the crunch play-off second leg at Grimsby.

Derby Co (From juniors on 17/9/88) FL 15+11/1 FLC 0+2 FAC 1 Others 3+4
Carlisle U (£100,000 on 13/3/95) FL 88+2/14 FLC 6/1 FAC 4 Others 15/1
Fulham (£175,000 on 23/6/97) FL 32+3/4 FLC 4 FAC 1+1 Others 3

HAZAN Alon
Born: Ashdod, Israel, 14 September 1967
Height: 6'0" Weight: 13.1
International Honours: Israel: 63

An Israeli international utility player signed by Watford from Ironi Ashdod last January, Alon suffered a hamstring injury almost immediately, which limited his opportunities, and found it difficult at first to adapt to the style and pace of the English game. However, he looks particularly stylish and comfortable on the ball and promises much for the future.

Watford (£200,000 from Ironi Ashdod on 13/1/98) FL 7+3

HEALD Gregory (Greg) James
Born: Enfield, 26 September 1971
Height: 6'1" Weight: 13.1
International Honours: E: Sch

Another player who followed John Still to Barnet, joining the club from Peterborough immediately prior to 1997-98 getting underway, he proved to be a no frills centre half who got down to business without fuss and stuck to the task throughout every match. Dangerous at set pieces, and a player you can rely upon to score more than his share from the back, Greg slammed in his fifth goal of the campaign in the first leg of the play-off match against Colchester. Despite Barnet winning the game 1-0 they failed to advance any further when losing the second leg.

Peterborough U (£35,000 from Enfield on 8/7/94) FL 101+4/6 FLC 8 FAC 8+1 Others 11/2
Barnet (Signed on 8/8/97) FL 43/3 FLC 4/1 FAC 1 Others 2/1

HEALD Paul Andrew
Born: Wath on Dearne, 20 September 1968
Height: 6'2" Weight: 14.0

A very popular Wimbledon goalkeeper, Paul made just two appearances for the club last season, both of them in the Coca Cola Cup, and both against Millwall, in 5-1 and 4-1 victories, respectively. Not a lot of work then for a man known for his quick-reaction saves and comfortable handling, but, nevertheless, at least it was something as he waited in the wings as Neil Sullivan's stand-in, having played just 25 games in the last three years.

Sheffield U (From trainee on 30/6/87)
Leyton Orient (Signed on 2/12/88) FL 176 FLC 13 FAC 9 Others 21
Coventry C (Loaned on 10/3/92) PL 2
Swindon T (Loaned on 24/3/94) PL 1+1
Wimbledon (£125,000 on 25/7/95) PL 20 FLC 5

HEANEY Neil Andrew
Born: Middlesbrough, 3 November 1971
Height: 5'9" Weight: 11.6
Club Honours: FAYC '88
International Honours: E: U21-6; Yth

A left winger with pace and skill, and the ability to deliver the ball into danger areas, his position at Manchester City in 1997-98 remained one of being available for transfer. Apart from coming into the side for the two home matches against Reading and Stoke in October, and being a surprise selection at Port Vale in March, that was it as far as first team selection was concerned in 1997-98 and he continued as a regular for the reserves. Although a proposed transfer to Charlton failed to come to fruition in February, he was loaned to the Addicks a month later and set up the vital winning home goal against Portsmouth with an exquisite cross that Steve Jones ably dealt with. Regarded as a left-sided player, Neil favours his right foot.

Arsenal (From trainee on 14/11/89) F/PL 4+3 FLC 0+1
Hartlepool U (Loaned on 3/1/91) FL 2+1
Cambridge U (Loaned on 9/1/92) FL 9+4/2 FAC 1
Southampton (£300,000 on 22/3/94) PL 42+19/5 FLC 4+2 FAC 6/2
Manchester C (£500,000 on 25/11/96) FL 13+5/1 FAC 2/1
Charlton Ath (Loaned on 26/3/98) FL 4+2 Others 3

HEARY Thomas Mark
Born: Dublin, 14 February 1979
Height: 5'10" Weight: 11.3
International Honours: Ei: Yth; Sch

Having been given a handful of opportunities for Huddersfield in 1996-97, the classy Irish youth international was expected to be challenging for a place in 1997-98 and, true to form, opened his playing account in the right-wing-back slot at Oxford on the first day of the season. Although spending most of his time in the reserves, he continued to impress with strong-running displays, allied to good touch and vision, and will be expected to challenge for a place in 1998-99.

Huddersfield T (From trainee on 17/2/96) FL 4+4 FLC 0+1 FAC 1

HEATH Robert
Born: Stoke, 31 August 1978
Height: 5'8" Weight: 10.0

In 1997-98 at long last a local product emerged from Stoke's youth team. It can never be easy for youngsters to develop in a relegation side, but Robert, a mobile, energetic midfield prospect with the ability to both dig in and play the ball, performed extremely well when called on and was properly rewarded with a new contract last February. There should be no surprise if this youngster claims a regular place in the side this coming season.

Stoke C (From trainee on 15/7/96) FL 4+2

HEATHCOTE Michael (Mick)
Born: Kelloe, 10 September 1965
Height: 6'2" Weight: 12.5

Although approaching the veteran stage the Plymouth captain, and ever dependable central defender, was still as determined and competent as ever in 1997-98. An excellent tackler, and commanding in the air, despite missing a large part of the season due to damaged knee ligaments in October, he

returned to shore up the defence in late December.

Sunderland (£15,000 from Spennymoor on 19/8/87) FL 6+3 Others 0+1
Halifax T (Loaned on 17/12/87) FL 7/1 FAC 1
York C (Loaned on 4/1/90) FL 3 Others 1
Shrewsbury T (£55,000 on 12/7/90) FL 43+1/6 FLC 6 FAC 5 Others 4
Cambridge U (£150,000 on 12/9/91) FL123+5/13 FLC 7/1 FAC 5+2/2 Others 7/2
Plymouth Arg (£100,000 on 27/7/95) FL 121+1/9 FLC 6/1 FAC 6/1 Others 7

HECKINBOTTOM Paul

Born: Barnsley, 17 July 1977
Height: 5'11" Weight: 12.0
A skilful, attacking left back, Paul spent most of last season at Scarborough on extended loan from Sunderland and impressed with some consistent performances as the team chased a play-off place. Unfortunate to miss the last few games of 1997-98 with a stress fracture of the foot, he will be looking to get back into action as early as possible, hopefully, with the Rokerites.

Sunderland (Free from Manchester U juniors on 14/7/95)
Scarborough (Loaned on 17/10/97) FL 28+1 Others 1

HEDMAN Magnus Carl

Born: Stockholm, Sweden, 19 March 1973
Height: 6'4" Weight: 14.5
International Honours: Sweden
A goalkeeper purchased from AIK Solna in the summer of 1997, Magnus possibly expected to walk into Coventry's first team immediately and was then probably surprised to find he had to displace a 40-year old. He finally came in for "Oggy" after the defeat at Villa in December and played 14 successive games before suffering a training injury, having rarely been put under intense pressure, and doing what was expected of him with a minimum of fuss. Magnus is a good shot-stopper, although looking a bit

vulnerable to the high cross, and has appeared for Sweden. However, with the former number one, Thomas Ravelli, having retired he has an opportunity to be the first choice for his country, but to do that he needs to be first choice at Highfield Road. Excellent in the final game, at Everton, when he saved a Nick Barmby penalty.

Coventry C (£500,000 from AIK Solna on 24/7/97) PL 14 FAC 3

Carl Heggs

HEGGS Carl Sydney

Born: Leicester, 11 October 1970
Height: 6'1" Weight: 12.10
An exciting and talented Northampton striker, who was signed from play-off final opponents, Swansea, for a tribunal set fee during the 1997 close season, Carl played

wide on the left and made many goals for his team mates. Unfortunate to miss a large portion of 1997-98, due to an hernia operation, before being struck down he scored the final penalty in the FA Cup match against Basingstoke, that saw the club into round three.

West Bromwich A (£25,000 from Leicester U on 22/8/91) FL 13+27/3 FLC 2 FAC 0+1 Others 6+3/1
Bristol Rov (Loaned on 27/1/95) FL 2+3/1
Swansea C (£60,000 on 27/7/95) FL 33+13/7 FLC 2 FAC 2 Others 4+1/1
Northampton T (£40,000 on 31/7/97) FL 21+12/4 FLC 1+1 FAC 4+1/1 Others 3+1/3

HEINOLA Antti Juhani

Born: Helsinki, Finland, 20 March 1973
Height: 5'10" Weight: 12.6
International Honours: Finland: 6
Signed from Heracles last January, the Finnish left-wing back made his debut as a substitute in the home game against Nottingham Forest and went on to make a further nine appearances from the bench before the campaign ended. Although requiring more experience of English football before he can be fully blooded, he looks to have good pace going forward, while remaining sound at the back.

Queens Park R (£150,000 from Heracles on 15/1/98) FL 0+10

HELLIWELL Ian

Born: Rotherham, 7 November 1962
Height: 6'3" Weight: 14.8
Unable to get a game at Burnley, being way down the pecking order, the big, strong, experienced target man was loaned out to Doncaster at the beginning of last November and stayed for three months. Scored in Rovers' first win in 1997-98, at home to Chester on 2 December, a tremendous right-footed shot into the roof of the net from the edge of the box sending the club on its way to a 2-1 victory, but, five games later, he was on his way back to Turf Moor after being sidelined with an injury. Was released during the summer.

York C (£10,000 from Matlock T on 23/10/87) FL 158+2/40 FLC 8/1 FAC 5 Others 9+1/7
Scunthorpe U (£80,000 on 16/8/91) FL 78+2/22 FLC 8/5 FAC 4/2 Others 9/2
Rotherham U (£50,000 on 1/8/93) FL 47+5/4 FLC 4+1 FAC 1+2/1 Others 2+1/1
Stockport Co (Signed on 12/1/95) FL 35+4/13 FLC 4/1 FAC 2/1 Others 1
Burnley (£30,000 on 9/2/96) FL 3+1
Mansfield T (Loaned on 6/9/96) FL 4+1/1
Chester C (Loaned on 11/10/96) FL 8+1/1
Doncaster Rov (Loaned on 3/11/97) FL 8/1 Others 1

HENCHOZ Stephane

Born: Billens, Switzerland, 7 September 1974
Height: 6'1" Weight: 12.3
International Honours: Switzerland: 13
Signed from Hamburg during the 1997 close season, the young Swiss international made a remarkable recovery from operations on both his ankles to take his place in the Blackburn side. Opinions on his worth varied, however. Seemingly leaden footed early on, in December, in the win at

Magnus Hedman

Highbury, he looked magnificent, but towards the end of the campaign he appeared jaded and ready for a rest. With his manager appearing to have had complete faith in his ability, fortunately, he managed to turn things around, and in the final three games looked calm, powerful, and competitive.

Blackburn Rov (£3,000,000 from Hamburg on 14/7/97) PL 36 FLC 0+1 FAC 4

HENDERSON Kevin Malcolm
Born: Ashington, 8 June 1974
Height: 5'11" Weight: 13.2

Signed from non-league Morpeth last December, the lightweight, but livewire striker proved a useful substitute in the latter stages of Burnley's season. He scored his first senior goal in the Auto Windscreens game against Carlisle, looked capable of grabbing several more, was not afraid of shooting from difficult positions, and may well be a player for the future.

Burnley (Signed from Morpeth T on 17/12/97) FL 0+7 Others 0+3/1

HENDON Ian Michael
Born: Ilford, 5 December 1971
Height: 6'0" Weight: 12.10
Club Honours: FAYC '90; CS '91; Div 3 '98
International Honours: E: U21-7; Yth

Appointed Notts County's club captain by manager, Sam Allardyce, in 1997-98, Ian had the distinction of leading the club into a season of outstanding success in which club and league records were broken as County became third division champions. A fast and powerful full back, wing back, and centre back, he was an inspirational leader during a truly exceptional campaign. Was selected for the PFA squad for the second successive year.

Tottenham H (From trainee on 20/12/89) FL 0+4 FLC 1 Others 0+2
Portsmouth (Loaned on 16/1/92) FL 1+3
Leyton Orient (Loaned on 26/3/92) FL 5+1
Barnsley (Loaned on 17/3/93) FL 6
Leyton Orient (£50,000 on 9/8/93) FL 130+1/5 FLC 8 FAC 7 Others 12/1
Birmingham C (Loaned on 23/3/95) FL 4
Notts Co (£50,000 on 24/2/97) FL 50 FLC 4/1 FAC 2+1

HENDRIE John Grattan
Born: Lennoxtown, 24 October 1963
Height: 5'8" Weight: 12.3
Club Honours: Div 3 '85, Div 2 '90, Div 1 '95
International Honours: S: Yth

Unfortunately, John's season at Barnsley in 1997-98 was ruined by a number of niggling injuries, although in between he proved himself well capable of competing at the top level. Will always be remembered by the fans for scoring in both cup games against Manchester United, and with a vicious late equaliser against Newcastle (one of his former clubs) at Oakwell. Still sharp around the box, his experience took defenders into areas of the pitch that they did not want to go. *Stop Press:* Immediately following the departure of Danny Wilson to Sheffield Wednesday on 6 July, John was announced as the new Barnsley player/manager, and

quickly appointed Peter Shirtliff as his assistant, and Eric Winstanley as chief coach.

Coventry C (From apprentice on 18/5/81) FL 15+6/2 FLC 2
Hereford U (Loaned on 10/1/84) FL 6
Bradford C (Free on 2/7/84) FL 173/46 FLC 17/3 FAC 11/6 Others 11/4
Newcastle U (£500,000 on 17/6/88) FL 34/4 FLC 2/1 FAC 4 Others 3
Leeds U (£600,000 on 20/6/89) FL 22+5/5 FLC 1 FAC 1 Others 2
Middlesbrough (£550,000 on 5/7/90) F/PL 181+11/44 FLC 22+2/6 FAC 10+2/2 Others 6/3
Barnsley (£250,000 on 11/10/96) F/PL 43+13/6 FAC 6/3

HENDRIE Lee Andrew
Born: Birmingham, 18 May 1977
Height: 5'10" Weight: 10.3
International Honours: E: B-1; U21-2; Yth

From a footballing family, being the son of a former Birmingham star, Paul, and the cousin of John, currently with Barnsley, Lee finally made the breakthrough at Aston Villa in 1997-98, becoming a regular player in the starting line-up at the end of January and playing a fundamental part in the club's run of good form. He also added to his England U21 caps, before coming off the bench for the England "B" team that played against the Russian equivalent. A hard-working, attacking midfielder, he scored his first-ever goal for the club at home to Coventry, when he weaved his way into the box to smash the ball home in a 3-0 win, and later scored twice more in away victories over Southampton and Sheffield Wednesday.

Aston Villa (From trainee on 18/5/94) PL 15+9/3 FAC 3+4 Others 2+1

HENDRY Edward Colin James
Born: Keith, 7 December 1965
Height: 6'1" Weight: 12.7
Club Honours: FMC '87; PL '95
International Honours: S: 35; B-1

1997-98 was not a vintage season for the man who has been the heartbeat of the Blackburn team over the last few years. The usual last-ditch tackles, brave headers, and ball-winning tackles were there but he was often hobbled by injury, while there remained the suspicion that he and Stephane Henchoz were not a natural combination. Despite all the problems, Colin was recognised by his fellow professionals as the best centre back in the business, when they elected him to the PFA award-winning Premiership side, and it would be almost too difficult to imagine him not being an integral part of Rovers' defence. *Stop Press:* As captain of Scotland in France '98, it was a huge disappointment to him that the side went out at the Group A stage, especially after drawing with Norway.

Dundee (Signed from Islavale on 1/7/83) SL 17+24/2 SC 2+3/1
Blackburn Rov (£30,000 on 11/3/87) FL 99+3/22 FLC 4 FAC 3 Others 13/1
Manchester C (£700,000 on 16/11/89) FL 57+6/5 FLC 4+1/1 FAC 5/2 Others 4/2
Blackburn Rov (£700,000 on 8/11/91) F/PL 229+5/12 FLC 23 FAC 17+1 Others 11

HENRIKSEN Tony Tim
Born: Hammel, Denmark, 25 April 1973
Height: 6'3" Weight: 13.9

A very tall goalkeeper, who joined Southend the previous season from the Dutch club, Randers Freja, Tony was forced into a United first team debut in the FA Cup match at Fulham when Simon Royce was sent off, and he marked the occasion with a fine penalty save. A good shot-stopper, he was subsequently deemed too inexperienced to cover for Royce's suspension, and Southend signed Neville Southall on loan, thus depriving him of any further appearances.*

Southend U (Free from Randers Freja on 18/10/96) FAC 0+1

HENRY Nicholas (Nicky) Ian
Born: Liverpool, 21 February 1969
Height: 5'6" Weight: 10.8
Club Honours: Div 2 '91

Known for his ability to keep things ticking over in midfield, Nicky holds the ball up well, is a good passer, and is always available when a team mate gets into difficulties. Unfortunately, he made only one appearance at Charlton last December, due to injury, and several abortive comeback attempts, which eventually necessitated a back operation, will keep him out until the start of 1998-98 at least.

Oldham Ath (From trainee on 6/7/87) F/PL 264+9/19 FLC 30+4/3 FAC 21 Others 5
Sheffield U (£500,000 on 28/2/97) FL 10 Others 2

HENSHAW Terrence (Terry) Robert
Born: Nottingham, 29 February 1980
Height: 5'10" Weight: 11.0

Still a trainee, and yet another young central defender from the Notts County youth Academy, Terry made his first team debut in the Auto Windscreen Shield, when he came off the bench during a 2-0 defeat at Burnley last January. Tall, quick, and skilful, with further physical fitness, he will no doubt be soon pressing for a regular squad place, maybe this coming term.

Notts Co (Trainee) Others 0+1

HERBERT Craig Justin
Born: Coventry, 9 November 1975
Height: 5'11" Weight: 12.0

As in the case of his team mate, Gareth Hanmer, the central defender was signed in the summer of 1997 from West Bromwich Albion and immediately went into the Shrewsbury first team. Was an ever present until suspension cost him his place in December and thereafter made only a handful of appearances. A hard worker, he probably suffered through being partnered by a succession of different players in early season.

West Bromwich A (Free from Torquay U juniors on 18/3/94) FL 8 FLC 2 Others 1/1
Shrewsbury T (Free on 23/7/97) FL 23+1 FLC 2 FAC 2/1 Others 1

HERRERA Roberto (Robbie)
Born: Torquay, 12 June 1970
Height: 5'7" Weight: 10.6

Having played every game for Fulham up to early last January, Robbie was injured and,

although having a couple of run outs for the reserves, was not a contender for a return to first team action for the rest of the campaign. As a talented left back or wing back, who is very popular with the fans, he is likely to be vying with the two former Queens Park Rangers clubmates, Rufus Brevett and Matthew Brazier, for the two left-flank spots in 1998-99.

Queens Park R (From trainee on 1/3/88) FL 4+2 FLC 1+2 Others 1+1
Torquay U (Loaned on 17/3/92) FL 11
Torquay U (Loaned on 24/10/92) FL 5
Fulham (Signed on 29/10/93) FL 143+2/1 FLC 15 FAC 13 Others 7+1

HESKEY Emile William Ivanhoe

Born: Leicester, 11 January 1978
Height: 6'2" Weight: 13.12
Club Honours: FLC '97
International Honours: E: B-1; U21-11; Yth

A two-footed Leicester striker with power and pace, Emile continued to develop in 1997-98, whilst shouldering the responsi-bility of being the main attacker for the Foxes. Although he found goals harder to come by this time round, he increased his all-round contribution considerably and still managed to hit the odd ferocious piledriver, as in home wins against both Tottenham and Chelsea. Also found his scoring touch at international level for both the England "B" and U21 teams, and was called into the full squad, though his progress was undoubtedly interrupted by the remarkable rise of Michael Owen. A massive handful for any defender, who will surely be given his chance at full international level soon, he finished the campaign as the club's leading scorer, following a brace of well-taken headers in the rout of Derby at Pride Park, and earned selection for the U21 squad that took part in the Toulon Tournament.

Leicester C (From trainee on 3/10/95) P/FL 91+10/27 FLC 9+2/2 FAC 5 Others 5

Emile Heskey

HESSENTHALER Andrew (Andy)

Born: Dartford, 17 August 1965
Height: 5'7" Weight: 11.5
International Honours: E: SP-1

A tireless worker for Gillingham in midfield in 1997-98, he also found himself at times in the unusual position of right-wing back and, unfortunately, had the dubious distinction of being booked more times than any other Gills' player. Terrier-like, and relentless, never knowing when he is beaten, Andy can be an inspiration to others needing direction.

Watford (£65,000 from Redbridge Forest on 12/9/91) FL 195/11 FLC 13/1 FAC 5/2 Others 4
Gillingham (£235,000 on 7/8/96) FL 80/2 FLC 9 FAC 5/1 Others 1

Andy Hessenthaler

HESSEY Sean Peter

Born: Whiston, 19 September 1978
Height: 5'10" Weight: 12.6

Released by Liverpool during the 1997 close season, having completed his time at Anfield as a trainee, Sean trialled at first Leeds, and then Wigan, before being awar-ded a one-year contract by Huddersfield in March. A central defender, cum midfielder, Sean made his Football League debut at Reading, when coming off the bench for the last four minutes. Strong in the air and on the ground, he shows good awareness, and looks to be one for the future.

Leeds U (Free from Liverpool juniors on 15/9/97)
Wigan Ath (Free on 24/12/97)
Huddersfield T (Free on 12/3/98) FL 0+1

HEWITT James (Jamie) Robert

Born: Chesterfield, 17 May 1968
Height: 5'10" Weight: 11.9

Chesterfield's Jamie had a quiet, steady season in 1997-98 in comparison to his previous one, with its Old Trafford semi-final heroics. But, for all that, the long-serving defender operated almost exclu-sively at right back, performing with familiar levels of skill, application, and

efficiency. Unflappable under pressure, and an excellent reader of the game, 1998-99 will be his testimonial year.

Chesterfield (From trainee on 22/4/86) FL 240+9/14 FLC 10/1 FAC 8+1 Others 11+2
Doncaster Rov (Free on 1/8/92) FL 32+1 FLC 3+1/1 FAC 1 Others 3
Chesterfield (Signed on 8/10/93) FL 169+7/10 FLC 11 FAC 13/1 Others 10

HEWLETT Matthew (Matt) Paul

Born: Bristol, 25 February 1976
Height: 6'2" Weight: 11.3
International Honours: E: Yth

No one more divides the Ashton Gate faithful than Matt, a midfield player with much natural ability, who, despite having made over 100 league appearances, has still not made the breakthrough from promising much to being the finished article. Has good vision and passing ability, with the energy to cover all areas of the pitch, but other aspects of his game gave the hecklers ammunition for their views in 1997-98, despite a welcoming four goals. Still a young man, there is plenty of time for him, especially with the side back in the first division.

Bristol C (From trainee on 12/8/93) FL 98+12/8 FLC 8+2 FAC 3+1/2 Others 5+1

HEY Antoine (Tony)

Born: Berlin, Germany, 19 September 1970
Height: 5'9" Weight: 11.6

Having signed from the German side, Fortuna Cologne, during the 1997 close season, Tony started 1997-98 in the Birmingham line-up, but after being troubled by calf and achilles problems lost his place on the right-hand side of midfield to another new signing, Jon McCarthy. However, during his time in the side, the German had shown a good appreciation of the game, to go with a useful turn of pace, and scored his one and only goal with a rasping drive in the Coca Cola Cup defeat at the hands of Arsenal in October.

Birmingham C (£300,000 from Fortuna Cologne on 16/7/97) FL 8+1 FLC 2/1

HICKS Stuart Jason

Born: Peterborough, 30 May 1967
Height: 6'1" Weight: 13.0

Signed from Scarborough during the 1997 close season as cover for the centre halves already at Leyton Orient, he was such an instant hit with the club, and the fans, that he remained in the team. Stuart, a big, strong, dominant defender, who is excellent in the air, even took over in goal at Shrewsbury when Chris Mackenzie was sent off.

Peterborough U (From apprentice on 10/8/84)
Colchester U (Free from Wisbech on 24/3/88) FL 57+7 FLC 2 FAC 5/1 Others 5
Scunthorpe U (Free on 19/8/90) FL 67/1 FLC 4 FAC 4/1 Others 8
Doncaster Rov (Free on 10/8/92) FL 36 FLC 2 FAC 1 Others 2
Huddersfield T (Signed on 27/8/93) FL 20+2/1 FLC 3 FAC 3 Others 1
Preston NE (Signed on 24/3/94) FL 11+1 FLC 2 Others 1/1
Scarborough (Signed on 22/2/95) FL 81+4/2 FLC 5 FAC 4 Others 3
Leyton Orient (Free on 5/8/97) FL 35 FLC 4 FAC 2

HIDEN Martin
Born: Stainz, Austria, 11 March 1973
Height: 6'0" Weight: 11.9
International Honours: Austria: 2
At £1.3 million this assured Austrian international defender looked to be an excellent acquisition for Leeds. Transferred from Rapid Vienna last February, in the face of competition from at least two other Premiership clubs, George Graham actually went to watch and sign him whilst Martin was playing a friendly in Dubai during the Austrian winter break. As a player who can play anywhere across the back four, after making his debut at home to Southampton in February at full back, he reverted to central defence. Excellent at reading the game, with good distribution, he is equally adept in the tackle. *Stop Press:* Selected for Austria's World Cup final 22, Martin failed to put in an appearance as the team went out at the Group B stage.
Leeds U (£1,300,000 from Rapid Vienna on 25/2/98) PL 11 FAC 1

HIGGINBOTTOM Daniel (Danny) John
Born: Manchester, 29 December 1978
Height: 6'0" Weight: 11.8
Having signed professional forms during the 1997 close season, on completion of his YTS stint, the young Manchester United defender enjoyed a rapid rise to progress, making his Premiership debut as a sixth-minute substitute against Barnsley in May, after just four outings with the reserve side up to the beginning of April. On that count alone, the future looks exceedingly bright for yet another of "Fergie's Fledglings."
Manchester U (From trainee on 10/7/97) PL 0+1

HIGGS Shane Peter
Born: Oxford, 13 May 1977
Height: 6'2" Weight: 12.12
A tall and agile goalkeeper, Shane, now in his third season as a Bristol Rovers' professional, had to be patient to add to his league appearances in 1997-98, his first of the season coming in September at Oldham in a remarkable match which ended 4-4. Eventually, he broke through again to claim the number one jersey, after starting against Walsall in the Auto Windscreen tie, and then played in the following seven league matches, displaying growing confidence in those performances. Contributes to Rovers' attacking options with his enormous goal kicks, which being pressure to opponents defences. Was surprisingly released during the summer.
Bristol Rov (From trainee on 17/7/95) FL 10 Others 2

HIGNETT Craig John
Born: Prescot, 12 January 1970
Height: 5'9" Weight: 11.10
Club Honours: Div 1 '95
A skilful and hard-working Middlesbrough midfielder, who played a key role in the club's fortunes since his arrival from Crewe Alexandra, "Higgy" is renowned for his exploitation of loose balls in and around the penalty area and has scored many vital goals for Boro. His powerful dead-ball kicking is

legendary and the fans were dismayed to hear that he was to leave at the end of last season. He will certainly be well remembered for his loyal service and it will be Boro's loss when he finally moves on.*
Crewe Alex (Free from Liverpool juniors on 11/5/88) FL 108+13/42 FLC 9+1/4 FAC 11+1/8 Others 6+1/3
Middlesbrough (£500,000 on 27/11/92) F/PL 126+30/33 FLC 19+3/12 FAC 9+2/3 Others 5+1

HILL Andrew (Andy) Rowland
Born: Maltby, 20 January 1965
Height: 5'11" Weight: 13.8
International Honours: E: Yth
A dependable Port Vale defender who, as usual, gave his all both at right back or in central defence, Andy used his experience well in 1997-98, but injuries caused him to miss over 20 games, which partly explained why the team had a struggling second half. An excellent passer, who likes to come out of defence with the ball, early on in the campaign he handed in a transfer request, expressing a wish to move nearer his Lancashire home, but later withdrew it, before being released during the summer.
Manchester U (From apprentice on 16/1/83)
Bury (Free on 4/7/84) FL 264/10 FLC 22/1 FAC 12 Others 19/1
Manchester C (£200,000 on 21/12/90) F/PL 91+7/6 FLC 11 FAC 2+1 Others 1
Port Vale (£150,000 on 25/8/95) FL 96+4/1 FLC 7 FAC 8 Others 6

HILL Clinton (Clint) Scott
Born: Knowsley, 19 October 1978
Height: 6'0" Weight: 11.6
Red was not this young man's favourite colour last season, as his over enthusiasm led to too many close encounters with the men in black! However, despite those problems, Clint, who broke through into the first team midway through the campaign, made enormous progress and was even recommended for an England U21 call-up. A solid and committed player, who is also assured, he is a strong and fearless tackler, and dominates in the air. Once he has settled down he could have a great future in the game.
Tranmere Rov (From trainee on 9/7/97) FL 13+1 FAC 2+1/1

HILL Colin Frederick
Born: Uxbridge, 12 November 1963
Height: 6'0" Weight: 12.11
Club Honours: FLC '97
International Honours: NI: 26
A central defender who signed for Northampton last November from Trelleborg in Sweden, he settled in well with the centre backs and was a regular first teamer following his arrival, often captaining the side in the absence of the regular skipper, Ray Warburton. He also became the first Town player for 30 years to win an international cap, while still on the clubs books, when selected yet again for Northern Ireland.
Arsenal (From apprentice on 7/8/81) FL 46/1 FLC 4 FAC 1 (Free to Maritimo during 1986 close season)
Colchester U (Free on 30/10/87) FL 64+5 FLC 2 FAC 7/2 Others 3+1

Sheffield U (£85,000 on 1/8/89) FL 77+5/1 FLC 5 FAC 10+2 Others 3
Leicester C (£200,000 on 26/3/92) F/PL 140+5 FLC 10+2/1 FAC 8 Others 9+1 (Free to Trelleborg during 1997 close season)
Northampton T (Free on 7/11/97) FL 27 FAC 3 Others 6

HILL Daniel (Danny) Ronald
Born: Enfield, 1 October 1974
Height: 5'9" Weight: 11.2
International Honours: E: U21-4; Yth
Having joined Cardiff City on loan from Spurs last February, after spending four seasons playing reserve team soccer, Danny had a major impact on City's midfield and showed the ability, composure, and calculating play the Bluebirds needed. With him in the side, City lost once in seven matches, but after he left they managed only two wins in ten games – both against Merthyr Tydfil in the FAW Invitation Cup. The club tried to extend his loan spell and when that failed they almost succeeded in agreeing a brand new loan deal with him, but a slight back injury sustained while moving furniture at home ended that possibility. Was released by Spurs during the summer. *Stop Press:* Signed for Oxford on 16 June.
Tottenham H (From trainee on 9/9/92) PL 4+6 FLC 0+2
Birmingham C (Loaned on 24/11/95) FL 5 FLC 2
Watford (Loaned on 15/2/96) FL 1
Cardiff C (Loaned on 19/2/98) FL 7

HILL Keith John
Born: Bolton, 17 May 1969
Height: 6'0" Weight: 12.6
Keith lost his regular centre-back partner, Alan Johnson, to injury before last season even started and was possibly Rochdale's most consistent defender, Dale losing six out of eight games in his absence through suspension and then injury around the turn of the year. Earlier he must have set a record when sent off after just 28 seconds at Orient, when he got in the way of a goal-bound shot and was adjudged to have deliberately handled. Is a player with good pace, and capable of playing right across the back four.*
Blackburn Rov (From juniors on 9/5/87) F/PL 89+7/4 FLC 6/1 FAC 5+1 Others 3+2
Plymouth Arg (Signed on 23/9/92) FL 117+6/2 FLC 9 FAC 10 Others 9
Rochdale (Free on 3/7/96) FL 79+1/5 FLC 4 FAC 3 Others 1

HILL Kevin
Born: Exeter, 6 March 1976
Height: 5'8" Weight: 10.3
Another inspired Kevin Hodges signing for Torquay, this left-sided midfielder made the giant step from the Great Mills (Western) League without any trouble at all in 1997-98. Having a terrific "engine", whether tackling back or popping up in the opposition penalty area to score valuable goals, he can run all day and is always looking for a shooting opportunity. Tap ins or long range shots, they all come the same to Kevin.
Torquay U (Free from Torrington on 8/8/97) FL 31+6/7 FLC 4 FAC 3 Others 1+1

HILLIER David
Born: Blackheath, 19 December 1969
Height: 5'10" Weight: 12.5
Club Honours: FAYC '88; Div 1 '91
International Honours: E: U21-1
David had a mediocre season at Portsmouth in 1997-98 until the arrival of Alan Ball, when his performances improved to the level he played at in 1996-97. When on form, the former Arsenal man proved a very effective midfield player and showed that he has the ability to play the ball around and also get stuck in when necessary. He also scored three goals during the campaign, including a 25 yarder against West Bromwich where he beat his former Arsenal team-mate, Alan Miller, to win a £20 bet.
Arsenal (From trainee on 11/2/88) F/PL 82+22/2 FLC 13+2 FAC 3+2 Others 5+4
Portsmouth (£250,000 on 2/11/96) FL 51/4 FLC 2/1 FAC 4/1

HILLS John David
Born: Blackpool, 21 April 1978
Height: 5'8" Weight: 11.2
Unable to further his career at Everton in 1997-98, with just three games under his belt in two years, John was loaned out first to Swansea (August) and then to Blackpool (January), his first club. In returning to Swansea for the second successive season, with an ability to deliver good crosses, he was used on the left side of midfield in seven games, while at Blackpool, where his loan deal was firmed up a month later, he was predominately seen as a left back, whose tackling and enthusiasm quickly made him popular with the fans.
Blackpool (From trainee on 27/10/95)
Everton (£90,000 on 4/11/95) PL 1+2
Swansea C (Loaned on 30/1/97) FL 11
Swansea C (Loaned on 22/8/97) FL 7
Blackpool (£75,000 on 16/1/98) FL 19/1 Others 2

HILTON Damian Alan
Born: Norwich, 6 September 1977
Height: 6'2" Weight: 12.6
A free transfer from Norwich City last March, the 20-year-old forward had not appeared in the League side at Carrow Road, but was plunged directly into first team duty with Brighton and Hove Albion. After a steady debut, Damian had little opportunity to impress so near to the end of the season, and only contracted until the end of the season, is sure to be playing his football elsewhere in 1998-99.
Norwich C (From trainee on 9/7/96)
Brighton & Hove A (Free on 12/3/98) FL 4+1

HILTON David
Born: Barnsley, 10 November 1977
Height: 5'11" Weight: 10.10
International Honours: E: Yth; Sch
Released by Manchester United during the 1997 close season, without ever being offered a first team opportunity, David called in at Darlington and made just one substitute appearance in the club's first home league game of last season, a 1-1 draw against Rotherham, while on trial. Although on a month-to-month contract until November, there were no further call

ups and the young defender subsequently moved north of the border to Ayr United.
Manchester U (From trainee on 19/12/94)
Darlington (Free on 22/8/97) FL 0+1

HILTON Maurice
Born: Stockton, 14 March 1979
Height: 5'9" Weight: 10.8
Another product of the Doncaster junior team, Maurice made his first team debut at full back in the F A Cup first round tie at Preston in 1997-98. In playing particularly well on the day, he made further appearances for the league side as the season progressed, and is highly regarded by all at Belle Vue, where his progress in the future will be keenly observed. Is still a trainee.
Doncaster Rov (Trainee) FL 9+1 FAC 1

HIMSWORTH Gary Paul
Born: Pickering, 19 December 1969
Height: 5'8" Weight: 10.6
1997-98 was a frustrating campaign for York's utility player, who missed a good deal of it owing to injuries. Quick and skilful, and best used on the left-hand side of the pitch, when called up for senior duty he was a reliable performer, either in defence or midfield.*
York C (From trainee on 27/1/88) FL 74+14/8 FLC 5 Others 5+2
Scarborough (Free on 5/12/90) FL 83+9/6 FLC 7+2/1 FAC 1+1 Others 6+1
Darlington (Free on 16/7/93) FL 86+8/8 FLC 5+1 FAC 6 Others 7/4
York C (£25,000 on 16/2/96) FL 48+8/3 FLC 4 FAC 5+1/1 Others 2/1

Andy Hinchcliffe

HINCHCLIFFE Andrew (Andy) George
Born: Manchester, 5 February 1969
Height: 5'10" Weight: 13.7
Club Honours: FAC '95; CS '95
International Honours: E: 6; U21-1; Yth
A classy, constructive left-wing back, Andy bounced back into action for Everton and

England in 1997-98, after recovering from an appalling cruciate knee ligament injury. Having recuperated for seven months, his first team recall was delayed by a thigh strain, then, when he finally returned, at Derby County on 13 September, he was sent off for a professional foul! However, he soon picked up where he had left off the season before, displaying his uncanny ability to swing in devastating corners and free kicks, before reclaiming his England place in the November friendly against Cameroon, when he played in an unfamiliar central defensive role, but looked more than comfortable. A well publicised difference of opinion with manager, Howard Kendall, meant that few were surprised when he was transferred to Sheffield Wednesday in January – a month after a proposed move to Tottenham had fallen through because of an achilles tendon injury. Quickly settling in at Hillsborough, scoring a goal against Liverpool in his third match, he added experience, stability, and skill to the left flank, and became the first Wednesday player for five years to represent England, when playing against Switzerland.
Manchester C (From apprentice on 13/2/86) FL 107+5/8 FLC 11/1 FAC 12/1 Others 4/1
Everton (£800,000 on 17/7/90) F/PL 170+12/6 FLC 21+2/1 FAC 12+2/1 Others 8
Sheffield Wed (£2,850,000 on 30/1/98) PL 15/1

David Hirst

HIRST David Eric
Born: Cudworth, 7 December 1967
Height: 5'11" Weight: 13.10
Club Honours: FLC '91
International Honours: E: 3; B-3; U21-7; Yth
An experienced former England international striker, David was signed by Southampton for a club record fee from Sheffield Wednesday last October and, having been troubled by injury for some time, Saints' fans wondered if it was money well spent. Undoubtedly, the question was

well and truly answered in positive fashion, when the record books showed him playing 30 games and scoring nine goals come the end of the season, including an unstoppable shot at the Dell against his former club in November. One of that rare breed of strikers who can run with the ball and finish strongly, he still has pace and a fine left foot, and will no doubt continue to score goals for some time to come.

Barnsley (From apprentice on 8/11/85) FL 26+2/9 FLC 1
Sheffield Wed (£200,000 on 11/8/86) F/PL 261+33/106 FLC 26+9/11 FAC 12+7/6 Others 8/5
Southampton (£2,000,000 on 17/10/97) PL 28/9 FLC 1 FAC 1

HISLOP Neil (Shaka)
Born: Hackney, 22 February 1969
Height: 6'4" Weight: 14.4
Club Honours: Div 2 '94
International Honours: E: U21-1

One of the tallest players ever to turn out for Newcastle, Shaka is a goalkeeper who uses his height to good effect in dealing with crosses, but whose agility and quick reflexes also enable him to get down quickly to deal with low shots. He started last season as third choice behind Shay Given and Pavel Srnicek, but worked hard in training as he waited his opportunity. This arrived when he was brought into the team in November when Given had been injured on international duty, and his consistent performances enabled him to retain his place, playing his part in the club's march to Wembley, when he made an outstanding save from Duncan Ferguson late in the FA Cup third round at Everton before being dropped in February, reputedly because he was delaying signing a new contract. Ironically, this occurred immediately after he had been selected for the England "B" squad for the game against Chile. Later, an injury to Tim Flowers saw Shaka drafted into the full England squad and, although he was not called upon to play, he did appear for the England U21 team against Switzerland in March. Out of contract during the summer, Shaka was due to leave the club under the Bosman ruling. *Stop Press:* Newspaper reports on 18 June confirmed that Shaka would be on his way to West Ham the moment his contract with Newcastle expired.

Reading (Signed from Howard University on 9/9/92) FL 104 FLC 10 FAC 3 Others 9
Newcastle U (£1,575,000 on 10/8/95) PL 53 FLC 8 FAC 6 Others 4

HITCHCOCK Kevin Joseph
Born: Canning Town, 5 October 1962
Height: 6'1" Weight: 13.4
Club Honours: AMC '87; FAC '97; FLC '98; ECWC '98

A loyal Chelsea goalkeeper, who found his opportunities limited behind international 'keepers, Ed de Goey and Dmitri Kharine, Kevin started just two matches in 1997-98, the third and fourth round Coca Cola Cup ties against Blackburn Rovers and Southampton, respectively. He distinguished himself in both matches, saving Chris

Sutton's penalty in the shoot-out and playing particularly well in the latter match, pulling off some good saves to keep the Blues on the path to Wembley. Was awarded a testimonial against Nottingham Forest in May in recognition of his services to Chelsea.

Nottingham F (£15,000 from Barking on 4/8/83)
Mansfield T (£14,000 on 1/2/84) FL 182 FLC 12 FAC 10 Others 20
Chelsea (£250,000 on 25/3/88) F/PL 90+3 FLC 12 FAC 14 Others 13
Northampton T (Loaned on 28/12/90) FL 17 Others 1

HITCHEN Steven (Steve) James
Born: Salford, 28 November 1976
Height: 5'8" Weight: 11.4

Steve was Macclesfield's first signing in the Football League, having been on the bench for Blackburn in their European campaign in 1995. Able to play at full back on either side, he could not force his way into a settled team until impressing as a substitute in mid-September and making his full debut the match after. Unfortunately pulled off with a hamstring injury, which dogged him for several months, he was unable to get a place in a settled defence.

Blackburn Rov (From trainee on 4/7/95)
Macclesfield T (Free on 14/7/97) FL 1+1

HJELDE Jon Olav
Born: Levanger, Norway, 30 April 1972
Height: 6'2" Weight: 13.7
Club Honours: Div 1 '98

This Norwegian central defender signed for Nottingham Forest from Rosenberg during the 1997 pre-season recess following an injury to Colin Cooper in a friendly game against Leeds. Big and strong, and especially good in the air, having made his Football League debut in the opening match of 1997-98 at Port Vale, he powered home two headed goals in the next match, an 8-0 win at Doncaster Rovers in the Coca Cola Cup. He also scored a vital equaliser at Sunderland in the league. Lost his place towards the end of September when Cooper returned to the fray, but was always available to slot in if required, and was well worth his first division championship medal.

Nottingham F (£600,000 from Rosenborg on 8/8/97) FL 23+5/1 FLC 2/2 FAC 1

HOBSON Gary
Born: Hull, 12 November 1972
Height: 6'1" Weight: 13.3

Although niggling injuries meant that he was absent for several short spells in 1997-98, Gary's contribution to Brighton and Hove Albion's third division survival cause was considerable. The classy central defender inherited the captaincy after the departure of Mark Morris in December, and was rewarded for his consistency with a new two-year contract by the delighted manager, Brian Horton, in March.

Hull C (From trainee on 17/7/91) FL 135+7 FLC 13+1 FAC 2+2/1 Others 6
Brighton & Hove A (£60,000 on 27/3/96) FL 74+5/1 FLC 4 FAC 3 Others 2

Gary Hobson

HOCKING Matthew (Matt) James
Born: Boston, 30 January 1978
Height: 5'11" Weight: 11.5

With Hull City beating off reported interest from Barnsley and Lincoln, Matt became the club's first money signing under Mark Hateley, following his switch from Sheffield United last September. Despite making only one senior appearance for the Blades, the young defender remained an ever present in the City line-up until suffering a nasty shoulder injury against Cardiff City in March. Although not the biggest of centre backs, he has good pace, reads the game well, and satisfies his new manager's insistence of playing the ball out of defence.

Sheffield U (From trainee on 16/5/96)
Hull C (£25,000 on 19/9/97) FL 31/1 FLC 2 FAC 1 Others 2

HOCKTON Daniel (Danny) John
Born: Barking, 7 February 1979
Height: 5'10" Weight: 11.11

Another fine product of Millwall's youth team, Danny has excellent potential as a centre forward with great pace and, having made his debut in 1996-97, acquitted himself well in his first full season in 1997-98, scoring some vital goals, four of them coming in three successive matches. Although he spent a lot of time on the subs' bench, when introduced he was of great nuisance value to many defences, and it was all part of the learning curve anyway. Has a good shot, and shows great awareness, especially in one-on-one situations with goalkeepers.

Millwall (From trainee on 8/3/97) FL 10+18/3 FLC 2+1/2 FAC 0+1 Others 0+2

HODGE John
Born: Skelmersdale, 1 April 1969
Height: 5'7" Weight: 11.3
Club Honours: AMC '94

Enjoyed a splendid first full season in 1997-98, with Walsall's main attacking threat coming time and again from his ability to take on defenders. He also had an eye for goal, his season's tally of ten including a volleyed match winner at Luton in November, and a last minute penalty equaliser against Preston in January. His excellent form was more than enough for his fellow professionals to select him for the award-winning PFA second division team.*

Exeter C (Signed from Falmouth T on 12/9/91) FL 57+8/10 FLC 3/1 FAC 2 Others 8+2/1
Swansea C (Signed on 14/7/93) FL 87+25/10 FLC 6+2/3 FAC 6 Others 13+4
Walsall (Free on 23/9/96) FL 67+9/12 FLC 5 FAC 7+1/2 Others 5+2

HODGE Stephen (Steve) Brian
Born: Nottingham, 25 October 1962
Height: 5'7" Weight: 10.3
Club Honours: FLC '89, '90; FMC '89; Div 1 '92
International Honours: E: 24; B-2; U21-8 (UEFAC '84)

Having left Watford in surprising circumstances early in 1996, the former England International joined Leyton Orient on a non-contract basis during the 1997 close season, thus returning to league football after 18 months out of the game. At his best, a naturally left-sided midfielder who could get forward to get a fair quota of goals, while defending with the best of them, Steve found it difficult to re-adjust and after a brief 59-minute appearance at Scunthorpe was released by the club.

Nottingham F (From apprentice on 25/10/80) FL 122+1/30 FLC 10/2 FAC 6 Others 11/4
Aston Villa (£450,000 on 27/8/85) FL 53/12 FLC 12/3 FAC 4/1 Others 1
Tottenham H (£650,000 on 23/12/86) FL 44+1/7 FLC 2 FAC 7/2
Nottingham F (£550,000 on 17/8/88) FL 79+3/20 FLC 20+1/6 FAC 11+1/2 Others 9/2
Leeds U (£900,000 on 25/7/91) F/PL 28+26/10 FLC 4+3 FAC 2+1 Others 0+3
Derby Co (£300,000 on 30/8/94) FL 10/2 Others 1/2
Queens Park R (£300,000 on 28/10/94) PL 15 FAC 1
Watford (Free on 15/12/95) FL 2 (Released on 13/1/96)
Leyton Orient (Free from Hong Kong on 15/8/97) FL 1

HODGES Glyn Peter
Born: Streatham, 30 April 1963
Height: 6'0" Weight: 12.3
Club Honours: Div 4 '83
International Honours: W: 18; B-1; U21-5; Yth

Returned to the Football League with Hull City at the start of last season, having spent a year with the Hong Kong based club, Sin Tao, and following trials at Chesterfield and Nottingham Forest. The former Welsh international's skills flourished in the third division, despite often being sidelined by niggling injuries, and, with the capacity to make things happen, his class regularly showed through, none more so than in the 5-4 defeat at Rotherham, when a tremendous double strike saw him reach 100 career league goals. In February, however, the left-sided midfielder exercised a clause in his contract to join Nottingham Forest and

provide experienced cover for former boss, Dave Bassett's Premiership bound side. Ultimately not required, he was released during the summer.

Wimbledon (From apprentice on 3/2/81) FL 200+32/49 FLC 14+2/3 FAC 13+2/2 Others 0+1
Newcastle U (£200,000 on 15/7/87) FL 7
Watford (£300,000 on 1/10/87) FL 82+4/15 FLC 5/2 FAC 8/1 Others 2+1/1
Crystal Palace (£410,000 on 16/7/90) FL 5+2 FLC 2+2/1
Sheffield U (£450,000 on 17/1/91) F/PL 116+31/19 FLC 4+3 FAC 13+3/3 Others 1
Derby Co (Free on 15/2/96) FL 1+8 (Freed during 1996 close season)
Hull C (Free from Sin Tao, Hong Kong on 22/8/97) FL 13+5/4 FLC 1 FAC 1 Others 2
Nottingham F (Free on 20/2/98)

HODGES Lee Leslie
Born: Plaistow, 2 March 1978
Height: 5'5" Weight: 10.2

Another promising West Ham youngster, Lee went on loan to Plymouth last November, playing ten games, and on returning he managed five first team appearances for the Hammers, when coming on as a substitute. Although small he is a bundle of energy and loves to be in the action, doing very well in tough FA Cup games against Blackburn and Arsenal. A very creative and attack minded midfielder, who has plenty of time on the ball and superb passing ability, and always willing to get a shot in, Lee should prove most useful this coming season as a member of Harry Redknapp's exciting young squad.

West Ham U (From trainee on 2/3/95) PL 0+2 FAC 0+3
Exeter C (Loaned on 13/9/96) FL 16+1
Leyton Orient (Loaned on 28/2/97) FL 3
Plymouth Arg (Loaned on 6/11/97) FL 9 Others 1

HODGES Lee Leslie
Born: Epping, 4 September 1973
Height: 6'0" Weight: 12.1
International Honours: E: Yth

Lee was signed from Barnet at half time, during the pre-season friendly against Southampton, and pitched straight into first team action, along with former team-mate, Linvoy Primus, signed at the same time. Although he struggled with a succession of injuries and played in only half the possible games, he showed ample evidence of his creative midfield ability, as well as the eye for goal which brought him an average of one in every four games. His campaign ended following an operation in February to repair cartilage damage in his left knee.

Tottenham H (From trainee on 29/2/92) PL 0+4
Plymouth Arg (Loaned on 26/2/93) FL 6+1/2
Wycombe W (Loaned on 31/12/93) FL 2+2 FAC 1 Others 1
Barnet (Free on 31/5/94) FL 94+11/26 FLC 6+1 FAC 6+1/4 Others 3+1
Reading (£100,000 on 29/7/97) FL 20+4/6 FLC 5+1 FAC 4+1

HODGSON Douglas (Doug) John
Born: Frankston, Australia, 27 February 1969
Height: 6'2" Weight: 13.10

Doug again played with typical Australian flair for Oldham, this time in 1997-98, a season which brought about a number of

bookings and also a bad injury which required two operations. A hard-tackling central defender who just hates to lose, and is an excellent header of the ball, he scored his first goals for the Latics when pushed up front, mainly as a stand-in for Sean McCarthy. Is also a good man to have on your side at set pieces.

Sheffield U (£30,000 from Heidelberg Alex on 22/1/94) FL 24+6/1 FLC 2+1 FAC 2+1 Others 1
Plymouth Arg (Loaned on 10/8/95) FL 3+2
Burnley (Loaned on 17/10/96) FL 1
Oldham Ath (Signed on 28/2/97) FL 33+7/4 FLC 0+2 FAC 3

HOGG Graeme James
Born: Aberdeen, 17 June 1964
Height: 6'1" Weight: 12.4
Club Honours: AIC '95
International Honours: S: U21-4; Yth

Having given way to Gary Strodder in the heart of Notts County's defence, playing just seven times in 1997-98, Graeme signed for Brentford in January. A centre half who wins virtually everything in the air, and has a strong left foot, he soon stiffened up the Bees' defence as he linked up with Jamie Bates and Danny Cullip, and his transfer fee was described by Bees' boss, Micky Adams, as "The best £5,000 I have ever spent". He also scored vital goals against Plymouth and Carlisle from headers, before being surprisingly released during the summer.

Manchester U (From apprentice on 1/6/82) FL 82+1/1 FLC 7+1 FAC 8 Others 12
West Bromwich A (Loaned on 3/11/87) FL 7 Others 1
Portsmouth (£150,000 on 25/8/88) FL 97+3/2 FLC 2 FAC 6 Others 2
Heart of Midlothian (£200,000 on 23/8/91) SL 50+8/3 SLC 6 SC 1/1 Others 4
Notts Co (£75,000 on 27/1/95) FL 66 FLC 4+1 FAC 4/1 Others 4
Brentford (£5,000 on 23/1/98) FL 17/2

HOGGETH Gary Denis
Born: South Shields, 7 October 1979
Height: 5'10" Weight: 10.8

Gary made his league debut in the Doncaster goal at Lincoln last November, when the club's other goalkeepers were unavailable for selection. Still a trainee, he did well on the night, following his unexpected promotion from the Rovers' youth team, and looks to be an excellent prospect for the future. It is to be hoped that the events of the last season will not have damaged his confidence overmuch.

Doncaster Rov (Trainee) FL 8

HOLCROFT Peter Ian
Born: Liverpool, 3 January 1976
Height: 5'9" Weight: 11.7

Still unable to break into the Swindon side in 1997-98, Peter was loaned out to Exeter City at the end of August, making three starts, coming off the bench on three further occasions, and equipping himself well before returning to reserve team football at the County Ground. A central midfielder who is skilful but slight, he played in roughly 50 per cent of the games, due to the odd injury, but faced with stiff competition for a place he was one of eight players transfer listed in March.

Everton (From trainee on 1/7/94)
Swindon T (Free on 11/11/96) FL 2+1
Exeter C (Loaned on 28/8/97) FL 3+3

HOLDSWORTH David Gary
Born: Walthamstow, 8 November 1968
Height: 6'1" Weight: 12.4
International Honours: E: U21-1; Yth

The Sheffield United skipper was once again a model of consistency at centre back in 1997-98, forging a strong partnership with Paul McGrath and Carl Tiler at the start, but performing equally well with a number of other partners, whether the team were playing with three centre backs or a flat back four. Scored the dramatic late equaliser against Coventry City in the F A Cup which enabled the club to progress to the semi-final stage, and was deservedly named the Blades' Away Travel Player of the Year. The twin brother of Bolton's Dean, he is good in the air, sound positionally, and rarely gets flustered.

Watford (From apprentice on 8/11/86) FL 249+9/10 FLC 20/2 FAC 14+1/1 Others 8+2
Sheffield U (£450,000 on 8/10/96) FL 77/3 FLC 5 FAC 9/1 Others 5

HOLDSWORTH Dean Christopher
Born: Walthamstow, 8 November 1968
Height: 5'11" Weight: 11.13
Club Honours: Div 3 '92
International Honours: E: B-1

Started the first four games for Wimbledon last season, and made two subs' appearances before joining Bolton in October for what was a club record transfer fee. As a member of the Dons' "crazy gang", it came as a bit of a surprise to most Wanderers' fans, but once the dust had settled they began to expect great things from the striker. Unfortunately, things did not quite work out as planned, as a series of niggling injuries and a poor start to the club's campaign conspired to make life difficult for the newcomer. Despite missing most of the Christmas period through injury, Dean still managed to appear in around half of the games, while managing just three goals. However, his partnership with Nathan Blake improved every time they played together and, with the first division looming up, this coming season would be the ideal setting to get things right if Bolton are to go back to the Premiership at the first time of asking. At his best, a natural goalscorer who invariably arrives in the box at the right time, and also well known as a male model and as the brother of Sheffield United's David.

Watford (From apprentice on 12/11/86) FL 2+14/3 Others 0+4
Carlisle U (Loaned on 11/2/88) FL 4/1
Port Vale (Loaned on 18/3/88) FL 6/2
Swansea C (Loaned on 25/8/88) FL 4+1/1
Brentford (Loaned on 13/10/88) FL 2+5/1
Brentford (£125,000 on 29/9/89) FL 106+4/53 FLC 7+1/6 FAC 6/7 Others 12+2/9
Wimbledon (£720,000 on 20/7/92) PL 148+21/58 FLC 16+3/11 FAC 13+7/7
Bolton W (£3,500,000 on 3/10/97) PL 17+3/3

HOLLAND Christopher (Chris) James
Born: Whalley, 11 September 1975
Height: 5'9" Weight: 11.5
International Honours: E: U21-10; Yth

Despite looking to be a certain starter in the Birmingham line-up in 1997-98, having had an impressive pre-season, Chris was unable to hold down a regular place and was confined mainly to the reserves. Although disappointed, he buckled down to produce much needed bite to his game when selected and will obviously be looking to mount a first team challenge in 1998-99. An attacking midfielder, who is quick with good energy levels, he is also inventive and skilful, especially in his passing and movement.

Preston NE (Trainee) FL 0+1 Others 1
Newcastle U (£100,000 on 20/1/94) PL 2+1 FLC 0+1
Birmingham C (£600,000 on 5/9/96) FL 30+12 FLC 3 FAC 3

HOLLAND Matthew (Matt) Rhys
Born: Bury, 11 April 1974
Height: 5'9" Weight: 11.12

Having joined Ipswich from Bournemouth during the 1997 close season, Matt soon became a firm favourite with the fans for his wholehearted endeavour in every match and, as an ever present, was influential in the club's second-half surge up the table, from his favoured position of central midfield. Interestingly, he started the season playing as a sweeper, or the central defender in a back three, and moved back and forth from defence to midfield as the injury situation dictated. Strong in the air, and a player who attacks the ball well, whether defending or attacking, he scored more than his fair share of goals, contributing a valuable 12, the highlights being a Coca Cola double at Torquay, the winner at Sheffield United, and a superb diving header against Sunderland. His most eventful experience was probably the home league game against Oxford, where he took over from Richard Wright in goal, while the 'keeper had stitches in a facial injury, and was powerless to prevent Kevin Francis from opening the scoring, scored the fourth goal himself, all before conceding a penalty! Was voted Player of the Year by the supporters.

West Ham U (From trainee on 3/7/92)
Bournemouth (Signed on 27/1/95) FL 97+7/18 FLC 6 FAC 3 Others 3
Ipswich T (£800,000 on 31/7/97) FL 46/10 FLC 7/2 FAC 4 Others 2

HOLLAND Paul
Born: Lincoln, 8 July 1973
Height: 5'11" Weight: 12.10
International Honours: E: U21-4; Yth; Sch

An intelligent, forceful midfielder, Paul enjoyed his best season at Saltergate to date in 1997-98, coming forward at corners, where his powerful headers from around the penalty spot were a welcome addition to Chesterfield's set-piece repertoire. He also revelled in the responsibility of being made captain, holding the midfield together, and performing well as a third centre back on occasions.

Mansfield T (From juniors on 4/7/91) FL 149/25 FLC 11 FAC 7/3 Others 9/1
Sheffield U (£250,000 on 20/6/95) FL 11+7/1 FLC 2/1
Chesterfield (Signed on 5/1/96) FL 72+5/8 FLC 5 FAC 10 Others 1

Paul Holland

HOLLOWAY Christopher (Chris) David
Born: Swansea, 5 February 1980
Height: 5'10" Weight: 11.7

Still a trainee, Chris made three starts for Exeter in 1997-98 and performed well. A midfielder who is expected to come right through the ranks, no doubt he would have had a longer run if the team were not in contention in the play offs for most of the season.

Exeter C (Trainee) FL 4+2

HOLLOWAY Darren
Born: Bishop Auckland, 3 October 1977
Height: 6'2" Weight: 12.2
International Honours: E: U21-1

One of the "finds" of Sunderland's promotion charge in 1997-98, the Bishop Auckland-born right back made his debut when filling in for the injured Chris Makin in a vital win at Stoke in October and never looked back. Also at home playing in the centre of the defence, Darren's ability to charge forward down the right flank and deliver telling crosses was vital to Sunderland's season. The 20-year old also made his England U21 debut against Switzerland in March, and received an England "B" call-up the following month. Earlier in the campaign, at the end of August, and before he had made a first team bow for Sunderland, he was loaned out to Carlisle, where his five-game spell coincided with one of the club's more successful times. Although there was some talk locally of him leaving, it was not to be and the rest is history.

Sunderland (From trainee on 12/10/95) FL 32 FAC 2 Others 3
Carlisle U (Loaned on 29/8/97) FL 5

HOLLOWAY Ian Scott
Born: Kingswood, 12 March 1963
Height: 5'8" Weight: 10.10
Club Honours: Div 3 '90

As Bristol Rovers' player/manager, Ian continued to enjoy his ball-winning midfield role, adding his experience, and passing the 350 league appearance mark during last season. His presence on the pitch was certainly useful in assisting some of the club's inexperienced youngsters, while his passing and all-round workrate was a revelation at times, and his spectacular late equalising goal in a first round FA Cup tie against Gillingham, his first of the season, was a personal highlight. The goal ensured a deserved replay, which was convincingly won at the Priestfield Stadium. So determined and passionate about the club, he was injured at Blackpool in the penultimate match of the campaign and missed the play offs, but was prompting his men from the dugout with his usual words of encouragement.
Bristol Rov (From apprentice on 18/3/81) FL 104+7/14 FLC 10/1 FAC 8/2 Others 5
Wimbledon (£35,000 on 18/7/85) FL 19/2 FLC 3 FAC 1
Brentford (£25,000 on 12/3/86) FL 27+3/2 FLC 2 FAC 3 Others 0+1
Torquay U (Loaned on 30/1/87) FL 5
Bristol Rov (£10,000 on 21/8/87) FL 179/26 FLC 5 FAC 10/1 Others 20/3
Queens Park R (£230,000 on 12/8/91) F/PL 130+17/4 FLC 12+1 FAC 7+1/1 Others 1+1
Bristol Rov (Free on 22/7/96) FL 63+7/1 FLC 4 FAC 4/1 Others 2

HOLLUND Martin
Born: Stord, Norway, 11 August 1975
Height: 6'0" Weight: 12.9

Signed by Hartlepool from Brann Bergen last November, in an attempt to solve the goalkeeping position which had been a problem since the start of the season, the classy Norwegian proved a good signing, showing himself to be agile for his size, and able to adapt to the English game. Popular with the supporters, he was given a contract to the end of the campaign and played in the last 28 games, giving a good account of himself, despite the club's promotion aspirations gradually disappearing.
Hartlepool U (Free from SK Brann Bergen on 21/11/97) FL 28 Others 2

HOLMES Matthew (Matty) Jason
Born: Luton, 1 August 1969
Height: 5'7" Weight: 11.0

Signed from Blackburn during the 1997 close season, having failed to get on Rovers' team sheet in 1996-97, Matty started badly for Charlton when he injured his knee in a summer testimonial game and did not make his league debut until last October. A fast, tricky, left-sided winger, who scored the winning goal against Crewe at The Valley in November, before a dreadful tackle broke his left leg just above the ankle in an FA Cup replay at Molineux in February. Hopefully, Matty will make a full recovery for 1998-99.
Bournemouth (From trainee on 22/8/88) FL 105+9/8 FLC 7 FAC 8+2 Others 5
Cardiff C (Loaned on 23/3/89) FL 0+1

West Ham U (£40,000 on 19/8/92) F/PL 63+13/4 FLC 4 FAC 6 Others 3/1
Blackburn Rov (£1,200,000 on 15/8/95) PL 8+1/1 Others 2+1
Charlton Ath (£250,000 on 24/7/97) FL 10+6/1 FAC 1+1

HOLMES Paul
Born: Stocksbridge, 18 February 1968
Height: 5'10" Weight: 11.3

Always willing to get into the opponents' half of the field, Paul had already lost his West Bromwich Albion right-back slot to Andy McDermott prior to the end of 1996-97, and he started 1997-98 in the same fashion before taking pole position in the third game of the season. With a surprise turn of pace, and comfortable on the ball, despite a certain inconsistency with his crossing, he is always good value. Dropping out of first team contention in mid-March, following a knee injury, and being placed on the transfer list soon afterwards he agreed to sign a new contract.
Doncaster Rov (From apprentice on 24/2/86) FL 42+5/1 FAC 3+1/1 Others 1
Torquay U (£6,000 on 12/8/88) FL 127+11/4 FLC 9 FAC 9+2 Others 13+3
Birmingham C (£40,000 on 5/6/92) FL 12 FAC 1
Everton (£100,000 on 19/3/93) PL 21 FLC 4 FAC 1 Others 0+2
West Bromwich A (£80,000 on 12/1/96) FL 85+1/1 FLC 5 FAC 3 Others 3

HOLMES Steven (Steve) Peter
Born: Middlesbrough, 13 January 1971
Height: 6'2" Weight: 13.0

The Lincoln defender converted into a central midfield role for the 1997-98 season with great effect, his ability to win the ball proving extremely valuable, and he was the club's only ever present player. Also netted some important goals, including both in the 2-1 home win over Exeter.*
Lincoln C (From trainee on 17/7/89)
Preston NE (£10,000 from Guisborough T, via Gainsborough Trinity, on 14/3/94) FL 13/1 FAC 3 Others 1
Hartlepool U (Loaned on 10/3/95) FL 5/2
Lincoln C (Loaned on 20/10/95) FL 12/1 Others 2
Lincoln C (£30,000 on 15/3/96) FL 84+1/9 FLC 6/2 FAC 4 Others 1

HOLSGROVE Paul
Born: Telford, 26 August 1969
Height: 6'1" Weight: 12.11

Having been released by Reading, following a loan period at Grimsby last September, Paul initially tied up with Crewe Alexandra on a non-contract basis and only a last-minute hitch between his agent and Dario Gradi thwarted a deal with Stoke. However, the new City manager, Chris Kamara, eventually got his man on a month-by-month contract until the end of the season. A good footballer, with vision and the ability to pass the ball, he conveniently slotted into an anchor role in midfield or as a sweeper, but was unlucky with injuries, which meant he missed a couple of key games in the relegation dog fight.*
Aldershot (From trainee on 9/2/87) FL 0+3 Others 1 (Free to Wokingham T in 1990 close season)
Luton T (£25,000 on 1/1/91) FL 1+1 (Free to Heracles in November 1991)

Millwall (Free on 13/8/92) FL 3+8 FLC 0+1 FAC 0+1 Others 2
Reading (Free on 10/8/94) FL 63+7/6 FLC 8+3/1 FAC 5
Grimsby T (Loaned on 12/9/97) FL 3+7
Crewe Alex (Free on 20/11/97) FL 7+1/1 FAC 1
Stoke C (Free on 27/1/98) FL 11+1/1

HOLT Andrew (Andy)
Born: Stockport, 21 April 1978
Height: 6'1" Weight: 12.7

As in 1996-97, Andy continued to show promise of things to come last season as he put together 15 games for Oldham, which included seven starts, and scored his first goal. As a strong tackler who is good in the air, and can be played in central defence or at full back with confidence, most of his appearances were made in the number three shirt following an injury to Carl Serrant. However, what really catches the eye is his massive long throw, which must be the longest in the game, and can be used effectively as a real attacking weapon.
Oldham Ath (From trainee on 23/7/96) FL 7+8/1 FAC 1

HOLT Michael Andrew
Born: Burnley, 28 July 1977
Height: 5'10" Weight: 11.12

A young forward who only appeared spasmodically for Preston last season, nevertheless, he continues to progress. Quick to pounce on the loose ball, he scored twice during the season, but will probably be best remembered for his missing the target during the single goal home defeat by Bournemouth.
Preston NE (Free from Blackburn Rov juniors on 16/8/96) FL 12+21/5 FLC 2+1/1 FAC 1+3 Others 0+1

HONE Mark Joseph
Born: Croydon, 31 March 1968
Height: 6'1" Weight: 12.7
International Honours: E: SP-4

A hard-tackling Lincoln midfield player, whose combative skills were not always appreciated by referees, Mark was out for two months early on last season after undergoing a hernia operation and when fit again missed several matches through suspensions. Skilful, and with a penchant to get forward, he broke his duck when scoring twice in the league in 1996-97. Was released during the summer.
Crystal Palace (From juniors on 3/11/85) FL 4 FLC 0+1
Southend U (£50,000 from Welling U on 11/8/94) FL 50+6 FLC 2+2 FAC 1 Others 2
Lincoln C (Free on 30/7/96) FL 48+5/2 FLC 7+1/1 FAC 4/1 Others 1

HOPE Christopher (Chris) Jonathan
Born: Sheffield, 14 November 1972
Height: 6'1" Weight: 12.7

The fact that Chris won all six Player of the Season trophies at the end of his fifth season with Scunthorpe shows what a tremendous campaign he had in 1997-98. A tall defender, who is virtually unbeatable in the air, he also developed more consistency and better distribution on the ground, as he remained a league ever-present for the

Chris Hope (right)

second successive season. Also able to play at right back, his aerial domination saw him get numerous goal assists from corners and throw-ins, and he also chipped in with a few goals himself.

Nottingham F (Free from Darlington juniors on 23/8/90)
Scunthorpe U (£50,000 on 5/7/93) FL 189+8/11 FLC 9+1 FAC 14/1 Others 13/2

HOPE Richard Paul
Born: Middlesbrough, 22 June 1978
Height: 6'2" Weight: 12.6

The son of the former Darlington goalkeeper, John, Richard played the majority of his first full season at Feethams in 1997-98 in the centre of defence, before ending at left back. Strong in the air, he scored his first ever goal in the last home game of the campaign with a rasping left-footed free kick from 25 yards out.

Blackburn Rov (From trainee on 9/8/95)
Darlington (Free on 17/1/97) FL 54+1/1 FLC 2 FAC 1 Others 0+1

HOPKIN David
Born: Greenock, 21 August 1970
Height: 5'9" Weight: 11.0
International Honours: S: 4; B-1

When Leeds' manager, George Graham was looking for a midfielder who could win the ball, pass it, do his share of tackling, and score some goals, the choice was obviously limited. However, it was little wonder, that David, arguably the best midfield player in the Nationwide League, became hot property once 1996-97 was over, and Graham had little hesitation in making him his record signing. He also made him club captain. Expected to be the mainstay of the new side, the Scotsman began last season well, though playing in a more central and deeper role than he had at Crystal Palace, scoring the winner at Blackburn in the 4-3 thriller in September on his way to establishing himself. In-and-out of the side in the New Year though, he suffered a bad eye injury in a reserve fixture with Birmingham in March, an injury that caused

him to miss more games. Even so, the flame-haired midfielder showed himself to be a fine all rounder, who combines an unwilting resilience with style and individuality. Despite being a member of Craig Brown's Scotland squad during the campaign, having played twice at full and "B" levels, he was not included among the final 22 who were booked for France '98.

Morton (Signed from Port Glasgow BC on 7/7/89) SL 33+15/4 SLC 2/2 SC 2/1
Chelsea (£300,000 on 25/9/92) PL 21+19/1 FLC 0+1 FAC 3+2
Crystal Palace (£850,000 on 29/7/95) FL 79+4/21 FLC 6/6 FAC 3 Others 4/2
Leeds U (£3,250,000 on 23/7/97) PL 22+3/1 FLC 4 FAC 1

HOPPER Anthony (Tony)
Born: Carlisle, 31 May 1976
Height: 5'11" Weight: 11.13
Club Honours: AMC '97

Tony was another member of the Carlisle squad to be sidelined through injury in 1997-98 and he did not make his debut until

December. Although more comfortable in midfield, most of his appearances were at full back and, though he sometimes found the going difficult, his positive attitude to the game was a continuing source of strength.
Carlisle U (From trainee on 18/7/94) FL 33+17/1 FAC 2+1/1 Others 4+2

HORLOCK Kevin
Born: Bexley, 1 November 1972
Height: 6'0" Weight: 12.0
Club Honours: Div 2 '96
International Honours: NI: 12; B-2
Following on from 1996-97 as an ever present for the first 22 Manchester City league and cup games last season, and having established himself in the Northern Ireland side, Kevin's excellent play was rewarded with the club captaincy at West Bromwich in December. However, fate struck, as within the first minute he received a bad knee injury which put him out of action for four months. Came back in April at Wolverhampton and had an excellent game that included scoring the second goal in a 2-2 draw with a superb free kick from 30 yards out and, despite picking up another injury at Sunderland which forced him to miss the Switzerland international, he was back for City's final two matches. Is an all-action midfielder who plays out of the left-back position, travelling far and wide.
West Ham U (From trainee on 1/7/91)
Swindon T (Free on 27/8/92) F/PL 151+12/22 FLC 15+2/1 FAC 12/3 Others 5+2
Manchester C (£1,250,000 on 31/1/97) FL 43/9 FLC 2/1

Barry Horne

HORNE Barry
Born: St Asaph, 18 May 1962
Height: 5'10" Weight: 12.2
Club Honours: WC '86; FAC '95; CS '95
International Honours: W: 59

Surplus to requirements at Birmingham, Barry, the PFA Chairman, was Huddersfield's first signing after the new management team took the reins and remained in the side from October, when he joined, until a first-time career pulled hamstring injury robbed him of first team duty for seven games. An industrious playmaker, and an instrumental figure in Town's midfield, covering every blade of grass and constantly making important tackles, his was the name that was recited repeatedly by the Kilner Bank faithful.*
Wrexham (Free from Rhyl on 26/6/84) FL 136/17 FLC 10/1 FAC 7/2 Others 15/3
Portsmouth (£60,000 on 17/7/87) FL 66+4/7 FLC 3 FAC 6
Southampton (£700,000 on 22/3/89) FL 111+1/6 FLC 15+2/3 FAC 15/3 Others 7/1
Everton (£675,000 on 1/7/92) PL 118+5/3 FLC 12+1 FAC 11+1 Others 3
Birmingham C (£250,000 on 10/6/96) FL 33 FLC 3 FAC 3
Huddersfield T (Free on 13/10/97) FL 29+1 FAC 2

HOTTE Mark Stephen
Born: Bradford, 27 September 1978
Height: 5'11" Weight: 11.1
Another young Oldham player on the first rung of the Football League ladder as a first-year professional in 1997-98, Mark could be one to watch out for this coming season. A centre half whose main asset is his speed, especially when challenging and coming out with the ball, he made his first team debut at Bristol Rovers as a sub, playing almost all of the second half. Also has very quick feet.
Oldham Ath (From trainee on 1/7/97) FL 0+1

HOUGHTON Raymond (Ray) James
Born: Glasgow, 9 January 1962
Height: 5'7" Weight: 10.10
Club Honours: FLC '86, '94; Div 1 '88, '90; CS '88; FAC '89, '92
International Honours: Ei: 73
An experienced Republic of Ireland international, he joined Reading from Crystal Palace on a free transfer as player/coach during the 1997 close season, and his influence soon became apparent as his penetrating passes from midfield started to unlock even the most determined of defences. His impact lessened as 1997-98 wore on, however, and he contributed just one goal, a neat strike in the 3-0 success over Manchester City. Featuring just once after the arrival of Tommy Burns, and with the Scot bringing in his own coaching staff and seven new players, Ray was told that he could leave the club during the summer.
West Ham U (From juniors on 5/7/79) FL 0+1
Fulham (Free on 7/7/82) FL 129/16 FLC 12/2 FAC 4/3
Oxford U (£147,000 on 13/9/85) FL 83/10 FLC 13/3 FAC 3 Others 6/1
Liverpool (£825,000 on 19/10/87) FL 147+6/28 FLC 14/3 FAC 26+1/4 Others 8/3
Aston Villa (£900,000 on 28/7/92) PL 83+12/6 FLC 11+2/2 FAC 7/2 Others 4+2/1
Crystal Palace (£300,000 on 23/3/95) P/FL 69+3/7 FLC 6 FAC 4 Others 4/1
Reading (Free on 21/7/97) FL 20+5/1 FLC 5+1 FAC 2+2

HOUGHTON Scott Aaron
Born: Hitchin, 22 October 1971
Height: 5'7" Weight: 12.4
Club Honours: FAYC '90
International Honours: E: Yth; Sch
1997-98 was an in-and-out season for Peterborough's Scott, with injury keeping him out for much of the time, but when he came back he showed what a busy wide player he could be, using his speed to keep defenders on the back foot and having the ability to go round to cross, or to cut inside and shoot. Able to play on either the left or right-hand sides of the pitch, he certainly impressed his fellow professionals who voted him into the PFA award-winning third division side.
Tottenham H (From trainee on 24/8/90) FL 0+10/2 FLC 0+2 Others 0+2
Ipswich T (Loaned on 26/3/91) FL 7+1/1
Gillingham (Loaned on 17/12/92) FL 3
Charlton Ath (Loaned on 26/2/93) FL 6
Luton T (Free on 10/8/93) FL 7+9/1 FLC 2+1 FAC 0+1 Others 2
Walsall (£20,000 on 2/9/94) FL 76+2/14 FLC 0+1/1 FAC 10/3 Others 4
Peterborough U (£60,000 + on 12/7/96) FL 50+12/12 FLC 5+2 FAC 7/1 Others 1+1/1

HOULT Russell
Born: Leicester, 22 November 1972
Height: 6'3" Weight: 14.9
Called upon just three times by Derby in 1997-98, this tall and agile goalkeeper spent virtually the whole of the season on the bench as back-up to Mart Poom, but if he can add consistency to his undoubted ability in the air he will continue to press for a return to the first team. Certainly, Russell never let the side down in his two Premiership games played, both 1-0 defeats at Coventry and at home to Chelsea, and made some excellent saves, especially in the first match, and obviously expects to press Poom for a place this coming term.
Leicester C (From trainee on 28/3/91) FL 10 FLC 3 Others 1
Lincoln C (Loaned on 27/8/91) FL 2 FLC 1
Bolton W (Loaned on 3/11/93) FL 3+1 Others 1
Lincoln C (Loaned on 12/8/94) FL 15 Others 1
Derby Co (£300,000 on 17/2/95) F/PL 88+2 FLC 5 FAC 4

HOUSHAM Steven (Steve) James
Born: Gainsborough, 24 February 1976
Height: 5'10" Weight: 12.7
1997-98 was expected to be the season when Steve established himself as a regular in the Scunthorpe side, but was again frustrated by injuries. An energetic, tough-tackling player, who likes to get forward from midfield or full back, he was a regular part of the squad for the first half of the campaign with a number of bigger clubs rumoured to be interested in him. However, switched to left-wing back for the FA Cup tie at Crystal Palace and proving a revelation in that role, a serious knee ligament injury saw his campaign end prematurely in mid-February.
Scunthorpe U (From trainee on 23/12/93) FL 73+17/4 FLC 3+1 FAC 5+1 Others 5+1/2

HOWARD Jonathan (Jon)
Born: Sheffield, 7 October 1971
Height: 5'11" Weight: 12.6

Having suffered a series of niggling injuries during the first months of last season, Jon had to wait until January before being fully able to remind Chesterfield fans of the kind of form that brought him to the fore during the 1996-97 FA Cup run. On his day, his pacy, persistent play across the forward line continued to cause plenty of problems for opponents and he was always likely to turn up with vital goals.

Rotherham U (From trainee on 10/7/90) FL 25+11/5 FLC 0+1 FAC 4/2 Others 3+1 (Free to Buxton on 11/11/94)
Chesterfield (Free on 9/12/94) FL 73+39/18 FLC 5 FAC 10+1/2 Others 5+3/2

HOWARD Michael Anthony
Born: Birkenhead, 2 December 1978
Height: 5'6" Weight: 10.4

After developing through Tranmere Rovers' junior ranks as a YTS to sign professional forms during the 1997 close season, Michael was unable to advance any further in 1997-98 and went on trial at Swansea, where he impressed. Having accepted a contract last February, the young defender quickly made his league debut as a sub at Notts County, before appearing as a left-wing back four days later at the Vetch against Exeter.

Tranmere Rov (From trainee on 9/7/97)
Swansea C (Free on 6/2/98) FL 2+1

HOWARD Steven (Steve) John
Born: Durham, 10 May 1976
Height: 6'2" Weight: 14.6

It was a mixed season for Hartlepool's powerful utility player. For most of 1997-98, Steve was played as an out-and-out centre forward, and there were signs that his awkward style of play could make him a real success in this position, but other times he was criticised for not being a regular goalscorer. However, there was no doubting that he had the right attitude, and few will forget the goal he scored with a tremendous 35-yard volley at Tranmere in the Coca Cola Cup.

Hartlepool U (Free from Tow Law on 8/8/95) FL 92+22/21 FLC 6/1 FAC 3 Others 5/2

HOWARTH Lee
Born: Bolton, 3 January 1968
Height: 6'2" Weight: 13.8

As captain and leader of Barnet, Lee never let anyone down in his role at centre half in 1997-98, and, perhaps the outstanding performer at Underhill last season, he will be sorely missed if he decides not to renew his contract in the summer. Is a no-nonsense, no-frills performer who gets on with the job in hand.*

Peterborough U (Free from Chorley on 16/8/91) FL 56+6 FLC 8 FAC 3 Others 3+2/1
Mansfield T (£15,000 on 5/8/94) FL 56+1/2 FLC 7 FAC 4 Others 5
Barnet (Signed on 26/1/96) FL 101+1/5 FLC 8 FAC 4 Others 4

HOWARTH Neil
Born: Farnworth, 15 November 1971
Height: 6'2" Weight: 12.12
Club Honours: GMVC '95, '97; FAT '96
International Honours: E: SP-2

Having proved to be a stalwart of the Macclesfield defence as the team captain for the past three seasons, due to new signings in 1997-98, Town's first experience of the Football League, he played in an unfamiliar role at left back, rather than his more comfortable position as a central defender. There is more to his game than out-and-out defending and, with a penchant to get forward and have a pop at goal, he scored a screamer from 35 yards against Scarborough in early February.

Burnley (From trainee on 2/7/90) FL 0+1
Macclesfield T (Free on 3/9/93) FL 38+3/3 FLC 2 FAC 1 Others 1

HOWE Edward (Eddie) John Frank
Born: Amersham, 29 November 1977
Height: 5'10" Weight: 11.10
International Honours: E: U21-2

Eddie established himself in the Bournemouth first team during 1997-98, earning himself the Player of the Year award, and proving to be a strong athletic player who can either play in midfield or defence, despite playing the majority of the season as a centre back, which looks to be his preferred role. Always committed, being strong in the air and an adept tackler who looks comfortable when carrying the ball forward, he was rewarded for his efforts by gaining a place in the England U21 squad to play in the Toulon tournament in France.

Bournemouth (From trainee on 4/7/96) FL 42+16/1 FLC 1+1 FAC 3 Others 3+2

HOWE Stephen Robert (Bobby)
Born: Annitsford, 6 November 1973
Height: 5'7" Weight 10.4
International Honours: E: Yth

After going stale in Nottingham Forest's reserves, Bobby joined Swindon last January for £30,000, payable in three instalments, and based on appearances. Ideally suited to a striking role, or tucking in just behind the front two, his Town career did not start well and he has yet to show his true form for the County Ground outfit. Despite having obvious skill and ability, he failed to make any real impression before being dropped prior to the home game against Portsmouth in March. An excellent passer of the ball, he is sure to play his way back.

Nottingham F (From trainee on 5/12/90) P/FL 6+8/2 FLC 2 Others 1+1
Ipswich T (Loaned on 17/1/97) FL 2+1 FLC 1
Swindon T (£30,000 on 16/1/98) FL 9+1

HOWELLS David
Born: Guildford, 15 December 1967
Height: 5'11" Weight: 12.4
Club Honours: FAC '91
International Honours: E: Yth

A hard-working midfield anchor man who is experienced playing just in front of the back four, or as a provider to strikers at Tottenham, 1997-98 was a season dogged

by injury, and prevented David from putting together a run of performances in which to demonstrate his great strength and stamina, along with his experience and tremendous organisational skills. Missing much of the campaign from November onwards, Spurs missed his ability to hold together the midfield, as demonstrated in the 3-2 home victory over Aston Villa in August. With competition for midfield places hotting up, rumours of a free transfer during the close season were compounded by David admitting that he would be looking elsewhere for first team football. A loyal servant of the club, he will be missed by everyone at White Hart Lane, and with him still having a tremendous amount to offer at Premiership level, he is sure to generate interest. *Stop Press:* Signed for Southampton on 2 July.

Tottenham H (From apprentice on 28/1/85) F/PL 238+39/22 FLC 26+5/4 FAC 18+4/1 Others 7

HOWEY Lee Matthew
Born: Sunderland, 1 April 1969
Height: 6'2" Weight: 13.9
Club Honours: Div 1 '96

Signed from Sunderland immediately prior to the start of 1997-98, Lee scored in his first game for Burnley, a Coca Cola Cup tie at Lincoln, but thereafter played mainly as a central defender. Effective in the early season, alongside the dominant Steve Blatherwick, he was less effective later on, when Gerry Harrison and Neil Moore bore the brunt of defensive duties, and faded out of the picture following an enforced injury absence just after Christmas.

Ipswich T (From trainee on 2/10/86 - Free to Blyth Spartans in March 1988)
Sunderland (Free from Bishop Auckland on 25/3/93) P/FL 39+30/8 FLC 1+4/2 FAC 2+4/1 Others 0+1
Burnley (£200,000 on 11/8/97) FL 21+2 FLC 3/1 FAC 2 Others 0+1

Lee Howey

HOWEY Stephen (Steve) Norman
Born: Sunderland, 26 October 1971
Height: 6'2" Weight: 11.12
Club Honours: Div 1 '93
International Honours: E: 4

Steve is the longest-serving player in Newcastle's squad, having started his career as a striker before developing into an international centre back. His natural pace and his ability to read the game mean that he is rarely exposed, and his coolness on the ball enables him to act as a launch pad for attacks, either by moving forward himself with the ball, or by using his fine passing ability. He returned to fitness during the summer of 1997, having missed most of the previous season with serious calf injuries, and came off the bench a number of times before making his first start of the campaign against Spurs in October, a year and four days since he last started a first team game. However, injuries continued to trouble him and he suffered an achilles tendon problem against Leicester in November. Returning to the side for the FA Cup tie at Stevenage, he was subsequently sidelined with a hamstring injury after only another nine appearances, thus missing the FA Cup semi final, although he recovered in time to play in the final.

Newcastle U (From trainee on 11/12/89) F/PL 146+22/6 FLC 14+2/1 FAC 16+2 Others 10+2

HOWIE Scott
Born: Glasgow, 4 January 1972
Height: 6'2" Weight: 13.7
Club Honours: S Div 2 '93
International Honours: S: U21-5

Scott became the fifth goalkeeper to be used by Reading in 1997-98, when he signed from Motherwell on transfer deadline day and played in the final seven games of Reading's stay in division one. Although letting in a couple of long-range goals in the 3-1 defeat at Wolves, apart from those lapses he showed himself to be a brave and agile 'keeper, who may well become first choice in 1998-99 under fellow Scot, Tommy Burns.

Clyde (Signed from Ferguslie U on 7/1/92) SL 55 SLC 3 SC 4 Others 1
Norwich C (£300,000 on 12/8/93) PL 1+1
Motherwell (£300,000 on 13/10/94) SL 69 SLC 4 SC 5 Others 1
Reading (£30,000 on 26/3/98) FL 7

HOYLAND Jamie William
Born: Sheffield, 23 January 1966
Height: 6'0" Weight: 14.0
International Honours: E: Yth

Although only an occasional player for Burnley in 1997-98, Jamie was still capable of hard-working and effective displays, either in central defence or midfield, but, when temporarily out of favour at Turf Moor, he had a loan spell with Carlisle in mid-November. Disappointingly, for the Cumbrians, a projected permanent move never materialised and he returned to Burnley, where he later regained a first team berth and played for the Clarets at Brunton Park at the end of February.*

Manchester C (From apprentice on 12/11/83) FL 2 FLC 0+1/1
Bury (Free on 11/7/86) FL 169+3/35 FLC 14+1/5 FAC 6 Others 12/2
Sheffield U (£250,000 on 4/7/90) F/PL 72+17/6 FLC 5+3/1 FAC 8+2/1 Others 5/1

Bristol C (Loaned on 4/3/94) FL 6
Burnley (£130,000 on 14/10/94) FL 77+10/4 FLC 5 FAC 7 Others 5+1
Carlisle U (Loaned on 20/11/97) FL 5

HREIDARSSON Hermann
Born: Iceland, 11 July 1974
Height: 6'0" Weight: 13.1
International Honours: Iceland: 10

The tall, blond, left-footed Icelandic international central defender signed for Crystal Palace immediately prior to the start of 1997-98, having had a trial the previous season, and quickly became a great crowd favourite, especially after his performance in containing Arsenal's Dennis Bergkamp at Selhurst Park. A great enthusiast, he can be seen smiling throughout the hardest of games, and there were many of these for Palace during a tough campaign that ended with relegation from Premiership. Not content to merely defend, he is adept at bringing the ball out of defence and looking to set up an attack. Excellent in the air, he began on the bench before coming into the side as a starter against Wimbledon, and was virtually a regular from thereon, apart from a handful of games towards the end of the season. Continued to add to his international caps.

Crystal Palace (Signed from IBV on 9/8/97) PL 26+4/2 FLC 2 FAC 4

HRISTOV Georgi
Born: Macedonia, 30 January 1976
Height: 5'10" Weight: 11.5
International Honours: Macedonia: 22

Brought in by Barnsley from Partizan Belgrade during the 1997 close season, in preparation for their first-ever assault on the Premiership, or old first division, Georgi showed in flashes why Danny Wilson had paid a club record fee for him. But, although able to beat people on the ground, being good in the air and making scoring sometimes look easy, he found the pace and intensity of the Premier League hard going, and it took him a long time to adjust to it. He therefore struggled to maintain a regular starting place in the team, despite being a regular scorer in the Mecedonian team, but should be a cut above first division defences in 1998-99.

Barnsley (£1,500,000 from Partizan Belgrade on 23/7/97) PL 11+12/4 FLC 1+2/1 FAC 1+1

HUCKERBY Darren Carl
Born: Nottingham, 23 April 1976
Height: 5'10" Weight: 11.12
International Honours: E: B-1; U21-4

Darren made a massive impact in 1997-98, his first full season with Coventry in the Premiership, and was rewarded by his nomination as PFA Young Player of the Year, and his selection for England "B" against Chile in February, when he set up Emile Heskey's goal. His speed and close control are his strength and seems to ghost past players and, despite being out for seven weeks in the autumn, he came back fitter and faster. There is no doubting that his game improved with coaching last season and he scored some classic goals, including

BBC's December Goal of the Month, his solo effort against Manchester United winning it. His goal at Anfield was runner up in January's competition, and his 30-yard chip at Southampton was third in February. However, the highlight of his season was the hat trick at Leeds, when he destroyed the home defence with his speed and strength, one of the goals coming third in the BBC's April Goal of the Month competition. Although his tendency to be caught offside seems to have been cured, he still needs to look up and pick out better-placed colleagues at times. Signed a new four-year contract in March.

Lincoln C From trainee on 14/7/93) FL 20+8/5 FLC 2 Others 1/2
Newcastle U (£400,000 on 10/11/95) PL 0+1 FAC 0+1
Millwall (Loaned on 6/9/96) FL 6/3
Coventry C (£1,000,000 on 23/11/96) PL 53+6/19 FLC 0+1 FAC 9/3

HUDSON Daniel (Danny) Robert
Born: Doncaster, 25 June 1979
Height: 5'9" Weight: 10.3

A young Rotherham midfielder who made big strides in 1997-98 towards carving himself out a good career, and showing that he had the ability to run all day, Danny scored his first ever senior goal in the resounding 6-0 FA Cup win against King's Lynn. Was rewarded with a contract, which could well see him become a force to be reckoned with this coming season.

Rotherham U (From trainee on 25/6/97) FL 6+4 FAC 0+2/1 Others 0+1

HUGHES Aaron William
Born: Magherafelt, 8 November 1979
Height: 6'0" Weight: 11.2
International Honours: NI: 3; B-2; Yth

Aaron is an Irish-born defender who has progressed through Newcastle's junior sides, having joined the club at 15 years of age. Given his initial taste of first team football in the pre-1997-98 season Irish International Tournament, and performing well enough to establish himself in the senior squad, he had a testing introduction to competitive football, in that he made his debut as a substitute in the Champions League match against Barcelona in the Nou Camp. His second appearance was again as substitute, again in the Champions League, this time at home to Dynamo Kiev, while his third was as a substitute in the FA Cup tie at Everton. Although primarily a central defender, he has demonstrated his flexibility by also playing at full back, and by acting as an effective man marker against Steve McManaman in the Coca Cola Cup game against Liverpool. Clearly a young man with a bright future, he has already broken into the Northern Ireland team, via the "B" side, playing against Slovakia, Switzerland, and Spain in the end of season games.

Newcastle U (From trainee on 11/3/97) PL 4 FLC 1 FAC 0+1 Others 0+2

HUGHES Andrew John
Born: Manchester, 2 January 1978
Height: 5'11" Weight: 12.1
Club Honours: Div 3 '98

Mainly a peripheral player at Oldham in 1997-98, playing 13 times, ten of them as sub, Andrew departed for Notts County, firstly on loan and then permanently on transfer deadline day, after impressing the management team at the County Ground. A pacy, hard-working central midfielder with plenty of stamina, he quickly endeared himself to the fans with his surging runs into the danger areas, scoring twice. With County achieving promotion, his 15 league games were enough for him to pick up a third division championship medal.

Oldham Ath (From trainee on 20/1/96) FL 18+15/1 FLC 1+1 FAC 3+1 Others 1+2
Notts Co (£150,000 on 29/1/98) FL 12+3/2

HUGHES Bryan

Born: Liverpool, 19 June 1976
Height: 5'10" Weight: 11.2
Club Honours: WC '95

Having shown Birmingham fans what he was capable of in the latter stages of 1996-97, the talented youngster blossomed in 1997-98, his first full season at the club, and it was no surprise when he was voted Young Player of the Year. Apart from possessing an excellent first touch, close control, and good passing skills, he can also score goals, something that became more than apparent when he cracked in a couple inside the first nine minutes at Stoke that sent City on their way to a memorable 7-0 win in January, followed a couple of weeks later by another brace that saw off Stockport 2-1 in the FA Cup. Used in central midfield or wide on the left, he will undoubtedly figure in the club's plans for 1998-99.

Wrexham (From trainee on 7/7/94) FL 71+23/12 FLC 2 FAC 13+3/7 Others 14+1/3
Birmingham C (£750,000 + on 12/3/97) FL 44+7/5 FLC 4/1 FAC 3/2

HUGHES Ceri Morgan

Born: Pontypridd, 26 February 1971
Height: 5'10" Weight: 12.7
International Honours: W: 8; B-2; Yth

Transferred from Luton to Wimbledon during the 1997 summer break, this tenacious of midfielders made his Premiership debut when coming off the bench in the opening game of 1997-98, at home to Liverpool, and was involved in the squad until the end of January in one form or another, before being ruled out for ten games due to a hamstring strain. That undoubtedly took the gloss off his season and, although coming back for the final seven games, he only made four of them. Comfortable on the ball and not lacking in pace, and capable of playing on either flank, the Welsh international should figure strongly in Joe Kinnear's plans for 1998-99. His only goal for the club to date, was a cracker in a 4-1 home win against Barnsley.

Luton T (From trainee on 1/7/89) FL 157+18/17 FLC 13/1 FAC 11/2 Others 6
Wimbledon (£400,000+ on 4/7/97) PL 13+4/1 FLC 2 FAC 2

HUGHES Robert David

Born: Wrexham, 1 February 1978
Height: 6'4" Weight: 13.6
International Honours: W: B-1; U21-9; Yth

After a highly encouraging end to 1996-97 at Aston Villa, David faced an often frustrating season in 1997-98. Unfortunate niggling injuries, including an ankle problem, and a thigh strain, hampered his progress, and after spending time on the subs' bench without a game, the tall, Welsh U21 central defender arrived at Carlisle on loan in March to make his Brunton Park debut in the defeat at the hands of Bournemouth. He did not last the full game and never re-appeared on first team duty, though he was selected as a substitute on three more occasions before going back to Villa Park. Played for the Welsh "B" side that met its Scottish counterparts in March.

Aston Villa (From trainee on 5/7/96) PL 4+3
Carlisle U (Loaned on 26/3/98) FL 1

HUGHES David Robert

Born: St Albans, 30 December 1972
Height: 5'10" Weight: 11.8
International Honours: W: U21-1. E: Sch

Unfortunately, a long-term injury meant just 15 appearances for the Southampton midfielder last season, eight of them coming from the bench, but he remained up beat and confident, despite his career being continually interrupted by injury and having yet to fulfil his undoubted potential. A hard-working midfielder who tackles back strongly, and who passes and moves well, showing excellent vision, David will be hoping for an injury-free run in 1998-99.

Southampton (From juniors on 2/7/91) PL 15+30/3 FLC 3+1 FAC 1+5/1

HUGHES Ian

Born: Bangor, 2 August 1974
Height: 5'10" Weight: 12.8
Club Honours: Div 2 '97
International Honours: W: U21-12; Yth

Having come through the ranks at Bury, and been a professional for six years, Ian struggled to gain a regular place in 1997-98, as in 1996-97, until an early season injury to Dean West gave him his chance, which he grasped with both hands, his height and strength being his main asset. He lost his place early in November, when a dismissal led to a five-match ban and, on coming back into contention, he was transferred to Blackpool, with Tony Ellis and cash going in the opposite direction. Missing just four games, and used both in defence and midfield, he proved to be an excellent buy and a player who gives everything and more.

Bury (From trainee on 19/11/91) FL 137+23/1 FLC 13+3 FAC 6+2 Others 14+4/1
Blackpool (£200,000 on 12/12/97) FL 20+1 Others 3

HUGHES Lee

Born: Birmingham, 22 May 1976
Height: 5'10" Weight: 11.6
International Honours: E: SP-4

An England semi-pro international, Lee was signed by West Bromwich Albion shortly after he had received the "Predator Award" at the non-league presentations evening, following his excellent scoring record, 34 goals in 30 outings, in the Vauxhall

Conference with Kidderminster Harriers during the 1996-97 campaign. A strong, purposeful player with an eye for goal, who had supported Albion since a child, he started on the bench in 1997-98, making his debut on the first day of the season, before opening his scoring account with two goals in a 3-2 win at Crewe in the second fixture, and becoming a permanent member of the Baggies' attack who finished the campaign as joint-top scorer on 14 with Andy Hunt.

West Bromwich A (£250,000+ from Kidderminster Hrs on 19/5/97) FL 18+19/14 FLC 0+2 FAC 2

HUGHES Leslie Mark

Born: Wrexham, 1 November 1963
Height: 5'11" Weight: 13.0
Club Honours: FAC '85, '90, '94, '97; ECWC '91, '98; ESC '91; FLC '92, '98; PL '93, '94; CS '93, '94
International Honours: W: 66; U21-5; Yth; Sch

This superb Chelsea centre forward had a memorable 1996-97 season, becoming the first 20th century player to win four FA Cup Winners' medals and finishing third in the Football Writers' Player of the Year poll, behind Gianfranco Zola and Juninho. His worth to Chelsea, however, was recognised by the Blues' supporters who voted him as Chelsea's Player of the Year, ahead of cult figures, Zola and Frank Leboeuf. "Sparky" began last season in great form – scoring against his old club Manchester United in the Charity Shield at Wembley, followed by a bullet-like header against Southampton, and a magnificent volley at Crystal Palace. He followed up by scoring against United again – his first goal at Old Trafford since his move to Chelsea. Rotating the striking positions, along with Gianluca Vialli and Tore Andre Flo, Mark then received the award that rounded off an incredible year – an MBE in the New Year's Honours List for his services to football. Following that, he dug Chelsea out of a hole in two cup semi finals; in the Coca Cola first leg at Highbury, Arsenal were cruising at 2-0 until he came off the bench on the hour mark and headed home to give the Blues a life-line. The second leg was Vialli's first match in charge, and Chelsea desperately needed an early goal to level the scores. Mark obliged with a firm drive from the edge of the box to set the team on the road to Wembley and Coca Cola Cup glory. If anything, his rescue act in the European Cup Winners' Cup semi was even more dramatic. The second leg against Vicenza at the Bridge was level at 2-2 on aggregate, but the Italians had a precious away goal – enter Mark Hughes. With just 20 minutes left he came off the bench and lashed home a trademark volley with his left foot to win the tie and put Chelsea into the final in Stockholm. "Hughsie" then scored twice against his favourite opposition, Liverpool – the second an acrobatic overhead bicycle kick. These exploits may well have been his "last hurrah" in the blue shirt of Chelsea as, since the triumph over Stuttgart, the club have signed continental strikers, Pierluigi Casiraghi and Brian Laudrup. With Mark's 35th birthday rapidly

approaching, whatever happens, his contribution to Chelsea's cause over the past three years has been immeasurable. *Stop Press:* Signed by Southampton for £500,000 on 10 July, the Welsh international moved in the knowledge that he had more chance of playing regular first team football at the Dell than at Stamford Bridge.

Manchester U (From apprentice on 5/11/80) FL 85+4/37 FLC 5+1/4 FAC 10/4 Others 14+2/2 (£2,500,000 to Barcelona on 1/7/86)
Manchester U (£1,500,000 on 20/7/88) F/PL 251+5/82 FLC 32/12 FAC 34+1/13 Others 27+1/8
Chelsea (£1,500,000 on 6/7/95) PL 88+7/25 FLC 7+3/3 FAC 13+1/9 Others 1+3/2

HUGHES Michael Eamonn
Born: Larne, 2 August 1971
Height: 5'7" Weight: 10.13
International Honours: NI: 42; U23-2; U21-1; Yth; Sch

Michael started at West Ham in 1997-98, being involved in six of the opening eight games, before being transferred across London to Wimbledon in a surprise move. He ended the campaign as the supporters' Player of the Year, having been instrumental in the team's survival and proving to be a powerful and effective winger with a great left foot, and a super buy for Joe Kinnear, the Dons' manager. With his killer passes and awareness, this Northern Ireland international was the most pleasing aspect of a very difficult campaign and the bonus was that he could score vital goals, two cracking efforts against Wrexham in the FA Cup replay seeing the club into the fourth round, while there were equalisers at Chelsea and Sheffield Wednesday, and a winner in the Leicester home game. Looks to be a key player in Dons' plans for 1998-99.

Manchester C (From trainee on 17/8/88) FL 25+1/1 FLC 5 FAC 1 Others 1 (£450,000 to RS Strasbourg in 1992 close season)
West Ham U (Loaned on 29/11/94) PL 15+2/2 FAC 2
West Ham U (Loaned on 2/10/95) PL 28 FLC 2 FAC 3/1
West Ham U (Free on 12/8/96) PL 33+5/3 FLC 5 FAC 2
Wimbledon (£800,000+ on 25/9/97) PL 29/4 FAC 4/2

HUGHES John Paul
Born: Hammersmith, 19 April 1976
Height: 6'0" Weight: 12.6
International Honours: E: Sch

The 1997-98 season was particularly frustrating for this very promising, locally-born Chelsea midfielder, who had created such a great impression in his debut season, 12 months earlier. Up until then, his career had been blighted by a series of injuries and, sadly, the injury jinx returned to haunt him, with a niggling ankle problem keeping him sidelined for the majority of the campaign. In managing just six starts, everybody at the Bridge will be hoping that his luck finally changes for the better in 1998-99.

Chelsea (From trainee on 11/7/94) PL 13+8/2 FAC 2 Others 1

HUGHES Stephen (Steve) John
Born: Reading, 18 September 1976
Height: 6'0" Weight: 12.12

Michael Hughes

Club Honours: FAYC '94; PL '98
International Honours: E: U21-8; Yth; Sch

A much vaunted young left-sided Arsenal midfielder who, despite limited opportunities in 1997-98, being in direct competition with the likes of Manu Petit and Marc Overmars, did well enough to be rewarded with a five-year contract. A youngster with a great left foot, who runs at defenders to put them under pressure, or is able to go wide or through the middle, and can produce superb crosses and great long passes, having come through the club's junior ranks he certainly does not look out of place among all the international stars now assembled at Highbury. His 17 Premiership appearances were good value for his championship medal, while his two goals both came in the same match, at Highbury against Chelsea, and were enough to secure a 2-0 victory over their London rivals, who were still very much in the title race at that particular time. Strangely, his only other goal of the campaign came in the Coca Cola Cup against – you've guessed it – Chelsea. Continued to add to his England U21 appearances during the campaign and is definitely one to watch our for, hopefully with the Gunners.

Arsenal (From trainee on 15/7/95) PL 17+16/3 FLC 3+3/1 FAC 5+3/1

HULBERT Robin James
Born: Plymouth, 14 March 1980
Height: 5'9" Weight: 10.5
International Honours: E: Yth; Sch

While still a second-year trainee, the classy Swindon midfielder was given a three-and-a-half year professional contract last September and was a regular member of the first team squad, despite making only one substitute appearance at Wolves in October. Joined Newcastle United on loan in February until the end of the season to gain some valuable experience, and was named in the provisional England squad of 30 players for the UEFA European Championships at U18 level to be held in Cyprus during the summer.

Swindon T (From trainee on 25/9/97) FLC 0+2

HUMES Anthony (Tony)
Born: Blyth, 19 March 1966
Height: 5'11" Weight: 12.0

Tony is the type of player any manager would be delighted to have on his staff. Like his co-Wrexham central defender, Brian Carey, he will always give you 100 per-cent effort with strong and aggressive, but fair, play, and is one of Brian Flynn's best signings. Also able to play in midfield as a ball winner, injuries seem to be part and parcel of his career, but, although he failed to start 1997-98, he eventually got into the side before being put out of action yet again and coming back strongly for the run in.

Ipswich T (From apprentice on 26/5/83) FL 107+13/10 FLC 6 FAC 4/1 Others 10/1
Wrexham (£40,000 on 27/3/92) FL 181+6/8 FLC 7 FAC 19/1 Others 13

HUMPHREY John

Born: Paddington, 31 January 1961
Height: 5'10" Weight: 11.12
Club Honours: FMC '91; Div 1 '94

Though released at the end of 1996-97, the veteran full-back rejoined Brighton and Hove Albion during the summer period and was one of the more successful members of the Seagulls' suspect defence last season. Placed on the transfer list with four other senior professionals in November, as part of an economy drive, John's contract was paid off the following month and he left for Chesham United in the Ryman's Isthmian League.

Wolverhampton W (From apprentice on 14/2/79) FL 149/3 FLC 8 FAC 7
Charlton Ath (£60,000 on 22/7/85) FL 194/3 FLC 13 FAC 9 Others 15/1
Crystal Palace (£400,000 on 16/8/90) F/PL 153+7/2 FLC 23+2 FAC 8+1 Others 8+1
Reading (Loaned on 9/12/93) FL 8 Others 1
Charlton Ath (Free on 13/7/95) FL 28 FLC 6 FAC 2
Gillingham (Free on 16/8/96) FL 9 FLC 3 Others 1
Brighton & Hove A (Free on 14/1/97) FL 22 FLC 2

HUMPHREYS Richard (Richie) John

Born: Sheffield, 30 November 1977
Height: 5'11" Weight: 14.6
International Honours: E: U21-3

Richie had a disappointing season at Sheffield Wednesday in 1997-98, his versatility under the previous manager, David Pleat, not doing him any favours in his efforts to impress Ron Atkinson. A natural striker, he was unable to force many opportunities up front, due to the galaxy of front men available at Hillsborough and, in just two starts and nine subs' appearances, he found himself playing in a left-wing back position, or left side of midfield, neither of which he looked at ease in. Hopefully, the new management will give him the chance to secure a front-line position this coming term.

Sheffield Wed (From trainee on 8/2/96) PL 17+24/3 FLC 1+2 FAC 3+4/2

HUNT Andrew (Andy)

Born: Thurrock, 9 June 1970
Height: 6'0" Weight: 12.0

West Bromwich Albion's leading scorer in 1997-98, despite carrying a leg injury and missing several games in February and March, Andy holds the ball up well, covers acres of ground each and every week, and is often used to being a lone raider up front. In short, he is an honest-to-goodness striker who never gives up the chase. Although starting the campaign well, scoring Albion's second in a 2-1 win against Tranmere, and following it up with another at Crewe, he was transfer listed at his own request, having become unsettled, but appeared to have had a change of heart towards the end of the season. Finished joint-top scorer on 14 with Lee Hughes. *Stop Press:* A free transfer under the Bosman ruling, Andy joined Charlton on 23 June.

Newcastle U (£150,000 from Kettering T on 29/1/91) FL 34+9/11 FLC 3/1 FAC 2/2 Others 3
West Bromwich A (£100,000 on 25/3/93) FL 201+11/76 FLC 12/4 FAC 7/2 Others 8+1/3

Andy Hunt

HUNT James Malcolm

Born: Derby, 17 December 1976
Height: 5'8" Weight: 10.3

A central midfielder with bags of energy and commitment, James was a free-transfer signing from Notts County during the 1997 close season, but initially found it hard to break into Northampton's first team. However, once he did only suspension and injury kept him out, and with pace and passing skills he looks to have a great future ahead of him.

Notts Co (From trainee on 15/7/94) FL 15+4/1 FAC 0+1 Others 2+2/1
Northampton T (Free on 7/8/97) FL 14+7 FAC 1+2 Others 6

HUNT Jonathan Richard

Born: Camden, 2 November 1971
Height: 5'10" Weight: 11.7
Club Honours: Div 2 '95; AMC '95

Signed from Birmingham in the 1997 close season as part of the deal which took Darren Wassall to St Andrews, although he started 1997-98 with a place in the first team he gradually became more of a squad player as Jim Smith made more signings. Despite being equally adept with either foot, and

having good vision, he will need to show more consistency in his play to force his way into the side this coming term, but feels confident that he can do just that. Always likely to pop up with a goal, there was only one for him during the campaign, the first in a 3-1 win over Everton at Pride Park.

Barnet (From juniors in 1989-90) FL 12+21 FLC 1 FAC 0+1 Others 6+2
Southend U (Free on 20/7/93) FL 41+8/6 FLC 1+3 FAC 1 Others 6+1
Birmingham C (£50,000 on 16/9/94) FL 67+10/18 FLC 10+5/2 FAC 3+1/1 Others 8/4
Derby Co (£500,000 on 23/5/97) PL 7+12/1 FLC 2+2

HUNTER Roy Ian

Born: Middlesbrough, 29 October 1973
Height: 5'10" Weight: 12.8

As Northampton's midfield dynamo, tenacious, aggressive and committed, Roy brought in the scouts from many Premiership clubs in 1997-98. Injured in the match at Wigan in February, it was first thought he would be back within a few weeks, but, unfortunately, it turned out to be more serious than first thought, and he missed the latter part of the campaign. A great favourite with the fans, he is both the

club's long-throw expert and the penalty taker, with a 100 per-cent record.

West Bromwich A (From trainee on 4/3/92) FL 3+6/1 Others 4+1
Northampton T (Free on 2/8/95) FL 80+18/9 FLC 6 FAC 8/2 Others 11/1

HURDLE Augustus (Gus) Athel
Born: Kensington, 14 October 1973
Height: 6'0" Weight: 11.4
International Honours: Barbados: 2

An extremely fast right back for Brentford, Gus, who is a Barbadian International, in common with many of his team mates, struggled for form in 1997-98 as the Bees fought against relegation. Despite making 23 appearances in the season, he was released from his contract by Micky Adams in January.

Fulham (From trainee on 3/7/92)
Brentford (Free on 5/10/93) FL 63+8 FLC 12 FAC 3+2 Others 5

HURST Christopher (Chris) Mark
Born: Barnsley, 3 October 1973
Height: 5'11" Weight: 11.6

The 24-year-old midfielder, having signed from Emley of Unibond League fame in the early part of last season, was thrust into action 24 hours after becoming a Huddersfield player, as a second-half substitute against Sheffield United. The former postman then made his full league debut in a 1•1 draw at Wolves, following another couple of appearances from the bench, before spending a brief spell on loan with Conference leaders, Halifax Town, in October.

Huddersfield T (£30,000 from Emley on 29/8/97) FL 1+2 FLC 0+1

HURST Paul Michael
Born: Sheffield, 25 September 1974
Height: 5'4" Weight: 9.4
Club Honours: AMC '96

Small in stature, but big in heart, Paul can play anywhere on the left side of the team, and filled in successfully both at the back and in midfield for Rotherham in 1997-98. Always a crowd favourite for his non-stop effort, he makes up for his lack of inches with his appetite for sheer hard work.

Rotherham U (From trainee on 12/8/93) FL 87+30/4 FLC 4 FAC 7/1 Others 9+1

HUTCHINGS Carl Emil
Born: Hammersmith, 24 September 1974
Height: 5'11" Weight: 11.0

A 100 per-cent Brentford utility player whose wholehearted effort and skill has made him a great favourite with the Bees fans, Carl commenced last season at centre back, switching into midfield, and then right back, before having another spell in the middle. He was eventually to play as a right-wing back, where his boundless energy would one minute see him as the furthest player forward and the next as the last man at the back, clearing his lines. He also scored five times, against Burnley, Bournemouth, Blackpool, Wrexham, and Luton, with three of the goals being converted within three minutes of the start of the match. *Stop Press:*

Announced as signing for Bristol City on 6 July, a fee of £130,000 settling the deal.

Brentford (From trainee on 12/7/93) FL 144+18/7 FLC 9+1 FAC 11+1 Others 11+3

HUTCHISON Donald (Don)
Born: Gateshead, 9 May 1971
Height: 6'1" Weight: 11.8
International Honours: S: B-1

Don was not expected to figure at Sheffield United in the early part of 1997-98, due to the shoulder injuries sustained in the play off-final of the previous season, however, he recovered to put in some strong midfield performances and was also called upon as a stand-in goalkeeper for 30 minutes, following the injury to Simon Tracey at Ipswich, only conceding a late goal when giving a stout display. After scoring his only goal of the campaign from the penalty spot in the F A Cup victory over Ipswich Town, he switched to Everton in an exchange deal which saw Jon O'Connor going in the opposite direction and, despite the stigma of being a former Liverpool player, began to endear himself to Evertonians. Possessing most of the qualities needed to become a top-class midfielder – good passing, snappy tackling, good workrate, and the ability to snatch decisive goals – he inherited the number ten shirt from Gary Speed and quickly became an integral member of the Blues' midfield.

Hartlepool U (From trainee on 20/3/90) FL 19+5/2 FLC 1+1 FAC 2 Others 1
Liverpool (£175,000 on 27/11/90) F/PL 33+12/7 FLC 7+1/2 FAC 1+2 Others 3+1/1
West Ham U (£1,500,000 on 30/8/94) PL 30+5/11 FLC 3/2 FAC 0+1
Sheffield U (£1,200,000 on 11/1/96) FL 70+8/5 FLC 3+2 FAC 5/1 Others 2+1
Everton (£1,000,000+ on 27/2/98) PL 11/1

HUTT Stephen Graham
Born: Middlesbrough, 19 February 1979
Height: 6'3" Weight: 12.0

One of Hartlepool's five first-year professionals, this tall midfielder began last season having played just 11 minutes of first team football in two substitute appearances, over two seasons. Recognised as a good all-round player, it looked like 1997-98 was going to be another year of disappointment, but late in the campaign he at last got another chance, and acquitted himself well in a four-match run.

Hartlepool U (From trainee on 8/7/97)) FL 4+1 Others 0+1

HUXFORD Richard John
Born: Scunthorpe, 25 July 1969
Height: 5'11" Weight: 12.2

A reliable and wholehearted player who can perform equally well in defence or midfield, Richard was first choice at right back for Burnley at the start of last season, before failing to settle into the wing-back role and being loaned out to Dunfermline in February. Quickly settled into the Scottish Premiership, as a regular, playing alongside Grant Brebner, on loan from Manchester United, before being released during the summer.

Barnet (Signed from Kettering T on 6/8/92) FL 33/1 FLC 2 FAC 2 Others 2+1

Millwall (Free on 16/7/93) FL 25+7 FLC 1+1/1 FAC 1 Others 3
Birmingham C (Loaned on 21/2/94) FL 5
Bradford C (£50,000 on 7/10/94) FL 55+6/2 FLC 5+1 FAC 3+1 Others 7+1
Peterborough U (Loaned on 4/10/96) FL 7
Burnley (Free on 21/1/97) FL 6+7 FLC 2+1 Others 1
Dunfermline (Loaned on 10/2/98) SL 9

HYDE Graham
Born: Doncaster, 10 November 1970
Height: 5'8" Weight: 11.11

1997-98 was another gritty, hard-working season for Sheffield Wednesday's Graham, with no little skill mixed in as well. As per usual, however, his contributions to the side went unnoticed until he was missing, although those in the game know otherwise. First and foremost, he is a midfielder with vision and excellent passing ability who knows when to release the ball and when not to, and has a good footballing brain. A consistent performer for so long, yet unlike some of lesser ability, he has never received representative honours, despite being admired by the fans at Hillsborough, who appreciate the tremendous workload he gets through on their behalf.

Sheffield Wed (From trainee on 17/5/88) F/PL 126+45/11 FLC 17+3/2 FAC 13+5/2 Others 4/1

HYDE Micah Anthony
Born: Newham, 10 November 1974
Height: 5'9" Weight: 11.5
Club Honours: Div 2 '98

Micah, a combative midfield player signed from Cambridge during the 1997 close season, settled quickly at Watford in 1997-98, missing only a handful of games, and was soon bringing out the best in his midfield partner, Richard Johnson. Sharp, tenacious, and a useful occasional scorer, his one real low point came when he failed to score a crucial penalty during the FA Cup shoot-out against Sheffield Wednesday. Was delighted to win a second division championship medal as the Hornets returned to division one after a two-year break.

Cambridge U (From trainee on 19/5/93) FL 89+18/13 FLC 3 FAC 7+2 Others 4+1
Watford (£225,000 on 21/7/97) FL 40/4 FLC 4/1 FAC 5

HYDE Paul David
Born: Hayes, 7 April 1963
Height: 6'1" Weight: 14.6
Club Honours: GMVC '93; FAT '93

Paul made the Leyton Orient number one shirt his own last season after joining the club towards the end of 1996-97, showing himself to be an excellent shot-stopper, saving two penalties, and being part of the best defensive record in the third division, until his campaign was ended by a broken leg in January at Exeter. Will be looking to regain his fitness and his first team place by this coming August.

Wycombe W (£15,000 from Hayes on 6/7/93) FL 105 FLC 10 FAC 13 Others 13
Leicester C (Free on 15/2/96)
Leyton Orient (Free on 3/2/97) FL 4
Leicester C (Free on 28/2/97)
Leyton Orient (Free on 14/3/97) FL 37 FLC 4 FAC 2 Others 1

We're a big supporter in all sorts of arenas.

At The Royal Bank of Scotland we're delighted to give our continued support to a wide variety of sporting events throughout the U.K.

The Royal Bank of Scotland

FOR MORE INFORMATION ON THE FULL RANGE OF SERVICES AVAILABLE FROM THE ROYAL BANK OF SCOTLAND PLEASE CONTACT BILL GILLINGS ON 01204 525474,

The Royal Bank of Scotland plc. Registered Office: 36 St. Andrew Square, Edinburgh EH2 2YB. Registered in Scotland No. 90312.

I

IGOE Samuel (Sammy) Gary
Born: Spelthorne, 30 September 1975
Height: 5'6" Weight: 10.0

Sammy started 1997-98 as a regular in the Portsmouth team, but a loss of form meant he was relegated to the bench, and then later in the season down to the reserves. An attacking midfielder, who is small in stature but big in heart and ability, with a good first touch and awareness of others, at that point he had been unable to reproduce his form from the previous season and 30 appearances was a poor return. However, coming back into the side for the final three games, he proved very effective and, in the 3-1 win at Bradford on the final day, set up two goals and scored himself as Pompey avoided the drop.
Portsmouth (From trainee on 15/2/94) FL 47+47/5 FLC 4+3 FAC 0+3

ILIC Sasa
Born: Melbourne, Australia, 18 July 1972
Height: 6'2" Weight: 14.0
International Honours: Macedonia: 3

Signed from St Leonards Stamcroft last October as goalkeeping cover, Sasa, who commands his area well and is very quick and agile for a big man, broke into the Charlton side in February when Andy Petterson suffered a loss of form, and Mike Salmon was injured. Big and strong, he had previously played in Yugoslavia at the top level, and had represented Macedonia, so Alan Curbishley had no qualms about bringing him into the side. Kept nine consecutive clean sheets to create a new club record, and made a penalty save in the Wembley play-off shoot-out that put the club into the Premiership.
Charlton Ath (Free from St Leonards Stamcroft on 5/10/97) FL 14 Others 3

ILLMAN Neil David
Born: Doncaster, 29 April 1975
Height: 5'7" Weight: 11.5

Released by Plymouth, due to opportunities being scarce at Home Park, Neil arrived at Exeter on a non-contract basis last December. A quick and lively forward, he proved popular with the Exeter fans for his determination and spirit, especially when chasing down defenders, and from seven starts he scored three goals. Moving on to Northwich Victoria, many felt it was a shame when personal terms could not be agreed for him to stay on a permanent basis.
Middlesbrough (From trainee on 23/3/93) FL 0+1 FLC 0+1 Others 3+1 (Free to Eastwood T on 26/2/94)
Plymouth Arg (£15,000 on 27/3/96) FL 13+18/4 FLC 0+1 FAC 2+1 Others 1+1/1
Cambridge U (Loaned on 28/3/96) FL 1+4
Exeter C (Free on 19/12/97) FL 6+2/2 Others 1/1

Andy Impey

IMPEY Andrew (Andy) Rodney
Born: Hammersmith, 30 September 1971
Height: 5'8" Weight: 11.2
International Honours: E: U21-1

With a hankering for a higher grade of football, Andy left Queens Park Rangers last September, bound for West Ham, having earlier failed a medical because of a foot injury. After arriving at Upton Park, he had a disrupted season, shaking off injuries while adapting to his new wing-back role. Primarily a right winger, he did well with his new defensive duties, being aggressive, strong, and very quick, and can look forward to an extended run in the side when properly fit.
Queens Park R (£35,000 from Yeading on 14/6/90) F/PL 177+10/13 FLC 15+1/3 FAC 7+3/1 Others 0+2/1
West Ham U (£1,300,000 on 26/9/97) PL 19 FLC 3 FAC 3

INCE Paul Emerson Carlyle
Born: Ilford, 21 October 1967
Height: 5'11" Weight: 12.2

Club Honours: CS '93, '94; FAC '90, '94; ECW '91; ESC '91; FLC '92; PL '93, '94
International Honours: E: 43; B-1; U21-2; Yth

After returning to England with Liverpool during the 1997 close season, having been with Inter Milan for the previous two years, the imposing central midfielder began to grow into the role of club skipper throughout 1997-98, toning down his impetuosity, and channelling his aggressive and competitive streak to the good of the team. A regular international, and proud to be in France with England's World Cup squad as we go to print, he scored an impressive eight goals for Liverpool during the campaign, including an equaliser against Everton, and two in the 4-0 win over Arsenal, both games being at Anfield. A midfield bundle of energy, he is both constructive and destructive in breaking up attacks and setting counter attacks in motion. *Stop Press:* Played in all four of England's World Cup games in France '98 and certainly enhanced his reputation with a

battling display against Argentine. Down to ten men for 73 minutes, the side eventually went out of the competition following the penalty shoot-out, which saw both Paul and David Batty failing to strike the target.

West Ham U (From apprentice on 18/7/85) FL 66+6/7 FLC 9/3 FAC 8+2/1 Others 4/1
Manchester U (£1,000,000 on 14/9/89) F/PL 203+3/24 FLC 23+1/2 FAC 26+1/1 Others 24/1 (£8,000,000 to Inter Milan on 13/7/95)
Liverpool (£4,200,000 on 22/7/97) PL 31/8 FLC 4 FAC 1 Others 4

INGHAM Gary
Born: Rotherham, 9 October 1964
Height: 5'11" Weight: 12.5

Gary was Doncaster's first-choice goal-keeper for the first two months of last season, despite having only joined the club on a part-time basis from non-league Gainsborough Trinity during the summer. After losing his place to Dean Williams in October, he was released by the club in November, when refusing to sign a full-time contract, and moved on to play for Stalybridge.

Rotherham U (Free from Bridlington T on 16/3/93)
Doncaster Rov (Free on 6/5/94) FL 1 (Freed during 1995 close season)
Doncaster Rov (Free from Gainsborough Trinity on 7/8/97) FL 10 FLC 2

INGLETHORPE Alexander (Alex) Matthew
Born: Epsom, 14 November 1971
Height: 5'11" Weight: 11.6

Although missing the first part of last season through injury, Alex returned for Leyton Orient in September to play as an attacking midfielder just behind the forwards, from where he could ghost in to the area unmarked. A scorer of valuable goals, he also returned briefly to his original position as a centre forward, netting twice in three games, at Hull and Colchester, the latter strike bringing a point in a 1-1 draw.

Watford (From juniors on 1/7/90) FL 2+10/2 FLC 1+2 Others 1+1/1
Barnet (Loaned on 23/3/95) FL 5+1/3
Leyton Orient (Signed on 19/5/95) FL 78+6/26 FLC 4/2 FAC 1+1 Others 2+1/1

INGRAM Stuart Denevan (Denny)
Born: Sunderland, 27 June 1976
Height: 5'10" Weight: 12.1

1997-98 was a better season for Hartlepool's long-serving utility player, his game maturing as he proved himself capable of doing a good job in any defensive or midfield position he was asked to play. His aggressive style, and keen will to win, were a definite asset to the club in the first half of the campaign, as a promotion challenge looked likely. Perhaps not fully appreciated by all supporters, he is a great team player who deserves to be part of a successful side.

Hartlepool U (From trainee on 5/7/94) FL 149+5/6 FLC 10+1 FAC 5 Others 5

INGRAM Rae
Born: Manchester, 6 December 1974
Height: 5'11" Weight: 12.8

With Manchester City under severe pressure for most of 1997-98, Rae slipped out of contention for a first team place and was

Paul Ince

happy to have a spell on loan at nearby Macclesfield in mid-March. Fitting straight in at left back, and making five appearances for a side pushing hard for promotion to the second division, he showed himself to be good on the overlap and an excellent crosser of the ball. Also capable of playing in central defence, he was one of 14 professionals released by City during the summer.

Manchester C (From trainee on 9/7/93) P/FL 18+5 FLC 1 FAC 4
Macclesfield T (Loaned on 19/3/98) FL 5

INMAN Niall Edward
Born: Wakefield, 6 February 1978
Height: 5'8" Weight: 11.6
International Honours: Ei: U21-5

Unable to get a first team opportunity at Peterborough early on last season, the young Republic of Ireland U21 international was loaned out to non-league Stevenage in December and impressed during their FA Cup run that ended at Newcastle. Back at London Road, however, he came into the team on the wide left for four of the remaining six games, scoring in a 2-0 home win over Cardiff, and looking to still have a future. Pace, trickery, and delivery are his main assets.

Peterborough U (From trainee on 3/7/96) FL 5+3/1 FLC 1 FAC 0+1

INNES Mark
Born: Glasgow, 27 September 1978
Height: 5'10" Weight: 12.1

A two-year professional at Oldham, Mark was finally unleashed in 1997-98 when making his Football League debut at Burnley in early September, and was given four further opportunities before the campaign ended. Very highly thought of at Boundary Park as a youngster of some quality who can play in midfield or as a full back, mainly down the left-hand side, he is both strong in the tackle and an excellent passer of the ball.

Oldham Ath (From trainee on 10/10/95) FL 2+2 Others 1

IRELAND Simon Piers
Born: Barnstaple, 23 November 1971
Height: 5'11" Weight: 11.2
International Honours: E: Sch

Simon was a popular figure at Doncaster and was a regular feature in the first team last season, usually playing at full back or on the wing. His was a dramatic and sudden departure as the Rovers sought to reduce their playing staff, around the transfer deadline and he moved on to join former Rovers' boss, Kerry Dixon, at Boreham Wood.

Huddersfield T (From juniors on 1/7/90) FL 10+9 FLC 1/1 FAC 0+1 Others 1+1
Wrexham (Loaned on 11/3/92) FL 2+3
Blackburn Rov (£200,000 on 3/11/92) PL 0+1
Mansfield T (£60,000 on 8/3/94) FL 89+5/11 FLC 9/1 FAC 6+1/1 Others 4+1
Doncaster Rov (Loaned on 18/10/96) FL 9/1
Doncaster Rov (£10,000 on 28/1/97) FL 52/1 FLC 1+1 FAC 1 Others 1

IRONS Kenneth (Kenny)
Born: Liverpool, 4 November 1970
Height: 5'10" Weight: 12.2
Kenny is at his most effective when playing just behind the attack, but his versatility means that he can be very effective in midfield, or even as an emergency full back, if the occasion arises. Contributed four goals to Tranmere's total last season, including an early gem against bottom-placed Huddersfield in November and, while he could never be described as having an incredible turn of speed, few players can read a game more comprehensively. Has rarely been known to hold back in the tackle.
Tranmere Rov (From trainee on 9/11/89) FL 270+38/39 FLC 19+7/4 FAC 13+2/3 Others 28+3/3

IRONSIDE Ian
Born: Sheffield, 8 March 1964
Height: 6'2" Weight: 13.10
Released by Scarborough during the 1997 close season, Ian was snapped up smartly by Oldham as the number two goalkeeper to Gary Kelly and got an early opportunity to shine when coming into the side at Grimsby in the Coca Cola Cup, following an injury to the latter. Unfortunately, that game was to be his last after he went on to suffer a combination of injuries that left the surgeons with no alternatives other than to bring his long and distinguished career to an end. Solid and reliable, he had followed his dad, Roy, the former Rotherham and Barnsley 'keeper, into football.
Barnsley (From juniors on 17/9/82)
Scarborough (Free from North Ferriby U on 8/3/88) FL 88 FLC 2 FAC 2 Others 10
Middlesbrough (£80,000 on 15/8/91) F/PL 12+1 FLC 2
Scarborough (Loaned on 5/3/92) FL 7
Stockport Co (Signed on 23/9/93) FL 17+2 FAC 1 Others 1
Scarborough (Free on 23/3/95) FL 88 FLC 4 FAC 4 Others 2
Oldham Ath (Free on 18/7/97) FLC 1

IRVINE Stuart Christopher
Born: Hartlepool, 1 March 1979
Height: 5'9" Weight: 11.10
Hartlepool's homegrown striker will probably be a little disappointed with his progress in 1997-98. After making an immediate impact the previous season, and signing a full professional contract, this time round he was forced to bide his time, mainly playing reserve team football. He finished the season by being named as a substitute in 15 of the last 18 games and, although he gained some important first team experience, he was unable to win a place in a starting line-up, bar one.
Hartlepool U (From trainee on 8/7/97) FL 3+10/1 FAC 0+1 Others 0+1

IRVING Richard James
Born: Halifax, 10 September 1975
Height: 5'7" Weight: 10.6
International Honours: E: Yth; Sch
Having been released by Nottingham Forest towards the end of 1996-97, Richard had trials at Aberdeen, Rochdale, and Bury, before being brought into the Macclesfield team last November to try and resolve a goal drought. Although the speedy little striker made intelligent runs and got into some great positions, the goals failed to materialise and he failed to maintain his place in the side, leaving to join non-league Runcorn by mutual consent in February.
Manchester U (From trainee on 1/10/92)
Nottingham F (£75,000 on 19/7/95) PL 0+1
Macclesfield T (Free on 7/10/97) FL 6+3 FAC 0+2

IRWIN Joseph Denis
Born: Cork, 31 October 1965
Height: 5'8" Weight: 11.0
Club Honours: CS '93, '96, '97; ECWC '91; ESC '91; FLC '92; PL '93, '94, '96, '97; FAC '94, '96
International Honours: Ei: 48; B-1; U23-1; U21-3; Yth; Sch
A highly experienced Manchester United defender, who is a model of consistency, and a specialist goalscorer from set plays, Denis started last season in excellent fashion, celebrating his first goal of the campaign in United's 3-0 victory over Kosice in the Champions' League in September. Then, having assumed the role of the regular penalty ace, following Teddy Sheringham's hat trick of misses, he scored his first in the vital Champions' League win against Feyenoord – his first penalty conversion since May 1995. In the return leg against the Dutch side in November, however, he was subjected to an horrendous tackle by Paul Bosvelt which, apart from an appearance against Wimbledon, kept him out of football until January. Fortunately, he made a remarkable recovery, showing no signs of complications in the FA Cup tie against Chelsea, and being an ever present for the remainder of the campaign, even captaining the side against Wimbledon in March. In signing a new two-year contract in October, he showed no signs of loosening his grip on that famous number three shirt. Continued to play for the Republic of Ireland in 1997-98, appearing against Lithuania, Belgium, and Argentine, and scoring the first goal in the 1-1 draw with Belgium.
Leeds U (From apprentice on 3/11/83) FL 72/1 FLC 5 FAC 3 Others 2
Oldham Ath (Free on 22/5/86) FL 166+1/4 FLC 19/3 FAC 13 Others 5
Manchester U (£625,000 on 20/6/90) F/PL 275+6/17 FLC 28+3 FAC 35+1/6 Others 38/2

ISMAEL Valerien
Born: Strasbourg, France, 28 September 1975
Height: 6'3" Weight: 13.0
Signed from Strasbourg early last January, the former French U21 international replaced Andy Roberts as Crystal Palace's most expensive signing and the jury is still out. A strong central defender who stands up well, and would be well backed to win supremacy in the air, he unfortunately came into a struggling side who leaked 25 goals in his first nine starts, making it nigh impossible for him to settle in partnership with Hermann Hreidarsson, having taken over from Andy Linighan. Despite being an experienced defender at European Cup level, he found the pace of the Premiership just too frenetic and required more time to adjust, but that was something the club did not have with relegation staring it in the face. Sent off in the penultimate game, at Bolton, he will reflect on the experience and, hopefully, come back well in 1998-99, as Palace prepare for yet another assault on the Premiership.
Crystal Palace (£2,750,000 from Strasbourg on 16/1/98) PL 13 FAC 3

IVERSON Steffen
Born: Oslo, Norway, 10 November 1976
Height: 6'1" Weight: 11.2
An extremely talented Tottenham striker whose season in 1997-98 was wrecked by injury, in the dozen or so appearances he made his fitness was obviously a doubt, as he lacked the pace and stamina which are his natural strengths. At his best, Steffen is instinctive and extremely intelligent in using his pace and vision to create space around him in which to attack the goal. However, his inclusion in the Norway squad, whilst not fully fit, brought criticism from his club and was compounded by the deterioration in the injuries when returning back from international duty, which effectively wrote his season off before Christmas. But, at only 22 years of age, he has the benefit of youth and an immense talent to re-establish his first team spot in the knowledge that Tottenham are keen to retain his skill.
Tottenham H (£2,700,000 from Rosenborg, via Nationalkam, on 7/12/96) PL 24+5/6

IZZET Mustafa (Muzzy) Kemmel
Born: Mile End, 31 October 1974
Height: 5'10" Weight: 10.12
Club Honours: FLC '97
The right-footed Leicester midfielder enjoyed an outstanding season in 1997-98, displaying boundless energy and exceptional skill. Unlucky not to have been called up to the England "B" squad, having finally rejected Turkey's claims for his services, he tormented the Athletico Madrid defence in the UEFA Cup without any reward. Scoring with a brilliant curled effort into the top corner to save a point in injury time against Palace, Muzzy was a vital cog in City's midfield unit, with only his lack of regular goals preventing him from gaining the recognition his obvious talent deserves. A popular choice as the club's Player of the Season, the aforementioned goal against Palace was accorded Goal of the Season status.
Chelsea (From trainee on 19/5/93)
Leicester C (£650,000 + on 28/3/96) P/FL 78+2/8 FLC 8/1 FAC 5 Others 5

Professional Footballers Association
Financial Management
Limited

The PFA has the job of looking after every aspect of a player's career: – his contract, advice on transfers, education and training, accident insurance, discipline and commercial matters. In line with these duties PFA Financial Management Limited was set up to provide the best possible financial and contractual advice to players during what is a very short-term career – an average of eight years.

Get in touch … you deserve the best financial advice.

PFA Financial Management Limited
91 Broad Street
Birmingham
B15 1AU

Tel: 0121 644 5277
Fax: 0121 644 5288

J

JACK Rodney Alphonso
Born: Kingstown, St Vincent, 28 September 1972
Height: 5'7" Weight: 10.9
International Honours: St Vincent: 65

As in previous seasons, this speedy and skilful St Vincent international striker scored some memorable goals for Torquay in 1997-98, and gave further indications that he is destined for football at a much higher level. Again topped the club's goalscoring charts and, more often than not, looked a class above the third division. Was delighted to be voted by his fellow professionals into the PFA award-winning third division team.

Torquay U (Free from Lambada, St Vincent on 10/10/95) FL 82+5/24 FLC 6/1 FAC 6 Others 6/3

JACKSON Elliot
Born: Swindon, 27 August 1977
Height: 6'2" Weight: 14.6

Rodney Jack

In 1997-98, Elliot, who had had a brief look at first team action in the previous campaign, had the chance to establish himself as first choice with regular 'keeper, Phil Whitehead, sidelined, having two spells, one of two games, and another of four. After perhaps his only "dodgy" game, he enjoyed an excellent display at York in the Coca Cola Cup, but was replaced by loan 'keeper, Arjan Van Heusden, and was unable to break back in after Whitehead's return. A good shot-stopper who takes crosses well, he is still learning and should feature again.

Oxford U (From trainee on 2/7/96) FL 6 FLC 3

JACKSON Justin Jonathan
Born: Nottingham, 10 December 1974
Height: 6'0" Weight: 11.6
Club Honours: Div 3 '98

Signed early last season from Woking, having earned an impressive reputation as a goalscorer, Justin eagerly took the chance to play full-time football at Notts County. His fitness and strength improved during the campaign, and with a full pre-season development he will undoubtedly develop his left-side attacking skills further. Despite making most of his appearances from the bench, his total sum of subs and starts were enough to warrant him a third division championship medal, as County romped away with the title.

Notts Co (£30,000 from Woking on 26/9/97) FL 4+11/1 FAC 0+1

JACKSON Kirk Stewart
Born: Doncaster, 16 October 1976
Height: 5'11" Weight: 12.0

The former Sheffield Wednesday and Scunthorpe forward joined Chesterfield for pre-season trials in the summer of 1997 and made a surprising, but creditable, debut as a substitute at Plymouth in August. An exquisite lob over their 'keeper very nearly brought about a goal, and earned Kirk a contract for the rest of the campaign, although he was farmed out on loan to Gainsborough in January.

Sheffield Wed (From trainee on 15/5/95)
Scunthorpe U (Free on 23/7/96) FL 0+4/1 Others 0+1
Chesterfield (Free on 6/8/97) FL 0+3 FLC 0+1 FAC 0+1 Others 1

JACKSON Mark Graham
Born: Leeds, 30 September 1977
Height: 6'0" Weight: 11.12
International Honours: E: Yth

After promising so much in 1996-97, last season was a bit of an anti-climax for Mark at Leeds, being only called up for just one first team appearance, and that as a substitute. Able to perform as well in central defence as in the midfield, he is good in the air, is a strong tackler who wins the ball and passes it to feet, and looks to have an all-round game. There is no doubt that he remains in George Graham's plans, being an unused sub for eight games, and he looks bound to be offered further opportunities in 1998-99.

Leeds U (From trainee on 1/7/95) PL 11+8 FAC 4

JACKSON Matthew (Matt) Alan
Born: Leeds, 19 October 1971
Height: 6'1" Weight: 12.12
Club Honours: FAC '95
International Honours: E: U21-10; Sch

Appointed club captain for 1997-98, Matt took to the role with great authority, confirming the promise of his performances of the previous campaign when giving a string of high quality displays at the heart of the Norwich defence. Able to play at right back or in the centre of defence, he is a composed, mature defender who copes well under pressure, is comfortable in possession, and strikes the ball well. Excellent at set pieces, he headed in a far post cross at Port Vale for City's second goal in a 2-2 draw. Also, his humourous columns in both the programme and local newspaper continued to be well received.

Luton T (From juniors on 4/7/90) FL 7+2 FLC 2 Others 0+1
Preston NE (Loaned on 27/3/91) FL 3+1 Others 1
Everton (£600,000 on 18/10/91) F/PL 132+6/4 FLC 9 FAC 14/2 Others 4
Charlton Ath (Loaned on 26/3/96) FL 8 Others 2
Queens Park R (Loaned on 20/8/96) FL 7
Birmingham C (Loaned on 31/10/96) FL 10
Norwich C (£450,000 on 24/12/96) FL 58+2/5 FAC 2

JACKSON Michael James
Born: Runcorn, 4 December 1973
Height: 6'0" Weight: 13.8
Club Honours: Div 2 '97
International Honours: E: Yth

A right-sided Preston central defender who started and finished last season strongly, Michael recovered well from a mid-term dip in form and confidence. He is cool under pressure and always goes for the safest option, his value to the side showing during a five-match absence through injury, four of which were lost. Quick to cover colleagues, he would appear ideally suited to a sweeper role, and also presents an aerial threat at set pieces, from which he scored on his 150th league appearance.
Crewe Alex (From trainee on 29/7/92) FL 5 FLC 1 FAC 1 Others 2
Bury (Free on 13/8/93) FL 123+2/9 FLC 9/1 FAC 3 Others 1
Preston NE (£125,000 on 26/3/97) FL 46+1/2 FLC 4 FAC 4 Others 4

JACKSON Richard
Born: Whitby, 18 April 1980
Height: 5'7" Weight: 9.4

Still a trainee until late in 1997-98, this promising young full back, and the only locally-born player in the Scarborough squad, made excellent progress with the reserves, enough so that he was given his Football League debut at right back in the home fixture against Doncaster last November, and followed it up with another appearance in the penultimate game of the season against Shrewsbury. Voted Boro's Young Player of the Year in recognition of his talent, Richard seems set for a good future in the game.
Scarborough (From trainee on 27/3/98) FL 2

JACOBS Wayne Graham
Born: Sheffield, 3 February 1969
Height: 5'9" Weight: 11.2

Ever present for Bradford City in 1997-98, playing in the first 18 games before an injury put him out of action in mid-November, Wayne came back strongly to feature in 21 of the remaining 22. As the captain, and leading by example from his favoured left-back spot, taking corners and set pieces generally, he scored with a tremendous 25-yard free kick in a 2-1 win at Stockport, his second game back, and later in the season, at Norwich, cracked in another one to start the scoring in a 3-2 win. A great favourite with the fans for his commitment and enthusiasm, not forgetting his powerful left foot, and liking to get forward, he is reckoned to be one of the club's best ever signings.
Sheffield Wed (From apprentice on 3/1/87) FL 5+1 FLC 3 Others 1
Hull C (£27,000 on 25/3/88) FL 127+2/4 FLC 7 FAC 8 Others 6
Rotherham U (Free on 5/8/93) FL 40+2/2 FLC 4 FAC 1 Others 2
Bradford C (Free on 5/8/94) FL 139+2/6 FLC 11 FAC 8/2 Others 5

JAGIELKA Stephen (Steve)
Born: Manchester, 10 March 1978
Height: 5'8" Weight: 11.5

Signed on a free transfer from Stoke in the summer of 1997, Steve was generally used as a substitute by Shrewsbury, despite a number of strikes in the Pontins League team. Scored his first senior goal in April at home to Brighton and looked very effective on the right when going forward, where his pace looks as if it can be productive.
Stoke C (From trainee on 15/7/96)
Shrewsbury T (Free on 30/7/97) FL 4+12/1 FLC 1+1

JAMES David Benjamin
Born: Welwyn Garden City, 1 August 1970
Height: 6'5" Weight: 14.5
Club Honours: FAYC '89; FLC '95
International Honours: E: 1; B-1; U21-10; Yth

1997-98 was another disappointing season for Liverpool's enigmatic goalkeeper, only this time, having started the first 27 Premiership games, he made way for Brad Friedel at the end of February. On his day a superb 'keeper, who is extremely agile for a big man and a great shot-stopper with good positional sense, and one who commands his area with great presence, on other days he appears indecisive and goals are conceded. Having pledged himself to the Reds, the purchase of Friedel may be just the spur he needs to find top form and win back his place between the sticks.
Watford (From trainee on 1/7/88) FL 89 FLC 6 FAC 2 Others 1
Liverpool (£1,000,000 on 6/7/92) PL 187+1 FLC 22 FAC 17 Others 17

JAMES Julian Colin
Born: Tring, 22 March 1970
Height: 5'10" Weight: 12.4
International Honours: E: U21-2

An uncompromising, fierce-tackling Luton full back, Julian suffered a season beset by injury, culminating in a badly double fractured leg against Bristol Rovers last April, which will keep him out for six months. As the club's first-choice right back when fit, the frequent absence of this reliable defender was a factor in Town's unsteady defence during much of the campaign.
Luton T (From trainee on 1/7/88) FL 262+20/13 FLC 16+1/1 FAC 21+1 Others 12+1
Preston NE (Loaned on 12/9/91) FL 6

JANSEN Matthew (Matt) Brooke
Born: Carlisle, 20 October 1977
Height: 5'11" Weight: 10.13
Club Honours: AMC '97
International Honours: E: Yth

As the most promising young player at Carlisle since Peter Bearsley, Matt was almost ever present for the club in 1997-98, scoring 12 goals in 30 outings, before being transferred to Crystal Palace in February for what was a record fee for the Cumbrians. A forward who is blessed with pace, ball control, and an eye for a goal, and is clearly destined to go to the top, he somewhat surprisingly chose to sign for Palace ahead of Manchester United. Started on the bench, scoring a stunner in a 3-1 defeat at Aston Villa, before making a full appearance at Newcastle and celebrating with the winner

in a 2-1 victory. After being selected for the England U21 squad's summer tournament, Matt said that he turned down United against much advice because he knew he would be in a queue for places at Old Trafford, despite there being a real chance that Palace would be relegated - something that ultimately happened. Strangely, Carlisle were also relegated to the third division.
Carlisle U (From trainee on 18/1/96) FL 26+16/10 FLC 4+1/3 FAC 1+3 Others 3+3
Crystal Palace (£1,000,000+ on 12/2/98) PL 5+3/3

JANSSON Jan
Born: Kalmar, Sweden, 26 January 1968
Height: 5'10" Weight: 12.4
International Honours: Sweden: 7

After firming up the loan tenure which existed in 1996-97, the skilful, left-sided Port Vale midfield player, with excellent dead ball ability, unfortunately missed a lot of the first half of the 1997-98 campaign due to a variety of injuries. Putting that behind him, Jan began to display good form when he became a regular in the team in the New Year, scoring five goals, all away from home, including two in the final game of the season at Huddersfield, which clinched safety from relegation. Made many a goal with his prowess from free kicks and corners.
Port Vale (£200,000 from Norrkoping on 4/11/96) FL 32+12/6 FLC 1+1 FAC 1

JARMAN Lee
Born: Cardiff, 16 December 1977
Height: 6'3" Weight: 13.3
International Honours: W: U21-7; Yth

Lee emerged from the wilderness at Cardiff City following the arrival of Frank Burrows as the new manager in February 1998. Initially, he seemed to lack confidence and rarely figured for some time, but Burrows picked him up, dusted him down, and urged him to start all over again. And what a response he got. The tall and talented right back showed far more aggression and consistency over the last three months of the season, and was even appointed captain when David Penney was injured. Having improved his basic defensive work under Burrows, both in the air and on the ground, Lee has been able to bring his ability on the ball and passing skills into focus and, for 1998-99, he has been urged to take responsibility for his own career and live up to the potential so many people know he has. Continued to play for the Welsh U21 side, appearing against Turkey and Belgium during the season.
Cardiff C (From trainee on 23/8/95) FL 76+11 FLC 3+1 FAC 3+3/1 Others 4+2

JEAN Earl Jude
Born: St Lucia, 9 October 1971
Height: 5'8" Weight: 11.4
International Honours: St Lucia: 4

Released by Rotherham during the 1997 close season, the diminutive striker spent most of 1997-98 at Plymouth as a substitute. Very quick, and always willing to try his luck on goal, the St Lucian international,

who missed some of the campaign due to international commitments, scored five goals, including a tremendous shot to open the scoring in Argyle's 2-2 home draw against Burnley.

Ipswich T (Free from Uniao de Coimbra Felguieras on 6/12/96) FL 0+1
Rotherham U (Free on 23/1/97) FL 7+11/6
Plymouth Arg (Free on 7/8/97) FL 16+20/4 FLC 1 FAC 2/1 Others 0+1

JEFFERS Francis

Born: Liverpool, 25 January 1981
Height: 5'10" Weight: 10.7
International Honours: E: Yth

Another of Everton's ever-increasing crop of talented teenagers to roll off the production line, when he became only the second 16-year old in the club's history to figure in a first team game. Certainly a baptism of fire, he was introduced a minute after half time at Manchester United last Boxing Day with the home team leading 2-0, but acquitted himself confidently. A clever, pacy striker, he committed himself to a long-term contract at the club in February, before being forced to sit out two months of the season after suffering from a mysterious heart virus. Bounced back to score a crucial goal in Everton's FA Youth Cup final defeat of Blackburn Rovers.

Everton (Trainee) PL 0+1

JEMSON Nigel Bradley

Born: Hutton, 10 August 1969
Height: 5'11" Weight: 12.10
Club Honours: FLC '90; AMC '96
International Honours: E: U21-1

A hard-working striker, and one who is always calling and urging his team mates on, prior to joining Bury from Oxford last February, Nigel had already got his goals tally into double figures, but with United short of cash he became a "necessary" sale. His early games for the Shakers saw him striking up a good understanding with another newcomer, Tony Ellis, and he laid on goals for the latter against West Bromwich and Port Vale. However, he subsequently struggled to come to terms with the club's style of play, and a penalty against Norwich was his only return in 15 games. Has a good first touch and holds the ball well for others.

Preston NE (From trainee on 6/7/87) FL 28+4/8 FAC 2/1 Others 5+1/5
Nottingham F (£150,000 on 24/3/88) FL 45+2/13 FLC 9/4 FAC 1+3/3 Others 1
Bolton W Loaned on 23/12/88) FL 4+1
Preston NE (Loaned on 15/3/89) FL 6+3/2 Others 2/1
Sheffield Wed (£800,000 on 17/9/91) F/PL 26+25/9 FLC 3+4 FAC 3+3/1 Others 2+2/1
Grimsby T (Loaned on 10/9/93) FL 6/2 Others 1
Notts Co (£300,000 on 8/9/94) FL 7+7/1 FLC 2+2/1 Others 1
Watford (Loaned on 12/1/95) FL 3+1
Rotherham U (Loaned on 15/2/96) FL 16/5 Others 3/4
Oxford U (£60,000 on 23/7/96) FL 68/27 FLC 12/6 FAC 2
Bury (£100,000 on 5/2/98) FL 11+4/1

JENKINS Iain

Born: Whiston, 24 November 1972
Height: 5'9" Weight: 11.10
International Honours: NI: 5; B-1

After attracting a number of scouts with some competent performances for Chester City in 1997-98, Iain left to join Dundee on transfer deadline day. It had certainly been a good season for him and he had looked equally at home in either full-back role, scoring his first ever league goal in a 3-1 win at Lincoln in January. Was again picked for international duties with Northern Ireland.

Everton (From trainee on 4/6/91) PL 3+2 FLC 0+1
Bradford C (Loaned on 31/12/92) FL 6 Others 1
Chester C (Free on 13/8/93) FL 155+5/1 FLC 7+2 FAC 11+1 Others 12

JENKINS Lee David

Born: Pontypool, 28 June 1979
Height: 5'9" Weight: 11.0
International Honours: W: U21-1; Yth; Sch

Lee struggled to make regular appearances for Swansea during the first half of last season, but came back strongly to show his versatility, when combining a wing back or midfield role during the second half. Almost back to his competitive best, a run of games towards the end of the campaign saw the youngster begin to display the kind of form that prompted the locals to think so highly of him in the first place. Made his Welsh U21 debut when coming on as a sub in Turkey during August.

Swansea C (From trainee on 20/12/96) FL 35+9/2 FAC 1 Others 2

JENKINS Stephen (Steve) Robert

Born: Merthyr, 16 July 1972
Height: 5'11" Weight: 12.3
Club Honours: AMC '94
International Honours: W: 10; U21-2; Yth

1997-98 was a frustrating season for Huddersfield's versatile Welsh international, as he missed the opening day defeat at Oxford United through suspension carried over from the previous campaign, followed by a stint on the sidelines through injury after being a regular at right back. That was followed by two further bans. However, there were some bright spots, including his continued selection for the Welsh squad, which saw him earn a cap against Jamaica, while his solid displays at the heart of Town's defence were rewarded with the captaincy of the team.

Swansea C (From trainee on 1/7/90) FL 155+10/1 FLC 12+1 FAC 10+1 Others 26
Huddersfield T (£275,000 on 3/11/95) FL 92+1/2 FLC 9 FAC 8

JEPSON Ronald (Ronnie) Francis

Born: Stoke, 12 May 1963
Height: 6'1" Weight: 13.7
Club Honours: Div 2 '97

An experienced striker, Ronnie started last season in Bury's colours before losing his place to Peter Swan and finding himself relegated to the subs' bench. Although prone to picking up injuries, he gained another run in the side following the sale of David Johnson, but come mid-January he was on his way to Oldham, where he arrived not fully match fit and took a while to get going. Known in the trade as "Rocket Ronnie", when he did get going he showed

his true worth, with four goals in the last three matches, and will obviously be looking for a few more in 1998-99.

Port Vale (Free from Nantwich T on 23/3/89) FL 12+10 FLC 1+1 FAC 1+1
Peterborough U (Loaned on 25/1/90) FL 18/5
Preston NE (£80,000 on 12/2/91) FL 36+2/8 FLC 2 Others 3/4
Exeter C (£60,000 on 29/7/92) FL 51+3/21 FLC 6/2 FAC 3/1 Others 4/1
Huddersfield T (£80,000 on 7/12/93) FL 95+12/36 FLC 6+1/2 FAC 4/3 Others 6/1
Bury (£40,000 on 27/7/96) FL 31+16/9 FLC 7/1 FAC 0+3 Others 1+1/2
Oldham Ath (£30,000 on 16/1/98) FL 9/4

JOACHIM Julian Kevin

Born: Peterborough, 20 September 1974
Height: 5'6" Weight: 12.2
International Honours: E: U21-9; Yth (UEFAC '93)

Up until last February, Julian had only made two starts for Aston Villa in 1997-98, despite being on the subs' bench in practically every other game, but when called upon he played well enough to deserve a bit of a run if nothing else. At that moment in time, it appeared that he was the club's fourth-choice striker and would only get a chance when others were unavailable but, after replacing the suspended Ian Taylor, the situation changed and he became a first team regular, finishing the campaign on par with Stan Collymore in the goalscoring stakes, with eight to his name. Able to play in a number of positions up front, or in midfield, pace is his biggest asset.

Leicester C (From trainee on 15/9/92) F/PL 77+22/25 FLC 7+2/3 FAC 4+1/1 Others 4+2/2
Aston Villa (£1,500,000 on 24/2/96) PL 23+29/13 FLC 1 FAC 2+1 Others 1+1

JOBLING Kevin Andrew

Born: Sunderland, 1 January 1968
Height: 5'9" Weight: 12.0
Club Honours: AMC '98

Although early last season, he shared the left-hand side, of Grimsby's defence almost equally with Tony Gallimore, the latter's consistency limited Kevin's opportunities in his customary left-back position in 1997-98. His adaptability, however, found him once again asked to operate in a midfield role when called upon and, as you would expect, he performed with all his usual determination. Released during the summer, he is still a strong tackler with an accurate passing range.

Leicester C (From apprentice on 9/1/86) FL 4+5 FAC 0+1 Others 3/2
Grimsby T (Signed on 19/2/88) FL 251+34/10 FLC 13+4/1 FAC 10+3/2 Others 7+7
Scunthorpe U (Loaned on 10/1/94) Others 1

JOBSON Richard Ian

Born: Holderness, 9 May 1963
Height: 6'1" Weight: 13.5
Club Honours: Div 2 '91
International Honours: E: B-2

Not part of Leeds' plans in 1997-98, having suffered two serious knee ligament injuries during the previous two years, the central defender was first loaned out to Southend towards the end of January and responded

with some good performances and a goal in his final game against Plymouth before being signed by Joe Royle for Manchester City on a free. A fine defender who goes about his work without fuss and ceremony, he made a good start, scoring in a 4-1 home win against Stockport, before receiving a nasty leg injury in the home game against Birmingham, which brought his campaign to an end. At 35 years of age it is difficult to know where Richard goes from here.

Watford (£22,000 from Burton A on 5/11/82) FL 26+2/4 FLC 2 FAC 0+1 Others 5+1
Hull C (£40,000 on 7/2/85) FL 219+2/17 FLC 12 FAC 13/1 Others 9
Oldham Ath (£460,000 on 30/8/90) F/PL 188+1/10 FLC 19/1 FAC 13 Others 4
Leeds U (£1,000,000 on 26/10/95) PL 22/1 FLC 3 FAC 1
Southend U (Loaned on 23/1/98) FL 8/1
Manchester C (Free on 12/3/98) FL 6/1

JOHANSEN Martin
Born: Glostrud, Denmark, 22 July 1972
Height: 5'8" Weight: 10.4
International Honours: Denmark: 1

A midfielder signed on a free transfer from FC Copenhagen under the Bosman ruling in the summer of 1997, and the twin brother of Bolton's Michael, Martin made only one start for Coventry in 1997-98, the Coca Cola away tie at Blackpool as a striker. There were to be two substitute appearances to add to that before he spent the rest of the season in the reserves.

Coventry C (Free from FC Copenhagen on 14/7/97) PL 0+2 FLC 1

JOHANSEN Michael Bro
Born: Glostrup, Denmark, 22 July 1972
Height: 5'6" Weight: 10.5
Club Honours: Div 1 '97
International Honours: Denmark: 4

A Danish international, Michael is a tricky winger who has become a firm favourite with the Bolton fans. Although his first team outings last season were mostly limited to substitute appearances, he did make a few starts and, despite his lack of height, he often proves to be a real handful for opposing teams, possessing a terrific turn of pace, and being able to take players on with apparent ease. His friendly, cheerful approach to the game (something of a rarity in these times) has earned him a lot of respect from Wanderers' fans and this was shown in the reception he got whenever playing at the Reebok.

Bolton W (£1,250,000 from FC Copenhagen on 14/8/96) F/PL 28+21/6 FLC 4+2 FAC 1+1

JOHANSEN Stig
Born: Norway, 13 June 1972
Height: 5'10" Weight: 12.1
International Honours: Norway

Signed from FK Bodo Glimt immediately prior to the start of 1997-98, the Norwegian international striker only appeared eight times for Southampton throughout the campaign and failed to find the back of the net. A prolific scorer in his home country, he was loaned to Bristol City in February in order to give him a further opportunity to find his feet, but in his three games, whilst exhibiting some skilful touches, he never looked likely to provide the goalscoring impetus that was required and returned to the Dell.

Southampton (£550,000 from FK Bodo Glimpt on 9/8/97) PL 3+3 FLC 1+1
Bristol C (Loaned on 12/2/97) FL 2+1

JOHNROSE Leonard (Lenny)
Born: Preston, 29 November 1969
Height: 5'10" Weight: 12.6
Club Honours: Div 2 '97

A midfield battler, Lenny is a particularly popular character at Bury and continues to surprise everyone at the club with his amazing stamina. His successful midfield partnership with Nick Daws continued once again throughout most of 1997-98, with his workrate and tough tackling making him a firm favourite with the fans. He also popped up with three important goals during the campaign, including a 90th-minute screamer, which earned an all-important point at Norwich.

Blackburn Rov (From trainee on 16/6/88) FL 20+22/11 FLC 2+1/1 FAC 0+3 Others 2
Preston NE (Loaned on 21/1/92) FL 1+2/1
Hartlepool U (£50,000 on 28/2/92) FL 59+7/11 FLC 5+1/4 FAC 5/1 Others 5
Bury (Signed on 7/12/93) FL 155+6/18 FLC 11+2 FAC 8/1 Others 9/1

JOHNSEN Jean Ronny
Born: Norway, 10 June 1969
Height: 6'2" Weight: 12.8
Club Honours: PL '97; CS '97
International Honours: Norway: 35

A classy Manchester United midfielder or central defender, Ronny started last season on a high note when he scored United's solitary goal against Chelsea in the FA Charity Shield at Wembley. Having then played in two of the Reds' opening Premiership games, he suffered the first of several long lay offs with calf injury problems. Coming back strongly, he enjoyed his most consistent spell during the months of December and January, celebrating his second goal of the campaign against Walsall in the fourth round of the FA Cup in January. But, just when he appeared to have put his injury woes behind him, he played in only two games during February, before coming back to kick-start United's vital end of season Championship challenge with a goal against Wimbledon at Old Trafford in March, and a superb header against Liverpool at Old Trafford on Good Friday. Unfortunately, he was carried off with an ankle injury following a tackle by Michael Owen in that game, and later underwent a successful operation to repair the damage. No doubt, the United faithful will be hoping that he has better luck with injuries during the 1998-99 campaign, and prove once again what an outstanding defender he is when on the top of his form. Signed a new five-year contract in December. *Stop Press:* Played in all four of Norway's World Cup games in France during the summer, before the team went out in the second round, beaten 1-0 by Italy.

Manchester U (£1,200,000 from Besiktas on 26/7/96) PL 44+9/2 FLC 1 FAC 5/1 Others 15/1

JOHNSON Andrew (Andy) James
Born: Bristol, 2 May 1974
Height: 6'0" Weight: 12.0
Club Honours: Div 1 '98
International Honours: E: Yth

Transferred to Nottingham Forest from Norwich during the summer of 1997, this strong and aggressive midfielder settled into the Forest team to eventually make the central midfield position his own, following the injury to another newcomer, Geoff Thomas. Fast off the mark, and a good passer, Andy linked up well with his team mates and, in getting forward whenever the opportunity arose, he scored four league goals, which included three in the last four games. Also able to play in defence, if required, he was delighted to win a first division championship medal, an honour which will see him back in the Premiership in 1998-99.

Norwich C (From trainee on 4/3/92) F/PL 56+10/13 FLC 6+1/2 FAC 2
Nottingham F (£2,200,000 on 4/7/97) FL 24+10/4 FLC 2+1

JOHNSON Damien Michael
Born: Lisburn, 18 November 1978
Height: 5'9" Weight: 10.0
International Honours: NI: U21-3; Yth

Having been blooded by Blackburn in the Coca Cola Cup game at Preston last season, the young Irishman was loaned out to Nottingham Forest at the end of January to further his football education. A very skilful, right-sided winger, he made his Football League debut at the City Ground against Oxford within a couple of days of arriving and was much admired for his ball-playing skills in the six games he played for Forest before going back to Ewood. Expected to be a star of the future by those who know about these things, Damien gained Northern Ireland U21 honours in 1997-98 to go with his youth caps, and signed a three-year contract with Rovers. Watch this space.

Blackburn Rov (From trainee on 2/2/96) FLC 1
Nottingham F (Loaned on 29/1/98) FL 5+1

JOHNSON David Anthony
Born: Kingston, Jamaica, 15 August 1976
Height: 5'6" Weight: 12.3
Club Honours: FAYC '95; Div 2 '97
International Honours: E: B-1

Just as the pint-sized striker was finally exhibiting the consistent lethal finishing which had been lacking at Bury for so long, the club's financial position meant that they were unable to hold on to their main asset and he became Ipswich's record signing in November. Despite the news being greeted by the fans with the question David who? It was not long, however, before they had revived a chant from the '70s – "Johnson, Born Is The King of Portman Road" – such was the impact he made. His greatest asset was his pace but, for a player of his stature, he was remarkably good in the air as well, frequently outjumping players much taller than himself and, although naturally left footed, was capable of scoring with either foot and was prepared to have a go from anywhere, which endeared him to the fans

David Johnson

Ever present for Huddersfield since his November move from Dundee United, this former Scotland U21 cap quickly settled down, adding an extra dimension to the midfield and flanks with his battling qualities and strong forward runs. He certainly celebrated in some style when he scored his first goal for Town in his 27th game, having drifted past his marker to fire past the Crewe 'keeper for the second goal in a 2-0 home win. All in all, it was an excellent start for the 26-year old.

Dundee U (Free from Broughty Ferry on 7/9/90) SL 72+13/7 SLC 5/2 SC 4 Others 4+1/2
Huddersfield T (£90,000 on 14/11/97) FL 28+1/1 FAC 2

JOHNSON Marvin Anthony
Born: Wembley, 29 October 1968
Height: 6'0" Weight: 13.6

Marvin was yet another member of the Luton squad to see his season ruined by injury in 1997-98. Although given to occasional errors, from which he often quickly recovers, Marvin remains a popular player at the club due to his commitment and enthusiasm, and formed his usual effective partnership with Steve Davis when fit, scoring two goals in his 16 appearances. Strong in the air, and deceptively good with his feet, he was sorely missed by the fans and team alike.

Luton T (From apprentice on 12/11/86) FL 246+14/6 FLC 19+2/1 FAC 11+1/1 Others 12

JOHNSON Michael Owen
Born: Nottingham, 4 July 1973
Height: 5'11" Weight: 11.12
Club Honours: AIC '95

A versatile and athletic Birmingham defender, Michael scored his first-ever goal after 250 games against Sheffield United last February and, as if to celebrate, followed it up with another in the very next game, against Bury. Played at left back, centre half, and as an emergency right back, and was singled out by the manager, Trevor Francis, as being one of the club's most improved performers of 1997-98. Nick-named "Magic", he has two good feet, looks to pass the ball, has impressive aerial strength, and is often used for a man-marking job. What else do you need?

Notts Co (From trainee on 9/7/91) FL 102+5 FLC 9 FAC 4 Others 15+1
Birmingham C (£225,000 on 1/9/95) FL 81+25/3 FLC 6+6 FAC 2+3 Others 4

JOHNSON Richard Mark
Born: Newcastle, Australia, 27 April 1974
Height: 5'10" Weight: 12.0
Club Honours: Div 2 '98

This midfielder was Watford's most improved player of last season, forging a fine understanding with newcomer, Micah Hyde, and proving to be a revelation, with his much-improved passing and new-found willingness to take responsibility. Happily, the long-range shooting that was previously his main claim to fame remained unimpaired, and he scored outstanding goals against Carlisle and Northampton. Although hampered by a knee injury in March, he recovered in time to top 50 appearances for

from the start. His striking partnership with Alex Mathie being an exciting aspect of the second half of the season. Made a sensational start to his Ipswich career, scoring in seven of his first nine games, including a double against Huddersfield and his first ever hat trick, against Oxford, which, in its way, mirrored his talents. Not surprisingly, his form attracted international recognition with call ups to the England U21 and "B" squads, while he also represented the Nationwide League side against a team from Italy's Serie "B". Is reportedly wanted, internationally, by Jamaica and Northern Ireland, as well as England, but is not rushing into a decision. Unusually, he finished the campaign as leading scorer at two clubs, as no Bury player surpassed his total of eight goals!

Manchester U (From trainee on 1/7/94)
Bury (Free on 5/7/95) FL 72+25/17 FLC 8+3/4 FAC 1+1 Others 3+2/1
Ipswich T (£800,000 on 14/11/97) FL 30+1/20 FAC 4/2 Others 2

JOHNSON Gavin
Born: Stowmarket, 10 October 1970
Height: 5'11" Weight: 11.12
Club Honours: Div 2 '92; Div 3 '97

Dogged by groin problems throughout last season, Gavin was restricted to just 20 league games for Wigan, but still showed himself to be a flexible player who can perform anywhere down the left flank, either at full back or in wide midfield. Released at the end of the season, he scored two goals during the campaign, including one in the home victory over Fulham.

Ipswich T (From trainee on 1/3/89) F/PL 114+18/11 FLC 10+1/2 FAC 12/2 Others 3+1/1
Luton T (Free on 4/7/95) FL 4+1
Wigan Ath (£15,000 on 15/12/95) FL 82+2/8 FLC 4 FAC 3 Others 1

JOHNSON Ian Grant
Born: Dundee, 24 March 1972
Height: 5'11" Weight: 11.0
International Honours: S: U21-6

the campaign, his 42 league games winning him a second division championship medal.
Watford (From trainee on 11/5/92) FL 144+20/13 FLC 12+1/1 FAC 11+1 Others 2+1

JOHNSON Ross Yorke
Born: Brighton, 2 January 1976
Height: 6'0" Weight: 12.12
Although playing in a struggling side in 1997-98, Ross continued to develop his game and was one of the successes in yet another traumatic campaign for Brighton and Hove Albion. The 22-year-old central defender missed only a handful of games and needs just one more outing to record a century of senior appearances for his hometown club. Is strong in the air and has a prodigious long throw.
Brighton & Hove A (From trainee on 22/7/94) FL 79+10 FLC 2+1 FAC 2 Others 3+1

JOHNSON Seth Art Maurice
Born: Birmingham, 12 March 1979
Height: 5'10" Weight: 11.0
International Honours: E: Yth
Another graduate of the Crewe Alexandra youth team, since coming into the side in 1996-97 Seth has become a regular in a midfield role and, in 1997-98, he continued to emphasise how far he has progressed in such a short period of time. Able to play in defence equally as well, he looks to become the complete player. Was also delighted to score for the England U18 team at Gresty Road last season and, at the end of a long, hard campaign, was looking forward to playing in the European Championships in Cyprus during the summer.
Crewe Alex (From trainee on 12/7/96) FL 47+4/2 FLC 2 FAC 1 Others 0+3

JOHNSTON Allan
Born: Glasgow, 14 December 1973
Height: 5'10" Weight: 11.0
International Honours: S: B-2; U21-3
A great favourite with the Sunderland fans, the tricky left winger was one of the club's outstanding performers last term, and a key figure in the promotion push. Enjoyed his best ever season for goals, as well as providing many others with his pin-point crossing ability. Aptly nicknamed "Magic", Allan's outstanding moments last season included a first-half hat trick at Huddersfield in February, and a brilliant winning goal at The Stadium of Light in March, against Portsmouth. Enjoyed a call up to the Scotland "B" squad the same month, and a first full cap must surely be just around the corner. Was voted Nationwide Player of the Month for March.
Heart of Midlothian (Free from Tynecastle BC on 23/6/90) SL 46+38/12 SLC 3+2/2 SC 4+1 (Signed for Rennes during 1996 close season)
Sunderland (£550,000 on 27/3/97) F/PL 42+4/12 FLC 2 FAC 2 Others 3

JONES Barry
Born: Prescot, 30 June 1970
Height: 5'11" Weight: 11.12
Club Honours: WC '95
Following 20 appearances for Wrexham at the start of last season, and the scorer of the opening goal in a 3-1 home win over Oldham, Barry signed for York in January 1998, after spending a month on loan at Bootham Crescent. Quickly impressing with his coolness and all-round ability, initially at right back, and then in the middle of the defence, he was made captain in the closing weeks and popped up with vital goals in wins at Brentford and Bristol Rovers.
Liverpool (Signed from Prescot Cables on 19/1/89) Others 0+1
Wrexham (Free from 10/7/92) FL 184+11/5 FLC 14+1/1 FAC 11+2 Others 21+1
York C (£40,000 on 17/12/97) FL 23/2

JONES Gary
Born: Huddersfield, 6 April 1969
Height: 6'1" Weight: 12.9
Club Honours: Div 3 '98
Gary produced one of the most dominant and outstanding turn-arounds in form ever seen at Notts County, when unable to rediscover his scoring touch before last Christmas, he subsequently found an amazing rich vein, in which he netted 23 goals in 23 games. A strong centre forward, who is both lively and flexible, he was the fans' Player of the Year, and winner of the division three Golden Boot award with a total of 28 goals. Without a doubt, his goals more than helped County to the title and he became the proud possessor of a third division championship medal.
Doncaster Rov (Free from Rossington Main Colliery on 26/1/89) FL 10+10/2 FLC 1 (Free to Grantham on 1/11/89)
Southend U (£25,000 from Boston U, via Kettering T, on 3/6/93) FL 47+23/16 FLC 3/1 FAC 2 Others 6+1/2
Lincoln C (Loaned on 17/9/93) FL 0+4/2 Others 0+1
Notts Co (£140,000 on 1/3/96) FL 80+9/36 FLC 3+1/1 FAC 4+1/1 Others 1+1
Scunthorpe U (Loaned on 21/2/97) FL 9+2/5

Allan Johnston (right)

Gary Jones (Notts County)

JONES Gary Roy
Born: Birkenhead, 3 June 1977
Height: 5'10" Weight: 12.0
Signed from the League of Wales side, Caernarfon Town, during the 1997 summer recess, Gary showed impressive form in Swansea's pre-season friendlies and started 1997-98 as a regular member of the first team squad, appearing nine times before going on loan to Rochdale in January. He immediately secured a midfield berth with his non-stop running and ability to get forward, and scored his first league goal in his fourth game, after which the deal was firmed up.
Swansea C (Signed from Caernarfon T on 11/7/97) FL 3+5 FLC 0+1
Rochdale (Free on 15/1/98) FL 17/2

JONES Gary Steven
Born: Chester, 10 May 1975
Height: 6'3" Weight: 14.0
Gary's versatility was neatly summed up by the Tranmere Rovers' programme contributor, who described him as "having performed in more positions than you know who"... and he did a good job in each of them. A manager's dream, if injuries or suspensions threaten the numbers, he is truly an all-rounder who can play in defence, in midfield just behind the front two, or as a centre forward. Often had to lead the front line alone during last season, and, despite a shortage of crosses from the wings, he still found the back of the net on 11 occasions, including a brace against Stockport on Easter Monday. Gary is a big man and, although not exceptionally fast, will always trouble opposing defenders.
Tranmere Rov (From trainee on 5/7/93) FL 75+46/20 FLC 9+2/3 FAC 4+2/2 Others 1+1

JONES Graeme Anthony
Born: Gateshead, 13 March 1970
Height: 6'0" Weight: 12.12
Club Honours: Div 3 '97
Unable to rediscover his 1996-97 goal-scoring record form for Wigan Athletic, the popular centre forward's season in 1997-98 was hampered by injuries which saw the former Player of the Year never enjoying an extended run in the side. Strong in the air, and having the ability to hold the ball up well, Graeme scored 14 goals during the campaign, including a brace against Lincoln and Rotherham in the Auto Windscreens Shield.
Doncaster Rov (£10,000 from Bridlington T on 2/8/93) FL 80+12/26 FLC 4+1/1 FAC 2+1/1 Others 5/1
Wigan Ath (£150,000 on 8/7/96) FL 67+6/40 FLC 2+1/1 FAC 4/1 Others 4/5

JONES Jason Andrew
Born: Wrexham, 10 May 1979
Height: 6'2" Weight: 12.7
International Honours: W: Yth
Released by Liverpool at the end of his YTS period, the young goalkeeper joined Swansea on an initial six-month contract last November, and was immediately loaned out to League of Wales side, Rhayader, to further his experience. Recalled after showing enough promise to be offered a further two-year contract, Jason made his Football League debut in the final game of last season, a 1-0 defeat at Mansfield.
Swansea C (Free from Liverpool juniors on 29/12/97) FL 1

JONES Jonathan (Jon) Berwyn
Born: Wrexham, 27 October 1978
Height: 5'11" Weight: 11.5
A young Chester City forward with a great deal of potential, his opportunities were limited last season, mainly due to the number of forwards at the club. Has tremendous pace and looks to have a bright future, and will no doubt be pushing for a regular first team place during 1998-99.
Chester C (From trainee on 27/3/97) FL 5+19/2 FAC 0+1 Others 1+2

JONES Keith Aubrey
Born: Dulwich, 14 October 1965
Height: 5'8" Weight: 11.2
International Honours: E: Yth; Sch
A hard-working, competitive right-sided midfield player, Keith had his best season yet for Charlton in 1997-98, as he built up a solid partnership with Mark Kinsella, while his dominance in the middle of the park set up many scoring opportunities for the front men. He also found the net on four occasions, including the winning goals against Manchester City at the Valley, and the one that earned a replay in the fourth round of the FA Cup against Wolverhampton Wanderers.
Chelsea (From apprentice on 16/8/83) FL 43+9/7 FLC 9+2/3 FAC 1 Others 4+1
Brentford (£40,000 on 3/9/87) FL 167+2/13 FLC 15/2 FAC 13/4 Others 16/1
Southend U (£175,000 on 21/10/91) FL 88+2/11 FLC 4 FAC 5 Others 9/1
Charlton Ath (£150,000 on 16/9/94) FL 113+6/4 FLC 3+1 FAC 4+2/1 Others 3

Keith Jones

JONES Philip Lee
Born: Wrexham, 29 May 1973
Height: 5'9" Weight: 10.8
International Honours: W: 2; B-1; U21-14
During the 1997 close season, Lee decided that his future lay with Tranmere rather than at nearby Anfield, and, apparently swayed by a fans' petition, he signed for the Birkenhead club, having already spent a loan period with them. Possessing impressive pace, and able to read the game well, Lee was troubled by injury throughout the campaign, the worst being cartilage damage sustained during the home game against Ipswich in December, but still managed to score ten goals and contribute many "assists". All in all, he proved beyond doubt what a valuable bargain buy he was, and continued to press for a place in the Welsh squad.
Wrexham (From trainee on 5/7/91) FL 24+15/10 FLC 2 FAC 1+2/1 Others 4+1/2
Liverpool (£300,000 on 12/3/92) PL 0+3 FLC 0+1
Crewe Alex Loaned on 3/9/93) FL 4+4/1
Wrexham (Loaned on 26/1/96) FL 20/8
Wrexham (Loaned on 31/1/97) FL 2+4
Tranmere Rov (£100,000 on 27/3/97) FL 37+5/14 FLC 5/1

JONES Lee
Born: Pontypridd, 9 August 1970
Height: 6'3" Weight: 14.4
Club Honours: AMC '94
After many years as Swansea's second-choice goalkeeper, Lee finally made the breakthrough when joining Bristol Rovers, initially on loan last January. Tall and commanding, he made a real impression in restoring confidence in Rovers' defence in the final two months of the season, and managed to keep a clean sheet against Southend, the club's first for 14 matches. Is reliable and assured under pressure, and his long-range goalkicking was a feature of his play, which helped Rovers finish in a creditable fifth spot and gave them a place in the second division play offs.
Swansea C (£7,500 from AFC Porth on 24/3/94) FL 6 Others 1
Bristol Rov (Signed on 7/3/98) FL 8 Others 2

JONES Nathan Jason
Born: Rhondda, 28 May 1973
Height: 5'7" Weight: 10.12
Signed in the 1997 close season after leaving Luton and spending two years in Spain, Nathan made a fine start in the Southend United midfield in 1997-98, operating on the left to good effect. His tenacious running and trickery made him a difficult opponent to cope with, although his transition into a more defensive role was not so successful, and after some lacklustre performances late on in the campaign he lost his first team place. Still young and has the ability to develop into a fine attacking midfielder.
Luton T (£10,000 from Merthyr on 30/6/95 - Freed on 20/12/95)
Southend U (Free from Nomincia on 5/8/97) FL 34+5 FLC 4 FAC 2/1 Others 0+1

JONES Paul Steven
Born: Chirk, 18 April 1967
Height: 6'3" Weight: 14.8
International Honours: W: 5

Possibly the surprise package of last season, having been instrumental in Stockport's promotion to the first division in 1996-97, the new Southampton manager, Dave Jones, went back to his former club for his namesake and it proved to be a master stroke. Outstanding throughout the campaign as an ever present, and voted the Supporters' Player of the Season, it was hard to pick the 'keeper's best save as there were so many, but the one against Newcastle when he dived to his left to keep out Alan Shearer's first-time shot was vitally important, Saints going on to win 2-1 and reach safety. In giving a previously nervous defence more confidence, Paul is now one of the Premiership's top custodians, playing in four of Wales' six matches last season, and looks set to shine for club and country for a good while yet.

Wolverhampton W (£40,000 from Kidderminster Harriers on 23/7/91) FL 33 FLC 2 FAC 5 Others 4
Stockport Co (£60,000 on 25/7/96) FL 46 FLC 11 FAC 4 Others 4
Southampton (£900,000 on 28/7/97) PL 38 FLC 4 FAC 1

JONES Robert (Rob) Marc
Born: Wrexham, 5 November 1971
Height: 5'10" Weight: 11.0
Club Honours: FAC '92; FLC '95
International Honours: W: Sch. E: 8; U21-2; Yth

Injuries again meant that Rob had mixed fortunes for Liverpool, this time in 1997-98, after he had begun the season so well and had begun to re-discover the form of two years ago. On his day, he is the complete right back, who is decisive in the tackle, wins balls cleanly, passes quickly and accurately over both short and long distances, and is not adverse to getting down

Rob Jones

the flank like a traditional winger to cross. Unfortunately, although the tactical awareness is still in place, injuries have slowed him down somewhat and he will be working on that aspect of his game with the view to starting 1998-99 in pole position. Interestingly, he has yet to score for the club since arriving from Crewe back in October 1991. Was ruled out of the last three matches due to him requiring a hernia operation and, at the same time, pledged his long-term future to the club.

Crewe Alex (From trainee on 20/12/88) FL 59+16/2 FLC 9 FAC 0+3 Others 3
Liverpool (£300,000 on 4/10/91) F/PL 182+1 FLC 21+1 FAC 27 Others 11

Paul Jones

JONES Scott
Born: Sheffield, 1 May 1975
Height: 5'10" Weight: 11.6

From Scott's point of view, 1997-98 went from a nightmare to a fairytale. Out of contract with Barnsley at the season's start, he spent the early part of it out on loan at Mansfield, where he made eight appearances, and at Notts County, (November) where he was not used, and nearly joined the former club after the clubs had agreed a deal. However, in deciding to stay, he signed a six-month contract and because of injuries found himself back in the first team. It was a situation he was to grasp. Strong tackling, and good in the air, despite his lack of inches, he became a regular in central defence, having changed from full back. His two goals against Manchester United made him an instant hero and his performances brought him an extended contract. Was the only Reds central defender to score during the season.

Barnsley (From trainee on 1/2/94) F/PL 28+6/1 FAC 1+2/2
Mansfield T (Loaned on 7/8/97) FL 6 FLC 2

JONES Stephen (Steve) Gary
Born: Cambridge, 17 March 1970
Height: 6'1" Weight: 13.3

Tall, strong and quick, Steve started last season as the first-choice Charlton striker alongside Clive Mendonca, but lost his place in October despite some impressive performances up front. He was then loaned to former club, Bournemouth, where he found the net four times in six appearances, before being recalled by Charlton, only to make spasmodic appearances until finishing the campaign as first choice again. In addition to some valuable goals, averaging one every three games, he generally created problems for defenders with his tireless running.

West Ham U (£22,000 from Billericay T on 16/11/92) PL 8+8/4 FAC 2+2/1 Others 1+1
Bournemouth (£150,000 on 21/10/94) FL 71+3/26 FLC 4/3 FAC 3/1 Others 3
West Ham U (Signed on 16/5/96) PL 5+3 FLC 0+1 FAC 2
Charlton Ath (£400,000 on 14/2/97) FL 20+5/7 FLC 2 FAC 1 Others 1+2
Bournemouth (Loaned on 24/12/97) FL 5/4 Others 1/1

JONES Vincent (Vinny) Peter
Born: Watford, 5 January 1965
Height: 6'0" Weight: 11.12
Club Honours: FAC '88 DIV 2 '90
International Honours: W: 9

A midfielder who is a great motivator on the field and hates to lose, always giving 100 per-cent effort, and well known for his intimidatory style, he is perhaps a better player than many have given him credit for. Controversial as he may be, Vinny is Queens Park Rangers' gain and Wimbledon's loss, having joined the former on transfer deadline day last March as the new player/coach. However, he will be sorely missed by the Wimbledon fans who have supported him through two spells at the club and strongly believe that one day "Jonah" will be back as the Dons' coach.

Missed few games up to his time of departure, and scored on his debut for Rangers at Huddersfield, his first league goal for 13 months, before going on to play the final six games of the season, being on the losing side just once as he helped to steer Rangers away from relegation. Continues to be dangerous from set pieces and long throws. Outside of football, he has many interests, including starring in a movie, and a television game and chat shows.

Wimbledon (£10,000 from Wealdstone on 20/11/86) FL 77/9 FLC 6+2 FAC 11+2/1 Others 3
Leeds U (£650,000 on 20/6/89) FL 44+2/5 FLC 2 FAC 1 Others 4
Sheffield U (£700,000 on 13/9/90) FL 35/2 FLC 4 FAC 1 Others 1
Chelsea (£575,000 on 30/8/91) F/PL 42/4 FLC 1 FAC 4/1 Others 5/2
Wimbledon (£700,000 on 10/9/92) F/PL 171+6/12 FLC 21+1/2 FAC 21+1/1
Queens Park R (£500,000 on 26/3/98) FL 7/1

JORDAN Scott Douglas
Born: Newcastle, 19 July 1975
Height: 5'10" Weight: 11.2
Despite looking to establish himself as a first team fixture, Scott was mostly on the sidelines for York City during the 1997-98 season. The midfielder, whose strengths are his passing ability and coolness, did, however, win his place back in the senior side during the closing weeks of the campaign, and will be looking to maintain that form in 1998-99.
York C (From trainee on 21/10/92) FL 64+31/5 FLC 4+1/1 FAC 2+2 Others 5+4

JOSEPH Marc Ellis
Born: Leicester, 10 November 1976
Height: 6'0" Weight: 12.5
Developing into a very good centre back at Cambridge in his first full season of league football, Marc had a shaky spell early on but had the strength to play through it. He has pace and a good understanding, and established himself in the side while forming a good central defensive partnership with Andy Duncan.
Cambridge U (From trainee on 23/5/95) FL 52+9 FLC 3 FAC 0+1 Others 1+1

JOSEPH Matthew (Matt) Nathan Adolphus
Born: Bethnal Green, 30 September 1972
Height: 5'8" Weight: 10.7
International Honours: E: Yth
A 1997 close season signing from Cambridge United, Matthew proved to be a good tackler who was equally comfortable playing at centre half or right back for Leyton Orient in 1997-98. Despite his lack of height, he is surprisingly good in the air and is a good overlapping player who likes to get into the opponents' area.
Arsenal (From trainee on 17/11/90)
Gillingham (Free on 7/12/92 - Free to Ilves during 1993 close season)
Cambridge U (Signed on 19/11/93) FL 157+2/6 FLC 6+1 FAC 7 Others 5
Leyton Orient (£10,000 on 22/1/98) FL 14/1

JOSEPH Roger Anthony
Born: Paddington, 24 December 1965
Height: 5'11" Weight: 11.10
International Honours: E: B-2

Signed from West Bromwich Albion during the 1997 close season, Roger rejoined Leyton Orient on a non-contract basis, once again proving a valuable squad member who could fit in anywhere across the defence. A good defender who is comfortable on the ball, he was unfortunate not to be a regular in 1997-98, but when called upon never let the team down.
Brentford (Free from Southall on 4/10/85) FL 103+1/2 FLC 7 FAC 1 Others 8
Wimbledon (£150,000 on 25/8/88) F/PL 155+7 FLC 17+2 FAC 11+1 Others 6
Millwall (Loaned on 2/3/95) FL 5
Leyton Orient (Free on 22/11/96) FL 15 Others 1
West Bromwich A (Free on 28/2/97) FL 0+2
Leyton Orient (Free on 7/8/97) FL 13+12 FLC 2+1 FAC 0+1 Others 1

Roger Joseph

JOYCE Warren Garton
Born: Oldham, 20 January 1965
Height: 5'9" Weight: 12.0
After incurring the disapproval of the Hull City faithful in 1996-97, last season Warren fought back to be the most consistent performer in a notably inconsistent team. The respect for the wholehearted midfielder extended beyond the terraces, as manager, Mark Hateley, handed him back the captain's armband in March and, in rejecting the overtures of Notts County and other clubs, offered him a new contract. Approaching 700 career appearances, but maintaining an amazing level of fitness in missing only one game in 1997-98, the son of Walter, a former manager at Rochdale, has enhanced his own coaching interests at Manchester United's Centre of Excellence. Swept the board with the club's Player of the Year awards.
Bolton W (From juniors on 23/6/82) FL 180+4/17 FLC 14+1/1 FAC 11/1 Others 11/2
Preston NR (£35,000 on 16/10/87) FL 170+7/34 FLC 8/2 FAC 6/1 Others 19/7
Plymouth Arg (£160,000 on 19/5/92) FL 28+2/3 FLC 6/1 FAC 2 Others 2

Burnley (£140,000 on 7/7/93) FL 65+5/9 FLC 8/1 FAC 4/1 Others 8/1
Hull C (Loaned on 20/1/95) FL 9/3
Hull C (£30,000 on 10/7/96) FL 90/9 FLC 6+1/1 FAC 4/1 Others 4/1

Warren Joyce

JULES Mark Anthony
Born: Bradford, 5 September 1971
Height: 5'8" Weight: 11.1
Mark began 1997-98 at Chesterfield in his customary left-wing-back position before missing several important games with injury. Upon his return, however, his ability to go past a man and deliver a fine cross featured in a midfield role that appeared to take a little getting used to, but he came through to link up well with Chris Perkins on the left.
Bradford C (From trainee on 3/7/90) FLC 0+1
Scarborough (Free on 14/8/91) FL 57+20/16 FLC 6+2/2 FAC 1+1 Others 6/4
Chesterfield (£40,000 on 21/5/93) FL 136+27/4 FLC 10+2/2 FAC 12+2 Others 9

JUPP Duncan Alan
Born: Haslemere, 25 January 1975
Height: 6'0" Weight: 12.12
International Honours: S: U21-10
The right back appeared mainly as a bit player for Wimbledon in 1997-98, appearing just six times intermittently, while sitting on the bench several times but not used. Composed on the ball, and with a liking to get forward, injuries apart, he looked more than adequate to deal with the Premiership, even in a campaign that saw the club in danger of being relegated, and is almost certain to play more than a passing role this time round. A Scottish U21 international, Duncan will be looking to go one better before too long.
Fulham (From trainee on 12/7/93) FL 101+4/2 FLC 10+2 FAC 9+1/1 Others 9+1/1
Wimbledon (£125,000 + on 27/6/96) PL 9 FLC 2 FAC 2+2

'When it's time to hang up your boots!'

If your playing days are coming to an end...
Let us help you with your retirement plans.

It pays to decide...

For more information call us FREE on
0500 302014 (quoting ref: LM35)

http://www.nationwide.co.uk

The World's No.1 Building Society

K

KALOGERACOS Vasilios (Vas)
Born: Perth, Australia, 21 March 1975
Height: 5'7" Weight: 11.0
A pint-sized striker, Vas was the "big-name" signing promised by the Stockport board last summer, moving from Perth Glory. Unfortunately, the transfer was not the success hoped for and, after four unremarkable displays, he was relegated to the reserves and "A" team before being sold back to Perth for an undisclosed fee in February.
Stockport Co (£80,000 from Perth Glory on 8/8/97) FL 0+2 FLC 1

KAMMARK Pontus Sven
Born: Vasteras, Sweden, 5 April 1969
Height: 5'11" Weight: 12.7
Club Honours: FLC '97
International Honours: Sweden: 34
The right-footed Leicester defender operated either as wing back or as a central defender in 1997-98 and, at the same time, developed a reputation as the best man-marker in the Premiership, nullifying the likes of Stan Collymore, Steve McManaman, and Ryan Giggs during the early weeks. Settling for a more orthodox central defensive role as the season progressed, he was also a regular choice for Sweden, and was disappointed when that nation just missed out on the trip to France during the summer. Unfortunate to miss the final home fixture against Barnsley, after aggravating an old back injury during the pre-match warm up, he missed only three other games.
Leicester C (£840,000 from IFK Gothenberg on 2/11/95) P/FL 45+1 FLC 4 FAC 4 Others 2

KATCHOURO Petr
Born: Urss, Belarus, 2 August 1972
Height: 5'11" Weight: 12.6
International Honours: Belarus: 22
The Sheffield United striker who was the previous year's Player of the Season, failed to register a single goal for the club in 1997-98. He even managed to miss in the dramatic penalty shoot-out against Coventry, when lifting his shot over the bar, despite scoring one for Belarus in their World Cup qualifying defeat in Scotland. Was linked with transfers and loan moves to various clubs during the campaign, including a swap deal with Queens Park Rangers, and a loan move to PAOK Salonika, which fell through due to a Greek FA technicality. However, in managing to lift his game towards the end of the campaign, he set up several goals for his fellow strikers with his pace.
Sheffield U (£650,000 from Dinamo Minsk on 19/7/96) FL 34+22/12 FLC 5+3/1 FAC 2+6 Others 3/1

KAVANAGH Graham Anthony
Born: Dublin, 2 December 1973
Height: 5'10" Weight: 12.11
International Honours: Ei: 1; B-1; U21-9; Yth; Sch
A creative Stoke midfield player who, on his day, can run a game from the centre of the park, Graham was clearly upset by the crowd reaction as the side tumbled down the table in the second half of last season. As the club's penalty taker, confidence is a huge part of his game and possessing one of the best dead-ball shots in the division, if not the hardest, he scored two terrific goals in the 4-0 win at Burnley in the Coca Cola Cup. He also added to his international CV when selected to play in a "B" match for the Republic of Ireland against Northern Ireland in February, and made his full debut against Czechoslovakia shortly afterwards.
Middlesbrough (Signed from Home Farm on 16/8/91) F/PL 22+13/3 FLC 1 FAC 3+1/1 Others 7
Darlington (Loaned on 25/2/94) FL 5
Stoke C (£250,000 + on 13/9/96) FL 76+6/9 FLC 6+1/5 FAC 1

KAVANAGH Jason Colin
Born: Meriden, 23 November 1971
Height: 5'9" Weight: 12.7
International Honours: E: Yth; Sch
1997-98 was a very consistent season for this versatile Wycombe defender as he coped admirably in his spells as wing back on both flanks, although more comfortable on his favoured right foot. Strong in the tackle, he liked to push forward whenever possible, and was rewarded with his first goal for the club at Blackpool in August.
Derby Co (From trainee on 9/12/88) FL 74+25/1 FLC 3+2 FAC 7 Others 8+8
Wycombe W (£25,000 on 1/11/96) FL 70+2/1 FLC 2 FAC 3+1 Others 3

KAY John
Born: Great Lumley, 29 January 1964
Height: 5'9" Weight: 11.6
Club Honours: Div 3 '88
A battling, no-nonsense full back, John enjoyed an excellent season with Scarborough in 1997-98, always putting in 100 per-cent commitment and, in missing just six games, made the right-back shirt his own. Assured and confident on the ball, and a great crowd favourite, he was voted the Away Supporters Player of the Year as a reward for his consistent display.
Arsenal (From apprentice on 7/8/81) FL 13+1
Wimbledon (£25,000 on 20/7/84) FL 63/2 FLC 3 FAC 3 Others 1
Middlesbrough (Loaned on 8/1/85) FL 8
Sunderland (£22,500 on 22/7/87) FL 196+3 FLC 19 FAC 12 Others 6
Shrewsbury T (Loaned on 28/3/96) FL 7 Others 1
Preston NE (Free on 23/8/96) FL 7 FLC 3
Scarborough (Free on 27/9/96) FL 74 FLC 2 FAC 2/1 Others 3

KEAN Robert Steven
Born: Luton, 3 June 1978
Height: 5'7" Weight: 10.2
One of a bunch of promising youngsters coming through the youth squad at Luton, Robert was a member of the team that won a South East Counties championship in consecutive seasons. Given a brief first team run out in 1997-98, and gaining in experience all the time, the young mid-fielder can be expected to appear more frequently in 1998-99.
Luton T (From trainee on 2/5/96) FL 0+1

KEANE Robert (Robbie) David
Born: Dublin, 8 July 1980
Height: 5'9" Weight: 10.0
International Honours: Ei: 3; B-1
A young forward who had a terrific 1996-97 for the juniors, but only started two reserve games, and was 17 in the summer, Robbie made a surprise opening day appearance at Norwich last season and was the first player to score two on his Wolves' debut since Ted Farmer in 1960. They were lovely goals, a dipping volley and a toe-poke after a good little run. Playing in the "hole" behind the front two, producing clever tricks and flicks, yet showing remarkable composure when presented with two chances against Bury, he scored three times for Eire at youth level, before returning from a tournament to lob the winner versus Middlesbrough. In the New Year he played more out on the right, being rested for the earlier FA Cup ties, but was booked against Wimbledon and then showed his inexperience when needlessly conceding a penalty at Leeds. Having progressed to the "B" team he then became Eire's second youngest full international ever, coming on for most of the second half in Czechoslovakia, before going on to play the whole 90 minutes against Argentina. Despite struggling to keep his place in the Wolves' team, Robbie was clearly the find of the season, being selected in the PFA divisional XI.
Wolverhampton W (From trainee on 26/7/97) FL 34+4/11 FLC 3+1 FAC 1+2

Robbie Keane

KEANE Roy Maurice
Born: Cork, 10 August 1971
Height: 5'10" Weight: 12.10
Club Honours: FMC '92; CS '93, '96, '97; PL '94, '96, '97; FAC '94, '96
International Honours: Ei: 38; U21-4; Yth; Sch

163

An inspirational Manchester United midfielder with excellent skills and a hardened edge, Roy started last season as United's new captain, having got into the habit of picking up trophies on the club's summer tour of the Far East. A regular first teamer throughout August and September, he scored two important Premiership goals against Coventry and West Ham but, although he was on the top of his form, and relishing his role as skipper, his campaign came to an abrupt end when he suffered cruciate knee ligament damage following a challenge with the Leeds inside-forward, Alf-Inge Haaland, at Elland Road in September. Despite openly admitting that the injury had provided him with the "biggest challenge of his life," he made such a good recovery from his operation that he was looking to make a first team return before the end of 1997-98. Although that was slightly ambitious, even by Roy's standards, he was hopeful of leading the club to further glories in 1998-99. Was named the Republic of Ireland's Player of the Year in October.

Nottingham F (£10,000 from Cobh Ramblers on 12/6/90) F/PL 114/22 FLC 17/6 FAC 18/3 Others 5/2

Manchester U (£3,750,000 on 22/7/93) PL 116+5/17 FLC 9+2 FAC 22+1/1 Others 19/4

KEARTON Jason Brett
Born: Ipswich, Australia, 9 July 1969
Height: 6'1" Weight: 11.10
Club Honours: FAC '95

Having understudied Neville Southall at Everton for so long, Jason put that experience to the test as the first-choice goalkeeper for Crewe in 1997-98, as he had done the previous season, and again came through with flying colours, keeping 13 clean sheets and only being displaced when injured. Is an excellent shot-stopper who stands up well and is confident on crosses.

Everton (Free from Brisbane Lions on 31/10/88) PL 3+3 FLC 1 FAC 1
Stoke C (Loaned on 13/8/91) FL 16 Others 1
Blackpool (Loaned on 9/1/92) FL 14
Notts Co (Loaned on 19/1/95) FL 10 Others 2
Crewe Alex (Free on 16/10/96) FL 73 FLC 1 FAC 5 Others 6

KEATES Dean Scott
Born: Walsall, 30 June 1978
Height: 5'5" Weight: 10.6

After playing only two previous first team appearances, Dean earned himself a regular place at Walsall in 1997-98 with some storming games in midfield, and was badly missed in the last month of the season after picking up a strain in the game against Gillingham. By that time, however, he had

scored an opportunist match winner at Millwall, and a fine Auto Windscreen goal against Brighton.

Walsall (From trainee on 14/8/96) FL 33+2/1 FLC 5+1 FAC 4 Others 5/1

KEEBLE Christopher (Chris) Mark
Born: Colchester, 17 September 1978
Height: 5'10" Weight: 10.6

A regular in the Ipswich reserve side in 1997-98, where he played in central midfield, Chris was included in the squad for the game at Port Vale and came off the substitutes' bench to make his first team debut – playing for the last two minutes. A youngster who favours his right foot, could he be another famous Keeble to emanate from Colchester!

Ipswich T (From trainee on 2/6/97) FL 0+1

KEEN Kevin Ian
Born: Amersham, 25 February 1967
Height: 5'7" Weight: 10.10
International Honours: E: Yth; Sch

A popular hard-working, right-sided Stoke midfield player, his early season performances in 1997-98 warranted a new contract and by Christmas he was one of the side's top performers. The change of manager to Chris Kamara did nothing for Kevin and he

Kevin Keen (left)

was quickly facing Pontins League football. Kamara's reign was short, however, and the new duo of Alan Durban and Chic Bates quickly restored him to the side.

West Ham U (From apprentice on 8/3/84) FL 187+32/21 FLC 21+1/5 FAC 15+7/1 Others 14+2/3
Wolverhampton W (£600,000 on 7/7/93) FL 37+5/7 FLC 2+1 FAC 5/1 Others 4/1
Stoke C (£300,000 on 19/10/94) FL 84+26/7 FLC 9+2/1 FAC 3 Others 2

KEISTER John Edward Samuel
Born: Manchester, 11 November 1970
Height: 5'8" Weight: 11.0
International Honours: Sierra Leone: 3

This tough-tackling Walsall midfielder, with an increasing degree of constructive ability, had some thing of an in-and-out season in 1997-98, but added to his Sierra Leone caps and always gave of his best when called into the first team. His general bad luck was summed up when in the midst of a battling display at Bristol City, during the final away match, he was harshly penalised for handball and City got the match winner from the free kick.

Walsall (Free from Faweh FC on 18/9/93) FL 76+27/2 FLC 3 FAC 10+2 Others 2+2

KELLER Kasey
Born: Washington, USA, 27 November 1969
Height: 6'2" Weight: 13.12
Club Honours: FLC '97
International Honours: USA: 31

As a cool, confident, and commanding goalkeeper, Kasey enhanced his growing international reputation at Leicester in 1997-98 with a series of outstanding displays for both club and country, in particular his performance to thwart Brazil that earned him rave reviews across the globe. Outstanding in the home draw with Sheffield Wednesday, he kept 16 clean sheets, three of them coming in the last four games, and continued to give the defence confidence throughout. Something of a joker off the field, he turned up for the club photocall sporting his glasses instead of the contact lenses he wears for games, and several frames were wasted before the photographer spotted the joke. *Stop Press:* Shared the goalkeeping duties with Liverpool's Brad Friedel in the Group F World Cup matches, playing against Germany and Iran, before the USA went out of the competition.

Millwall (Free from Portland University on 20/2/92) FL 176 FLC 14 FAC 8 Others 4
Leicester C (£900,000 on 17/8/96) PL 63 FLC 9 FAC 6 Others 2

KELLY Alan Thomas
Born: Preston, 11 August 1968
Height: 6'2" Weight: 14.3
International Honours: Ei: 20; U23-1; Yth

Alan suffered another injury-hit season after starting 1997-98 as second choice when Simon Tracey was given his chance following his run at the end of 1996-97. Then, after making three penalty saves in the FA Cup replay against Coventry City, which were instrumental in taking United to the semi final, Alan reckoned his last

penalty save came in the shoot-out against Blackburn in the 1993 cup run. Appearing once again in the Republic of Ireland squad, when contesting the goalkeeping spot with Shay Given, he missed the run in to the end of the campaign due to a knee injury, which necessitated a cartilage operation.

Preston NE (From apprentice on 25/9/85) FL 142 FLC 1 FAC 8 Others 13
Sheffield U (£200,000 on 24/7/92) P/FL 191+3 FLC 13 FAC 17 Others 2

KELLY David Thomas
Born: Birmingham, 25 November 1965
Height: 5'11" Weight: 12.1
Club Honours: Div '93
International Honours: Ei: 26; B-3; U23-1; U21-3

Seen by John Aldridge as his natural successor, this hard-working striker was signed by Tranmere from Sunderland in the 1997 close season and mid-way through last term, became club captain. His many and varied duties included having to race from his Midlands home to St Andrews in order to hand the Rovers' team sheet, for the

league game against Birmingham, to the referee just before the deadline, the line-up having been dictated to him over John Aldridge's mobile phone from the team coach stuck in traffic on the M6! "Ned", as he is known, often turned out when less than 100 per-cent fit, in deference to his own welfare, in order to bolster the team cause, and made an invaluable contribution. Finished 1997-98 as Rovers' top scorer. Added to his Republic of Ireland caps with three further appearances during the season.

Walsall (Signed from Alvechurch on 21/12/83) FL 115+32/63 FLC 11+1/4 FAC 12+2/3 Others 14+3/10
West Ham U (£600,000 on 1/8/88) FL 29+12/7 FLC 11+3/5 FAC 6 Others 2+1/2
Leicester C (£300,000 on 22/3/90) FL 63+3/22 FLC 6/2 FAC 1 Others 2/1
Newcastle U (£250,000 on 4/12/91) FL 70/35 FLC 4/2 FAC 5/1 Others 4/1
Wolverhampton W (£750,000 on 23/6/93) FL 76+7/26 FLC 5/2 FAC 11/6 Others 4/2
Sunderland (£1,000,000 on 19/9/95) P/FL 32+2/2 FLC 2+1 FAC 3
Tranmere Rov (£350,000 on 5/8/97) FL 28+1/11 FLC 5/3 FAC 3

Alan Kelly

KELLY Garry
Born: Drogheda, 9 July 1974
Height: 5'8" Weight: 13.3
International Honours: Ei: 28; U21-5; Yth; Sch

Is still regarded as one of the best right-sided full backs in the Premier League. Even so, he began last season on the right side of Leeds' midfield, where his searing pace was used to good effect. Due to his versatility proving invaluable, once again, Garry was also deployed in central defence when Lucas Radebe was away at the African Nations Cup. Having had a really consistent 1997-98, he was justifiably rewarded with a recall to the Republic of Ireland team. Still only 23-years old, he has already amassed over 200 games for the club, and during the campaign, signed a new four-and-a-half-year contract. As the skipper in the 5-0 victory at Derby in March, he really epitomised the spirit at Elland Road and is a "true" professional.
Leeds U (Signed from Home Farm on 24/9/91) PL 186+4/2 FLC 18+1 FAC 19+1 Others 4

Garry Kelly

KELLY Gary Alexander
Born: Preston, 3 August 1966
Height: 5'11" Weight: 13.6
Club Honours: FAYC '85
International Honours: Ei: B-1; U23-1; U21-8

The son of Alan (senior) and brother to Alan (junior), both Republic of Ireland international goalkeepers, Gary would surely have joined them had it not been for his distinct lack of inches. A good shot-stopper as normal for Oldham, he was unfortunately forced to miss a large chunk of 1997-98 due to a knee injury sustained in the opening match of the season. Somewhat a specialist in keeping clean sheets, he managed ten during his 32 matches played, three of them in succession.
Newcastle U (From apprentice on 20/6/84) FL 53 FLC 4 FAC 3 Others 2
Blackpool (Loaned on 7/10/88) FL 5
Bury (£60,000 on 5/10/89) FL 236 FLC 14 FAC 13 Others 29
Oldham Ath (£10,000 on 27/8/96) FL 68 FLC 4 FAC 5 Others 1

KELLY Patrick (Paddy)
Born: Kirkcaldy, 26 April 1978
Height: 6'2" Weight: 12.0
International Honours: S: Yth

Released by Glasgow Celtic during the 1997 close season, Paddy moved to Newcastle under the wing of Kenny Dalglish, but, unable to get first team action, and looking to get match fit, he was loaned to Reading, where he played at centre back in three of the last seven games, finishing on the losing side each time, and being substituted in the final match at home to Norwich City. Despite only giving glimpses of his undoubted ability, the Royals' manager, Tommy Burns, announced his intention to try and sign the lanky defender on a permanent contract.
Glasgow Celtic (From juniors on 3/8/95) SL 1
Newcastle U (Free on 9/8/97)
Reading (Loaned on 26/3/98) FL 3

KELLY Raymond (Ray)
Born: Athlone, 29 December 1976
Height: 5'11" Weight: 12.0
International Honours: Ei: U21-4

Signed from Athlone Town in the 1994 close season, this promising young striker came through Manchester City's "A" and reserve sides to gain selection for the Republic of Ireland's U21 side before being loaned out to Wrexham last October. After making eight appearances, during which he scored one of the goals in a 3-1 home win over Southend, he was recalled due to a striker crisis to make his City debut at home to Huddersfield and, despite being subbed, was praised for his efforts. Placed on the transfer list in February, he went back on loan to Wrexham and came off the bench twice before the campaign drew to a close.
Manchester C (£30,000 from Athlone T on 1/8/94) FL 1
Wrexham (Loaned on 3/10/97) FL 5+1/1
Wrexham (Loaned on 26/3/98) FL 0+4

KENNA Jeffrey (Jeff) Jude
Born: Dublin, 27 August 1970
Height: 5'11" Weight: 12.2
International Honours: Ei: 24; B-1; U21-8; Yth; Sch

After two and a half seasons at Blackburn, Jeff finally made the transition in 1997-98 to being an accepted member of the team. Initially required to fill in at left back when Graeme Le Saux was not replaced, he performed well, but when switched to right back he blossomed and by the end of the campaign had become the club's most reliable defender. He also gained a regular position with the Eire national side. In the club's 4-4-2 system he is not required to attack, but has pace, can tackle, and reads the game well.
Southampton (From trainee on 25/4/89) F/PL 110+4/4 FLC 4 FAC 10+1 Others 3
Blackburn Rov (£1,500,000 on 15/3/95) PL 115/1 FLC 8 FAC 8 Others 6

KENNEDY John Neil
Born: Newmarket, 19 August 1978
Height: 5'8" Weight: 10.5

An ever present for Ipswich reserves last season, John's solid performances earned him a place in the first team squad for the trip to Port Vale and he made his debut as a substitute, coming on for the final ten minutes. Showed some useful touches while playing in his normal position of left back, keeping the balance of left-footed players, and could be one for the future.
Ipswich T (From trainee on 2/6/97) FL 0+1

KENNEDY Mark
Born: Dublin, 15 May 1976
Height: 5'11" Weight: 11.9
International Honours: Ei: 18; U21-7; Yth; Sch

With just one appearance from the Liverpool bench last season, and with a hankering to get back to the capital, Mark was loaned out to Queens Park Rangers in January. Having made his debut at Stockport, he went on to score two goals in their next game, a 3-2 win against Crewe, and played in six more matches for the club, being Man of the Match in nearly all of them, before returning north when the Pool had an injury crisis. With Rangers still trying to sign the talented left-sided winger, Wimbledon surprisingly stepped in to buy him on transfer deadline day in March, despite him carrying a broken wrist which prevented him playing in all but the final four games. A quality player with great skill and pace, who loves going past defenders as if they did not exist, great things are expected of the Republic of Ireland international.
Millwall (From trainee on 6/5/92) FL 37+6/9 FLC 6+1/2 FAC 3+1/1
Liverpool (£1,500,000 on 21/3/95) PL 5+11 FLC 0+2 FAC 0+1 Others 0+2
Queens Park R (Loaned on 27/1/98) FL 8/2
Wimbledon (£1,750,000 on 27/3/98) PL 4

KENNEDY Peter Henry James
Born: Lurgan, 10 September 1973
Height: 5'11" Weight: 11.11
Club Honours: Div 2 '98
International Honours: NI: B-1

A left-sided winger or wing back, who was transferred to Watford from Notts County in July 1997, a deal which already looks like a bargain, Peter was on the verge of leaving the game after a depressing spell in County's reserves, but was signed unseen by Graham Taylor and soon endeared himself to the Watford faithful with his pace, skill on the ball, and powerful shooting. A formidable scorer, especially away from home, the Irishman scored his first-ever hat trick at Southend, a pair at Luton to guarantee instant immortality, and a Goal of the Month contender against Sheffield Wednesday in the FA Cup. In February, his progress was halted by a cracked bone in his leg, but he had already done enough to secure selection for the PFA second division team at left back, still finish as the club's leading scorer with 13 goals, and win a second division championship medal. Is a Northern Ireland "B" cap, with further honours sure to follow.
Notts Co (£100,000 from Portadown on 28/8/96) FL 20+2 FLC 1 FAC 2+1/1 Others 0+1
Watford (£130,000 on 10/7/97) FL 34/11 FLC 4/1 FAC 5/1

Peter Kennedy

KENTON Darren Edward
Born: Wandsworth, 13 September 1978
Height: 5'11" Weight: 11.11

A first-year professional, having come through the ranks as a YTS, Darren made his league debut for Norwich as a substitute at Tranmere last October. Obviously inexperienced and under pressure, he then dropped away from the senior scene to produce several Man of the Match displays for the reserves before winning a recall in February, when coming into the side for his first start, against Manchester City at Carrow Road. Primarily a central defender, but thus far playing in midfield and at full back, his future looks both assured and bright.

Norwich C (From trainee on 3/7/97) FL 7+4

KEOWN Martin Raymond
Born: Oxford, 24 July 1966
Height: 6'1" Weight: 12.4
Club Honours: PL '98; FAC '98
International Honours: E: 18; B-1; U21-8; Yth

In making club history when becoming the first player since the war to re-sign for Arsenal, returning to Highbury in 1993, he now knows that the decision was the right one, having won championship and FA Cup winners' medals in 1997-98 after the Gunners raced to the double with a late run. A superb man marker, Martin moved ahead of Steve Bould in the centre-back pecking order, having been out of the Premiership side until towards the end of November, when restored following injury. A commanding defender with plenty of pace, who reads the situation well, is strong in the air, and one of the best tacklers around, he was given far more freedom of movement under the watchful eye of Arsene Wenger than he had been given before, and he flourished. Continued to play for England, being named in the final 22 that were to travel to France in the summer to contest the World Cup Finals, and looks good for a number of years to come. *Stop Press:* Not called upon during the World Cup games in France '98, he could only watch as England bravely departed from the competition.

Arsenal (From apprentice on 2/2/84) FL 22 FAC 5
Brighton & Hove A (Loaned on 15/2/85) FL 21+2/1 FLC 2/1 Others 2/1
Aston Villa (£200,000 on 9/6/86) FL 109+3/3 FLC 12+1 FAC 6 Others 2
Everton (£750,000 on 7/8/89) F/PL 92+4 FLC 11 FAC 12+1 Others 6
Arsenal (£2,000,000 on 4/2/93) PL 147+18/2 FLC 16+2/1 FAC 15+2 Others 11+5

KERNAGHAN Alan Nigel
Born: Otley, 25 April 1967
Height: 6'1" Weight: 14.1
International Honours: NI: Sch. Ei: 22

Following a disappointing 1996-97 when he was dogged by injuries, Alan came back into the Manchester City side for the second and third games of last season, mainly due to an injury to Kit Symons, but was sent off in the latter, at Sunderland, and a few weeks later joined St Johnstone on a three-month loan. Still a reliable central defender, he settled in well and the move was firmed up just before Christmas.

Middlesbrough (From apprentice on 8/3/85) F/PL 172+40/16 FLC 22+7/1 FAC 7+4/3 Others 14+2/2
Charlton Ath (Loaned on 17/1/91) FL 13
Manchester C (£1,600,000 on 20/9/93) P/FL 55+8/1 FLC 8 FAC 7/1
Bolton W (Loaned on 18/8/94) FL 9+2
Bradford C (Loaned on 2/2/96) FL 5

KERR David William
Born: Dumfries, 6 September 1974
Height: 5'11" Weight: 12.7

Having suffered a double fracture of the leg in Mansfield's cause in 1996-97, the midfielder came back hesitantly last season and though used carefully, often in a substitute role, did not let the side down. A strong tackler, who can also play in defence, David scored his first goals for the club, both at home, and both in 1-0 victories, against Scunthorpe and Swansea, the last named being the final game of the campaign.

Manchester C (From trainee on 10/9/91) PL 4+2
Mansfield T (Loaned on 22/9/95) FL 4+1 Others 1
Mansfield T (£20,000 on 31/7/96) FL 16+11/2 FLC 1 Others 2

KERRIGAN Steven (Steve) John
Born: Baillieston, 9 October 1972
Height: 6'1" Weight: 12.4

A forward signed in mid-last season from Ayr United, Steve made his Shrewsbury league debut in January at Torquay. Although a niggling injury hampered his progress, towards the end of the campaign, he began to build a formidable partnership with Lee Steele, scoring his first goal in March at Home to Hull. His strength so far has been making, rather than scoring goals, but effective in the air and on the ground, 1998-99 should see him blossom further.

Albion Rovers (Free from Newmains Juveniles on 22/7/92) SL 46+7/14 SLC 2/1 SC 1 Others 1
Clydebank (Signed on 11/2/94) SL 17+13 SLC 1+1 Others 2+1/2
Stranraer (Signed on 4/11/95) SL 19+2/5 SC 1
Albion Rov (Free from Newmains Juveniles on 22/7/92) SL 46+7/14 SLC 2/1 SC 1 Others 1
Clydebank (Signed on 11/2/94) SL 17+13 SLC 1+1 Others 2+1/2
Ayr U (Signed on 25/6/96) SL 26+7/17 SLC 2/2 SC 1 Others 2/2
Shrewsbury T (£25,000 on 21/1/98) FL 11+3/2

Martin Keown

KERSLAKE David
Born: Stepney, 19 June 1966
Height: 5'9" Weight: 12.3
International Honours: E: U21-1; Yth; Sch

After being released by Tottenham during the 1997 close season, David moved across London to trial with Charlton before signing for Ipswich in the opening month of last season. However, although featuring regularly on the subs' bench he could not establish himself in Town's first team and went on loan to Wycombe in December, where he acquitted himself well in 11 games, his pace and close control from his right-wing-back slot causing problems for opposing defenders. Then it was back to Portman Road and a permanent transfer to Swindon in March. Into his third spell at the County Ground, David was mainly deployed to great effect as a sweeper, and the fans, especially those in the south stand who have enjoyed watching him since he first joined the club in 1989, will be looking for more of the same this coming term.

Queens Park R (From apprentice on 1/6/83) FL 38+20/6 FLC 6+2/4 FAC 2+2 Others 2+2
Swindon T (£110,000 on 24/11/89) FL 133+2/1 FLC 12 FAC 8 Others 10
Leeds U (£500,000 on 11/3/93) PL 8
Tottenham H (£450,000 on 24/9/93) PL 34+3 FLC 5 FAC 1+1
Swindon T (Loaned on 29/11/96) FL 8
Charlton Ath (Free on 8/8/97)
Ipswich T (Free on 22/8/97) FL 2+5 FLC 1+1
Wycombe W (Loaned on 12/12/97) FL 9+1 Others 1
Swindon T (Free on 10/3/98) FL 10

Temur Ketsbaia

KETSBAIA Temuri
Born: Georgia, 18 March 1968
Height: 6'0" Weight: 13.0
International Honours: Georgia: 25

A Georgian international, Temuri had offers from Germany, Spain, and Italy when he became available through freedom of contract in the summer of 1997, but chose to join Newcastle instead. An attacking midfielder with a tremendous engine, who displays a dynamic combination of speed and skill, when on the ball he tends to favour the direct approach, making a bee-line for goal with deep penetrating runs, which is exciting to watch, but which can be frustrating for sometimes better placed colleagues. Unable to secure a regular first team place at United, he was used primarily as a substitute, one of his rare full appearances being in the FA Cup quarter final against Barnsley, when he scored the opening goal and turned in a Man of the Match performance. Made a habit of scoring late goals, usually followed by eccentric celebrations, including the last-minute strike against Croatia Zagreb, which won the place in the Champions League, after he came on as a substitute, and points winners against Bolton and Leeds.

Newcastle U (Free from AEK Athens on 10/7/97) PL 16+15/3 FLC 1+1 FAC 2+4/1 Others 3+5/1

KEWELL Harold (Harry)
Born: Smithfield, Australia, 22 September 1978
Height: 6'0" Weight: 11.10
Club Honours: FAYC '97

Quite easily Leeds' find of last season, and what a talent, Harry was the first member of the 1997 FA Youth Cup winning side to gain a regular place in the first team, while at the same time, taking the Premiership by storm. Very strong, and exceptionally quick, his bursts of speed left many Premiership defenders in his wake. Promoted from left-wing back for the youth side to a more striking position in the first team, he scored some excellent goals with his magical left foot, including a blistering drive from just inside the box in the 4-3 victory over Derby County, and two excellent goals against Oxford in the FA Cup. Unfortunately, Harry was sent off at Blackburn in his second full game in what must rank as one of the craziest decisions of the season – requesting a free kick to be taken in the correct place. For Leeds' supporters, the only downside of his season were the number of call ups to the Australian national side, although it was his goals that almost took them to the 1998 World Cup Finals. This precocious 19-year-old sensation should have a huge future in the game, having captured the imagination of all United supporters with his impact on the Premiership, and being duly rewarded with an improved four-year contract during the season.

Leeds U (Signed from the Australian Academy of Sport on 23/12/95) PL 28+4/5 FLC 2/1 FAC 4/2

KEY Lance William
Born: Kettering, 13 May 1968
Height: 6'2" Weight: 14.6

Having been released by Sheffield United during the summer, and having earlier been at Rochdale on a loan spell, Lance re-signed for Dale on the eve of last season when Ian Gray left for Stockport. The big goalkeeper was a popular figure with the fans, but in mid-season he lost his place to newcomer, Neil Edwards, thereafter appearing only when the former Stockport man was injured. Agile for such a big man, and brave, he is a recognised shot-stopper.

Sheffield Wed (£10,000 from Histon on 14/4/90) FAC 0+1
Oldham Ath (Loaned on 12/10/93) PL 2
Oxford U (Loaned on 26/1/95) FL 6
Lincoln C (Loaned on 11/8/95) FL 5
Hartlepool U (Loaned on 15/12/95) FL 1
Rochdale (Loaned on 1/3/96) FL 14
Dundee U (Free on 26/7/96) SL 4
Sheffield U (Free on 14/3/97)
Rochdale (Free on 6/8/97) FL 19 FLC 2

KHARINE Dmitri Victorvitch
Born: Moscow, Russia, 16 August 1968
Height: 6'2" Weight: 13.9
International Honours: Russia: 38

The popular Russian 'keeper made his return to first team action last February, after spending 17 months on the sidelines with a ruptured cruciate ligament in his left knee. He made his re-appearance at Leicester as part of new manager, Luca Vialli's controversial policy of rotating goalkeepers – Dmitri playing league matches and Ed de Goey being favoured for cup matches. He proved that he had lost none of his sharpness and agility during his long lay off, with a string of impressive performances, and having been resident in this country since December 1992, has applied for British citizenship.

Chelsea (£200,000 from CSKA Moscow on 22/12/92) PL 117 FLC 8 FAC 12 Others 4

KIDD Ryan Andrew
Born: Radcliffe, 6 October 1971
Height: 6'1" Weight: 13.0
Club Honours: Div 3 '96

Once again Preston's most consistent performer over a season in 1997-98, Ryan has developed into a thoroughly reliable left-sided centre half or full back, only missing matches through injury or suspension. Strong in the tackle, and a decisive header of the ball, he continued with his run of bad luck at attacking set pieces, scoring only twice during the campaign, one of these being the only goal of the game versus Luton – and that with his right foot! As the campaign progressed, he became increasingly dangerous on the overlap, and completed 150 Football League appearances for the club, playing well until an operation on a niggling ankle injury ended his season early in April.

Port Vale (From trainee on 12/7/90) FL 1 FLC 0+2 Others 0+1
Preston NE (Free on 15/7/92) FL 168+13/6 FLC 12+1/1 FAC 11 Others 13+1/1

KIELY Dean Laurence
Born: Salford, 10 October 1970
Height: 6'1" Weight: 13.5
Club Honours: Div 2 '97
International Honours: E: Yth; Sch

One of three ever-present players for Bury in 1997-98, the goalkeeper continued to turn in consistent performances in each game for

the Shakers, and a succession of fine displays of agility and bravery did much to ensure that Bury retained their division one status. His season included two penalty saves and ended with a much-deserved international call-up for the Republic of Ireland squad in May.

Coventry C (From trainee on 30/10/87)
York C (Signed on 9/3/90) FL 210 FLC 9 FAC 4 Others 16
Bury (Signed on 15/8/96) FL 92 FLC 8 FAC 3 Others 3

KILBANE Kevin Daniel
Born: Preston, 1 February 1977
Height: 6'0" Weight: 12.10
International Honours: Ei: 3; U21-8

In joining West Bromwich Albion from Preston during the 1997 close season, Kevin became Albion's record signing, beating the previous record of £748,000 paid to Manchester City for Peter Barnes in 1979. Quickly becoming a crowd favourite, the left winger showed he had the ability to go past defenders with pace to spare in order to get in telling crosses while still on the run. Very strong and mobile, the Irishman scored Albion's first goal of 1997-98, a fierce 18-yard left-footed drive past the 'keeper that set up a 2-1 win over Tranmere. Continuing to turn out for the Republic of Ireland U21 side, and upgraded to full international with three caps during the season, he is definitely a player with a future.

Preston NE (From trainee on 6/7/95) FL 39+8/3
West Bromwich A (£1,000,000 on 13/6/97) FL 42+1/4 FLC 5 FAC 2/1

KILFORD Ian Anthony
Born: Bristol, 6 October 1973
Height: 5'10" Weight: 11.0
Club Honours: Div 3 '97

A graceful midfielder who is comfortable on the ball, the Wigan Athletic player ended last season as the second top league scorer for the club. Once again called upon to fill a variety of roles, from right back to left wing, his attacking ability netted 10 goals, including winners in the home games against Oldham Athletic and Watford.*

Nottingham F (From trainee on 3/4/91) FL 0+1
Wigan Ath (Loaned on 23/12/93) FL 2+1/2 FAC 0+1
Wigan Ath (Free on 13/7/94) FL 111+19/27 FLC 6+1 FAC 6+2/1 Others 6+1/1

KIMBLE Alan Frank
Born: Dagenham, 6 August 1966
Height: 5'9" Weight: 12.4
Club Honours: Div 3 '91

A very reliable Wimbledon left back, who likes to come forward and is very fast, Alan can produce some excellent crosses and corners, and is recognised as a bit of a set-piece expert. Fitted into the team very well in 1997-98, being pushed up into midfield on a few occasions, where he added another dimension to the Dons' attack. Has a superb left foot, and is noted for his long kicks into the channels and throws to match. His twin brother, Gary, started out with him at Charlton, Exeter (loan), and Cambridge, before they parted company.

Charlton Ath (From juniors on 8/8/84) FL 6
Exeter C (Loaned on 23/8/85) FL 1 FLC 1
Cambridge U (Free on 22/8/86) FL 295+4/24 FLC 23+1 FAC 29/1 Others 22
Wimbledon (£175,000 on 27/7/93) PL 122+5 FLC 14+1 FAC 20

KINDER Vladimir (Vlad)
Born: Bratislava, Czechoslovakia, 9 March 1969
Height: 5'10" Weight: 13.0
International Honours: Czechoslovakia: 29

This confident and passionate defender breezed into the Cellnet from Slovan Bratislava during Middlesbrough's Premiership survival fight in 1996-97 and, although unable to prevent the "drop", acquitted himself well enough to establish his right to a permanent defensive role in 1997-98, making over 30 appearances. Able to play in both full-back slots, Vlad is a fully committed defender with the determination to get into scoring positions on the break, hence his valuable brace of league goals.

Middlesbrough (£1,000,000 from Slovan Bratislava on 18/1/97) F/PL 29+3/3 FLC 6 FAC 3+1

KING Philip (Phil) Geoffrey
Born: Bristol, 28 December 1967
Height: 5'8" Weight: 12.7
Club Honours: FLC '91
International Honours: E: B-1

Out of favour at Swindon in 1997-98, Phil was not used in the first team at all, and was

Kevin Kilbane

one of eight players transfer listed by Steve McMahon in March. Earlier, he had played six games on loan at Blackpool in October and, although impressing with his skilful play, was unable to agree terms for a permanent move. As an attacking left back, he can often be used as an extra forward, and still possesses a superb left foot which is capable of delivering quality passes and crosses. May lack the speed of yesteryear, but has a football brain that compensates.

Exeter C (From apprentice on 7/1/85) FL 24+3 FLC 1 Others 1+2
Torquay U (£3,000 on 14/7/86) FL 24/3 FLC 2 FAC 1 Others 2
Swindon T (£155,000 on 6/2/87) FL 112+4/4 FLC 11 FAC 5 Others 13
Sheffield Wed (£400,000 on 30/11/89) F/PL 124+5/2 FLC 17 FAC 9 Others 4
Notts Co (Loaned on 22/10/93) FL 6 Others 2
Aston Villa (£250,000 on 1/8/94) PL 13+3 FLC 3 Others 4
West Bromwich A (Loaned on 30/10/95) FL 4 Others 1
Swindon T (Free on 26/3/97) FL 5
Blackpool (Loaned on 20/10/97) FL 6

KINKLADZE Georgiou

Born: Tbilisi, Georgia, 6 November 1973
Height: 5'8" Weight: 10.9
International Honours: Georgia: 30

Following on from 1996-97, he of the brilliant dribbling ability, spent the summer in the gym to strengthen his frame and started last season in good form, turning on his skills much to the excitement of the crowd. At the end of October, he was involved in a car crash where he was lucky to walk away without having been seriously injured, and missed the next two games, mainly through shock and having had 30 stitches in his back. During the next three months, despite playing in 16 of the 18 available games, he only scored two goals, the second, a gem at Maine Road against West Ham was often shown on television, but, following this, his form and involvement appeared to go down and with the new manager, Joe Royle, in place selection was no longer automatic. However, there was still another great goal to come, a beautifully flighted ball from 30 yards out beating the Queens Park Rangers' 'keeper in a 2-2 home draw, before he flew off to play for Georgia in Tunisia. Completed his English career being honoured by his fellow professionals, when selected for the award-winning PFA first division team. *Stop Press:* According to press reports, the little Georgian midfielder signed for the Dutch giants, Ajax, early in May, a £5,000,000 fee changing hands.

Manchester C (£2,000,000 from Dinamo Tbilisi on 17/8/95) P/FL 105+1/20 FLC 6 FAC 9/2

KINSELLA Mark Anthony

Born: Dublin, 12 August 1972
Height: 5'8" Weight: 11.4
Club Honours: GMVC '92; FAT '92
International Honours: Ei: 2; B-1; U21-8; Yth

1997-98 was another tremendous season for Charlton's Mark, and culminated in a well deserved call up to the full Republic of Ireland side for the Czechoslovakia and Argentine games, having earlier played for the "B" side. Comfortable on the ball, and able to pass accurately, his trusty right foot provided several goals from midfield. Also a free-kick specialist, who can score spectacular goals from long range, he was made team captain during the campaign and led the side by example. The only ever present in a season that saw Athletic reach the Premiership via the play offs, Mark was deservedly voted the Supporters' Club Player of the Year.

Colchester U (Free from Home Farm on 18/8/89) FL 174+6/27 FLC 11/3 FAC 11/1 Others 9+1/5
Charlton Ath (£150,000 on 23/9/96) FL 83/12 FLC 2 FAC 4/1 Others 3

KITSON Paul

Born: Murton, 9 January 1971
Height: 5'11" Weight: 10.12
International Honours: E: U21-7

The nimble West Ham striker suffered a miserable season in 1997-98 as he fought against a persistent groin injury. He first got injured at Huddersfield in the Coca Cola Cup in September and returned to the side in December, scoring winning goals against Sheffield Wednesday and Wimbledon to show everyone what they were missing. Unfortunately, further groin problems returned and he had to miss the rest of the campaign, apart from a couple of games where he was still not match fit. It is hoped that his problem will have been cured during the summer to allow him to return to partner John Hartson as the main Hammers' strike force. *Stop Press:* Was ruled out of action until October following further surgery on his groin injury.

Leicester C (From trainee on 15/12/88) FL 39+11/6 FLC 5/3 FAC 1+1/1 Others 5/1
Derby Co (£1,300,000 on 11/3/92) FL 105/36 FLC 7/3 FAC 5/1 Others 13+1/9
Newcastle U (£2,250,000 on 24/9/94) PL 26+10/10 FLC 3+2/1 FAC 6+1/3 Others 0+1
West Ham U (£2,300,000 on 10/2/97) PL 26+1/12 FLC 2 FAC 2/1

KIWOMYA Andrew (Andy) Derek

Born: Huddersfield, 1 October 1967
Height: 5'10" Weight: 10.10
International Honours: E: Yth

Unable to get a place in Bradford's 1997-98 squad, Andy was loaned out to Burnley at the beginning of September, but failed to make an impact in his three games and went back to Valley Parade before being freed to join Notts County on a month-by-month contract in early December. Very unfortunate to arrive at a time when the County juggernaut was beginning to roll, this restricted his opportunities, but he showed signs of being a talented and speedy winger prior to being released in February. Is the brother of the former Ipswich and Arsenal player, Chris.

Barnsley (From apprentice on 16/7/85) FL 1
Sheffield Wed (£5,000 on 7/10/86)
Dundee (Free ON 29/9/92) SL 11+10/1 SC 0+1
Rotherham U (Free on 1/10/93) FL 4+3 FLC 0+1 Others 0+2 (Free to Halifax during 1994 close season)
Scunthorpe U (Free on 23/3/95) FL 9/3
Bradford C (Free on 4/7/95) FL 27+16/3 FLC 1+1 FAC 3 Others 2+1
Luton T (Loaned on 27/3/97) FL 5/1

Burnley (Loaned on 1/9/97) FL 1+2
Notts Co (Free on 4/12/97) FL 0+2 Others 1

KLINSMANN Jurgen

Born: Geopingen, Germany, 30 July 1964
Height: 6'2" Weight: 12.12
International Honours: West Germany/ Germany: 108

Returning to White Hart Lane last December, on loan from Sampdoria, and making his debut in the London derby at home to Arsenal, Jurgen set about the task of saving Tottenham from the drop. Although the pacy striker was slow to start, admitting to himself that he was lacking match fitness, his inclusion alone seemed to inspire the team, bouncing back from a heavy 4-1 defeat at Aston Villa, with a 1-1 draw against Arsenal, in a game that they dominated for most of the 90 minutes. Three games later in the home tie against West Ham, the German found the net with typical tenacity to earn a much-needed three points. However, whilst Tottenham's performances were improving, results were not, and it seemed that his dream return was going to end in a nightmare, but just as relegation beckoned with only two games remaining, Jurgen found his form and contributed to the survival with a fine goal in the 2-0 victory over Newcastle. And, in what was already confirmed as his penultimate performance for the club, he produced an individual display of sheer brilliance, linking with Les Ferdinand in the 6-2 demolition of Wimbledon, and netting four marvellous goals. His mission complete, and with differences of opinion with coach, Christian Gross, unresolved, Jurgen left White Hart Lane a hero once more, with Tottenham's Premiership status intact, bound for France '98, and his German international team mates. *Stop Press:* Played in all five World Cup games for Germany during the summer, scoring three times, before the side departed from the competition at the quarter-final stage.

Tottenham H (£2,000,000 from Monaco on 1/8/94) PL 41/20 FLC 3/4 FAC 6/5 (Transferred to Bayern Munich on 6/7/95)
Tottenham H (Loaned from Sampdoria on 23/12/97) PL 15/9 FAC 3

KNIGHT Alan Edward

Born: Balham, 3 July 1961
Height: 6'1" Weight: 13.11
Club Honours: Div 3 '83
International Honours: E: U21-2; Yth

Apart from the opening game, Alan started 1997-98 as the number two goalkeeper behind Aaron Flahaven, but when the latter was dropped midway through the season he stepped in, and for the most part played well. Unfortunately, a couple of bad performances, resulting in a loss of form, meant new manager, Alan Ball, having no option but to replace him with Flahaven again. Still an excellent shot-stopper, despite having made his debut for Pompey as long ago as 1997-98, he ended the campaign with 773 first team appearances for his only club.*

Portsmouth (From apprentice on 12/3/79) FL 662 FLC 49 FAC 41 Others 21

KNILL Alan Richard
Born: Slough, 8 October 1964
Height: 6'3" Weight: 13.0
Club Honours: WC '89
International Honours: W: 1; Yth

Signed by Rotherham from Scunthorpe during the 1997 close season, Alan was brought in to add strength to the centre of defence. He did just that and was always dominating in the air, while he was more than useful with dead-ball situations in the opponents' penalty area. His two headed goals inside two minutes rescued a point against Mansfield after United had gone two down.

Southampton (From apprentice on 14/10/82)
Halifax T (Free on 13/7/84) FL 118/6 FLC 6 FAC 6 Others 6
Swansea C (£15,000 on 14/8/87) FL 89/3 FLC 4 FAC 5 Others 7
Bury (£95,000 on 18/8/89) FL 141+3/8 FLC 7 FAC 8/1 Others 14+1/1
Cardiff C (Loaned on 24/9/93) FL 4
Scunthorpe U (Signed on 5/11/93) FL 131/8 FLC 5 FAC 10 Others 8
Rotherham U (Free on 7/7/97) FL 38/3 FLC 2 FAC 3/1 Others 1

KNOWLES Darren Thomas
Born: Sheffield, 8 October 1970
Height: 5'6" Weight: 11.1

A battling right back who is small in stature but whose never-say-die attitude makes him a real favourite with the Hartlepool supporters. Seemingly fearless, excelling as a tough-tackling defender who is also able to play an overlapping role to good effect, he was the club's only ever-present in 1997-98, and was playing just as well at the end of the season as he had been at the start.

Sheffield U (From trainee on 1/7/89)
Stockport Co (£3,000 on 14/9/91) FL 51+12 FLC 2+4 Others 14+1
Scarborough (Free on 4/8/93) FL 139+5/2 FLC 11+1 FAC 9 Others 7
Hartlepool U (Free on 27/3/97) FL 53/1 FLC 2 FAC 1 Others 2

KONCHESKY Paul Martyn
Born: Barking, 15 May 1981
Height: 5'9" Weight: 10.12
International Honours: E: Yth

A left-sided defender, Paul made his debut for Charlton in the second league match of last season against Oxford United at the Valley when only 16 years and 93 days old, making him the youngest ever player to make a senior appearance for the club. Very self assured for one so young, he created a good impression and should become a first team regular in the near future.

Charlton Ath (Trainee) FL 2+1 FLC 1

KOORDES Rogier
Born: Haarlem, Holland, 13 June 1972
Height: 6'1" Weight: 12.11

Rogier, a left-sided midfield player with Port Vale, was unable to hold down a regular place in 1997-98, firstly through injury, and then, when moving down the pecking order behind Jan Jansson and Wayne Corden. despite featuring regularly at reserve level, he did not make another first team

appearance after Boxing Day and is still searching for his first goal in Vale colours.

Port Vale (£75,000 from Telstar on 12/2/97) FL 16+7

KOZLUK Robert
Born: Mansfield, 5 August 1977
Height: 5'8" Weight: 11.7
International Honours: E: U21-2

Having come through the ranks at Derby, 1997-98 saw the talented right-wing back gain his first taste of senior football, including a four-game spell in late autumn, following on from a promising debut at Southend in the Coca Cola Cup earlier. Displayed great composure for one so young, and has a lethal shot, allied to a great deal of pace. Definitely one for the future, he made two England U21 appearances in the end of season Toulon tournament.

Derby Co (From trainee on 10/2/96) PL 6+3 FLC 2 FAC 1

KRIZAN Ales
Born: Slovenia, 25 July 1971
Height: 5'11" Weight: 13.4
International Honours: Slovenia: 25

Signed from Marbor Branik, a leading Slovakian side, during the 1997 close season, this left-sided defender, or wing back, had to wait for his chance to break into the Barnsley first team. A good reader of the game, and a solid defender, he also was capable of producing a long throw, but the rigours of the Premier League made it hard for him to settle, and he suffered a number of niggling injuries which interrupted his chances of gaining a regular place.

Barnsley (£400,000 from Marbor Branik on 30/7/97) PL 12 FLC 3 FAC 1

KUBICKI Dariusz
Born: Warsaw, Poland, 6 June 1963
Height: 5'10" Weight: 11.12
Club Honours: Div 1 '96
International Honours: Poland: 49

Signed from Sunderland during the 1997 close season, the full back made his debut on the left side, despite normally playing on the right. With a reputation for being a tough tackler, Dariusz settled in well, apart from the visit to Oxford in which the whole team seemed to have an off day. Received a good reception from his previous supporters at Sunderland, the Wolves' goal coming from his centre. However, unfortunately conceded a penalty against Swindon and was then taken out of the team, playing just once more at Portsmouth, his only appearance at right-back for Wolves, and in March he was loaned to Tranmere, before being released during the summer.

Aston Villa (£200,000 from Legia Warsaw on 28/8/91) F/PL 24+1 FLC 3 FAC 4+1 Others 1
Sunderland (£100,000 on 4/3/94) P/FL 135+1 FLC 7 FAC 7
Wolverhampton W (Free on 8/8/97) FL 12 FLC 4
Tranmere Rov (Loaned on 3/3/98) FL 12

KULCSAR George
Born: Budapest, Hungary, 12 August 1967
Height: 6'2" Weight: 13.4
International Honours: Australia: 3

A strong ball-winning midfielder, who controls the middle very well, and was a

great crowd favourite at Bradford, it came as a shock to the fans when he was transferred to Queens Park Rangers last December. However, despite starting for City on the opening day of 1997-98, he had missed the following nine games after Peter Beagrie came into the side and, although recovering somewhat, the management obviously thought they could dispense with his services. Interestingly, as Ray Harford's first buy, he made his debut against Bradford, being injured after 30 minutes, and then ruled out until early February. Coming back to add stability, appearing in 11 of the last 17 games, with Rangers having secured their place in the first division, George might find things easier in 1998-99.

Bradford C (£100,000 from Royal Antwerp on 7/3/97) FL 23+3/1
Queens Park R (£250,000 on 17/12/97) FL 11+1

KVARME Bjorn Tore
Born: Trondheim, Norway, 17 June 1972
Height: 6'2" Weight: 12.9
International Honours: Norway:1

1997-98 was a season of mixed fortunes for the Norwegian, who had quickly established himself in the back line at Liverpool. His strong tackling and raiding down the flanks proved a useful asset for the club, but after the manager, Roy Evans, reverted to a flat back four midway through the campaign, he struggled to retain his place and was in and out of the side from thereon. Many had expected him to make the international breakthrough for his country, especially with the World Cup being held in France during the summer, but the fact that he was not a regular fixture at club level would not have helped his cause and he was ignored.

Liverpool (Free from Rosenborg on 17/1/97) PL 37+1 FLC 2 FAC 2 Others 4

KYD Michael Robert
Born: Hackney, 21 May 1977
Height: 5'8" Weight: 12.10

Started 1997-98 at Cambridge with five goals in his first eight games, and was going like a train until a cartilage operation kept him out for five weeks, which disrupted both his and the team's season. When the striker returned he struggled to regain form and it was not until the last games of the campaign that he regained the scoring touch. Has the skills to play at a higher level, but will need to add more consistency to his game.

Cambridge U (From trainee on 18/5/95) FL 71+23/20 FLC 3+1/1 FAC 5+2/1 Others 1+2

KYRATZOGLOU Alexandros (Alex) Bassilios
Born: Armidale, Australia, 27 August 1974
Height: 5'10" Weight: 12.1

An Australian signed for Oldham from a Greek club, IEK Athens, last October, Alex made his Football League debut when coming off the bench a few days later at Millwall. Reportedly a forward of some stature, he was not quite what the Latics were looking for and he returned from whence he came a week later.

Oldham Ath (Free from IEK Athens on 7/10/97) FL 0+1

LACEY Damien James
Born: Ogur, 3 August 1977
Height: 5'9" Weight: 11.3

Having recovered well from his illness of the previous season, Damien came back well for Swansea in 1997-98, showing himself to be a tremendous worker in midfield. A strong tackler with good passing ability, he also impressed everybody when switched to a right-sided wing-back role. Scored his first goal for the senior side in the 3-0 win at Doncaster in October.

Swansea C (From trainee on 1/7/96) FL 25+7/1 FLC 2 Others 1

LAMA Bernard Pascal
Born: St Symphorien, France, 7 April 1963
Height: 6'3" Weight: 12.5
International Honours: France: 37

The French international goalkeeper joined West Ham on loan from Paris St Germain last December, although he did not make his debut, however, until the beginning of March, following an injury to Craig Forrest. Despite being 35 years of age, Bernard was hoping to be chosen for the French World Cup squad and his confident and agile displays for the Hammers in 14 appearances convinced the national manager to name him in the final 22. After giving two excellent performances against Arsenal in the FA Cup, he kept his place for the remainder of the season and West Ham were hoping to sign him on a permanent basis at the time of going to press. *Stop Press:* Selected for France's 22-strong World Cup squad, but not called upon, he was reported earlier to have signed for Paris St Germain on 19 May.

West Ham U (Loaned from St Paris Germain on 24/12/97) PL 12 FAC 2

James Lambert

LAMBERT Christopher James
Born: Henley, 14 September 1973
Height: 5'7" Weight: 11.2

Enjoyed his best season at Reading so far in 1997-98, in terms of goals scored as well as first team appearances. At last he seemed to have made a permanent spot for himself as a wide left midfield player, and his exciting runs and pin-point crosses did much to brighten a generally drab campaign for the club. The highlight, for him, was the televised goal he scored in the 3-3 draw with Nottingham Forest, when he dribbled past three players before sliding the ball under the goalkeeper. Has now signed an extended contract with his hometown club.

Reading (From juniors on 3/7/92) FL 76+48/16 FLC 8+3/2 FAC 9+2/1 Others 2+3/1

LAMBOURDE Bernard
Born: Guadaloupe, 11 May 1971
Height: 6'1" Weight: 11.8
Club Honours: FLC '98

This impressive right-sided central defender joined Chelsea from Bordeaux during the 1997 close season to give extra cover in defence, following the departure of Erland Johnsen, and long-term injuries to David Lee and Michael Duberry. Unfortunately, in his first outing for the club, a pre-season friendly at Kingstonian, he picked up a painful hip injury which sidelined him for seven matches, prior to his league debut for Chelsea in the pressure cooker atmosphere of Old Trafford, where he gave an assured performance as the Blues extended their remarkable record there. Sadly, for Bernard, he was sent off three matches later at Anfield and never had a long run in the first team thereafter. He also played in midfield, in a holding position, where his tackling and thoughtful distribution made a useful contribution. Having learned his footballing trade at Cannes, where he played alongside current team-mate, Laurent Charvet, as well as Patrick Vieira and Zinedine Zidane, before switching to Bordeaux, his second term in England will surely go more smoothly than his first, and he has the ability to be a very valuable acquisition.

Chelsea (£1,600,000 from Bordeaux on 10/7/97) PL 5+2 FLC 3 Others 1+2

LAMPARD Frank James
Born: Romford, 21 June 1978
Height: 6'0" Weight: 12.6
International Honours: E: B-1; U21-6; Yth

1997-98 was a great season for the 19-year-old West Ham midfielder, and must have warmed the heart of his dad, Frank senior, who, having once played for the club, is now the assistant manager. In making remarkable progress, when establishing himself in the first team, he went on to make his debut for both England "B" and the U21 teams. Very talented, and with an eye for goal, as his ten from midfield show, he scored his first-ever hat trick against Walsall in the Coca Cola Cup, and is surely destined for a big future in the game.

West Ham U (From trainee on 1/7/95) PL 30+16/5 FLC 6+1/4 FAC 7/1
Swansea C (Loaned on 6/10/95) FL 8+1/1 Others 1+1

Frank Lampard

LANCASHIRE Graham
Born: Blackpool, 19 October 1972
Height: 5'10" Weight: 11.12
Club Honours: Div 4 '92, Div 3 '97

Having started 1997-98 at Wigan, the striker was an expensive signing by Rochdale standards when joining in October, but looked to be the answer to the Dale's goalscoring problem when he netted twice on his home debut and struck up a successful partnership with Robbie Painter. Unfortunately, injured soon afterwards, he missed a number of games and his season stuttered along as he spent a spell restricted to the substitute's role, before a return to form in March as he and Painter netted ten goals in the last six home games.

Burnley (From trainee on 1/7/91) FL 11+20/8 FLC 1+1 FAC 2+2/1 Others 2+4
Halifax T (Loaned on 20/11/92) FL 2 Others 1+1
Chester C (Loaned on 21/1/94) FL 10+1/7
Preston NE (£55,000 on 23/12/94) FL 11+12/2 Others 1+1
Wigan Ath (£35,000 on 12/1/96) FL 20+10/2 FLC 2+1/4
Rochdale (£40,000 on 2/10/97) FL 20+7/9 Others 1

LANDON Richard John
Born: Worthing, 22 March 1970
Height: 6'3" Weight: 13.5

Having had a successful loan spell with Macclesfield during the Conference championship season, Richard was signed in the 1997 close season to create a strong strike force for a team ready to experience its first taste of life in the Football League. Despite being squeezed out by new arrivals, as manager, Sammy McIlroy, tried to find a goal scoring formation, the tall striker remained one of the team's top scorers, with seven goals from six starts.

Plymouth Arg (£30,000 from Bedworth U on 26/1/94) FL 21+9/12 FLC 0+1 FAC 0+1 Others 4

Stockport Co (£50,000 on 13/7/95) FL 7+6/4 FLC 0+1 FAC 0+1
Rotherham U (Loaned on 3/3/97) FL 7+1
Macclesfield T (Free on 11/7/97) FL 6+12/7 FLC 2 FAC 0+1 Others 0+1

LANGAN Kevin
Born: Jersey, 7 April 1978
Height: 6'0" Weight: 11.2
This Bristol City right back only made four playing appearances as a substitute in 1997-98 to add to his solitary game of the previous term, but he again proved to be a solid performer who is waiting for further opportunities, while turning in many good displays with the reserves in their South West Trophy winning side. Many feel he is certain to establish himself if given a run of games.
Bristol C (From trainee on 4/7/96) FL 0+3 FAC 0+1 Others 1

LARKIN James (Jim) Thomas
Born: Canada, 23 October 1975
Height: 6'0" Weight: 13.7
Brought over from Canada on trial, the goalkeeper made just one first team appearance for Cambridge, a 2-2 draw at Rotherham, before being released to look for another club. His next stop was Walsall, whom he also joined on non-contract terms in March, but, with James Walker ever present for the Saddlers, there was no joy there either.
Cambridge U (Free from Canada on 16/1/98) FL 1
Walsall (Free on 20/3/98)

LARSEN Stig Olav
Born: Bergen, Norway, 26 September 1973
Height: 6'1" Weight: 13.4
An old-fashioned centre forward, with a good physique, and with a reputation for being dangerous in the box, Hartlepool's third Norwegian import began well after arriving last September by scoring a hat trick in a friendly against Chester le Street. Admittedly not fully match fit, he made a handful of substitute appearances but, unable to prove that he had adapted to the English game, he was allowed to leave the club before the season ended.
Hartlepool U (Free from Fana IL on 19/12/97) FL 0+4 Others 0+1

LAURSEN Jacob
Born: Denmark, 6 October 1971
Height: 5'11" Weight: 12.0
International Honours: Denmark: 22
As one of the unsung heroes in Derby's commendable season in 1997-98, the Danish international defender showed that he could operate either as one of three centre backs, or anywhere in a flat back four. Not noted for joining in attacking moves, his strength lying in the timing of tackles and distribution, he was unfortunate to sustain a knee injury against Chelsea in April which put an early end to his season. However, all of that was put behind him as he was fit enough to travel to France during the summer as a member of Denmark's much vaunted World Cup squad. *Stop Press:* Although called upon just once in the World

Cup Finals, the first round defeat at the hands of France, he will treasure the memory.
Derby Co (£500,000 from Silkeborg on 17/7/96) PL 62+2/2 FLC 4 FAC 3

LAVIN Gerard
Born: Corby, 5 February 1974
Height: 5'10" Weight: 11.0
International Honours: S: U21-7
As in 1996-97, Gerard's season in 1997-98 was severely disrupted by a knee injury and it remains to be seen whether he can recapture the fitness that saw him shine for the Scotland U21 side. Got back into the Millwall side for the final few matches of the campaign and showed up well. A tough-tackling player with good control, who reads the game well, and likes to get forward, Gerard is equally at home at full back or in midfield and, hopefully, can get a run of games under his belt in 1998-99.
Watford (From trainee on 11/5/92) FL 121+5/3 FLC 11/1 FAC 6 Others 2+1
Millwall (£500,000 on 23/11/95) FL 29+7 FAC 2+1 Others 1

LAW Brian John
Born: Merthyr Tydfil, 1 January 1970
Height: 6'2" Weight: 14.0
International Honours: W: 1; U21-2; Yth; Sch
Released by Wolves during the 1997 summer recess, Brian quickly got himself sorted at Millwall, and, apart from suspension, was a regular at the heart of their defence in 1997-98. His experience was invaluable and he became a reliable captain who led by example, never accepting anything less than 110 per cent. Nicknamed "Mr Consistency", and readily accepted by the faithful due to his hard, but sure tackling and motivation, he also displays great vision when often able to turn defence into attack by means of his excellent long passing ability.
Queens Park R (From trainee on 15/8/87) FL 19+1 FLC 2+1 FAC 3 Others 1
Wolverhampton W (£134,000 on 23/12/94) FL 26+5/1 FLC 1+1 FAC 7
Millwall (Free on 31/7/97) FL 40/4 FLC 3 FAC 1 Others 2

LAWRENCE James (Jamie) Hubert
Born: Balham, 8 March 1970
Height: 6'0" Weight: 12.11
Club Honours: FLC '97
A 1997 close season signing from Leicester, Jamie got his Bradford career away on the opening day of 1997-98 and, apart from three games, was rarely absent, his pace and longing to beat player after player being a joy to watch for the fans. Although starting as an orthodox right winger, he showed that he was equally as comfortable in a wing-back position, where his ability to tackle back as well as his running, coupled to no small amount of skill, made him a great crowd pleaser.
Sunderland (Signed from Cowes on 15/10/93) FL 2+2 FLC 0+1
Doncaster Rov (£20,000 on 17/3/94) FL 16+9/3 FLC 2 FAC 1 Others 3

Leicester C (£125,000 on 6/1/95) P/FL 21+26/1 FLC 3+4/2 FAC 1+1
Bradford C (£50,000 on 17/6/97) FL 38+5/3 FLC 2 FAC 1

LAWRENCE Matthew (Matty) James
Born: Northampton, 19 June 1974
Height: 6'1" Weight: 12.12
If someone had said that by last January only one of Fulham's promotion winning squad of 1996-97 would be a regular, that would have been unbelievable enough, but for that one to be Matty Lawrence it would have been nothing short of fantasy. This is meant as no criticism of Matty, who filled in at right back, and, when necessary, the left-back position extremely well, using his pace to get down the flanks to put over fine crosses. It was just that so many of the stars in the promotion run were discarded or relegated to the reserves as soon as the new regime of Kevin Keegan/Ray Wilkins took over. Appeared in 54 matches during the season, more than any other Fulham player and will be delighted to be playing first division football in 1998-99.
Wycombe W (£20,000 from Grays Ath on 19/1/96) FL 13+3/1 FLC 4 FAC 1 Others 0+1
Fulham (Free on 7/2/97) FL 56+2 FLC 4 FAC 2 Others 5

LAWS Brian
Born: Wallsend, 14 October 1961
Height: 5'9" Weight: 11.5
Club Honours: Div 3 '82; FLC '89, '90; FMC '89
International Honours: E: B-1
Reduced fitness led to the Scunthorpe player/manager making only a handful of first team appearances last season as he preferred to have control from the touchlines. Still a tremendous passer of the ball, and great competitor, he played as sweeper for the first team, where his experience and ability to bring the ball out of defence helped stabilise a young team.
Burnley (From apprentice on 19/10/79) FL 125/12 FLC 14/2 FAC 15/1 Others 3
Huddersfield T (£10,000 on 26/8/83) FL 56/1 FLC 7 FAC 3
Middlesbrough (£30,000 on 15/3/85) FL 103+5/12 FLC 6+1/2 FAC 8+1 Others 6+1
Nottingham F (£120,000 on 7/7/88) F/PL 136+11/4 FLC 28+4 FAC 16+2/1 Others 11+1
Grimsby T (Free on 1/12/94) FL 30+16/2 FLC 2 FAC 4/1
Darlington (Free on 18/11/96) FL 10 FAC 1
Scunthorpe U (Free on 27/1/97) FL 11+7 FLC 1+1 FAC 0+2 Others 2

LAWSON Ian James
Born: Huddersfield, 4 November 1977
Height: 5'11" Weight: 11.5
A product of Huddersfield's youth policy who made his debut in 1996-97, Ian was expected to get an extended run last season, but, apart from the odd injury problem, he continued to be a regular on the substitutes' bench. Often thrust into action late on in games in order to add pace to the front line, he proved very good in the air and showed a nice variety of skilful touches. He will definitely be looking for more starting opportunities this coming term.
Huddersfield T (From trainee on 26/1/95) FL 11+25/3 FLC 1+4 FAC 1+1

LAZARIDIS Stanley (Stan)
Born: Perth, Australia, 16 August 1972
Height: 5'9" Weight: 11.12
International Honours: Australia: 21

The flying Australian winger added consistency to his play at West Ham last season and proved a handful for the opposing defenders. Stan has lightening pace and also likes to cut inside and shoot, and, at Newcastle in February, he hit a 35 yarder past a stunned Shay Given to earn the Hammers a 1-0 win. A regular in the Australian national side, he was disappointed when the team lost to Iran in the World Cup play offs and ruined his dream of France '98. When on song, he is one of the most exciting wingers in the country and, hopefully, will remain consistent.
West Ham U (£300,000 from West Adelaide on 8/9/95) PL 42+12/3 FLC 5+1 FAC 7+1

LEABURN Carl Winston
Born: Lewisham, 30 March 1969
Height: 6'3" Weight: 13.0

The tall striker was out of contract at Charlton at the beginning of 1997-98 and did not start a game until October when he was surprisingly chosen for the visit to Tranmere. Then, in another equally surprising move, he was transferred to Wimbledon early in January, having just scored against Nottingham Forest in the FA Cup. Playing in 16 of the last 21 games of the campaign, this big, powerful, old-fashioned centre forward, not unlike John Fashanu in style and physique, and also excellent in the air, scored four important goals, particularly in the Selhurst derby when he netted two in a 3-0 win. Looking to be worth every penny of the fee paid, Carl is a real handful at set pieces with his presence, and holds the ball up for others to arrive.
Charlton Ath (From apprentice on 22/4/87) FL 276+46/53 FLC 19/5 FAC 19+2/4 Others 9+5/4
Northampton (Loaned on 22/3/90) FL 9
Wimbledon (£300,000 on 9/1/98) PL 15+1/4

LEADBITTER Christopher (Chris) Jonathan
Born: Middlesbrough, 17 October 1967
Height: 5'9" Weight: 10.6
Club Honours: Div 3 '91

Released by Plymouth during the 1997 close season, Chris began 1997-98 at non-league Dorchester before signing for Torquay in November, where he emerged from a career threatening injury suffered at Argyle to provide hard graft and skill to the left side of midfield. A tough tackler who can play in a number of positions, Chris celebrated his "comeback" with a goal in his second start, a 1-1 draw at Exeter.*
Grimsby T (From apprentice on 4/9/85)
Hereford U (Free on 21/8/86) FL 32+4/1 FLC 2 FAC 2 Others 3
Cambridge U (Free on 2/8/88) FL 144+32/18 FLC 12/3 FAC 16+2/3 Others 11+2/1
Bournemouth (£25,000 on 16/8/93) FL 45+9/3 FLC 6+1 FAC 5 Others 2
Plymouth Arg (Free on 27/7/95) FL 46+6/1 FLC 2 FAC 6/1 Others 5+1/1 (Free to Dorchester T during 1997 close season)
Torquay U (Free on 27/11/97) FL 21+5/1 FAC 0+2 Others 4

LEANING Andrew (Andy) John
Born: Goole, 18 May 1963
Height: 6'1" Weight: 14.7

In 1997-98, Andy again patiently played second fiddle to Billy Mercer, and Chesterfield certainly benefited from having such an experienced 'keeper in reserve, not least for his willingness to watch Billy and help with his game. With an ability to work with others in a competitive environment, a career as a coach must be on the cards when he decides that his playing days are over.*
York C (Free from Rowntree Mackintosh on 1/7/85) FL 69 FLC 4 FAC 8 Others 5
Sheffield U (Free on 28/5/87) FL 21 FLC 2 FAC 2
Bristol C (£12,000 on 27/9/88) FL 75 FLC 5 FAC 7 Others 2
Lincoln C (Free on 24/3/94) FL 36 FLC 6 FAC 3 Others 6 (Freed during 1996 season)
Dundee (Free on 19/7/96)
Chesterfield (Free on 1/10/96) FL 14 FAC 2 Others 1

LEBOEUF Frank
Born: France, 22 January 1968
Height: 6'0" Weight: 12.6
Club Honours: FAC '97; FLC '98; ECWC '98
International Honours: France: 16

By his own admission, Frank learned some painful lessons about the physical side of the Premiership during his first season in England, and he became a better player because of it. Although highly respected for his constructive counter attacking, some opponents felt that he was vulnerable under a long-ball assault, but he worked hard to eliminate this perceived weakness from his game in 1997-98. Combining his Gallic attacking flair with this more robust approach, he continued to trigger explosive Chelsea counter attacks with raking 40-yard passes to the front players – two of these pin-point passes created goals in Chelsea's 6-1 victory at White Hart Lane. One of the modern games' most successful penalty takers, he has a 100 per-cent record from the spot since joining the club, and also packs a rocket shot with his right foot, being deadly when linking up with the attack. With Leicester City tenaciously clinging to a goalless scoreline at Stamford Bridge, and just a few minutes remaining, Frank galloped forward to lash an unstoppable 30-yard drive past brave 'keeper Pegguy Arphexad, to score one of the most spectacular goals of the campaign – the second season running that he has broken Leicester hearts with a late winner. His calm authority in defence, and all-round ability on the ball, has made him a crucial element in Chelsea's cup successes over the past two seasons, and, as a consequence, a cult figure with the Chelsea crowd. He returned to home soil for France '98 as part of Aimee Jacquet's squad, where his cultured attacking from deep defensive positions was expected to add a valuable dimension to France's tactics. *Stop Press:* Although appearing twice for France during the World Cup Finals, prior to the final itself Frank was not expected to play against Brazil and did so only because Laurent Blanc was suspended. Marking Ronaldo was a tough

order, but the Chelsea man came through with flying colours in France's great 3-0 victory and, while it is easy in hindsight to say that the great Brazilian was not match fit, Frank did what he had to superbly. He also gave Blues' fans a taste of what to expect this coming term when partnering the Londoner's latest acquisition, Marcel Desailly.
Chelsea (£2,500,000 from Strasbourg on 12/7/96) PL 58/11 FLC 6 FAC 8/1 Others 10/1

LEE Christian
Born: Aylesbury, 8 October 1976
Height: 6'2" Weight: 11.7

A lanky striker, who burst into Northampton's first team in 1996-97 with nine goals, Christian found it very hard to hold down a first team spot last season, although he was yet another player to lose out through injury. Hopefully, there are further opportunities around the corner for him.
Northampton T (Free from Doncaster Rov juniors on 13/7/95) FL 16+24/7 FLC 2/2 FAC 2+3 Others 6+2

LEE David John
Born: Kingswood, 26 November 1969
Height: 6'3" Weight: 14.7
Club Honours: Div 2 '89; FLC '98
International Honours: E: U21-10; Yth

This popular sweeper made a successful comeback for Chelsea in 1997-98 after sustaining a nasty broken leg in October 1996. He made two substitute appearances, replacing player/manager, Ruud Gullit, in the Coca Cola Cup ties against Blackburn Rovers and Southampton, before joining Sheffield United on loan to regain match fitness. The Blades' then-boss, Nigel Spackman, was a former team mate of David's and was aware that the talented sweeper had the necessary ability to help their play-off push. He then returned to Samford Bridge to make one more league start – against Leeds United at Elland Road. This year marks David's tenth at Chelsea and he has been awarded a richly-deserved testimonial.
Chelsea (From trainee on 1/7/88) F/PL 119+32/11 FLC 13+7/1 FAC 10+4 Others 6+2/1
Reading (Loaned on 30/1/92) FL 5/5
Plymouth Arg (Loaned on 26/3/92) FL 9/1
Portsmouth (Loaned on 12/8/94) FL 4+1
Sheffield U (Loaned on 19/12/97) FL 5

LEE David Mark
Born: Manchester, 5 November 1967
Height: 5'7" Weight: 11.0
Club Honours: Div 1 '97

One of the most exciting wingers in the second division on his day, David took some time to settle in at Wigan, following his 1997 close season transfer from Bolton Wanderers. A speedy player who can run all day and take his markers on with ease, one of his five league goals came with a spectacular lob from the edge of the penalty box in the away victory over Burnley.
Bury (From juniors on 8/8/86) FL 203+5/35 FLC 15/1 FAC 6 Others 19+1/4
Southampton (£350,000 on 27/8/91) F/PL 11+9 FAC 0+1 Others 1+1

Bolton W (£300,000 on 2/11/92) P/FL 124+31/17 FLC 19+1/2 FAC 13+2 Others 8+1/1
Wigan Ath (£250,000 on 16/7/97) FL 41+2/5 FLC 2/1 FAC 3/2 Others 3

LEE Graeme Barry
Born: Middlesbrough, 31 May 1978
Height: 6'2" Weight: 13.7
1997-98 was a great season for Hartlepool's 19-year-old central defender, as he built on his successes of the previous campaign, and was often outstanding in the middle of a three-man central defence. Although scoring two goals against Swansea on his debut as a striker, realistically this was only a temporary diversion from his best position, and he appeared content to learn the game at the Victoria Park. Not surprisingly, towards the end of the term it was reported that he was attracting the attention of bigger clubs.
Hartlepool U (From trainee on 2/7/96) FL 61+6/3 FLC 1+2/1 FAC 3 Others 3+1/1

LEE Jason Benedict
Born: Forest Gate, 9 May 1971
Height: 6'3" Weight: 13.8
Club Honours: Div 2 '98
Signed from Nottingham Forest in June 1997, the powerfully-built striker in the tradition of Watford centre forwards, proved to be a graceful mover with good first touch. Despite these assets, Jason's goal return was disappointing until a late flurry of four goals in the last five matches, including the strike at Bristol City that ensured promotion, and the winner at Fulham that clinched the championship. His luck obviously changing, he was delighted to win a second division championship medal as the Hornets returned to division one after a break of two years.
Charlton Ath (From trainee on 2/6/89) FL 0+1 Others 0+2
Stockport Co (Loaned on 6/2/91) FL 2
Lincoln C (£35,000 on 1/3/91) FL 86+7/21 FLC 6 FAC 2+1/1 Others 4
Southend U (Signed on 6/8/93) FL 18+6/3 FLC 1 FAC 1 Others 5+3/3
Nottingham F (£200,000 on 4/3/94) F/PL 41+35/14 FLC 4+3/1 FAC 0+5 Others 4+2
Charlton Ath (Loaned on 5/2/97) FL 7+1/3
Grimsby T (Loaned on 27/3/97) FL 2+5/2 FAC 1
Watford (£200,000 on 16/6/97) FL 35+1/10 FLC 3 FAC 4 Others 1

LEE Robert Martin
Born: West Ham, 1 February 1966
Height: 5'11" Weight: 11.13
Club Honours: Div 1 '93
International Honours: E: 18; B-1; U21-2

Robert continued to demonstrate his dependability, with a string of consistent performances as an essential part of the Newcastle midfield alongside David Batty in 1997-98. An energetic and influential box-to-box player, he was appointed club captain on Peter Beardsley's departure, a responsibility he accepted with relish. Physically strong, and difficult to knock off the ball, he allied his considerable skill to a high workrate that enabled him to move into goalscoring positions, although successful strikes were rarer than in previous seasons. While recovering from the disappointment of missing Euro '96 to win back his place in the England squad and add to his tally of caps, he was disappointed to miss the FA Cup semi final with a hamstring injury, although obviously delighted to lead the side out at Wembley. *Stop Press:* As a member of England's World Cup squad in action during the summer, Rob was only called up for ten minutes, during a 2-0 win over Colombia, and then it was back to the bench.
Charlton Ath (Free from Hornchurch on 12/7/83) FL 274+24/59 FLC 16+3/1 FAC 14/2 Others 10+2/3
Newcastle U (£700,00 on 22/9/92) F/PL 206+3/43 FLC 15/3 FAC 20/4 Others 18/4

Jason Lee (centre)

LEESE Lars

Born: Germany, 18 August 1969
Height: 6'5" Weight: 14.5

Another Barnsley 1997 close season signing in an effort to bolster their Premiership assault, this time a goalkeeper from the German side, Bayern Leverkusen, for much of 1997-98 Lars was understudy to Dave Watson, although when given his chance he showed why he had been brought to the club. Having kept goal in five games and conceded eight goals, his moment of glory came at Anfield, where he defied Liverpool for the entire 90 minutes as the Tykes produced a remarkable 1-0 victory. His height made him good on crosses and he also showed himself to be a good shot-stopper.

Barnsley (£250,000 from Bayer Leverkusen on 23/7/97) PL 8+1 FLC 2

LEGG Andrew (Andy)

Born: Neath, 28 July 1966
Height: 5'8" Weight: 10.7
Club Honours: WC '89, '91; AIC '95
International Honours: W: 4

After failing to agree terms with Birmingham on a new two-year contract, Andy went on loan to Ipswich last November and played in seven games, scoring with a header against Sheffield United, and producing a long throw that led to the winning goal at Oxford in the Coca Cola Cup. Despite Ipswich also offering him a permanent contract, he returned to St Andrews before signing permanently for Reading in February. There, the Welsh international enjoyed a run of ten games at left back until being sidelined with a pulled hamstring at Charlton. Prior to that, he had shown a predilection for moving upfield in support of the strikers, coupled to his best-known skill – the huge throw to the near post.

Swansea C (Signed from Britton Ferry on 12/8/88) FL 155+8/29 FLC 9+1 FAC 16/4 Others 15+3/5
Notts Co (£275,000 on 23/7/93) FL 85+4/9 FLC 11 FAC 7+1 Others 13+2/6
Birmingham C (Signed on 29/2/96) FL 31+14/5 FLC 3+1 FAC 2+1
Ipswich T (Loaned on 3/11/97) FL 6/1 FLC 1
Reading (£75,000 on 20/2/98) FL 10

LEITCH Donald **Scott**

Born: Motherwell, 6 October 1969
Height: 5'9" Weight: 11.8

Unfortunately, Scott's 1997-98 season was disrupted by injuries which prevented him reaching any real consistency for Swindon. The left-footed Scots-born midfield anchor-man was only at his best when he was able to string a few games together, but he scored a couple of memorable goals – the first in the Coca Cola Cup tie at Watford, though it could not prevent Swindon's early exit, and then a long-range special at Stockport in November. Troubled by a groin strain towards the end of the season, he missed the final seven matches.

Dumfermline Ath (Free from Shettleston Juniors on 4/4/90) SL 72+17/16 SLC 6+1/3 SC 3 Others 1

Heart of Midlothian (Signed on 6/8/93) SL 46+9/2 SLC 1+2/1 SC 3 Others 2
Swindon T (£15,000 on 29/3/96) FL 68+1/1 FLC 7/2 FAC 1

LENAGH Steven Michael

Born: Durham, 21 March 1979
Height: 6'3" Weight: 13.9

Released from Sheffield Wednesday, where he had been a trainee, the tall central defender signed for Chesterfield on monthly terms last November and put in some promising reserve performances before being given first team action in the Auto Windscreens Shield, and then as a substitute. Having signed a contract for 1998-99, there will obviously be more opportunities in the pipeline for the young man this coming season.

Chesterfield (Free from Sheffield Wed juniors on 3/11/97) FL 0+3 Others 0+1

LENNON Neil Francis

Born: Lurgan, 25 June 1971
Height: 5'9" Weight: 12.7
Club Honours: FLC '97
International Honours: NI: 21; B-1; U23-1; U21-2; Yth

In 1997-98, the fiery, right-footed Leicester midfield dynamo continued to develop as a key member of the midfield units for both his club and Northern Ireland. A consistent performer throughout the season, he rattled in a scorcher from 25 yards in the home clash with Southampton on Easter Tuesday, having previously had the task of rolling the ball into an empty net for his previous strike at Highbury. Unfortunately, a fifth booking robbed him of his ever-present tag and he ended the campaign in the headlines due to a well documented incident concerning Alan Shearer.

Manchester C (From trainee on 26/8/89) FL 1
Crewe Alex (Free on 9/8/90) FL 142+5/15 FLC 8+1/1 FAC 16/1 Others 15+1
Leicester C (£750,000 on 23/2/96) P/FL 86+1/4 FLC 8/1 FAC 4 Others 5

LEONARD Mark Anthony

Born: St Helens, 27 September 1962
Height: 6'0" Weight: 13.3

The veteran ex-striker was an automatic choice in the Rochdale side in 1997-98, injury and suspension apart, and generally figured as the strong man in midfield, using his power as the ball winner. However, after the serious injury to John Pender, he was switched to one of his earlier roles, that of central defender, where his aerial prowess certainly helped a sometimes lightweight back four, Dale conceding only one goal in his first four games at the back, before he too fell victim to the club's number five jinx. Following his defensive move, "Lenny" also took over the skipper's armband.*

Everton (Signed from Witton A on 24/2/82)
Tranmere Rov (Loaned on 24/3/83) FL 6+1
Crewe Alex (Free on 1/6/83) FL 51+3/15 FLC 4/2 FAC 2 Others 3+1
Stockport Co (Free on 13/2/85) FL 73/23 FLC 5/2 FAC 1 Others 2/3
Bradford C (£40,000 on 27/9/86) FL 120+37/29 FLC 13+5/6 FAC 6+3/1 Others 6+5/3
Rochdale (£40,000 on 27/3/92) FL 9/1

Preston NE (£40,000 on 13/8/92) FL 19+3/1 FLC 2
Chester C (Free on 13/8/93) FL 28+4/8 FLC 2 FAC 3/1 Others 3
Wigan Ath (Signed on 15/9/94) FL 60+4/12 FLC 2 FAC 6/2 Others 6/2
Rochdale (Free on 3/7/96) FL 72/6 FLC 4 FAC 2 Others 1

LEONHARDSEN Oyvind

Born: Norway, 17 August 1970
Height: 5'10" Weight: 11.2
International Honours: Norway: 58

Signed from Wimbledon during the 1997 summer recess, Oyvind was seen by Liverpool to be another piece of the missing jigsaw, a player who can get up and down the park, provide support to both defence and the forwards, and be on the scoresheet with effective regularity. Although he netted six times for the Pool, most of them came in high-scoring games, while as a right-footed midfielder he spent most of his time on the left. That aside, he is strong, holds the ball up well, and should become an integral part of the Liverpool side once the team settles. At the time of going to press was one of several Premiership stars who were looking for World Cup success with Norway. *Stop Press:* Played three times for Norway in France '98, before the side were eliminated in the second round by Italy.

Wimbledon (£660,000 from Rosenborg on 8/11/94) PL 73+3/13 FLC 7+2/1 FAC 17/2
Liverpool (£3,500,000 on 3/6/97) PL 26+1/6 FLC 3+2 FAC 1 Others 2

LE SAUX Graeme Pierre

Born: Jersey, 17 October 1968
Height: 5'10" Weight: 12.2
Club Honours: PL '95; FLC '98
International Honours: E: 29; B-2; U21-4

Celestine Babayaro's bizarre broken leg injury just four days before the start of last season left the Chelsea boss, Ruud Gullit, with a real dilemma. Short of cover for the left-wing-back position, following Scott Minto's summer transfer to Benfica, he moved quickly to snap up England star, Graeme le Saux, from Blackburn Rovers for a club record £5 million – clinching the deal with just over 24 hours before the big kick off. A former Chelsea junior, Graeme had left the club in acrimonious circumstances in 1993, but under the tutelage of Kenny Dalglish he had developed into a world class left-wing back after being used by the Blues as a left-sided utility player. Chelsea beat off opposition from Arsenal, Juventus, and Barcelona, for the Channel Islander's signature, but the transfer fee represented something of a loss for the club as they had originally sold him for £650,000! A somewhat prickly customer, Graeme had become disenchanted with life at Ewood Park after bravely battling back from a serious leg injury to reclaim his England berth from Stuart Pearce and Andy Hinchcliffe. Scored his first goal back at Chelsea with a stunning 30-yard piledriver at Crystal Palace in September and, one month later, was a member of England's heroic team which clinched World Cup qualification in Rome. Following that, he badly dislocated an elbow against Leicester

Graeme le Saux

City, which sidelined him for eight matches. Coming back, he scored goals in successive matches in January, against Manchester United and Ipswich Town – a delightful chip over Peter Schmeichel, and a neatly-taken sidefooter at Portman Road in the Coca Cola Cup quarter final – before collecting his first medal with Chelsea in the Coca Cola Cup final. Unfortunately, a calf injury sustained against his old club, Blackburn, kept him out of the European Cup Winners' Cup final, though he recovered in time to take his place in Glenn Hoddle's World Cup squad, where his overlapping and pin-point crossing was reckoned to be a vital part of England's attacking strategy. Was also delighted to be recognised by his fellow professionals when named among the PFA award-winning Premiership select. *Stop Press:* Appeared in all four of England's World Cup games during the summer, but will probably be best remembered for his 90th-minute tousle with his Chelsea team mate, Dan Petrescu, which led to a 2-1 win for Romania.

Chelsea (Free from St Paul's, Jersey, on 9/12/87) F/PL 77+13/8 FLC 7+6/1 FAC 7+1 Others 8+1
Blackburn Rov (Signed on 25/3/93) PL 127+2/7 FLC 10 FAC 8 Others 6+1
Chelsea (£5,000,000 on 8/8/97) PL 26/1 FLC 4/1 FAC 1/1 Others 3

LESTER Jack William
Born: Sheffield, 8 October 1975
Height: 5'10" Weight: 12.0
Club Honours: AMC '98
International Honours: E: Sch

Having broken into the Grimsby senior squad at the end of 1996-97, he firmly established himself last season with an eight-minute hat trick in a Coca Cola Cup tie against Oldham. Unfortunately, a mid-season injury kept him out of the side for a long period and after his return he had difficulty in recapturing his old form, often appearing as a second-half substitute.

However, during both the second division and AWS run in, Jack returned to his best, playing a vital part in both competitions as the club swept towards a return to the first division, via the play offs, and won the latter trophy following a 2-1 victory over Bournemouth at Wembley. Is a striker who relies on speed and skill to drop defenders.

Grimsby T (From juniors on 8/7/94) FL 44+30/9 FLC 3+4/3 FAC 4+2/2 Others 4+4
Doncaster Rov (Loaned on 20/9/96) FL 5+6/1

LE TISSIER Matthew (Matt) Paul
Born: Guernsey, 14 October 1968
Height: 6'1" Weight: 13.8
International Honours: E: 8; B-6; Yth

What can be added to what has already been said about the enigmatic Southampton midfielder? His 1997-98 started on a low note, when he was missing until late September, having broken his arm in a pre-season friendly, and, on his return, he injured his groin and was missing for a further two matches. Returning again, he was substituted ten times before he regained something like his old best form and fitness, and it appeared that he had done enough to get into England's World Cup squad when he scored a hat trick, hit the woodwork twice, and completely dominated a "B" international against Russia. Added to this was a club goalscoring run at the end of term, making him Saints' top scorer with 14, and one can understand both his and his fans' disappointment at his omission. However, if he stays fit he is going to remain one of the games most creative players for years to come. Brilliant with the ball at his feet, often beating defenders for "fun", Matt can both score and create, and often opens the door when others cannot find the key.

Southampton (From apprentice on 17/10/86) F/PL 346+37/151 FLC 39+6/26 FAC 30+1/12 Others 11+1/9

LEVER Mark
Born: Beverley, 29 March 1970
Height: 6'3" Weight: 13.5
Club Honours: AMC '98

Following a dismal 1996-97, when his opportunities were limited by suspension and injury, Mark returned to full fitness and assumed his usual commanding role at the centre of Grimsby's defence last season, where his strength in the air and sound tackling contributed greatly to the Mariners' Wembley wins in the AWS competition and the second division play-off final. Now into his testimonial having spent ten years at Blundell Park, he is still young enough to complete another ten.*

Grimsby T (From trainee on 9/8/88) FL 293+9/8 FLC 21+1 FAC 15+2 Others 18

LEWIS Benjamin (Ben)
Born: Chelmsford, 22 June 1977
Height: 6'1" Weight: 12.3

Picked up after being released by Colchester during the 1997 close season, Ben made his full Southend debut in September 1997 at home to Fulham, and scored in a 1-0 victory. A strong and dominant centre half, he performed with a maturity well above his years over the next three months, but a sending off in the FA Cup against Fulham saw him drop out of the first team picture, before he was released during the summer.

Colchester U (From trainee on 24/3/96) FL 1+1 Others 1
Southend U (Free on 18/8/97) FL 14/1 FLC 1+1 FAC 1+1 Others 1

LEWIS Neil Anthony
Born: Wolverhampton, 28 June 1974
Height: 5'8" Weight: 11.1
Club Honours: FLC '97

A 1997 close season signing from Leicester, Neil was an immediate starter for Peterborough in 1997-98, playing either as a left-wing back or more forward in midfield, his excellent dribbling skills allowing him to play in any number of positions. With great potential, but with occasional lapses, it will be interesting to see where he settles in 1998-99.

Leicester C (From trainee on 9/7/92) F/PL 53+14/1 FLC 6+1 FAC 2 Others 2
Peterborough U (£75,000 on 26/6/97) FL 31+3 FLC 4 FAC 3 Others 0+1

LIBURD Richard John
Born: Nottingham, 26 September 1973
Height: 5'9" Weight: 11.1

Having been released by his previous club, Bradford City, after failing to make a first team appearance in 1997-98, Richard made his Carlisle debut in the vital end of February clash with Burnley, and gave an excellent display in that game which the Cumbrians won 2-1. Playing mainly as a right-wing back, and strong in the tackle, lack of match fitness sometimes showed in later appearances, but his raw ability was obvious and if he stays at Brunton Park he will certainly be an asset in the coming term.*

Middlesbrough (£20,000 from Eastwood T on 25/3/93) FL 41/1 FLC 4 FAC 2 Others 5
Bradford C (£200,000 on 2l/7/94) FL 75+3/3 FLC 6+2 FAC 2+2 Others 2
Carlisle U (Free on 26/2/98) FL 9

LIDDELL Andrew Mark
Born: Leeds, 28 June 1973
Height: 5'7" Weight: 10.9
International Honours: S: U21-11

In Barnsley's first-ever season of Premiership football, Andrew found his chances more and more limited as 1997-98 progressed, as the manager decided that it was his attack that needed strengthening. When selected, however, he still showed a good appetite for work, and was always a fierce competitor, never giving less than 100 per-cent effort. Despite suffering a badly broken nose, which hampered him late in the campaign, he came back into the side to score at Newcastle in the FA Cup quarter final, but, in the main, was consigned to the subs' bench more often than not.
Barnsley (From trainee on 6/7/91) F/PL 139+51/34 FLC 10+1/3 FAC 5+7/1 Others 2+1

LIDDLE Craig George
Born: Chester le Street, 21 October 1971
Height: 5'11" Weight: 12.7

A much sought after young Middlesbrough defender, cum midfielder, Craig made just eight appearances last season for the club, but whenever called upon he could be relied to put in a solid performance. However, with first team prospects dwindling, he was loaned out to Darlington in February and spent the rest of the term at Feethams, his hard tackling and composure seeing him slot easily into their defence. Is also powerful in the air.
Aston Villa (From trainee on 4/7/90 - Free to Blyth Spartans in August 1991)
Middlesbrough (Free on 12/7/94) P/FL 20+5 FLC 3+2 FAC 2 Others 2
Darlington (Loaned on 20/2/98) FL 15

LIGHTBOURNE Kyle Lavince
Born: Bermuda, 29 September 1968
Height: 6'2" Weight: 12.4
International Honours: Bermuda: 6

Purchased from Walsall in the summer of 1997, it was never envisaged that the striker would be a Coventry regular, and he appeared as a substitute in five early league games. Making his first start in the away leg of the Blackpool Coca Cola tie, he then played in the home leg and the third round tie against Everton, having a good game in the latter, linking well with Simon Haworth, and was unlucky not to score. Keeping his place for the following game against Barnsley, in what turned out to be his one and only Premiership start, his final appearance was at West Ham on Boxing Day, as a substitute, before he went on loan to Fulham for a month and scored three goals. Returned to City for a short spell, but was then sold to Stoke City in March, and almost immediately was struck down by a virus, which showed up after a series of lethargic displays. Blood tests tracked down the problem and, following an enforced rest, he regained a spot in the squad, albeit on the

subs' bench, netting an injury-time goal in the 2-1 win over Portsmouth.
Scarborough (Signed on 11/12/92) FL 11+8/3 FLC 1 Others 0+1
Walsall (Free on 17/9/93) FL 158+7/65 FLC 8/3 FAC 16+2/12 Others 7/5
Coventry C (£500,000+ on 18/7/97) PL 1+6 FLC 3
Fulham (Loaned on 13/1/98) FL 4/2 Others 1/1
Stoke City (£500,000 on 16/2/98) FL 9+4/2

LIGHTFOOT Christopher (Chris) Ian
Born: Warrington, 1 April 1970
Height: 6'2" Weight: 13.6

A versatile Crewe defender who can also play in central midfield, Chris' season in 1997-98, as in 1996-97, was spoiled by several injuries, which was the reason he made just 15 appearances, six of them as a sub. Aggressive and strong in possession, with good passing technique, and extremely popular with the crowd, he can always be relied upon to fill in whatever role is required. Scored in the 2-0 home win against Stoke for his customary goal.
Chester C (From trainee on 11/7/88) FL 263+14/32 FLC 15+2/1 FAC 16+2/1 Others 14+2/5
Wigan Ath (£87,500 on 13/7/95) FL 11+3/1 FLC 2 FAC 2 Others 3
Crewe Alex (£50,000 on 22/3/96) FL 28+16/2 FLC 1+1 FAC 1+1/1 Others 3+2

LILLEY Derek Symon
Born: Paisley, 9 February 1974
Height: 5'11" Weight: 12.7
International Honours: S: Yth

A strong and speedy Leeds' striker, Derek had to be content with a place on the substitutes' bench last season, but his all-round play developed and he was a regular goalscorer in the reserves before suffering a groin injury in January. Came on and scored his first goal for the first team, the winner in a 3-2 fightback at Barnsley.
Greenock Morton (Free from Everton BC on 13/8/91) SL 157+23/56 SLC 5+1/4 SC 9+4/4 Others 6+4/5
Leeds U (£500,000+ on 27/3/97) PL 4+15/1 FLC 0+3 FAC 0+1

LING Martin
Born: West Ham, 15 July 1966
Height: 5'8" Weight: 10.8
Club Honours: Div 2 '96

An excellent passer of the ball, who recaptured the form that made him a Premiership player a couple of years ago, much of the Leyton Orient team play centred on Martin in 1997-98, making him one of the best midfielders in the league, a fact recognised by his fellow players when casting their votes for the PFA award-winning third division team. In 1998-99, Martin will be looking to add to his strike rate, but he did make a scoring return to Exeter during the campaign. An ever present in the league, his great balance allows him to often drift past defenders with ease.
Exeter C (From apprentice on 13/1/84) FL 109+8/14 FLC 8 FAC 4 Others 5
Swindon T (£25,000 on 14/7/86) FL 2 FLC 1+1
Southend U (£15,000 on 16/10/86) FL 126+12/31 FLC 8/2 FAC 7/1 Others ll+1/3

Mansfield T (Loaned on 24/1/91) FL 3
Swindon T (£15,000 on 28/3/91) F/PL 132+18/10 FLC 11+1/1 FAC 10+1/1 Others 12+1/1
Leyton Orient (Free on 23/7/96) FL 85+5/3 FLC 6 FAC 4 Others 2/1

LINGER Paul Hayden
Born: Stepney, 20 December 1974
Height: 5'6" Weight: 10.5

Released by Charlton last September, despite overcoming a broken leg suffered the previous April, the diminutive midfielder moved on to Leyton Orient in order to kick-start his career. However, being very much in the mould of Martin Ling, Paul was unable to hold down a place and signed for Brighton in December. Skilful in control, with the ability to get forward, and a good passer, he was drafted straight into first team duty, making an impressive debut against Shrewsbury and becoming a regular member of the squad for the remainder of the campaign, prior to being released in the summer.
Charlton Ath (From trainee on 1/7/93) FL 5+18/1 FLC 0+1 Others 0+3
Leyton Orient (Free on 25/9/97) FL 1+2 FAC 0+1
Brighton & Hove A (Free on 17/12/97) FL 17+2 Others 1

LINIGHAN Andrew (Andy)
Born: Hartlepool, 18 June 1962
Height: 6'3" Weight: 13.10
Club Honours: FLC '93; FAC '93; ECWC '94
International Honours: E: B-4

A first team ever present in the centre of Crystal Palace's defence last season until giving way to Ismael Valerien in February, despite the precarious position of the team, the rearguard was never quite the same again, conceding over 30 goals without him. However, back for the final game against his old team, Sheffield Wednesday, which resulted in a 1-0 win for the Eagles, it was only the sixth time during the Premiership campaign that Palace had completed a shut out and Andy was on the field for all six. Although his age is against him, he is still a consistent, tough-tackling defender who controls the back line well, misses little in the air, and comes out with the ball looking for the pass. Is the brother of David (Blackpool) and Brian (Bury).
Hartlepool U (Free from Henry Smiths BC on 19/9/80) FL 110/4 FLC 7+1/1 FAC 8 Others 1/1
Leeds U (£20,000 on 15/5/84) FL 66/3 FLC 6/1 FAC 2 Others 2
Oldham Ath (£65,000 on 17/1/86) FL 87/6 FLC 8/2 FAC 3 Others 4
Norwich C (£350,000 on 4/3/88) FL 86/8 FLC 6 FAC 10 Others 4
Arsenal (£1,250,000 on 4/7/90) F/PL 101+17/5 FLC 13+1/1 FAC 12+2/1 Others 9+1/1
Crystal Palace (£150,000 on 27/1/97) F/PL 45/2 FLC 2 FAC 2+1 Others 3

LINIGHAN Brian
Born: Hartlepool, 2 November 1973
Height: 6'3" Weight: 12.12

Signed from Sheffield Wednesday during the 1997 close season, the young centre half captained Bury's reserves throughout 1997-98 but seldom looked like gaining a first

team opportunity, with competition for places tight. However, although not appearing in the league side, he showed up as a late substitute in both of the Coca Cola Cup games against Sunderland and, throughout the season, showed himself to be both solid and reliable in everything he did, especially in the air. From a footballing family, Brian (senior) played one game for Darlington in 1958, while brothers, David and Andy, are still active centre backs.

Sheffield Wed (From trainee on 16/7/92) PL 1 FLC 1 FAC 1
Bury (Free on 2/7/97) FLC 0+2

LINIGHAN David
Born: Hartlepool, 9 January 1965
Height: 6'2" Weight: 13.0
Club Honours: Div 2 '92

The experienced central defender and Blackpool club captain missed several games through injury in 1997-98 but, when available, he showed he was still a force to be reckoned with. In forming a solid partnership with Tony Butler, the brother of Andy is commanding in the air and competitive on the deck, and is always likely to pop up with the odd goal or two. Interestingly, two of his three goals last season came in the home and away legs of the Coca Cola Cup games against Coventry. Was released during the summer.

Hartlepool U (From juniors on 3/3/82) FL 84+7/5 FLC 3+1/1 FAC 4 Others 2
Derby Co (£25,000 on 11/8/86)
Shrewsbury T (£30,000 on 4/12/86) FL 65/1 FLC 5 FAC 3 Others 1
Ipswich T (£300,000 on 23/6/88) F/PL 275+2/12 FLC 21 FAC 18/1 Others 11
Blackpool (£80,000 on 17/11/95) FL 97+3/5 FLC 6/2 FAC 2/1 Others 8

LINTON Desmond (Des) Martin
Born: Birmingham, 5 September 1971
Height: 6'1" Weight: 13.10

Started last season at Peterborough's regular right back, but gave way to the improving Chris McMenamin before coming back strongly in the final six games. Able to play in midfield, and a good tackler who enjoys linking up with the forwards, Des always looks to have time on the ball.

Leicester C (From trainee on 9/1/90) FL 6+5 FLC 0+1 Others 1
Luton T (Signed on 22/10/91) FL 65+18/1 FLC 4+1 FAC 8 Others 7
Peterborough U (£25,000 on 26/3/97) FL 33+5 FLC 2 FAC 2+1 Others 2

LISBIE Kevin Anthony
Born: Hackney, 17 October 1978
Height: 5'8" Weight: 10.12
International Honours: E: Yth

An exciting young Charlton striker who is exceptionally quick, has good ball control, and a prolific goalscorer in youth and reserve team football, Kevin only started one game for the Addicks last season, but was named as substitute on numerous occasions, scoring in the home win over Oxford United in August. Can also play wide on the right.

Charlton Ath (From trainee on 24/5/96) FL 5+37/2 FLC 0+4 FAC 0+1

LITTLE Colin Campbell
Born: Wythenshawe, 4 November 1972
Height: 5'10" Weight: 11.0

Always a danger in the opposition penalty area, especially when he runs at defenders, Colin rewarded his manager by topping Crewe's scoring charts in 1997-1998 with 13 goals to his credit, after having to work extremely hard to gain a regular spot in the side up front. Came off the bench to score twice in 3-0 win at Tranmere and, when grabbing a hat trick in the 5-0 win over Bradford towards the end of the season, he became the first man to attain three in a match for the Alex in over two years.

Crewe Alex (£50,000 from Hyde U on 7/2/96) FL 39+30/14 FLC 1+1 FAC 3 Others 5/3

Colin Little

LITTLE Glen Matthew
Born: Wimbledon, 15 October 1975
Height: 6'3" Weight: 13.0

Glen had few chances in the first team before last Christmas, but grabbed his opportunity when given it and was a key player for Burnley in most games from then on. Nominally a right-sided midfielder, his unorthodox style incorporates speed, the ability to confuse an opponent in the process of taking the ball past him, and an explosive shot, his first senior goal, against Notts County in the Auto Windscreens Shield, being a strong Goal of the Season contender. Many fans wondered how different the Clarets' season might have been if his chance had come earlier.

Crystal Palace (From trainee on 1/7/94 - Free to Glentoran on 11/11/94)
Burnley (£100,000 on 29/11/96) FL 24+9/4 FLC 0+2 FAC 1+1 Others 3+1/1

LITTLEJOHN Adrian Sylvester
Born: Wolverhampton, 26 September 1970
Height: 5'9" Weight: 11.0
International Honours: E: Yth

A very quick and direct forward who is at his most dangerous when given the ball to feet and running at defenders, either through the middle or down the flanks, Adrian was also used by Plymouth during last season as an emergency left-wing back. With this leading to a difference of opinion with the management, he joined Oldham on transfer deadline day in a straight swap for Phil Starbuck and quickly showed what he was capable of, scoring three goals in his five Latics' appearances. When fully fit he will be a great asset to the side with his pace.

Walsall (Free from West Bromwich A juniors on 24/5/89) FL 26+18/1 FLC 2+1 FAC 1+1 Others 4+1
Sheffield U (Free on 6/8/91) F/PL 44+25/12 FLC 5+1 FAC 3+2/1 Others 2/1
Plymouth Arg (£100,000 on 22/9/95) FL 100+10/29 FLC 6 FAC 6+2/3 Others 6
Oldham Ath (Signed on 20/3/98) FL 5/3

LIVINGSTONE Stephen (Steve)
Born: Middlesbrough, 8 September 1969
Height: 6'1" Weight: 12.7
Club Honours: AMC '98

Strong and physical in the old centre-forward mould, Steve is a tireless worker, with good timing in the air, deft touches, and a sense of awareness in the box. Once again, 1997-98 was a season in which Steve served not only up front for Grimsby, but also as an emergency central defender, a role which he has filled to good effect with his usual enthusiasm and determination, and which gave the side flexibility. Scored twice in a 2-0 win at Fulham, another side looking for a return to the first division. Came off the bench for both Wembley visits, the AWS win over Bournemouth, and the second division play-off victory over Northampton.*

Coventry C (From trainee on 16/7/86) FL 17+14/5 FLC 8+2/10 Others 0+1
Blackburn Rov (£450,000 on 17/1/91) F/PL 25+5/10 FLC 2 FAC 1/1
Chelsea (£350,000 on 23/3/93) PL 0+1
Port Vale (Loaned on 3/9/93) FL 4+1
Grimsby T (£140,000 on 29/10/93) FL 140+32/33 FLC 7+4/4 FAC 6+5/2 Others 4+3

LJUNG Per-Ola
Born: Almhult, Sweden, 7 November 1967
Height: 5'9" Weight: 11.10

Signed from Helsingborg on non-contract terms last December, the Swedish wing back made one appearance for Watford in the Auto Windscreens Shield, while on trial, before returning to Sweden, without obtaining a contract, in February.

Watford (Free from Helsingborg on 4/12/97) Others 1

LLEWELLYN Christopher (Chris) Mark
Born: Merthyr, 29 August 1979
Height: 5'11" Weight: 11.6
International Honours: W: 2; B-1; U21-3; Yth

Still eligible for the Norwich youth team, what a big season 1997-98 was for Chris.

Already a Welsh U18 international, he went on to win three U21 caps, as well as gaining "B" recognition also, and after making his first team debut in an FA Cup tie at Grimsby early in the New Year, he scored his first senior goal in a remarkable 3-3 home draw against Birmingham in March. A very level-headed youngster, who appears to have the ability to go all the way, he was called up to the Welsh full squad during the summer, playing against Malta and Tunisia. Although preferring to play up front, it would seem that he poses a danger from any position in the last third, scoring three goals in the last six games from an attacking midfield role.
Norwich C (From trainee on 21/1/97) FL 10+5/4 FAC 0+1

LLOYD Kevin Gareth
Born: Llanidloes, 26 September 1970
Height: 6'0" Weight: 12.1
When 1997-98 got underway, Cardiff City expected Kevin and Chris Beech to be in contention for the left-wing back position throughout. Unfortunately, injuries meant that he was unable to start one league or cup match, making just four subs' appearances, suffering severe back problems which eventually needed an operation and, when getting back to fitness, the season was ending. After an horrendous time of it, he was given a free transfer, but offered the option to start training with City in 1998-99 to prove his fitness, while several clubs in non-League and League of Wales soccer immediately showed strong interest when he became available. Is a steady and determined player.
Hereford U (Free from Caersws on 7/11/94) FL 49+2/3 FLC 2 FAC 1 Others 6
Cardiff C (Free on 2/8/96) FL 27+6/1 FLC 2+2 Others 3

LOCK Anthony (Tony) Charles
Born: Harlow, 3 September 1976
Height: 5'11" Weight: 13.0
Another homegrown Colchester starlet, Tony had an excellent pre-1997-98 season, when he formed a productive partnership with Mark Sale, before picking up a collarbone injury which cost him a starting place for the league campaign. Largely used as substitute, when he provided late winners against Scarborough and Torquay, he finally got a run in the team from February and certainly did not let his many advocates down, finishing the campaign with six goals. Will be looking to hold down a permanent place in the side this coming term.
Colchester U (From trainee on 18/4/95) FL 15+26/8 FLC 0+2 FAC 0+3 Others 0+5

LOCKE Adam Spencer
Born: Croydon, 20 August 1970
Height: 5'11" Weight: 12.7
A free-transfer signing from Colchester in the summer of 1997, Adam was Bristol City's find of last season. A right-wing back, with great commitment, and the ability to run at the opposition, he made the position his own at Ashton Gate with many fine performances. Unfortunately, he did not

match the goalscoring return he achieved with Colchester in 1996-97, though he was robbed of a fine long-range goal in a 1-0 defeat at Burnley, when the referee ruled another City player offside.
Crystal Palace (From trainee on 21/6/88)
Southend U (Free on 6/8/90) FL 56+17/4 FLC 5 FAC 2+1 Others 6+1
Colchester U (Loaned on 8/10/93) FL 4 Others 1
Colchester U (Free on 23/9/94) FL 64+15/8 FLC 5+1 FAC 5 Others 8+5
Bristol C (Free on 23/7/97) FL 35+2/1 FLC 3 FAC 2 Others 2/1

LOCKWOOD Matthew (Matt) Dominic
Born: Southend, 17 October 1976
Height: 5'9" Weight: 10.12
This talented and versatile player really established himself in the Bristol Rovers' team in 1997-98 as a confident and natural left footer, who was extremely comfortable in possession. Although able to play equally well at left back, where he made most of his appearances, or as a left-sided midfielder, he prefers the central midfield role. And, as a creator of goals, his accurate crosses provided many opportunities for the strikers, none more important than his superb cross four minutes from the end of the final league match of the season against Brentford, from which Rovers scored the winner and secured a place in the second division play offs.
Queens Park R (Free from Southend U juniors on 2/5/95)
Bristol Rov (Free on 24/7/96) FL 58+5/1 FLC 2+1 FAC 6 Others 4+2

LOGAN Richard Anthony
Born: Barnsley, 24 May 1969
Height: 6'1" Weight: 13.3
A very strong player who is extremely versatile and was therefore a very valuable member of the Plymouth squad in 1997-98. Once again used in a variety of roles in defence and midfield, he scored his fair share of goals, including three in consecutive games against Grimsby, Wigan, and Oxford, in August.*
Huddersfield T (Free from Gainsborough Trinity on 15/11/93) FL 35+10/1 FLC 3 FAC 1 Others 9
Plymouth Arg (£20,000 on 26/10/95) FL 67+19/12 FLC 4/1 FAC 2+2 Others 8

LOMAS James Duncan
Born: Chesterfield, 18 October 1977
Height: 5'11" Weight: 12.0
Tall and elegant, this right-sided midfielder, and graduate of Chesterfield's youth scheme, broke into the first team at the end of 1997-98. With good turn of speed, and an excellent crosser, he did not seem unwilling to try things for fear that they might go wrong and took his promotion in his stride, holding great promise for the future.
Chesterfield (From trainee on 16/9/96) FL 2+4 Others 1+1

LOMAS Stephen (Steve) Martin
Born: Hanover, Germany, 18 January 1974
Height: 6'0" Weight: 12.8
International Honours: NI: 26; B-1; Yth; Sch
The West Ham captain was excellent throughout last season and deservedly

finished as runner up in the fans' Hammer of the Year competition. Steve is a good ball winner, has good passing skills, and possesses a long throw, which always causes problems, even for Premiership defences. A regular in the Northern Ireland squad, his aggression in midfield provided the driving force, and in the FA Cup he scored the winner against his former club, Manchester City, before becoming the hero of the hour when sinking the vital penalty against Blackburn to put West Ham into the quarter finals.
Manchester C (From trainee on 22/1/91) P/FL 102+9/8 FLC 15/2 FAC 10+1/1
West Ham U (£1,600,000 on 26/3/97) PL 40/2 FLC 4 FAC 5/1

LOMBARDO Attilio
Born: Maria la Fossa, Italy, 6 January 1966
Height: 5'11" Weight: 12.6
International Honours: Italy: 18
Signed from Juventus just before the start of 1997-98, this quality midfielder quickly became the "darling" of the Crystal Palace crowd in the opening game, a 2-1 win over Everton, when he scored the first and had an "assist" for the second. Elegant in all he does and a great long passer of the ball, his new manager, Steve Coppell, described him thus: "His sheer class gives everyone a buzz. He does things that are not spectacular, but simply efficient. The way he controls the ball and sees space is an inspiration and sets the standard for everyone else in the team." There was certainly an air of expectancy before it all went wrong. Starting with the match at Selhurst Park against Newcastle, a 2-1 defeat, the team went 16 games before it achieved another victory and, surprisingly, it came in the shape of a 2-1 win at Newcastle on 18 March, which coincided with it being the Italian's first game as the player/manager, and Coppell having moved upstairs as Director of Football. many of those games, however, he had missed through injury and, although he played well when available, it was all too much, even for him, needing an interpreter to give instructions, and with many players just not up to the task at hand – averting relegation. Interestingly, in the matches Attilio scored, Palace never lost. An Italian international, and still on the verge of the squad, he had been hoping to make the World Cup Finals in France during the summer, having been used in a qualifying game, but was ultimately not selected for the final 22.
Crystal Palace (£1,600,000 from Juventus on 9/8/97) PL 21+3/5

LONGWORTH Steven Paul
Born: Preston, 6 February 1980
Height: 5'9" Weight: 11.3
Introduced from the bench by Blackpool in the 90th minute of their FA Cup game against Blyth Spartans last November, the second-year trainee midfielder hardly got much time to find out about life as a professional footballer. However, the club

obviously have faith in the youngster, who was due to sign professional forms during the summer, as he was a named sub on seven more occasions and came on twice.

Blackpool (Trainee) FL 0+2 FAC 0+1

LORMOR Anthony (Tony)
Born: Ashington, 29 October 1970
Height: 6'0" Weight: 13.6

An experienced goalscorer, tall and rangy in the traditional mould, with persistence and pace to match, Tony kicked off 1997-98 at Chesterfield with a goal on the opening day in a 3-1 home win against Walsall. He then scored seven, four of them being penalties, in 17 games before being transferred to Preston as part of the deal that involved David Reeves going in the opposite direction. However, despite a goal on his debut, and a brace at Southend, he was never able to repeat his Chesterfield goalscoring exploits at Deepdale, and was loaned to Notts County in February. Although given a chance at County, playing a number of times, mainly as a sub, and being unlucky not to score, he soon headed back to North End, where he failed to make any further appearances.

Newcastle U (From trainee on 25/2/88) FL 6+2/3
Lincoln C (£25,000 on 29/1/90) FL 90+10/30 FLC 1+2/3 FAC 4/2 Others 6
Peterborough U (Free on 4/7/94) FL 2+3 FAC 1 Others 1+1
Chesterfield (Free on 23/12/94) FL 97+16/35 FLC 8/4 FAC 5/3 Others 7+1/3
Preston NE (£130,000+ on 5/11/97) FL 9+3/3 FAC 3 Others 3
Notts Co (Loaned on 20/2/98) FL 2+5

LOVELL Stuart Andrew
Born: Sydney, Australia, 9 January 1972
Height: 5'10" Weight: 12.2
Club Honours: Div 2 '94

A local-born, wholehearted Reading striker who, because of injury, did not come into the team until last December, and even then failing to find his form, scoring just once in 18 appearances, a brave header in a 2-0 away win at Swindon being the high point of his season. He certainly proved more popular with the fans than either manager, Terry Bullivant frequently using him as substitute, and Tommy Burns finding it difficult to accommodate him, employing him in a totally alien role as right-wing back in the last game of the campaign, after which, he was released during the summer.

Reading (From trainee on 13/7/90) FL 177+50/58 FLC 13/5 FAC 7+9/2 Others 7+3/2

LOW Joshua (Josh) David
Born: Bristol, 15 February, 1979
Height: 6'1" Weight: 12.0
International Honours: W: Yth

A tall, tricky winger, Josh broke through with Bristol Rovers in 1997-98 and enjoyed a good season, making a number of first team appearances, his pace and ability to cross the ball into dangerous areas always being a threat. Yet to open his goal account, his only other disappointment was his dismissal at Wigan Athletic in December, when three more of his team mates were sent off, thus equalling a league record.

Although losing his place, following his suspension, he was rewarded for his progress as a young professional with a further two-year contract.

Bristol Rov (From trainee on 19/8/96) FL 6+8 FLC 0+2 FAC 2+1 Others 2

LOWE David Anthony
Born: Liverpool, 30 August 1965
Height: 5'10" Weight: 11.9
Club Honours: AMC '85; Div 2 '92, Div 3 '97
International Honours: E: U21-2; Yth

A hard-working striker, David completed a memorable season for Wigan in 1997-98, ending up the top scorer with 18 goals and setting up a new club aggregate scoring record, his goal in the home victory over Burnley being his 60th for the Springfield Park side. Celebrated by sweeping the board with the Player of the Year awards, collecting both the supporters and club's trophies. Captained Athletic in the final six games and was never on the losing side.

Wigan Ath (From apprentice on 1/6/83) FL 179+9/40 FLC 8 FAC 16+1/4 Others 18/9
Ipswich T (£80,000 on 26/6/87) FL 121+13/37 FLC 10/2 FAC 3 Others 10+2/6
Port Vale (Loaned on 19/3/92) FL 8+1/2
Leicester C (£250,000 on 13/7/92) F/PL 68+26/22 FLC 4+3/1 FAC 2+2 Others 3
Port Vale (Loaned on 18/2/94) FL 18+1/5
Wigan Ath (£125,000 on 28/3/96) FL 80+12/25 FLC 4 FAC 3+1/1 Others 4/1

David Lowe

LOWE Kenneth (Kenny)
Born: Sedgefield, 6 November 1961
Height: 6'1" Weight: 11.13
Club Honours: FAT '90
International Honours: E: SP-2

Having made just nine appearances in Darlington's midfield during the early months of 1997-98, this much-travelled journeyman returned to Gateshead in November to take up the post of player/coach with the Conference side, after coming from Tyneside the previous March. At the age of 36, the man who was once described as the "Glenn Hoddle of non-league football" finally returned to his roots.

Hartlepool U (From apprentice on 14/11/78) FL 50+4/3 FLC 1+1 FAC 2 Others 1 (Free to Billingham during 1984 close season)
Scarborough (Free from Barrow, via Spearwood, Australia, Gateshead and Morecambe, on 15/1/88) FL 4 (Free to Barrow in April 1989)
Barnet (£40,000 on 1/3/91) FL 55+17/5 FLC 2+1 FAC 5 Others 4
Stoke C (Free on 5/8/93) FL 3+6 FLC 2 Others 2
Birmingham C (£75,000 on 17/12/93) FL 14+7/3 FLC 0+1 FAC 3+1 Others 2+1 (Free to Gateshead on 10/1/96)
Carlisle U (Loaned on 22/9/94) FL 1+1
Hartlepool U (Loaned on 28/8/95) FL 13/3 FLC 2
Darlington (Free on 26/3/97) FL 10+4 FAC 2

LOWNDES Nathan Peter
Born: Salford, 2 June 1977
Height: 5'11" Weight: 10.6

Having shown his potential in 1996-97, the flame-haired, slightly-built Watford striker again impressed with his close control and ability to turn, in his few first team appearances in 1997-98. One of these was the FA Cup third round tie against Sheffield Wednesday - a chance he seized with alacrity, showing up well against Premiership opponents.

Leeds U (From trainee on 1/4/95)
Watford (£40,000 on 3/10/95) FL 1+6 FLC 0+1 FAC 1+1 Others 1

LOWTHORPE Adam
Born: Hull, 7 August 1975
Height: 5'7" Weight: 11.3

On the transfer list since last August, as Mark Hateley aimed to trim down the Hull City squad, Adam remained determined to establish himself with his hometown club. Recalled to the team in the latter part of the season, he responded with a superb run of form in an orthodox right-back berth, looking more confident when going forward, and capping his re-emergence with his first goal at Boothferry Park, against Leyton Orient in March.

Hull C (From trainee on 2/7/93) FL 70+11/3 FLC 5 FAC 2 Others 2+3

LUCAS David Anthony
Born: Preston, 23 November 1977
Height: 6'2" Weight: 13.10
International Honours: E: Yth

An injury relegated David to second choice in goal for Preston for most of last season – this despite playing in the England U20 squad in Malaysia during the summer of 1997. Brought in early in the New Year, when Tepi Moilanen struggled, playing seven matches before giving way again, he gets down well, although not always appearing to command his area as much as he could. However, he is still very young for a 'keeper, and has bags of potential for the future, as evidenced by his selection in the Nationwide representative squad for the match against Italy's Serie "B" side, the England U21 squad in March versus Switzerland, and the England "B" squad against Portugal.

Preston NE (From trainee on 12/12/94) FL 9 FLC 1 FAC 1 Others 3
Darlington (Loaned on 14/12/95) FL 6
Darlington (Loaned on 3/10/96) FL 7
Scunthorpe U (Loaned on 23/12/96) FL 6 Others 2

LUCAS Richard
Born: Chapeltown, 22 September 1970
Height: 5'10" Weight: 12.6

An enthusiastic player, Richard was a fixture at left back for Hartlepool for most of 1997-98. In the first half of the season he was a consistent performer who was dependable, yet received little credit, but in the latter stages of the campaign his game went a little stale, although he can justifiably feel aggrieved to have been given a free transfer. Previously never having scored a league goal, he will be pleased to remember two particular games when he scored late goals to earn draws, when a Pool's defeat seemed inevitable.

Sheffield U (From trainee on 1/7/89) FL 8+2 FAC 1 Others 0+1
Preston NE (£40,000 on 24/12/92) FL 47+3 FAC 4 Others 4+1
Lincoln C (Loaned on 14/10/94) FL 4 Others 2
Scarborough (Free on 5/7/95) FL 63+9 FLC 6 FAC 3+1 Others 2
Hartlepool U (Free on 27/3/97) FL 49/2 FLC 2 FAC 1 Others 1

LUCKETTI Christopher (Chris) James
Born: Littleborough, 28 September 1971
Height: 6'0" Weight: 13.6
Club Honours: Div 2 '97

A commanding central defender, and Bury's captain, Chris was ever-present for the Shakers in 1997-98 as he continued to enhance his growing reputation with a string of consistent performances at the heart of the defence. Powerful in the air, and good with the ball at his feet, he was also one of a now small band of defenders in the Football League to stay clear of suspension, when picking up a minimal number of yellow cards during his 52 league and cup games.

Rochdale (Trainee) FL 1
Stockport Co (Free on 23/8/90)
Halifax T (Free on 12/7/91) FL 73+5/2 FLC 2/1 FAC 2 Others 4
Bury (£50,000 on 1/10/93) FL 192/7 FLC 11 FAC 10/1 Others 15/1

LUMSDON Christopher (Chris)
Born: Newcastle, 15 December 1979
Height: 5'11" Weight: 10.6

A first-year Sunderland professional, having come through the junior ranks, the 18-year-old left winger from Killingworth had been earning rave reviews for his performances in the reserves at Sunderland and was rewarded with his first team debut at Wolves last February. Despite being substituted late on, Chris played his part in an important 1-0 win for the team, and will undoubtedly be heard from again before too long.

Sunderland (From trainee on 3/7/97) FL 1

LUNDEKVAM Claus
Born: Norway, 22 February 1973
Height: 6'3" Weight: 12.10
International Honours: Norway: 5

A very cultured Southampton central defender, Claus continued to be an outstanding performer in 1997-98, being as comfortable in attacking positions as well as in defence, often pushing forward in support, and continued to establish a formidable partnership with Ken Monkou. In missing only eight games last season, it would be difficult to imagine the Saints without him and it was a surprise that he did not establish himself at the heart of Norway's defence, especially with the World Cup in the offing. Strong on the ball and a good passer.

Southampton (£400,000 from SK Brann on 3/9/96) PL 59+1 FLC 11+1 FAC 1

LUNT Kenneth (Kenny) Vincent
Born: Runcorn, 20 November 1979
Height: 5'10" Weight: 10.0
International Honours: E: Yth; Sch

A graduate from the FA school at Lilleshall, Kenny has been capped at schoolboy and youth level for England and aims to extend his international honours to senior level. Having signed professional forms for Crewe during the 1997 close season, the young midfielder started in the number eight shirt on the opening day at Swindon, scored the club's first goal of the campaign in the next match at home to Bury in the Coca Cola Cup, and made excellent progress that was rewarded by 43 appearances. Is yet another great prospect for Alex.

Crewe Alex (From trainee on 12/6/97) FL 29+12/2 FLC 2/1

LYDIATE Jason Lee
Born: Manchester, 29 October 1971
Height: 5'11" Weight: 12.3

Able to perform at full back or centre half, Jason actually opened the scoring for Blackpool in 1997-98, when volleying home the winner against Luton in the first match of the season. Figuring in half of the club's games, usually as a filler for someone missing, he could always be relied upon, his pace, power, and aerial ability often getting him out of trouble. Was released during the summer.

Manchester U (From trainee on 1/7/90)
Bolton W (Free on 19/3/92) FL 29+1 FLC 4 FAC 2 Others 1
Blackpool (£75,000 on 3/3/95) FL 81+5/2 FLC 7+2 FAC 6/1 Others 4+1

LYTTLE Desmond (Des)
Born: Wolverhampton, 24 September 1971
Height: 5'9" Weight: 12.13
Club Honours: Div 1 '98

Started 1997-98 in sound form for Nottingham Forest and played in the first 35 league matches before losing his place to the Frenchman, Thierry Bonalair, due to suspension. Despite not figuring in the final 11 matches of the campaign, Des was good value for his first division championship medal and will be looking forward with some relish to a return to the Premiership this coming term. Prior to losing his place, however, the right back again proved to be both solid and reliable in the tackle, and a player who liked to get forward to service the front men. Also has excellent powers of recovery.

Leicester C (From trainee on 1/9/90)
Swansea C (£12,500 from Worcester C on 9/7/92) FL 46/1 FLC 2 FAC 5 Others 5
Nottingham F (£375,000 on 27/7/93) F/PL 172+3/3 FLC 18 FAC 15 Others 8

Chris Lucketti

PFA Enterprises Ltd

Commercial Opportunities
with the Professional Footballers Association

The Professional Footballers Association has access to over 4,000 current and ex-players and has an enormously influential marque which provides the strongest possible accreditation, adding the status and appeal of the world's most popular sport to your own product, promotion or event.

PRODUCT ENDORSEMENTS

PERSONAL APPEARANCES

SPONSORSHIP OPPORTUNITIES

AFTER DINNER SPEAKERS

CORPORATE HOSPITALITY PACKAGES

BUSINESS PARTNERSHIPS

FOOTBALL IN THE COMMUNITY

AWARDS DINNER

For more information on commercial opportunities with the Professional Footballers Association, please contact:

PFA Enterprises Ltd

London
Garry Nelson
Tel: 0171-839-8663 Fax: 0171-839-2097
or e-mail:gnelson@thepfa.co.uk

Manchester
George Berry
Tel: 0161-228-2733 Fax: 0161-236-4496
or e-mail: gberry@thepfa.co.uk

www.thepfa.co.uk

MABBUTT Gary Vincent
Born: Bristol, 23 August 1961
Height: 5'10" Weight: 12.9
Club Honours: UEFA '84; FAC '91
International Honours: E: 16; B-9; U21-7;
Yth

Coming back from the injury which had kept him out of the 1996-97 campaign, bar one game, Gary struggled to hold a regular first team spot for Tottenham in 1997-98, but proved strong and reliable when called upon. His experience and long service at the club ensured a warm welcome from the fans and opponents alike for this widely respected professional. Unfortunately, the side lacked his organisational skills at crucial times throughout the season, and the news that Gary would be leaving the club after 16 years, was greeted with sorrow at the Lane. However, this most loyal of players enjoyed the moment of being handed the captain's armband once again for his farewell appearance in the final home game against Southampton. Stating his intention to play on for another two years brought rumours of a move to the Valley and newly promoted Charlton, but wherever he goes, this cool, commanding defender will always be fondly remembered at Tottenham. Still has a tremendous attitude to the game.
Bristol Rov (From apprentice on 9/1/79) FL 122+9/10 FLC 10/1 FAC 5+1/1
Tottenham H (£105,000 on 11/8/82) F/PL 458+19/27 FLC 60+2/2 FAC 45+2/3 Others 29+4/4

McALINDON Gareth Edward
Born: Hexham, 6 April 1977
Height: 5'10" Weight: 12.9
Club Honours: AMC '97

"Macca" was another forward who made many of his Carlisle appearances coming off the bench in 1997-98, although he did also notch up 16 league starts in the campaign. A goal tally of only four was perhaps disappointing for a player who, at times, looked a natural goalscorer, but these included a 20-yard last-minute strike against Wigan that brought the first league win of the season. While his extra-time effort against Oldham in the AWS was the Cumbrians' first ever "Golden Goal".
Carlisle U (Free from Newcastle U juniors on 10/7/95) FL 19+24/5 FLC 3 FAC 1+1/1 Others 1+4/2

McALLISTER Brian
Born: Glasgow, 30 November 1970
Height: 5'11" Weight: 12.5
International Honours: S: 3

This tall Scottish international central defender has spent his entire career with Wimbledon and has always performed well, never letting the side down. Unfortunately, he was ruled out of all but ten games in

1997-98, mainly due to an achilles heel injury, but will undoubtedly be challenging for a first team place once fully fit. Good at making powerful runs into the opposing half, excellent in the air, and, with a strong left foot, he is well capable of hitting wonderful long passes behind the full backs.
Wimbledon (From trainee on 1/3/89) F/PL 74+11 FLC 8+1 FAC 5+3 Others 1
Plymouth Arg (Loaned on 5/12/90) FL 7+1
Crewe Alex (Loaned on 8/3/96) FL 13/1 Others 2

McALLISTER Gary
Born: Motherwell, 25 December 1964
Height: 6'1" Weight: 11.8
Club Honours: S Div 1 '85; Div 1 '92; CS '92
International Honours: S: 56; B-2; U21-1

1997-98 was a sad season for Coventry's Scottish international captain. He injured his knee in the Leicester home game in November and, despite recovering to return against Spurs two weeks later, he collapsed before half time and never appeared in the first team again. The problem was a torn cruciate ligament, which was not operated on immediately in the hope that he could still make France '98. However, having rested up, he returned for a reserve game in early March, but collapsed again, and the operation was finally carried out. In the early part of the campaign, Gary had played well, his dead-ball activity being of a high level, and he had an outstanding game at Wimbledon, playing in a more forward role. City fans can only speculate how he might have performed alongside a "minder" like George Boateng.
Motherwell (Signed from Fir Park BC on 5/9/81) SL 52+7/6 SLC 3+1 SC 7/2
Leicester C (£125,000 on 15/8/85) FL 199+2/47 FLC 14+1/3 FAC 5/2 Others 4
Leeds U (£1,000,000 on 2/7/90) F/PL 230+1/31 FLC 26/5 FAC 24/6 Others 14/4
Coventry C (£3,000,000 on 26/7/96) PL 52/6 FLC 8/3 FAC 4

McANESPIE Stephen (Steve)
Born: Kilmarnock, 1 February 1972
Height: 5'9" Weight: 10.7
Club Honours: S Div 1 '95; SLC '95; Div 1 '97
International Honours: S: Yth

Started 1997-98 at Bolton where he found it difficult to break into the first team, making just four senior appearances before signing for Kevin Keegan's Fulham at the end of November. Surprisingly, he played mainly in the Capital League at right back and in midfield for his new team and went to Bradford on loan on transfer deadline day, where he impressed as an overlapping right back who loved getting up the line to deliver a steady flow of crosses to the front men in his seven games played. Is confident on the ball and steady in defence.
Aberdeen (From juniors on 12/5/88. Transferred to Vasterhauringe on 30/6/93)
Raith Rov (Signed on 25/1/94) SL 37+3 SLC 4 SC 3 Others 5
Bolton W (£900,000 on 30/9/95) F/PL 19+5 FLC 6
Fulham (£100,000 on 28/11/97) FL 2+2 FAC 1 Others 2+1
Bradford C (Loaned on 26/3/98) FL 7

McAREAVEY Paul
Born: Belfast, 3 December 1980
Height: 5'10" Weight: 11.0

An emerging talent at the County Ground, Paul earned a call into the Swindon first team squad towards the end of 1997-98 after giving a series of impressive displays for the reserves – most notably against a Tottenham side which had Darren Anderton and David Howells lining up in midfield against him. Having made his debut as a substitute at Carrow Road in the penultimate match, although it was a harsh baptism as Swindon went down 5-0, he is expected to challenge some of the more established players for a place in the coming season. Amazingly, the youngster did not arrive at the club as a trainee until last September and looks to be a precocious talent.
Swindon T (Trainee) FL 0+1

McAREE Rodney (Rod) Joseph
Born: Dungannon, 19 August 1974
Height: 5'7" Weight: 10.9
International Honours: NI: Yth; Sch

A hard-working Fulham midfielder, Rod had what for him must have been a very disappointing season in 1997-98, taking part in only two league matches. As a regular member of the Capital league side, before being loaned out to Conference club, Woking, for the last two months of the campaign, the euphoria over his wonderful goal at Carlisle, which virtually clinched promotion a year earlier, must have seemed a long time ago.
Liverpool (From trainee on 21/8/91)
Bristol C (Free on 26/7/94) FL 4+2 FLC 2 (Free to Dungannon Swifts on 6/11/95)
Fulham (Free on 29/12/95) FL 22+6/3 FLC 2+2 Others 0+2

MACARI Paul
Born: Manchester, 23 August 1976
Height: 5'8" Weight: 11.6

A summer of recuperation after an operation on his back was hardly the best start to a season's preparation for Paul, who was looking to break into the Stoke first team after a prolific goalscoring record in the reserves. His father's exit from the club also seemed to effect his progress, as well as that of his brother Mike. Whilst he eventually made the subs' bench, and made his league debut in a 1-1 draw at Charlton last October, he was made available for transfer in January and was told he would be freed at the end of an unhappy season.
Stoke C (From juniors on 26/8/93) FL 0+3

McATEER Jason Wynn
Born: Birkenhead, 18 June 1971
Height: 5'10" Weight: 11.12
International Honours: Ei: 25; B-1

Jason had an amazingly difficult season at Liverpool in 1997-98, first when breaking his left fibula in the end of January game at home to Blackburn and then, just one game after returning, he detached a muscle when playing against Arsenal. Following the first injury, the Republic of Ireland international had made a perfect comeback when notching two goals in a 5-0 rout of West

Ham at Anfield, and immediately set his sights on holding down his favourite midfield role, having spent the majority of his Pool career battling with Rob Jones for the right-wing-back slot. It was not to be though. As a player who is capable of making brave and aggressive runs into the opposition's danger areas, it is not surprising to know that he comes from the famous McAteer boxing family, his uncles, Pat and Les, both being British champions.

Bolton W (Signed from Marine on 22/1/92) P/FL 109+5/8 FLC 11/2 FAC 11/3 Others 8+1/2
Liverpool (£4,500,000 on 6/9/95) PL 78+9/3 FLC 10+1 FAC 10/3 Others 9

McAULEY Sean
Born: Sheffield, 23 June 1972
Height: 5'11" Weight: 11.12
International Honours: S: U21-1

Sean struggled during his first full season at Scunthorpe, often becoming a target for terrace criticism for his performances at left back. A regular until Christmas, he then lost form before coming back to have an excellent closing two months, when showing that he was far better suited to a flat back four than a five-man defence, his defensive skills of tackling and covering being more in evidence as he began to win the fans over.

Manchester U (From trainee on 1/7/90)
St Johnstone (Signed on 22/4/92) SL 59+3 SLC 3/1 SC 3 Others 1
Chesterfield (Loaned on 4/11/94) FL 1/1 FAC 1+1 Others 2
Hartlepool U (Free on 21/7/95) FL 84/1 FLC 6 FAC 3 Others 3
Scunthorpe U (Signed on 26/3/97) FL 39+5/1 FLC 3 FAC 2 Others 1

McCALL Stephen (Steve) Harold
Born: Carlisle, 15 October 1960
Height: 5'11" Weight: 12.6
Club Honours: UEFAC '81
International Honours: E: B-1; U21-6; Yth

Torquay's player/coach. Despite missing part of last season through injury, Steve returned to display all the midfield passing skills for which he has become synonymous and, at the same time, inspired those around him. Will have had 20 years as a professional this coming October.*

Ipswich T (From apprentice on 5/10/78) FL 249+8/7 FLC 29 FAC 23+1/1 Others 18+1/3
Sheffield Wed (£300,000 on 3/6/87) FL 21+8/2 FLC 2+3 FAC 1 Others 0+1
Carlisle U (Loaned on 8/2/90) FL 6
Plymouth Arg (£25,000 on 26/3/92) FL 97+3/5 FLC 5 FAC 6 Others 6
Torquay U (Free on 12/7/96) FL 43+8/2 FLC 3+1 Others 4/1

McCAMMON Mark Jason
Born: Barnet, 7 August 1978
Height: 6'5" Weight: 14.5

Signed on non-contract terms in December 1996, the tall, pacy striker made his debut for Cambridge United when coming off the bench during the home FA Cup draw against Stevenage Borough last December. Then, in the club's next fixture, he stepped up for a full appearance at Bristol Rovers in the Auto Windscreen Shield. Still only 19, despite making two further subs' appearances for

United, he spent much of last season gaining valuable experience, playing non-league football at neighbouring, Cambridge City.
Cambridge U (Free from Cambridge C on 31/12/96) FL 0+2 FAC 0+1 Others 1

McCANN Gavin Peter
Born: Blackpool, 10 January 1978
Height: 5'11" Weight: 11.0

A sharp, snappy Everton central midfielder, with a good range of passing skills and a fine shot, Gavin caused a stir when he appeared in a senior line-up for the first time in a pre-1997-98 season friendly against Glasgow Rangers. His first involvement of the game after coming as a substitute was a challenge which left Brian Laudrup in a heap on the floor! After making substitute appearances against Newcastle, Arsenal, and Liverpool in the Premiership, just as he seemed set to earn a first team opportunity, he injured his ankle. Recovered from that setback, only to suffer a hairline fracture of his leg in a reserve team game, the youngster overcame that obstacle too, to make his full debut at Tottenham, and hold his place for a further four matches.
Everton (From trainee on 1/7/95) PL 5+6

McCARTHY Jonathan (Jon) David
Born: Middlesbrough, 18 August 1970
Height: 5'9" Weight: 11.5
International Honours: NI: 7; B-2

Began 1997-98 playing in six of Port Vale's opening seven games, operating on the right wing, before being transferred to Birmingham in September and going straight into the side at the expense of Tony Hey. Had an up-and-down start at St Andrews, his unselfish tracking back and high workrate going largely uncredited by a demanding crowd, although when going forward he provided numerous assists, improved City's attacking thrusts, and chipped in with some important goals, none more so than the winner at Ipswich, and the opener in a home 1-1 draw against Middlesbrough. Continuing to play for Northern Ireland, making appearances against Portugal, Slovakia, and Spain, as well as having a "B" outing against the Republic in February, Jon has great pace and skill to match his persistence.
Hartlepool U (From juniors on 7/11/87) FL 0+1 (Free to Shepshed Charterhouse in March 1989)
York C (Free on 22/3/90) FL 198+1/31 FLC 8/1 FAC 11/3 Others 15/3
Port Vale (£450,000 on 1/8/95) FL 93+1/12 FLC 10/2 FAC 7/1 Others 8/2
Birmingham C (£1,850,000 on 11/9/97) FL 41/3 FAC 3

McCARTHY Paul Jason
Born: Cork, 4 August 1971
Height: 5'10" Weight: 13.12
International Honours: Ei: U21-10; Yth; Sch

A strong central defender for Wycombe Wanderers, Paul began last season as captain before losing his place in November to new signing, Nicky Mohan. Eventually regained his place, and the captaincy soon after, but then missed the last ten games of the season after a hernia operation. Very comfortable

on the ball, preferring to play constructively out of defence when possible, his only goal was the winner against Burnley in February, and he is always dangerous in the box at set pieces.
Brighton & Hove A (From trainee on 26/4/89) FL 180+1/6 FLC 11/1 FAC 13 Others 12/1
Wycombe W (£100,000 on 5/7/96) FL 64+7/1 FLC 6/1 FAC 5 Others 2

McCARTHY Sean Casey
Born: Bridgend, 12 September 1967
Height: 6'1" Weight: 12.12
International Honours: W: B-1

A hard-running, bustling striker who never gives up trying, and continually keeps defenders on their toes, Sean scored eight goals from his 30 appearances for Oldham last season but, after losing form, was loaned out to Bristol City on transfer deadline day. In attempting to fill the void left by the departure of Shaun Goater, there was no doubt about his sterling efforts on behalf of City, but he did not have much luck in front of goal and his only strike in seven games came in the final fixture at Preston. Is now back at Boundary Park and raring to go under the new management team.
Swansea C (Signed from Bridgend T on 22/10/85) FL 76+15/25 FLC 4+1/3 FAC 5+2/4 Others 9+1/6
Plymouth Arg (£50,000 on 18/8/88) FL 67+3/19 FLC 7/5 FAC 3/1 Others 0+1/1
Bradford C (£250,000 on 4/7/90) FL 127+4/60 FLC 10+2/10 FAC 8/2 Others 8+1/7
Oldham Ath (£500,000 on 3/12/93) P/FL 117+23/43 FLC 10/1 FAC 6+1/1 Others 4/1
Bristol C (Loaned on 26/3/98) FL 7/1

McCLAIR Brian John
Born: Airdrie, 8 December 1963
Height: 5'10" Weight: 12.13
Club Honours: SC '85; SPD '86; FAC '90, '94; CS '94; ECWC '91; ESC '91; FLC '91; PL '93, '94, '96, '97
International Honours: S: 30; B-1; U21-8; Yth

A very experienced Manchester United midfielder, or out-and-out striker, Brian took up his perennial role as United's "main man on the bench" when the 1997-98 campaign got under way and, having made his first full appearance of the season against Ipswich in the Coca Cola Cup in October, he became one of only three United players to play in all competitions. *Stop Press:* Although one of United's greatest ever servants, on approaching his 11th year at Old Trafford, he was given a free transfer during the summer and reportedly signed for Motherwell, the club he started out with in 1981.
Motherwell (Free from Aston Villa juniors on 1/8/81) SL 32+7/15 SLC 9+1/4 SC 2/1
Glasgow Celtic (£100,000 on 1/7/83) SL 129+16/99 SLC 19+1/9 SC 14+4/11 Others 13+2/3
Manchester U (£850,000 on 30/7/87) F/PL 296+59/88 FLC 44+1/19 FAC 39+6/14 Others 23+6/7

McCONNELL Barry
Born: Exeter, 1 January 1977
Height: 5'10" Weight: 10.3

A promising Exeter youngster who has

come through the ranks, Barry made only a handful of starts last season, despite his goals per game ratio being very good. Able to perform as a wing back, or up front, he will be looking for a longer run in the team in 1998-99, especially after picking up the club's Young Player of the Year award.
Exeter C (From trainee on 4/8/95) FL 31+27/6 FLC 1+2 FAC 2+1 Others 0+1

McDERMOTT Andrew (Andy)
Born: Sydney, Australia, 24 March 1977
Height: 5'9" Weight: 11.3
Started last season at West Bromwich Albion in possession of the right-back slot until relinquishing it to Paul Holmes three games into the campaign, following a period of uncertainty. Fast, with good composure, and also capable of playing in midfield, Andy occasionally deputised for his rival before coming back into contention during the run-in, having excelled with the reserves. His ability to pass the ball is a real asset, one of his biggest fans being Ray Harford, the manager who initially signed him.
Queens Park R (Signed from Australian Institute of Sport on 4/8/95) FL 6/2
West Bromwich A (£400,000 on 27/3/97) FL 19 FLC 2/1

McDERMOTT John
Born: Middlesbrough, 3 February 1969
Height: 5'7" Weight: 11.0
Club Honours: AMC '98
In his 11th season with Grimsby there is little new one can say about this consummate professional. Once again, firmly established as an automatic choice at right back in 1997-98, he is surprisingly fast for a defender, is a strong tackler who provides excellent service for the front runners, and is not averse to going forward with the ball. He also worked well to establish a partnership with whoever of the midfield players he was teamed up with, an asset that could not be underestimated as the team produced a quick return to the first division, via the play offs, and won the Auto Windscreen Shield.*
Grimsby T (From trainee on 1/6/87) FL 359+15/7 FLC 24+1 FAC 26+1/1 Others 21

McDONALD Alan
Born: Belfast, 12 October 1963
Height: 6'2" Weight: 13.11
International Honours: NI: 52; Yth; Sch
The vastly experienced former Northern Ireland captain, an imposing and likeable stopper, joined Swindon during the 1997 close season on a free transfer after 17 years loyal service at Queens Park Rangers, and made an immediate impact as he helped to tighten up the Town rearguard which had leaked so many goals towards the end of 1996-97. Despite a loss of form costing him his place after Christmas, he soon bounced back into the frame, his finest hour coming on his return to Rangers as a stand-in goalkeeper, following the first-half dismissal of Fraser Digby. Alan simply would not be beaten as the ten men and the

unlikely goalkeeping star recorded a vital away win.
Queens Park R (From apprentice on 12/8/81) F/PL 395+7/13 FLC 43/2 FAC 33/2 Others 5
Charlton Ath (Loaned on 24/3/83) FL 9
Swindon T (Free on 8/7/97) FL 30+3/1 FLC 2 FAC 1

Alan McDonald

McDONALD Christopher (Chris)
Born: Edinburgh, 14 October 1975
Height: 6'1" Weight: 13.0
International Honours: S: Sch
A brave central defender who made a great comeback for Hartlepool after 11 months out with a cruciate knee ligament injury, Chris performed well in his few appearances in 1997-98, but was unable to gain a regular place, such was the competition in what was Pool's strongest position. Unfortunately, he received a toe injury late in the campaign and, with this question mark over his fitness, he was only offered a three-month contract to prove himself for the coming season.
Arsenal (From trainee on 13/12/93)
Stoke C (Free on 31/8/95)
Hartlepool U (Free on 17/8/96) FL 13+2 FLC 2

MacDONALD David (Dave) Hugh
Born: Dublin, 2 January 1971
Height: 5'11" Weight: 12.12
International Honours: Ei: B-1; U21-3; Yth; Sch
Played in the first game of last season for Barnet, but did not figure from there on, due to the form of the back five, and was released during the summer. If given the opportunity, Dave is a tough, strong-tackling, no-nonsense full back, who is also a good long passer, especially into the channels.
Tottenham H (From trainee on 5/8/88) PL 2
Gillingham (Loaned on 27/9/90) FL 10 Others 2

Bradford C (Loaned on 28/8/92) FL 7
Reading (Loaned on 6/3/93) FL 11
Peterborough U (Free on 13/8/93) FL 28+1 FLC 4 FAC 2 Others 1
Barnet (Free on 24/3/94) FL 86+10 FLC 8+2 FAC 5 Others 4

McDONALD Martin Joseph
Born: Irvine, 4 December 1973
Height: 6'1" Weight: 11.12
A former favourite with Macclesfield before signing for Southport, Sammy McIlroy finally got him back last December from Doncaster after several months of negotiations, and admitted that he did not want him to leave in the first place. A midfielder with a tremendous engine, and an ability to run from box to box, Martin is also a tenacious tackler and his return coincided with the team's ascent from mid-table towards a promotion position.
Stockport Co (Free from Bramhall on 5/8/92 - Free to Macclesfield T during 1993 close season)
Doncaster Rov (£20,000 from Southport on 1/8/96) FL 48/4 FLC 4 FAC 2
Macclesfield T (£20,000 on 10/12/97) FL 22/1 Others 1

McDONALD Paul Thomas
Born: Motherwell, 20 April 1968
Height: 5'7" Weight: 10.0
Club Honours: S Div 1 '88; B&QC '92, '93
The nippy little winger failed to reproduce the form he showed in 1996-97 as Brighton and Hove Albion struggled from the outset of last season. Transfer listed in November, as the club desperately sought to cut its wage bill, Paul's contract was paid off in December and, after a brief trial with his home-town club Motherwell, he joined Premier League, Dunfermline Athletic, in January.
Hamilton Academical (Signed from Merry Street BC on 30/6/86) SL 187+28/26 SLC 8+2/2 SC 8+1 Others 8/3
Southampton (£75,000 on 8/6/93) PL 0+3 FAC 0+1
Burnley (Loaned on 15/9/95) FL 8+1/1 Others 2
Brighton & Hove A (£25,000 on 16/2/96) FL 52+9/5 FLC 4 FAC 3 Others 2/1

McDONALD Rodney (Rod)
Born: Westminster, 20 March 1967
Height: 5'10" Weight: 12.7
After being given a 12-month contract for 1997-98, Rod could not hold down a regular place in Chester City's attack, coming into the side mainly to cover for injuries, and of 33 appearances ten were from the bench. A hard-working striker, who scored five goals in all, and a maker as well as being a taker of chances, he was released by City at the end of the season.
Walsall (Signed from Colne Dynamoes on 24/8/90) FL 142+7/40 FLC 9/2 FAC 8/2 Others 10/1
Partick Thistle (£30,000 on 23/9/94) SL 34+7/10 SLC 2+1/1 SC 2 Others 0+1(Free to Southport during 1996 close season)
Chester C (Free on 25/11/96) FL 43+10/11 FLC 1 FAC 1 Others 3/1

McELHATTON Michael (Mike)
Born: Killarney, 16 April 1975
Height: 6'1" Weight: 12.8
International Honours: Ei: Sch

As one of Scarborough's most consistent performers throughout 1997-98, and a wholehearted competitor, Mike had a wonderful season in the midfield, showing himself to be a strong tackler, while chipping in with some spectacular goals, the first coming in a 4-0 home win against Doncaster. A versatile player, who has been known to don the goalkeeper's jersey, and can also play in defence if required, he was surprisingly released during the summer.

Bournemouth (From trainee on 5/7/93) FL 21+21/2 FLC 3+1 FAC 1+2/1 Others 1
Scarborough (£15,000 on 20/9/96) FL 64+6/7 FLC 3 FAC 3+1 Others 4

McFARLANE Andrew (Andy) Antonie
Born: Wolverhampton, 30 November 1966
Height: 6'3" Weight: 12.8
Club Honours: AMC '94

Unfortunately, Andy missed a large part of last season with an achilles tendon injury, but returned at the tail-end of the campaign to provide height and strength to Torquay's rather lightweight attack. Although ungainly at times, his persistence often reaped dividends and he was rewarded with seven goals.

Portsmouth (£20,000 from Cradley T on 20/11/90) FL 0+2
Swansea C (£20,000 on 6/8/92) FL 33+22/8 FLC 3/1 FAC 0+6 Others 3+4/3
Scunthorpe U (£15,000 on 4/8/95) FL 48+12/19 FLC 4/1 FAC 2+2/2 Others 3/2
Torquay U (£20,000 on 10/1/97) FL 37+4/8 FLC 3/1 Others 3/1

McGAVIN Steven (Steve) James
Born: North Walsham, 24 January 1969
Height: 5'9" Weight: 12.8
Club Honours: GMVC '92; FAT '92; Div 2 '95

A skilful Wycombe midfielder with high workrate, Steve continued to play a very influential role, linking midfield with the strikers in 1997-98. Strong with both feet, as his superb curling left-foot goal against Luton testified, his close control always posing problems for defences in his roving role, he had an outstanding game on Boxing Day against the leaders, Watford.

Ipswich T (From trainee on 29/1/87 - Free to Thetford T in August 1987)
Colchester U (£10,000 from Sudbury T on 28/7/92) FL 55+3/17 FLC 2 FAC 6/2 Others 4
Birmingham C (£150,000 on 7/1/94) FL 16+7/2 FLC 1+1/1 FAC 3+1/2 Others 1+3
Wycombe W (£140,000 on 20/3/95) FL 102+13/14 FLC 4+2 FAC 6+1/3 Others 4+1

McGHEE David Christopher
Born: Worthing, 19 June 1976
Height: 5'11" Weight: 12.4

David is a wholehearted Brentford utility player who can play in any position and is specifically dangerous from set pieces. Despite suffering a succession of injuries in 1997-98, namely a torn cartilage (August), a knee (December), and ending the campaign requiring a hernia operation, David appeared in over 30 games, but, not surprisingly, was unable to match his usual level of performance in a struggling side.

Brentford (From trainee on 15/7/94) FL 95+22/8 FLC 5+2/1 FAC 9/1 Others 8+1

McGIBBON Patrick (Pat)
Born: Lurgan, 6 September 1973
Height: 6'2" Weight: 13.12
International Honours: NI: 6; B-4; U21-1; Sch

A strong, reliable Wigan Athletic central defender, who is dominant in the air and strong in the tackle, Pat was a virtual ever present during 1997-98, his first full season with the club following his move from Manchester United, which was made permanent during the previous summer. Once again, his poised performances were recognised at international level, when being called up by Northern Ireland for their World Cup matches.

Manchester U (£100,000 from Portadown on 1/8/92) FLC 1
Swansea C (Loaned on 20/9/96) FL 1
Wigan Ath (£250,000 on 3/3/97) FL 42+3/1 FLC 2 FAC 3 Others 1

McGINLAY John
Born: Inverness, 8 April 1964
Height: 5'9" Weight: 11.6
Club Honours: Div 1 '97
International Honours: S: 13; B-2

After being Bolton's leading goalscorer for the fourth time in succession, the strong,

John McGinlay

determined, hard-running striker found the pace of the Premiership a little difficult at the beginning of last season, making ten appearances in all, and scoring two goals, before being transferred to Bradford at the start of November. Signed for a record-breaking fee, as far as City were concerned, John had a terrible time of it with injuries and his career came to a temporary halt in March when he was forced to have an operation for an achilles tendon. With the news, unfortunately, came the realisation that he had no hope of being selected for Scotland's World Cup side, and he concentrated his efforts on getting fit for the coming term.

Shrewsbury T (Signed from Elgin C on 22/2/89) FL 58+2/27 FLC 4 FAC 1/2 Others 3/2
Bury (£175,000 on 11/7/90) FL 16+9/9 FLC 1 FAC 1 Others 1+1
Millwall (£80,000 on 21/1/91) FL 27+7/10 FLC 2+1 FAC 2 Others 2/1
Bolton W (£125,000 on 30/9/92) P/FL 180+12/87 FLC 23+2/14 FAC 16+1/10 Others 11/7
Bradford C (£625,000 on 6/11/97) FL 12+5/3 FAC 0+1

McGINTY Brian

Born: East Kilbride, 10 December 1976
Height: 6'1" Weight: 12.6

The classy right-footed midfielder initially joined Hull City on a short-term contract last November, having been released from Rangers' massive squad, and, despite only a handful of games for the Glasgow giants, he soon proved his worth with some inspiring performances in a struggling Hull team. Once he had reached match fitness, such was his impact that the boss, Mark Hateley, a former Ibrox colleague, was delighted when Brian accepted a three-year contract, describing him as "the steal of the season". Is definitely one to look out for in 1998-99.

Glasgow R (From juniors on 1/7/93) SL 3 SLC 0+1
Hull C (Free on 28/11/97) FL 21/2 Others 1+1

McGLEISH Scott

Born: Barnet, 10 February 1974
Height: 5'10" Weight: 11.7

Started last season as a regular in Leyton Orient's colours, but, despite producing plenty of workrate, he was unable to rediscover his scoring touch and was transferred to Barnet where his delightful goal celebrations were seen on a regular basis. Brave as a lion, and with a prodigious leap for a small man, Scott is highly rated by his manager, John Still.

Charlton Ath (Free from Edgware T on 24/5/94) FL 0+6
Leyton Orient (Loaned on 10/3/95) FL 4+2/1 Others 1/1
Peterborough U (Free on 4/7/95) FL 3+10 FLC 0+1 FAC 0+1 Others 3+1/2
Colchester U (Loaned on 23/2/96) FL 10+5/6 Others 2
Cambridge U (Loaned on 2/9/96) FL 10/7 FLC 1
Leyton Orient (£50,000 on 22/11/96) FL 36/7 FLC 3/1 FAC 1 Others 1
Barnet (£70,000 on 1/10/97) FL 37/13 FAC 1 Others 2+1

McGOLDRICK Edward (Eddie) John

Born: Islington, 30 April 1965
Height: 5'10" Weight: 11.7
Club Honours: Div 4 '87; FMC '91; ECWC '94
International Honours: Ei: 15; B-1

After such a good season at Manchester City in 1996-97, when he was such a steadying influence in midfield, 1997-98 was a huge disappointment for Eddie. Niggling injuries and a bout of sciatica continuously kept him from being available for regular selection, his first home appearance coming against Reading as a sub in October, and from his six starts he had to be substituted four times, either due to injury or tactical reasons.

Having last appeared in late November, and one of the players made available for transfer, in March he was loaned to Stockport, a side suffering a severe injury crisis. Strangely, within nine days he was back at Maine Road as a member of the County side that were thumped 4-1.

Northampton T (£10,000 from Nuneaton Borough on 23/8/86) FL 97+10/9 FLC 9 FAC 6+1/1 Others 7/1
Crystal Palace (£200,000 on 10/1/89) FL 139+8/11 FLC 21+1/2 FAC 5 Others 13+2/3
Arsenal (£1,000,000 on 18/6/93) PL 32+6 FLC 7+2 FAC 1+1 Others 4+4/1
Manchester C (£300,000 on 20/9/96) FL 39+1 FLC 1+1 FAC 3
Stockport Co (Loaned on 26/3/98) FL 2

Scott McGleish

McGOWAN Gavin Gregory
Born: Blackheath, 16 January 1976
Height: 5'8" Weight: 11.10
Club Honours: FAYC '94
International Honours: E: Yth; Sch

Unable to get many opportunities at Arsenal in 1997-98, Gavin started last season at Luton, thus having his second spell on loan with the Hatters, but injuries once again restricted his value to Town and he played just eight games before returning to Highbury. A full back who can play on either side, but is happier on the right and is very quick, he came off the bench in the home Premiership game against Crystal Palace in February for his only Gunners' outing of the campaign, before being released during the summer. Is both skilful and a sound tackler.

Arsenal (From trainee on 1/7/94) PL 3+3 FAC 1
Luton T (Loaned on 27/3/97) FL 2
Luton T (Loaned on 11/7/97) FL 6+2

McGRATH Paul
Born: Ealing, 4 December 1959
Height: 6'2" Weight: 14.0
Club Honours: FAC '85; FLC '94, '96
International Honours: Ei: 83

A veteran defender signed by Sheffield United from Derby County on a monthly contract, immediately prior to 1997-98 getting underway, he was a revelation at the beginning of the season with his uncanny ability to be in the very place where the ball was arriving, a skill which earned him a full contract to the end of the campaign. Played 14 games until his dodgy knees caught up with him and, despite hopes that he could return for the run in, he was eventually advised to retire before any permanent damage was caused. His successful testimonial in Dublin was a timely reward for a fine player.

Manchester U (f30,000 from St Patricks on 30/4/82) FL 159+4/12 FLC 13/2 FAC 15+2/2 Others 9
Aston Villa (£400,000 on 3/8/89) F/PL 248+5/9 FLC 29+1/1 FAC 23+1 Others 15+1
Derby Co (£100,000 + on 12/10/96) PL 23+1 FAC 2
Sheffield U (Free on 8/8/97) FL 12 FLC 2

McGREAL John
Born: Liverpool, 2 June 1972
Height: 5'11" Weight: 12.8

There was widespread relief among Tranmere fans in the 1997 close season when this cool and confident central defender decided to sign a new contract and stay with the club, rather than pursue a rumoured move to France. Possessing the enviable ability to read a pass, and take the ball from an opponent's feet before the adversary realises fully what has happened, John is very rarely flustered under pressure, a trait which often leads to comparisons with his hero, Alan Hansen. A cultured and visionary player, who loves to carry the ball out of defence to set up an attack, his confidence is blossoming as he matures. Is still rumoured to be a target for a number of Premier League clubs.

Tranmere Rov (From trainee on 3/7/90) FL 157+2/1 FLC 15+1 FAC 7 Others 7+2

McGREGOR Mark Dale Thomas
Born: Chester, 16 February 1977
Height: 5'11" Weight: 11.5

Mark is becoming more impressive with every season, attracting the attention of many leading club scouts with his assured and mature displays at right back for Wrexham. Can also fill in a central defensive position more than adequately. Cool and composed, he often combines defence and attack down the right, and always adds an extra option, which was seen to advantage when he scored the last-minute equaliser against Watford at the Racecourse in December. A player to watch.

Wrexham (From trainee on 4/7/95) FL 106+7/4 FLC 3 FAC 13+1 Others 4

Mark McGregor

McINTOSH Martin Wyllie
Born: East Kilbride, 19 March 1971
Height: 6'2" Weight: 12.0
International Honours: S: B-2

The bargain of the decade for Stockport, the big defender was snapped up at the beginning of last season after leading Hamilton Academicals to promotion in Scotland. Injury to the Stockport skipper, Mike Flynn, handed him a debut against Middlesbrough in September and only suspension kept him out of the first team. After that, with his transfer value increasing ten-fold in a few months, he was rewarded with two Scottish "B" caps, against Wales and Norway, scoring the first goal in a 4-0 win over Wales. Powerful and commanding in the air, he is also assured on the deck, and blessed with great passing ability.

St Mirren (Free from Tottenham H juniors on 30/11/88) SL 2+2
Clydebank (Signed on 17/8/91) SL 59+6/10 SLC 2 SC 4+1/1 Others 3/1
Hamilton Accademical (Signed on 1/2/94) SL 99/12 SLC 5 SC 5 Others 5/1
Stockport Co (£80,000 on 15/8/97) FL 38/2 FLC 2 FAC 2

McINTYRE James (Jim)
Born: Dumbarton, 24 May 1972
Height: 5'11" Weight: 11.5

As the Reading manager, Tommy Burns' most expensive signing of the seven he made on deadline day, after being transferred from Kilmarnock, the Scottish forward played in six games, was substituted in five of them, and failed to score as the team headed out of the first division. However, he was selected for Scotland "B" versus Norway "B" after joining the Royals and, now that he has moved his family to Reading, will be able to give a better account of himself in the coming season.

Bristol C (Free from Duntocher BC on 10/10/91) FL 1 Others 0+1
Exeter C (Loaned on 11/2/93) FL 12+3/3 Others 4/1
Airdrie (Signed on 23/9/93) SL 32+22/10 SLC 3+3/1 SC 1+4 Others 2+2/2
Kilmarnock (Signed on 22/3/96) SL 42+3/9 SLC 2+1 SC 5+1/2 Others 2/1
Reading (£420,000 on 26/3/98) FL 6

McINTYRE Kevin
Born: Liverpool, 23 December 1977
Height: 5'10" Weight: 12.0

A product of Tranmere's much admired youth scheme, Kevin made his first team debut at the City ground in October 1997, coming on as a substitute against Nottingham Forest. A stalwart of the club's Pontins League side, where his solid performances have marked him out as one to watch for the future, his usual position is in midfield, but he is equally happy to drop back to cover the defence. Plays in contact lenses.

Tranmere Rov (From trainee on 6/11/96) FL 0+2

McKAY Matthew (Matty) Paul
Born: Warrington, 21 January 1981
Height: 6'0" Weight: 12.0

A product of Chester City's youth policy, Matty progressed through the School of Excellence to make his league debut as a substitute against Darlington last December, while still a trainee. After another sub appearance, this time against Barnet, he made three starts in City's midfield before amazingly signing for Everton on transfer deadline day in a deal which eased the club's financial worries. A very skilful midfielder, this young man has been tipped to go all the way to the top by City manager, Kevin Ratcliffe.

Chester C (Trainee) FL 3+2
Everton (£500,000+ on 27/3/98)

MACKEN Jonathan Paul
Born: Manchester, 7 September 1977
Height: 5'10" Weight: 12.8
International Honours: E: Yth

A young striker signed from Manchester United from the summer of 1997, Jonathan soon became a favourite of the Preston fans with his commitment and bustling style. Obviously modelling himself on his hero, Mark Hughes, he is hard to shake off the ball, lays it off well, and will always have a strike at goal. Never a regular starter until

late on in the season, he nevertheless featured in the majority of squads and contributed much to the team.

Manchester U (From trainee on 10/7/96)
Preston NE (£250,000 on 31/7/97) FL 20+9/6 FLC 2+2/2 FAC 2+1 Others 0+3

McKENNA Paul Stephen
Born: Chorley, 20 October 1977
Height: 5'7" Weight: 11.12

A young midfielder who made his first appearance for Preston in over a year, when coming on as a substitute against Southend on Easter Saturday, he followed this up with his first start two days later at Northampton, where his tenacious tackling and positive distribution were well demonstrated. Remained a regular until the end of the campaign, and will be looking for more opportunities to develop in the first team next season.

Preston NE (From trainee on 2/2/96) FL 8+2/1 Others 2

MacKENZIE Christopher (Chris) Neil
Born: Northampton, 14 May 1972
Height: 6'0" Weight: 12.6

Having joined Leyton Orient on a non-contract basis from Hereford last October, Chris made his debut in the Auto Windscreen Shield game against Colchester and saved a penalty, but in his first league appearance he was unfortunate to be shown the red card for handling outside his area. Another excellent shot-stopper, whom despite not being the biggest of 'keepers, commands his area well, he signed on a permanent contract before the end of the campaign.

Hereford U (£15,000 from Corby on 20/7/94) FL 59+1/1 FLC 1 FAC 4 Others 8
Leyton Orient (Free on 17/10/97) FL 4 Others 1

McKENZIE Leon Mark
Born: Croydon, 17 May 1978
Height: 5'11" Weight: 11.2

From a famous boxing family, his uncle Duke being a world champion at three different weights, Leon made just four subs' appearances for Crystal Palace in 1997-98 and was loaned to Fulham for match practice in October. In the event, the young striker impressed with his pace and close control, but was unfortunate to receive an injury after only three games which forced him to return to Selhurst Park. Fast off the mark, with neat control, he is an ideal player to introduce late in a game when defenders are tiring.

Crystal Palace (From trainee on 7/10/95) F/PL 8+28/2 FLC 4/1 FAC 1+4
Fulham (Loaned on 3/10/97) FL 1+2

MacKENZIE Neil David
Born: Birmingham, 15 April 1976
Height: 6'2" Weight: 12.5

Although unlucky with injuries, 1997-98 was another season of promise and progress for this tall, gifted Stoke midfielder. A playmaker with some tackling abilities he proved the doubters wrong when he secured an extended run in the side, but, unfortunately, the team's decline saw a change of

manager, particularly after the heavy defeat at home to Birmingham, and Neil fell from favour under the Chris Kamara regime. Blessed with a powerful shot, he is one of the best dead-ball strikers in the club.

Stoke C (Free from West Bromwich A juniors on 9/11/95) FL 12+22/1 FLC 1+1 FAC 0+1

McKINLAY Thomas (Tosh) Valley
Born: Glasgow, 3 December 1964
Height: 5'7" Weight: 11.10
International Honours: S: 22; B-2; U21-6; Yth

It was a master stroke by Stoke manager, Chris Kamara, to secure a three-month loan signing of Tosh from Celtic last January, and he was quick to show his abilities in a City shirt, while still holding out hopes of a place in the Scotland squad for France '98. Unfortunately sent off in his debut against Middlesbrough at home, which led to a three-match ban after he had played only three games for the club, as the replacement for Andrew Griffin, just as the suspension was starting, however, he was recalled to the Celtic squad and that was the last the City fans saw of a top-class left back who was at his best breaking forward. *Stop Press:* Twice came off the bench for Scotland in first round games before the side were eliminated from the World Cup at that stage.

Dundee (Free from Celtic BC on 7/8/81) SL 161+1/8 SLC 18+1/1 SC 23
Heart of Midlothian (Signed on 7/12/88) SL 200+6/7 SLC 12/1 SC 15 Others 8/1
Glasgow Celtic (Signed on 4/11/94) SL 74+7 SLC 4+1 SC 15 Others 11
Stoke C (Loaned on 28/1/98) FL 3

McKINLAY William (Billy)
Born: Glasgow, 22 April 1969
Height: 5'9" Weight: 11.6
International Honours: S: 28; B-1; U21-6; Yth; Sch

With his bleached blond hair, aggressive and energetic, Billy is always likely to be noticed, and several referees took the opportunity of recording his name in their books in 1997-98. Consequently, he missed several games, but still emerged as one of Blackburn's outstanding players, patrolling the area in front of the back four, winning tackles, and covering a huge area of the centre field. Although suspensions and injuries did not help to establish him in the Scottish team, he remained on the fringe of their side and, at the time of going to press, had been named among the 22-strong party bound for the World Cup Finals in France during the summer. *Stop Press:* Used just once, as a 78th-minute sub in a 2-1 defeat at the hands of Brazil, he could only watch in despair as the Scots crashed out of the World Cup at the end of the first round games.

Dundee U (Free from Hamilton Thistle on 24/6/85) SL 210+10/23 SLC 21/3 SC 23+3/4 Others 17/2
Blackburn Rov (£1,750,000 on 14/10/95) PL 62+12/3 FLC 3/1 FAC 6+1

McLAREN Paul Andrew
Born: High Wycombe, 17 November 1976
Height: 6'0" Weight: 13.4

In adding aggression to his play in 1997-98,

and establishing himself as a regular fixture in the Luton midfield, Paul seems to have improved every aspect of his game, except his shooting. Although he possesses a powerful shot, and uses it frequently, he failed to find the net once during the season, despite going close on several occasions. However, his surging runs, his ability to win the ball, and his excellent crosses, marked him out as one of the few successes in a mostly poor Town side and he could well become a target for a bigger club, especially if he could get his name on the scoresheet occasionally.

Luton T (From trainee on 5/1/94) FL 63+17/1 FLC 4+1 FAC 2 Others 7

McLEARY Alan Terry
Born: Lambeth, 6 October 1964
Height: 5'11" Weight: 11.9
Club Honours: FLT '83; Div 2 '88
International Honours: E: B-2; U21-1; Yth

Having been a trainee at Millwall in the early 1980s, Alan came home for his second spell at the end of 1996-97 and added vital experience to the Lions' defence at the start of 1997-98, until injury kept him out for the rest of the season. In completing 400 games for the club, he just seemed to get better and better as time went on and, although a good reader of the game, with good passing ability, his greatest attribute was the way he motivated all those around him.

Millwall (From apprentice on 12/10/81) FL 289+18/5 FLC 16+1 FAC 24+1/2 Others 22+1/2
Sheffield U (Loaned on 23/7/92) PL 3
Wimbledon (Loaned on 16/10/92) PL 4 FLC 2
Charlton Ath (Free on 27/5/93) FL 66/3 FLC 2 FAC 6 Others 3
Bristol C (Free on 31/7/95) FL 31+3 FLC 5
Millwall (Free on 21/2/97) FL 34 FLC 2 FAC 1

McLOUGHLIN Alan Francis
Born: Manchester, 20 April 1967
Height: 5'8" Weight: 10.10
International Honours: Ei: 34; B-3

Alan was an integral part of the Portsmouth midfield for the most part of last season, although his return of four goals in over 30 games was not up to his usual standard. Again a regular member of the Republic of Ireland team, and hoping to stay in the squad for at least another couple of years, he remains a skilful midfielder with great passing technique, awareness of team mates, and an ability to get forward into good attacking positions.*

Manchester U (From apprentice on 25/4/85)
Swindon T (Free on 15/8/86) FL 101+5/19 FLC 11+3/5 FAC 4+2 Others 10/1
Torquay U (Loaned on 13/3/87) FL 21+3/4
Southampton (£1,000,000 on 13/12/90) FL 22+2/1 FLC 0+1 FAC 4 Others 1
Aston Villa (Loaned on 30/9/91) Others 1
Portsmouth (£400,000 on 17/2/92) FL 238+11/42 FLC 21/3 FAC 13+1/7 Others 9/1

McMAHON Gerard (Gerry) Joseph
Born: Belfast, 29 December 1973
Height: 5'11" Weight: 11.12
International Honours: NI: 17; B-3; U21-1; Yth; Sch

Last season started with Gerry on the Stoke bench, although his regular contributions were still greatly appreciated and, indeed,

the win at Maine Road was probably his finest performance in a City shirt, when playing as a front man with support from Paul Stewart. However, listed in the New Year, and with his contract expiring in the summer of 1998, St Johnstone from the Scottish Premier League stepped in and purchased him for £85,000. Continued to play for Northern Ireland, making three further appearances in 1997-98, as well as playing in a "B" match against the Republic.

Tottenham H (£100,000 from Glenavon on 31/7/92) PL 9+7 FLC 3 FAC 0+1
Barnet (Loaned on 20/10/94) FL 10/2 FAC 2/1 Others 1
Stoke C (£450,000 on 17/9/96) FL 38+14/3 FLC 5+3 FAC 1

McMAHON Samuel (Sam) Keiron
Born: Newark, 10 February 1976
Height: 5'10" Weight: 11.9
The right-footed Leicester midfielder found his opportunities at Filbert Street in 1997-98 limited by the emergence of the two Stuarts, Campbell and Wilson, but still managed a couple of appearances from the bench. A classy young player who could still make it big, given the right breaks, he came on to try and rescue something in the League Cup debacle at Grimsby, before getting a run out in the home draw with Palace.
Leicester C (From trainee on 10/7/94) P/FL 1+4/1 FLC 0+2

McMAHON Stephen (Steve)
Born: Liverpool, 20 August 1961
Height: 5'9" Weight: 12.1
Club Honours: Div 1 '86, '88, '90; Div 2 '96; FAC '86, '89; CS '88, '89
International Honours: E: 17; B-2; U21-6
Swindon's player/manager is not doing too much of the former these days, indeed, he only laced his boots up once last term for a substitute appearance in the home draw with Huddersfield Town in September. A persistent back problem now looks likely to finally end the playing career of one of England's best midfield players of recent years, enabling him to concentrate on the demands of management.
Everton (From apprentice on 29/8/79) FL 99+1/11 FLC 11/3 FAC 9
Aston Villa (£175,000 on 20/5/83) FL 74+1/7 FLC 9 FAC 3 Others 4
Liverpool (£375,000 on 12/9/85) FL 202+2/29 FLC 27/13 FAC 30/7 Others 16/1
Manchester C (£900,000 on 24/12/91) F/PL 83+4/1 FLC 8 FAC 3
Swindon T (£100,000 on 1/12/94) FL 38+4 FLC 4 FAC 3+1 Others 0+1

McMANAMAN Steven (Steve)
Born: Bootle, 11 February 1972
Height: 6'0" Weight: 10.10
Club Honours: FAC '92; FLC '95
International Honours: E: 22; U21-7; Yth
Articulate and intelligent off the pitch, Steve brings those same qualities to Liverpool and England when playing, and is reckoned to be a possible manager of the future. Continued to score brilliant individual goals in 1997-98, the one against Celtic in the UEFA Cup having all the hallmarks of this lively and dangerous old-fashioned winger.

A good dribbler, with close control and great balance, with the ability to go past defenders as if they do not exist, while some fans bemoan him being too much of an individual, his speed, and accurate shooting, which resulted in 12 goals, added to a high workrate, would make it difficult for any manager to leave him out. At the time of going to press, he was looking forward to helping England progress in the World Cup. *Stop Press:* Called upon just once during World Cup '98 in France during the summer, Steve came on for the last 16 minutes of the first round, with the instruction to run at the Colombian defence, and that was that.
Liverpool (From trainee on 19/2/90) F/PL 233+11/42 FLC 32+1/10 FAC 28+1/5 Others 27/4

McMENAMIN Christopher (Chris)
Born: Donegal, 27 December 1973
Height: 5'10" Weight: 11.12
Coming into the Peterborough side to make his Football League debut in a 5-0 win at Doncaster three games into last season, having been released by Coventry during the summer, the young right back made a good impression, so much so that he made 34 further appearances. A skilful player who was always looking to create something, and equally capable of playing in midfield, Chris is expected to make up for lost time.
Coventry C (Signed from Hitchin T on 20/9/96)
Peterborough U (Free on 8/8/97) FL 25+3 FLC 2 FAC 2 Others 3

McMILLAN Lyndon Andre (Andy)
Born: Bloemfontein, South Africa, 22 June 1968
Height: 5'11" Weight: 11.9
1997-98 was another good season for York City's "Mr Consistency" at right back, despite him missing almost three months through injury. There were also two firsts for the ever reliable defender - he captained the side on a couple of occasions and then, to everyone's amazement, was sent off in a game at Walsall for two 'alleged' fouls which earned yellow cards. Late in the campaign, Andy netted his first goal for over two years, his fifth in over ten years at Bootham Crescent, when he hit the winner at Carlisle, and that with his left foot! In 1998-99, Andy will deservedly be celebrating his testimonial in the knowledge that only two men have ever played more games for the Minstermen - Barry Jackson and Chris Topping.
York C (Signed on 17/10/87) FL 376+12/5 FLC 25 FAC 16 Others 25

McNALLY Mark
Born: Motherwell, 10 March 1971
Height: 5'9" Weight: 11.2
Club Honours: SC '95
International Honours: S: U21-2
Despite playing under three managers at Stoke last season, Mark was never given a meaningful chance in the first team, either at right back or in the heart of the defence. Indeed, he spent the season in the reserves prior to being listed in January. While a

move to Dundee United looked on the cards in March, and Mark made the trip to Dundee, there was apparent confusion with Stoke wanting a small fee and the Scottish club believing he was available on a free. A sturdy defender, who tackles well and is good in the air, despite his lack of height, he is likely to find a first team spot away from the Britannia Stadium.
Glasgow Celtic (From juniors on 15/5/87) SL 112+10/3 SLC 11+2/1 SC 10 Others 6+1
Southend U (£100,000 on 8/12/95) FL 52+2/2 FLC 2 FAC 2
Stoke C (£120,000 on 27/3/97) FL 6+1

McNALLY Ross Jonathan
Born: Dublin, 6 September 1978
Height: 6'1" Weight: 12.5
Having come through the ranks as a junior, the young central defender made two substitute appearances for Brighton and Hove Albion, before making the starting line-up for the first time last February, in the absence of Ross Johnson. The Seagulls were eclipsed 1-4 by Torquay United at Gillingham, but the Irish teenager at least had the pleasure of registering his first senior goal for the club, prior to being released in the summer.
Brighton & Hove A (From trainee on 10/7/97) FL 1+1/1 Others 0+1

McNIVEN David Jonathan
Born: Leeds, 27 May 1978
Height: 5'11" Weight: 12.0
As in 1996-97, David's appearances from the bench far outweighed his starts for Oldham in 1997-98, but he has a good footballing pedigree, his dad, David senior, having played for Leeds back in the 1970s, while his twin brother, Scott, is with him at Boundary Park, and there are high hopes for the both of them. As a forward who can hold up play well and mixes up his attacking intent with good running both on and off the ball, given a proper run in the side might do wonders for him. Scored his first goal for the club in the 2-0 home win over Southend in April.
Oldham Ath (From trainee on 25/10/95) FL 4+12/1 FLC 0+2

McNIVEN Scott Andrew
Born: Leeds, 27 May 1978
Height: 5'10" Weight: 10.6
International Honours: S: U21-1; Yth
The twin of David, while his brother tries to score goals, Scott tries to prevent them, being a solid Oldham full back who favours the right-hand side. Able to play further forward if required, where he is full of running and an excellent passer, he could eventually turn out to be a versatile all-rounder, but it is more than likely that he will concentrate on a defensive role in the short term. Came to the fore in 1997-98, with 30 starts in 40 appearances, and scored his first goal for the club, the second in a 2-2 draw at home to Northampton in September.
Oldham Ath (From trainee on 25/10/95) FL 51+9/1 FLC 4+1 FAC 5+1 Others 5

McPHAIL Stephen
Born: London, 9 December 1979
Height: 5'10" Weight: 12.0
Club Honours: FAYC '97

The 18-year-old Leeds' midfielder, who is already a precocious talent, became yet another member of the victorious youth side to break into the first team picture in 1997-98, and deservedly so. Reminiscent of Liam Brady, and possessing such a sweet left foot, Stephen made his full debut at Leicester in February as a substitute, and also came on at Derby, where his first touch was a superb 40-yard pass to set up Jimmy Hasselbaink for the fifth goal. His all-round display augered well for a young man with a big future in the game.

Leeds U (From trainee on 23/12/96) PL 0+4

McPHERSON Keith Anthony
Born: Greenwich, 11 September 1963
Height: 6'1" Weight: 12.0
Club Honours: FAYC '81; Div 4 '87, Div 2 '94

The veteran centre back was a regular in the Reading side in 1997-98, and also skipper up until December, when he was rested following the 4-0 defeat at Middlesbrough and a recurrence of his pelvic problem. He did not return until March, when he played twice more, then after another big loss – 5-1 at Stockport – again had to visit the treatment room. The groin injury that had troubled him earlier then kept him out until the end of the campaign, but, hopefully, with the summer rest behind him he can come back strongly in 1998-99.

West Ham U (From apprentice on 12/9/81) FL 1
Cambridge U (Loaned on 30/9/85) FL 11/1
Northampton T (£15,000 on 23/1/86) FL 182/8 FLC 9/1 FAC 12 Others 13
Reading (Signed on 24/8/90) FL 251+5/8 FLC 19+1/1 FAC 11+1 Others 9+1

McPHERSON Malcolm
Born: Glasgow, 19 December 1974
Height: 5'10" Weight: 12.0

The right-sided Brentford midfielder or attacker received few opportunities at Griffin Park in 1997-98 until the arrival of Micky Adams as manager saw him selected as a right-wing back. Although Malcolm showed promise there, a leg injury ruled him out and by the time he recovered Carl Hutchings had made the position his own. Was released during the summer.

West Ham U (£30,000 from Yeovil on 4/1/94)
Brentford (Free on 31/7/96) FL 9+3 FAC 1 Others 1+1

McROBERT Lee Peter
Born: Bromley, 4 October 1972
Height: 5'9" Weight: 10.12

Having found it hard to hold down a place in Millwall's midfield in 1997-98, Lee went on loan to non-league Dover before returning to first team duty in late January. The change seemed to have done him some good and he had an excellent game on the left-hand side of midfield at York to help the side to a 3-2 win. Although there was only three more starts and a sub appearance from thereon, niggling injuries obviously affecting his performances, he still looked more than useful with his ability to win the ball in tight situations. Was released during the summer.

Millwall (£35,000 from Sittingbourne on 17/2/95) FL 12+11/1 FLC 1 FAC 1 Others 0+1

MADAR Mickael Raymond
Born: Paris, France, 8 May 1968
Height: 6'0" Weight: 13.2
International Honours: France: 3

Arriving at Everton from Spanish side, Deportivo la Coruna, on a free transfer last January, Mickael made an immediate impact on the side, forging an instant and profitable partnership up front with Duncan Ferguson and Nick Barmby, and it was no coincidence that both players enjoyed an upturn in their own scoring fortunes following his arrival. Having scored on his debut at Crystal Palace, and adding goals regularly after that, despite occasionally looking uncomfortable with the physical edge to the British game, the French international will be looking to step up a gear in 1998-99, especially with the Blues remaining in the Premiership.

Everton (Free from Deportivo la Coruna on 31/12/97) PL 15+2/5

MADDISON Neil Stanley
Born: Darlington, 2 October 1969
Height: 5'10" Weight: 11.8

Signed from Southampton last October, after starting the opening five matches at the Dell, Neil returned to his native north east to enjoy the power and the glory of the club's triumphant return to the Premiership, having played no small part himself in the campaign. His performances were inspired and intelligent, and he was sorely missed when sidelined though injury. The epitome of the midfield powerhouse, the three goals with which he was credited speak volumes for his opportunism in attack, and his fans expect more of the same in the Premiership.

Southampton (From trainee on 14/4/88) F/PL 149+20/19 FLC 9+5 FAC 8+5 Others 1
Middlesbrough (£250,000 on 31/10/97) FL 16+6/4 FLC 4 FAC 3

MADDIX Daniel (Danny) Shawn
Born: Ashford, 11 October 1967
Height: 5'11" Weight: 11.7
International Honours: Jamaica: 1

Still a strong-tackling central defender who

Mickael Madar

is good in the air, and a more than useful man marker if required, Danny's 1997-98 season at Queens Park Rangers was disrupted first by a knee injury and then, later on, his ambition to play for Jamaica in the World Cup finals in France '98. Although selected for Jamaica, and playing, he was not included in the final 22 players and found it hard to hide his disappointment. Having been at Rangers for over ten years, he shows no signs of making way for others.

Tottenham H (From apprentice on 25/7/85)
Southend U (Loaned on 1/11/86) FL 2
Queens Park R (Free on 23/7/87) F/PL 204+34/8 FLC 19/2 FAC 21+2/2 Others 2+3

MAGILTON Jim
Born: Belfast, 6 May 1969
Height: 6'0" Weight: 14.2
International Honours: NI: 39; U23-2; U21-1; Yth; Sch

A regular in Southampton's midfield at the start of 1997-98, Jim was signed by Sheffield Wednesday's David Pleat, seemingly assured of a midfield slot, and even captaining the side for several games, before fading from the scene on the arrival of Ron Atkinson as manager. However, he eventually came back, via several sittings on the bench, to score a vital equalising goal against West Ham, his first start for nearly three months, and virtually maintained a first team slot from thereon in. Still a member of the Northern Ireland squad, he works hard for the team, has good vision, and, on the face of it, appears to be the ideal midfield man.

Liverpool (From apprentice on 14/5/86)
Oxford U (£100,000 on 3/10/90) FL 150/34 FLC 9/1 FAC 8/4 Others 6/3
Southampton (£600,000 on 11/2/94) PL 124+6/13 FLC 12+2/2 FAC 12/3
Sheffield Wed (£1,600,000 on 10/9/97) PL 13+8/1 FLC 2 FAC 1

MAHER Kevin Andrew
Born: Ilford, 17 October 1976
Height: 6'0" Weight: 12.5
International Honours: Ei: U21-4

Signed from Spurs last January, Kevin showed all the abilities of a player who had been with a Premiership club, with his control and passing reminiscent of the now-departed Mike Marsh, as he fitted into the Southend midfield easily. Despite not asserting himself in the way that his skill suggested he could do, the Blues' fans will be keen to see a lot more from him this coming season. Added to his Republic of Ireland U21 appearances when playing in the two European Championship qualifying games against Lithuania during the season.

Tottenham H (From trainee on 1/7/95)
Southend U (Free on 23/1/98) FL 18/1

MAHER Shaun Patrick
Born: Dublin, 20 June 1978
Height: 6'2" Weight: 12.3

Amidst a plethora of expensive signings, Shaun joined Fulham last December on a free transfer from Irish club, Bohemians. A right back, or central defender, the 19-year old was signed as one for the future and,

apart from a couple of outings in the Auto Windscreen Shield, his season was spent in the reserve side which finished runners up in the Capital League.

Fulham (Signed from Bohemians on 18/12/97) Others 2

MAHON Alan Joseph
Born: Dublin, 4 April 1978
Height: 5'10" Weight: 11.5
International Honours: Ei: U21-8; Yth; Sch

After an impressive and explosive arrival onto the first team scene at Tranmere in 1996-97, this young Irishman would be the first to admit that last term was something of an anti-climax and a season probably best forgotten. The combination of a recurring stomach injury, plus the burden of expectancy, conspired to give him a frustrating time, and he was unable to make the progress he had wished for. Nicknamed "Ronan" for his resemblance to the Boyzone lead singer, Alan is undoubtedly talented and possesses a good first touch, vision, and a real turn of pace. Matters improved towards the end of the campaign, with an excellent goal and a solid performance against Oxford, which should have gone some way towards restoring his confidence and better things are expected of him in the coming season. Continued to add to his Republic of Ireland caps with six more appearances in 1997-98.

Tranmere Rov (From trainee on 7/4/95) FL 17+28/3 FLC 0+5 FAC 0+1

MAHONEY-JOHNSON Michael Anthony
Born: Paddington, 6 November 1976
Height: 5'10" Weight: 12.0

A pacy Queens Park Rangers' striker who had been given a couple of opportunities at the club in 1996-97, Michael failed to build upon them, making just one substitute appearance in 1997-98 when called from the bench during the home game against Sunderland in December. Coming along quite nicely in the reserves though, to further his footballing education he was loaned to Brighton in mid-February, becoming Steve Gritt's last signing before he was controversially sacked. Unfortunately it went from bad to worse, and the inexperienced 21-year old did not enjoy the best of times with the struggling Seagulls before returning to Loftus Road.

Queens Park R (From trainee on 11/4/95) FL 0+3
Wycombe W (Loaned on 30/8/96) FL 2+2/2
Brighton & Hove A (Loaned on 13/2/98) FL 3+1

MAHORN Paul Gladstone
Born: Leyton, 13 August 1973
Height: 5'10" Weight: 13.0

A striker who feeds off the target man, and one who is fast around the box, Paul was signed by Port Vale on trial last March after being released by Spurs. Only appeared in the first team once, when coming off the substitutes' bench for the final two minutes at West Bromwich, but in that time he won the corner that led to a crucial equaliser. As a non-contract player it will be interesting to see where he turns up next. Earlier in the

campaign, with Steffen Iverson, Chris Armstrong, and Les Ferdinand all out injured, he was used on four separate occasions, coming off the bench against Carlisle in the Coca Cola Cup game at White Hart Lane and scoring the goal that ensured victory for the Premiership side.

Tottenham H (From trainee on 31/1/92) PL 3 FLC 0+1/1 FAC 0+1
Fulham (Loaned on 23/9/93) FL 1+2 Others 1
Burnley (Loaned on 28/3/96) FL 3+5/1
Port Vale (Free on 13/3/98) FL 0+1

MAINWARING Carl Andrew
Born: Swansea, 15 March 1980
Height: 6'0" Weight: 11.13

The top scorer for Swansea's youth side, Carl was given a first team opportunity in a re-arranged game at Chester last November and showed enough promise to be afforded more games as the season wore on. Still a trainee, the young striker has been offered a professional contract on completion of his YTS period.

Swansea C (Trainee) FL 2+1 FAC 0+1

MAKEL Lee Robert
Born: Sunderland, 11 January 1973
Height: 5'10" Weight: 11.7

The quietly spoken Geordie started last season as a regular in Huddersfield's midfield, showing up well with his silky defence-splitting passes until Town began to struggle. Injury kept him out of the side for a couple of months, and when he returned it was mainly as a substitute as the regular first team fought to grind out results. Clearly not in the plans of the new manager, Lee was placed on the transfer list, signing for Scottish Premier League side, Hearts, in March for £75,000.

Newcastle U (From trainee on 11/2/91) FL 6+6/1 FLC 1 Others 0+1
Blackburn Rov (£160,000 on 20/7/92) PL 1+5 FLC 0+3 Others 1+3
Huddersfield T (£300,000 on 13/10/95) FL 62+3/5 FLC 7 FAC 6+1

MAKIN Christopher (Chris) Gregory
Born: Manchester, 8 May 1973
Height: 5'10" Weight: 11.2
International Honours: E: U21-5; Yth; Sch

Having been away from the English soccer scene since the 1996 close season, Chris joined Sunderland last August from the French club, Marseille, quickly establishing himself in the first team as a strong tackler who used the ball intelligently. Unfortunate to sustain a leg injury at home to Swindon in October, which gave Darren Holloway his chance, further injuries to the squad allowed the right back to return in the New Year to play his part in the club's promotion push, which ultimately "blew up" in the play-off final, in which he took part. Has plenty of stamina with which to pressure opponents and two good feet.

Oldham Ath (From trainee on 2/11/91) F/PL 93+1/4 FLC 7 FAC 11 Others 1+1 (Transferred to Marseille during 1996 close season)
Wigan Ath (Loaned on 28/8/92) FL 14+1/2
Sunderland (£500,000 on 5/8/97) FL 23+2/1 FLC 3 FAC 1 Others 1+1

MALKIN Christopher (Chris) Gregory
Born: Hoylake, 4 June 1967
Height: 6'3" Weight: 12.9
Club Honours: AMC '90

Although Blackpool's record signing, as in 1996-97, Chris was constantly plagued by injury last season. Full of running and tireless up front at his best, in 1997-98 the tall striker will be remembered mainly by the supporters for his spectacular strike against Gillingham after he had come on as a sub. Although there was only to be one more to add to his account, he scored a number of goals for the reserves, including a hat trick against Stockport. Will hope to be fully recovered and back on song this coming term.

Tranmere Rov (Free from Stork AFC on 27/7/87) FL 184+48/60 FLC 20+5/6 FAC 9+4/3 Others 26+7/7
Millwall (£400,000 on 13/7/95) FL 46+6/13 FLC 5/1 FAC 2/1
Blackpool (£275,000 on 14/10/96) FL 21+14/5 FLC 0+3 FAC 2+1 Others 0+3

MANN Neil
Born: Nottingham, 19 November 1972
Height: 5'10" Weight: 12.1

As a player who thrives on confidence, the left-sided midfielder found it difficult to perform consistently last season as Hull City continued to struggle to string a good run of results together. Undoubtedly one of the most skilful players at the club, his form was also not helped by injury, which saw him undergoing a hernia operation in September, and he was placed on the transfer list in March. Was voted by the travelling supporters as the Away Match Player of the Year.

Grimsby T (Free from Notts Co juniors on 6/9/90)
Hull C (Free from Grantham T, via Spalding, on 30/7/93) FL 109+31/8 FLC 8+3 FAC 5+2/1 Others 8+2/1

MANNINGER Alexander (Alex)
Born: Austria, 4 June 1977
Height: 6'2" Weight: 13.3
Club Honours: FAC '98

An Austrian U21 international goalkeeper with massive potential, Alex was signed from Cazino Salzburg during the 1997 close season to learn the business from David Seaman with a view to eventually taking over from the England 'keeper at Arsenal. In the event, he jumped in front of all the other recognised men at the club – John Lukic, Vince Bartram, and Lee Harper, who were all released or transferred – when standing in for the injured Seaman on 16 occasion, keeping several clean sheets in the process, including a shut out at Manchester United, the only blemish being the 4-0 defeat at Liverpool. He also excelled in the FA Cup quarter-final penalty shoot-out at West Ham when saving from Eyal Berkovic and, although not playing in the Wembley 2-0 win over Newcastle, he was presented with a winners' medal as a named substitute. As a shot-stopper who stands up well, his strength allowing him to come a long way for crosses, barring accidents, he is thought to be a star of the future without a doubt.

Arsenal (£500,000 from Cazino Salzburg on 17/6/97) PL 7 FLC 4 FAC 5

MANUEL William (Billy) Albert James
Born: Hackney, 28 June 1969
Height: 5'8" Weight: 12.0
Club Honours: Div 3 '92

Released by Gillingham during the 1997 close season, this fiesty, lively midfielder only played a bit part in the Barnet first team in 1997-98. Having recovered from a broken ankle the previous January, what he lacked in pace he made up for in determination. Can also be used at full back with some confidence, being a worthy tackler.

Tottenham H (From trainee on 28/7/87)
Gillingham (Signed on 10/2/89) FL 74+13/5 FLC 2 FAC 3 Others 5
Brentford (£60,000 on 14/6/91) FL 83+11/1 FLC 7+1/1 FAC 4 Others 8+2
Peterborough U (Free on 16/9/94)
Cambridge U (Free on 28/10/94) FL 10 FAC 2
Peterborough U (Free on 28/2/95) FL 27/2 FLC 4/3 FAC 1+1 Others 2
Gillingham (Free on 26/1/96) FL 9+12 FAC 1 Others 1
Barnet (Free on 18/7/97) FL 10+7 FLC 2+1 FAC 1 Others 0+3

MARCELLE Clinton (Clint) Sherwin
Born: Trinidad, 9 November 1968
Height: 5'4" Weight: 10.0
International Honours: Trinidad & Tobago: 8

Clint took time to come to terms with the Premier League at Barnsley in 1997-98 and was used mainly as a substitute by the manager. However, his pace always caused problems and, when given a run in the team, he produced some fine performances, which gained him to further selection for the Trinidad & Tobago international team, although on his return he found himself out of the team and his chances even more limited. Without any goals to his credit last season, hopefully, he will find first division defences more to his liking in 1998-99, as in 1996-97.*

Barnsley (Free from Felgueiras on 8/8/96) F/PL 35+25/8 FLC 3+3 FAC 5+1/1

[MARCELO] Cipriano Dos Santos
Born: Miteroi, Brazil, 11 October 1969
Height: 6'0" Weight: 13.8

Signed from the Portuguese club, Deportivo Alaves, last October, following a trial period, his chances at Sheffield United were limited until the sales of Brian Deane and Jan-Aage Fjortoft removed the competition for the striking berth, although he had managed a debut goal against Queens Park Rangers. Despite never looking fully convincing in the physical side of the English game, he nonetheless scored some vital goals, including the equaliser at Coventry City, followed by the famous shirt in the crowd incident, which continued the amazing cup run of the club.

Sheffield U (£400,000 from Dep Aleves on 6/10/97) FL 12+9/6 FAC 5+1/1 Others 1+1/1

MARDON Paul Jonathan
Born: Bristol, 14 September 1969
Height: 6'0" Weight: 12.0
International Honours: W: 1

After such a poor season in 1996-97, having

been on the treatment table from October to March, Paul was hoping for a better time of it at West Bromwich Albion in 1997-98, especially as he had managed a handful of games at the end of the previous campaign and had got his confidence back. Unfortunately, after a steady start he was absent for some nine games before coming back strongly to produce some excellent displays until struck down again and being absent from the side after December. Capable of playing in midfield or defence, he is very powerful in the air, sound and composed on the ground, has fair pace, and will be back, hopefully, stronger than ever.

Bristol C (From trainee on 29/1/88) FL 29+13 FLC 3+3/1 Others 1
Doncaster Rov (Loaned on 13/9/90) FL 3
Birmingham C (£115,000 on 16/8/91) FL 54+10 FLC 11+1 FAC 1 Others 3
West Bromwich A (£400,000 on 18/11/93) FL 113+8/3 FLC 8 FAC 3 Others 2

MARGETSON Martyn Walter
Born: Neath, 8 September 1971
Height: 6'0" Weight: 14.0
International Honours: W: B; U21-7; Yth; Sch

Into the last season of his contract at Manchester City, with Tommy Wright injured, the goalkeeper made an impressive start to 1997-98, playing in the first 14 games, and, in the latter, performing excellently, despite the team winning only three times during that period. A shot-stopper who excels under the back-pass ruling, his clearances being long and normally accurate, although eventually giving way to Wright, he continued to perform well when called upon. Having understudied 16 various 'keepers during his time at Maine Road, it was a huge disappointment to be told that his contract was not to be renewed on the eve of the match at Port Vale, especially as he was enjoying the best spell of his career.

Manchester C (From trainee on 5/7/90) F/PL 51 FLC 2+2 FAC 3 Others 1
Bristol Rov (Loaned on 8/12/93) FL 2+1

MARKER Nicholas (Nicky) Robert
Born: Budleigh Salterton, 3 May 1965
Height: 6'0" Weight: 12.11

Able to play both in defence and midfield, this most versatile of players is a good all-rounder, who is more than capable of doing a man-marking job at the back if required. Good in the air, and in the passing side of the game, where he likes to get forward, Nicky left Blackburn during the 1997 close season and deservedly won Sheffield United's Player of the Year award for his strong performances right across the pitch. Undoubtedly the most consistent performer at the club throughout 1997-98, strangely, his only goals of the campaign came in both home and away games against Charlton in the league.

Exeter C (From apprentice on 4/5/83) FL 196+6/3 FLC 11/1 FAC 8 Others 8/3
Plymouth Arg (£95,000 on 31/10/87) FL 201+1/13 FLC 15/3 FAC 9/1 Others 7/1

Blackburn Rov (£500,000 on 23/9/92) PL 41+13/1 FLC 3+1 FAC 4+1 Others 1+1
Sheffield U (£400,000 on 29/7/97) FL 43/2 FLC 4 FAC 8 Others 2

Nicky Marker

MARKSTEDT Peter

Born: Vasteras, Sweden, 11 January 1972
Height: 5'11" Weight: 13.10

With Barnsley's backs against the wall during their first attempt at Premier League football, and in a bid to stiffen their defence, Peter was signed from Vasteras SK last November. A stylish centre back, he made his debut at Anfield and his defensive qualities were put to the test as Barnsley gave an against the odds display to win 1-0. Strong in the air, and calm and composed on the floor, unfortunately the rest of his season was disrupted by injuries, firstly to the back, and then to the neck, which forced an early end to his efforts.

Barnsley (£250,000 from Vasteras SK on 21/11/97) PL 6+1 FAC 1

MARRIOTT Andrew (Andy)

Born: Sutton in Ashfield, 11 October 1970
Height: 6'1" Weight: 12.6
Club Honours: Div 4 '92; FMC '92; WC '95
International Honours: E: U21-1; Yth; Sch. W: 5

Now recognised as the Welsh number two, Andy continued to be a superb shot-stopper for Wrexham in 1997-98, despite asking to be put on the transfer list as he would like a higher grade of football if the opportunity arose. No club has come in for him to date and, while he has many natural qualities, he would no doubt be the first to admit that certain aspects of his game still need to be worked on, like most 'keepers. Regarded as one of the best custodians in the lower

division, his long goal kicks often spelt danger for the opposition, one such kick reaching Karl Connolly, who headed home from inside the six-yard box during the 2-2 home draw against Carlisle.

Arsenal (From trainee on 22/10/88)
Nottingham F (£50,000 on 20/6/89) F/PL 11 FLC 1 Others 1
West Bromwich A (Loaned on 6/9/89) FL 3
Blackburn Rov (Loaned on 29/12/89) FL 2
Colchester U (Loaned on 21/3/90) FL 10
Burnley (Loaned on 29/8/91) FL 15 Others 2
Wrexham (£200,000 on 8/10/93) FL 213 FLC 10 FAC 22 Others 21

MARSDEN Christopher (Chris)

Born: Sheffield, 3 January 1969
Height: 5'11" Weight: 10.12

One of the Stockport kingpins in their promotion campaign of 1996-97, Chris' busy and effective displays in 1997-98 earned him a move to Birmingham in October, but, at the same time, left a large hole in County's midfield. Brought to the club in order to add a better balance to the side, and to act as an orchestrator in setting up attacks, he started in style by scoring what turned out to be the winner just eight minutes into his debut at St Andrews against Wolves. Rarely missing from the action, his slick passing and clever positional play helped City tick far better during the last two thirds.

Sheffield U (From apprentice on 6/1/87) FL 13+3/1 FLC 1 Others 1
Huddersfield T (Signed on 15/7/88) FL 113+8/9 FLC 15+1 FAC 6+2 Others 10
Coventry C (Loaned on 2/11/93) PL 5+2
Wolverhampton W (£250,000 on 11/1/94) FL 8 FAC 3
Notts Co (£250,000 on 15/11/94) FL 10 FLC 1 Others 1/1
Stockport Co (£70,000 on 12/1/96) FL 63+2/3 FLC 13 FAC 4 Others 4/1
Birmingham C (£500,000 on 9/10/97) FL 31+1/1 FAC 2

Andy Marriott

MARSH Christopher (Chris) Jonathan
Born: Sedgley, 14 January 1970
Height: 5'11" Weight: 13.2

After an early-season spell out of action in 1997-98, Walsall's longest-serving player returned to make the number three spot his own and, though earlier in his career he had been better known for his effectiveness when going forward, he gave some outstanding displays as a man-for-man marker. For the record, as in 1996-97, Chris stepped up to take his place in goal after Jimmy Walker was carried off after 29 minutes at Northampton and, although unable to be faulted, conceded three goals in a 3-2 defeat.
Walsall (From trainee on 11/7/88) FL 268+34/21 FLC 17+2/1 FAC 29+1/3 Others 19+1/3

MARSH Michael (Mike) Andrew
Born: Liverpool, 21 July 1969
Height: 5'8" Weight: 11.0
Club Honours: FAC '92

Mike finally succumbed to the knee injury that had dogged him for his whole Southend career and retired in October 1997. The passing and tackling, allied to a fine shot, were sorely missed at Roots Hall, and his absence was one of the reasons the team struggled so badly during 1997-98. Although no longer able to cope with the rigours of league football, he joined Barrow, showing that a half-fit Mike Marsh is still worth having around.
Liverpool (Free from Kirby T on 21/8/87) F/PL 42+27/2 FLC 10+1/3 FAC 6+2 Others 12+1/1
West Ham U (Signed on 17/9/93) PL 46+3/1 FLC 6 FAC 6/1
Coventry C (£450,000 on 30/12/94) PL 15/2 FAC 4 (£500,000 to Galatasaray on 13/7/95)
Southend U (£500,000 on 4/9/95) FL 84/11 FLC 8/1 FAC 2 Others 3/1

MARSH Simon Thomas Peter
Born: Ealing, 29 January 1977
Height: 5'11" Weight: 11.6
International Honours: E: U21-1

Simon virtually doubled his appearances for Oxford during 1997-98, most of them coming towards the end of the season when Mike Ford was injured. Appeared a very competent player in the left-back berth, so much so that he was called into the provisional England U21 squad for the summer tournament in France, and looks good for a regular spot in the forthcoming season. Was one of only four outfield (of 24) players at United who started a game and did not manage a goal.
Oxford U (From trainee on 22/11/94) FL 29+6/1 FLC 4+2 FAC 2 Others 2

MARSHALL Andrew (Andy) John
Born: Bury St Edmunds, 14 April 1975
Height: 6'2" Weight: 13.7
International Honours: E: U21-4

Handed the position of first-choice custodian at Norwich at the start of 1997-98, with Bryan Gunn relegated to the role of deputy, Andy quickly proved his worth in giving some outstanding displays, while missing just four games throughout the campaign and keeping ten clean sheets. Gaining in confidence all the time, he was strong on crosses, coming for the ball well, and kicked hard and long. Despite City being under pressure in the bottom half of the first division, he held his nerve and, at the same time, added to his collection of England U21 caps.
Norwich C (From trainee on 6/7/93) P/FL 72+1 FLC 4 FAC 3+1
Bournemouth (Loaned on 9/9/96) FL 11
Gillingham (Loaned on 21/11/96) FL 5 FLC 1 Others 1

Andy Marshall

MARSHALL Dwight Wayne
Born: Jamaica, WI, 3 October 1965
Height: 5'7" Weight: 11.8

Injured for much of the early part of last season, causing him to miss a call up to the Jamaican World Cup squad training session, he recovered to become a key member of the Luton squad which avoided relegation by virtue of a late season recovery. During this period, he scored some important goals to help win valuable points and, still capable of bursts of speed and fast reactions, he is a dangerous opponent to ignore, even when appearing not to be making a great contribution. Available on a free transfer for much of the season, his late return to goalscoring form may attract enquiries from other clubs, but came too late for the Reggae Boyz.
Plymouth Arg (£35,000 from Grays Athletic on 9/8/91) FL 93+6/27 FLC 8/1 FAC 7+2/4 Others 7+1/4
Middlesbrough (Loaned on 25/3/93) PL 0+3
Luton T (£150,000 on 15/7/94) FL 87+37/27 FLC 5+1/2 FAC 7+1/5 Others 6+3/3

MARSHALL Ian Paul
Born: Liverpool, 20 March 1966
Height: 6'1" Weight: 12.12
Club Honours: Div 2 '91

The left-footed Leicester striker continued to be injury prone throughout last season, requiring a hernia operation, and also suffering from a separate groin problem. Nevertheless, he continued to add to his goal tally regularly, even when pressed into action as an emergency central defender, and scored the early goal in Madrid that gave City hopes of a European upset, and a double at St James Park that helped the Foxes to a well-earned point. Always lively when fit, but the time he spent on the treatment table eventually proved crucial to City's bid for a UEFA place through their league position. Excellent in the air, Ian is a key player when it comes to set pieces, at both ends of the park.
Everton (From apprentice on 23/3/84) FL 9+6/1 FLC 1+1/1 Others 7
Oldham Ath (£100,000 on 24/3/88) F/PL 165+5/36 FLC 17 FAC 14/3 Others 2+1/1
Ipswich T (£750,000 on 9/8/93) P/FL 79+5/32 FLC 4/3 FAC 9/3
Leicester C (£875,000 on 31/8/96) PL 41+11/15 FLC 1/1 FAC 6/3 Others 2/1

MARSHALL Lee Alan
Born: Nottingham, 1 August 1975
Height: 5'9" Weight: 9.12

After a year out of league football, the former Nottingham Forest junior appeared to make the most of a second chance with Scunthorpe in 1997-98. Consistent performances in the reserves led to a number of first team opportunities, and he can expect to figure in the team regularly during 1998-99. Only slightly built, with good close control when running at defenders, he also proved versatile, playing right back, in midfield, and as a striker.
Nottingham F (From trainee on 3/8/92)
Stockport Co (Free on 20/3/95) FL 1 (Free to Eastwood T on 24/8/96)
Scunthorpe U (£5,000 on 6/6/97) FL 12+9/1 FLC 0+1 FAC 1 Others 1

MARSHALL Lee Keith
Born: Islington, 21 January 1979
Height: 6'0" Weight: 11.11

Lee made a very impressive start to 1997-98, his first full season as a professional at Norwich after arriving from non-league Enfield at the tail end of 1996-97, and soon forced his way into first team reckoning. Having made his Football League debut against Bury at Carrow Road in early November, and giving an impressive display, he unfortunately broke his ankle four days later, at West Bromwich, and was forced to miss the next three months. Returning to the squad for two subs' appearances in March, his attacking right-back play will have marked him down as one to watch out for in 1998-99.
Norwich C (Signed from Enfield on 27/3/97) FL 2+2

MARSHALL Scott Roderick
Born: Edinburgh, 1 May 1973
Height: 6'1" Weight: 12.5
International Honours: S: U21-5; Yth

An Arsenal central defender, Scott found himself way down the pecking order at Highbury in 1997-98, behind Tony Adams, Martin Keown, Steve Bould, and the new signing from Luton, Matthew Upson. Very good in the air, and a player who will come

out of defence looking to pass the ball, he made just five appearances, three of them from the bench, before going back to the reserves. Strangely, goalkeepers seem to run in his family, his father being a former Hearts' goalkeeper, while his brother, Gordon, more recently kept goal for Celtic. *Stop Press:* Was a free transfer signing for Southampton on 13 July.

Arsenal (From trainee on 18/3/91) PL 19+5/1 FLC 1+1
Rotherham U (Loaned on 3/12/93) FL 10/1 Others 1
Sheffield U (Loaned on 25/8/94) FL 17

MARSHALL Shaun Andrew
Born: Fakenham, 3 October 1978
Height: 6'1" Weight: 12.12
Now in his second year as a professional at Cambridge, the promising young goalkeeper stepped in for two games to replace the injured Scott Barrett last October and, although conceding one goal in each game, Shaun could be well pleased with his performance, especially in the first match, against Hull City, after which he was given the star rating by Match Magazine. Not yet 20, he is Barrett's understudy and, in time, can make the number one spot his permanent property.

Cambridge U (From trainee on 21/2/97) FL 3

MARTIN Jae Andrew
Born: Hampstead, 5 February 1976
Height: 5'11" Weight: 11.10
A lively winger, Jae had a disappointing season for Lincoln in 1997-98. Ruled out early on after a hernia operation and later used as a substitute, he failed to make the starting line-up at all during the campaign, but did score with a cracking shot in the victory at Doncaster. Was released during the summer.

Southend U (From trainee on 7/5/93) FL 1+7 FLC 1+1 Others 0+1
Leyton Orient (Loaned on 9/9/94) FL 1+3 Others 1
Birmingham C (Free on 1/7/95) FL 1+6 Others 0+2
Lincoln C (Signed on 21/8/96) FL 29+12/5 FLC 5/1 FAC 1 Others 0+1

MARTIN John
Born: London, 15 July 1981
Height: 5'6" Weight: 9.12
Despite being a first-year trainee, the young Leyton Orient midfielder's progress through the youth team and reserves in 1997-98 was so impressive that he was deservedly given a first team opportunity at the end of last season and regardless of his age, did not look out of place. Thought very highly of at Brisbane Road, there is every chance that John will progress even further this coming term.

Leyton Orient (Trainee) FL 0+1

MARTIN Kevin
Born: Bromsgrove, 22 June 1976
Height: 6'1" Weight: 12.9
A promising young 'keeper, Kevin began last season as first team regular at Scarborough, opening up with two clean sheets and giving some impressive displays as his team launched a strong challenge for

promotion. Unfortunately, however, he suffered a bad knee injury in October, which sidelined him for the remainder of the season, and he was released during the summer.

Scarborough (From trainee on 5/7/95) FL 23 FLC 2 FAC 3+1 Others 1

MARTIN Lee Andrew
Born: Hyde, 5 February 1968
Height: 5'11" Weight 12.6
Club Honours: FAC '90; ESC '91
International Honours: E: U21-2
An experienced utility defender, Lee did not make any further first team appearances for Bristol Rovers in the 1997-98 season, but did spend a month on loan at Huddersfield Town during October, where he played three times at left back. Unfortunately, a degenerative back injury halted his progress, and currently training to be a physiotherapist, he hopes to continue in the game as a part-time player at non-league level.

Manchester U (From trainee on 14/5/86) F/PL 56+17/1 FLC 8+2 FAC 13+1/1 Others 7+6
Glasgow Celtic (£1,000,000 on 18/1/94) SL 19 SLC 1
Bristol Rov (Free on 8/8/96) FL 25 FLC 2 Others 1
Huddersfield T (Loaned on 1/9/97) FL 2+1 FLC 1

MARTINDALE Gary
Born: Liverpool, 24 June 1971
Height: 6'0" Weight: 12.1
Club Honours: Div 3 '98
A Rotherham target at the start of 1997-98, he had to wait until mid-March before he eventually joined the club from Notts County. After playing in the reserves for most of the season, he took some time to adjust to the pace of first team football but he could well find his previous scoring touch again this coming season. Unusual for a striker is the fact that he possesses excellent distribution qualities. Interestingly, his 22 appearances for Notts County guaranteed him a third division championship medal as his former team raced away with the title.

Bolton W (Signed from Burscough on 24/3/94)
Peterborough U (Signed on 4/7/95) FL 26+5/15 FLC 4/1 FAC 4 Others 4/2
Notts Co (£175,000 on 6/3/96) FL 34+32/13 FLC 3+1 FAC 3+1 Others 5+1/3
Mansfield T (Loaned on 7/2/97) FL 5/2
Rotherham U (Signed on 12/3/98) FL 7+1/2

MARTINEZ Roberto
Born: Balaguer Lerida, Spain, 13 July 1973
Height: 5'10" Weight: 12.2
Club Honours: Div 3 '97
A cultured right-footed Wigan midfielder, who completed a century of league starts for the club during last season, Roberto is a superbly skilful player with excellent passing ability. Surprisingly, for the first time since he arrived from Spain, he failed to be named in the PFA award-winning divisional team. Scored just two goals in 1997-98, a cracking angled drive in a 2-1 win at Wycombe, and a tremendous 25 yarder that opened the scoring in the 2-1 FA Cup win over York.

Wigan Ath (Free from Balaguer on 25/7/95) FL 106+12/14 FLC 5/1 FAC 7/4 Others 4+2/1

MARTYN Antony Nigel
Born: St Austell, 11 August 1966
Height: 6'2" Weight: 14.7
Club Honours: Div 3 '90; FMC '91; Div 1 '94
International Honours: E: 7; B-6; U21-11
Coming into last season, Nigel was the "form" 'keeper of 1996-97, with 19 clean sheets from 37 games. Continued his astounding record of consistency in 1997-98, although at least he had the comfort of being protected by a more solid Leeds' team than the one he was exposed by and given a torrid time in his early days. The odd mistake, which resulted in goals for the opposition, was more than offset by vital and brilliant saves made throughout the campaign such as the diving one-handed stop delivered by a vicious volley from inside the box, from Spurs' Allan Nielsen at Elland Road in the 1-0 victory. Unfortunate to miss just one league game, owing to being controversially sent off in the last minute of the FA Cup victory over Oxford United, in the wake of David Seaman's injury he began to establish himself as England's clear second-choice 'keeper, and was one of three goalies selected for England's final 22 bound for the World Cup Finals in France '98. His manager, George Graham, rates him as one of the best he has worked with, as did his fellow professionals who voted him into the award-winning PFA Premiership side. *Stop Press:* With David Seaman an ever present for England in the World Cup games during the summer, Nigel was not called upon.

Bristol Rov (Free from St Blazey on 6/8/87) FL 101 FLC 6 FAC 6 Others 11
Crystal Palace (£1,000,000 on 21/11/89) F/PL 272 FLC 36 FAC 22 Others 19
Leeds U (£2,250,000 on 26/7/96) PL 74 FLC 7 FAC 8

MASKELL Craig Dell
Born: Aldershot, 10 April 1968
Height: 5'10" Weight: 11.11
As Brighton and Hove Albion's leading goalscorer in 1996-97, Craig was a regular in the number ten shirt again last season, but managed to score only three times in 20 outings before being placed on the transfer list in November, when the hard-up Seagulls off-loaded five senior professionals as part of a massive cost-cutting exercise. Craig's contract was paid up in December and, after a brief trial with Dunfermline Athletic, he left for Hong Kong to join the Happy Valley club. Returned to the Football League with Leyton Orient in March, scoring his first goal for the club in a 3-2 home defeat at the hands of Shrewsbury.

Southampton (From apprentice on 15/4/86) FL 2+4/1
Huddersfield T (£20,000 on 31/5/88) FL 86+1/43 FLC 6/4 FAC 8/3 Others 7/4
Reading (£250,000 on 7/8/90) FL 60+12/26 FLC 2 FAC 5+1 Others 1
Swindon T (£225,000 on 9/7/92) F/PL 40+7/22 FLC 3+1/1 FAC 2+1 Others 4+1/4
Southampton (£250,000 on 7/2/94) PL 8+9/1 FAC 1+1
Bristol C (Loaned on 28/12/95) FL 5/1
Brighton & Hove A (£40,000 on 1/3/96) FL 68+1/20 FLC 4+1 FAC 3/1 Others 2/1 (Free to Happy Valley on 20/12/97)
Leyton Orient (Free on 26/3/98) FL 7+1/2

MASON Andrew (Andy) John
Born: Bolton, 22 November 1974
Height: 6'0" Weight: 12.0
Andy was signed after being released by Chesterfield at the end of 1996-97 and producing stunning strike displays in pre-season friendlies. Unfortunately, the goals did not materialise and he failed to keep a first team place after October, while late call ups still failed to produce goals. However, he did have a successful scoring time while on loan at non-league Boston United, prior to being released during the summer.
Bolton W (From trainee on 21/5/93)
Hull C (Free on 27/6/95) FL 14+12/4 FLC 1+3 Others 1+2
Chesterfield (Signed on 26/3/97) FL 1+1
Macclesfield T (Free on 7/8/97) FL 7+5 FLC 2/1 FAC 0+1

MASON Paul David
Born: Liverpool, 3 September 1963
Height: 5'8" Weight: 12.1
Club Honours: SLC '90; SC '90
Unfortunately, Paul managed only two appearances for Ipswich during 1997-98, a season in which his goals from midfield were sadly missed after injury took its toll. A routine x-ray after the Coca Cola Cup game at Charlton revealed that he had broken his hand and an operation was required to pin it. This kept him on the sidelines for a month, before he aggravated an old achilles tendon injury in a reserve game. He eventually learnt that an operation was required to correct the problem, which meant that his season was finished in December. Hopefully, he will be back as good as new this coming campaign.*
Aberdeen (£200,000 from FC Groningen on 1/8/88) SL 138+20/27 SLC 13+2/8 SC 11+1/1 Others 7/1
Ipswich T (£400,000 on 18/6/93) P/FL 103+10/25 FLC 10/4 FAC 4+3/3 Others 4/3

MASSEY Stuart Anthony
Born: Crawley, 17 November 1964
Height: 5'11" Weight: 12.7
Stuart ended last season in plaster after suffering a knee ligament injury in the game at Manchester City, but being a great team man in the Oxford midfield, and a battler, he will be sure to get back playing again, hopefully by the New Year. Prior to that, he was out of the side for the first part of the season, but regained his place and scored his only goal at Tranmere. Was somewhat surprisingly released during the summer.
Crystal Palace (£20,000 from Sutton U on 17/7/92) F/PL 1+1 Others 1
Oxford U (Free on 5/7/94) FL 82+21/8 FLC 9+4/1 FAC 8+1/4 Others 3

MASTERS Neil Bradley
Born: Ballymena, 25 May 1972
Height: 6'1" Weight: 14.2
International Honours: NI: Yth
Signed from Wolves too late to get a game for Gillingham in 1996-97, although given the opportunity last season, and proving to be a cultured left back with a superb left foot from dead-ball situations, Neil had so many injuries that he was never able to string a proper run together. Hopefully, 1998-99 will bring the Irishman better fortune.

Bournemouth (From trainee on 31/8/90) FL 37+1/2 FLC 4/1 FAC 5+2/1 Others 1
Wolverhampton W (£300,000 on 22/12/93) FL 10+2
Gillingham (Signed on 2/4/97) FL 11 Others 1

MATHIE Alexander (Alex)
Born: Bathgate, 20 December 1968
Height: 5'10" Weight: 11.7
International Honours: S: Yth
Although Alex ensured he had a place in Ipswich folklore on 21 February 1998, when he scored a first-half hat trick against Norwich, overall it was a mixed season for him. Having completely recovered from the shoulder problems, he then picked up a groin injury in a pre-season friendly at Rushden & Diamonds, which kept him out until October, before coming back to score the winner against Manchester City, followed three days later by the opening goal of the Coca Cola win over Manchester United – a notable Manchester double. Despite forming a lethal and exciting partnership with David Johnson, which helped spark Ipswich's revival, he often found himself the odd man out as George Burley juggled his three strikers around, but still managed to score some excellent goals, being particularly adept at the art of volleying. Has the ability to hold up play and bring others into the game, to match the skill that enables him to beat opponents on the inside and the outside.
Glasgow Celtic (From juniors on 15/5/87) SL 7+4 SC 1 Others 0+1
Morton (£100,000 on 1/8/91) SL 73+1/31 SLC 2/1 SC 5/3 Others 7/9
Port Vale (Loaned on 30/3/93) FL 0+3
Newcastle U (£285,000 on 30/7/93) PL 3+22/4 FLC 2+2
Ipswich T (£500,000 on 24/2/95) P/FL 88+13/37 FLC 9+2/7 FAC 2+2 Others 6/1

MATTEO Dominic
Born: Dumfries, 28 April 1974
Height: 6'1" Weight: 11.12
International Honours: E: B-1; U21-4; Yth
1997-98 was yet another season in which he promised much for Liverpool, but failed to have an extended run in the side in which to fulfil his rich promise as a central defender, who can break down attacks and then set up counter attacks with sudden swiftness. His skill also allows him to play in any number of positions, especially out wide, where he runs at defenders to express himself in attacking areas. Still on the verge of full England international honours, having played for the "B" side against Chile last February and as an over-age player for the U21s the following month, a settled run could see him called up in 1998-99.
Liverpool (From trainee on 27/5/92) PL 64+11 FLC 9 FAC 4+1 Others 9
Sunderland (Loaned on 28/3/95) FL 1

MATTHEW Damian
Born: Islington, 23 September 1970
Height: 5'11" Weight" 10.10 Club Honours: Div 1 '94
International Honours: E: U21-9
After a run in the Burnley first team early on last season, Damian was almost transferred to Northampton, but failed to agree terms.

However, he returned to make a major contribution to the Clarets' good form after Christmas, and continued to be a constructive member of a sometimes undermanned midfield unit. Although the possessor of a good shot, this aspect of his game failed to get him results in 1997-98.*
Chelsea (From trainee on 13/6/89) F/PL 13+8 FLC 5 Others 1
Luton T (Loaned on 25/9/92) FL 3+2 Others 1
Crystal Palace (£150,000 on 11/2/94) F/PL 17+7/1 FLC 2+1 FAC 1
Bristol Rov (Loaned on 12/1/96) FL 8 Others 2/1
Burnley (£65,000 on 23/7/96) FL 50+9/7 FLC 6+1/1 FAC 2/1 Others 3

MATTHEWS Lee Joseph
Born: Middlesbrough, 16 January 1979
Height: 6'3" Weight: 12.6
Club Honours: FAYC '97
International Honours: E: Yth
A 19-year-old striker, and another former member of the successful youth team at Leeds, Lee was a regular member of the reserve side in 1997-98 and made his full debut as a substitute in the 2-0 victory at Crystal Palace in January. He then maintained his place on the bench, making further appearances. Very quick, and with a good touch for a tall striker, he looks to have a big future at Elland Road. Is also a member of the England set up at U19 level.
Leeds U (From trainee on 15/2/96) PL 0+3 FLC 0+1

MATTHEWS Robert (Rob) David
Born: Slough, 14 October 1970
Height: 6'0" Weight: 13.0
Club Honours: Div 2 '97
International Honours: E: Sch
A cruciate ligament operation the previous April kept Rob sidelined throughout the summer of 1997 and early season months, but, following much hard work and determination, the winger battled back to full fitness, making his long-awaited comeback at Charlton last January, and immediately recaptured his best form, playing in 15 games during the run-in. Tricky and direct, his return was a godsend for the Shakers, he revitalised the attacking options available to the manager.
Notts Co (Free from Loughborough University on 26/3/92) FL 23+20/11 FLC 0+2 FAC 3+2/2 Others 4+3
Luton T (£80,000 on 17/3/95) FL 6+5 FLC 0+1
York C (£90,000 on 8/9/95) FL 14+3/1 FAC 1 Others 3
Bury (£100,000 on 12/1/96) FL 42+16/9 FLC 1+3 FAC 1 Others 3

MAUGE Ronald (Ronnie) Carlton
Born: Islington, 10 March 1969
Height: 5'10" Weight: 11.10
A strong and combative Plymouth midfielder, Ronnie gets through a lot of tackles in midfield, and also has a very good eye for goal. Unfortunately troubled with injuries throughout last season, this reduced his first team appearances and he spent most of the latter part of the campaign as a substitute, always giving his all when introduced, and being a player you could rely upon.
Charlton Ath (From trainee on 22/7/87)
Fulham (Free on 21/9/88) FL 47+3/2 FLC 4 FAC 1 Others 2

Bury (£40,000 on 30/7/90) FL 92+16/10 FLC 8+2/2 FAC 8/2 Others 10+2
Manchester C (Loaned on 26/9/91) Others 0+1
Plymouth Arg (£40,000 on 22/7/95) FL 88+15/10 FLC 4 FAC 8/2 Others 4+1/1

MAUTONE Steven (Steve)
Born: Myrtleford, Australia, 10 August 1970
Height: 6'1" Weight: 13.2
Having firmed up his temporary transfer from West Ham on a permanent basis during the 1997 close season, Steve retained his position as Reading's first-choice goalkeeper at the start of 1997-98, and his form varied between competent and good during a run of 19 matches. However, after injuring a cartilage in his left knee, whilst warming up 20 minutes before the kick off in the league match at Port Vale, he had to be replaced by Nicky Hammond at the last minute and, despite extensive physiotherapy and treatment at Lilleshall, apart from making a handful of reserve team appearances, that was it.
West Ham U (£30,000 from Canberra Cosmos on 29/3/96) PL 1 FLC 2
Crewe Alex (Loaned on 6/9/96) FL 3
Reading (Signed on 17/2/97) FL 29 FLC 5

MAXFIELD Scott
Born: Doncaster, 13 July 1976
Height: 5'9" Weight: 11.6
Having fought back from a knee injury, which kept him out of Hull City's pre-season games, only to need keyhole surgery on a cartilage in his right knee last November, it was not until February that Scott was given an extended run. Back in harness, he appeared at his best in a conventional left-back role, his strong tackling and sensible distribution taking the eye. Was released during the summer.
Doncaster Rov (From trainee on 8/7/94) FL 22+7/1 FLC 0+1 Others 1
Hull C (Signed on 27/3/96) FL 23+12 FLC 1+1 FAC 1 Others 0+1

MAY David
Born: Oldham, 24 June 1970
Height: 6'0" Weight: 12.10
Club Honours: CS '94, '96; PL '96, '97; FAC '96
A very able Manchester United central defender, with good recovery skills and excellent heading ability, David had a frustrating start to 1997-98 when he sustained a torn thigh muscle during the club's pre-season warm-up campaign. With only two appearances on the bench as a non-playing substitute against Juventus and Crystal Palace in October, his first full game of the season came against Ipswich in the Coca Cola Cup in October. Having then failed to make another appearance until the FA Cup replay against Barnsley in February, because of a persistent knee injury problem, it was only during the latter half of the campaign that he began to regain full fitness. Despite Alex Ferguson shoring up his defence with the acquisition of David's former Blackburn team-mate, Henning Berg, in August, at least he had the consolation of being offered a new six-year contract in October.

Blackburn Rov (From trainee on 16/6/88) F/PL 123/3 FLC 12+1/2 FAC 10/1 Others 5
Manchester U (£1,400,000 on 1/7/94) PL 61+12/6 FLC 5/1 FAC 5 Others 13+1/1

MAYBURY Alan
Born: Dublin, 8 August 1978
Height: 5'11" Weight: 11.7
Club Honours: FAYC '97
International Honours: Ei: 1; B-1; U21-3; Yth
The 20-year-old right back and captain of the Leeds' youth side that won the FA Youth Cup in 1996-97, Alan made his home first team debut in the 4-3 victory over Derby County last November, before being substituted at half time after being given a hard time by Aljosa Asanovic. To his credit, he remained in the first team picture and performed very commendably, and is highly thought of by George Graham and his staff. One for the future, he was awarded his first full cap for the Republic of Ireland in the game against Czechoslovakia in April, having earlier appeared for both the "B" side and the U21s.
Leeds U (Free from St Kevin's BC on 17/8/95) PL 10+3 FLC 1 FAC 2

MAYO Kerry
Born: Haywards Heath, 21 September 1977
Height: 5'10" Weight: 12.8
The 20-year-old local lad continued where he left off the previous campaign and had a fine season in Brighton and Hove Albion's uphill struggle to retain Football League status in 1997-98. The flame-haired dynamo was an automatic choice in the Seagulls' midfield, and scored two excellent goals in the 3-2 defeat of Chester City at Gillingham on 28 February, which ensured that the newly-installed manager, Brian Horton, got off to a winning start.
Brighton & Hove A (From trainee on 3/7/96) FL 65+3/6 FLC 2 FAC 1+1 Others 1+2

MAYRLEB Christian
Born: Austria, 8 June 1972
Height: 5'10" Weight: 11.7
A pacy forward who was signed on a six-month contract from the Austrian club, FC Tyrol, last January, Christian made his Sheffield Wednesday Premiership debut two days later when coming off the bench to take part in a 1-1 home draw against Wimbledon. Although showing a good appetite for the game, he obviously needed more time to settle down to adjust to the hurly-burly pace of the English game, two more subs' appearances not nearly enough to form a proper opinion of his capabilities. Prior to FC Tyrol, he was with Admira FC.
Sheffield Wed (Free on 28/1/98) PL 0+3

MEAKER Michael John
Born: Greenford, 18 August 1971
Height: 5'11" Weight: 12.0
International Honours: W: B-1; U21-2
As in 1996-97, Michael's career at Reading failed to take off as he completed yet another season where he was unable to command a regular place on either the right or left-hand side of midfield, despite his pace and undoubted ability to run at players.

Although he doubled his goal tally of the previous campaign, scoring twice, against Wolves and Stoke City, he was frequently substituted by manager, Terry Bullivant, and then failed to complete a full 90 minutes for his replacement, Tommy Burns, before being told he could leave the club during the summer.
Queens Park R (From trainee on 7/2/90) F/PL 21+13/1 FLC 2/1 FAC 3/1 Others 0+1
Plymouth Arg (Loaned on 20/11/91) FL 4 Others 1
Reading (£550,000 on 19/7/95) FL 46+21/2 FLC 3/1 FAC 0+3

MEAN Scott James
Born: Crawley, 13 December 1973
Height: 5'11" Weight: 13.8
A stylish midfielder who makes penetrating runs into the danger areas, Scott finally made his league debut for West Ham, when coming on as a substitute against Leeds last March, and followed up with two further appearances from the bench before the curtain came down on another Premiership campaign. Happily, Scott was able to prove that he was back to full fitness after a couple of injury plagued seasons, and it is hoped that he will now be able to replay the faith shown in him by Harry Redknapp, when signing him from Bournemouth during the 1996 summer recess.
Bournemouth (From trainee on 10/8/92) FL 52+22/8 FLC 7+1 FAC 2+1 Others 4
West Ham U (£100,000 on 18/7/96) PL 0+3

MEDLIN Nicholas (Nicky) Ryan Maxwell
Born: Camborne, 23 November 1976
Height: 5'7" Weight: 10.7
An Exeter ball winner who keeps things ticking over in midfield, Nicky had a varied season in 1997-98 with few appearances, although he equipped himself well with the chances he had prior to being released during the summer. A real battler is this youngster, having already come back strongly from a broken leg.
Exeter C (From trainee on 4/8/95) FL 20+17/1 FAC 1 Others 2+2

MEECHAN Alexander (Alex) Thomas
Born: Plymouth, 29 January 1980
Height: 5'10" Weight: 10.10
Still a trainee, the teenage striker was called upon just once by Swindon in 1997-98, making his first team bow as a second-half substitute at Wolves in October, and although often included in the Town squad, being on the bench on two more occasions, he was not used. Surprisingly released by the club at the end of his two-year apprenticeship in the summer, he will obviously be looking to get back into the league at the earliest opportunity.
Swindon T (Trainee) FL 0+1

MELLON Michael (Micky) Joseph
Born: Paisley, 18 March 1972
Height: 5'9" Weight: 11.3
Signed from Blackpool last October, Micky proved to be a lively midfield player for Tranmere, who liked to make early passes and telling forward runs. Hard working, if his early performances for Rovers were a

little subdued, he improved rapidly as the season progressed and soon settled into the side. Although not an out-and-out goalscorer, he possesses a fearsome shot, opening his account with a powerful volley against a Stoke side with Neville Southall in goal, and can be relied upon to contribute a few goals to the seasonal tally. Also delights in popping up in dangerous positions.

Bristol C (From trainee on 6/12/89) FL 26+9/1 FLC 3 FAC 1+1 Others 5+3
West Bromwich A (£75,000 on 11/2/93) FL 38+7/6 FLC 3+2 FAC 0+1 Others 6/1
Blackpool (£50,000 on 23/11/94) FL 123+1/14 FLC 9/1 FAC 4 Others 7/2
Tranmere Rov (£285,000 on 31/10/97) FL 24+9/2 FAC 2+1

MELVANG Lars Mandrup
Born: Seattle, USA, 3 April 1969
Height: 5'9" Weight: 11.10
Arriving at Watford from Silkeborg last August, the Danish right back, or wing back, initially came on a months trial period, which was extended because of injury problems. Despite scoring on his debut against Brentford, Lars eventually left in March, having been unable to secure a contract.

Watford (Loaned from Silkeborg on 21/8/97) FL 4/1 FLC 1

MELVILLE Andrew (Andy) Roger
Born: Swansea, 29 November 1968
Height: 6'0" Weight: 13.10
Club Honours: WC '89; Div 1 '96
International Honours: W: 32; B-1; U21-2
The Welsh international centre back's reign as a stalwart in the Sunderland defence was ended last term as a new generation of young defenders emerged, his hamstring injury in October giving Jody Craddock his chance, leaving first team opportunities limited thereafter. Allowed to join Bradford on loan in February, Andy proved very solid and reliable in his six games, and was well liked by the fans, especially after his bullet-like header set up a 2-1 win for City at the Valley Parade against Port Vale. Won his 32nd Welsh cap in August against Turkey – a game in which he also scored.

Swansea C (From trainee on 25/7/86) FL 165+10/22 FLC 10 FAC 14+1/5 Others 13/2
Oxford U (£275,000 on 23/7/90) FL 135/13 FLC 12/1 FAC 6 Others 6/1
Sunderland (Signed on 9/8/93) P/FL 160/12 FLC 12+1 FAC 9 Others 2
Bradford C (Loaned on 13/2/98) FL 6/1

MENDES-RODRIGUEZ Alberto
Born: Nurnberg, Germany, 24 October 1974
Height: 5'11" Weight: 11.9
A Portuguese striker who was plucked from the lower reaches of the German League during the 1997 summer recess, as a player for the future, Alberto made his first team debut for Arsenal in the third round of the Coca Cola Cup at home to Birmingham last October. Very direct, skilful, strong, and pacy, put through by Stephen Hughes in extra time, he fired a low drive into the right-hand corner to score the third goal in a 4-1 win. There were four more oppor-

tunities, including a showing from the bench at Anfield in the penultimate game of the season, the club having already won the Premiership and content to blood one or two of the younger players. Looks useful.

Arsenal (£250,000 from FC Feucht on 21/7/97) PL 1+2 FLC 2/1

MENDONCA Clive Paul
Born: Islington, 9 September 1968
Height: 5'10" Weight: 12.6
Signed from Grimsby Town in the summer of 1997, Clive made an immediate impact, finishing last season as top scorer with 28, the best haul for a Charlton player for 22 years, and beating his own personal record. Very comfortable on the ball, with the ability to turn a defender and gain a yard, he is deadly in front of goal, and is also able to hold play up to bring others into the game. Scored a hat trick against Norwich at Carrow Road in September, and another in the play-off final at Wembley that saw the club reach the Premiership at the expense of Sunderland.

Sheffield U (From apprentice on 10/9/86) FL 8+5/4 FLC 0+1 Others 1
Doncaster Rov (Loaned on 26/2/88) FL 2
Rotherham U (£35,000 on 25/3/88) FL 71+13/27 FLC 5+2/1 FAC 4+1/2 Others 4+2/1
Sheffield U (£110,000 on 1/8/91) FL 4+6/1 FLC 0+2 Others 0+1
Grimsby T (Loaned on 9/1/92) FL 10/3
Grimsby T (£85,000 on 13/8/92) FL 151+5/57 FLC 10+1/3 FAC 8/2 Others 2/1
Charlton Ath (£700,000 on 23/5/97) FL 40/23 FLC 2/1 FAC 2/1 Others 2/3

MERCER William (Billy)
Born: Liverpool, 22 May 1969
Height: 6'2" Weight: 13.5
Billy was kept busy in the Chesterfield goal last season, as the team often set aside their broad "safety-first" outlook in favour of a more attacking style, but he acquitted himself well. Although he may have looked a little shaky on occasions, he played through bouts of nagging injury in a selfless fashion and, while lesser men might have cried off, as always, he put the team's needs before his own reputation and emerged with great credit. Has good positional sense, stands up well, and is a recognised shot stopper.

Liverpool (From trainee on 21/8/87)
Rotherham U (Signed on 16/2/89) FL 104 FLC 12 FAC 12 Others 10
Sheffield U (Signed on 12/10/94) FL 4
Chesterfield (£93,000 on 5/9/95) FL 105 FLC 6 FAC 9 Others 5

MERSON Paul Charles
Born: Harlesden, 20 March 1968
Height: 6'0" Weight: 13.2
Club Honours: Div 1 '89, '91; FLC '93; FAC '93; ECWC '94
International Honours: E: 19; B-4; U21-4; Yth
In one of the most surprising transfer deals since his appointment as manager of Middlesbrough, the fans were delighted when "Robbo" obtained Paul's signature from Arsenal during the 1997 close season. He arrived in a blaze of excitement, pledging his avowed intent to take the Boro

back into the Premiership at the first attempt, and the fans loved him for that. They loved him even more when the final whistle blew in the concluding match of the campaign, Boro being promoted with Paul's allegiance to the cause having been tremendous. Almost an ever present in the team, he gave his all for the Boro, scoring some fantastic goals, and, by popular acclaim, winning many Man of the Match awards along the way, something that was well recognised by his fellow professionals when they voted him into the award-winning PFA first division select. An examination of his personal stats read like pure fantasy, such was his commitment and dedication. By this time, the faithful had endowed him with cult status, and when a local radio commentator dubbed him "Magic Man" the name stuck. "Magic" looks set the serve the Boro well into the next century and the fans are delighted at the prospect. His captaincy of the England "B" team, and subsequent inclusion in the World Cup squad, merely confirmed the resurrection of his career, and his determination to compete again at the highest level. *Stop Press:* One of the surprise choices for France '98, Paul came on for the final 41 minutes of the back-to-the-wall game against Argentina, scored a penalty in the shoot-out, but then saw ten-man England ultimately lose 4-3 on penalties.

Arsenal (From apprentice on 1/12/85) F/PL 289+38/78 FLC 38+2/9 FAC 28+3/4 Others 27+2/7
Brentford (Loaned on 22/1/87) FL 6+1 Others 1+1
Middlesbrough (£4,500,000+ on 15/7/97) FL 45/12 FLC 7/3 FAC 3/1

MESSER Gary Michael
Born: Consett, 22 September 1979
Height: 6'1" Weight: 12.0
Gary was rewarded for his sterling efforts in the Doncaster junior teams with a number of substitute appearances at first team level, before making his full league debut last March. Proving to be a player with some promise, the young striker notched his first goal against the eventual champions, Notts County, a month later.

Doncaster Rov (Trainee) FL 4+10/1

MIDDLETON Craig Dean
Born: Nuneaton, 10 September 1970
Height: 5'10" Weight: 11.5
The energy and athleticism of Craig persuaded the Cardiff City manager, Frank Burrows, to offer him a new contract for 1998-99 on condition he moved to South Wales. Craig was among only three players offered new contracts at Cardiff City, his enthusiasm for the task, wherever he played in 1997-98, being infectious, although his aggression occasionally got him into trouble with referees. Playing in a number of positions, shining as a central defender, and in a role just behind the front two strikers, he also performed in midfield and at right back, and was named Most Improved Player by Cardiff City Supporters' Club.*

Coventry C (From trainee on 30/5/89) F/PL 2+1 FLC 1

Cambridge U (Free on 20/7/93) FL 55+4/10 FLC 3 FAC 1 Others 1
Cardiff C (Free on 30/8/96) FL 68+6/4 FLC 2+1 FAC 8/1 Others 3+1

MIDGLEY Craig Steven
Born: Bradford, 24 May 1976
Height: 5'8" Weight: 10.13

A bustling forward who can also play in midfield, and is effective running at defences and creating chances for others, Craig was a rare money signing for Hartlepool, having joined them last March to further his career after languishing in Bradford City's reserves for rather too long. On the small side, he showed a good attitude and proved he could be a real handful to opposition defences when playing in the last nine games of the season. Earlier, in December, he had a spell on loan at Darlington, scoring once in two appearances, before returning to Valley Parade.

Bradford C (From trainee on 4/7/95) FL 0+11/1 FAC 0+4 Others 1
Scarborough (Loaned on 7/12/95) FL 14+2/1
Scarborough (Loaned on 14/3/97) FL 6/2
Darlington (Loaned on 1/12/97) FL 1 Others 0+1/1
Hartlepool U (£10,000 on 13/3/98) FL 9/3

MIDWOOD Michael Adrian
Born: Burnley, 19 April 1976
Height: 5'11" Weight: 13.4

As a former Huddersfield player who had been released two years earlier without being given a first team run, Michael's performance for Halifax in a pre-1997-98 season friendly against Town was duly noted and he was signed up for a second chance. A striker with the strength and ability to make space for himself, and take up good positions, he made his Football League debut on the opening day at Oxford as a sub, before being released in October. Now playing with non-league Emley.

Huddersfield T (From trainee on 6/7/94 - Free to Halifax during 1995 close season)
Huddersfield T (Free on 8/8/97) FL 0+1

MIKE Adrian (Adie) Roosevelt
Born: Manchester, 16 November 1973
Height: 6'0" Weight: 11.9
International Honours: E: Yth; Sch

Released by Stockport during the 1997 close season, Adie proved to be one of the few Doncaster success stories of 1997-98, working hard for his team mates, whether as an out-and-out striker, or, more often than not, as a central defender. He only missed a handful of league games during the whole term, and weighed in occasionally with a welcome goal as the Rovers strove to preserve their fragile league status.

Manchester C (From trainee on 15/7/92) F/PL 5+11/2 FLC 1+1 FAC 0+1
Bury (Loaned on 25/3/93) FL 5+2/1
Stockport Co (£60,000 on 18/8/95) FL 4+5 FAC 0+1 Others 1+1
Hartlepool U (Loaned on 4/10/96) FL 7/1
Doncaster Rov (Loaned on 14/2/97) FL 5/1
Doncaster Rov (Free on 5/8/97) FL 42/4 FLC 2 FAC 1/1 Others 1

MIKLOSKO Ludek (Ludo)
Born: Ostrava, Czechoslovakia, 9 December 1961
Height: 6'5" Weight: 14.0
International Honours: Czechoslovakia: 44

The experienced Czech 'keeper, in his ninth season at West Ham, will not look back with happy memories of 1997-98. Having had a remarkable run of consistency, and been a great servant to the club, during November he had a couple of poor games and then, unfortunately, was injured and had to have knee surgery. When fully fit, he found that Craig Forrest and later, Bernard Lama, had grabbed their chances as first-choice 'keepers. Big and strong, making difficult saves look easy, and a good kicker, sadly the campaign ended with Ludo picking up a calf injury.

West Ham U (£300,000 from Banik Ostrava on 19/2/90) F/PL 315 FLC 25 FAC 25 Others 8

MILDENHALL Stephen (Steve) James
Born: Swindon, 13 May 1978
Height: 6'5" Weight: 13.5

Spent much of 1997-98 at Swindon in the reserves before moving into the spotlight in October when he made his full league debut in a live televised game at Portsmouth. Suffered a terrible injury in the first half, which later required stitches for a gash in his groin but, with no 'keeper on the bench, he bravely battled on to the end of the game, pulling off a series of brilliant saves to keep

Adie Mike

a clean sheet and earn the Man of the Match award. To complete a wonderful night for the 19-year old, the result put Swindon on top of the table for 24 hours. Was voted Young Player of the Year in an end of season poll.

Swindon T (From trainee on 19/7/96) FL 4+1 FLC 2

MILLEN Keith Derek
Born: Croydon, 26 September 1966
Height: 6'2" Weight: 12.4
Club Honours: Div 3 '92; Div 2 '98

This central defender has now made more than 450 league appearances for Watford and Brentford, his only other club. As usual, a model of consistency and professionalism, despite a string of minor injuries in 1997-98, his partnership with Robert Page at the heart of the Watford defence had much to do with the team's generally sound defensive record, and was a major factor in the club's second division championship success, his 38 games winning him a medal.

Brentford (From apprentice on 7/8/84) FL 301+4/17 FLC 26/2 FAC 18/1 Others 30+1
Watford (Signed on 22/3/94) FL 153+1/5 FLC 9 FAC 14 Others 1

MILLER Alan John
Born: Epping, 29 March 1970
Height: 6'3" Weight: 14.6
Club Honours: FAYC '88; ECWC '94; Div 1 '95
International Honours: E: U21-4; Sch

Started in West Bromwich Albion's goal in 1997-98, playing in 47 of the first 48 games, before being operated on for a double hernia that allowed young Chris Adamson and Paul Crichton the opportunity of first team football. Well built and commanding, with good reflexes and safe hands, Alan has become a big favourite with the fans and played exceedingly well both home and away last season, his presence giving the defence a real solid look. Often the difference between winning and losing, he was most impressive in the 3-1 win at Bury and the 1-0 victory over arch rivals, Birmingham, at the Hawthorns, keeping 12 clean sheets in all. Was recognised by his fellow professionals when elected for the PFA award-winning first division side, and by the club who awarded him the Player of the Year trophy.

Arsenal (From trainee on 5/5/88) PL 6+2
Plymouth Arg (Loaned on 24/11/88) FL 13 FAC 2
West Bromwich A (Loaned on 15/8/91) FL 3
Birmingham C (Loaned on 19/12/91) FL 15 Others 1
Middlesbrough (£500,000 on 12/8/94) P/FL 57 FLC 3 FAC 2 Others 2
Grimsby T (Loaned on 28/1/97) FL 3
West Bromwich A (£400,000 on 28/2/97) FL 53 FLC 4 FAC 2

MILLER Kevin
Born: Falmouth, 15 March 1969
Height: 6'1" Weight: 13.0
Club Honours: Div 4 '90

Signed from Watford during the 1997 summer break, in doing so Kevin broke Nigel Martyn's Crystal Palace record

Alan Miller

signing fee for a goalkeeper, and went straight into the side on the opening day where he remained as the club's only ever present in 1997-98. Despite keeping just nine clean sheets and conceding 75 goals, he performed well and fully deserved his Premiership status, showing himself to be an excellent shot-stopper and good at coming for crosses. Rated by Match Magazine as Palace's Man of the Match on several occasions, one of his best performances came in the 6-2 defeat at Chelsea, despite the scoreline he superbly saved at least another six goal-bound efforts to deny the club's local rivals from winning by a "cricket" score.

Exeter C (Free from Newquay on 9/3/89) FL 163 FLC 7 FAC 12 Others 18
Birmingham C (£250,000 on 14/5/93) FL 24 FLC 4 Others 2
Watford (£250,000 on 7/8/94) FL 128 FLC 10 FAC 10 Others 3

Crystal Palace (£1,000,000+ on 21/7/97) PL 38 FLC 2 FAC 4

MILLER Paul Anthony
Born: Woking, 31 January 1968
Height: 6'0" Weight: 11.7

An experienced player signed in the 1997 close season from Bristol Rovers, Paul proved both skilful and hard working at Lincoln and was used in midfield and up front, despite being plagued by a back injury for much of the campaign. Scored in the 1-0 home victory against Shrewsbury, a goal which came in useful when deciding which three sides would achieve automatic promotion from the third division.

Wimbledon (From Yeovil T on 12/8/87) F/PL 65+15/10 FLC 3+3 FAC 3 Others 1
Newport Co (Loaned on 20/10/87) FL 6/2
Bristol C (Loaned on 11/1/90) FL 0+3 Others 2
Bristol Rov (£100,000 on 16/8/94) FL 100+5/22 FLC 7/1 FAC 5/4 Others 11/2
Lincoln C (Free on 8/8/97) FL 20+4/2 FLC 2

MILLER Thomas (Tommy) William
Born: Easington, 8 January 1979
Height: 6'0" Weight: 11.8

The most successful of Hartlepool's five first-year professionals, Tommy had something to live up to, having been voted the Young Player of the Year for 1996-97. Although benefiting from full-time training, he was unfortunate to get an ankle injury on his full debut against Doncaster but, biding his time, he eventually gained a regular first team place in midfield towards the end of the season, when he showed himself to be a good passer and a good reader of the game. Looks to be an exciting prospect.
Hartlepool U (From trainee on 8/7/97) FL 11+2/1

MILLIGAN Michael (Mike) Joseph
Born: Manchester, 20 February 1967
Height: 5'8" Weight: 11.0
International Honours: Ei: 1; B-2; U23-1; U21-1

A knee injury sustained during the summer games, and a hernia operation early in the New Year, badly hampered the ever-willing Norwich midfielder in 1997-98, and his presence was sorely missed when he was unavailable. Too much of an influence to the team to be sitting on the bench, when fit all of his appearances were starts, and he remains a competitive, tenacious, all-action midfield general who is at his best when breaking down the opposition's rhythm.
Oldham Ath (From apprentice on 2/3/85) FL 161+1/17 FLC 19+1/1 FAC 12/1 Others 4
Everton (£1,000,000 on 24/8/90) FL 16+1/1 FLC 0+1 FAC 4+1/1
Oldham Ath (£600,000 on 17/7/91) P/FL 117/6 FLC 11/1 FAC 9 Others 1/1
Norwich C (£800,000 on 27/6/94) P/FL 103+8/5 FLC 11 FAC 6

MILLIGAN Ross
Born: Dumfries, 2 June 1978
Height: 6'0" Weight: 12.10

A full back who was recruited from Glasgow Rangers in the 1997 close season, Ross found it difficult to break into the first team at Carlisle in 1997-98. However, when he did so, he was yet another defender who often looked more comfortable going forward. Having been signed on a one-year contract, he was released at the end of the campaign.
Glasgow R (Free from Maxwelton Thistle on 3/9/95)
Carlisle U (Free on 22/7/97) FL 2+5 FLC 0+1 Others 1

MILLS Daniel (Danny) John
Born: Norwich, 18 May 1977
Height: 5'11" Weight: 11.9
International Honours: E: Yth

Although a consistent member of the Norwich squad in 1997-98, there were not too many opportunities going for his preferred central defensive position, his appearances being mainly restricted to right back, and he was granted a transfer in November. With no offers as such, Danny remained at Carrow Road, but after captaining the Nationwide U21 side at Charlton against their Italian counterparts in March, he caught the eye of Alan

Curbishley, who was looking after the side that night, enough to sign him for Charlton. Impressing all those at his new club as a strong and skilful defender, who likes to get down the flank to get in crosses, he scored on his debut at Crewe and looks to be a shrewd buy.
Norwich C (From trainee on 1/11/94) FL 46+20 FLC 3+2/1 FAC 2
Charlton Ath (£350,000 on 19/3/98) FL 9/1 Others 2

MILLS Daniel (Danny) Raymond
Born: Sidcup, 13 February 1975
Height: 6'0" Weight: 11.6

Having suffered badly from a hamstring injury in the 1996-97 season, Danny came back to play in the opening three games of 1997-98, but never fitted into the manager's plans and was released during the summer. Able to play on either flank, and both pacy and tricky, he will benefit from a run of games and better fortune.
Charlton Ath (From trainee on 1/7/93) Others 0+2
Barnet (Free on 29/9/95) FL 10+17 FLC 1 FAC 1+2 Others 0+1

MILLS Rowan Lee
Born: Mexborough, 10 July 1970
Height: 6'1" Weight: 12.11

In finishing last season as top scorer for Port Vale for the first time in his career, with 16 goals, the strong striker, who is good in the air, and who never misses an opportunity to shoot, led the front line excellently. Tended to score in bursts and one of the memorable variety came when he lashed in a tremendous strike from a free kick against Norwich. Although he suffered a bit of a lean spell towards the end of the campaign, he was on the mark in the final game at Huddersfield, helping to secure a crucial win that meant safety from relegation.
Wolverhampton W (Signed from Stocksbridge on 9/12/92) FL 12+13/2 FLC 1 FAC 3+1/1 Others 3/1
Derby Co (£400,000 on 24/2/95) FL 16/7
Port Vale (£200,000 on 1/8/95) FL 81+28/35 FLC 7+3/5 FAC 0+3 Others 6/4

MILNER Andrew (Andy) John
Born: Kendal, 10 February 1967
Height: 6'0" Weight: 11.0

After being the leading scorer in 1996-97, Andy became victim to a whole glut of strikers at Chester City in 1997-98 and made just one full and two subs' appearances at the start of the season before losing his place. Following a loan spell at Hereford United, he joined another Vauxhall Conference side, Morecambe, on a part-time basis in November, leaving City for a small fee.
Manchester C (£7,000 from Netherfield on 24/1/89)
Rochdale (£20,000 on 18/1/90) FL 103+24/25 FLC 9+4/5 FAC 6+2/1 Others 4/2
Chester C (Free on 12/8/94) FL 106+19/24 FLC 5+3/3 FAC 5+1/4 Others 4+1

MILNER Jonathan Robert
Born: Mansfield, 30 March 1981
Height: 5'9" Weight: 10.12

A young striker, and yet another product of Mansfield's youth policy, Jonathan made his

first team debut in the third match of last season, at home to Cardiff, whilst still a trainee. Following several more appearances from the bench, he made his full debut at Colchester in February, when Steve Whitehall was unavailable, and if maintaining his initial promise, he should go far.
Mansfield T (Trainee) FL 1+6

MILOSEVIC Savo
Born: Bijeljina, Yugoslavia, 2 September 1973
Height: 6'1" Weight: 13.4
Club Honours: FLC '96
International Honours: Yugoslavia: 28

Savo had a disappointing start to the season at Aston Villa in 1997-98, failing to secure a regular place in the starting line-up. In fact, his first run of games came at the end of September, when he scored the winning goal in extra time to give Villa victory over Bordeaux in the first round of the UEFA Cup. This came at a time when he emerged from what he described as the lowest point of his entire career. Had his best spell around November and December, when he showed some good form and, at the same time, managed to hold down a place until the middle of January. At this juncture, the Yugoslavian international was transfer listed, following a much publicised incident during the match at Blackburn, and only made a handful of appearances from thereon before being transferred to Real Zaragoza during the summer for a fee of £3.7 million. A striker with huge potential, who has terrific touch and presence, and should score many more goals than he does, he continued to play for his country throughout and was one of the final 22 selected for the World Cup Finals in France.
Aston Villa (£3,500,000 from Partizan Belgrade on 17/7/95) PL 84+6/27 FLC 8+1/1 FAC 10/2 Others 8/2

MILTON Simon Charles
Born: Fulham, 23 August 1963
Height: 5'10" Weight: 11.5
Club Honours: Div 2 '92

Able to play wide on the right, or in central midfield, and with a fair goalscoring ratio down the years, Simon was unable to re-establish himself in the Ipswich side in 1997-98, despite making the odd appearance here and there, and his testimonial season proved to be his last at Portman Road as he was given a free transfer at the end of it. At his best, a player capable of scoring explosive goals after breaking through from midfield, hopefully, his experience will not be lost to the game.
Ipswich T (£5,500 from Bury T on 17/7/87) F/PL 217+64/48 FLC 15+8/3 FAC 12/1 Others 14+2/3
Exeter C (Loaned on 1/11/87) FL 2/3 Others 1
Torquay U (Loaned on 1/3/88) FL 4/1

MIMMS Robert (Bobby) Andrew
Born: York, 12 October 1963
Height: 6'3" Weight: 14.4
Club Honours: Div 1 '87; CS '87
International Honours: E: U21-3

A vastly experienced goalkeeper who, when he joined Rotherham from Preston during

the 1997 close season, returned to the club where he made his league debut. Although at times he lacked confidence in coming out, he proved he is still an excellent shot-stopper and made a string of crucial saves, particularly late in games.

Halifax T (From apprentice on 5/8/81)
Rotherham U (£15,000 on 6/11/81) FL 83 FLC 7 FAC 3 Others 1
Everton (£150,000 on 30/5/85) FL 29 FLC 2 FAC 2 Others 4
Notts Co (Loaned on 13/3/86) FL 2 Others 1
Sunderland (Loaned on 11/12/86) FL 4
Blackburn Rov (Loaned on 23/1/87) FL 6
Manchester C (Loaned on 24/9/87) FL 3
Tottenham H (£325,000 on 25/2/88) FL 37 FLC 5 FAC 2
Aberdeen (Loaned on 16/2/90) SL 6 SC 2
Blackburn Rov (£250,000 on 22/12/90) F/PL 126+2 FLC 15 FAC 9 Others 4
Crystal Palace (Free on 30/8/96) FL 1
Preston NE (Free on 5/9/96) FL 27 FLC 2 FAC 2
Rotherham U (Free on 8/8/97) FL 43 FAC 4

MINETT Jason

Born: Peterborough, 12 August 1971
Height: 5'10" Weight: 10.2

Able to be used either in defence or midfield, and a tough tackler, Jason only managed six league starts for Exeter in 1997-98 before a thigh muscle injury saw his season come to a premature end. At his best, a skilful player with good distribution, he was released during the summer.

Norwich C (From trainee on 4/7/89) F/PL 0+3
Exeter C (Free on 19/3/93) FL 83+5/3 FLC 4 FAC 6 Others 7/2
Lincoln C (Free on 10/7/95) FL 41+5/5 FLC 2+4 FAC 1 Others 4+1
Exeter C (Free on 17/1/97) FL 19 FLC 1+1

MINTON Jeffrey (Jeff) Simon Thompson

Born: Hackney, 28 December 1973
Height: 5'6" Weight: 11.10
Thompson-Minton Jeffrey Simon

Brighton and Hove Albion's talented midfielder had an unsettled campaign in 1997-98, but, at his best, he remained a highly influential member of the team. In his fourth season with the Seagulls, Jeff clocked up his 150th senior appearance in the goalless draw with fellow strugglers, Doncaster Rovers, at Gillingham in February. However, his finest hour came when he bagged both goals in an important 2-1 "home" win over Scunthorpe United early in April, which brought to an end a goal drought for the Albion that had lasted for almost eight and a half hours. Voted Player of the Season by the fans, he also finished the campaign as the club's leading goalscorer, with a modest total of seven.*

Tottenham H (From trainee on 11/1/92) FL 2/1 FLC 0+1
Brighton & Hove A (Free on 25/7/94) FL 132+7/22 FLC 10/1 FAC 7 Others 4

MISSE-MISSE Jean-Jacques

Born: Yaounde, Camaroon, 7 August 1968
Height: 5'9" Weight: 11.4
International Honours: Cameroon: 10

A Cameroon international, Jean-Jacques joined Chesterfield on non-contract forms last March after two unsuccessful months at Dundee United, and made a surprise debut days after arriving. As you would expect

from a man who had played more than 50 times for his country, he showed some good touches before being withdrawn injured, but returned to Scotland to await approaches from other clubs before considering any permanent move to Saltergate.

Dundee U (Free from Trazonspor on 8/1/98) SL 4 SC 0+1
Chesterfield (Free on 13/3/98) FL 1

MITCHELL James (Jamie)

Born: Glasgow, 6 November 1976
Height: 5'6" Weight: 9.10

A talented young Scarborough striker who spent much of 1997-798 on the substitutes' bench, Jamie is capable of jinking his way past defenders, although his lack of "bulk" probably restricted his progress. Despite his ball skills being a joy to watch, and scoring three times, including one at Brighton when he came off the bench to equalise, he was released on a free transfer at the end of the season.

Norwich C (From trainee on 4/7/95)
Scarborough (Free on 2/8/96) FL 31+47/10 FLC 2+4 FAC 4 Others 0+2

MITCHELL Neil Nicholas

Born: Lytham, 7 November 1974
Height: 5'7" Weight: 11.1
Club Honours: GMVC '97
International Honours: E: Sch

Having been a valued member of Macclesfield's Conference winning team of 1996-97, Neil was expected to be a key player in the club's first taste of life in the Football League. Unfortunately, despite showing early promise in the pre-season friendlies, the midfielder never came up to expectations and failed to feature in the first team line-up after the early games in August, until a squad shortage let him in for a place in the FA Cup second round game, prior to him leaving for Morecambe in January.

Blackpool (From trainee on 28/11/92) FL 39+28/8 FLC 0+3 FAC 2+1/1 Others 5+1/1
Rochdale (Loaned on 8/12/95) FL 3+1
Macclesfield T (Free on 17/7/96) FL 2+4 FLC 0+2 FAC 1+1

MITCHELL Paul Robert

Born: Nottingham, 8 November 1978
Height: 5'8" Weight: 10.8

Having made his first team debut at Notts County while still a trainee in 1996-97, Paul added to that with two more appearances in 1997-98, this time round as a bright prospect who has developed well from the youth system into a reserve player. Although very confident and comfortable with the ball, and versatile enough to play in both midfield or defence, he was released during the summer.

Notts Co (From trainee on 16/7/97) FL 1+1 Others 1

MITCHELL Paul Robert

Born: Bournemouth, 20 October 1971
Height: 5'9" Weight: 12.0
International Honours: E: Yth; Sch

Having been released by Torquay at the end of 1996-97, Paul was re-signed immediately prior to the start of 1997-98 and took possession of Torquay's number eight shirt,

playing in the opening nine games before losing his place to the newcomer, Kevin Hill. A utility player who could be used in a number of roles in midfield or defence, but had suffered a number of injuries during his stay at Plainmoor, he later joined non-league Barry Town, thus joining up with former United colleague, Lee Barrow.

Bournemouth (From trainee on 7/8/89) FL 6+6 Others 1+1
West Ham U (£40,000 on 6/8/93) PL 0+1
Bournemouth (Free on 28/3/96) FL 2+2
Torquay U (Free on 9/8/96) FL 33+5/1 FLC 4 FAC 0+1 Others 2

MOHAN Nicholas (Nicky)

Born: Middlesbrough, 6 October 1970
Height: 6'1" Weight: 14.0

Having joined Wycombe from Bradford on a month's loan in the second week of last season, he immediately impressed as a big, strong central defender who dominated in the air. Unable to get a game at Valley Parade, he returned to Wycombe in October as a permanent signing, and, apart from eight games, played the rest of the campaign, being a major factor in the team's 18 clean sheets in 1997-98.

Middlesbrough (From juniors on 18/11/87) F/PL 93+6/4 FLC 11 FAC 9+1 Others 11
Hull C (Loaned on 26/9/92) FL 5/1
Leicester C (£330,000 on 7/7/94) PL 23 FLC 2 FAC 1
Bradford C (£225,000 on 13/7/95) FL 83/4 FLC 8 FAC 5 Others 5
Wycombe W (Loaned on 14/8/97) FL 6
Wycombe W (£75,000 on 10/10/97) FL 27 FAC 2 Others 1

Nicky Mohan

MOILANEN Teuvo (Tepi) Johannes

Born: Oulu, Finland, 12 December 1973
Height: 6'5" Weight: 13.12
International Honours: Finland: 1

Started 1997-98 as first-choice goalkeeper for Preston, only missing one game – when

winning his first full cap for Finland in the World Cup qualifier against Norway – until being dropped in January after some inconsistent performances. Returned strongly as Man of the Match at Brentford, after missing seven games, and showed he had returned to his early-season form. Excellent on crosses, and a long kicker, his ground work showed great improvement as the campaign progressed.

Preston NE (£120,000 from FF Jaro on 12/12/95) FL 46 FLC 5 FAC 3 Others 1
Scarborough (Loaned on 12/12/96) FL 4
Darlington (Loaned on 17/1/97) FL 16

MOLBY Jan

Born: Kolding, Jutland, 4 July 1963
Height: 6'1" Weight: 15.10
Club Honours: Div 1 '86, '90; FAC '86, '92; FLC '95
International Honours: Denmark: 67

The Swansea player/manager played his first game of the 1997-98 season at Peterborough on 4 October, but three days later was sacked following a dismal run of results – one win in eight league games. It was a disappointing end for the former Danish international, who had always believed in good football and bringing the youngsters through, but had little cash at his disposal to put things right quickly.

Liverpool (£575,000 from Ajax on 24/8/84) F/PL 195+23/44 FLC 25+3/9 FAC 24+4/4 Others 16+2/4

Barnsley (Loaned on 22/9/95) FL 5
Norwich C (Loaned on 22/12/95) FL 3 FLC 2/1
Swansea C (Free on 22/2/96) FL 39+2/8 FLC 1 Others 1+1

MOLDOVAN Viorel Dinu

Born: Bistrita, Romania, 8 July 1972
Height: 5'9" Weight: 11.4
International Honours: Romania: 28

A striker purchased by Coventry from the Swiss club, Grasshoppers of Zurich, last January, Viorel had already earned a scoring reputation with several goals in Romania's World Cup qualifying games and two prolific seasons in Switzerland. In his fourth substitute appearance, he scored the winning goal at Villa Park in the FA Cup, and followed up with a goal at Palace ten days later. Struggled, however, in the FA Cup ties with Sheffield United and missed a glorious chance in the replay before limping off. His arrival coincided with the upturn in form, even though he was not selected, and many fans argued that it created sufficient pressure to spark City's other strikers into better form. *Stop Press:* Had an excellent World Cup during the summer, scoring twice in four games, including the first in a 2-1 win over England, and generally impressing before Romania went out of the competition, beaten by Croatia.

Coventry C (£3,250,000 from Grasshoppers on 9/1/98) PL 5+5/1 FAC 2+2/1

Viorel Moldovan

MOLENAAR Robert

Born: Zaandam, Holland, 27 February 1969
Height: 6'2" Weight: 14.4

Signed the previous season from the Dutch Premier League, this strong, powerful Leeds' defender immediately found himself an Elland Road favourite, being christened the "terminator". Robert began last season in the first team picture, and scored in successive away wins – a rasping volley at Blackburn, and a powerful header at Southampton. Unfortunately, he began to incur the wrath of referees and was omitted from the first team at the end of September until December, where, on his return, he produced a superb performance in the 2-0 victory over Bolton. He appeared then to have adapted fully to the demands of the Premiership and deservedly remained in the first team picture. Very powerful in the air, he is a menace to opposing defences at the set piece.

Leeds U (£1,000,000 from FC Volendam on 11/1/97) PL 30+4/3 FLC 2+1 FAC 5/1

MONCRIEFFE Prince

Born: Jamaica, 27 February 1977
Height: 5'10" Weight: 11.0

Signed from Hyde during the summer of 1997, Prince ended his first season at Doncaster in 1997-98 as the club's leading goalscorer in the league, although his final total of eight was modest. Towards the end of the campaign, he moved from his usual position of central striker to full back with a degree of success, and, still very much a raw talent, he could go on to better things with the right guidance.

Doncaster Rov (Free from Hyde U on 18/7/97) FL 30+8/8 FLC 2 FAC 1 Others 1

MONCUR John Frederick

Born: Stepney, 22 September 1966
Height: 5'7" Weight: 9.10

Despite being unlucky with calf and groin injuries at West Ham in 1997-98, John still did a good job when called upon, and his battling qualities were prominent in outstanding displays at both Coventry and Bolton, which earned valuable points. A talented midfielder with excellent passing skills, he can never get enough of the ball and always makes himself available by finding space for himself. Although used mainly as a starter, he came off the bench four times, scoring in the 6-0 win over Barnsley on one such occasion. Is a player you can rely on.

Tottenham H (From apprentice on 22/8/84) FL 10+11/1 FLC 1+2
Doncaster Rov (Loaned on 25/9/86) FL 4
Cambridge U (Loaned on 27/3/87) FL 3+1
Portsmouth (Loaned on 22/3/89) FL 7
Brentford (Loaned on 19/10/89) FL 5/1 Others 1
Ipswich T (Loaned on 24/10/91) FL 5+1
Swindon T (£80,000 on 30/3/92) F/PL 53+5/5 FLC 4 FAC 1 Others 4/1
West Ham U (£900,000 on 24/6/94) PL 92+5/5 FLC 11/2 FAC 6+1/1

MONINGTON Mark David

Born: Bilsthorpe, 21 October 1970
Height: 6'1" Weight: 14.0
Club Honours: AMC '96

The Rotherham central defender was injured in the first game of last season and did not play again until January. A strong tackler, and good in the air, Mark was sent up front on a few occasions when the team were chasing the game and came up with a last-minute winner against Leyton Orient. In the last few weeks of the campaign, however, he had to battle for a place, but always gave maximum effort, before being released in the summer.

Burnley (From juniors on 23/3/89) FL 65+19/5 FLC 5 FAC 4+1/1 Others 4+2
Rotherham U (Signed on 28/11/94) FL 75+4/3 FLC 3 FAC 1 Others 4

MONKOU Kenneth (Ken) John
Born: Surinam, 29 November 1964
Height: 6'3" Weight: 14.4
Club Honours: FMC '90
International Honours: Holland: U21

Having had a disappointing 1996-97 season, the Southampton player re-established himself at the heart of Saints' defence in 1997-98, again proving to be very strong in the air and on the ground. Also very dangerous in front of goal, he scored twice and had a hand in a number of other goals, his excellent form being a major factor in Southampton's improved league position. His partnership with Claus Lundekvam also went from strength to strength and, for a big defender, he shows good skill on the ground, where he is quite capable of hitting quality long balls behind opposing defences.

Chelsea (£100,000 from Feyenoord on 2/3/89) FL 92+2/2 FLC 12 FAC 3 Others 10
Southampton (£750,000 on 21/8/92) PL 168+8/9 FLC 18+1/2 FAC 14/1

MOODY Paul
Born: Portsmouth, 13 June 1967
Height: 6'3" Weight: 14.9

One of the success stories of Fulham's 1997-98 season, Paul was, for three months, Fulham's record signing, having arrived from Oxford during the summer and, despite missing several games through injury, was top scorer with 16 goals. His aerial ability brought about other goals, which included a hat trick in a 4-1 win at Luton in January, and his wholehearted approach to the game often caused panic in opposition defences. It was unfortunate that the only blemish on his record was the sending off for a late challenge, after only 36 minutes, in the first leg of the play off against Grimsby.

Southampton (£50,000 from Waterlooville on 15/7/91) F/PL 7+5 FLC 1 FAC 0+1
Reading (Loaned on 9/12/92) FL 5/1 Others 1
Oxford U (£60,000 on 19/2/94) FL 98+38/49 FLC 10+4/4 FAC 7+1/5 Others 3/3
Fulham (£200,000 on 4/7/97) FL 27+6/15 FLC 2+1 FAC 1+1 Others 2/1

Ken Monkou

Paul Moody

Tommy Mooney

MOONEY Thomas (Tommy) John
Born: Middlesbrough, 11 August 1971
Height: 5'11" Weight: 12.6
Club Honours: Div 2 '98

Probably the first name to be written on the Watford team sheet in 1997-98, both because of his dauntless attitude and his willingness and ability to appear anywhere on the left-hand side of the pitch. Tommy started the season in central defence, despite being the previous season's leading scorer, but was frequently deployed further upfield and contributed his usual quota of goals, including an important last-gasp winner against Bristol Rovers. In appearing in all but one league game, he was delighted to pick up his first medal as a professional, as the Hornets stormed to the second division title.

Aston Villa (From trainee on 23/11/89)
Scarborough (Free on 1/8/90) FL 96+11/30 FLC 11+2/8 FAC 3 Others 6/2
Southend U (£100,000 on 12/7/93) FL 9+5/5 FLC 1+1 Others 2+3
Watford (Signed on 17/3/94) FL 155+8/30 FLC 15/1 FAC 10+1/1 Others 1

MOORE Alan
Born: Dublin, 25 November 1974
Height: 5'10" Weight: 11.4
Club Honours: Div 1 '95
International Honours: Ei: 8; U21-4; Yth; Sch

The speedy Middlesbrough winger started brightly enough in 1997-98, before his early promise faded when injuries forced prolonged absences from first team duty, his last appearance being at the end of September. Mainly left sided, Alan can provide pure magic on his day as a quick-witted flankman who not only enjoys running at defences to deliver super crosses, but one who is armed with the ability to score from all kinds of angles himself. Continues to add to his Republic of Ireland caps, and if he can put in a run of games together he could do well in the Premiership.

Middlesbrough (From trainee on 5/12/91) F/PL 95+19/14 FLC 8+6/1 FAC 3+2/2 Others 3+1

MOORE Darren Mark
Born: Birmingham, 22 April 1974
Height: 6'2" Weight: 15.6

Signed from Doncaster during the 1997 summer recess, the fee being settled by a tribunal, "Bruno" proved to be a powerfully-built centre half who was impressive in the air, awesome in the tackle, and a frightening opponent for any attacker. Unfortunate to miss over five months of last season, due to hamstring and groin injuries, he first came into the Bradford side following the injury to John Dreyer and quickly became a crowd favourite. If fit, he will undoubtedly be a regular this coming term, although, at the time of going to press, it is unclear as to who his defensive partner might be.

Torquay U (From trainee on 18/11/92) FL 102+1/8 FLC 6 FAC 7/2 Others 8/2
Doncaster Rov (£62,500 on 19/7/95) FL 76/7 FLC 4 FAC 1 Others 3/1
Bradford C (£310,000+ on 18/6/97) FL 18

MOORE Ian Ronald
Born: Birkenhead, 26 August 1976
Height: 5'11" Weight: 12.0
International Honours: E: U21-7; Yth

Unable to establish himself at Nottingham Forest in 1997-98, the son of a former footballer, Ronnie, who is probably best remembered for playing over 300 games for Tranmere, was used more in a substitute role for the club, with Pierre van Hooijdonk and Kevin Campbell proving unassailable as the front two. He was also loaned out to West Ham at the end of September, but made only one appearance from the bench before returning to the City Ground. However, the young striker did score a vital goal at Stoke in the league, his looping 87th-minute header bringing about a 1-1 draw, and keeping the club in touch with Middlesbrough at the top of the first division. Good in the air and on the ground, he will be looking for first team football in 1998-99.

Tranmere Rov (From trainee on 6/7/94) FL 41+17/12 FLC 3+2/1 FAC 1+1 Others 0+1
Bradford C (Loaned on 13/9/96) FL 6
Nottingham F (£1,000,000 on 15/3/97) F/PL 3+12/1 FLC 0+2 FAC 1
West Ham U (Loaned on 26/9/97) PL 0+1

MOORE Mark Steven
Born: Bradford, 9 July 1972
Height: 5'11" Weight: 13.0

Despite being born in England, Mark arrived at Cambridge on a non-contract basis last March following trials with Ipswich, via South Africa, and then New Hampshire College in America, where he had been spotted by former United favourite, Graham Smith. A 25-year-old midfielder, who is equally proficient in a sweeper role, he made his debut when coming off the bench for the last three minutes in a 4-1 win over Swansea at the Abbey, and was hoping that he had done enough to impress the United management.

Cambridge U (Free from New Hampshire College on 19/3/98) FL 0+1

MOORE Neil
Born: Liverpool, 21 September 1972
Height: 6'1" Weight: 12.9

Freed by Norwich during the 1997 close season, Neil was one of the few real successes of Burnley's campaign. As a centre back of the thoughtful and cultured variety, his consistency made him almost ever present after arriving initially on trial. As well as his cool interceptions and quick thinking at the back, he was a useful man up front from set pieces, most notably with the header that provided the Clarets' last-minute winner at Preston.

Everton (From trainee on 4/6/91) PL 4+1 FLC 0+1
Blackpool (Loaned on 9/9/94) FL 7 Others 1
Oldham Ath (Loaned on 16/2/95) FL 5
Carlisle U (Loaned on 25/8/95) FL 13 Others 2
Rotherham U (Loaned on 20/3/96) FL 10+1
Norwich C (Free on 8/1/97) FL 2
Burnley (Free on 29/8/97) FL 38+2/3 FLC 2 FAC 2/1 Others 4

MORALEE Jamie David
Born: Wandsworth, 2 December 1971
Height: 5'11" Weight: 11.0

A talented striker who is comfortable on the ball, and who takes up good positions, Jamie has never been able to recapture his early promise during his time at Crewe, due to continually missing games through injury. Again, in 1997-98, he was subjected to the same problems, managing just four starts and seven subs' appearances before being released at the end of the season, and it is difficult to see where he goes from here.

Crystal Palace (From trainee on 3/7/90) FL 2+4
Millwall (Free on 3/9/92) FL 56+11/19 FLC 3+1/1 FAC 1 Others 3+1
Watford (£450,000 on 13/7/94) FL 40+9/7 FLC 6+1 FAC 5
Crewe Alex (Free on 8/8/96) FL 10+6 FLC 1+1 FAC 2

MOREIRA Fabio da Silva
Born: Brazil, 14 March 1972
Height: 5'10" Weight: 11.6
A talented Brazilian midfielder in his own right, despite happening to be Emerson's brother in law, Fabio arrived at Middlesbrough from Chavez in February 1997, and was not called upon for first team duty until last October, when he started the Huddersfield match at the Cellnet. Flashy, with flicks and tricks, but not relishing the tackling side of the game, he was not used again and left the club before the season's end.

Middlesbrough (Free from Chavez on 24/2/97) FL 1

MOREIRA Joao Manuel Silva
Born: Angola, 30 June 1970
Height: 6'2" Weight: 14.0
Although starting 1997-98 in the first team at Swansea, the strong, left-sided defender, with attacking tendencies, soon gave way to others following a change of management, and after just seven games was given a free transfer by Alan Cork at the end of March.

Swansea C (£50,000 from Benfica on 3/7/96) FL 15 FLC 2+1 FAC 2 Others 5

MORENO Jaime (Jamie) Morales
Born: Bolivia, 19 January 1974
Height: 5'10" Weight: 11.9
Club Honours: Div 1 '95
International Honours: Bolivia: 55
A skilful Bolivian forward with superb ball control, Jamie returned to Middlesbrough last December for his second spell as a loan signing from his current club, Washington United, for the duration of their mid-season recess in 1997. He came back looking fitter and sharper than previously, and his seven appearances produced one goal, that allowed Boro to claim three points in the away game at Stoke, before he returned to Washington for the resumption of their season.

Middlesbrough (£250,000 from Blooming on 20/9/94) P/FL 8+13/1 FLC 3 FAC 0+1 Others 3/1 (£100,000 to Washington UDC on 11/8/96)
Middlesbrough (Loaned on 1/12/97) FL 1+4/1 FAC 2

MORGAN Alan Meredith
Born: Aberystwyth, 2 November 1973
Height: 5'10" Weight: 11.4
International Honours: W: U21-2; Yth; Sch

Enjoyed a better season than last for Tranmere in 1997-98, but must have been disappointed not to have enjoyed a more extended first team run. A versatile performer, he continued to turn in many solid displays for the Pontins' League side and, with the possible exception of goalkeeper, he can operate effectively on his day in all the outfield positions. If he can only steer clear of injury, Alan will hope for a better and more consistent campaign this time round.

Tranmere Rov (From trainee on 8/5/92) FL 14+10/1 FLC 0+2 FAC 2

MORGAN Christopher (Chris) Paul
Born: Barnsley, 13 February 1978
Height: 5'10" Weight: 11.11
The latest in a long line of Barnsley players to come from the juniors, Chris forced his way into the team last season after being the captain of the reserves, immediately endearing himself to the crowd with his never-say-die performances. An aggressive competitor, who settled into the Premier League instantly, as a combative centre back, once he settles to the pace of the game he has what it takes to go to the very top.

Barnsley (From trainee on 3/7/96) PL 10+1 FAC 3

MORGAN Simon Charles
Born: Birmingham, 5 September 1966
Height: 5'10" Weight: 12.5
International Honours: E: U21-2
After leading Fulham to promotion in 1996-97 (and writing a best-selling book about it!), last season was a bitter disappointment to their inspirational skipper. The newly arrived Paul Bracewell was given the captaincy at a time when Simon missed a couple of matches with a minor injury, before he picked up a major one in November and was out of action for several months. That he came back to do a superb job in central defence in both play-off legs was a great credit to him and, whether in midfield, or at the back, he always gave 100 per cent.

Leicester C (From apprentice on 15/11/84) FL 147+13/3 FLC 14/1 FAC 4+1 Others 3
Fulham (£100,000 on 12/10/90) FL 285+5/43 FLC 23/1 FAC 14/1 Others 17/4

MORGAN Stephen (Steve) Alphonso
Born: Oldham, 19 September 1968
Height: 5'11" Weight: 12.0
Club Honours: Div 3 '97
A well-built hard-tackling Wigan Athletic left back, who can play in central midfield when required, Steve spent two early months of last season on loan at Bury, as a replacement for David Pugh, but returned to the club following an achilles injury. He came back to first team action in the third round FA Cup tie against Blackburn Rovers and scored his only goal in the 1-1 home draw against Northampton, before losing his place towards the end of the campaign.

Blackpool (From apprentice on 12/8/86) FL 135+9/10 FLC 13/2 FAC 16/1 Others 10+1/1
Plymouth Arg (£115,000 on 16/7/90) FL 120+1/6 FLC 7 FAC 6 Others 5
Coventry C (£110,000 on 14/7/93) PL 65+3/2 FLC 5/3 FAC 5

Bristol Rov (Loaned on 1/3/96) FL 5 Others 2
Wigan Ath (Free on 10/7/96) FL 31+5/2 FLC 2 FAC 1 Others 4
Bury (Loaned on 26/9/97) FL 5

MORLEY Benjamin (Ben)
Born: Hull, 22 December 1980
Height: 5'9" Weight: 10.1
The first-year trainee stormed on to the Boothferry scene when making his senior debut for Hull City last December in the AWS win against Scarborough. A regular in the league squad in the New Year, when he was also a leading member of the club's successful FA Youth Cup team, Ben was usually employed as a right-wing back, displaying the energy to get up and down to put in a telling cross.

Hull C (Trainee) FL 5+3 Others 1

MORLEY David Thomas
Born: St Helens, 25 September 1977
Height: 6'2" Weight: 12.7
Having been in the wings as a professional at Manchester City since early 1996, David finally made his debut at Bury last September and celebrated by scoring the equaliser with a fine header. Then, apart from a couple of subs' appearances in November, it was back to the reserves for the tall young midfielder, followed by a period on loan with Ayr United in Scotland. Reckoned to be a very good young central player with a fine career ahead of him, he is expected to be challenging for a regular first team place before too long.

Manchester C (From trainee on 3/1/96) FL 1+2/1
Ayr U (Loaned on 14/3/98) SL 4

MORLEY Trevor William
Born: Nottingham, 20 March 1961
Height: 5'11" Weight: 12.1
Club Honours: Div 4 '87
International Honours: E: SP-6
The distinguished career in English football of the veteran striker came to an end at Reading in 1997-98 after three seasons with the Elm Park club, with the news that he was moving to Norway where his wife was born, and will play his future football in that country. Age and a succession of serious injuries finally caught up with the brave front player, who still managed a respectable return of nine goals from 24 starts. His best form came in cup games, as he netted in the surprise 3-2 Coca Cola Cup win at Leeds, in both FA Cup games against Cheltenham, and also in normal time as well as in the penalty shoot out against Cardiff City.

Northampton T (£20,000 from Nuneaton Borough on 21/6/85) FL 107+1/39 FLC 10/4 FAC 6/2 Others 7
Manchester C (£175,000 on 22/1/88) FL 69+3/18 FLC 7/3 FAC 1 Others 2
West Ham U (£500,000 on 28/12/89) F/PL 159+19/57 FLC 10+1/5 FAC 14+5/7 Others 5+1/1 (Free to Brann Bergen on 17/5/95)
Reading (Free on 1/8/95) FL 67+10/31 FLC 5/2 FAC 9/5

MORRIS Andrew (Andy) Dean
Born: Sheffield, 17 November 1967
Height: 6'4" Weight: 15.12
A powerfully built, hard-running forward, who can create panic in opposition penalty areas with flick ons and sheer bulk, Andy

suffered a wretched testimonial season in 1997-98, that saw his opportunities restricted by two operations on his left knee, and was released during the summer. The big man, known as "Bruno", richly deserved his benefit year, which is set to culminate with a testimonial match this August, but his enforced lay off has allowed him to dabble in the media world, with a weekly column in a local newspaper.

Rotherham U (From juniors on 29/7/85) FL 0+7 FLC 0+1
Chesterfield (Signed on 12/1/88) FL 225+40/56 FLC 15+2/8 FAC 15+2/4 Others 18+4/3
Exeter C (Loaned on 4/3/92) FL 4+3/2

MORRIS Jody

Born: Hammersmith, 22 December 1978
Height: 5'5" Weight: 9.7
Club Honours: ECWC '98
International Honours: E: U21-3; Yth; Sch

This highly promising Chelsea midfielder's career has been interrupted by a long-standing ankle injury, which restricted him to just 12 starts in 1997-98, although one of these came at Wembley in the Charity Shield against Manchester United, a great thrill for a young player of just 18. The third of these matches, a fourth round Coca Cola Cup tie against Southampton, saw Jody dramatically snatch an extra-time winner when he spectacularly curled home from 20 yards after 117 minutes. He then underwent surgery in an attempt to cure his ankle problem, before coming back for a run in the first team towards the end of the season, to give an impressive performance in the European Cup Winners' Cup semi final, second leg against Vicenza. Scored his first league goal in the final match against Bolton, which extinguished Wanderers' flickering survival hopes. A level-headed, mature young man, he made a favourable impression on the Channel 4 "Fly-on-the-Wall" documentary, featuring the Chelsea youth squad, and is clearly a player with a bright future.

Chelsea (From trainee on 8/1/96) PL 15+10/1 FLC 3/2 Others 2+1

MORRIS Lee

Born: Blackpool, 30 April 1980
Height: 5'10" Weight: 11.2
International Honours: E: Yth

The son of Sheffield United's former winger, Colin, who played nearly 250 league games during the 1980's, Lee followed his dad to Bramall Lane as a schoolboy and graduated through the ranks to turn professional at the end of 1997. Made his debut shortly afterwards, when coming off the bench at home to Wolves, and was given a further seven subs' appearances before the season was over. Used to give the side pace and width up front, the youngster also played for the England youth side and looks certain to be one for the future.

Sheffield U (From trainee on 24/12/97) FL 0+5 FAC 0+2 Others 0+1

MORRIS Mark John

Born: Carshalton, 26 September 1962
Height: 6'2" Weight: 14.2
Club Honours: Div 4 '83

Brighton's much-travelled central defender clocked up his 500th Football League appearance in the 2-1 win over Rochdale at Gillingham last September, the Seagull's first win of the season at the eleventh attempt. Bagged the first goal in the crucial victory, but was surprisingly one of five senior players transfer listed in November. His contract was paid up just before Christmas and he moved along the Sussex coast to Dr Martens Premier side, Hastings Town.

Wimbledon (From apprentice on 26/9/80) FL 167+1/9 FLC 11 FAC 11 Others 1+1
Aldershot (Loaned on 5/9/85) FL 14 FAC 1
Watford (£35,000 on 21/7/87) FL 41/1 FLC 5/1 FAC 7
Sheffield U (£175,000 on 11/7/89) FL 53+3/3 FLC 5 FAC 5 Others 2
Bournemouth (£100,000 on 31/7/91) FL 190+4/8 FLC 15/2 FAC 17/1 Others 9
Gillingham (Loaned on 23/9/96) FL 6 FLC 2
Brighton & Hove A (Free on 31/10/96) FL 30+1/2 FLC 2 FAC 2

MORRISON Andrew (Andy) Charles

Born: Inverness, 30 July 1970
Height: 6'1" Weight: 13.10

Just when Huddersfield supporters were seeing the best out of the commanding defender and captain, injury struck again when the influential Scot, playing solidly at centre back, required surgery after limping off from an FA Cup tie against the Premiership side, Wimbledon. Up to then, Andy had made the number five shirt his own berth, missing only a handful of games through suspensions and minor injuries, and had been on the verge of a call up to the Scotland "B" squad. Resolute tackling and 100 per-cent commitment are his forte.

Plymouth Arg (From trainee on 6/7/88) FL 105+8/6 FLC 10+1/1 FAC 6 Others 2+1
Blackburn Rov (£500,000 on 5/8/93) PL 1+4 FAC 1
Blackpool (£245,000 on 9/12/94) FL 47/3 FAC 2 Others 4
Huddersfield T (£500,000 on 4/7/96) FL 31+2/2 FLC 5 FAC 2

MORRISON Clinton Hubert

Born: Wandsworth, 4 May 1979
Height: 5'10" Weight: 10.0

With Crystal Palace on their way back to the first division, Clinton, a former trainee who had scored many goals in the youth and reserve teams alongside Leon McKenzie, was given an early opportunity as a sub in the last game of 1997-98. The young striker certainly took advantage. In coming on for the last eight minutes, he scored the only goal of the match in the 90th minute of the game, being in the right place at the right time to convert. An exciting prospect, he has good first touch, holds the ball up well, and has good pace, especially when twisting and turning around the area to lose his marker.

Crystal Palace (From trainee on 29/3/97) PL 0+1/1

MORRISON David (Dave) Ellis

Born: Waltham Forest, 30 November 1974
Height: 5'11" Weight: 12.10

An excellent crosser with both feet, and a player who likes taking defenders on, Dave

started Leyton Orient's first game of last season before being carried off after five minutes with a cruciate knee ligament injury, which ruled him out for the rest of the season. Hopefully, the likeable left winger will return back to his best in time for the beginning of the new campaign.

Peterborough U (£30,000 from Chelmsford C on 12/5/94) FL 59+18/12 FLC 4+1/1 FAC 5+3 Others 6+2
Leyton Orient (£25,000 on 21/3/97) FL 9+1

MORRISSEY John Joseph

Born: Liverpool, 8 March 1965
Height: 5'8" Weight: 11.9
International Honours: E: Yth

As Tranmere's longest serving player, and granted a testimonial in the forthcoming season, John may be considered something of a veteran, but his skill and division have barely diminished. Has made more first team appearances as a winger than any other player in Rovers' history, and there are few, if any, better old-fashioned wingmen in the first division, it being exhilarating to see him take on a defender and pass him, and then send in an accurate cross. Able to give the side real width, and invaluable when someone is needed to hold the ball in a tight situation, he is the son of the former Everton star of the 1960s, John (senior). Always supplies a few memorable goals himself each season.*

Everton (From apprentice on 10/3/83) FL 1 Others 0+1
Wolverhampton W (Free on 2/8/85) FL 5+5/1 FLC 1
Tranmere Rov (£8,000 on 2/10/85) FL 391+55/50 FLC 38+2/2 FAC 28+2/5 Others 39+3/6

MORROW Stephen (Steve) Joseph

Born: Belfast, 2 July 1970
Height: 6'0" Weight: 11.6
Club Honours: FAYC '88; FLC '93; ECEC '94
International Honours: NI: 32; B-1; U23-2; Yth; Sch

Began last season at the heart of Queens Park Rangers' defence, before losing his place when the management team of Stewart Houston and Bruce Rioch left the club. However, having returned to the side in mid-January, he scored his only goal of the campaign, an important last-minute equaliser in the 2-2 draw at Sheffield United. A Northern Ireland international, playing five games in 1997-98, Steve has an assured left foot that can link defence with attack with a single, accurate pass.

Arsenal (From trainee on 5/5/88) F/PL 39+23/1 FLC 7+4/2 FAC 5+2 Others 1+4
Reading (Loaned on 16/1/91) FL 10
Watford (Loaned on 14/8/91) FL 7+1 Others 1
Reading (Loaned on 30/10/91) FL 3
Barnet (Loaned on 4/3/92) FL 1
Queens Park R (£1,000,000 on 27/3/97) FL 36/3 FLC 2 FAC 1

MORTIMER Paul Henry

Born: Kensington, 8 May 1968
Height: 5'11" Weight: 12.7
International Honours: E: U21-2

A gifted left-sided Charlton midfield player, Paul missed most of last season with a persistent hamstring injury. Comfortable on

the ball, with good vision, he can pass with pin-point accuracy and, when on song, there are few to match him in the entire league. Has the ability to go past players and score spectacular goals, which he did on four occasions last season, and is a real asset to the club if he can stay free from injury.*

Charlton Ath (Free from Farnborough T on 22/9/87) FL 108+5/17 FLC 4+1 FAC 8 Others 3+1
Aston Villa (£350,000 on 24/7/91) FL 10+2/1 FLC 2
Crystal Palace (£500,000 on 18/10/91) F/PL 18+4/2 FLC 1 FAC 1 Others 3
Brentford (Loaned on 22/1/93) FL 6 Others 2
Charlton Ath (£200,000 on 5/7/94) FL 57+12/14 FLC 2 FAC 3/1 Others 0+1

MOSES Adrian Paul
Born: Doncaster, 4 May 1975
Height: 5'10" Weight: 12.8
International Honours: E: U21-2

Although one of Barnsley's most improved players throughout last season, he took some time to settle in at the top level, but once this was achieved he became a mainstay at the heart of the Reds' defence. A good tackler, and one of their quickest players, it was because of this that he was used as a man marker on a number of occasions. Was the star defender in the club's 1-0 win at Aston Villa, and also gave excellent displays at Liverpool and Manchester United, in the FA Cup, all matches where Barnsley got a result when the odds were heavily stacked against them. Also added to his solitary England U21 cap with an appearance against Greece.
Barnsley (From juniors on 2/7/93) F/PL 81+10/3 FLC 4 FAC 10

MOSS Neil Graham
Born: New Milton, 10 May 1975
Height: 6'2" Weight: 13.10

A still promising Southampton goalkeeper, who established himself as the number two to Paul Jones after the departure of Maik Taylor to Fulham, he started 1997-98 on loan at Gillingham, appearing in the first 12 games before giving way to Jim Stannard and returning to the Dell. Although the form of the ever-present Jones prevented him from appearing at senior level last season, his retention by the manager shows he is confident that Neil will be a more than adequate deputy when called upon.
Bournemouth (From trainee on 29/1/93) FL 21+1 FLC 1 FAC 3+1 Others 2
Southampton (£250,000 on 20/12/95) PL 3 FLC 2
Gillingham (Loaned on 8/8/97) FL 10 FLC 2

MOUNTFIELD Derek Neal
Born: Liverpool, 2 November 1962
Height: 6'1" Weight: 13.6
Club Honours: FAC '84; CS '84, '85; Div 1 '85, '87, Div 3 '95; ECWC '85
International Honours: E: B-1; U21-1

Re-signed for Walsall during the summer, after being initially released at the end of the previous season, Derek soon made his presence felt with a late equaliser against Fulham in the opening home league game of 1997-98. Though he felt the pace at times, he played in more than half the league programme and did a fine marshalling job in defence, before being again released by new manager, Ray Graydon, in May.

Tranmere Rov (From apprentice on 4/11/80) FL 26/1 FLC 2 FAC 1
Everton (£30,000 on 2/6/82) FL 100+6/19 FLC 16/3 FAC 17/2 Others 14+1/1
Aston Villa (£450,000 on 6/6/88) FL 88+2/9 FLC 13/2 FAC 6/1 Others 11/5
Wolverhampton W (£150,000 on 7/11/91) FL 79+4/4 FLC 4/1 FAC 2 Others 2
Carlisle U (Free on 3/8/94) FL 30+1/3 FLC 4+1 FAC 4/1 Others 6/1
Northampton T (Free on 6/10/95) FL 4
Walsall (Free on 6/11/95) FL 96+1/2 FLC 8 FAC 9+1 Others 4

MOWBRAY Anthony (Tony) Mark
Born: Saltburn, 22 November 1963
Height: 6'1" Weight: 13.2
International Honours: E: B-2

As in 1996-97, Tony's season in 1997-98 was interrupted by his troublesome groin problem, which flared up a couple of times and caused him to miss the run in. Earlier, however, the resurgence in form of the team after Christmas coincided with his return to the side, and his captaincy inspired those around him, his mastery in the air there for all to see. And, although lacking in pace, he more than compensates by his anticipation and positional play. Underwent an operation on his groin injury in the close season and has been offered a new contract, subject to a clean bill of health.*
Middlesbrough (From apprentice on 27/11/81) FL 345+3/25 FLC 28+2/2 FAC 23/1 Others 23+1/1
Glasgow Celtic (£1,000,000 on 8/11/91) SL 75+3/6 SLC 7 SC 5 Others 6
Ipswich T (£300,000 on 6/10/95) FL 50+2/2 FLC 5/1 FAC 6 Others 3/1

MOYES David William
Born: Glasgow, 25 April 1963
Height: 6'1" Weight: 12.12
Club Honours: SPL '82; AMC '86; Div 3 '96
International Honours: S: Yth; Sch

Started last season as assistant manager to Gary Peters at Preston, before taking on the full manager's position himself in January. Before then, he had continued to show his experience in the centre of defence, when younger players were left out through lack of form or confidence, and let no-one down, reaching 400 FL games at Grimsby over the Christmas period. Continued to play in the reserves, but made only one more first team start after becoming manager, and had the dubious distinction of being booked whilst a non-playing substitute at Northampton.
Glasgow Celtic (From juniors in 1980) SL 19+5 SLC 7+1 Others 2+1
Cambridge U (Free on 28/10/83) FL 79/1 FLC 3 FAC 1 Others 3
Bristol C (£10,000 on 10/10/85) FL 83/6 FLC 6 FAC 5 Others 15
Shrewsbury T (£30,000 on 30/10/87) FL 91+5/11 FLC 4 FAC 3/1 Others 5
Dunfermline Ath (Signed on 1/8/90) SL 105/13 SLC 17/1 SC 5
Hamilton Academical (£42,500 on 27/8/93) SL 5
Preston NE (Free on 20/9/93) FL 142+1/15 FLC 5/1 FAC 11+1/2 Others 13+1/1

MUGGLETON Carl David
Born: Leicester, 13 September 1968
Height: 6'2" Weight: 13.4
International Honours: E: U21-1

Started last season well at Stoke, reinforcing his qualities as an excellent shot-stopper. His ability to deal with crosses also looked much improved, but defensive problems as the side slipped down division one affected his confidence and he lost his place to Neville Southall, prior to an injury to his right thumb in training in March ending his season early.
Leicester C (From apprentice on 17/9/86) FL 46 FAC 3 Others 5
Chesterfield (Loaned on 10/9/87) FL 17 Others 2
Blackpool (Loaned on 1/2/88) FL 2
Hartlepool U (Loaned on 28/10/88) FL 8 Others 2
Stockport Co (Loaned on 1/3/90) FL 4
Stoke C (Loaned on 13/8/93) FL 6 FLC 1 Others 2
Glasgow Celtic (£150,000 on 11/1/94) SL 12 SC 1
Stoke C (£150,000 on 21/7/94) FL 97 FLC 12 FAC 1 Others 4
Rotherham U (Loaned on 1/11/95) FL 6 Others 1
Sheffield U (Loaned on 28/3/96) FL 0+1

MULLIN John
Born: Bury, 11 August 1975
Height: 6'0" Weight: 11.10

The powerful Sunderland striker endured a frustrating season at the Stadium of Light in 1997-98, finding himself well down the forward pecking order and, in an effort to keep match fit, had loan spells at Preston (February) and Burnley (March). Unfortunately, in trying to improve North End's poor scoring rate, his pace and strength in the air was not fully exploited by his team mates, despite creating some good opportunities, while at Burnley he looked more like the finished article than during his first period at the club. Playing just behind the two Andys, Cooke and Payton, he proved to be an effective supply line for his fellow strikers. However, his time at Turf Moor was ended prematurely, following a dismissal against Blackpool.
Burnley (From trainee on 18/8/92) FL 7+11/2 FAC 2
Sunderland (£40,000+ on 12/8/95) P/FL 15+11/2 FLC 1 FAC 2+1
Preston NE (Loaned on 13/2/98) FL 4+3 Others 1
Burnley (Loaned on 26/3/98) FL 6

MULRYNE Phillip Patrick
Born: Belfast, 1 January 1978
Height: 5'8" Weight: 10.11
Club Honours: FAYC '95
International Honours: NI: 5; B-1; U21-3

A young Manchester United forward with excellent all-round skills, Philip made a promising start to his senior career at Old Trafford with an excellent performance against Ipswich in the Coca Cola Cup last October. Later, Alex Ferguson said of him, "Mulryne did very well for us. He always wanted the ball, and that's a very good habit." Already a full international with Northern Ireland, playing twice in 1997-98 as well as making his debut for the "B" side, the future looks exceedingly bright for yet another of "Fergie's Fledglings".
Manchester U (From trainee on 17/3/95) PL 1 FLC 1 FAC 0+1

MUNROE Karl Augustus
Born: Manchester, 23 September 1979
Height: 6'0" Weight: 10.11

Still a trainee, the young defender was

considered promising enough to warrant a run out in the last game of 1997-98 and came off the bench for the final 26 minutes at Mansfield. Karl is yet another of a good band of juniors to have been offered a professional contract on completion of his YTS period.

Swansea C (Trainee) FL 0+1

MUNTASSER Jehad
Born: Libya, 26 July 1978
Height: 5'10" Weight: 9.12

Although born in Libya, Jehad learnt his football in Italy where he grew up, and was brought to England by Arsenal during the 1997 close season, having been seen playing for the little-known Pro Seslo side. Showing a fair bit of promise in the reserves, he was introduced in mid-October against Birmingham in the Coca Cola Cup at Highbury, when coming off the bench in the 29th minute of extra time. He was then surprisingly freed and joined Bristol City in January. Yet to make an appearance for the Robins, the club hold high hopes for him, that is if he can build himself up. Able to play in midfield or up front, both wide and through the middle, he has excellent first touch, great awareness, two good feet, balance, and can feint and dribble like all continentals. Watch this space....

Arsenal (Signed from Pro Seslo on 9/7/97) FLC 0+1
Bristol C (Free on 30/1/98)

MURDOCK Colin James
Born: Ballymena, 2 July 1975
Height: 6'3" Weight: 13.0
International Honours: NI: B-3; Yth; Sch

The young Northern Ireland "B" international centre half joined Preston during the summer of 1997 – one of a trio of Manchester United players to do so – and developed over the season into a useful left-sided defender. His partnership with Michael Jackson blossomed towards the end of the campaign, and he obviously benefited from regular first team football. With this experience behind him, he is expected to play an integral part in Preston's defence for several years to come.

Manchester U (From juniors on 21/7/92)
Preston NE (£100,000 on 23/5/97) FL 27/1 FLC 2 FAC 1+1 Others 2

MURPHY Daniel (Danny) Benjamin
Born: Chester, 18 March 1977
Height: 5'9" Weight: 10.8
International Honours: E: U21-2; Yth; Sch

It took some time for the Liverpool manager, Roy Evans, to pick this bargain up from Crewe, but, after signing him in the 1997 close season, the lad eventually gained a reasonably regular place in 1997-98, and his worth to the team proved to be immense, despite his lack of goals. Fast, fierce, and highly competitive for a small player, Danny's greatest asset, apart from his large heart, is creativity, something that had been missing from the side during the absence of Jamie Redknapp. Looked confident and sharp when in the team and Jan Molby

described him as the club's best passer of the ball over 15 or 20 yards. His ideal position at present is in central midfield, but do not be surprised if he moves on to an attacking partnership alongside Michael Owen in the future. Added to his international honours when capped twice by England at U21 level last season, against Moldova and Greece.

Crewe Alex (From trainee on 21/3/94) FL 110+24/27 FLC 7 FAC 7/4 Others 15+3/3
Liverpool (£1,500,000+ on 17/7/97) PL 6+10 FAC 0+1

MURPHY John James
Born: Whiston, 18 October 1976
Height: 6'1" Weight: 14.0

A tall, strong central striker, now in his fourth season as a professional at Chester City after coming through the youth team, injury once again restricted his appearances in the early part of 1997-98. Having recovered, however, John only missed one of the last 16 games of the campaign and was playing the best football of his career thus far. Signed a new deal for the club during the summer.

Chester C (From trainee on 6/7/95) FL 24+37/8 FLC 2+3/1 FAC 0+2 Others 2+1

MURPHY Matthew (Matt) Simon
Born: Northampton, 20 August 1971
Height: 6'0" Weight: 12.2

Having joined Scunthorpe on loan from Oxford last December, with a £30,000 fee reportedly agreed between both clubs, he did well on his debut against Scarborough, but was ineligible for the following FA Cup game and lost his place in the starting line-up. Finding further opportunities limited, he returned to the Manor Ground to enjoy the final two months of the season as a regular, and scored twice in a big win over Stoke. Preferring an attacking midfield role, although sometimes used as a striker, those were to be his only league goals, although he did score at York in the Coca Cola Cup.

Oxford U (£20,000 from Corby T on 12/2/93) FL 52+65/17 FLC 2+8/2 FAC 2+3 Others 3+3/3
Scunthorpe U (Loaned on 12/12/97) FL 1+2 Others 1

MURPHY Shaun Peter
Born: Sydney, Australia, 5 November 1970
Height: 6'1" Weight: 12.0
Club Honours: AIC '95
International Honours: Australia: 1

A firm figure in West Bromwich Albion's back division in 1996-97, the tall, raven-haired Shaun underwent a hernia operation early on last season but, after regaining full fitness, he reclaimed his place, performing well alongside the new signing, Matt Carbon. Strong and reliable, as good in the air as on the ground, he was unfortunate to suffer further injury before coming back immediately prior to the end of the campaign and promising to be as competitive as ever in 1998-99.

Notts Co (Signed from Perth Italia on 4/9/92) FL 100+9/5 FLC 5+2 FAC 6/1 Others 12+1/1
West Bromwich A (£500,000 on 31/12/96) FL 30+4/3 FLC 1 FAC 3

MURRAY Paul
Born: Carlisle, 31 August 1976
Height: 5'9" Weight: 10.5
International Honours: E: B-1; U21-4; Yth

An excellent season for Paul ended dramatically when he broke his leg in two places after just ten minutes of Queens Park Rangers' away game at Norwich last February. Having earlier played for the England U21 side against Italy and Greece, and for the "B" team versus Chile, the classy midfielder had outside hopes of furthering his international honours, but the injury ended any chance of that. Cool and composed on the ball, and a versatile player who can play equally well in defence if required, he has a great future ahead of him and will be back, hopefully, as good as new.

Carlisle U (From trainee on 14/6/94) FL 27+14/1 FLC 2 FAC 1 Others 6+1
Queens Park R (£300,000 on 8/3/96) P/FL 58+7/6 FLC 4/1 FAC 5

MURRAY Robert (Rob) James
Born: Hammersmith, 21 October 1974
Height: 5'11" Weight: 12.7
International Honours: S: U21-1

Expected to build on his previous appearances for Bournemouth, Rob had a disappointing time of it in 1997-98, making just six appearances, all from the bench, prior to being released the summer. A very strong player, with good aerial ability to go with robust tackling, and able to play in defence or attack, it would be a surprise if he did not come back into league football, having promised much at an earlier stage of his career.

Bournemouth (From trainee on 11/1/93) FL 88+59/12 FLC 6+6 FAC 2+7 Others 2+4/2

MURRAY Scott George
Born: Aberdeen, 26 May 1974
Height: 5'10" Weight: 11.0

Unable to get a game at Aston Villa in 1997-98, Scott moved to Bristol City in December and quickly settled in to overcome early impressions when a wag christened him as "too good to hurry". The right back, who is extremely confident in possession, impressed many with his play when going forward and it was a surprise that he did not make the starting line-up more often than he did, despite suffering the odd lack of composure in front of goals. It is confidently expected, however, that he will come to the fore this coming season and prove what an excellent piece of business the City manager, John Ward, did in securing his services.

Aston Villa (£35,000 from Fraserburgh on 16/3/94) PL 4
Bristol C (£150,000 on 12/12/97) FL 10+13 Others 2

MURRAY Shaun
Born: Newcastle, 7 December 1970
Height: 5'8" Weight: 11.2
International Honours: E: Yth; Sch

A very skilful Bradford midfielder, Shaun had a good season in 1997-98, despite injuries, his ability to retain the ball being priceless at times and, with a liking to dictate a game, and always on the go, his

vision and passing skills set up a good many attacks. Despite having a preference for the left-hand side, he is quite at home on the right, but regardless of which flank he plays on he is always comfortable. At the end of his contract, and not offered a new deal, Shaun will be looking for a new club this coming term.

Tottenham H (From trainee on 10/12/87)
Portsmouth (£100,000 on 12/6/89) FL 21+13/1 FLC 2+1/1 FAC 1+3 Others 2+2
Scarborough (Signed on 1/11/93) FL 29/5 FAC 2 Others 2
Bradford C (£200,000 on 11/8/94) FL 105+25/8 FLC 7+2/1 FAC 4+2 Others 4/2

MURTY Graeme Stuart
Born: Saltburn, 13 November 1974
Height: 5'10" Weight: 11.10

York City's "Mr Versatile", Graeme was equally at home in either full-back positions or wide on the flanks in midfield in 1997-98. A very enthusiastic and energetic player, one of his best displays of the campaign was at left back in a home game against Bristol City in February. Unfortunately, he missed the last few games owing to a hernia operation. *Stop Press:* Signed for Reading on 6 July, a fee of £700,000 changing hands.
York C (From trainee on 23/3/93) FL 106+11/7 FLC 10/2 FAC 5+1 Others 6+2

MUSCAT Kevin Vincent
Born: Crawley, 7 August 1973
Height: 5'11" Weight: 12.2
International Honours: Australia: 9

A right back, who was part of the transfer exchange last October that saw Jamie Smith go to Palace, Kevin went straight into Smith's former Wolves' position and showed that he liked to go forward, running half the length of the field to score at Crewe. In the next match he conceded a penalty at Stoke, and a combination of a suspension and international duty kept him out until after Christmas. The Australian proved to be a good tackler, although four bookings in six games meant more suspension, but, nevertheless, he remained a key defender for Wolves.
Crystal Palace (£35,000 from South Melbourne on 16/8/96) FL 51+2/2 FLC 4/1 FAC 2 Others 2
Wolverhampton W (£200,000 on 22/10/97) FL 22+2/3 FAC 5

MUSSELWHITE Paul Stephen
Born: Portsmouth, 22 December 1968
Height: 6'2" Weight: 14.2
Club Honours: AMC '93

Although having another consistent season in the Port Vale goal, despite the team's battle against relegation from the first division in 1997-98, Paul was left out for five games in March when the manager rang the changes after some poor results. However, the commanding 'keeper returned refreshed and made a last-minute penalty save at Birmingham City, that ultimately proved costly for both teams, and has now made more league appearances in the Vale goal than any other custodian.*
Portsmouth (From apprentice on 1/12/86)
Scunthorpe U (Free on 21/3/88) FL 132 FLC 11 FAC 7 Others 13
Port Vale (£20,000 on 30/7/92) FL 244 FLC 12 FAC 20 Others 19

MUSTAFA Tarkan
Born: London, 28 August 1973
Height: 5'10" Weight: 11.7

Signed from non-league Kettering, prior to the start of 1997-98, Tarkan was introduced to the Barnet side in the third game of the season, at home to Exeter, when coming off the bench for the final 20 minutes. A pacy, attacking right winger who likes to run at defenders, and can go on the inside or the outside to get in crosses, he made 12 appearances in all, ten of them as a sub, and looked to be useful.
Barnet (Free from Kettering T on 5/8/97) FL 2+9 FLC 0+1

MUSTOE Neil John
Born: Gloucester, 5 November 1976
Height: 5'9" Weight: 12.10

A left-sided midfield player signed by Wigan Athletic from Manchester United last January, Neil made his debut for the club in the second round of the Auto Windscreens Shield victory over Rotherham United, but failed to make any other first team appearances. Contracted until the end of the coming season, and having once been a "Fergie Fledgling" at Old Trafford, he will be looking to kick-start his career.
Manchester U (From trainee on 1/7/95)
Wigan Ath (Signed on 7/1/98) Others 0+1

MUSTOE Robin (Robbie)
Born: Witney, 28 August 1968
Height: 5'11" Weight: 11.12
Club Honours: Div 1 '95

A powerhouse Middlesbrough midfielder with a "never say die" attitude to every game, Robbie has worn the captain's arm band with distinction on several occasions, his strong tackling, powerful running, and positional anticipation, leading to his involvement in many spectacular goals, five of them last season, including two in the FA Cup that were instrumental in making sure it was the Boro that progressed to the fourth round, and not Queens Park Rangers. An inspired signing from Oxford by the then manager, Colin Todd, he has become a firm favourite with the fans and his long service must soon be rewarded with a testimonial match.
Oxford U (From juniors on 2/7/86) FL 78+13/10 FLC 2 FAC 2 Others 3
Middlesbrough (£375,000 on 5/7/90) F/PL 233+10/18 FLC 39+1/7 FAC 20/2 Others 12+1/1

MUTCH Andrew (Andy) Todd
Born: Liverpool, 28 December 1963
Height: 5'10" Weight: 11.3
Club Honours: Div 4 '88, Div 3 '89; AMC '88
International Honours: E: B-3; U21-1

The old Wolves and Swindon warhorse, Andy continued to sit on the sidelines for Stockport in 1997-98, and continued to delight his army of Edgeley Park fans by climbing off the bench to score the odd goal. However, as the season wore on, the striker's appearances became less frequent and less effective, and with his contract up during the summer there is a real chance that this will be his last term of league soccer.

Wolverhampton W (Signed from Southport on 25/2/86) FL 277+12/96 FLC 14/4 FAC 11+1/1 Others 23/4
Swindon T (£250,000 on 16/8/93) F/PL 34+16/6 FLC 6+1/3 FAC 4/1 Others 3/2
Wigan Ath (Loaned on 24/8/95) FL 7/1
Stockport Co (Free on 15/3/96) FL 28+36/10 FLC 4+3/6 FAC 1+2/1 Others 3+1

MYALL Stuart Thomas
Born: Eastbourne, 12 November 1974
Height: 5'10" Weight: 12.12

Released by Brighton during the 1996 close season, and signed for Brentford by David Webb, the central midfielder with good passing ability, was finally given his Bees' debut by another manager, Eddie May, on 1 November 1997, at Bournemouth, and played well. Although selected again for the next game, against Carlisle, following the sacking of May, Stuart was released in January without having played again.
Brighton & Hove A (From trainee on 9/7/93) FL 69+11/4 FLC 4 FAC 4 Others 4+1
Brentford (Free on 31/7/96) FL 2

MYERS Andrew (Andy) John
Born: Hounslow, 3 November 1973
Height: 5'10" Weight: 12.11
Club Honours: FAC '97; ECWC '98
International Honours: E: U21-4; Yth

A very accomplished left-sided Chelsea player, who can play either as wing back or the left side of central defence, Andy found his opportunities limited in 1997-98 by the club's new signings and a troublesome hamstring strain picked up in the Coca Cola Cup quarter final at Portman Road against Ipswich Town. He is particularly quick off the mark, and his pace is a great asset when either attacking or covering back in defence. Despite starting just 13 matches last season, he never let the team down with his wholehearted, battling attitude.
Chelsea (From trainee on 25/7/91) F/PL 73+10/2 FLC 2+1 FAC 9+1 Others 4+2

MYHRE Thomas
Born: Sarpsborg, Norway, 16 October 1973
Height: 6'4" Weight: 13.12
International Honours: Norway: 1

A tall, commanding goalkeeper with outstanding reflexes, Thomas proved to be a worthy successor to the great Neville Southall at Everton in 1997-98, having arrived in November from Viking Stavangar, after weeks of haggling over his transfer fee. Handed his debut the following week at Leeds, Thomas went on to keep a clean sheet in each of his first three games and never looked back – despite a scare during an away match at Barnsley when he received lengthy treatment after a goalmouth skirmish, and later revealed he wore contact lenses which had been dislodged! Hugely popular with the Everton supporters, especially for his ecstatic celebrations when goals go in at the opposite end to the one he is defending, he was rewarded for an excellent season with a place in Norway's World Cup 22 for France '98, but was not called upon.
Everton (£800,000 from Viking Stavanger on 28/11/97) PL 22 FAC 1

Professional Footballers Association
2 Oxford Court
Bishopsgate
Manchester
M2 3WQ

Tel: 0161 236 0575
Fax: 0161 228 7229

* * * * *

PFA Financial Management
91 Broad Street
Birmingham
B15 1AU

Tel: 0121 644 5277
Fax: 0121 644 5288

* * * * *

PFA Enterprises Ltd
Suite 9, 4th Floor
52 Haymarket
London
SW1Y 4RP

Tel: 0171 839 8663
Fax: 0171 839 2097
email: gnelson@thepfa.co.uk

NASH Marc
Born: Newcastle, 13 May 1978
Height: 5'9" Weight: 11.7
A regular goalscorer for Hartlepool's reserve team, Marc played through last season on a month-to-month contract after being discovered turning out for Northern Alliance team, Benfield Park, in September. He made one brief appearance for the first team, coming on as a substitute at Shrewsbury, but, having just three minutes on the pitch, he was unable to make a great impression. Subsequently, he was hampered by an ankle injury and did not get any further chances, although he remains on a monthly contract.
Hartlepool U (Signed from Benfield Park on 8/9/97) FL 0+1

NASH Martin
Born: Regina, Canada, 27 December 1975
Height: 5'11" Weight: 12.5
International Honours: Canada: 10
The Canadian international became Stockport's most capped player in 1997-98 after playing in his country's World Cup qualifying campaign. Despite having the pace and crossing ability to make a name for himself on either flank, his jaunts abroad hindered his Edgeley Park development, keeping him on the fringes of the first team for the entire season. Was released during the summer.
Stockport Co (Free from Regina on 27/11/96) FL 0+11 FLC 0+1 Others 2+1/1

NAYLOR Anthony (Tony) Joseph
Born: Manchester, 29 March 1967
Height: 5'7" Weight: 10.8
The small, nippy Port Vale striker did not quite live up the the standards set in the previous season, but began the 1997-98 campaign well, scoring a superb goal against Sunderland after a run from the halfway line that remained one of Sky TV's Goals of the Season. Unfortunately, the goals dried up after early November, Tony adding just two more from then onwards that sneaked him into double figures.
Crewe Alex (£20,000 from Droylsden on 22/3/90) FL 104+18/45 FLC 7+2/5 FAC 9/7 Others 12/9
Port Vale (£150,000 on 18/7/94) FL 127+26/47 FLC 10/4 FAC 9/1 Others 5+1/3

NAYLOR Dominic John
Born: Watford, 12 August 1970
Height: 5'10" Weight: 12.6
Club Honours: FAYC '89
The Leyton Orient club captain started 1997-98 in his normal left-back position, but played equally well when asked to perform in midfield, again showing himself to be a good tackler and passer of the ball who got through a tremendous amount of work during the game. Out of contract at the end of the season, under the Bosman ruling, Dominic left on a free transfer.
Watford (From trainee on 20/9/88)
Halifax T (Loaned on 6/12/89) FL 5+1/1 Others 1+1 (Free to Hong Kong in October 1990)
Barnet (Free on 12/8/91) FL 50+1 FLC 2 FAC 5/1 Others 4
Plymouth Arg (Free on 16/7/93) FL 84+1 FLC 2 FAC 8 Others 4+1/1
Gillingham (Free on 11/8/95) FL 30+1/1 FLC 2/1 FAC 3 Others 1
Leyton Orient (£25,000 on 15/8/96) FL 87/4 FLC 6 FAC 4 Others 3

NAYLOR Glenn
Born: Goole, 11 August 1972
Height: 5'10" Weight: 11.10
This quick and skilful Darlington forward appeared in more league games during 1997-98 than anyone, but for goalkeeper, David Preece. His endless running was rewarded with ten goals in all competitions and he ended as third-top scorer behind Darren Roberts and Mario Dörner.*
York C (From trainee on 5/3/90) FL 78+33/30 FLC 2+4 FAC 4+1/2 Others 3+4
Darlington (Loaned on 13/10/95) FL 3+1/1 Others 1+1
Darlington (Signed on 26/9/96) FL 68+11/18 FLC 1+1/1 FAC 6/2 Others 2

NAYLOR Lee Martyn
Born: Walsall, 19 March 1980
Height: 5'10" Weight: 11.3
A young Wolves' left back, Lee made his debut at the age of 17, doing as well as his colleagues in a rugged encounter with Birmingham. It took him a few months to claim a regular place, beginning with a win over Charlton in which he scored with a splendid header, before making 12 successive appearances. Fully tested, he defended calmly and provided some useful centres at the other end and looks to be an excellent discovery.
Wolverhampton W (From trainee on 10/10/97) FL 14+2 FLC 1 FAC 4/1

NAYLOR Martyn Paul
Born: Walsall, 2 August 1977
Height: 5'9" Weight: 10.2
A right-sided full back signed by Shrewsbury in the 1997 close season from Telford, Martyn proved to be very speedy in launching attacks. Restricted to a small number of appearances early on, he has a further year left of a two-year contract and will be hoping to be offered more opportunities in 1998-99.
Shrewsbury T (Free from Telford on 2/7/97) FL 2 FLC 1

NAYLOR Richard Alan
Born: Leeds, 28 February 1977
Height: 6'1" Weight: 13.7
The knee problems which caused him to miss part of the previous campaign in Ipswich's colours showed no respite in 1997-98, and this, combined with the fantastic form of David Johnson, Alex Mathie, and Jamie Scowcroft, meant that he was restricted to just five substitute appearances for Ipswich. He did, however, score two goals when he came on as a substitute against Reading and Huddersfield, but it was a season he would rather put behind him as he strives for full fitness this coming term. Although recognised as a striker these days, he actually started out as a central defender and could prove to be highly versatile as his career pans out.
Ipswich T (From trainee on 10/7/95) FL 19+13/6 FLC 1+3/1 FAC 0+1

NAYLOR Stuart William
Born: Wetherby, 6 December 1962
Height: 6'4" Weight: 12.10
International Honours: E: B-3; Yth
The previous season's regular first-choice 'keeper, it looked as though Stuart would never get an opportunity for Bristol City in 1997-98, it taking an injury to Keith Welch to allow him to demonstrate his excellent shot-stopping abilities in the final two games of the campaign. Placed on the transfer list by the City during the campaign, it was fitting that he had the opportunity to bid a possible farewell by again performing in the first team.*
Lincoln C (Free from Yorkshire Amateurs on 19/6/80) FL 49 FLC 4 FAC 2 Others 6
Peterborough U (Loaned on 23/2/83) FL 8
Crewe Alex (Loaned on 6/10/83) FL 38
Crewe Alex (Loaned on 23/8/94) FL 17 FLC 2 FAC 2 Others 3
West Bromwich A (£100,000 on 18/2/86) FL 354+1 FLC 22 FAC 13 Others 20
Bristol C (Free on 13/8/96) FL 37 FLC 4 FAC 4 Others 1

NDAH George Ehialimolisa
Born: Dulwich, 23 December 1974
Height: 6'1" Weight: 11.4
International Honours: E: Yth
After failing to get a call up for Crystal Palace at the start of 1997-98, George went out on loan to Gillingham, playing four times, before going back to Selhurst Park and scoring against Hull City in the Coca Cola Cup. With opportunities still scarce, in November he became Steve McMahon's biggest signing for Swindon, and made a sensational start when he scored after just 12 minutes on his debut at home to Middlesbrough. Unfortunately, a run of goalless games was followed by a knee injury and the striker was seldom seen at his very best, his only other goal coming from the penalty spot in a local derby defeat at Oxford. His tremendous pace is a real asset at this level and, fully fit, he is expected to torment opposition defences this coming term.
Crystal Palace (From trainee on 10/8/92) F/PL 33+45/8 FLC 7+6/2 FAC 3+1/1 Others 4+1
Bournemouth (Loaned on 13/10/95) FL 12/2 Others 1
Gillingham (Loaned on 29/8/97) FL 4
Swindon T (£500,000 on 21/11/97) FL 14/2 FAC 1

N'DIAYE Sada (Pepe)
Born: Dakar, Senegal, 27 March 1975
Height: 5'8" Weight: 11.1
Signed at the same time as fellow Frenchman, Regis Coulbault, Pepe had a dream debut for Southend away to Plymouth last October, scoring the winner in a 3-2 victory. Incredibly fast and tricky, he is also

215

fairly slight, proving easy for opposition defenders to brush off the ball and, after a short spell of first team football, found himself on the sidelines before he departed during the summer.

Southend U (Free from Troyes on 17/10/97) FL 15+2/2 FAC 1 Others 1

NDLOVU Peter

Born: Buluwayo, Zimbabwe, 25 February 1973
Height: 5'8" Weight: 10.2
International Honours: Zimbabwe: 20

Signed on a pay-as-you-play deal from Coventry during the 1997 close season, the Zimbabwean international scored four times in his first six games for Birmingham before suffering a loss of form in mid-term. Came back to prominence with a stunning goal – a scorching 30-yard drive which beat the 'keeper all ends up – in City's 3-2 defeat at Leeds, and was later described as being too good for the first division by his manager, Trevor Francis, after he had produced a devastating spell of form up front. With two great feet, and comfortable either in midfield or up front, at his best, he can produce amazing pace and control, which takes him past defenders as if they do not exist.

Coventry C (£10,000 from Highlanders on 16/8/91) F/PL 141+36/37 FLC 10/2 FAC 5+4/2 Others 0+1
Birmingham C (£1,600,000 on 15/7/97) FL 29+10/9 FLC 5/1 FAC 1+1/1

Peter Ndlovu

NEAL Ashley James

Born: Northampton, 16 December 1974
Height: 6'0" Weight: 14.6

Formerly on non-contract terms at Peterborough, the son of the former Liverpool and England full back, Phil, signed professional forms during the 1997 close season and was expecting to be in contention for a first team place. In the event, he was unable to get a game, other than being called in as defensive cover on a handful of occasions. Is strong and uncompromising, and able to play at full back or in a more central role.

Liverpool (From trainee on 27/4/93)
Brighton & Hove A (Loaned on 27/9/96) FL 8
Huddersfield T (Free on 13/12/96)
Peterborough U (Free on 27/3/97) FL 6+2 FAC 0+1

NEIL James (Jimmy) Darren

Born: Bury St Edmunds, 28 February 1976
Height: 5'8" Weight: 11.7

Having turned down a new contract with Grimsby, Jimmy joined Scunthorpe for the start of last season and immediately won a first team place at left-wing back. A left-sided player who loves to get forward, he seemed well suited to the role, but ran into injury problems in September which meant he needed a hernia operation. Although getting back into the side for two matches at Christmas, he then found himself spending the remainder of the campaign in the reserves. Was offered a three-month contract for the start of the coming term.

Grimsby T (From trainee on 13/7/94) FL 1+1
Scunthorpe U (Free on 7/8/97) FL 6+1 FLC 1

NEILL Lucas Edward

Born: Sydney, Australia, 9 March 1978
Height: 6'1" Weight: 12.0

Still only 20 years old, Lucas was expected to advance his career at Millwall in 1997-98, having been a success since arriving at the New Den from the Australian Football academy in 1995, but, unfortunately, he played very few games due to differing injuries, and was sorely missed. Performs equally well in defence, as he does in midfield, and has a penchant for scoring great goals from outside the area. Hopefully, when fully recovered, he will become the driving force that was expected of him.

Millwall (Free from AIS on 13/11/95) FL 43+15/4 FLC 1+1 FAC 2 Others 2

NEILSON Alan Bruce

Born: Wegburg, Germany, 26 September 1972
Height: 5'11" Weight: 12.10
International Honours: W: 5; B-2; U21-7

Having played ten games for Southampton in 1997-98, Alan became one of Ray Wilkins' first signings for Fulham, in November, and his consistent displays in central defence alongside Chris Coleman had much to do with the club reaching third place in the league by January. Unfortunately, injuries restricted his appearances later in the season, but his cool confidence, and passing ability, should ensure stability in the Cottagers' defence for years to come.

Newcastle U (From trainee on 11/2/91) F/PL 35+7/1 FLC 4 Others 4
Southampton (£500,000 on 1/6/95) PL 42+13 FLC 7 FAC 1+1
Fulham (£250,000 on 28/11/97) FL 17 FAC 2 Others 1

NELSON Fernando

Born: Portugal, 5 November 1971
Height: 5'11" Weight: 12.3
International Honours: Portugal: 6

As Aston Villa's most experienced player in terms of European experience, Fernando was a regular squad member in 1997-98, being named for all but one of the 51 games, while actually appearing in only 34 of them. Able to play as a right-wing back, or even further forward, he switched to a midfield role in late October, mainly to accommodate a returning Gary Charles and, at the same time, continued to be available for Portugal, being called up to play against Northern

Ireland. Not only good when running the opposition, Fernando has proved to be sound defensively, with an excellent recovery rate, and good tackling ability.

Aston Villa (£1,750,000 from Sporting Lisbon on 26/7/96) PL 54+5 FLC 3 FAC 1+1 Others 7+2

NETHERCOTT Stuart David

Born: Ilford, 21 March 1973
Height: 6'1" Weight: 13.8
International Honours: E: U21-8

Unable to break into the Spurs' side in 1997-98, Stuart went out on loan to Millwall at the end of January, being drafted into the centre of the defence, following injuries to both Alan McLeary and Scott Fitzgerald. Unfortunately, having impressed all around him as the man for the job, he too was put out of action for the remainder of the campaign, after suffering a bad shoulder injury. Proving to be an excellent header, and a strong, robust defender who gave no quarter, he signed permanent forms on transfer deadline day. Also showed good awareness and passing ability.

Tottenham H (From trainee on 17/8/91) PL 31+23 FAC 5+3/1
Maidstone U (Loaned on 5/9/91) FL 13/1 Others 1
Barnet (Loaned on 13/2/92) FL 3
Millwall (Signed on 22/1/98) FL 10

NEVILLE Gary Alexander

Born: Bury, 18 February 1975
Height: 5'10" Weight: 11.10
Club Honours: FAYC '92; PL '96, '97; FAC '96; CS '96
International Honours: E: 30; Yth (UEFAC '93)

A hard-tackling Manchester United full back, who is equally as effective in the centre of defence, Gary was given a relaxing start to last season by Alex Ferguson, following his exertions for England in the summer. Having sat on the bench as a non-playing substitute in United's opening three Premiership games, he made his bow against Leicester at Filbert Street in August. A model of consistency throughout the course of the campaign, he relinquished his familiar right-back slot for United's short-lived Coca Cola Cup run, and was a named substitute in the FA Cup ties against Walsall and Barnsley – though he played in the replay which United lost 3-2. Reaffirming his commitment to United's cause before flying out to Italy on England duty he said, "Manchester United is as big as any club in Europe, and the players at Old Trafford have no reason to go to Italy. I do not feel anywhere I could go from United being a step up." Having captained the club in their European Cup quarter-final game against Monaco in March, there are few better rivals for the right-back spot in the country, and there were no surprises when he was selected for England's World Cup Final campaign during the summer. Was selected by his fellow professionals for the PFA award-winning Premiership side. *Stop Press:* Played in three of England's World Cup games in France, having missed the first, and enhanced his reputation, especially in the match against Argentine.

Manchester U (From trainee on 29/1/93) PL 111 FLC 4+1 FAC 14+2 Others 20+4

Gary Neville (right)

NEVILLE Philip (Phil) John
Born: Bury, 21 January 1977
Height: 5'11" Weight: 12.0
Club Honours: FAYC '95; PL '96, '97; FAC
'96: CS '96, '97
International Honours: E: 12; U21-7; Yth;
Sch

A superb right back who is equally as adaptable as a central defender, Phil made an excellent start to last season when he gave a sterling performance in the Charity Shield against Chelsea, and played in Manchester United's opening three Premiership games. Confined to the bench for most of September, he enjoyed a more consistent run during the months of November and December, when Denis Irwin was out through injury. His adaptability, however, kept him in the team even when Irwin returned, and he produced some excellent performances in the centre of defence. Having celebrated his first goal in senior football against Chelsea at Stamford Bridge in February, his next big goal was to emulate his brother Gary as a regular in the England team.
Manchester U (From trainee on 1/6/94) PL 61+13/1 FLC 3+1 FAC 10+1 Others 10+4

Phil Neville

NEVLAND Erik
Born: Stavanger, Norway, 10 November 1977
Height: 5'9" Weight: 11.2
International Honours: Norway: 3

A highly talented striker with an eye for a goal, Erik was the latest Viking to arrive at Manchester United, from Stavanger in the summer of 1997. Although he had to wait six months before making his first team debut against Southampton in January, he was a named substitute in United's next match against Walsall in the FA Cup. Having replaced Ben Thornley in the second half, he was a likely scorer when Brian McClair put him through for a one to one with goalkeeper, James Walker, but he unselfishly laid the ball off for Andy Cole to score. His appearance in that game certainly got the statisticians searching through their reference books, it being the first time that four Norwegians had played together for United in one game. "That was a bit special," said Erik. "The others have been an inspiration to me."
Manchester U (Signed from Viking Stavanger on 15/7/97) PL 0+1 FLC 0+1 FAC 2+1

NEWELL Justin James
Born: Germany, 8 February 1980
Height: 5'9" Weight: 11.0
Given his Football League debut at Plainmoor against Doncaster last September, Torquay's YTS striker impressed on his brief appearance as a 74th minute sub, but injury and the consistency of the regular forwards denied him further first team chances. Big and strong, Justin scored a lot of goals in junior football and with good first touch looks to bring that ability to senior level.
Torquay U (Trainee) FL 0+1

NEWHOUSE Aidan Robert
Born: Wallasey, 23 May 1972
Height: 6'2" Weight: 13.5
International Honours: E: Yth

Signed on a free transfer from Wimbledon during the 1997 close season before Mr Al Fayed took over at Fulham, Aidan had spent most of his years with the Dons in their Football Combination side, but quickly acclimatised again to league football. His most successful games for his new club came in the Coca Cola Cup, in which he scored three goals in the two matches against Wycombe, before he followed Micky Adams and Alan Cork when they left for Swansea City in October. Unfortunately, after just four games, the tall striker had to undergo surgery for a ruptured achilles heel tendon and, despite coming back prior to the season ending, found the damage had been done. Has two good feet and is at his best when getting into wide positions.
Chester C (From trainee on 1/7/89) FL 29+15/6 FLC 5+1 FAC 0+2 Others 2+3/1
Wimbledon (£100,000 on 22/2/90) F/PL 7+16/2 FLC 1+1 FAC 2 Others 0+1
Port Vale (Loaned on 21/1/94) FL 0+2 FAC 0+1
Portsmouth (Loaned on 2/12/94) FL 6/1
Torquay U (Loaned on 7/12/95) FL 4/2
Fulham (Free on 20/6/97) FL 7+1/1 FLC 3+1/3
Swansea C (£30,000 on 31/10/97) FL 3+5 FAC 1

NEWMAN Richard (Ricky) Adrian
Born: Guildford, 5 August 1970
Height: 5'10" Weight: 12.6

Missing just ten games for Millwall in 1997-98, Ricky continued to show the good form that he brought with him from Crystal Palace two seasons earlier, and celebrated with his 100th league game. An excellent utility man who, although appearing mainly as a full back, can play just as well in central defences and midfield. Strong in the tackle, good in the air, and pacy, when unavailable he was sorely missed.
Crystal Palace (From juniors on 22/1/88) F/PL 43+5/3 FLC 5 FAC 5+2 Others 2
Maidstone U (Loaned on 28/2/92) FL 9+1/1
Millwall (£500,000 on 19/7/95) FL 108+4/5 FLC 9 FAC 5 Others 3

NEWMAN Robert (Rob) Nigel
Born: Bradford on Avon, 13 December 1963
Height: 6'2" Weight: 13.4
Club Honours: AMC '86

Used sparingly last season at Norwich, the big, strong defender spent three months on loan at Scottish Premier Division outfit, Motherwell, and there were rumours of a possible permanent move. However, that did not come to fruition and he came back to remain a valuable squad member at City, his versatility giving Mike Walker many more options, before being recruited on a loan deal on transfer deadline day by Wigan Athletic. The veteran central defender endeared himself to the Springfield Park crowd with some fine end of season displays, showing himself to be both strong in the air and tackle in steadying Latics' defence, which saw just one defeat during the last nine games. Was released by Norwich during the summer.
Bristol C (From apprentice on 5/10/81) FL 382+12/52 FLC 29+1/2 FAC 27/2 Others 33/5
Norwich C (£600,000 on 15/7/91) F/PL 181+24/14 FLC 22+2/2 FAC 13/1 Others 7
Motherwell (Loaned on 12/12/97) SL 11 SC 3
Wigan Ath (Loaned on 26/3/98) FL 8

NEWSOME Jonathan (Jon)
Born: Sheffield, 6 September 1970
Height: 6'2" Weight: 13.11
Club Honours: Div 1 '92; CS '92

Despite Sheffield Wednesday being up against it in 1997-98, Jon had a fairly steady season in his central defensive role until picking up a knee injury which put him out of the last eight matches. A very unassuming type of player, he very rarely attracts the limelight, but is a man you can rely upon to always give 100 per-cent effort. Is a good all-round defender who is not easy to pass, has a good recovery rate, is a decisive tackler, and can use the ball well. His best moment would have been in scoring one of the goals that beat Leeds, one of his old teams, at Elland Road, despite it being a simple tap in at the far post.
Sheffield Wed (From trainee on 1/7/89) FL 6+1 FLC 3
Leeds U (£150,000 on 11/6/91) F/PL 62+14/3 FLC 3 FAC 3+1 Others 5
Norwich C (£1,000,000 on 30/6/94) P/FL 61+1/7 FLC 9 FAC 5/1
Sheffield Wed (£1,600,000 on 16/3/96) PL 43/4 FLC 2 FAC 6

NEWTON Edward (Eddie) John Ikem
Born: Hammersmith, 13 December 1971
Height: 5'11" Weight: 12.8
Club Honours: FAC '97; FLC '98; ECWC '98
International Honours: E: U21-2

In a team which contains top-class attacking midfield players it is essential to have a man sitting "in the hole", mopping up counter attacks, covering, tackling, and man marking. This is the role that Eddie performed to perfection for Chelsea in 1997-98, but, unfortunately, as in the previous two season, injuries restricted his appearances. After recovering from a broken leg sustained in 1996, his troublesome knee was operated upon during the summer of 1997, which sidelined him for the first part of the campaign. He returned for the stricken Gustavo Poyet, until suffering a broken bone in his foot, but battled back to appear in the Coca Cola Cup final against Middlesbrough, and to make a substitute appearance in the European Cup Winners' Cup final against VFB Stuttgart in Stockholm. This made it three winning cup finals within 12 months for a player who had come up through the ranks at Stamford Bridge, and during a season that saw Eddie make his 200th first team appearance.
Chelsea (From trainee on 17/5/90) F/PL 138+20/8 FLC 15+2/1 FAC 15+2/1 Others 11+1
Cardiff C (Loaned on 23/1/92) FL 18/4

NEWTON Shaun O'Neill
Born: Camberwell, 20 August 1975
Height: 5'8" Weight: 11.7
International Honours: E: U21-3

An extremely fast, right-sided Charlton winger who can also play at right back, Shaun is at his best when getting down to the byline and cutting back crosses for the strikers to run on to. Scored some great goals himself in 1997-98, including two in the 3-0 home win over Middlesbrough and probably had his best season yet for the Addicks. Netted a decisive shoot-out penalty in the Wembley play-off final, and is now considered a regular in the side.
Charlton Ath (From trainee on 1/7/93) FL 134+38/15 FLC 14/2 FAC 7+2 Others 7+1/2

NICHOLLS Kevin John Richard
Born: Newham, 2 January 1979
Height: 6'0" Weight: 11.0
International Honours: E: Yth

A fierce-tackling Charlton midfield player, who can also play in defence, Kevin began last season as a substitute in the first three games, before starting the next two, but then only featured twice more on the bench until missing the rest of the campaign with a knee injury. Has good ball control, is confident, and should establish himself in the side during the coming term.
Charlton Ath (From trainee on 29/1/96) FL 4+8/1 FLC 2+2

NICHOLLS Mark
Born: Hillingdon, 30 May 1977
Height: 5'10" Weight: 10.4
Club Honours: FLC '98

Although in direct competition with four

top-class internationals for a striker's berth at Chelsea in 1997-98, this confident, locally-developed, young centre forward still managed to grab his fair share of the headlines – earning a reputation as a "super sub" into the bargain. In December, he came on at White Hart Lane to score his first senior goal in the 6-1 rout of Spurs and, the following month, with the Blues 1-0 down at half time at home to Coventry City, he again came off the bench to score two superb goals within five minutes to turn the match in his side's favour. Despite Chelsea's much publicised worldwide transfer dealings, the emergence of talented young players such as Mark, just goes to prove that the Blues still have one of the best youth policies in the game.
Chelsea (From trainee on 1/7/95) PL 11+16/3 FLC 2+2 FAC 1 Others 0+2

Mark Nicholls

NICHOLSON Shane Michael
Born: Newark, 3 June 1970
Height: 5'10" Weight: 12.2
Club Honours: GMVC '88

A good tackler who enjoys going forward to link up with the forwards, and is always ready to supply a steady flow of accurate crosses, Shane started the first nine games of 1997-98 for West Bromwich Albion before suffering a bad leg injury and being forced out of action until mid-December. He was then the subject of a drugs enquiry, but with that cleared up he returned to first team action and played 11 times, performing well, until admitting to being a frequent user of amphetamines and being suspended from all football for three months of rehabilitation, prior to being released during the summer.
Lincoln C (From trainee on 19/7/88) FL 122+11/6 FLC 8+3 FAC 6/1 Others 7+1
Derby Co (£100,000 on 22/4/92) FL 73+1/1 FLC 4 FAC 4/1 Others 5
West Bromwich A (£150,000 on 9/2/96) FL 50+2 FLC 4 Others 4

NICOL Stephen (Steve)
Born: Irvine, 11 December 1961
Height: 5'10" Weight: 12.8
Club Honours: Div 1 '84, '86, '88, '90; FAC '86, '89, '92; EC '84; CS '89
International Honours: S: 27; U21-14

An experienced trouper, Steve played only a minor role at Sheffield Wednesday in 1997-98, appearing in just seven games, but proved himself a solid professional when helping out a very young reserve side prior to being loaned out to West Bromwich Albion in March. At the Hawthorns, however, his vast experience stood out during the last six weeks of the campaign when he skippered the team from his midfield role. Acting as the anchorman, he was outstanding as Albion finished with a flourish, while remaining unbeaten against four of the top six clubs. Was released by Wednesday in the summer and is now a free agent.

Ayr U (From juniors in 1979) SL 68+2/7 SLC 16/1 SC 3
Liverpool (£300,000 on 26/10/81) F/PL 328+15/36 FLC 42/4 FAC 50/3 Others 32+2/3
Notts Co (Free on 20/1/95) FL 32/2 FLC 1 FAC 1 Others 3/1
Sheffield Wed (Free on 25/11/95) PL 41+8 FLC 0+2 FAC 2+1
West Bromwich A (Loaned on 12/3/98) FL 9

NIELSEN Allan
Born: Esbjerg, Denmark, 13 March 1971
Height: 5'8" Weight: 11.2
International Honours: Denmark: 20

This versatile, attacking midfielder spent much of last season hindered by minor injuries which were aggravated by the need to play in a patched-up Tottenham line-up, even as an out-and-striker, when not fully fit. Allan is quick and intelligent in his role of supporting the forwards and provides accurate through balls in the build up to attacks. Has a keen eye for goal too, and scored a tremendous effort in the 1-1 home draw with arch-rivals Arsenal in December. Similar in style to his team mate, David Howells, he too has great tenacity and gives 100 per-cent effort in every game he plays in. Strong in the tackle, and a difficult player to beat, he keeps the ball at his feet well, showing great confidence in doing so. As strong in the air as on the ground, Allan remains a first choice for the Danish international side and has the ability to be a key figure at White Hart Lane, providing he stays injury free. *Stop Press:* Played in all of Denmark's World Cup games during the summer and, having scored against South Africa, further impressed before the side went out to Brazil in the quarter finals.

Tottenham H (£1,650,000 from Brondby on 3/9/96) PL 49+5/9 FLC 3+1 FAC 1

NIELSEN John Schmidt
Born: Aarhus, Denmark, 7 April 1972
Height: 5'8" Weight: 11.5

A tireless worker and strong tackler, John never managed to find his way into the team-selection policy of Alvin Martin at Southend United during 1997-98, and spent most of his time on the sidelines, making the odd substitute appearance. The lack of a reserve team at Roots Hall meant that when he did get an opportunity, he appeared a little "match-rusty", and did not do his talents justice.

Southend U (Free from Ikaast on 2/8/96) FL 18+11/3 FLC 2/1 FAC 1 Others 1

NIELSEN Martin Ulrich
Born: Aarhus, Denmark, 24 March 1973
Height: 5'11" Weight: 12.4

Sacrificed as part of FC Copenhagen's push for the Danish title, Martin became Huddersfield's 36th player used in 1997-98, when signing a three-month contract in March, and the club's first Scandinavian import since Karl Hansen turned out in 1948-49. Although capable of playing equally well in central or wide positions, where he showed pace, good dribbling, and crossing skills, and was keen to make a good impression, the midfielder had to settle for a place on the subs' bench as Town continued the fight to avoid relegation. Released at the end of the season and returned to Denmark.

Huddersfield T (Free from FC Copenhagen on 19/3/98) FL 0+3

NILSEN Roger
Born: Tromso, Norway, 8 August 1969
Height: 5'11" Weight: 12.6
International Honours: Norway: 31

This classy Sheffield United defender whose season in 1997-98 was disrupted by injury and the need to perform in a number of positions, both at full back, and centre back, scored his first goal for the club in the penalty shoot-out against Coventry in the sixth round of the F A Cup. A possible £500,000 move to an unnamed Premier League club was turned down by United at the start of the campaign, and a projected move to Wolverhampton Wanderers then fell through due to his injury and, although he remained in contention for a Norwegian international slot, he failed to make the final 22 that represented the country in the World Cup during the summer. Possesses a long throw, which continued to be used to good effect.

Sheffield U (£550,000 from Viking Stavanger on 2/11/93) P/FL 143+6 FLC 6+1 FAC 9+2 Others 2+1

NILSSON Nilsennart Roland
Born: Helsingborg, Sweden, 27 November 1963
Height: 6'0" Weight: 11.6
Club Honours: FLC '91
International Honours: Sweden: 94

The Swedish international full back returned to England with Coventry after three years in his home country, signing from Helsingborg during the 1998 close season. His impact was immediate and the problem right-back position suddenly looked secure, as he missed only two games after making his debut at Old Trafford, being Man of the Match in his first two appearances. Roland's strengths, as ever, were his excellent positional play, his fitness, and his strong passing skill, while his partnership with Paul Telfer was one of the highlights of City's season.

Sheffield Wed (£375,000 from IFK Gothenburg on 8/12/89) F/PL 151/2 FLC 16/1 FAC 15 Others 3+1 (Transferred to Helsingborg on 9/5/94)
Coventry C (£200,000 on 29/7/97) PL 32 FLC 3 FAC 4

NIXON Eric Walter
Born: Manchester, 4 October 1962
Height: 6'4" Weight: 14.6
Club Honours: AMC '90

Signed from Tranmere early last season, the veteran 'keeper was drafted in to bolster Stockport's goalkeeping resources, and soon became a first team regular, his traditional combination of breathtaking brilliance and eccentricity making him hero and villain in turns with the Edgeley Park fans. Tall and dominating, his all-round performances kept the younger Ian Gray down to a handful of appearances, and reserve team football.

Manchester C (£1,000 from Curzon Ashton on 10/12/83) FL 58 FLC 8 FAC 10 Others 8
Wolverhampton W (Loaned on 29/8/86) FL 16
Bradford C (Loaned on 28/11/86) FL 3
Southampton (Loaned on 23/12/86) FL 4
Carlisle U (Loaned on 23/1/87) FL 16
Tranmere Rov (£60,000 on 24/3/88) FL 341 FLC 34 FAC 19 Others 45+1
Reading (Loaned on 9/1/96) FLC 1
Blackpool (Loaned on 5/2/96) FL 20 Others 2
Bradford C (Loaned on 13/9/96) FL 12
Stockport Co (£100,000 on 28/8/97) FL 43 FLC 2 FAC 2

NOEL-WILLIAMS Gifton Ruben Elisha
Born: Islington, 21 January 1980
Height: 6'1" Weight:13.6
Club Honours: Div 2 '98
International Honours: E: Yth

The young striker has now clocked up over 50 appearances for Watford, despite the fact he is still only 18. After sporadic appearances the previous season, Gifton became a regular in the first team squad in 1997-98, showing improved control and vision, and undoubtedly benefiting from the experience of playing alongside Jason Lee and Ronnie Rosenthal. Mysteriously, he always does well against west country teams, scoring against Swindon, Plymouth, Torquay, and both Bristol clubs, while his seasonal tally of 11 goals put him into double figures for the first time. Won a second division championship medal as the team went back to the first division after a two-year break.

Watford (From trainee on 13/2/97) FL 36+27/9 FLC 3+1/1 FAC 6/4

NOGAN Kurt
Born: Cardiff, 9 September 1970
Height: 5'11" Weight: 12.7
International Honours: W: U21-2

An experienced Preston striker, Kurt again failed to live up to his reputation during 1997-98, despite finally breaking his duck for the club with a brace against Watford, and a typical goal at former club, Burnley. Hardly ever finishing a full game, he flitted in and out of both the side and the squad, and will surely be looking to kick-start his career this coming season.

Luton T (From trainee on 11/7/89) FL 17+16/3 FLC 1+3/1 Others 1+1
Peterborough U (Free on 30/9/92) Others 1
Brighton & Hove A (Free on 17/10/92) FL 97/49 FLC 10/7 FAC 5+1 Others 7/4

Burnley (£250,000 on 24/4/95) FL 87+5/33 FLC 8/5 FAC 3 Others 5/4
Preston NE (£150,000 + on 13/3/97) FL 19+10/5 FLC 1+1 FAC 0+1 Others 3/1

NOGAN Lee Martin
Born: Cardiff, 21 May 1969
Height: 5'9" Weight: 11.0
Club Honours: AMC '98
International Honours: W: 2; B-1; U21-1
A 1997 close season signing from Reading, as Alan Buckley began rebuilding Grimsby for a quick return to the first division, Lee had the difficult task of stepping into the boots of departed Blundell Park favourite, Clive Mendonca, and took some time to establish his credentials with the supporters. However, as an intelligent, hard-working player, and difficult to mark, he was the club's second highest scorer in 1997-98, and was a member of the side that returned to the first division at the first attempt, via the play offs, and won the Auto Windscreen Shield.
Oxford U (From trainee on 25/3/87) FL 57+7/10 FLC 4+1 FAC 2+1/1 Others 4+1/1
Brentford (Loaned on 25/3/87) FL 10+1/2
Southend U (Loaned on 17/9/87) FL 6/1 FLC 2 Others 1/1
Watford (£350,000 on 12/12/91) FL 97+8/26 FLC 5+2/3 FAC 2/1 Others 1+2
Southend U (Loaned on 17/3/94) FL 4+1
Reading (£250,000 on 12/1/95) FL 71+20/26 FLC 5+1/1 FAC 2 Others 3/2
Notts Co (Loaned on 14/2/97) FL 6
Grimsby T (£170,000 on 24/7/97) FL 33+3/8 FLC 6/1 FAC 4/2 Others 8/2

Lee Nogan

NOLAN Ian Robert
Born: Liverpool, 9 July 1970
Height: 6'0" Weight: 12.1
International Honours: NI: 7
Ian was enjoying what was probably his best ever season at Sheffield Wednesday in 1997-98, playing in his preferred position of right back, and adding to his Northern Ireland caps, until suffering a badly-broken leg when challenged by Spurs' Justin Edinburgh during the Owls' 1-0 win on 21 February. Although it seemed fairly innocuous at the time, the clash broke both tibia and fibia, meaning that this immensely hard-working and spirited player will be out for some while yet. His mobility and attacking flair was certainly missed by all and sundry, while his absence gave the team fewer options.
Preston NE (From trainee on 31/8/88)
Tranmere Rov (£10,000 from Marine, via Northwich Victoria, on 2/8/91) FL 87+1/1 FLC 10/1 FAC 7 Others 9
Sheffield Wed (£1,500,000 on 17/8/94) PL 136/4 FLC 12 FAC 11

NOTTINGHAM Steven Edward
Born: Peterborough, 21 June 1980
Height: 6'0". Weight: 11.3
Still a trainee, the young defender made his Football League debut in Scunthorpe's closing match of last season, at Shrewsbury Town. Although a regular in the club's reserves and juniors as a central defender, he made his first team bow as a right back and will now be looking for further chances after turning professional in the summer.
Scunthorpe U (Trainee) FL 1

NOWLAND Adam Christopher
Born: Preston, 6 July 1981
Height: 5'11" Weight: 11.6
Yet another first-year trainee introduced by Blackpool at the end of 1997-98, the 16-year-old striker came off the bench for the last six minutes in the final game of the campaign, at Chesterfield. Obviously highly rated at Bloomfield Road, Adam top scored for the juniors and aims to go all the way.
Blackpool (Trainee) FL 0+1

NUGENT Kevin Patrick
Born: Edmonton, 10 April 1969
Height: 6'1" Weight: 13.3
International Honours: Ei: Yth
Cardiff City were delighted with the capture of Kevin from Bristol City at the start of last season, and although he was unable to play in pre-season friendlies while the fee was sorted out by a tribunal, he teamed up with Carl Dale for the opening league match and they looked sharp and incisive together. Unfortunately, Dale badly injured an ankle in that first game after scoring the only goal, but the newcomer impressed and went into the second match, against Southend in the Coca Cola Cup, full of confidence. This time, Steve White was his partner, and once again they looked a useful pairing. But then he injured his ankle during the clash with Southend and, although finishing the game, was ruled out for months. Scarcely fit all season, carrying a number of niggling injuries, playing just seven times, and, having started 1997-98 with so much optimism, Kevin finished it desperately frustrated by his run of bad luck. Capable of leading a line superbly well, with good ability in the air, he is aiming to start afresh in 1998-99 when he pulls the Bluebirds' shirt back on.
Leyton Orient (From trainee on 8/7/87) FL 86+8/20 FLC 9+3/6 FAC 9/3 Others 9+1/1
Plymouth Arg (£200,000 on 23/3/92) FL 124+7/32 FLC 11/2 FAC 10/3 Others 5+3
Bristol C (Signed on 29/9/95) FL 48+22/14 FLC 2+2 FAC 3+2/1 Others 2+1
Cardiff C (£65,000 on 4/8/97) FL 2+2 FLC 1 FAC 2/1

NURSE David John
Born: Kings Lynn, 12 October 1976
Height: 6'3" Weight: 12.6
Having been at Millwall since signing from Manchester City during the 1995 summer period, following a recommendation from the club's former 'keeper, Alex Stepney, David finally made his first team debut for the club at the New Den against Wimbledon in the Coca Cola Cup last October. Although beaten four times, the young goalie would have benefitted from the experience but, with Tim Carter and Nigel Spink ahead of him, he failed to break back in and was loaned to Brentford on transfer deadline day, without appearing in their first team. Released during the summer, he is sound in the air and a good shot-stopper.
Manchester C (From trainee on 17/10/95)
Millwall (Free on 28/6/96) FLC 1

NWADIKE Chukweumeka (Emeka) Ibezimife
Born: Camberwell, 9 August 1978
Height: 6'0" Weight: 12.7
Despite all the changes at the club, this central defender, now in his second year at Shrewsbury was unable to break into the first team, apart from briefly early on in 1997-98. Although still well thought of at Gay Meadow, he was released during the summer.
Wolverhampton W (From trainee on 3/7/96)
Shrewsbury T (Free on 10/12/96) FL 2+1 FLC 0+1

NYAMAH Kofi
Born: Islington, 20 June 1975
Height: 5'9" Weight: 11.10
1997-98 was a further season of opportunity for Kofi at Stoke and, although principally used as a left back, his great strength was going forward as either an overlapping wing back or as a left-sided midfielder. An excellent crosser of the ball, and tricky in one-to-one situations, he was on occasions caught out in defensive situations at times which marred good performances. Despite being transfer listed in January, he stuck to his task manfully and won back his place in the first team once Alan Durban took over as caretaker boss. Kofi was not the only one to benefit, as Stoke paid Kettering every time he played in the first team.
Cambridge U (From trainee on 19/5/93) FL 9+14/2 FLC 0+2 FAC 3+1/1 Others 4) Free to Kettering T during 1995 close season
Stoke C (£25,000 on 24/12/96) FL 9+8 FLC 1+1

NZAMBA Guy Roger
Born: Port Gentil, Gabon, 13 July 1970
Height: 5'9" Weight: 12.7
A French trialist brought to Southend last September by manager, Alvin Martin, Roger had what turned out to be one of the shortest careers of all time at Roots Hall. A well-built and fast forward, he came on in the 41st minute of the 1-0 home victory over Fulham, but was injured and replaced in the 65th minute, after which he returned to France, his career in the blue of Southend lasting just 24 minutes.
Southend U (Free from Trieste on 19/9/97) FL 0+1

O

OAKES Michael Christian
Born: Northwich, 30 October 1973
Height: 6'2" Weight: 14.6
International Honours: E: U21-6

The son of Alan, the former Manchester City record appearance holder, this young goalkeeper has the unenviable distinction of standing in for Mark Bosnich at Aston Villa, a task he has carried out for several years now. A professional at Aston Villa since the summer of 1991, Michael is brave, comes out well for crosses, and is a good shot-stopper in his own right. He is also a great kicker, which is very important these days. His only opportunities in 1997-98, and there were nine of them, came when Bosnich was unavailable, either through injury or away on international duty, and he could not be blamed for the fact that only two of the games were won. Hopefully, his main chance will come before too long.
Aston Villa (From juniors on 16/7/91) PL 26+2 FLC 2 Others 3
Scarborough (Loaned on 26/11/93) FL 1 Others 1

OAKES Scott John
Born: Leicester, 5 August 1972
Height: 5'11" Weight: 11.13
International Honours: E: U21-1

A versatile player who can perform well, either in midfield or up front, he was on Sheffield Wednesday's first team bench on 16 occasions last season, but came on to the field of play just six times and never once made a start. Always shows great composure on the ball, is enthusiastic enough, and possesses skill and a great shot, but needs a proper run in the side to bring the best out of him. As the son of a member of the famous pop group, Showaddywaddy, with his super ability Scott is too good to be constantly on the sidelines and will surely take the bull by the horns to force his way into the side this coming term.
Leicester C (From trainee on 9/5/90) FL 1+2 Others 1
Luton T (Signed on 22/10/91) FL 136+37/27 FLC 3+3/1 FAC 12+2/5 Others 3+3/1
Sheffield Wed (£425,000 + on 1/8/96) PL 7+16/1 FLC 0+1 FAC 0+2

OAKLEY Matthew
Born: Peterborough, 17 August 1977
Height: 5'10" Weight: 12.1
International Honours: E: U21-4

A Southampton wide midfielder who can also play at full back, Matthew's good form in 1997-98 saw him return to the England U21 squad and establish himself at club level in 38 league and cup games. Although only scoring once – a great goal at Crystal Palace earning a 1-1 draw – his versatility and forceful play made him a valuable member of a side that showed good improvement under the new manager, Dave Jones. Another feature of his play is his

ability to get a lot of distance on long throws.
Southampton (From trainee on 1/7/95) PL 60+12/5 FLC 10+1 FAC 3+2/1

OATWAY Anthony (Charlie) Philip David Terry Frank Donald Stanley Gerry Gordon Stephen James
Born: Hammersmith, 28 November 1973
Height: 5'7" Weight: 10.10

Signed by Brentford from Torquay at the start of last season, the tigerish midfield ball winner, who was named after Queens Park Rangers players of the 70s, joined the club as Eddie May's first signing, the third time May had signed him, after previously securing his services for Cardiff and Torquay. A regular in midfield until the New Year, when a knee injury forced him to miss games, his season came to a halt when he finally had to submit to an operation, before re-appearing as a sub for the final two games.
Cardiff C (Free from Yeading on 4/8/94) FL 29+3 FLC 2/1 FAC 1+1 Others 3+1
Torquay U (Free on 28/12/95) FL 65+2/1 FLC 3 FAC 1
Brentford (£10,000 on 21/8/97) FL 30+3 FAC 2

O'BRIEN Andrew (Andy) James
Born: Harrogate, 29 June 1979
Height: 6'3" Weight: 11.9
International Honours: E: Yth

As the Young Player of the Year for 1996-97, Andy, known as "Rash" because of his man-marking ability, was expected to hold down a regular place in the Bradford side last season, but, in the event, did not make a first team start until early December. An extremely mobile central defender, who can also play in midfield if the need be, his good form saw him selected for the Football League U21 side that played its Italian counterparts at Charlton. Continued to take the eye of the scouts and is developing all the time.
Bradford C (From trainee on 28/10/96) FL 41+7/2 FAC 4

O'BRIEN Liam Francis
Born: Dublin, 5 September 1964
Height: 6'1" Weight: 12.6
Club Honours: Div 1 '93
International Honours: Ei: 16; U23-1; Yth; Sch

Uncertain as to where his career was going in the summer of 1997, but having committed his immediate future to Tranmere, Liam seemed to enjoy a new lease of life in the Rovers' midfield in 1997-98 as dependable and consistent as ever during the campaign, he continued to enjoy and exploit his ability to dictate the flow and pace of a game. Having a right-foot shot that can be ferocious when he can get forward from his favoured position just in front of the back four, he is especially dangerous at set pieces. He particularly enjoyed Rovers' FA Cup fifth round visit to Newcastle, being a former Magpie.*
Manchester U (£60,000 from Shamrock Rov on 14/10/86) FL 16+15/2 FLC 1+2 FAC 0+2

Newcastle U (£250,000 on 15/11/88) F/PL 131+20/19 FLC 9/1 FAC 12+2/1 Others 9+2/1
Tranmere Rov (£300,000 on 21/1/94) FL 151+7/10 FLC 15+1/1 FAC 7+1/1 Others 5+1

Liam O'Brien

O'CONNELL Brendan
Born: Lambeth, 12 November 1966
Height: 5'10" Weight: 12.1

Signed from Charlton at the start of 1997-98, this hard-working, non-stop midfielder made a dream start for Wigan Athletic when scoring a hat trick in the opening match, at home against Wycombe Wanderers. Having quickly settled in with his new side, scoring two more league goals, unfortunately, a serious blood clot on the knee was to end his season in December.
Portsmouth (From apprentice on 1/7/85)
Exeter C (Free on 4/8/86) FL 73+8/19 FLC 3+1/2 FAC 3 Others 4
Burnley (Free on 1/7/88) FL 62+2/17 FLC 6/3 FAC 3/1 Others 5/2
Huddersfield T (Loaned on 30/11/89) FL 11/1
Barnsley (£50,000 on 23/3/90) FL 212+28/35 FLC 10+1/1 FAC 14/1 Others 7+1/2
Charlton Ath (£125,000 on 26/7/96) FL 33+5/2 FLC 2 FAC 2
Wigan Ath (£120,000 on 8/8/97) FL 17/5 FLC 2 FAC 1

O'CONNOR Derek Peter Luke
Born: Dublin, 9 March 1978
Height: 5'11" Weight: 12.1
International Honours: Ei: U21-3; Yth; Sch

Having come through the ranks as a Huddersfield trainee goalkeeper, the 20-year-old Dubliner was given his full league debut in front of the Sky TV cameras at home to Nottingham Forest early last October. Capped for the Republic of Ireland at U21 level, and a member of a successful side which finished third in the World Youth Championships in Malaysia, he has since been released from the club after making a promising start.
Huddersfield T (From trainee on 16/5/95) FL 1 FLC 0+1

O'CONNOR Jonathan (Jon)
Born: Darlington, 28 October 1976
Height: 5'10" Weight: 11.3
International Honours: E: U21-3; Yth

A highly promising defender, unfortunately, Jon's career stalled at Everton due to a series of serious injuries and, following his only appearance of last season when coming off the bench for the final 15 minutes at Aston Villa, he was allowed to join the ever-expanding colony of old Evertonians at Sheffield United in February. As part of the deal that took Don Hutchison in the opposite direction, he made just two powerful subs' appearances, in which he looked to be a player for the future, his ability being recognised when selected for the Nationwide U21 side that played against its Italian counterparts at Charlton in March. Is equally at home at right back, or in central defence, where his ability to marshal those around him is excellent for one so young.

Everton (From trainee on 28/10/93) PL 3+2
Sheffield U (Signed on 10/2/98) FL 0+2

O'CONNOR Mark Andrew
Born: Thundersley, 10 March 1963
Height: 5'8" Weight: 10.10
Club Honours: Div 3 '87

More than capable as an attacking midfielder, or wing back, with good control and ball-passing skills, last season was a wretched one for Gillingham's Mark. Although playing in the Coca Cola Cup at home to Birmingham, his broken leg from two years ago could not stand up to regular league football and, in October 1997, he announced his retirement. A sad loss to the game, he had a well-deserved testimonial match in April, which included the likes of Glenn Hoddle, and former Gills' favourite, Steve Bruce, before departing for pastures new.

Queens Park R (From apprentice on 1/6/80) FL 2+1
Exeter C (Loaned on 7/10/83) FL 38/1 FAC 2/1 Others 3/1
Bristol Rov (£20,000 on 13/8/84) FL 79+1/10 FLC 8/1 FAC 7/1 Others 4/1
Bournemouth (£25,000 on 27/3/86) FL 115+13/12 FLC 5+3 FAC 7 Others 4+1
Gillingham (£70,000 on 15/12/89) FL 107+9/8 FLC 8 FAC 7+1 Others 6+2/1
Bournemouth (Free on 5/7/93) FL 56+2/3 FLC 7+1 FAC 4 Others 1
Gillingham (Free on 4/8/95) FL 36+4/1 FLC 3+1 FAC 5

O'CONNOR Martyn John
Born: Walsall, 10 December 1967
Height: 5'9" Weight: 11.8

Martyn was used in more of a holding role at Birmingham in 1997-98, unlike previously, but showed an intelligence to adapt well and produced a series of outstanding displays during the run-in. A hard worker, although unspectacular, he was steady and reliable in everything he did and linked play well, while effectively breaking down the opposition's attacks. The only missing ingredient from his normal game was a lack of goals, one being his sum total for the season, but what a goal it was. With Blues 1-0 down at home to Manchester City, and into injury time, first Nicky Forster scrambled an equaliser and then Martyn,

with slide-rule precision, slotted in a 25 yarder to bring about a memorable 2-1 victory. His exceptional stamina has to be his number one asset.

Crystal Palace (£25,000 from Bromsgrove Rov on 26/6/92) FL 2 Others 1+1
Walsall (Loaned on 24/3/93) FL 10/1 Others 2/1
Walsall (£40,000 on 14/2/94) FL 94/21 FLC 6/2 FAC 10/2 Others 3/1
Peterborough U (£350,000 on 12/7/96) FL 18/3 FLC 4 FAC 2
Birmingham C (£500,000 + on 29/11/96) FL 56+1/5 FLC 3 FAC 3

O'GORMAN David (Dave)
Born: Chester, 20 June 1972
Height: 5'8" Weight: 11.10

Returning to the Football League after six long years, Dave signed for Swansea immediately prior to the start of last season, having come to notice while at non-league Barry Town. A wide midfielder or forward, he was influential in scoring five goals and producing crosses for others, before knee ligament problems restricted him during the latter part of the campaign. Although his subs' appearances almost doubled his starts, Dave looks to be a welcome addition at the Vetch Field.

Wrexham (From trainee on 6/7/90) FL 8+9 FAC 1 Others 1 (Free to Northwich Vic during 1991 close season)
Swansea C (£20,000 from Barry T on 8/8/97) FL 11+23/5 FLC 2 Others 1

Steve Ogrizovic

OGRIZOVIC Steven (Steve)
Born: Mansfield, 12 September 1957
Height: 6'4" Weight: 15.0
Club Honours: FAC '87

The long-standing Coventry 'keeper was under pressure in 1997-98 from Swedish international signing, Magnus Hedman, but he kept his place until the 3-0 defeat at Villa Park in December, rarely letting the side down during that period, with his agility unimpaired by his age. Returning to the first team against Sheffield United in the FA Cup, when Hedman was injured, he made a dramatic last-minute dash back to distract

Peter Katchouro from scoring what would have been the winner. However, he could do nothing about the replay defeat at Bramall Lane, keeping his place when Hedman returned to fitness, and at Filbert Street he made two world class saves, being awarded the PFA Merit award for achievements to the game the following day, a fitting tribute to a great servant. Having broken George Curtis' all-time appearance record for the club, Steve played his 500th league game at Tottenham on Easter Monday, celebrating with a finger tip round the post from Ramon Vega's header.

Chesterfield (Signed from ONRYC on 28/7/77) FL 16 FLC 2
Liverpool (£70,000 on 18/11/77) FL 4 Others 1
Shrewsbury T (£70,000 on 11/8/82) FL 84 FLC 7 FAC 5
Coventry C (£72,000 on 22/6/84) F/PL 502/1 FLC 49 FAC 34 Others 11

O'HAGAN Daniel (Danny) Alexander Nicholas
Born: Padstow, 24 April 1976
Height: 6'1" Weight: 13.8

Having been released by Plymouth the previous season and plying his trade with Weston super Mare, Danny earned a surprise recall to league football with his former club when coming back to Home Park last November. Having impressed with his development in non-league football, the strong centre forward was re-signed on a short-term contract by Mick Jones, and justified the manager's faith in him when scoring in a 1-1 draw at Northampton in the Auto Windscreen Shield.

Plymouth Arg (From trainee on 29/6/94) FL 1+8/1 FLC 0+1 Others 1 (Free to Weston super Mare on 20/9/96)
Plymouth Arg (Free on 6/11/97) FL 5+4 Others 1/1

O'KANE John Andrew
Born: Nottingham, 15 November 1974
Height: 5'10" Weight: 12.2
Club Honours: FAYC '92; Div 2 '97

Unable to progress at Manchester United in 1997-98, John went out on loan to Bradford last October, standing in for Chris Wilder at right back, and then Wayne Jacobs at left back, in seven games, during which time he showed himself to be a versatile player who was both comfortable on the ball and able to produce excellent forays deep into an opponent's half. Back at Old Trafford, and still a Central League player, in January, Everton tempted him to Goodison where he looked neat and tidy on the right-hand side of a five-man defence when figuring in ten of the Toffees' last 11 matches. Is also capable of playing in midfield.

Manchester U (From trainee on 29/1/93) PL 1+1 FLC 2+1 FAC 1 Others 1
Bury (Loaned on 25/10/96) FL 2+2/2
Bury (Loaned on 16/1/97) FL 9/1 Others 1
Bradford C (Loaned on 31/10/97) FL 7
Everton (£250,000+ on 30/1/98) PL 12

OLDFIELD David Charles
Born: Perth, Australia, 30 May 1968
Height: 5'11" Weight: 13.4
International Honours: E: U21-1

Not surprisingly named as the Luton Supporters' Player of the Year, this hard-

working, attacking midfielder enjoyed an outstanding 1997-98 in what was otherwise a bleak time for the Kenilworth faithful. Tackling back, using the ball well, especially long through balls, reading the game, and finishing coolly, at the start of the campaign he played as a support striker to Tony Thorpe, who once again shot to the top of the division's goalscoring charts. After Thorpe left, he found himself cast as the main striker and, although this was not his best position, he responded well and his total of 11 goals made him second highest scorer at the club. At the end of the season, he found himself playing alongside the prolific Rory Allen, and five goals from the final eight games from David, and six from Allen ensured safety and saw the Aussie-born player at his very best. *Stop Press:* Released under the Bosman ruling, David signed for Stoke on 21 June.

Luton T (From apprentice on 16/5/86) FL 21+8/4 FLC 4+2/2 FAC 0+1 Others 2+1/2
Manchester C (£600,000 on 14/3/89) FL 18+8/6 FLC 2+1/2 Others 0+1/1
Leicester C (£150,000 on 12/1/90) F/PL 163+25/26 FLC 10+1/1 FAC 6/3 Others 11+3/2
Millwall (Loaned on 24/2/95) FL 16+1/6
Luton T (£150,000 on 21/7/95) FL 99+18/18 FLC 11/2 FAC 2 Others 7+2/4

David Oldfield

O'LEARY Kristian Denis
Born: Port Talbot, 30 August 1977
Height: 6'0" Weight: 13.4
International Honours: W: Yth

A strong tackler with good passing ability, who can play in the centre of defence or in midfield, Kristian's form for Swansea last season was a revelation, and was one of the reasons that the club allowed Christian Edwards to leave for Nottingham Forest in March. Definitely one to watch out for this coming term, an improvement in his overall fitness made all the difference.

Swansea C (From trainee on 1/7/96) FL 35+7/1 FLC 1 FAC 2+1 Others 1

OLIVER Michael
Born: Cleveland, 2 August 1975
Height: 5'10" Weight: 12.4

A strong-running and skilful Darlington midfielder, Michael enjoyed himself in 1997-98, his second full season at the club, despite his goal touch deserting him after hitting nine in 1996-97. Always covering every inch of the pitch with his energetic running, his ability to burst through from midfield kept defences on their toes.

Middlesbrough (From trainee on 19/8/92) Others 0+1
Stockport Co (£15,000 on 7/7/94) FL 17+5/1 FLC 0+2 FAC 2 Others 1
Darlington (Free on 30/7/96) FL 67+11/11 FLC 6 FAC 6 Others 1+1

OMIGIE Joseph (Joe) Eghodalo
Born: Hammersmith, 13 June 1972
Height: 6'2" Weight: 13.0

Joe, a tall, gangly striker, who unsettles defenders with his awkward style, played just five minutes for Brentford in 1997-98, as a substitute against Chesterfield in August, before being released by the Bees' new manager, Micky Adams, in January.

Brentford (Free from Donna FC on 26/8/94) FL 10+14/1 FAC 0+3 Others 2+1/1

OMOYINMI Emmanuel (Manny)
Born: Nigeria, 28 December 1977
Height: 5'6" Weight: 10.7
International Honours: E: Sch

Loaned to Dundee last February, where he played well, on his return to West Ham he got his first team chance when coming on as a substitute in the live televised game against Leeds in March. A right winger, with lightening pace, one run in the match saw him pick out John Hartson, who hit the post. He was in the headlines after coming on as a sub again, this time at Crystal Palace, when scoring two well-taken goals which gave West Ham a point. Now Manny has made the breakthrough, his pace and goalscoring abilities should bring him further success.

West Ham U (From trainee on 17/5/95) PL 1+5/2
Bournemouth (Loaned on 30/9/96) FL 5+2
Dundee U (Loaned on 20/2/98) SL 1+3 SC 0+1

O'NEILL John Joseph
Born: Glasgow, 3 January 1974
Height: 5'11" Weight: 12.0

Although arriving at Bournemouth as a quick and lively striker, John settled down well last season as an attacking midfielder, who was occasionally used up front, scoring four goals, including a spectacular effort that helped put Bristol City out of the FA Cup. Despite 1997-98 being in stark contrast to the previous campaign, when he struggled to find his form, he was released during the summer.

Queens Park (From school on 25/7/91) SL 70+21/30 SLC 2+1 SC 2 Others 0+1
Glasgow Celtic (Signed on 16/5/94) SL 0+2
Bournemouth (Free on 29/3/96) FL 42+24/4 FLC 2+2 FAC 3+1/1 Others 4+2

O'NEILL Keith Padre Gerard
Born: Dublin, 16 February 1976
Height: 6'1" Weight: 12.7
International Honours: Ei: 9; U21-1; Yth; Sch

The mercurial Irishman endured a dreadfully disappointing season at Norwich in 1997-98, in terms of injuries, starting just six games as minor niggles, then a fractured foot deprived the Canaries of one of their prized possessions. At the start of the campaign, Keith had been the subject of a £4 million bid and went on to be selected for the Republic of Ireland squad on two occasions, but, unfortunately, it was the foot injury that dominated the news. Able to play at wing back, but more dangerous in an advanced left-sided midfield position, he provides great pace, power, and accurate crosses to the forwards, something the fans can only hope will be unimpaired in 1998-99.

Norwich C (From trainee on 1/7/94) P/FL 40+15/8 FLC 6+2 FAC 3

O'NEILL Michael Andrew Martin
Born: Portadown, 5 July 1969
Height: 5'11" Weight: 11.10
International Honours: NI: 31; B-1; U23-1; U21-1; Yth; Sch

Michael started just three games for Coventry in 1997-98 and was substitute in two others, only appearing when there were injuries and suspensions, before going on an extended loan to Aberdeen in January, where he joined the former City assistant manager, Alex Miller. From there, the Northern Ireland international was loaned to Reading until the end of the campaign, playing either on the left-hand side or centre of midfield. Despite not being an immediate success, his performances improved under the new manager, Tommy Burns, who announced that he would like to sign him on a permanent contract if terms could be agreed.

Newcastle U (Signed from Coleraine on 23/10/87) FL 36+12/15 FLC 2 FAC 3+2/1 Others 1
Dundee U (Signed on 15/8/89) SL 49+15/11 SLC 3+2/1 SC 2 Others 3+2/1
Hibernian (Signed on 20/8/93) SL 96+2/19 SLC 9/3 SC 6/2
Coventry C (£500.000 on 26/7/96) PL 3+2 FLC 1
Aberdeen (Loaned on 22/1/98) SL 4+1 SC 0+1
Reading (Loaned on 2/3/98) FL 9/1

ONUORA Ifem (Iffy)
Born: Glasgow, 28 July 1967
Height: 6'1" Weight: 13.10

Having started 1997-98 in Gillingham's colours, scoring three times in 25 appearances, Iffy was seen by Swindon as the ideal replacement for Wayne Allison, who was missed so much following his move to Huddersfield, and he signed for the Robins in March. Big and strong, and able to hold the ball up well, exactly the qualities the club needed in a frontman, he became an instant crowd favourite by scoring the winner on his debut – flying full length to net a diving header in the 2-1 victory at QPR – before suffering a bizarre facial injury against Charlton, when an accidental clash with the referee left him nursing a depressed fracture of the cheekbone. That injury was expected to rule him out for the rest of the season, but the club's mounting casualty list saw the brave striker back in action for the final two games with a protective mask covering the injury.

Huddersfield T (Signed from Bradford University on 28/7/89) FL 115+50/30 FLC 10+6/4 FAC 11+3/3 Others 13+3/3
Mansfield T (£30,000 on 20/7/94) FL 17+11/8 FAC 0+1 Others 1
Gillingham (£25,000 on 16/8/96) FL 53+9/23 FLC 6/1 FAC 4/2 Others 1
Swindon T (£120,000 on 13/3/98) FL 6/1

ONWERE Udo Alozie
Born: Hammersmith, 9 November 1971
Height: 6'0" Weight: 11.7

Released by Blackpool during the 1997 summer break, Udo arrived at Barnet prior to 1997-98 getting underway and made his first start against Swansea in the seventh game of the new campaign, after being used as a sub on three earlier occasions. Showing himself to be a ball-playing midfielder, who is also a hard tackler, he will undoubtedly improve with another season's experience of first team football.

Fulham (From trainee on 11/7/90) FL 66+19/7 FLC 4+2 FAC 1+1 Others 9
Lincoln C (Free on 12/8/94) FL 40+3/4 FLC 5 FAC 1 Others 4/1 (Free to Dover Ath in August 1996)
Blackpool (Free on 13/9/96) FL 5+4 FLC 1 FAC 1 Others 0+2
Barnet (Free on 5/8/97) FL 11+6 FLC 2+1 FAC 0+1 Others 1

ORD Richard John
Born: Murton, 3 March 1970
Height: 6'2" Weight: 13.5
Club Honours: Div 1 '96
International Honours: E: U21-3

Unfortunately, the central defender was plagued by a back injury early on in Sunderland's promotion campaign during 1997-98 and when he returned to fitness, found his way blocked by Darren Williams and Jody Craddock. However, Sunderland's longest serving player was always ready when needed and turned in a typically gutsy display at Wolves in February in a vital 1-0 win. Good in the air, and on the ground, especially in the tackle, his long legs retrieving many a ball, and also surprisingly skilful for a big man, Richard will no doubt feel he still has plenty to offer the club.

Sunderland (From trainee on 14/7/87) P/FL 223+20/7 FLC 17+5 FAC 11+1/1 Others 5+2
York C (Loaned on 22/2/90) FL 3

ORLYGSSON Thorvaldur (Toddy)
Born: Iceland, 2 August 1966
Height: 5'11" Weight: 11.3
International Honours: Iceland: 41

Although starting the first three games for Oldham in 1997-98, he fell out of favour under manager, Neil Warnock, and only came back into the team when there were shortages in April. However, he performed so well that the manager had no option other than to keep playing him. A midfielder who is effective both in the centre or on the wide right, where he can make penetrating runs to get into the danger areas, he also enjoys dead-ball situations.

Nottingham F (£175,000 from KA Akureyri on 9/12/89) F/PL 31+6/2 FLC 5+1/2 FAC 1 Others 0+1
Stoke C (Free on 5/8/93) FL 86+4/16 FLC 7/1 FAC 6/1 Others 7/1
Oldham Ath (£180,000 on 22/12/95) FL 46+8/1 FLC 5+1 FAC 3+1

ORMEROD Anthony
Born: Middlesbrough, 31 March 1979
Height: 5'10" Weight: 11.8
International Honours: E: Yth

A gifted young Middlesbrough winger who can play on either flank, Anthony looks set to make the grade at the highest level after being blooded last season. Having made his debut at Bradford in September, and scoring the equaliser with a magnificent curved drive, he went on to play a further 22 games, while scoring two more goals, before a hernia operation put him out of action towards the end of the campaign. But, during that time, he showed a maturity which belied his years and an unspoilt confidence that augurs well for the future. Able to go on the inside or the outside, with fine control, he has the choice of getting in superb crosses or going on himself. Scheduled to be fit in time for the coming season, he is tipped to surprise many a Premiership defence.

Middlesbrough (From trainee on 16/5/96) FL 8+10/3 FLC 2+1 FAC 2

ORMEROD Brett Ryan
Born: Blackburn, 18 October 1976
Height: 5'11" Weight: 11.4

Having played four times as a sub for Blackpool the previous season, the young striker was looking forward to making his full debut and scoring his first goal for the club in 1997-98. In the event he achieved both targets, although not becoming a regular. After making four appearances from the bench, he was again brought on, this time at Carlisle on Boxing Day for the injured Chris Malkin, scoring the equaliser, and two days later he started the home game against Wrexham, heading in the Seasiders' only goal in a 3-1 defeat. Rested after seven more starts, Brett will be looking to come good in 1998-99.

Blackpool (£50,000 from Accrington Stanley on 21/3/97) FL 5+8/2 FAC 0+1 Others 3

ORMEROD Mark Ian
Born: Bournemouth, 5 February 1976
Height: 6'0" Weight: 12.11

Mark was first choice beneath the bar for Brighton and Hove Albion in 1997-98 until early November when a loss of form let in his friendly rival, Nicky Rust. Possibly, his finest performance of the season came in the match at Walsall, in the Auto Windscreens Shield competition, when he played superbly to keep the scoreline to a "respectable" 0-5. Having regained the number one jersey at the end of February, he certainly played his part in keeping the Seagulls off the bottom rung of the third division.

Brighton & Hove A (From trainee on 21/7/94) FL 51 FLC 2 Others 2

ORMONDROYD Ian
Born: Bradford, 22 September 1964
Height: 6'4" Weight: 13.9

A well-travelled striker, Ian arrived at Scunthorpe from Oldham early last September and had a very disappointing season, having to carry an ankle injury, and

never getting near his top form with third division defences being too strong for him. Still good in the air though, he only managed seven league starts and only scored one goal, and that came in a reserve match. Unfortunately, with his ankle problem persisting, he did not appear in any games after the end of March and was released during the summer.

Bradford C (Signed from Thackley on 6/9/85) FL 72+15/20 FLC 12+2/4 FAC 7/2 Others 7+2/1
Oldham Ath (Loaned on 27/3/87) FL 8+2/1
Aston Villa (£600,000 on 2/2/89) FL 41+15/6 FLC 4+2/2 FAC 5/2 Others 6+1
Derby Co (£350,000 on 19/9/91) FL 25/8 FLC 3 FAC 3/1
Leicester C (Signed on 11/3/92) F/PL 67+10/7 FLC 6/2 FAC 1+1 Others 11/3
Hull C (Loaned on 27/1/95) FL 10/6
Bradford C (£75,000 on 13/7/95) FL 28+10/6 FLC 7/3 FAC 2+1/1 Others 2+2
Oldham Ath (Free on 20/9/96) FL 26+5/8 FAC 1
Scunthorpe U (£25,000 on 5/9/97) FL 7+13 FAC 0+3 Others 0+3

OSBORN Simon Edward
Born: Croydon, 19 January 1972
Height: 5'9" Weight: 11.4

The left-footed midfielder was felt to be the man most likely to prompt those around him into making Wolves "click" as a team in 1997-98. However, he had been struggling for fitness during the summer and his knee problems had not settled down by August, forcing a bone graft operation, thus his season did not get underway until as a sub versus Ipswich. Starting the next eight matches, scoring against Queens Park Rangers in the initial outing, he then missed a further seven through another injury. His next absence was to be self-inflicted. Having been sent off at Ipswich, he scored with a beautifully measured lob against Portsmouth, but the celebrations were low key, as he faced suspension for the FA Cup semi final, a game in which Wolves were outclassed in the centre of the park.

Crystal Palace (From trainee on 3/1/90) F/PL 47+8/5 FLC 11/1 FAC 2 Others 1+3
Reading (£90,000 on 17/8/94) FL 31+1/5 FLC 4 Others 3
Queens Park R (£1,100,000 on 7/7/95) PL 6+3/1 FLC 2
Wolverhampton W (£1,000,000 on 22/12/95) FL 77+3/9 FLC 1/1 FAC 8 Others 2

OSTENSTAD Egil
Born: Haugesvad, Norway, 2 January 1972
Height: 6'0" Weight: 12.6
International Honours: Norway: 13

Reported to be the subject of a substantial bid from another club at the start of 1997-98, this Southampton striker had a great season, scoring 11 goals in 22 starts, plus nine as sub. In fact, not being fully fit, he came off the bench to score on three occasions. A great favourite with the fans, the Norwegian international formed a very good striking partnership with David Hirst after the injury to Kevin Davies, scoring braces on three separate occasions. Strong running and full of purpose, his best goal was probably the drag back, turn and shot at West Ham, which took the Saints to a 4-2 victory. If you want to pack your team with defenders and play a lone striker, Egil would

be your man. *Stop Press:* As a member of Norway's World Cup squad, he appeared just once, against Scotland, before the side went out to Italy in the second round.

Southampton (£800,000 from Viking Stavanger on 3/10/96) PL 50+9/21 FLC 7/3 FAC 1+1/1

Egil Ostenstad

OSTER John Morgan
Born: Boston, 8 December 1978
Height: 5'9" Weight: 10.8
International Honours: W: 3; U21-7; Yth

Having been signed from Grimsby during the 1997 close season, this gifted out-and-out winger, with the ability to play on either the right or left, nearly scored a goal with his first touch in an Everton shirt – a ferocious shot in a summer testimonial match against Glasgow Rangers, which flew narrowly wide. Like so many other young players at Goodison Park, he struggled to impress in a side constantly battling against relegation, but he clearly possesses a huge degree of natural talent and had been tracked by Manchester United and Newcastle before Howard Kendall swooped. In boasting the distinction of winning his first international cap for Wales without touching the ball, after coming on as a late substitute in Belgium, he went on to win full caps against Brazil and Jamaica, but was strangely sent off when playing for the U21 team against Italy. Finished on a high, with the distinction of having made more appearances for the club than any other player during the Blues' troubled campaign.

Grimsby T (From trainee on 11/7/96) FL 21+3/3 FAC 0+1/1
Everton (£1,500,000 on 21/7/97) PL 16+15/1 FLC 3/1 FAC 0+1

O'SULLIVAN Wayne St John
Born: Akrotiri, Cyprus, 25 February 1974
Height: 5'9" Weight: 11.2
Club Honours: Div 2 '96
International Honours: Ei: U21-2

Wayne O'Sullivan

Having arrived at Cardiff City from Swindon last August and making an immediate impact with some tricky runs down the right, Wayne came through a period where his form faded, to finish 1997-98 strongly, showing himself to be determined and hard working to keep the number 11 shirt for the last 14 matches. An attacking player who loves to run at defenders and fool them with sheer trickery, he was always willing to work, but occasionally had to lift himself as the team struggled to find form. Is a gutsy type of player who will put this behind him and aim to put things right in 1998-99, and should thrive under Frank Burrows' guidance.

Swindon T (From trainee on 1/5/93) FL 65+24/3 FLC 11/1 FAC 1+3 Others 3+2
Cardiff C (£75,000 on 22/8/97) FL 40+3/2 FLC 0+1 FAC 5/1 Others 1

OTTO Ricky
Born: Hackney, 9 November 1967
Height: 5'10" Weight: 11.10
Club Honours: Div 2 '95; AMC '95

Unable to find a place at Birmingham in 1997-98, Ricky was loaned to Notts County early in September with a view to a permanent transfer. With a unique talent as devastating wingman, and very special at set pieces, he quickly became a first teamer at County until suffering serious knee ligament damage that put him out of action for the rest of the campaign after just six games. To describe him as a crowd pleaser would be an understatement, and all and sundry at Meadow Lane were both saddened and shocked by his long-term enforced absence from the game. Was released from his contract at Birmingham by mutual consent in December.

Leyton Orient (Free from Haringey Borough on 7/11/90) FL 41+15/13 FLC 3 FAC 2+1 Others 5+1/2
Southend U (£100,000 on 9/7/93) FL 63+1/17 FLC 3 FAC 1 Others 8/2
Birmingham C (£800,000 on 19/12/94) FL 25+21/6 FLC 3+3 FAC 2/1 Others 8/1
Charlton Ath (Loaned on 19/9/96) FL 5+2 FLC 2
Peterborough U (Loaned on 6/2/97) FL 15/4 Others 2/2
Notts Co (Loaned on 3/9/97) FL 4 FLC 2

OVERMARS Marc
Born: Ernst, Holland, 29 March 1973
Height: 5'8" Weight: 11.4
Club Honours: PL '98; FAC '98
International Honours: Holland: 46

A 1997 summer signing for Arsenal, Marc turned out to be a terrific buy from the Dutch side, Ajax, missing just seven games throughout 1997-98 and ending the season with both Premiership and FA Cup winners' medals after the side had stormed to the double. Interestingly, on arriving at Highbury, there were many who felt that the manager, Arsene Wenger, had taken too much of a gamble on a man who had suffered such an horrendous knee injury that he had been forced to miss Holland's Euro '96. However, such was Wenger's faith in the Dutchman that the crowd favourite, Paul Merson, was allowed to join Middlesbrough. Although taking him a little while to find his feet, possibly due to the narrowness of the Highbury pitch, there was eventually just no stopping him, missing just seven games and scoring 16 goals being testament to his durability. Apart from helping the Dutch international side to qualify for France '98, his highlights of a brilliant start to his English career came with the vital Premiership winner at Manchester United and the opening goal at Wembley in a 2-0 FA Cup final win over Newcastle. Great when getting down the left flank, his wonderful pace and trickery often seeing him go past even the best of full backs as if they were transparent, a good many goals came from his pin-point crosses. *Stop Press:* Although having an excellent World Cup, scoring in the 5-0 win over South Korea, he was unfortunate to be forced to miss Holland's semi-final match against Brazil

225

when suffering damage to a hamstring. Back as a substitute for the third place game against Croatia, a 2-1 defeat made it a sad end after promising so much.

Arsenal (£7,000,000 from Ajax on 10/7/97) PL 32/12 FLC 3/2 FAC 8+1/2 Others 2

OVERSON Vincent (Vince) David
Born: Kettering, 15 May 1962
Height: 6'2" Weight: 15.0
Club Honours: Div 3 '82, Div 2 '93; AMC '91, '92

A big, strong, and forceful central defender, Vince was signed on loan from Burnley last September as Shrewsbury were looking for some experience at the back. Unfortunately, having begun to provide that in his play and organisation, a possible permanent move was thwarted by the return of an injury, which had curtailed much of 1996-97 season, and he played just twice before being laid up and returning to Turf Moor.

Burnley (From apprentice on 16/11/79) FL 207+4/6 FLC 9/1 FAC 19 Others 10
Birmingham C (Free on 11/6/86) FL 179+3/3 FLC 11+1 FAC 8 Others 11/1
Stoke C (£55,000 on 29/8/91) FL 167+3/6 FLC 13/1 FAC 10 Others 23
Burnley (Free on 15/8/96) FL 6+2 FLC 1 Others 1
Shrewsbury T (Loaned on 18/9/97) FL 2

OWEN Gareth
Born: Chester, 21 October 1971
Height: 5'8" Weight: 12.0
Club Honours: WC '95
International Honours: W: B-1; U21-8

It was far more like the "real" Gareth in 1997-98 than in previous seasons, as he at last showed his true potential for Wrexham, often producing form which should see the Welsh team manager, Bobby Gould, at least taking a look at the player. Although enjoying the long-passing game, strong foraging is also a prominent feature of his play, and often brought him success in front of goal. One such effort which jogs the memory was his goal at Dean Court against Bournemouth, after a mazy run.

Wrexham (From trainee on 6/7/90) FL 210+44/28 FLC 7+1 FAC 20+5 Others 30+1

Marc Overmars (background)

OWEN Michael James
Born: Chester, 14 December 1979
Height: 5'9" Weight: 10.4
Club Honours: FAYC '96
International Honours: E: 9; U21-1; Yth; Sch

Having got his Liverpool career underway in 1996-97, Michael proceeded to get his full international career underway on 11 February 1998, against Chile at Wembley, and, in doing so, at the age of 18 years and 59 days, became the youngest player this century to play for England, surpassing Duncan Edwards record by 124 days. He had earlier played for the England U21 side against Greece. In short, it was a superlative season for the goalscoring wizard, usurping even the great heights to which Robbie Fowler and Ian Rush had aspired. He is younger, much quicker, more mentally alert, and more imposing than any youngster of recent years. Despite a lack of height, he is phenomenally fast, his quicksilver pace being too much for all but the finest of defenders, and he is deadly when running at people, particularly in the area. Regarded by Pele as the best player in England, he scored

23 goals for Liverpool last season, which included hat tricks at home to Grimsby (Coca Cola Cup) and at Sheffield Wednesday in the Premiership, and, as we go to press, he awaits World Cup glory in France '98. Was also delighted to be named as the PFA Young Player of the Year, as well as being included in the PFA Premiership select. *Stop Press:* Held back purposely by Glenn Hoddle during England's opening game of the World Cup Finals, Michael was introduced in the 73rd minute of the Romanian match and scored an equaliser ten minutes later, before the Romanians snatched a winner in the 90th minute. Then, having started against Colombia, he showed his true worth against Argentine in the second round, his ability to run at defenders bringing about a penalty for the equaliser, and one of the goals of the competition when he raced past two defenders to shoot across the 'keeper into the top corner. Although England went out, following a penalty shoot-out, the youngest player on view was one of the bright spots of the tournament and was acknowledged by all and sundry as being a future "great".

Liverpool (From juniors on 18/12/96) PL 35+3/19 FLC 4/4 Others 3+1/1

OWERS Gary
Born: Newcastle, 3 October 1968
Height: 5'11" Weight: 12.7
Club Honours: Div 3 '88

Unfortunately, injury brought Gary's lengthy ever-present run to an end last October, thus disrupting his season, and he did not really establish himself back in the Bristol City side until the last quarter of the campaign, when his experience in midfield did much to help the team through the difficult time following Shaun Goater's departure. It was therefore fitting that his goal against Walsall in the penultimate game allowed him to maintain his record of having scored in every season of his professional career.

Sunderland (From apprentice on 8/10/86) FL 259+9/25 FLC 25+1/1 FAC 10+2 Others 11+1/1
Bristol C (£250,000 on 23/12/94) FL 121+5/9 FLC 9/1 FAC 9 Others 9/2

Gary Owers

PAATELAINEN Mika (Mixu) Matti
Born: Helsinki, Finland, 3 February 1967
Height: 6'0" Weight: 13.11
International Honours: Finland: 55

This big striker was signed from Bolton immediately prior to the start of last season, mainly because Wolves had nobody who could hold the ball efficiently up front. His first outing saw him come on as a sub at Queens Park Rangers in the Coca Cola Cup, and take just 21 minutes to score, a sweet left-foot drive from just outside the area. Finding the pace of the derby at West Bromwich difficult, Mixu was used as cover in an 11-match spell, making eight appearances as sub yet not starting. Despite his first goal at Molineux not coming until February against Charlton, his well-taken strike at Wimbledon kept Wolves in the FA Cup, though he later had his nose broken after an incident that involved Vinnie Jones. Four goals were enough to make him top scorer for Wolves in that competition, yet he had failed to score for them in the league.
Dundee U (Signed from Valkeakosken on 30/10/87) SL 101+32/33 SLC 7+2/5 SC 20+1/8 Others 8+1/1
Aberdeen (Signed on 31/3/92) SL 53+22/23 SLC 6/3 SC 7+1/1 Others 3/1
Bolton W (£300,000 on 29/7/94) P/FL 58+11/15 FLC 8+1/2 FAC 1+1 Others 3/1
Wolverhampton W (£250,000 on 8/8/97) FL 10+13 FLC 4+1/1 FAC 4+1/4

PADOVANO Michele
Born: Turin, Italy, 28 August 1966
Height: 5'10" Weight: 10.10
International Honours: Italy: 1

An Italian international striker languishing in the Juventus reserve side, Michele joined up with his former team mate, Attilio Lombardo, at Crystal Palace last November, being bought for the sole purpose to score the goals that would get the side out of a "hole" in the Premiership. In the event, he played just ten times - being withdrawn in all of his eight starts and twice coming off the bench - due to injury, and was unable to put together a run of more than two games at a time, scoring just one goal, at Leicester in a 1-1 draw. There was no doubting his talent, super touches on the ball, and speed to react to situations, but he was just not fit enough to do himself and the club justice. Hopefully, he can put 1997-98 behind him and be ready to go this coming term.
Crystal Palace (£1,700,000 from Juventus on 18/11/97) PL 8+2/1

PAGAL Jean Claude
Born: Cameroon, 15 September 1964
Height: 5'11" Weight: 12.3
International Honours: Cameroon: 17

The 33-year-old Cameroon-born midfielder boasted an impressive pedigree that included an appearance in the 1990 World Cup quarter final against England. Having

spent a period of time in Austrian football, he arrived at Carlisle from St Etienne last February, following trials at Oxford and Derby, but made only one league appearance, in which he was substituted, before being released.
Carlisle U (Free from St Etienne on 17/2/98) FL 1

PAGE Robert John
Born: Llwynpia, 3 September 1974
Height: 6'0" Weight: 12.5
Club Honours: Div 2 '98
International Honours: W: 6; U21-6; Yth; Sch

As Watford's central defender and captain, and a consistent performer who is strong in the air, and times his tackles well, Robert showed improved discipline to lead the team with a calm authority in 1997-98. Has now played more than 100 league matches for Watford, but has yet to score a goal. Last season, he had the unusual distinction of playing against Brazil (for Wales) and Barnet (for Watford in the FA Cup) in the same week, before winning a second division championship medal when the Hornets finished top of the table.
Watford (From trainee on 19/4/93) FL 100+5 FLC 8 FAC 9+1 Others 3/1

PAINTER Peter Robert (Robbie)
Born: Wigan, 26 January 1971
Height: 5'11" Weight: 12.2

Rochdale's most consistent forward, by far, the hard-working Robbie scored in each of the first three games of last season and had 11 goals to his credit by the half-way point. His non-stop chasing continued to worry opponents, even when the goals dried up and he had to play as a lone striker. Returning to the goal charts after a near three-month drought, when teamed up again with Graham Lancashire, he remained easily the side's top scorer, missing just one game and being voted Player of the Year by the fans.

Chester C (From trainee on 1/7/88) FL 58+26/8 FLC 2+2 FAC 7+1/3 Others 3+3
Maidstone U (£30,000 on 16/8/91) FL 27+3/5 FLC 2 FAC 1+1 Others 0+2
Burnley (£25,000 on 27/3/92) FL 16+10/2 FLC 2 FAC 1
Darlington (Signed on 16/9/93) FL 104+11/28 FLC 2+4/1 FAC 5+1/2 Others 9/3
Rochdale (Signed on 10/10/96) FL 66+6/24 FLC 2/1 FAC 3 Others 3

PALLISTER Gary Andrew
Born: Ramsgate, 30 June 1965
Height: 6'4" Weight: 14.13
Club Honours: FAC '90, '94, '96; CS '93, '94, '96, '97; ECWC '91; ESC '91; FLC '92; PL '93, '94, '96, '97
International Honours: E: 22; B-9

A superb central defender, whose excellent reading of the game makes him difficult to pass, Gary was one of Manchester United's most consistent performers until he suffered a recurrence of his back injury problems in the latter stages of last season. Having previously formed an excellent understanding with new recruit, Henning Berg, he gave some typically solid performances, notably in the Champion's League, where he played like a colossus. Having mistakenly been sent off at Bolton in September, following a fracas with Nathan Blake, it seemed that a three-match ban might interrupt his season, but he was later exonerated from any blame by the FA. Having been rested for the Coca Cola Cup tie against Ipswich in October, then again in the FA Cup against Walsall in January, it was during United's Premiership game at Chelsea in February that he sustained his old back injury problem. Sorely missed by United during the second leg of their vital European tie against Monaco in March, he made his comeback against Blackburn at Ewood Park in April, confident that his injury woes were well and truly behind him. Was also recognised by his fellow professionals when he was named in the

Gary Pallister

PFA Premiership award-winning selection. *Stop Press:* Re-joined Middlesbrough on 8 July in a deal thought to be worth £2.5 million.

Middlesbrough (Free from Billingham T on 7/11/84) FL 156/5 FLC 10 FAC 10/1 Others 13
Darlington (Loaned on 18/10/85) FL 7
Manchester U (£2,300,000 on 29/8/89) F/PL 314+3/12 FLC 36 FAC 38/1 Others 45+1/1

PALMER Carlton Lloyd
Born: Rowley Regis, 5 December 1965
Height: 6'2" Weight: 12.4
International Honours: E: 18; B-5; U21-4

Out of favour at Leeds, the former England player had been subject to much crowd and press criticism before joining Southampton last September, but his form for the Saints was outstanding and he was only narrowly beaten to the Player of the Season award by goalkeeper, Paul Jones. His arrival, in fact, totally transformed the midfield with his all-action style and surging runs forward, and he was an inspiration to all around him, scoring three goals in 30 games, the best being an amazing shot from the most acute of angles in the home match against Sheffield Wednesday, one of his former clubs. Able to play equally well as a full back, in central defence, or midfield, his long legs making him a difficult opponent to pass, he can run forever and often produces tremendous surges into the box from seemingly nowhere.

West Bromwich A (From apprentice on 21/12/84) FL 114+7/4 FLC 7+1/1 FAC 4 Others 6
Sheffield Wed (£750,000 on 23/2/89) F/PL 204+1/14 FLC 31/1 FAC 18/2 Others 8+1/1
Leeds U (£2,600,000 on 30/6/94) PL 100+2/5 FLC 12/1 FAC 12/1 Others 4/1
Southampton (£1,000,000 on 26/9/97) PL 26/3 FLC 3 FAC 1

PALMER Stephen (Steve) Leonard
Born: Brighton, 31 March 1968
Height: 6'1" Weight: 12.13
Club Honours: Div 2 '92, '98
International Honours: E: Sch

Steve is a versatile player, equally accomplished in central defence or in midfield, who turned in a series of sterling performances, particularly when the team was faltering towards the end of last season. His versatility was such that he actually started a league match in every shirt from number one to 14 during the campaign, a unique feat that required only a little help from the manager. Having occupied ten different shirts by the end of January, he replaced the previously ever-present Richard Johnson at number ten during March and turned out at number seven soon afterwards. And, with promotion secured and a second division championship medal, he started the home match against Bournemouth in goal, keeping a clean sheet for all of ten seconds before changing places with regular 'keeper, Alex Chamberlain. An invaluable team man, he completed the set by playing in the number nine shirt against Fulham on the last day.*

Ipswich T (Free from Cambridge University on 1/8/89) F/PL 87+24/2 FLC 3 FAC 8+3/1 Others 4+2
Watford (£135,000 on 28/9/95) FL 107+10/4 FLC 8+1 FAC 7+1 Others 4

PAPACONSTANTINOU Loukas
Born: Toronto, Canada, 10 May 1974
Height: 6'2" Weight: 12.0

One of three Canadians at Darlington in 1997-98, having signed from Alabama Saints during the summer of 1997, the goalkeeper played only one first team game, at home to Mansfield, when he kept a clean sheet. Unable to shift the existing 'keeper, David Preece, following a foot injury he returned to Canada in December.

Darlington (Free from Alabama Saints on 4/7/97) FL 1

PARKER Garry Stuart
Born: Oxford, 7 September 1965
Height: 5'11" Weight: 13.2
Club Honours: FLC '89, '90, '97; ESC '89
International Honours: E: B-1; U21-6; Yth

Once again, the right-footed Leicester midfielder was the main playmaker for the team, even though he had to settle for periods on the bench as last season unfolded and injuries prevailed. Remaining deadly from the spot to secure a win against Leeds, and vital points against Villa and Southampton, and possessing a sharp footballing brain that he uses to save his legs, he can still split a defence with a single pass, as demonstrated in the FA Cup win over Northampton. His sending off, effectively for taking a free kick too quickly, against Athletico Madrid, took the steam out of City's efforts to topple the Spaniards and merely emphasised how influential he was to Martin O'Neill's team framework. Is a player who will not be hurried and hates to give the ball away.

Luton T (From apprentice on 5/5/83) FL 31+11/3 FLC 1+3/1 FAC 6+2
Hull C (£72,000 on 21/2/86) FL 82+2/8 FLC 5 FAC 4 Others 2/1
Nottingham F (£260,000 on 24/3/88) FL 99+4/17 FLC 22+1/4 FAC 16/5 Others 9/3
Aston Villa (£650,000 on 29/11/91) F/PL 91+4/13 FLC 12 FAC 10/1 Others 0+2
Leicester C (£300,000 on 10/2/95) P/FL 87+20/10 FLC 13/1 FAC 9/2 Others 4+1/2

PARKER Scott Matthew
Born: Lambeth, 13 October 1980
Height: 5'8" Weight: 11.0
International Honours: E: Yth

Scott proved himself to be an extremely skilful young midfield player when making his Charlton debut last August, coming on as a substitute against Bury. Unfortunately, a knee injury restricted his first team appearances, but when in the side he looked very assured and self confident. Has excellent touch, reads the game well, and is a very exciting prospect who should soon become a regular.

Charlton Ath (From trainee on 22/10/97) FL 0+3 FAC 0+1

PARKIN Brian
Born: Birkenhead, 12 October 1965
Height: 6'3" Weight: 14.7
Club Honours: Div 3 '90

Despite being a very experienced 'keeper, with nearly 300 league games under his belt, Brian failed to gain a regular place as Wycombe's number one in 1997-98 and

made just the one appearance in a 2-0 defeat at York when Martin Taylor was suspended. An excellent shot-stopper, and in one-on-one situations, he was released during the summer.

Oldham Ath (From juniors on 31/3/83) FL 6 FLC 2
Crewe Alex (Free on 30/11/84) FL 98 FLC 7 FAC 2 Others 6
Crystal Palace (Free on 1/7/88) FL 20 FLC 3 Others 2
Bristol Rov (Free on 11/11/89) FL 241 FLC 15 FAC 12 Others 23
Wycombe W (Free on 24/7/96) FL 25 FLC 4

PARKINSON Andrew (Andy) John
Born: Liverpool, 27 May 1979
Height: 5'8" Weight: 10.12

Having already made his first team debut, as a sub, at Wolves last October, and go on to make four further appearances, an injury to Lee Jones saw the 18-year-old Andy taking his place in the Tranmere starting line-up for the FA Cup tie against Sunderland last January. And, amid great scenes, 90 minutes later he was the toast of Birkenhead, his goal putting the club into the fifth round draw for only the second time in its history. A regular member of the reserve team competing in the Pontins League, he had already shown signs of his raw talent and potential and, despite there still being plenty to learn, he is expected by those in the know to succeed at the higher level. Is a forward who can play on both sides, and loves taking defenders on, possessing great pace, skill, and much enthusiasm.

Tranmere Rov (From Liverpool juniors on 12/4/97) FL 8+10/1 FAC 2+1/1

Gary Parkinson

PARKINSON Gary Anthony
Born: Thornaby, 10 January 1968
Height: 5"11" Weight: 13.5

A surprise capture from Burnley during the summer of 1997, Gary finally provided the solution to Preston's long-standing right-

back slot. Vastly experienced (with over 450 senior games to his credit), he enjoys over-lapping and is a threat at set pieces, as a series of tremendous efforts at Carlisle and Watford (the latter from over 35 yards), and at home to York and Southend testify. He also scored from a similar distance in open play against Notts County in the FA Cup and Blackpool in the league, his exploits being a useful adjunct to his defensive capabilities; a fact recognised when he was selected for the PFA Divisional award-winning side.

Middlesbrough (Free from Everton juniors on 17/1/86) FL 194+8/5 FLC 20/1 FAC 17/1 Others 19
Southend U (Loaned on 10/10/92) FL 6
Bolton W (Free on 2/3/93) FL 1+2 Others 4
Burnley (Signed on 27/1/94) FL 134+1/4 FLC 12 FAC 10 Others 6/1
Preston NE (£50,000 on 30/5/97) FL 44+1/5 FLC 4 FAC 4/1 Others 4

PARKINSON Philip (Phil) John
Born: Chorley, 1 December 1967
Height: 6'0" Weight: 12.8
Club Honours: Div 2 '94

Far and away Reading's most committed and consistent player during a long and difficult season in 1997-98, skippering the side after Keith McPherson's injury, and being a runaway winner in the fans' vote for Player of the Season. He also picked up several Evening Post Player of the Month awards, and his bravery shone through many gloomy afternoons and evenings as Royals were rooted to the bottom of the division one table. Having to operate in defence, as well as midfield as injuries took their toll, he always led the side by example and signed a contract which will keep him at the club until 2000. Predominately a ball winner, he played more first team games than anyone else, scoring one goal, a stunning volley in the Coca Cola Cup success against Wolves.

Southampton (From apprentice on 7/12/85)
Bury (£12,000 on 8/3/88) FL 133+12/5 FLC 6+1 FAC 4/1 Others 13/1
Reading (£37,500 on 10/7/92) FL 192+23/8 FLC 20+1/2 FAC 13/1 Others 4+2

PARKS Anthony (Tony)
Born: Hackney, 28 January 1963
Height: 5'10" Weight: 11.5

Having been released by Blackpool during the 1997 close season, Tony moved on to Burnley before joining Doncaster on loan last February. Whilst he did well to finish on the winning side in his six league appearances, he also did well at times to keep the goals against him down to a reasonable level, conceding just ten – a credible record with all things considered. An experienced goalkeeper, the former Tottenham player still has much to offer.*

Tottenham H (From apprentice on 22/9/80) FL 37 FLC 1 FAC 5 Others 5
Oxford U (Loaned on 1/10/86) FL 5
Gillingham (Loaned on 1/9/87) FL 2
Brentford (£60,000 on 24/8/88) FL 71 FLC 7 FAC 8 Others 5
Fulham (Free on 27/2/91) FL 2
West Ham U (Free on 15/8/91) FL 6 FAC 3
Stoke C (Free on 21/8/92) FL 2 FLC 1
Falkirk (Free on 14/10/92) SL 112 SLC 8 SC 4 Others 4
Blackpool (Free on 6/9/96)
Burnley (Free on 13/8/97)
Doncaster Rov (Loaned on 13/2/98) FL 6

PARLOUR Raymond (Ray)
Born: Romford, 7 March 1973
Height: 5'10" Weight: 11.12
Club Honours: FLC '93; PL '98; FAC '98
International Honours: E: B-1; U21-12

Without doubt, the most improved player at Arsenal in 1997-98, having earlier been expected to move to West Ham, Ray shone in 47 games for the club, missing just six, and finishing the campaign with Premiership and FA Cup winners' medals as the Gunners stormed to the double. Such was his progress as a reformed character under Arsene Wenger, he was named in the 30-strong England squad before it was watered down to the 22 who would go to France during the summer to contest the World Cup. This followed an excellent performance for the England "B" side against Chile in February. A hard-working, hard-tackling, hustling midfielder, and a good passer of the ball, until last season many saw him as just another player, but that all changed as he developed further with the added confidence that success brings. And, if you add to that the fact that he scored six goals, which almost equalled his career total, then the improvement can be seen clearly. Of the goals, in terms of importance, there was one in a 1-1 home draw against Spurs, the second in a 2-1 FA Cup win at Middlesbrough, and two inside the first 15 minutes in a 4-1 win at Blackburn. Whatever the future holds for him, the experience gained during the last 12 months will hold him in good stead.

Arsenal (From trainee on 6/3/91) F/PL 135+35/11 FLC 17+3 FAC 19/2 Others 10+3

Ray Parlour

PARMENTER Steven (Steve) James
Born: Chelmsford, 22 January 1977
Height: 5'9" Weight: 11.0

Steve, a lively Bristol Rovers' forward, opened last season with a first half appearance against Plymouth Argyle before

being substituted, and then had to be content with a few, sporadic appearances from the bench. However, following a successful loan spell with Conference club, Yeovil, in September, he returned to Rovers full of confidence and was given further oppor-tunities, making a start in an Auto Windscreen tie victory over Cambridge United. An unsuccessful trial at Southend United, where he had been a youth trainee, was followed by a non-contract place at Yeovil Town in March.

Queens Park R (Free from Southend U juniors on 2/5/95)
Bristol Rov (Free on 15/7/96) FL 11+7/2 FLC 1+1 FAC 0+2/1 Others 1+1

PARRIS George Michael
Born: Ilford, 11 September 1964
Height: 5'9" Weight: 13.0
International Honours: E: Sch

George came to Southend on a trial basis at the start of 1997-98, having been freed by Brighton, but made only one full appearance before being released by his old colleague, Alvin Martin. Still full of effort and heart, he could not be faulted for his commitment, but, at 33 years of age, he had lost the sharpness required to perform at this level, and was unable to convince Alvin that he had a long-term future at Roots Hall.

West Ham U (From apprentice on 9/9/82) FL 211+28/12 FLC 27+3/1 FAC 21/4 Others 7+1/1
Birmingham C (£150,000 on 12/3/93) FL 36+3/1 FLC 2 FAC 1 (Free to Norrkoping during 1996 close season)
Brentford (Loaned on 8/8/94) FL 5 FAC 2/1
Bristol C (Loaned on 1/12/94) FL 6
Brighton & Hove A (Loaned on 9/2/95) FL 18/2
Brighton & Hove A (Free on 29/9/95) FL 55+1/3 FLC 2 FAC 6 Others 6
Southend U (Free on 5/8/97) FL 1

PARRISH Sean
Born: Wrexham, 14 March 1972
Height: 5'10" Weight: 11.8

The Northampton midfielder ran the middle of the park with Roy Hunter at the start of 1997-98, but like Roy, his campaign ended early, when he was carried off against Gillingham in October, and was out for the rest of the season, spending most of his time on crutches. A hard-working, hard-tackling player, who can also score important goals, witness the one that put paid to Luton in September, he intends to be raring to go for 1998-99.

Shrewsbury T (From trainee on 12/7/90) FL 1+2 FLC 1 Others 3 (Free to Telford during 1992 close season)
Doncaster Rov (£20,000 on 28/5/94) FL 64+2/8 FLC 3+1 FAC 2/1 Others 3
Northampton T (£35,000 + on 2/8/96) FL 49+2/9 FLC 5+1 FAC 1 Others 3/1

PARTRIDGE Scott Malcolm
Born: Leicester, 13 October 1974
Height: 5'9" Weight: 11.2

The classy midfielder spent just over a year with Cardiff City, having signed in February 1997, and left at the end of last March on a free transfer to Torquay. The key asset for Scott was his pace, and he made an early impact in 1997-98, playing in the first ten matches and being influential in wins at

Leyton Orient and Mansfield Town, before gradually dropping out of favour. In signing for United, he returned to a club where he had been on loan in 1995 but found it hard to discover his best form, although his undoubted talent should manifest itself in 1998-99.

Bradford C (From trainee on 10/7/92) FL 0+5 FLC 1+1
Bristol C (Free on 18/2/94) FL 24+33/7 FLC 2+3/1 FAC 1+3
Torquay U (Loaned on 13/10/95) FL 5/2
Plymouth Arg (Loaned on 22/1/96) FL 6+1/2
Scarborough (Loaned on 8/3/96) FL 5+2
Cardiff C (£50,000 on 14/2/97) FL 29+8/2 FLC 2 FAC 2 Others 1
Torquay U (Signed on 26/3/98) FL 4+1

PASCOLO Marco

Born: Sion, Switzerland, 9 May 1966
Height: 6'2" Weight: 14.4
International Honours: Switzerland: 40

Signed from Cagliari during the 1997 close season, the Swiss international goalkeeper came as competition and cover for Mark Crossley, but found himself pushed into action for the opening three games of 1997-98 and keeping three clean sheets. He was then injured, joining the club's other two 'keepers, Alan Fettis and Crossley, on the sidelines, and when recovered found the way to the first team barred after Dave Beasant, brought in from Southampton, had made the position his own. Played just six times in all and will be looking to challenge both Beasant and Crossley for a place in the Premiership this coming term.

Nottingham F (£750,000 from Cagliari on 24/7/97) FL 5 FLC 1

PATERSON Scott

Born: Aberdeen, 13 May 1972
Height: 5'11" Weight: 12.10

Scott is a composed and skilful central defender who impressed greatly during his one-month loan at Cardiff City last November, and if the Bluebirds could have persuaded Bristol City to part with the defender for the right price there is no doubt he would have been snapped up. His ability on the ground and in the air, gave City's defence a new air of authority and assurance, and he fitted in well with Mark Harris before going back to Ashton Gate after just five appearances. However, although having started the first six games at City in 1997-98, he was freed during the summer, which would have allowed Cardiff the opportunity to sign him on a permanent basis.

Liverpool (£15,000 from Cove R on 19/3/92)
Bristol C (Free on 4/7/94) FL 40+10/1 FLC 6 FAC 2 Others 3
Cardiff C (Loaned on 7/11/97) FL 5

PATTERSON Darren James

Born: Belfast, 15 October 1969
Height: 6'2" Weight: 12.10
International Honours: NI: 11; B-3; U21-1; Yth

An ankle injury at the start of last season kept him out of contention, but once fit he alternated between full back and central defence, depending upon the needs of the club. Would probably not be a first choice in either position if all the squad were fit but, with so many injuries at Luton, he got plenty of first team chances. Sent off in April against Gillingham, as Town were fighting for second division survival, two weeks later he hit his personal highlight when he scored the only goal of the game for Northern Ireland against Switzerland, having been called into the national team as a replacement, following a good display for the "B" team against the Republic of Ireland in February. Was surprisingly released during the summer.

West Bromwich A (From trainee on 5/7/88)
Wigan Ath (Free on 17/4/89) FL 69+28/6 FLC 7+1/3 FAC 5+4/1 Others 7
Crystal Palace (£225,000 on 1/7/92) PL 22/1 FLC 4 FAC 6
Luton T (£100,000 on 21/8/95) FL 52+4 FLC 0+1 FAC 2+1 Others 9
Preston NE (Loaned on 4/10/96) FL 2

PATTERSON Mark

Born: Leeds, 13 September 1968
Height: 5'10" Weight: 12.4

Having failed to get off the mark with Plymouth in 1997-98, the attacking full back signed for Gillingham in October. Unfortunately, his few months with the club were tempered with a bad hamstring injury, but he came back strongly towards the end of the season to show that he had lost none of his verve, supplying quality crosses to the forwards at one end of the park, while proving to be quick and strong in the tackle at the other end.

Carlisle U (From trainee on 30/8/86) FL 19+3 FLC 4 Others 1
Derby Co (£60,000 on 10/11/87) FL 41+10/3 FLC 5+2 FAC 4 Others 5+1/2
Plymouth Arg (£85,000 on 23/7/93) FL 131+3/3 FLC 3 FAC 8 Others 9
Gillingham (£45,000 on 30/10/97) FL 23 FAC 2

PATTERSON Mark Andrew

Born: Darwen, 24 May 1965
Height: 5'7" Weight: 11.4
Club Honours: FMC '87

Following the breakdown of proposed moves to both Southend and Burnley in 1996-97, Mark began last season at the back in the Sheffield United team and was an ever present until his failure to agree to a new contract led to his transfer to Bury in December. However, before leaving Bramall Lane, he scored the Blades' 600th Football League goal in the 1-0 win at Reading. Returning to Gigg Lane for a second stretch, following a six-year absence, the midfield battler gave maximum effort, while his experience proved crucial to Bury's second-half recovery that saw the club maintain its first division status.

Blackburn Rov (From apprentice on 1/5/83) FL 89+12/20 FLC 4/1 FAC 3+1 Others 2+4/1
Preston NE (£20,000 on 15/6/88) FL 54+1/19 FLC 4+1 FAC 4 Others 7/2
Bury (Signed on 1/2/90) FL 42/10 FLC 2 FAC 1 Others 4
Bolton W (£65,000 on 10/1/91) P/FL 158+11/11 FLC 16+4/2 FAC 17/1 Others 9
Sheffield U (£300,000 on 22/12/95) FL 72+2/4 FLC 9 FAC 3
Southend U (Loaned on 27/3/97) FL 4
Bury (£125,000 on 11/12/97) FL 18/2 FAC 1

PATTIMORE Michael Richard

Born: Newport, 15 March 1979
Height: 5'8" Weight: 10.13
International Honours: W: Yth

Despite having made his Football League debut while still a trainee in 1996-97, before signing pro forms during the following summer, this young forward enjoyed few chances to show what he could do for Swindon Town in 1997-98. Successive substitute appearances against Queens Park Rangers and Bradford in November were the sum total of his contribution to the first team and, although he could boast a 100 percent record, as both games were won, he was handed a free transfer at the end of the season.

Swindon T (From trainee on 1/7/97) FL 0+3

PATTON Aaron Anthony

Born: London, 27 February 1979
Height: 5'7" Weight: 12.1

A left back in his first season as a professional at Wycombe after progressing from the youth team, Aaron had to wait until the final minute of the final game of the season at Walsall before making his senior debut and was unfortunate not to get a touch of the ball. Will obviously want to build on that experience in 1998-99.

Wycombe W (From trainee on 1/7/97) FL 0+1

PAYNE Derek Richard

Born: Edgware, 26 April 1967
Height: 5'6" Weight: 10.8

A small, battling midfielder in his second season at Peterborough in 1997-98, despite his aggression occasionally getting him into trouble, his hard-working displays, coupled to good distribution, made him a must. Popped up with a couple of goals, including a late equaliser in a 2-2 draw at Brighton in September, before becoming unavailable for selection during the final stages of the campaign.

Barnet (£12,000 from Hayes on 1/12/88) FL 50+1/6 FLC 2 FAC 2 Others 3+1
Southend U (Free on 15/7/93) FL 32+3 FLC 2 FAC 1 Others 8/1
Watford (Signed on 21/7/94) FL 33+3/1 FLC 3 FAC 0+1 Others 2
Peterborough U (Free on 8/8/96) FL 71+2/4 FLC 7 FAC 9 Others 8

PAYNE Stephen (Steve) John

Born: Pontefract, 1 August 1975
Height: 5'11" Weight: 12.5
Club Honours: GMVC '95, '97; FAT '96
International Honours: E: SP-1

As the backbone of the Macclesfield side since his arrival in December 1994, Steve held the defence together last season in the club's first experience of the Football League, proving to be a strong central defender who liked to get forward for set pieces. Good in the tackle, with an excellent turn of pace, and a player who can provide pin-point crosses to the wings, he was unlucky to miss a month of the season, in October, with ankle ligament damage.

Huddersfield T (From trainee on 12/7/93)
Macclesfield T (Free on 23/12/94) FL 39 FLC 2 FAC 2 Others 1

PAYTON Andrew (Andy) Paul
Born: Whalley, 23 October 1967
Height: 5'9" Weight: 11.13

Having started last season at Huddersfield, and scoring the club's first goal of the new campaign, he found himself in and out of the side before being exchanged for Burnley's Paul Barnes in January. Finally arriving at his hometown club, after years as a prolific striker in both England and Scotland, he continued to provide a steady stream of goals as the Clarets battled against relegation. Andy's game is based mainly on his finishing ability and, while he is unlikely to collect many Man of the Match awards, his strike rate all but guarantees his selection. Particularly good in one-on-one situations, he rarely misses a decent chance.

Hull C (From apprentice on 29/7/85) FL 116+28/55 FLC 9+2/1 FAC 8 Others 3/1
Middlesbrough (£750,000 on 22/11/91) FL 8+11/3 FAC 1+3
Glasgow Celtic (Signed on 14/8/92) SL 20+16/15 SLC 3+2/5 SC 1+1 Others 3
Barnsley (Signed on 25/11/93) FL 100+8/41 FLC 7/3 FAC 6+1/1
Huddersfield T (£350,000 on 4/7/96) FL 42+1/17 FLC 7/3 FAC 2
Burnley (Signed on 16/1/98) FL 19/9 Others 5/3

PEACOCK Lee Anthony (Tony)
Born: Paisley, 9 October 1976
Height: 6'0" Weight: 12.8
Club Honours: AMC '97
International Honours: S: Yth

The powerful, hardworking Scottish-born forward was injured in Carlisle's opening fixture of the 1997-98 campaign at Southend and, having made one substitute appearance at the end of September, he joined Mansfield the following month in what was a record fee for the Stags. Initially, Tony disappointed many supporters, but then started to show the skills for which he was bought, especially alongside Steve Whitehall, and looks to make a big impact in 1998-99.

Carlisle U (From trainee on 10/3/95) FL 52+24/11 FLC 2+3 FAC 4+1/1 Others 6+4
Mansfield T (£150,000 on 17/10/97) FL 25+7/5 FAC 2 Others 2

PEACOCK Darren
Born: Bristol, 3 February 1968
Height: 6'2" Weight: 12.12
Club Honours: WC '90

Pony-tailed Darren is a centre back, who, as in previous seasons, was a regular in Newcastle's defence in 1997-98 through his consistent performances, using his pace and his ability to read the game to command the heart of back division, and his skilful distribution to turn defence into attack. After struggling with a niggling injury towards the end of the 1996-97 season, he had operations to his knee and groin during the summer, which delayed his start to the new season. His first game was as a substitute in the home Champions League game against Barcelona, and he quickly re-established himself as first choice until he was disturbed by an ankle injury and lost his place to Steve Howey in late January. Was then offered the opportunity to move to Everton as part of the Gary Speed transfer, but declined as he

preferred to stay and fight for his place at St James' Park. Out of contract during the summer, Darren was looking for another club under the Bosman ruling. *Stop Press:* According to press reports, Darren agreed to join Blackburn on 11 June.

Newport Co (From apprentice on 11/2/86) FL 24+4 FLC 2 FAC 1 Others 1+1
Hereford U (Free on 23/3/89) FL 56+3/4 FLC 6 FAC 6/1 Others 6
Queens Park R (£200,000 on 22/12/90) F/PL 123+3/6 FLC 12/1 FAC 3 Others 2
Newcastle U (£2,700,000 on 24/3/94) PL 131+2/2 FLC 13+1/2 FAC 11 Others 17+1

PEACOCK Gavin Keith
Born: Eltham, 18 November 1967
Height: 5'8" Weight: 11.8
Club Honours: Div 1 '93
International Honours: E: Yth; Sch

Having turned out to be an excellent acquisition since joining from Chelsea, Gavin had another superb season in which he ended the 1997-98 campaign as second top scorer at Queens Park Rangers with ten goals, after getting the club underway in the third game. Injury, unfortunately, ruled him out of seven of the last 11 games as Rangers battled to avoid relegation, something they ultimately managed to avoid by just one point. Able to play up front, or in midfield, Gavin is always a menace to opposing defences with his ability to play one-twos that will often take him into scoring positions, and he seems to have the knack of putting away vital goals. The son of Keith, the former Charlton player, he shared the penalty duties with Simon Barker and is almost certain to be a key man for Rangers in 1998-99.

Queens Park R (From apprentice on 19/11/84) FL 7+10/1 FAC 0+1
Gillingham (£40,000 on 5/10/87) FL 69+1/11 FLC 4 FAC 2 Others 5/1
Bournemouth (£250,000 on 16/8/89) FL 56/8 FLC 6 FAC 2 Others 2
Newcastle U (£275,000 on 30/11/90) FL 102+3/35 FLC 6/5 FAC 6/2 Others 3/4
Chelsea (£1,250,000 on 12/8/93) PL 92+11/17 FLC 6/1 FAC 14+4/9 Others 7
Queens Park R (£1,000,000 on 22/11/96) FL 65+1/14 FLC 2/1 FAC 6/2

Tony Peacock

PEACOCK Richard (Rich) John
Born: Sheffield, 29 October 1972
Height: 5'10" Weight: 11.5

A troublesome stomach strain was eventually resolved with a double hernia operation last November, just as Rich had completed his 150th league appearance for Hull City. Unfortunately, just as he neared full fitness, the injury jinx struck again as he damaged ankle ligaments in training, and it was March before the popular Tiger returned to action and displayed the ball skills that had been so badly missed. Regularly used wide on the right, a more central role has allowed him to give vent to his full range of abilities.

Hull C (Signed from Sheffield FC on 14/10/93) FL 131+29/19 FLC 9+2/2 FAC 7/1 Others 3+1

PEAKE Jason William
Born: Leicester, 29 September 1971
Height: 5'11" Weight: 12.10
International Honours: E: Yth; Sch

A free transfer signing from Brighton last October, Jason found himself unable to break into Bury's midfield in 1997-98. He did, however, gain an early chance deputising in the problematic left-wing-back position for three games soon after his arrival, only to subsequently fall behind Gordon Armstrong and Bryan Small in the pecking order. Possesses good control and passing qualities.

Leicester C (From trainee on 9/1/90) FL 4+4/1 Others 1+1
Hartlepool U (Loaned on 13/2/92) FL 5+1/1
Halifax T (Free on 26/8/92) FL 32+1/1 FAC 1 Others 2
Rochdale (Signed on 23/3/94) FL 91+4/6 FLC 3 FAC 5/2 Others 7/1
Brighton & Hove A (Signed on 30/7/96) FL 27+3/1 FLC 2 FAC 2 Others 1
Bury (Free on 8/10/97) FL 3+3

PEAKE Trevor
Born: Nuneaton, 10 February 1957
Height: 6'0" Weight: 12.9
Club Honours: FAC '87
International Honours: E: SP-2

As the reserve team coach at Luton Town, and already in the history books as the club's oldest league player, he made a surprise substitute 57th-minute appearance against Wrexham last September. The appearance, forced upon the club by mounting injuries, proved a disaster as Trevor, once one of the steadiest performers in league football, was run ragged by the opposition who took the score from 2-2 to 5-2 after his introduction. Later left Luton to take up a coaching opportunity at Premier League, Coventry, the club with whom he won an FA Cup winner's medal in 1987.

Lincoln C (£27,500 from Nuneaton Borough on 15/6/79) FL 171/7 FLC 16/2 FAC 7
Coventry C (£100,000 on 6/7/83) FL 277+1/6 FLC 30 FAC 17/1 Others 10
Luton T (£100,000 on 27/8/91) FL 175+4 FLC 7 FAC 13 Others 3

PEARCE Dennis Anthony
Born: Wolverhampton, 10 September 1974
Height: 5'9" Weight: 11.0
Club Honours: Div 3 '98

Having left Wolves on a free transfer in the summer of 1997, without having established himself in first team football, Dennis at last made the big breakthrough in 1997-98, with over 40 appearances for Notts County. A delightfully skilful left back and wing back, whose attacking talents developed as the season progressed, he was yet another player from Meadow Lane who was selected by his fellow professionals of being worthy of a place in the PFA award-winning third division side, an award that will sit nicely alongside his third division championship medal.

Aston Villa (From trainee on 7/6/93)
Wolverhampton W (Free on 3/7/95) FL 7+2 FLC 1 FAC 1
Notts Co (Free on 21/7/97) FL 27+1/2 FLC 3 FAC 2+1 Others 1

PEARCE Alexander **Gregory (Greg)**
Born: Bolton, 26 May 1980
Height: 5'10" Weight: 11.7

Having already made his first team debut for Chesterfield in 1997-98, much is hoped for from this tall central defender. Graduating from Chesterfield's Centre of Excellence, Greg signed a one-year professional contract last April, and looks to further establish himself this coming term.

Chesterfield (From trainee on 24/3/98) Others 0+1

Ian Pearce

PEARCE Ian Anthony
Born: Bury St Edmunds, 7 May 1974
Height: 6'3" Weight: 14.4
Club Honours: PL '95
International Honours: E: U21-3; Yth

The forgotten man of Blackburn's championship winning side of 1995, Ian returned from long-term injury to play five games early last season, before being sold to West Ham in September. Settling in well as a central defender at Upton Park, he proved to be good in the air, strong in the tackle,

and, for such a big man, very fast. He also continued to improve throughout the campaign, culminating in him giving a storming display in the 3-0 defeat of Leeds, and an excellent showing at Arsenal in the FA Cup, where he scored the Hammers goal. Is very skilful on the ground, where he looks to make the right pass.

Chelsea (From juniors on 1/8/91) F/PL 0+4 Others 0+1
Blackburn Rov (£300,000 on 4/10/93) PL 43+19/2 FLC 4+4/1 FAC 1+2 Others 6+1
West Ham U (£1,600,000+ on 19/9/97) PL 30/1 FLC 3 FAC 6/1

PEARCE Stuart
Born: Hammersmith, 24 April 1962
Height: 5'10" Weight: 13.0
Club Honours: FLC '89, '90; FMC '89, '92
International Honours: E: 76; U21-1

Following Nottingham Forest's relegation, Stuart joined Newcastle in the summer of 1997 to continue playing at Premiership level in the hope of prolonging his international career. He quickly settled into the team, showing that he still has plenty to offer at the top level, adding a welcome element of controlled aggression to the defence, but he strained his right hamstring in the away Champions League game against Croatia Zagreb. Unfortunately, aggravated the hamstring again in training as he was about to come back, and then burst a blood vessel in it when next ready to return, which saw him missing for three months before re-appearing as a substitute in the away tie at Barcelona, whereafter he became a regular, either in his recognised left-back position, or at the centre of defence. His enthusiasm for the game remained undiminished, and his inspiring play quickly won the hearts of the Tyneside public, while the quality of his performances led to Barry Davies stating on Match of the Day that he was playing as well as ever, which Stuart quickly invited him to repeat to England manager, Glenn Hoddle! His first goal for Newcastle was a typical thunderous drive in the home tie with Kiev, which was also his first-ever goal in a European club competition.

Coventry C (£25,000 from Wealdstone on 20/10/83) FL 52/4 FAC 2
Nottingham F (£200,000 on 3/6/85) F/PL 401/63 FLC 60/10 FAC 37/9 Others 24/6
Newcastle U (Free on 21/7/97) PL 25 FAC 7 Others 3+1/1

PEARCEY Jason Kevin
Born: Leamington, 23 July 1971
Height: 6'1" Weight: 13.12

After losing his place in goal at Grimsby to new signing, Aidan Davison, at the start of last season, Jason, despite consistent performances for the reserves, was unable to win back his place and appeared only occasionally for the senior side, before being released in the summer. However, he is a good man to have for an emergency, having been tried and tested in league football, being recognised for his control of the area and excellent shot-stopping qualities.

Mansfield T (From trainee on 18/7/89) FL 77 FLC 5 FAC 2 Others 7
Grimsby T (£10,000 on 15/11/94) FL 49 FLC 3 FAC 1

PEARSON Nigel Graham
Born: Nottingham, 21 August 1963
Height: 6'1" Weight: 14.5
Club Honours: FLC '91; Div 1 '95
The inspirational captain of Middlesbrough in 1997-98, Nigel once again lead by example, wringing every ounce of effort out of his charges, and fittingly leading them back into the Premiership in his final season as a player. In doing so, the old war-horse endured a season of agony, courtesy of his battle scarred legs and injured knees. He has always said he would know when it was time to go and like everything else he does, he timed his exit to perfection - the triumphant return to Premiership status for Boro. The occasion quite simply, the concluding game of the season and a very convincing 4-1 victory before his adoring fans, centre stage, ensuring that no one missed out on their share of the accolades (nor the champagne), constantly acknow-ledging every section of the crowd and, if he was not, he most certainly should have been, "savouring" the sobriquet bestowed upon him by his fans as that of "Captain Fantastic". Whilst at Boro "Big Nige" has tasted the bitter sweet sensations of promotion and relegation, alongside three Wembley appearances, and it would be naive to think that a talent like his would be lost to the game, so do not be surprised if his next sobriquet isn't that of "Monumental Manager". Some players aspire to it, Nigel exudes it. Another honour came when his fellow professionals voted him into the award winning PFA first division select.
Shrewsbury T (£5,000 from Heanor T on 12/11/81) FL 153/5 FLC 19 FAC 6 Others 3
Sheffield Wed (£250,000 on 16/10/87) F/PL 176+4/14 FLC 17+2/5 FAC 15/1 Others 10
Middlesbrough (£500,000 on 19/7/94) P/FL 115+1/5 FLC 14 FAC 9

PEDERSEN Jan Ove
Born: Oslo, Norway, 12 November 1968
Height: 5'8" Weight: 11.1
International Honours: Norway: 13
A classy midfielder, Jan became the first of Hartlepool's many foreign imports when signed on loan from Norwegian team, SK Brann, last October, and quickly settled into English football, showing real quality with his precise passing game and time on the ball. A remarkable transfer coup, he has been described as one of the best players to play for the club in recent years, and having enjoyed his spell with the club there are high hopes he will be back at Victoria Park in 1998-99.
Hartlepool U (Loaned from Brann Bergen on 31/10/97) FL 17/1 FAC 1/1 Others 2/1

PEDERSEN Per Werner
Born: Aalberg, Denmark, 30 March 1969
Height: 6'0" Weight: 13.8
International Honours: Denmark: 8
Left out of Blackburn's plans at the start of last season, following the arrival of a new manager, the Danish international striker was then given a run out in both legs of the Coca Cola Cup against Preston, coming on as a sub in the first and starting the second, before being loaned to Borussia Munchengladbach. Not an out-and-out striker, he only scored one goal in Germany prior to returning to Ewood at the end of the campaign, and hopes for better in 1998-99. Has fair pace and is comfortable on the ball.
Blackburn Rov (£2,500,000 from Odense on 22/2/97) PL 6+5/1 FLC 1+1

PEDERSEN Tore
Born: Norway, 29 September 1969
Height: 6'0" Weight: 12.6
International Honours: Norway: 46
Unclaimed by several European sides in the 1997 close season, he came to Blackburn at the downturn of a very good career and when given the opportunity he appeared assured, had typical Norwegian aplomb, and coped with Premiership football with some ease. Unfortunately handicapped by injury and illness, and at a club where the centre-back partnership was established, he could not gain a regular place and will be looking for better in 1998-99.
Blackburn Rov (£500,000 from St Pauli on 15/9/97) PL 3+2 FLC 3

PEEL Nathan James
Born: Blackburn, 17 May 1972
Height: 6'1" Weight: 13.3
Released by Rotherham towards the end of 1996-97, the big forward made a couple of appearances from the bench for Macclesfield in the Conference before signing up for the start of the club's first experience of the Football League. Despite having to wait a month for a first team call up, he linked up well with the other front men, scoring two goals in his first three games, hammering both home from the edge of the box. Then, apart from one other goal, he lost his strike form and his first team place, following the arrival of new faces, before joining Winsford United at the end of December.
Preston NE (From trainee on 9/7/90) FL 1+9/1 FLC 1 Others 1+1
Sheffield U (£50,000 on 1/8/91) FL 0+1
Halifax T (Loaned on 3/2/93) FL 3
Burnley (£60,000 on 24/9/93) FL 4+12/2 FLC 1 FAC 0+3 Others 0+2
Rotherham U (Loaned on 23/3/95) FL 9/4
Mansfield T (Loaned on 27/10/95) FL 2 Others 1
Doncaster Rov (Loaned on 23/2/96) FL 2
Rotherham U (Free on 15/7/96)
Macclesfield T (Free on 9/1/97) FL 10+4/3 FAC 2

PEER Dean
Born: Stourbridge, 8 August 1969
Height: 6'2" Weight: 12.4
Club Honours: AMC '91
Although a recognised central midfield player, last season Dean was used in the middle of Northampton's defence in emergency and gave the impression he had played there all his days. While he may not be one of the most skilful players on the club's books, he is certainly one of the most committed and, despite being in and out of the first team throughout 1997-98, he always gave his all, and will be remembered for his equalising goal against Watford at Vicarage Road.*
Birmingham C (From trainee on 9/7/87) FL 106+14/8 FLC 14+1/3 FAC 2+1 Others 11+1/1
Mansfield T (Loaned on 18/12/92) FL 10 Others 1
Walsall (Free on 16/11/93) FL 41+4/8 FLC 2 FAC 4+2 Others 3
Northampton T (Free on 22/8/95) FL 70+23/4 FLC 3+2/1 FAC 6 Others 7+5

PELL Robert Anthony
Born: Leeds, 5 February 1979
Height: 6'1" Weight: 13.1
In failing to make a first team appearance for Rotherham last season, Robert joined Doncaster on extended loan last November, and made league appearances as a central defender, and as a central striker in the last few matches of the campaign. Released during the summer, despite being young and raw he shows good heart, something which should stand him in good stead in the future.
Rotherham U (From trainee on 25/6/97) FL 2
Doncaster Rov (Loaned on 21/11/97) FL 6+4/1

PEMBERTON John Matthew
Born: Oldham, 18 November 1964
Height: 5'11" Weight: 12.12
Released by Leeds immediately prior to the start of 1997-98, after being incapacitated throughout much of the previous campaign, and failing to make a first team start, John joined Crewe as a player/coach and started the opening two matches. Unfortunately, injuries struck again, and the much ex-perienced, tough-tackling central defender saw no more action for the senior side.
Rochdale (Free from Chadderton on 26/9/84) FL 1
Crewe Alex (£1,000 on 29/3/85) FL 116+5/1 FLC 7/1 FAC 3 Others 7
Crystal Palace (£80,000 on 24/3/88) FL 76+2/2 FLC 6+1 FAC 8 Others 12
Sheffield U (£300,000 on 27/7/90) F/PL 67+1 FLC 4 FAC 4 Others 1
Leeds U (£250,000 on 12/11/93) PL 44+9 FLC 3+1 FAC 5+1 Others 4
Crewe Alex (Free on 8/8/97) FL 1 FLC 1

PEMBERTON Martin Calvin
Born: Bradford, 1 February 1976
Height: 5'11" Weight: 12.6
Martin spent much of last season for Doncaster at full back, despite a preferred position in the forward line, but missed a large part of the campaign through a troublesome back injury. However, fit and back in the first team, he left the club, along with many other players, shortly before the transfer deadline, bound for Scunthorpe, where he broke into the side as a striker who showed a penchant for running at defenders.
Oldham Ath (From trainee on 22/7/94) FL 0+5 FLC 0+1 Others 0+1
Doncaster Rov (Free on 21/3/97) FL 33+2/3 FLC 0+1
Scunthorpe U (Free on 26/3/98) FL 3+3

PEMBRIDGE Mark Anthony
Born: Merthyr Tydfil, 29 November 1970
Height: 5'8" Weight: 11.12
International Honours: W: 28; B-2; U21-1; Sch

1997-98 was another excellent season for Sheffield Wednesday's Mark, despite the club suffering in the Premiership, as he supplied his own brand of skill and combative workrate down the Owl's left side. However, when David Pleat left as manager, he had to work hard to convince Pleat's replacement, Ron Atkinson, that he was indispensible to the team, as the latter had set up a swap deal with Coventry involving David Burrows. In the event, Mark rejected his part of the deal and was eventually rewarded with a new, improved contract. A terrific striker of the ball with his left foot, there were two spectacular long-range efforts among his four goals, against Chelsea, as per 1996-97, and at Everton, where he hit a brace in a 3-1 victory. Continued to be a vital cog in the Welsh international side.*

Luton T (From trainee on 1/7/89) FL 60/6 FLC 2 FAC 4 Others 4
Derby Co (£1,250,000 on 2/6/92) FL 108+2/28 FLC 9/1 FAC 6/3 Others 15/5
Sheffield Wed (£900,000 on 19/7/95) PL 88+5/12 FLC 6/1 FAC 7/1

PENDER John Patrick
Born: Luton, 19 November 1963
Height: 6'0" Weight: 13.12
Club Honours: Div 4 '92, Div 3 '97
International Honours: Ei: U21-5; Yth

Having moved from Wigan during the 1997 close season, the imposing and experienced centre half was another Rochdale signing to be put out of action through injury, even before 1997-98 got underway. With the man he should have teamed up with, Alan Johnson, out for the season, John eventually made his debut in November and was given the captain's armband. Tragically, though, a missed tackle in the game at Scunthorpe in February left him with a severely damaged knee, ruling him out for a year and thus putting his future playing career in jeopardy.

Wolverhampton W (From apprentice on 8/11/81) FL 115+2/3 FLC 5 FAC 7/1
Charlton Ath (£35,000 on 23/7/85) FL 41 FLC 1 FAC 1 Others 2/1
Bristol C (£50,000 on 30/10/87) FL 83/3 FLC 11 FAC 8 Others 12
Burnley (£70,000 on 18/10/90) FL 171/8 FLC 11/1 FAC 17/1 Others 21/1
Wigan Ath (£30,000 on 22/8/95) FL 67+3/1 FLC 2 FAC 5 Others 4
Rochdale (Signed on 22/7/97) FL 14 FAC 0+1 Others 2

PENNEY David Mark
Born: Wakefield, 17 August 1964
Height: 5'10" Weight: 12.0
Club Honours: WC '91

Signed from Swansea during the 1997 summer break, the strong, hard-working midfielder was appointed Cardiff City captain on arrival at the start of what was planned as a chase for promotion. Instead, his personal form dipped and Cardiff struggled throughout. For his part, he wants the chance to show the City fans what he can do during 1998-99. "I feel for the fans after the way Cardiff City's season went," says David. "It was an awful season and I am determined to really show what I can do during the second year of my contract." A

full badge FA Coach, who says he wants to keep playing "as long as possible", in tests conducted by the club he was the quickest player at Ninian Park over 30 metres.
Derby Co (£1,500 from Pontefract Collieries on 26/9/85) FL 6+13 FLC 2+3/1 FAC 1/1 Others 1+3/1
Oxford U (£175,000 on 23/6/89) FL 76+34/15 FLC 10+1 FAC 2+2/1 Others 3+1
Swansea C (Loaned on 28/3/91) FL 12/3
Swansea C (£20,000 on 24/3/94) FL 112+7/20 FLC 5+1/2 FAC 7/1 Others 14
Cardiff C (£20,000 on 24/7/97) FL 32+2/5 FLC 1 FAC 6

PENNOCK Adrian Barry
Born: Ipswich, 27 March 1971
Height: 6'1" Weight: 13.5

Unfortunate to miss most of the first part of last season through a knee operation, Adrian came back for Gillingham's Boxing Day clash at his former club, Bournemouth, only to be sent off within 20 minutes! A steady performer in the right-back or sweeper position in the latter of the campaign, he continued to impress as a player who is always looking to pass the ball.*
Norwich C (From trainee on 4/7/89) FL 1
Bournemouth (£30,000 on 14/8/92) FL 130+1/9 FLC 9 FAC 12/1 Others 8
Gillingham (£30,000 on 4/10/96) FL 46/2 FLC 1 FAC 2 Others 1

PENRICE Gary Kenneth
Born: Bristol, 23 March 1964
Height: 5'8" Weight: 10.6

Signed from Watford during the 1997 close season, the skilful, local-born midfielder returned to his hometown club, Bristol Rovers, after an absence of eight years, in which he had played at the highest level. Gary's ability to hold the ball and use it to good advantage was a major reason why the player/manager, Ian Holloway, wanted his former team mate to return and help him develop his young side. And, in an injury-free season, he completed his 400th league appearance and was eventually given the responsibility to coach the first team squad, along with scouting duties. One of two players to have played on five different home grounds for Rovers, he uncharacteristically got himself sent off in the final league game, against Brentford, before appearing in the two play-off legs against Northampton.
Bristol Rov (Free from Mangotsfield on 6/11/84) FL 186+2/54 FLC 11/3 FAC 11/7 Others 13+2/2
Watford (£500,000 on 14/11/89) FL 41+2/18 FAC 4/1 Others 1/1
Aston Villa (£1,000,000 on 8/3/91) FL 14+6/1
Queens Park R (£625,000 on 29/10/91) F/PL 55+27/20 FLC 5+2/2 FAC 2+2/1 Others 1
Watford (£300,000 on 15/11/95) FL 26+13/2 FLC 2+1 FAC 1 Others 1+1
Bristol Rov (Free on 18/7/97) FL 38+2/5 FLC 2 FAC 5/1 Others 3

PEPPER Colin **Nigel**
Born: Rotherham, 25 April 1968
Height: 5'10" Weight: 12.4

An extremely hard-tackling, competitive Bradford player, whose great strength is in closing attackers down, although that part of his game saw him serve four separate suspensions in 1997-98, it did not stop him

from being the club's most consistent midfielder throughout the campaign. However, notwithstanding that, it was his long-range shooting and ability to get into scoring positions that mainly took the eye, as he picked up five goals, including a brace at Reading early on. Also sets up chances for others with unselfish play.
Rotherham U (From apprentice on 26/4/86) FL 35+10/1 FLC 1/1 FAC 1+1 Others 3+3
York C (Free on 18/7/90) FL 223+12/39 FLC 16+2/3 FAC 12/2 Others 15+1
Bradford C (£100,000 on 28/2/97) FL 42+1/10 FLC 2 FAC 1

PEREIRA Luis Boa Morte
Born: Lisbon, Portugal, 4 August 1977
Height: 5'10" Weight: 11.5
Club Honours: PL '98

Spotted by Arsene Wenger, the Arsenal manager, playing for Portugal in the Toulon U21 tournament during the summer of 1997, he was signed from Sporting Lisbon a few weeks later in time to prepare for the Gunners' 1997-98 campaign. A pacy right-sided winger, cum striker, who is very direct and shoots on sight of the goal, he did very well in his first season of English football, despite not scoring a Premiership goal in 15 appearances (11 from the bench). In what is probably the most thankless and difficult task at Highbury, competing for places with Dennis Bergkamp, Nicolas Anelka, Ian Wright, and Marc Overmars, to name but a few, he scored twice for a depleted side in a 4-1 Coca Cola Cup win over Birmingham in October and looked promising. Just turned 21, and obviously bought with an eye on the future, he is expected to do very well indeed.
Arsenal (£1,750,000+ from Sporting Lisbon on 25/6/97) PL 4+11 FLC 1/2 FAC 1+3 Others 0+1

PEREZ Lionel
Born: Bagnols Coze, France, 24 April 1967
Height: 5'11" Weight: 13.4

Having arrived at Sunderland in 1996 as an "unknown" and establishing himself between the sticks and as a cult hero with the fans, Lionel was expected to be under pressure last term, following the arrival of Edwin Zoetebier. Typical of the flamboyant Frenchman, though, he played in every league game, performing his usual brand of heroics, especially in the vital away game at Charlton in March, when he made two world-class saves late on to secure a priceless promotion point. Occasionally suspect on crosses, the Frenchman proved to be an excellent servant to Sunderland, and with his current contractual situation in doubt, the fans at the Stadium of Light were keeping their fingers crossed that he remains on Wearside. *Stop Press:* Released by the club during the summer, Lionel joined Newcastle United on a free transfer on 2 June.
Sunderland (£200,000 from Bordeaux on 21/8/96) F/PL 74+1 FLC 2 FAC 4 Others 3

PERKINS Christopher (Chris) Paul
Born: Stepney, 1 March 1980
Height: 5'11" Weight: 12.11

Still a trainee, Chris made the transition

from youth football to Southend's first team in the most dramatic of manners, when injuries led to him teaming up at the heart of the defence with fellow youngster, Ben Lewis, last season. Although he only managed a handful of appearances, he impressed with his cool head and strong tackling, allied to some impressive distribution. Along with Leo Roget, he could form the basis of a very secure defence in the not-too-distant future.

Southend U (Trainee) FL 3+2 Others 1

Chris Perkins (Chesterfield)

PERKINS Christopher (Chris) Peter
Born: Nottingham, 9 January 1974
Height: 5'11" Weight: 11.0
A quiet and undemonstrative "team" player, Chris's best work for Chesterfield in 1997-98 came from his progress as a wing-back who linked well with both midfield and forwards. Awareness and an excellent workrate were again important features of his play, and an added bonus was his ability to deliver accurate, telling free kicks into danger areas.

Mansfield T (From trainee on 19/11/92) FL 3+5 Others 0+1
Chesterfield (Free on 15/7/94) FL 104+9/2 FLC 5+1/1 FAC 12 Others 8+3

PERON Jean (Jeff) Francois
Born: France, 11 October 1965
Height: 5'9" Weight: 11.0
Signed from Lens early in 1997-98, this experienced midfielder, who had earlier played for Caen and RC Strasbourg, gave some outstanding displays on the left flank of Walsall's midfield, and ended the campaign being voted Player of the Season. After going close on numerous occasions throughout the season, he finally opened his goal account with a superb volley to win the game against Wigan in March and, despite

seeking a transfer in the closing months, continued to give of his best.
Walsall (Free from Lens on 22/8/97) FL 38/1 FLC 5 FAC 4 Others 5

PERRETT Russell
Born: Barton on Sea, 18 June 1973
Height: 6'3" Weight: 13.2
Russell came back into Portsmouth's starting line-up at the end of last August, but struggled to maintain the level of his performances the previous season, and was unable to hold down a regular place. A centre back with good ability on the ground, having a liking to play the ball away to feet, and strong in the air as you would expect from someone of his height, unfortunately, his loss of form coincided with others regaining theirs, and he only really came into contention when injuries and suspensions hit the team.
Portsmouth (Signed from Lymington on 30/9/95) FL 54+3/2 FLC 3 FAC 4

PERRY Christopher (Chris) John
Born: Carshalton, 26 April 1973
Height: 5'8" Weight: 11.1
Ever present for Wimbledon in 1997-98, bar just three games due to suspension, his continued availability was a welcome relief for a club struggling badly with injuries. A central defender with much pace, who reads situations well and is a good competitive tackler, as a boy he followed the club and has come through the ranks to not only play for them but to be recognised among the best defenders the Dons have ever had, and unlucky not to have been capped at any level. Perceptive and well known for his marking skills, Chris reads the game well, something that helps him keep the country's top strikers under control. Appreciated by the fans no end, he scored his second ever Premiership goal in the great 3-1 at Newcastle in mid-September.
Wimbledon (From trainee on 2/7/91) PL 124+9/2 FLC 13 FAC 22/1

PERRY Jason
Born: Newport, 2 April 1970
Height: 5'11" Weight: 11.12
Club Honours: WC '92, '93; Div 3 '93
International Honours: W: 1; B-2; U21-3; Yth; Sch
Freed by Cardiff during the 1997 close season, the all-action, hard-tackling right back became an instant cult figure with Bristol Rovers' supporters in 1997-98. Having made his league debut as substitute in the first match of the season, against Plymouth Argyle, and despite sustaining a nasty head injury before completing the match, he proved to be a wholehearted player who added steel to Rovers' back line until suspensions ruined his run of appearances. Released during the summer, Jason also deputised in the centre of the defence against Cambridge in an Auto Windscreen tie.
Cardiff C (From trainee on 21/8/87) FL 278+3/5 FLC 22 FAC 14+1 Others 25+1
Bristol Rov (Free on 4/7/97) FL 24+1 FLC 2 FAC 2+1 Others 2

PERRY Mark James
Born: Ealing, 19 October 1978
Height: 5'11" Weight: 11.11
International Honours: E: Yth; Sch
The young midfielder began 1997-98 on the bench for Queens Park Rangers and was in the starting line-up for four of the next five games. However, he only appeared occasionally from thereon, and was injured after just seven minutes of the home game against Middlesbrough at the beginning of March, which ended his season. An excellent reader of the game, and comfortable on the ball, Mark can also play on the right-hand side of three at the back, where he tackles and passes well.
Queens Park R (From trainee on 26/10/95) FL 8+2/1 FLC 2

Paul Peschisolido

PESCHISOLIDO Paolo (Paul) Pasquale
Born: Scarborough, Canada, 25 May 1971
Height: 5'7" Weight: 10.12
International Honours: Canada: 35
Started 1997-98 the way he ended the previous campaign at West Bromwich, his purposeful running being a constant threat to defenders, and scored a splendid hat trick in Albion's 3-1 win at Bury before he surprisingly became Fulham's first £1 million signing in October. Paul's tremendous acceleration and ball control continued to make him a constant menace to all defenders and 13 goals in 32 league matches, including a hat trick in the 5-0 home win over Carlisle in April, was a good ratio for any striker, especially when the majority of the scoring chances he created for himself. Being sent off for a reckless challenge in the second leg of the play offs against Grimsby was an isolated incident, due to frustration, and should be seen as such. Is married to

Karren Brady, Birmingham City's managing director.

Birmingham C (£25,000 from Toronto Blizzards on 11/11/92) FL 37+6/16 FLC 2/1 FAC 0+1 Others 1+1
Stoke C (£400,000 on 1/8/94) FL 59+7/19 FLC 6/3 FAC 3 Others 5+1/2
Birmingham C (£400,000 on 29/3/96) FL 7+2/1
West Bromwich A (£600,000 on 24/7/96) FL 36+9/18 FLC 4+1/3 FAC 1
Fulham (£1,100,000 on 24/10/97) FL 32/13 FAC 3 Others 2

PETERS Mark

Born: St Asaph, 6 July 1972
Height: 6'0" Weight: 11.3

Having come back from a nasty leg fracture that had kept him out of the game since March 1996, to play a dominant role at the heart of Mansfield's defence in 1997-98, the central defender obviously breathed a sigh of relief. Prior to the injury, Mark had shown exceptional form for Town and by the end of the campaign he was virtually back in harness, his tackling game intact.

Manchester C (From trainee on 5/7/90)
Norwich C (Free on 2/9/92)
Peterborough U (Free on 10/8/93) FL 17+2 FLC 2 Others 2
Mansfield T (Free on 30/9/94) FL 70+1/8 FLC 3 FAC 6 Others 5

PETHICK Robert (Robbie) John

Born: Tavistock, 8 September 1970
Height: 5'10" Weight: 11.12

Robbie made more appearances for Portsmouth than anyone else during the course of 1997-98, playing as a right-wing back, and for the most part performing well, although, like others, he struggled with loss of form and a lack of confidence. An attacking player who loves to get forward down the flank to deliver telling crosses, and a good passer of the ball, he scored his second goal in five seasons when a thundering 25-yard shot opened the scoring in a 3-1 home win over Queens Park Rangers.

Portsmouth (£30,000 from Weymouth on 1/10/93) FL 153+26/3 FLC 12+3 FAC 9 Others 3+1

PETIT Emmanuel (Manu)

Born: Dieppe, France, 22 September 1970
Height: 6'1" Weight: 12.7
Club Honours: PL '98; FAC '98
International Honours: France: 26

Signed from the French champions, AS Monaco, during the 1997 close season, although Manu was an unknown as far as the Arsenal fans were concerned, there was little doubt that Arsene Wenger knew plenty about him, having been there as the manager. And, given a central midfield role alongside his French compatriot, Patrick Vieira, the two of them were probably the main influence on a side that ultimately won the Premiership and the FA Cup in 1997-98. Despite making a slow start, possibly due to the fact that he had been playing as a central defender in France, and obviously new to his team mates, he just got better and better, and was good value for his championship and FA Cup winners' medals. A tough tackler with the most cultured left foot seen at Highbury since the days of Liam Brady,

Manu Petit

his and Vieira's midfield supremacy at Manchester United in mid-March, in a side minus Dennis Bergkamp, was the moment when the Arsenal faithful realised that United were not the certainties that people thought they were. Having established himself at international level with France, along with Vieira, he was selected for the final 22 who would carry the country's hopes in the World Cup Finals during the summer. *Stop Press:* After playing brilliantly in every match for France, from the first round games through to the final itself, words could not express his delight when getting his hands on the World Cup, following the 3-0 win over Brazil – especially as he had dreamt of a 2-0 victory and had scored the third goal himself.

Arsenal (£3,500,000 from AS Monaco on 25/6/97) PL 32/2 FLC 3 FAC 7 Others 2

PETRESCU Daniel (Dan) Vasile

Born: Bucharest, Romania, 22 December 1967
Height: 5'9" Weight: 11.9
Club Honours: FAC '97; FLC '98; ECWC '98
International Honours: Romania: 72

A superbly talented right-wing back, Dan began last season for Chelsea in tremendous form, scoring in three consecutive Premiership matches within seven days – away at Barnsley and Wimbledon, followed by a stunning edge-of-the-box chip against Southampton at Stamford Bridge. Given licence by Chelsea boss, Ruud Gullit, to play further forward, he continued his hot-scoring streak with a brace against Tromso, and an audacious volley with the outside of his foot in the 6-1 rout against Tottenham, a match in which he gave a superb perform-

ance and earned Man of the Match plaudits from the national press. This gave him the remarkable tally, for a wing back, of six goals before Christmas. Arguably, his most important goal came in the Coca Cola Cup semi final against Arsenal, when he turned on a sixpence, dribbled past two defenders, and calmly placed a sidefooter past the 'keeper. This was the deciding goal which sent Chelsea to Wembley on a 4-3 aggregate. Having played in both the Coca Cola and Cup Winners' Cup finals, Dan's next big occasion was to come in France '98 as captain of Romania's World Cup side. *Stop Press:* Played in all four of Romania's World Cup games during the summer, which included a 2-1 victory over England – Dan scored the winner in the 90th minute after hoodwinking his Chelsea team mate, Graeme le Saux, who was in direct competition with him down the flank.

Sheffield Wed (£1,250,000 from Genoa, via Foggia, on 6/8/94) PL 28+9/3 FLC 2 FAC 0+2
Chelsea (£2,300,000 on 18/11/95) PL 87+2/10 FLC 5/2 FAC 14/1 Others 7+1/2

PETTA Robert (Bobby) Alfred Manuel
Born: Rotterdam, Holland, 6 August 1974
Height: 5'7" Weight: 11.3

In his second season in England, in 1997-98, Bobby started to show the form which persuaded George Burley to bring him across the North Sea to Ipswich. He also proved that he had learned to adjust to the English game and hone his skills accordingly, playing on the left of midfield where he had the option of going wide and getting in a cross, or cutting inside for a shot. He also became more aware of his defensive duties, culminating in a superb display in the home game with Sunderland, in which he contributed to the win by tracking back with the opposition midfield players. It was, however, as an attacking player that he made most of an impression and was the club's leading "assister", several goals coming from his pin-point crosses. He appeared to be able to glide past defenders with ease – as several found to their cost, and scored his first goal for the club at Swindon, before notching a notable double in the local "demolition derby" with Norwich.

Ipswich T (Free from Feyenoord on 12/6/96) FL 29+9/7 FLC 4+2 FAC 3+1 Others 2

PETTERSON Andrew (Andy) Keith
Born: Freemantle, Australia, 26 September 1969
Height: 6'2" Weight: 14.7

Started last season as Charlton's first-choice 'keeper, before losing his place to Mike Salmon in November after a loss of form. A good shot-stopper, who is prepared to come off his line when necessary, and also having a very powerful and accurate kick which can put opposing defences under pressure, Andy got back into the side in January when Salmon was injured, but after another five games was replaced by Sasa Ilic.

Luton T (Signed on 30/12/88) FL 16+3 FLC 2 Others 2
Ipswich T (Loaned on 26/3/93) PL 1

Charlton Ath (£85,000 on 15/7/94) FL 61+1 FLC 5 FAC 1 Others 4
Bradford C (Loaned on 8/12/94) FL 3
Ipswich T (Loaned on 26/9/95) FL 1
Plymouth Arg (Loaned on 19/1/96) FL 6
Colchester U (Loaned on 8/3/96) FL 5

PETTINGER Paul Allen
Born: Sheffield, 1 October 1975
Height: 6'1" Weight: 13.7
Club Honours: FAYC '93
International Honours: E: Yth; Sch

Having been kept out of the Carlisle side for the whole of 1996-97, due to the excellent form of Tony Caig, Paul joined Rotherham during the 1997 close season. Still an up-and-coming goalkeeper, he was given a few first team opportunities, but whenever he came into the side he did not let anyone down, being a reliable back up for Bobby Mimms. He also played a starring role in a successful campaign for the reserve team.

Leeds U (From trainee on 16/10/92)
Torquay U (Loaned on 23/12/94) FL 3
Rotherham U (Loaned on 11/8/95) FL 0+1
Gillingham (Free on 28/3/96)
Carlisle U (Free on 2/8/96)
Rotherham U (Free on 1/8/97) FL 3 FLC 2 Others 1

PHELAN Terence (Terry) Michael
Born: Manchester, 16 March 1967
Height: 5'8" Weight: 10.0
Club Honours: FAC '88
International Honours: Ei: 38; B-1; U23-1; U21-1; Yth

A sharp tackling, pacy left back, Terry has proved enormously popular with the Everton fans but, like so many players at Goodison in 1997-98, he suffered from the injury curse which blighted the club. First choice at the beginning of the campaign, featuring in the first four matches until a calf strain sidelined him for the first time, he made another four appearances before the end of November, prior to a knee injury effectively ending his season. Although the gritty Republic of Ireland international battled his way steadily back to fitness, he then suffered a recurrence in a reserve team match against Liverpool in December, but, come the spring, he was back to full fitness again and was hoping to reclaim his first team place in 1998-99.

Leeds U (From apprentice on 3/8/84) FL 12+2 FLC 3 Others 2
Swansea C (Free on 30/7/86) FL 45 FLC 4 FAC 5 Others 3
Wimbledon (£100,000 on 29/7/87) FL 155+4/1 FLC 13+2 FAC 16/2 Others 8
Manchester C (£2,500,000 on 25/8/92) PL 102+1/2 FLC 11 FAC 8/1
Chelsea (£900,000 on 15/11/95) PL 13+2 FLC 0+1 FAC 8
Everton (£850,000 on 1/1/97) PL 23+1 FLC 0+1 FAC 1

PHILLIPS David Owen
Born: Wegburg, Germany, 29 July 1963
Height: 5'10" Weight: 12.5
Club Honours: FAC '87
International Honours: W: 62; U21-4; Yth

A free transfer from Nottingham Forest last October gave David a new lease of life and changed the fortunes of Huddersfield in a difficult campaign as he knocked ten years off his age with his energy-packed perform-

ances. There was no doubting that brought a touch of versatility and class to the first team, something that was evident in his first eight games, when he was used in four different positions, although predominately a midfielder. In displaying genuine quality, a good awareness of the game, being comfortable with both feet, and an excellent striker of the ball, both his Town goals were sweeping volleys from the edge of the box.*

Plymouth Arg (From apprentice on 3/8/81) FL 65+8/15 FLC 2+1 FAC 12+1 Others 4/1
Manchester C (£65,000 on 23/8/84) FL 81/13 FLC 8 FAC 5 Others 5/3
Coventry C (£150,000 on 5/6/86) FL 93+7/8 FLC 8 FAC 9/1 Others 5+1/2
Norwich C (£525,000 on 31/7/89) F/PL 152/18 FLC 12 FAC 14/1 Others 8/1
Nottingham F (Signed on 20/8/93) F/PL 116+10/5 FLC 16+1 FAC 10+2 Others 4
Huddersfield T (Free on 14/11/97) FL 29/2 FAC 2

PHILLIPS Gareth Russell
Born: Pontypridd, 19 August 1979
Height: 5'8" Weight: 9.8
International Honours: W: Yth; Sch

Still a second-year YTS, Gareth skippered Swansea's successful youth side during 1997-98, and, despite being a bit on the short side, his workrate in midfield was enough to see him earn half a dozen subs' league appearances for the first team during the campaign, his debut coming in the home fixture against Notts County in October. A Welsh youth international, he was due to sign professional forms in the summer.

Swansea C (Trainee) FL 0+6

PHILLIPS James (Jimmy) Neil
Born: Bolton, 8 February 1966
Height: 6'0" Weight: 12.7
Club Honours: Div 1 '97

The only Bolton-born member of the first team last season, Jimmy must have thought his days were numbered when Colin Todd signed Robbie Elliott at the start of the campaign, and then Mike Whitlow when Elliott was ruled out in September. True to his totally professional approach, however, the veteran did not let this affect him, deservedly getting his chance in January when an injury forced Whitlow out of the picture for the rest of the term, and taking the opportunity to produce some fantastic displays, particularly as a wing back in a new formation, which proved a godsend for his new-found attacking style of play. With his runs on the left wing causing problems for opposing teams, he even scored his first goal for four years in the 5-2 defeat of Crystal Palace in May, a scintillating half volley, after taking the ball down on his chest and turning to hammer the ball home – an effort which helped him deservedly win the Man of the Match award for that particular game!

Bolton W (From apprentice on 1/8/83) FL 103+5/2 FLC 8 FAC 7 Others 14
Glasgow R (£95,000 on 27/3/87) SL 19+6 SLC 4 Others 4
Oxford U (£110,000 on 26/8/88) FL 79/8 FLC 3 FAC 4 Others 2/1
Middlesbrough (£250,000 on 15/3/90) F/PL 139/6 FLC 16 FAC 10 Others 5/2
Bolton W (£250,000 on 20/7/93) P/FL 181+2/2 FLC 23+1 FAC 10 Others 9/2

Kevin Phillips

PHILLIPS Kevin
Born: Hitchin, 25 July 1973
Height: 5'7" Weight: 11.0
International Honours: E: B-1

Surely one of the bargains of the decade, Kevin signed for Sunderland from Watford for £300,000 in the summer of 1997 and went on to become the Wearsiders' most potent goalscorer since Marco Gabbiadini ten years earlier. Possessing tremendous pace, and surprising aerial ability for a small man, he struck up a tremendous partnership with Niall Quinn, being voted Nationwide Player of the Month for December, and earned a call up to the England "B" squad in April. Scored in a record breaking nine consecutive home games between November and March and hit four in the 5-1 FA Cup romp at Rotherham in January, the former non-leaguer was a key man in Sunderland's promotion run, also having the pleasure of scoring on his home debut in August against

Manchester City, in what was the first league game at the Stadium of Light. Capped an incredible first season by breaking Brian Clough's 36-year-old goal-scoring record, when notching his 35th goal of the season in the ill-fated Wembley play-off final, and was voted Nationwide Player of the Season.

Watford (£10,000 from Baldock on 19/12/94) FL 54+5/24 FLC 2/1 FAC 2 Others 0+2
Sunderland (£325,000+ on 17/7/97) FL 42+1/29 FAC 2/4 Others 3/2

PHILLIPS Lee
Born: Aberdare, 18 March 1979
Height: 6'1" Weight: 11.9
International Honours: W: Yth

Having turned professional during the 1997 close season, after appearing for Cardiff in 1996-97 while still a trainee, Lee was another of City's youngsters given further opportunities, following the arrival of new manager, Frank Burrows, playing in the last

seven matches of the campaign, all at right back. As a player who made his Nationwide League debut at Hartlepool in February 1997, showing great composure for a youngster, his good form earning him call-ups to the Welsh U21 squad, 1998-99 will be crucial to him, having spent much of last season sitting in the stands watching Cardiff, as they did not have a reserve team. In many ways it was a waste until Burrows arrived and gave him the chance to show what he can do, and, although he took his chance reasonably well, he now needs to press forward and earn a regular first team spot in 1998-99.

Cardiff C (From trainee on 14/7/97) FL 9+2 Others 0+1

PHILLIPS Lee Paul
Born: Penzance, 16 September 1980
Height: 5'11" Weight: 12.0

Considered an excellent prospect for the future, the young Plymouth centre forward possesses good pace and a very mature all-round game. Having missed a lot of 1996-97 with a broken leg, he unfortunately repeated the same feat in the final weeks of last season, having come back at the beginning of the year. Hopefully, these breaks will not knock his confidence and, with time on his side, he can still fulfil his potential.

Plymouth Arg (Trainee) FL 3+9 Others 0+1

PHILLIPS Martin John
Born: Exeter, 13 March 1976
Height: 5'10" Weight: 11.10

Out of contention for a place at Manchester City in 1997-98, Martin went out on loan to Scunthorpe at the beginning of 1998, but failed to win an immediate place in the starting line-up. An out-and-out winger with good ball skills, he arrived at Glanford Park when the team was struggling and appeared in just four matches before returning to Maine Road. His next port of call was Exeter, his old club, in March, and he stayed on for the duration, playing in eight matches and again showing himself to be a tricky winger with an accurate cross. Still a great favourite at St James, many fans would love to see him move back permanently.

Exeter C (From trainee on 4/7/94) FL 36+16/5 FLC 1+2 FAC 2+2 Others 1+5
Manchester C (£500,000 on 25/11/95) P/FL 3+12 FLC 0+1
Scunthorpe U (Loaned on 5/1/98) FL 2+1 Others 1
Exeter C (Loaned on 19/3/98) FL 7+1

PHILLIPS Wayne
Born: Bangor, 15 December 1970
Height: 5'10" Weight: 11.2
International Honours: W: B-2

In and out of the Wrexham side in 1997-98, Wayne was handed a chance to resurrect his flagging career when he was transferred to Stockport in February. At his best, a central midfielder who likes to be involved in the thick of it, with stamina to spare that takes him from one end of the park to the other, he needed the challenge and responded to it well, in giving a series of workmanlike, if unspectacular displays that earned him a

recall to the Welsh set-up and a second "B" cap in March.

Wrexham (From trainee on 23/8/89) FL 184+23/16 FLC 17+1 FAC 12+2/1 Others 18+6/1
Stockport Co (£200,000 on 13/2/98) FL 7+6

PHILLISKIRK Anthony (Tony)
Born: Sunderland, 10 February 1965
Height: 6'1" Weight: 13.3
International Honours: E: Sch

Having been a regular with Cardiff in 1996-97 when the Bluebirds reached the third division play offs, and still having a year left to run on his contract, Tony was mystified to find he was not in the reckoning for a first team place in 1997-98. Instead, he trained with Burnley, and spent loan spells with non-league Halifax and Macclesfield, before being released at the end of the season. A proven goalscorer, he went to Macclesfield in mid-February with a view to providing experience for a side aiming to climb out of the third division at the first attempt, having just come up from the Conference. Unfortunately, he was unable to gain a regular starting place and was used to chase a late goal or two as a sub, when coming off the bench in nine of his ten appearances.

Sheffield U (From juniors on 16/8/83) FL 62+18/20 FLC 4+1/1 FAC 5/1 Others 3+2
Rotherham U (Loaned on 16/10/86) FL 6/1
Oldham Ath (£25,000 on 13/7/88) FL 3+7/1 FLC 0+2/1 Others 1
Preston NE (Signed on 10/2/89) FL 13+1/6
Bolton W (£50,000 on 22/6/89) FL 139+2/51 FLC 18/12 FAC 10/7 Others 13/5
Peterborough U (£85,000 on 17/10/92) FL 37+6/15 FLC 2/1 FAC 4/1 Others 2/1
Burnley (£80,000 on 21/1/94) FL 33+7/9 FLC 4+1
Carlisle U (Loaned on 26/10/95) FL 3/1
Cardiff C (£60,000 on 7/12/95) FL 55+6/5 FLC 2 FAC 2 Others 1+2
Macclesfield T (Loaned on 12/2/98) FL 1+9/1

PHILPOTT Lee
Born: Barnet, 21 February 1970
Height: 5'10" Weight: 12.9
Club Honours: Div 3 '91

In and out of the Blackpool side in 1997-98, dependant on which system used, it was an unsettling time for the wide left-sided midfielder, especially after overcoming injury problems. More of a provider of chances, via his crossing ability, and not noted as a scorer, he still managed to net his customary couple, both at home, in a 2-2 draw with Oldham and the second goal in a 2-1 win over Preston. Can also play as a wing back if required.*

Peterborough U (From trainee on 17/7/86) FL 1+3 FAC 0+1 Others 0+2
Cambridge U (Free on 31/5/89) FL 118+16/17 FLC 10/1 FAC 19/3 Others 15/2
Leicester C (£350,000 on 24/11/92) F/PL 57+18/3 FLC 2+1 FAC 6+2 Others 4+1
Blackpool (£75,000 on 22/3/96) FL 51+20/5 FLC 5/1 FAC 4 Others 0+2

PICKERING Albert (Ally) Gary
Born: Manchester, 22 June 1967
Height: 5'10" Weight: 11.1

Still a strong tackler, Ally had a season of high and lows at Stoke in 1997-98. His flat crosses were always dangerous and indeed, when Chris Kamara arrived at the club Ally

stepped up to captain in the absence of Larus Sigurdsson and appeared to relish the challenge. But in the dark days of that era he seemed to lose confidence and was substituted on more than one occasion. However, the attacking right back's first goal for the club, in the home game against Portsmouth, will live in the memory despite it being an undistinguished season.

Rotherham U (£18,500 from Buxton on 2/2/90) FL 87+1/2 FLC 6 FAC 9 Others 7
Coventry C (£80,000 on 27/10/93) PL 54+11 FLC 5+1 FAC 4/1
Stoke C (£280,000 on 15/8/96) FL 81+1/1 FLC 9 FAC 2

PILKINGTON Kevin William
Born: Hitchin, 8 March 1974
Height: 6'1" Weight: 13.0
Club Honours: FAYC '92
International Honours: E: Sch

A young Manchester United goalkeeper, who is good on crosses and stands up well against forwards, Kevin spent most of his time in 1997-98 playing in United's reserve side until he was briefly called up as cover for Peter Schmeichel in the Premiership games against Everton and Coventry in December. With Rai van der Gouw commandeering the subs' bench, however, he went on loan to Glasgow Celtic in April, before being released during the summer.

Manchester U (From trainee on 6/7/92) PL 4+2 FLC 1 FAC 1
Rochdale (Loaned on 2/2/96) FL 6
Rotherham U (Loaned on 22/1/97) FL 17

PINNOCK James Edward
Born: Dartford, 1 August 1978
Height: 5'9" Weight: 11.5

Despite being a regular goalscorer for Gillingham's Capital League side in 1997-98, he was out of contention for a league position owing to the number of players in the pecking order, his only appearance coming as a four-minute sub in the vital 1-0 victory at Plymouth, at the end of April. Now a full-time professional, James will be looking for a better run this coming season.

Gillingham (From trainee on 2/7/97) FL 0+3 Others 0+1

PIPER Leonard (Lenny) Henry
Born: Camberwell, 8 August 1977
Height: 5'8" Weight: 11.6
International Honours: E: Yth

Restricted to just two substitute showings for Gillingham early in 1997-98, before fading into the obscurity of reserve team football, Lenny's season finished in February when he broke his leg in a Capital League game against Fulham, prior to being released in the summer. With good control, and a liking to take on the opposition from midfield, the youngster will be looking to get back into action as soon as possible.

Wimbledon (From trainee on 1/6/95)
Gillingham (£40,000 on 22/7/96) FL 4+16/1 FLC 2+3 FAC 1 Others 1/1

PISTONE Alessandro
Born: Milan, Italy, 27 July 1975
Height: 5'11" Weight: 12.1

Alessandro was rated one of the brightest

young prospects in Serie "A" when he joined Newcastle during the 1997 close season as a wing back with a fine reputation, having appeared on the left for Inter Milan and on the right for the Italy U21's, a side he also captained. He quickly impressed the Geordies with his evident class, cool demeanour, assured control, and his flair for speeding down the wing and delivering quality crosses. However, the early season injury situation at Newcastle led to him playing as one of a back three, where he instantly settled, marshalling his colleagues, displaying his ability in the air, and his strength in the tackle. Despite a wealth of talent at the club, he appeared regularly throughout the season, although a foot injury sidelined him during October, and a back injury kept him out of the FA Cup semi final, a competition in which he had made his mark earlier when supplying the cross from which Alan Shearer headed the winner in the tie against Tranmere. Recovered in time to play in the final at Wembley.

Newcastle U (£4,300,000 from Inter Milan on 31/7/97) PL 28 FLC 1 FAC 5 Others 5

PITCHER Darren Edward
Born: Stepney, 12 October 1969
Height: 5'9" Weight: 12.2
International Honours: E: Yth

Having had an operation to repair damage to a cruciate knee ligament early into 1996-97, Darren was devastated when, after seven months out of action, he came back in two reserve matches only to be told that the operation would have to be carried out again. Out of action until the end of 1997, this hard-tackling Crystal Palace midfield dynamo was loaned to Leyton Orient last January in an effort of play his way back to full fitness and, despite showing glimpses of his range of passing skills in a couple of games played, he was unfortunate to pick up another injury, which sadly led to his retirement from the game.

Charlton Ath (From trainee on 12/1/88) FL 170+4/3 FLC 11 FAC 12/3 Others 8
Crystal Palace (£700,000 on 5/7/94) P/FL 60+4 FLC 5+1/1 FAC 10/1 Others 3
Leyton Orient (Loaned on 5/1/98) FL 1 Others 1

PLATT Clive Linton
Born: Wolverhampton, 27 October 1977
Height: 6'4" Weight: 12.7

This splendidly built young Walsall striker opened last season in fine style with goals in both the first two games, but subsequently did not have much luck with his finishing and was out of the team more than in it. However, there is still plenty of time for the young man who, with great strength in the air and on the ground, will surely be able to harness it to good account before too long.

Walsall (From trainee on 25/7/96) FL 12+13/3 FLC 1+2/1 FAC 0+1 Others 1+3

PLATT David Andrew
Born: Chadderton, 10 June 1966
Height: 5'10" Weight: 11.12
Club Honours: PL '98; FAC '98
International Honours: E: 62; B-3; U21-3

David's decision to stay at Arsenal for 1997-98, rather than sign for Middlesbrough

along with Paul Merson during the summer of 1997, was a wise one for he finally won the championship and FA Cup medals that had eluded him throughout his long and successful career, as the Gunners came with a late run to "do" the double. They also came close to picking up the Coca Cola Cup as well, having taken a 2-1 semi-final lead to Stamford Bridge, only to be wiped out 3-1 in the return leg. Denied a regular place in central midfield by the Patrick Vieira and Manu Petit combination, and by the inspired form of Ray Parlour on the right, he still continued hugely with his numerous forays from the bench and 14 starts, most notably when scoring the winner in a 3-2 Highbury thriller against Manchester United in November. *Stop Press:* It was reported on 8 July that David would be retiring from the game in order to learn the ropes before embarking on a career in management.

Manchester U (Signed from Chadderton on 24/7/84)
Crewe Alex (Free on 25/1/85) FL 134/55 FLC 8/4 FAC 3/1 Others 7
Aston Villa (£200,000 on 2/2/88) FL 121/50 FLC 14/10 FAC 4/2 Others 6/6 (£5,500,000 to Bari on 20/7/91)
Arsenal (£4,750,000 from Sampdoria, via Juventus, on 14/7/95) PL 65+23/13 FLC 7+3/2 FAC 3+3 Others 2+2

PLUCK Colin Ian
Born: London, 6 September 1978
Height: 6'0" Weight: 12.10

A first-year professional and former youth captain, Colin made his first team debut for Watford at Gillingham last season, playing in the centre of defence, and showing fair composure. Sure to be a part of the Hornets' future plans, he will be looking for further opportunities in 1998-99.

Watford (From trainee on 13/2/97) FL 1 Others 1

PLUMMER Dwayne Jermaine
Born: Bristol, 12 May 1978
Height: 5'9" Weight: 11.0

A winger of undoubted ability, but one who still has to fulfil his potential for Bristol City, Dwayne managed only one appearance during last season, when coming off the bench in a 2-0 win at Southend United in October. Still only 20 years of age, with limited experience, 1998-99 could bring about the opportunity he seeks, and the chance to run at first division defences.

Bristol C (From trainee on 5/9/95) FL 1+13 FLC 1+2 Others 0+1

POBORSKY Karel
Born: Prague, Czechoslovakia, 30 March 1972
Height: 5'9" Weight: 11.6
Club Honours: PL '97; CS '96
International Honours: Czechoslovakia: 35

An exciting Manchester United winger, whose speed with the Czechoslovakian international side during Euro '96 earned him the nickname of "The Express Train," Karel enjoyed an extended run during the early part of last season, and scored in United's 3-0 victory over Coventry at the end of August. However, despite being a regular on the bench and a scorer in United's

7-0 victory over Barnsley in October, Alex Ferguson decided to sell him to Benfica in December, the fee being £3m. It was a disappointing end to what had promised to be a great signing for the club, but, ultimately, although having lots of ability, the player was unable to force himself into the team week in and week out.

Manchester U (£3,500,000 from Slavia Prague on 8/8/96) PL 18+14/5 FLC 3/1 FAC 2 Others 5+6

POLLITT Michael Francis
Born: Farnworth, 29 February 1972
Height: 6'4" Weight: 14.0

Unable to displace the talented Darren Ward at Notts County in 1997-98, this most capable of goalkeepers lived out of a suitcase during the season, being loaned to Oldham (August), Gillingham (December), and Brentford (January), before joining Sunderland on a permanent basis in February. Certainly, he never let anyone down, despite having to cover for short-term injuries, and impressed wherever he went with his positional sense, his ability to command the area, especially with crosses, and reflex shot-stopping. Was released during the summer without making an appearance for Sunderland.

Manchester U (From trainee on 1/7/90)
Bury (Free on 10/7/91)
Lincoln C (Free on 1/12/92) FL 57 FLC 5 FAC 2 Others 4
Darlington (Free on 11/8/94) FL 55 FLC 4 FAC 3 Others 5
Notts Co (£75,000 on 14/11/95) FL 10 Others 2
Oldham Ath (Loaned on 29/8/97) FL 16
Gillingham (Loaned on 12/12/97) FL 6
Brentford (Loaned on 22/1/98) FL 5
Sunderland (£75,000 on 23/2/98)

Jamie Pollock

POLLOCK Jamie
Born: Stockton, 16 February 1974
Height: 5'11" Weight: 14.0
Club Honours: Div 1 '95, '97
International Honours: E: U21-3; Yth

As one of the most tenacious, terrier-like players in the game, and one who always performs with total dedication and a passion for the game that endears him to the fans, Jamie was played on the right, rather than in his favoured centre-of-midfield position at Bolton in 1997-98, but was still a real crowd pleaser. Transferred to Manchester City in March, in an ill-fated attempt to help the club avoid the clutches of the second division, he started at Maine Road with a swashbuckling display against Sheffield United, before being made captain in his third game, at home to Stockport, and leading from the front. This was defined perfectly in the 2-2 draw at Wolves when he received the ball deep in midfield, ran forward along the byline, forcing himself through two or three tackles, before finding the net from an acute angle. It was a terrific example of enthusiasm and spirit, and the same again is called for if City are to come back at the first attempt.

Middlesbrough (From trainee on 18/12/91) F/PL 144+11/17 FLC 17+2/1 FAC 13+1/1 Others 4+1 (Free to Osasuna on 6/9/96)
Bolton W (£1,500,000 on 22/11/96) F/PL 43+3/5 FLC 4+1/1 FAC 4/2
Manchester C (£1,000,000 on 19/3/98) FL 8/1

POLSTON John David
Born: Walthamstow, 10 June 1968
Height: 5'11" Weight: 11.12
International Honours: E: Yth

Yet another Norwich player to endure a nightmare campaign in 1997-98, John started as the first-choice centre back before a succession of injuries, which began with an ankle, then his back, and then a serious groin strain, kept him out of action until early March. From then on though it was just subs' appearances and he was released during the summer. Strength in the air and on the ground, and without frills, is what you can expect from this defender.

Tottenham H (From apprentice on 16/7/85) FL 17+7/1 FLC 3+1
Norwich C (£250,000 on 24/7/90) F/PL 200+15/8 FLC 20+1/2 FAC 17+1/1 Others 9/1

POOLE Kevin
Born: Bromsgrove, 21 July 1963
Height: 5'10" Weight: 12.11

Released during the 1997 close season, having managed just eight games in the Leicester goal as the understudy to Kasey Keller throughout 1996-97, on joining Birmingham as the number two to Ian Bennett he might have been forgiven for thinking that things might get better. Sound on crosses, an excellent shot-stopper, and a recognised saver of penalties, he saved three of them while performing admirably in Blues' reserve side, but the first team call, with Bennett in tremendous form, did not come. Finally making his debut on the last day, due to an injury to the latter, he kept a clean sheet and had little to do as Brum agonisingly missed out on a play-off place, when drawing 0-0 against Charlton in front of a rousing 26,000 sell-out at St Andrews.

Aston Villa (From apprentice on 26/6/81) FL 28 FLC 2 FAC 1 Others 1
Northampton T (Loaned on 8/11/84) FL 3

Middlesbrough (Signed on 27/8/87) FL 34 FLC 4 FAC 2 Others 2
Hartlepool U (Loaned on 27/3/91) FL 12
Leicester C (£40,000 on 30/7/91) F/PL 163 FLC 10 FAC 8 Others 12
Birmingham C (Free on 4/8/97) FL 1

POOM Mart
Born: Tallin, Estonia, 3 February 1972
Height: 6'4" Weight: 13.6
International Honours: Estonia: 59

Almost ever present in 1997-98, missing just three games, the current Estonian international goalkeeper, in his second season at Derby, became firmly established in the first team. His height and agility allow him to command the penalty area at set pieces and, despite the odd mistake, he produced a series of exceptional saves, especially in the first half of the campaign when County were looking to climb the Premiership at the expense of the more fancied sides. Kept 15 clean sheets in all, three of them in succession, and looks set to again make it difficult for the club's number two, Russell Hoult, to further his appearances.
Portsmouth (£200,000 from FC Wil on 4/8/94) FL 4 FLC 3 (Signed by Tallin SC on 9/5/96)
Derby Co (£500,000 on 26/3/97) PL 40 FLC 3 FAC 2

Mart Poom

POPE Steven Anthony
Born: Stoke, 8 September 1976
Height: 5'11" Weight: 12.3
With only one first team appearance for Crewe to his name prior to the start of 1997-97, and that three years earlier, the young defender, came off the subs' bench on the opening day of the season at Swindon and eventually made his full league debut at Sheffield United. However, with competition keen for defensive places, it was back to

the reserves until he was loaned out to Kidderminster Harriers in February.
Crewe Alex (From trainee on 3/6/95) FL 2+4 FLC 0+1

PORIC Adem
Born: Kensington, 22 April 1973
Height: 5'9" Weight: 11.13
Once again unable to get a proper run at Sheffield Wednesday, this time in 1997-98, appearing just four times, all in the role of a sub, the tenacious, hard-working midfielder was freed and moved to Rotherham on a month-by-month contract. However, after looking to be an accomplished player on his debut, he could not reproduce the same form and consequently did not have his term extended. Moving down the road to Notts County, he arrived just prior to the transfer deadline with the unenviable task of trying to win a place in a prospective title-winning team and, after experiencing some difficulty adjusting to the rough and tumble of the third division, he was released during the summer.
Sheffield Wed (£60,000 from St George's Budapest on 1/10/93) PL 3+11 FLC 0+3
Southend U (Loaned on 7/2/97) FL 7
Rotherham U (Free on 10/2/98) FL 4
Notts Co (Free on 26/3/98) FL 3+1

PORTER Andrew (Andy) Michael
Born: Holmes Chapel, 17 September 1968
Height: 5'9" Weight: 12.0
Club Honours: AMC '93
A Port Vale midfield player who was not an automatic choice for the first time in a number of years, Andy was as aggressive as ever, and when in the team he always gave everything, filling in both full-back positions when injuries dictated. Very good at man-to-man marking, he was once again successful in that role when dealing with Georgiou Kinkladze at Manchester City, where the Vale gained an important 3-2 victory. Scored just the one goal, a penalty against Crewe Alexandra.*
Port Vale (From trainee on 29/6/87) FL 313+44/22 FLC 22+1 FAC 20+4/3 Others 26+2/1

PORTER Gary Michael
Born: Sunderland, 6 March 1966
Height: 5'6" Weight: 11.0
Club Honours: FAYC '82
International Honours: E: U21-12; Yth
Signed by Walsall during the 1997 close season after 14 seasons with Watford, for whom he had scored a spectacular League Cup goal against the Saddlers in September 1996, he steadily gained confidence after breaking a leg in 1996-97, and gave some excellent displays in midfield during the mid-part of the campaign. His constructive work was enhanced by his eye for goal, and in the 7-0 hammering of Macclesfield in the FA Cup he netted both a powerful header and a fine rising shot.
Watford (From apprentice on 6/3/84) FL 362+38/47 FLC 30+2/5 FAC 25+2/3 Others 12+1/2
Walsall (Free on 25/7/97) FL 25+4/1 FLC 2+2 FAC 3/2 Others 5

POTTER Graham Stephen
Born: Solihull, 20 May 1975
Height: 6'1" Weight: 11.12
International Honours: E: U21-1; Yth
Able to play on the left-hand side of the defence, or in midfield, being predominately a wing back, Graham has had little luck at West Bromwich Albion, having been sidelined through injury for the last six weeks of 1996-97 and then, with Albion having so many left-sided players available, not able to force his way into the side in 1997-98. Even when loaned to Northampton at the end of October for an extended two-month run he only managed six appearances before returning to the Hawthorns. However, he finally got an opportunity when replacing Shane Nicholson, and will hope to build on that this coming term.
Birmingham C (From trainee on 1/7/92) FL 23+2/2 FAC 1 Others 6
Wycombe W (Loaned on 17/9/93) FL 2+1 FLC 1 Others 1
Stoke C (£75,000 on 20/12/93) FL 41+4/1 FLC 3+1 FAC 4 Others 5
Southampton (£250,000 + on 23/7/96) FL 2+6 FLC 1+1
West Bromwich A (£300,000 + on 14/2/97) FL 6+5
Northampton T (Loaned on 24/10/97) FL 4 Others 1

POTTS Steven (Steve) John
Born: Hartford, USA, 7 May 1967
Height: 5'8" Weight: 10.11
International Honours: E: Yth
Although not a first team regular at West Ham these day, when called upon in 1997-98, Steve never put a foot wrong. Still a very dependable defender, and a good reader of the game. At the start of the season he played in a well-deserved testimonial match against Queens Park Rangers, and a week later made his 400th first team appearance for West Ham in their 2-1 win at Barnsley. Unfortunate to be out injured for the last three games, he was sorely missed as the Hammers' defence conceded 11 goals, which spoilt their European hopes.
West Ham U (From apprentice on 11/5/84) F/PL 333+22/1 FLC 34+2 FAC 39+1 Others 14+1

POUNEWATCHY Stephane Zeusnagapa
Born: Paris, France, 10 February 1968
Height: 6'1" Weight: 15.12
Club Honours: AMC '97
As in 1996-97, Stephane was a commanding presence in the heart of the Carlisle defence in 1997-98, and, as one of the most technically accomplished performers on the club's books, the Frenchman continued to radiate an air of solidity, while clearly playing well within himself. A player who likes to get forward, his occasional forays upfield were always welcome, and he netted three goals in the campaign before being released.
Carlisle U (Free from Gueugnon on 6/8/96) FL 81/3 FLC 7 FAC 5 Others 9/2

POUNTNEY Craig Frank
Born: Bromsgrove, 23 November 1979
Height: 5'7" Weight: 9.10
Coming through the Shrewsbury Town

ranks as a YTS to sign professional forms at the end of last April, Craig celebrated with a Football League debut when coming off the bench for the final game of the season, at home to Scunthorpe. A wide, right-sided type who has progressed well, he is one for the future.

Shrewsbury T (From trainee on 27/4/98) FL 0+1

POUTON Alan

Born: Newcastle, 1 February 1977
Height: 6'0" Weight: 12.8

The young York midfielder continued to make good progress in 1997-98, and was a virtual ever present in the side. At his best in the centre of midfield, he is a strong and determined player who likes to run at defences. He also scored six goals, all away from home, the best being a spectacular solo effort in an end-of-season win at Carlisle.

Oxford U (Free from Newcastle U juniors on 7/11/95)
York C (Free on 8/12/95) FL 55+8/6 FLC 3+1 FAC 5/1 Others 2

POWELL Christopher (Chris) George Robin

Born: Lambeth, 8 September 1969
Height: 5'10" Weight: 11.7

As Derby's first-choice left-wing back, who maintained his consistent progress under Jim Smith in 1997-98, Chris is equally adept with both the defensive and creative implications of his role and missed just one game during a tough campaign. Has excellent control, can use both feet, and can read the game well. He also scored his first Premiership goal for the club in the 3-1 win over Everton at Pride Park in mid-September. *Stop Press:* Charlton were reported to have broken their transfer record when Chris signed from Derby for £825,000 on 22 June.

Crystal Palace (From trainee on 24/12/87) FL 2+1 FLC 0+1 Others 0+1
Aldershot (Loaned on 11/1/90) FL 11
Southend U (Free on 30/8/90) FL 246+2/3 FLC 13 FAC 8 Others 21
Derby Co (£750,000 on 31/1/96) F/PL 89+2/1 FLC 5 FAC 5/1

POWELL Darryl Anthony

Born: Lambeth, 15 November 1971
Height: 6'0" Weight: 12.10
International Honours: Jamaica: 5

A left-sided Derby midfielder who can also operate as an extra defender if needed, although 1997-98 brought a real bonus to this unassuming player, with promotion to the Jamaican squad for the France '98 World Cup, he struggled to hold down a regular place at County as competition increased for places. Highly dependable in whatever position he is asked to play, he picked up an ankle injury towards the end of the season, but was recovered in time to be available for World Cup selection in the summer. Is strong in the tackle and a good passer of the ball. *Stop Press:* Played twice for Jamaica, against Croatia and Argentina, before the side crashed out of the World Cup at the end of the first round.

Portsmouth (From trainee on 22/12/88) FL 83+49/16 FLC 11+3/3 FAC 10 Others 9+5/4
Derby Co (£750,000 on 27/7/95) F/PL 76+17/6 FLC 3+1 FAC 5

POWELL Paul

Born: Wallingford, 30 June 1978
Height: 5'8" Weight: 11.6

After a season of reserve team football and sitting on the bench, Paul made a welcome return to first team action in a big way, appearing in 22 games for Oxford in 1997-98. Playing down the left-hand side, and one of four left wingers at the club, he also appeared at left back, and in midfield, and gave a number of very impressive displays, so much so that he (with Simon Marsh) was called into the provisional England U21 squad for the summer tournament in Toulon. A good long throw is another asset for the local lad, who scored his first goal at Norwich.

Oxford U (From trainee on 2/7/96) FL 12+12/1 FLC 0+1 FAC 1 Others 0+2

POWER Graeme Richard

Born: Harrow, 7 March 1977
Height: 5'10" Weight: 10.10
International Honours: E: Yth

The competent Bristol Rovers' left back, cum central defender, made a miserable start to 1997-98, sustaining a dislocated collar bone in the opening 36 minutes of the first match of the season against Plymouth Argyle, the team he had made his league debut against 11 months earlier. The injury necessitated surgery and he was absent for six months. Back in harness, his surging runs were another attacking aspect of Rovers' play which helped them become the second division's top goalscorers but, after playing as a sub in the second leg of the play-off defeat at Northampton, he was released during the summer.

Queens Park R (From trainee on 11/4/95)
Bristol Rov (Free on 15/7/96) FL 25+1 FAC 1 Others 1+2

POWER Philip (Phil) Damian

Born: Salford, 25 July 1967
Height: 5'7" Weight: 11.7
Club Honours: GMVC '95, '97; FAT '96
International Honours: E: SP-2

One of the leading scorers for Macclesfield since joining them in their non-league days,

Phil Power

Phil is a tricky striker, who is fast on the ball, adept at holding and twisting around his opponents, and can score well in a scrambled situation, or find the net from opportunist positions. Unfortunately, he was unable to command a settled starting place in the team last season, but will obviously hope for better fortune in 1998-99.*

Crewe Alex (Signed from Witton A on 1/8/85) FL 18+9/3 FLC 1 Others 0+1 (Freed during 1987 close season)
Macclesfield T (Signed from Stalybridge on 8/10/93) FL 21+17/7 FLC 0+2 FAC 2 Others 1

POYET Gustavo Augusto

Born: Montevideo, Uruguay, 15 November 1967
Height: 6'2" Weight: 13.0
Club Honours: ECWC '98
International Honours: Uruguay: 21

Chelsea confirmed their cosmopolitan reputation when Gustavo, their first South American international, and occasional captain of Uruguay, arrived at Stamford Bridge in June 1997 to join the host of continental stars already at the club. The tall, elegant midfielder moved to Chelsea on a free transfer from Real Zaragoza after being swayed by a quote from Diego Maradona, who stated that Ruud Gullit and Gianfranco Zola were two of the best players he had ever seen. Gustavo had indeed played against Chelsea previously, for Zaragoza in the 1995 European Cup Winners' Cup semi final, and was a member of the Zaragoza team which defeated Arsenal in the final. As one of that rare breed of midfield player, a prolific goalscorer – particularly with his head – he scored 14 Spanish League goals in his last season at Zaragoza, of which nine were headers. Settled quickly into English football, scoring four goals in the Blues' first nine Premiership matches, before snapping his cruciate ligaments in a freak training ground accident in mid-October. He then made an incredible recovery, returning as a substitute against Spurs on Easter Sunday, starting against Vicenza in the European Cup Winners' Cup semi final and scoring the vital equaliser when Chelsea looked dead and buried, before playing in the final against VFB Stuttgart, when his control of the midfield, alongside Dennis Wise, Roberto Di Matteo, and Dan Petrescu was crucial as Chelsea won their second cup during a memorable season. Chelsea's aim for 1998-99 is a sustained challenge for the Premiership title and a fully-fit Gustavo Poyet is an essential part of those plans.

Chelsea (Free from Real Zaragoza on 15/7/97) PL 11+3/4 Others 5/1

PREECE Andrew (Andy) Paul

Born: Evesham, 27 March 1967
Height: 6'1" Weight: 12.0

Picking up where he left off in 1996-97, Andy scored 14 goals for Blackpool last season and ran Phil Clarkson close for the leading goalscorer title. Well known for his strike partnership with Chris Armstrong at both Wrexham and Crystal Palace, all of his strikes came in singles and, as you would expect, several were match winners. Was released during the summer.

Northampton T (Free from Evesham on 31/8/88)
FL 0+1 FLC 0+1 Others 0+1 (Free to Worcester C
during 1989 close season)
Wrexham (Free on 22/3/90) FL 44+7/7 FLC
5+1/1 FAC 1/2 Others 5/1
Stockport Co (£10,000 on 18/12/91) FL 89+8/42
FLC 2+1 FAC 7/3 Others 12+2/9
Crystal Palace (£350,000 on 23/6/94) PL 17+3/4
FLC 4+2/1 FAC 2+3
Blackpool (£200,000 on 5/7/95) FL 114+12/35
FLC 8+2/1 FAC 2+3/2 Others 12/2

PREECE David

Born: Sunderland, 26 August 1976
Height: 6'2" Weight: 12.3

Out of luck with first team opportunities at
Sunderland, having been a professional at
the club for three years, the young goalkeeper signed for Darlington during the
1997 close season and missed just one game
throughout 1997-98, and that when
suspended after being sent off against
Brighton. A tremendous shot-stopper who
saved a number of penalties during the
campaign, David was often the difference
between winning and losing.
Sunderland (From trainee on 30/6/94)
Darlington (Free on 28/7/97) FL 45 FLC 2 FAC 4
Others 1

PREECE David William

Born: Bridgnorth, 28 May, 1963
Height: 5'6" Weight: 11.6
Club Honours: FLC '88
International Honours: E: B-3

As Cambridge's player/coach, David is one
of the most respected midfielders in the
lower divisions and, although first team
appearances were limited last season, his
experience showed whenever he played. A
good passer of the ball, who is able to dictate
and control the tempo of the game, the
younger players at the club learn a lot from
his experience.
Walsall (From apprentice on 22/7/80) FL 107+4/5
FLC 18/5 FAC 6/1 Others 1
Luton T (£150,000 on 6/12/84) FL 328+8/21 FLC
23/3 FAC 27/2 Others 8+1/1
Derby Co (Free on 11/8/95) FL 10+3/1 FLC 2
Birmingham C (Loaned on 24/11/95) FL 6 Others 1
Swindon T (Loaned on 21/3/96) FL 7/1
Cambridge U (Free on 6/9/96) FL 34+13 FLC
3+1 Others 0+1

PREECE Roger

Born: Much Wenlock, 9 June 1968
Height: 5'8" Weight: 10.11

Signed from Telford in the 1997 close
season as the Shrewsbury player/coach,
Roger struggled with injury early on. Vastly
experienced, the hard-working, hard-
tackling midfielder was uncompromising in
the tackle and always in the action, taking
on responsibility easily.*
Wrexham (Free from Coventry C juniors on
15/8/86) FL 89+21/12 FLC 2+1 FAC 5 Others
8+1/1
Chester C (Free to Southport on 14/8/90) FL
165+5/4 FLC 10 FAC 8/1 Others 11 (Freed on
18/10/96)
Shrewsbury T (Free from Telford on 4/7/97) FL
25+2/1 FAC 2

PRESSMAN Kevin Paul

Born: Fareham, 6 November 1967
Height: 6'1" Weight: 14.12
International Honours: E: B-3; U21-1; Yth;
Sch

David Preece (Darlington)

Kevin had yet another good time in goal at
Sheffield Wednesday in 1997-98, his
reliability helping the team enormously to
keep just above the relegation zone. Was
rewarded for his good form when selected
for the England "B" team, and remains
desperately unlucky not to have gained a full
cap, despite being named for the last two
full squads. In missing just two games
through injury, his one great memory of
the season would have to be the FA Cup
third round replay against Watford at
Hillsborough when, having saved a penalty,
he blasted home one himself during a 5-3
shoot-out victory. Quick off his line for a big
man, he does not commit himself too often
and excels in one-to-one confrontations.

Kevin Pressman

Sheffield Wed (From apprentice on 7/11/85) F/PL
232 FLC 29 FAC 15 Others 4
Stoke C (Loaned on 10/3/92) FL 4 Others 2

PRICE Jason Jeffrey

Born: Pontypridd, 12 April 1977
Height: 6'2" Weight: 11.5
International Honours: W: U21-1

Having signed a new contract with Swansea
during the 1997 close season, Jason started
1997-98 as the first-choice right-sided wing
back, showing an ability to attack the
opposition in order to get his crosses in. Still
gaining in experience, his good work being
rewarded with an appearance for the Welsh
U21 side in Italy in April, he could
eventually make his mark in central defence.
Swansea C (Free from Aberaman on 17/7/95) FL
32+4/3 FLC 2 FAC 1

PRICE Ryan

Born: Stafford, 13 March 1970
Height: 6'4" Weight: 14.0
Club Honours: AMC '95; GMVC '97; FAT
'96
International Honours: E: SP-6

Having spent a full season as a deputy
'keeper for Birmingham, Ryan returned to
non-league football with Macclesfield to get
regular first team games. To that end, he
succeeded well in Town's goal in their first
Football League season, having lost none of
his fearlessness, despite an accident on the
pitch in 1996-97 which left him needing a
face rebuild with titanium plates and screws
being fitted. Very agile, and an excellent
shot-stopper, as an ever present, the giant
goalie was one of the key factors in the

club's drive towards the second division, especially with 19 clean sheets under his belt.

Birmingham C (£40,000 from Stafford R on 9/8/94) Others 1
Macclesfield T (£15,000 on 3/11/95) FL 46 FLC 2 FAC 2 Others 1

PRIEST Christopher (Chris)
Born: Leigh, 18 October 1973
Height: 5'10" Weight: 10.10
A talented Chester City midfielder with great stamina, Chris is one of the main assets in the side's midfield, being a strong tackler and a great passer of the ball. He also has the ability to pop up in the box to score vital goals, three of his seven in 1997-98, being either match winners or match savers.
Everton (From trainee on 1/6/92)
Chester C (Loaned on 9/9/94) FL 11/1 Others 2
Chester C (Free on 11/1/95) FL 116+5/21 FLC 3 FAC 5/1 Others 6

PRIMUS Linvoy Stephen
Born: Forest Gate, 14 September 1973
Height: 6'0" Weight: 14.0
Signed from Barnet just before the start of last season, along with Lee Hodges, and valued at £400,000 in the combined £500,000 fee which brought the two players to Elm Park, was a regular at centre back, except for a mid-season spell of 14 games which he missed due to an injured shin, and proved to be one of the more reliable members of a struggling side. Strong in the air, he scored once, a televised header in the 3-3 draw at home to Nottingham Forest. However, he needs a settled defence around him to fulfil his obvious potential.
Charlton Ath (From trainee on 14/8/92) FL 4 FLC 0+1 Others 0+1
Barnet (Free on 18/7/94) FL 127/7 FLC 9+1 FAC 8/1 Others 4
Reading (£400,000 on 29/7/97) FL 36/1 FLC 6 FAC 1

PRIOR Spencer Justin
Born: Southend, 22 April 1971
Height: 6'3" Weight: 13.4
Club Honours: FLC '97
The Leicester central defender, once again proved to be solid and dependable at the heart of the Foxes' three-man rearguard throughout 1997-98, before suffering three-broken ribs in a collision with the Southampton 'keeper, Paul Jones, on Easter Tuesday, an injury that brought his season to a premature end. Great in the air, with a fine recovery rate, and extremely mobile, there are few strikers who continue to get the better of him, and there are few defences better than Citys.
Southend U (From trainee on 22/5/89) FL 135/3 FLC 9 FAC 5 Others 7/1
Norwich C (£200,000 on 24/6/93) P/FL 67+7/1 FLC 10+1/1 FAC 0+2 Others 2
Leicester C (£600,000 on 17/8/96) PL 61+3 FLC 7 FAC 5 Others 2

PRITCHARD David Michael
Born: Wolverhampton, 27 May 1972
Height: 5'8" Weight: 11.5
International Honours: W: B-1
A contract dispute was finally resolved last December when the tough-tackling Bristol

Rovers' full back signed a new 18-month deal. Started 1997-98 in the more uncustomary left-back spot for seven games, but returned to right back for the remainder of the campaign. Unfortunate to have received his first red card of his career in the highly controversial match at Wigan in December, which saw four Rovers' players and one opponent dismissed, but managed to stay injury free to complete a century of appearances for the club. Was also rewarded with his first Welsh "B" cap against Scotland.
West Bromwich A (From trainee on 5/7/90) FL 1+4 (Free to Telford during 1992 close season)
Bristol Rov (£15,000 on 25/2/94) FL 124+1 FLC 7 FAC 10 Others 9

PROKAS Richard
Born: Penrith, 22 January 1976
Height: 5'9" Weight: 11.4
Club Honours: Div 3 '95; AMC '97
Now one of the diminishing band of survivors from the third division championship side of three years ago, Richard had one of his best seasons at Carlisle, after two years of restricted appearances. A combative performer in the midfield, who wears his heart on his sleeve, his determined attitude is appreciated by the home fans, if not always by opposing forwards! Despite occasional injury problems, he made a total of 40 appearances, scoring his only goal in the AWS at Burnley.
Carlisle U (From trainee on 18/7/94) FL 97+9/2 FLC 7+1 FAC 5 Others 15+3/1

PRUDHOE Mark
Born: Washington, 8 November 1963
Height: 6'0" Weight: 14.0
Club Honours: GMVC '90; Div 4 '91
Transferred from Stoke during the 1997 close season to Bradford as a replacement for Aidan Davison, who had been released, Mark started at Valley Parade as first-choice goalkeeper, but was dropped after four games to make way for the Australian, Robert Zabica. Strangely, the latter himself was replaced by Mark after four appearances, only for the club to bring in Gary Walsh from Middlesbrough within two weeks. An excellent clubman, and liked by the fans, there were to be just three more appearances as a stand in for Walsh before the campaign ended. Remains an excellent shot stopper, however.
Sunderland (From apprentice on 11/9/81) FL 7
Hartlepool U (Loaned on 4/11/83) FL 3
Birmingham C (£22,000 on 24/9/84) FL 1 FLC 4
Walsall (£22,000 on 27/2/86) FL 26 FLC 4 FAC 1
Doncaster Rov (Loaned on 11/12/86) FL 5
Grimsby T (Loaned on 26/3/87) FL 8
Hartlepool U (Loaned on 29/8/87) FL 13
Bristol C (Loaned on 6/11/87) FL 3 Others 2
Carlisle U (£10,000 on 11/12/87) FL 34 FLC 2
Darlington (£10,000 on 16/3/89) FL 146 FLC 8 FAC 9 Others 6
Stoke C (£120,000 on 24/6/93) FL 82 FLC 6+1 FAC 5 Others 7
Peterborough U (Loaned on 30/9/94) FL 6
York C (Loaned on 14/2/97) FL 2
Bradford C (£70,000 on 17/7/97) FL 8 FLC 1

PUGH David
Born: Liverpool, 19 September 1964
Height: 5'10" Weight: 13.0
Club Honours: Div 2 '97

Having made the journey from division three to division one with Bury it was cruel for the Shakers' skipper to suffer an injury in the opening game of last season at home to Reading. A serious knee problem meant that he was destined only to ever play 48 minutes in the first division, as he spent the remainder of the campaign attempting to regain fitness, after a number of operations, before being forced to announce his retirement as a direct result of the injury. A goalscoring midfield man and wing back, he was a model professional and will sadly be missed at Gigg Lane.
Chester C (£35,000 from Runcorn on 21/7/89) FL 168+11/23 FLC 13 FAC 11+1 Others 9
Bury (£22,500 on 3/8/94) FL 101+2/28 FLC 7/1 FAC 6 Others 9/3

PURSE Darren John
Born: Stepney, 14 February 1977
Height: 6'2" Weight: 12.8
International Honours: E: U21-2
Developing into a very useful centre back, Darren quickly became Oxford's major asset in 1997-98, and it was hardly surprising that a number of clubs were running the rule over him, especially after he had scored six goals by mid-October, including a spectacular strike at West Bromwich. Reckoned by a few good judges to be a future England player if he keeps progressing at the current rate, and with United short of cash, he became their third man to be sold during the campaign when signing for Birmingham in February, a deal that saw Kevin Francis moving in the opposite direction. Competent on the ball, with a penchant to look for the right pass, and strong in the air, he was eased into the City side mainly as a sub, rather than exposing him to the promotion push. Although an obvious buy for the future, his ability was recognised at England U21 level, playing twice in the end of season Toulon tournament, and he could well be Steve Bruce's eventual successor.
Leyton Orient (From trainee on 22/2/94) FL 48+7/3 FLC 2 FAC 1 Others 7+1/2
Oxford U (£100,000 on 23/7/96) FL 52+7/5 FLC 10+1/2 FAC 2
Birmingham C (£800,000 on 17/2/98) FL 2+6

PUTTNAM David Paul
Born: Leicester, 3 February 1967
Height: 5'10" Weight: 12.2
Released by Gillingham during the 1997 summer recess, having earlier spent a couple of months on loan at non-league Yeovil, the skilful, wide left-sided midfielder started 1997-98 on trial at Swansea, making six appearances, before moving on in September when not offered a contract. A tricky player who can pass defenders with ease on occasion, the last few seasons have seen him inundated with injury problems.
Leicester C (£8,000 from Leicester U on 9/2/89) FL 4+3 FLC 0+1
Lincoln C (£35,000 on 21/1/90) FL 160+17/21 FLC 13+1/1 FAC 4 Others 8+1
Gillingham (£50,000 on 6/10/95) FL 15+25/2 FLC 1+5/1 FAC 0+5 Others 2
Swansea C (Free on 7/8/97) FL 4 FLC 2

QUAILEY Brian Sullivan
Born: Leicester, 24 March 1978
Height: 6'1" Weight: 13.11
Signed from non-league Nuneaton Borough early last season, Brian was not expected to figure for West Bromwich Albion in the immediate future, but after giving a series of fine performances for the reserves he came off the bench to make his debut at Manchester City at the end of February. A versatile forward, with strength, pace, and a good shot, the youngster should get further opportunities this coming term.
West Bromwich A (Signed from Nuneaton Borough on 22/9/97) FL 0+5

QUASHIE Nigel Francis
Born: Peckham, 20 July 1978
Height: 5'9" Weight: 11.0
International Honours: E: B-1; U21-4; Yth
Having returned from injury and illness in 1997-98, the Queens Park Rangers central midfielder's form really improved once Ray Harford had been installed as manager. Good when going forward, always looking to make the right pass, or to get a powerful shot on target, Nigel scored two goals in the 2-1 home win over Huddersfield Town, his only goals of the season, and was included in the England U21 and "B" squads in recognition of his good work. Is strong on the ball, has good control, and does not give possession up without a struggle.
Queens Park R (From trainee on 1/8/95) P/FL 50+7/3 FLC 0+1 FAC 4/2

QUIGLEY Michael Anthony
Born: Manchester, 2 October 1970
Height: 5'7" Weight: 11.4
Transfer listed by Hull City last September, "Quigs" found himself on the fringe of the Boothferry action for much of 1997-98, a rare highlight being his goal in the 3-0 win over Scarborough in October. Having fought back into contention in January, he was then struck down by a knee injury suffered in an AWS match at Grimsby, and must be praying for better luck in 1998-99.
Manchester C (From trainee on 1/7/89) F/PL 3+9 Others 1
Wrexham (Loaned on 17/2/95) FL 4
Hull C (Free on 5/7/95) FL 36+15/3 FLC 3+4/1 FAC 3 Others 2

QUINN Alan
Born: Dublin, 13 June 1979
Height: 5'9" Weight: 10.6
Having been signed by Sheffield Wednesday from the quaintly named Cherry Orchard, an Irish side, last December, the 18-year-old midfielder quickly became a regular in the Owls' youth team that ultimately won the FA Premier Northern Youth League. Obviously making quite an impression at Hillsborough, at the end of April he was selected for the first team squad at Everton and made his Premiership debut when coming off the bench in the last minute. This lad is definitely a comer.
Sheffield Wed (Signed from Cherry Orchard on 6/12/97) PL 0+1

QUINN James (Jimmy) Martin
Born: Belfast, 18 November 1959
Height: 6'0" Weight: 13.10
Club Honours: Div 2 '94
International Honours: NI: 48; B-1
Having resigned his post as joint player/manager at Reading shortly before the 1996-97 campaign came to a halt, at the age of 37 Jimmy joined up with Barry Fry at Peterborough during the 1997 close season. In being in the right place at the right time, the former Northern Ireland international striker had managed 19 goals before Christmas, including a hat trick in a 5-1 home win over Barnet, but added just six more before finishing the club's leading goalscorer and being honoured by his fellow professionals with selection to the PFA award-winning third division team. Missed just four games in 1997-98.
Swindon T (£10,000 from Oswestry on 31/12/81) FL 34+15/10 FLC 1+1 FAC 5+3/6 Others 1/2
Blackburn Rov (£32,000 on 15/8/84) FL 58+13/17 FLC 6+1/2 FAC 4/3 Others 2/1
Swindon T (£50,000 on 19/12/86) FL 61+3/30 FLC 6/8 FAC 5 Others 10+1/5
Leicester C (£210,000 on 20/6/88) FL 13+18/6 FLC 2+1 FAC 0+1 Others 0+1
Bradford (Signed on 17/3/89) FL 35/14 FLC 2/1 Others 1
West Ham U (£320,000 on 30/12/89) FL 34+13/19 FLC 3/1 FAC 4+2/2 Others 1
Bournemouth (£40,000 on 5/8/91) FL 43/19 FLC 4/2 FAC 5/2 Others 2/1
Reading (£55,000 on 27/7/92) FL 149+33/71 FLC 12+4/12 FAC 9/5 Others 6+3/6
Peterborough U (Free on 15/7/97) FL 40+2/20 FLC 4/1 FAC 3/3 Others 3+1/1

QUINN Stephen James (Jimmy)
Born: Coventry, 14 December 1974
Height: 6'1" Weight: 12.10
International Honours: NI: 12; B-2; U21-1; Yth
An exciting Northern Ireland international striker, Jimmy started last season at Blackpool, as he had done for the past four years, playing in most of the matches up until early November before an enforced lay off saw him put out of action. Back in early February, within weeks he had signed for West Bromwich Albion, being introduced on the right-hand side, and quickly made an impact, especially when scoring twice against Middlesbrough. With pace and height, he looks to trouble the best of defences.
Birmingham C (Trainee) FL 1+3
Blackpool (£25,000 on 5/7/93) FL 128+23/36 FLC 10+4/5 FAC 5+1/4 Others 7+4/2
Stockport Co (Loaned on 4/3/94) FL 0+1
West Bromwich A (£500,000 on 20/2/98) FL 12+1/2

QUINN Niall John
Born: Dublin, 6 October 1966
Height: 6'4" Weight: 15.10
Club Honours: FLC '87
International Honours: Ei: 61; B-1; U23-1; U21-6; Yth; Sch
Following a third knee operation in a year last September, big Niall must have thought his Sunderland injury jinx was going to continue throughout 1997-98. However, the striker's luck was to deservedly change when he returned to the first team and, in tandem with Kevin Phillips, he set about terrorising division one defences as the team surged up the table. The Irishman's aerial ability was the perfect foil for the nippy Phillips' pace, and Niall himself weighed in with his quota of goals, including a hat trick against Stockport in March, and braces in successive games against Queens Park Rangers and West Bromwich in April. Most significantly, the likeable striker scored the first ever goal at the Stadium of Light in the 3-1 defeat of his former club, Manchester City, in August, a month in which he also won his 62nd cap for Eire. Scored twice in the play-off final at Wembley.
Arsenal (From juniors on 30/11/83) FL 59+8/14 FLC 14+2/4 FAC 8+2/2 Others 0+1
Manchester C (£800,000 on 21/3/90) F/PL 183+20/66 FLC 20+2/7 FAC 13+3/4 Others 3/1
Sunderland (£1,300,000 on 17/8/96) F/PL 41+6/16 FLC 1/1 FAC 2/1 Others 2/2

QUINN Robert John
Born: Sidcup, 8 November 1976
Height: 5'11" Weight: 11.2
International Honours: Ei: U21-5
Unable to break into the Crystal Palace first team in 1997-98, apart from one appearance from the bench at home to Bolton early on, despite being an unused sub on 12 other occasions, Robert was confined mainly to the reserves, while continuing the learning process. With the defence suffering badly in the Premiership it was probably a wise move to hold him back, especially as he is a promising defender who could go far in the game. Strong and tenacious in the tackle, and a good passer, he continued to be called up by the Republic of Ireland U21 side during the campaign and, with Palace back in the first division, expect him to be in the side before too long.
Crystal Palace (From trainee on 11/3/95) F/PL 18+5/1 FLC 2+1/1 Others 2+1

QUINN Wayne Richard
Born: Truro, 19 November 1976
Height: 5'10" Weight: 11.12
International Honours: E: B-1; U21-2; Yth
A left-wing back, Wayne was undoubtedly the find of last season for Sheffield United. Came into the team at the start of 1997-98, due to an injury to Mitch Ward, and was a fixture until a knee injury led to an enforced absence. His performances saw him being immediately offered a three-year contract and progress through the England U21 squad (called up after only four first team appearances) to the "B" team. Also played for the England Nationwide U21 side. Tracked at the end of the campaign by several Premier clubs, who were prepared to pay up to £3 million for his services, he showed commendable coolness in scoring the decisive penalty in the exciting shoot-out victory over Coventry City, and also scored an excellent volley against Reading, his first goal for the club.
Sheffield U (From trainee on 6/12/94) FL 28/2 FLC 5 FAC 4+1 Others 2

PFA Enterprises Ltd
18 Oxford Court
Bishopsgate
Manchester
M2 3WQ

Tel: 0161 228 2733
Fax: 0161 236 4496
email: gberry@thepfa.co.uk

* * * * *

Football in the Community
11 Oxford Court
Bishopsgate
Manchester
M2 3WQ

Tel: 0161 236 0583
Fax: 0161 236 4459

* * * * *

F.F.E. & V.T.S. Ltd
2 Oxford Court
Bishopsgate
Manchester
M2 3WQ

Tel: 0161 236 0637
Fax: 0161 228 7229

RADEBE Lucas
Born: Johannesburg, South Africa, 12 April 1969
Height: 6'1" Weight: 11.8
International Honours: South Africa: 44

Lucas is now one of George Graham's more experienced squad players, his versatility giving the Leeds' manager the range of quality options he required, and is invaluable to the set up at Elland Road. His combination of skill, strength, and determination making him one of the top defenders in the Premier League, if not the best man marker. Able to play in a number of positions, including goalkeeper, he has now become the lynchpin of the United defence. Had a very consistent season in 1997-98 and scored his first goal for the club in the FA Cup victory over Oxford. The downside was that the club was badly affected by his number of call ups to the South African side, which meant him missing a number of games. *Stop Press:* Captained South Africa in their three World Cup matches in France '98 and impressed, despite the side not qualifying from Group C, drawing with Denmark and Saudi Arabia, but losing to France.

Leeds U (£250,000 from Kaizer Chiefs on 5/9/94) PL 73+11 FLC 6+3 FAC 9+2/1

RAE Alexander (Alex) Scott
Born: Glasgow, 30 September 1969
Height: 5'9" Weight: 11.12
International Honours: S: B-4; U21-8

The Scottish schemer enjoyed a prolonged run in the Sunderland first team in 1997-98 for the first time since joining the club in 1996. Following an injury to Kevin Ball in October, Alex was able to form an excellent central midfield partnership with Lee Clark that was vital to the club's promotion push. Possessing good passing and tackling skills, his combative style sometimes landed him in trouble with officials, but his willingness to "get stuck in" and compete was a key factor in the team's successes last season. Alex also made two appearances for the Scotland "B" team last term.

Falkirk (Free from Bishopbriggs on 15/6/87) SL 71+12/20 SLC 5/1 SC 2+1
Millwall (£100,000 on 20/8/90) FL 205+13/63 FLC 13+2/1 FAC 13/6 Others 10/1
Sunderland (£750,000 on 14/6/96) F/PL 37+15/5 FLC 3+1/2 FAC 2 Others 0+2

RAMAGE Craig Darren
Born: Derby, 30 March 1970
Height: 5'9" Weight: 11.8
International Honours: E: U21-3

Released by Watford during the summer of 1997, Craig joined Bradford on a two-year contract and, after sitting on the bench for the opening few games of last season, began to establish himself in the Bantams' midfield. This, despite suffering from first

shingles, and then a cartilage problem. Conversely, recognised as a battling, tigerish tackler, on the other side of his coin in the same match you can see him stroking the ball about with real aplomb and exhibiting delightful touches. Once a goalscorer, he only got the one in 1997-98, waiting until the final day, a home 3-1 defeat at the hands of Portsmouth, to open his account with a consolation header.

Derby Co (From trainee on 20/7/88) FL 33+9/4 FLC 6+1/2 FAC 3+1/1 Others 0+3
Wigan Ath (Loaned on 16/2/89) FL 10/2 Others 0+1
Watford (£90,000 on 21/2/94) FL 99+5/27 FLC 8+1/2 FAC 7
Peterborough U (Loaned on 10/2/97) FL 7 Others 1
Bradford C (Free on 24/6/97) FL 24+8/1 FLC 0+1

RAMASUT Mahan William **Thomas (Tom)**
Born: Cardiff, 30 August 1977
Height: 5'10" Weight: 11.2
International Honours: W: B-1; U21-4; Yth

A slightly built, but deceptive Bristol Rovers' left winger, Tom scored a memorable second league goal against Wrexham last October, with a superb free kick around the defensive wall, and another, a stunning 35-yard left-foot strike, that was a candidate for Goal of the Season in Rovers' impressive 5-0 victory over Wigan. Having improved his stamina and strength on the ball, which helped to establish himself in the

team, he won further Welsh U21 caps in Turkey and Italy and made his Welsh "B" debut as a substitute against Scotland. Was also honoured by being voted the Supporters' Club Young Player of the Season.

Norwich C (Signed on 28/7/95)
Bristol Rov (Free on 12/9/96) FL 30+12/6 FAC 3 Others 2

RAMMELL Andrew (Andy) Victor
Born: Nuneaton, 10 February 1967
Height: 6'1" Weight: 13.12

Once again, Andy had a difficult season at Southend, as he was unable to retain a regular place in the starting line-up in 1997-98, his lack of goals seeing him constantly in a fight with at least three other players for a place alongside Jeroen Boere up front. A player you could never accuse of giving less than 100 per-cent effort, his first touch occasionally let him down, but he did have an inspired game as an emergency centre half, putting his excellent aerial abilities to good use, before being released in the summer.

Manchester U (£40,000 from Atherstone U on 26/9/89)
Barnsley (£100,000 on 14/9/90) FL 149+36/44 FLC 11+3/1 FAC 12+1/4 Others 8/1
Southend U (Signed on 22/2/96) FL 50+19/13 FLC 3+3/1 FAC 2+1 Others 1

Craig Ramage

RAMSAY John William
Born: Sunderland, 25 January 1979
Height: 5'8" Weight: 9.10
Fresh out of the YTS ranks, John rarely made the starting line-up for Doncaster last season, his first team involvement being largely as a substitute who generally dropped into midfield when the occasion arose. He, too, had his contract cancelled prior to the transfer deadline and will be hoping to rebuild his career elsewhere.
Doncaster Rov (From trainee on 31/10/97) FL 2+2 FLC 0+1 FAC 0+1 Others 0+1

RANDALL Adrian John
Born: Amesbury, 10 November 1968
Height: 5'11" Weight: 12.4
Club Honours: Div 4 '92, Div 2 '97
International Honours: E: Yth
With competition for places in Bury's midfield department particularly fierce in 1997-98, Adrian found himself out of favour and was unable to earn any kind of extended run in the side, as he struggled to recapture his best form. A six-match ban to fellow midfield man, Andy Gray, allowed the opening for a brief two-match stretch in the starting line-up during November, appearing against Huddersfield and Sunderland, but he was mainly to be found kicking around on the Shakers' substitutes bench in what must have been a frustrating time for a player making 16 substitute appearance in total.
Bournemouth (From apprentice on 2/9/86) FL 3 Others 1+2
Aldershot (Signed on 15/9/88) FL 102+5/12 FLC 3 FAC 11/3 Others 10/2
Burnley (£40,000 on 12/12/91) FL 105+20/8 FLC 6/1 FAC 8+2/1 Others 3
York C (£140,000 on 28/12/95) FL 26+6/2 FLC 5 FAC 0+1
Bury (£140,000 on 12/12/96) FL 16+18/3 FLC 1+3 Others 0+2

RANDALL Dean
Born: Nottingham, 15 May 1979
Height: 6'1" Weight: 12.0
A first-year professional at Notts County in 1997-98, this young centre half had the benefit of a number of experienced defenders coaching him, and helping him develop from youth player to the ranks of full timer. Having always impressed with his commitment, which won him the accolade of Reserve Team Player of the Year from the supporters, Dean was given a first team opportunity when coming off the bench at Burnley in a 2-0 Auto Windscreen Shield defeat last January, before being released at the end of the season.
Notts Co (From trainee on 16/7/97) Others 0+1

RANKIN Isaiah (Izzy)
Born: London, 22 May 1978
Height: 5'10" Weight: 11.0
An Ian Wright look-alike striker who spent three months on loan at Colchester from Arsenal last September, Izzy showed devastating pace and a good eye for goal. Although his stay was disrupted by injury, and the rule banning loan players from FA Cup ties, so that he never had a settled run in the team, Izzy still produced five goals in his

12 games, signing off on Boxing Day with a brace against Brighton at Gillingham.
Arsenal (From trainee on 12/9/95) PL 0+1
Colchester U (Loaned on 25/9/97) FL 10+1/5 Others 1

RANKINE Simon Mark
Born: Doncaster, 30 September 1969
Height: 5'9" Weight: 12.11
Originally listed during the summer of 1997, his early season form in Preston's midfield in 1997-98 was a revelation for the fans, whom he had failed to impress the previous term. A hard-working player, he supported both attack and defence well, often getting into good scoring positions, but, unfortunately, his lack of true finishing ability resulted in only one goal. Following an injury sustained in a freak DIY accident in December, almost resulting in the loss of a finger, he found his first team opportunities restricted from then on, as Simon Davey and Michael Appleton adopted the midfield mantle, and only returned towards the end of the campaign.
Doncaster Rov (From trainee on 4/7/88) FL 160+4/20 FLC 8+1/1 FAC 8/2 Others 14/2
Wolverhampton W (£70,000 on 31/1/92) FL 112+20/1 FLC 9+1 FAC 14+2 Others 7+2
Preston NE (£100,000 on 17/9/96) FL 53+5/1 FLC 6 FAC 4 Others 2

RAPLEY Kevin John
Born: Reading, 21 September 1977
Height: 5'9" Weight: 10.8
A fast and tricky right-footed Brentford striker who bears more than a little resemblance in style to former Bee, Nicky Forster, Kevin was given his first start of last season at Shrewsbury in the Coca Cola Cup, and responded with two goals. Remained in the side throughout Eddie May's reign as boss and, in that time, scored a last-minute winner with an overhead kick against Burnley, after which he removed his shirt waving it above his head all the way back to the centre circle! Initially left out by new manager, Micky Adams, he forced his way back into the squad in January and was a regular for the rest of the campaign, scoring in successive games against Bristol City and Bournemouth in March, having come off the bench on each occasion. Also scored after coming off the bench in the last game of the season, at Bristol Rovers, but it was not enough to prevent the Bees being relegated to the third division.
Brentford (From trainee on 8/7/96) FL 24+15/9 FLC 3+1/2 FAC 0+1 Others 1

RATCLIFFE Simon
Born: Urmston, 8 February 1967
Height: 6'0" Weight: 13.0
Club Honours: Div 3 '92
International Honours: E: Yth; Sch
A hardworking midfielder, Simon started the first ten games in 1997-98 and continued to produce good performances until his season effectively was ended at the end of 1997, when he sustained several niggling injuries which resulted in him requiring an operation. Although known for his strong right foot, his one goal came via a header in a 4-1 win at Wigan.

Manchester U (From apprentice on 13/2/85)
Norwich C (£40,000 on 16/6/87) FL 6+3 FLC 2
Brentford (£100,000 on 13/1/89) FL 197+17/14 FLC 13+3 FAC 9+1 Others 26+2/2
Gillingham (Free on 4/8/95) FL 100+5/10 FLC 11/2 FAC 5+2/1 Others 1

RAVANELLI Fabrizio
Born: Italy, 11 December 1968
Height: 6'1" Weight: 13.4
International Honours: Italy: 22
A controversial world-class striker who arrived at Middlesbrough amidst great expectations, winning instant admiration from all and sundry, he scored many great goals and created club records for "hat-tricks" and goals scored, before leaving under a cloud to join Marseilles for £5.3 million last September. Still a great player, and still a class act, his three goals in five games went a long way to ensure that Italy reached the World Cup Finals.
Middlesbrough (£7,000,000 from Juventus on 15/8/96) F/PL 35/17 FLC 8/9 FAC 7/6

RAVEN Paul Duncan
Born: Salisbury, 28 July 1970
Height: 6'1" Weight: 12.12
International Honours: E: Sch
Having played well for West Bromwich Albion throughout 1996-97, Paul was looking forward to doing likewise in 1997-98, but sadly, injuries robbed him of all bar a dozen appearances. Although playing through the pain barrier after suffering a bad knock early on, he was forced out of the fray in mid-October, and was out of first team action from then on, despite attempting a comeback with the reserves. The son-in-law of a former Doncaster player, Brian Makepeace, he is both confident and strong in the air and on the ground, and is always a danger at set pieces, scoring from close range in the 4-2 Coca Cola Cup win over Luton in September.
Doncaster Rov (From juniors on 6/6/88) FL 52/4 FLC 2 FAC 5 Others 2
West Bromwich A (£100,000 on 23/3/89) FL 216+4/14 FLC 16/1 FAC 8/3 Others 15/1
Doncaster Rov (Loaned on 27/11/91) FL 7

RAWLINSON Mark David
Born: Bolton, 9 June 1975
Height: 5'10" Weight: 11.4
As a central midfielder who is a good passer of the ball, and able to play in defence if required, Mark did not have a consistent run in the Bournemouth first team last season, managing only 20 starts and ten substitute appearances. However, his ability to get forward, as well as producing the goods as a man-to-man marker, should see him back on song in 1998-99.
Manchester U (From trainee on 5/7/93)
Bournemouth (Free on 1/7/95) FL 41+28/2 FLC 2+1 FAC 2+1 Others 3

RAYNOR Paul James
Born: Nottingham, 29 April 1966
Height: 6'0" Weight: 12.11
Club Honours: WC '89, '91
Paul joined Leyton Orient last February on a non-contract basis from Guang Deong, having played for a brief spell in China after

being released by Cambridge during the previous summer, and made his return to the Football League in February. Is a good, attacking, wide-right midfielder and an excellent passer of the ball.

Nottingham F (From apprentice on 2/4/84) FL 3 FLC 1
Bristol Rov (Loaned on 28/3/85) FL 7+1
Huddersfield T (Free on 15/8/85) FL 38+12/9 FLC 3 FAC 2+1 Others 1
Swansea C (Free on 27/3/87) FL 170+21/27 FLC 11+1/3 FAC 8+1/1 Others 15+1/3
Wrexham (Loaned on 17/10/88) FL 6
Cambridge U (Free on 10/3/92) FL 46+3/2 FLC 5 FAC 1 Others 2+1/1
Preston NE (£36,000 on 23/7/93) FL 72+8/9 FLC 4+1 FAC 7/1 Others 10/2
Cambridge U (Signed on 12/9/95) FL 78+1/7 FLC 1+1 FAC 2 Others 1 (Free to Guang Deong during 1997 close season)
Leyton Orient (Free on 26/2/98) FL 5+5

READ Paul Colin
Born: Harlow, 25 September 1973
Height: 5'11" Weight: 12.6
International Honours: E: Sch

A nimble right-footed striker, with good control and a cool head in the box, Paul found it difficult to establish himself at Wycombe last season. Began well with three goals in his first three starts but, in spite of 17 goals in 19 reserve games, he was mainly used as a substitute. Played in the final four games of the campaign when his confidence returned, scoring the winning goal at Walsall with a well-taken lob.

Arsenal (From trainee on 11/10/91)
Leyton Orient (Loaned on 10/3/95) FL 11 Others 1
Southend U (Loaned on 6/10/95) FL 3+1/1 Others 1
Wycombe W (£35,000 + on 17/1/97) FL 21+20/8 FLC 2/1 FAC 1+1

Karl Ready

READY Karl
Born: Neath, 14 August 1972
Height: 6'1" Weight: 13.3
International Honours: W: 5; B-2; U21-5; Sch

A central defender who can play equally well at full back if required, the Welsh international had an excellent season at Queens Park Rangers in 1997-98 after being brought back into the first team in mid-September, missing just two games during the rest of the campaign, and scoring three goals in the process. Good in the air and very steady, Karl was appointed captain during Gavin Peacock's absence from the side.

Queens Park R (From trainee on 13/8/90) F/PL 115+14/6 FLC 4+2/1 FAC 7

REDFEARN Neil David
Born: Dewsbury, 20 June 1965
Height: 5'9" Weight: 12.8
Club Honours: Div 2 '91

After a career in the lower divisions, Neil was never going to let his chance to play in the Premiership pass him by and was always at the heart of Barnsley's battle for survival in 1997-98. Leading by example, never hiding from the action, even when things were not going right for him or the team, and a model professional, he yet again led the goals' chart, having the distinction of scoring the club's first ever goal at the top level, his will to win and explosive shooting being just two of his many attributes. Despite his age, his 11 Premiership goals will be sending out alarm bells to many managers this coming term. *Stop Press:* Joined newly-promoted Charlton on 25 June in a transfer deal thought to be worth £1 million.

Bolton W (Free from Nottingham F juniors on 23/6/82) FL 35/1 FLC 2 FAC 4
Lincoln C (£8,250 on 23/3/84) FL 96+4/13 FLC 4 FAC 3/1 Others 7
Doncaster Rov (£17,500 on 22/8/86) FL 46/14 FLC 2 FAC 3/1 Others 2
Crystal Palace (£100,000 on 31/7/87) FL 57/10 FLC 6 FAC 1 Others 1
Watford (£150,000 on 21/11/88) FL 22+2/3 FLC 1 FAC 6/3 Others 5/1

Neil Redfearn

Oldham Ath (£150,000 on 12/1/90) FL 56+6/16 FLC 3/1 FAC 7+1/3 Others 1
Barnsley (£150,000 on 5/9/91) F/PL 289+3/72 FLC 21/6 FAC 20/6 Others 5

REDKNAPP Jamie Frank
Born: Barton on Sea, 25 June 1973
Height: 6'0" Weight: 12.10
Club Honours: FLC '95
International Honours: E: 8; B-1; U21-19; Yth; Sch

The son of the West Ham manager, Harry, Jamie signed a five-year contract at the end of 1997-98, and is clearly in Roy Evans' plans to build a championship winning team at Liverpool. The midfielder was a major influence on the side, and Liverpool looked more settled, more determined, and more difficult to beat when he was in the line-up. Although prone to the odd injury, making 26 appearances from a possible 47 last season, his masterful passing ability, and tough tackling, were such positive attributes that the Reds appeared to struggle without him. Most likely a possible captain for the future, he would almost certainly gone to France with England's World Cup squad had he not suffered a knee ligament injury at Coventry with five games to go, having had a run out with the England U21 side as a sweeper against Switzerland and been in the final 30. Was reported to have married the "pop star", Louise, during the summer.

Bournemouth (From trainee on 27/6/90) FL 6+7 FLC 3 FAC 3 Others 2
Liverpool (£350,000 on 15/1/91) F/PL 154+23/19 FLC 25/5 FAC 15+1/2 Others 15+4/1

REDMILE Matthew Ian
Born: Nottingham, 12 November 1976
Height: 6'3" Weight: 14.10
Club Honours: Div 3 '98

Began last season at Notts County as an instant hero with his goalscoring exploits from set pieces. A huge and powerful

central defender, who is gifted with quite exceptional ball-playing ability, Matthew admits to having been less than consistent in the latter part of the campaign, despite winning a third division championship medal, but has promised himself, and the supporters, to add greater fitness and speed in 1998-99. The result could be formidable.

Notts Co (From trainee on 4/7/95) FL 55+2/5 FLC 4 FAC 6 Others 3

REDMOND Stephen (Steve)

Born: Liverpool, 2 November 1967
Height: 5'11" Weight: 11.7
Club Honours: FAYC '86
International Honours: E: U21-14; Yth

Although a loss of form saw him miss a number of games for Oldham in 1997-98, when he did play he was as reliable as ever. An extremely experienced central defender with over 500 games under his belt, as you would expect he reads the game well, is cool under pressure, and is a good passer of the ball. Is currently contracted on a week-to-week basis.*

Manchester C (From apprentice on 3/12/84) FL 231+4/7 FLC 24 FAC 17 Others 11
Oldham Ath (£300,000 on 10/7/92) P/FL 195+10/4 FLC 20 FAC 10+2 Others 1+1

REED Adam Maurice

Born: Bishop Auckland, 18 February 1975
Height: 6'0" Weight: 12.0

Unable to get a game at Blackburn in 1997-98, Adam was loaned out to Rochdale in December and impressed enough to be likened to the former Dale hero, Alan Reeves. A regular at centre back in his two months at Spotland, his later appearances unfortunately coincided with the club's form slumping to such an extent that six games in a row were lost, before he returned to Ewood Park, from where he was released during the summer. Still only a youngster as defenders go, Adam combines great aerial strength with positional ability.

Darlington (From trainee on 16/7/93) FL 45+7/1 FLC 1+1 FAC 1 Others 3
Blackburn Rov (£200,000 on 9/8/95)
Darlington (Loaned on 21/2/97) FL 14
Rochdale (Loaned on 5/12/97) FL 10 Others 2/1

REED John Paul

Born: Rotherham, 27 August 1972
Height: 5'10" Weight: 10.11

Released by Sheffield United during the 1997 close season, having failed to get a first team game the previous season due to injuries, John signed for Blackpool and although playing regularly for the reserves registered just one start and three subs' appearances in 1997-98. Somewhat disappointed, the right-sided midfielder with good ball skills was released during the summer.

Sheffield U (From trainee on 3/7/90) FL 11+4/2 FLC 1 Others 1/1
Scarborough (Loaned on 10/1/91) FL 14/6
Scarborough (Loaned on 26/9/91) FL 5+1 FLC 1
Darlington (Loaned on 19/3/93) FL 8+2/2
Mansfield T (Loaned on 23/9/93) FL 12+1/2 FAC 1 Others 3/2
Blackpool (Free on 21/7/97) FL 0+3 Others 1

REED Martin John

Born: Scarborough, 10 January 1978
Height: 6'0" Weight: 11.6

A strong-tackling and determined central defender, Martin had an extended run in the York senior side during the first half of last season, and again showed himself to be a most promising young player. Standing in for the injured Steve Tutill, he maintained his place until the arrival of Barry Jones from Wrexham and it will not be too long before he is a regular.

York C (From trainee on 4/7/96) FL 23+1 FLC 2 FAC 2 Others 1

REES Jason Mark

Born: Aberdare, 22 December 1969
Height: 5'5" Weight: 10.2
International Honours: W: 1; U21-3; B-1; Yth; Sch

Freed by Portsmouth during the 1997 summer recess, Jason played well in pre-season trials at Cambridge to earn a contract and made an excellent start to 1997-98. A tenacious, hard-working ball winner, he showed his class when running the midfield at Orient, and was the key player in the team, but his form later took a dip and he struggled to regain his place in the side, being released during the summer.

Luton T (From trainee on 1/7/88) FL 59+23 FLC 3+2 FAC 2+1 Others 5+1/2
Mansfield T (Loaned on 23/12/93) FL 15/1 Others 1
Portsmouth (Free on 18/7/94) FL 30+13/3 FLC 2+1 FAC 0+1
Exeter C (Loaned on 31/1/97) FL 7
Cambridge U (Free on 8/8/97) FL 17+3 FLC 2 Others 1

REEVES Alan

Born: Birkenhead, 19 November 1967
Height: 6'0" Weight: 12.0

A typical old-fashioned centre half, despite not being in line for Wimbledon places in 1997-98, appearing just once as a sub in the Coca Cola Cup, one could not fault him for his enthusiasm and drive. Tough tackling and aerial strengths are also among his main attributes and he is as good as any at the latter, his ability to head the ball powerfully being well known and a skill that brought him to the club in the first place. Dangerous at set pieces, he was freed during the summer and will have spent the break looking for a new club.

Norwich C (Signed from Heswall on 20/9/88)
Gillingham (Loaned on 9/2/89) FL 18
Chester C (£10,000 on 18/8/89) FL 31+9/2 FLC 1+1 FAC 3 Others 3
Rochdale (Free on 2/7/91) FL 119+2/9 FLC 12/1 FAC 6 Others 5
Wimbledon (£300,000 on 6/9/94) PL 52+5/4 FLC 2+2 FAC 8

REEVES David Edward

Born: Birkenhead, 19 November 1967
Height: 6'0" Weight: 12.6
Club Honours: Div 3 '95

Despite notching four early season goals for Preston in 1997-98, David hit a barren patch and was exchanged for Chesterfield's Tony Lormor in November. Made an immediate impact at Saltergate, scoring winners in his first two games and building an instant

rapport with the fans, he played well with his back to the goal and worked his socks off for his team mates, while proving tricky and difficult to dispossess when going through on goal. It is interesting to note that if the player plus cash deal that brought him to Chesterfield was expressed as a money figure alone, it would be a record for a fee paid by the Spireites. David is the twin brother of Alan Reeves, of Wimbledon and Rochdale.

Sheffield Wed (Free from Heswall on 6/8/86) FL 8+9/2 FLC 1+1/1 FAC 1+1 Others 0+1
Scunthorpe U (Loaned on 17/12/86) FL 3+1/2
Scunthorpe U (Loaned on 1/10/87) FL 6/4
Burnley (Loaned on 20/11/87) FL 16/8 Others 2/1
Bolton W (£80,000 on 17/8/89) FL 111+23/29 FLC 14+1/1 FAC 8+5/5 Others 9+2/7
Notts Co (£80,000 on 25/3/93) FL 9+4/2 FLC 1+1
Carlisle U (£121,000 on 1/10/93) FL 127/47 FLC 9/5 FAC 9/4 Others 23/7
Preston NE (Signed on 9/10/96) FL 45+2/12 FLC 3+1/3 FAC 2/3 Others 1
Chesterfield (Signed on 6/11/97) FL 26/5 FAC 1+1/1

REGIS David (Dave)

Born: Paddington, 3 March 1964
Height: 6'1" Weight: 13.8
Club Honours: Div 2 '93

Unable to get much of an opportunity in the Premiership with Barnsley in 1997-98, the veteran striker was loaned out to Scunthorpe at the start of the season, proving to be a handful for third division defences during the opening five matches, before returning to Oakwell. Unsuccessful loan spells followed at Leyton Orient and Lincoln and he was just about to move into non-league football when Scunthorpe finally got their man on non-contract terms in February. Scoring twice in four games before rupturing knee ligaments, Dave will be on the sidelines until October, at least.

Notts Co (£25,000 from Barnet on 28/9/90) FL 31+15/15 FLC 0+2 Others 6/2
Plymouth Arg (£200,000 on 7/11/91) FL 28+3/4 FLC 2/3 FAC 1
Bournemouth (Loaned on 13/8/92) FL 6/2
Stoke C (£100,000 on 23/10/92) FL 49+14/15 FLC 2/1 FAC 4+1/2 Others 7+1/2
Birmingham C (£200,00 on 1/8/94) FL 4+2/2 FLC 1
Southend U (Signed on 16/9/94) FL 34+4/9 FLC 1 FAC 1 Others 1+2/1
Barnsley (Signed on 21/2/96) FL 4+12/1 FLC 0+3
Peterborough U (Loaned on 30/9/96) FL 4+3/1
Notts Co (Loaned on 7/2/97) FL 7+3/2
Scunthorpe U (Loaned on 3/8/97) FL 5
Leyton Orient (Free on 30/10/97) FL 4
Lincoln C (Free on 19/12/97) FL 0+1
Scunthorpe U (Free on 6/2/98) FL 4/2

REID Paul Robert

Born: Oldbury, 19 January 1968
Height: 5'9" Weight: 11.8

Again playing down the left-hand side for Oldham, missing just three games throughout 1997-98, there was no doubting at times that his leadership qualities were the biggest single plus at the club in a sometimes difficult season. An excellent tackler, and a hard-running midfielder, among his other qualities is the ability to score spectacular and often vital goals, five coming from him during the campaign, two of them in a 3-1 home win over Gillingham.

Leicester C (From apprentice on 9/1/86) FL 140+22/21 FLC 13/4 FAC 5+1 Others 6+2
Bradford C (Loaned on 19/3/92) FL 7
Bradford C (£25,000 on 27/7/92) FL 80+2/15 FLC 3/2 FAC 3 Others 5/1
Huddersfield T (£70,000 on 20/5/94) FL 70+7/6 FLC 9/1 FAC 5+1 Others 1
Oldham Ath (£100,000 on 27/3/97) FL 53/6 FLC 2 FAC 4

REID Steven John
Born: Kingston, 10 March 1981
Height: 5'11" Weight: 11.10
International Honours: E: Yth

A product of Millwall's youth team, and still a trainee, Steven was introduced to the first team on the final day of last season, when he came on for the last 21 minutes at the New Den against Bournemouth. An England youth cap, the club felt that he warranted the opportunity on the basis of excellent performances he had earlier given at both youth and reserve team levels. A powerful front runner, with a good turn of speed, and good in the air, he can also play in midfield, where he impresses with strong tackling.
Millwall (Trainee) FL 0+1

REINA Enrique (Ricky) Iglesias
Born: Folkestone, 2 October 1971
Height: 6'0" Weight: 13.5

The tall striker with a powerful long throw finally broke into the Football League when signing for the Bees from Dover last September. Having made his debut as sub against Southampton in the Coca Cola Cup in September, and scoring on his first full appearance against Bristol City in November, when hooking the ball home, he was unfortunately diagnosed as carrying severe knee problems, and formally retired from the game in April.
Brentford (£50,000 + from Dover on 15/9/97) FL 2+4/1 FLC 0+1 FAC 2

REINELT Robert (Robbie) Squire
Born: Loughton, 11 March 1974
Height: 5'11" Weight: 12.0

The scorer of Brighton and Hove Albion's equaliser at Hereford in the last game of the 1996-97 campaign, which kept the Seagulls in the Football League, he found it difficult to find the net last season. Hampered by a poor disciplinary record, and a knee injury sustained in February, Robbie was as enthusiastic as ever, but struggled to find his touch in Albion's continually changing front line, before being released during the summer.
Aldershot (Trainee) FL 3+2
Gillingham (Free from Wivenhoe T on 19/3/93) FL 34+18/5 FLC 3/1 FAC 5+2/2 Others 5
Colchester U (Signed on 22/3/95) FL 22+26/10 FLC 4+1/2 FAC 1 Others 3/1
Brighton & Hove A (£15,000 on 13/2/97) FL 32+12/7 FLC 2 Others 1

REMY Christophe Philippe
Born: Besancon, France, 6 August 1971
Height: 5'10" Weight: 12.6

Christophe joined Oxford during the 1997 close season, following a short trial, having earlier trialled unsuccessfully with Derby County. Starting last season as a regular wing back, he looked very competent on the ball and, with the side playing a new formation, he proved to be a good attacking option. Unfortunately, however, not being used to playing so many games he began to suffer with a few injuries, most notably a back problem, which sidelined him for some time. Prior to arriving at United, he had played all his football in France with Auxerre, whom he helped to win the French League and Cup in his last term with them.
Oxford U (Signed from Auxerre on 25/7/97) FL 13+3 FLC 4 FAC 0+1

RENNIE David
Born: Edinburgh, 29 August 1964
Height: 6'0" Weight: 13.0
International Honours: S: Yth;

A central defender, cum midfielder, with an eye for the long ball, David did not figure too highly at Northampton after the manager brought in David Brightwell and Colin Hill, and after six appearances in 1997-98 he was released to join Peterborough in December. Having got off to a flier at Posh, unfortunately, his season was disrupted due to a hernia operation, but if he can get back to full fitness during the summer he could be a great asset to the club. Is excellent at set pieces.
Leicester C (From apprentice on 18/5/82) FL 21/1 FLC 2
Leeds U (£50,000 on 17/1/86) FL 95+6/5 FLC 7 FAC 7/1 Others 4/1
Bristol C (£175,000 on 31/7/89) FL 101+3/8 FLC 8 FAC 9 Others 5
Birmingham C (£120,000 on 20/2/92) FL 32+3/4 FLC 1 Others 1
Coventry C (£100,000 on 11/3/93) PL 80+2/3 FLC 6 FAC 3+1
Northampton T (Free on 5/8/96) FL 45+3/4 FLC 4 FAC 1 Others 5
Peterborough U (Free on 1/12/97) FL 18 Others 4

RENNISON Graham Lee
Born: York, 2 October 1978
Height: 6'0" Weight: 12.8

Still a trainee, the young central defender made a traumatic Football League debut for York City last April, when he was sent off at Luton for deliberate hand ball after just 34 minutes. However, due to sign a full-time contract for the Minstermen during the summer, upon completion of his time as a YTS, the promising youngster can hopefully look forward to further first team opportunities in 1998-99.
York C (Trainee) FL 1

RESCH Franz
Born: Vienna, Austria, 4 May 1969
Height: 6'0" Weight: 12.0
International Honours: Austria: 2

A cultured Austrian international left back, Franz arrived at Darlington from Motherwell, along with fellow-countryman, Mario Dörner, last October, but never really established himself in the first team and returned home before the end of the season. Before leaving though, he left the fans with the memory of an excellent strike in a 3-1 win over Peterborough at Feethams, which had followed his assist cross for the opening goal.
Motherwell (Free from VFB Modling on 1/7/97) SL 3 SLC 2
Darlington (Free on 17/10/97) FL 15+2/1 FAC 1+2
Motherwell (Free from VFB Modling on 1/7/97) SL 3 SLC 2

RHODES Andrew (Andy) Charles
Born: Askern, 23 August 1964
Height: 6'1" Weight: 12.9

A vastly experienced 'keeper, Andy joined Scarborough on loan from the Scottish club, Airdrie, following an injury to Kevin Martin last November, and performed well in his spell at the seaside, before returning to Scotland. Later joined Halifax Town, where he was a star performer during the run-in to their Conference title success.
Barnsley (From apprentice on 24/8/82) FL 36 FLC 2 FAC 1
Doncaster Rov (£25,000 on 22/10/85) FL 106 FLC 6 FAC 6 Others 7
Oldham Ath (£55,000 on 11/3/88) FL 69 FLC 7 FAC 1 Others 2
Dunfermline (Signed on 23/7/90) SL 79 SLC 6 SC 4
St Johnstone (Signed on 2/7/92) SL 107 SLC 9 SC 9 Others 2
Airdrie (Signed on 12/12/95) SL 30 SLC 1 SC 1 Others 1
Scarborough (Loaned on 27/11/97) FL 11 Others 1

RIBEIRO Bruno
Born: Setubal, Portugal, 22 October 1975
Height: 5'8" Weight: 12.2

The Leeds' management team of George Graham and David O'Leary were on a 1997 close season visit to check the form of Jimmy Hasselbaink when they spotted Bruno playing for the opposition, signing him up almost immediately from Vittoria Setubal, and earmarking him as "one for the future". Bruno, though, had other ideas, and settled into the side from the off, becoming an instant favourite with the fans, providing flair and ingenuity from midfield, and scoring important goals, including his volley at Sheffield Wednesday in the second game of the campaign. In fact, the Portuguese youngster made such an impression that he was offered and accepted an improved extension to his original contract. Finding himself on the verge of a call up to the Portuguese national side, this extremely talented and dogged midfielder must be classed as one of the finds of the season.
Leeds U (£500,000 from Vittoria Setubal on 18/7/97) PL 28+1/3 FLC 2+1/1 FAC 3

RICARD Cuesta Hamilton
Born: Colombia, 12 January 1974
Height: 6'2" Weight: 14.5
International Honours: Colombia: 18

Signed from Deportivo Cali last March, and looking every inch the archetypal striker, Hamilton made his Middlesbrough debut in the 3-0 demolition of Norwich City at the Cellnet on 22 March, acquitting himself well, and giving the fans much to enthuse over. Another late arrival in "Robbo's" ongoing search for lasting success, the Colombian appeared in every game from his debut to the end of the season, but, sadly, he was unable to produce the form suggested

by his reputation and consequently did not claim 100 per-cent popularity with the fans. However, he scored a vital goal in the 1-1 home draw against Wolves in the penultimate match, a goal that kept Boro one point clear of the chasing play-off group and helped ease the passage to the Premiership. *Stop Press:* Selected for Colombia's final 22 bound for France '98, he came off the bench for the second half against England to no avail as the team crashed out of the World Cup at the Group G stage.

Middlesbrough (£2,000,000+ from Deportivo Cali on 13/3/98) FL 4+5/2 FLC 1

RICHARDS Dean Ivor
Born: Bradford, 9 June 1974
Height: 6'2" Weight: 13.5
International Honours: E: U21-4

A Wolves' central defender who often shows Premier League class but also suffers lapses of concentration, major knee problems prevented him playing from January 1997 until Boxing Day, when he was booked in the second minute. Settling down to some competent performances, it was no coincidence that Wolves did not concede a goal in his first four outings, and his form attracted some big clubs, scoring with a fine header at Charlton. The old inconsistencies then crept back in, before a hamstring injury eventually put him on the sidelines.

Bradford C (From trainee on 10/7/92) FL 82+4/4 FLC 7/1 FAC 4/1 Others 3+2
Wolverhampton W (£1,850,000 on 25/3/95) FL 78+3/4 FLC 7 FAC 9/1 Others 2

RICHARDS Tony Spencer
Born: Newham, 17 September 1973
Height: 5'11" Weight: 13.1

Having joined Leyton Orient from Cambridge during the summer of 1997, Tony started last season trying to play through an injury and, consequently, was unable to show his true ability. Finally succumbing, he was forced out between September and Christmas, before returning to score twice in the 8-0 victory against Doncaster. A good crosser of the ball, who will be looking for an injury-free run in the side to show his full potential in 1998-99, he took over from Paul Hyde in goal at Exeter for the last ten minutes after the 'keeper broke his leg.

West Ham U (From trainee on 14/8/92. Free to Hong Kong R during 1993 close season)
Cambridge U (Signed from Sudbury T on 10/8/97) FL 29+13/5 FLC 1 Others 3
Leyton Orient (£10,000 on 21/7/97) FL 10+7/2 FLC 1+2 Others 1

RICHARDSON Barry
Born: Wallsend, 5 August 1969
Height: 6'1" Weight: 12.1

The popular Lincoln goalkeeper began last season out of favour but won his place back after John Vaughan suffered a back injury, keeping seven clean sheets in 15 consecutive appearances. An excellent shot-stopper who produced some tremendous saves, his campaign ended early after he was red-carded at Macclesfield in April.*

Sunderland (From trainee on 20/5/88)
Scarborough (Free on 21/3/89) FL 30 FLC 1 Others 1
Stockport Co (Free on 16/8/91)
Northampton T (Free on 10/9/91) FL 96 FLC 4 FAC 5 Others 8
Preston NE (£20,000 on 25/7/94) FL 20 FLC 2 FAC 3 Others 2
Lincoln C (£20,000 on 20/10/95) FL 96 FLC 5 FAC 6 Others 1

RICHARDSON Craig Thomas
Born: Newham, 8 October 1979
Height: 5'8" Weight: 10.3

Signed up as a trainee by Leyton Orient in June 1997, having been released by Charlton, the left-wing back made one brief appearance in the starting line-up against Rochdale, and one substitute appearance in 1997-98, before going back to reserve team football. Looking quietly comfortable on the ball, and good at attacking the opposing defence, he seems sure to be offered professional terms during the summer..

Leyton Orient (Trainee) FL 1

RICHARDSON Ian George
Born: Barking, 22 October 1970
Height: 5'10" Weight: 11.1
Club Honours: Div 3 '98
International Honours: E: SP-1

Brought to Notts County by the previous manager as a ball-winning midfielder, but recognised by his new manager to have potential as a left-sided central defender in a three-man back line, despite being reluctantly converted to his new role, he made the position his own for the second half of last season and, as well as winning a third division championship medal, won the admiration of team mates and fans alike with his superb displays. Has great energy, which allows him to patrol all the pitch and is a constant aerial danger at set pieces.

Birmingham C (£60,000 from Dagenham & Redbridge on 23/8/95) FL 3+4 FLC 3+1 FAC 2 Others 1+2
Notts Co (£200,000 on 19/1/96) FL 56+8/3 FLC 4 FAC 1/1 Others 5

RICHARDSON Jonathan (Jon) Derek
Born: Nottingham, 29 August 1975
Height: 6'0" Weight: 12.6

Jon had another good season for Exeter in 1997-98 and was virtually an ever present in the centre of defence. Good in the air and on the ground, his passing and tactical awareness must mean that it will not be long before a big club makes a bid for the City captain, who has now made well over 150 league appearances for the club.

Exeter C (From trainee on 7/7/94) 168+4/4 FLC 7/1 FAC 7 Others 8

RICHARDSON Kevin
Born: Newcastle, 4 December 1962
Height: 5'7" Weight: 11.7
Club Honours: FAC '84; CS '84; Div 1 '85, '89; ECWC '85; FLC '94
International Honours: E: 1

The veteran midfielder played in three early games for Coventry last season when Gary McAllister was injured and, despite being on a week-to-week contract, performed well

enough to persuade Southampton to move for him in September, as a replacement for the outgoing Jim Magilton. Following the transfer, Kevin was a revelation, covering a tremendous amount of ground and, along with Carlton Palmer, was an integral part of the Saints' midfield engine room as they rose up the table to safety. An underrated player for most of his career, he has proved to be a great competitor, a decisive tackler, and a good man to get to take corners and free kicks, with his ability to swerve the ball.

Everton (From apprentice on 8/12/80) FL 95+14/16 FLC 10+3/3 FAC 13/1 Others 7+2
Watford (£225,000 on 4/9/86) FL 39/2 FLC 3 FAC 7 Others 1
Arsenal (£200,000 on 26/8/87) FL 88+8/5 FLC 13+3/2 FAC 9/1 Others 3 (£750,000 to Real Sociedad on 1/7/90)
Aston Villa (£450,000 on 6/8/91) F/PL 142+1/13 FLC 15/3 FAC 12 Others 10
Coventry C (£300,000 on 16/2/95) PL 75+3 FLC 8/1 FAC 7
Southampton (£150,000 on 10/9/97) PL 25+3 FLC 4 FAC 1

RICHARDSON Lee James
Born: Halifax, 12 March 1969
Height: 5'11" Weight: 11.0

Starting last season on loan at Stockport, where he impressed the fans with a series of neat displays, he returned to Oldham from where he was transferred to Huddersfield at the end of October. When 1997-98 closed and reflections were made on how the campaign went, nobody would doubt that the money spent on Lee made him an absolute bargain by today's standards. However, his time at Town was very much start-stop-start. A cracking long-range volley in the win against Stoke, followed by a spell on the sidelines due to suspensions, many of these arriving at reserve team level, and injury problems, before coming back to display a handy knack of ball-winning skills. This ability was coupled to defence-splitting passes, which contributed to a Man of the Match award against Tranmere Rovers, and a one-man display in the 2-2 draw against Bury, when he scored his 13th consecutive penalty to go with another hallmarked volley.

Halifax T (From trainee on 6/7/87) FL 43+13/2 FLC 4 FAC 4+2 Others 6
Watford (£175,000 on 9/2/89) FL 40+1/1 FLC 1+1 FAC 1
Blackburn Rov (£250,000 on 15/8/90) FL 50+12/3 FLC 1 Others 2+2
Aberdeen (£152,000 on 16/9/92) SL 59+5/6 SLC 2/1 SC 8/2 Others 3/1
Oldham Ath (£300,000 on 12/8/94) FL 82+6/21 FLC 6/2 FAC 3 Others 4
Stockport Co (Loaned on 15/8/97) FL 4+2
Huddersfield T (£65,000 on 24/10/97) FL 16+5/3 FAC 0+2

RICHARDSON Lloyd Matthew
Born: Dewsbury, 7 October 1977
Height: 5'11" Weight: 11.12
International Honours: E: Yth

Having got his career underway at Oldham in 1996-97, a good many people expected Lloyd to mount a challenge for a regular first team place in 1997-98, but all he could manage was an appearance from the bench in the Auto Windscreen Shield at Carlisle in

December. A wide midfielder who, at his best, is tricky, and confident on the ball, he was released during the summer.

Oldham Ath (From trainee on 11/10/94) FL 0+1 Others 0+1

RICHARDSON Neil Thomas
Born: Sunderland, 3 March 1968
Height: 6'0" Weight: 13.9
Club Honours: AMC '96

In his ninth year at Rotherham, Neil had his best ever season and was as reliable as ever in defence, whether he played as a sweeper or in the middle of the back line. Still recognised as just about the best passer of a ball in the club, he demonstrated his ability at taking free kicks on several occasions, a talent which helped him to his highest goals tally.*

Rotherham U (Signed from Brandon U on 18/8/89) FL 164+15/10 FLC 13+1/1 FAC 8+1/1 Others 11+2/1
Exeter C (Loaned on 8/11/96) FL 14 Others 2

Nick Richardson

RICHARDSON Nicholas (Nick) John
Born: Halifax, 11 April 1967
Height: 6'1" Weight: 12.6
Club Honours: Div 3 '93; WC '93

Being voted both Chester City's Player of the Year and Away Player of the Year for 1997-98 was a tremendous feat for Nick, as he missed all of the previous season due to a bad knee injury. Having battled well to return to the side, he missed just two games and again proved to be a very stylish midfielder who provided the catalyst for City's attacking moves. He also gave several memorable performances when covering at right back.*

Halifax T (Free from Emley on 15/11/88) FL 89+12/17 FLC 6+4/2 FAC 2+1/1 Others 6/1
Cardiff C (£35,000 on 13/8/92) FL 106+5/13 FLC 4 FAC 6 Others 12+2/2

Wrexham (Loaned on 21/10/94) FL 4/2
Chester C (Loaned on 16/12/94) FL 6/1
Bury (£22,500 on 8/8/95) FL 3+2 FLC 1
Chester C (£40,000 on 7/9/95) FL 86+4/6 FLC 4 FAC 3/1 Others 3/1

RICKERS Paul Steven
Born: Leeds, 9 May 1975
Height: 5'10" Weight: 11.0

A busy right-sided Oldham midfielder who never shirks a tackle, Paul again missed very few games in 1997-98, his great stamina seeing him prominent at both ends of the pitch, a talent that again got him his normal quota of goals for the team. Skilful and comfortable in possession, and always looking to hurt the opposition, you can rely on him to be in the thick of the action.

Oldham Ath (From trainee on 16/7/93) FL 107+6/9 FLC 6 FAC 6+1 Others 1+1

Paul Rickers

RICKETTS Michael Barrington
Born: Birmingham, 4 December 1978
Height: 6'2" Weight: 11.12

Still in his teens, Michael spent much of last season on the Walsall substitutes' bench, having mixed Auto Windscreen experiences when being sent off unluckily at Barnet in December, and then coming off the bench to score a fine winner at Peterborough in February. With good feet, and aerial ability to match, there is no reason why the youngster cannot make it.

Walsall (From trainee on 13/9/96) FL 8+28/3 FLC 0+2 FAC 1+1 Others 3+1/1

RIDLER David (Dave) George
Born: Liverpool, 12 March 1976
Height: 6'1" Weight: 12.2

In 1997-98, Dave showed that he was fast becoming a valuable asset among Wrexham's central defensive personnel after coming in as Tony Humes' replacement, when the latter was injured for a long spell.

A controlled type of player who does not get ruffled easily, and one who formed a more than useful partnership at the heart of the defence alongside Brian Carey, he was unlucky to miss the last few games due to injury, but can only improve. The qualified "chef and baker" looks to "cook up" a very healthy team selection problem for his manager in 1998-99.

Wrexham (Free from Rockys on 3/7/96) FL 25+6 FAC 4 Others 2

RIEDLE Karl-Heinz
Born: Weiler, Germany, 16 September 1965
Height: 5'10" Weight: 11.6
International Honours: Germany: 42

A German international forward of immense ability, particularly in the air, Karl-Heinz scored two of the goals for Borussia Dortmund that helped defeat Juventus 3-1 in the 1997 European Cup final, before signing for Liverpool immediately prior to the start of 1997-98. Certainly, on paper it appeared to be a brilliant transfer coup, but, in reality, although he was strong going forward, at 32 years of age the German will have great difficulty holding up the progress of Michael Owen and Robbie Fowler, even in the short term. However, with Fowler probably out until this coming December, he can still do a good job for Liverpool, although the club would undoubtedly like more goals from him this coming term.

Liverpool (£1,600,000 from Borussia Dortmund on 4/8/97) PL 18+7/6 FLC 2+3 FAC 1 Others 1+2/1

RIEPER Marc
Born: Rodoure, Denmark, 5 June 1968
Height: 6'4" Weight: 14.2
International Honours: Denmark: 57

The likeable Danish defender played in the first five league games for West Ham last season before leaving the club on 12 September, after scoring in the defeat of Wimbledon. With his contract due to expire, and Celtic having shown an interest, he was allowed to depart, despite him having been a regular in the line-up for the past three years, and his height and strength being badly missed. Arriving at Celtic Park, he immediately went into the first team and played a big part in their Premier League success as they pipped their rivals, Rangers, to clinch the championship. *Stop Press:* Played for Denmark in the World Cup in France '98.

West Ham U (£500,000 from Brondby on 8/12/94) PL 83+7/5 FLC 6+1 FAC 4

RIGBY Anthony (Tony) Angelo
Born: Ormskirk, 10 August 1972
Height: 5'7" Weight: 12.12
Club Honours: Div 2 '97

Undoubtedly the fans hero at Gigg Lane with his dazzling array of close ball skills, the midfield maestro's appearance in the Bury starting line-up against Wolves last January was the first time that he had received the nod from manager, Stan Ternent, in more than 18 months, having previously been consigned to the substitutes' bench. With February bringing him

an extended run, it also coincided in an upturn in the Shakers' fortunes as they fought their way clear of the relegation zone in division one, and the fans will be hoping for more of the same in 1998-99.

Crewe Alex (From trainee on 16/5/90)
Bury (Free from Barrow, via Lancaster C and Runcorn & Burscough, on 6/1/93) FL 119+45/19 FLC 5+2/2 FAC 5+3/1 Others 13+3/2
Scarborough (Loaned on 14/2/97) FL 5/1

RIMMER Stuart Alan

Born: Southport, 12 October 1964
Height: 5'7" Weight: 11.0
International Honours: E: Yth

As Chester City's all-time record league goalscorer (134 in total over two spells at the club), Stuart was surprisingly given a free transfer at the end of last season. Although not as pacy as in previous campaigns, he worked hard throughout when re-creating his partnership with Gary Bennett. Scored eight goals for City, including the equaliser in the last game, against Scarborough.

Everton (From apprentice on 15/10/82) FL 3
Chester C (£10,000 on 17/1/85) FL 110+4/67 FLC 6/6 FAC 4+3 Others 11+1/3
Watford (£205,000 on 18/3/88) FL 10/1 FLC 0+1/1
Notts Co (£200,000 on 10/11/88) FL 3+1/2 FAC 2 Others 3
Walsall (£150,000 on 2/2/89) FL 85+3/31 FLC 6/4 FAC 5/2 Others 7/7
Barnsley (£150,000 on 5/3/91) FL 10+5/1 Others 1
Chester C (£150,000 on 15/8/91) FL 213+34/67 FLC 14+2/3 FAC 10+3/2 Others 10+4/1
Rochdale (Loaned on 2/9/94) FL 3
Preston NE (Loaned on 5/12/94) FL 0+2

RIOCH Gregor (Greg) James

Born: Sutton Coldfield, 24 June 1975
Height: 5'11" Weight: 12.10

Mark Hateley's surprise choice as the new Hull City captain in 1997-98, Greg's undoubted enthusiasm was there for all to see and, when concluding the remarkable 7-4 September win against Swansea by being sent off, in a way it merely underlined his total commitment to the cause. Bruce Rioch's son does not know how to give less than 100 per-cent effort, while his manager also values his versatility, and he was used in central midfield, left-wing back, as well as in his recognised left-back berth. Although relinquishing the captaincy in March, when he suffered a dip in form, he is bound to be back.

Luton T (From trainee on 19/7/93)
Barnet (Loaned on 17/9/93) FL 3 FLC 2 Others 1
Peterborough U (Free on 11/8/95) FL 13+5 FLC 2 FAC 2+1 Others 2+1
Hull C (Free on 10/7/96) FL 76+2/6 FLC 6/2 FAC 3 Others 2

RIPLEY Stuart Edward

Born: Middlesbrough, 20 November 1967
Height: 5'11" Weight: 13.0
Club Honours: PL '95
International Honours: E: 2; U21-8; Yth

With a blistering start to last season for Blackburn, Stuart saw off the challenge of the Greek, Georgios Donis, gained a call up for the England team, and evoked memories of his arrival from Middlesbrough. His England appearance lasted five minutes,

Greg Rioch

until he tore a hamstring, and his season disappeared with it because he returned the player of old, whose chief asset was his tackling and covering. However, three goals was a dizzy return for a player who is not noted for getting on the scoresheet that often, but two headers and a pile driver were more than welcome, even if unexpected. Despite losing his place at the end of the season, he was recalled for the crucial final game, but pulled his hamstring again after only two minutes. *Stop Press:* Signed for Southampton on 6 July, a fee of £1.5 million making the move possible.

Middlesbrough (From apprentice on 23/12/85) FL 210+39/26 FLC 21+2/3 FAC 17+1/1 Others 20+1/1
Bolton W (Loaned on 18/2/86) FL 5/1 Others 0+1
Blackburn Rov (£1,300,000 on 20/7/92) PL 172+15/13 FLC 18 FAC 14/3 Others 8+1

Stuart Ripley

RITCHIE Andrew (Andy) Timothy
Born: Manchester, 28 November 1960
Height: 5'10" Weight: 12.9
Club Honours: Div 2 '91
International Honours: E: U21-1; Yth; Sch

Andy thought throughout last season that his services as Oldham's player/coach under Neil Warnock were not being fully utilised, something that was remedied come the end of the campaign when he was installed as the new manager. Known to the fans as "God", although this coming term will be his first in management, as far as the faithful are concerned he cannot fail. In short, they are probably thinking ahead to the first division. On a playing front in 1997-98, he scored three goals in 18 appearances and, while not having the pace of yesteryear, he proved he was still capable of finding great positions in and around the box.

Manchester U (From apprentice on 5/12/77) FL 26+7/13 FLC 3+2 FAC 3+1
Brighton & Hove A (£500,000 on 17/10/80) FL 82+7/23 FLC 3+1/1 FAC 9/2
Leeds U (£150,000 on 25/3/83) FL 127+9/40 FLC 11/3 FAC 9/1 Others 2+1
Oldham Ath (£50,000 on 14/8/87) F/PL 187+30/82 FLC 18+2/18 FAC 8+2/4 Others 3
Scarborough (Free on 3/8/95) FL 59+9/17 FLC 4+1/2 FAC 4/1 Others 1
Oldham Ath (Free on 21/2/97) FL 14+11/2 FLC 1/1 FAC 1+1

RIVERS Mark Alan
Born: Crewe, 26 November 1975
Height: 5'11" Weight: 11.2

Now a regular at Crewe, usually playing in a wide position on either flank, Mark has overcome several injury problems in the past after coming through from the club's exceptional youth academy, and can be relied upon to score a reasonable quota of goals each season. Eight goals, which placed him equal second in the goalscoring charts, was the return for his 38 games in 1997-98, but obviously the manager would like some more. His height can make him a danger, especially at set pieces.

Crewe Alex (From trainee on 6/5/94) FL 78+17/22 FLC 4+1/1 FAC 8/3 Others 6+3/3

ROACH Neville
Born: Reading, 29 September 1978
Height: 5'10" Weight: 11.1

The powerfully-built Reading striker continued where he had left off in 1996-97, scoring in pre-season friendlies against Bournemouth and Wycombe, and then in the Coca Cola Cup tie against Swansea. After that his form dipped and he was relegated to the role of substitute for long periods of the season, following which, a loss of confidence ensued and he was allowed to join Kingstonian on loan in a bid to regain his goalscoring reputation. He did so with Reading, albeit at reserve level, and looks to have a great future with the club as he is still only 19.

Reading (From trainee on 10/5/97) FL 2+9/1 FLC 1+4/1

ROBERTS Andrew (Andy) James
Born: Dartford, 20 March 1974
Height: 5'10" Weight: 13.0
Club Honours: FAYC '91
International Honours: E: U21-5

Having started last season at Crystal Palace as the club captain and a regular in the side as a midfield general, while not being quite at his best, it still came as a major shock to Palace fans when he signed for their local rivals, Wimbledon, for a reduced fee early in March. Going straight into the Dons' line-up for the game against Arsenal, Andy saw out the rest of the campaign without missing a match, and impressed all of his new fans that he was more than just a useful acquisition. Able to perform as a sweeper, as well as in midfield, his sound, solid displays, coupled with good positional sense, awareness, and passing ability, should be invaluable to the club in 1998-99. Scored the first goal in a vital 2-1 against Leicester to open his account.

Millwall (From trainee on 29/10/91) FL 132+6/5 FLC 12/2 FAC 7 Others 4/1
Crystal Palace (£2,520,000 on 29/7/95) F/PL 106+2/2 FLC 7+1 FAC 8 Others 6/1
Wimbledon (£1,200,000+ on 10/3/98) PL 12/1

ROBERTS Anthony (Tony) Mark
Born: Holyhead, 4 August 1969
Height: 6'0" Weight: 13.11
International Honours: W: 2; B-2; U21-2; Yth

Although playing over 100 league games for Queens Park Rangers during a ten-year career at the club, Tony has nearly always been the second-choice goalkeeper at the club and, true to form, started 1997-98 as the number two to Lee Harper, before being recalled to the side when the management team of Stewart Houston and Bruce Rioch left Queens Park Rangers. A good shot-stopper, and a very good kicker of the ball, he was playing well but lost his place back to Harper on breaking a hand in January, and was released during the summer.

Queens Park R (From trainee on 24/7/87) F/PL 122 FLC 10 FAC 10+1 Others 2

ROBERTS Benjamin (Ben) James
Born: Bishop Auckland, 22 June 1975
Height: 6'1" Weight: 12.11
International Honours: E: U21-1

An aspiring young Middlesbrough goalkeeper, Ben put aside the nightmare of conceding the fastest-ever Wembley cup final goal in 1996-97 to get on with life as the deputy to Mark Schwarzer in 1997-98. Despite starting the first seven games of the new campaign, before giving way to Schwarzer and going back to the reserves, he is still a recognised shot-stopper, and aims to get the chance to prove it in the Premiership. Has an excellent attitude to the game, and the temperament to rise above disappointment.

Middlesbrough (From trainee on 24/3/93) F/PL 15+1 FLC 2+1 FAC 6 Others 1
Hartlepool U (Loaned on 19/10/95) FL 4 Others 1
Wycombe W (Loaned on 8/12/95) FL 15
Bradford C (Loaned on 27/8/96) FL 2

ROBERTS Christian (Chris) John
Born: Cardiff, 22 October 1979
Height: 5'10" Weight: 12.8
International Honours: W: Yth

Made his Nationwide League debut for Cardiff last September, while still a trainee,

when he went on as substitute during the home match against Rochdale and sparked a recovery with an outstanding display, laying on goals for Steve White and Jeff Eckhardt in a 2-1 City win. Then aged 17, Chris lined up alongside 39-year-old veteran, Steve White, there being an age gap of 22 years between the two strikers. Unfortunately, he twisted a knee in the next training session and eventually needed an operation before coming back strongly in the second half of the season, finishing with three goals from five starts and six substitute appearances. Fast and strong, with a willingness to learn, and a great attitude, the youngster was already on a senior contract when Frank Burrows arrived, but he soon agreed a new and improved offer.

Cardiff C (From trainee on 8/10/97) FL 5+6/3

ROBERTS Darren Anthony
Born: Birmingham, 12 October 1969
Height: 6'0" Weight: 12.4

A popular all-action centre forward who, despite leaving on loan to Peterborough last February, still ended 1997-98 as Darlington's top scorer, his total of 14 goals in 30 outings well up in percentage terms on his 18 in 50 in 1996-97. Full of enthusiasm for the game, and a player who always gave his all for the full 90 minutes – having scored several vital goals – there was speculation towards the end of January that he would be on his way, due to him going through a lean spell. Interestingly, he came back to score a brace in a 2-2 draw at Hartlepool, returned to the bench, and then departed for London Road. Unfortunately, taken on for the last three months of the campaign, he was unable to show Barry Fry what he could do for Posh as he was injured in his second game and never really returned to full fitness thereafter.

Wolverhampton W (£20,000 from Burton A on 23/4/92) FL 12+9/5 FLC 0+1 Others 1+1
Hereford U (Loaned on 18/3/94) FL 5+1/5
Chesterfield (Free on 18/7/94) FL 10+15/1 FAC 3/1 FAC 1+1 Others 2+5/3
Darlington (Free on 30/7/96) FL 66+6/28 FLC 6/3 FAC 4/1 Others 2
Peterborough U (Loaned on 20/2/98) FL 2+1

ROBERTS Iwan Wyn
Born: Bangor, 26 June 1968
Height: 6'3" Weight: 14.2
International Honours: W: 7; B-1; Yth; Sch

Transferred from Wolves to Norwich during the 1997 close season, Iwan's move to Carrow Road failed to bring the flood of goals that he, Mike Walker, and the fans had hoped for. A powerful, bustling, brave striker who has excellent aerial ability, he was kept out of action at various times during the campaign by a badly bruised toe and a gashed shin and, when fit, his hopes of having a great supply line were dashed by the long-term injuries to Darren Eadie and Keith O'Neill. Although five goals was a scant return for his endeavour, he remained in the Welsh manager, Bobby Gould's thoughts, being called into the "B" squad in mid-March.

Watford (From trainee on 4/7/88) FL 40+23/9 FLC 6+2/3 FAC 1+6 Others 5

Huddersfield T (£275,000 on 2/8/90) FL 141+1/50 FLC 13+1/6 FAC 12/4 Others 14/8
Leicester C (£100,000 on 25/11/93) F/PL 92+8/41 FLC 5/1 FAC 5/2 Others 1
Wolverhampton W (£1,300,000 + on 15/7/96) FL 24+9/12 FLC 2 FAC 0+1 Others 2
Norwich C (£900,000 on 9/7/97) FL 29+2/5 FLC 2/2

ROBERTS Jason Andre Davis

Born: Park Royal, 25 January 1978
Height: 5'11" Weight: 12.7
International Honours: Grenada: 3

Plucked from non-league Hayes by Wolves early last season, but unable to immediately make his mark at Molineux and to further his experience, he was loaned out to Torquay in December. He certainly made his mark with the third division side, scoring six times in 15 matches, before having another loan spell, this time with Bristol City in March. At Ashton Gate, he quickly showed himself to be a player of promise and great pace, and looked an ideal replacement for Shaun Goater but, after scoring the winner at Oldham, he chose to play for Grenada in an international tournament, where he demonstrated his talents as the country's leading goalscorer. Could well make the desired breakthrough for his club this coming term.

Wolverhampton W (£250,000 from Hayes on 12/9/97)
Torquay U (Loaned on 19/12/97) FL 13+1/6 Others 1
Bristol C (Loaned on 26/3/98) FL 1+2/1

ROBERTS Neil Wyn

Born: Wrexham, 7 April 1978
Height: 5'10" Weight: 11.0
International Honours: W: Yth

A product of the much respected youth system at Wrexham, Neil was the club's find of 1997-98. Coming into the side at the end of September, he set the place alight with five goals in four games, and while never as prolific after that he has continued to show immense promise for one so young in his first full season in the Football League. A phenomenal workrate is just one aspect of his play which takes the eye, whilst his chasing of lost causes is more than appreciated by the fans. Another notable skill is an ability to use his body to lay the ball off, often with his chest, and similar in many ways to a certain Mark Hughes who originated from just up the road! Is always alive to a half chance.

Wrexham (From trainee on 3/7/96) FL 29+5/8 FAC 3+1/1 Others 0+1

ROBERTSON David

Born: Aberdeen, 17 October 1968
Height: 5'11" Weight: 11.0
International Honours: S: 3; B-1; U21-7

The left back arrived at Leeds on the last day of 1996-97. Apparently George Graham had been tracking the Scottish international defender ever since he went to Elland Road and feared he may move abroad for free as his contract at Rangers was due to expire. David took a little while to adjust to the game in the Premiership and became a target for the terraces at first. Initially, better at going forward than defending, as the season progressed he began to really settle down and produce more consistent performances, before being unfortunate to tear a cartilage in training in February, and being sidelined going into April. There is no doubt that the best is yet to come from this experienced wing back.

Aberdeen (Free from Deeside BC on 19/7/85) SL 71/2 SLC 14/1 SC 3 Others 6
Glasgow R (Signed on 2/7/91) SL 182+1/15 SLC 18+1/1 SC 26/3 Others 18
Leeds U (£500,000 on 23/5/97) PL 24+2 FLC 4 FAC 1

David Robertson

ROBERTSON Graham Stuart

Born: Edinburgh, 2 November 1976
Height: 5'11" Weight: 10.10

Persuaded to move to London by Jimmy Nichol in the summer of 1996, Graham has yet to break into the Millwall side, having made just three subs' appearances in two years, one of them coming last season at Preston. However, he impressed in the reserves with some good starts, playing either in midfield or further forward, where he showed a good turn of pace, control, and a powerful shot.

Raith Rov (Free from Balgonie Juniors on 3/8/93)
Millwall (Signed on 21/8/96) FL 0+2 Others 0+1

ROBERTSON John Nicholas

Born: Liverpool, 8 January 1974
Height: 6'2" Weight: 13.2

Having spent most of last season in the reserves, apart from three games, it was a disappointing campaign for Lincoln's solid central defender, especially as the club finally achieved promotion to the second division without requiring his services. At his best, a wholehearted, tough tackler, with a never-say-die approach, he was released during the summer.

Wigan Ath (From trainee on 6/7/92) FL 108+4/4 FLC 12 FAC 8+1 Others 8+1
Lincoln C (£15,000 on 5/12/95) FL 38+2/1 FLC 1 FAC 1 Others 2

ROBERTSON Mark William

Born: Sydney, Australia, 6 April 1977
Height: 5'9" Weight: 12.4

Burnley's Australian-born utility man, who was signed last October from Marconi, made almost all of his first team appearances in midfield, where he was tenacious and showed good distribution, but occasionally seemed rather lightweight in a section of the team that often lacked bite. Now acclimatised, 1998-99 should be a little easier.

Burnley (Free from Marconi on 3/10/97) FL 8+3 Others 3+1

ROBINS Mark Gordon

Born: Ashton under Lyme, 22 December 1969
Height: 5'8" Weight: 11.11
Club Honours: FAC '90; ECWC '91; ESC '91; FLC '97
International Honours: E: U21-6

A nippy, experienced striker, Mark joined Reading on loan from Leicester City last August after a run of injuries had hit the club, and played in five games without scoring. His passing, though, was exemplary, and his best performance came against Oxford, where he set up both of Royals' goals in the 2-1 win over their local rivals. However, his last game in his month at Elm Park was the disastrous 6-0 reverse at Tranmere, and, with other players coming back after regaining fitness, he returned to Filbert Street, where he failed to make an appearance during the campaign.

Manchester U (From apprentice on 23/12/86) FL 19+29/11 FLC 0+7/2 FAC 4+4/3 Others 4+3/1
Norwich C (£800,000 on 14/8/92) PL 57+10/20 FLC 6+3/1 Others 1+1
Leicester C (£1,000,000 on 16/1/95) P/FL 40+16/12 FLC 5+4/5 FAC 4+2 Others 1+1
Reading (Loaned on 29/8/97) FL 5

ROBINSON Carl Phillip

Born: Llandrindod Wells, 13 October 1976
Height: 5'10" Weight: 12.10
International Honours: W: B-1; U21-6; Yth

The young right-footed Wolves' midfielder was not selected for the first four games last season, but then had three Molineux outings in eight days. Remaining in the team during September, and rewarded with a three-year contract, his competitive nature led to some bookings, but his performances gradually improved and he scored against Tranmere. After briefly losing his place, he scored the winner against Forest in December, the first of 22 successive games he was to participate in. That strike was surpassed by a fine half volley against Bradford and then a lunging header versus Wimbledon, while a defence-splitting pass gave Don Goodman the chance to knock Leeds out of the FA Cup. With Welsh "B" recognition following, perhaps he will develop into the ball winner Wolves have long required.

Wolverhampton W (From trainee on 3/7/95) FL 28+6/3 FLC 4 FAC 7/1
Shrewsbury T (Loaned on 28/3/96) FL 2+2 Others 1

ROBINSON Jamie
Born: Liverpool, 26 February 1972
Height: 6'1" Weight: 12.8
Club Honours: Div 3 '95

Released by Carlisle during the 1997 close season, prior to moving south to Plainmoor, this central defender proved to be yet another shrewd signing by Torquay's Kevin Hodges. A highly efficient and unfussy stopper who missed only the AWS game, he can also play in midfield when required and menaces when pushed up for set pieces.*

Liverpool (From trainee on 4/6/90)
Barnsley (Free on 17/7/92) FL 8+1 Others 3
Carlisle U (Signed on 28/1/94) FL 46+11/4 FLC 1+2 FAC 3 Others 7+6/1
Torquay U (Free on 2/7/97) FL 46 FLC 4 FAC 3 Others 3

ROBINSON John Robert Campbell
Born: Bulawayo, Rhodesia, 29 August 1971
Height: 5'10" Weight: 11.7
International Honours: W: 10; U21-5

A right-sided Charlton winger who is equally comfortable on the left, John has also been used as an emergency full back and, in fact, made his Welsh international debut in this position. With an ability to run at players, and a good crosser of the ball, he scored some useful goals in 1997-98, and was a regular in the side until he suffered a hairline fracture of his right leg in April, which ruled him out until the play-off final at Wembley, when he came on as a sub. Is now a regular in the full Welsh international side, and was recognised by his fellow professionals when they voted him into the award-winning PFA first division select.

Brighton & Hove A (From trainee on 21/4/89) FL 57+5/6 FLC 5/1 FAC 2+1 Others 1+2/2
Charlton Ath (£75,000 on 15/9/92) FL 179+8/23 FLC 11+2/4 FAC 10+2/2 Others 5+1

ROBINSON Leslie (Les)
Born: Shirebrook, 1 March 1967
Height: 5'9" Weight: 12.4

An ever present in the Oxford defence in 1997-98, Les deservedly won the club's Player of the Year award after another season of 110 per-cent effort and ultra consistency. He even managed a couple of goals, rarities for him, although he does like the League Cup, where one of his cracking strikes came. Ending the campaign as captain, due reward for a player who is now approaching 350 games for the club, he reads the game well and, always prepared to get forward, he fought off the challenge of Christophe Remy, firstly by playing as a sweeper, and then in excelling at full back.

Mansfield T (Free from Chesterfield juniors on 6/10/84) FL 11+4 Others 1
Stockport Co (£10,000 on 27/11/86) FL 67/3 FLC 2 FAC 4 Others 4
Doncaster Rov (£20,000 on 24/3/88) FL 82/12 FLC 4 FAC 5 Others 5/1
Oxford U (£150,000 on 19/3/90) FL 289+5/3 FLC 31/8 FAC 14+1 Others 10

ROBINSON Spencer Liam
Born: Bradford, 29 December 1965
Height: 5'7" Weight: 12.7

Signed from Burnley during the 1997 close season, the industrious and experienced lower division striker was expected to provide the goals for Scarborough's anticipated promotion push in 1997-98. However, despite showing flashes of his undoubted ability, he struggled to make an impact, having been dogged by illness early on, and will hope for better fortunes in the coming season.

Huddersfield T (Free from Nottingham F juniors on 5/1/84) FL 17+4/2
Tranmere Rov (Loaned on 18/12/85) FL 4/3
Bury (£60,000 on 8/7/86) FL 248+14/89 FLC 17+3/6 FAC 9/1 Others 24/4
Bristol C (£130,000 on 14/7/93) FL 31+10/4 FLC 2/1 FAC 5 Others 1
Burnley (£250,000 on 26/7/94) FL 43+20/9 FLC 5+1/2 FAC 5/1 Others 1+1
Scarborough (Free on 5/8/97) FL 28+8/4 FLC 1+1 FAC 1/1 Others 1+2

ROBINSON Mark James
Born: Rochdale, 21 November 1968
Height: 5'9" Weight: 12.4
Club Honours: Div 2 '96

One of the few players to have joined the club before current manager, Steve McMahon, took charge, Swindon's "Mr Utility" filled a variety of positions across the back line and in midfield throughout last season. Having started in the sweeper role, looking very accomplished, a bad knee injury ruled him out until November and he never quite got back to his best after that setback, though he could always be relied upon to show great enthusiasm and commitment. Defends well, and very good going forward to cross quality balls into the middle, his only goal of the season was a match winner against Stoke.

West Bromwich A (From apprentice on 10/1/87) FL 2 FLC 0+1
Barnsley (Free on 23/6/87) FL 117+20/6 FLC 7+2 FAC 7+1 Others 3+2/1
Newcastle U (£450,000 on 9/3/93) F/PL 14+11 FAC 1
Swindon T (£600,000 on 22/7/94) FL 155+1/3 FLC 15 FAC 10 Others 6+1

ROBINSON Matthew Richard
Born: Exeter, 23 December 1974
Height: 5'11" Weight: 11.8

Unable to hold down a first team place at Southampton in 1997-98, making just one subs' appearance in the second match of the season, at Manchester United, Matthew made the rare transfer down the M27 to join Portsmouth in February, and become one of only a handful of players to have done so. Coming into the side straight away, he slotted in at left back and proved a very effective player going forward, while linking up well with his fellow defenders. Has a sweet left foot and a great touch on the ball to match.

Southampton (From trainee on 1/7/93) PL 3+11 FAC 1+2
Portsmouth (£50,000 on 20/2/98) FL 15

ROBINSON Paul Derrick
Born: Sunderland, 20 November 1978
Height: 5'11" Weight: 12.11

Having made nine first team appearances from the bench for Darlington, while still a trainee, this promising, confident young forward signed professional forms during the 1997 close season, but was initially used sparingly. However, at the end of last February he went on to score in three successive games, a feat which brought him to the attention of bigger clubs, although it was still quite a surprise when he signed for Newcastle in a £500,000 deal that also involved the England youth international, James Coppinger, a first-year trainee and a player who had yet to appear for Darlington's first team. Obviously bought for the future, neither of the youngsters have been called upon as yet.

Darlington (From trainee on 14/7/97) FL 7+19/3 FLC 0+1 FAC 2+4/1 Others 0+1
Newcastle U (£250,000+ on 27/3/98)

ROBINSON Paul Peter
Born: Watford, 14 December 1978
Height: 5'9" Weight: 11.6
Club Honours: Div 2 '98

The locally-born full back adapted well to the new challenge presented by the wing-back role at Watford in 1997-98, when drawing on his schoolboy experience as a striker. He also showed improved discipline in his tackling, and got off the mark with his first goals for the club, his 22 league appearances good enough to win him a second division championship medal as the Hornets went back to the first division after a two-year break.

Watford (From trainee on 13/2/97) FL 22+12/2 FAC 3+2 Others 3

Phil Robinson

ROBINSON Phillip (Phil) John
Born: Stafford, 6 January 1967
Height: 5'10" Weight: 11.7
Club Honours: Div 4 '88, Div 3 '89, '98; AMC '88, '91

Every team striving for promotion requires the experience of people who have seen it and done it all before, and Phil brought this quality to the 1997-98 division three champions, having returned in August 1996 to Notts County, a club where he had been

involved in two promotions previously. Always a competitive and intelligent midfielder, he sealed a good season's work with the final goal in the final minute of the final match, before collecting his third division championship medal.

Aston Villa (From apprentice on 8/1/85) FL 2+1/1
Wolverhampton W (£5,000 on 3/7/87) FL 63+8/8 FLC 6 FAC 3/1 Others 8+2
Notts Co (£67,500 on 18/8/89) FL 65+1/5 FLC 6/1 FAC 1+1 Others 9+1
Birmingham C (Loaned on 18/3/91) FL 9 Others 2+1
Huddersfield T (£50,000 on 1/9/92) FL 74+1/5 FLC 4 FAC 8/1 Others 8
Northampton T (Loaned on 2/9/94) FL 14 FLC 1 FAC 1 Others 2
Chesterfield (£15,000 on 9/12/94) FL 60+1/17 FLC 1 FAC 2 Others 8/4
Notts Co (£80,000 on 16/8/96) FL 63+14/5 FLC 4 FAC 6+1/1 Others 1

Steve Robinson (Bournemouth)

ROBINSON Stephen (Steve)
Born: Lisburn, 10 December 1974
Height: 5'9" Weight: 11.3
International Honours: NI: 1; B-4; U21-1; Yth; Sch

Steve played the majority of last season in the centre of Bournemouth's midfield, but was also employed on the left and right-hand sides, looking comfortable in all of these positions. As an attacking midfielder, and a good finisher, having been the club's leading scorer during 1997-98 with 13 goals, he continued to be on the fringes of the Northern Ireland squad, making yet another "B" team appearance, this time against the Republic in February.

Tottenham H (From trainee on 27/1/93) PL 1+1
Bournemouth (Free on 20/10/94) FL 145+13/29 FLC 6 FAC 8+1/3 Others 11/2

ROBINSON Steven (Steve) Eli
Born: Nottingham, 17 January 1975
Height: 5'9" Weight: 11.3

A professional for four years at Birmingham, but with limited experience, Steve finally became a first team squad regular in 1997-98, and celebrated his newly-found opportunities by scoring his first-ever goal, the first in a 4-1 Coca Cola Cup win over Stockport at St Andrews in September. A hard-working midfielder who never stops running, his workrate being phenomenal, he gradually added a surer pass to his repertoire, and appears to be on the verge of stepping up a class. Has proved his mettle, having overcome a debilitating illness to force himself into contention.

Birmingham C (From trainee on 9/6/93) FL 28+12 FLC 4/1 FAC 0+1 Others 1
Peterborough U (Loaned on 15/3/96) FL 5

ROBSON Glenn Alan
Born: Sunderland, 25 September 1977
Height: 5'11" Weight: 11.7

Despite making regular appearances up front for the reserve side in 1997-98, the promising young Rochdale striker was again restricted to a few first team outings as substitute, even being denied a first senior goal by a superb save by Swansea's Roger Freestone near the end of Dale's 3-0 victory over the Swans. Is bound to get more opportunities before too long.

Rochdale (Signed from Murton on 13/11/96) FL 0+10

ROBSON Mark Andrew
Born: Newham, 22 May 1969
Height: 5'7" Weight: 10.2
Club Honours: Div 3 '98

Snapped up on a free transfer from Charlton during the 1997 close season to fill the position of winger, Mark had a wonderful season at Notts County in 1997-98, playing as a winger, midfielder, or in the slot just behind the two strikers. Probably one of the best passers of a ball in the league, when County were at their best he was almost always the outstanding catalyst, and it came as no surprise to anyone watching football at that level that the oldest club in the Football League won the third division title last season.

Exeter C (From apprentice on 17/12/86) FL 26/7 FAC 2 Others 2
Tottenham H (£50,000 on 17/7/87) FL 3+5 FLC 1
Reading (Loaned on 24/3/88) FL 5+2
Watford (Loaned on 5/10/89) FL 1
Plymouth Arg (Loaned on 22/12/89) FL 7
Exeter C (Loaned on 3/1/92) FL 7+1/1 Others 3/1
West Ham U (Free on 14/8/92) F/PL 42+5/8 FLC 2 FAC 2/1 Others 4+1
Charlton Ath (£125,000 on 17/11/93) FL 79+26/9 FLC 4+2 FAC 10/2 Others 2
Notts Co (Free on 23/6/97) FL 26+2/4 FLC 1 FAC 3 Others 1

ROCASTLE David Carlyle
Born: Lewisham, 2 May 1967
Height: 5'9" Weight: 12.10
Club Honours: FLC '87; Div 1 '89, '91
International Honours: E: 14; B-2; U21-14

The former England international came out of his Chelsea wilderness last October with

a sensational loan move to third division, Hull City, following an enquiry made by Tigers' boss, Mark Hateley, a close friend and former next door neighbour. Having received a rapturous welcome from the City fans, David rewarded them with a memorable scoring debut against Scarborough at Boothferry, and made a total of 11 appearances, despite missing seven games during his three-month stay, mainly due to the over zealous efforts of the opposition. In displaying the silky skills that made him a championship winner at Arsenal in 1989 and 1991, he is sure to be in demand with his Chelsea contract now completed.

Arsenal (From apprentice on 31/12/84) FL 204+14/24 FLC 32+1/6 FAC 18+2/4 Others 9
Leeds U (£2,000,000 on 4/8/92) PL 17+8/2 FLC 0+3 FAC 0+3 Others 2+1
Manchester C (£2,000,000 on 22/12/93) PL 21/2 FAC 2
Chelsea (£1,250,000 on 12/8/94) PL 27+2 FLC 3/1 Others 7+1/1
Norwich C (Loaned on 9/1/97) FL 11
Hull C (Loaned on 9/10/97) FL 10/1 FLC 1

ROCHE Stephen (Steve) Michael
Born: Dublin, 2 October 1978
Height: 5'11" Weight: 11.2
International Honours: Ei: Yth; Sch

Another Millwall youngster who had very few chances to shine in 1997-98, the young Irishman made just one start to go with a subs' appearance, being confined mainly to the reserves. Is a hard-working left-sided midfielder who can perform equally well as a defender or as a forward, being strong in the challenge, and a good passer of the ball.

Millwall (Free from Belvedere on 6/10/94) FL 4+4 FLC 1

ROCKETT Jason
Born: London, 26 September 1969
Height: 6'1" Weight: 13.6

Jason is a powerful central defender who has been a terrific servant since joining Scarborough five years ago. Despite being troubled by a knee injury in 1997-98, he once again stood out as one of the best centre backs in division three, and also chipped in with some vital goals as Boro chased promotion. Unfortunately, he looks set to hang up his boots because of his injury problems.

Rotherham U (Signed from British Universities on 25/3/92)
Scarborough (Free on 4/8/93) FL 171+1/11 FLC 10 FAC 7 Others 7/2

RODGER Graham
Born: Glasgow, 1 April 1967
Height: 6'2" Weight: 13.8
Club Honours: FAC '87
International Honours: E: U21-4

A Grimsby right-footed central defender who is exceptionally strong in the air and very useful in the box during set pieces, he was displaced at the start of last season by the return to fitness of Peter Handyside and Mark Lever. Graham regained his place for a couple of months late in 1997, during another injury spell for Lever, and showed that he had lost none of the skill that had contributed to his most successful 1996-97 campaign. However, his own long-term

injury problems kept him out of the game for the latter half of 1997-98, and he was released during the summer.

Wolverhampton W (Apprentice) FL 1
Coventry C (Free on 18/2/85) FL 31+5/2 FLC 3+1 FAC 1+1 Others 0+1
Luton T (£150,000 on 1/8/89) FL 27+1/2 FLC 2 Others 3
Grimsby T (£135,000 on 8/1/92) FL 134+12/11 FLC 4+1 FAC 12/1 Others 3

RODGER Simon Lee
Born: Shoreham, 3 October 1971
Height: 5'9" Weight: 11.9
Club Honours: Div 1 '94

A tough-tackling, hard-working, left-sided Crystal Palace midfielder, and their longest-serving player, who has been dreadfully unlucky with injuries down the years, Simon came back in 1997-98 to make 33 appearances, his best season since 1993-94. Despite the team having a rough time of it, he appeared to relish the challenge, taking free kicks and corners with all his old spirit, and scoring two goals, both long-range efforts from the edge of the box - at Sheffield Wednesday and at home to West Ham in the penultimate game. Has a sweet left foot, and is more than capable of running with the ball while looking to create goalscoring chances.

Crystal Palace (£1,000 from Bognor Regis T on 2/7/90) F/PL133+22/7 FLC 15+1 FAC 5+3 Others 5+2
Manchester C (Loaned on 28/10/96) FL 8/1
Stoke C (Loaned on 14/2/97) FL 5

Simon Rodger

RODOSTHENOUS Michael
Born: Islington, 25 August 1976
Height: 5'11" Weight: 11.2
Not in line for first team duties at West
Bromwich in 1997-98, Michael was
released and joined Cambridge on non-
contract forms in October. An attacking
midfielder, who had also played as a striker
for Albion's reserves, he was limited to just
three appearances at the Abbey, despite his
obvious abilities which included pace, good
first touch, and an eye for goal, before being
freed in the New Year.
West Bromwich A (From trainee on 19/7/95) FL
0+1
Cambridge U (Free on 10/10/97) FL 0+2 Others 1

ROGAN Anthony (Anton) Gerard Patrick
Born: Belfast, 25 March 1966
Height: 6'0" Weight: 13.0
Club Honours: SPD '88; SC '88, '89
International Honours: NI: 18
Released by Millwall during the 1997 close
season, having suffered a series of injuries,
including one to his calf which was slow to
mend, Anton joined Blackpool with a view
to kick-starting his career. Unfortunately, the
tough-tackling left back, with a penchant to
get forward, played just two early games,
picked up another bad injury almost as soon
as he arrived, and saw no more action in
1997-98 until appearing in a few reserve
games at the end of the campaign.
Glasgow Celtic (Signed from Distillery on 9/5/86)
SL 115+12/4 SLC 12+1 SC 18/1 Others 8
Sunderland (£350,000 on 4/10/91) FL 45+1/1
FLC 1 FAC 8 Others 2
Oxford U (Signed on 9/8/93) FL 56+2/3 FLC 4
FAC 4 Others 2
Millwall (Free on 11/8/95) FL 30+6/8 FLC 1 FAC
2 Others 1
Blackpool (Free on 18/7/97) FL 1 FLC 1

ROGERS Alan
Born: Liverpool, 3 January 1977
Height: 5'10" Weight: 11.8
Club Honours: Div 1 '98
International Honours: E: U21-3
With Stuart Pearce joining Newcastle
during the 1997 summer period, Nottingham
Forest moved quickly to sign this promising
youngster from first division rivals,
Tranmere. Having been thrust in and out of
first team action at Tranmere in 1995-96,
Alan had impressed as a young wing back
who could go a long way in the game, his
ability to get down the line to feed the
forwards, and his rate of recovery being
excellent, and he accepted the challenge
offered by Forest with some alacrity. As the
club's only ever present, he exceeded all
hopes, and was well worth his first division
championship medal as both he and Forest
headed for Premiership football in 1998-99.
Scored just the one goal, at Bury in a 3-0
win, and was rewarded for his overall
performances with three England U21 caps
in the end of season Toulon tournament.
Tranmere Rov (From trainee on 1/7/95) FL
53+4/2 FLC 1 FAC 1
Nottingham F (£2,000,000 on 10/7/97) FL 46/1
FLC 4 FAC 1

Alan Rogers

ROGERS Darren John
Born: Birmingham, 9 April 1970
Height: 6'0" Weight: 13.0
After making a useful start to last season on
the left flank of Walsall's defence, following
a cruciate injury suffered in 1996-97, Darren
moved to Stevenage at the beginning of
October, where he was unfortunately injured
early on. At his best, a skilful, overlapping
wing back, and a real crowd pleaser, it is
difficult to see him getting back.
West Bromwich A (From trainee on 5/7/88) FL
7+7/1 FAC 0+1 Others 1/1
Birmingham C (Free on 1/7/92) FL 15+3 FLC 2
FAC 0+1 Others 5
Wycombe W (Loaned on 5/11/93) FL 0+1 Others 1
Walsall (Free on 19/7/94) FL 48+10 FLC 6 FAC
5+2 Others 5

ROGERS Lee Julian
Born: Doncaster, 28 October 1966
Height: 5'11" Weight: 12.1
Yet again, "Nobby" was blighted by injury.
It started in Chesterfield's first pre-1997-98
season friendly, when he turned an ankle
and missed two months. Having regained
fitness, and becoming aware that his first
team opportunities were limited, the
experienced defender, who can operate in
either full-back position, asked for his name
to be circulated to other clubs in November.
Was released during the summer.
Doncaster Rov (From trainee on 27/7/84) Others 1
Chesterfield (Free on 29/8/86) FL 310+24/1 FLC
17+1 FAC 11+1 Others 27+1

ROGERS Paul Anthony
Born: Portsmouth, 21 March 1965
Height: 6'0" Weight: 12.0
Club Honours: Div 3 '97
International Honours: E: SP-6

A combative and hard-working Wigan
Athletic midfielder, Paul completed a half
century of league appearances last season
and, at his best, is an unspectacular ball
winner who rarely captures the headlines.
There is no doubting that he relishes a
challenge, and he saved his best perform-
ances for the end of the campaign as the club
steered themselves away from a relegation
spot. Can run for 90 minutes if the need be.
Sheffield U (£35,000 from Sutton U on 29/1/92)
F/PL 120+5/10 FLC 8+1/1 FAC 4 Others 1
Notts Co (Signed on 29/12/95) FL 21+1/2 FAC 1
Others 6/1
Wigan Ath (Loaned on 13/12/96) FL 7+2/3
Wigan Ath (£50,000 on 7/3/97) FL 43+6 FLC 2
FAC 1 Others 2

ROGET Leo Thomas Earl
Born: Ilford, 1 August 1977
Height: 6'1" Weight: 12.2
Leo's Southend season in 1997-98 was
almost totally written off by a severe back
injury, which meant he was out of action
from mid-September until April. His
undoubted quality led to manager, Alvin
Martin, fighting to keep him at the start of
the campaign, after he had trials with two top
Dutch clubs, who spotted the centre half's
dominating skills. His relaxed manner hides
a reading of the game which is second to
none, and he must surely have a better time
in 1998-99.
Southend U (From trainee on 5/7/95) FL 40+4/1
FLC 3 FAC 1

ROLLING Franck Jacques
Born: Colnar, France, 23 August 1968
Height: 6'1" Weight: 13.0
Club Honours: FLC '97
Having joined Bournemouth from Leicester
during the 1997 close season, Franck
showed up well in 1997-98 as a central
defender who could also play at full back.
Although in and out of the team, battling
with Eddie Howe for a place, he looked to
be a classy defender who, whilst being
strong in the air and an excellent tackler, is
also a good passer of the ball and able to
move forward dangerously. This resulted in
him scoring eight goals, with three of them
helping the club to the Auto Windscreens
Shield final.
Ayr U (Signed from FC Pau on 8/8/94) SL 35/2
SLC 2 SC 1 Others 4
Leicester C (£100,000 on 4/9/95) P/FL 18 FLC 5
FAC 0+1
Bournemouth (Free on 8/8/97) FL 26+4/4 FLC
2/1 FAC 0+2 Others 3/3

ROLLO James (Jimmy) Stuart
Born: Wisbech, 22 May 1976
Height: 5'11" Weight: 11.5
Scored his first ever goal at full-time level,
when he sent a bullet-like header into the net
for Cardiff against Southend in the Coca
Cola Cup last August, but, unfortunately, he
could not remember a thing, having collided
head-on with a defender and being taken to
hospital. Thankfully, somebody provided a
video of his goal so that he could watch it. A
useful utility player, who perhaps needs to
settle into one position as quickly as

possible, over the season he struggled to break through and was eventually given a free transfer by manager, Frank Burrows.

Walsall (From trainee on 26/5/95) Others 0+1 (Free to Yate T in September 1995)
Cardiff C (Free from Bath C on 1/3/97) FL 6+9 FLC 0+1/1 FAC 0+2 Others 1+1

ROONEY Mark John
Born: Lambeth, 19 May 1978
Height: 5'10" Weight: 10.10

Having spent a year in the reserves, following a trainee spell, Mark finally made his Watford first team debut against Fulham in the Auto Windscreens Shield in 1997-98. A wing back, who also played a number of reserve matches in midfield, he was given a free transfer at the end of the season.

Watford (From trainee on 5/7/96) Others 1

ROPER Ian Robert
Born: Nuneaton, 20 June 1977
Height: 6'3" Weight: 14.0

Ian had mixed experiences at Walsall in 1997-98, as he sought to establish himself at the heart of the defence, and this was epitomised by his experiences in the two games at Bristol Rovers. In September, he was sent off at the Beeches for holding back ace goalscorer, Barry Hayles, but in the Auto Windscreen Shield win there in January, he shut the self same striker out of the game. Strong and uncompromising, he should continue to improve.

Walsall (From trainee on 15/5/95) FL 26+11 FLC 0+2 FAC 2+1 Others 5+1

ROSCOE Andrew (Andy) Ronald
Born: Liverpool, 4 June 1973
Height: 5'11" Weight: 12.0
Club Honours: AMC '96

Andy made more appearances for Rotherham than any other player last season and, at the same time, added goalscoring to his repertoire with his best ever tally. A good left-footed player, who is equally at home playing as a wing back, tucked inside in midfield, or as a winger, and an excellent taker of free kicks and corners, he always brings balance to the side, although he rarely got the credit he deserved from the crowd.

Bolton W (Free from Liverpool juniors on 17/7/91) FL 2+1 Others 1+1
Rotherham U (£70,000 on 27/10/94) FL 157+7/13 FLC 8 FAC 6/2 Others 9/2

ROSE Andrew (Andy) Mark
Born: Ascot, 9 August 1978
Height: 5'9" Weight: 12.2

Despite being on Oxford's bench for several games towards the end of last season, Andy, a young first-year professional full back, appeared just once in a defeat at Port Vale, where he played for five minutes. With manager, Malcolm Shotton, willing to give opportunities to talented youngsters, he may well have the chance in 1998-99 to make more of a breakthrough, although he must first displace the reliable Les Robinson to do so.

Oxford U (From trainee on 1/7/97) FL 0+1

ROSE Colin James
Born: Winsford, 22 January 1972
Height: 5'8" Weight: 11.1
International Honours: E: SP-2

Signed from Witton Albion in time for Macclesfield's first taste of soccer in the Football League, despite making a promising start in midfield Colin lost his first team place following the arrival of Martin McDonald. A useful man to have around, in the early games he showed a good turn of pace, provided pin-point crosses from the corner flag, and proved to be a tough little tackler in central midfield, working well on the overlap down the wing.

Crewe Alex (From trainee on 3/4/90) FL 17+5/1 FLC 1+1 FAC 3 Others 3 (Free to Witton A during 1992 close season)
Macclesfield T (Free on 8/8/97) FL 15+4 FLC 2 FAC 2

ROSE Matthew
Born: Dartford, 24 September 1975
Height: 5'11" Weight: 11.1
Club Honours: FAYC '94
International Honours: E: U21-2

Signed from Arsenal during the 1997 close season, Matthew started 1997-98 in Queens Park Rangers' first team in the right-back slot but, following the departure of the management duo of Stewart Houston and Bruce Rioch in November, he was dropped from the side and did not return until making two substitute appearances in the last few games. Despite his inexperience, he remains a young player with potential, who can perform equally well in the centre of defence, being sound positionally and a good tackler.

Arsenal (From trainee on 19/7/94) PL 2+3
Queens Park R (£500,000 on 20/5/97) FL 13+3 FLC 2

ROSENTHAL Ronny
Born: Haifa, Israel, 11 October 1963
Height: 5'10" Weight: 12.13
Club Honours: Div 2 '98
International Honours: Israel: 60

An inspired free transfer signing from Tottenham in August 1997, whose class and experience proved vital to Watford's promotion challenge, Ronny showed exemplary commitment and enthusiasm to go with that touch of Premiership class that made all the difference at second division level. Having scored a first-minute goal at Grimsby, and a memorable "rocket" against Blackpool, after a series of niggling injuries he finally succumbed to a knee operation in March and was sadly missed for the remainder of the season. However, his 25 league games saw him well worth his second division championship medal as the Hornets raced to the top of the table and stayed there.

Liverpool (Loaned from Standard Liege on 22/3/90) FL 5+3/7
Liverpool (£1,000,000 on 29/6/90) F/PL 27+39/14 FLC 2+7/1 FAC 5+3 Others 2+4
Tottenham H (£250,000 on 26/1/94) PL 55+33/4 FLC 3/1 FAC 7+2/6
Watford (Free on 12/8/97) FL 24+1/8 FLC 3+1/1 FAC 2/2

ROSLER Uwe
Born: Attenburg, Germany, 15 November 1968
Height: 6'0" Weight: 12.4
International Honours: East Germany: 5

After three successful seasons at Manchester City as the club's leading goalscorer, and a firm favourite with the fans, Uwe started 1997-98 by declining to sign a new contract, and was made available for transfer. Although starting the opening six games, he was subbed four times, and showed up disappointingly before suffering an ankle injury that kept him out of action until early December. Back to a tumultuous welcome at West Bromwich, however, he began as new, foraging and running like his old self, and scoring six times in a run of 21 games, until being relegated to the bench and finishing as either a used substitute or being out injured. In a sorry end to four exciting campaigns, Uwe signed a three-year contract with Kaiserslautern and left Maine Road on a free.

Manchester C (£375,000 from FC Nurnberg on 2/3/94) P/FL 141+11/50 FLC 10+1/5 FAC 14/9

ROWBOTHAM Darren
Born: Cardiff, 22 October 1966
Height: 5'10" Weight: 12.13
Club Honours: Div 4 '90
International Honours: W: Yth

1997-98 was a fantastic season for Exeter's Darren, as he became the first person to top 20 goals in a season since he did it in his first spell here in 1989-90, while his strike partnership with Steve Flack really took off. An enthusiastic character, his good control and vast experience meant that he also brought other players into the action, and thus contributed a lot to the overall team play. Was delighted to be named the club's Player of the Year.

Plymouth Arg (From juniors on 7/11/84) FL 22+4/2 FLC 1 FAC 0+3/1 Others 1+1
Exeter C (Signed on 31/10/87) FL 110+8/47 FLC 11/6 FAC 8/5 Others 5/1
Torquay U (£25,000 on 13/9/91) FL 14/3 FAC 3/1 Others 2
Birmingham C (£20,000 on 2/1/92) FL 31+5/6 FLC 0+1 Others 3+1
Mansfield T (Loaned on 18/12/92) FL 4
Hereford U (Loaned on 25/3/93) FL 8/2
Crewe Alex (Free on 6/7/93) FL 59+2/21 FLC 3/1 FAC 4/3 Others 6+2/1
Shrewsbury T (Free on 28/7/95) FL 31+9/9 FLC 3+2/2 FAC 4/1 Others 1+3
Exeter C (Free on 24/10/96) FL 67+1/31 FLC 2 FAC 4/2 Others 2/1

ROWBOTHAM Jason
Born: Cardiff, 3 January 1969
Height: 5'9" Weight: 11.6
Club Honours: S Div 1 '95; SLC '95

A very gifted Plymouth defender with the ability to carry the ball out of defence, Jason occupied many positions in the defence throughout the course of last season. Most accomplished as a sweeper, he unfortunately missed a large part of the campaign due to ruptured knee ligaments.

Plymouth Arg (From trainee on 20/7/87) FL 8+1 FLC 0+1
Shrewsbury T (Free on 26/3/92)
Hereford U (Free on 17/10/92) FL 3+2/1 FAC 1

Raith Rov (Free on 31/7/93) SL 47+9/1 SLC 3+2 SC 2+1 Others 1
Wycombe W (£40,000 on 14/9/95) FL 27 FLC 2 FAC 2 Others 2
Plymouth Arg (Free on 11/10/96) FL 35+5 FLC 2 FAC 0+1 Others 2+1

ROWE Ezekiel (Zeke) Bartholomew
Born: Stoke Newington, 30 October 1973
Height: 5'11" Weight: 12.8

1997-98 was another season of unfulfilled promise for the former Chelsea man, and he again made more substitute appearances than starts for Peterborough, due to more experienced colleagues keeping him out of the side. A speedy forward, who looks good when running at defences, he was loaned out to Doncaster in February and worked hard, often being the lone man up front. Despite Rovers being earmarked for the Conference, Zeke let nobody down and weighed in with a couple of goals before returning to London Road and turning out in the final two games of the campaign.*

Chelsea (From trainee on 12/6/92)
Barnet (Loaned on 12/11/93) FL 9+1/2 FAC 2/1
Brighton & Hove A (Loaned on 28/3/96) FL 9/3
Peterborough U (Free on 4/7/96) FL 13+15/3 FLC 2 FAC 3+2 Others 0+3
Doncaster Rov (Loaned on 20/2/98) FL 6/2

ROWE Rodney Carl
Born: Huddersfield, 30 July 1975
Height: 5'8" Weight: 12.8

1997-98 was a season of two halves for York City's top scorer. In October and early November he netted eight goals in a run of nine games, being one of the leading marksmen in the second division, but from mid-November to the end of the campaign, however, his scoring touch deserted him and he only added a further four in 24 games, which included two in a defeat at Preston in March. Can also play on the wide right, where his pace makes it difficult for the opposition.

Huddersfield T (From trainee on 12/7/93) FL 14+20/2 FLC 0+2 FAC 6+1/2 Others 3/1
Scarborough (Loaned on 11/8/94) FL 10+4/1 FLC 4/1
Bury (Loaned on 20/3/95) FL 1+2
York C (£80,000 on 19/2/97) FL 47+4/14 FLC 3/1 FAC 2/3 Others 1/1

ROWETT Gary
Born: Bromsgrove, 6 March 1974
Height: 6'0" Weight: 12.10

A Derby right-sided defender who can play as part of a three-man defence, or in a flat back four, these days Gary is noted for being perhaps the most consistent player at the club, and had another superb season in 1997-98, maintaining his progress as a regular in a side which has gained in confidence during his four years at the club. Does not tend to join the attacking moves, playing the last man at the back role with reliability, he reads the game well and has the vision to pick out the forwards with good early balls. Is also an impressive tackler.

Cambridge U (From trainee on 10/9/91) FL 51+12/9 FLC 7/1 FAC 5+2 Others 5/3
Everton (£200,000 on 21/5/94) PL 2+2
Blackpool (Loaned on 23/1/95) FL 17
Derby Co (£300,000 on 20/7/95) P/FL 101+4/3 FLC 8/2 FAC 5+2

ROWLAND Keith
Born: Portadown, 1 September 1971
Height: 5'10" Weight: 10.0
International Honours: NI: 12; B-3; Yth

This Irish defender played in some of the early season games for West Ham in 1997-98, but could not maintain a regular place and to keep his Northern Ireland international interest alive he needed first team football. It was on that basis that he reluctantly left the Hammers to join Queens Park Rangers in January, where he made his debut against Stockport. Part of the deal that involved Trevor Sinclair going in the opposite direction, he joined Rangers, along with Iain Dowie, and played seven times in the left-back slot before gashing his leg in the away game at Norwich. An excellent crosser of the ball, with a great left foot, Keith played for the "B" team against the Republic in February.

Bournemouth (From trainee on 2/10/89) FL 65+7/2 FLC 5 FAC 8 Others 3
Coventry C (Loaned on 8/1/93) PL 0+2
West Ham U (£110,000 on 6/8/93) PL 63+17/1 FLC 3+2 FAC 5+1
Queens Park R (Signed on 30/1/98) FL 7

ROYCE Simon Ernest
Born: Forest Gate, 9 September 1971
Height: 6'2" Weight: 12.8

1997-98 was another good season for Simon in the Southend goal, his shot-stopping being again called into serious use in a struggling team, and he responded magnificently. Sent off at Fulham in the FA Cup in December, and with the on-loan Neville Southall retaining his place for nine matches, he did not return until February. The layoff did not dull his reactions, however, with United winning the first two matches he returned for, the first time in the campaign the club had won consecutively.

Rodney Rowe

Was surprisingly released during the summer.

Southend U (£35,000 from Heybridge Swifts on 15/10/91) FL 147+2 FLC 9 FAC 5 Others 6

RUDDOCK Neil
Born: Wandsworth, 9 May 1968
Height: 6'2" Weight: 12.12
Club Honours: FLC '95
International Honours: E: 1; B-1; U21-4; Yth

Although the big central defender started the opening game of last season for Liverpool, he appeared to have had his best days in the famous red shirt and was loaned to Queens Park Rangers on transfer deadline day, after making only four appearances for the club at that point in time. When he arrived at Loftus Road, Rangers were lying in 18th spot in the first division with only four points separating them from the bottom club, Reading, and seven games to play. However, to show what a difference he made, Rangers lost just once in the remaining matches and steered themselves clear of relegation. Very strong, and a player who attacks the ball to head bravely, despite losing a little pace, his ability at that level was there for all to see. At the time of going to press, Rangers were still trying to negotiate his transfer on a permanent basis.

Millwall (From apprentice on 3/3/86) Others 3+1/1
Tottenham H (£50,000 on 14/4/86) FL 7+2 FAC 1+1/1
Millwall (£300,000 on 29/6/88) FL 0+2/1 FLC 2/3 Others 1+1
Southampton (£250,000 on 13/2/89) FL 100+7/9 FLC 14+1/1 FAC 10/3 Others 6
Tottenham H (£750,000 on 29/7/92) PL 38/3 FLC 4 FAC 5
Liverpool (£2,500,000 on 22/7/93) PL 111+4/11 FLC 19+1/1 FAC 11 Others 5+1
Queens Park R (Loaned on 26/3/98) FL 7

RUDI Petter
Born: Norway, 17 September 1973
Height: 6'3" Weight: 12.10
International Honours: Norway: 16

Brought to Sheffield Wednesday by David Pleat from Molde last October, this young Norwegian international proved to be a big hit with the fans, who admired his attitude of getting up and getting on with it, regarding midfield tousles and knocks. Playing first out on the left side of midfield, and then on the right, due to an injury to Niclas Alexandersson, Petter showed skill and determination until a niggling leg strain halted his run of appearances in March. However, making a quick recovery he was back near the end of a tough first campaign and, although hoping to be selected for Norway in the World Cup, he was not among the final 22 names.

Sheffield Wed (£800,000 from Molde on 17/10/97) PL 19+3 FAC 3

RUFUS Richard Raymond
Born: Lewisham, 12 January 1975
Height: 6'1" Weight: 11.10
International Honours: E: U21-6

Good in the air, and a strong tackler, who reads the game well and is very calm under pressure, Richard is very fast and has improved his distribution, making him one of the most accomplished defenders in the first division in 1997-98. Scored his first senior goal for Charlton in the first division play-off final at Wembley, a game that saw Athletic reach the Premiership at the expense of Sunderland. It took a long time coming, 165 games to be precise, having gone close on many occasions from set pieces and corners, but rarely has a more important goal been scored.

Charlton Ath (From trainee on 1/7/93) FL 142+3 FLC 8 FAC 7 Others 5/1

RUSH David
Born: Sunderland, 15 May 1971
Height: 5'7" Weight: 11.4

Having suffered with illness and injury during his first season at York in 1996-97, playing just three times, it was thought that the effervescent striker would be up for it in 1997-98, but, after making just three further appearances, his contract was cancelled in September after serious breaches of club rules.

Sunderland (From trainee on 21/7/89) FL 40+19/12 FLC 1+1 FAC 9/1 Others 1+1
Hartlepool U (Loaned on 15/8/91) FL 8/2
Peterborough U (Loaned on 27/10/93) FL 2+2/1 FLC 1/1
Cambridge U (Loaned on 12/9/94) FL 2
Oxford U (£100,000 on 23/9/94) FL 67+25/21 FLC 3+3 FAC 2+3/1 Others 6+1/2
York C (£80,000 on 31/1/97) FL 2+3 Others 1

RUSH Ian James
Born: St Asaph, 20 October 1961
Height: 6'0" Weight: 12.6
Club Honours: Div 1 '82, '83, '84, '86, '90; FLC '81, '82, '83, '84, '95; FAC '86, '89, '92; EC '84; CS '82, '89
International Honours: W: 73; U21-2; Sch

Arch goalscorer, Ian, joined Newcastle from Liverpool in the 1997 close season on a 12-month contract, expecting to be used as a squad player, but the club's early season striker crisis led to him playing more often than he expected. Although some of his pace and sharpness has eroded, he was as enthusiastic as ever and his positional awareness remained a lesson for younger strikers. His first goal for Newcastle came in the Coca Cola Cup against Hull, taking his career total to 49, and equalling Geoff Hurst's competition record. Although a torn cartilage required an operation in October, he returned in time to send Newcastle on their way to Wembley with the FA Cup third round winner against old rivals, Everton, extending his record as the top FA Cup goalscorer this century. He went to Sheffield United on loan in February, but turned down the chance of a permanent move and returned to St James Park, stating that he wanted to try and win a fourth FA Cup winners medal. Was released during the summer.

Chester C (From apprentice on 25/9/79) FL 33+1/14 FAC 5/3
Liverpool (£300,000 on 1/5/80) FL 182/109 FLC 38/21 FAC 22/20 Others 31+1/17 (£3,200,000 to Juventus on 1/7/86)
Liverpool (Loaned on 1/7/86) FL 42/30 FLC 9/4 FAC 3 Others 3/6

Liverpool (£2,800,000 on 23/8/88) F/PL 223+22/90 FLC 30/23 FAC 30+6/19 Others 16+1/7
Leeds U (Free on 24/5/96) PL 34+2/3 FLC 2 FAC 2+2
Newcastle U (Free on 15/8/97) PL 6+4 FLC 2/1 FAC 0+1/1 Others 1
Sheffield U (Loaned on 24/2/98) FL 4

RUSH Matthew James
Born: Hackney, 6 August 1971
Height: 5'11" Weight: 12.10
International Honours: Ei: U21-4

Matthew was forever injured last season, thus allowing only 20 appearances of sorts for Oldham, and has never really fully recovered from the cruciate knee ligament operation he had a year or two ago. At his best as a pacy right winger with two good feet, who can go both sides, he will, hopefully, stand up to the rigours of 1998-99 and give the fans something to shout about. Is also useful in aerial situations.

West Ham U (From trainee on 24/3/90) F/PL 29+19/5 FLC 4 Others 2+1
Cambridge U (Loaned on 12/3/93) FL 4+6
Swansea C (Loaned on 10/1/94) FL 13 Others 4
Norwich C (£330,000 on 18/8/95) FL 0+3
Northampton T (Loaned on 28/10/96) FL 6/2
Northampton T (Loaned on 19/12/96) FL 8/1 Others 1/1
Oldham Ath (£165,000 on 27/3/97) FL 17+7/3 FAC 0+3 Others 0+1

RUSSELL Alexander (Alex) John
Born: Crosby, 17 March 1973
Height: 5'9" Weight: 11.7

The son of a former Southport star, he passed 100 league games for Rochdale during last season but, after continuing his great form of the previous term when scoring four goals from midfield in the first dozen games, injuries disrupted his progress. Although reclaiming a first team spot, when Mark Leonard was switched to defence, Alex appeared to have slipped behind the other youngsters, Mark Bailey and Gary Jones, in the battle for the midfield slots, and was released during the summer.

Rochdale (£4,000 from Burscough on 11/7/94) FL 83+19/14 FLC 5/1 FAC 1+1 Others 2+3

RUSSELL Craig Stewart
Born: South Shields, 4 February 1974
Height: 5'10" Weight: 12.6
Club Honours: Div 1 '96

Out of favour at Sunderland following the arrival of Kevin Phillips during the 1997 close season, Craig, who had been tracked throughout the summer by Frank Clark, the Manchester City manager, arrived at Maine Road last November, with Nicky Summerbee going in the opposite direction in a straight swop. Signed on a Thursday, a medical on Friday, and in the first team on Saturday at Sheffield United, that was his introduction to the club. Although brought in as a hard-running, direct sort of player, with pace and spirit, and an ability to make room for shooting opportunities in the area, he eventually settled into a wing-back position. His one and only goal for City came at Portsmouth.

Sunderland (From trainee on 1/7/92) P/FL 103+47/31 FLC 7+6/1 FAC 6+3/2 Others 2
Manchester C (£1,000,000 on 14/11/97) FL 17+7/1 FAC 2

RUSSELL Darel Francis Roy
Born: Stepney, 22 October 1980
Height: 6'0" Weight: 11.9
International Honours: E: Yth

A trainee at the start of 1997-98, Darel signed professional forms at Norwich in November, following some very impressive early displays for both the reserve and youth teams. Highly thought of at Carrow Road, there are those who feel that the youngster is another Andy Johnson in the making, he has played for the England U18 side and is a forceful midfielder with a capacity to burst through into shooting distance. Also comfortable on the ball, and a good passer, he came off the bench during the final game at Reading and could well force his way into senior reckoning in 1998-99.
Norwich C (From trainee on 29/11/97) FL 0+1

RUSSELL Kevin John
Born: Portsmouth, 6 December 1966
Height: 5'9" Weight: 10.12
Club Honours: Div 2 '93
International Honours: E: Yth

The former Wrexham front-line goalscorer who nowadays plays in midfield, had a "quiet season", due to an injury suffered in January, which restricted his appearances from then on. "Rooster" has been around for a long time, and his experience would have been an asset in the club's unsuccessful quest to reach the play offs, especially as he always provides an attacking option (a legacy of his former striker days), something that was sadly lacking in the final run in.
Portsmouth (Free from Brighton & Hove A juniors on 9/10/84) FL 3+1/1 FLC 0+1 FAC 0+1 Others 1+1
Wrexham (£10,000 on 17/7/87) FL 84/43 FLC 4/1 FAC 4 Others 8/3
Leicester C (£175,000 on 20/6/89) FL 24+19/10 FLC 0+1 FAC 1 Others 5/2
Peterborough U (Loaned on 6/9/90) FL 7/3
Cardiff C (Loaned on 17/1/91) FL 3
Hereford U (Loaned on 7/11/91) FL 3/1 Others 1/1
Stoke C (Loaned on 2/1/92) FL 5/1
Stoke C (£95,000 on 16/7/92) FL 30+10/5 FLC 3 FAC 2 Others 4+1/1
Burnley (£150,000 on 28/6/93) FL 26+2/6 FLC 4/1 FAC 4 Others 1/1
Bournemouth (£125,000 on 3/3/94) FL 30/1 FLC 3/1 FAC 2/1
Notts Co (£60,000 on 24/2/95) FL 9+2
Wrexham (£60,000 on 21/7/95) FL 85+12/7 FLC 4/1 FAC 10+2/3 Others 3

RUSSELL Lee Edward
Born: Southampton, 3 September 1969
Height: 5'11" Weight: 12.0

Lee had another campaign wrecked by injury, and managed to start only nine games for Portsmouth in 1997-98 as a left-wing back. Unfortunately, for both him and the club, Pompey managed to win just one of those nine games and he will therefore be hoping that he can rid himself of his injury problems before the start of the coming season. Capable of playing in midfield and

central defence, where he can use his good aerial ability to effect, he would have made many more appearances had it not been for injuries.*
Portsmouth (From trainee on 12/7/88) FL 103+20/3 FLC 8+2 FAC 4+2 Others 5+2
Bournemouth (Loaned on 9/9/94) FL 3

RUSSELL Matthew Lee
Born: Dewsbury, 17 January 1978
Height: 5'11" Weight: 11.5

The young striker continued to progress through the ranks to the brink of a first team place at Scarborough in 1997-98, making two subs' appearances in the third division, and performing well in the reserve team's successful Pontins League campaign. Also had a loan spell with Doncaster Rovers towards the end of the season, impressing many with his energy and commitment in a midfield role.
Scarborough (From trainee on 3/7/96) FL 1+6 FLC 0+1
Doncaster Rov (Loaned on 26/3/98) FL 4/1

RUST Nicholas (Nicky) Charles Irwin
Born: Ely, 25 September 1974
Height: 6'1" Weight: 13.1
International Honours: E: Yth

As in the previous season, Nicky shared the goalkeeping duties for Brighton and Hove Albion with Mark Ormerod throughout 1997-98. Taking over in early November, he had a lengthy run in the side until relinquishing his place to the less experienced Ormerod in February, having been particularly impressive in the excellent 2-1 win at Peterborough at Christmas, when he performed heroics to keep the league leaders at bay. Though not quite enjoying the pinnacle of form, the 23-year old remained a great favourite with the Seagulls' supporters, who will be sad to see him leave the club, following his release during the summer.
Brighton & Hove A (Free from Arsenal juniors on 9/7/93) FL 177 FLC 14 FAC 9 Others 9

RYAN Darragh Joseph
Born: Cuckfield, 21 May 1980
Height: 5'10" Weight: 10.4

The skipper of Brighton and Hove Albion's youth team, Darragh broke into the first team squad in late November last, and scored a goal in only his second appearance, a 2-0 win at Scunthorpe. The trainee forward looked set for a run in the side, but bad fortune struck during the 2-1 win over promotion favourites, Peterborough United, at the end of December. Having come on as a sub with a quarter of an hour to go, seven minutes later he suffered a badly broken leg after a poorly-timed tackle by a Peterborough defender, which sidelined him for the remainder of the season. Ironically, a similar incident some 12 years earlier had ended the career of Darragh's father, the former Brighton and Republic of Ireland star, Gerry Ryan. Despite the disappointment, young Ryan was awarded a one-year contract by manager, Brian Horton, in March.
Brighton & Hove A (From trainee on 25/3/98) FL 1+3/1

RYAN Keith James
Born: Northampton, 25 June 1970
Height: 5'11" Weight: 12.8
Club Honours: FAT '91, '93; GMVC '93

After just four months playing in the last three years, due to bad knee injuries, Keith's bad luck at Wycombe continued when he picked up a back strain on the opening day of last season. However, when he re-established himself five weeks later in an unfamiliar central defensive position, he quickly became the club's great success story of the campaign, playing a full part in every match from then on. His great pace and fierce, but fair tackling attracted the attention of Premiership clubs, and when Neil Smillie became temporary manager in February, he was made captain and immediately responded, scoring the only goal in three out of the next four games, all headers, this after his previous manager prevented him from going up at set pieces. Right footed and strong in the air, and formerly a striker, cum midfielder, he is therefore comfortable going forward. Was the winner in all three of the club's Player of the Year awards and is a model professional in every way, proving that there is a way back after career threatening injuries.
Wycombe W (Signed from Berkhamstead T in 1989-90) FL 124+5/12 FLC 7/2 FAC 8+3/3 Others 12+1

RYAN Robert (Robbie) Paul
Born: Dublin, 16 May 1977
Height: 5'10" Weight: 12.0
International Honours: Ei: U21-5; Yth; Sch

As a member of the Irish U21 squad, having featured in the World Youth Championships held in Malaysia in the summer of 1997, Robbie was expected to break through into the Huddersfield side last season on a more regular basis. In the event he did, when deputising for Tom Cowan at left back, before being surprisingly transferred to Millwall in January. Fitted in well with the Lions as a naturally left-footed player, his outstanding level of fitness allowing him to join in with the attack and then recover rapidly if required. Shows good awareness, and seems to have an excellent future ahead of him.
Huddersfield T (Free from Belvedere on 26/7/94) FL 12+3 FLC 2
Millwall (£10,000 on 30/1/98) FL 16

RYDER Stuart Henry
Born: Sutton Coldfield, 6 November 1973
Height: 6'0" Weight: 12.6
International Honours: E: U21-3

After suffering serious injury problems over the previous two campaign, Stuart began last season in Walsall's first team, lost his place, and then came back to give the sort of polished displays that suggested he was back to the form that made him an England youth cap a few years earlier. A cool, calm, and collected central defender, who looks to play the ball out of defence, many fans were disappointed when he was released in May.
Walsall (From trainee on 16/7/92) FL 86+15/5 FLC 5+1 FAC 9 Others 7+1

SADLIER Richard Thomas
Born: Dublin, 14 January 1979
Height: 6'2" Weight: 12.10
International Honours: Ei: Yth
Started last season well at Millwall, with three goals in three games, and looked set for a promising time of it up front until injury sidelined him for the rest of the campaign. His pace and ability to shoot with either foot have seen him excel at reserve team level and, once fit again, he is expected to become a scourge of defences, especially in the second division. Is also good in the air, his extra height menacing 'keepers.
Millwall (Signed from Belvedere on 14/8/96) FL 10+4/3 FLC 1

SAIB Moussa
Born: Algeria, 6 March 1969
Height: 5'9" Weight: 11.8
International Honours: Algeria: 39
Signed from Valencia last February, Moussa made his debut for Tottenham in the home clash with Bolton Wanderers on 1 March, proving to be a talented midfielder with the ability to hold the midfield together and slow the game down in order to stabilise play when under attack. A player of great experience, the Algerian international delivers accurate crosses and through balls to the front line, and is understandably confident with the ball at his feet when going forward. An all rounder, while having the ability to read the game and cut out offensive balls delivered into his own half, and strong in the challenge, on the other side of the coin he likes to get forward, and demonstrated his striking ability with a goal in the 6-2 defeat of Wimbledon in May. Having signed a four-year deal with the club, Moussa promises to provide the experience and commitment that Tottenham need if they are to challenge for honours in 1998-99.
Tottenham H (£2,300,000 from Valencia on 25/2/98) PL 3+6/1

SALAKO John Akin
Born: Nigeria, 11 February 1969
Height: 5'10" Weight: 12.8
Club Honours: FMC '91; Div '94
International Honours: E: 5
1997-98 was a make-or-break season for John at Coventry and, despite playing well on occasions, especially in the Coca Cola Cup against Everton when he scored twice, he failed to grab other opportunities. Eventually, with his contract due to expire during the summer, he turned down new terms and moved to Bolton on transfer deadline day to help ease the recent departure of Jamie Pollock to Manchester City. Although his appearances all came from the substitute's bench, the tricky left winger showed the Reebok faithful some glimpses that the old magic was still there,

particularly when making rapid runs into the opponents half, before he was released during the summer. *Stop Press:* Signed for Fulham on 8 July.
Crystal Palace (From apprentice on 3/11/86) F/PL 172+43/22 FLC 19+5/5 FAC 20/4 Others 11+3/2
Swansea C (Loaned on 14/8/89) FL 13/3 Others 2/1
Coventry C (£1,500,000 on 7/8/95) PL 68+4/4 FLC 9/3 FAC 4/1
Bolton W (Free on 26/3/98) PL 0+7

SALE Mark David
Born: Burton on Trent, 27 February 1972
Height: 6'4" Weight: 14.4
An extremely tall centre forward, and target man, Mark took some time before opening his account for Colchester last season, with a goal against Doncaster in late October. From then on, they began to flow more frequently, although "Car-Boot's" role in the team demanded that he set up more chances than he received himself, carrying out a lot of the unglamorous, physical work, often against two opposition centre backs, and being the unsung hero of the team. Deceptively good on the ground at times, he finished with eight goals in the season, including two in the 5-1 demolition of Macclesfield – the second a spectacular 20-yard drive.
Stoke C (From trainee on 10/7/90) FL 0+2
Cambridge U (Free on 31/7/91. Free to Rocester in December 1991)
Birmingham C (Free on 26/3/92) FL 11+10 FLC 2/1 Others 3+1/2
Torquay U (£10,000 on 5/3/93) FL 30+14/8 FLC 1 FAC 2/1 Others 3+1
Preston NE (£20,000 on 26/7/94) FL 10+3/7 FLC 1+1 FAC 0+1 Others 4
Mansfield T (£50,000 on 31/7/95) FL 36+9/12 FLC 4/1 FAC 2 Others 1
Colchester U (£23,500 on 10/3/97) FL 48+1/10 FLC 2 FAC 3/1 Others 6+1

SALMON Michael (Mike) Bernard
Born: Leyland, 14 July 1964
Height: 6'2" Weight: 14.0
An experienced goalkeeper, Mike started last season as understudy to Andy Petterson, before regaining his place in the Charlton side in December and playing 11 consecutive games until damaging a knee at Manchester City, and requiring an operation, which kept him out for the rest of the campaign. Ironically, as a good shot-stopper who is reasonably good on crosses, and very laid back in approach, he was probably having his best ever spell for the club before the injury occurred.*
Blackburn Rov (From juniors on 16/10/81) FL 1
Chester C (Loaned on 18/10/82) FL 16 FAC 2
Stockport Co (Free on 3/8/83) FL 118 FLC 10 FAC 3 Others 3
Bolton W (Free on 31/7/86F) FL 26 FLC 2 FAC 4 Others 4
Wrexham (£18,000 on 7/3/87) FL 100 FLC 4 FAC 4 Others 9
Charlton Ath (£100,000 on 6/7/89) FL 148 FLC 11 FAC 10 Others 6

SALT Phillip (Phil) Thomas
Born: Oldham, 2 March 1979
Height: 5'11" Weight: 11.9
Another of the Oldham youngsters to make his first team debut in 1997-98, Phil is an intelligent right-sided midfielder, who

impresses as an excellent passer of the ball, and who hates to give it away. He is also highly thought of at Boundary Park and it was that confidence that saw him introduced three times last season, his initial appearance coming when he was selected for the side that played at Carlisle in the Auto Windscreen Shield in December. Watch out for him to be further blooded this coming term.
Oldham Ath (From trainee on 1/7/97) FL 1+1 Others 1

SAMPSON Ian
Born: Wakefield, 14 November 1968
Height: 6'2" Weight: 13.3
Central defender "Sammo" is one of Northampton's defensive "Rocks", together with Ray Warburton and Colin Hill. In what was his fourth season with the club, reliable in defence, good in the air, with the ability to "pinch" goals when moving up for set pieces, and despite missing two months of 1997-98 through injury, his return coincided with the goals against tally dropping.
Sunderland (Signed from Goole T on 13/11/90) FL 13+4/1 FLC 1 FAC 0+2 Others 0+1
Northampton T (Loaned on 8/12/93) FL 8
Northampton T (Free on 5/8/94) FL 154+3/13 FLC 10 FAC 4 Others 15/2

SAMUELS Dean Walter
Born: Hackney, 29 March 1973
Height: 6'2" Weight: 12.6
A tall, quick Barnet centre forward, Dean is never happier than when running with the ball at pace, at defenders. Often used late in games to take advantage of tiring defences, all of his 27 appearances in 1997-98 were from the bench.
Barnet (Signed from Boreham Wood on 24/12/96) FL 13+26/3 FLC 0+3 FAC 0+1 Others 1+1/1

SAMWAYS Mark
Born: Doncaster, 11 November 1968
Height: 6'2" Weight: 14.0
Appointed York's first-choice 'keeper at the start of last season, after signing from Scunthorpe during the summer, Mark gave a number of commanding displays when helping the club rise to third in the second division table early in November. Later that month, however, he was injured in a game at Blackpool, which sidelined him for a couple of months, but returned to first team duty in February, before losing his place to Andy Warrington later in the campaign and being released during the summer.
Doncaster Rov (From trainee on 20/8/87) FL 121 FLC 3 FAC 4 Others 10
Scunthorpe U (Signed on 26/3/92) FL 180 FLC 10 FAC 16 Others 16
York C (Free on 18/7/97) FL 29 FLC 4 FAC 1

SANDERS Steven (Steve)
Born: Halifax, 2 June 1978
Height: 5'10" Weight: 12.0
Unable to get a first team opportunity at Huddersfield, Steve signed for Doncaster during the 1997 close season, but never seemed to be able to cement a regular place at Rovers, although he featured in more than half of the league fixtures to some degree. Usually given a full-back berth, he was

released from his contract prior to the transfer deadline, along with a number of other players.

Huddersfield T (From trainee on 3/7/96)
Doncaster Rov (Free on 8/8/97) FL 19+6 FLC 2 Others 1

SANDFORD Lee Robert
Born: Basingstoke, 22 April 1968
Height: 6'1" Weight: 13.4
Club Honours: AMC '92; Div 2 '93
International Honours: E: Yth

In what was undoubtedly the comeback of last season for Sheffield United fans, Lee, having spent September on loan at Reading, while out of the picture at United and transfer listed, came back into the side following injuries and transfers, to form a solid and reliable centre back partnership with David Holdsworth. At Reading, his arrival at left back coincided with the Berkshire club's best spell, as they won three of the five games in which he played. Ironically, his only goal of 1997-98 was a vital late header against Reading that took United through to the sixth round of the FA Cup at the expense of his old team mates. Is a strong tackler and good in the air.

Portsmouth (From apprentice on 4/12/85) FL 66+6/1 FLC 11 FAC 4 Others 2+1
Stoke C (£140,000 on 22/12/89) FL 255+3/8 FLC 19 FAC 16/2 Others 31/4
Sheffield U (£500,000 on 22/7/96) FL 40+5/2 FLC 3 FAC 7/1 Others 3+1
Reading (Loaned on 5/9/97) FL 5

Lee Sandford

SANDWITH Kevin
Born: Workington, 30 April 1978
Height: 5'11" Weight: 12.5

A second-year Carlisle professional, and a tough-tackling left back, Kevin made his Football League debut at Plymouth last February and followed that up with two more appearances, one of them being from the bench. Having come through the ranks, first as a junior and then as a reserve, the coming term may give him more prospect of a regular first team berth.

Carlisle U (From trainee on 16/7/96) FL 2+1

SANETTI Francesco
Born: Rome, Italy, 11 January 1979
Height: 6'1" Weight: 12.6

This 19-year-old striker came to Sheffield Wednesday under the freedom of contract stipulation, from the Italian club, Genoa, at the end of April, and made his Premiership debut at Hillsborough as a second-half sub against Aston Villa in the penultimate game of 1997-98. Francesco certainly created an excellent impression, despite Wednesday losing 3-1, when scoring a fine individual goal in the 88th minute to give the score some sense of respectability. In looking to be a hit for the coming season, it transpired that Ron Atkinson had wanted to sign the youngster earlier, but Genoa would not release his clearance papers until made to by EUFA. Hopefully, he should have no difficulty settling in Sheffield, with Benito Carbone and Paolo Di Canio to look after him.

Sheffield Wed (Free from Genoa on 30/4/98) PL 1+1/1

SAN JUAN Jesus Garcia
Born: Zaragoza, Spain, 22 August 1971
Height: 5'10" Weight: 11.13

The Spanish midfielder was hired by Wolves for three months last September, with a view to a permanent move, coming on as sub at Fulham after 13 minutes and scoring 20 minutes later with a neat right-foot shot, though he was not renowned for his scoring exploits. Although his name was pronounced "Hesus" the goal prompted choruses of "Hallelujah" from the Wolves' fans that night. Started the next six games but struggled to make an impact, having not proved to be the hard tackler the club were seeking.

Wolverhampton W (Loaned from Real Zaragoza on 16/9/97) FL 4 FLC 2+1/1

SAUL Eric Michael
Born: Dublin, 28 October 1978
Height: 5'7" Weight: 10.10

A versatile former trainee, Eric was included in Brighton and Hove Albion's first team squad from last October, having impressed with his performances in the reserves. The diminutive Dubliner was used entirely in a substitute role, before making the starting line-up for the first time for the Auto Windscreens Shield match at Walsall, in January, when the Seagulls were soundly beaten 5-0. Was released during the summer.

Brighton & Hove A (From trainee on 10/7/97) FL 0+4 Others 1

SAUNDERS Dean Nicholas
Born: Swansea, 21 June 1964
Height: 5'8" Weight: 10.6
Club Honours: FAC '92; FLC '94
International Honours: W: 63

Having gone well for Nottingham Forest in 1996-97, Dean was confidently expected to continue the good work at the City Ground in 1997-98, but found himself unable to get the opportunity to shine due to the good form of Kevin Campbell and Pierre van Hooijdonk. After 12 games and four goals, when standing in for the two players in question, the Welsh international striker was allowed to move to Sheffield United on a free transfer in December, and immediately proved his ability in taking over the goalscoring mantle from Brian Deane and Jan Aage Fjortoft. Scored one of the goals of the season when volleying past the Port Vale 'keeper from the touchline, and regularly showed his awareness and quicksilver thinking in the United cause throughout the campaign.*

Swansea C (From apprentice on 24/6/82) FL 42+7/12 FLC 2+1 FAC 1 Others 1+1
Cardiff C (Loaned on 29/3/85) FL 3+1
Brighton & Hove A (Free on 7/8/85) FL 66+6/21 FLC 4 FAC 7/5 Others 3
Oxford U (£60,000 on 12/3/87) FL 57+2/22 FLC 9+1/8 FAC 2/2 Others 2/1
Derby Co (£1,000,000 on 28/10/88) FL 106/42 FLC 12/10 FAC 6 Others 7/5
Liverpool (£2,900,000 on 19/7/91) F/PL 42/11 FLC 5/2 FAC 8/2 Others 6/10
Aston Villa (£2,300,000 on 10/9/92) F/PL 111+1/37 FLC 15/7 FAC 9/4 Others 8/1 (£2,350,000 to Galatasaray on 1/7/95)
Nottingham F (£1,500,000 on 16/7/96) F/PL 39+4/5 FLC 5+1/2 FAC 2/2
Sheffield U (Free on 5/12/97) FL 23+1/10 FAC 6/2 Others 2

Mark Saunders

SAUNDERS Mark Philip
Born: Reading, 23 July 1971
Height: 5'11" Weight: 11.12

Probably the most improved Plymouth player of last season, Mark, in his third year of professional football, showed that he had adapted well. With fewer injury set backs than previously, he made great progress in keeping more senior professionals out of the team and showed himself to be a good, strong central midfielder who was well able

to get forward positions. Finished the campaign with seven league goals, many of them vital to Argyle's cause.

Plymouth Arg (Signed from Tiverton T on 22/8/95) FL 60+12/11 FLC 1+1 FAC 2+3 Others 2

SAVAGE David (Dave) Thomas Patrick
Born: Dublin, 30 July 1973
Height: 6'1" Weight: 12.7
International Honours: Ei: 5; U21-5

Yet another Millwall player whose 1997-98 was blighted by injury, a lower back problem hampering his performances, Dave is at home either in midfield or up front. Predominantly right sided, he is, however, very effective on the opposite side, where he can cut inside to put defences under great pressure, and has a stunning shot that the fans would love to see more of. One such instance, in November, saw him unleash a 20-yard right footer that won the match at Burnley.

Brighton & Hove A (Signed from Kilkenny on 5/3/91 - Free to Longford T in May 1992)
Millwall (£15,000 on 27/5/94) FL 104+26/6 FLC 11/2 FAC 6+2/2 Others 2/1

Robbie Savage

SAVAGE Robert (Robbie) William
Born: Wrexham, 18 October 1974
Height: 5'11" Weight: 10.7
Club Honours: FAYC '92
International Honours: W: 9; U21-5; Yth; Sch

A right-footed midfielder, or wing back, who is full of energy and self confidence, Robbie signed from Crewe in July 1997 and started last season on Leicester's bench, before forcing his way into the starting line-up with a series of committed performances. Converted successfully to the right-wing-back role, where his attacking qualities were able to be given full rein, he opened his account for the club with a rasping 25 yarder

into the top corner at the Dell, and added to his repertoire by rounding the 'keeper to score in the FA Cup tie against Northampton. Also established himself in the Welsh team during 1997-98, scoring against Turkey.

Manchester U (From trainee on 5/7/93)
Crewe Alex (Free on 22/7/94) FL 74+3/10 FLC 5 FAC 5 Others 8/1
Leicester C (£400,000 on 23/7/97) PL 28+7/2 FLC 1 FAC 2/1 Others 0+1

SAVILLE Andrew (Andy) Victor
Born: Hull, 12 December 1964
Height: 6'0" Weight: 12.13
Club Honours: Div 3 '96

Faced with heavy competition for forward places at Wigan, the rugged, shaven-headed centre forward faded out of the picture after making just six subs' appearances, and signed for Cardiff at the end of last October, City finally ending their long quest for a striker, following injuries to Kevin Nugent and Carl Dale. After a spell in Wigan Reserves, Andy looked out of touch and struggled to produce his best, but he improved gradually, though, and proved his doubters wrong by really turning on the form, following the arrival of manager, Frank Burrows, in February, scoring all three goals in a 3-3 draw at Scunthorpe. Has a two-year contract with Cardiff City and seems to be thriving under Burrows, leading the line well, bringing midfield players into the action, and scoring goals, 13 of them to be precise.

Hull C (Signed on 23/9/83) FL 74+27/18 FLC 6/1 FAC 3+2/1 Others 4+2
Walsall (£100,000 on 23/3/89) FL 28+10/5 FLC 2 Others 1+1
Barnsley (£80,000 on 9/3/90) FL 71+11/21 FLC 5+1 FAC 2+1 Others 4/1
Hartlepool U (£60,000 on 13/3/92) FL 37/14 FLC 4/1 FAC 4/5 Others 3/1
Birmingham C (£155,000 on 22/3/93) FL 51+8/17 FLC 4/1 FAC 1 Others 1
Burnley (Loaned on 30/12/94) FL 3+1/1 FAC 1
Preston NE (£100,000 on 29/7/95) FL 56/30 FLC 6 FAC 2 Others 2/1
Wigan Ath (£125,000 on 25/10/96) FL 17+8/4 FLC 0+1 FAC 1 Others 1
Cardiff C (£75,000 on 31/10/97) FL 32+1/11 FAC 4+1/2

SAWYERS Robert (Rob)
Born: Dudley, 20 November 1978
Height: 5'10" Weight: 11.3

Formerly a trainee at Wolves, Rob signed for Barnet last October, having failed to be offered professional terms at Molineux, and made his first team debut in the Auto Windscreens competition. Appearing once more, this time in the league, and acquitting himself well, he is predominantly a left-wing back who is pacy, can dribble, and has a good left foot.

Barnet (Free from Wolverhampton W juniors on 22/10/97) FL 1 Others 1

SCALES John Robert
Born: Harrogate, 4 July 1966
Height: 6'2" Weight: 13.5
Club Honours: FAC '88; FLC '95
International Honours: E: 3; B-2

In what had promised to be an exciting season for John, who had put himself back

into the reckoning for an England spot under Glenn Hoddle, apart from a dozen games, Tottenham fans were deprived through injury in 1997-98 of the great aerial ability and precision passing which had made him a favourite at Wimbledon and Liverpool alike. His sheer presence is enough to lift any team, and his self confidence is sure to be instrumental in his comeback this coming term. At his best, a pacy central defender with the build of an athlete, he can play across most defensive positions, is powerful in the air, has two good feet, and is dangerous at set plays.

Bristol Rov (Free from Leeds U juniors on 11/7/85) FL 68+4/2 FLC 3 FAC 6 Others 3+1
Wimbledon (£70,000 on 16/7/87) F/PL 235+5/11 FLC 18+1 FAC 20+1 Others 7+1/4
Liverpool (£3,500,000 on 2/9/94) PL 65/2 FLC 10/2 FAC 14 Others 4+1
Tottenham H (£2,600,000 on 11/12/96) PL 19+3 FLC 2

SCHMEICHEL Peter Boleslaw
Born: Gladsaxe, Denmark, 18 November 1963
Height: 6'4" Weight: 16.0
Club Honours: ESC '91; FLC '92; PL '93, '94, '96, '97; FAC '94, '96; CS '93, '94, '96, '97
International Honours: Denmark (UEFAC '92): 104

A highly influential Manchester United goalkeeper with great presence, Peter made history on two counts during the course of 1997-98. Having first blanked out Coventry at Old Trafford in United's fifth game of the season, it registering the best-ever start by a Reds' defence since Newton Heath entered the old-style Football League 105 years earlier, and against Derby in February, he became the first goalkeeper to keep 100 clean sheets since the Premiership kicked off in August 1992. His achievements certainly impressed his team-mate, Gary Pallister, who said: "Peter Schmeichel is the best in the world bar none," whilst former United legend, George Best, added: "Peter is up there with the greats. I have seen them all starting with Lev Yashin." Although now one of the elder members of the side at 34, he remains an unmoveable force in the team and, made captain in the absence Roy Keane, he missed only two Premiership games before the turn of the year, against Everton and Coventry. However, an injury against Arsenal in March meant that he was an absentee from United's vital European Cup tie with Monaco in the following game. Although picking out outstanding individual performances during the course of the season is always difficult in Peter's case, he played an inspired role against Juventus in the Champions' League game in Italy, and against Newcastle at St James' Park in the Premiership in December. The only mute point was his lack of a first team goal. Well he does normally score one a season! *Stop Press:* Ever present in all five of Denmark's World Cup games during the summer, he played his 100th international against Saudi Arabia before the side went out of the competition at the hands of Brazil.

Manchester U (£550,000 from Brondby on 12/8/91) F/PL 258 FLC 17 FAC 33 Others 34/1

SCHOFIELD John David
Born: Barnsley, 16 May 1965
Height: 5'11" Weight: 11.8

Signed from Doncaster immediately prior to the start of last season, this strong player was disappointing in Mansfield's midfield during the early stages of 1997-98, but following the injury to Stuart Watkiss he was moved into the heart of defence and finished the campaign in outstanding form. Twice had to deputise in goal, and even there did not concede a goal.

Lincoln C (Free from Gainsborough Trinity on 10/11/88) FL 221+10/11 FLC 15/2 FAC 5+2 Others 13+1
Doncaster Rov (Free on 18/11/94) FL 107+3/12 FLC 4 FAC 2 Others 3
Mansfield T (£10,000 on 8/8/97) FL 44 FLC 2 FAC 2 Others 2

John Schofield

SCHOLES Paul
Born: Salford, 16 November 1974
Height: 5'7" Weight: 11.0
Club Honours: PL '96, '97; FAC '96; CS '96, '97
International Honours: E: 11; Yth (UEFAC '93)

A prolific goalscorer who can play as an out-and-out striker, or in central midfield for Manchester United, Paul certainly came of age on the international front even before the 1997-98 campaign began. Elevated to full England status by Glenn Hoddle at the end of the previous campaign, he scored against Italy in Turin on his debut, then found the net again whilst making his World Cup debut against Moldova at Wembley in August. Although the signing of Teddy Sheringham in the summer appeared to bar his way to a permanent place in United's starting line-up, he actually played alongside him for most of the season, apart from three short spells out of the side at the turn of the year. Always a danger in front of goal,

his most prolific scoring spell came during September and November, when he averaged a goal every three games. His most notable strikes coming in the Champions' League against Juventus and Feyenoord. Awarded the prestigious Manchester Evening News – Boddington's Bitter Sports Personality of the Year trophy in January, a persistent knee problem, which he aggravated in the vital European Cup quarter final against Monaco at Old Trafford in March, appeared to have ended his season. But, having made a remarkable recovery, he came back to score the vital winner against Blackburn in the Premiership in March and was looking forward to France '98 as the campaign came to a close. *Stop Ptess:* Man of the Match for England in their opening World Cup game against Tunisia, scoring the second goal in a 2-0 win, he played in all four games before the side went out of the competition on penalties.

Manchester U (From trainee on 29/1/93) PL 66+32/26 FLC 6+1/5 FAC 5+3/3 Others 9+8/3

SCHREUDER Jan-Dirk (Dick)
Born: Holland, 2 August 1971
Height: 5'8" Weight: 11.5

A Dutch U21 international spotted by Chic Bates on an end of season scouting mission in Holland, he was signed by Stoke under the Bosman ruling in the 1997 close season and the club management clearly had high hopes for his midfield abilities. Unfortunately, his early season form lacked promise, while a recurring ankle injury ruled him out of contention for the first half of the campaign, and he returned to Holland for an operation. Although he came back he was unable to regain fitness, being transfer listed without response in January, and freed during the summer.

Stoke C (Free from RKC Waalwijk on 4/7/97) FLC 0+2

SCHWARZER Mark
Born: Sydney, Australia, 6 October 1972
Height: 6'5" Weight: 13.6
International Honours: Australia: 4

With just under 14 stones contained in his cat-like 6'5" frame, Mark has all of the attributes of the legendary 'keepers who have won the adulation of soccer fans everywhere by their bravery and contempt for the flying boot. If goalies have to be crazy then here is the epitome of madness. Fortunately, his "madness" is tempered with intelligence and calculated risk, concluding usually with a clean, calm, and clinical collection of the ball, followed by swift and efficient distribution to a colleague, thus launching a counter attack to present the opposition with defensive problems of their own. The Australian is a great crowd pleaser, and much loved by the faithful, who look forward with great anticipation to the coming examination of his ability by the finest sharp-shooters in the Premiership.

Bradford C (£350,000 from Kaiserslautern on 22/11/96) FL 13 FAC 3
Middlesbrough (£1,500,000 on 26/2/97) F/PL 42 FLC 10 FAC 3

SCIMECA Riccardo
Born: Leamington Spa, 13 June 1975
Height: 6'1" Weight: 12.9
Club Honours: FLC '96
International Honours: E: B-1; U21-9

A highly versatile player, Riccardo not only played in the centre of Aston Villa's defence in 1997-98, but also performed in a wing-back role and in midfield. One of the highlights for him was when making his full European debut against Athletico Bilbao, before a head injury suffered against West Ham in November, ended a sequence of ten successive starts and the longest run of first team games chalked up thus far. Unfortunately, after returning to the side on Boxing Day, and appearing in 11 out of 13 games, a hamstring injury put him on the sidelines for five weeks and when he came back as a sub for three games, the same injury re-occurred to put him out of action for the campaign. On the international front, he regained the captaincy of the England U21 side, playing in several European qualifying games, and was also selected for England "B" against Chile.

Aston Villa (From trainee on 7/7/93) PL 34+21 FLC 3+3 FAC 7+1 Others 4

Riccardo Scimeca

SCOTT Andrew (Andy)
Born: Epsom, 2 August 1972
Height: 6'1" Weight: 11.5

Signed from Sheffield United last November, the tall, stylish Brentford striker lashed home an unstoppable right-foot shot on his debut at Oldham to secure the Bees a point. Although finding it difficult to establish himself as a force up front in a struggling team, he produced another super performance in the return match against Oldham in March, when, firstly, he clinically converted a Scott Canham through ball and, secondly, he beat his marker before

making an inch perfect cross for Robert Taylor to score the clincher. Is the brother of Fulham's Rob.

Sheffield U (£50,000 from Sutton U on 1/12/92) P/FL 39+36/6 FLC 5/2 FAC 2+1 Others 3+1/3
Chesterfield (Loaned on 18/10/96) FL 4+1/3
Bury (Loaned on 21/3/97) FL 2+6
Brentford (£75,000 on 21/11/97) FL 24+2/5 Others 1

SCOTT Andrew (Andy) Michael
Born: Manchester, 27 June 1975
Height: 6'0" Weight: 12.11

Released by Cardiff during the 1997 close season, having suffered a whole range of injuries during his two-year stay at Ninian Park, and failing to do himself justice, he signed on with Rochdale immediately prior to the start of 1997-98 and came on a as a sub in the opening game. Although given a year's contract, he was unable to reach full match fitness thereafter, and it was not until the second half of the campaign that he made his only full appearance, at left back, followed by another from the bench, before being freed during the summer.

Blackburn Rov (From trainee on 4/1/93)
Cardiff C (Free on 9/8/94) FL 14+2/1 FLC 0+1 FAC 1 Others 1
Rochdale (Free on 8/8/97) FL 1+2

SCOTT Gary Craig
Born: Liverpool, 3 February 1978
Height: 5'8" Weight: 11.2

Having been released by Tranmere during the 1997 close season, without a first team game under his belt, he joined Rotherham and became yet another United player who did not have the best of luck, twice suffering injuries after making it into the league. However, this right-wing back should get more opportunities in the near future, and could well make the position his own.

Tranmere Rov (From trainee on 18/10/95)
Rotherham U (Free on 7/8/97) FL 6+1 FAC 1 Others 1

SCOTT Keith
Born: Westminster, 9 June 1967
Height: 6'3" Weight: 14.3
Club Honours: GMVC '93; FAT '93

A big, strong target man for Wycombe Wanderers, Keith was signed on a permanent basis from Norwich in the summer of 1997, following up a loan period at the end of 1996-97. Normally injury free, he had four spells out of the team with knocks, two of these being picked up on the training ground, one of which turned his elbow septic. In spite of that, he still managed 12 goals in 30 starts, and remained a handful for any defence, being excellent at holding off challenges, and strong in the air where he puts defenders under pressure. His most memorable goal was a superb right-footed snap shot on the turn, at home to Plymouth.

Lincoln C (Free from Leicester U on 22/3/90) FL 7+9/2 FLC 0+1 Others 1+1
Wycombe W (£30,000 in March 1991) FL 15/10 FLC 4/2 FAC 6/1 Others 2/2
Swindon T (£375,000 on 18/11/93) P/FL 43+8/12 FLC 5/3 Others 3/1
Stoke C (£300,000 on 30/12/94) FL 22+3/3 FAC 2/1 Others 0+1

Norwich C (Signed on 11/11/95) FL 10+15/5 FLC 0+2 FAC 0+2
Bournemouth (Loaned on 16/2/96) FL 8/1
Watford (Loaned on 7/2/97) FL 6/2 Others 2
Wycombe W (£55,000 on 27/3/97) FL 37+1/14 FLC 1/1 FAC 2 Others 0+1

Keith Scott

SCOTT Kevin Watson
Born: Easington, 17 December 1966
Height: 6'3" Weight: 14.5
Club Honours: FAYC '85; Div 1 '93

Having formed a formidable central defensive partnership with Matt Jackson during Norwich's best period in 1997-98, the giant centre back unfortunately fell victim to the club's injury jinx when his knee required surgery in February. Solid and reliable, strong in the air and on the ground, with the ability to come out with the ball, Kevin was back for the last four games as the club successfully pulled away from the relegation zone. Is particularly dangerous at set plays.

Newcastle U (From apprentice on 19/12/84) F/PL 227/8 FLC 18 FAC 15+1/1 Others 12+1/2
Tottenham H (£850,000 on 1/2/94) PL 16+2/1 FLC 0+1
Port Vale (Loaned on 13/1/95) FL 17/1
Charlton Ath (Loaned on 20/12/96) FL 4
Norwich C (£250,000 on 21/1/97) FL 31+2 FLC 1 FAC 1

SCOTT Martin
Born: Sheffield, 7 January 1968
Height: 5'9" Weight: 11.7
Club Honours: Div 4 '89; Div 1 '96

The popular Sunderland left back began last season as the club's first choice but, following injury, he returned to find Michael Gray in superb form and played just 11 games in all. "Scotty" is still highly thought of at the Stadium of Light for his over-lapping, attacking wing play, but it remains to be seen whether or not he will be able to displace his rival in 1998-99, as the side once again eyes the Premiership. Capable of

scoring important goals and dangerous at free kicks.

Rotherham U (From apprentice on 10/1/86) FL 93+1/3 FLC 11/2 FAC 7+2 Others 7/2
Bristol C (£200,000 on 5/12/90) FL 171/14 FLC 10/1 FAC 10 Others 8/1
Sunderland (£750,000 on 23/12/94) P/FL 90/7 FLC 8/1 FAC 5

SCOTT Richard Paul
Born: Dudley, 29 September 1974
Height: 5'9" Weight: 12.8

A hard-working, right-sided Shrewsbury midfielder, who can also play at full back, Richard was not always an automatic choice early last season but he set about successfully winning a regular place after the turn of the year. Very effective when moving forward through the middle, he has a good eye for the net, finding it on ten occasions, many through spectacular shots or moving through the defence quickly to beat the 'keeper one on one. Times his runs to perfection.

Birmingham C (From trainee on 17/5/93) FL 11+1 FLC 3+1 Others 3
Shrewsbury T (Signed on 22/3/95) FL 91+14/18 FLC 6 FAC 8+1/3 Others 8+1/1

SCOTT Robert (Rob)
Born: Epsom, 15 August 1973
Height: 6'1" Weight: 11.10

Rob, whose long throws and nine league goals helped Fulham win promotion in 1996-97 was very much a fringe player last season, playing a dozen reserve games and starting only ten times in the first team. With a lack of match practice, he also seemed to have lost the extra yard of pace which took him into dangerous positions but, hopefully, this will return with regular football.

Sheffield U (£20,000 from Sutton U on 1/8/93) FL 2+4/1 FLC 0+1 Others 2+1
Scarborough (Loaned on 22/3/95) FL 8/3
Northampton T (Loaned on 24/11/95) FL 5 Others 1
Fulham (£30,000 on 10/1/96) FL 63+18/17 FLC 3+5 FAC 3/1 Others 2+2/1

SCOWCROFT James (Jamie) Benjamin
Born: Bury St Edmunds, 15 November 1975
Height: 6'1" Weight: 12.2
International Honours: E: U21-5

1997-98 was rather a mixed season for Jamie, having started it as Ipswich's main striker because of Alex Mathie's injuries, he ended it on the bench because of Mathie's form! In between, he was badly injured at Norwich and was carried from the field in a neck brace, being paralysed down one side. Although recovering completely within a few days, later in the season he tore a cartilage in his knee which required surgery. His main problem, however, was caused by suspensions for a sending off and bookings, because it was while he was sidelined that the David Johnson-Mathie partnership blossomed and, when he was ready to return, he could not get back in the side. This lack of regular first team football ultimately affected his international call ups, although he was asked to join the England "B" squad for the Chile game, appeared for

the U21s against Greece, and also played for the Nationwide League team.

Ipswich T (From trainee on 1/7/94) FL 72+23/17 FLC 11+1/2 FAC 7 Others 3+4/1

SCULLY Anthony (Tony) Derek Thomas
Born: Dublin, 12 June 1976
Height: 5'7" Weight: 11.12
International Honours: Ei: U21-10; Yth; Sch

Having moved to Manchester City from Crystal Palace in time for the start of 1997-98, Tony found to his cost that City had no real need for an out-and-out left-sided wingman and, following nine appearances, of which eight were as a sub, he was loaned to Stoke at the end of January. Spotted by Chris Kamara in City's reserve side, he went straight into the team at Stoke and showed impressive form in seven games before returning to Maine Road. With his contract up for grabs during the coming summer, he moved to Queens Park Rangers in March, making his debut at Stoke, and went on to play for the rest of the season, except the away game at Manchester City, due to a contract restriction imposed when signing. At his best when running at defenders, Tony could prove to be a great acquisition for Rangers. Continued to add to his Republic of Ireland U21 appearances.

Crystal Palace (From trainee on 2/12/93) FL 0+3
Bournemouth (Loaned on 14/10/94) FL 6+4 Others 2
Cardiff C (Loaned on 5/1/96) FL 13+1
Manchester C (£80,000 on 12/8/97) FL 1+8
Stoke C (Loaned on 27/1/98) FL 7
Queens Park R (£155,000 on 17/3/98) FL 7

SEABURY Kevin
Born: Shrewsbury, 24 November 1973
Height: 5'9" Weight: 11.11

A right-sided versatile defender, this local lad has now played in excess of 140 games for Shrewsbury and made the full-back spot his own last season. A very popular player with the fans, he has an uncanny knack of turning up on the goal line to make countless last-ditch clearances. Is equally happy defending or joining the attack and was delighted to score his first ever league goal in 1997-98.

Shrewsbury T (From trainee on 6/7/92) FL 122+20/2 FLC 6+2/1 FAC 8 Others 7+2

SEAGRAVES Mark
Born: Bootle, 22 October 1966
Height: 6'0" Weight: 13.12
Club Honours: Div 2 '96
International Honours: E: Yth

Swindon Town's vastly experienced club captain had a torrid 1997-98 season, despite beginning the campaign in good form, striking up an excellent partnership with Alan McDonald, and playing the opening seven games. But shortly afterwards a long-term pelvic injury was diagnosed and needed three month's complete rest. The centre back's hopes of a comeback were then dashed by a calf strain and finally a knee problem, which eventually required surgery. A wonderful ambassador for the club off the field, it was with much regret that Steve McMahon told his fellow scouser that he was to be released in the summer.

Liverpool (From apprentice on 4/11/83) FLC 1 FAC 1
Norwich C (Loaned on 21/11/86) FL 3
Manchester C (£100,000 on 25/9/87) FL 36+6 FLC 3 FAC 3 Others 2
Bolton W (£100,000 on 24/9/90) FL 152+5/7 FLC 8 FAC 17/1 Others 13/1
Swindon T (£100,000 on 6/6/95) FL 57+4 FLC 10+1 FAC 4+1 Others 2

SEAL David
Born: Penrith, Australia, 26 January 1972
Height: 5'11" Weight: 12.4

An out-and-out enthusiastic striker who joined Northampton on loan from Bristol City last August, and by October had signed for a club record fee, David showed that he had the knack of being in the right place at the right time, starting the season with seven goals in nine games. Although the goals dried up and his appearances became fewer, he had already become a firm favourite with the fans, and is still very much part of the Town set up.

Bristol C (£80,000 from Aalst on 7/10/94) FL 24+27/10 FLC 4+1/3 FAC 1+1 Others 2+1/1
Northampton T (£90,000 on 11/8/97) FL 30+7/12 FLC 2/1 FAC 2+1/1 Others 1+3

David Seaman

SEAMAN David Andrew
Born: Rotherham, 19 September 1963
Height: 6'4" Weight: 14.10
Club Honours: Div 1 '91; PL '98; FAC '93, '98; FLC '93; ECWC '94
International Honours: E: 44; B-6; U21-10

Having had somewhat of a roller coaster ride earlier on in 1997-98, seeming to not be his old self in Arsenal's goal as the Gunners slipped up here and there, conceding a few soft goals, he was put out of action in mid-January after suffering a broken finger during the 2-2- draw at Coventry. Came back refreshed at the end of March and although young Alex Manninger had done exceptionally well in his absence, keeping

Manchester United at bay at Old Trafford just two weeks earlier, he stepped straight back into the side, keeping eight clean sheets in 11 games, as the Gunners marched to both the Premiership title and the FA Cup, when beating Newcastle 2-0 at Wembley, to seal an amazing season. He also secured his England place in readiness for the World Cup Finals to be held in France during the summer, despite playing in just four of the previous nine fixtures. *Stop Press:* Appeared in all four games in France '98, before a ten-men England were beaten on penalties by Argentina after David had saved one of the five taken, having earlier been booked for bringing down Diego Simeone for a dubious fifth-minute penalty that was converted by Gabriel Batistuta.

Leeds U (From apprentice on 22/9/81)
Peterborough U (£4,000 on 13/8/82) FL 91 FLC 10 FAC 5
Birmingham C (£100,000 on 5/10/84) FL 75 FLC 4 FAC 5
Queens Park R (£225,000 on 7/8/86) FL 141 FLC 13 FAC 17 Others 4
Arsenal (£1,300,000 on 18/5/90) F/PL 280 FLC 31 FAC 36 Others 30

SEARLE Damon Peter
Born: Cardiff, 26 October 1971
Height: 5'11" Weight: 10.4
Club Honours: WC '92, '93; Div 3 '93
International Honours: W: B-1; U21-6; Yth

The former Welsh "B" and U21 international continued his return to form after claiming the left-back berth at Stockport for long stretches of last season, despite strong competition from Colin Woodthorpe. More of an attacking player than out-and-out defender, his jinking runs from a wing-back position took him closer to the hearts of the fans as he set up chances for others.*

Cardiff C (From trainee on 20/8/90) FL 232+2/3 FLC 9/1 FAC 13 Others 29
Stockport Co (Free on 28/5/96) FL 34+7 FLC 2+1 FAC 2 Others 1

SEARLE Stephen (Stevie)
Born: Lambeth, 7 March 1977
Height: 5'10" Weight: 11.2

Signed from non-league Sittingbourne immediately prior to the start of 1997-98, Stevie became a bigger influence as the season went on, after making his first team debut in the seventh game against Swansea, when coming off the bench. A creative, attacking midfielder who likes the ball on the ground and is a good passer, he has a big future ahead of him.

Barnet (Free from Sittingbourne on 1/8/97) FL 26+4/2 FAC 1 Others 3

SEDGEMORE Benjamin (Ben) Redwood
Born: Wolverhampton, 5 August 1975
Height: 5'11" Weight: 12.10
International Honours: E: Sch

Having started last season with Mansfield, the big, talented midfielder, whose enthusiasm is infectious, transferred to Macclesfield just before deadline day and made an immediate impact on the team. Unfortunately, he was sent off on his third appearance for getting involved in an ugly

incident in the match against Lincoln, but came back strongly as Town stepped up the pace for a crack at second division football in 1998-99.

Birmingham C (From trainee on 17/5/93)
Northampton T (Loaned on 22/12/94) FL 1
Mansfield T (Loaned on 25/8/95) FL 4+5 Others 1
Peterborough U (Free on 10/1/96) FL 13+4 FAC 1
Mansfield T (Free on 6/9/96) FL 58+9/6 FLC 1 FAC 2+1 Others 2
Macclesfield T (£25,000 on 19/3/98) FL 5

SEDGLEY Stephen (Steve) Philip
Born: Enfield, 26 May 1968
Height: 6'1" Weight: 13.13
Club Honours: FAC '91
International Honours: E: U21-11

Arriving at Wolves from Ipswich during the 1997 close season, in exchange for Mark Venus and cash, being seen mainly as a midfielder, the versatile left-footed player was immediately required to form a central defensive partnership with Keith Curle. He was doing very well until the sixth game, when he limped off and had to have an operation to remove a small piece of bone in his knee, missing 18 matches. After making a confident return at Maine Road, he then got sent off at Portsmouth, before being plagued by a foot injury, a London specialist having to be consulted. Played well in the FA Cup semi final, despite a lapse of concentration that resulted in the Arsenal goal, and was then unluckily dismissed against Manchester City, to continue his season of interruptions.

Coventry C (From apprentice on 2/6/86) FL 81+3/3 FLC 9/2 FAC 2+2 Others 5+1
Tottenham H (£750,000 on 28/7/89) F/PL 147+17/8 FLC 24+3/1 FAC 22+1/1 Others 5+3
Ipswich T (£1,000,000 on 15/6/94) P/FL 105/15 FLC 10/2 FAC 5 Others 1
Wolverhampton W (£700,000 on 29/7/97) FL 18+1 FLC 2 FAC 6

SEDGWICK Christopher (Chris) Edward
Born: Sheffield, 28 April 1980
Height: 5'11" Weight: 10.10

As a Rotherham youngster, Chris showed outstanding promise as a winger of the future, with his ability to run at defences and supply good crosses. Unfortunately, just as he looked as if he might break into the first team on a regular basis in 1997-98, he suffered an ankle injury at the end of October, which kept him out for the rest of the season.

Rotherham U (From trainee on 16/8/97) FL 0+4 FLC 0+1

SEDLAN Jason Mark
Born: Peterborough, 5 August 1979
Height: 5'9" Weight: 11.2

Still a trainee, the young attacking midfielder was called up by Mansfield for the final game of last season against Swansea, and given nine minutes of first team experience when coming off the bench. A strong runner with skill, who looks to probe defences, Jason, who has scored a fair amount of goals for the youth team from midfield, has been offered a professional contract for this coming term.

Mansfield T (Trainee) FL 0+1

SEDLOSKI Goce
Born: Macedonia, 10 April 1974
Height: 6'1" Weight: 13.3
International Honours: Macedonia: 14

This big, powerful Macedonian international central defender was signed by Sheffield Wednesday from the Croatian club, Hadjuk Split, last March, after a trial period, with the possibility that his transfer fee might rise to £1 million depending on appearances. He quickly made his Premiership debut at Bolton, when coming off the bench, and followed that up with three starts, including a visit to Arsenal, before a cartilage injury suffered earlier forced him on to the sidelines. It was such a shame, because having come into a shaky defence, he had looked strong, even if lacking a little in sharpness, and appeared to be exactly what the Owls were looking for. Will be lucky to be back in time for the start of 1998-99.

Sheffield Wed (£750,000+ from Hadjuk Split on 13/3/98) PL 3+1

SEGERS Johannes (Hans)
Born: Eindhoven, Holland, 30 October 1961
Height: 5'11" Weight: 12.12

This goalkeeper's off-the-field problems have been well publicised, and having been on Wolves' staff during 1996-97 he finally got his chance in March 1998, when Mike Stowell was ill. The agility of the Dutchman made up for his lack of height and he kept his place for the FA Cup quarter final, making a penalty save in the closing minutes to ensure the club went through. Showed his quality when stopping another penalty the following week against Crewe. Was freed during the summer.

Nottingham F (£50,000 from PSV Eindhoven on 14/8/84) FL 58 FLC 4 FAC 5
Stoke C (Loaned on 13/2/87) FL 1
Sheffield U (Loaned on 19/11/87) FL 10 Others 1
Dunfermline Ath (Loaned on 1/3/88) SL 4
Wimbledon (£180,000 on 28/9/88) F/PL 265+2 FLC 26 FAC 22 Others 7
Wolverhampton W (Free on 30/8/96) FL 11 FAC 2

SEGURA Victor Abascal
Born: Zaragoza, Spain, 30 March 1973
Height: 6'0" Weight: 12.3

Signed from the Spanish side, Lleida, immediately prior to the start of 1997-98, Victor spent much of the season at Norwich playing out of position, but when appearing in his favoured central defensive role he looked far more comfortable and assured. Made his Football League debut on the opening day at Carrow Road against Wolves and, as a whole, apart from falling foul of officialdom and suffering two spells of suspension, the former Spanish U21 international adapted well to the English game.

Norwich C (Free from Lleida on 2/8/97) FL 22+3 FLC 2 FAC 1

SELLARS Scott
Born: Sheffield, 27 November 1965
Height: 5'8" Weight: 10.0
Club Honours: FMC '87; Div 1 '93, '97
International Honours: E: U21-3

An inspirational left-sided Bolton midfielder who missed the last three months of 1997-98 through injury, Scott had been one of the side's most effective players until that time, turning in a number of top-class performances. His mazy runs must make him a nightmare to play against, and he was part of a very effective midfield unit, along with Alan Thompson and Per Frandsen. He also pitches in with a fair amount of goals (despite last season's poor tally by his own standards of two), and will be sure to add to that when fit again. A fit Scott Sellars is a vital part of the Reebok set up.

Leeds U (From apprentice on 25/7/83) FL 72+4/12 FLC 4/1 FAC 4 Others 2/1
Blackburn Rov (£20,000 on 28/7/86) FL 194+8/35 FLC 12/3 FAC 11/1 Others 20/2
Leeds U (£800,000 on 1/7/92) PL 6+1 FLC 1+1 Others 1
Newcastle U (£700,000 on 9/3/93) F/PL 56+5/5 FLC 6+1/2 FAC 3 Others 4/1
Bolton W (£750,000 on 7/12/95) P/FL 84+2/13 FLC 6+1 FAC 4

SELLEY Ian
Born: Chertsey, 14 June 1974
Height: 5'9" Weight: 10.1
Club Honours: FLC '93; FAC '93; ECWC '94
International Honours: E: U21-3; Yth

What a miserable 1997-98 season Ian had. Having joined Fulham from Arsenal in October, the midfielder broke his leg badly in only his third game for the club against Northampton Town and, at this moment in time, seems unlikely that he will be able even to start 1998-99. And, having suffered a similar injury in February 1995, he must think there is a jinx on him. Obviously, Fulham have yet to see the best of him but as a man marker and a ball-winner, he will surely be a potent force at the Cottage when his recovery is complete.

Arsenal (From trainee on 6/5/92) PL 35+6 FLC 5+1 FAC 3 Others 8+2/2
Southend U (Loaned on 3/12/96) FL 3+1
Fulham (£500,000 on 17/10/97) FL 3

SEPP Dennis
Born: Appledoorn, Holland, 5 June 1973
Height: 5'11" Weight: 11.12

Signed on a free transfer from the Dutch second division side, HSC 21, where he was working in a bank during the week, Dennis arrived at Bradford during the 1997 close season looking to pick up where he had left off in Holland – scoring goals. Unfortunately, it was not to be as his 1997-98 campaign was ruined by injuries, his Football League debut not coming until he appeared as a sub in mid-February. In two more appearances from the bench, he was used in a left-wing role, showing plenty of speed, skill, and crossing ability.

Bradford C (Free from HSC 21 on 24/6/97) FL 0+3

SERRANT Carl
Born: Bradford, 12 September 1975
Height: 6'0" Weight: 11.2
International Honours: E: B-1; U21-2; Yth

1997-98 was another terrific season for the Oldham youngster, despite him missing 14

games due to a nasty knee injury. Valued highly by the club, this classy left back also impressed Glenn Hoddle so much so that he upgraded from the England U21 side to "B" international honours. Strong in the tackle, and reliable in the air, Carl's great asset is his lightning pace which allows him to recover rapidly and also to link with the midfield in setting up attacking situations. Definitely Premiership material this one. *Stop Press:* Out of contract, Carl signed for Newcastle on 7 July for a cut-price £500,000 to stop him from going abroad under the Bosman ruling.

Oldham Ath (From trainee on 22/7/94) FL 84+6/1 FLC 7 FAC 6/1 Others 3

SERTORI Mark Anthony
Born: Manchester, 1 September 1967
Height: 6'2" Weight: 14.2
Club Honours: GMVC '88

An ever-present in the Scunthorpe side until last March, Mark had a very good season with his no-nonsense style of defending making him a big crowd favourite. Switched to centre forward on a number of occasions during the campaign, he showed signs of being a good target man as he never stopped running, and showed improved ability on the ground. Ended the campaign disappointingly, with a back injury sidelining him for a while and then a red card forcing him to miss the closing two matches, before he was released during the summer.

Stockport Co (Signed from East Manchester on 7/2/87) FL 3+1 FLC 1
Lincoln C (Free on 1/7/88) FL 43+7/9 FLC 6 FAC 4/1 Others 5/2
Wrexham (£30,000 on 9/2/90) FL 106+4/3 FLC 8+1 FAC 6 Others 9+1
Bury (Free on 22/7/94) FL 4+9/1 FLC 1 FAC 2+1 Others 1+2/1
Scunthorpe U (Free on 22/7/96) FL 82+1/2 FLC 6 FAC 7 Others 4+1

SHAIL Mark Edward David
Born: Sandviken, Sweden, 15 October 1966
Height: 6'1" Weight: 13.3
International Honours: E: SP-1

Injury problems continued to disrupt this cool central defender's career in 1997-98, and he only managed two appearances for Bristol City before being sidelined yet again. At his best, authoritative, and reliable, whether the ball is in the air or on the ground, it is to be hoped that he will be fit for the challenge of division one soccer in the forthcoming campaign, as the reliance on this talented player is likely to be much required.

Bristol C (£45,000 from Yeovil on 25/3/93) FL 96+7/4 FLC 5+1 FAC 10/1 Others 4

SHAKESPEARE Craig Robert
Born: Birmingham, 26 October 1963
Height: 5'10" Weight: 13.6

Freed by Grimsby during the summer of 1997, Craig was expected to be a first team regular when he arrived at Scunthorpe, but a disappointing pre-season saw him start the campaign on the substitutes' bench. Got a chance in the starting line-up in mid-September, but only managed three starts before reverting back to the bench and being

loaned to Telford United on transfer deadline day until the end of the season. A solid midfielder with a good left foot, and passing ability, he still has another year to run of his contract at Glanford Park.

Walsall (From apprentice on 5/11/81) FL 276+8/45 FLC 31/6 FAC 22/6 Others 18/2
Sheffield Wed (£300,000 on 19/6/89) FL 15+2 FLC 3/1 Others 0+1
West Bromwich A (£275,000 on 8/2/90) FL 104+8/12 FLC 6/1 FAC 5/2 Others 5/1
Grimsby T (£115,000 on 14/7/93) FL 84+22/10 FLC 6+1 FAC 5+2 Others 0+1
Scunthorpe U (Free on 7/7/97) FL 3+1 FLC 1+2 FAC 0+1 Others 1

SHARP Kevin Phillip
Born: Ontario, Canada, 19 September 1974
Height: 5'9" Weight: 11.11
Club Honours: FAYC '93; Div 3 '97
International Honours: E: Yth (UEFAYC '93); Sch

A classy and dependable left back with vision, who is also a good tackler, Kevin enjoyed a solid season in 1997-98, despite feeling that he was often being made the scapegoat for some poor team performances, something which ultimately saw him ask for a transfer. Made 38 league appearances during the campaign and became a firm favourite with the fans who are desperate for him to stay at Springfield Park.

Leeds U (£60,000 from Auxerre on 20/10/92) PL 11+6 Others 0+1
Wigan Ath (£100,000 on 30/11/95) 84+9/8 FLC 2+1 FAC 3+1 Others 2+1

Paul Shaw

SHAW Paul
Born: Burnham, 4 September 1973
Height: 5'11" Weight: 12.4
International Honours: E: Yth

Signed during the 1997 close season from Arsenal, the striker proved to be well worth the fee paid by Millwall, scoring 13 goals to become the club's leading scorer in 1997-

98. At the same time, he showed a willingness to tackle back in order to both re-possess and allow his team mates to regroup. However, his tireless running that allowed him to get into great positions is his greatest asset and, coupled with his excellent first touch, could see him becoming a prolific scorer at this level.

Arsenal (From trainee on 18/9/91) PL 1+11/2 FAC 0+1
Burnley (Loaned on 23/3/95) FL 8+1/4
Cardiff C (Loaned on 11/8/95) FL 6
Peterborough U (Loaned on 20/10/95) FL 12/5 Others 2
Millwall (£250,000 on 15/9/97) FL 40/11 FLC 2/1 Others 2/1

SHAW Richard Edward
Born: Brentford, 11 September 1968
Height: 5'9" Weight: 12.8
Club Honours: FMC '91; Div 1 '94

The experienced Coventry defender was a regular in the centre of defence until last Christmas, when he made way for Gary Breen's return from suspension. Regained a place at right back against Chelsea away, but looked uncomfortable and, although Paul Williams' suspension gave him the opportunity to return to his normal position, he suffered a groin strain in the Villa Park cup tie and was out for a few games. A strong competitor, with a good turn of speed, he was prone to the occasional mistake, but on balance his all-round game was greatly improved last season.

Crystal Palace (From apprentice on 4/9/86) F/PL 193+14/3 FLC 28+2 FAC 18 Others 12+1
Hull C (Loaned on 14/12/89) FL 4
Coventry C (£1,000,000 on 17/11/95) PL 89 FLC 7 FAC 10

SHAW Simon Robert
Born: Middlesbrough, 21 September 1973
Height: 6'0" Weight: 12.0

As Darlington's longest-serving player, despite his young age, after spending his first three seasons at the club in midfield, Simon then held the right-back spot for the next three. A good passer, who is comfortable on the ball, and a tackler when the need be, he came back into the side to take over from Alan Gray towards the end of last September before giving way to the on-loan Ashley Fickling in March and being released during the summer.

Darlington (From trainee on 14/8/92) FL 144+32/12 FLC 5+1 FAC 10/2 Others 6+1

SHEARER Alan
Born: Newcastle, 13 August 1970
Height: 6'0" Weight: 12.6
Club Honours: PL '95
International Honours: E: 43; B-1; U21-11; Yth

After captaining England to victory in Le Tournoi in France in the summer of 1997, Alan was seriously injured in the pre-season Umbro international tournament, playing for Newcastle against Chelsea at Goodison Park. Stretching for a through ball in injury time, he fractured the fibula in his right ankle, ruptured the ligaments on both sides of the bone, and displaced the joint. It was a grave blow to both club and country, as witnessed by the column inches devoted to

the injury, and his recovery progress. His excellent scoring record is testament to his finishing, being clinical in close, spectacular from long range, two footed, and powerful in the air. His game is much more than just goals, however. His body strength is such that he can resist the most physical of challenges, holding up the ball before laying it off to colleagues, and he created space for others with intelligent use of the flanks, from where he crosses like an accomplished winger. He also inspires and lifts his team mates with his tremendous workrate and drive, his excellent attitude and temperament, his unselfishness, and his will to win. These same qualities, plus the fact that he is a hometown boy, have made him a hero on Tyneside. He returned to action after only 172 days absence, appearing as a substitute against Bolton in January, although the club later admitted that with hindsight he should have been given longer to recover. However, making his first full appearance eight days later in the FA Cup tie at Stevenage and scoring after 153 seconds, he played his part in taking his club to Wembley by netting five times on the way, including his first ever FA Cup brace in the Stevenage replay. Goals in the Premiership proved more elusive, but he did grab a late winner in the vital game against Barnsley on Easter Monday, and remains the Premiership's leading all-time goalscorer. Recalled to the England side, initially as substitute against Chile, he was then re-installed as captain against Switzerland, and he also captained his club when Robert Lee was absent. *Stop Press:* Playing in all four of England's World Cup games during the summer, a competition that ended in a penalty shoot-out defeat at the hands of Argentine, Alan started the ball rolling with the first goal in a 2-0 win over Tunisia, and scored a penalty against the "Argies", before coming home to recharge his batteries.

Southampton (From trainee on 14/4/88) FL 105+13/23 FLC 16+2/11 FAC 11+3/4 Others 8/5
Blackburn Rov (£3,600,000 on 24/7/92) PL 132+6/112 FLC 16/14 FAC 8/2 Others 9/2
Newcastle U (£15,000,000 on 30/7/96) PL 46+2/27 FLC 1/1 FAC 9/6 Others 5/1

SHEFFIELD Jonathan (Jon)
Born: Bedworth, 1 February 1969
Height: 5'11" Weight: 12.10
Signed in the 1997 close season from Peterborough, Jon proved an excellent asset to Plymouth as a strong and very agile goalkeeper, and superb shot-stopper. Played in every game throughout last season and remained extremely consistent, despite the lack of a genuine understudy to keep him on his toes.

Norwich C (From apprentice on 16/2/87) FL 1
Aldershot (Loaned on 22/9/89) FL 11 Others 1
Aldershot (Loaned on 21/8/90) FL 15 Others 1
Cambridge U (Free on 18/3/91) FL 56 FLC 3 FAC 4 Others 6
Colchester U (Loaned on 23/12/93) FL 6
Swindon T (Loaned on 28/1/94) PL 2
Hereford U (Loaned on 15/9/94) FL 8 FLC 2
Peterborough U (£150,000 on 20/7/95) FL 62 FLC 8 FAC 6 Others 5
Plymouth Arg (£100,000 on 28/7/97) FL 46 FLC 2 FAC 2 Others 1

SHELDON Gareth Richard
Born: Barnsley, 8 May 1980
Height: 5'11" Weight: 12.0
A young striker who made his Football League debut as a substitute in Scunthorpe's closing game of last season at Shrewsbury Town, Gareth arrived at Glanford Park on trial in September 1997 and scored a hat trick on his youth team debut to win a year's contract as a trainee. Very quick, with a liking to run at opponents, he will be looking for further first team opportunities this coming season.

Scunthorpe U (Trainee) FL 0+1

SHELIA Murtaz
Born: Tbilisi, Georgia, 25 March 1969
Height: 6'2" Weight: 13.6
International Honours: Georgia: 25
Despite arriving from Alana Vladikavkas last October, the big, strong Georgian defender had to wait until December for a work permit before he was able to get a game for Manchester City, but when it came he was quickly into action, scoring on his debut at Birmingham. Although elated to be heading in what he thought was the winner in the 88th minute, unfortunately, for him and City, the Brummies came back to score twice, deep into injury time. As a well-established Georgian international, he looked to be just what the doctor had ordered, but, having scored another goal, almost an identical one, against Nottingham Forest, the good times came to an end when a bad knee injury sustained at Maine Road against Oxford saw him sidelined until 1998-99. Badly missed, he might just have been the difference between first and second division football.

Manchester C (£400,000 from Alana Vladikavkas on 26/11/97) FL 12/2 FAC 2

SHELTON Andrew (Andy) Marc
Born: Sutton Coldfield, 19 June 1980
Height: 5'10" Weight: 12.0
As the son of Chester City assistant manager, Gary, Andy has progressed through the club's youth teams during the past couple of seasons, turning in some good performances in midfield on the way. Having made his Football League debut as a substitute against Colchester last April, and then coming off the bench in the last game of the campaign, versus Scarborough, he was offered a full-time contract for 1998-99.

Chester C (Trainee) FL 0+2

SHELTON Gary
Born: Nottingham, 21 March 1958
Height: 5'7" Weight: 11.2
International Honours: E: U21-1
As assistant manager to Kevin Ratcliffe at Chester, and still registered as a player last season, Gary made just three league appearances and, in doing so, became the oldest man to ever play for the club. At his best, a skilful midfield playmaker, it was a pity that he did not appear in the same side as his son, Andy, and equal another record held by the Herds, Alec (father) and David (son), who played for Stockport back in 1951-52.

Walsall (From apprentice on 1/3/76) FL 12+12 FLC 0+1 FAC 2+2/1
Aston Villa (£80,000 on 18/1/78) FL 24/7 FLC 2+1/1
Notts Co (Loaned on 13/3/80) FL 8
Sheffield Wed (£50,000 on 25/3/82) FL 195+3/18 FLC 19/3 FAC 23+1/3 Others 1
Oxford U (£150,000 on 24/7/87) FL 60+5/1 FLC 7+1/2 FAC 5 Others 1
Bristol C (Signed on 24/8/89) FL 149+1/24 FLC 12 FAC 9 Others 9/3
Rochdale (Loaned on 11/2/94) FL 3
Chester C (Free on 22/7/94) FL 62+7/6 FLC 4+1 FAC 3 Others 2/2

SHERIDAN Darren Stephen
Born: Manchester, 8 December 1967
Height: 5'5" Weight: 10.12
Although this combative midfielder was probably the best passer of the ball at Barnsley in 1997-98, he was yet another who found the Premier League a hard place to play. Yet he never gave less than 100 percent and, as one of the characters of the team, his infectiousness rubbed off to great effect on the rest of the players. Is the brother of Bolton's John, having followed him into the game via non-league football.

Barnsley (£10,000 from Winsford U on 12/8/93) F/PL 134+12/4 FLC 7+1/1 FAC 7+2 Others 1+1

SHERIDAN John Joseph
Born: Stretford, 1 October 1964
Height: 5'9" Weight: 12.0
Club Honours: FLC '91; Div 1 '97
International Honours: Ei: 34; B-1; U23-2; U21-2; Yth
Having missed the majority of 1997-98 through injury, his first appearance of a troubled season came in Bolton's 5-1 hammering at the hands of Coventry in January. Following on from that minor set-back, John figured prominently in the closing stages of the campaign, producing some sparkling performances which coincided with the club's change of league form. Although released during the summer, he must still be considered as one of the best passers of a ball in the game today, possessing a right foot capable of splitting the tightest of defences, and an awareness and ability to hold the ball for what seems like ages.

Leeds U (Free from Manchester C juniors on 2/3/82) FL 225+5/47 FLC 14/3 FAC 11+1/1 Others 11/1
Nottingham F (£650,000 on 3/8/89) FLC 1
Sheffield Wed (£500,000 on 3/11/89) F/PL 187+10/25 FLC 24/3 FAC 17+1/3 Others 4/2
Birmingham C (Loaned on 9/2/96) FL 1+1 FLC 2
Bolton W (£180,000 on 13/11/96) F/PL 24+8/2 FLC 2 FAC 2

SHERINGHAM Edward (Teddy) Paul
Born: Highams Park, 2 April 1966
Height: 5'11" Weight: 12.5
Club Honours: Div 2 '88; FMC '92; CS '97
International Honours: E: 35; U21-1; Yth
A natural goalscorer, who is widely acclaimed as the most intelligent striker in the Premiership, Teddy's arrival from Spurs in the summer of 1997, as a direct replacement for Eric Cantona, certainly raised a few eyebrows at Manchester

273

United. Despite missing a penalty against his former club, Spurs, on the opening day of the campaign, he notched his first goal in United's scintillating 2-0 win against Everton at Goodison Park in August and, although he managed to play in that game with cracked ribs, sustained at Leicester the week before, the injury prevented him from appearing in England's World Cup qualifying game against Moldova. A first team absentee during September, he came back with a vengeance, with goals in successive games against Juventus, Crystal Palace, and Derby, and continued his goalscoring spree during November, with double strikes in the Premiership against Sheffield Wednesday and Arsenal. After scoring his 11th goal of the campaign, in United's 5-3 victory over Chelsea in the FA Cup, he had another short lay off with injury problems, before returning to score two more against Barnsley in the FA Cup. Described by former teammate, Jurgen Klinsmann, as the best forward he has ever played with, Teddy was hoping to give Alan Shearer the same sort of star-studded service for England in the World Cup Finals during the summer. *Stop Press:* Sadly, though, following a well documented incident immediately prior to France '98, Teddy appeared out of sorts against Tunisia and Romania and was replaced by Michael Owen for the remainder of the competition.

Millwall (From apprentice on 19/1/84) FL 205+15/93 FLC 16+1/8 FAC 12/5 Others 11+2/5
Aldershot (Loaned on 1/2/85) FL 4+1 Others 1
Nottingham F (£2,000,000 on 23/7/91) FL 42/14 FLC 10/5 FAC 4/2 Others 6/2
Tottenham H (£2,100,000 on 28/8/92) PL 163+3/76 FLC 14/10 FAC 17/13
Manchester U (£3,500,000 on 1/7/97) PL 28+3/9 FAC 2+1/3 Others 8/2

SHERON Michael (Mike) Nigel
Born: Liverpool, 11 January 1972
Height: 5'10" Weight: 11.13
International Honours: E: U21-16

In transferring from Stoke during the 1997 close season, Mike became Queens Park Rangers' record signing, but then had to wait to make his debut, due to a back injury. Once fit, however, he came into the side at Reading, showing himself to be the striker that both the club and the fans expected, and his first goal came in the next game at home to West Bromwich Albion. Although he struggled with his form midway through the campaign, he finished strongly, scoring two important goals in the 2-2 draw at Sunderland and, more importantly, a goal to earn a vital point against his old club, Manchester City, in the penultimate game. A player with vision and skill to go with his sharpness around the box, he finished top scorer at Rangers with 11 goals.

Manchester C (From trainee on 5/7/90) F/PL 82+18/24 FLC 9+1/1 FAC 5+3/3 Others 1
Bury (Loaned on 28/3/91) FL 1+4/1 Others 2
Norwich C (£1,000,000 on 26/8/94) P/FL 19+9/2 FLC 6/3 FAC 4/2
Stoke C (£450,000 on 13/11/95) FL 64+5/34 FLC 4/5 FAC 1 Others 2
Queens Park R (£2,750,000 on 2/7/97) FL 36+4/11 FAC 2

Tim Sherwood

SHERWOOD Timothy (Tim) Alan
Born: St Albans, 6 February 1969
Height: 6'0" Weight: 12.9
Club Honours: PL '95
International Honours: E: B-1; U21-4

As captain and spokesman for the Blackburn team, Tim seldom failed to produce a highly energetic performance in 1997-98, as in previous seasons. And, as the one midfield fixture, he is also the one player from that area who gets forward enough to score, his

goal in the FA Cup at Sheffield Wednesday being a model of energy and desire. Although capable of constructive play, especially when making himself available and transferring possession quickly, he continues, in the main, to earn his place by his energy, self belief, and total commitment.

Watford (From trainee on 7/2/87) FL 23+9/2 FLC 4+1 FAC 9 Others 4+1
Norwich C (£175,000 on 18/7/89) FL 66+5/10 FLC 7/1 FAC 4 Others 5+1/2
Blackburn Rov (£500,000 on 12/2/92) F/PL 220+7/22 FLC 22+1/1 FAC 15+2/4 Others 10

SHIELDS Anthony (Tony) Gerald
Born: Londonderry, 4 June 1980
Height: 5'7" Weight: 10.10

A first-year trainee, Tony came on as substitute for Peterborough's final game of last season at home to Hartlepool, looking useful as a strong-running striker. He had earlier come to notice as a member of United's FA Youth Cup side that reached the semi-final stages before getting beaten by Blackburn, and playing on in that game after having stitches put in a head wound.

Peterborough U (Trainee) FL 0+1

SHILTON Samuel (Sam) Roger
Born: Nottingham, 21 July 1978
Height: 5'10" Weight: 11.6

The son of Peter Shilton, Sam, a left-sided midfield player who is tipped for a bright future, played a handful of games for Plymouth Argyle before he joined Coventry in October 1995. Finally made his City debut at home to Crystal Palace last season, but struggled with the pace of the game, before later playing at West Ham when injuries hit the club. Was a regular for the reserves and is sure to come again.

Plymouth Arg (Trainee) FL 1+2 FAC 0+1
Coventry C (£12,500 on 31/10/95) PL 2

Mike Sheron

SHIPPERLEY Neil Jason
Born: Chatham, 30 October 1974
Height: 6'1" Weight: 13.12
International Honours: E: U21-7

The former England U21 international striker started last season for Crystal Palace on the subs' bench before coming alive in a spell of six goals in eight games, forgetting the two he scored at West Ham before the floodlights failed. Unfortunately, he was then injured and out of action for three months, and although coming back the damage had been done. there was no doubt that Palace missed his goals, five of them having come in successive matches, and they probably missed his workrate, especially his chasing of lost causes and of harrying defenders into mistakes. The son of a former professional, Dave, who played for Charlton, Gillingham, and Reading in the 1970's, Neil packs a good shot in both feet and is always looking to test the 'keeper, something he is bound to be doing again this coming term.
Chelsea (From trainee on 24/9/92) PL 26+11/7 FLC 4+2/1 FAC 3/1 Others 2
Watford ((Loaned on 7/12/94) FL 5+1/1
Southampton (£1,250,000 on 6/1/95) PL 65+1/11 FLC 5+1/2 FAC 10/5
Crystal Palace (£1,000,000 on 25/10/96) F/PL 46+12/19 FLC 2 FAC 2 Others 3/1

SHIRTLIFF Peter Andrew
Born: Hoyland, 6 April 1961
Height: 6'2" Weight: 13.3
Club Honours: FLC '91

Early last season, the manager used the big central defender's experience at Premiership level to try and settle the rest of Barnsley's defence, but, after suffering a hamstring injury, his opportunities were very limited and he accepted a coaching role early on. Later, when Malcolm Shotton left to become manager of Oxford, Peter became coach of the reserves, thus bringing into play his near 20 years of professional football.
Sheffield Wed (From apprentice on 31/10/78) FL 188/4 FLC 17+1 FAC 17+1/1
Charlton Ath (£125,000 on 6/8/86) FL 102+1/7 FLC 10 FAC 5 Others 7/2
Sheffield Wed (£500,000 on 26/7/89) F/PL 104/4 FLC 18/1 FAC 9/2 Others 4
Wolverhampton W (£250,000 on 18/8/93) FL 67+2 FLC 4 FAC 7 Others 5
Barnsley (£125,000 on 25/8/95) F/PL 48+1 FLC 1 FAC 1
Carlisle U (Loaned on 25/10/96) FL 5

SHORT Christian (Chris) Mark
Born: Munster, Germany, 9 May 1970
Height: 5'10" Weight: 12.2
Club Honours: AIC '95

Chris was another Sheffield United defender whose season in 1997-98 was wrecked, first by the ankle injury which caused him to miss the previous season's play offs, and then by the good form of Vas Borbokis, managing only one substitute appearance in the Coca Cola Cup in the first part of the campaign, before coming back against Ipswich in the F A Cup match in January and being sent off. Although there were a further eight games for him, that was it for the tall and commanding centre back. *Stop Press:* Signed for Stoke under the Bosman ruling on 21 June.

Scarborough (Free from Pickering T on 11/7/88) FL 42+1/1 FLC 5 FAC 1 Others 3+1
Notts Co (£100,000 on 5/9/90) FL 77+17/2 FLC 7 FAC 4+1 Others 8+1/1
Huddersfield T (Loaned on 23/12/94) FL 6 Others 1
Sheffield U (Signed on 29/12/95) FL 40+4 FLC 3+1 FAC 7 Others 1+1

SHORT Craig Jonathan
Born: Bridlington, 25 June 1968
Height: 6'1" Weight: 13.8

A tall, commanding centre half, with the ability to bring the ball out of defence like a continental sweeper, Craig enjoyed his most consistent season in an Everton jersey in 1997-98. After starting on the substitutes' bench, he quickly reclaimed his place and was almost ever present from mid-October. Ironically, that run started following an infamous post-match disagreement with manager, Howard Kendall, on the pitch at Coventry, after a Coca Cola Cup mauling. The pair made up afterwards and he went on to become the defensive mainstay for the Blues.
Scarborough (Free from Pickering T on 15/10/87) FL 61+2/7 FLC 6 FAC 2 Others 7/1
Notts Co (£100,000 on 27/7/89) FL 128/6 FLC 6/1 FAC 8/1 Others 16/2
Derby Co (£2,500,000 on 18/9/92) FL 118/9 FLC 11 FAC 7/4 Others 7
Everton (£2,700,000 on 18/7/95) PL 68+9/4 FLC 5 FAC 4 Others 3

SHOWLER Paul
Born: Doncaster, 10 October 1966
Height: 5'7" Weight: 11.6
International Honours: E: SP-2

Injured throughout 1997-98, rumours of a return to first team action with Luton continued to circulate, but, apart from a 16-minute substitute appearance against Oldham, early on, the return never came as he failed to reach match fitness. His natural position as a left-sided midfielder, able to provide width on that flank, remained a problem for Town, who diced with relegation all season after making the play offs the previous term. Now apparently recovered, he was training throughout the summer in the hope of re-establishing himself in 1998-99.
Barnet (Free from Altrincham on 15/8/91) FL 69+2/12 FLC 2 FAC 3+1/1 Others 7
Bradford C (Free on 4/8/93) FL 72+16/15 FLC 8+1/5 FAC 6/2 Others 4+1
Luton T (£50,000 on 19/8/96) FL 21+3/6 FLC 3+1 FAC 3 Others 1+1

SHUTT Carl Steven
Born: Sheffield, 10 October 1961
Height: 5'10" Weight: 12.10
Club Honours: Div1 '90; Div 1 '92

The much experienced Darlington striker, cum midfielder made more subs' appearances in 1997-98 than he started games, but he continued to be a vital clubman, despite being 35 years of age. A hard-working player, who can still call on his pace to get away from the opposition, and who is still good in tight situations, his versatility knew no bounds last season, when twice coming off the bench to deputise for David Preece in the Quakers' goal and keeping clean sheets on both occasions.

Sheffield Wed (Free from Spalding on 13/5/85) FL 36+4/16 FLC 3/1 FAC 4+1/4
Bristol C (£55,000 on 30/10/87) FL 39+7/10 FLC 5+2/4 FAC 7+1/4 Others 10+1/4
Leeds U (£50,000 on 23/3/89) F/PL 46+33/17 FLC 6+2/2 FAC 10/1 Others 4+5/4
Birmingham C (£50,000 on 23/8/93) FL 18+8/4 FLC 3
Manchester C (Loaned on 31/12/93) PL 5+1
Bradford C (£75,000 on 11/8/94) FL 60+28/15 FLC 8+2/1 FAC 3+2 Others 5+2/1
Darlington (Signed on 27/3/97) FL 20+19/7 FLC 2 FAC 1+1

SHUTTLEWORTH Barry
Born: Accrington, 9 July 1977
Height: 5'8" Weight: 11.0

Signed from Bury during the 1997 close season, Barry appeared at left back or on the left wing on a regular basis for Rotherham's reserve team, but was unable to break through to Football league level and was restricted to just one start, that coming in the Auto Windscreens Shield. Was released during the summer.
Bury (From trainee on 5/7/95)
Rotherham U (Free on 1/8/97) FAC 0+1 Others 1

SIGURDSSON Larus Orri
Born: Akureyri, Iceland, 4 June 1973
Height: 6'0" Weight: 12.8
International Honours: Iceland: 16

By the very high standards he had set himself in the two previous seasons, Larus had a disappointing 1997-98 campaign and, as the Stoke captain, he was clearly unsettled by the club's problems both on and off the field of play. Admired by the supporters, he is good in the air, extremely quick, and has the skill to make further substantial progress, although he did seem to miss the presence of a strong partner in the heart of defence, such as an Ian Cranson or a Vince Overson. Showed his commitment to the challenge, when he flew back by private jet from international duty in Iceland to play 24 hours later in a derby game against Port Vale.
Stoke C (£150,000 from Thor on 21/10/94) FL 156+1/2 FLC 12 FAC 4+1 Others 4

SIMONSEN Steven (Steve) Preben
Born: South Shields, 3 April 1979
Height: 6'2" Weight: 12.8
International Honours: E: U21-1; Yth

Having kept goal for England U18s against Russia one Friday night last November, Steve found himself rushing back north to the Pulse Stadium to make his first team debut for Tranmere against Bradford City the following day. Third-choice 'keeper at the start of 1997-98, an injury to Danny Coyne and the sale of Eric Nixon to Stockport County, conspired to give Steve his chance, and he remained ever present until the end of the season. Made an immediate name for himself by keeping seven consecutive clean sheets, a feat never achieved by any Rovers' player before, and which set a new club record. Brave, athletic, and blessed with exceptional positional and distribution skills, Steve is now rated in the multi-million pound bracket. Particularly enjoyed playing in the FA Cup fourth round tie against his boyhood heroes, Sunderland.

Won his first England U21 cap when selected for the game against France, a 1-1 draw, in the end of season Toulon tournament.

Tranmere Rov (From trainee on 9/10/96) FL 30 FAC 3

Steve Simonsen

SIMPSON Colin Robertson
Born: Oxford, 30 April 1976
Height: 6'1" Weight: 11.5
Signed by Leyton Orient on a free transfer from Hendon last December, Colin had impressed everybody at the O's after scoring twice against them in the FA Cup. Having been rejected earlier in his career by Watford, the big, strong target man who made a goalscoring debut for the club at Shrewsbury, will be looking to become a regular in the team next season.

Watford (From trainee on 6/7/94) FL 0+1 (Free to Hendon during 1997 close season)
Leyton Orient (Free on 8/12/97) FL 9+5/3 Others 1+1

SIMPSON Fitzroy
Born: Bradford on Avon, 26 February 1970
Height: 5'7" Weight: 10.7
International Honours: Jamaica: 21
Like his team mate, Paul Hall, Fitzroy spent most of last season away from Portsmouth on international duty with Jamaica and was unable to hold down a regular place in the team on his return, for the most part, having to settle for substitute appearances. A tough-tackling midfielder, who can also take defenders on, he has both pace and stamina, and is not afraid to shoot from distance. *Stop Press:* Like his team-mate, Paul Hall, he saw duty with Jamaica in the Group H World Cup games in France during the summer, playing three times before the Reggae Boyz crashed out of the competition at the end of the first round.

Swindon T (From trainee on 6/7/88) FL 78+27/9 FLC 15+2/1 FAC 2+1 Others 3+2
Manchester C (£500,000 on 6/3/92) F/PL 58+13/4 FLC 5+1 FAC 4+1
Bristol C (Loaned on 16/9/94) FL 4
Portsmouth (£200,000 on 17/8/95) FL 84+6/9 FLC 6 FAC 6

SIMPSON Karl Edward
Born: Newmarket, 14 October 1976
Height: 5'11" Weight: 11.9
Yet another Norwich player to miss much of 1997-98 through injury, hamstring and knee problems halting his progress, Karl made just six appearances, four of them from the bench, and failed to make his mark at the club. Despite being a right winger with pace, and a good physique, who is both direct and positive, he was not offered another contract and would have been looking for another club during the summer. Another attribute is a long throw.

Norwich C (From juniors on 4/7/95) FL 4+6 FLC 1

SIMPSON Michael
Born: Nottingham, 28 February 1974
Height: 5'9" Weight: 10.8
Club Honours: AIC '95
1997-98 was a rather frustrating season for this talented, right-footed Wycombe midfielder, who, after starting the first five games, only began seven more and spent much of the time on the substitutes' bench. Nippy, and with excellent passing skills, he is definitely one of the most talented mid-fielders at his level, and is unlucky to be challenging the established pairing of Dave Carroll and Steve Brown for a midfield spot.

Notts Co (From trainee on 1/7/92) FL 39+10/3 FLC 4+1 FAC 2+1 Others 7+3
Plymouth Arg (Loaned on 4/10/96) FL 10+2
Wycombe W (£50,000 on 5/12/96) FL 26+15/1 FLC 2 FAC 0+2 Others 2

SIMPSON Paul David
Born: Carlisle, 26 July 1966
Height: 5'7" Weight: 11.12
International Honours: E: U21-5; Yth
Having started last season with Derby, following his October temporary transfer to Wolves, this busy left-footed player proved to be more of a midfielder than a winger. No wonder the loan deal became a permanent one when, on his home debut, he created two goals against Swindon, then scored a memorable one himself from 40 yards. Harshly given his first red card at Reading, which meant a three-match suspension when the team were doing well, he was a surprise choice for the FA Cup semi final, but made little impression in a tough game. However, his liking for free kicks was still in evidence, as he curled one in to earn a point from Manchester City.

Manchester C (From apprentice on 4/8/83) FL 99+22/18 FLC 10+1/2 FAC 10+2/4 Others 8+3
Oxford U (£200,000 on 31/10/88) FL 138+6/43 FLC 10/3 FAC 9/2 Others 5/2
Derby Co (£500,000 on 20/2/92) P/FL 134+52/48 FLC 12+3/6 FAC 4+4/1 Others 14+2/2
Sheffield U (Loaned on 6/12/96) FL 2+4
Wolverhampton W (£75,000 on 10/10/97) FL 23+5/4 FAC 2+2

SIMPSON Phillip (Phil) Mark
Born: Lambeth, 19 October 1969
Height: 5'8" Weight: 11.12
A tough-tackling Barnet midfielder, Phil is also a powerful runner with the ball who scores spectacular goals, four of them hitting the net in 1997-98. And, in linking play well from defence to attack, he is an important member of a side that went well enough to reach the third division play offs.

Barnet (Signed from Stevenage Borough on 27/10/95) FL 80+7/7 FLC 6/2 FAC 3+1/1 Others 3+1

SIMPSON Robert (Robbie) Anthony
Born: Luton, 3 March 1976
Height: 5'10" Weight: 11.6
International Honours: E: Yth
Released by Tottenham during the 1996 summer recess, Robbie joined Portsmouth, but before he could create an impression was unfortunate to suffer a badly-broken ankle during pre-season training. Out of action for some 15 months, he fought his way back through the reserves as an attacking midfielder, scoring seven goals, to make his Football League debut when coming off the bench at Fratton Park against Ipswich. With one more subs' appearance under his belt before 1997-98 ended, and having impressed Alan Ball with his determination to succeed, he looks to be in line for selection this coming term.

Tottenham H (From trainee on 1/11/93)
Portsmouth (Free on 16/7/96) FL 0+2

SINCLAIR Frank Mohammed
Born: Lambeth, 3 December 1971
Height: 5'9" Weight: 12.9
Club Honours: FAC '97; FLC '98
International Honours: Jamaica: 13
Frank became the second Chelsea player within five bizarre days last August whose eccentric post-goal celebrations cost him dearly. Following Celestine Babayaro's broken leg in a friendly at Slough after Tore Andre Flo's hat-trick goal, Frank scored one of his rare goals in the season's opener at Highfield Road and landed in hot water with the Football Association after being reported to the FA by referee, Paul Danson. In the next match at Barnsley, he cleverly created Gustavo Poyet's first Premiership goal, but in the fourth match against Southampton he was sent off for a rash piece of retaliation, which resulted in a suspension. He then had a 23-match run in the first team, often playing on the right of a flat back four, as the Blues occasionally switched to a 4-4-2 formation. In January, having opted to become one of the "Reggae Boyz" when making himself eligible for Jamaica's World Cup '98 squad, he was immediately drafted into their side for the Gold Cup match against world champions, Brazil, in Miami and played heroically as Jamaica held out for a shock goalless draw. Returned to score crucial goals in successive matches for Chelsea. In the European Cup Winners' Cup quarter-final second leg at the Bridge, Real Betis had stunned Chelsea by grabbing an early goal to level the aggregate scores until Frank stepped up to meet Gianfranco Zola's free kick with an unstoppable header after 30 minutes. He chose Wembley for his next goalscoring exploit ten days later, in the Coca Cola Cup final against Middlesbrough. With a tense match into extra time, he intercepted the ball in midfield, continued his run into the penalty area and met Dennis Wise's cross

with a firm downward header to give Chelsea a vital breakthrough. Sadly, for Frank, that was to be his last first team appearance of the season, as a calf strain prevented his involvement in Chelsea's European triumph, although it did not keep him away from France '98 as Jamaica needed him in their difficult Group H matches. *Stop Press:* Played in all three of Jamaica's World Cup games during the summer, two defeats by Argentina and Croatia, being followed by a 2-1 victory over Japan.

Chelsea (From trainee on 17/5/90) F/PL 163+6/7 FLC 17+1/2 FAC 18/1 Others 13/3
West Bromwich A (Loaned on 12/12/91) FL 6/1

SINCLAIR Ronald (Ronnie) McDonald
Born: Stirling, 19 November 1964
Height: 5'11" Weight: 12.3
Club Honours: Div 2 '93
International Honours: S: Yth; Sch

Ronnie, a vastly experienced goalkeeper who was voted Chester City's Player of the Year in 1996-97, lost his place to Wayne Brown last October and was placed on the transfer list at his own request. Came back to regain the number one spot in December, but then missed the last five games of the season due to an operation on his arm. Was given a free transfer during the summer.

Nottingham F (From apprentice on 30/10/82)
Wrexham (Loaned on 1/3/84) FL 11 Others 1
Leeds U (£10,000 on 27/6/86) FL 8 FLC 1
Halifax T (Loaned on 1/3/87) FL 4
Halifax T (Loaned on 23/12/88) FL 10 Others 1
Bristol C (Free on 1/9/89) FL 44 FLC 3 FAC 5 Others 3
Walsall (Loaned on 5/9/91) FL 10 Others 1
Stoke C (£25,000 on 21/11/91) FL 78+2 FLC 2 FAC 4 Others 10
Chester C (Free on 12/8/96) FL 70 FLC 3 FAC 3 Others 3

SINCLAIR Trevor Lloyd
Born: Dulwich, 2 March 1973
Height: 5'10" Weight: 12.5
International Honours: E: B-1; U21-14; Yth

Began last season on the bench at Queens Park Rangers, although he was in the first team for the next game, and ever present then on until his transfer to West Ham in January. Despite scoring two goals in the 2-1 home win against Stockport, and the winner at Crewe, transfer speculation surrounded his time at Loftus Road last season. However, once at Upton Park, Trevor wasted no time in making an impact, scoring twice on his debut against Everton, and since Harry Redknapp brought him back into the Premiership he has been sensational. With tremendous pace, and the ability to play either down the right flank or through the middle, when the regular strikers, John Hartson and Paul Kitson, were out injured, he weighed in with seven league goals. He was also called up for both the England "B" and U21 squads, and further honours should follow.

Blackpool (From trainee on 21/8/90) FL 84+28/15 FLC 8 FAC 6+1 Others 8+5/1
Queens Park R (£750,000 on 12/8/93) P/FL 162+5/16 FLC 13/3 FAC 10/2
West Ham U (£2,300,000+ on 30/1/98) PL 14/7

SINNOTT Lee
Born: Pelsall, 12 July 1965
Height: 6'1" Weight: 13.7
International Honours: E: U21-1; Yth

A central defender who, at his best, attacks the ball in the air and shows great presence in both boxes, Lee is now in the veteran stage, but utilised his great experience for Oldham in 1997-98, despite injury, when standing in on 15 occasions and never letting the side down. Loaned to Bradford on transfer deadline day, and into his third spell with City, he impressed the locals with his distribution and reading of a game in seven appearances before returning to Boundary Park.

Walsall (From apprentice on 16/11/82) FL 40/2 FLC 3 FAC 4
Watford (£100,000 on 15/9/83) FL 71+7/2 FLC 6 FAC 11
Bradford C (£130,000 on 23/7/87) FL 173/6 FLC 19 FAC 9 Others 12/1
Crystal Palace (£300,000 on 8/8/91) F/PL 53+2 FLC 9+1 FAC 1 Others 2
Bradford C (£50,000 on 9/12/93) FL 34/1 FLC 2 FAC 2 Others 2
Huddersfield T (£105,000 on 23/12/94) FL 86+1/1 FLC 6 FAC 4 Others 3
Oldham Ath (£30,000+ on 7/7/97) FL 11+2 FLC 1
Bradford C (Loaned on 26/3/98) FL 7

SINTON Andrew (Andy)
Born: Cramlington, 19 March 1966
Height: 5'8" Weight: 11.5
International Honours: E: 12; B-3; Sch

Andy was yet another Tottenham player whose talents in midfield were missed for much of last season, due to injury and the introduction of David Ginola and Nicola Berti to the side. Accurate crosses and tremendous vision are amongst his strengths, as well as the ability to beat opponents with his pace, and while most at home playing wide on the wing he is versatile enough to fill a central role when required. Recognised for a capacity to keep the ball closely controlled at his feet is another attribute, and with his enthusiasm in the tackle he still has a great deal to offer when fully fit. Is an experienced campaigner, who will be hoping to retain his fitness and stay injury free in order to regain his regular first team spot in 1998-99.

Cambridge U (From apprentice on 13/4/83) FL 90+3/13 FLC 6/1 FAC 3 Others 2/1
Brentford (£25,000 on 13/12/85) FL 149/28 FLC 8/3 FAC 11/1 Others 14/2
Queens Park R (£350,000 on 23/3/89) F/PL 160/22 FLC 14 FAC 13/2 Others 3/1
Sheffield Wed (£2,750,000 on 19/8/93) PL 54+6/3 FLC 13 FAC 5
Tottenham H (£1,500,000 on 23/1/96) PL 54+7/6 FLC 3 FAC 2

SISSOKO Habib
Born: Juvisy Orge, France, 24 May 1971
Height: 6'3" Weight: 14.6

Unknown to the Preston fans when signed from French football last February, on the strength of one reserve game, Habib quickly won the fans over with his obvious talent and commitment. Good in the air, he showed strength and skill on the ground, laying the ball off well, and keen to run at players, although a little naive about offside

at first. Sadly, he was released after only seven weeks at the club, following a much publicised off-field incident.

Preston NE (Free from Louhans on 19/2/98) FL 4+3

SISSONS Michael Anthony
Born: Sutton in Ashfield, 24 November 1978
Height: 5'9" Weight: 10.0

Another of Mansfield's promising youngsters from the YTS ranks, who signed a professional contract last January, Michael was given an early taste of first team football when coming off the bench at Colchester a few weeks later. A midfield workhorse, he closes down the opposition well, is strong in the tackle, and is neat and tidy in distribution.

Mansfield T (From trainee on 27/1/98) FL 0+1

SKELTON Aaron Matthew
Born: Welwyn Garden City, 22 November 1974
Height: 5'11" Weight: 12.6

A former Luton trainee whose professional career there was dogged by injury, Aaron was snapped up on a free transfer by Steve Wignall in the 1997 close season, and proved to be an excellent acquisition for Colchester in 1997-98. Essentially a skilful midfielder, he also had to fill in as an emergency centre back at times, and contributed seven vital goals – almost all of which were spectacular long-range strikes, including a volley against Shrewsbury, and a 35 yarder against Macclesfield. He also had the honour of scoring United's first ever winning goal against their bogey side, Rotherham, and is a player who will undoubtedly do well in division two in 1998-99.

Luton T (From trainee on 16/12/92) FL 5+3 FLC 0+1 FAC 2 Others 2
Colchester U (Free on 3/7/97) FL 37+2/7 FLC 1 FAC 3+1 Others 3+1

SKINNER Craig Richard
Born: Heywood, 21 October 1970
Height: 5'10" Weight: 11.6

Competed with Martin Chalk for the old outside-right slot at Wrexham in 1997-98. Similar to the former, in having plenty of pace and trickery, he does not score many goals from a position which has not always borne fruit in recent years, but funnels back well to help his team mates.

Blackburn Rov (From trainee on 13/6/89) FL 11+5 FLC 0+1 FAC 1 Others 3/1
Plymouth Arg (Signed on 21/8/92) FL 42+11/4 FLC 4 FAC 5+2/1 Others 3+1
Wrexham (£50,000 on 21/7/95) FL 58+17/8 FLC 3+1/1 FAC 8+1 Others 3+1

SKINNER Justin
Born: Hounslow, 30 January 1969
Height: 6'0" Weight: 12.0

An experienced central midfielder, Justin made just four further league appearances for Bristol Rovers in 1997-98 before joining Scottish club, Hibernian in March, having earlier spent two months on loan at Walsall, and scored the winning goal for the Saddlers

in an impressive Coca Cola Cup victory over Nottingham Forest. Before going north of the border, he had completed over 300 league appearances for his two English clubs.

Fulham (From apprentice on 17/11/86) FL 111+24/23 FLC 10+1/4 FAC 5+1 Others 10+1/1
Bristol Rov (£130,000 on 27/8/91) FL 174+13/12 FLC 11 FAC 8+1 Others 14+2/2
Walsall (Loaned on 12/9/97) FL 10 FLC 3/1

Justin Skinner

SLADE Steven (Steve) Anthony
Born: Hackney, 6 October 1975
Height: 6'0" Weight: 10.10
International Honours: E: U21-4

Following his run of games for Queens Park Rangers at the end of 1996-97, Steve might have been forgiven for thinking that he would be making the starting line-up on more occasions in 1997-98, but it continued to be more of the same, with 26 appearances, 22 of them from the bench. Despite there being no goals, he is a hard-running forward who looks to create opportunities for others with good movement on and off the ball. Is also good in the air.

Tottenham H (From trainee on 1/7/94) PL 1+4 FLC 0+1 FAC 0+2
Queens Park R (£350,000 on 12/7/96) FL 14+25/4 FLC 1+1 FAC 0+2
Brentford (Loaned on 13/2/97) FL 4

SLATER Robert (Robbie) David
Born: Ormskirk, 22 November 1964
Height: 5'10" Weight: 13.0
Club Honours: PL '95
International Honours: Australia: 17

Although starting last season in Southampton's opening two games, prior to being out of action for quite some time following a hernia operation, Robbie never really got going, making just 12 appearances in all, before becoming a surprise signing for Wolves on transfer deadline day. Despite coming into the side immediately and proving to be at home on the right-hand side of midfield, where he produced some powerful runs and was never afraid to shoot, he will be all the better for the summer respite. Very competitive, he could do a useful job in Wolves' midfield as they again strive to make it to the Premiership. *Stop Press:* Citing family reasons for wanting to move back to his home near Lens in France, Wolves released Robbie from his contract on 7 July.

Blackburn Rov (£300,000 from Lens on 4/8/94) PL 12+6 FLC 1 FAC 1 Others 2
West Ham U (£600,000 on 15/8/95) PL 18+7/2 FLC 3 FAC 1
Southampton (£250,000 on 3/9/96) PL 25+16/2 FLC 5+3 FAC 1
Wolverhampton W (£75,000 on 26/3/98) FL 4+2 FAC 0+1

SLATER Stuart Ian
Born: Sudbury, 27 March 1969
Height: 5'9" Weight: 11.6
Club Honours: Div 2 '98
International Honours: E: B-2; U21-3

An experienced winger or wide midfield player with exceptional skills, yet again Stuart suffered more than his share of injuries, including an achilles operation in 1997-98. A great favourite with the Watford crowd, who always lifts the team when he plays, his ability to use the ball to everyone's advantage was sorely missed. Despite the disappointment of being unavailable, his 14 league games were enough to win him a second division championship medal as the Hornets returned to division one after a two-year break.

West Ham U (From apprentice on 2/4/87) FL 134+7/11 FLC 16+1/2 FAC 16/3 Others 5/2
Glasgow Celtic (£1,500,000 on 14/8/92) SL 40+3/3 SLC 3+2 SC 3 Others 4
Ipswich T (£750,000 on 30/9/93) P/FL 61+11/4 FLC 6 FAC 6 Others 2+2
Leicester C (Free on 24/10/96)
Watford (Free on 28/11/96) FL 22+8/1 FLC 3 FAC 3 Others 1

SMALL Bryan
Born: Birmingham, 15 November 1971
Height: 5'9" Weight: 11.9
International Honours: E: U21-12; Yth

Unable to get a first team opportunity at Bolton last season, the tenacious, nippy, overlapping left-wing back enjoyed a three-month loan period at Luton early on, but was unable to agree personal terms and returned to the Reebok after making 15 appearances. The next loan stop was at Bradford in December, where he played five games, before moving on to Bury at the end of January. At Gigg Lane, Bryan met with immediate success as the sixth player to appear in the left-wing-back position during the campaign and, after two months on loan, he signed for the Shakers, playing in the closing 18 league games, while helping them pull clear of the relegation zone. A naturally left-footed player, who demonstrated the ability to cross well, in addition to defensive duties, he scored the first goal of his career at Sunderland's Stadium of Light.*

Aston Villa (From trainee on 9/7/90) F/PL 31+5 FLC 2 FAC 2+1 Others 4
Birmingham C (Loaned on 9/9/94) FL 3
Bolton W (Free on 20/3/96) F/PL 11+1 FLC 1 FAC 3
Luton T (Loaned on 8/9/97) FL 15
Bradford C (Loaned on 19/12/97) FL 5
Bury (Free on 30/1/98) FL 18/1

SMART Allan Andrew Colin
Born: Perth, 8 July 1974
Height: 5'11" Weight: 12.10
Club Honours: AMC '97

A forward who both makes and takes goalscoring opportunities, and probably one of the most skilful players at Carlisle, Allan began last season with two goals in three games before injury sidelined him for six months. Back in action in late February, he helped the Cumbrians win 3-0 at Preston,

Stuart Slater (foreground)

his former club, and then kept his place until the end of the campaign. Something of a touch player, all at Brunton Park will be hoping he can sustain his fitness in the return to division three.

Preston NE (£15,000 from Caledonian Thistle on 22/11/94) FL 17+4/6 FAC 2/1 Others 1+1
Carlisle U (Loaned on 24/11/95) FL 3+1
Northampton T (Loaned on 13/9/96) FL 1
Carlisle U (Signed on 9/10/96) FL 41+3/17 FLC 1/1 FAC 4 Others 4+1

SMEETS Jorg
Born: Amsterdam, Holland, 5 November 1970
Height: 5'6" Weight: 10.4

Recruited from the Dutch club, Heracles, last October, Jorg made his Football League debut in the away game at Grimsby Town. Used mainly as a substitute, his best position was just behind the front two strikers and he scored a spectacular goal, his first in the English league, in a 4-0 victory over Brentford. You might also be interested to know that he possesses the smallest feet in the league with a shoe size of 4½.

Wigan Ath (£100,000 from Heracles on 3/10/97) FL 10+13/3 FAC 1 Others 3

SMITH Alexander (Alex) Philip
Born: Liverpool, 15 February 1976
Height: 5'8" Weight: 10.6

Never managing to establish himself as a regular at Swindon, after promising much the previous year, his only two starts in 1997-98 came in successive away games at West Bromwich and Manchester City – the latter ending in a disastrous 6-0 drubbing which cost several players, including Alex, their places. Despite having a good left foot, he never really discovered his best position and was therefore regarded as a squad player, and, transfer listed in the spring, he eventually joined Huddersfield in February and impressed on his full debut at Nottingham Forest on the left wing. Certainly a useful addition to the Terriers' squad, having regularly shown well at left back in the reserves as a strong tackler and good passer, with a liking for getting into forward positions, he was surprisingly released during the summer.

Everton (From trainee on 1/7/94)
Swindon T (Free on 12/1/96) FL 17+14/1
Huddersfield T (Free on 6/2/98) FL 4+2

SMITH Carl Paul
Born: Sheffield, 15 January 1979
Height: 5'7" Weight: 11.4

Carl started last season as a Burnley trainee, before turning professional early in September and celebrating when coming off the bench just five days later for the last 20 minutes of a league match at Chesterfield. That was his lot for 1997-98 and he went back to develop his midfield skills in the reserves.

Burnley (From trainee on 2/9/97) FL 0+1

SMITH Craig
Born: Mansfield, 2 August 1976
Height: 6'1" Weight: 13.7

Taken on loan from Derby last August, the young striker was unable to make much impression while at Rochdale, managing just one start at left back and three brief substitute appearances, with all his league games unfortunately ending in defeat. Is still awaiting a first team debut for County.

Derby Co (From trainee on 9/8/95)
Rochdale (Loaned on 29/8/97) FL 1+2 FLC 0+1

SMITH David
Born: Stonehouse, 29 March 1968
Height: 5'8" Weight: 10.7
Club Honours: AMC '98
International Honours: E: U21-10

Last January, David became yet another of Grimsby manager, Alan Buckley's signings from his previous club West Bromwich Albion, as he strengthened his promotion-seeking squad. Able to play anywhere on the left flank, although his favoured position was on the wing, and a hard and willing worker, he formed an effective partnership with left back, Tony Gallimore. Marked his Town debut with a 25 yard volley that was arguably the goal of the season, and was delighted to be a member of the side that returned to the first division, via the play offs, and won the Auto Windscreen Shield.

Coventry C (From apprentice on 7/7/86) F/PL 144+10/19 FLC 17 FAC 6 Others 4+1
Bournemouth (Loaned on 8/1/93) FL 1
Birmingham C (Signed on 12/3/93) FL 35+3/3 FLC 4 FAC 0+1 Others 1
West Bromwich A (£90,000 on 31/1/94) FL 82+20/2 FLC 4 FAC 1+3 Others 4+1
Grimsby T (£200,000 on 16/1/98) FL 17/1 FAC 1 Others 7/1

SMITH David Alan
Born: Stockport, 2 May 1973
Height: 5'10" Weight: 16.0

David was given his chance in the Doncaster goal against Brighton last October, after showing up well in a reserve game some days earlier following his non-contract move from non-league Bramhall. With Rovers beaten 3-1 at home, this was to be his only game for the club and he was released within a few weeks.

Doncaster Rov (Free from Bramhall on 3/10/97) FL 1

SMITH David (Dave) Christopher
Born: Liverpool, 26 December 1970
Height: 5'9" Weight: 12.9

Oxford's midfield anchorman again was virtually an ever present, this time in 1997-98, and he doubled his league goal tally with his only goal of the season, the winner, against Ipswich Town. Now approaching 220 appearances in his four seasons with the club, he remains a steadying influence, linking both with the defence and the rest of the side. Can sometimes be seen coming late into the box, and came close to adding to his goal tally.

Norwich C (From trainee on 4/7/89) F/PL 13+5 FAC 2+1 Others 1+1
Oxford U (£100,000 on 5/7/94) FL 174+2/2 FLC 22/1 FAC 9 Others 7

SMITH Dean
Born: West Bromwich, 19 March 1971
Height: 6'1" Weight: 12.10

Having joined Leyton Orient from Hereford during the 1997 close season, Dean started 1997-98 at centre half before switching to central midfield in an emergency, but was so comfortable in that position that he remained there. A strong player who is equally good in the air as along the ground, possesses a good shot, and is capable of scoring valuable goals, Dean is the club penalty taker. Took over as captain at the end of the campaign.

Walsall (From trainee on 1/7/89) FL 137+5/2 FLC 10 FAC 4 Others 10
Hereford U (£75,000 on 17/6/94) FL 116+1/19 FLC 10/3 FAC 7 Others 11+1/4
Leyton Orient (£42,500 on 16/6/97) FL 43/9 FLC 4 FAC 2/1 Others 2

Dean Smith

SMITH James (Jamie) Jade Anthony
Born: Birmingham, 17 September 1974
Height: 5'7" Weight: 10.8

Started the first 16 games for Wolves last season and was only prevented from appearing in number 17, against Swindon at Molineux, because he was the key man in a complicated transfer deal, which ultimately saw him go to Crystal Palace, with Dougie Freedman and Kevin Muscat travelling in the opposite direction. An enthusiastic and exciting right back, Jamie had impressed Palace when scoring against them in the 1996-97 play offs, and with Steve Coppell looking for a right-wing back to give the side more width during their Premiership campaign, he had come to mind. Unfortunately, after making his debut at Sheffield Wednesday, he was sent off late in the next game, at home to Aston Villa, who equalised moments later. Involved in the majority of the games from thereon, in what was a very difficult season for Palace, the experience would have done him no harm. Good at providing early crosses for the front men.

Wolverhampton W (From trainee on 7/6/93) FL 71+6 FLC 10+1 FAC 2 Others 4/1
Crystal Palace (Signed on 22/10/97) PL 16+2 FAC 4

SMITH Mark Jonathan
Born: Bristol, 13 September 1979
Height: 5'11" Weight: 11.5

A second-year trainee, and a central

defender who is best at man marking, Mark has pace to match his positional play, and improved distribution from defence. Having experienced first team football when making his debut in November in an Auto Windscreen Shield tie against Cambridge at the Memorial Ground, he was given another outing in the next round tie at Exeter. Will hopefully gain further experience when he is expected to be loaned out to Conference clubs during the season.

Bristol Rov (Trainee) Others 2

SMITH Martin Geoffrey
Born: Sunderland, 13 November 1974
Height: 5'11" Weight: 12.6
Club Honours: Div 1 '96
International Honours: E: U21-1; Sch

One of the most naturally gifted players at Sunderland, the midfielder, cum striker, spent the summer of 1997 losing weight and regaining full fitness for the forthcoming campaign. Despite alternating between the starting line-up and the substitutes' bench early in the term, Martin's performances were much improved, and he scored a brilliantly headed goal against Wolves last September. However, following a foot injury sustained at Portsmouth in November, he returned to find the team in excellent form and opportunities limited. One hopes that "Smithy's" luck will eventually change, and that his undoubted ability will be rewarded with a regular first team place.

Sunderland (From trainee on 9/9/92) P/FL 86+25/22 FLC 6+4/1 FAC 7+2/1

SMITH Michael (Mike) Robert
Born: Liverpool, 28 September 1973
Height: 5'11" Weight: 11.7

Always a popular figure with the home supporters, Mike was never more than a figure on the fringe of first team affairs during 1997-98. As the season progressed, his attractive wing play became no more than a distant memory, and he was repeatedly left out when younger, less experienced players were thrown into the fight against relegation to the Conference.

Tranmere Rov (From trainee on 22/5/92 - Free to Derry C during 1993 close season)
Doncaster Rov (Signed from Runcorn on 5/1/96) FL 33+17/5 FLC 1+1 FAC 1 Others 1

SMITH Neil James
Born: Lambeth, 30 September 1971
Height: 5'9" Weight: 12.12
Club Honours: FAYC '90

A 1997 close season signing from Gillingham, Neil was second only to Matt Lawrence in the Fulham appearance charts, with 52 in all competitions, missing only two league matches. Considering the number of midfield players purchased during the campaign, that shows his commitment and consistency and, while he is first and foremost a ball winner he also played a wing-back role when required. Has one of the longest throws in the business.

Tottenham H (From trainee on 24/7/90)
Gillingham (£40,000 on 17/10/91) FL 204+9/10 FLC 14+1/1 FAC 18/2 Others 7+1/2
Fulham (Signed on 4/7/97) FL 42+2 FLC 3 FAC 3/1 Others 1+1

SMITH Ian Paul
Born: Easington, 22 January 1976
Height: 6'0" Weight: 13.3

1997-98 was a season to forget for Burnley's highly-talented winger. Out at the beginning with a broken foot bone, Paul was subsequently sidelined with an ankle injury, and then a thigh strain. In between times, he seemed to find it difficult to convince Chris Waddle of his undoubted potential, and his speed and passing skills were seen all too seldom at Turf Moor.

Burnley (From trainee on 10/7/94) FL 41+21/4 FLC 1+1 FAC 4+1 Others 5

SMITH Paul Antony
Born: Hastings, 25 January 1976
Height: 5'11" Weight: 11.7

Signed on loan from Nottingham Forest last October, before the move to Lincoln was made permanent two months later, Paul proved to be a winger with plenty of skill and pace who was always keen to take on defenders. Badly missed when a hamstring injury kept him out for 12 games, he returned for the final four matches of the season, scoring his third goal in the league in the 3-0 win over Peterborough.

Nottingham F (£50,000 from Hastings T on 13/1/95)
Lincoln C (£30,000 on 17/10/97) FL 15+2/3 Others 1

SMITH Paul William
Born: Lenham, 18 September 1971
Height: 5'11" Weight: 14.0

Signed during the 1997 close season from Brentford, Paul was Gillingham's only ever present last season, while showing himself to be a good passer and ball-winning central midfielder. He also scored the club's most vital goal, netting the winner in injury time at Plymouth, a goal which put the Gills into the play-off position with one game to go. Without a doubt the Player of the Year, he was often the difference between winning and losing.

Southend U (From trainee on 16/3/90) FL 18+2/1 Others 0+1
Brentford (Free on 6/8/93) FL 159/11 FLC 12/1 FAC 12/3 Others 15/2
Gillingham (Signed on 25/7/97) FL 46/3 FLC 2 FAC 2 Others 1

Paul Smith (Gillingham)

SMITH Peter John
Born: Stone, 12 July 1969
Height: 6'1" Weight: 12.7

The lanky right back's progress was thwarted by injury and loss of form in the early part of last season, but, on regaining his place in Brighton and Hove Albion's side in mid-November, Peter retained the number two shirt for most of the remainder of the campaign. The popular Midlander scored a long-range beauty in the 1-1 draw with Scarborough at Gillingham in January, his first goal in 15 months. A good tackler, he enjoys using his pace to get forward.

Brighton & Hove A (Free from Alma Swanley on 8/8/94) FL 114+12/4 FLC 8+2 FAC 6/1 Others 7+1

SMITH Peter Lee
Born: Rhyl, 18 September 1978
Height: 5'10" Weight: 10.8
International Honours: E: Yth; Sch

Despite his Welsh birthplace, Peter is a graduate from the FA School of Excellence at Lilleshall, and has represented England at both schoolboy and youth level. With one subs' appearance for Crewe under his belt prior to 1997-98, and then five further appearances from the bench throughout the season, the young forward had to be patient before making his full debut in the final game, at Ipswich. Full of running and skill, he is sure to be a player you will hear more of in the future.

Crewe Alex (From trainee on 12/7/96) FL 1+6

SMITH Gareth Shaun
Born: Leeds, 9 April 1971
Height: 5'10" Weight: 11.0

In missing just three games in 1997-98, Shaun once again proved his value to a Crewe side that was playing in the first division for the first time in its history, having signed a long-term contract at the start of the campaign. A naturally strong left-footed player, who has made the number three position his own at Gresty Road, the club captain once again weighed in with important goals, eight of them making him joint second in the scoring charts. The regular penalty taker tackles well, enjoys his surging runs up the flank, and is deadly from set pieces.

Halifax T (From trainee on 1/7/89) FL 6+1 Others 1 (Free to Emley in May 1991)
Crewe Alex (Free on 31/12/91) FL 219+19/30 FLC 7+1/2 FAC 12+2/3 Others 19+2/3

SMITH Thomas (Tommy) Edward
Born: Northampton, 25 November 1977
Height: 5'9" Weight: 10.10

Freed by Manchester United last April, having been relegated way down the pecking order at Old Trafford, Tommy signed non-contract terms for Cambridge and played 25 minutes as a second-half substitute in the final game of the season at Hull. Like his famous namesake, a tough-tackling defender who possesses a sweet left foot, this youngster could yet still make it. Was the third Red to have appeared at the Abbey in 1997-98, following Grant Brebner and Andy Duncan.

Manchester U (From trainee on 3/5/95)
Cambridge U (Free on 27/4/98) FL 0+1

SMITH Thomas William
Born: Hemel Hempstead, 22 May 1980
Height: 5'8" Weight: 11.4
International Honours: E: Yth
Starting last season at Watford as a trainee, the young winger, cum striker, signed full professional forms in October and made his first team debut soon afterwards. A member of the England U18 squad, he possesses speed and skill, and is a prolific scorer at reserve and junior level.
Watford (From trainee on 21/10/97) FL 0+1 FAC 0+1

SNEEKES Richard
Born: Amsterdam, Holland, 30 October 1968
Height: 5'11" Weight: 12.2
As in 1996-97, Richard was a key figure in midfield for West Bromwich Albion in 1997-98, having a splendid first half to the season, and being the cog around which Sean Flynn, Ian Hamilton, Peter Butler, Kevin Kilbane and company functioned. As a fine footballer with good skills, and a powerful shot, he also scored some cracking goals, while, at the same time, set up chances galore for his team mates. Unfortunately, he went off the boil towards the end of February and was omitted from the line-up before coming back to add both flair and commitment in a more forward role, alongside Lee Hughes.
Bolton W (£200,000 from Fortuna Sittard on 12/8/94) P/FL 51+4/7 FLC 11+1/3 FAC 2/1
West Bromwich A (£385,000 on 11/3/96) FL 92+8/21 FLC 7/1 FAC 3/2

SNIJDERS Mark Werner
Born: Holland, 12 March 1972
Height: 6'2" Weight: 13.0
A classy central defender who impressed Port Vale in pre-season trials before signing on a permanent basis a month later, he is a ball player with typical Dutch tendencies when in possession. Unfortunately, he tended to be in and out of the side through a variety of injuries, and his campaign ended at Queens Park Rangers in February after he complained of feeling ill during the kick around. Scored two goals, versus Queens Park Rangers at home, and at Manchester City.
Port Vale (Free from AZ Alkmaar on 8/9/97) FL 22+2/2 FAC 2

SNODIN Ian
Born: Rotherham, 15 August 1963
Height: 5'10" Weight: 11.0
Club Honours: Div 1 '87
International Honours: E: B-2; U21-4; Yth
Freed by Oldham during the summer of 1997, this vastly experienced midfielder added a touch of class to the Scarborough side in 1997-98, while giving 100 per-cent effort in every game he played. Comfortable, either defending or further forward, his outstanding skills were a key ingredient in Boro's push for promotion, although his enthusiasm to compete for every ball led to him receiving two red cards. His older brother, Glynn, also joined Scarborough last summer, taking on the role of youth team coach.

Doncaster Rov (From apprentice on 18/8/80) FL 181+7/25 FLC 9/1 FAC 11+1/1 Others 3
Leeds U (£200,000 on 22/5/85) FL 51/6 FLC 3/2 FAC 1
Everton (£840,000 on 16/1/87) F/PL 142+6/3 FLC 19+4/2 FAC 26/2 Others 3
Sunderland (Loaned on 13/10/94) FL 6
Oldham Ath (Free on 9/1/95) FL 55+2 FAC 1 Others 1
Scarborough (Free on 8/8/97) FL 33+2 FLC 1 FAC 1 Others 1

SOBIECH Jorg
Born: Gelsenkirchen, Germany, 15 January 1969
Height: 5'10" Weight: 10.9
Jorg was brought to Chris Kamara's attention at Stoke last March by a Dutch contact, who had followed the German's progress at Nijmegen, and a small loan fee secured his services for the rest of the season. A dream debut saw him make significant contributions for both goals in the win over Queens Park Rangers, the only victory in the Kamara reign, and he proved to be a superb crosser of the ball, being intelligent both in defence and going forward until an injury interrupted his run of games.
Stoke C (Loaned from NEC Nijmegen on 20/3/98) FL 3

SODJE Efetobore (Efe)
Born: Greenwich, 5 October 1972
Height: 6'1" Weight: 12.0
Club Honours: GMVC '96
Signed from Stevenage Borough during the 1997 close season, the big central defender is renowned for wearing a bandanna at the request of his mother, who believes it will bring him luck. Ability wise, he has a great turn of pace, is a tenacious tackler, likes to move up for set pieces, and quickly hit the headlines when he scored Macclesfield's first-ever Football League goal. An ambitious player who hopes for a Nigerian international call up in the near future, he has attracted a host of scouts throughout 1997-98.
Macclesfield T (£30,000 from Stevenage Borough on 11/7/97) FL 41/3 FLC 2 FAC 2 Others 1

SOLBAKKEN Stele
Born: Norway, 27 February 1968
Height: 6'2" Weight: 13.7
International Honours: Norway: 36
Signed from Lillestrom last October, the Norwegian international immediately made his Premiership debut for Wimbledon at Leicester and was involved in 14 consecutive matches, scoring in the home fixture against West Ham, before being left out of the side to play Crystal Palace. Although he came back as a sub three matches later, it had already been agreed that he could join FC Molde in a £300,000 transfer deal and that was the last time he was seen in the Dons' colours. Has great enthusiasm for the game. *Stop Press:* A member of Norway's successful international squad, he was selected for the World Cup tournament in France during the past summer and performed well in central midfield, in three of the side's four games,

holding the ball up, while looking to find his team mates, and occasionally getting himself forward into shooting positions.
Wimbledon (£250,000 from Lillestrom on 17/10/97) PL 4+2/1 FAC 1+1

SOLIS Mauricio Mora
Born: Costa Rica, 13 December 1972
Height: 5'8" Weight: 11.10
International Honours: Costa Rica: 34
A full Costa Rican international, and in to his second season at Derby in 1997-98, unlike his compatriot, Pablo Wanchope, he could not find a way into the side with several players ahead of him in the pecking order for a midfield position. Very skilful, although not over-physical, he began to make his mark with a number of substitute appearances as the season came to an end, but basically needs a run of games to bring the best out of him.
Derby Co (£600,000 from CS Heridiano on 27/3/97) PL 3+8 FLC 1+2

SOLSKJAER Ole Gunnar
Born: Norway, 26 February 1973
Height: 5'10" Weight: 11.10
Club Honours: PL '97
International Honours: Norway: 14
A well-balanced Manchester United striker with a powerful shot in either foot, Ole had a torrid time with injuries during the course of last season, having initially sustained ankle ligament problems during a friendly against Inter Milan at Old Trafford in July. Confined mostly to the substitutes' bench, after a lengthy spell out of the side he showed that he had lost none of his goalscoring touch when he returned briefly in September, and, having scored against Chelsea at the end of that month, he hit a brace against Sheffield Wednesday and Blackburn in November. With further strikes against Coventry in the Premiership and Walsall in the FA Cup, his solitary goal against Monaco in the European Cup quarter finals in March could not prevent United from going out of the competition. In showing his loyalty to the club at the start of last season by signing a new seven-year contract, Alex Ferguson said of his contribution: " He deserves it because he's done fantastically well." *Stop Press:* Was a member of the Norwegian side that qualified from Group A after defeating Brazil 2-1, only to go out of the competition in the next round following a 1-0 defeat at the hands of Italy.
Manchester U (£1,500,000 from Molde on 29/7/96) PL 40+15/24 FAC 1+4/2 Others 11+5/2

SOLTVEDT Trond Egil
Born: Vos, Norway, 15 February 1967
Height: 6'1" Weight: 12.8
International Honours: Norway: 4
A midfield player signed from Rosenborg Trondheim in the summer of 1997, after starring in their European Champions League side, he made his Coventry debut against Chelsea on the opening day as a ball winner in midfield. With a liking to get forward at every opportunity, he showed why, with a superb winning goal at home to

Southampton, but probably had his best game of the season in the home draw with Liverpool in April. Won his fourth cap as a substitute against Belgium and ended the campaign on the fringe of the Norwegian World Cup squad, having begun to make a real impression on the English game.

Coventry C (£500,000 from Rosenborg on 24/7/97) PL 26+4/1 FLC 1+1 FAC 3+1

Trond Soltvedt

SONNER Daniel (Danny) James
Born: Wigan, 9 January 1972
Height: 5'11" Weight: 12.8
International Honours: NI: 1; B-3

1997-98 proved to be a frustrating season for Danny as he was unable to command a regular place in the Ipswich side and the majority of his appearances were as a substitute. Preferring to play in a central midfield role, with the ability to produce defence splitting passes, he also possesses a good right-foot shot, which he used to effect when netting the winning goal in the Swindon home game, after coming on as a substitute. Despite his problems, he was able to further his Northern Ireland career during the term and made his full international debut against Albania, when coming off the bench. Also played for the "B" team against the Republic in February.*

Burnley (Free from Wigan Ath juniors on 6/8/90) FL 1+5 FLC 0+1/1 Others 0+2 (Free to Preussen Koln during 1993 close season)
Bury (Loaned on 21/11/92) FL 5/3 FAC 3 Others 1/1
Ipswich T (Free on 12/6/96) FL 28+24/3 FLC 6+2/1 FAC 1+1 Others 0+1

SORVEL Neil Simon
Born: Whiston, 2 March 1973
Height: 6'0" Weight: 12.9
Club Honours: GMVC '95, '97; FAT '96

A quiet unassuming character off the park, Neil turns into a strong midfield dynamo on it, with tough tackles and good distribution, and will tirelessly run for a full 90 minutes. However, as the second longest serving Macclesfield player, who has almost been ever present since his arrival from Crewe

back in the summer of 1991, he has yet to reach his best in the Football League.

Crewe Alex (From trainee on 31/7/91) FL 5+4 FAC 1+1 Others 4
Macclesfield T (Free on 21/8/92) FL 41+4/3 FLC 2 FAC 2 Others 0+1

SOUTHALL Neville
Born: Llandudno, 16 September 1958
Height: 6'1" Weight: 14.0
Club Honours: FAC '84, '95; CS '84, '85, '95; Div 1 '85, '87; ECW '85
International Honours: W: 92

Neville's place in the Everton Hall of Fame is already secure, but the legendary Welsh international goalkeeper continued to establish new records at Goodison in 1997-98 before losing out to new signing, Thomas Myhre. Having become the first footballer to play in 200 Premiership matches, when he kept goal at Derby County on 13 September, on 29 November he made his 750th appearance in an Everton jersey, a figure never likely to be matched. Allowed to join Southend United on loan in December, he made his debut for them on Boxing Day and spent two months at Roots Hall before joining Stoke City on loan. When that move became permanent in March, apart from relieving an edgy Carl Muggleton in the first team, he brought an air of composure to a leaky defence, and combined playing with additional coaching duties in the reserves, along with specialist training for all the club's 'keepers. Still a fine shot-stopper, his contribution at City in a difficult run in should not be under-estimated.

Bury (£6,000 from Winsford U on 14/6/80) FL 39 FAC 5
Everton (£150,000 on 13/7/81) F/PL 578 FLC 65 FAC 70 Others 37
Port Vale (Loaned on 27/1/83) FL 9
Southend U (Loaned on 24/12/97) FL 9
Stoke C (Free on 27/2/98) FL 12

SOUTHALL Leslie Nicholas (Nicky)
Born: Stockton, 28 January 1972
Height: 5'10" Weight: 12.12

Having struggled to hold a first team place down at Grimsby in 1997-98, as the new manager, Alan Buckley, rebuilt, Nicky moved to Gillingham in December, and quickly settled as an attacking midfielder. Adaptable on either wing, where he is a tireless worker, he scored on his debut for the Gills after just four minutes in the 2-1 home defeat by Southend, and proved to be good value as the side pushed its way towards the play-off places.

Hartlepool U (Free from Darlington juniors on 21/2/91) FL118+20/24 FLC 6+1/3 FAC 4+4 Others 6+2
Grimsby T (£40,000 on 12/7/95) FL 55+17/6 FLC 3+3/1 FAC 4+3/2
Gillingham (Free on 9/12/97) FL 22+1/2 Others 1

SOUTHGATE Gareth
Born: Watford, 3 September 1970
Height: 6'0" Weight: 12.8
Club Honours: Div 1 '94; FLC '96
International Honours: E: 27

Following the transfer of Andy Townsend at the end of last August, Gareth took over the captain's armband at Aston Villa and proceeded to lead by example as one of the most consistent players at the club, missing

Gareth Southgate

just eight games throughout the campaign. Cool, classy, and composed at the heart of the defence, there are not many strikers who can knock him out of his stride, something well recognised at international level, where he continues for England in a similar role. And, with two good feet, he is more than comfortable when bringing the ball out of defence, while he is always available to support his team mates when they need a passing option. The season ended on a personal high note, with him booking his place in the squad of 22 that would represent England in the World Cup in France during the summer. *Stop Press:* Having been injured in England's opening game of the World Cup in France '98, he came back stoically for the last 50 minutes of the Argentinian match, following David Beckham's dismissal, only to have another bad experience of the penalty shoot-out system.

Crystal Palace (From trainee on 17/1/89) F/PL 148+4/15 FLC 23+1/7 FAC 9 Others 6
Aston Villa (£2,500,000 on 1/7/95) PL 91/2 FLC 10/1 FAC 10 Others 9

SPARROW Paul

Born: Wandsworth, 24 March 1975
Height: 6'1" Weight: 11.4
Club Honours: Div 3 '96

As the captain of Preston's reserve team in 1997-98, Paul again played all along the back four, although his best position was undoubtedly at right back. Having made six first team appearances the previous season, he was expected to add to that considerably, but, in the event, he failed to feature until the penultimate game, at Wrexham, where he gave a steady performance at left back before being released in the summer.

Crystal Palace (From trainee on 13/7/93) FL 1 FLC 0+1
Preston NE (Signed on 8/3/96) FL 20 FAC 1 Others 1

SPEDDING Duncan

Born: Camberley, 7 September 1977
Height: 6'1" Weight: 11.1

Joined Southampton as a schoolboy and made the senior team for the first time last season, when coming straight into the side for the home game against Arsenal in August. Echoing his name, Duncan is a speedy left-sided player who had four first team outings, plus four as sub, and can play anywhere up the left flank, taking on players and producing useful crosses. Also delivers a very good corner kick.

Southampton (From trainee on 24/5/96) PL 4+3 FLC 0+1

SPEED Gary Andrew

Born: Deeside, 8 September 1969
Height: 5'10" Weight: 12.10
Club Honours: Div 2 '90, Div 1 '92; CS '92
International Honours: W: 47; U21-3; Yth

Howard Kendall sprung a surprise on the eve of last season when he named Gary as the new Everton captain. The goalscoring midfielder responded to the added responsibility with some of the most consistently influential displays of his career and, employed in a more central midfield role, he

found himself as more of a tackling anchorman than he had been previously used to, but revelled in the role. However, midway through the campaign there were rumours that he was unhappy at the club he had supported since a boy, and the situation reached a head when he refused to travel for an away match at West Ham. Soon after, in February, he was sold to Newcastle. Obviously, his departure from Goodison was fractious, but he was prevented from giving his side of the story by signing a non-disclosure agreement. On Tyneside, however, playing in midfield, he added welcome pace and width down the left flank, whilst his prowess in the air gave United an extra dimension near goal, his finishing sharpness being demonstrated by his first goal for the club when he squeezed the ball under the 'keeper at pace in the FA Cup tie against Barnsley. And, in looking to pursue his ambition for more club honours, he was ultimately rewarded with a runners-up medal following the FA Cup final defeat at the hands of Arsenal. Continued to appear for the Welsh national side, playing in five of their six matches.

Leeds U (From trainee on 13/6/88) F/PL 231+17/39 FLC 25+1/11 FAC 21/5 Others 14+3/2
Everton (£3,500,000 on 1/7/96) PL 58/15 FLC 5/1 FAC 2/1
Newcastle U (£5,500,000 on 6/2/98) PL 13/1 FAC 4/1

SPENCER John

Born: Glasgow, 11 September 1970
Height: 5'6" Weight: 11.7
International Honours: S: 14; U21-3; Yth; Sch

Much was expected of John at Queens Park Rangers last season, after his successes in 1996-97, but injury and behind the scenes disruption affected his form and, although the bustling little striker scored six goals, and whenever he scored Rangers did not lose, he was allowed to go on loan to Everton in March. However, he made such an impression on Howard Kendall that the Toffees' manager felt obliged to make the move permanent and, following a scare over a heart scan, the player was eventually given the all-clear to complete the move. Although failing to register a goal, he is expected to become the perfect foil for big Duncan Ferguson in 1998-99, with his ability to retain possession in tight corners giving defenders all kinds of problems.

Glasgow R (From juniors on 11/9/86) SL 7+6/2 SLC 2 Others 1+1/1
Morton (Loaned on 4/3/89) FL 4/1
Chelsea (£450,000 on 1/8/92) PL 75+28/36 FLC 5+4/2 FAC16+4/4 Others 4+1/1
Queens Park R (£2,500,000 on 22/11/96) FL 47+1/22 FLC 1 FAC 6/2
Everton (Loaned on 9/3/98) PL 3+3

SPENCER Simon Dean

Born: Islington, 10 September 1976
Height: 5'10" Weight: 11.4
International Honours: E: Yth

Freed by Spurs during the 1997 close season, this neat, right-footed midfielder made his Brentford debut in the opening game of last season at Millwall, and was

selected again three days later for the Coca Cola Cup tie against Shrewsbury. That was unfortunately it as far as first team football was concerned and he was released by new manager, Micky Adams, in January.

Tottenham H (From trainee on 1/7/95)
Brentford (Free on 14/7/97) FL 1 FLC 1

SPINK Dean Peter

Born: Birmingham, 22 January 1967
Height: 6'0" Weight: 14.8
Club Honours: Div 3 '94

Signed from Shrewsbury during the 1997 close season, Dean showed the Wrexham faithful that he was very good at holding the ball up, with strength being a vital asset of his play, despite having an in-and-out sort of time of it in 1997-98, and wishing that his goals tally was better. Will obviously be hoping for a better reward in 1998-99, although the playing system adopted at the Racecourse these days limits opportunities.

Aston Villa (£30,000 from Halesowen T on 1/7/89)
Scarborough (Loaned on 20/11/89) FL 3/2 Others 1
Bury (Loaned on 1/2/90) FL 6/1
Shrewsbury T (£75,000 on 15/3/90) FL 244+29/53 FLC 22+2/1 FAC 18+2/6 Others 19+2/3
Wrexham (£65,000 on 15/7/97) FL 33+3/6 FLC 2/1 FAC 1+1 Others 1

SPINK Nigel Philip

Born: Chelmsford, 8 August 1958
Height: 6'2" Weight: 14.6
Club Honours: EC '82; ESC '82; FLC '94
International Honours: E: 1; B-2

Having stood in for Alan Miller at West Bromwich in a Coca Cola Cup game at home to Cambridge last August, a few weeks later, this very experience goalkeeper was transferred to Millwall, who were short of cover for the injured Tim Carter. Despite his age, his ability to command his area at all times gave solace to an often beleaguered defence until it was discovered in January that he needed a hernia operation. Came back into the side for the last few matches and again showed his value as a shot-stopper, excelling in one-on-one situations, and difficult to get the better of in the air.

Aston Villa (£4,000 from Chelmsford C on 1/1/77) F/PL 357+4 FLC 45 FAC 28 Others 25+1
West Bromwich A (Free on 31/1/96) FL 19 FLC 3 Others 2
Millwall (£50,000 on 26/9/97) FL 21 FAC 1 Others 2

SPRING Matthew John

Born: Harlow, 17 November 1979
Height: 5'11" Weight: 11.5

Matthew made an impressive debut for Luton in a 3-0 home win over Plymouth Argyle last October, a result that ended a run of 11 winless games and four consecutive defeats. However, this normally controlled, but tenacious midfielder was sent off late in the game for an impetuous tackle and thereafter used sparingly for the remainder of the season. A star in the club's successful youth team, who has great vision and the ability to read a game, he was voted joint Young Player of the Year. Will surely be given further chances in 1998-99, as he

looks to join the impressive list of youngsters developed by Town in recent years.

Luton T (From trainee on 2/7/97) FL 6+6 FAC 1

SQUIRES James (Jamie) Alexander
Born: Preston, 15 November 1975
Height: 6'2" Weight: 13.11
Unable to make his mark at Preston, Jamie was loaned to Mansfield early last season and made his debut for the Stags as a replacement for the indisposed Stuart Watkiss in a central defensive role. That was it as far as appearances went and, having returned to Deepdale, the once promising Jamie was released at the end of March.

Preston NE (From trainee on 26/4/94) FL 24+7 FLC 1 FAC 0+1 Others 5+1
Mansfield T (Loaned on 22/8/97) FL 1

SRNICEK Pavel (Pav)
Born: Ostrava, Czechoslovakia, 10 March 1968
Height: 6'2" Weight: 14.9
Club Honours: Div 1 '93
International Honours: Czechoslovakia: 19
Goalkeeper Pav is one of Newcastle's longest-serving players, but lost out to the competition of Shaka Hislop and newly arrived Shay Given in 1997-98, making a single appearance, at home to Blackburn, during the campaign. A very popular figure on Tyneside, his agility and reflexes make him a fine shot-stopper, while he has worked hard to improve his all-round game and, although out of favour at United, is still appreciated in his homeland, and added to his tally of Czech Republic caps during the season. Out of contract during the summer, Pavel was looking for a new club under the Bosman ruling.

Newcastle U (£350,000 from Banik Ostrava on 5/2/91) F/PL 148+1 FLC 10+1 FAC 11 Others 17

STALLARD Mark
Born: Derby, 24 October 1974
Height: 6'0" Weight: 12.10
The Wycombe Wanderers striker began last season in explosive form, with 11 goals in his first 16 games, including a hat trick at home to Walsall, and finished with 18 in 46 starts, 17 in the league, which is just one behind the club's Football League record. With great upper body strength, he finds it easy to turn his marker and has a knack of finding good goalscoring positions, while his trusty right foot sends in very hard, accurate shots. He also has a useful left foot as well, volleying a goal with it against Blackpool.

Derby Co (From trainee on 6/11/91) FL 19+8/2 FLC 2+1/2 FAC 2+1 Others 3/2
Fulham (Loaned on 23/9/94) FL 4/3
Bradford C (£110,000 on 12/1/96) FL 33+10/10 FLC 2/1 FAC 0+1 Others 3/2
Preston NE (Loaned on 14/2/97) FL 4/1
Wycombe W (£100,000 on 7/3/97) FL 55/21 FLC 1+1 Others 2/1

STAMP Darryn Michael
Born: Beverley, 21 September 1978
Height: 6'3" Weight: 12.0
Spotted by Paul Wilson playing in the East Riding County side, while still at school,

Darryn's first season with a professional club saw him get few chances in the Scunthorpe first team in 1997-98, although he has been given another year's contract. A tall, slim striker, he has great ball skills and looks good when running at opposing defenders, but needs to add some strength to his play. However, the United management have high hopes that he can make the breakthrough.

Scunthorpe U (Signed from Hessle on 7/7/97) FL 4+6/1 FLC 0+1

STAMP Philip (Phil) Lawrence
Born: Middlesbrough, 12 December 1975
Height: 5'10" Weight: 13.5
International Honours: E: Yth
A determined young Middlesbrough midfielder, full of running and enthusiasm, Phil came through the club's production line of training and development, and is a credit to the system. Never one to shirk a tackle, he has always given full value, and won several Man of the Match awards for his performances in 1997-98. Possesses good vision and his distraction to the opposition when running off the ball has created many scoring chances for his colleagues. Is a genuine 100 per center, and is cool and decisive in front of goal.

Middlesbrough (From trainee on 4/2/93) P/FL 43+16/3 FLC 9+2/1 FAC 5+3/1 Others 5+1

STAMPS Scott
Born: Birmingham, 20 March 1975
Height: 5'11" Weight: 11.0
A left back, or wing back, Scott enjoyed an impressive season up to last season at Colchester, before losing his place to the fit-again Simon Betts in November, and never fully reclaiming it, although he did score his first goal for United against Brighton at Priestfield on Boxing Day. He then suffered a cartilage injury which needed surgery, and brought his campaign to a premature end, causing him to miss out on Wembley again, having been cup tied in 1996-97.

Torquay U (From trainee on 6/7/93) FL 80+6/5 FLC 5 FAC 2 Others 2+1/1
Colchester U (£10,000 on 26/3/97) FL 33+2/1 FLC 2 FAC 2+1 Others 1

STANNARD James (Jim) David
Born: Harold Hill, 6 October 1962
Height: 6'2" Weight: 16.2
Jim's place as Gillingham's number one was constantly under threat throughout last season, and that the manager, Tony Pulis, brought in four other goalkeepers on loan merely emphasised the fact. However, when called upon, he never let the side down, and his performance in the 2-0 victory at top-of-the-table, Bristol City, was rated by many as the finest display by a Gillingham 'keeper for many a year. Released during the summer, although less agile than previous, he is still an excellent shot-stopper.

Fulham (Signed from Ford U on 5/6/80) FL 41 FLC 3 FAC 1
Southend U (Loaned on 17/9/84) FL 6
Charlton Ath (Loaned on 1/2/85) FL 1
Southend U (£12,000 on 28/3/85) FL 103 FLC 6 FAC 4 Others 5

Fulham (£50,000 on 14/8/87) FL 348/1 FLC 22 FAC 13 Others 18
Gillingham (Free on 4/8/95) FL 104 FLC 8 FAC 9 Others 2

STANT Phillip (Phil) Richard
Born: Bolton, 13 October 1962
Height: 6'0" Weight: 13.4
Club Honours: Div 3 '93; WC '93
Unfortunately, for both Phil, a vastly experienced striker, and Lincoln, his goals inexplicably dried up after netting twice in the first four league and cup games for 1997-98. Dropped in November, and making only occasional appearances during the rest of the season, he became part of the Lincoln management team following the dismissal of John Beck in March, as assistant to caretaker manager, Shane Westley.

Reading (Signed from Camberley on 19/8/82) FL 3+1/2
Hereford U (Free from Army on 25/11/86) FL 83+6/38 FLC 3/2 FAC 3/2 Others 11/7
Notts Co (£175,000 on 18/7/89) FL 14+8/6 FLC 2/1 FAC 0+1 Others 3+2
Blackpool (Loaned on 5/9/90) FL 12/5
Lincoln C (Loaned on 22/11/90) FL 4
Huddersfield T (Loaned on 3/1/91) FL 5/1
Fulham (£60,000 on 8/2/91) FL 19/5 Others 1
Mansfield T (£50,000 on 1/8/91) FL 56+1/32 FLC 4/1 FAC 2 Others 2
Cardiff C (£100,000 on 4/12/92) FL 77+2/34 FLC 2/2 FAC 6+1/4 Others 10/3
Mansfield T (Loaned on 12/8/93) FL 4/1 FLC 1/1
Bury (£90,000 on 27/1/95) FL 49+13/23 FLC 5+1/4 FAC 1 Others 5
Northampton T (Loaned on 22/11/96) FL 4+1/2
Lincoln C (£30,000 on 26/12/96) FL 39+4/18 FLC 2/1 FAC 2+2 Others 1

STANTON Nathan
Born: Nottingham, 6 May 1981
Height: 5'9" Weight: 11.3
International Honours: E: Yth
A first-year trainee who marked a superb season in the juniors and reserves by coming on as a second-half substitute for his league debut at Scarborough last Easter Monday, Nathan became only the fourth 16-year old to ever play in the league for Scunthorpe. A compact defender, who is very quick, and strong on the floor, he is expected to figure regularly in 1998-99 and to have a big future in the game.

Scunthorpe U (Trainee) FL 0+1

STARBUCK Philip (Phil) Michael
Born: Nottingham, 24 November 1968
Height: 5'10" Weight: 13.3
Released by Sheffield United during the 1997 close season, Phil joined Oldham on the opening day of 1997-98 and within two minutes of stepping on to the training pitch damaged his knee to such an extent that his first appearance was not until January. Nine games and one goal later, however, he was transferred to Plymouth, in March, in a deal that saw Adrian Littlejohn travelling in the opposite direction. Formerly a forward, he was used in an attacking midfield role, supporting the two central strikers, but due to niggling injuries he failed to make the impact the management expected and was released during the summer.

Nottingham F (From apprentice on 19/8/86) FL 9+27/2 FLC 1+3 FAC 2+5 Others 0+4
Birmingham C (Loaned on 7/3/88) FL 3
Hereford U (Loaned on 19/2/90) FL 6 Others 1
Blackburn Rov (Loaned on 6/9/90) FL 5+1/1
Huddersfield T (£100,000 on 17/8/91) FL 120+17/36 FLC 13+2/4 FAC 5+1 Others 16+3/7
Sheffield U (£150,000 on 28/10/94) FL 26+10/2 FLC 0+2 FAC 1+1
Bristol C (Loaned on 15/9/95) FL 5/1 Others 1
Oldham Ath (Free on 9/8/97) FL 7+2/1
Plymouth Arg (Signed on 20/3/98) FL 6+1

STATHAM Brian

Born: Zimbabwe, 21 May 1969
Height: 5'9" Weight: 11.7
Club Honours: Div 3 '92
International Honours: E: U21-3

Signed from Brentford last August, Gillingham's midfield ball winner, cum defender, had the misfortune to be sent off on his return to Griffin Park the following month! A player who is good in the air, despite his lack of inches, he was a regular in the side up until Christmas, before losing his place due to difficulties in settling at the club, being mainly used as a substitute thereafter.

Tottenham H (From trainee on 3/8/87) FL 20+4 FLC 2 FAC 0+1
Reading (Loaned on 28/3/91) FL 8
Bournemouth (Loaned on 20/11/91) FL 2 Others 1
Brentford (£70,000 on 16/1/92) FL 148+18/1 FLC 12 FAC 6 Others 22
Gillingham (£10,000 on 22/8/97) FL 16+4 FAC 2 Others 1

STAUNTON Stephen (Steve)

Born: Dundalk, 19 January 1969
Height: 6'1" Weight: 12.12
Club Honours: FAC '89; Div 1 '90; FLC '94, '96
International Honours: Ei: 74; U21-4; Yth

A left-sided Aston Villa player of real quality, the Irish international is at his most dangerous when pushing forward from deep positions on the wide left to deliver telling crosses into the danger areas. He also spells danger to goalkeepers from anywhere around the box and, with one such strike against Sheffield Wednesday, he sent a 30-yard shot crashing into the net off both posts with such force that the 'keeper never stood a chance. That then is his forte. An excellent passer of the ball, who always seems to have plenty of time and space, he thrived on a central defensive role in 1997-98, showing fine form and being second choice as captain when Gareth Southgate was unavailable. Just as effective as a wing back, or in midfield, he also had a relatively injury-free season, missing a few games because of a jarred knee and then a hamstring injury, but was a regular for the Republic. *Stop Press:* Re-joined Liverpool on 2 July under the Bosman ruling.

Liverpool (£20,000 from Dundalk on 2/9/86) FL 55+10 FLC 6+2/4 FAC 14+2/1 Others 1/1
Bradford C (Loaned on 13/11/87) FL 7+1 FLC 2 Others 1
Aston Villa (£1,100,000 on 7/8/91) F/PL 205+3/16 FLC 17+2/1 FAC 19+1/1 Others 15+1

STEELE Lee Anthony

Born: Liverpool, 7 December 1973
Height: 5'8" Weight: 12.7

A goalscoring forward who signed from Northwich in the summer of 1997, Lee made his debut for Shrewsbury on the opening day of last season and quickly became a firm crowd favourite, with his busy style of play always pressing defenders. Thriving on taking defenders on and turning them inside out, he proved to be a tireless worker who, in his first season, netted two hat tricks, at home to Brentford (Coca Cola Cup) and at Leyton Orient in the league, and shot himself into the leading goalscoring charts of division three.

Shrewsbury T (£30,000 + from Northwich Vic on 23/7/97) FL 37+1/13 FLC 2/3 FAC 1 Others 1

STEFANOVIC Dejan

Born: Yugoslavia, 28 October 1974
Height: 6'2" Weight: 12.10
International Honours: Yugoslavia: 10

Although a classy defender who is calm and composed on the ball, with excellent passing skills, he was again unable to claim a regular place at Sheffield Wednesday, either at left back or in central defence, in 1997-98. Expecting to go to the World Cup Finals in France, the Yugoslav international appeared in a new scheming midfield role for the Owls at the end of the campaign and did well but, having played too few games, there were rumours that it was going to be difficult for him to renew his work permit in time for 1998-99 and, hopefully, Hillsborough has not seen the last of the classy strolling gait of Dejan! *Stop Press:* According to press reports, Dejan's application for a new work permit was turned down on 7 July.

Sheffield Wed (£2,000,000 from Red Star Belgrade on 22/12/95) PL 51+4/4 FLC 2 FAC 2

STEIN Mark Earl Sean

Born: Capetown, South Africa, 29 January 1966
Height: 5'6" Weight: 11.10
Club Honours: FLC '88; AMC '92; Div 2 '93
International Honours: E: Yth

Unable to get a game at Chelsea, the little striker joined Ipswich on loan for two months at the start of last season as cover for Alex Mathie, leading the line well and linking up with James Scowcroft, while being able to feed off the tall striker's flick-ons. Although he scored three times during his stay – all from close in – there was never any question of him joining Town on a permanent basis and he went back to Stamford Bridge before being loaned to Bournemouth early in March. Still quick, and always dangerous inside the box, Mark notched four goals during his stay at Dean Court, two of them spectacular efforts, and will be looking for more regular football in 1998-99.

Luton T (From juniors on 31/1/84) FL 41+13/19 FLC 4+1 FAC 9/3 Others 3/1
Aldershot (Loaned on 29/1/86) FL 2/1
Queens Park R (£300,000 on 26/8/88) FL 20+13/4 FLC 4/2 FAC 2+1/1 Others 4
Oxford U (Signed on 15/9/89) FL 72+10/18 FLC 4 FAC 2+1 Others 3
Stoke C (£100,000 on 15/9/91) FL 94/50 FLC 8/8 FAC 4 Others 17/10

Chelsea (£1,500,000 on 28/10/93) PL 46+4/21 FLC 0+1 FAC 9/2 Others 2+1/2
Stoke C (Loaned on 22/11/96) FL 11/4
Ipswich T (Loaned on 22/8/97) FL 6+1/2 FLC 3+1/1
Bournemouth (Loaned on 4/3/98) FL 11/4 Others 3

STEINER Robert Herman

Born: Finsprong, Sweden, 20 June 1973
Height: 6'2" Weight: 13.5

Having spent a period on loan at Bradford during 1996-97, the fans were delighted to hear that the bustling Norrkoping forward had agreed to sign a permanent contract in the summer of 1997 and he, in turn, was delighted to score the winner on the opening day of 1997-98. More goals followed and he finished the campaign at the top of the charts with 11, equal to that of Edinho. Yet another of the Bradford contingent that suffered a whole run of injuries, Robert, who has a great attitude to the game, takes a lot of knocks but gets up and gets on with it. Is strong on the ground and in the air.

Bradford C (Loaned from Norrkoping on 31/10/96) FL 14+1/3 FAC 1/1
Bradford C (£500,000 from Norrkoping on 31/7/97) FL 26+11/10 FLC 2/1 FAC 1

STEPHENSON Paul

Born: Wallsend, 2 January 1968
Height: 5'10" Weight: 12.12
International Honours: E: Yth

A great late-season signing for Hartlepool from York last March, unfortunately a medial ligament injury meant he had to wait several weeks to make his debut for his new club. Although not fully match fit, he was impressive, playing an attacking wide role in the last three games, and there are high expectations that he will be a key player in Pool's 1998-99 promotion push. Prior to leaving Bootham Crescent, he probably had his best spell at the club, hitting five goals, including strikes against two of his former clubs, Millwall and Brentford, and a brace in a dramatic home win over Carlisle in October.

Newcastle U (From apprentice on 2/1/86) FL 58+3/1 FLC 3+1 FAC 2 Others 2
Millwall (£300,000 on 10/11/88) FL 81+17/6 FLC 3/1 FAC 9/2 Others 8/1
Gillingham (Loaned on 21/11/92) FL 12/2 Others 2
Brentford (£30,000 on 4/3/93) FL 70/2 FLC 6/1 FAC 1+1 Others 5
York C (Signed on 7/8/95) FL 91+6/8 FLC 9+2 FAC 5 Others 2+2/1
Hartlepool U (Free on 20/3/98) FL 3

STEVENS Michael Gary

Born: Barrow, 27 March 1963
Height: 5'11" Weight: 12.7
Club Honours: FAC '84; Div 1 '85, '87; ECWC '85; CS '84, '85; SPD '89, '90, '91, '92, '93, '94; SLC '89, '91, '94; SC '92
International Honours: E: 46; B-1

As a vastly experienced right back with plenty of top flight and international football behind him, Gary proved invaluable in helping the Tranmere youngsters through the club's injury crisis, when leading by example in the sweeper's role in 1997-98. Continued to turn in neat, mature, and sensible performances, when not sidelined by niggling injuries, and showed himself to

be as reliable as ever when called upon to perform in a number of positions. Calm, assured, and respected, he was released by Rovers on a free transfer during the summer.

Everton (From apprentice on 8/4/81) FL 207+1/8 FLC 30/1 FAC 39/3 Others 10
Glasgow R (£1,000,000 on 19/7/88) SL 186+1/8 SLC 22 SC 22/1 Others 14
Tranmere Rov (£350,000 on 22/9/94) FL 126+1/2 FLC 15 FAC 4 Others 4

STEVENS Ian David
Born: Malta, 21 October 1966
Height: 5'10" Weight: 12.6
Club Honours: AMC '89

Recruited in the summer of 1997 from Shrewsbury, illness kept Ian out of the side until late October, and his first goal did not arrive until early November. As full fitness returned, he emerged as a consistent striker, and perhaps the most natural goalscorer to have worn a Carlisle shirt in recent years. Very sharp in and around the box, his hat trick against Bristol Rovers was the first by a Carlisle player in the league since 1989, and the first at Brunton Park for over a decade.

Preston NE (From apprentice on 22/11/84) FL 9+2/2 Others 1
Stockport Co (Free on 27/10/86) FL 1+1 FAC 0+1 Others 0+1 (Free to Lancaster C on 27/11/86)
Bolton W (Free on 25/3/87) FL 26+21/7 FLC 1+2 FAC 4/2 Others 3+1
Bury (Free on 3/7/91) FL 100+10/38 FLC 3+1 FAC 2+2 Others 7+1/2
Shrewsbury T (£20,000 on 11/8/94) FL 94+17/37 FLC 2+1 FAC 4+2/2 Others 10+2/12
Carlisle U (£100,000 on 13/5/97) FL 33+4/17 FAC 1 Others 3/2

STEVENS Keith Henry
Born: Merton, 21 June 1964
Height: 6'0" Weight: 12.12
Club Honours: FLT '83; Div 2 '88

Nicknamed "Rhino" by the Millwall faithful, Keith has been an inspirational figure at the club for the past 17 years and is Millwall through and through. As a tough-tackling defender who gave no quarter, he returned after a cruciate ligament injury to play a handful of games in 1997-98, before taking on the role of reserve team coach. And, although keeping fit in case further first team football beckoned, his loyalty saw him rewarded with the manager's post in succession to Billy Bonds at the end of the season.

Millwall (From apprentice on 23/6/81) FL 451+8/9 FLC 36/1 FAC 28 Others 29+1

STEVENS Mark Richard
Born: Swindon, 3 December 1977
Height: 6'5" Weight: 12.7
International Honours: E: Sch

A second-year professional, Mark made his only first team appearance in a very young, injury-hit Oxford side which took on Nottingham Forest at the start of last season, coming on late in the game as a centre back. Prior to that time, he had been playing in the reserve side as a striker, but has remained at the back since then. With more experience, he could well become effective at both ends of the park.

Oxford U (From juniors on 2/7/96) FL 0+1

STEVENS Shaun Delano
Born: London, 28 September 1978
Height: 5'7" Weight: 10.4

Having been released by Millwall, where he had been a YTS, he was given a short contract by Notts County, prior to 1997-98 getting underway, with the opportunity to prove his worth. A very fast and able striker, who always impressed with his willingness to run, sadly the financial regime at County precluded any extension of his contract, and he left the club in October after just one appearance as a sub at Tranmere in the Coca Cola Cup.

Notts Co (Free from Millwall juniors on 5/8/97) FLC 0+1

STEWART William Paul Marcus
Born: Bristol, 7 November 1972
Height: 5'10" Weight: 11.0
International Honours: E: Sch

Fully recovered from shin surgery, Marcus started last season with high hopes of finding the form that made him Huddersfield's record signing, but much too often he was given little or no service in the early part of the campaign, thus affecting his goalscoring contributions. An upturn in fortunes coincided with Town finding him a new strike partner, Wayne Allison, and he blossomed in his new surroundings, becoming the club's top scorer for 1997-98. A skilful striker who knows where the goal is, and very fast around the box, Allison was an excellent foil for his talents.

Bristol Rov (From trainee on 18/7/91) FL 137+34/57 FLC 11/5 FAC 7+1/3 Others 16+1/14
Huddersfield T (£1,200,000 + on 2/7/96) FL 57+4/23 FLC 8/4 FAC 3/1

Marcus Stewart

STEWART Paul Andrew
Born: Manchester, 7 October 1964
Height: 5'11" Weight: 12.4
Club Honours: FAC '91; Div 1 '94, '96
International Honours: E: 3; B-5; U21-1; Yth

Released by Sunderland during the 1997

close season and signing for Stoke, Paul, who had often played in midfield previously, quickly settled into a striking role at his new club. Initially dubious at the prospect of an ageing striker come to finish his professional time, the supporters were won over by his commitment to the cause and professionalism, as he forged a striking pairing with Peter Thorne. Suffering more than his share of injuries, particularly a recurring thigh problem, he had some fine games to look back on in a difficult season, most notably an excellent showing in the 1-0 win at Manchester City, one of his earlier clubs.

Blackpool (From apprentice on 13/10/81) FL 188+13/56 FLC 11/3 FAC 7/2 Others 6/1
Manchester C (£200,000 on 19/3/87) FL 51/26 FLC 4/2 FAC 6/1 Others 2/1
Tottenham H (£1,700,000 on 21/6/88) FL 126+5/28 FLC 23/7 FAC 9/2 Others 9
Liverpool (£2,300,000 on 29/7/92) PL 28+4/1 FLC 6 FAC 1 Others 3/2
Crystal Palace (Loaned on 24/1/94) FL 18/3
Wolverhampton W (Loaned on 2/9/94) FL 5+3/2 Others 2
Burnley (Loaned on 8/2/95) FL 6
Sunderland (Loaned on 29/8/95) FL 1+1
Sunderland (Free on 5/3/96) P/FL 30+4/5 FLC 3
Stoke C (Free on 25/6/97) FL 22/3 FLC 2 FAC 1

STIMAC Igor
Born: Croatia, 6 September 1967
Height: 6'2" Weight: 13.0
International Honours: Croatia: 34

A tall and imposing Croatian international centre half, whose place in the Derby defence in 1997-98 was interrupted on several occasions by a back injury – a similar situation to the previous season – he is very much the typical continental defender, tough in the tackle and comfortable in distribution of the ball. Most definitely one of the men to build your team around, when fit his calmness under pressure, and ability to retain the ball, is inspirational. Once again a key member of the Croatian side, Igor was looking forward with anticipation to an eventual meeting with England in France '98. *Stop Press:* Appeared in all of Croatia's World Cup games in France during the summer, the country's first time on the big stage, and impressed all the way to the semi-final and then the third place, following a 2-1 win over Holland.

Derby Co (£1,570,000 from Hadjuk Split on 31/10/95) F/PL 70/3 FLC 1 FAC 4

STIMSON Mark
Born: Plaistow, 27 December 1967
Height: 5'11" Weight: 12.6

After the opening game of last season, injury forced Mark out of the Southend side until December, but as an amazingly committed and wholehearted left back, who never shirks a challenge, possibly the reason he spends so much time on the physio's couch, he came back strongly. His defensive qualities are good, as are his attacking tendencies, and his overlapping and crossing was shown to good effect on his return to the team.

Tottenham H (From apprentice on 15/7/85) FL 1+1

Leyton Orient (Loaned on 15/3/88) FL 10
Gillingham (Loaned on 19/1/89) FL 18
Newcastle U (£200,000 on 16/6/89) FL 82+4/2 FLC 5 FAC 7/1 Others 6
Portsmouth (Loaned on 10/12/92) FL 3+1
Portsmouth (£100,000 on 23/7/93) FL 57+1/2 FLC 9/1 FAC 3 Others 3
Barnet (Loaned on 21/9/95) FL 5 Others 1
Southend U (£25,000 on 15/3/96) FL 34+5 Others 1

STOCKDALE Robert (Robbie) Keith
Born: Middlesbrough, 30 November 1979
Height: 5'11" Weight: 11.3

Still a trainee at Middlesbrough, and extremely well thought of, Robbie was surprisingly blooded in the FA Cup replay against Queens Park Rangers in January and followed that up with a Football League debut at the Cellnet against Tranmere three weeks later. A hard-tackling, aggressive right back, and an out-and-out defender, he has progressed through the Boro youth set up, along with other youngsters like Anthony Ormerod, to prove that there is more to the club than the foreign legion.
Middlesbrough (Trainee) FL 1 FAC 1

STOCKLEY Samuel (Sam) Joshua
Born: Tiverton, 5 September 1977
Height: 5'10" Weight: 12.0

Sam missed very few games for Barnet last season as he continued to prove both tough and tenacious, and the ideal man to fill the right-wing back role. Young, and still improving, he can run all day long in his quest to win the ball.
Southampton (From trainee on 1/7/96)
Barnet (Free on 31/12/96) FL 61+1 FLC 4 FAC 1 Others 4

Micky Stockwell

STOCKWELL Michael (Micky) Thomas
Born: Chelmsford, 14 February 1965
Height: 5'9" Weight: 11.4
Club Honours: Div 2 '92

Micky continued to amaze all at Ipswich in 1997-98 with his stamina and energy, as he celebrated his 500th appearance for the club during the season, still running up and down the pitch like a youngster. Once again he started a campaign in the right-back berth, but played most games on the right-hand side of the midfield four, and continued to cause problems for opposition defences down their left flank. Having missed just one game although ever present in the league, he was runner up in the Supporters' Player of the Year poll and, although his goalscoring was not as prolific, there was the equaliser at Bristol Rovers, which enabled Ipswich to earn a replay in the FA Cup.
Ipswich T (From apprentice on 17/12/82) F/PL 420+21/31 FLC 36+4/4 FAC 26+3/2 Others 22+2/2

STOKER Gareth
Born: Bishop Auckland, 22 February 1973
Height: 5'9" Weight: 10.10

A genuine 100 per-cent character who, in the right circumstances, is capable of inspiring his team, Gareth is enthusiastic and willing to run all day for Cardiff. At Shrewsbury, when the Bluebirds were struggling badly, he was sent on to try and pep things up, producing the desired effect following a stirring tackle on Devon White, the big Shrewsbury striker, the team's performance being visibly lifted by the young man's intervention. A ball winner who then gives a simple pass to a team mate, his season ended in bitter disappointment after he injured a knee during a midweek friendly against a college side. Initially, the injury did not look too bad, but he needed an operation on cruciate ligament damage and was ruled out for months. Still under contract at Cardiff City, though, hopefully, he will be back during 1998-99.
Hull C (Free from Leeds U juniors on 13/9/91) FL 24+6/2 FLC 3 FAC 2+1 Others 0+2 (Released during 1993 close season)
Hereford U (Signed from Bishop Auckland on 16/3/95) FL 65+5/6 FLC 5+1 FAC 3+1/1 Others 6+1/1
Cardiff C (£80,000 on 29/1/97) FL 29+8/4 FLC 1+1 FAC 1+3 Others 2+1

STOKES Dean Anthony
Born: Birmingham, 23 May 1970
Height: 5'9" Weight: 11.2

Dean, a reserve left back for Port Vale, was limited to just six starts last season, but, as usual, he gave 100 per cent every time he pulled the shirt on, once again proving to be strong in the tackle. Suffered a bad facial injury at Sheffield United (the ground at which he was carried off in 1996-97) when he lost a couple of teeth, before being released during the summer.
Port Vale (Signed from Halesowen T on 15/1/93) FL 53+7 FLC 1+1 FAC 4 Others 5+3

STONE Steven (Steve) Brian
Born: Gateshead, 20 August 1971
Height: 5'9" Weight: 12.7
Club Honours: Div 1 '98
International Honours: E: 9

Started 1997-98 for Nottingham Forest after

missing most of the previous season with a serious knee injury and appeared in the opening two league games before going down with a hernia problem. Came back in October and stayed on throughout the campaign, returning to full fitness and top form, and playing a major part in helping Forest to the first division title, and a further taste of the Premiership. With the ability to run all day, whether defending or linking up with the forwards, this hard-working, right-sided midfielder is also comfortable on the ball, passes well, and occasionally gets into good scoring positions. If he remains injury free, Steve is certain to go well in 1998-99.
Nottingham F (From trainee on 20/5/89) F/PL 163+4/20 FLC 11+1 FAC 8 Others 12/2

STONES Craig
Born: Scunthorpe, 31 May 1980
Height: 5'11" Weight: 11.2

The teenager signed on a three-year contract in the summer of 1997 after completing his first year as a trainee at Lincoln, having been a regular in the first team squad in 1997-98, where he showed plenty of ability for a player of such a young age. Appearing 18 times in all, 12 of them starts, the midfielder will undoubtedly have the scouts flocking to Sincil Bank in 1998-99.
Lincoln C (From trainee on 1/7/97) FL 10+7 FAC 1+1 Others 1

Stuart Storer

STORER Stuart John
Born: Rugby, 16 January 1967
Height: 5'11" Weight: 12.13
Club Honours: AMC '89

No player contributed more to Brighton and Hove Albion's survival battle in 1997-98 than Stuart. The enthusiastic, pacy forward continued to play despite a hernia problem, but was eventually forced to submit to

surgery in early January. Typically, he returned to first team action just five weeks after the operation, and quickly regained his form. With the departure of five of the club's top earners as part of an economy drive in December, the 31-year old became the Seagulls' senior professional.

Mansfield T (Juniors) FL 0+1 (Freed in March 1984)
Birmingham C (Free from VS Rugby on 10/1/85) FL 5+3 FLC 1
Everton (Signed on 6/3/87)
Wigan Ath (Loaned on 23/7/87) FL 9+3 FLC 4
Bolton W (£25,000 on 24/12/87) FL 95+28/12 FLC 9+2 FAC 7+3/2 Others 16+5/1
Exeter C (£25,000 on 25/3/93) FL 75+2/8 FLC 4/1 FAC 4+1/1 Others 6
Brighton & Hove A (£15,000 on 2/3/95) FL 100+19/11 FLC 5+1 FAC 4+1/1 Others 4/1

STOWELL Michael (Mike)
Born: Portsmouth, 19 April 1965
Height: 6'2" Weight: 14.2

The Wolves' goalkeeper did not concede anything for 199 minutes of last season, only to advance too far and be beaten by a back pass. Despite some inconsistency, he made some stunning saves and when he stopped an Ipswich penalty there was a follow-up shot which saw him produce an even better stop. In the FA Cup he helped Wolves beat Wimbledon 2-1, showing fine reflexes to push powerful close-in efforts to safety, and before an illness ended his run in the team he had appeared in all 43 matches.

Preston NE (Free from Leyland Motors on 14/2/85)
Everton (Free on 12/12/85) Others 1
Chester C (Loaned on 3/9/87) FL 14 Others 2
York C (Loaned on 24/12/87) FL 6
Manchester C (Loaned on 2/2/88) FL 14 FAC 1
Port Vale (Loaned on 21/10/88) FL 7 Others 1
Wolverhampton W (Loaned on 17/3/89) FL 7
Preston NE (Loaned on 8/2/90) FL 2
Wolverhampton W (£250,000 on 28/6/90) FL 313 FLC 23 FAC 19 Others 11

STRACHAN Gavin David
Born: Aberdeen, 23 December 1978
Height: 5'11" Weight: 11.7
International Honours: S: U21-2; Yth

Gavin is a combative Coventry midfielder who models himself on Gary McAllister more than his father, Gordon, the City manager. Regardless of that, following several substitute appearances, he was thrown into the deep end at Villa Park in the FA Cup because of Paul Telfer's suspension, and did not let the side down, his was the pass which set George Boateng away for the move which led to the goal. A great prospect for the future, and recognised by the Scottish U21 selectors in 1997-98 with two caps, he played in the first cup tie against Sheffield United and won the penalty with a great surge into the area.

Coventry C (From trainee on 28/11/96) PL 2+7 FAC 2+2

STREET Kevin
Born: Crewe, 25 November 1977
Height: 5'10" Weight: 10.8

Introduced to the Crewe subs' bench early on in 1997-98, after making steady progress through the youth and reserve sides at Gresty Road, the young forward soon became a regular member of the first team squad after scoring the winner against Tranmere just 14 minutes into his first appearance. Able to play right across the front line, with good feet, and developing as the season progressed, Kevin looks to be a real prospect.

Crewe Alex (From trainee on 4/7/96) FL 15+17/4

Kevin Street

STREETER Terence (Terry) Stephen
Born: Brighton, 26 October 1969
Height: 6'1" Weight: 13.0

A talented Brighton and Hove Albion YTS trainee, the big and strong 18-year-old striker's performances in the reserve team were impressive, and he was given his chance in the senior squad towards the end of last season, after the Seagulls had ensured that their Football League place was secure. Was rewarded for his endeavours at the end of the campaign when the manager, Brian Horton, advised him that he would be receiving a one-year contract on completing his YTS period.

Brighton & Hove A (Trainee) FL 0+2

STRODDER Gary John
Born: Cleckheaton, 1 April 1965
Height: 6'1" Weight: 13.3
Club Honours: Div 3 '98

The rock and foundation around which the highly successful 1997-98 Notts County team that ultimately won the third division title was built, Gary's tough, uncompromising style often inspired the younger players around him. Powerful in the air, and always a danger at set pieces, he was another County man who was chosen for the PFA division three select by his fellow professionals. Is a great enthusiast with an amusing literary style in the club programme.*

Lincoln C (From apprentice on 8/4/83) FL 122+10/6 FLC 7+1 FAC 2+1 Others 5+1
West Ham U (Signed on 20/3/87) FL 59+6/2 FLC 8 FAC 4+2 Others 2
West Bromwich A (£190,000 on 22/8/90) FL 123+17/8 FLC 8+1 FAC 7/1 Others 10
Notts Co (£145,000 on 14/7/95) FL 108+2/9 FLC 8 FAC 9 Others 6

STRONG Gregory (Greg)
Born: Bolton, 5 September 1975
Height: 6'2" Weight: 11.12
International Honours: E: Yth; Sch

A powerful central defender who was bought for the future and had failed to make an appearance for Bolton in 1996-97, Greg at least managed three games in 1997-98, one of them being his full debut, at Leyton Orient in the Coca Cola Cup. Following that, in an effort to keep him active, and to further his experience, he was loaned to Blackpool in November as a stand-in for the injured David Linighan, and made an immediate impact when scoring the only goal of the game against York on his way to winning the Man of the Match award. Back at the Reebok, he will be hoping that the breakthrough is not far away.

Wigan Ath (From trainee on 1/10/92) FL 28+7/3 FLC 5 FAC 1 Others 3+1
Bolton W Signed on 10/9/95) PL 0+1 FLC 1+1
Blackpool (Loaned on 21/11/97) FL 11/1 Others 1

STUART Graham Charles
Born: Tooting, 24 October 1970
Height: 5'9" Weight: 11.10
Club Honours: FAC '95
International Honours: E: U21-5; Yth

A versatile and talented player, at home in midfield or up front, Graham was ever present at Everton last season until being sold to Sheffield United at the end of November. His value to the club had been inestimable, scoring a number of significant goals, including the winner in Everton's first win in 1997-98, against West Ham. As part of the deal that took Mitch Ward and Carl Tiler in the opposite direction, he took some time to win the fans over, mainly because he was playing away from his favourite position but, following his first goal for his new club, at Queens Park Rangers, all that changed. Having ended the longest spell of his career without a goal, his form improved and he ended the campaign very strongly until a broken hand forced him to miss the play offs, an injury which may have been significant in United's failure to progress beyond the semi-final stage. With workrate to spare, he is certain to give United more of the same in 1998-99.

Chelsea (From trainee on 15/6/89) F/PL 70+17/14 FLC 11/2 FAC 5+2/1 Others 3+2/1
Everton (£850,000 on 19/8/93) PL 116+20/23 FLC 9/3 FAC 10+3/5 Others 2+1/1
Sheffield U (£850,000 on 28/11/97) FL 27+1/5 FAC 6 Others 0+1

STUART Jamie Christopher
Born: Southwark, 15 October 1976
Height: 5'10" Weight: 11.0
International Honours: E: U21-4; Yth

A left-footed defender, Jamie only made one appearance for Charlton during last season, when he came on as substitute for the

second half against Ipswich at the Valley in the Coca Cola Cup. Normally a left back, he played in central defence, and looked very assured. Quick, and a good passer of the ball, with a penchant to get forward and put early crosses into the box, his contract was cancelled by the club in December after he failed a routine drugs test.

Charlton Ath (From trainee on 18/1/95) FL 49+1/3 FLC 8+1 FAC 3 Others 0+1

STUART Mark Richard
Born: Chiswick, 15 December 1966
Height: 5'10" Weight: 11.10
International Honours: E: Sch

As Rochdale's longest-serving player, Mark was again a regular on the left flank in 1997-98 and, although starting a number of games on the bench, he almost always came on at some point, as when netting the winner against Hull. Still a tricky, classy wingman on his day, his best performance was probably in Dale's rare away success, also against Hull, when he scored with a trademark free kick, his 40th league goal for the club.*

Charlton Ath (From juniors on 3/7/84) FL 89+18/28 FLC 7+3/2 FAC 1/1 Others 9+1
Plymouth Arg (£150,000 on 4/11/88) FL 55+2/11 FLC 4 FAC 3 Others 2/1
Ipswich T (Loaned on 22/3/90) FL 5/2
Bradford C (£80,000 on 3/8/90) FL 22+7/5 FLC 6/1 FAC 0+1 Others 1+1
Huddersfield T (Free on 30/10/92) FL 9+6/3 FAC 2 Others 4/1
Rochdale (Free on 5/7/93) FL 157+26/41 FLC 9+1/1 FAC 6/1 Others 6+4/2

STURGESS Paul Christopher
Born: Dartford, 4 August 1975
Height: 5'11" Weight: 12.5

Transferred from Charlton during the 1997 summer period, Paul started the first 11 matches at left back for Millwall in 1997-98 and played a few more times prior to Christmas, before becoming yet another Lion to be sidelined for the remainder of the campaign. Predominately a left back, but equally at home in midfield, he is quick, hard tackling, difficult to pass, and a player who loves to get forward to deliver quality crosses. In short, the club will eventually find him to be an asset.

Charlton Ath (From trainee on 1/7/93) FL 43+8 FLC 4+1 FAC 1 Others 5
Millwall (Free on 3/7/97) FL 12+2 FLC 4 FAC 1 Others 0+1

STURRIDGE Dean Constantine
Born: Birmingham, 26 July 1973
Height: 5'8" Weight: 12.1

The ever-popular, strong and direct striker began last season at Derby recovering from the effects of a cartilage operation, but soon regained his regular first team spot, forming an exciting and effective partnership with Pablo Wanchope. Despite his sharpness and ability to run at defenders in danger areas, he still needs to build on the undoubted potential which earned him a long-term contract with the club, especially when finding goals harder to come by in the second half of the campaign. However, Dean showed that he was becoming more positionally aware and interacted well with

the Rams' more recent tactics, when picking out better placed colleagues.

Derby Co (From trainee on 1/7/91) P/FL 102+20/41 FLC 5+1/2 FAC 3/2 Others 2+1
Torquay U (Loaned on 16/12/94) FL 10/5

Dean Sturridge

STURRIDGE Simon Andrew
Born: Birmingham, 9 December 1969
Height: 5'6" Weight: 11.8
Club Honours: AMC '91

Having recovered from a cruciate ligament knee injury from the previous campaign, Simon made two very short substitute appearances for Stoke in 1997-98 before damaging the cruciate in his other knee at Rochdale. While recovery looks to be on course, and no doubt his confidence was boosted by the club's decision to extend his contract for another term, it was an awesome injury and destroyed any chance of his return to the side last season. The brother of Derby's Dean, and a speedy little striker who enjoys running at defences, surely luck will change for this very popular player.

Birmingham C (From trainee on 8/7/88) FL 129+21/30 FLC 10+4/1 FAC 8/2 Others 14/5
Stoke C (£75,000 on 24/9/93) FL 42+26/14 FLC 2+1 FAC 3+3/1 Others 7+3

SULLIVAN Neil
Born: Sutton, 24 February 1970
Height: 6'0" Weight: 12.1
International Honours: S: 3

The one-time Wimbledon trainee bloomed into one of the best goalkeepers in the Premiership in 1997-98 and was picked for the Scottish squad to play in the World Cup

in France during the summer. Good at shot-stopping and dealing with crosses, whilst organising his defence well, Neil continued to pull off some fine saves as an ever present to keep the Dons in the game when the pressure was almost unbearable during this past tricky season. Kept 15 clean sheets, four of them in succession, and six out of the final nine games that were interspersed by uncharacteristic defeats, 5-0 at Arsenal, who were riding high and went on to win the Premiership, and 6-2 at home to a desperate Tottenham who were fighting to avoid relegation. Possesses an excellent long kick. *Stop Press:* Despite playing twice for Scotland during the season, he was out of luck in the World Cup Finals during the summer and could only sit and watch as Jim Leighton saw out all three games.

Wimbledon (From trainee on 26/7/88) F/PL 105+1 FLC 8 FAC 20
Crystal Palace (Loaned on 1/5/92) FL 1

SUMMERBEE Nicholas (Nicky) John
Born: Altrincham, 26 August 1971
Height: 5'11" Weight: 12.8
International Honours: E: B-1; U21-3

It was quite a surprise for many in the football world when Manchester City decided on a direct swop involving Nicky and Sunderland's Craig Russell last November, but as it turned out it could not have been better. A right-sided player who is adept at bringing the ball out of defence, drifting past defenders as if they do not exist, or performing further forward, he made an immediate impact, scoring on his debut at Portsmouth, and going on to play a key role in the club's 17-match mid-season unbeaten run. He also forged a fine partnership with Darren Holloway down the right flank, where his crossing ability provided good service for Niall Quinn and Kevin Phillips as the club stormed into the play-off positions. This was never better emphasised than when he returned to Maine Road with his new club and crossed a beautifully flighted ball for Phillips to net the winner.

Swindon T (From trainee on 20/7/89) F/PL 89+23/6 FLC 9+1/3 FAC 2+4 Others 7/1
Manchester C (£1,500,000 on 24/6/94) P/FL 119+12/6 FLC 11+2/2 FAC 12/2
Sunderland (£1,000,000 on 14/11/97) FL 22+3/3 FAC 2 Others 3/1

SUMMERBELL Mark
Born: Durham, 30 October 1976
Height: 5'10" Weight: 11.9

An aspiring young Middlesbrough midfielder, Mark followed up his three substitute appearances made in 1996-97 with a further 12 games in 1997-98, including eight starts. He also scored his first goal for the club, the opener in a 2-1 win over Bolton and one that ensured Boro progressed in the Coca Cola Cup. Still highly thought of at the club as a prospect who could go a long way in the game, he buzzes around midfield, reads the game well, passes incisively, and loves to go forward with the ball.

Middlesbrough (From trainee on 1/7/95) F/PL 7+7 FLC 1/1

SUNDGOT Ole Bjorn
Born: Olsmund, Norway, 21 March 1972
Height: 6'1" Weight: 11.4
International Honours: Norway: 1

Having had a run in the Bradford side during 1996-97, and getting among the goals, Ole was expected to be one of the club's leading marksman last season, but, in the event, he did not come up to expectation and, after becoming homesick, returned to Norway with Molde at the end of November. A strong, burly striker, there were just six subs' appearances and no goals prior to him leaving.

Bradford C (Free from Molde on 1/11/96) FL 11+14/6 FLC 0+1

SUTCH Daryl
Born: Beccles, 11 September 1971
Height: 6'0" Weight: 12.0
International Honours: E: U21-4; Yth

Apart from Andy Marshall, the only other Norwich player to start in more than 40 league games in 1997-98, Daryl signed a new contract which takes him through to June 2001 and, having been at the club for over ten years, if you allow for his YTS time, 1998-99 has been designated for his testimonial campaign. Consistent at either right or left back, with pace and good engines, and his ability to play in a more attacking role being very useful to his manager, he continued to mature last season. Can also be used in a man-marking role.

Norwich C (From trainee on 6/7/90) F/PL 132+33/7 FLC 11+3 FAC 6+3 Others 2+3

SUTHERLAND Colin
Born: Glasgow, 15 March 1975
Height: 5'11" Weight: 11.10

A useful squad player at Scarborough in 1997-98, Colin is primarily a left back, but his strength and heading ability enable him to adapt to a central defensive role when required. One of the few players at the McCain Stadium to cost a fee, he was surprisingly released on a free transfer at the end of the season.

Clydebank (Free from Kilpatrick Juniors on 24/2/95) SL 42+1/2 SLC 2+1 SC 1 Others 3
Scarborough (Signed on 20/12/96) FL 35+8 FLC 2 FAC 1 Others 1+1

SUTTON Christopher (Chris) Roy
Born: Nottingham, 10 March 1973
Height: 6'3" Weight: 13.5
Club Honours: PL '95
International Honours: E: 1; B-2; U21-13

The controversy about Chris refusing to play for the England "B" side in 1997-98, having earlier played for the full side against the Cameroon, overshadowed a fine season in which the striker not only scored goals, but led the Blackburn line in a manner that brought the best from those alongside him. Mobile, able to hold the ball and turn, and bring others into the game, he looked the genuine article, a complete footballer, and his hat trick against Leicester was a sample of all that is good about English football, goals scored with skill and intelligence. He also struck another hat trick in a 4-0 win at Aston Villa on 13 August. Carling player of

the month in February, he finished tied with Michael Owen and Dion Dublin as the Premiership's leading scorer, and his final goal, a blistering free kick two minutes from the end of the final game, took the side into Europe.

Norwich C (From trainee on 2/7/91) F/PL 89+13/35 FLC 8+1/3 FAC 10/5 Others 6
Blackburn Rov (£5,000,000 on 13/7/94) PL 108+5/44 FLC 10+1/6 FAC 8/4 Others 6+3/1

SVENSSON Mathias (Matt)
Born: Boras, Sweden, 24 September 1974
Height: 6'0" Weight: 12.4
International Honours: Sweden: 1

Matt was unable to reproduce his form from the previous season in 1997-98 at Portsmouth, scoring only five goals in 29 appearances, despite starting the campaign well when striking four in his first five games. However, injury and loss of form did not help his cause and, after failing to link effectively with John Aloisi up front, when Alan Ball arrived as manager he was used only as a fringe player. A strong, bustling striker, though, with Pompey staring relegation in the face, he returned for the last two games, replacing John Aloisi, and formed an effective partnership with John Durnin, which saw the latter score three goals, thus helping to avert the drop into division two. *Stop Press:* Joined the Austrian club, Innsbruck, for £100,000 on 7 July.

Portsmouth (£200,000 from Elfsborg on 6/12/96) FL 34+11/10 FLC 1/1 FAC 3+2/1

SWAILES Christopher (Chris) William
Born: Gateshead, 19 October 1970
Height: 6'2" Weight: 12.11

Having performed so well at the end of 1996-97, it seemed natural that Chris would begin 1997-98 at the heart of the Ipswich defence, but the close season signing of Mark Venus changed all that and he was to be found on the substitutes' bench on the opening day of the season. After deputising for Jason Cundy in four games at the start of September, and making one further appearance as a substitute, he moved to Bury as part of the David Johnson deal in November. Initially, his luck changed at his new abode, scoring against Oxford on his debut and enjoying a run of nine successive games before losing his place to Gordon Armstrong. Still quick for a big man, the last four months of the campaign proved frustrating as he seldom featured, even among those on the subs' bench.

Ipswich T (From trainee on 23/5/89)
Peterborough U (£10,000 on 28/3/91 - Free to Boston in August 1991)
Doncaster Rov (Free from Bridlington T on 27/10/93) FL 49 FLC 2/1 FAC 1 Others 2
Ipswich T (£225,000 on 23/3/95) P/FL 34+3/1 FLC 3 Others 2
Bury (£200,000 on 14/11/97) FL 12+1/1 FAC 2

SWALES Stephen (Steve) Colin
Born: Whitby, 26 December 1973
Height: 5'8" Weight: 10.6

A left-wing back with pace and good tackling ability, Steve enjoyed the best possible start to last season as he lashed in a

left-wing cross from Lee Hodges to score Reading's first goal of 1997-98 after 12 minutes of the opening day's fixture at Bury. After that everything was going to be something of an anti-climax, but he had the satisfaction of keeping a fairly regular place in the team, though he was only selected as substitute by the new manager, Tommy Burns. However, he signed a new two-year deal with the club which will keep him playing for the Royals until the summer of 2000.

Scarborough (From trainee on 3/8/92) FL 51+3/1 FAC 5 Others 3
Reading (£70,000 on 13/7/95) FL 33+10/1 FLC 6+1 FAC 6

SWAN Peter Harold
Born: Leeds, 28 September 1966
Height: 6'2" Weight: 15.9
Club Honours: AMC '93

An eve of season capture from Burnley, the experienced central defender proved to be an integral part of Bury's team in 1997-98, whether performing heroics in defence or using the strength of his near 16-stone frame to advantage in attack. Indeed, in certain instances he switched roles during the same games. While "Swaney" may have lost much of his speed these days, he still proved to be a handful for first division defenders and ended the campaign with six goals.

Leeds U (From trainee on 6/8/84) FL 43+6/11 FLC 3/2 FAC 3 Others 1+2
Hull C (£200,000 on 23/3/89) FL 76+4/24 FLC 2+3/1 FAC 2 Others 1
Port Vale (£300,000 on 16/8/91) FL 105+6/5 FLC 6 FAC 9/1 Others 12/1
Plymouth Arg (£300,000 on 22/7/94) FL 24+3/2 FLC 2/1 FAC 2
Burnley (£200,000 on 4/8/95) FL 47+2/7 FLC 2 FAC 3 Others 6
Bury (£50,000 on 8/8/97) FL 26+11/6 FLC 1+1 FAC 1

SYMONS Christopher (Kit) Jeremiah
Born: Basingstoke, 8 March 1971
Height: 6'2" Weight: 13.7
International Honours: W: 27; B-1; U21-2; Yth

Having played the previous two seasons for Manchester City without missing a game, other than two through injury and one when getting married in Portsmouth Cathedral, Kit was looking forward to 1997-98 with some relish. Started as captain but, with the club always seeming to be fighting an uphill battle to avoid the drop into division two, his form suffered and he relinquished the responsibility in an effort to regain some stability back into his game. However, when the new manager, Joe Royle, arrived in February he was re-instated as captain, but before long he was relegated to the subs' bench and, although coming back for the final three games, there was no respite as City were ultimately relegated. A central defender with foresight and skill, he will be one of the men that Royle will be looking to if the club is to make an immediate return.*

Portsmouth (From trainee on 30/12/88) FL 161/10 FLC 19 FAC 10 Others 13+1/1
Manchester C (£1,600,000 on 17/8/95) P/FL 124/4 FLC 6 FAC 9

TAAFFE Steven Lee
Born: Stoke, 10 September 1979
Height: 5'5" Weight: 9.0
Whilst of only small physique, the former trainee showed enough in a number of startling reserve and youth team performances last season to earn a place, initially on the Stoke first team bench from where he made his debut, playing the last 20 minutes of a home defeat at the hands of Tranmere in March. A young, very competitive, and mobile striker, his goalscoring record in 1997-98 in all competitions exceeded 30.
Stoke C (From trainee on 8/8/96) FL 0+3

TAGGART Gerald (Gerry) Paul
Born: Belfast, 18 October 1970
Height: 6'1" Weight: 13.12
Club Honours: Div 1 '97
International Honours: NI: 45; U23-2; Yth; Sch
Last season was a somewhat frustrating one for Gerry, who, injured at the end of October, was out of action for almost six months after forming a strong centre-back pairing with Mark Fish. A Northern Ireland international, with a considerable amount of experience, he returned to action in the vital away win at Aston Villa in April, and promptly won the Man of the Match award, his no-nonsense, tough-tackling style making him a formidable opponent. Contract disagreements were reported at the end of 1997-98, and if the problem is not resolved the Trotters could have a lot of potential buyers vying for Gerry's signature come the new season. Is particularly dangerous at the other end of the field, especially at set pieces.
Manchester C (From trainee on 1/7/89) FL 10+2/1 Others 1
Barnsley (£75,000 on 10/1/90) FL 209+3/16 FLC 15/1 FAC 14/2 Others 6/1
Bolton W (£1,500,000 on 1/8/95) F/PL 68+1/4 FLC 8/1 FAC 4

TAIT Paul Ronald
Born: Sutton Coldfield, 31 July 1971
Height: 6'1" Weight: 10.10
Club Honours: Div 2 '95; AMC '95
Unable to reach match fitness at Birmingham in 1997-98, having pulled a hamstring in pre-season, the combative midfielder was loaned out to Northampton in December with a view to putting a few games under his belt. In the event, however, he had to return to St Andrews after a couple of starts, due to a stomach muscle injury, and from then on it meant battling against a series of niggling problems in order to get him fit in time for 1998-99, his testimonial year. Once described as "the new Trevor Francis", Paul's career has been a constant struggle against injury.
Birmingham C (From trainee on 2/8/88) FL 135+35/14 FLC 13+2 FAC 6+2 Others 13+5/4
Northampton T (Loaned on 24/12/97) FL 2+1

TALBOT Stewart
Born: Birmingham, 14 June 1973
Height: 5'11" Weight: 13.7
An energetic Port Vale midfield player who led the club's appearance charts last season, Stewart has a good engine in motoring from box to box and his eye for goal is evidenced by his six strikes last season. Good in the air, his enthusiasm holds no bounds, which sometimes brings him more bookings than he deserves and he missed only three games last season, two of them due to suspension.
Port Vale (Signed from Moor Green on 10/8/94) FL 77+21/12 FLC 2+3 FAC 4+1 Others 2+3/1

TALBOYS Steven (Steve) John
Born: Bristol, 18 September 1966
Height: 5'10" Weight: 11.10
A mobile left-sided player who enjoys getting into crossing and shooting positions, Steve started last season in Watford's first team squad, but was unable to clinch a place. Although leaving Vicarage Road in January, in order to pursue a career outside football, he remains involved at non-league level, where his stamina and pace can still be put to good advantage.
Wimbledon (£10,000 from Gloucester C on 10/1/92) PL 19+7/1 FLC 2+1 FAC 1+1
Watford (Free on 25/7/96) FL 2+3 FLC 0+1 Others 1

TALIA Francesco (Frank)
Born: Melbourne, Australia, 20 July 1972
Height: 6'1" Weight: 13.6
Club Honours: Div 2 '96
As second choice behind Fraser Digby at the start of last season, Frank's only appearance before Christmas came in a Coca Cola Cup tie at Watford. Later troubled by a persistent knee injury, he made just two starts in the league in February/March – both ending in defeat by a single goal, before undergoing surgery in a bid to cure the problem. Expected to challenge new Town signing, Jimmy Glass, for the number one jersey in 1998-99, he is extremely agile, and a good shot-stopper, who also comes out well for crosses.
Blackburn Rov (Free from Sunshine George Cross on 28/8/92)
Hartlepool U (Loaned on 29/12/92) FL 14 Others 1
Swindon T (£150,000 on 8/9/95) FL 33 FLC 6

TALLON Gerrit (Gary) Thomas
Born: Drogheda, 5 September 1973
Height: 5'10" Weight: 12.7
Gary, a bubbly young Irish player, was taken on trial at Mansfield last December after giving an impressive performance against them in a reserve match, having earlier been released by Kilmarnock. Rapidly improving with every game, he showed himself to be a talented left-sided midfielder who was skilful in going forward to produce superb crosses for the target men. Opened his scoring account in the 2-0 home win over Peterborough.
Blackburn Rov (£30,000 from Drogheda U on 27/11/91)
Kilmarnock (Free on 20/6/96) SL 4 SLC 1 SC 1
Chester C (Loaned on 26/3/97) FL 1
Mansfield T (Free on 1/12/97) FL 26/1 Others 2

TANKARD Allen John
Born: Islington, 21 May 1969
Height: 5'10" Weight: 12.10
Despite being the regular left back for Port Vale in 1997-98, Allen would probably admit that it was not one of his best campaigns. With a penchant to get forward to supplement the attack, which sometimes meant that the team were caught on the break, he was the unfortunate player who missed the decisive penalty in the FA Cup shoot-out defeat against Arsenal, after having had one of his best games of the season.
Southampton (From apprentice on 27/5/87) FL 5 Others 2
Wigan Ath (Free on 4/7/88) FL 205+4/4 FLC 15/1 FAC 13 Others 20
Port Vale (£87,500 on 26/7/93) FL 165+5/2 FLC 16 FAC 13/1 Others 8+1

TANNER Adam David
Born: Maldon, 25 October 1973
Height: 6'0" Weight: 12.1
Putting all the troubles of the previous season behind him, Adam got on with being a valuable member of the Ipswich first team squad in 1997-98, without ever establishing a permanent place. When he did play, it was usually in the central defensive position, which he appeared to have adopted in preference to his original midfield role, and managed to put that to good use as his distribution from the back was usually very good. Scored his only goal from the penalty spot against Bury and then proceeded to miss one at Wolverhampton. Recently signed a new two-year contract with the club.
Ipswich T (From trainee on 13/7/92) P/FL 36+18/7 FLC 1+1 FAC 5+1 Others 3+1/1

TARICCO Mauricio Ricardo
Born: Buenos Aires, Argentine, 10 March 1973
Height: 5'9" Weight: 11.7
Began last season in the left-back position at Ipswich, but the injury to Paul Mason meant their partnership was broken and it took a while to establish similar links with Bobby Petta. However, the arrival of Jamie Clapham saw him switched to right back and it was this formation that produced the wonderful unbeaten run which took Town to the play offs, Mauricio's contribution being recognised when he was named in the PFA Nationwide division one select team. Scored just two goals, both against Premiership opposition in the Coca Cola Cup, the first of which being the second in the 2-0 defeat of Manchester United, when he drove in a screamer of a shot from outside the area that fairly flew into the top corner of the net to earn him the Goal of the Season award from the supporters.
Ipswich T (£175,000 from Argentinos on 9/9/94) FL 118+3/3 FLC 14/2 FAC 8 Others 7

TATE Christopher (Chris) Douglas
Born: York, 27 December 1977
Height: 6'0" Weight: 11.10
Unable to get anywhere at Sunderland, Chris signed for Scarborough during the 1997 close season and proved to be a

promising young striker who is good in the air, while scoring regularly for the reserve team that won the Pontins League third division championship. Impressed when called into first team action, despite 23 of his 27 appearances coming from the bench, he should be pushing for a regular place in 1998-99.

Sunderland (Free from York C juniors on 17/7/96)
Scarborough (Free on 5/8/97) FL 3+2/1 FAC 0+1 Others 1+1

TAYLOR Craig

Born: Plymouth, 24 January 1974
Height: 6'1" Weight: 13.2

Signed from non-league Dorchester at the end of 1996-97, Craig was very disappointed when a groin injury picked up in the summer delayed his Football League debut for Swindon in 1997-98. But when the moment finally arrived – at home to Port Vale in October – it was the proverbial dream come true. Not only did he help Town record a 4-2 home win, he also scored a stunning goal from all of 30 yards. Older brother Shaun, now at Bristol City, had once been a big favourite with the fans, but the young defender had shown that Taylor "Mark II" could be just as big a hit with the County Ground faithful. Contributed just one more goal over the season, but benefited tremendously from playing alongside the likes of Alan McDonald and Brian Borrows, to enjoy a good first season.

Swindon T (£25,000 from Dorchester T on 15/4/97) FL 28+4/2 FAC 1

TAYLOR Gareth Keith

Born: Weston super Mare, 25 February 1973
Height: 6'2" Weight: 13.8
International Honours: W: 8; U21-7

The Sheffield United striker experienced an in-and-out season in 1997-98, when starting behind Brian Deane and Jan Aage Fjortoft in the queue for the starting strikers' role, and having to be content with a place on the bench. A string of impressive substitute appearances, including a stunning volley for the winner against Forest in September led to a call up to the Welsh squad, before a proposed £750,000 transfer to Huddersfield Town, fell through due to an alleged injury which would require keyhole surgery. Later linked with moves to Utrecht, Stoke City, Genoa, and Sochaux, he stayed to fight for a starting spot and remained a popular figure with the fans, who voiced their disapproval at the proposed transfers.

Bristol Rov (Free from Southampton juniors on 29/7/91) FL 31+16/16 FLC 3+1 FAC 1+1 Others 5
Crystal Palace (£750,000 on 27/9/95) FL 18+2/1 FAC 2/1
Sheffield U (Signed on 8/3/96) FL 49+23/23 FLC 5+2/1 FAC 5+2 Others 1+1

TAYLOR Ian Kenneth

Born: Birmingham, 4 June 1968
Height: 6'1" Weight: 12.4
Club Honours: AMC '93; FLC '96

An extremely versatile player, Ian had another excellent season for Aston Villa and scored some crucial goals, none more so than his effort against Steaua Bucharest in the UEFA Cup. In fact, goals were a real feature of his game in 1997-98, nine of them hitting the back of the net in all. One of the most popular players at Villa Park for the amount of hard work and effort he puts into every performance, he suffered a hamstring injury which kept him out for a couple of games in October and November, followed by a two-match suspension in February. In accepting that his committed style of play, and tenacious tackling will inevitably mean him picking up cautions along the way, at the same time he will be working on timing his tackles to better effect. Capable of playing in midfield, or as a forward, being good in the air and composed on the ball, he is a useful man for Villa to be able to call upon.

Port Vale (£15,000 from Moor Green on 13/7/92) FL 83/28 FLC 4/2 FAC 6/1 Others 13/4
Sheffield Wed (£1,000,000 on 12/7/94) PL 9+5/1 FLC 2+2/1
Aston Villa (£1,000,000 on 21/12/94) PL 105+8/12 FLC 8+1/2 FAC 7+1/1 Others 9/3

TAYLOR John Patrick

Born: Norwich, 24 October 1964
Height: 6'3" Weight: 13.12
Club Honours: Div 3 '91

Now in his second spell at Cambridge, "Shaggy" is an extremely popular player with both the fans and fellow professionals alike, and gave invaluable experience to the youngsters around him in 1997-98. an intelligent striker, who is good in the air, and always looks to help the defence out when it is under pressure, despite making just 19 full league appearances, he scored ten goals – an excellent strike rate. Will be taking on the responsibility for the reserve side in the Combination League in 1998-99.*

Colchester U (From juniors on 17/12/82)
Cambridge U (Signed from Sudbury T on 24/8/88) FL 139+21/46 FLC 9+2/2 FAC 21/10 Others 12+2/2
Bristol Rov (Signed on 28/3/92) FL 91+4/44 FLC 4/1 FAC 3 Others 5
Bradford C (£300,000 on 5/7/94) FL 35+1/11 FLC 4/2 FAC 2 Others 3
Luton T (£200,000 on 23/3/95) FL 27+10/3 FLC 2 Others 1/1
Lincoln C (Loaned on 27/9/96) FL 5/2
Colchester U (Loaned on 8/11/96) FL 8/5 Others 1
Cambridge U (Free on 10/1/97) FL 38+17/14 FLC 0+2 FAC 3+1

TAYLOR Lee Vincent

Born: Hammersmith, 24 February 1976
Height: 5'11" Weight: 12.0

Shrewsbury full back or central defender. The promise shown in his first season remained generally unfulfilled in 1997-98 as he was limited to only a handful of appearances in emergencies, spending most of the campaign in the reserve team, before being released during the summer. A player who is comfortable on the ball, further experience should do him the world of good.

Shrewsbury T (Free from Southwark Faweh on 14/8/96) FL 14+3 FLC 2 FAC 2

Ian Taylor

TAYLOR Maik Stefan
Born: Germany, 4 September 1971
Height: 6'4" Weight: 14.2
International Honours: NI: U21-1

Out of favour at Southampton, due to the good form shown by Paul Jones after his arrival from Stockport, the big goalkeeper was Ray Wilkins choice to backstop Fulham's promotion drive, signing for the club in November. A good shot-stopper, Maik kept 12 clean sheets in his 28 league matches and to think that only three years ago he won a Beazer Homes League championship medal for Farnborough Town. His many assets include shot-stopping, sound positional play, and good, safe hands. Despite being born in Germany and being 26 years of age, Maik was delighted to gain his first international honour as an over-age player for the Northern Ireland U21 side that beat Switzerland 2-1 in April.

Barnet (Free from Farnborough on 7/6/95) FL 70 FLC 6 FAC 6 Others 2
Southampton (£500,000 on 1/1/97) PL 18
Fulham (£800,000+ on 17/11/97) FL 28 FAC 2 Others 3

TAYLOR Robert Mark
Born: Birmingham, 22 February 1966
Height: 5'9" Weight: 12.5
Club Honours: Div 3 '94

With over 350 league appearances under his belt, on his day Mark can be a very influential midfielder, having just completed his eighth season at Shrewsbury. His appearances in 1997-98 were limited to some extent by injury and he was released during the summer. However, as a player who can both create and defend, being able to play at full back if required, there is every chance he could come back to the league as good as new.

Walsall (From trainee on 24/7/84) FL 100+13/4 FLC 7+1 FAC 3+4 Others 10
Sheffield Wed (£50,000 on 22/6/89) FL 8+1 FLC 2
Shrewsbury T (Loaned on 7/2/91) FL 19/2 FAC 1
Shrewsbury T (£70,000 on 13/9/91) FL 244+5/13 FLC 19 FAC 15 Others 17+2/3

TAYLOR Martin James
Born: Tamworth, 9 December 1966
Height: 6'0" Weight: 13.6

Signed on a free from Derby in the summer of 1997, after four loan appearances at the end of 1996-97, the Wycombe goalkeeper's form, particularly in the second half of 1997-98, was outstanding, and he pulled off some truly extraordinary saves, several defying belief. He was particularly good at point-blank saves, his value to the team being underlined by his 18 clean sheets.

Derby Co (Signed from Mile Oak Rov on 2/7/86) F/PL 97 FLC 7 FAC 5 Others 11
Carlisle U (Loaned on 23/9/87) FL 10 FLC 1 FAC 1 Others 2
Scunthorpe U (Loaned on 17/12/87) FL 8
Crewe Alex (Loaned on 20/9/96) FL 6
Wycombe W (Free on 27/3/97) FL 49 FLC 2 FAC 2 Others 2

TAYLOR Robert (Bob)
Born: Horden, 3 February 1967
Height: 5'10" Weight: 12.0

Started 1997-98 playing in four of West Bromwich Albion's first eight games, and gave his all, but with Andy Hunt and Lee Hughes leading the race for the attacking places, he was loaned out to Bolton in January, in a bid to pep up their front line. At the Reebok, Bob proved to be so popular and successful that he was signed for a second loan period in March, as cover until the end of the season, his endless running and commitment to Wanderers' cause making him an instant hit. With relegation staring the club in the face, he will be most fondly remembered for scoring the goal against Manchester United, at Old Trafford in February, that had the reigning champions panicking until a last-gasp equaliser saved their blushes! He also scored a vital goal in the 2-1 win against Blackburn at the Reebok in April. A centre forward with a vast amount of experience, a large proportion of the Reebok faithful would be more than happy to see him complete a permanent deal, as the side attempts to rejoin the Premiership at the first time of asking.*

Leeds U (Free from Horden Colliery on 27/3/86) FL 33+9/9 FLC 5+1/3 FAC 1 Others 4+1/1
Bristol C (£175,000 on 23/3/89) FL 96+10/50 FLC 6+1/2 FAC 9+1/5 Others 3/1
West Bromwich A (£300,000 on 31/1/92) FL 211+27/96 FLC 16/6 FAC 6+2/3 Others 16+3/8
Bolton W (Loaned on 8/1/98) PL 10+2/3

TAYLOR Robert Anthony
Born: Norwich, 30 April 1971
Height: 6'1" Weight: 13.8

A Brentford target man with deft flicks from both head and feet, good passing ability, and a useful right-foot shot, Robert had a tremendous start to last season with two goals at Shrewsbury (CCC), and against Grimsby (NL) and Colchester (FAC). Most of his strikes were spectacular and the three around Christmas time were possibly the best. A lob over Neville Southall against Southend, a 35 yarder at Gillingham, and a 20 yarder over the defensive wall against Millwall. However, the second half of the campaign saw him struggle, following constant press speculation about his future and tight marking by opponents, who realised if they stopped him scoring they would probably stop Brentford scoring too. Picked up an ankle injury late in the season that kept him out of action for three games before returning for the final game, at Bristol Rovers, following which, the Bees were relegated to the third division.

Norwich C (From trainee on 26/3/90)
Leyton Orient (Loaned on 28/3/91) FL 0+3/1
Birmingham C (Signed on 31/8/91)
Leyton Orient (Free on 21/10/91) FL 54+19/20 FLC 1+1 FAC 2+1 Others 2+1
Brentford (£100,000 on 24/3/94) FL 172+1/56 FLC 16/6 FAC 10/8 Others 14/4

TAYLOR Scott James
Born: Chertsey, 5 May 1976
Height: 5'10" Weight: 11.4

Unable to get a first team opportunity at Bolton in 1997-98, with the side under threat of relegation for most of the time, the young striker was loaned to first Rotherham (December) and then Blackpool (March),

just to keep him match fit in case of a call up. A clever ball player, who was good at making space for himself with well-timed runs, he scored three goals in 11 outings at Rotherham, while being involved in the making of several others, and his return to Wanderers was regarded by the locals as premature, since his departure signalled a dip in United's form. Joining Blackpool on transfer deadline day, he scored in his first full game, against Brentford, on Easter Monday, making five appearances in all before returning to the Reebok. Hopefully, with the pressure off, there should be further opportunities at Bolton in 1998-99.

Millwall (£15,000 from Staines on 8/2/95) FL 13+15 FLC 0+2/2 FAC 1+1
Bolton W (£150,000 on 29/3/96) P/FL 2+10/1 FLC 0+3/1 FAC 1/1
Rotherham U (Loaned on 12/12/97) FL 10/3 Others 1
Blackpool (Loaned on 26/3/98) FL 3+2/1

TAYLOR Shaun
Born: Plymouth, 26 February 1963
Height: 6'1" Weight: 13.0
Club Honours: Div 4 '90; Div 2 '96

The inspiration of Bristol City in 1997-98, this central defender was the single most important reason for City's promotion and his massive contribution to their success was recognised by the fans who voted him as their Player Of The Season for the second consecutive year. his single-minded commitment was much missed in the concluding matches, which he was forced to miss when suffering a ruptured cruciate ligament in the home game with Watford on 13 April, an injury that is likely to sideline him for at least eight months. Deservedly selected as a member of the PFA second division side, it was the fourth time he has been recognised by his fellow professionals.*

Exeter C (Free from Bideford T on 10/12/86) FL 200/16 FLC 12 FAC 9 Others 12
Swindon T (£200,000 on 26/7/91) F/PL 212/30 FLC 22+1/2 FAC 14 Others 10/1
Bristol C (£50,000 + on 6/9/96) FL 72/3 FLC 4/2 FAC 5/1 Others 5

TEATHER Paul
Born: Rotherham, 26 December 1977
Height: 5'11" Weight: 11.8
International Honours: E: Yth Sch

As one of Manchester United's youngsters, and a third-year professional who had yet to be given a first team opportunity at Old Trafford, Paul spent a three-month loan spell at Bournemouth, starting last December. A midfielder who can play in the centre or on either flank, despite being substituted in four of his six starts, he impressed during his 12 games as a youngster who might just make it.

Manchester U (From trainee on 1/8/94)
Bournemouth (Loaned on 19/12/97) FL 5+5 Others 1+1

TEDALDI Domenico Arch
Born: Aberystwyth, 12 August 1980
Height: 5'9" Weight: 9.12
International Honours: W: Yth

Welsh born, despite his exotic name, this

YTS boy was given his Doncaster league debut at Rochdale last March, and scored with his first touch after coming on as a substitute. Surprisingly, he was later released, as the club sought to unload their playing staff towards the end of the season, but you are sure to hear of him before too long.

Doncaster Rov (Trainee) FL 0+2/1

TELFER Paul Norman
Born: Edinburgh, 21 October 1971
Height: 5'9" Weight: 11.6
International Honours: S: B-2; U21-3
Having had a superb season in 1997-98, Coventry's Paul was called into the Scotland "B" squad, although many thought him more than worthy of the full team. Mainly used as a right-sided midfield player who excels with his energy, persistence, and excellent first touch, he is the one man who has obviously benefited from Gordon Strachan's one-to-one coaching methods, and who plays the same role that his mentor played. Although injured in the autumn, with the side missing his industry badly, he returned to play a key part in the resurgence after Christmas, scoring three goals, including the 45-second effort at Palace and a stinging free kick at Bramall Lane. Was selected for Scotland "B", but had to pull out with injury.
Luton T (From trainee on 7/11/88) FL 136+8/19 FLC 5 FAC 14/2 Others 2/1
Coventry C (£1,500,000 on 11/7/95) PL 95+3/4 FLC 10/2 FAC 11/3

TEN HEUVEL Laurens
Born: Amsterdam, Holland, 6 June 1976
Height: 6'0" Weight: 12.3
Because of the influx of a number of strikers at Barnsley in 1997-98, Laurens saw his first team opportunities restricted to a bare minimum, making just two starts, both of them in FA Cup games. A skilful striker with a powerful shot, he was again one of the leading lights in the successful reserve team. Spent a month on loan at Northampton, without being called up, and was eventually released in the summer.
Barnsley (£75,000 from FC Den Bosch on 12/3/96) F/PL 1+7 FLC 0+1

TERRIER David
Born: Verdun, France, 4 August 1973
Height: 5'11" Weight: 11.6
Having joined West Ham on a free transfer from Metz during the 1997 close season, the 25-year-old left back was expected to be a key defender, while deputising for the injured Julian Dicks. Although making his debut on the opening day of 1997-98, when coming on as a late substitution against Barnsley, this was to be his only game for the club and, after spending an unhappy six months at Upton Park, he joined Newcastle in January, but never made an appearance during his six-month stay, before being released in the summer.
West Ham U (Signed from Metz on 18/7/97) PL 0+1
Newcastle U (Free on 16/1/98)

Ben Thatcher

THATCHER Benjamin (Ben) David
Born: Swindon, 30 November 1975
Height: 5'10" Weight: 12.7
International Honours: E: U21-4; Yth
After recovering from his ankle injury of the previous season, Ben came back into the Wimbledon side for the game against Newcastle last September and was a regular until suffering further damage early in the New Year, and being put out of action for another month. A young defender who reads situations well, and copes in a way that fully justified the fee paid for him, while looking comfortable in a centre-back or left-back role, although coming back gingerly, by the end of a tough campaign he looked to have completely shaken off his earlier problems and, hopefully, will be raring to go in 1998-99. Added to his England U21 international caps with an appearance against Italy during the season.
Millwall (From trainee on 8/6/92) FL 87+3/1 FLC 6 FAC 7 Others 1
Wimbledon (£1,840,000 on 5/7/96) PL 32+3 FLC 3 FAC 3

THOLOT Didier
Born: France, 2 April 1964
Height: 5'9" Weight: 11.6
Signed on loan from Swiss club, Sion, last March, along with Jean-Jacques Eydelie, after previous experience with Bordeaux, Didier made the best possible start for Walsall with a goal on his debut in the 2-1 win at champions elect, Watford. At a time when goals had almost dried up from the rest of the side, he got four more before the end of the season, including one with the coolest of finishes at Bristol City's Ashton Gate. However, his future was still uncertain at the time of going to press.*
Walsall (Loaned from Sion on 3/3/98) FL 13+1/4 Others 1+1/1

THOM Stuart Paul
Born: Dewsbury, 27 December 1976
Height: 6'2" Weight: 11.12
Having been a professional at Nottingham Forest for some four years without receiving a first team opportunity, Stuart was loaned out to Mansfield last December to further his footballing education. Reckoned to have a good future, his seven games at Town showed him to be a strong central defender who, as you would expect of a Forest man, had two good feet and looked to play the ball from the back. Is also good in the air.
Nottingham F (From trainee on 11/1/94)
Mansfield T (Loaned on 24/12/97) FL 5 Others 2

THOMAS Anthony (Tony)
Born: Liverpool, 12 July 1971
Height: 5'11" Weight: 13.0
Club Honours: AMC '90
An attacking right back with the ability to deliver damaging crosses into the opposition penalty area, Tony was signed from Tranmere last August, just two weeks after starring against Everton in a pre-season friendly. A childhood Evertonian, he was delighted by the switch to Goodison, only to find his campaign interrupted by a stream of injuries, managing just nine appearances, only three in succession, before a thigh injury ended 1997-98 for him in February. Not just an attacking full back, but one that can defend well, and powerfully built, he can tackle with the best of them.
Tranmere Rov (From trainee on 1/2/89) FL 254+3/12 FLC 23+1/1 FAC 7 Others 26/1
Everton (£400,000+ on 7/8/97) PL 6+1 FLC 1 FAC 1

THOMAS David (Dai) John
Born: Caerphilly, 26 September 1975
Height: 5'10" Weight: 12.7
Club Honours: Div 2 '98
International Honours: W: U21-2

After coming to the fore at Swansea in 1996-97, and continuing to work hard at improving his first touch throughout the summer of 1997, the centre forward signed for Watford in time for the start of the new season. Although securing Welsh U21 honours, and proving himself to be a useful squad man, Dai was unable to command a regular place, although his 16 league games were good enough to win him a second division championship medal as the Hornets went to the top of the table and stayed there.

Swansea C (From trainee on 25/7/94) FL 36+20/10 FLC 2 FAC 0+1 Others 5+3/3
Watford (£100,000 on 17/7/97) FL 8+8/3 FAC 1+3

THOMAS Geoffrey (Geoff) Robert
Born: Manchester, 5 August 1964
Height: 6'1" Weight: 13.2
Club Honours: FMC '91; Div 1 '98
International Honours: E: 9; B-3

Released by Wolves during the 1997 close season, the former England midfielder was snapped up by Nottingham Forest and given a one-year contract, starting 1997-98 on the left side of midfield, and scoring three goals in the opening three games. Unfortunately, the injury jinx struck again when he suffered back problem in September which put him out of action until after Christmas and, on coming back, it was either as cover for Andy Johnson or Scot Gemmill. At his best, a hard-running, powerful player with a great left foot, despite his injury, his 20 league games earned him a first division championship medal and, if he stays on at the City Ground, another crack at the Premiership.*

Rochdale (Free from Littleborough on 13/8/82) FL 10+1/1 Others 0+1
Crewe Alex (Free on 22/3/84) FL 120+5/20 FLC 8 FAC 2 Others 2+1
Crystal Palace (£50,000 on 8/6/87) F/PL 192+3/26 FLC 24/3 FAC 13+1/2 Others 15+1/4
Wolverhampton W (£800,000 on 18/6/93) FL 36+10/8 FLC 1 FAC 1 Others 6
Nottingham F (Free on 18/7/97) FL 13+7/3 FLC 2/1

THOMAS Glen Andrew
Born: Hackney, 6 October 1967
Height: 6'1" Weight: 13.3

A player who can perform equally well in the centre of defence or at left back, injury forced him to miss nearly all of last season, although he made a surprise appearance at Wrexham in December, only to break down once again. Forced to limp off with another long-term injury problem after returning in early April, Glen was released during the summer.

Fulham (From apprentice on 9/10/85) FL 246+5/6 FLC 21 FAC 8 Others 14+1
Peterborough U (Free on 4/11/94) FL 6+2 FAC 0+1 Others 2
Barnet (Free on 23/3/95) FL 22+1 FLC 2 Others 1
Gillingham (£30,000 on 15/1/96) FL 20+8 FAC 1 Others 1

THOMAS James Alan
Born: Swansea, 16 January 1979
Height: 5'10" Weight: 11.4
International Honours: W: U21-7; Yth

As a second-year professional at Blackburn who was not quite ready for the Premiership, but had a need to further his footballing education, the young Welsh U21 international was loaned to West Bromwich Albion last August. Given his Football League debut as a sub at Stoke, James followed the experience up with another appearance from the bench against Reading at the Hawthorns, before making a start at Queens Park Rangers, where he was unlucky not to get on the scoresheet. Highly rated at Ewood as a left-sided centre forward who has pace and shooting ability to match, he is expected to come through in the near future.

Blackburn Rov (From trainee on 2/7/96)
West Bromwich A (Loaned on 29/8/97) FL 1+2

THOMAS Martin Russell
Born: Lymington, 12 September 1973
Height: 5'8" Weight: 12.6

Martin made just seven appearances for Fulham in 1997-98, and five of them were from the bench, making it a frustrating season for a man looking to get his career off the ground. Even a couple of goals against Wycombe Wanderers in the Auto Windscreen Shield, and being equal top scorer in the reserves with five, was a poor reward for a wholehearted player who never gives less than 100 per cent, whatever level he is playing. Either in midfield, at right back, or up front, he does a good job and now that Fulham have given him a free transfer he should have no difficulty finding a new club.

Southampton (From trainee on 19/6/92)
Leyton Orient (Free on 24/3/94) FL 5/2
Fulham (Free on 21/7/94) FL 59+31/8 FLC 6+1 FAC 4/1 Others 7+1/2

THOMAS Michael Lauriston
Born: Lambeth, 24 August 1967
Height: 5'10" Weight: 12.4
Club Honours: FLC '87, 95; Div 1 '89, '91; FAC '92
International Honours: E: 2; B-5; U21-12; Yth; Sch

No longer an automatic choice for a squad place at Liverpool in 1997-98, although he did play 13 games and score one goal, he was loaned out to Middlesbrough in February, possibly with a view to a permanent transfer. An experienced midfielder, Michael was immediately pitched in to the promotion fray on his arrival at the Cellnet, and his ten consecutive appearances brought some stability to a side that was struggling due to the absence of seven key players through injury. Is capable of mixing up tough tackling with fine attacking moves, which often culminate in goals.

Arsenal (From apprentice on 31/12/84) FL 149+14/24 FLC 21+2/5 FAC 14+3/1 Others 5+2/1
Portsmouth (Loaned on 30/12/86) FL 3
Liverpool (£1,500,000 on 16/12/91) F/PL 96+28/9 FLC 7+3/1 FAC 15+2/2 Others 10+2
Middlesbrough (Loaned on 3/2/98) FL 10

THOMAS Mitchell Anthony
Born: Luton, 2 October 1964
Height: 6'2" Weight: 13.0
International Honours: E: B-1; U21-3; Yth

Although now entering the veteran stage and hampered at the start of last season with hernia problems, Mitchell again proved a tower of strength for Luton at the back, taking his total appearances for the club over the 300 mark and over 550 in first-class football. An awkward opponent, with long legs, aggressive, and tenacious, he often appears awkward, but is hard to get round and is an excellent passer out of defence. Also a nuisance to opposing defences when joining in attacks, he provides many important knock ons for the forwards to feed off.

Luton T (From apprentice on 27/8/82) FL 106+1/1 FLC 5 FAC 18
Tottenham H (£233,000 on 7/7/86) FL 136+21/6 FLC 28+1/1 FAC 12/1
West Ham U (£525,000 on 7/8/91) FL 37+1/3 FLC 5 FAC 4 Others 2
Luton T (Free on 12/11/93) FL 144+9/5 FLC 9+1 FAC 6 Others 5+1

Mitchell Thomas

THOMAS Roderick (Rod) Clive
Born: Brent, 10 October 1970
Height: 5'6" Weight: 11.0
Club Honours: FAYC '89; Div 3 '95; AMC '97
International Honours: E: U21-1; Yth; Sch

Having joined Chester City during the 1997 close season on a free transfer from Carlisle, Rod showed himself to be a very skilled ball player and soon became a great favourite with the crowd. Unfortunately, he was unable to maintain a level of consistency and 13 of his 42 appearances were as a substitute. Has the ability to create panic in opposing defences.

Watford (From trainee on 3/5/88) FL 63+21/9 FLC 3+2 FAC 0+1 Others 3+1
Gillingham (Loaned on 27/3/92) FL 8/1 Others 1
Carlisle U (Free on 12/7/93) FL 124+22/16 FLC 11+1/3 FAC 9+4 Others 22+4/9
Chester C (Free on 4/7/97) FL 25+13/4 FLC 2 FAC 2

THOMAS Scott Lee
Born: Bury, 30 October 1974
Height: 5'11" Weight: 11.4
Brought in on loan by Brian Horton from the manager's former club, Manchester City, last March, Scott had been out of first team action for some time but was immediately drafted into Brighton and Hove Albion's league side for the 0-0 draw at Cardiff. Capable of playing on either wing as an out-and-out winger, or as a wing back, he showed considerable skills, especially in taking defenders on and making a beeline for goal. On returning to Maine Road, he was released during the summer.
Manchester C (From trainee on 26/3/92) PL 0+2
Brighton & Hove A (Loaned on 25/3/98) FL 7

THOMAS Wayne
Born: Walsall, 28 August 1978
Height: 5'8" Weight: 12.2
Wayne was loaned to Kidderminster for a spell last season, but returned to score a spectacular goal in the Auto Windscreen southern final at Bournemouth and, with age on his side, is one of Walsall's bright hopes for the future in midfield. A player who is always looking for the pass, and comfortable in possession, he is known at the Bescot for his ability to hit excellent long balls to feet.
Walsall (From trainee on 25/7/96) FL 17+8 FLC 0+1 FAC 2 Others 1/1

THOMAS Wayne Junior Robert
Born: Gloucester, 17 May 1979
Height: 5'11" Weight: 11.12
With two seasons of occasional first team football already under his belt at Torquay, Wayne was yet another first-year pro who improved his CV during last season. Despite appearing in a number of positions, including goalkeeper, the youngster is more at home up front or in central defence, which will probably prove to be his best position in the longer run.
Torquay U (From trainee on 4/7/97) FL 7+32/1 FLC 0+1 FAC 2 Others 1+4

THOME Emerson August
Born: Porto Alegra, Brazil, 30 March 1972
Height: 6'1" Weight: 13.4
Signed from the famed Portuguese side, Benfica, from mid-March until the end of last season, due to injuries to others at Sheffield Wednesday, he was given an earlier debut than expected and took his chance with open arms. First came into the team at Barnsley because of the short-term absence of Peter Atherton, but immediately moved over as cover for Goce Sedloski, following his injury, and then played through to the end of the campaign. Having shown a good awareness of his defensive duties, and proving to be a strong tackler, allied to very good distribution, Ron Atkinson was so impressed that he offered him a long-term contract. Watch this space.
Sheffield Wed (Free from Benfica on 23/3/98) PL 6

THOMPSON Alan
Born: Newcastle, 22 December 1973
Height: 6'0" Weight: 12.8
Club Honours: Div 1 '97
International Honours: E: U21-2; Yth
1997-98 was another excellent season for "Thommo", who will go down in the history books as the scorer of the first ever goal in the Reebok Stadium, netting a penalty for Bolton in the match against Spurs in September. After going through a somewhat lean patch just before Christmas, Alan exploded into life in the New Year with some outstanding performances and some equally outstanding goals as well, particularly his piledrivers against Liverpool and Leeds. His all-action displays prompted interest from a number of other Premiership clubs, and rumours of an England call up continued to circulate. *Stop Press:* Joined Aston Villa on 5 June for a transfer fee amounting to £4.5 million.
Newcastle U (From trainee on 11/3/91) FL 13+3 FAC 1 Others 3
Bolton W (£250,000 on 22/7/93) P/FL 143+14/34 FLC 24+1/5 FAC 6+2/2 Others 7+1/1

THOMPSON Andrew (Andy) Richard
Born: Cannock, 9 November 1967
Height: 5'6" Weight: 10.11
Club Honours: Div 4 '88, Div 3 '89; AMC '88
Signed from Wolves on a free transfer just before the start of 1997-98, this compact and consistent full back soon settled into the Tranmere team and was the nearest that the club had to an ever present, missing just two games in mid-season due to injury. Andy's first goal for the club came against Reading in September and, in the absence of John Aldridge, he assumed the role of regular penalty taker. A controller, rather than a creator, his never-say-die attitude and tenacity endeared him to the Prenton Park faithful.
West Bromwich A (From apprentice on 16/11/85) FL 18+6/1 FLC 0+1 FAC 2 Others 1+1
Wolverhampton W (£35,000 on 21/11/86) FL 356+20/43 FLC 22 FAC 20/1 Others 33/1
Tranmere Rov (Free on 21/7/97) FL 44/3 FLC 5 FAC 3

THOMPSON David Anthony
Born: Birkenhead, 12 September 1977
Height: 5'7" Weight: 10.0
Club Honours: FAYC '96
International Honours: E: U21-2; Yth
Unable to grab himself a regular slot in Liverpool's central midfield as yet, David went on loan to Swindon last November and impressed the manager, Steve McMahon, a former Anfield hero, with his attitude and commitment. Was a massive success at Town during his two-month stint, turning in several outstanding performances, the best of the lot coming when he inspired Swindon to a 4-1 home win over their local rivals, Oxford. Skilful on the ball, and an excellent passer, he was just the type of player Steve would love to have signed, and showed himself to be potentially one of the Premiership's stars of the future.
Liverpool (From trainee on 8/11/94) PL 1+6/1
Swindon T (Loaned on 21/11/97) FL 10

THOMPSON Neil
Born: Beverley, 2 October 1963
Height: 5'10" Weight: 12.8
Club Honours: GMVC '87; Div 2 '92
International Honours: E: SP-4
Neil lost his place in the Barnsley team to new signing, Darren Barnard, at the start of last season, but came back when Barnard was tried in midfield. Although as solid as ever, he soon found himself out again, and spent much of the second half of the campaign out on loan at first Oldham and then York. After eight appearances at Oldham, he spent the last two months of the campaign at York, playing at left back and in the centre of the defence, where he impressed with his strength and quality. Was appointed City's player/coach for the coming term.
Hull C (Free from Nottingham F juniors on 28/11/81) FL 29+2
Scarborough (Free on 1/8/83) FL 87/15 FLC 8/1 FAC 4 Others 9/1
Ipswich T (£100,000 on 9/6/89) F/PL 199+7/19 FLC 14+1/1 FAC 17/1 Others 8/2
Barnsley (Free on 14/6/96) F/PL 27/5 FLC 4 FAC 1
Oldham Ath (Loaned on 24/12/97) FL 8
York C (Loaned on 2/3/98) FL 12/2

THOMPSON Niall Joseph
Born: Birmingham, 16 April 1974
Height: 6'0" Weight: 12.0
Having experienced league football earlier in his career with Colchester, this neat and tidy striker, with good passing ability, joined Brentford last February from Seattle and made his debut as a substitute in the home defeat at York the same month. Although completing a number of further appearances as a striker, or playing just behind the front two, despite his general play being good he found it difficult to pose any real goal threat and, subsequently, failed to make the scoring charts.
Crystal Palace (From juniors on 16/7/92)
Colchester U (Free from Hong Kong on 4/11/94) FL 5+8/5 FAC 0+1 (Freed during 1995 close season)
Brentford (Free from Seattle on 27/2/98) FL 6+2

THOMPSON Philip Paul
Born: Blackpool, 1 April 1981
Height: 5'11" Weight: 12.0
Given a run out in Blackpool's penultimate game of last season, at home to Bristol Rovers, the young central defender with a famous name stood in for Tony Butler and showed promise in a 1-0 win. A first-year trainee, he is strongly built, and could have a future in the game.
Blackpool (Trainee) FL 1

THOMPSON Steven (Steve) James
Born: Oldham, 2 November 1964
Height: 5'10" Weight: 13.5
Club Honours: AMC '89
Just one of 15 1997 close season signings made by Rotherham, in joining from Burnley, Steve brought experience to the team with his ability to pass the ball and, at the same time, also helped to provide several goals with his cleverly flighted corners. Invariably, when he was on song in

midfield the team played well, although he occasionally found two games in a week difficult to cope with.

Bolton W (From apprentice on 4/11/82) FL 329+6/49 FLC 27/2 FAC 21/4 Others 39/2
Luton T (£180,000 on 13/8/91) FL 5 FLC 2
Leicester C (Signed on 22/10/91) F/PL 121+6/18 FLC 6/2 FAC 8/1 Others 11+3/4
Burnley (£200,000 on 24/2/95) FL 44+5/1 FLC 2 Others 1+1
Rotherham U (Free on 24/7/97) FL 32+7/3 FLC 1 FAC 3 Others 1

THOMSEN Claus

Born: Aarhus, Denmark, 31 May 1970
Height: 6'3" Weight: 13.6
International Honours: Denmark: 16

A Danish international midfielder who can also play central defence, it soon became clear after 1997-98 got underway that Claus did not feature in Howard Kendall's long term plans at Everton. Although starting the first match of the season against Crystal Palace, he did not play again until January and, while he scored his first goal for the club with an acrobatic overhead kick against Derby County in February, after coming on as a substitute, his departure to AB Copenhagen on 5 March for a fee of £500,000 was no great surprise.

Ipswich T (£250,000 from Aarhus on 15/6/94) P/FL 77+4/7 FLC 8/1 FAC 5 Others 2+1
Everton (£900,000 on 18/1/97) PL 17+7/1 FAC 1

THOMSON Andrew (Andy)

Born: Motherwell, 1 April 1971
Height: 5'10" Weight: 10.13

A lack of confidence in his own striking ability caused Andy, and Southend United, problems during 1997-98, and he tended to flit in and out of the team until a spell of four goals in three games in March 1998 saw him return to something like his own self. Released during the summer, he is a tireless worker who will be hoping to continue his league career with a new club this coming season.

Queen of the South (Free from Jerviston BC on 28/7/89) SL 163+12/93 SLC 8/3 SC 7+2/5 Others 9/8
Southend U (£250,000 on 4/7/94) FL 87+35/28 FLC 4+1 FAC 3+2 Others 1+2

THOMSON Andrew (Andy) John

Born: Swindon, 28 March 1974
Height: 6'3" Weight: 14.12

A tall, powerful, tough-tackling central defender, with reliable aerial ability, Andy managed to cement a place in the centre of Portsmouth's defence in 1997-98, and played well alongside Adrian Whitbread and Andy Awford. A steady performer throughout the season, like a number of his team mates he seemed to improve with the arrival of Alan Ball as manager and, with the club at the wrong end of the table and staring relegation in the face, he scored two vital goals in the run-in, including a last-minute equaliser against Birmingham at Fratton Park, a goal which ultimately proved to be crucial.

Swindon T (From trainee on 1/5/93) P/FL 21+1 FLC 5/1 Others 3
Portsmouth (£75,000 on 29/12/95) FL 71+8/3 FLC 2 FAC 5+1

THOMSON Scott Yuill

Born: Edinburgh, 8 November 1966
Height: 6'0" Weight: 11.9

A former team mate of Hull City assistant manager, Billy Kirkwood, at Dundee United, Scott took his first goalkeeping steps south of the border, despite interest from a number of senior Scottish clubs, when starting last season at Boothferry Park. It was not all roses, however, and he soon lost out to the impressive Steve Wilson, his only appearance after September being the 5-1 St Valentine's Day massacre at Torquay. Loaned to Motherwell for the rest of the campaign, he is best known for his heroics in Raith Rovers' penalty shoot-out success against Celtic in the 1994 Scottish Coca Cola Cup Final.

Dundee U (Free from Hutchison Vale BC on 18/6/84) SL 5 SLC 1
Raith Rov (Loaned on 10/8/85) SL 1
Forfar Ath (Signed on 21/6/91) SL 88 SLC 3 SC 5 Others 2
Raith Rov (Signed on 8/9/93) SL 122 SLC 8 SC 8 Others 8
Hull C (Free on 8/8/97) FL 9 FLC 3
Motherwell (Loaned on 23/3/98) SL 1

THORN Andrew (Andy) Charles

Born: Carshalton, 12 November 1966
Height: 6'0" Weight: 12.10
Club Honours: FAC '88
International Honours: E: U21-5

Always one to relish a physical tussle with a big striker, and never afraid to talk his Tranmere colleagues through a game, Andy rarely shirked a challenge or tackle, but, sadly, last February, he was forced to announce his retirement at the age of 32. The premature end to his playing career was brought about by a series of injuries which worsened his long-time knee problems, and made continuation unadvisable. Always gave 100 per-cent effort in every game, and his leadership, both on and off the pitch, is bound to be missed.

Wimbledon (From apprentice on 13/11/84) FL 106+1/2 FLC 7 FAC 9 Others 1
Newcastle U (£850,000 on 1/8/88) FL 36/2 FLC 4/1 Others 3
Crystal Palace (£650,000 on 5/12/89) F/PL 128/3 FLC 19/4 FAC 10 Others 11
Wimbledon (Free on 5/10/94) PL 33+4/1 FLC 2 FAC 3
Heart of Midlothian (Free on 17/9/96) SL 1
Tranmere Rov (Free on 27/9/96) FL 36/1 FLC 3 FAC 1

THORNE Peter Lee

Born: Manchester, 21 June 1973
Height: 6'0" Weight: 12.10
Club Honours: Div 2 '96

Peter was Chic Bates' only 1997 close season cash signing for Stoke, the deal being settled by a tribunal-fixed fee of £350,000, rising to a maximum of £550,000 linked to appearances, from Swindon. Robins' boss, Steve McMahon, made his legendary comment that you could not get a good pie lady for that, let alone a striker with Thorne's track record. After a slow start "Pistol Pete" soon commenced amassing his goals. However, like many Stoke players he was unsettled by the goings on behind the

scene and then fell badly in a game and damaged his ribs, which were slow to heal. Whilst he returned, his goalscoring consistency was not helped by a badly-cut knee in the 2-1 win over Portsmouth, but to his great credit he was one of the few players in the horrendous 7-0 home defeat by Birmingham to come out of the game with pride, as he battled on alone in a vain effort to stem the tide.

Blackburn Rov (From trainee on 20/6/91) Others 0+1
Wigan Ath (Loaned on 11/3/94) FL 10+1
Swindon T (£225,000 on 18/1/95) FL 66+11/27 FLC 5+1/4 FAC 4+2 Others 1+1/1
Stoke C (£350,000+ on 25/7/97) FL 33+3/12 FLC 4/4 FAC 0+1

Peter Thorne

THORNLEY Benjamin (Ben) Lindsay

Born: Bury, 21 April 1975
Height: 5'9" Weight: 11.12
Club Honours: FAYC '92
International Honours: E: U21-3; Sch

A tricky Manchester United right winger, who is essentially left footed, Ben made several appearances on the bench as a non-playing substitute in 1997-98, before making his full bow against Crystal Palace last October. His most important contribution of the season, however, came against Wimbledon in the Premiership in March, when his fantastic run down the left flank helped to set up a goal for Paul Scholes. With rumours circulating Manchester about the possible return of Andrei Kanchelskis to the club during the summer, Ben's speedy wing play might tempt Alex Ferguson to think again.

Manchester U (From trainee on 29/1/93) PL 1+8 FLC 4 FAC 1
Stockport Co (Loaned on 6/11/95) FL 8+2/1 Others 1
Huddersfield T (Loaned on 22/2/96) FL 12/2

THORNLEY Roderick (Rod)
Born: Bury, 2 April 1977
Height: 5'9" Weight: 10.5

Rod was yet another Doncaster non-contract signing from an obscure non-league club in 1997-98, joining from Warrington Town last October. Having made his debut in the Rovers' attack against Brighton in October, he was substituted at half time and left shortly afterwards.

Doncaster Rov (Free from Warrington on 3/10/97) FL 1

THORP Hamilton
Born: Australia, 21 August 1973
Height: 6'2" Weight: 14.7

Yet another of Portsmouth's Australian imports in 1997-98, arriving from West Adelaide, the tall, gangling centre forward found it hard to adjust to the pace of English football and suffered with injuries throughout the season. Came off the bench to make his Football League debut in the opening fixture, a 2-2 draw at Manchester City, and then scored the opening goal in a 2-2 Coca Cola Cup draw at Peterborough, his only start for Pompey, before having his contract terminated by mutual consent during the summer.

Portsmouth (£75,000 from West Adelaide on 8/8/97) FL 34+1/2 FLC 2 FAC 2

THORP Michael Stephen
Born: Wallington, 5 December 1975
Height: 6'0" Weight: 12.0

Michael ended an 11-year association with Reading when he was given a free transfer at the end of last season, having originally joined the club's Centre of Excellence in 1987. With only a handful of appearances behind him since signing as a professional, and following loans to both Slough Town and Cheltenham, a change of club may be just what is needed to kick-start his career. Still a relative youngster, at 23 years of age, his play at centre back has gradually improved as he has added aggression to his composure and passing skills.

Reading (From trainee on 12/1/95) FL 2+3 FLC 2 FAC 1+1

THORPE Andrew (Andy)
Born: Stockport, 15 September 1960
Height: 5'11" Weight: 12.0

Andy played his first league game for five seasons when he appeared in the Doncaster defence for their home game with Cambridge United, late last September. Signed from non-league Chorley on a non-contract basis, he was injured in the next game, at Torquay, and was released a few weeks later.

Stockport Co (From juniors on 2/8/78) FL 312+2/3 FLC 23 FAC 8 Others 4/1
Tranmere Rov (Free on 1/8/86) FL 51+2 FLC 4/1 FAC 2 Others 3
Stockport Co (Free on 25/1/88) FL 172+3 FLC 9+1 FAC 5 Others 14+1/1 (Moved to Australia during 1992 close season)
Doncaster Rov (Free from Chorley on 19/9/97) FL 2

THORPE Anthony (Tony) Lee
Born: Leicester, 10 April 1974
Height: 5'9" Weight: 12.6

An excellent opportunist striker who is never afraid to go for goal or to let misses put him off trying again, he is a constant worry to defences, his quick reactions, especially on the turn, causing problems to all but the very best. However, one of the mysteries of last season was why Tony, having been signed by Fulham from Luton in February to score goals, following a recent hat trick in a 3-0 win over Blackpool, spent the last eight league matches on the bench with only cameo appearances on the field. Although scoring twice in the five games he started after joining Fulham, a superb solo effort when coming on as sub against Carlisle being one of them, he did not start again until the second leg of the play offs when Paul Moody was suspended. Having been an attacking midfielder with Luton until his last full season, when he netted 31 goals and was elected to the PFA second division XI, Tony should be a valuable asset to Fulham in their 1998-99 drive for automatic promotion. *Stop Press:* Signed for Bristol City, where he is expected to link up with Ade Akinbiyi, for £1 million on 4 June.

Luton T (Free from Leicester C juniors on 18/8/92) FL 93+27/50 FLC 5+4/5 FAC 4+3/2 Others 4+3/3
Fulham (£800,000 on 26/2/98) FL 5+8/3 Others 1+1

THORPE Jeffrey (Jeff) Roger
Born: Whitehaven, 17 November 1972
Height: 5'10" Weight: 12.8
Club Honours: Div 3 '95

Still only 25, but now the longest serving player at Carlisle in 1997-98, Jeff again found his appearances restricted by injury. However, his commitment was never in doubt and he gave some gutsy performances both at left back and in midfield and, being one of the few left-sided players at the club, it looked likely that he would sign a new contract during the past summer. Decidedly pacy, he can be used anywhere where he can get at the opposition.*

Carlisle U (From trainee on 2/7/91) FL 94+56/6 FLC 7+3 FAC 4+2 Others 8+8/1

THORPE Lee Anthony
Born: Wolverhampton, 14 December 1975
Height: 6'1" Weight: 12.4

Signed by Lincoln after a successful trial in which he scored a superb goal in a pre-season friendly against Nottingham Forest, having had limited previous experience at Blackpool, he quickly became a first choice at Sincil Bank in 1997-98. An aggressive player with the ability to score plenty of goals, Lee finished leading scorer and netted with a spectacular volley to clinch promotion in the final fixture against Brighton.

Blackpool (From trainee on 18/7/94) FL 2+10 FLC 0+1 FAC 1 Others 1
Lincoln C (Free on 4/8/97) FL 44/14 FLC 2 FAC 4 Others 1

TIATTO Daniele (Danny) Amadio
Born: Melbourne, Australia, 22 May 1973
Height: 5'7" Weight: 12.0
International Honours: Australia: 9

Danny came to Stoke last November on long-term loan from FC Baden in the Swiss League, searching to make his name in English football so as to attract the eye of Aussie soccer boss, Terry Venables. Having joined Baden from Melbourne Knights in Australia, and almost immediately been put out on loan to Salernitana in Serie "B", he made an immediate impact at Stoke, whether as a wide left-sided midfielder or as a left back. With a gifted left foot and timing and strength to make this a potent weapon, he was taken easily to the hearts of an appreciating City faithful.

Stoke C (Loaned from FC Baden on 25/11/97) FL 11+4/1

TIERNEY Francis (Fran)
Born: Liverpool, 10 September 1975
Height: 5'10" Weight: 11.0
International Honours: E: Yth

Since the disappointment of the transfer to Liverpool that did not happen a couple of seasons ago, Fran has found it difficult to hold down a regular place in the Crewe line-up and he fared no different in 1997-98. A wide player who can be influential in the front line, with good ball control and temperament to match, he made only one start last season, at home to first division champions elect, Nottingham Forest, and was released during the summer.

Crewe Alex (From trainee on 22/3/93) FL 57+30/10 FLC 6 FAC 1+4 Others 5+6/3

Carl Tiler

TILER Carl
Born: Sheffield, 11 February 1970
Height: 6'3" Weight: 13.10
International Honours: E: U21-13

A tall, commanding central defender who uses his height to good effect in both penalty areas, Carl was ever present at Sheffield

United last season, forming a formidable threesome with David Holdsworth and Paul McGrath, until being surprisingly transferred to Everton in November. Although decidedly unimpressed initially, the fans were soon won over by him following a string of impressive performances, while playing on the left of a three-man central defensive triangle. Consistently solid and reliable, he was usually the first name on the team sheet and, apart from an absence due to suspension, he became a regular and ended the season as an Evertonian favourite.

Barnsley (From trainee on 2/8/88) FL 67+4/3 FLC 4 FAC 4+1 Others 3+1
Nottingham F (£1,400,000 on 30/5/91) F/PL 67+2/1 FLC 10+1 FAC 6 Others 1
Swindon T (Loaned on 18/11/94) FL 2
Aston Villa (£750,000 on 28/10/95) PL 10+2/1 FLC 1 FAC 2
Sheffield U (£650,000 on 26/3/97) FL 23/2 FLC 5 Others 3
Everton (£500,000 on 28/11/97) PL 19/1 FAC 1

TILLSON Andrew (Andy)
Born: Huntingdon, 30 June 1966
Height: 6'2" Weight: 12.10
The Bristol Rovers' central defender and captain performed consistently in 1997-98, and was reliable as ever at the centre of their defence, missing just a handful of league games, three of which were at Christmas, due to suspension, following his dismissal at Wigan in the game which saw the referee produce an unprecedented five red cards. Andy's aerial strength and excellent positional play makes him one of the best defenders outside the top flight, and has now completed almost 200 league appearances for Rovers in his six years, while remaining as popular as ever with the supporters.

Grimsby T (Free from Kettering T on 14/7/88) FL 104+1/5 FLC 8 FAC 10 Others 5
Queens Park R (£400,000 on 21/12/90) FL 27+2/2 FLC 2 Others 1
Grimsby T (Loaned on 15/9/92) FL 4 Others 1
Bristol Rov (£370,000 on 7/11/92) FL 189+2/8 FLC 12/1 FAC 10 Others 18+1/2

Eric Tinkler

TINKLER Eric
Born: Capetown, South Africa, 30 July 1970
Height: 6'2" Weight: 12.8
International Honours: South Africa: 29
Signed from Cagliari during the 1997 close season, with a view to strengthening the Barnsley midfield in view of their move up in class, Eric was another who found the Premier League a very unforgiving place in 1997-98. However, he maintained his place in the team until an injury to the sciatic nerve forced him to miss a number of matches, and was always a threat in the air from set pieces. Although playing most of his matches in midfield, the manager tried him as sweeper on a couple of occasions, but the injury and a drop in form lost him his place in the South African team, for which he had been a regular.

Barnsley (£650,000 from Cagliari on 23/7/97) PL 21+4/1 FLC 2 FAC 2

TINKLER Mark Roland
Born: Bishop Auckland, 24 October 1974
Height: 5'11" Weight: 13.3
Club Honours: FAYC '93
International Honours: E: Yth (UEFAC '93); Sch

Having settled in well at York, following his arrival towards the end of 1996-97, Mark led the club's appearance charts in 1997-98, when missing just two games. Although playing mainly in midfield, he also made a number of appearances in the centre of defence, where his strength and ability to read the game in a sweeper's role was impressive. Also scored four goals, including winners against Preston and Walsall.

Leeds U (From trainee on 29/11/91) PL 14+11 FLC 1 Others 0+1
York C (£100,000 on 25/3/97) FL 52+1/5 FLC 4 FAC 2 Others 1

TINNION Brian
Born: Stanley, 23 February 1968
Height: 6'0" Weight: 13.0
1997-98 was a good season for this left-sided player, whose cultured left foot contributed to creating many of Bristol City's goalscoring opportunities, though only managing three successful strikes himself. His workrate was much better than in the previous campaign and this, allied to his creativity, would probably have been enough to allow him to lay claim as being City's best player of the season if it was not

Brian Tinnion

for the outstanding form of Shaun Taylor, Keith Welch, Greg Goodridge, and Adam Locke.*

Newcastle U (From apprentice on 26/2/86) FL 30+2/2 FLC 5 Others 1+1
Bradford C (£150,000 on 9/3/89) FL 137+8/22 FLC 12/1 FAC 9/4 Others 7+1/2
Bristol C (£180,000 on 23/3/93) FL 185+8/16 FLC 12 FAC 13+2/3 Others 6+2

TINSON Darren Lee
Born: Birmingham, 15 November 1969
Height: 6'0" Weight: 12.12
Club Honours: GMVC '97

Darren was one of the most improved players at Macclesfield last season, having taken well to league football. Physically very strong, with a good turn of speed, he played at right back, coming forward quickly, and was good on the overlap with the winger. He can also easily revert to the central defence, which was his more normal position before joining Town from Northwich during their Conference days.

Macclesfield T (£10,000 from Northwich Vic on 14/2/96) FL 44 FLC 2 FAC 2

TIPTON Matthew John
Born: Conway, 29 June 1980
Height: 5'10" Weight: 10.7
International Honours: W: U21-1; Yth

Yet another gem unearthed from the Oldham youth system, Matthew made three further appearances for the club in 1997-98, following his first team debut as a sub at Carlisle in the Auto Windscreen Shield last December, and impressed. A centre forward who hustles and bustles, and who has scored a lot of goals at reserve and youth level, he is expected to bring that ability to the first team. Two footed and a bit of an all-rounder, his promise was recognised by the Welsh U21 selectors and resulted in him making his debut against Italy in April.

Oldham Ath (From trainee on 1/7/97) FL 1+2 Others 0+1

TISDALE Paul Robert
Born: Malta, 14 January 1973
Height: 5'9" Weight: 11.13
International Honours: E: Sch

Signed on a free transfer from Southampton in the close season of 1997, this creative midfield player was unable to impress enough to gain a regular place in the Bristol City team in 1997-98, and went on loan to Exeter in December. Althouth performing well, during a crisis, he eventually chose to return to Ashton Gate, where he made an unsuccessful effort to fight his way back into the Robins' side. Put on City's open to transfer list, Paul can look back on a campaign where he collected medals as a member of the club's successful reserve side, who secured the South West Trophy League without losing a match, as well as winning the trophy final by beating Bristol Rovers Reserves (league runners-up) over two legs. He also scored his first ever league goal while at Exeter.

Southampton (From juniors on 5/6/91) PL 5+11/1 FLC 0+1 FAC 0+1
Northampton T (Loaned on 12/3/92) FL 5

Huddersfield T (Loaned on 29/11/96) FL 1+1
Bristol C (Free on 2/6/97) FL 2+3 FLC 1+1 FAC 1
Exeter C (Loaned on 23/12/97) FL 10/1

TODD Andrew (Andy) John James
Born: Derby, 21 September 1974
Height: 5'10" Weight: 11.10
Club Honours: Div 1 '97

A revelation at the heart of the Bolton defence last season, Andy, the son of the manager, Colin, has developed into one of the most promising centre backs in the game. Making his first start in 1997-98 against Crystal Palace at the end of September, his outstanding form was enough to make him a permanent fixture at the heart of the Wanderers' defence for the rest of the campaign. His consistently top-class performances prompted fans and journalists to compare him with his father – a compliment of the highest nature – while his solid, dependable style of play made him the most improved performer at the club over the last two terms. Deservedly winning a Player of the Year award with the Trotters, he will certainly be one to watch in the coming months.

Middlesbrough (From trainee on 6/3/92) FL 7+1 FLC 1+1 Others 5
Swindon T (Loaned on 27/2/95) FL 13
Bolton W (£250,000 on 1/8/95) P/FL 38+14/2 FLC 7+5/1 FAC 1

TODD Lee
Born: Hartlepool, 7 March 1972
Height: 5'5" Weight: 10.3

Signed from Stockport by Southampton at the beginning of last season, Lee was an outstanding full back with County, as they gained promotion to the first division in 1996-97, but found it difficult to establish

himself at Premiership level, making just 11 appearances. Equally at home on the left or right-hand sides, and a former winger, he is a bubbly character who is always in the thick of the action and could make a name for himself, given the opportunity.

Stockport Co (Free from Hartlepool U juniors on 23/7/90) FL 214+11/2 FLC 24+2 FAC 17/2 Others 33+1
Southampton (£500,000 on 28/7/97) PL 9+1 FLC 1

TOLSON Neil
Born: Walsall, 25 October 1973
Height: 6'2" Weight: 12.4

After being York's leading scorer the previous term, Neil had a difficult and frustrating time of it in 1997-98, chiefly due to injuries that kept him sidelined for long periods. The highlight of his season was a goal at Watford in September, which earned City a 1-1 draw against the division two champions elect. Using his height well, and extremely quick, there should be plenty of goals yet to come.

Walsall (From trainee on 17/12/91) FL 3+6/1 FAC 0+1/1 Others 1+2
Oldham Ath (£150,000 on 24/3/92) PL 0+3
Bradford C (Signed on 2/12/93) FL 32+31/12 FLC 1+4/1 FAC 3+1/1 Others 2+2/3
Chester C (Loaned on 6/1/95) FL 3+1
York C (Free on 15/7/96) FL 49+7/15 FLC 7+1/3 FAC 4/2 Others 0+1

TOMASSON Jon Dahl
Born: Copenhagen, Denmark, 29 August 1976
Height: 6'0" Weight: 11.8
International Honours: Denmark: 4

Jon Dahl was something of a scoring sensation in Holland, being tall, fast, and skilful, and proving himself a clinical

Andy Todd (left)

finisher with a cool head. Already capped by Denmark, he was courted by some of the big names of Europe, including Ajax and Barcelona, but he chose to join Newcastle during the 1997 close season. He looked a good buy, scoring four times in summer games, including two on his debut against the Dutch champions, PSV Eindhoven. However, following the sale of Les Ferdinand and the injury to Alan Shearer, he was pressed into service as an out-and-out striker, rather than his favoured position, playing off the front players, and he found this a difficult challenge at Premiership level. A shortage of goals that led to a loss of confidence saw him spend most of his time on the bench in the latter part of the season. *Stop Press:* Transferred to Feyenoord on 19 June for £2.5 million.

Newcastle U (£2,200,000 from Herenveen on 14/7/97) PL 17+6/3 FLC 2+1/1 FAC 2 Others 6+1

TOMLINSON Graeme Murdoch
Born: Watford, 10 December 1975
Height: 5'9" Weight: 11.7

Yet another youngster loaned to Bournemouth by Manchester United in 1997-98, Graeme arrived at Dean Court at the start of the new campaign, having recovered from a seriously broken leg. A striker with good awareness around the box, and a good touch on the ball, he soon got down to business and acquitted himself well during his stay, scoring in the 2-0 win over Blackpool, before going back to Old Trafford. Was later loaned out to Millwall to further his experience and scored on his debut. At the New Den, he showed good close control, to go with an ability to get at defenders, and generally created goalscoring opportunities for both himself and his team mates. Released by United during the summer, he still looks a good prospect.

Bradford C (Trainee) FL 12+5/6 FAC 0+1
Manchester U (£100,000 on 12/7/94) FLC 0+2
Luton T (Loaned on 22/3/96) FL 1+6
Bournemouth (Loaned on 8/8/97) FL 6+1/1
Millwall (Loaned on 26/3/98) FL 2+1/1

TORPEY Stephen (Steve) David James
Born: Islington, 8 December 1970
Height: 6'3" Weight: 14.13
Club Honours: AMC '94

Transferred to Bristol City from Swansea just prior to the start of last season, Steve suffered a sickening head injury on his debut at Grimsby, after he had scored in a 1-1 draw. He bravely came back much quicker than was expected, but, in not being up to his old form, the striker became the butt of criticism from the Ashton Gate crowd and, whilst his overall play had much improved, a further injury disappointingly ended his season in the 2-0 home win over Bristol Rovers on 14 March. Known as a battler in his Swansea days, and a player used to being a solitary front man, he will undoubtedly win over the City fans before too long, hopefully, in 1998-99.

Millwall (From trainee on 14/2/89) FL 3+4 FLC 0+1
Bradford C (£70,000 on 21/11/90) FL 86+10/22 FLC 6 FAC 2+1 Others 8/6

Swansea C (£80,000 on 3/8/93) FL 151+11/44 FLC 9+2/2 FAC 10/5 Others 18+3/6
Bristol C (£400,000 on 8/8/97) FL 19+10/8 FLC 2 FAC 1 Others 2

TOWN David Edward
Born: Bournemouth, 9 December 1976
Height: 5'8" Weight: 11.13

Although not tall for a striker, the Bournemouth man is quick and lively in pursuit of half chances around the box, being a good foil alongside a tall target man such as Steve Fletcher. Having made the breakthrough in 1996-97, many thought that David would become a regular in 1997-98, but, in the event, he was only called upon eight times as a substitute when in need of chasing a game. Is always involved and never afraid to run at defenders.

Bournemouth (From trainee on 11/4/95) FL 17+29/2 FLC 0+5 Others 0+2

TOWNLEY Leon
Born: Loughton, 16 February 1976
Height: 6'2" Weight: 13.6

The big, strong centre half was one of Eddie May's early signings for Brentford when joining from Tottenham last September, but initially found the pace of the second division fast and furious and tired towards the end of games. After a month out of the side, he was recalled by new Bees' manager, Micky Adams, and showed some good form, scoring with headers against Blackpool and Luton, before being replaced by another new signing, Graeme Hogg, at the end of January. From then on, apart from an occasional selection as substitute, he did not appear again, but is bound to come back next season.

Tottenham H (From trainee on 1/7/94)
Brentford (£50,000 on 18/9/97) FL 15+1/1 FLC 1 FAC 1 Others 1/1

TOWNSEND Andrew (Andy) David
Born: Maidstone, 23 July 1963
Height: 5'11" Weight: 13.6
Club Honours: FLC '94, '96
International Honours: Ei: 70; B-1

Andy Townsend

Signed from Aston Villa two or three weeks into the 1997-98 season, Andy was fully committed to the cause of ensuring a rapid return to the Premiership for Middlesbrough, and settled quickly into the club's midfield to earn immediate acclaim for his spirited performances. Rated third in the final analysis of Boro's "star" players of the season, he fully merited his placing, and inspired many of the youngsters who were being introduced to first team football during the campaign. Vastly experienced, having over 400 league appearances to his credit with Southampton, Norwich, Chelsea, and Villa, and honoured with over 40 caps for the Republic of Ireland, he served the Boro well and fully justified his signing. Is the son of Don, the former Charlton and Crystal Palace full back.

Southampton (£35,000 from Weymouth on 15/1/85) FL 77+6/5 FLC 7+1 FAC 2+3 Others 3+2
Norwich C (£300,000 on 31/8/88) FL 66+5/8 FLC 3+1 FAC 10/2 Others 3
Chelsea (£1,200,000 on 5/7/90) F/PL 110/12 FLC 17/7 FAC 7 Others 4
Aston Villa (£2,100,000 on 26/7/93) PL 133+1/8 FLC 20/2 FAC 12 Others 10/1
Middlesbrough (£500,000 on 29/8/97) FL 35+2/2 FLC 6 FAC 3

TRACEY Simon Peter
Born: Woolwich, 9 December 1967
Height: 6'0" Weight: 13.8

An extremely agile goalkeeper, who is a superb shot-stopper, he started last season as first choice at Sheffield United, playing in 24 of the first 25 games, and showing excellent form, before making way for his great rival at Bramall Lane, Alan Kelly. He then alternated with Kelly, who continued to be injury prone, and during one spell in February kept three clean sheets in consecutive games. However, when the Irish international finally had to stand down towards the end of the campaign in order to have a cartilage operation, Simon stepped up to play the remaining five fixtures, including the two play-off games which ultimately saw Sunderland reach Wembley at the expense of United. Is known for his ability to dribble out of the area to get extra distance on his kicks.

Wimbledon (From apprentice on 3/2/86) FL 1 Others 1
Sheffield U (£7,500 on 19/10/88) F/PL 186+2 FLC 11 FAC 14 Others 10
Manchester C (Loaned on 27/10/94) PL 3
Norwich C (Loaned on 31/12/94) PL 1 FAC 2
Wimbledon (Loaned on 2/11/95) PL 1

TRAVIS Simon Christopher
Born: Preston, 22 March 1977
Height: 5'10" Weight: 11.0

Simon was another of Stockport's promising youngsters who were thrown into the first team fray in 1997-98 as an injury crisis bit deep. The 21-year old, a signing from Welsh League side, Holywell Town, came to the club as a full back with a pacy reputation and, bearing that in mind, the management employed his speed in a more forward role, mainly from the subs' bench, where he memorably scored two important goals after coming on against Port Vale on Boxing Day. Looks to be a good bet for the future.

Torquay U (Trainee) FL 4+4 FLC 1 FAC 1 (Freed on 5/1/96)
Stockport Co (£10,000 from Holywell T on 14/8/97) FL 3+10/2 FLC 0+1 FAC 0+1

TRETTON Andrew David
Born: Derby, 9 October 1976
Height: 6'0" Weight: 12.9

Shrewsbury Town central defender. Signed on a free transfer from Derby last December, following a trial at Chesterfield, Andrew made his league debut just before Christmas, scoring his first goal at the end of February in a 1-1 draw at Barnet. He quickly grasped the opportunity of first team football, turning in some increasingly assured performances, and looking equally at home in the air or on the ground. Unfortunate to suffer an injury after 14 consecutive games that cut his season short, all at Gay Meadow will be looking forward to his return in 1998-99.

Derby Co (From trainee on 18/10/93)
Shrewsbury T (Free on 12/12/97) FL 14/1

TREVITT Simon
Born: Dewsbury, 20 December 1967
Height: 5'11" Weight: 12.9

Transfer listed by Hull City last September, after featuring in the early games of the campaign in the influential right-back berth, an instantly forgettable season was compounded in December when a loan move to Swansea City (he was prepared to uproot his family and start afresh) came to an abrupt end after just one game, as he pulled a hamstring in training. Remaining out of favour on his return to Hull, Simon will be looking for better luck in 1998-99.

Huddersfield T (From apprentice on 16/6/86) FL 216+13/3 FLC 23/1 FAC 13 Others 19+1
Hull C (Free on 24/11/95) FL 50+1/1 FLC 3 Others 1
Swansea C (Loaned on 12/12/97) FL 1

TROLLOPE Paul Jonathan
Born: Swindon, 3 June 1972
Height: 6'0" Weight: 12.6
International Honours: W: 5

With 13 Premiership games for Derby behind him in 1997-98, the Welsh international signed for Fulham in late November and made his debut in a 1-1 draw at home to Micky Adams' new team, Brentford. A left-sided midfield player, he scored three goals during the season and contributed some excellent crosses. Despite appearing more comfortable in a left-of-centre midfield role, rather than as a wide player, the competition in midfield meant that he was on the subs' bench for the final six league matches, although being brought back for the play offs. Is the son of the former Swindon appearance record holder, John.

Swindon T (From trainee on 23/12/89)
Torquay U (Free on 26/3/92) FL 103+3/16 FLC 9+1/1 FAC 7 Others 8+1
Derby Co (£100,000 on 16/12/94) F/PL 47+18/5 FLC 3+2/1 FAC 3+1
Grimsby T (Loaned on 30/8/96) FL 6+1/1
Crystal Palace (Loaned on 11/10/96) FL 0+9
Fulham (£600,000 on 28/11/97) FL 19+5/3 FAC 2 Others 3

TSKHADADZE Kakhaber
Born: Rustavi, Georgia, 7 September 1968
Height: 6'2" Weight: 12.7
International Honours: CIS/Georgia: 26

Signed last February from Alana Vladikavkaz, after waiting three weeks for his work permit to arrive, the Georgian international lent his weight to Manchester City's relegation battle, proving to be an impressive defender, with central sweeper being his best position. Despite not playing competitively for more than two months, he soon got the hang of things, and able to get involved in opposing penalty area battles, he scored a cracking goal at Huddersfield with a bullet-force header from 20 yards. Although he appeared to be part of the team, his contribution good, he began to be left out on occasions before picking up an ankle injury which brought his campaign to an end. Was then very disappointed to be told he could leave the club during the summer, having settled in well with his family.

Manchester C (£300,000 from Alana Vladikavkaz on 6/2/98) FL 10/1

TUCK Stuart Gary
Born: Brighton, 1 October 1974
Height: 5'11" Weight: 11.7

As in the previous season, Brighton and Hove Albion's tenacious and popular left-back was again plagued with troublesome injuries during 1997-98. Having missed the opening of the campaign through injury, Stuart had the honour of skippering his home-town club for a spell in the absence of several senior players in November, and remained first choice in the number three shirt when fit. However, the injury jinx struck yet again in March though, and the unlucky 23-year old missed the run in with a recurrent groin problem that required surgery.

Brighton & Hove A (From trainee on 9/7/93) FL 76+3/1 FLC 6 FAC 2 Others 6+1

TUCKER Dexter Calbert
Born: Pontefract, 22 February 1979
Height: 6'2" Weight: 12.0

Dexter impressed the new Hull City manager, Mark Hateley, to such an extent in 1997-98 that he allowed the highly-rated Gavin Gordon to leave, so clearing the way for the young forward to have some early senior opportunities. His height and strength also received notable praise during the Tigers' FA Youth Cup run, and he was duly offered professional terms at the end of the season.

Hull C (Trainee) FL 1+6

TULLY Stephen (Steve) Richard
Born: Torbay, 10 February 1980
Height: 5'7" Weight: 10.4

Despite his slight of build, Steve is very strong and aggressive and it was this factor that convinced the Torquay management that the lad had a future in the game. Still a second year YTS, the local-born right-wing back, who is highly talented and comfortable on the ball, and possibly the best crosser at the club, made 11 appearances for last season after coming on at Barnet in

November. Highly thought of, he has accepted senior contract for 1998-99.
Torquay U (Trainee) FL 4+5 FAC 0+1 Others 1

TURLEY William (Billy) Lee
Born: Wolverhampton, 15 July 1973
Height: 6'4" Weight: 14.10
With the form of Andy Woodman restricting the crowd-pleasing custodian's chances of first team football at Northampton last season, he was loaned to Leyton Orient in February as a replacement for Paul Hyde, who had broken his leg. On making his debut in the Sky TV game against Peterborough, Billy showed up well as a commanding goalkeeper who could kick the ball with both feet, as well as having good distribution skills.
Northampton T (Free from Evesham on 10/7/95) FL 3 Others 3
Leyton Orient (Loaned on 5/2/98) FL 14

TURNBULL Lee Mark
Born: Stockton, 27 September 1967
Height: 6'0" Weight: 13.0
Released by Scunthorpe during the 1997 summer recess, this much-travelled utility player signed for Darlington, but found his time at Feethams dogged by injury and made few appearances, all in the first half of the campaign, before being allowed to leave during the close season. A tough and competitive midfielder, cum target man, Lee has been dreadfully unlucky with injuries over the past two or three seasons and, hopefully, he can get back on track.
Middlesbrough (From trainee on 7/9/85) FL 8+8/4 FLC 0+1 Others 1+1/1
Aston Villa (Signed on 24/8/87)
Doncaster Rov (£17,500 on 3/11/87) FL 108+15/21 FLC 3+1/2 FAC 5+1 Others 9+1/2
Chesterfield (£35,000 on 14/2/91) FL 80+7/26 FLC 2+3/1 FAC 3/1 Others 5
Doncaster Rov (Signed on 8/10/93) FL 10+1/1 FAC 2 Others 1
Wycombe W (£20,000 on 21/1/94) FL 8+3/1 FLC 0+1/1 FAC 1 Others 1
Scunthorpe U (£12,000 on 6/3/95) FL 37+10/7 FLC 2 FAC 2 Others 1
Darlington (Free on 11/7/97) FL 4+5 FLC 0+1 FAC 0+2

TURNER Andrew (Andy) Peter
Born: Woolwich, 23 March 1975
Height: 5'10" Weight: 11.7
International Honours: Ei: U21-7. E: Yth; Sch
As in 1996-97, Andy again failed to establish himself as a regular first team player at Portsmouth in 1997-98, although his season was not helped by injuries. In 18 appearances during the campaign he managed just one goal, but definitely one to remember as he finished a 40-yard run with a tremendous shot from the edge of the box to open the scoring in a 1-1 home draw against Norwich. At his best, very quick and skilful from the left flank, and a great crosser, with a knack for getting the ball over from seemingly impossible positions.
Tottenham H (From trainee on 8/4/92) PL 8+12/3 FLC 0+2/1 FAC 0+1
Wycombe W (Loaned on 26/8/94) FL 3+1
Doncaster Rov (Loaned on 10/10/94) FL 4/1 Others 1/1

Huddersfield T (Loaned on 28/11/95) FL 2+3/1
Southend U (Loaned on 28/3/96) FL 4+2
Portsmouth (£250,000 on 4/9/96) FL 34+6/3 FLC 2+2 FAC 1

TUTILL Stephen (Steve) Alan
Born: York, 1 October 1969
Height: 5'10" Weight: 12.6
International Honours: E: Sch
Injured on the second Saturday of last season, York's longest-serving player was out of action for several months and took no more part in the club's campaign prior to being transferred to Darlington in February. A vastly experienced hard-tackling, commanding central defender, Steve was called upon to bolster the Quakers' flagging defence and soon won over the fans with his committed approach, before giving way to injury after seven games.
York C (From trainee on 27/1/88) FL 293+8/6 FLC 21 FAC 18+1 Others 22+3/1
Darlington (Free on 20/2/98) FL 7

David Tuttle

TUTTLE David Philip
Born: Reading, 6 February 1972
Height: 6'1" Weight: 12.10
Club Honours: FAYC '90
International Honours: E: Yth
Having signed a new contract for Crystal Palace last August, David started the first eight games of the club's Premiership campaign in robust form until breaking his leg against Wimbledon at Selhurst Park. There was no doubt that the strong central defender was badly missed, his tackling and aerial strength alongside Andy Linighan or Hermann Hreidarsson could have made all the difference, while his ability to find the front men with well-struck passes was also lost. Surprisingly, he came back as a sub at Arsenal in February and started at Chelsea a couple of games later before breaking down again, his season finished. One of the bravest players in the game, Palace fans can only hope that he continues to defy the injury jinx.

Tottenham H (From trainee on 8/2/90) F/PL 10+3 FLC 3+1 Others 1/1
Peterborough U (Loaned on 21/1/93) FL 7
Sheffield U (£350,000 on 1/8/93) P/FL 63/1 FLC 2 FAC 3
Crystal Palace (Signed on 8/3/96) F/PL 56+2/3 FLC 4 FAC 1 Others 5

TWEED Steven (Steve)
Born: Edinburgh, 9 August 1972
Height: 6'3" Weight: 13.2
International Honours: S: B-2; U21-3
Steve's early season form for Stoke in 1997-98 seemed to verify what an astute piece of business manager, Chic Bates, pulled off in the summer of 1997 in attracting him to the Britannia Stadium, via his agent, Steve Archibald. Having been released by Greek club, Ionikos, for no fee, by Christmas he was being touted as a possible for Craig Brown's Scotland World Cup squad for France. The problems off the field leading to the home defeat by Birmingham clearly affected his form to such an extent that the new boss, Chris Kamara, dropped him after the home game against Middlesbrough. With yet a further change in manager he was recalled and the confidence was clearly rebuilding as the campaign drew to its close.
Hibernian (Free from Hutchison Vale BC on 25/8/90) (Freed during 1996 close season) SL 105+3/6 SLC 9/1 SC 9/1
Stoke C (Free from Ionikos on 8/8/97) FL 35+3 FLC 5 FAC 1

TWISS Michael John
Born: Salford, 26 December 1977
Height: 5'11" Weight: 12.8
A talented Manchester United player, who started his career as a forward before reverting to left back, Michael was so thrilled to be named as a substitute for United's Champions' League game against Koscice in November, he said: "I just sat there with a dazed look on my face trying to take it all in. Choccy (Brian McClair) told me the next day, he had never seen somebody so happy to be sat on the bench!" Having then made an appearance in the FA Cup replay against Barnsley in February, as a substitute for Denis Irwin, he showed himself to be yet another young player with an excellent future.
Manchester U (From trainee on 5/7/96) FAC 0+1

TYLER Mark Richard
Born: Norwich, 2 April 1977
Height: 6'0" Weight: 12.9
International Honours: E: Yth
Mark finally made it last season at Peterborough, having been a professional at the club since 1994-95, and playing not more than a handful of games during that time. In keeping Bart Griemink in the wings, the young goalkeeper was the only ever present in the side, other than Andy Edwards, and kept 16 clean sheets as he grabbed his chance with both hands. Tall, and a good shot-stopper, he was called up for the England "B" squad and for the U21s in Toulon this summer in acknowledgement of his displays.
Peterborough U (From trainee on 7/12/94) FL 53+1 FLC 4 FAC 3 Others 7

GEORGE DAVIES & CO

SOLICITORS

Solicitors to the PFA

SPORTS

SPONSORSHIP AGREEMENTS
CLUB / COMPANY FORMATION
MEDIA / ADVERTISING

COMPANY

COMPANY DISPUTES
INSOLVENCY
CHARITY SPECIALISTS

LITIGATION

FOOTBALL INJURIES
MATRIMONIAL

EMPLOYMENT

SERVICE CONTRACTS
INDUSTRIAL TRIBUNALS

COMMERCIAL

LEASES / GRANTS
TERMS OF BUSINESS

PROPERTY

HOUSE PURCHASES
INHERITANCE AND WILLS

*George Davies & Co are proud
to have been solicitors to the PFA for over 25 years.*

*Whatever your legal problem telephone us
and we will explain how we can help you.*

INVESTOR IN PEOPLE

0161-236-8992

FOUNTAIN COURT, 68 FOUNTAIN STREET, MANCHESTER, M2 2FB

UV

Lee Unsworth

UHLENBEEK Gustav (Gus) Reinier
Born: Paramaribo, 20 August 1970
Height: 5'9" Weight: 12.6

A broken foot sustained in the 1996-97 play-off game with Sheffield United, did not heal properly during the 1997 close season and Gus was forced to have surgery to resolve the problem. The aftermath of this meant complete rest for a month, which saw the wing back miss the first half of the campaign and, when fit to return, the team were playing well so he had to wait his chance. However, his opportunity came when Mauricio Taricco was suspended and he showed that he had lost none of his tremendous pace – there was always a buzz of anticipation in the crowd when he ran at the opposition's defence. One of his appearances came in the local derby with Norwich and he provided the pass which enabled Alex Mathie to score his second goal. *Stop Press:* Much to the chagrin of his manager, Gus signed for Fulham on a free transfer under the Bosman ruling on 8 July.
Ipswich T (£100,000 from Top Ost on 11/8/95) FL 77+12/4 FLC 5+3 FAC 4+3 Others 7+1

ULLATHORNE Robert
Born: Wakefield, 11 October 1971
Height: 5'8" Weight: 11.3
International Honours: E: Yth

A left-sided Leicester wing back, Robert battled back from a broken ankle on his debut the previous season to full fitness midway through the 1997-98 campaign and scored from the bench in the bizarre defeat at Blackburn, before finding his progress halted by a red card at Bolton two games later. Clearly an accomplished performer, of whom Foxes' fans have yet to see the best, he has the ability to get at defenders in order to produce telling crosses, via a super left foot. Happy to play anywhere down the left-hand side, his enthusiasm rubs off on team mates.
Norwich C (From trainee on 6/7/90) F/PL 86+8/7 FLC 10+2/1 FAC 7+1 Others 1 (Free to Osasuna during 1996 close season)
Leicester C (£600,000 on 18/2/97) PL 3+3/1 FLC 1

UNSWORTH David Gerald
Born: Chorley, 16 October 1973
Height: 6'1" Weight: 13.7
Club Honours: FAC '95; CS '95
International Honours: E: 1; U21-7; Yth

Signed from Everton last September, the powerful left-sided central defender had an excellent season at West Ham and reached the form that gained him an England cap. Strong in the tackle, and good in the air, his presence brought a determined look to the Hammers' rearguard. Pleased to be on the scoresheet twice, in victories over Chelsea and Crystal Palace, there was talk of him being unsettled in the south, but all the fans hope that he will be staying.

Everton (From trainee on 25/6/92) F/PL 108+8/11 FLC 5+2 FAC 7 Others 4/1
West Ham U (£1,000,000+ on 18/8/97) PL 32/2 FLC 5 FAC 4

UNSWORTH Lee Peter
Born: Eccles, 25 February 1973
Height: 5'11" Weight: 11.8

Able to play in central defence or on either flank, and showing steady improvement, Lee has proved to be highly adaptable during his time at Crewe, his pace often helping him recover situations right across the defensive spectrum. Started 1997-98 at right back before the arrival of Marcus Bignot, and stood in for a number of players down with injury, including Shaun Smith, Ashley Westwood, and Chris Lightfoot, while further proving his adaptability. Is sound in the air and a good tackler.
Crewe Alex (Signed from Ashton U on 20/2/95) FL 75+19 FLC 5+1/1 FAC 4+1/1 Others 8+2

UPSON Matthew James
Born: Stowmarket, 18 April 1979
Height: 6'1" Weight: 11.4
International Honours: E: Yth

Signed from Luton at the end of 1996-97, the young centre back was definitely brought in as one for the future, but still managed to put in eight full appearances in 1997-98, making his debut for Arsenal in the second game of the season, a 2-2 draw at Coventry. Later, with the Premiership already won, Matthew played alongside Steve Bould at Anfield and was stunned by a 12-minute blitz that saw Liverpool score three times on their way to a 4-0 win. Cool and confident, strong in the air, and a player with good passing ability who likes to come out with the ball, that would have been an invaluable lesson as to what football at this level is all about. He is certainly in the right

place though, having Tony Adams, Martin Keown and Steve Bould to point the way.
Luton T (From trainee on 24/4/96) FL 0+1 Others 1
Arsenal (£1,000,000 on 14/5/97) PL 5 FLC 2 FAC 1

Matthew Upson

UTLEY Darren
Born: Barnsley, 28 September 1977
Height: 6'0" Weight: 11.7

Darren was very much the forgotten man of Belle Vue during 1997-98, when he was largely ignored by the Doncaster hierarchy

after refusing a move during the previous summer. Subsequently, the young defender was released during the spring, and it is to be hoped that he will not drift out of the professional game for he has much to offer and will do an excellent job for anyone prepared to give him a chance.

Doncaster Rov (From trainee on 9/12/95) FL 22+6/1 FLC 1 FAC 1

VALERY Patrick Jean Claude
Born: Brignoles, France, 3 July 1969
Height: 5'11" Weight: 11.5

A French star with Monaco, and a former U21 international, he left his native country bound for Blackburn during the 1997 close season, having more recently played for Bastia. Although performing at wing back he never appeared comfortable on the overlap, but is a sound, if rugged defender, whose main defensive problem is in coping with the high cross. Unfortunate to lose his place at right back when Jeff Kenna was moved to his stronger side, he unexpectedly came in at left back in the final games of the season. Although reportedly not happy with reserve team football, Patrick has signed a year's extension to his contract.

Blackburn Rov (Free from Bastia on 1/7/97) PL 14+1 FLC 2 FAC 1+1

Patrick Valery

VAN BLERK Jason
Born: Sydney, Australia, 16 March 1968
Height: 6'1" Weight: 13.0
International Honours: Australia: 22

Signed from Millwall during the 1997 close season, following prolonged negotiations delayed by work permits, Jason finally arrived at Manchester City immediately prior to the start of 1997-98. An Australian international who can play at left back, or as an attacking midfielder, after making his debut at Sunderland he spent the campaign in and out of the starting line-up before being transferred to West Bromwich Albion

in March. Coming from a side which ultimately failed to avoid relegation, he showed himself to be strong and forceful, and confident, both in the air and on the ground.

Millwall (£300,000 from Go Ahead Eagles on 8/9/94) FL 68+5/2 FLC 5 FAC 6+1 Others 1+1
Manchester C (Free on 9/8/97) FL 10+9 FLC 0+1 FAC 0+1
West Bromwich A (£250,000 on 13/3/98) FL 8

VAN DER GOUW Raimond (Rai)
Born: Oldenzaal, Holland, 24 March 1963
Height 6'3" Weight 13.1

A highly experienced goalkeeper with a safe pair of hands, Rai continued to spend most of his time on the Manchester United substitutes' bench during the course of last season, as understudy to Peter Schmeichel. Having played against Ipswich in the Coca Cola Cup tie at Portman Road in October, however, he was suddenly thrust into the side for the crunch battle against Monaco in the European Cup in March. Although desperately unlucky to have been beaten by an unstoppable shot by David Trezeguet in that match, he tried his best to salvage the Reds' ill-fated European campaign with a couple of brilliant saves. On the goal that put United out of the competition at the quarter-final stage he said, "It was certainly very fast. They are saying 96mph! That's fast!" On a more positive note, he was delighted to have been appointed United's goalkeeping coach on the backroom staff, which will undoubtedly extend his career at Old Trafford.

Manchester U (Signed from Vitesse Arnhem on 12/7/96) PL 6+1 FLC 3 Others 2

Rai van der Gouw

VAN DER LAAN Robertus (Robin) Petrus
Born: Schiedam, Holland, 5 September 1968
Height: 6'0" Weight: 13.8
Club Honours: AMC '93

Having begun 1997-98 as club captain at Derby, an ankle injury received in October saw him out of action until returning to the first team squad in mid-April, after match practice with the reserves, and fitting well into the squad system. A midfielder who prefers a right-sided position, and has commendable battling qualities, he is robust in the tackle, and likes nothing better than driving forward to encourage the forwards. An imposing figure, his ability at set pieces often creates chances for others.

Port Vale (£80,000 from Wageningen on 21/2/91) FL 154+22/24 FLC 11+1/1 FAC 9+1/1 Others 11+1/1
Derby Co (£675,000 on 2/8/95) F/PL 61+4/8 FLC 6+2 FAC 3+1/3
Wolverhampton W (Loaned on 11/10/96) FL 7

VAN DER VELDEN Carel
Born: Arnhem, Holland, 3 August 1972
Height: 5'11" Weight: 13.7

Freed by Barnsley during the 1997 close season, this talented Dutch-born midfielder, of whom Scarborough boss, Mick Wadsworth, had high hopes of when he signed him, unfortunately encountered problems in his personal life and was released after just three months, by mutual consent, so that he could return to Holland. Appearing in just ten games, his great 15-yard shot that brought about the third goal in a 3-3 draw at Lincoln, merely emphasised his loss to the side.

Barnsley (£75,000 from FC Den Bosch on 12/3/96) FL 7+2 FLC 1
Scarborough (Free on 5/8/97) FL 5+3/1 FLC 2

VAN DULLEMEN Raymond Robert
Born: Gravenhage, Holland, 6 May 1973
Height: 6'1" Weight: 14.0

Having come to Northampton on trial from Dutch non-league football at the beginning of last season, and being given a one-year contract on the strength of his performances in the summer friendlies, he was unfortunately hospitalised with a hernia injury after a couple of substitute appearances. Later loaned out to Kettering Town, the Dutch lad became a popular figure at Rockingham Road, but on his return to Sixfields found it hard to hold down a regular place, even in the reserves, with so many strikers on the books.

Northampton T (Free from VIOS on 8/8/97) FL 0+1 FLC 0+1

VAN GOBBEL Ulrich
Born: Surinam, 16 January 1971
Height: 5'11" Weight: 13.8
International Honours: Holland: 9

Unable to settle with Southampton, this powerful and athletic Dutch defender, or wing back, made just two appearances last season before being sold to Feyenord in September. A year earlier he had arrived at the Dell after his £1.3 million fee had broken the club transfer record, this time round, he departed for the sum of £800,000. What a difference a year makes!

Southampton (£1,300,000 from Galatasaray on 19/10/96) PL 25+2/1 FLC 6/1 FAC 1

VAN HEUSDEN Arjan
Born: Alphen, Holland, 11 December 1972
Height: 6'3" Weight: 13.12

Once again spending most of his time as Port Vale's reserve 'keeper, Arjan was loaned to Oxford last September on an extended spell to cover for the injured Phil Whitehead, and took over from the youngster, Elliot Jackson. He kept a clean sheet on his debut, saving a penalty against Bradford, and later on kept three shut outs in a row, as he adhered himself to the United fans. Prior to that he had been the penalty hero in the Coca Cola Cup, when he made vital saves in the shoot-out against Tranmere. Returning to Vale Park after United were unable to meet the transfer fee needed to make the move permanent, he had to wait until February before donning a Vale jersey, which he claimed for five games until a leg injury sidelined him once again. Was released during the summer.

Port Vale (£4,500 from Noordwijk on 15/8/94) FL 27 FLC 4 Others 2
Oxford U (Loaned on 26/9/97) FL 11 FLC 2

VAN HOOIJDONK Pierre
Born: Steenbergen, Holland, 29 November 1969
Height: 6'4" Weight: 13.12
Club Honours: Div 1 '98
International Honours: Holland: 15

Having joined Nottingham Forest towards the end of 1996-97, with the club already destined to play first division football, the big, powerful Dutch striker came into his own last season, having a terrific time of it when scoring 34 league and cup goals to fall just two short of Wally Ardron's all-time Forest scoring record set in 1951. Good on the ground, and in the air, his real asset is his pace and control when latching on to the ball well outside the area and, on occasion, he appeared to terrorise even the best of well-drilled defences. Needless to say, his strike partnership with a revitalised Kevin Campbell was probably the biggest single factor in the club going back to the Premiership at the first time of asking, while his scoring statistics showed two hat tricks, at the City Ground, against Queens Park Rangers and Charlton, and seven braces. Apart from becoming the new hero in succession to Stuart Pearce, he also took over the latter's role as the club's free-kick specialist. Was recognised by his fellow professionals when elected to the PFA award-winning first division team. *Stop Press:* Selected for Holland's World Cup squad, Pierre made three appearances in France '98 – scoring in the 5-0 win over South Korea, going close against Brazil in the semi-final match, but being rather quiet against Croatia in the third place play off.

Glasgow Celtic (£1,200,000 from NAC Breda on 7/1/95) SL 66+3/44 SLC 5+1/3 SC 10/9 Others 5+2
Nottingham Forest (£4,500,000 on 11/3/97) F/PL 49+1/30 FLC 4/4 FAC 0+1/1

VARTY John William (Will)
Born: Workington, 1 October 1976
Height: 6'0" Weight: 12.4
Club Honours: AMC '97

After a successful debut campaign in 1996-97, Will was again a fixture in the Carlisle defence in 1997-98, missing only two games all season. Very much a back-four player, who would have gained vastly in experience during the last term, a rare foray upfield brought a last-minute equaliser against Walsall – his first ever goal for the club.

Carlisle U (From trainee on 10/7/95) FL 74+2/1 FLC 8 FAC 3 Others 9+1

VAUGHAN Anthony (Tony) John
Born: Manchester, 11 October 1975
Height: 6'1" Weight: 11.2
International Honours: E: Sch; Yth

Manchester born, Tony signed for City during the 1997 close season, having spent the whole of his career at Ipswich, and, although starting 1997-98 well, he appeared to slip from the limelight following the opening five games and missed the next nine before coming back at the end of October. Settling in well at full back, or centre back, he was delighted to score at Maine Road against Wolves, but having been booked for the third time, and subbed against Nottingham Forest, he was sidelined for 17 games during the first three months of the New Year. However, coming back for the remaining six fixtures, despite the club's eventual fall from grace, he had an excellent spell, showing commitment and flair from midfield, a position he appeared to be more than comfortable in.

Ipswich T (From trainee on 1/7/94) P/FL 56+11/3 FLC 4+2 FAC 2 Others 4
Manchester C (£1,350,000 on 9/7/97) FL 19/1 FLC 2

VAUGHAN John
Born: Isleworth, 26 June 1964
Height: 5'10" Weight: 13.1
Club Honours: Div 3 '91, '96

John, a veteran who competed with Barry Richardson for the Lincoln goalkeeper's jersey throughout last season, began as first choice but was kept out by injuries and then dropped after conceding five goals at home to Notts County in January. Won his place back following Richardson's suspension, playing in the final four games as the side dropped just two points on its way to automatic promotion from the third division.

West Ham U (From apprentice on 30/6/82)
Charlton Ath (Loaned on 11/3/85) FL 6
Bristol Rov (Loaned on 11/3/85) FL 6
Wrexham (Loaned on 23/10/85) FL 4
Bristol C (Loaned on 4/3/86) FL 2
Fulham (£12,500 on 21/8/86) FL 44 FLC 4 FAC 4 Others 3
Bristol C (Loaned on 21/1/88) FL 3
Cambridge U (Free on 6/6/88) FL 178 FLC 13 FAC 24 Others 16
Charlton Ath (Free on 5/8/93) FL 5+1 FAC 2 Others 1+1
Preston NE (Free on 26/7/94) FL 65+1 FLC 2 FAC 2 Others 5
Lincoln C (Free on 14/8/96) FL 29 FLC 3 Others 1
Colchester U (Loaned on 3/2/97) FL 5 Others 1

VEART Thomas Carl
Born: Whyalla, Australia, 21 May 1970
Height: 5'11" Weight: 12.8
International Honours: Australia: 15

Another player to arrive at Millwall in 1997-98 from another London side, this time from Crystal Palace in December, despite being a member of the first team squad, Carl had failed to make more than two starts during the campaign and was allowed to leave. He started well enough at the New Den, scoring at Bristol City in his third appearance, showing good control and the ability to use either foot, before becoming yet another Lion to fall victim to injury and being sidelined for the remainder of the season. Is able to perform equally well in midfield or defence.

Sheffield U (£250,000 from Adelaide C on 22/7/94) FL 47+19/16 FLC 2+1/1 FAC 2+1/1 Others 2
Crystal Palace (£225,000 on 8/3/96) F/PL 41+16/6 FLC 4+1/3 FAC 2/1 Others 2+2/1
Millwall (£50,000+ on 11/12/97) FL 7+1/1 Others 1

VEGA Ramon
Born: Zurich, Switzerland, 14 June 1971
Height: 6'3" Weight: 13.0
International Honours: Switzerland: 20

A strong, athletic Tottenham full back who is deadly in the air from set pieces, Ramon started last season with a disastrous own goal against Manchester United in the curtain raiser. However, it was not long before he found the form which has made him a regular in the Switzerland international side. For his build, he is unusually agile and skilful, with tight turns and pin-point, accurate crosses, and loves to deliver the long ball from his own half as much as he enjoys getting forward in raiding down the wings. Consecutive headed goals in the game at Everton and a first-half equaliser in the 6-1 home drubbing by Chelsea, demonstrated that he has the predatory instincts of a natural striker when in the opponents penalty box. This was also confirmed with the opening goal for Switzerland in the friendly international against England, a game which ended in a 1-1 draw. Another Spurs' player who suffered from injury, which interrupted his form in 1997-98, Ramon continued to be solid in defence alongside either Sol Campbell, John Scales, or Colin Calderwood, a line-up which should prove extremely difficult to beat when all are fit and fielded together.

Tottenham H (£3,750,000 from Cagliari on 11/1/97) PL 30+3/4 FLC 2 FAC 3

VENUS Mark
Born: Hartlepool, 6 April 1967
Height: 6'0" Weight: 13.11
Club Honours: Div 3 '89

A 1997 summer signing from Wolves, Mark joined Ipswich as part of the deal that saw Steve Sedgley move in the opposite direction, in order to give Town a better ratio of left-footed players. Went straight into the team, partnering Jason Cundy in central defence, and scored his first goal in only his second game, at Charlton in the Coca Cola Cup. Charlton's goalkeeper was harshly penalised under "the six second rule" and the newcomer scored direct from the resultant free kick. However, his season took a turn for the worse. Having left the

field during the game at Norwich, in September, with what was thought to be a minor thigh injury, it proved more serious and he did not come back until the end of December at Swindon, lasting just three games before breaking a toe against Chelsea. This again proved difficult to heal and it was not until mid-April that he returned to the side.

Hartlepool U (From juniors on 22/3/85) FL 4 Others 0+1
Leicester C (Free on 6/9/85) FL 58+3/1 FLC 3 FAC 2 Others 2+1
Wolverhampton W (£40,000 on 23/3/88) FL 271+16/7 FLC 17+1/1 FAC 15+1 Others 17/2
Ipswich T (£150,000 on 29/7/97) FL 12+2/1 FLC 5/1 FAC 1 Others 2

VERITY Daniel Richard
Born: Bradford, 19 April 1980
Height: 6'0" Weight: 11.3

A former Bradford YTS, Daniel signed professional forms for the club last March and celebrated with a Football League debut when coming off the bench for ten minutes at Bury a couple of weeks later. Thought highly of at Valley Parade, he is a strong, hard-working central defender, who has represented Great Britain's Catholic Schools in competition, and who now hopes to make a career in football.

Bradford C (From trainee on 28/3/98) FL 0+1

VERNAZZA Paulo Andrea Pietro
Born: London, 1 November 1979
Height: 6'0" Weight: 11.10
International Honours: E: Yth

Despite his Italian name which he owed to his parenthood, Paulo was born in London and came through Arsenal's junior ranks to turn professional last November. A right-sided player who can play up front or on the flank, he is both fast, tricky, and direct, and appears to have an eye for a goal. Certainly well thought of at Highbury, he made his first team debut in the home Coca Cola Cup tie against Birmingham, alongside Chris Wreh, while still a trainee, and later, with nine first teamers out of action, partnered Nicolas Anelka at Crystal Palace in the Premiership. Watch this space....

Arsenal (From trainee on 18/11/97) PL 1 FLC 1

VEYSEY Kenneth (Ken) James
Born: Hackney, 8 June 1967
Height: 5'11" Weight: 12.7

Ken proved a revelation in 1997-98, his second spell at Torquay earning the respect of the defenders in front of him. Much experienced, and with a calm authority allied to agile shot-stopping, he unluckily missed the Wembley play-off final after his dismissal at Leyton Orient. Has a great attitude to the game.

Torquay U (Signed from Dawlish T on 19/11/87) FL 72 FLC 2 FAC 10 Others 9
Oxford U (£110,000 on 29/10/90) FL 57 FLC 2 FAC 4 Others 4
Reading (Free on 17/8/93)
Exeter C (Free on 14/10/93) FL 11+1 Others 3
(Free to Dorchester T on 17/9/94)
Torquay U (Free on 11/8/97) FL 27 FAC 2 Others 3

VIALLI Gianluca (Luca)
Born: Italy, 9 July 1964
Height: 5'11" Weight: 13.6
Club Honours: FAC '97; FLC '98; ECWC '98
International Honours: Italy: 59

We're all familiar with the phrase "Football's a funny old game", but rarely has this marvellous game, even with all its glorious uncertainties, thrown up such a reversal of fortune for a footballer. For much of the 1996-97 season, Luca looked a forlorn figure on the Chelsea substitutes' bench, and a fleeting two-minute appearance in the FA Cup final as a substitute was perceived by many pundits to have been his swan song in the famous blue shirt. Who would have thought that nine months later he would have replaced the charismatic Ruud Gullit as the Blues' player/manager! After a summer of press speculation linking Luca with clubs all over Europe, the popular centre forward stayed on to battle for a place in Chelsea's powerful strike force. He replaced Mark Hughes for the second Premiership fixture at Barnsley and scored a classic "four-timer" in the televised 6-0 drubbing of the newcomers – Chelsea's best away win for seven years, and their highest in top-flight football. However, he saved his best form for the European Cup Winners' campaign, where his vast experience of continental football was invaluable. After scoring with his backside in Bratislava, in Chelsea's 4-0 aggregate triumph over Slovan in the first round, the next round saw the team travel beyond the Arctic Circle to play Tromso in farcical conditions, and Luca rescued the Blues with two late, superb individual goals as the Norwegian club looked set to send Chelsea slithering out of the competition. The 3-2 deficit was potentially difficult to overcome, but Chelsea played some magnificent attacking football to win 7-1 with Vialli to the fore, scoring a tremendous hat trick. Continuing to score consistently throughout the season, leading the Chelsea scoring chart, Luca's first match in charge, following Ruud Gullit's departure, was the second leg Coca Cola Cup semi final at home to Arsenal when Chelsea needed to overturn a 2-1 deficit. After a pre-match champagne toast, he led from the front, inspiring the team to a 3-1 victory in a bristling performance. This clinched a 4-3 aggregate victory and a Wembley Cup final appearance after his first match as manager – surely some sort of record! Having left himself out of the Coca Cola Cup final squad altogether, it was a mark of the squad's esteem for the man that they forced him up the Royal Box to lift the trophy after the victory over Middlesbrough. To win one cup competition as a new manager is incredible, but two is just unbelievable! Yet that is what Luca achieved. Taking a leaf from the Gullit manual for success, he also rotated the squad to telling effect, picking himself for the semi final and final of the Cup Winners' Cup as the Blues collected their second cup in their most successful season ever – thanks to inspired substitutions against Vicenza and

Stuttgart. A genuinely modest, popular man, whose avowed ambition is to lead Chelsea to the Premiership title, he finished the season with 19 goals, and it remains to be seen how often he plays in the future, especially now that Chelsea have signed Brian Laudrup and Pierluigi Casiraghi.

Chelsea (Free from Juventus, via Sampdoria and Cremonese, on 10/7/96) PL 37+12/20 FLC 3+1 FAC 1+4/4 Others 8+1/6

VICKERS Ashley James Ward
Born: Sheffield, 14 June 1972
Height: 6'3" Weight: 12.10

Signed from the non-league side, Heybridge Swifts, last December, as a player for the future, Ashley made his Football League debut for Peterborough six days later in a 2-1 home defeat at the hands of Brighton, being sent off with nine minutes to go. Following that, the tall central defender went back to the reserves to regroup and will be looking for a more auspicious start to 1998-99.

Peterborough U (£5,000 from Heybridge Swifts on 22/12/97) FL 1

VICKERS Stephen (Steve)
Born: Bishop Auckland, 13 October 1967
Height: 6'1" Weight: 12.12
Club Honours: AMC '90; Div 1 '95

A versatile and powerful defender, Steve is now considered to be a cornerstone of Middlesbrough's well-established rearguard making 42 appearances in 1997-98 out of a possible 57, only being absent when injured or non-available for duty. Strong in the air, and fearless in the tackle, his reputation is that of a "no nonsense" type who cuts out the threat and then finds a better placed team mate with a ball-to-feet delivery. Extremely popular with the Boro fans, who know a good player when they see one, he was one of the keys that unlocked the Premiership door at the first time of asking last season.

Tranmere Rov (Signed from Spennymoor U on 11/9/85) FL 310+1/11 FLC 20+1/5 FAC 19/3 Others 36/1
Middlesbrough (£700,000 on 3/12/93) P/FL 157+7/7 FLC 20+1/2 FAC 15+1 Others 2

VIEIRA Patrick
Born: Dakar, Senegal, 23 June 1976
Height: 6'4" Weight: 13.0
Club Honours: PL '98; FAC '98
International Honours: France: 9

A great acquisition for Arsenal, Patrick was arguably the most influential central midfielder in the Premiership in 1997-98, his telescopic legs being used to tremendous effect for both club and country. Bullet-like shooting also brought him two goals, the 35-yard drive for the third in the 3-1 Premiership victory over Newcastle at Highbury in mid-April was right out of the mould. Very consistent, missing just seven games in all, he was good value for his championship and FA Cup winners' medals as Arsenal took the campaign, especially the last third of it, by storm to "do" the double for the second time in their history. With a good "engine" that allows him a lot of freedom, if you add his vision and passing abilities, along with hard but fair tackling, to

the equation there is not much else you would be looking for. Just 22 years of age, it is unbelievable to think that his former club, Inter Milan, failed to recognise his great talent and let him go without ever giving him a first team opportunity. Mind you, they did try to buy him back once they realised the error of their ways. *Stop Press:* Having played just once in the France '98 competition prior to the World Cup Final, due to the excellent form of Laurent Blanc and Marcel Desailly, when the latter was sent off in the final against Brazil Patrick was called from the bench and was delighted to be part of the French 3-0 victory. It was a great end to a great year.

Arsenal (£3,500,000 from AC Milan on 14/8/96) PL 61+3/4 FLC 5 FAC 11+1 Others 3

VINCENT Jamie Roy
Born: Wimbledon, 18 June 1975
Height: 5'10" Weight: 11.8

As first choice at left back for Bournemouth during 1997-98, Jamie had a very consistent season, being quick and not afraid to move forward when the opportunity arose. He is also an accomplished defender who is an excellent tackler and dangerous at dead-ball situations.

Crystal Palace (From trainee on 13/7/93) FL 19+6 FLC 2+1/1 FAC 1
Bournemouth (Loaned on 18/11/94) FL 8
Bournemouth (£25,000 + on 30/8/96) FL 71+2/3 FLC 2+1 FAC 4 Others 6/1

VINNICOMBE Christopher (Chris)
Born: Exeter, 20 October 1970
Height: 5'9" Weight: 10.12
Club Honours: SPD '91
International Honours: E: U21-12

At last enjoying an injury-free season, in 1997-98, Chris was employed by Burnley in a more forward position than hitherto, taking over the left-sided wing-back role, following the departure of David Eyres. However, the classy, and still pacy former England U21 international lost his place when Chris Waddle rearranged the defensive formation and moved Mark Winstanley to the left.*

Patrick Vieira

Exeter C (From trainee on 1/7/89) FL 35+4/1 FLC 5/1 Others 2
Glasgow R (£150,000 on 3/11/89) SL 14+9/1 SLC 1+2 Others 1
Burnley (£200,000 on 30/6/94) FL 90+5/3 FLC 9 FAC 2 Others 7+1/1

VIVEASH Adrian Lee
Born: Swindon, 30 September 1969
Height: 6'2" Weight: 12.13

Walsall's tall, dominant central defender missed his first game for nearly two years when suspended last December, an absence that allowed Stuart Ryder to deputise for a couple of games, but on coming back he carried on where he had left off in steadying a defence that conceded less goals than Wigan, eight league places above the Saddlers in the second division table. A player who must be the club's best-ever free-transfer signing, he can perform confidently anywhere across the back four, pass long and short with accuracy, and continued to get his name on the scoresheet.

Swindon T (From trainee on 14/7/88) FL 51+3/2 FLC 6+1 FAC 0+1 Others 2
Reading (Loaned on 4/1/93) FL 5 Others 1/1
Reading (Loaned on 20/1/95) FL 6
Barnsley (Loaned on 10/8/95) FL 2/1
Walsall (Free on 16/10/95) FL 119/12 FLC 8 FAC 13/2 Others 8/1

VLACHOS Michail
Born: Athens, Greece, 20 September 1967
Height: 5'11" Weight: 12.10
International Honours: Greece: 1

A Greek international, Michail was signed from AEK Athens last January and became manager Alan Ball's first permanent signing on joining Portsmouth, first slotting in as a left-wing back, before moving into a central midfield roll for which he proved most effective. It was this positional change which was part of Pompey's best run of the season, despite him being forced to miss four of the last eight games following an injury at Sunderland. Is a tough tackler who can be used to great advantage in a man-marking role.

Portsmouth (Signed from AEK Athens on 30/1/98) FL 15

VONK Michel Christian
Born: Alkmaar, Holland, 28 October 1968
Height: 6'3" Weight: 13.3

A good, solid central defender who, at his best, is excellent in the air and a good man to have on your side for a man-marking job, Michel had a rough time of it at Sheffield United in 1997-98. Not fit for the start of the season, while still recovering from a cruciate knee ligament operation the previous November, he finally came back at the beginning of December, at Norwich, and was sent off, as well as conceding an own goal. Following two more appearances, sadly, the injury re-occurred to put him out of action for the rest of the campaign. A popular player, United fans are keeping their fingers crossed that he makes a sound recovery.

Manchester C (£300.000 from SVV Dordrecht on 11/3/92) F/PL 87+4/3 FLC 3+2/1 FAC 6+1/1
Oldham Ath (Loaned on 17/11/95) FL 5/1
Sheffield U (£350,000 on 21/12/95) FL 37/2 FLC 4/2 FAC 2

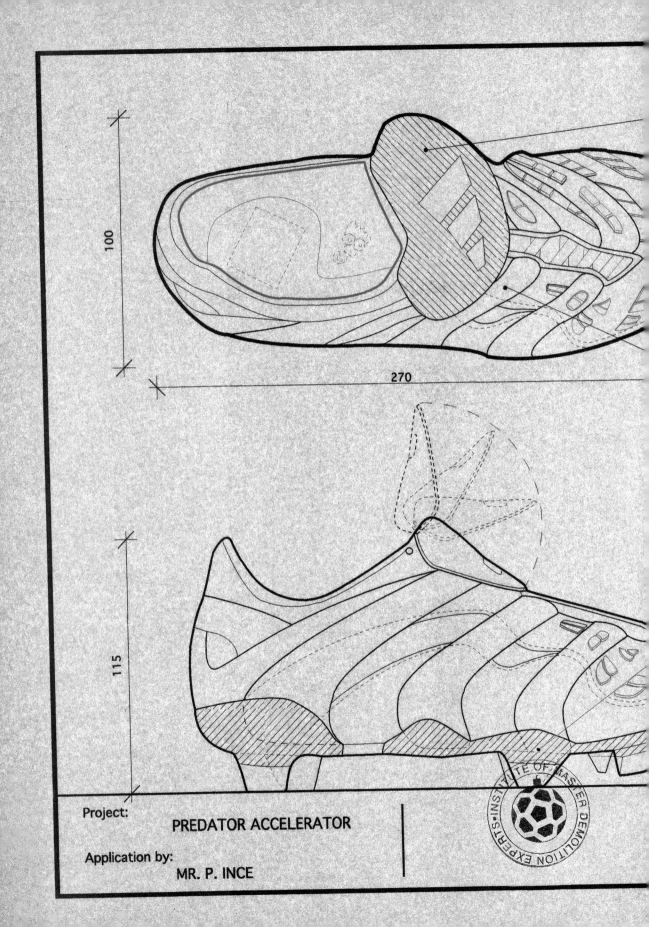

100

270

115

Project:

PREDATOR ACCELERATOR

Application by:

MR. P. INCE

INSTITUTE OF MASTER DEMOLITION EXPERTS

TONGUE AREA TO BE
PANTONE REF 032

RUBBER AREAS MAXIMISE
SWERVE ON DEMOLITION
BALL AND INCREASE POWER.

3 WHITE STRIPES ON
EACH ELEVATION.

CONSTRUCTION ALLOWS
IMPROVED SPEED OF
MOVEMENT AROUND ALL
GRASSED AREAS.

WORK TO BE COMPLETED
IN UNDER 90 MINUTES

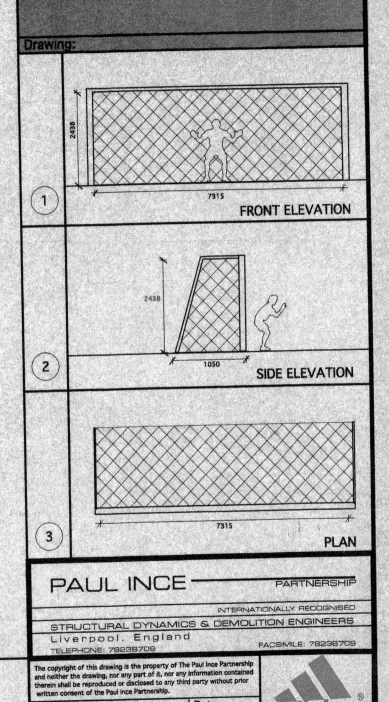

STRUCTURE TO BE DEMOLISHED

Drawing:

1 — 2438 — 7315 — **FRONT ELEVATION**

2 — 2438 — 1050 — **SIDE ELEVATION**

3 — 7315 — **PLAN**

PAUL INCE ——— PARTNERSHIP

INTERNATIONALLY RECOGNISED

STRUCTURAL DYNAMICS & DEMOLITION ENGINEERS
Liverpool, England
TELEPHONE: 78238709   FACSIMILE: 78238709

The copyright of this drawing is the property of The Paul Ince Partnership
and neither the drawing, nor any part of it, nor any information contained
therein shall be reproduced or disclosed to any third party without prior
written consent of the Paul Ince Partnership.

Scale	1:50, 1:1	Date	98/99
Drawn	Job No. 2155	Drg No. 01	

adidas®
Soccer Re-Invented

Dennis Wise

W

WADDLE Christopher (Chris) Roland
Born: Felling, 14 December 1960
Height: 6'2" Weight: 13.3
International Honours: E: 62; U21-1
Released by Sunderland during the 1997 close season in order to take over at Burnley as the player/manager, Chris was a regular in the side for the first half of 1997-98, but following an injury absence his appearances became less frequent. Still capable of magical sleight of foot and inch-perfect passing, his football brain sometimes appeared too far ahead of his team mates, while at other times his managerial duties seemed to compromise his effectiveness on the field. *Stop Press:* Parted company with Burnley on 12 May.
Newcastle U (£1,000 from Tow Law on 28/7/80) FL 169+1/46 FLC 8/2 FAC 12/4
Tottenham H (£590,000 on 1/7/85) FL 137+1/33 FLC 21/4 FAC 14/5 Others 4 (£4,250,000 to Marseilles on 1/7/89)
Sheffield Wed (£1,000,000 on 1/7/92) PL 94+15/10 FLC 19 FAC 12+1/3 Others 3+1/1
Falkirk (Free on 13/9/96) SL 3/1
Bradford C (Free on 12/10/96) FL 25/6 FAC 3/1
Sunderland (£75,000 on 20/3/97) PL 7/1
Burnley (Free on 17/7/97) FL 26+5/1 FLC 2+1 FAC 2

WADDOCK Gary Patrick
Born: Kingsbury, 17 March 1962
Height: 5'10" Weight: 12.5
Club Honours: Div 2 '83
International Honours: Ei: 21; B-1; U23-1; U21-1

As club captain, Gary's value to the team can best be gauged by Luton's performances when he is missing and he needed all his fighting spirit and high workrate qualities to lift an often uninspiring Luton team, beset by injuries throughout 1997-98. An excellent ball winner, this defensive midfielder had few opportunities to show his attacking skills, but finally led the club to safety at the end of a tough campaign, mainly through determination and personal example. Was yet another Luton man to be released during the summer.
Queens Park R (From apprentice on 26/7/79) FL 191+12/8 FLC 21+1/2 FAC 14 Others 1 (Free to Charleroi in December 1987)
Millwall (£130,000 on 16/8/89) FL 51+7/2 FLC 5+1 FAC 5 Others 3/1
Queens Park R (Free on 20/12/91)
Swindon T (Loaned on 19/3/92) FL 5+1
Bristol Rov (£100,000 on 7/11/92) FL 71/1 FLC 2 FAC 2 Others 2
Luton T (Free on 9/9/94) FL 146+7/3 FLC 10 FAC 8 Others 4+3

WAINWRIGHT Neil
Born: Warrington, 4 November 1977
Height: 6'0" Weight: 11.5
A slim wide man who can set the crowd alight, Neil broke onto the Football League scene in 1997-98, after coming through Wrexham's junior ranks so ably marshalled by Cliff Sear and his youth development staff. Scored some spectacular goals in his first season, such as the one at Blackpool in December, when coming on as sub and cracking the match winner from some 25 yards. Can play on either wing, but prefers the left flank in order to cut inside and shoot with his better right foot. Definitely a player to watch, he has a good first touch, and loves taking on the opposition, hoping to press the panic button and make things happen.
Wrexham (From trainee on 3/7/96) FL 7+4/3 FAC 1 Others 1

WALKER Andrew (Andy) Francis
Born: Glasgow, 6 April 1965
Height: 5'8" Weight: 11.6
Club Honours: S Div 1 '85; SPD '88; SFAC '88
International Honours: S: 3; U21-1

Having been made available for transfer prior to 1997-98 getting underway, the Sheffield United man managed just one appearance from the bench before being loaned to Hibernian and Raith Rovers, for three months apiece, in order for him to at least be match fit. It was a far cry from the days that he was feted at Bolton and Glasgow Celtic, but at the age of 33, injuries seem to have caught up with him. At his best, a top-class striker with a great first touch, and great acceleration, who could score important goals and create havoc in the tightest of defences, there could still be a sting in the tail.
Motherwell (From Baillieston Juniors on 31/7/84) SL 65+12/17 SLC 2+4/1 SC 9+2/2

Glasgow Celtic (£350,000 on 1/7/87) SL 86+22/40 SLC 9+6/8 SC 8+3/6 Others 5+2/3
Newcastle U (Loaned on 1/9/91) FL 2 FLC 1
Bolton W (£160,000 on 9/1/92) FL 61+6/44 FLC 3/1 FAC 9+3/8 Others 5/2
Glasgow Celtic (£550,000 on 1/7/94) SL 26+16/9 SLC 6+1/2 SC 3+2 Others 2+1/1
Sheffield U (£500,000 on 23/2/96) FL 32+20/20 FLC 2/2 FAC 1 Others 0+2/1
Hibernian (Loaned on 12/12/97) SL 6+2/2 SC 1
Raith Rov (Loaned on 13/3/98) SL 8+1/3

WALKER Desmond (Des) Sinclair
Born: Hackney, 26 November 1965
Height: 5'11" Weight: 11.13
Club Honours: FLC '89, '90; FMC '89, '92
International Honours: E: 59; U21-7

What more can this fine, pacy central defender do to get his deserved place back in the England squad, the Sheffield Wednesday fans were asking of Glenn Hoddle last season. An ever present, Des once again showed his astute covering of colleagues, decisive tackling and timely interceptions, which frustrate even the best of opponents, and all the while he worked on any weaknesses in his footballing make-up in an effort to eradicate them. A pleasure to work with, he rarely loses his cool and just gets on with the job in hand. However, there were still no goals for him, having gone five seasons at Wednesday without one, but look at his record closely and you will find just one in a career that began in 1983-84.
Nottingham F (From apprentice on 2/12/83) FL 259+5/1 FLC 40 FAC 27 Others 14 (£1,500,000 to Sampdoria on 1/8/92)
Sheffield Wed (£2,700,000 on 22/7/93) PL 190 FLC 17 FAC 15

Des Walker

WALKER Ian Michael
Born: Watford, 31 October 1971
Height: 6'1" Weight: 13.1
Club Honours: FAYC '90
International Honours: E: 3; B-1; U21-9;
Yth

1997-98 was a disappointing season for this goalkeeper who, for much of the time, found himself relying on a patched-up defence which changed from week to week due to Tottenham's well-reported injury problems. At his best, he showed glimpses of the agility and athleticism which had made him the regular England deputy to David Seaman, keeping clean sheets against some of the most prolific Premiership strike forces, in Arsenal and Blackburn. These were amongst the high points of his season, but were unfortunately overshadowed by the nightmare of the 6-1 home defeat at the hands of Chelsea, and a total of 12 goals conceded to Liverpool, Coventry, and Aston Villa. After picking up a shoulder injury in the FAC third round home tie against Fulham, Ian was forced to recover whilst watching a competent Espen Baardsen challenge for the number one spot at Spurs with a fine run of performances, while the injury, and drop in form, resulted in him losing his England spot in the final squad of 22 for the World Cup Finals in France. He had earlier played for the England "B" side against Russia. The son of Mike, the former Norwich manager, Ian will be looking forward to this coming term and the chance to answer his critics.
Tottenham H (From trainee on 4/12/89) F/PL 191+1 FLC 16 FAC 16 Others 2
Oxford U (Loaned on 31/8/90) FL 2 FLC 1

Jimmy Walker

WALKER James (Jimmy) Barry
Born: Sutton in Ashfield, 9 July 1973
Height: 5'11" Weight: 13.5
As Walsall's only ever present in 1997-98, playing in all 62 games despite being carried

off at Northampton on Boxing Day when the victim of a flying boot, Jimmy kept five clean sheets in the opening 11 games and was an inspiration to his colleagues with his bravery and agility, both seen to best effect in the FA Cup defeat at Manchester United, when he saved the Saddlers from a real hammering. Known as "Whacker", due to his prodigious kicking ability, he also skippered the side on a number of occasions.
Notts Co (From trainee on 9/7/91)
Walsall (Free on 4/8/93) FL 142+1 FLC 10 FAC 15 Others 10

WALKER John
Born: Glasgow, 12 December 1973
Height: 5'6" Weight: 11.6
International Honours: S: Yth
Dogged by multiple knee injuries all of last season, this talented Mansfield midfielder made only a couple of subs' appearances throughout the campaign, but should be fully fit for the start of 1998-99. His main attributes are ball control, distribution, and positional awareness.
Glasgow R (From Clydebank BC on 29/8/90)
Clydebank (Signed on 31/7/93) SL 18+9/2 Others 4+3
Grimsby T (Signed on 19/9/95) FL 1+2/1
Mansfield T (£50,000 on 6/9/96) FL 33+4/3 FAC 2 Others 1+1

Justin Walker

WALKER Justin
Born: Nottingham, 6 September 1975
Height: 5'10" Weight: 12.12
International Honours: E: Yth
Having firmed up his loan transfer from Nottingham Forest, Justin's first full season in league football saw him establish himself as a regular member of the Scunthorpe midfield in 1997-98. A good passer and a strong tackler, he settled quickly to the demands of third division football and showed good ability at driving the midfield forward. Also filled in as a central defender, giving one of his best performances in that position in the match against Hull in September.

Nottingham F (From juniors on 10/9/92)
Scunthorpe U (Signed on 26/3/97) FL 46+3/1 FLC 4 FAC 3 Others 2

WALKER Keith Cameron
Born: Edinburgh, 17 April 1966
Height: 6'0" Weight: 12.8

Appointed captain at the start of last season, following his signing a three-year contract during the summer, Keith had one of his most injury-free campaigns since joining Swansea from St Mirren nearly nine years ago. An inspirational figure in the City rearguard, the central defender scored one of his finest ever goals in the televised 1-0 win at Cardiff in November. A strong tackler, he also has an ability to hit the forwards with long-range passes out of defence.
Stirling A (Signed from ICI in 1984) SL 82+9/17 SLC 5/3 SC 5/2
St Mirren (Signed during 1987 close season) SL 41+2/6 SLC 3 SC 1 Others 3
Swansea C (£80,000 on 23/11/89) FL 261+8/9 FLC 10 FAC 21/1 Others 26

Keith Walker

WALKER Richard Martin
Born: Birmingham, 8 November 1977
Height: 6'0" Weight: 12.0
A professional at Aston Villa for two years, this young forward finally made his debut when coming off the bench at Leeds last December but, despite being a named sub on three further occasions, that was to be his sole appearance for the club to date. As a regular in the reserves, and having scored a fair number of goals, it was only fitting that Richard should be given a first team opportunity and if he continues to progress at the same rate he is bound to further his experience in the near future.
Aston Villa (From trainee on 13/12/95) PL 0+1

Ray Wallace

WALLACE Raymond (Ray) George
Born: Greenwich, 2 October 1969
Height: 5'6" Weight: 11.4
International Honours: E: U21-4

One of three footballing brothers, Rod (Leeds) and Danny (once of England), being the other two, Ray was yet another of the Stoke players clearly unsettled by the problems visited on the club during a difficult 1997-98 season. "Razor" remained a great crowd pleaser for his performances as a hard tackling central midfielder and it was hardly surprising that his competitive style was missed by the side when he was absent, due to suspension or being out of favour.
Southampton (From trainee on 21/4/88) FL 33+2 FLC 8 FAC 2 Others 2
Leeds U (£100,000 on 8/7/91) F/PL 5+2
Swansea C (Loaned on 20/3/92) FL 2
Reading (Loaned on 11/3/94) FL 3
Stoke C (Free on 11/8/94) FL 141+7/12 FLC 13 FAC 5 Others 11/1
Hull C (Loaned on 16/12/94) FL 7

WALLACE Rodney (Rod) Seymour
Born: Greenwich, 2 October 1969
Height: 5'7" Weight: 11.3
Club Honours: Div 1 '92; CS '92
International Honours: E: B-2; U21-11

Rod began last season as Leeds' longest-serving player and, above all others, blossomed under George Graham. In fact, he and Jimmy Floyd Hasselbaink had already struck up a good partnership in the summer friendlies. Began the campaign in superb fashion, and his lightning pace began to exploit defences, especially away from home. Prior to March, all but two of Rod's goals were on away soil, including his glorious curling drive in the 4-3 victory at Blackburn, and his volley that gained a point at Newcastle. Performed at a very high standard throughout 1997-98, his display at Barnsley being instrumental in the side

coming from 2-0 down to win 3-2. As well as scoring, Rod also set up his fair share of chances for his team mates. Unfortunately, United struggled to persuade him to sign a new contract, and he was eventually placed on the transfer list because of his refusal to open negotiations, being able to leave on a "free" under the Bosman ruling in the summer.
Southampton (From trainee on 19/4/88) FL 111+17/45 FLC 18+1/6 FAC 10/3 Others 3+1/2
Leeds U (£1,600,000 on 7/6/91) F/PL 187+25/53 FLC 18+1/8 FAC 16+5/4 Others 1+4/1

WALLING Dean Anthony
Born: Leeds, 17 April 1969
Height: 6'0" Weight: 11.10
Club Honours: Div 3 '95; AMC '97
International Honours: St Kitts

Dean, who became Lincoln's record signing last September on arriving from Carlisle, quickly settled down in the centre of the defence as the team captain, while showing himself to be a solid and reliable defender, as well as being the source of a steady supply of goals. Was selected for the PFA division three representative team, having already won international honours, when playing for St Kitts and Nevis against the British Virgin Islands and Guadeloupe in the Shell Caribbean Cup.
Rochdale (Free from Leeds U juniors on 30/7/87) FL 43+22/8 FLC 3 FAC 0+1 Others 1+1 (Free to Kitchener (Toronto), during 1990 close season)
Carlisle U (Free from Guiseley, via Franklin (Toronto), on 1/7/91) FL 230+6/21 FLC 18/3 FAC 14+1/1 Others 35/5
Lincoln C (£75,000 on 30/9/97) FL 35/5 FAC 4/3

Dean Walling

WALLWORK Ronald (Ronnie)
Born: Manchester, 10 September 1977
Height: 5'9" Weight: 12.9
Club Honours: FAYC '95
International Honours: E: Yth

A highly-talented Manchester United central defender, who is a brilliant striker of the ball, especially with his left foot, Ronnie gave an excellent account of himself when coming on as a substitute for Gary Pallister in the Premiership game against Barnsley at Old Trafford in October. Following what was his first team debut, he was loaned first to Carlisle United (December) and then Stockport County (March), in order to further his experience. At Carlisle he gave some accomplished displays in central defence, during what turned out to be the club's best form of the campaign, and headed a fine goal in the 5-0 drubbing of Southend, while at County he continued the good work as a firm and effective stopper, before going back to Old Trafford. Earned rave reviews in 1997-98 from Manchester United's reserve boss, Jimmy Ryan, who feels that the youngster has an excellent future ahead of him.
Manchester U (From trainee on 17/3/95) PL 0+1
Carlisle U (Loaned on 22/12/97) FL 10/1 Others 2
Stockport Co (Loaned on 18/3/98) FL 7

WALSH Gary
Born: Wigan, 21 March 1968
Height: 6'3" Weight: 15.10
Club Honours: ECWC '91; ESC '91; FAC '94
International Honours: E: U21-2

Unable to get a shout at Middlesbrough, Gary was loaned to Bradford last September in order to keep match fit and, at the same time, to resolve a goalkeeping problem at Valley Parade. Having kept four clean sheets in his first five games, the giant 'keeper was signed up permanently on the last day of October and went on to keep eight more clean sheets, while missing just three games. Spectacular, agile, and tall and commanding, with the strength to secure crosses, he made the art of goalkeeping look easy, and it was no surprise that he was voted the club's Player of the Year.
Manchester U (From juniors on 25/4/85) F/PL 49+1 FLC 7 Others 6
Airdrie (Loaned on 11/8/88) SL 3 SLC 1
Oldham Ath (Loaned on 19/11/93) PL 6
Middlesbrough (£500,000 on 11/8/95) PL 44 FLC 9 FAC 4
Bradford C (£500,000+ on 26/9/97) FL 35 FAC 1

WALSH Michael Shane
Born: Rotherham, 5 August 1977
Height: 6'0" Weight: 12.8

The young defender has now completed a century of league appearances for Scunthorpe, despite being just 21 years of age. Had another solid season in 1997-98 playing anywhere across the back five, though at his best as a right back, using his considerable pace and strength to get forward. Very composed on the ball, with a terrific long throw which leads to a number of goals, he is tipped to progress to a higher level of football.
Scunthorpe U (From trainee on 3/7/95) FL 94+9/1 FLC 4 FAC 9 Others 5

WALSH Steven (Steve)
Born: Preston, 3 November 1964
Height: 6'3" Weight: 14.9
Club Honours: AMC '85; FLC '97

Leicester's left-footed central defender and club captain suffered from a number of injuries throughout last season, particularly with hamstring and knee problems. Despite that, he remained an inspirational figure, when available, contributing vital goals to earn a draw deep into injury time against Arsenal and one to win the fixture at Elland Road, ironically before departing with hamstring trouble. He also cracked his ribs when colliding with the post in attempting to prevent a goal in the League Cup tie at Grimsby, thus ending the evening in hospital. Approaching the end of his career, but still a colossus at Filbert Street where his place in the Hall of Fame is assured, in passing the 400 appearance mark he moved up into eighth place on City's all-time list.

Wigan Ath (From juniors on 11/9/82) FL 123+3/4 FLC 7 FAC 6 Others 10+2
Leicester C (£100,000 on 24/6/86) F/PL 330+5/50 FLC 32/3 FAC 12/1 Others 23/4

WALTERS Mark Everton

Born: Birmingham, 2 June 1964
Height: 5'10" Weight: 12.8
Club Honours: FAYC '80; ESC '82; SPD '89, '90, '91; SLC '89, '91; FAC '92
International Honours: E: 1; B-1; U21-9; Yth; Sch

Arguably Swindon's best player when on top form, Mark is still capable of tormenting the best defenders around with his silky dribbling skills and trademark stepover, and continues to deliver a mean corner and cross when allowed time and "spec" to pick out his man. Scored some brilliant goals again last season, including a 30 yarder against Stevenage in the FA Cup, and a curler into the top corner in the final game against Sunderland, but assumed penalty taking responsibility with mixed fortunes – scoring against QPR, and missing against Stockport. Agreed a new contract in the summer which should keep him at Swindon to the year 2000.

Aston Villa (From apprentice on 18/5/82) FL 168+13/39 FLC 20+1/6 FAC 11+1/1 Others 7+3/2
Glasgow R (£500,000 on 31/12/87) SL 101+5/32 SLC 13/11 SC 14/6 Others 10/2
Liverpool (£1,250,000 on 13/8/91) F/PL 58+36/14 FLC 10+2/4 FAC 6+3 Others 8+1/1
Stoke C (Loaned on 24/3/94) FL 9/2
Wolverhampton W (Loaned on 9/9/94) FL 11/3
Southampton (Free on 18/1/96) PL 4+1 FAC 4
Swindon T (Free on 31/7/96) FL 49+12/13 FLC 5+1/1 FAC 2/1

WALTON David (Dave) Lee

Born: Bedlington, 10 April 1973
Height: 6'2" Weight: 14.8
Club Honours: Div 3 '94

The central defender played just seven games for Shrewsbury in 1997-98 before a well-deserved big-money transfer saw him signed by first division Crewe in October. Dominant at the back, and showing tremendous commitment and effort, he settled in well at the heart of Alex's defence, in partnership with Ashley Westwood and Lee Unsworth, and looks certain to progress even further. Poses a constant danger at set pieces.

Sheffield U (Free from Ashington on 13/3/92)
Shrewsbury T (Signed on 5/11/93) FL 127+1/10 FLC 7 FAC 10/1 Others 11/1
Crewe Alex (£500,000+ on 20/10/97) FL 27 FAC 1

WALTON Mark Andrew

Born: Merthyr Tydfil, 1 June 1969
Height: 6'4" Weight: 14.7
International Honours: W: U21-1

Mark began last season in fine form for Fulham and kept the South African international 'keeper, Andre Arendse, waiting for his debut until the tenth game. Having kept four clean sheets in the first seven league games, he then shared goalkeeping duties with Andre until the arrival of Maik Taylor from Southampton. Neither got a look in after that and he had a short loan spell at Gillingham, during which he gave a brilliant display in a 2-0 victory against champions-to-be Watford at Vicarage Road. A commanding figure in the box, he is also a good stopper and a long-kick specialist.

Luton T (From juniors on 21/2/87)
Colchester U (£15,000 on 5/11/87) FL 40 FLC 3 FAC 8 Others 5
Norwich C (£75,000 on 15/8/89) FL 22 FLC 1 FAC 5
Wrexham (Loaned on 27/8/93) FL 6
Dundee (Free on 27/1/94)
Bolton W (Free on 2/3/94) FL 3 (Free to Wroxham on 9/9/94)
Fulham (Free from Fakenham T on 12/8/96) FL 40 FLC 5 Others 3
Gillingham (Loaned on 6/2/98) FL 1

WANCHOPE Pablo Cesar

Born: Costa Rica, 31 July 1976
Height: 6'4" Weight: 12.6
International Honours: Costa Rica: 20

An eccentric Costa Rican international striker who is now a household name for his unusual style of play, belying his background as a basketball player, Pablo is very tall, but skilful with it, and built on his initial success with Derby to form a potent partnership with Dean Sturridge, their contrasting styles making life very difficult for opposing defenders in 1997-98. At times, even his team mates are unsure what he is going to do next, but the comedy moments are cancelled out by some wonderful individual skills. A real character, and a great favourite with the home fans, who was voted Carling Player of the Month in October, he came back well from a close season knee operation and netted four times for his country in a 7-2 victory over Cuba in the Americas Gold Cup.

Derby Co (£600,000 from CS Heridiano on 27/3/97) PL 32+5/14 FLC 4/4 FAC 2

WANLESS Paul Steven

Born: Banbury, 14 December 1973
Height: 6'1" Weight: 13.4

A very important player in Cambridge's midfield in 1997-98, he made a clean sweep of all the supporters' Player of the Year awards, such was his importance to the team. As ever, he was a ball winner who got forward to score goals – eight being a good total in anyone's book – was strong and brave, and always put in 100 per-cent effort as he patrolled the pitch from box to box. The obvious choice for team captain, it would be difficult to imagine the side without him.

Oxford U (From trainee on 3/12/91) FL 12+20 FLC 0+3/1 Others 2+2

Lincoln C (Free on 7/7/95) FL 7+1 Others 2
Cambridge U (Free on 8/3/96) FL 83+3/12 FLC 3 FAC 5 Others 1

Paul Wanless

WARBURTON Raymond (Ray)

Born: Rotherham, 7 October 1967
Height: 6'0" Weight: 12.13

As Northampton's centre half and club captain, Ray is acknowledged by many as being one of the best players to ever wear a Cobblers' shirt. Yet another key man to be out of contention in 1997-98 through injury, in the ten games he missed only two clean sheets were kept, and only ten points were picked up from a possible 30. Good on the floor, powerful in the air, and dangerous around the opponents' goal area, he is one of the main reasons that Town were chasing a first division place.

Rotherham U (From apprentice on 5/10/85) FL 3+1 FAC 2 Others 2
York C (Free on 8/8/89) FL 86+4/9 FLC 8/1 FAC 6/1 Others 7
Northampton T (£35,000 on 4/2/94) FL 174/11 FLC 6 FAC 7/1 Others 17/3

WARD Ashley Stuart

Born: Manchester, 24 November 1970
Height: 6'1" Weight: 13.0

With opportunities sparse at Derby in 1997-98, Ashley, who transferred to Barnsley at the beginning of September, must be rated as one of the bargain buys of the season. A centre forward of the old brigade, he led the line with non-stop effort and no shortage of skill, even returning from an attack of meningitis to produce a match-winning display at Liverpool. His main attributes were his strength and his ability to work across the full width of the field, also his eye for a goal which brought Barnsley a number of wins, starting with a 90th-minute winner at Chesterfield in the Coca Cola Cup. Apart from the goals at Chesterfield and

Liverpool, Ashley scored winners at Aston Villa, and at Oakwell against Derby, his old club, and Crystal Palace. Later in the campaign he suffered a hamstring injury, but would still not lie down.

Manchester C (From trainee on 5/8/89) FL 0+1 FAC 0+2
Wrexham (Loaned on 10/1/91) FL 4/2 Others 1
Leicester C (£80,000 on 30/7/91) FL 2+8 FLC 2+1 FAC 0+1 Others 0+1
Blackpool (Loaned on 21/11/92) FL 2/1
Crewe Alex (£80,000 on 1/12/92) FL 58+3/25 FLC 4/2 FAC 2/4 Others 7/5
Norwich C (£500,000 on 8/12/94) P/FL 53/18 FLC 6/3 FAC 1
Derby Co (£1,000,000 on 19/3/96) F/PL 32+8/9 FLC 1+1 FAC 2/1
Barnsley (£1,300,000+ on 5/9/97) PL 28+1/8 FLC 3/1 FAC 6/1

WARD Darren

Born: Worksop, 11 May 1974
Height: 5'11" Weight: 12.9
Club Honours: Div 3 '98
International Honours: W: U21-2

The 1997-98 season saw not only a return to form for this quite exceptional young Notts County 'keeper, but further development and improvement. Called into the Welsh "B" squad, and a player who must surely go on to gain full international honours, his performances contributed points galore to his team as they marched to the third division title. So much so, that his fellow professionals selected him for the PFA award-winning divisional team.

Mansfield T (From trainee on 27/7/92) FL 81 FLC 5 FAC 5 Others 6
Notts Co (£160,000 on 11/7/95) FL 128 FLC 10 FAC 10 Others 8

WARD Darren Philip

Born: Kenton, 13 September 1978
Height: 6'0" Weight: 12.6

As a cultured Watford central defender with excellent passing skills, Darren had hoped to press home his first team claim last season, but, unfortunately, he was particularly unlucky with injuries, a heel problem requiring surgery in October, and a broken leg sustained during a reserve match in February finally putting him out of action for the remainder of the campaign. However, he is young enough and good enough to come again.

Watford (From trainee on 13/2/97) FL 8 FAC 1 Others 0+1

WARD Gavin John

Born: Sutton Coldfield, 30 June 1970
Height: 6'4" Weight: 14.12
Club Honours: Div 3 '93; WC '93

As Bolton's number two 'keeper behind the ever dependable Keith Branagan, Gavin made just six starts for Bolton last season, mainly when Branagan was injured in December, but, in conceding 14 goals, it was not a particularly happy time for him. Despite this, he is still an assured goalkeeper, who is more than capable of filling in for Branagan when required, as was proven when he won a first division championship medal in 1997.

Shrewsbury T (Free from Aston Villa juniors on 26/9/88)

West Bromwich A (Free on 18/9/89)
Cardiff C (Free on 5/10/89) FL 58+1 FAC 1 Others 7
Leicester C (£175,000 on 16/7/93) F/PL 38 FLC 3 FAC 0+1 Others 4
Bradford C (£175,000 on 13/7/95) FL 36 FLC 6 FAC 3 Others 2
Bolton W (£300,000 on 29/3/96) F/PL 19+3 FLC 2 FAC 4

WARD Mitchum (Mitch) David

Born: Sheffield, 19 June 1971
Height: 5'8" Weight: 11.7

With just six appearances behind him at Sheffield United in 1997-98, Mitch followed his old manager, Howard Kendall, to Everton in November, with Graham Stuart going in the opposite direction. A versatile performer who played on the left and right-hand side of defence, his introduction to Goodison was constantly interrupted by injury, suffering the misfortune to concede a penalty on his debut at Chelsea, and making only three more appearances before an ankle injury sidelined him. A brief comeback was interrupted by a hamstring injury, before a knee injury effectively curtailed his season before it had really started. Has two good feet and is an excellent striker of the ball.

Sheffield U (From trainee on 1/7/89) F/PL 135+19/11 FLC 8+3/2 FAC 7+2/2 Others 5+1/1
Crewe Alex (Loaned on 1/11/90) FL 4/1 FAC 1/1 Others 2
Everton (£850,000 on 25/11/97) PL 8

Paul Warhurst

WARD Nicholas (Nic) John
Born: Wrexham, 30 November 1977
Height: 5'9" Weight: 11.9
Despite progressing from the YTS ranks, and thought to be one for the future in 1996-97, the busy, speedy forward struggled to fulfill his potential at Shrewsbury in 1997-98, having just three starts, and left the club by mutual consent in mid-season.
Shrewsbury T (From trainee on 12/7/96) FL 8+12/1 FAC 0+2 Others 0+2

WARD Peter
Born: Durham, 15 October 1964
Height: 5'11" Weight: 11.10
Always an important "cog in the wheel" of Wrexham's midfield engine room, a fit Peter Ward is essential to the present side, with his specialist free kicks always a problem for the opposition. Manager, Brian Flynn, insists on a patient passing game which fits in well with Peter's style of play, but injuries at vital times in the past have always seemed to dog him, however. Last season was no different, his play being affected towards the latter end of the campaign when his influence was so badly needed.
Huddersfield T (Signed from Chester le Street on 7/1/87) FL 24+13/2 FLC 1+1 FAC 2 Others 1
Rochdale (Free on 20/7/89) FL 83+1/10 FLC 5 FAC 7/1 Others 5
Stockport Co (Signed on 6/6/91) FL 140+2/10 FLC 8/1 FAC 7 Others 26/6
Wrexham (Signed on 19/7/95) FL 92+3/13 FLC 5 FAC 17/1 Others 2/1

WARHURST Paul
Born: Stockport, 26 September 1969
Height: 6'1" Weight: 12.10
Club Honours: PL '95
International Honours: E: U21-8
Having suffered a whole range of injuries during a career that at one stage looked as if he would play at full international level, Paul joined Crystal Palace from Blackburn during the 1997 close season with a view to making a fresh start. However, after scoring three goals in six games, he broke a leg for the third time in the third round FA Cup game in January against Scunthorpe, before coming back for the final few matches, playing in a sweeper role. A most versatile player who can be used with confidence in defence, as a central defender or full back with good powers of recovery, or up front where he is a danger with his aerial ability and all-round strength. Always looking to make the right pass when coming out of defence with the ball, and able to read the game well, if he can remain injury free, within reason, he can do a great job for Palace. From a footballing family, Paul is the son of Roy, who was a tough, uncompromising wing half for Sheffield United, Birmingham, and Manchester City, among others, during the 1940s and 1950s.
Manchester C (From trainee on 1/7/88)
Oldham Ath (£10,000 on 27/10/88) FL 60+7/2 FLC 8 FAC 5+4 Others 2
Sheffield Wed (£750,000 on 17/7/91) F/PL 60+6/6 FLC 9/4 FAC 7+1/5 Others 5/3
Blackburn Rov (£2,700,000 on 17/8/93) PL 30+27/4 FLC 6+2 FAC 2+1 Others 4+2
Crystal Palace (£1,250,000 on 31/7/97) PL 22/3 FLC 1 FAC 1

WARNE Paul
Born: Norwich, 8 May 1973
Height: 5'9" Weight: 11.2
A prolific goalscorer for one of manager, John Deehan's former clubs, non-league Wroxham, Paul was one of Wigan's pre-1997-98 season signings. Having made his Football League debut as a substitute at Bristol City in late August, his first league start saw him net the only goal in a victory at Blackpool, which ultimately collected the supporters' award for the Away Goal of the Season. Very quick, especially around the box, he made 27 appearances for Athletic, of which 24 were from the bench.
Wigan Ath (£25,000 from Wroxham on 30/7/97) FL 3+22/2 Others 0+2

WARNER Anthony (Tony) Randolph
Born: Liverpool, 11 May 1974
Height: 6'4" Weight: 13.9
Signed on loan from Liverpool last November, at a time when all three goalkeepers on Swindon Town's books were simultaneously struck down by injury, Tony, a David James look-alike, had a trouble-free first appearance in a 1-0 home win over Bradford City. But a disappointing performance next time out, when top-of-the-table Town slumped to a 4-2 defeat at Stockport, cost him his place in the side and he went back to Anfield without adding to his two starts.
Liverpool (Signed from juniors on 1/1/94)
Swindon T (Loaned on 5/11/97) FL 2

WARNER Michael James
Born: Harrogate, 17 January 1974
Height: 5'9" Weight: 10.10
As a former Northampton winger, now converted to wing back, Michael had restricted first team appearances in 1997-98, due to the large playing squad. Despite this, however, when called upon he always gave of his best, and in his substitute appearance against Grimsby he was voted Man of the Match. Manager, Ian Atkins, has earmarked him as another one for the future.*
Northampton T (Free from Tamworth on 10/7/95) FL 4+15 FAC 0+2 Others 1+3

WARNER Philip
Born: Southampton, 2 February 1979
Height: 5'10" Weight: 11.7
Another of Southampton's local-born talents to come through the junior ranks, signing professional forms during the 1997 close season, Philip was introduced by the Saints on the final day of last season at Tottenham in a 1-1 draw. Able to play in the centre of defence or at full back, as a named sub he came off the bench in the 39th minute to replace Jason Dodd and did reasonably well, showing up as being quick, a good jumper, and a tackler. Is expected to make further progress.
Southampton (From trainee on 23/5/97) PL 0+1

WARNER Vance
Born: Leeds, 3 September 1974
Height: 6'0" Weight: 13.2
International Honours: E: Yth

Vance looked to be a bargain buy for Rotherham when he was plucked from Nottingham Forest's reserves at the start of 1997-98, and he proved a major asset at the back with his tremendous pace and tackling ability, before unfortunately missing several games through injury at vital times in the season. However, there is no doubting that he could make his mark at a higher level and could be a vital key to future United promotion hopes.
Nottingham F (From trainee on 14/9/91) F/PL 4+1 FLC 1+1
Grimsby T (Loaned on 2/2/96) FL 3
Rotherham U (Signed on 29/8/97) FL 21 FAC 3

WARREN Christer Simon
Born: Dorchester, 10 October 1974
Height: 5'10" Weight: 11.10
Unable to get further opportunities at Southampton in 1997-98, Christer moved along the coast to Bournemouth in October to look for a change of luck. Very quick, and not afraid to take on defenders, he played either in a strike role or wide on the left-hand side of midfield, where he looked most effective, and after scoring the winner at Preston on his debut he notched a further five goals. Ending the campaign as an automatic choice for the Cherries, just watch him go in 1998-99.
Southampton (£40,000 from Cheltenham T on 31/3/95) PL 1+7 FLC 1
Brighton & Hove A (Loaned on 11/10/96) FL 3
Fulham (Loaned on 6/3/97) FL 8+3/1
Bournemouth (£50,000 on 8/10/97) FL 29+1/6 FAC 3 Others 4

WARREN Lee Anthony
Born: Manchester, 28 February 1969
Height: 6'0" Weight: 12.2
Despite Doncaster Rovers' eventual League demise, Lee could look back on the 1997-98 season with a degree of personal satisfaction, having won the Supporters Club Player of the Year award. This was most deserved, following his consistent performances at the heart of the defence, where he normally featured in a sweeper role.
Leeds U (From trainee on 27/7/87)
Rochdale (Free on 28/10/87) FL 31/1 FAC 1 Others 2
Hull C (£40,000 on 25/8/88) FL 141+12/1 FLC 8 FAC 5+1 Others 3+2/1
Lincoln C (Loaned on 20/9/90) FL 2+1/1
Doncaster Rov (Free on 21/7/94) FL 115+10/3 FLC 3 FAC 2+1 Others 5+1

WARREN Mark Wayne
Born: Clapton, 12 November 1974
Height: 6'0" Weight: 12.2
International Honours: E: Yth
Leyton Orient's Player of the Year in 1996-97 carried on where he left off in 1997-98 and had yet another excellent season. As a player with tremendous pace, who never gives less than 100 per cent, a good tackler, and comfortable when coming forward with the ball, he was often pushed forward in emergencies and scored the equaliser in the 4-4 draw with Bolton at the Reebok.
Leyton Orient (From trainee on 6/7/92) FL 124+18/5 FLC 7/1 FAC 5 Others 9+4/1

Lee Warren

WARRINGTON Andrew (Andy) Clifford
Born: Sheffield, 10 June 1976
Height: 6'3" Weight: 12.13

Andy started last season as second choice 'keeper for York, but following an injury to Mark Samways he was recalled to first team action. Then losing his place, following a 7-2 defeat at Burnley in January, he returned to senior duty in the last six weeks of the campaign, during which he showed impressive form. Hit the headlines in January in an Auto Windscreens Shield match at Blackpool, when, after a 1-1 draw, the game went into a marathon penalty shoot out, which involved all 22 players. Unfortunately, he was the last City player to take a spot kick and missed, City going out of the competition 10-9.

York C (From trainee on 11/6/94) FL 50 FLC 6 FAC 2 Others 4

WASSALL Darren Paul
Born: Birmingham, 27 June 1968
Height: 6'0" Weight: 12.10
Club Honours: FMC '92

Having firmed up his loan transfer from Derby at the end of 1996-97, the Birmingham fans were looking forward to Darren being a key member of the defence in 1997-98, in a side aiming for promotion. In the event, his season was ruined by an achilles injury that ruled him out of action from November, but prior to that his pace and man-marking ability figured high in City's early form. Having had another operation in March that was to keep him out for the rest of the campaign, he will be desperate to get back early in 1998-99.

Nottingham F (From apprentice on 1/6/86) FL 17+10 FLC 6+2 FAC 3+1 Others 4+2/1
Hereford U (Loaned on 23/10/87) FL 5 FAC 1 Others 1
Bury (Loaned on 2/3/89) FL 7/1

Derby Co (£600,000 on 15/6/92) FL 90+8 FLC 9 FAC 4 Others 11
Manchester C (Loaned on 11/9/96) FL 14+1 FLC 2
Birmingham C (£100,000 on 26/3/97) FL 22 FLC 5

WATERMAN David (Dave) Graham
Born: Guernsey, 16 May 1977
Height: 5'10" Weight: 13.2
International Honours: NI: U21-3

Having come right through the ranks at Portsmouth to make four subs' appearances in 1996-97, despite having to contend with injury Dave jumped straight into the first team at the start of last season, although his inexperience showed early on when he was sent off against Peterborough in the Coca Cola Cup. However, learning from that, he proved a very effective defender when called upon and, as the campaign went on, his performances steadily improved. Certainly comfortable in the right-back position, he also found himself deputising in the centre of the defence on the odd occasions that Adrian Whitbread was not available, and it was there that he celebrated the last day 3-1 victory at Bradford that averted relegation. Kick-started his international career with three appearances for the Northern Ireland U21 side in 1997-98.

Portsmouth (From trainee on 4/7/95) FL 11+8 FLC 1 FAC 1

WATKIN Stephen (Steve)
Born: Wrexham, 16 June 1971
Height: 5'10" Weight: 11.10
Club Honours: WC '95
International Honours: W: B-2; Sch

Signed by Jan Molby for Swansea last September, having made just six subs' appearances for Wrexham in 1997-98, Steve struggled to make his mark at the Vetch

Field, following an injury sustained against Leyton Orient on his debut for City, and took three months to score his first goal. However, showing good control and beginning to hold the ball up well for his new colleagues, he started to perform more consistently towards the end of the campaign, something which should augur well for 1998-99.

Wrexham (From juniors on 24/7/89) FL 167+33/55 FLC 11+3/4 FAC 16+6/12 Others 17+5/4
Swansea C (£108,000 on 26/9/97) FL 24+8/3 FAC 0+1

WATKISS Stuart Paul
Born: Wolverhampton, 8 May 1966
Height: 6'2" Weight: 13.7

Yet another of Mansfield's major casualties last term, this central defender came back in March, having played six of the opening seven games, only for his injury to recur after just four appearances. Should be fully fit for the start of 1998-99, when his stout defending and intelligent use of the ball will be invaluable.

Wolverhampton W (From trainee on 13/7/84) FL 2
Crewe Alex (Free on 28/2/86) FL 3
Walsall (Free from Rushall Olympic on 5/8/93) FL 60+2/2 FLC 8/1 FAC 5 Others 2
Hereford U (Free on 16/2/96) FL 19 Others 2
Mansfield T (Free on 17/7/96) FL 40+1/1 FLC 3 FAC 1

Alex Watson

WATSON Alexander (Alex) Francis
Born: Liverpool, 5 April 1968
Height: 6'1" Weight: 12.0
Club Honours: CS '88
International Honours: E: Yth

As Torquay's centre half and skipper, Alex has not missed a match since joining the club in November 1995 and, in doing so, has become part of Plainmoor folklore. He also

missed very little in the air, while his tackling ability and positional play along-side Jon Gittens, was the backbone behind United's run to the play-off final.*

Liverpool (From apprentice on 18/5/85) FL 3+1 FLC 1+1 FAC 1+1 Others 1
Derby Co (Loaned on 30/8/90) FL 5
Bournemouth (£150,000 on 18/1/91) FL 145+6/5 FLC 14/1 FAC 12/1 Others 5
Gillingham (Loaned on 11/9/95) FL 10/1
Torquay U (£50,000 on 23/11/95) 121/4 FLC 6 FAC 6 Others 5/1

WATSON Andrew (Andy) Anthony
Born: Leeds, 1 April 1967
Height: 5'9" Weight: 11.2
Club Honours: WC '91

The hero of Walsall's 1997-98 Coca Cola Cup win over Nottingham Forest, with two late goals in the second leg, and the scorer of both goals at Peterborough that earned a fourth round FA Cup tie at Manchester United, Andy's opportunism was sadly missed in the last two and a half months when he was out of action with a ligament injury. Quick and sharp around the box, the striker has the knack of being in the right place at the right time and finished as runner up to Roger Boli in the club's goalscoring charts.*

Halifax T (Free from Harrogate T on 23/8/88) FL 75+8/15 FLC 5+1/2 FAC 6/1 Others 7/1
Swansea C (£40,000 on 31/7/90) FL 9+5/1 FLC 0+1 Others 1+1
Carlisle U (£30,000 on 19/9/91) FL 55+1/22 FLC 4/5 FAC 3 Others 1/1
Blackpool (£55,000 on 5/2/93) FL 88+27/43 FLC 6/5 FAC 3+2 Others 7+1/1
Walsall (£60,000 on 5/9/96) FL 45+18/12 FLC 5/4 FAC 4+3/3 Others 4/1

WATSON David (Dave)
Born: Liverpool, 20 November 1961
Height: 6'0" Weight: 12.4
Club Honours: FLC '85; Div 2 '86; Div 1 '87, CS '87, '95; FAC '95
International Honours: E: 12; U21-7 (UEFAC '84)

A defensive rock and inspirational once again for Everton, Dave suffered the misfortune to lose his club captaincy to Gary Speed on the opening day of last season. Typically, he shrugged off the disap-pointment to establish himself yet again as one of the most consistent performers at Goodison. Despite celebrating his 36th birthday during the campaign, he remained one of the fittest players at the club, although age began to catch up with him in the shape of a series of niggling injuries. Now moving more and more into the coaching side of things, and helping out with the reserve team when not involved with first team duties, his future seems certain to be as a manager.

Liverpool (From juniors on 25/5/79)
Norwich C (£100,000 on 29/11/80) FL 212/11 FLC 21/3 FAC 18/1
Everton (£900,000 on 22/8/86) F/PL 392+3/24 FLC 38/6 FAC 44/5 Others 16+1/3

WATSON David (Dave) Neil
Born: Barnsley, 10 November 1973
Height: 6'0" Weight: 12.3
International Honours: E: U21-5; Yth

Dave Watson (Barnsley)

Despite conceding many goals in the Premiership in 1997-98, Dave not only maintained his position as number one goalkeeper at Barnsley, but enhanced his reputation as one of the best 'keepers in the league. A superb shot-stopper, who gained more confidence in the command of his area as the season developed, he missed a few games, having sustained an injury to the kidneys early in the season, but came back strongly as the side tightened up consider-ably at the back, and was excellent at Aston Villa as the last line of defence that came away with a 1-0 win.

Barnsley (From trainee on 4/7/92) F/PL 172 FLC 14 FAC 11 Others 1

WATSON Kevin Edward
Born: Hackney, 3 January 1974
Height: 6'0" Weight: 12.6

A skilful midfielder with a lovely touch on the ball and creative passing ability, Kevin was rewarded with a new one-year contract last March, despite again failing to hold down a regular slot at Swindon. His longest

run of games was eight, when he found his best form of the season in the autumn, but a thigh injury halted his progress and his services were rarely called upon again. His potential is there for all to see and he just needs to get more consistency into his game to really make the breakthrough.

Tottenham H (From trainee on 15/5/92) PL 4+1 FLC 1+1/1 FAC 0+1
Brentford (Loaned on 24/3/94) FL 2+1
Bristol C (Loaned on 2/12/94) FL 1+1
Barnet (Loaned on 16/2/95) FL 13
Swindon T (Free on 15/7/96) FL 30+15/1 FLC 1+1 FAC 1+1

WATSON Paul Douglas
Born: Hastings, 4 January 1975
Height: 5'8" Weight: 10.10

Unable to make too much of an impact at Fulham in 1997-98, Paul, a compact left-wing back who loves getting forward to support the attack, was signed by Micky Adams for the second time, when joining Brentford in December. Apart from being absent on occasion through ineligibility he played in every match from the day he

signed until the end of the season, becoming the regular corner taker from both sides. Having taken over from Ijah Anderson, who suffered a broken leg, it will be interesting to see if there is room for both of them in the side this coming season.

Gillingham (From trainee on 8/12/92) FL 57+5/2 FLC 4 FAC 6 Others 5+3
Fulham (£13,000 on 30/7/96) FL 48+2/4 FLC 3/1 FAC 2 Others 2
Brentford (£50,000 on 12/12/97) FL 25

Steve Watson

WATSON Stephen (Steve) Craig
Born: North Shields, 1 April 1974
Height: 6'0" Weight: 12.7
International Honours: E: B-1; U21-12; Yth
A homegrown product, Steve firmly established himself as a key part of the Newcastle defence in 1997-98, alongside the galaxy of British and foreign stars. Blessed with an ideal temperament, his high level of skills, his reading of the game, and his composure on the ball, enable him to cope comfortably with the demands of playing at the top level. Although performing most often at right back, his versatility is one of his assets, and he gave an outstanding performance at centre back in the home Champions League game against Barcelona, before he was called up to join the England squad for the game against Cameroon, his first such experience. He was then selected for the "B" squad for the Chile game, but had to withdraw when he broke a bone in his right foot in the FA Cup replay against Stevenage, at a time when he was the club's only ever present. Following his recovery, he subsequently played for the England "B" team against Russia, but was disappointed to make just a subs' appearance in the FA Cup final against Arsenal.
Newcastle U (From trainee on 6/4/91) F/PL 172+29/12 FLC 10+6/1 FAC 13+4 Others 17+4/1

WATTS Julian
Born: Sheffield, 17 March 1971
Height: 6'3" Weight: 13.7
Club Honours: FLC '97
The right-footed Leicester central defender found his opportunities limited in 1997-98 and enjoyed most of his first team action on loan at Crewe, where he played five times, and Huddersfield. Appeared eight times for Town as cover for injuries, showing himself to be competent and comfortable on the ball, before being recalled to Filbert Street just when an extension had been agreed. Answered the call whenever needed, and even got a taste of European action when stepping into the line-up for the return leg against Athletico Madrid, but never let the team down and remained a popular and valued squad member throughout the campaign, prior to being released in the summer.
Rotherham U (Signed from Frenchville CA on 10/7/90) FL 17+3/1 FLC 1 FAC 4 Others 2
Sheffield Wed (£80,000 on 13/3/92) PL 12+4/1 FLC 1 Others 1
Shrewsbury T (Loaned on 18/12/92) FL 9 Others 1
Leicester C (£210,000 on 29/3/96) P/FL 31+7/1 FLC 6+1 FAC 2+1 Others 4
Crewe Alex (Loaned on 29/8/97) FL 5
Huddersfield T (Loaned on 5/2/98) FL 8

WDOWCZYK Dariusz
Born: Warsaw, Poland, 21 September 1962
Height: 5'11" Weight: 11.11
International Honours: Poland : 52
The former Polish international captain ended his career in British football following a disappointing season at Reading in 1997-98, which saw him make just eight first team appearances, four of them as substitute. There were still signs of his obvious class and ability to hit long, raking passes, but a series of hamstring and knee injuries meant that he did not figure in the starting line-up from October, and made only occasional reserve appearances after that. Is returning to Poland, where he hopes to become a coach.
Glasgow Celtic (£400,000 from Legia Warsaw on 17/11/89) SL 112+4/4 SLC 11 SC 13/2 Others 6+1
Reading (Free on 12/8/94) FL 77+5 FLC 7+1 FAC 1 Others 3

WEATHERSTONE Simon
Born: Reading, 26 January 1980
Height: 5'10" Weight: 11.12
Simon did not make the breakthrough he would have hoped for in 1997-98, but remains on the fringes of the Oxford first team. Having been made up to a professional with over a year of his YT scheme still to finish, much was expected of the young striker, and he showed that he had talent with a superb chip over Dave Beasant, in Oxford's excellent win at Nottingham Forest, to clinch the game. It was his only first team goal so far, but more can be expected if he gets a prolonged run this coming season.
Oxford U (From trainee on 27/3/97) FL 2+10/1

WEBBER Damien John
Born: Littlehampton, 8 October 1968
Height: 6'4" Weight: 14.0

Due to a bad injury suffered early in 1997-98, having made just three appearances for Millwall during the campaign, Damien's playing career was prematurely ended. An obvious tragedy for both club and player alike, the big central defender had been expected to compete strongly for a regular first team slot and thus build on his impressive performances of 1996-97, when he showed himself to be good in the air, pacy, and with an ability to come out of defence with the ball to set up attacks.
Millwall (Signed from Bognor Regis on 27/10/94) FL 52+13/4 FLC 3+3 FAC 3+2 Others 2

WELCH Keith James
Born: Bolton, 3 October 1968
Height: 6'2" Weight: 13.7
Recognised as one of the best goalkeepers in the lower leagues last season, it was a surprise to many at Bristol City that this accomplished player was not selected for the second division PFA award-winning side. "Mr Cool" would be a deserving nickname for this custodian par-excellence, whose skill and composure with the ball at his feet sets him apart from most of the goalies operating in the Premier and the Football League. Unfortunately, a serious groin injury suffered in a 1-0 defeat at Chesterfield, during the penultimate away game, ended his campaign and all at Ashton Gate are now keeping their fingers crossed that he will be fit for 1998-99.
Rochdale (Free from Bolton W juniors on 3/3/87) FL 205 FLC 12 FAC 10 Others 12
Bristol C (£200,000 on 25/7/91) FL 250 FLC 16 FAC 13 Others 14

WELLER Paul Anthony
Born: Brighton, 6 March 1975
Height: 5'8" Weight: 11.0
Never one to abandon the pursuit of seemingly lost causes, Paul was one of the more consistent performers in Burnley's struggling side last season, sometimes employed on the right side of midfield, and sometimes as a right-wing back. Often making up in sheer effort what he lacked in silky skills, no bad thing at second division level, he scored the all-important third goal in the 3-3 draw at Rotherham in the FA Cup.
Burnley (From trainee on 30/11/93) FL 78+17/5 FLC 4+2 FAC 4+2/1 Others 6

WEST Colin
Born: Wallsend, 13 November 1962
Height: 6'1" Weight: 13.11
Started last season as first choice for Leyton Orient, but was unfortunate to lose his place after three games, making a couple of brief appearances as substitute, before joining Northampton on loan in September, playing twice. Next stop was Rushden & Diamonds, initially on loan, and then permanently after Christmas. Although not always a crowd favourite, his goalscoring record over almost 20 years speaks for itself.
Sunderland (From apprentice on 9/7/80) FL 88+14/21 FLC 13+4/5 FAC 3+1/2
Watford (£115,000 on 28/3/85) FL 45/20 FLC 2+1 FAC 8/3

Glasgow R (£180,000 on 23/5/86) SL 4+6/2 SLC 2/1 SC 0+1 Others 0+2
Sheffield Wed (£150,000 on 7/9/87) FL 40+5/8 FLC 6/3 FAC 6/1 Others 3/1
West Bromwich A (Signed on 24/2/89) FL 64+9/22 FLC 2 FAC 4/1 Others 2/1
Port Vale (Loaned on 1/11/91) FL 5/1
Swansea C (Free on 5/8/92) FL 29+4/12 FLC 0+1 FAC 5/2 Others 3+2/1
Leyton Orient (Free on 26/7/93) FL 132+10/42 FLC 6/2 FAC 7+1/2 Others 9/4
Northampton T (Loaned on 19/9/97) FL 1+1

WEST Dean

Born: Morley, 5 December 1972
Height: 5'10" Weight: 12.2
Club Honours: Div 2 '97

Nicknamed "Fred", Dean's influence as an overlapping right-wing back was sorely missed by Bury in 1997-98, after he had appeared in the opening four league games and both Coca Cola Cup games against Crewe. Unfortunate to suffer a groin injury, which subsequently involved complications and required more than one operation, the lay-off eventually encompassed the entire season, despite a couple of failed comebacks at reserve level. A wholehearted player, he will be itching to get back into action in 1998-99.
Lincoln C (From trainee on 17/8/91) FL 93+26/20 FLC 11/1 FAC 6/1 Others 5+2/1
Bury (Signed on 29/9/95) FL 82+5/5 FLC 6 FAC 2 Others 2+1

WESTCOTT John Peter James

Born: Eastbourne, 31 May 1979
Height: 5'6" Weight: 10.4

Having come through the club's junior ranks, the diminutive, speedy winger was blooded in his first season as a professional with his local club, Brighton and Hove Albion, in 1997-98. It was not an ideal time for any player to attempt to establish himself with the Seagulls, but the youngster came through a difficult baptism with credit. Initially confined to the substitute's bench, John went on to enjoy runs in the side under both Steve Gritt and his successor, Brian Horton, and was rewarded with a new two-year contract in March. Unfortunately, a torn hamstring kept him out of the side in the latter stages of the campaign.
Brighton & Hove A (From trainee on 10/7/97) FL 19+5 FLC 0+2 FAC 1 Others 0+1

WESTWOOD Ashley Michael

Born: Bridgnorth, 31 August 1976
Height: 6'0" Weight: 11.3
Club Honours: FAYC '95
International Honours: E: Yth

Following his arrival from Manchester United two seasons earlier, Ashley became a regular member of Crewe's defence, his ability to read the game and tackle well standing the club in good stead, until having to receive remedial surgery towards the end of 1996-97. Although back in time for the start of 1997-98, injuries continued to reduce his appearances and his 23 games saw him share defensive duties with Lee Unsworth and a couple of others. Despite his lack of height, is excellent in the air.
Manchester U (From trainee on 1/7/94)
Crewe Alex (£40,000 on 26/7/95) FL 93+5/9 FLC 8 FAC 9/2 Others 10

WESTWOOD Christopher (Chris) John

Born: Dudley, 13 February 1977
Height: 6'0" Weight: 12.2

A central defender who originally joined Wolves as a YTS in 1993, Chris had been in the reserves a long time before beginning last season on the fringe of the first team. Injuries to players in his position actually delayed his debut, as it was preferable for him to have more experienced back-up, but when the on-loan Simon Coleman was refused permission to play in the Coca Cola Cup his chance finally came, and he was also involved in the next two games. Despite his lack of height, his timing helped him frequently head the ball clear and he had another brief flurry in the team in November, being blamed for a Portsmouth goal, but making amends by scoring for Wolves that night. Was released during the summer.
Wolverhampton W (From trainee on 3/7/95) FL 3+1/1 FLC 1+1

WETHERALL David

Born: Sheffield, 14 March 1971
Height: 6'3" Weight: 13.12
International Honours: E: Sch

This reliable and often underrated Leeds' central defender had an excellent season in 1997-98 at Elland Road. Still only 26, David has matured into a fine Premiership centre half and played in all but one game up to the home match against Southampton in March, where he began a two-match suspension. However, on coming back, he found his position challenged by the in-form Robert Molenaar. As well as being a commanding figure at the back, he is also a useful weapon in attack, thanks to his power in the air. Scored the decisive winner versus Manchester United at Elland Road, with a glorious diving header, and followed this up with another headed goal in the rout of Newcastle. David is Leeds "through and through", and captained the side on the occasions when David Hopkin was not available. Has now signed an improved contract which should see him remain at the club until 2002.
Sheffield Wed (From trainee on 1/7/89)
Leeds U (£125,000 on 15/7/91) F/PL 174+7/12 FLC 19+1/2 FAC 17+3/3 Others 4

WHALLEY Gareth

Born: Manchester, 19 December 1973
Height: 5'10" Weight: 11.6

An influential Crewe midfielder, Gareth seemed destined for the Premiership in 1997-98, having been assessed by both Liverpool and Spurs, but due to it being an unsettling period, apart from a couple of early games, he only came back into the side last January. Quickly got down to business, scoring the second goal in a 3-2 win at Port Vale, and was soon back to his best, always looking to set up attacks, and excellent in possession. Out of contract at the end of 1998-99, he can also fill in at full back if required.
Crewe Alex (From trainee on 29/7/92) FL 174+6/9 FLC 10+1/1 FAC 15+1/4 Others 24/3

WHARTON Paul William

Born: Newcastle, 26 June 1977
Height: 5'4" Weight: 10.2
International Honours: E: Yth

Having overcome the prolonged shoulder injury that ruined his 1996-97 campaign, Paul featured in Hull City's pre-1997-98 season games but made way when the league action began and was placed on the transfer list last August, his only senior appearances coming in the home defeat by Rochdale in February. Despite his City frustrations, the diminutive former Leeds' junior still has plenty to offer as he buzzes around midfield.
Leeds U (From trainee on 27/6/94)
Hull C (Free on 13/2/96) FL 8+3

Noel Whelan

WHELAN Noel

Born: Leeds, 30 December 1974
Height: 6'2" Weight: 12.3
Club Honours: FAYC '93
International Honours: E: U21-2; Yth (UEFAC '93)

Injured in a pre-season game, and then involved in an off-the-field incident where he damaged his ankle, Noel's return to the Coventry side early last December coincided with the start of an excellent run. And, in becoming a more mature player than previous, he was played as a left-sided midfielder who caused opponents a lot of problems with his runs from deep, thus complimenting his silky skills to the full. His ability to get forward, and his nose for goal, also ensured he scored regularly, and there were good goals at Southampton, Leicester, and Bolton, to go with a blinder at home to Aston Villa. With Dion Dublin and Darren Huckerby playing so well up front, he seemed happy in the deeper role, and there was even talk of a possible England call up as the club once again proved the critics wrong when successfully defending its Premiership status.
Leeds U (From trainee on 5/3/93) PL 28+20/7 FLC 3+2/1 FAC 2 Others 3
Coventry C (£2,000,000 on 16/12/95) PL 76+1/20 FLC 4 FAC 11/3

WHELAN Philip (Phil) James
Born: Stockport, 7 March 1972
Height: 6'4" Weight: 14.7
International Honours: E: U21-3
Oxford's 1997 summer signing had a nightmare time of it in 1997-98, following his move from Middlesbrough. The big centre back, who had been signed to replace Matt Elliott, received a back injury on the opening day, after a collision with a team mate, which kept him out for nine games. Then, having battled his way back, he had the misfortune to suffer a bad leg break at West Bromwich, which kept him out for the remainder of the season. He came back to make a couple of reserve appearances towards the end of April, and should be fit and raring to go come the new season.
Ipswich T (From juniors on 2/7/90) F/PL 76+6/2 FLC 6+1 FAC 3+1 Others 1
Middlesbrough (£300,000 on 3/4/95) PL 18+4/1 FLC 5 FAC 3
Oxford U (£150,000 on 15/7/97) FL 6+2 FLC 1

WHELAN Spencer Randall
Born: Liverpool, 17 September 1971
Height: 6'2" Weight: 13.0
Spencer probably had his best ever season in the centre of the Chester City defence in 1997-98, again proving to be particularly commanding in the air and a great favourite with the fans. Very useful at set pieces, he scored four goals during the campaign, two of them coming in successive matches in April, against Colchester (home) and Macclesfield (away).
Chester C (Free from Liverpool juniors on 3/4/90) FL 196+19/8 FLC 11+1/2 FAC 9+3 Others 5+2

WHITBREAD Adrian Richard
Born: Epping, 22 October 1971
Height: 6'1" Weight: 11.13
As the Portsmouth team captain, he led by example throughout last season, being solid and dependable alongside Andy Awford and Andy Thomson in the centre of defence, and one of the few players to hold a regular place in the team, bar injury. It was Adrian's leadership that held the team together, while board wranglings and management changes were going on, and he was certainly the hero of the hour at Reading in February, when his late shot brought about a 1-0 win.
Leyton Orient (From trainee on 13/11/89) FL 125/2 FLC 10+1 FAC 11/1 Others 8
Swindon T (£500,000 on 29/7/93) P/FL 35+1/1 FAC 2
West Ham U (£650,000 on 17/8/94) PL 3+7 FLC 2+1 FAC 1
Portsmouth (Loaned on 9/11/95) FL 13
Portsmouth (£250,000 on 24/10/96) FL 62/1 FLC 2 FAC 2

WHITE Alan
Born: Darlington, 22 March 1976
Height: 6'1" Weight: 13.2
After a two-week trial period, Luton signed this reliable central defender from Middlesbrough last September, when the injury-hit club was particularly short in that position. He began repaying some of the fee back with some sound performances and, in October, scored the only goal of the game at Carlisle, which won three valuable points for the Town. Sound in the air, quick on the ground, and a good striker of the ball, he was bought for the future as well as to cover the immediate need, and could play an important role in the club's recovery as they put this relegation threatened season behind them.
Middlesbrough (From trainee on 8/7/94) Others 1
Luton T (£40,000 on 22/9/97) FL 26+2/1 FLC 1 FAC 1 Others 3

WHITE David
Born: Manchester, 30 October 1967
Height: 6'1" Weight: 12.9
International Honours: E: 1; B-2; U21-6; Yth
David was yet another Sheffield United player to lose almost all of 1997-98 to injury, his only full appearance coming at Bramall Lane against Wrexham in the Coca Cola Cup, when he lasted an hour before being substituted after injuring his ankle. Unfortunately, there followed an operation with a long recovery rate, which meant that he would take no further interest in the season, and left United fans wondering what kind of difference a fully-fit David White might have made to a campaign that ended with the club still in the first division. At his best, one of the most exciting forwards in the modern game, who terrorised defences with his hard running and ability to score spectaculars from distance or from acute angles, the fans would be happy for a lot less than that.
Manchester C (From apprentice on 7/11/85) F/PL 273+12/79 FLC 24+2/11 FAC 22/4 Others 9/2
Leeds U (£2,000,000 on 22/12/93) PL 28+14/9 FLC 1 FAC 6/1 Others 1+1
Sheffield U (Signed on 17/11/95) FL 55+11/13 FLC 3+1/1 FAC 4 Others 3

WHITE Devon Winston
Born: Nottingham, 2 March 1964
Height: 6'3" Weight: 14.0
Club Honours: Div 3 '90; AIC '95
A fully committed centre forward, Devon joined Shrewsbury from Notts County last September and immediately gained terrace popularity. He was the target man Town had been seeking, and a steady goalscorer, especially before the New Year, bagging a hat trick against Macclesfield. Difficult to knock off the ball, he never really received the service in the box to use his height and power in order to convert more goals.
Lincoln C (From Arnold FC on 14/12/84) FL 21+8/4 Others 2+1/2 (Free to Boston U in October 1986)
Bristol Rov (Free on 21/8/87) FL 190+12/53 FLC 9/2 FAC 10/3 Others 19/2
Cambridge U (£100,000 on 28/3/92) FL 15+7/4 FLC 4/1 FAC 1 Others 1/1
Queens Park R (£100,000 on 26/1/93) PL 16+10/9 FLC 1+1

Adrian Whitbread

Notts Co (£110,000 on 23/12/94) FL 34+6/15 FLC 4/6 FAC 2+1/2 Others 4/1
Watford (£100,000 on 16/2/96) FL 28+10/7 FLC 4 FAC 2/1 Others 1
Notts Co (£20,000 on 14/3/97) FL 11+4/2 FLC 3/1
Shrewsbury T (35,000 on 23/9/97) FL 30+2/10 FAC 2 Others 1

WHITE Jason Gregory
Born: Meriden, 19 October 1971
Height: 6'0" Weight: 12.10

Having joined Rotherham from Northampton last September, Jason kept up his remarkable sequence of scoring for all of his clubs on his debut, when netting against Lincoln, and he went on to become second highest scorer, helped by his pace and strength. Had a number of different partners up front, and his absence due to injury for a spell from mid-January could well have cost the team automatic promotion.
Derby Co (From trainee on 4/7/90)
Scunthorpe U (Free on 6/9/91) FL 44+24/16 FLC 2 FAC 3+3/1 Others 4+4/1
Darlington (Loaned on 20/8/93) FL 4/1
Scarborough (Free on 10/12/93) FL 60+3/20 FLC 2+1 FAC 5/1 Others 1
Northampton T (£35,000 on 15/6/95) FL 55+22/18 FLC 1+4 FAC 3 Others 5+2
Rotherham U (£25,000 on 9/9/97) FL 26+1/12 FAC 2/1 Others 1

WHITE Stephen (Steve) James
Born: Chipping Sodbury, 2 January 1959
Height: 5'11" Weight: 12.6
Club Honours: Div 2 '82

The popular striker finally called a halt to his career at the end of 1997-98, after 21 years in full-time football, having helped Swindon Town to the division two title, and promotion to the old first division, in 1982, and twice played in front of full houses at Wembley Stadium in play-off finals. Still played a full part at Cardiff City last season, even though he was the oldest outfield player in the Nationwide League, and remained exceptionally fit, scoring a crucial FA Cup goal to help City beat Slough on their way to the fourth round. Steve sees his future in coaching or management, and during last season had talks with both Bath City and Yeovil, but he would love to remain in the Nationwide League now he has called a halt to his playing days. "I still feel fit and able to play well, but I want people to remember me as a reasonable player," says Steve, "I feel now is the right time to stop. Cardiff City fans have been good to me – perhaps they liked a trier."
Bristol Rov (Free from Mangotsfield on 11/7/77) FL 46+4/20 FLC 2/1 FAC 3/3
Luton T (£200,000 on 24/12/79) FL 63+9/25 FLC 3+1/1 FAC 2+1
Charlton Ath (£150,000 on 30/7/82) FL 29/12 FLC 2
Lincoln C (Loaned on 28/1/83) FL 2+1
Luton T (Loaned on 24/2/83) FL 4
Bristol Rov (£45,000 on 26/8/83) FL 89+12/24 FLC 8/2 FAC 7+1/2 Others 5+2/1
Swindon T (Free on 8/7/86) FL 200+44/83 FLC 21+8/11 FAC 9+2/2 Others 22+6/15
Hereford U (Free on 26/8/94) FL 70+6/44 FLC 5/2 FAC 6/4 Others 9+2/3
Cardiff C (Free on 9/8/96) FL 44+23/15 FLC 4 FAC 2+1/2 Others 3+2

WHITE Thomas (Tom) Matthew
Born: Bristol, 26 January 1976
Height: 6'0" Weight: 13.6

The Bristol Rovers' central defender developed a good defensive partnership in 1997-98 with firstly, the experienced Brian Gayle, and later Steve Foster, before finally losing his place to club captain, Andy Tillson. Good in the air, and improving his distribution, Tom has developed into an effective man-to-man marker, and is cool under pressure. After he was left out of the team in March he subsequently decided a cartilage operation could not be put off until the summer, which meant he missed Rovers' final run in of the season. When he returns to full fitness, he will again take up the challenge for a first team spot.
Bristol Rov (From trainee on 13/7/94) FL 44+7/1 FAC 5 Others 1+1

WHITEHALL Steven (Steve) Christopher
Born: Bromborough, 8 December 1966
Height: 5'10" Weight: 11.5

Having been signed from Rochdale during the summer of 1997, although starting 1997-98 for Mansfield slowly, Steve's campaign really took off with a magnificent goal at Lincoln, and thereafter he never looked back. Despite just missing out on the "Golden Boot" award for the division, the strong-running striker proved to be a bargain buy who should score many more goals for Town, and scooped every Player of the Year award on offer at the club.
Rochdale (£20,000 from Southport on 23/7/91) FL 212+26/75 FLC 10+3/4 FAC 13+2/3 Others 15+1/10
Mansfield T (£20,000 on 8/8/97) FL 42+1/24 FLC 2 FAC 2/1 Others 2/1

WHITEHEAD Philip (Phil) Matthew
Born: Halifax, 17 December 1969
Height: 6'3" Weight: 15.4

Phil had another consistently good season in Oxford's goal in 1997-98, although he did miss two months with a knee injury. Big and strong, he commands his area well and is a good kicker of the ball, even claiming an assist in the home win over Norwich with a big clearance. Had a good run towards the end of the campaign, when he conceded just one goal in five matches, as United rose up the table. The popular 'keeper looks set to be the number one for a while yet.
Halifax T (From trainee on 1/7/88) FL 42 FLC 2 FAC 4 Others 3
Barnsley (£60,000 on 9/3/90) FL 16
Halifax T (Loaned on 7/3/91) FL 9
Scunthorpe U (Loaned on 29/11/91) FL 8 Others 2
Scunthorpe U (Loaned on 4/9/92) FL 8 FLC 2
Bradford C (Loaned on 19/11/92) FL 6 Others 4
Oxford U (£75,000 on 1/11/93) FL 186 FLC 13 FAC 13 Others 3

WHITEHOUSE Dane Lee
Born: Sheffield, 14 October 1970
Height: 5'9" Weight: 12.8

Undoubtedly one of the factors in the Sheffield United team missing promotion was the loss of Dane to injury, sustained in the match at Port Vale last November. His tremendous form on the left-hand side of midfield, and also in central midfield, had

been one of the reasons why the team started last season so well, added to which his goals were sorely missed. Having turned down a big money move to an unnamed Premier League club at the start of the season, as he is a Blade through and through, he went on to win one of the Nationwide Player of the Month awards in recognition of his hard-working displays in linking defence with attack, and his all-round value to the side. Likely to be out until this coming Christmas, he is a great loss to the club in their quest for Premiership football.
Sheffield U (From trainee on 1/7//89) F/PL 204+27/38 FLC 20+1/8 FAC 14+3/2 Others 6/2

WHITLEY James (Jim)
Born: Zambia, 14 April 1975
Height: 5'9" Weight: 11.0
International Honours: NI: 1

As the elder brother of Jeff, Jim has made the slower progress of the two but, after signing a three-year contract last December, his luck changed and he made his Manchester City debut as a first-half substitute against Bradford City, the press voting him Man of the Match. In going on to play in 20 of the next 22 games, it was also the first time that two brothers had been on the field at the same time for City. A midfielder with a nice turn of pace to go with good distribution, and already under the microscope of the Northern Ireland manager, having made his debut against Spain, with added maturity and strength he can look forward to a good future.
Manchester C (From juniors on 1/8/94) FL 17+2 FAC 1+1

WHITLEY Jeffrey (Jeff)
Born: Zambia, 28 January 1979
Height: 5'8" Weight: 10.0
International Honours: NI: 3; B-1; U21-3

As the younger brother of Jim, having established himself at Manchester City in 1996-97 and, at the same time, making two international appearances as a sub for Northern Ireland, Jeff was expecting to have a big season in 1997-98. In the event, it was not quite what he would have wished for. Making a late start in October, and with the club continually looking towards the second division, he was unable to cement a regular place in the side, despite winning the Man of the Match award against Crewe, and showing much energy, maturity, and confidence in midfield. And even when he scored his second goal for City, at Bradford, his day was spoiled when he was sent off. Made a further appearance for Northern Ireland as a 90-minute sub against Spain, as well as playing at "B" and U21 level, and is sure to be an asset as City look to come back at the first time of asking in 1998-99.
Manchester C (From trainee on 19/2/96) FL 26+14/2 FLC 1 FAC 1

WHITLOW Michael (Mike) William
Born: Northwich, 13 January 1968
Height: 6'0" Weight: 12.12
Club Honours: Div 2 '90, Div 1 '92; FLC '97

A vastly experienced left back, Mike provided a much-needed sense of stability

and confidence to a shaky looking Bolton defence, when signing from Leicester last September as a hasty replacement for the injured Robbie Elliott, his experience shining through in the calm and controlled performances he gave. Fitting into the team instantly, he is one of football's typical unsung heroes – a player who does his job effectively, without being a headline grabber, yet sure to be appreciated by their team mates. Although he possesses a terrific left foot, which can unleash a thunderbolt of a shot when required, he has yet to score for the Wanderers, but it should not be too long before he breaks that duck.

Leeds U (£10,000 from Witton A on 11/11/88) FL 62+15/4 FLC 4+1 FAC 1+4 Others 9
Leicester C (£250,000 on 27/3/92) F/PL 141+6/8 FLC 12/1 FAC 6 Others 14
Bolton W (£500,000+ on 19/9/97) PL 13 FLC 3 FAC 1

WHITNEY Jonathan (Jon) David
Born: Nantwich, 23 December 1970
Height: 5'10" Weight: 13.8

Jon, a left-sided Lincoln defender, won his place back for the start of last season, after eight months out with a cruciate knee ligament injury, and missed just two league games as the club gained promotion from the third division. Tough tackling, with the knack of scoring, he even substituted in goal for the last half hour at Macclesfield, following the dismissal of Barry Richardson, and did well until beaten by a late goal.*

Huddersfield T (£10,000 from Winsford, via Wigan Ath YTS and Skelmersdale, on 21/10/93) FL 17+1 FLC 0+1 Others 4/1
Wigan Ath (Loaned on 17/3/95) FL 12
Lincoln C (£20,000 on 31/10/95) FL 85+3/6 FLC 7/1 FAC 6/2 Others 4

WHITTAKER Stuart
Born: Liverpool, 2 January 1975
Height: 5'7" Weight: 9.6

A free transfer signing from Bolton during the 1997 close season, as Macclesfield looked to strengthen the side for the start of their first ever Football League campaign, Stuart ultimately proved to be a fast out-and-out left winger who switched over to the right for spells, while confusing the opposition. Despite having to wait until October before getting a first team run out, he soon impressed, running the Notts County defence ragged on his third appearance and going on to gain a regular place for the remainder of the season, apart from when he was out injured in December with ankle ligament trouble. Was delighted to score two tremendous goals in the FA Cup first round at Hartlepool, and went on to create many of the chances for others to take advantage of during the run in to promotion.

Bolton W (Free from Liverpool juniors on 14/5/93) FL 2+1 FLC 0+1
Wigan Ath (Loaned on 30/8/96) FL 2+1
Macclesfield T (Free on 8/8/97) FL 29+2/4 FAC 2/2 Others 1

WHITTINGHAM Guy
Born: Evesham, 10 November 1964
Height: 5'10" Weight: 12.2

Guy had a difficult season at Sheffield Wednesday in 1997-98 in fighting to maintain his right-sided midfield role, being put under a lot of pressure by Benito Carbone and the Swedish international, Niclas Alexandersson. A great team player, who has always shown good spirit, and has always been good for a few goals, he scored four during the campaign, three in successive matches, the other being the effective equaliser in a 2-2 draw at Aston Villa. Despite being a frustrated striker at heart, you can rely on him to deliver 100 per-cent effort wherever he plays.

Portsmouth (Free from Yeovil on 9/6/89) FL 149+11/88 FLC 7+2/3 FAC 7+3/10 Others 9/3
Aston Villa (£1,200,000 on 1/8/93) PL 17+8/5 FLC 4+1/1 Others 2+1
Wolverhampton W (Loaned on 28/2/94) FL 13/8 FAC 1
Sheffield Wed (£700,000 on 21/12/94) PL 89+22/22 FLC 7+1/2 FAC 7+1/1

WHITTLE Justin Phillip
Born: Derby, 18 March 1971
Height: 6'1" Weight: 12.12

Whilst he lost his place in the Stoke side with the emergence of Steve Tweed in the first part of last season, he kept his form in the reserves – a side he captained – and was an almost permanent substitute. With a change of manager in the mid-season and a loss of form in defence, in the main Justin was preferred by the new manager, Chris Kamara, and he never let him down. Although late to the game, following his Army career, Justin has proved a joy to work with at the Britannia Stadium and his late term form had many wondering whether his parental qualifications might not see him into the Jamaican World Cup squad.

Glasgow Celtic (Free from Army during 1994 close season)
Stoke C (Free on 20/10/94) FL 57+8 FLC 2+4 FAC 2 Others 2

WHITTON Stephen (Steve) Paul
Born: East Ham, 4 December 1960
Height: 6'1" Weight: 13.7
Club Honours: Div 2 '92

A vastly experienced forward with plenty of top league experience at a variety of clubs, "Whitts" began 1997-98 as player/assistant manager at Colchester, with the idea that he would not be playing too often as the young guns got their chances. However, a combination of injuries and loss of form led to an early recall, and saw Steve playing a holding role in midfield for the middle part of the season – scoring one goal, at Scarborough, before a niggling neck injury, which had been troubling him for over two years, finally won the day and caused him to retire as a player in the spring.

Coventry C (From apprentice on 15/9/78) FL 64+10/21 FLC 3+2 FAC 3/2
West Ham U (£175,000 on 11/7/83) FL 35+4/6 FLC 6/2 FAC 1
Birmingham C (Loaned on 31/1/86) FL 8/2
Birmingham C (£60,000 on 28/8/86) FL 94+1/28 FLC 7+1/4 FAC 5 Others 3/1
Sheffield Wed (£275,000 on 3/3/89) FL 22+10/4 FLC 3/4 FAC 0+1 Others 0+1
Ipswich T (£150,000 on 11/7/91) F/PL 80+8/15 FLC 7+1/2 FAC 8+1/2 Others 4
Colchester U (£10,000 on 24/3/94) FL 105+11/21 FLC 6+1 FAC 6/2 Others 7+2/1

WHITWORTH Neil Anthony
Born: Wigan, 12 April 1972
Height: 6'2" Weight: 12.6
International Honours: E: Yth

Returning to his hometown club on a short-term contract, after being released by Kilmarnock last March, Neil made his second debut for Wigan Athletic when he came on as a substitute in the home victory over Oldham Athletic. At his best a dominant centre back and a sound tackler who leads by example, he made just one league start before being released at the end of the season.

Wigan Ath (Trainee) FL 1+1
Manchester U (£45,000 on 1/7/90) FL 1
Preston NE (Loaned on 16/1/92) FL 6
Barnsley (Loaned on 20/2/92) FL 11
Rotherham U (Loaned on 8/10/93) FL 8/1 Others 2
Blackpool (Loaned on 10/12/93) FL 3
Kilmarnock (£265,000 on 2/9/94) SL 73+1/3 SLC 3 SC 4 Others 1
Wigan Ath (Free on 11/3/98) FL 1+3

WHYTE David Antony
Born: Greenwich, 20 April 1971
Height: 5'9" Weight: 10.7
Club Honours: Div 1 '94

Released by Charlton early last season, despite having commanded a hefty transfer fee just three years earlier, David returned to league action with Ipswich last November following injury problems and an unsuccessful trial at Reading. Unfortunately, after making just one appearance, against his old club, his knee flared up again and, with his monthly contract not being renewed, he rested up before moving on to Bristol Rovers in January. There, given a short-term contract, the striker showed glimpses of his talent, in that he was still quick in the box, and still possessed his ball-playing skills, before he finished 1997-98 at Southend on non-contract forms, scoring on his debut in a 3-1 win at Wigan and missing just one match in nine possible appearances.

Crystal Palace (Free from Greenwich Borough on 15/2/89) FL 17+10/4 FLC 5+2/2 FAC 0+1 Others 0+3/1
Charlton Ath (Loaned on 26/3/92) FL 7+1/2
Charlton Ath (£450,000 on 5/7/94) FL 65+20/28 FLC 5+2/4 FAC 3+1/1 Others 0+2
Reading (Free on 19/9/97)
Ipswich T (Free on 31/10/97) FL 2
Bristol Rov (Free on 22/1/98) FL 0+4 Others 0+1
Southend U (Free on 13/3/98) FL 3+5/1

WHYTE Derek
Born: Glasgow, 31 August 1968
Height: 5'11" Weight: 12.12
Club Honours: SPD '88; SC '88, '89; Div 1 '95
International Honours: S: 11; B-3; SU21-9; Yth; Sch

Transferred to Aberdeen last December, Derek will surely look back at his sojourn at Middlesbrough as one of the best periods of his distinguished career. His polished displays in sharing the central defensive roles with captain, Nigel Pearson, and Steve Vickers, being exemplified by his ability to clear his defensive lines, using his speciality overhead kick, and usually finding a well-placed colleague in the process. Strong and

aggressive in the tackle, the Scot did enough to ensure that his reputation will rank alongside that of other Boro legends in the Hall of Fame and his performances most certainly caught the eye of national coach, Craig Brown, who selected him for the final 22 bound for France '98, having earlier used him for the qualifying match against Finland. *Stop Press:* Although sitting on the bench, he failed to make an appearance as Scotland crashed out of the World Cup at the Group A stage.

Glasgow Celtic (From juniors on 13/5/85) SL 211+5/7 SLC 18+1 SC 26 Others 15/1
Middlesbrough (£500,000 on 1/8/92) F/PL 160+7/2 FLC 15+1/1 FAC 4+2 Others 6

WIDDRINGTON Thomas (Tommy)
Born: Newcastle, 1 October 1971
Height: 5'9" Weight: 11.12

1997-98 was not a brilliant season for the ex-Southampton left-sided midfielder as he found himself in and out of the Grimsby side during the first half of the campaign, as the manager, Alan Buckley, sought the right combination for a quick return to first division status. His dilemma was partly resolved when long-term injury problems kept Tommy out of the side from the New Year, but this most versatile of players is sure to be back in harness, whether it be performing in midfield as a tough-tackling ball winner, as a full back, or even in the sweeper role.

Southampton (From trainee on 10/5/90) F/PL 67+8/3 FLC 3+1 FAC 11
Wigan Ath (Loaned on 12/9/91) FL 5+1 FLC 2
Grimsby T (£300,000 on 11/7/96) FL 56+7/7 FLC 7+1 FAC 3 Others 1

WIEKENS Gerard
Born: Holland, 25 February 1973
Height: 6'0" Weight: 13.4

After nine years in Dutch football, Gerard signed for Manchester City in March 1997 and was allowed to play out the remainder of the 1996-97 season in Holland before making his Football League debut on the opening day of 1997-98 against Portsmouth at Maine Road, and scoring in a 2-2 draw. Able to perform in central defence, or midfield, he showed impressive style as a quick, skilful, and technically correct, typically Dutch type of player. And, apart from a spell of six weeks out injured, he was a regular throughout the campaign, scoring five goals, captaining the side for a short-term period, and generally relishing the challenge that life at the bottom of division one brought.

Manchester C (£500,000 from SC Veendam on 28/7/97) FL 35+2/5 FLC 2 FAC 1

WILBRAHAM Aaron Thomas
Born: Manchester, 21 October 1979
Height: 6'2" Weight: 11.5

As a promising young YTS striker at Stockport, the tall 18-year old was quickly snapped up on professional forms by the new manager, Gary Megson, early in 1997-98. As the season progressed, and having established something of a reputation at the club with 28 goals in 25 games for the "A" team, he then made an impressive first team

bow as a sub against Crewe late in the season, a performance that earned him a full debut in the derby match at Maine Road. Despite County ultimately losing 4-1, the youngster scored a stunning equaliser just six minutes into the match and appears to be definitely one for the future.

Stockport Co (From trainee on 29/8/97) FL 6+1/1

WILCOX Jason Malcolm
Born: Farnworth, 15 July 1971
Height: 5'11" Weight: 11.10
Club Honours: PL '95
International Honours: E: 1; B-2

1997-98 was a frustrating season for the Blackburn left winger who played one game for the England "B" side and was always a fringe candidate for the World Cup. The emergence of Damien Duff, and the huge void left by le Saux, saw him continually shuffled from wide left to left back, often in the game itself. Known not to favour

Gerard Wiekens

playing at the back, the truth is that he was probably the best equipped man at the club for the role, even if he was uncomfortable with the off side trap. At his best a player with pace, and the ability to send in raking angled crosses, who contributes well to flowing movements.

Blackburn Rov (From trainee on 13/6/89) F/PL 198+21/28 FLC 16+1/1 FAC 15+2/1 Others 5

WILCOX Russell (Russ)
Born: Hemsworth, 25 March 1964
Height: 6'0" Weight: 12.12
Club Honours: Div 4 '87; Div 3 '96
International Honours: E: SP-3

A 1997 summer signing from Preston, Russ quickly became the key defensive organiser for Scunthorpe until an early season calf injury in training sidelined him for over two months. Took a while to rediscover his best form, but had a superb closing three months, adding a wealth of experience to the

defence. Superb in the air, and a good tackler, his ability to bring the ball out of defence also helps the team's attacking game.

Doncaster Rov (Apprentice) FL 1
Northampton T (£15,000 from Frickley Ath on 30/6/86) FL 137+1/9 FLC 6 FAC 10 Others 8/1
Hull C (£120,000 on 6/8/90) FL 92+8/7 FLC 5 FAC 5/1 Others 5+1
Doncaster Rov (£60,000 on 30/7/93) FL 81/6 FLC 5/2 FAC 3 Others 3
Preston NE (£60,000 on 22/9/95) FL 62/1 FLC 4 FAC 3/1 Others 2
Scunthorpe U (£15,000 on 8/7/97) FL 30+1/2 FLC 2+1 FAC 4/2 Others 3

WILDE Adam
Born: Southampton, 22 May 1979
Height: 5'10" Weight: 11.8
Having signed professional forms for Cambridge during the latter part of the previous campaign, 1997-98 was a disappointing season for Adam at the Abbey, being limited to just two subs' appearances in February. An attacking left winger, he had a spell on loan at non-league Wisbech, in an effort to get back on track and, hopefully, 1998-99 will see him back to his best. Still only 19, there is plenty of time for this exciting youngster.

Cambridge U (From trainee on 21/2/97) FL 0+3

WILDER Christopher (Chris) John
Born: Stocksbridge, 23 September 1967
Height: 5'11" Weight: 12.8
A very consistent full back, who also played a few times for Bradford as a sweeper, or centre back, Chris was a big favourite with the fans who were dismayed when he was transferred to Sheffield United last March, immediately prior to the transfer deadline. Signed by Steve Thompson, although playing mainly at right back he also performed in midfield as the club reached the play offs and, after missing the first leg against Sunderland, he came back in to a side that failed to progress any further. Able to support the forwards when required, and dangerous from free kicks anywhere around the penalty area, he is a good man to have in your side.

Southampton (From apprentice on 26/9/85)
Sheffield U (Free on 20/8/86) FL 89+4/1 FLC 8+1 FAC 7 Others 3
Walsall (Loaned on 2/11/89) FL 4 FAC 1 Others 2
Charlton Ath (Loaned on 12/10/90) FL 1
Charlton Ath (Loaned on 28/11/91) FL 2
Leyton Orient (Loaned on 27/2/92) FL 16/1 Others 1
Rotherham U (£50,000 on 30/7/92) FL 129+3/11 FLC 11 FAC 6+2/1 Others 6+1
Notts Co (£150,000 on 2/1/96) FL 46 FLC 2 FAC 4 Others 1
Bradford C (£150,000 on 27/3/97) FL 35+7 FLC 2 FAC 1
Sheffield U (£150,000 on 25/3/98) FL 7+1 Others 1

WILDING Peter John
Born: Shrewsbury, 28 November 1968
Height: 6'1" Weight: 12.12
After signing for Shrewsbury from Telford in the summer of 1997, the local lad became an instant hit. Hard working and powerful, if in the early stages a little raw, Peter showed to advantage when moving forward to with ball and formed a formidable partnership

with any of the other central defenders he played alongside. It is a crying shame that he broke into league football so late in his career.

Shrewsbury T (£10,000 from Telford on 10/6/97) FL 33+1/1 FLC 2 FAC 2 Others 1/1

WILKINS Ian John
Born: Lincoln, 3 April 1980
Height: 6'0" Weight: 12.7
Still a second-year YTS player when making his Football League debut as a substitute at Barnet last September, the promising homegrown Lincoln defender was rewarded with a full contract in March. Well worth his opportunity, the youth team captain is definitely another Imp for the future.

Lincoln C (From trainee on 28/3/98) FL 1+1

Richard Wilkins

WILKINS Richard John
Born: Lambeth, 28 May 1965
Height: 6'0" Weight: 12.3
Club Honours: Div 3 '91
An inspirational club and first team captain, "Wilky" has just cleaned up in all of the Player of the Year awards, as due reward for an outstanding season at Colchester in 1997-98. Starting off in his accustomed position of central midfield, he soon had to fill in as emergency centre half, as injuries and suspensions hit, but looked so comfortable in this new role that the management decided not to buy a new centre half once Peter Cawley was injured, and kept him there instead. Despite his new, deeper role, Richard still provided five goals for the cause, and his reward was to lift the division three play-off trophy at Wembley.

Colchester U (Free from Haverhill Rov on 20/11/86) FL 150+2/22 FLC 6 FAC 7+2/4 Others 9+3/3
Cambridge U (£65,000 on 25/7/90) FL 79+2/7 FLC 6 FAC 8+1 Others 9
Hereford U (Free on 20/7/94) FL 76+1/5 FLC 6 FAC 6 Others 8/2
Colchester U (£30,000 on 3/7/96) FL 77/7 FLC 5 FAC 3/1 Others 8

WILKINSON John Colbridge
Born: Exeter, 24 August 1979
Height: 5'9" Weight: 11.0
A young YTS left winger who has graduated through Exeter's youth team, John was given his first taste of league football last season in the final match, against Macclesfield, when coming on after 71 minutes. Due to be offered a professional contract, the youngster will be looking to make as big an impact at senior level as he has in the junior ranks.

Exeter C (Trainee) FL 0+1

WILKINSON Paul
Born: Louth, 30 October 1964
Height: 6'1" Weight: 12.4
Club Honours: CS '86; Div 1 '87, '95
International Honours: E: U21-4
Despite being one of the men who took Barnsley into the Premiership, the big centre forward found himself making way for newcomers when the manager decided that the team needed strengthening and he signed for Millwall last September. Always a threat to defences with his presence, Paul scored the winner at Grimsby on his debut for the Lions and generally acted as the target man for others, such as Paul Shaw and Kim Grant. Has good control, quick feet, and is still excellent in the air. *Stop Press:* Joined Northampton on a free transfer during the summer.

Grimsby T (From apprentice on 8/11/82) FL 69+2/27 FLC 10/5 FAC 4+2/1
Everton (£250,000 on 28/3/85) FL 19+12/7 FLC 3+1/7 FAC 3/1 Others 6+2/1
Nottingham F (£200,000 on 26/3/87) FL 32+2/5 FLC 3/1 FAC 4+1/1/2 Others 1
Watford (£300,000 on 16/8/88) FL 133+1/52 FLC 4/1 FAC 8+1 Others 8/3
Middlesbrough (£550,000 on 16/8/91) F/PL 161+5/49 FLC 16/8 FAC 5+1/4 Others 5+1/4
Oldham Ath (Loaned on 26/10/95) FL 4/1 Others 1/1
Watford (Loaned on 1/12/95) FL 4
Luton T (Loaned on 28/3/96) FL 3
Barnsley (Free on 19/7/96) F/PL 48+1/9 FLC 4/2 FAC 2
Millwall (£150,000 on 18/9/97) FL 22+8/3 FLC 1 FAC 1 Others 1

WILKINSON Stephen (Steve) John
Born: Lincoln, 1 September 1968
Height: 6'0" Weight: 11.12
Club Honours: Div 3 '96
Well known from his days in a Mansfield shirt, Steve joined Chesterfield from Preston during the 1997 close season, but was probably on to a loser from the start as far as fitting in with the crowd was concerned. Having recorded his 100th league goal in his second full appearance for the Spireites, he then found scoring opportunities severely limited, and fans who saw only the "goals for" column freely abused him, further

reducing his confidence and his effectiveness. However, his tireless work paid off, though, and the old Steve began to emerge from January as his scoring touch returned.

Leicester C (From apprentice on 6/9/86) FL 5+4/1 FAC 1
Crewe Alex (Loaned on 8/9/88) FL 3+2/2
Mansfield T (£80,000 on 2/10/89) FL 214+18/83 FLC 13+1/4 FAC 10/2 Others 17/1
Preston NE (£90,000 on 15/6/95) FL 44+8/13 FLC 4/4 FAC 3/1 Others 3
Chesterfield (£70,000+ on 4/7/97) FL 24+6/6 FLC 1 FAC 3 Others 1

WILLEMS Ron

Born: Epe, Holland, 20 September 1966
Height: 6'0" Weight: 13.0

The Dutch striker, who prefers the linkman role between midfield and attack, could not dislodge Francesco Baiano from this position in the Derby side in 1997-98, but, still a useful squad player, he made numerous telling appearances in this role in the second half of the season. An unassuming player, who puts a lot of hard work and tracking back into his role when called upon, Ron has been at the club since the summer of 1995 and looks good for some time yet.

Derby Co (£300,000 from Grasshoppers, Zurich, via PEC Zwolle, Twente Enschede and Ajax, on 28/7/95) F/PL 41+18/13 FLC 2/1 FAC 4+2/2

WILLIAMS Adrian

Born: Reading, 16 August 1971
Height: 6'2" Weight: 13.2
Club Honours: Div 2 '94
International Honours: W: 9

The solid Wolves' central defender did not join proceedings until 20 September last, playing well at Sunderland, but was then given the captaincy against Fulham, though Keith Curle returned to the role the next match. Had a bad night in his home town of Reading, having conceded a penalty against Ipswich he ventured forward to hit the post at the other end. After a 14-match run he suffered a hamstring strain, which, coupled with a recurrence of his ankle problem, kept him out of the next 14, but he gradually worked his way back, doing well in the FA Cup. On the international front, however, his highlight was to come as a sub for Wales against Brazil.

Reading (From trainee on 4/3/89) FL 191+5/14 FLC 16/1 FAC 16/2 Others 14/2
Wolverhampton W (£750,000 on 3/7/96) FL 26 FLC 2 FAC 2+2 Others 2/1

WILLIAMS Andrew Phillip

Born: Bristol, 8 October 1977
Height: 5'10" Weight: 10.10
International Honours: W: 2; U21-2

A pacy young Southampton winger who made his first team debut in the first game of last season at home to Bolton, all in all he appeared on 24 occasions, 20 of them when coming off the bench. His excellent progress also saw him make a full international debut for Wales, having previously played at U21 level, and, able to operate on either flank, he would appear to be an exciting youngster with many more outings in prospect.

Southampton (From trainee on 24/5/96) PL 3+17 FLC 1+2 FAC 0+1

WILLIAMS Darren

Born: Middlesbrough, 28 April 1977
Height: 5'9" Weight: 11.2
International Honours: E: B-1; U21-1

The 20-year-old Sunderland utility man established himself as a solid central defender in partnership with Jody Craddock in 1997-98. Quick, and good in the air, Darren was rewarded for his fine performances with a first England U21 cap in March and a call up to the England "B" squad in April, when he went on to win his first cap at this level against Russia. His willingness to bring the ball out of defence and link up with the midfield was a crucial factor in the team's successes as the promotion campaign gathered momentum. Continued to find the net, three goals helping the cause.

York C (From trainee on 21/6/95) FL 16+4 FLC 4+1 FAC 1 Others 3/1
Sunderland (£50,000 on 18/10/96) F/PL 45+2/4 FLC 3/1 FAC 2+1 Others 3

WILLIAMS Dean Paul

Born: Lichfield, 5 January 1972
Height: 6'0" Weight: 12.8

Dean began last season at Doncaster by refusing to train, although Rovers still held his registration. He did eventually agree to play, making his first appearance at Darlington in October, but following seven games without a win a subsequent falling out with the then manager, Danny Bergara, saw this most capable goalkeeper leave for Gateshead after just a few weeks.

Birmingham C (From trainee on 11/7/90) FL 4 FAC 1 (Free to Tamworth in March 1992)
Brentford (£2,000 on 8/8/93) FL 6+1
Doncaster Rov (Free on 12/8/94) FL 83+2 FLC 3 FAC 2 Others 5

WILLIAMS Gareth James

Born: Isle of Wight, 12 March 1967
Height: 6'0" Weight: 12.2

A skilful striker with excellent ball control, Gareth was Scarborough's top scorer with 15 goals in 1997-98, even though an injury at Notts County in February affected his form and the goals dried up. Unfortunately, from then on, he had a miserable time, especially in the play-off semi finals against Torquay, when he missed a penalty in the first leg, and was sent off in the second. Overall though, he had a very impressive season.

Aston Villa (£30,000 from Gosport Borough on 9/1/88) FL 6+6 FLC 0+1 FAC 2 Others 0+1
Barnsley (£200,000 on 6/8/91) FL 23+11/6 FLC 1 FAC 1+1 Others 1+1
Hull C (Loaned on 17/9/92) FL 4
Hull C (Loaned on 6/1/94) FL 16/2
Wolverhampton W (Free on 23/8/94)
Bournemouth (Free on 16/9/94) FL 0+1
Northampton T (Free on 27/9/94) FL 38+12/1 FLC 2 FAC 2 Others 5+1
Scarborough (Free on 9/8/96) FL 85+3/25 FLC 6/1 FAC 4 Others 4

WILLIAMS David Geraint (George)

Born: Treorchy, 5 January 1962
Height: 5'7" Weight: 12.6
Club Honours: Div 2 '87
International Honours: W: 13; U21-2; Yth

Despite still being an excellent tackler and a great battler, George lost his place in the

Ipswich side last season when the manager decided to pair Keiron Dyer and Matt Holland in central midfield, and he was unable to regain it. At his best in midfield skirmishes, but now into the veteran stage of his career, he was given a free transfer during the summer following a stint as summariser for local radio, where he came across rather well.

Bristol Rov (From apprentice on 12/1/80) FL 138+3/8 FLC 14 FAC 9+2/2 Others 5
Derby Co (£40,000 on 29/3/85) FL 276+1/9 FLC 26+1/1 FAC 17 Others 11
Ipswich T (£650,000 on 1/7/92) P/FL 217/3 FLC 24+1 FAC 18 Others 4

WILLIAMS John Nelson

Born: Birmingham, 11 May 1968
Height: 6'1" Weight: 13.12

Released by Hereford during the 1997 close season, the tall, speedy striker, once known as "the flying postman", joined Walsall on trial, but left after coming off the bench in the opening game of 1997-98. He quickly moved on to Exeter, where he showed real power and pace, before a series of niggling injuries, and the form of Darren Rowbotham and Steve Flack, restricted his opportunities and saw him unable to make an impact.

Swansea C (£5,000 from Cradley T on 19/8/91) FL 36+3/11 FLC 2+1 FAC 3 Others 1
Coventry C (£250,000 on 1/7/92) PL 66+14/11 FLC 4 FAC 2
Notts Co (Loaned on 7/10/94) FL 3+2/2
Stoke C (Loaned on 23/12/94) FL 1+3
Swansea C (Loaned on 3/2/95) FL 6+1/2
Wycombe W (£150,000 on 15/9/95) FL 34+14/8 FLC 4+1/2 FAC 5/4 Others 2
Hereford U (Free on 14/2/97) FL 8+3/3
Walsall (Free on 21/7/97) FL 0+1
Exeter C (Free on 29/8/97) FL 16+20/4

WILLIAMS Lee

Born: Birmingham, 3 February 1973
Height: 5'7" Weight: 11.13
International Honours: E: Yth

A useful passer of the ball with two good feet, and a player who gets forward well to link up with the forwards, Lee came on in leaps and bounds for Mansfield last term. Following the injury to Tony Ford in October, he was switched to wing back and soon made the position his own, prior to being allowed to leave during the summer.

Aston Villa (From trainee on 26/1/91)
Shrewsbury T (Loaned on 8/11/92) FL 2+1 FAC 1+1/1 Others 2
Peterborough U (Signed on 23/3/94) FL 83+8/1 FLC 4+1 FAC 5+1/1 Others 7 (Free to Shamrock Rov during 1996 close season)
Tranmere Rov (Free on 26/2/97)
Mansfield T (Free on 27/3/97) FL 36+8/3 FAC 2 Others 2

WILLIAMS Mark

Born: Bangor, 10 December 1973
Height: 5'11" Weight: 13.6

A forward signed in the 1997 close season from Telford United, his second spell at Shrewsbury, Mark never really got started as he suffered injury for almost the entire campaign. With very limited involvement, supporters will need to wait until next season to judge his performances.

Shrewsbury T (From trainee on 6/7/92) FL 0+3 (Freed on 8/3/93)
Shrewsbury T (Signed from Telford on 2/7/97) FL 0+5

WILLIAMS Mark Stuart
Born: Stalybridge, 28 September 1970
Height: 6'0" Weight: 13.0
Club Honours: Div 3 '94
Mark began 1997-98 for Chesterfield in the same commanding form as he finished the previous season, coping well with the arrival of a new centre-half partner, to run the defence in his usual determined and uncompromising fashion. Voted the Supporters' Club Player of the Year, one of the fans' favourite features of his play is his work in getting forward at set pieces, where flick ons caused panic and led to goals.
Shrewsbury T (Free from Newtown on 27/3/92) FL 96+6/3 FLC 7+1 FAC 6 Others 6/1
Chesterfield (£50,000 on 7/8/95) FL 128/9 FLC 7 FAC 12/1 Others 6

WILLIAMS Martin Keith
Born: Luton, 12 July 1973
Height: 5'9" Weight: 11.12
Martin played some of the best football of his career under Terry Bullivant at Reading in 1997-98, proving to be a regular goalscorer in a struggling side, his pace, spirit, and willingness to take players on making him a vital member of the midfield. Although failing to impress the incoming manager, Tommy Burns, and failing to feature in any of his line-ups, despite scoring in six consecutive reserve team appearances, he is still under contract, however, and should still have the opportunity to play an important role as the club attempts to regain division one status.
Luton T (Free from Leicester C juniors on 13/9/91) FL 12+28/2 FLC 1 FAC 0+1 Others 2+1
Colchester U (Loaned on 9/3/95) FL 3
Reading (Free on 13/7/95) FL 57+16/10 FLC 6+3/2 FAC 3+1

WILLIAMS Michael (Mike) Anthony
Born: Bradford, 21 November 1969
Height: 5'10" Weight: 11.6
Having suffered from a whole range of injuries over the previous couple of seasons, including a broken leg, Mike was freed by Sheffield Wednesday during the 1997 close season and moved over the Pennines to join Burnley. Expected to replace Gary Parkinson at right back, he played almost exclusively in midfield where, despite his pace often bothering the opposition, he was not a regular due to recurring injury problems.
Sheffield Wed (Free from Maltby MW on 13/2/91) F/PL 16+7/1 FLC 3+2 Others 1
Halifax T (Loaned on 18/12/92) FL 9/1
Huddersfield T (Loaned on 18/10/96) FL 2
Peterborough U (Loaned on 27/3/97) FL 6
Burnley (Free on 18/7/97) FL 13+1/1 FLC 2 FAC 2 Others 1

WILLIAMS Michael John
Born: Stepney, 9 October 1978
Height: 6'1" Weight: 12.5
A first-year Leyton Orient professional who performs equally well up front or in central defence, Michael made his debut as a substitute against Rotherham last October and showed himself to be a big, strong player with a penchant for getting stuck in. Was surprisingly released during the summer.
Leyton Orient (From trainee on 8/7/97) FL 0+1

WILLIAMS Paul Anthony
Born: Stratford, 16 August 1965
Height: 5'7" Weight: 10.9
Club Honours: FLC '91; Div 1 '94
International Honours: E: B-3; U21-4
After a brief Southend first team run, Paul was injured last September, and a subsequent disagreement with manager, Alvin Martin, saw him spend the final three months of the season on loan to Canvey Island, before being released during the summer. A team player with a lot to offer, and hoping to get his league career back on track in 1998-99, his lightning speed and good close control is almost certain to be put to good use elsewhere in the league.
Charlton Ath (£12,000 from Woodford T on 23/2/87) FL 74+8/23 FLC 6/3 FAC 6+1/3
Brentford (Loaned on 20/10/87) FL 7/3 Others 1/3
Sheffield Wed (£700,000 on 15/8/90) F/PL 78+15/25 FLC 10+3/3 FAC 3+2 Others 3
Crystal Palace (Signed on 11/9/92) F/PL 38+8/7 FLC 4+1 Others 2/2
Sunderland (Loaned on 19/1/95) FL 3
Birmingham C (Loaned on 13/3/95) FL 8+3 Others 1/1
Charlton Ath (Free on 29/9/95) FL 2+7
Torquay U (Loaned on 28/3/96) FL 9
Southend U (Free on 30/8/96) FL 30+9/7 FLC 1+2/2 FAC 1

WILLIAMS Paul Darren
Born: Burton, 26 March 1971
Height: 6'0" Weight: 13.0
International Honours: E: U21-6
A hard-tackling Coventry midfield player, who can also play in the centre of defence, Paul had a hard time with referees in 1997-98, being booked five times in the first six games, and suspended before the end of September. Following being sent off at Villa Park for two yellow cards, and at Highfield Road in a controversial incident with Dennis Bergkamp, he used his enforced absence to have a minor operation on a niggling hernia injury, but, despite being up and running again, was unable to regain a starting place before the end of the season.
Derby Co (From trainee on 13/7/89) FL 153+7/26 FLC 10+2/2 FAC 8/3 Others 14+1/2
Lincoln C (Loaned on 9/11/89) FL 3 FAC 2 Others 1
Coventry C (£975,000 on 6/8/95) PL 76+8/4 FLC 10/1 FAC 6

WILLIAMS Paul Richard Curtis
Born: Leicester, 11 September 1969
Height: 5'7" Weight: 11.0
An ever dependable Plymouth left back/ wing back, not only is Paul a strong tackler, but is extremely quick, a feature of his play that allows him to cover his defensive colleagues. Always willing to go forward, and often one of the most potent attacking

options in the team, he looks to take on the opposition and supplies excellent crosses into the danger zone. A player whose future is in the balance, he missed a number of vital games during the relegation dogfight and the outcome might have been more favourable with his services intact.*
Leicester C (From trainee on 1/7/88)
Stockport Co (Free on 5/7/89) FL 61+9/4 FLC 3 FAC 4 Others 7+5/1
Coventry C (£150,000 on 12/8/93) PL 8+6 FLC 1+1 FAC 3
West Bromwich A (Loaned on 19/11/93) FL 5
Huddersfield T (Loaned on 17/11/94) FL 2 Others 1
Huddersfield T (Loaned on 17/3/95) FL 7
Plymouth Arg (£50,000 on 10/8/95) FL 131/4 FLC 6 FAC 8 Others 7/1

WILLIAMS Scott John
Born: Bangor, 7 August 1974
Height: 6'0" Weight: 12.0
International Honours: W: U21-5; Yth
True to form in 1997-98, Scott remained Wrexham's unluckiest player with injuries, which leads one to forget at times that he was still involved at the Racecourse, as his appearances were very rare. However, this is doing him an injustice, as he is still young and can still make an impression. Tall and slim for a full back, the Welsh U21 cap is composed and skilful on the ball with good distribution and can play in any number of other positions in both midfield and defence. Was released during the summer.
Wrexham (From trainee on 2/7/93) FL 26+6 FLC 1 Others 2+2

WILLIAMSON Daniel (Danny) Alan
Born: West Ham, 5 December 1973
Height: 5'11" Weight: 12.3
A polished midfielder from the east end of London, Danny became missing in action throughout most of his first season at Everton, following a 1997 summer move from West Ham. A regular in the Everton line-up until December, when he sustained hamstring and foot injuries which kept him out for the rest of the campaign, he is clearly a promising player and Evertonians are still waiting to see the best of him. Hopefully, in 1998-99, he will shake off the injury hoodoo of the past two years, and get the trouble-free run that his passing abilities and skill on the ball deserve.
West Ham U (From trainee on 3/7/92) PL 47+4/5 FLC 0+2 FAC 5
Doncaster Rov (Loaned on 8/10/93) FL 10+3/1 FAC 2/2 Others 1
Everton (Signed on 14/8/97) PL 15 FLC 2

WILLIAMSON David (Davey) Francis
Born: Hong Kong, 15 December 1975
Height: 5'6" Weight: 10.3
A free transfer signing from Motherwell in August 1996, having failed to make a first team start for Cambridge in 1996-97, this nippy, attacking midfielder was looking for a breakthrough last season but struggled to make the necessary impact, being limited to nine appearances, four of them from the bench. Disappointingly, he was released in mid-March and moved to non-league Kingstonian.

329

Motherwell (Free from Irvine Vic on 7/9/95)
Cambridge U (Free on 3/8/96) FL 2+4 FLC 2
Others 1

WILLIS Roger Christopher
Born: Sheffield, 17 June 1967
Height: 6'1" Weight: 12.0
Club Honours: GMVC '91
International Honours: E: SP-1

Transferred to Chesterfield from Peterborough during the 1997 close season, as befits a player of Roger's experience, he has a good footballing brain and is always looking to get other forwards going with astute passes. He can also be a bit of a handful in the air too. Signed as "utility" player, he was expected to fill a midfield or wing-back berth, but emerged as an unlikely scorer after three games, before being laid low by injury. Subsequently, he found opportunities rather limited and became a regular substitute until reclaiming a place in the forward line in March, and finishing as the Spireites' top scorer.
Grimsby T (Signed from Dunkirk on 20/7/89) FL 1+8 FLC 0+1
Barnet (£10,000 on 1/8/90) FL 39+5/13 FLC 2 FAC 5+1/3 Others 1+4/1
Watford (£175,000 on 6/10/92) FL 30+6/2 FAC 1
Birmingham C (£150,000 on 31/12/93) FL 12+7/5 FAC 0+1
Southend U (Signed on 16/9/94) FL 30+1/7 FAC 1 Others 1
Peterborough U (Free on 13/8/96) FL 34+6/6 FLC 3 FAC 5+1 Others 5
Chesterfield (£100,000 on 11/7/97) FL 19+15/8 FLC 3/2 FAC 1+1/1 Others 1

WILSON Clive Euclid Aklana
Born: Manchester, 13 November 1961
Height: 5'7" Weight: 11.4
Club Honours: Div 2 '89

An experienced fringe player who made his breakthrough into the Tottenham side last November as injuries took their toll on the back four, Clive is capable of playing on the right or left flank, and in maintaining a tremendous level of personal fitness, his experience could always be relied on when called upon. A busy player, who is confident on the ball, and likes to get into the opponents half, he remained an important squad player who can deliver quality crosses and long balls with great accuracy. With competition for places in the back four hotting up, rumours of a move in the close season surfaced, fuelled by Clive's enthusiasm to play regular first team football for as long as possible. Still has a great deal to offer, and is versatile enough to fill a midfield role if called upon.*
Manchester C (From juniors on 8/12/79) FL 96+2/9 FLC 10/2 FAC 2 Others 5
Chester C (Loaned on 16/9/82) FL 21/2
Chelsea (£250,000 on 19/3/87) FL 68+13/5 FLC 3+3 FAC 4 Others 10+2
Manchester C (Loaned on 19/3/87) FL 11
Queens Park R (£450,000 on 4/7/90) F/PL 170+2/12 FLC 16/1 FAC 8/1 Others 2+1
Tottenham H (Free on 12/6/95) PL 67+3/1 FLC 7 FAC 7+1/1

WILSON Kevin James
Born: Banbury, 18 April 1961
Height: 5'8" Weight: 11.4
Club Honours: Div 2 '89; FMC '90
International Honours: NI: 42

Having been turned down for the job of manager at Walsall, the former Northern Ireland international striker joined Northampton during the 1997 close season as assistant to Ian Atkins, while still keeping his playing options open. Although first team appearances were few and far between, when called upon, Kevin always gave his best and, despite being 37 this year, still held his own against many who are younger. His enthusiasm cannot be questioned, and throughout the campaign he could often be seen leaping from his place on the bench, offering instructions.
Derby Co (£20,000 from Banbury U on 21/12/79) FL 106+16/30 FLC 8+3/8 FAC 8/3
Ipswich T (£100,000 on 5/1/85) FL 94+4/34 FLC 8/8 FAC 10/3 Others 7/4
Chelsea (£335,000 on 25/6/87) FL 124+28/42 FLC 10+2/4 FAC 7+1/1 Others 14+5/8
Notts Co (£225,000 on 27/3/92) FL 58+11/3 FLC 3+1 FAC 2 Others 5+1
Bradford C (Loaned on 13/1/94) FL 5
Walsall (Free on 4/8/94) FL 124+1/38 FLC 8/3 FAC 13/7 Others 6/1
Northampton T (Free on 28/7/97) FL 1+8 FAC 0+1

WILSON Mark Antony
Born: Scunthorpe, 9 February 1979
Height: 5'11" Weight: 12.2
International Honours: E: Yth; Sch

As you would probably expect, the Manchester United starlet was by far the pick of the three loan players on view at Wrexham during 1997-98. Skilful and direct, Mark was the club's leading goalscorer during his two-and-a-half month stay, netting several of the memorable variety, such as on his Football League debut at Burnley when he cut in from the right wing to beat the 'keeper from 15 yards for the winner, and against Brentford at the Racecourse, when a weaving run saw him confound a number of defenders before unleashing a powerful shot into the corner of the net. Back at United in time for 1998-99, the young central midfielder, cum forward, could be a future star.
Manchester U (From trainee on 16/2/96)
Wrexham (Loaned on 23/2/98) FL 12+1/4

WILSON Patrick (Padi)
Born: Manchester, 9 November 1971
Height: 5'8" Weight: 10.5

Signed from non-league football just before the start of last season, the strong forward started 1997-98 as a consistent member of the Plymouth first team squad, but gradually fell out of favour with the management and moved to Doncaster early in the New Year. Having scored his first senior goal for Argyle against Oxford in the Coca Cola Cup, Padi was signed with a view to solving Rovers' goalscoring problems and looked a tricky customer in his initial outings. Unfortunately, his first spell at Belle Vue was truncated due to a custodial sentence awarded for motoring offences, while his second spell saw him as a member of a side relegated to the Conference.
Plymouth Arg (£45,000 from Ashton U on 9/8/97) FL 7+4/1 FLC 1+1/1 FAC 1+1
Doncaster Rov (Free on 22/1/98) FL 10/1

WILSON Paul Anthony
Born: Bradford, 2 August 1968
Height: 5'11" Weight: 12.2

Having been at Cambridge at the end of 1996-97, on loan from Scunthorpe, the move became permanent during the 1997 close season on Paul becoming a free agent. A regular in the side at left back until the first week in February, scoring six goals, all from penalties or free kicks, he lost his place to Ian Ashbee and spent the remainder of the campaign on the bench, before being freed at the end of June.
Huddersfield T (From apprentice on 12/6/86) FL 15 FLC 1
Norwich C (£30,000 on 23/7/87)
Northampton T (£30,000 on 12/2/88) FL 132+9/6 FLC 10/1 FAC 7 Others 6+3
Halifax T (£30,000 on 19/12/91) FL 45/7 FLC 2 FAC 1 Others 2
Burnley (Signed on 1/2/93) FL 31 FAC 0+1
York C (Signed on 6/10/94) FL 21+1 FAC 2 Others 1
Scunthorpe U (Signed on 9/8/95) FL 77/2 FLC 4 FAC 6 Others 4
Cambridge U (Free on 27/3/97) FL 38/5 FLC 2 FAC 4/1

WILSON Paul Robert
Born: Forest Gate, 26 September 1964
Height: 5'9" Weight: 12.0
Club Honours: GMVC '91

As Barnet's longest-serving player, Paul continued to keep younger men on the sidelines in 1997-98, missing just ten games throughout a long and arduous campaign that ended at the semi-final stage of the third division play offs. Uncompromising in the tackle, and the club's spot-kick king, he can also score goals away from set pieces, and is the only man remaining from Barnet's non-league side.
Barnet (Signed from Barking on 1/3/88) FL 201+12/21 FLC 11+1/1 FAC 21+1 Others 9+3/1

WILSON Stephen (Steve) Lee
Born: Hull, 24 April 1974
Height: 5'10" Weight: 10.12

The current longest serving Tiger has had to battle for Hull City goalkeeping supremacy with Alan Fettis and Roy Carroll (both Northern Ireland internationals) in the past and lost his senior place again when the club's only 1997 close season signing was the experienced custodian, Scott Thomson. However, "Wilo" regained the number one shirt in September, missing only one more game, giving a string of fine displays, and grabbing wider attention with an astonishing performance at Selhurst Park that saw Crystal Palace knocked out of the Coca Cola Cup. His slender frame will always leave him at a disadvantage, but improved distribution has backed up his dependable shot-stopping ability.
Hull C (From trainee on 13/7/92) FL 130+1 FLC 9 FAC 8 Others 9+1

WILSON Stuart Kevin
Born: Leicester, 16 September 1977
Height: 5'8" Weight: 9.12

A promising young Leicester midfielder, Stuart made regular appearances from the bench as 1997-98 progressed, displaying plenty of potential, and contributing goals at

Blackburn when he charged down the 'keeper's clearance to score, and at home to Coventry. Definitely one for the future, of whom Martin O'Neill has great hopes for the coming season, he was voted the Young Player of the Season by the Supporters' Club. Excellent speed and crossing ability are other features of his game.

Leicester C (From trainee on 4/7/96) PL 0+13/3 FLC 0+1 FAC 0+4

WILSTERMAN Brian Hank
Born: Surinam, 19 November 1966
Height: 6'1" Weight: 12.8

Brian enjoyed a better season at Oxford in 1997-98, especially following the injury to Phil Whelan, when he notched up nine of his 16 starts in a short-time period. A centre back, he was perhaps unlucky not to appear more often, but now sees his chances of games being limited by the Steve Davis/Phil Gilchrist partnership, which Oxford ended the season successfully with. A steady all-rounder, built on a career in Holland and Belgium, he will no doubt work hard to regain a place. Has yet to score a first team goal.

Oxford U (£200,000 from Beerschot on 28/2/97) FL 16+9 FLC 1

WINSTANLEY Mark Andrew
Born: St Helens, 22 January 1968
Height: 6'1" Weight: 12.7
Club Honours: AMC '89

Burnley's defensive formation was changed many times during last season, and Mark, after losing his normal place in central defence, unexpectedly re-emerged on the left with a licence to go forward, in addition to his duties at the back. Solid in the tackle at his best, although occasionally prone to defensive lapses, he did reasonably well when fit, in a side which spent most of the campaign staring relegation in the face.*

Bolton W (From trainee on 22/7/86) FL 215+5/3 FLC 19+1 FAC 19 Others 26/3
Burnley (Signed on 5/8/94) FL 150+1/5 FLC 13 FAC 8 Others 8+1

WINTERBURN Nigel
Born: Nuneaton, 11 December 1963
Height: 5'9" Weight: 11.4
Club Honours: Div 1 '89, '91; PL '98; FAC '93, '98; FLC '93; ECWC '94
International Honours: E: 2; B-3; U21-1; Yth

Despite strong rumours during the summer of 1997 that Arsenal were about to sign Graeme le Saux from Blackburn, the long-serving Gunners' left back made more Premiership appearances than any other player and, at the same time, took home a championship medal for his pains. He would also have been delighted to have won an FA Cup winners' medal, following the 2-0 win over Newcastle at Wembley. Not one of the game's great scorers, his one league goal was not only a stunner, but a vital one at that, securing both points at Chelsea with a long-range 89th minute drive that took the score to 3-2. A tough-tackling left back who likes nothing better than getting down the line to supply accurate crosses to the

forwards, and noted for his long throws, he is also recognised for his ability to pass long balls into the channels. As assured as ever, Nigel developed a good understanding with Marc Overmars.

Birmingham C (From apprentice on 14/8/81)
Wimbledon (Free on 22/9/83) FL 164+1/8 FLC 13 FAC 12 Others 2
Arsenal (£407,000 on 26/5/87) F/PL 380+2/8 FLC 48/3 FAC 41 Others 34

WISE Dennis Frank
Born: Kensington, 16 December 1966
Height: 5'6" Weight: 10.10
Club Honours: FAC '88, '97; FLC '98; ECWC '98
International Honours: E: 12; B-3; U21-1

The past 12 months have been remarkable for Dennis Wise. In May 1997 he became the first Chelsea captain to lift the FA Cup at Wembley, the first of three trophies, and then began 1997-98 playing the best football of his career. Such was his outstanding form as the "dynamo" in Chelsea's vibrant midfield, that even that hard taskmaster, Ruud Gullit, expressed astonishment that "Wisey" was not part of Glenn Hoddle's England plans. As the debate rages over the foreign influx into the Premiership, it is obvious that playing alongside such class midfielders as Roberto di Matteo, Gustavo Poyet, and Dan Petrescu has brought an added dimension to Dennis's game. Despite that, however, his robust approach incurred the wrath of referees, and 14 bookings brought two lengthy suspensions and, coupled with a toe injury, meant another enforced lay off. It is an indication of the skipper's value to the team that his periods on the sidelines coincided with a slump in Chelsea's form. Having produced outstanding performances in the Coca Cola and Cup Winners' Cup finals, creating crucial goals in each match before lifting the trophies, this sparky, ebullient character epitomises the spirit of Chelsea.

Wimbledon (Free from Southampton juniors on 28/3/85) FL 127+8/27 FLC 14 FAC 11/3 Others 5
Chelsea (£1,600,000 on 3/7/90) F/PL 237+7/46 FLC 27/6 FAC 25/6 Others 20/3

WITTER Anthony (Tony) Junior
Born: London, 12 August 1965
Height: 6'1" Weight: 13.0

Despite still being one of the quickest defenders around, and equally good with either foot, Tony found it hard to hold down a regular spot in the centre of Millwall's defence in 1997-98, due to much competition. However, in the final months, he got back into the side because of suspension and injuries to others and saw out the season on a high, prior to being released in the summer. A player with great pace, who loves to get forward, and is good in the challenge, he is also a great favourite with the crowd.

Crystal Palace (£10,000 from Grays Ath on 24/10/90)
Queens Park R (£125,000 on 19/8/91) PL 1
Plymouth Arg (Loaned on 9/1/92) FL 3/1
Reading (Loaned on 11/2/94) FL 4
Millwall (£100,000 on 14/10/94) FL 99+3/2 FLC 8 FAC 8

WOAN Ian Simon
Born: Heswall, 14 December 1967
Height: 5'10" Weight: 12.4
Club Honours: Div 1 '98

Never first choice on the wide left at Nottingham Forest in 1997-98, due to the excellent form shown by Chris Bart-Williams, and injuries, but when he was called up for first team duty he rarely let the side down. Still a talented left-footed player, who can perform anywhere down the left flank, he can both play or drive balls in, has a lovely touch, a wide range of passing skills, and rarely allows himself to be hurried, something which is sometimes mistakenly taken for laziness. Scored in the 5-2 home win over Charlton, his lone goal of the campaign.

Nottingham F (£80,000 from Runcorn on 14/3/90) F/PL 188+20/31 FLC 15+3/1 FAC 20+1/6 Others 13/2

WOOD Steven (Steve) Ronald
Born: Oldham, 23 June 1963
Height: 5'9" Weight: 10.10

The veteran of the Macclesfield team, having always played for fringe teams around the east Manchester area, Steve is the fearless terrier of the midfield, the team's highest scorer in the Conference championship side, and also in their first season in the Football League. Despite fracturing a cheekbone last September, requiring an operation to relieve a trapped eye nerve, he missed only three matches and, in December, he fractured the other cheek, but was back after only one match wearing a "Zoro" style face mask. Is the joker of the team, both on and off the field.*

Macclesfield T (Free from Ashton U on 22/7/93) FL 43/13 FLC 2 FAC 1/2 Others 1

WOODHOUSE Curtis
Born: Beverley, 17 April 1980
Height: 5'8" Weight: 11.0

Called into the England U18 squad during 1997-98, Curtis also made his Football League debut for Sheffield United while still a trainee, mainly due to injuries suffered by Dane Whitehouse and Wayne Quinn, both left-sided players. Rushed into action, he came off the bench at Bramall Lane against Crewe at the end of November and was then involved in the next eight games as a wing back before going down with a knee injury himself. Having signed professional forms on the last day of 1997, this very promising youngster recovered well to come back for one subs' appearance before the season ended.

Sheffield U (From trainee on 31/12/97) FL 4+5 FAC 1

WOODMAN Andrew (Andy) John
Born: Camberwell, 11 August 1971
Height: 6'3" Weight: 13.7

As Northampton's first team goalkeeper, with a larger than life personality, Andy is confident on crosses and a fine shot-stopper, and complimented a good back four by making the defence one of the best in the division in 1997-98. Often getting the crowd

behind him when "conducting" their singing, and acknowledging their encouragement, once again his name was linked with several Premiership clubs, but he still firmly remains a Cobbler, being the club's only ever present during the campaign.

Crystal Palace (From trainee on 1/7/89)
Exeter C (Free on 4/7/94) FL 6 FLC 1 FAC 1 Others 2
Northampton T (Free on 10/3/95) FL 145 FLC 8 FAC 8 Others 13

WOODS Christopher (Chris) Charles Eric
Born: Boston, 14 November 1959
Height: 6'2" Weight: 14.12
Club Honours: Div 2 '86; FLC '78, '85; SPD '87, '89, '90, '91; SLC '87, '89, '91
International Honours: E: 43; B-2; U21-6; Yth

Joining Burnley during the 1997 close season, having been released by Sunderland, the former England 'keeper unexpectedly returned to league action following the March departure of Marlon Beresford. Playing in a side facing relegation, he proved that much of the old ability was still in place, a spectacular double save against Grimsby showing him at his best.*

Nottingham F (From apprentice on 1/12/76) FLC 7
Queens Park R (£250,000 on 4/7/79) FL 63 FLC 8 FAC 1
Norwich C (£225,000 on 12/3/81) FL 216 FLC 26 FAC 19 Others 6
Glasgow R (£600,000 on 2/7/86) SL 173 SLC 21 SC 15 Others 21
Sheffield Wed (£1,200,000 on 15/8/91) F/PL 106+1 FLC 13 FAC 10 Others 5
Reading (Loaned on 27/10/95) FL 5 (Free to Colorado Rapids on 10/5/96)
Southampton (Free on 2/11/96) PL 4 FLC 2
Sunderland (Free on 27/3/97)
Burnley (Free on 17/7/97) FL 12 Others 2

WOODS Matthew (Mattie) James
Born: Gosport, 9 September 1976
Height: 6'1" Weight: 12.13

Mattie completed his second season with Chester City in 1997-98, having made 31 appearances, mainly in defence. Also capable of operating in midfield to good effect, with a penchant to get forward and have a crack at goal, he scored a 70th-minute equaliser at Shrewsbury, following a tremendous 20-yard shot.

Everton (From trainee on 1/7/95)
Chester C (Free on 12/8/96) FL 33+17/3 FLC 0+3/1 FAC 3 Others 2+1

WOODS Neil Stephen
Born: York, 30 July 1966
Height: 6'0" Weight: 12.11

The right-footed, old-style centre forward, who is particularly adept at holding the ball up, shielding it, and then laying it off, was unable to regain a regular place at Grimsby, following a change of managership, and spent abortive loans spells at Wigan, Scunthorpe, and Mansfield, before returning to Blundell Park. At Wigan he played just once before suffering a hamstring injury, at Scunthorpe he arrived into a struggling team and managed just two starts before a change in style did not suit his abilities, while at Mansfield there was no permanent transfer

to be had after six appearances. A tried and trusted target man, he was released by Town during the summer.

Doncaster Rov (From apprentice on 31/8/83) FL 55+10/16 FLC 4/1 FAC 5/2 Others 5+2/3
Glasgow R (£120,000 on 22/12/86) SL 0+3
Ipswich T (£120,000 on 3/8/87) FL 15+12/5 Others 4/1
Bradford C (Signed on 1/3/90) FL 13+1/2
Grimsby T (£82,000 on 23/8/90) FL 175+51/42 FLC 11+3/2 FAC 8+2/3 Others 8/1
Wigan Ath (Loaned on 6/11/97) FL 1
Scunthorpe U (Loaned on 19/1/98) FL 2
Mansfield T (Loaned on 16/2/98) FL 5+1

WOODS Stephen (Steve) John
Born: Davenham, 15 December 1976
Height: 5'11" Weight: 11.13

After serving a long apprenticeship in Stoke's reserve and junior sides, Steve's patience was finally rewarded with a substitute appearance in the home game against Huddersfield Town. He had caught manager Chris Kamara's eye in the reserves and, despite being on the transfer list, was happy with the call. Acquitted himself well, but jumped at the chance of a loan spell at Plymouth on transfer deadline day, where he performed admirably, looking comfortable on the ball, before returning to the Victoria Ground.

Stoke C (From trainee on 3/8/95) FL 0+1
Plymouth Arg (Loaned on 26/3/98) FL 4+1

WOODTHORPE Colin John
Born: Ellesmere Port, 13 January 1969
Height: 5'11" Weight: 11.8

Signed during the 1997 close season from Aberdeen, having spent the last three years, almost to the day, in the Scottish Premiership, the seasoned defender was picked up by his former Norwich team mate and current Stockport manager, Gary Megson, with a view to stabilising the defence of a club that was due to get its first-ever taste of first division football. Unfortunately, troublesome back and calf injuries, and competition from a resurgent Damon Searle, restricted his opportunities at left back, but his experience showed through when filling in as a useful midfielder. Still has a year left to run on his contract.

Chester C (From trainee on 23/8/86) FL 154+1/6 FLC 10 FAC 8+1 Others 18/1
Norwich C (£175,000 on 17/7/90) F/PL 36+7/1 FLC 0+2 FAC 6 Others 1+1
Aberdeen (£400,000 on 20/7/94) SL 43+5/1 SLC 5+1/1 SC 4 Others 5+2
Stockport Co (£200,000 on 29/7/97) FL 29+3/1 FLC 4/1

WOODWARD Andrew (Andy) Stephen
Born: Stockport, 23 September 1973
Height: 5'11" Weight: 13.6
Club Honours: Div 2 '97

After patiently waiting in the wings in 1997-98, Bury's versatile defender found himself given a regular chance in Stan Ternent's first division side, and he grasped the opening with both hands. Able to perform equally well at centre half, or at full back, he chipped in with a string of consistent performances, mainly at right back, showing himself to be solid in the

tackle and eager to forage forward. With the relegation battle over, "Woody" is now an integral and highly respected member of the Shakers' squad.

Crewe Alex (From trainee on 29/7/92) FL 9+11 FLC 2 Others 0+3
Bury (Signed on 13/8/95) FL 45+19 FLC 1+2 FAC 2 Others 5

WOOLSEY Jeffrey (Jeff) Alexander
Born: Upminster, 8 November 1977
Height: 5'11" Weight: 12.3

Released by Arsenal during the 1997 close season, the young defender spent several months on Queens Park Ranger's books without an opportunity before being signed by Brighton manager, Brian Horton, on a one-month contract in March, and making his debut as a late substitute for skipper, Gary Hobson, in the tremendous 2-2 draw with the new champions, Notts County, at Meadow Lane. Jeff will obviously be looking to firm up his contract with Albion this summer.

Arsenal (From trainee on 4/7/96)
Queens Park R (Free on 30/8/97)
Brighton & Hove A (Free on 25/3/98) FL 1+2

WORMULL Simon James
Born: Crawley, 1 December 1976
Height: 5'10" Weight: 12.3

Signed from Spurs during the 1997 close season, Simon showed himself to be a hard-working Brentford right-sided midfielder with good passing ability in 1997-98. After making his debut for the Bees on the opening day, and playing in the next two matches before a few appearances as a sub, he was left out of the side for four months before being recalled in January by new manager, Micky Adams, for three games. Was released by the club in March and joined Brighton on a monthly contract.

Tottenham H (From trainee on 1/7/95)
Brentford (Free on 14/7/97) FL 3+2 FLC 1+1 Others 1
Brighton & Hove A (Free on 25/3/98)

WORRALL Benjamin (Ben) Joseph
Born: Swindon, 7 December 1975
Height: 5'7" Weight: 11.6
International Honours: E: Yth

One of the smallest players currently playing in the Football League, Ben was hugely popular with Scarborough supporters in 1997-98 for his tremendous workrate. A real midfield dynamo, and the kind of player every team needs, both of his goals last season came in a 3-1 home win over Cardiff in April, as the Boro pushed for a play-off place.

Swindon T (From trainee on 8/7/94) FL 1+2
Scarborough (Free on 2/8/96) FL 20+16/3 FLC 2+2 Others 2+1

WORTHINGTON Nigel
Born: Ballymena, 4 November 1961
Height: 5'11" Weight: 12.6
Club Honours: FLC '91
International Honours: NI: 66; Yth

Having joined Blackpool from Stoke in the summer of 1997 as player/manager, the former Northern Ireland international was not expecting to see too much action, but

due to both Anton Rogan and Darren Bradshaw being unavailable he appeared a few times in the problem left-back spot until managing to sort out something more permanent. That dealt with, and at 38 years of age, Nigel decided it was better to concentrate on the management side of things and saw no more action after the end of November.

Notts Co (£100,000 from Ballymena on 1/7/81) FL 62+5/4 FLC 11 FAC 4 Others 3
Sheffield Wed (£125,000 on 6/2/84) F/PL 334+4/12 FLC 41/1 FAC 29 Others 9/1
Leeds U (£325,000 on 4/7/94) PL 33+10/1 FLC 4+1 FAC 6+1
Stoke C (Free on 18/7/96) FL 12 FLC 3/1
Blackpool (Free on 14/7/97) FL 4+5

WOTTON Paul Anthony
Born: Plymouth, 17 August 1977
Height: 5'11" Weight: 12.0
Having come through the Plymouth ranks as a trainee, Paul established himself as a valuable member of the first team squad in 1997-98 after deciding that central defence was his best position. Settling into the role, using his fine speed to curtail opposition forays, and comfortable on the ball, he was a good link between defence and midfield. And, getting stronger in the air, it appears that he will develop into a very talented defender. Scored a superb goal against Preston North End in the 2-0 home victory, when driving home from the edge of the area.

Plymouth Arg (From trainee on 10/7/95) FL 41+10/2 FLC 2 FAC 4 Others 4+1/2

WRACK Darren
Born: Cleethorpes, 5 May 1976
Height: 5'9" Weight: 12.2
After a bleak 1996-97 season, the change of managership at Grimsby in 1997-98 did little to revive this locally born player's career, a handful of appearances as substitute being his only first team outings during the campaign. However, as a lively right-footed wingman with the ability to put over excellent crosses, he is bound to be back.

Derby Co (From trainee on 12/7/94) FL 4+22/1 FLC 0+3 FAC 0+2
Grimsby T (£100,000 + on 19/7/96) FL 5+8/1 Others 0+1
Shrewsbury T (Loaned on 17/2/97) FL 3+1 Others 1

WRAIGHT Gary Paul
Born: Epping, 5 March 1979
Height: 5'7" Weight: 11.11
A young right-footed midfielder, promoted from Wycombe's youth team of the previous season, Gary made three appearances in 1997-98, one of them starting as a left-wing back, and the other two while substituting as a right-wing back, and acquitted himself well.

Wycombe W (From trainee on 1/7/97) FL 1 Others 0+2

WREH Christopher (Chris)
Born: Liberia, 14 May 1975
Height: 5'7" Weight: 11.13
Club Honours: PL '98; FAC '98
International Honours: Liberia: 7

Another signing from Monaco, Arsene Wenger's former club, the Liberian striker moved to Arsenal at the start of the 1997-98 Premiership season and made his debut as a 70th-minute sub in the club's opening UEFA Cup fixture against POAK Salonika. Obviously needing more time to settle, Chris failed to impress in the early games but, called back into the side for what turned out to be the championship run-in, he scored the only goals of the games at Wimbledon and Bolton, and then booked his place in the FA Cup final with the winner in the 1-0 semi-final clash against Wolves. The cousin of George Weah, the brilliant AC Milan striker, and like his famous relative a Liberian international, following the 2-0 FA Cup final win over Newcastle at Wembley he could boast of winning both championship and FA Cup medals in his first English campaign, as the Gunners raced to the double. Very fast, skilful, and two footed, the biggest compliment you could pay him is to say that he is similar in style to Ian Wright, the man he kept on the sidelines on FA Cup Final day.

Arsenal (£300,000 from Monaco on 14/8/97) PL 7+9/3 FLC 1+2 FAC 2+4/1 Others 0+1

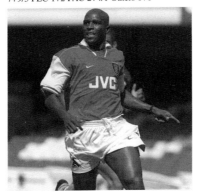

Chris Wreh

WRIGHT Alan Geoffrey
Born: Ashton under Lyne, 28 September 1971
Height: 5'4" Weight: 9.9
Club Honours: FLC '96
International Honours: E: U21-2; Yth; Sch
As always a player you can rely upon for being consistency personified, this left-sided Aston Villa full back, cum wing back, was ever present in 1997-98, bar one game, and never wavered, despite the side being in the bottom half for most of the campaign. In short, he has an excellent attitude, which was best portrayed when he stated that the club were good enough to get into the top six, having won just seven of their opening 23 league games. On the verge of an England cap at one stage of his career, Alan linked well with the likes of Steve Staunton down the left flank, producing all the skill and pace of a winger when getting forward to deliver superb crosses and, in doing so, continued to show all the traits of a natural footballer. Is also great in the air for one so small.

Blackpool (From trainee on 13/4/89) FL 91+7 FLC 10+2 FAC 8 Others 11+2
Blackburn Rov (£400,000 on 25/10/91) F/PL 67+7/1 FLC 8 FAC 5+1 Others 3
Aston Villa (£1,000,000 on 10/3/95) PL 119+2/3 FLC 11 FAC 12 Others 10

WRIGHT Anthony (Tony) Allan
Born: Swansea, 19 September 1979
Height: 5'9" Weight: 11.8
International Honours: W: B-1; U21-2; Yth
A midfielder, Tony made a brief first team debut for Oxford in 1997-98, when appearing for 12 minutes against Tranmere towards the end of the campaign, having already made a dramatic entry into international football when called into the Wales U21 side against Belgium, and adding to that cap later on, as well as being recognised at "B" level. Another of United's exciting youngsters, of which much will be expected in the new season, he was rewarded for his good work with a professional contract before the end of his YTS contract.

Oxford U (From trainee on 10/12/97) FL 0+1

WRIGHT Darren
Born: Warrington, 7 September 1979
Height: 5'6" Weight: 10.0
Yet another product of Chester City's youth policy, Darren made his Football League debut as a substitute in the 5-0 defeat at Exeter last April, prior to making his full debut at Darlington a couple of games later. A fast, strong running forward, he is sure to be a crowd pleaser in the future.

Chester C (Trainee) FL 3+2 Others 0+1

WRIGHT David
Born: Warrington, 1 May 1980
Height: 5'11" Weight: 10.8
A first-year Crewe professional, the young defender had a run out last season as a sub, making his first team debut when coming off the bench in a 2-0 win at Norwich in August. Thought of very highly at Gresty Road, this was followed by two further subs' appearances towards the end of the campaign and, all in all, he showed himself to be a very capable youngster.

Crewe Alex (From trainee on 18/6/97) FL 0+3

WRIGHT Ian Edward
Born: Woolwich, 3 November 1963
Height: 5'10" Weight: 11.8
Club Honours: PL '98; FMC '91; FLC '93; FAC '93, '98
International Honours: E: 31; B-3
1997-98 was a strange season for the Arsenal striker in many ways. He started it with the club's opening goal of the campaign, at Leeds, scored the next two at home to Coventry, before cracking in a hat trick during the 4-1 win at Highbury against Bolton that propelled him into the Gunners' record books as their greatest goalscorer of all time – overtaking Cliff Bastin's 178 league and cup goals total that had stood since 1938-39. A few days earlier he had scored two of England's goals in the World Cup qualifier 4-0 win over Moldova at Wembley. However, from thereon it was

almost downhill, despite playing three more times for England, as the goals gradually dried up just before Christmas, and a series of niggling injuries, including a hamstring problem, saw him in and out of the side for the rest of the campaign. Even when fit, he often lost out to the emerging Nicolas Anelka, and with Dennis Bergkamp leading the way to goals, it looked as thought the Gunners could maybe manage without him. Although coming back as a sub in the 4-0 home win over Everton – the game that saw Arsenal clinch the championship – he was surprisingly not called off the bench during the FA Cup final victory over Newcastle, even though Bergkamp was out injured. Then, having finished 1997-98 on a high, collecting both championship and FA Cup winners' medals, a recurrence of the hamstring injury kept him out of France '98. He later announced on ITV that it was time to explore different avenues and that he would be meeting Arsene Wenger to discuss such matters. *Stop Press:* According to press reports, Ian transferred to West Ham on 13 July, a £750,000 fee securing a two-year deal.

Crystal Palace (Free from Greenwich Borough on 2/8/85) FL 206+19/89 FLC 19/9 FAC 9+2/3 Others 19+3/16
Arsenal (£2,500,000 on 24/9/91) F/PL 212+9/128 FLC 29/29 FAC 16/12 Others 22/16

WRIGHT Ian Matthew
Born: Lichfield, 10 March 1972
Height: 6'1" Weight: 13.4

Cartilage trouble last December and an ankle knock in January brought "the other" Ian Wright's season to a stuttering halt. Having hit the national headlines in September, when he headed home the all-important away goal for third division Hull City, that dumped Premiership, Crystal Palace, out of the Coca Cola Cup, the solid, uncomplicated centre half, refused new terms and was set to leave the club at the end of the campaign.*

Stoke C (From trainee on 11/7/90) FL 6 FLC 1+1 Others 1
Bristol Rov (Signed on 23/9/93) FLC 2+1 FAC 2 Others 5+1
Hull C (Free on 2/7/96) FL 65+8/2 FLC 7/1 FAC 4 Others 3/1

WRIGHT Jermaine Malaki
Born: Greenwich, 21 October 1975
Height: 5'9" Weight: 11.9
International Honours: E: Yth

Primarily a winger, but able to occupy a more central role if required, Jermaine's first team chances at Wolves last season were again limited, mainly to that of a substitute. Having come on four times in the club's first nine matches, making an impact against Bury when his right-footed cross gave Steve Bull the chance to convert, he went back to the reserves before signing for Crewe in February. Made five appearances for Alex in a variety of positions, and will give Dario Gradi further options in 1998-99.

Millwall (From trainee on 27/11/92)
Wolverhampton W (£60,000 on 29/12/94) FL 4+16 FLC 1+3/1 Others 0+1
Doncaster Rov (Loaned on 1/3/96) FL 13
Crewe Alex (£25,000 on 19/2/98) FL 3+2

WRIGHT Mark
Born: Dorchester, 1 August 1963
Height: 6'3" Weight: 13.3
Club Honours: FAC '92
International Honours: E: 45; U21-4

Injuries and non-selection saw the centre back have a season of mixed fortunes in 1997-98, his age beginning to count against him, even though he still looks a class act when wearing the red shirt of Liverpool. His tackling was as tough as ever, while his positional sense and tactical awareness make him difficult to replace, though these days younger men force him on to the sidelines not by their ability but by their youth. Just seven games being his sum total. At his best, Mark was a player who always appeared to have plenty of time of the ball.

Oxford U (From juniors on 26/8/80) FL 8+2 FAC 1
Southampton (£80,000 on 25/3/82) FL 170/7 FLC 25/2 FAC 17/1 Others 10/1
Derby Co (£760,000 on 27/8/87) FL 144/10 FLC 15 FAC 5 Others 7
Liverpool (£2,200,000 on 15/7/91) F/PL 156+2/5 FLC 14+2/1 FAC 18 Others 18/1

WRIGHT Nicholas (Nick) John
Born: Derby, 15 October 1975
Height: 5'9" Weight: 11.7

After arriving on loan from Derby County and making his Football League debut against Bristol City at the end of last November, Nick's skilful wing play, allied to a willingness to battle for the cause, made him one of the most popular loanees ever to pull on a Carlisle jersey, and he signed a permanent contract three months later. Scored United's final league goal of 1997-98, the second in a 3-2 defeat at Luton, having earlier weighed in with some important goals, including a brace in the victory at Preston, and created several others, notably for centre forward, Ian Stevens.

Derby Co (From trainee on 12/7/94)
Carlisle U (£35,000 on 28/11/97) FL 25/5 Others 2/2

WRIGHT Richard Ian
Born: Ipswich, 5 November 1977
Height: 6'2" Weight: 13.0
International Honours: E: U21-8; Yth; Sch

Richard continued to blossom at Ipswich in 1997-98, maintaining a high level of consistency between the posts, which helped to further his international career with call-ups to the England U21 and "B" sides. He was also asked to train with the England first team squad for the Chile game. An ever present, although it would seem that during Town's unbeaten run he often had little to do, it was sometimes quite the opposite - his saves protected the run. Showed his bravery in the Oxford home game, when he had a boot in the face which saw him leave the pitch for treatment and play the next few games in a mask, looking as if he had strayed from the "Phantom of the Opera". Is extremely agile for a big man, getting down to low shots very quickly, and also kicks long and hard.

Ipswich T (From trainee on 2/1/95) P/FL 112 FLC 13 FAC 8 Others 6

WRIGHT Stephen
Born: Bellshill, 27 August 1971
Height: 5'10" Weight: 11.6
International Honours: S: 2; B-2; U21-14

Signed by Wolves on loan from Glasgow Rangers last March, this very experienced Scottish international right back failed to achieve as much as he would have liked, mainly due to injuries. Despite making a torrid debut at Ipswich, where Wolves were beaten 3-0, he looked more composed in the next match before returning to Ibrox.

Aberdeen (Free from Eastercraigs on 28/11/87) SL 141+7/1 SLC 11+1 SC 13 Others 3
Glasgow R (Signed on 5/7/95) SL 7 SLC 5 Others 6+1
Wolverhampton W (Loaned on 20/3/98) FL 3

WRIGHT Thomas (Tommy) Elliott
Born: Dunfermline, 10 January 1966
Height: 5'7" Weight: 11.4
International Honours: S: U21-1; Yth

Signed from Bradford early on in 1997-98, Tommy made 13 appearances for Oldham while still on a month-by-month contract but, unable to agree terms on a permanent basis, he departed for Kilmarnock at the end of November. As a fast and tricky attacking right winger, who is capable of providing good service to the front men, he is also capable of getting a few goals himself and, before departing, he had added another two to his collection.

Leeds U (From apprentice on 15/1/83) FL 73+8/24 FLC 3+2/1 FAC 4/3
Oldham Ath (£80,000 on 24/10/86) FL 110+2/23 FLC 7+1/2 FAC 3/2 Others 3
Leicester C (£350,000 on 14/8/89) FL 122+7/22 FLC 7+1 FAC 4 Others 10/7
Middlesbrough (£650,000 on 1/7/92) F/PL 44+9/5 FLC 3+1 FAC 3/1 Others 5+1
Bradford C (Free on 4/7/95) FL 30+15/5 FLC 6+1/2 FAC 1+1 Others 2+1
Oldham Ath (Free on 29/8/97) FL 10+2/2 FAC 1

WRIGHT Thomas (Tommy) James
Born: Belfast, 29 August 1963
Height: 6'1" Weight: 14.5
Club Honours: Div 1 '93
International Honours: NI: 29; U23-1

Having missed the end of the 1996-97 campaign because of an injury, the Manchester City goalkeeper was hoping to be available for selection at the start of 1997-98, but, unfortunately injured in a pre-season friendly at Falkirk, he was sidelined for the opening games. Although match fit by mid-September, he could not get back into the side, due to the excellent form shown by Martyn Margetson and, despite playing for Northern Ireland against Albania, had to bide his time at club level. Having come back at the end of October to play just three times before breaking again, he next returned in December to put in a run of 17 games until a knee injury finally ended his season. A highly experienced shot-stopper, Tommy is known for setting up attacks with quick throws and excellent long kicks.

Newcastle U (£30,000 from Linfield on 27/1/88) F/PL 72+1 FLC 6 FAC 4 Others 3
Hull C (Loaned on 14/2/91) FL 6
Nottingham F (£450,000 on 24/9/93) P/FL 11 FLC 2
Reading (Loaned on 4/10/96) FL 17
Manchester C (Loaned on 17/1/97) FL 5
Manchester C (£450,000 on 3/3/97) FL 26 FAC 2

XAUSA Davide
Born: Vancouver, Canada, 10 March 1976
Height: 6'0" Weight: 12.7
In having one of the shortest careers in length of time in Stoke's history, Davide, a Canadian junior international who had been freed by Port Vale after a trial, was signed up by Chris Kamara on a similar basis last February. Following an injury crisis, he was quickly called up to play in the first team at Bury, and then made the bench for the next game, but showed nothing of consequence and was released, joining St Johnstone until the end of the season.
Port Vale (Free from Vancouver on 14/1/98)
Stoke C (Free on 12/2/98) FL 1

YATES Dean Richard
Born: Leicester, 26 October 1967
Height: 6'2" Weight: 12.6
Club Honours: AIC '95
International Honours: E: U21-5
This tall Derby central defender, who possesses the control and vision more associated with continental sweepers, would be a regular first team choice if fit, but had another injury hit season in 1997-98, only managing three full months in the side. Tending to play on the left of a three-man central defence, the team looked much more secure upon his return, keeping three clean sheets in succession in December, but the spell failed to last and Dean was out of action from early February onwards, before being given a free transfer during the summer.
Notts Co (From apprentice on 14/6/85) FL 312+2/33 FLC 24 FAC 20 Others 36/4
Derby Co (£350,000 on 26/1/95) F/PL 65+3/3 FLC 3 FAC 3

YATES Stephen (Steve)
Born: Bristol, 29 January 1970
Height: 5'11" Weight: 12.2
Club Honours: Div 3 '90
Until last November he had only been used as a substitute for Queens Park Rangers in 1997-98, but once installed in the side he rediscovered his excellent form of the previous season and became one of the key men who successfully fought off relegation to the second division. Capable of playing in the centre of the defence, or in both full-back slots, Steve is a hard-tackling, but fair defender who works hard for the team and rarely gets flustered. Is also good in the air.
Bristol Rov (From trainee on 1/7/88) FL 196+1 FLC 9 FAC 11 Others 21
Queens Park R (£650,000 on 16/8/93) P/FL 116+12/2 FLC 5 FAC 7

YORKE Dwight
Born: Canaan, Tobago, 3 November 1971
Height: 5'10" Weight: 12.4
Club Honours: FLC '96
International Honours: Trinidad & Tobago: 16

Starting 1997-98 off in a midfield role for Aston Villa, playing behind Savo Milosevic and Stan Collymore, mainly to accommodate the latter, Dwight looked rather uncomfortable for a while and took some time to settle down. Despite him describing his season as "so,so", especially during the time when he had a lean spell in terms of goals, and was out of action for a number of games due to a calf operation, on his day he still looked an exciting player who used his pace to advantage when running at defenders. A natural athlete with great balance and a lovely left foot, he continued to pick up goals, 16 in league and cup games making him Villa's leading scorer, several of them vital to the cause. Among them were winners at Derby and Southampton, and at Villa Park against Leeds and Arsenal, to go with braces at Everton and Coventry, and seven goals in the last seven games went a long way towards pushing the club from 11th in the table to a respectable seventh. Continued to play for Trinidad and Tobago.
Aston Villa (£120,000 from Signal Hill on 19/12/89) F/PL 194+36/75 FLC 20+2/8 FAC 22+2/13 Others 10/3

YOUDS Edward (Eddie) Paul
Born: Liverpool, 3 May 1970
Height: 6'1" Weight: 13.0
A hero at Bradford, after missing the whole of 1996-97 with serious knee injuries he came back to play every game bar one in 1997-98 before being transferred to Charlton on transfer deadline day. Having shown such excellent form, the transfer came as a bitter blow to many at Valley Parade, but for the big, strong central defender it was business as usual, and he immediately won over the Addicks' supporters with his rugged, no-nonsense style. Good in the air, and a ferocious tackler, Eddie marshals the defence well, likes to get forward for corners and set pieces, and in building a good understanding with Richard Rufus, looks to be a shrewd investment.
Everton (From trainee on 10/6/88) FL 5+3 FLC 0+1 Others 1
Cardiff C (Loaned on 29/12/89) FL 0+1 FAC 0+1
Wrexham (Loaned on 8/2/90) FL 20/2
Ipswich T (£250,000 on 15/11/91) F/PL 38+12/1 FLC 1+2 FAC 5+1
Bradford C (£175,000 on 2/1/95) FL 85/8 FLC 7/2 FAC 3 Others 4
Charlton Ath (£550,000 on 26/3/98) FL 8 Others 3

YOUNG Neil Anthony
Born: Harlow, 31 August 1973
Height: 5'9" Weight: 12.0
Neil had another consistent season at right back for Bournemouth in 1997-98, producing some fine displays and breaking his scoring duck for the club when finishing the season with two goals. An athletic full back, who is adept at moving forward to support the attacking players, his surging runs down the wing often end in dangerous crosses being delivered into dangerous areas.
Tottenham H (From trainee on 17/8/91)
Bournemouth (Free on 11/10/94) FL 159+2/2 FLC 7 FAC 9 Others 11

YOUNG Scott
Born: Pontypridd, 14 January 1976
Height: 6'2" Weight: 12.6
International Honours: W: B-1; U21-5
Dependable and solid, good on the ground, and in the air, the Welshman is strong and consistent, and a player who will surely play a big part in Frank Burrows' plans for Cardiff in 1998-99. Not at his best in 1997-98, but worked hard to put things right, he played at centre half, right back, in a more forward role just behind midfield, and in midfield during last season, but his favoured position is at centre half. There will be plenty of competition for that spot this coming season, though, with Lee Jarman, Jeff Eckhardt, and Lee Phillips all ready to stake their claims as well, but Scott, in the middle of a two-year contract, is ready to bounce back. Played for the Welsh "B" side in March against the Scottish equivalent.
Cardiff C (From trainee on 4/7/94) FL 118+14/4 FLC 7+1 FAC 10 Others 12+3/1

YOUNGS Thomas (Tom) Anthony John
Born: Bury St Edmunds, 31 August 1979
Height: 5'9" Weight: 10.4
With Cambridge since the age of ten, this intelligent forward made his first team debut last September as a substitute at the Abbey against Colchester, and nearly scored with his first touch. Having been given his first start in the Auto Windscreen Shield at Bristol Rovers, followed by another in the home league game against Doncaster, he is expected to be one of United's stars of the future.
Cambridge U (From juniors on 3/7/97) FL 1+3 Others 1

ZABEK Lee Kevin
Born: Bristol, 13 October 1978
Height: 6'0" Weight: 12.0
Having made a breakthrough to replace the experienced Bristol Rovers' player/manager, Ian Holloway in 1997-98, Lee, who has a Polish grandfather, proved to be a good ball winner and distributor from central midfield, and scored his first league goal, a powerful header, in the last minute at Millwall. Rewarded with a four-year contract, he will provide strong competition for a first team place in 1998-99, especially after appearing in the final few matches of the season and then being involved in the second division play offs.
Bristol Rov (From trainee on 28/7/97) FL 9+5/1 Others 3

ZABICA Robert
Born: Perth, Australia, 9 April 1964
Height: 6'5" Weight: 12.10
International Honours: Australia: 20
A former Australian international goalkeeper, Robert joined Bradford from Spearwood Dalminatic just as last season was getting underway, and came into the side as a replacement for Mark Prudhoe to make his first team debut in a 1-1 home draw against Huddersfield in the Coca Cola Cup. Unfortunately, having lost his place after just four games, he suffered a whole range of injuries that ultimately saw his

contract terminated by mutual consent in February.

Bradford C (£175,000+ from Spearwood Dalmatinac on 21/8/97) FL 3 FLC 1

ZAGORAKIS Theodoros (Theo)
Born: Kavala, Greece, 27 October 1971
Height: 5'9" Weight: 11.6
International Honours: Greece: 35

A right-footed midfielder and captain of the Greek national team, Theo was signed from PAOK Salonika last February after a brief trial period at Leicester. Keen to sample life in the Premiership, he soon impressed the Filbert Street faithful with his hard running and powerful shot, and showed signs of settling quickly into English football, whilst still learning the language. Likely to be a key player for City next season, his first goal for them was the strike that, mathematically at least, ended Barnsley's Premiership tenure.

Leicester C (£750,000 from PAOK Salonika on 6/2/98) PL 12+2/1

ZOETEBIER Eduard (Ed) Andreas
Born: Permerend, Holland, 7 May 1970
Height: 6'3" Weight: 13.7

A Dutch goalkeeper, signed from Volendam during the 1997 close season, Ed was expected to seriously pressurise Lionel Perez for the Sunderland goalkeeping jersey in 1997-98. However, the Frenchman's good form restricted him to just two Coca Cola Cup appearances and, frustrated, he returned to Holland in mid-January, joining Feyenoord.

Sunderland (£325,000 from FC Volendam on 22/7/97) FLC 2

ZOHAR Itzhak (Itzy)
Born: Tel Aviv, Israel, 31 October 1970
Height: 6'2" Weight: 12.4
International Honours: Israel: 30

An interesting signing from Antwerp a week into 1997-98, having had a great deal of difficulty over a work permit, this ball-winning midfielder, and an experienced Israeli international, made his first team bow as a sub for Crystal Palace in a 3-0 Premiership defeat at Chelsea, six games into the new season. However, although he sat on the bench in a good many games he only made four starts and four subs' appearances before having his contract cancelled and leaving for Maccabi Haifa in January. Never happy playing in the reserves, where he missed two penalties, prior to moving on, Itzhak came off the bench in the Christmas game at Selhurst Park against Southampton and missed an 82nd minute penalty, which would have given the side its first win for seven matches. Never really settling to show off his passing skills, Steve Coppell stated: "Itzy fell a long way short of what I expected and I accept total responsibility."

Crystal Palace (£1,000,000 from Antwerp on 20/8/97) PL 2+4 FLC 2

ZOIS Peter
Born: Australia, 21 April 1978
Height: 6'0" Weight: 12.2

With Jon Hallworth out through injury, Peter arrived unexpectedly one February evening in 1997 from non-league Purfleet, and played in goal for Cardiff City against Rotherham United at home, having earlier trialled at Spurs and West Ham. After all, following the departure of Tony Elliott to Scarborough, City did not have a senior back-up 'keeper with experience. However, on the night, the Australian did not look at all happy at any time, and his eccentric goalkeeping, in a game that ended 2-2, led manager, Frank Burrows, to end his trial period immediately. Surely, the Cardiff City career of Zois will become a quiz question – the player whose name began with Z who only played once for the club.

Cardiff C (Free from Purfleet on 23/2/98) FL 1

ZOLA Gianfranco
Born: Sardinia, Italy, 5 July 1966
Height: 5'6" Weight: 10.10
Club Honours: FAC '97; FLC '98; ECWC '98
International Honours: Italy: 35

Chelsea's first-ever Player of the Year began last season in fairly subdued fashion, quietly concerned over his own lack of form, before returning to his very best in November and grabbing the headlines dramatically. After Italy's qualification for France '98 was confirmed, he curled home two of his unstoppable free kicks in consecutive matches – against Tromso and West Ham, and then, on the last Saturday of the month, scored his first hat trick in senior football as the Blues demolished Derby County 4-0 to draw level on points with Manchester United at the top of the Premiership. In the New Year, the little Italian hit a purple patch in Chelsea's Cup Winners' Cup campaign, scoring with a sweet left-foot drive against Real Betis in the quarter final, second leg at the Bridge. Then, with Chelsea trailing to Vicenza in the semi final, second leg, he sent a bullet of a header past the 'keeper to level the scores, prior to Mark Hughes grabbing the winner. Despite sustaining a groin injury against Liverpool, and looking certain to miss the final against VFB Stuttgart 19 days later, he returned to Italy for intensive treatment and, incredibly, was passed fit to play, although he spent 70 goalless minutes on the substitutes' bench. However, called on to replace Tore Andre Flo, with his second touch he slammed Dennis Wise's through ball past the goalkeeper for the only goal of the game. Gianfranco has made an incalculable contribution to Chelsea's success over the past 12 months and his love affair with Chelsea's fans continues. Sadly, though, Cesare Maldini seems less enamoured, and from being a certainty for the Italian's World Cup squad, after his outstanding performances in the qualifiers, he slipped down the pecking order, despite his dazzling ball skills and dead-ball ability, which allows him to compete with the very best.

Chelsea (£4,500,000 from Parma, via Napoli, Torres and Nuorese, on 15/11/96) PL 45+5/16 FLC 4 FAC 8/4 Others 8+1/4

Gianfranco Zola

FA Carling Premiership and Nationwide League Clubs : Summary of Appearances and Goals for 1997-98.

KEY TO TABLES: P/FL = Premier/Football League. FLC = Football League Cup. FAC = FA Cup. Others = Other first team appearances.
Left hand figures in each column list number of full appearances + appearances as substitute. Right hand figures list number of goals scored.

ARSENAL (PREM: 1st)

	P/FL App	P/FL Goals	FLC App	FLC Goals	FAC App	FAC Goals	Others App	Others Goals
Adams	26	3	2		6		2	
Anelka	16+10	6	3		8+1	3	1+1	
Bergkamp	28	16	4	2	7	3	1	1
Bould	21+3		3		4+1		2	
Crowe			0+1		0+1			
Dixon	26+2		3		7		2	
Garde	6+4				1			
Grimandi	16+6	1	4		3+2			
Hughes	7+10	2	3+2	1	3+3			
Keown	18		2		7			
McGowan	0+1							
Manninger	7		4		5			
Marshall	1+2		1+1					
Mendes -Rodriguez	1+2		2	1				
Muntasser			0+1					
Overmars	32	12	3	2	8+1	2	2	
Parlour	34	5	4		7	1	2	
Pereira	4+11		1	2	1+3		0+1	
Petit	32	2	3		7		2	
Platt	11+20	3	2+2	1	1+3		0+2	
Rankin	0+1							
Seaman	31		1		4		2	
Upson	5		2		1			
Vernazza	1							
Vieira	31+2	2	2		8+1		2	
Winterburn	35+1	1	3		8		2	
Wreh	7+9	3	1+2		2+4	1	0+1	
Wright	22+2	10	1	1	1		2	

ASTON VILLA (PREM: 7th)

	P/FL App	P/FL Goals	FLC App	FLC Goals	FAC App	FAC Goals	Others App	Others Goals
Barry	1+1							
Bosnich	30		1		4		7	
Byfield	1+6				0+1			
Charles	14+4	1	0+1		0+1		2+3	
Collymore	23+2	6	1		4	1	6+1	1
Curcic	3+4		0+1				0+1	
Draper	31	3	1		4		7	
Ehiogu	37		1		4		6	
Grayson	28+5		0+1		4	2	4+2	
Hendrie	13+4	3			2+2		2+1	
Joachim	16+10	8			1+1		1+1	
Milosevic	19+4	7	1		2	1	6	2
Nelson	21+4		1		1		5+2	
Oakes	8						1	
Scimeca	16+5		1		2+1		4	
Southgate	32		1		3		7	
Staunton	27	1			4	1	7+1	
Taylor	30+2	6	1		3		8	3
Townsend	3							
Walker	0+1							
Wright	35+2		1		4		8	
Yorke	30	12	1		2	2	7	2

BARNET (DIV 3: 7th)

	P/FL App	P/FL Goals	FLC App	FLC Goals	FAC App	FAC Goals	Others App	Others Goals
Adams	4+7	1						
Basham	19+1	1					3	
Charlery	18+14	6	4		1	1	2+1	
Devine	37+3	16	4	2			2	
De Vito	0+1							
Doolan	17							
Ford	19		4		1			
Goodhind	22+13	1	3+1				3	1

BARNET cont.

	P/FL App	P/FL Goals	FLC App	FLC Goals	FAC App	FAC Goals	Others App	Others Goals
Harle	42+1	2	4		1		2	
Harrison	46		4		1		3	
Heald	43	3	4	1	1		2	1
Howarth	45	4	4		1		3	
McDonald	1		0+1					
McGleish	37	13			1		2+1	
Manuel	10+7		2+1		1		0+3	
Mills	5+1		1					
Mustafa	2+9		0+1					
Onwere	11+6		2+1		0+1		1	
Samuels	0+22	2	0+3		0+1		0+1	
Sawyers	1						1	
Searle	26+4	2			1		3	
Simpson	27+4	4	3				2+1	
Stockley	40+1		4		1		3	
Wilson	34+5	5	1+1		1		1+1	1

BARNSLEY (PREM: 19th)

	P/FL App	P/FL Goals	FLC App	FLC Goals	FAC App	FAC Goals	Others App	Others Goals
Appleby	13+2		1+1		1+1			
Barnard	33+2	2	3		5	2		
Bosancic	13+4	2			3+1			
Bullock	23+10		1+1		3+2			
De Zeeuw	26		2		5			
Eaden	32+3		2		5			
Fjortoft	12+3	6						
Hendrie	7+13	1			4	2		
Hristov	11+12	4	1+2	1	1+1			
Jones	12				1		2	
Krizan	12		3		1			
Leese	8+1		2					
Liddell	13+13	1	2	2	1+4	1		
Marcelle	9+11		0+2		3+1			
Markstedt	6+1				1			
Morgan	10+1				3			
Moses	32+3		2		6			
Redfearn	37	11	3	2	6	2		
Sheridan	20+6		3	1	3+1			
Shirtliff	4		1					
Ten Heuvel	0+2		0+1					
Thompson	3		1					
Tinkler	21+4	1	2		2			
Ward	28+1	8	3	1	6	1		
Watson	30		1		6			
Wilkinson	3+1							

BIRMINGHAM CITY (DIV 1: 7th)

	P/FL App	P/FL Goals	FLC App	FLC Goals	FAC App	FAC Goals	Others App	Others Goals
Ablett	34+2		5		3		1	
Adebola	16+1	7						
Bass	30		3+1		3			
Bennett	45		5		3			
Bruce	40	2	2		3			
Charlton	23+1				1			
Cottee	4+1	1						
Devlin	13+9	5	5	3	0+1			
Forinton	0+1							
Forster	12+16	3			3			
Francis	2+18	1	0+5	1	0+2			
Furlong	24+1	15	4	2	2	2		
Gill	3							
Grainger	27+6	2	4+1		3			
Hey	8+1		2	1				
Holland	2+8		3					
Hughes	34+6	5	4	1	3	2		

BIRMINGHAM CITY cont.

	P/FL App	P/FL Goals	FLC App	FLC Goals	FAC App	FAC Goals	Others App	Others Goals
Johnson	22+16	3	1+4		0+2			
McCarthy	41	3			3			
Marsden	31+1	1			2			
Ndlovu	29+10	9	5	1	1+1	1		
O'Connor	32+1	1	3		3			
Poole	1							
Purse	2+6							
Robinson	17+8		4	1	0+1			
Wassall	14		5					

BLACKBURN ROVERS (PREM: 6th)

	P/FL App	P/FL Goals	FLC App	FLC Goals	FAC App	FAC Goals	Others App	Others Goals
Andersson	1+3		3	1	0+1			
Beattie	0+3		1		0+1			
Bohinen	6+10	1	1+1	1	0+1			
Broomes	2+2		1					
Coleman			1					
Croft	19+4	1	3		2			
Dahlin	11+10	4	2	2	0+1			
Davidson	1							
Duff	17+9	4	2+1		3+1	1		
Fettis	7+1				1			
Filan	7							
Flitcroft	28+5		1+1		2+1			
Flowers	24+1		3		3			
Gallacher	31+2	16	0+1	1	4	3		
Henchoz	36		0+1		4			
Hendry	34	1	1		4			
Johnson			1					
Kenna	37		1		4			
McKinlay	26+4		2	1	3			
Pearce	1+4							
Pedersen P			1+1					
Pedersen T	3+2		3					
Ripley	25+4	2			3	1		
Sherwood	29+2	5	1+1		4	2		
Sutton	35	18	2	1	4	2		
Valery	14+1		2		1+1			
Wilcox	24+7	4	1		2+2			

Chris Sutton (Blackburn Rovers)

BLACKPOOL (DIV 2: 12th)

	P/FL App	P/FL Goals	FLC App	FLC Goals	FAC App	FAC Goals	Others App	Others Goals
Banks	45		4		2		3	
Barnes	1							
Bent	25+11	3			2		3	
Bonner	32	3	4		2		1	
Brabin	15+9	3	2		1		0+2	
Bradshaw	6		3					
Bryan	43	1	4		1		3	
Butler	37		2		2		2	
Carlisle	8+3	2					1	
Clarkson	42+3	13	3		2	2	3	1
Conroy	5+1							
Dixon	6+1				2		1	
Ellis	18	8	2+1		2	1		
Foster	1							
Greenacre	2+2							
Haddow	0+1							
Hills	19	1			2			
Hughes	20+1						3	
King	6							
Linighan	26+3		3	2	1	1	2	
Longworth	0+2				0+1			
Lydiate	22+1	1	3+1		2		1	
Malkin	13+7	2	0+3		0+1		0+1	
Mellon	9+1		3					
Nowland	0+1							
Ormerod	5+4	2			0+1		3	
Philpott	27+8	2	3		2		0+1	
Preece	42+2	11	4	1	1	1	3	1
Quinn	11+3	4	3				0+1	
Reed	0+3				1			
Rogan	1		1					
Strong	11	1					1	
Taylor	3+2	1						
Thompson	1							
Worthington	4+5							

BOLTON WANDERERS (PREM: 18th)

	P/FL App	P/FL Goals	FLC App	FLC Goals	FAC App	FAC Goals	Others App	Others Goals
Aljofree	2							
Beardsley	14+3	2	3		0+1			
Bergsson	34+1	2	3		1			
Blake	35	12	3	2	1			
Branagan	34		3					
Carr	0+5							
Cox	20+1	1			0+1			
Elliott	4							
Fairclough	10+1							
Fish	22	2	1		1			
Frandsen	38	2	4	1	1			
Giallanza	0+3							
Gunnlaugsson	2+13		0+3	1	1			
Holdsworth	17+3	3						
Johansen	4+12	1	1+2					
McAnespie	1+1		2					
McGinlay	4+3		2+1	2				
Phillips	21+1	1	1+1					
Pollock	25+1	1	4	1	1			
Salako	0+7							
Sellars	22	2	3		1			
Sheridan	12							
Strong			1+1					
Taggart	14+1		1					
Taylor	10+2	3						
Thompson	33	9	4	1	1			
Todd	23+2		4	1	1			
Ward	4+2		1		1			
Whitlow	13		3		1			

BOURNEMOUTH (DIV 2: 9th)

	P/FL App	P/FL Goals	FLC App	FLC Goals	FAC App	FAC Goals	Others App	Others Goals
Bailey	30+2	1	2		1+1		5	1
Beardsmore	28+1	1	1		2	1	3	1
Brissett	13+18	1	0+2		1		2+2	
Cox	46	3	2		3		6	
Dean	3+5						1	
Fletcher C	0+1							
Fletcher S	42	12	2		3	1	6	
Glass	46		2		3		6	
Harrington	4+4		0+1		1+1			
Hayter	0+5							
Howe	31+9	1	1+1		3		3+2	
Jones	5	4					1	1
Murray	0+4		0+1		0+1			
O'Neill	34+9	3	2		3	1	4+2	
Rawlinson	16+9		2		1+1		1	
Robinson	45	10	2		3	2	6	1
Rolling	26+4	4	2	1	0+2		3	3
Stein	11	4					3	
Teather	5+5						1+1	
Tomlinson	6+1	1						
Town	0+7		0+1					
Vincent	43+1	3	2		3		5	1
Warren	29+1	6			3		4	
Young	43+1	2	2		3		6	

BRADFORD CITY (DIV 1: 13th)

	P/FL App	P/FL Goals	FLC App	FLC Goals	FAC App	FAC Goals	Others App	Others Goals
Beagrie	31+3		2		1			
Blake	23+11	7	0+2		1			
Bolland	2+8							
Bower	1+2							
Davies	1+3							
Dreyer	15+2		2					
Edinho	34+7	10	2	1				
Grant	1+2							
Jacobs	36	2	2		1			
Kulcsar	14+3	1						
Lawrence	38+5	3	2		1			
McAnespie	7							
McGinlay	12+5	3			0+1			
Melville	6	1						
Midgley	0+2				0+1			
Moore	18							
Murray	29+9		2		1			
O'Brien	23+3				1			
O'Kane	7							
Pepper	31+1	5	2		1			
Prudhoe	8		1					
Ramage	24+8	1	0+1					
Sepp	0+3							
Sinnott	7							
Small	5							
Steiner	26+11	10	2	1	1			
Sundgot	0+5		0+1					
Verity	0+1							
Walsh	35				1			
Wilder	31+4		2		1			
Youds	38	1	2		1			
Zabika	3		1					

BRENTFORD (DIV 2: 21st)

	P/FL App	P/FL Goals	FLC App	FLC Goals	FAC App	FAC Goals	Others App	Others Goals
Adams							0+1	
Anderson	17		4					
Aspinall	24	3					1	
Barrowcliff	5+6		3		2			
Bates	40	1	4		2		1	
Benstead	1							
Bent	19+5	4	3	1	2			
Blaney	4+1							
Bryan	2+9	2			0+1			

BRENTFORD cont.

	P/FL App	P/FL Goals	FLC App	FLC Goals	FAC App	FAC Goals	Others App	Others Goals
Canham	11+11		2+2		0+1		1	
Clark	0+4						0+1	
Cockerill	23				2			
Colgan	5							
Cullip	13							
Dearden	35		4		2		1	
Dennis	0+5						0+1	
Denys	12+7	1	4	1			1	
Gleghorn	11	1					1	
Goddard -Crawley			0+2					
Hall	6							
Hogg	17	2						
Hurdle	17		4		1+1			
Hutchings	43	5	4		2			
McGhee	19+10	1	2		2			
McPherson	7+2				1			
Myall	2							
Oatway	30+3				2			
Omigie	0+1							
Pollitt	5							
Rapley	23+14	9	3+1	2	0+1		1	
Reina	2+4	1	0+1		2			
Scott	24+2	5					1	
Spencer	1		1					
Taylor	39+1	13	4	3	1	2	1	
Thompson	6+2							
Townley	15+1	1	1		1		1	1
Watson	25							
Wormull	3+2		1+1				1	

BRIGHTON & HOVE ALBION (DIV 3: 23rd)

	P/FL App	P/FL Goals	FLC App	FLC Goals	FAC App	FAC Goals	Others App	Others Goals
Allan	17+2	1			1		1	
Andrews	2+1							
Ansah	7+7	3			0+1		1	
Armstrong	12+8						1	
Atkinson	9							
Baird	9	1					1	
Barker	15+2	2			1			
Barnes	12							
Emblen	15	4						
Gislason	7							
Hilton	4+1							
Hobson	30+3		2		1			
Humphrey	11		2					
Johnson	38		2					
Linger	17+2						1	
McDonald	7+4	1	2		1			
McNally	1+1	1					0+1	
Mahoney -Johnson	3+1							
Maskell	16+1	2	2	1	1			
Mayo	43+1	6	2		1		0+1	
Minton	36	6	2	1	1			
Morris	19	1	2					
Ormerod	30		2				1	
Reinelt	25+7	4	2				1	
Rust	16				1			
Ryan	1+3	1						
Saul	0+4						1	
Smith	25+2	1	0+1		1		1	
Storer	33+4	2	2		1	1	1	
Streeter	0+2							
Thomas	7							
Tuck	19+3	1			1		1	
Westcott	19+15		0+2		1		0+1	
Woolsey	1+2							

BRISTOL CITY (DIV 2: 2nd)

	P/FL App	Goals	FLC App	Goals	FAC App	Goals	Others App	Goals
Barclay	0+8		0+1		0+1			
Bell	44	10	4		2		2	
Bent	0+2		0+2	1				
Brennan	4+2				1			
Carey	37+1		1+1		2		2	
Cramb	34+6	9	2		1	1	1+1	
Doherty	22+8	2	1		1			
Dyche	10+1		1					
Edwards	34+3	2	3		1		1	
Goater	28+5	17	3	1	2		1+1	
Goodridge	28+3	6	1+1	1	2		0+1	
Hewlett	27+7	4	3		1		1+1	
Johansen	2+1							
Langan	0+3				0+1			
Locke	35+2	1	3		2		2	1
McCarthy	7	1						
Murray	10+13				2			
Naylor	2							
Owers	20+2	1	4				2	
Paterson	7+3		3					
Plummer	0+1							
Roberts	1+2	1						
Shail	2							
Taylor	43	2	4	2	2	1	2	
Tinnion	44	3	4		1+1		2	
Tisdale	2+3		1+1		1			
Torpey	19+10	8	2		1		2	
Welch	44		4		2		2	

BRISTOL ROVERS (DIV 2: 5th)

	P/FL App	Goals	FLC App	Goals	FAC App	Goals	Others App	Goals
Alsop	10+7	1	2	1	1	1	2	
Basford	5+2						3	
Beadle	36+4	15	1+1		4	2	4+1	1
Bennett	8+11	2	1+1		0+2		3	2
Collett	30		2		5		1	
Cureton	39+4	13	2		2		2	1
Foster	32+2		1		3		4	
French	2+1				0+2			
Gayle	16		2					
Hayfield	9+9				3+1		1+2	
Hayles	45	23	2		5	2	3+2	2
Higgs	8						2	
Holloway	34+5		2		3	1	2	
Jones	8						2	
Lockwood	22+2		0+1		5		4+1	
Low	6+4				2+1		2	
Parmenter	1+3				0+1		1	
Penrice	38+2	5	2		5	1	3	
Perry	24+1		2		2+1		2	
Power	9+1						0+2	
Pritchard	32+1	1	1		5		3	
Ramasut	25+6	6			2		2	
Skinner	4							
Smith							2	
Tillson	32+1	3	2		3		3+1	1
White	22+2	1			5		1	
Whyte	0+4						0+1	
Zabek	9+4	1					3	

BURNLEY (DIV 2: 20th)

	P/FL App	Goals	FLC App	Goals	FAC App	Goals	Others App	Goals
Barnes	24+1	6	3		2			
Beresford	34		4		2		3	
Blatherwick	13+8		3		1+1		3	
Brass	37+3	1	3		2		3+1	
Carr-Lawton	0+1							
Cooke	26+8	16	2	1	2	1	5	2
Cowans	5+1		1		2			
Creaney	9+1	8	1					
Duerden	1							

BURNLEY cont.

	P/FL App	Goals	FLC App	Goals	FAC App	Goals	Others App	Goals
Eastwood	1+2							
Eyres	13	1	4	1				
Ford	32+4	1	2		0+1		4+1	
Gentile			1					
Gleghorn	1							
Harrison	33+2				0+2		3	
Henderson	0+7						0+3	1
Howey	21+2		3	1	2		0+1	
Hoyland	2+7						2+1	
Huxford	4		2+1					
Kiwomya	1+2							
Little	19+5	4	0+2				3	1
Matthew	21+6	1	3+1				2	
Moore	38+2	3	2		2	1	4	
Mullin	6							
Payton	19	9					5	3
Robertson	8+3						3+1	
Smith C	0+1							
Smith P	8+6				0+1		3	
Vinnicombe	20+3		2		1		3+1	1
Waddle	26+5	1	2+1		2			
Weller	32+7	2	2+1		2	1	2	
Williams	13+1	1	2		2		1	
Winstanley	27		2				4	
Woods	12						2	

BURY (DIV 1: 17th)

	P/FL App	Goals	FLC App	Goals	FAC App	Goals	Others App	Goals
Armstrong	33+4	2	3	1	2			
Barrass			0+1					
Battersby	28+9	6	3+1	1	2			
Butler	43	2	4		1			
Dalglish	1+11				1			
Daws	46	2	4	1	2			
Ellis	21+1	6						
Gray AA	21	1	3	1	2	2		
Gray AD	4+2	1						
Hughes	12+1		2+2					
Jemson	11+4	1						
Jepson	7+9		4	1	0+2			
Johnrose	44	3	4		2			
Johnson	17	5	4	3				
Kiely	46		4		2			
Linighan			0+2					
Lucketti	46	2	4		2			
Matthews	9+6							
Morgan	5							
Patterson	18	2			1			
Peake	3+3							
Pugh	1							
Randall	2+13		1+3					
Rigby	8+16	1			0+1			
Small	18	1						
Swailes	12+1	1			2			
Swan	26+11	6	1+1		1			
West	4		2					
Woodward	20+12		1+1		2			

CAMBRIDGE UNITED (DIV 3: 16th)

	P/FL App	Goals	FLC App	Goals	FAC App	Goals	Others App	Goals
Ashbee	27	1			4		1	
Barnwell	11+5	4			0+1		0+1	
Barrett	43		2		4		1	
Beall	25+5	1			4	1		
Benjamin	16+9	4	0+2		2+1	1		
Brebner	6	1						
Butler	28+3	10	2	1	2+2	2 1		
Campbell	46	2	2		4		1	
Charles	7	1						
Chenery	36	2	2		4			
Duncan	18+1							

CAMBRIDGE UNITED cont.

	P/FL App	Goals	FLC App	Goals	FAC App	Goals	Others App	Goals
Finney	4+3	2						
Foster	26	1	2		4			
Hayes	5+3						1	
Joseph Marc	37+4		2		0+1			
Joseph Matt	5+2		0+1				1	
Kyd	36+2	11	2	1	3+1		0+1	
Larkin	1							
McCammon	0+2				0+1		1	
Marshall	2							
Moore	0+1							
Preece	15+7				2		0+1	
Rees	17+3		2				1	
Rodesthenous	0+2						1	
Smith	0+1							
Taylor	19+15	10	0+2		3+1			
Wanless	42	8	2		4			
Wilde	0+2							
Williamson	2+4		2				1	
Wilson	31	5	2		4	1	1	
Youngs	1+3						1	

CARDIFF CITY (DIV 3: 21st)

	P/FL App	Goals	FLC App	Goals	FAC App	Goals	Others App	Goals
Beech	46	1	2		6			
Cadette	0+4							
Carss	36+6	1	2		5+1		1	
Crowe	7+1	1						
Dale	16+9	4			6	4		
Earnshaw	0+5						0+1	
Eckhardt	19+2	3			2+1			
Elliott	2+1				1		1	
Fowler	38	5	2	1	3+1	1		
Greenacre	11	2						
Hallworth	43		2		5			
Harriott								
Harris	38	1	2		6			
Hill	7							
Jarman	18+5		1+1		0+3		1	
Lloyd	0+2		0+2					
Middleton	28+5		2		6			
Nugent	2+2		1		2	1		
O'Sullivan	40+3	2	0+1		5	1	1	
Partridge	15+7	2	2		2		1	
Paterson	5							
Penney	32+2	5	1		6			
Phillips	7+1						0+1	
Roberts	5+6	3						
Rollo	3+2		0+1	1	0+2		1	
Saville	32+1	11			4+1	2		
Stoker	12+8	1	1+1		1+3		1	
White	12+17	2	2		0+1	1	1	
Young	31	3	2		6		1	
Zois	1							

CARLISLE UNITED (DIV 2: 23rd)

	P/FL App	Goals	FLC App	Goals	FAC App	Goals	Others App	Goals
Anthony	25	2					3	1
Archdeacon	18	4	4		1			
Aspinall	18		4	1	1			
Barr	39	3	4		1		2	
Boertien	8+1		0+2		1		1	
Bowman	6+1	1					1	
Caig	46		4		1		3	
Couzens	18+9	2	3	1			0+3	
Croci	1							
Delap	8+1		1				2	
Dobie	9+14	1	0+4		0+1		1+1	
Foster	7							
Gray	0+1							
Harrison	6+4		2					
Holloway	5							

CARLISLE UNITED cont.

	P/FL App	P/FL Goals	FLC App	FLC Goals	FAC App	FAC Goals	Others App	Others Goals
Hopper	16+ 3				0+1		1+1	
Hoyland	5							
Hughes	1							
Jansen	22+ 1	9	4	3	1		2	
Liburd	9							
McAlindon	16+12	3	3		1		1+2	1
Milligan	2+ 5		0+1				1	
Pagal	1							
Peacock	1+ 1							
Pounewatchy	39	2	3		1		2	1
Prokas	33+ 1		4		1		2	1
Sandwith	2+ 1							
Smart	16	6	1	1				
Stevens	33+ 4	17			1		3	2
Thorpe	12+ 2		1				1	
Varty	43+ 1	1	4		1		3	
Walling	6		2	1				
Wallwork	10	1					2	
Wright	25	5					2	2

CHARLTON ATHLETIC (DIV 1: 4th)

	P/FL App	P/FL Goals	FLC App	FLC Goals	FAC App	FAC Goals	Others App	Others Goals
Allen	7+ 5	2					0+2	
Balmer	13+ 3		2				0+1	
Barness	21+ 8	1	1		0+1		1+1	
Bowen	34+ 2				3		3	
Bright	13+ 3	7	0+2		2+1		3	
Brown	27+ 7	2	2		3	1	0+2	
Chapple	29+ 6	4	1		3			
Emblen	0+ 4							
Heaney	4+ 2						3	
Holmes	10+ 6	1			1+1			
Ilic	14						3	
Jones K	44	3	1		2+1	1	3	
Jones S	18+ 5	7	2		1		1+2	
Kinsella	46	6	2		3			
Konchesky	2+ 1		1					
Leaburn	13+ 1	3			1	1		
Lisbie	1+16	1	0+1					
Mendonca	40	23	2	1	2	1	2	3
Mills	9	1					2	
Mortimer	8+ 5	4					0+1	
Newton	33+ 8	5	2		3		3	1
Nicholls	1+ 5		1+1					
Parker	0+ 5				0+1			
Petterson	23		2		1			
Robinson	37+ 1	8	2		3	1	0+1	
Rufus	42		1		3		3	1
Salmon	9				2			
Stuart	0+ 1		0+1					
Youds	8						3	

CHELSEA (PREM: 4th)

	P/FL App	P/FL Goals	FLC App	FLC Goals	FAC App	FAC Goals	Others App	Others Goals
Babayaro	8		1+1				2+1	
Charvet	7+ 4	2	0+1				0+1	
Clark	22+ 4	1	4+2		1		7+1	
Crittenden	0+ 2		1					
De Goey	28		4		1		10	
Di Matteo	28+ 2	4	4	3	1		9	3
Duberry	23		3		1		6	
Flo	16+18	11	3+1	2	1		3+2	2
Granville	9+ 4		3				4+1	1
Gullit	0+ 6		3+1					
Hampshire			0+1					
Harley	3							
Hitchcock			2					
Hughes M	25+ 4	9	3+3	2	1		1+3	2
Hughes P	5+ 4						1	
Kharine	10							
Lambourde	5+ 2		3				1+2	

CHELSEA cont.

	P/FL App	P/FL Goals	FLC App	FLC Goals	FAC App	FAC Goals	Others App	Others Goals
Leboeuf	32	5	4		1		10	1
Lee	1		0+2					
Le Saux	26	1	4	1	1	1	3	
Morris	9+ 3	1	1	1			2+1	
Myers	11+ 1		1		0+1		1+2	
Newton	17+ 1		3+1				6+1	
Nicholls	8+11	3	2		1		0+2	
Petrescu	31	5	3	1	1		7+1	2
Poyet	11+ 3	4					5	1
Sinclair	20+ 2	1	4+1				6	1
Vialli	14+ 7	11	2+1		0+1	2	8+1	6
Wise	26	3	4				10	
Zola	23+ 4	8	4		1		8+1	4

CHESTER CITY (DIV 3: 14th)

	P/FL App	P/FL Goals	FLC App	FLC Goals	FAC App	FAC Goals	Others App	Others Goals
Alsford	39	4	2		2		1	
Bennett	37+ 4	11	2		2			
Brown	13				2		1	
Davidson	24	2	2		0+1		1	
Dobson	6							
Fisher	29+ 6	1	2		2		1	
Flitcroft	43+ 1	4	2		2		1	1
Giles	8+ 2							
Jenkins	34	1	2		2		1	
Jones	2+ 5	1			0+1		1	
McDonald	21+10	5	1		1			
McKay	3+ 2							
Milner	1		0+2					
Murphy	19+ 8	4	0+1		0+1			
Priest	37	6			2	1	1	
Richardson	41+ 3	2	2		2	1	1	
Rimmer	26+ 8	8	1		1+1		1	
Shelton A	0+ 2							
Shelton G	3							
Sinclair	33		2					
Thomas	25+13	4	2		2			
Whelan	35	4	2		2		1	
Woods	24+ 5	2	0+2	1				
Wright	3+ 2						0+1	

CHESTERFIELD (DIV 2: 10th)

	P/FL App	P/FL Goals	FLC App	FLC Goals	FAC App	FAC Goals	Others App	Others Goals
Allardyce	0+ 1							
Beaumont	32+ 7	1	3+1		3			
Breckin	40+ 3	1	3		3	1		
Carr	8+ 2	1	1		0+1		1	
Creaney	3+ 1							
Curtis	34+ 2	1	4				0+1	
Dunn	0+ 7				0+1		1	
Ebdon	29+ 4	2	2		3		1	
Garvey	2+ 1							
Gaughan	2		0+1					
Gayle	5							
Hewitt	44	1	4		3			
Holland	32+ 3	3	3		3			
Howard	30+ 5	6	2		2			
Jackson	0+ 3		0+1		0+1		1	
Jules	29+ 4	1	3		3		1	
Leaning	5				2			
Lenagh	0+ 3						0+1	
Lomas	2+ 2						1	
Lormor	11+ 2	4	4	3			1	
Mercer	36		4		1		1	
Misse-Misse	1							
Morris	3+ 1	1						
Pearce							0+1	
Perkins	43	2	3		2		1	
Reeves	26	5			1+1	1		
Rogers	2+ 1							
Wilkinson	24+ 6	6	1		3		1	

CHESTERFIELD cont.

	P/FL App	P/FL Goals	FLC App	FLC Goals	FAC App	FAC Goals	Others App	Others Goals
Williams	44	3	4		3		1	
Willis	19+15	8	3	2	1+1	1	1	

COLCHESTER UNITED (DIV 3: 4th)

	P/FL App	P/FL Goals	FLC App	FLC Goals	FAC App	FAC Goals	Others App	Others Goals
Abrahams	16+ 9	7	2		1+1		1	
Adcock	19+ 6	5	0+2		3+1		1	
Betts	17				2+1		3	
Branston	12						1	
Brown	0+ 2							
Buckle	33+ 5	5	2		1		4	
Cawley	27		2		3		1	
Duguid	6+15	3			3+1		0+3	
Dunne	22+ 3	2			3+1		4	
Emberson	46		2		4		4	
Forbes	25+10	1	1+1		2	1	3+1	
Greene	38	4	2		4		3	1
Gregory D	42+ 2	5	2		4	2	4	1
Gregory N	12+ 3	7					3	2
Hathaway	5+ 7		2	1	1+1			
Haydon	9+ 8				1+1		1	
Lock	14+18	6	0+2		0+3		0+4	
Rankin	10+ 1	5						
Sale	38+ 1	7	2		3	1	4	
Skelton	37+ 2	7	1		3+1		3+1	
Stamps	26+ 1	1	2		2+1		1	
Whitton	15+ 6	1			2			
Wilkins	37	5	2		2		2	

COVENTRY CITY (PREM: 11th)

	P/FL App	P/FL Goals	FLC App	FLC Goals	FAC App	FAC Goals	Others App	Others Goals
Boateng	14	1			5			
Boland	8+11		1+1		0+1			
Breen	30	1	3+1		5			
Burrows	33		4		5			
Dublin	36	18	2	1	5	4		
Ducros	1+ 2		0+1					
Hall	20+ 5	1	3+1	1	2+2			
Haworth	4+ 6		2	1	0+1			
Hedman	14				3			
Huckerby	32+ 2	14	0+1		5	1		
Johansen	0+ 2		1					
Lightbourne	1+ 6		3					
McAllister	14		4	2				
Moldovan	5+ 5	1			2+2	1		
Nilsson	32		3		4			
Ogrizovic	24		4		2			
O'Neill	2+ 2		1					
Richardson	3							
Salako	11		2	2				
Shaw	33		4		3			
Shilton	2							
Soltvedt	26+ 4	1	1+1		3+1			
Strachan G	2+ 7				2+2			
Telfer	33	3	2		4	2		
Whelan	21	6			4			
Williams	17+ 3		4		1			

CREWE ALEXANDRA (DIV 1: 11th)

	P/FL App	P/FL Goals	FLC App	FLC Goals	FAC App	FAC Goals	Others App	Others Goals
Adebola	26+ 1	7	1+1		1			
Anthrobus	27+ 3	6	1					
Bankole	3							
Bignot	42				1			
Charnock	33	3	2		1			
Collins	0+ 1		0+1					
Foran	10+ 2	1						
Garvey	8+ 5	2	0+2					
Guinan	3							
Holsgrove	7+ 1	1			1			
Johnson	39+ 1	1	2		1			
Kearton	43		1					

CREWE ALEXANDRA cont.

	P/FL App	Goals	FLC App	Goals	FAC App	Goals	Others App	Goals
Lightfoot	7+6	1	1+1					
Little	29+11	13	1		1			
Lunt	29+12	2	2	1				
Moralee	3+6		1+1					
Pemberton	1		1					
Pope	2+4							
Rivers	31+4	6	2	1	1	1		
Smith P	1+5							
Smith S	43	6	2	2	1			
Street	15+17	4						
Tierney	1+3							
Unsworth	31+5		1		1			
Walton	27				1			
Watts	5							
Westwood	19+2	3	2					
Whalley	18	1	1					
Wright D	0+3							
Wright J	3+2							

CRYSTAL PALACE (PREM: 20th)

	P/FL App	Goals	FLC App	Goals	FAC App	Goals	Others App	Goals
Bent	10+6	5						
Billio	1+2							
Bonetti	0+2							
Boxall	0+1		1					
Brolin	13				3			
Burton -Godwin	1+1				0+1			
Curcic	6+2	1						
Davies	0+1							
Dyer	21+3	4	0+1		4	4		
Edworthy	33+1		1		4			
Emblen	8+5				1+1	2		
Folan	0+1							
Freedman	2+5		1+1					
Fullarton	19+6	1	2		3			
Ginty	2+3				0+1			

CRYSTAL PALACE cont.

	P/FL App	Goals	FLC App	Goals	FAC App	Goals	Others App	Goals
Gordon	36+1	2	2		4			
Hreidarsson	26+4	2	2		4			
Ismael	13				3			
Jansen	5+3	3						
Linighan	26		2		2+1			
Lombardo	21+3	5			0+1			
McKenzie	0+3				0+1			
Miller	38		2		4			
Morrison	0+1	1						
Muscat	9		1					
Ndah	2+1		0+1	1				
Padavano	8+2	1						
Quinn	0+1							
Roberts	25		1		4			
Rodger	27+2	2	0+1		3			
Shipperley	17+9	7	2					
Smith	16+2				4			
Tuttle	8+1		1					
Veart	1+5		1+1	1				
Warhurst	22	3	1		1			
Zohar	2+4		2					

DARLINGTON (DIV 3: 19th)

	P/FL App	Goals	FLC App	Goals	FAC App	Goals	Others App	Goals
Atkinson	29+3	1	1		4	1	1	1
Barnard	30+6		2		3+1		1	
Brumwell	26+9				0+3			
Brydon	11+4		1		1+1			
Campbell	4+2		1					
Crosby	32+2	1	2		4		1	
Davey	10+1							
Davies	2						1	
De Vos	24	3	1		3		1	
Di Lella	0+5							
Dorner	25+2	10			3	1		
Ellison	4+4	3						
Fickling	8							

DARLINGTON cont.

	P/FL App	Goals	FLC App	Goals	FAC App	Goals	Others App	Goals
Gaughan	23+1	1			2		1	
Gray	6		2					
Giummarra	0+4							
Hilton	0+1							
Hope	34+1	1	2		1		0+1	
Liddle	15							
Lowe	5+2		2					
Midgley	1						0+1	1
Naylor	38+4	8	1+1		4	1	1	
Oliver	33+6	2	2		4		1	
Papaconstantinou								
Preece	45		2		4		1	
Resch	15+2	1			1+2			
Roberts	24+4	12	2	1	3	1	1	
Robinson	7+12	3	0+1		2+2	1	0+1	
Shaw	28+3	2			4		1	
Shutt	15+18	5	2		1+1			
Turnbull	4+5		0+1		0+2			
Tutill	7							

DERBY COUNTY (PREM: 9th)

	P/FL App	Goals	FLC App	Goals	FAC App	Goals	Others App	Goals
Asanovic	3+1	1	1					
Baiano	30+3	12	1		2	1		
Bohinen	9		1					
Burton	12+17	3	1		2			
Carbon	3+1							
Carsley	34	1	2		2			
Dailly	30	1	4		0+1			
Delap	10+3							
Elliott	3		2		0+1			
Eranio	23	5	1		1			
Hoult	2		1					
Hunt	7+12	1	2+2					
Kozluk	6+3		2		1			
Laursen	27+1	1	2		1			
Poom	36		3		2			
Powell C	35+2	1	4		2	1		
Powell D	12+11		1		2			
Rowett	32+3	1	4	2	1+1			
Simpson	1		0+2					
Solis	3+6		1+2					
Stimac	22	1			2			
Sturridge	24+6	9	4	1				
Trollope	4+6		2+1	1				
Van der Laan	7+3		2+1					
Wanchope	30+2	13	4	4	2			
Ward	2+1							
Willems	3+7				0+2			
Yates	8+1				2			

DONCASTER ROVERS (DIV 3: 24th)

	P/FL App	Goals	FLC App	Goals	FAC App	Goals	Others App	Goals
Betts	2+1							
Borg	1							
Brookes	9+2		2		1		0+1	
Clark	1+1							
Conlon	4+10	1						
Cunningham	32+1	1	1+1				1	
Davis	15						1	
Debenham	4+2							
Dobbin	28+3				1		1	
Donnelly	8+1	1						
Dowell	1							
Edwards	5+4							
Esdaille Darren	21+1		1					
Esdaille David	10+3		2					
Finley	6+1		1					
George	16+2	1						
Gore	25		2		1		1	
Hammond	1				0+1	1		
Hawes	8+3							

Neil Shipperley (Crystal Palace)

DONCASTER ROVERS cont.

	P/FL App	Goals	FLC App	Goals	FAC App	Goals	Others App	Goals
Hawthorne	7+1							
Helliwell	8	1					1	
Hilton	9+1				1			
Hoggeth	8							
Ingham	10	2						
Ireland	34		1+1		1		1	
McDonald	15	2	2		1			
Messer	4+9	1						
Mike	42	4	2		1	1	1	
Moncrieffe	30+8	8	2		1		1	
Parks	6							
Pell	6+4	1						
Pemberton	24+2	1	0+1					
Ramsay	2+9		0+1		0+1			
Rowe	6	2						
Russell	4+1							
Sanders	19+6		2				1	
Smith D	1							
Smith M	9+10	3	1		1		1	
Tedaldi	0+2	1						
Thornley	1							
Thorpe	2							
Utley	2+2							
Warren	44	1	1		1		1	
Williams	6				1			
Wilson	10	1						

EVERTON (PREM: 17th)

	P/FL App	Goals	FLC App	Goals	FAC App	Goals	Others App	Goals
Allen	2+3							
Ball	21+4	1	1+1		1			
Barmby	26+4	2	1+1	3	1			
Barrett	12+1							
Beagrie	4+2							
Bilic	22+2		3					
Branch	1+5							
Cadamarteri	15+11	4	1+2	1	1			
Dunne	2+1				1			
Farrelly	18+8	1	1		1	1		
Ferguson	28+1	12	2		1			
Gerrard	4		2					
Grant	7	1	1		1			
Hinchcliffe	15+2		3					
Hutchison	11	1						
Jeffers	0+1							
McCann	5+6							
Madar	15+2	5						
Myhre	22				1			
O'Connor	0+1							
O'Kane	12							
Oster	16+15	1	3	1	0+1			
Phelan	8+1		0+1					
Short	27+4		2					
Southall	12		1					
Speed	21	6	3					
Spencer	3+3							
Stuart	14	2	3	1				
Thomas	6+1				1			
Thomsen	2+6	1			1			
Tiler	19	1			1			
Ward	8							
Watson	25+1	1	3					
Williamson	15		2					

EXETER CITY (DIV 3: 15th)

	P/FL App	Goals	FLC App	Goals	FAC App	Goals	Others App	Goals
Baddeley	29+3	1			1		0+1	
Bayes	45		2		2		1	
Birch	31+2	5	1		2			
Blake	36+2		2		2		1	
Braithwaite	0+5	1	1		0+1			

EXETER CITY cont.

	P/FL App	Goals	FLC App	Goals	FAC App	Goals	Others App	Goals
Breslan	0+1							
Clark	31	3			2	1	1	
Curran	9		2					
Cyrus	17+4		2		1+1			
Devlin	31+2	2					1	
Dungey	1							
Flack	37+4	14	2		1		0+1	
Fry	16+12	1	0+2		1		1	
Gale	42+1	4	2		2		1	
Gardner	19+4	1	2		1		1	
Ghazghazi	1+8				1+1		1	
Hare	5+2		0+1					
Holcroft	3+3							
Holloway	4+2							
Illman	6+2	2					1	1
McConnell	10+6	6	1		1		0+1	
Medlin	11+9				1		1	
Minett	6		1+1					
Phillips	7+1							
Richardson	41	1	2		2		1	
Rowbotham	42+1	22	2		2	1		
Tisdale	10	1						
Wilkinson	0+1							
Williams	16+20	4						

FULHAM (DIV 2: 6th)

	P/FL App	Goals	FLC App	Goals	FAC App	Goals	Others App	Goals
Arendse	6		2		1			
Arnott	0+1						0+2	
Beardsley	8	1					1	1
Blake	24+2	2			2	1	2+1	
Bracewell	36		3				2	
Brazier	3+4	1						
Brevett	11						2	
Brooker	4+5		1+1				2+1	
Carpenter	15+9	2	4	1	1	1	2	
Cockerill	5+3		2+1					
Coleman	26	1			1		3	
Collins	10+3	1					3	
Conroy	10+1	2	3	2				
Cullip	18+3	1	4		1			
Cusack	1+1		1+1					
Freeman	0+7						2	1
Hayward	32+3	4	4		1+1		3	
Herrera	26		4		3		1	
Lawrence	43		4		2		5	
Lightbourne	4	2					1	1
McAnespie	2+2				1		2+1	
McAree	1+1		1+2				0+1	
McKenzie	1+2							
Maher	1						2	
Moody	27+6	15	2+1		1+1		2	1
Morgan	18+1	1	4		1		2	
Neilson	17				2		1	
Newhouse	7+1	1	3+1	3				
Peschisolido	32	13			3		2	
Scott	6+11	3	0+4		2	1	2+1	
Selley	3							
Smith	42+2		3		3		1+1	
Taylor	28				2		3	
Thomas	0+4						2+1	2
Thorpe	5+8	3					1+1	
Trollope	19+5	3			2		3	
Walton	12		2				2	
Watson	4+2	1			1		1	

GILLINGHAM (DIV 2: 8th)

	P/FL App	Goals	FLC App	Goals	FAC App	Goals	Others App	Goals
Akinbiyi	44	21	2		2	1	0+1	
Ashby	43		1		2		1	
Bailey	7+6	1						

GILLINGHAM cont.

	P/FL App	Goals	FLC App	Goals	FAC App	Goals	Others App	Goals
Bartram	9							
Bryant	25+10		2		1		1	
Butler	30+13	6	2		2		1	
Butters	31	7	2		2			
Chapman			1					
Corbett	8+8	2	0+1				0+1	
Fortune-West	5+15	4	0+1		0+1			
Galloway	32+7	1	2		1+1			
Green	17+8		1+1				0+1	
Hessenthaler	42		2		2		1	
Masters	11						1	
Moss	10		2					
Ndah	4							
O'Connor			1					
Onuora	16+6	2			2	1	1	
Patterson	23		2					
Pennock	20							
Pinnock	0+1							
Piper	0+1		0+1					
Pollitt	6							
Ratcliffe	16+5	1	2		0+2		1	
Smith	46	3	2		2		1	
Southall	22+1	2					1	
Stannard	20				2		1	
Statham	16+4				2		1	
Thomas	2+1							
Walton	1							

GRIMSBY TOWN (DIV 2: 3rd)

	P/FL App	Goals	FLC App	Goals	FAC App	Goals	Others App	Goals
Black	24+15	2	5		4		2+5	1
Bloomer							0+1	
Burnett	20+1	1					8	3
Butterfield	4+3		1		0+1		1+1	1
Chapman							0+1	
Clare	8+14	3			1+4		4+2	
Davison	42		5		6		10	
Dobbin	1+1							
Donovan	46	16	6	1	6	1	9	3
Gallimore	34+1	2	5		6		10	
Gilbert	5		1					
Groves	46	7	6	2	6	1	10	2
Handyside	40+2		6		6		9+1	
Holsgrove	3+7							
Jobling	17+13	1	1+3	1	5	1	2+3	
Lester	27+13	4	3+2	3	4	2	4+4	
Lever	37+1	5					9	
Livingstone	28+13	5	3+3	4	2+3		4+3	
McDermott	40+1	1	5		6	1	10	
Nogan	33+3	8	6	1	4	2	8	2
Pearcey	4		1					
Rodger	10+1		1+1		5	1	1	
Smith	17	1			1		7	1
Southall	4+1		1+1		1+1	1		
Widdrington	15+6	3	5+1		2		1	
Woods	1+9		0+2		0+1	1	1	
Wrack	0+1						0+1	

HARTLEPOOL UNITED (DIV 3: 17th)

	P/FL App	Goals	FLC App	Goals	FAC App	Goals	Others App	Goals
Allon	3+1	2						
Baker	16	5	2	1				
Barron	32+1		1		1		2	
Beech	34+2	6	1		1	1	2	1
Bradley	43		1				2	
Clark	19+5	7			0+1		1	
Connor	4+1							
Cullen	28	12	2		1		2	
Davies	18+2		1		1			
Davis	2				1			
Di Lella	1+4	2						

HARTLEPOOL UNITED cont.

	P/FL App	P/FL Goals	FLC App	FLC Goals	FAC App	FAC Goals	Others App	Others Goals
Dobson	1		1		1			
Elliott	0+4				0+1			
Gavin	0+3							
Halliday	21+10	5	1+1		0+1		2	
Harper	15							
Hollund	28						2	
Howard	34+9	7	2	1	1		2	
Hutt	4							
Ingram	35+1	3	2		1			
Irvine	1+8							
Knowles	46	1	2		1		2	
Larsen	0+4						0+1	
Lee	35+2	3	1	1	1		2	1
Lucas	42	2	2		1		1	
McDonald	4+2							
Midgley	9	3						
Miller	11+2	1						
Nash	0+1							
Pedersen	17	1			1	1	2	1
Stephenson	3							

HUDDERSFIELD TOWN (DIV 1: 16th)

	P/FL App	P/FL Goals	FLC App	FLC Goals	FAC App	FAC Goals	Others App	Others Goals
Allison	27	6			2			
Baldry	8+3	1	1+1					
Barnes	11+4	1						
Bartram	12							
Beresford	5+3		1					
Browning	10+4		1					
Burnett	11+4		3+1	1				
Collins	9+1		1					
Dalton	26+5	13	1		2			
Dyer	8+4	1	3	1				
Dyson	35+1	1	3		2			
Edmondson	15+4		2		0+1			
Edwards	26+12	1	2		0+1			
Facey	1+2							
Francis	9		4					
Gray	34+1	1	2		2			
Harper	24				2			
Heary	2+1		0+1					
Hessey	0+1							
Horne	29+1				2			
Hurst	1+2		0+1					
Jenkins	28+1	1	4		2			
Johnson	28+1	1			2			
Lawson	3+15		0+1					
Makel	10+3		4		0+1			
Martin	2+1		1					
Midwood	0+1							
Morrison	22+1	1	3		2			
Nielsen	0+3							
O'Connor	1		0+1					
Payton	4+1		2	1				
Phillips	29	2			2			
Richardson	16+5	3			0+2			
Ryan	10		2					
Smith	4+2							
Stewart	38+3	16	4		2	1		
Watts	8							

HULL CITY (DIV 3: 22nd)

	P/FL App	P/FL Goals	FLC App	FLC Goals	FAC App	FAC Goals	Others App	Others Goals
Bettney	28+2	1	2				1	
Boyack	12	3						
Brien	14+1		5					
Brown A	0+3		0+1					
Brown D	7	2						
Darby	27+2	13	3	1	1		2	1
Dewhurst	24	3	3				2	
Dickinson	2+1		1					

HULL CITY cont.

	P/FL App	P/FL Goals	FLC App	FLC Goals	FAC App	FAC Goals	Others App	Others Goals
Doncel	8+4		3					
Edwards	20+1						1	
Ellington	4+3	2	0+1		0+1		0+1	
Fewings	13+5		1+2		0+1		0+1	
Gage	8+2				1		1	
Gordon	0+5	2	0+1					
Greaves	17+8	2	2		1			
Hateley	4+5		4+1					
Hocking	31	1	2		1		2	
Hodges	13+5	4	1		1		2	
Joyce	45	4	4+1	1	1		2	
Lowthorpe	18+5	2	1				0+2	
McGinty	21	2					1+1	
Mann	20+14	3	2+1		1		2	
Maxfield	10+4							
Morley	5+3						1	
Peacock	26+1	2	4+1	1	1			
Quigley	4+5	1	1+3				1	
Rioch	38+1	5	4		1		1	
Rocastle	10	1	1					
Thomson	9		3					
Trevitt	4		1					
Tucker	1+6							
Wharton	1							
Wilson	37		2		1		2	
Wright	25+8	2	5	1	1		1	

IPSWICH TOWN (DIV 1: 5th)

	P/FL App	P/FL Goals	FLC App	FLC Goals	FAC App	FAC Goals	Others App	Others Goals
Brown	1							
Clapham	22						1	
Cundy	40+1	3	6		3		2	
Dozzell	8	1	2	1				
Dyer	41	4	7	1	2		2	
Gregory	2+6	1	0+2					
Holland	46	10	7	2	4		2	
Johnson	30+1	20			4	2	2	
Keeble	0+1							
Kennedy	0+1							
Kerslake	2+5		1+1					
Legg	6	1	1					
Mason	1		1					
Matthie	25+12	13	3+2	2	0+2		2	
Milton	7+13		1+1					
Mowbray	23+2		4	1	2			
Naylor	0+5	2						
Petta	28+4	7	3+2		3+1		2	
Scowcroft	19+12	6	5	1	4		0+2	
Sonner	6+17	1	1+1		0+1		0+1	
Stein	6+1	2	3+1	1				
Stockwell	46	3	6	1	4	1	2	
Swailes	3+2		1					
Tanner	14+4	1	0+1		3+1			
Taricco	41		6		4		2	
Uhlenbeek	6+5				2		1+1	
Venus	12+2	1	5		1		2	
Whyte	2							
Williams	23		7		4			
Wright	46		7		4		2	

LEEDS UNITED (PREM: 5th)

	P/FL App	P/FL Goals	FLC App	FLC Goals	FAC App	FAC Goals	Others App	Others Goals
Beeney	1				0+1			
Bowyer	21+4	3	2+1	1	3			
Haaland	26+6	7	3		2			
Halle	31+2	2	2+1		3			
Harte	12				1+2			
Hasselbaink	30+3	16	3	2	4	4		
Hiden	11				1			
Hopkin	22+3	1	4		1			
Jackson	0+1							

LEEDS UNITED cont.

	P/FL App	P/FL Goals	FLC App	FLC Goals	FAC App	FAC Goals	Others App	Others Goals
Kelly	34		3		3+1			
Kewell	26+3	5	2	1	4	2		
Lilley	0+13	1	0+3		0+1			
McPhail	0+4							
Martyn	37		4		4			
Matthews	0+3		0+1					
Maybury	9+3		1		2			
Molenaar	18+4	2	2+1		3	1		
Radebe	26+1		4		2	1		
Ribeiro	28+1	3	2+1	1	3			
Robertson	24+2		4		1			
Wallace	29+2	10	4	2	4	1		
Wetherall	33+1	3	4	2	3			

LEICESTER CITY (PREM: 10th)

	P/FL App	P/FL Goals	FLC App	FLC Goals	FAC App	FAC Goals	Others App	Others Goals
Arphexad	6							
Campbell	6+5		1					
Claridge	10+7						0+1	
Cottee	7+12	4	1		0+2	1	0+1	
Elliott	37	7	1		2		2	
Fenton	9+14	3	1		0+1		0+2	
Guppy	37	2	1		2		2	
Heskey	35	10			2		2	
Izzet	36	4			2		2	
Kammark	35				2		2	
Keller	32				2		2	
Lennon	37	2	1		2		2	
McMahon	0+1		0+1					
Marshall	22+2	7	1	1	2	1	2	1
Parker	15+7	3			2	1	2	
Prior	28+2				1		2	
Savage	28+7	2	1		2	1	0+1	
Ullathorne	3+3	1						
Walsh	23+3	3	1		1		1	
Watts	0+3				1		1	
Wilson	0+11	2	0+1		0+2			
Zagorakis	12+2	1						

LEYTON ORIENT (DIV 3: 11th)

	P/FL App	P/FL Goals	FLC App	FLC Goals	FAC App	FAC Goals	Others App	Others Goals
Baker	4+27	3	1+1	2	0+1		1+1	
Bennett	1+1						1	
Channing	29+5		2+1		2		2	
Clark	39	5	3		2		1	
Colkin	5+6		0+1					
Cooper	0+1						1	
Fenn	3							
Griffiths	31+2	18	4	3	2	1	2	
Hanson	4+8	1			1+1		0+2	
Harris	21+14	6	1		2		1+1	
Hicks	35		4		2			
Hodge	1							
Hyde	28		4		2		1	
Inglethorpe	38	9	2	2	1		1	1
Joseph M	14	1						
Joseph R	13+12		2+1		0+1		1	
Ling	46	2	4		2		1	
McGleish	8		3	1				
McKenzie	4						1	
Martin	0+1							
Maskell	7+1	2						
Morrison	1+1							
Naylor	43	1	4		2		2	
Pitcher	1						1	
Raynor	5+5							
Regis	4							
Richards	10+7	2	1+2				1	
Richardson	1							
Simpson	9+5	3					1+1	

	P/FL App	P/FL Goals	FLC App	FLC Goals	FAC App	FAC Goals	Others App	Others Goals
LEYTON ORIENT cont.								
Smith	43	9	4		2	1	2	
Turley	14							
Warren	41		4	1	2		1	
West	2+ 5		1		0+ 1			
Williams	0+ 1							
LINCOLN CITY (DIV 3: 3rd)								
Ainsworth	6	3	2	1				
Alcide	25+ 4	12	1		0+ 2	1	0+ 1	
Austin	46		1		4		1	
Bailey	1+ 4	1						
Barnett	33		2		4		1	
Bimson	7+ 5				0+ 1		0+ 1	
Brown G	15							
Brown Simon	1							
Brown Steve	16+15	3			2+ 1		0+ 1	
Chandler			1					
Finnigan	6							
Flash	2+ 3							
Fleming	40	3	1+ 1		4	2		
Gordon	9+ 4	3			4		1	
Harris	0+ 1							
Holmes	46	4	2		4		1	
Hone	22+ 2	2	2		3	1	1	
Martin	0+ 7	1						
Miller	20+ 4	2	2					
Regis	0+ 1							
Richardson	26				4			
Robertson	2						1	
Smith	15+ 2	3					1	
Stant	17+ 4	2	2	1	2+ 2			
Stones	10+ 5				1+ 1		1	
Thorpe	44	14	2		4		1	
Vaughan	19		2				1	
Walling	35	5			4	3		
Whitney	42+ 2	1	2		4	2	1	
Wilkins	1+ 1							
LIVERPOOL (PREM: 3rd)								
Babb	18+ 1		2				1	
Berger	6+16	3	2+ 1	1	0+ 1		1+ 1	
Bjornebye	24+ 1		3				4	
Carragher	17+ 3		2				1	
Fowler	19+ 1	9	4	3	1		3	1
Friedel	11							
Harkness	24+ 1		3+ 1		1		1	
Ince	31	8	4		1		4	
James	27		5		1		4	
Jones	20+ 1		2				3	
Kennedy	0+ 1							
Kvarme	22+ 1		2		1		4	
Leonhardsen	27+ 1	6	3+ 2		1		2	
McAteer	15+ 6	2	3		1		1	
McManaman	36	11	5		1		4	1
Matteo	24+ 2		4		1		2	
Murphy	6+10				0+ 1			
Owen	34+ 2	18	4	4			3+ 1	1
Redknapp	20	3	3	1	1	1	2	
Riedle	18+ 7	6	2+ 3		1		1+ 2	1
Ruddock	2		1				1	
Thomas	10+ 1	1	1				1	
Thompson	1+ 4	1						
Wright	6						1	
LUTON TOWN (DIV 2: 17th)								
Abbey			1					
Alexander	39	8	2		1		2	
Allen C	14	1					3	
Allen R	8	6						

	P/FL App	P/FL Goals	FLC App	FLC Goals	FAC App	FAC Goals	Others App	Others Goals
LUTON TOWN cont.								
Davies	8+12	1	3+ 1		0+ 1		3	
Davis K	32						1	
Davis S	38	5	4	1			2	
Dibble	1		2					
Doherty	1+ 9				0+ 1			
Douglas	5+12	1	3+ 1	1				
Evers	14+ 9	3	2				3	
Feuer	13		1		1		2	
Fotiades	5+10	1			1			
Fraser	1							
George	1		0+ 2				0+ 1	
Gray	14+ 3	2	1				0+ 1	
Harvey	5+ 1		2+ 1		1		1	
James	23+ 1		1		1			
Johnson	13+ 1	2	3					
Kean	0+ 1							
McGowan	6+ 2							
McLaren	41+ 2		4		1		2	
Marshall	19+10	3	2				2	1
Oldfield	45	10	4		1		3	1
Patterson	23				0+ 1		3	
Peake	0+ 1							
Showler	0+ 1							
Small	15							
Spring	6+ 6				1			
Thomas	27+ 1	1	2				2	
Thorpe	27+ 1	14	2+ 1	3			1+ 1	2
Waddock	36+ 2		4		1		0+ 2	
White	26+ 2	1	1		1		3	
MACCLESFIELD TOWN (DIV 3: 2nd)								
Askey	37+ 2	6	2				1	
Brown	2							
Chambers	17+ 4	4					1	
Cooper	8	2						
Davenport	2+ 2	1						
Durkan	2+ 2							
Edey	9+ 4						1	
Gardiner	7	2			1			
Hitchen	1+ 1							
Howarth	38+ 3	3	2		1		1	
Ingram	5							
Irving	6+ 3				0+ 2			
Landon	6+12	7	2		0+ 1		0+ 1	
McDonald	22		1				1	
Mason	7+ 5		2	1	0+ 1			
Mitchell	2+ 4		0+ 2		1+ 1			
Payne	39		2		2		1	
Peel	10+ 4	3			2			
Philliskirk	1+ 9	1						
Power	21+17	7	0+ 2		2		1	
Price	46		2		2		1	
Rose	15+ 4		2		2			
Sedgemore	5							
Sodje	41	3	2		2		1	
Sorvel	41+ 4	3	2		2		0+ 1	
Tinson	44		2		2			
Whittaker	29+ 2	4			2	2	1	
Wood	43	13	2		1	2	1	
MANCHESTER CITY (DIV 1: 22nd)								
Beardsley	5+ 1							
Beesley	4+ 3							
Bishop	4+ 2							
Bradbury	23+ 4	7	2					
Brannan	27+ 5	3	2		1			
Brightwell	19+ 2		2		2			
Briscoe	5	1						
Brown	18+ 8				2	1		

	P/FL App	P/FL Goals	FLC App	FLC Goals	FAC App	FAC Goals	Others App	Others Goals
MANCHESTER CITY cont.								
Conlon	1+ 6							
Creaney	1							
Crooks	3+ 2							
Dickov	21+ 9	9	0+ 1		2			
Edghill	36				1			
Goater	7	3						
Greenacre	2+ 1	1			0+ 1			
Heaney	3							
Horlock	25	5	2	1				
Jobson	6	1						
Kelly	1							
Kernaghan	1		1					
Kinkladze	29+ 1	4	2		2	1		
McGoldrick	6+ 1		0+ 1					
Margetson	28		2					
Morley	1+ 2	1						
Pollock	8	1						
Rosler	23+ 6	6	2		2	1		
Russell	17+ 1				2			
Scully	1+ 8							
Shelia	12	2			2			
Summerbee	4+ 5		2					
Symons	42	1	1		1			
Tskhadadze	10	1						
Van Blerk	10+ 9		0+ 1		0+ 1			
Vaughan	19	1	2					
Whitley Jeff	14+ 3	1			1			
Whitley Jim	17+ 2				1+ 1			
Wiekens	35+ 2	5	2		1			
Wright	18		2					
MANCHESTER UNITED (PREM: 2nd)								
Beckham	34+ 3	9			3+ 1	2	8+ 1	
Berg	23+ 4	1			2		5+ 2	1
Brown	1+ 1						8	
Butt	31+ 2	3			1		8	
Clegg	1+ 2				2+ 1		0+ 1	
Cole	31+ 2	15	1		3	5	7+ 1	5
Cruyff	3+ 2		1		0+ 1		0+ 1	
Curtis	3+ 5		1					
Giggs	28+ 1	8			2		6	1
Higginbottom	0+ 1							
Irwin	23+ 2	2	0+ 1		3+ 1		7	2
Johnsen	18+ 4	2	1		3	1	6	1
Keane	9	2					2	
McClair	2+11		1		3		0+ 3	
May	7+ 2		1		1			
Mulryne	1		1		0+ 1			
Neville G	34				2+ 1		8	
Neville P	24+ 6	1	1		3		6+ 2	
Nevland	0+ 1		0+ 1		2+ 1			
Pallister	33				3		7	
Pilkington	2							
Poborsky	3+ 7	2	1				2+ 2	
Schmeichel	32				4		8	
Scholes	28+ 3	8	0+ 1		2		7+ 1	2
Sheringham	28+ 3	9			2+ 1	3	8	2
Solskjaer	15+ 7	6			1+ 1	2	3+ 3	1
Thornley	0+ 5		1		2			
Twiss					0+ 1			
Van der Gouw	4+ 1		1				1	
Wallwork	0+ 1							
MANSFIELD TOWN (DIV 3: 12th)								
Bowling	33		2		2		2	
Christie	26+13	10	2	4	0+ 2		0+ 1	
Clarke	26+ 9	4	1		1		0+ 1	
Doolan	24	1	2	1	2			
Eustace	24+ 5	1	2		2		0+ 1	

MANSFIELD TOWN cont.

	P/FL App	Goals	FLC App	Goals	FAC App	Goals	Others App	Goals
Ford	33 + 1	3	2	1			2	
Gibson	13							
Hackett	23	1			2			
Hadley	0 + 2							
Harper	46	5	2		2		2	
Hassell	8 + 1							
Jones	6		2					
Kerr	7 + 11	2					2	
Milner	1 + 6							
Peacock	25 + 7	5			2		2	
Peters	24	2			2			
Schofield	44		2		2		2	
Sedgemore	21 + 7	2	1		1 + 1		2	
Sedlan	0 + 1							
Sissons	0 + 1							
Squires	1							
Tallon	26	1					2	
Thom	5						2	
Walker	0 + 1						0 + 1	
Watkiss	10		2					
Whitehall	42 + 1	24	2		2	1	2	1
Williams	33 + 5	3			2		2	
Woods	5 + 1							

MIDDLESBROUGH (DIV 1: 2nd)

	P/FL App	Goals	FLC App	Goals	FAC App	Goals	Others App	Goals
Armstrong	7 + 4	7						
Baker	5 + 1		2 + 2		0 + 1			
Beck	31 + 8	14	6 + 1	1	0 + 1			
Beresford	3							
Blackmore	1 + 1							
Branca	11	9	2	1				
Campbell	5 + 2		3 + 1	1	2	1		
Dibble	2							
Emerson	21	4	4					
Festa	38	2	7		2			
Fleming	28 + 3	1	2					
Freestone	0 + 2		1 + 1	1				
Gascoigne	7		0 + 1					
Harrison	16 + 4		3 + 1		2			
Hignett	28 + 8	7	4 + 1	3	1 + 1	1		
Kinder	25 + 1	2	5		1			
Liddle	2 + 4		1 + 1					
Maddison	16 + 6	4	4		3			
Merson	45	12	7	3	3	1		
Moore	3 + 1		0 + 1					
Moreira	1							
Moreno	1 + 4	1			2			
Mustoe	31 + 1	3	7		3	2		
Ormerod	8 + 10	3	2 + 1		2			
Pearson	29	2	4		1			
Ravanelli	2	1						
Ricard	4 + 5	2	1					
Roberts	6		1					
Schwarzer	35		7		3			
Stamp	8 + 2		1		1			
Stockdale	1							
Summerbell	7 + 4		1	1				
Thomas	10							
Townsend	35 + 2	2	6		3			
Vickers	30 + 3		6		3			
Whyte	4 + 4		1					

MILLWALL (DIV 2: 18th)

	P/FL App	Goals	FLC App	Goals	FAC App	Goals	Others App	Goals
Allen	21 + 7		3		1		1 + 1	
Bircham	3 + 1				0 + 1		2	
Black	13						1	
Bowry	41 + 2	2	2		1			
Brown	45		4		1		2	
Cahill	1							

MILLWALL cont.

	P/FL App	Goals	FLC App	Goals	FAC App	Goals	Others App	Goals
Carter	12		3					
Cook	3							
Crossley	13							
Doyle	8 + 12		1		1		1 + 1	
Fitzgerald	16 + 2		1				2	
Grant	31 + 8	8	3	1	0 + 1		2	1
Gray	12	1						
Harris	2 + 1							
Hockton	10 + 16	3	2 + 1	2	0 + 1		0 + 2	
Lavin	4 + 3							
Law	40	4	3		1		2	
McLeary	19		2		1			
McRobert	4 + 1							
Neill	3 + 3						1	
Nethercott	10							
Newman	35	1	4		1		1	
Nurse			1					
Reid	0 + 1							
Robertson	0 + 1							
Roche	0 + 1		1					
Ryan	16							
Sadlier	3 + 1	3	1					
Savage	24 + 7	1	3	1	1		1	
Shaw	40	11	2	1			2	1
Spink	21				1		2	
Stevens	3 + 1						0 + 1	
Sturgess	12 + 2		4		1		0 + 1	
Tomlinson	2 + 1	1						
Veart	7 + 1	1					1	
Webber	0 + 1		1 + 1					
Wilkinson	22 + 8	3	1		1		1	
Witter	10 + 1		2					

NEWCASTLE UNITED (PREM: 13th)

	P/FL App	Goals	FLC App	Goals	FAC App	Goals	Others App	Goals
Albert	21 + 2		3		3 + 1		7 + 1	
Andersson	10 + 2	2			2 + 1			
Asprilla	8 + 2	2			1		5	4
Barnes	22 + 4	6	3		3 + 2		5	1
Barton	17 + 6	3	2		4 + 1		5	
Batty	32	1	2		6	1	7	
Beresford	17 + 1	2	3		2 + 1		7	4
Brayson			0 + 1					
Dabizas	10 + 1	1			2			
Gillespie	25 + 4	4	2		5		5 + 2	
Given	24				4		6	
Griffin	4							
Hamilton	7 + 5		1 + 1	1	1		2	
Hislop	13		3		3		2	
Howey	11 + 3		1		5		1 + 2	
Hughes	4		1		0 + 1		0 + 2	
Ketsbaia	16 + 15	3	1 + 1		2 + 4	1	3 + 5	1
Lee	26 + 2	4	2		6		6	
Peacock	19 + 1		2 + 1		1		4 + 1	
Pearce	25				7		3 + 1	1
Pistone	28		1		5		5	
Rush	6 + 4		2	1	0 + 1	1	1	
Shearer	15 + 2	2			6	5		
Speed	13	1			4	1		
Srnicek	1							
Tomasson	17 + 6	3	2 + 1	1	2		6 + 1	
Watson	27 + 2	1	2 + 1		3 + 1		8	

NORTHAMPTON TOWN (DIV 2: 4th)

	P/FL App	Goals	FLC App	Goals	FAC App	Goals	Others App	Goals
Bishop	7				1		1	
Brightwell	34 + 1	1	2		5		2 + 1	
Clarkson	42	1	2		5		4	1
Colkin							1 + 1	
Conway	2 + 1		1					
Dozzell	18 + 3	4			1		3	

NORTHAMPTON TOWN cont.

	P/FL App	Goals	FLC App	Goals	FAC App	Goals	Others App	Goals
Drysdale	1							
Frain	45	1	2		5		6	1
Freestone	23 + 2	11			1		5 + 1	2
Gayle	26 + 9	6	1 + 1	2	4		4 + 1	2
Gibb	6 + 29	1	0 + 2		2 + 3		2 + 2	
Gleghorn	3 + 5	1						
Heggs	21 + 12	4	1 + 1		4 + 1	1	3 + 1	3
Hill	27				3		6	
Hunt	14 + 7				1 + 2		6	
Hunter	28	3	2		5	2	3	
Lee	3 + 3		1		1 + 1		1	
Parrish	12	1	2					
Peer	26 + 4	2			4		2 + 1	
Potter	4						1	
Rennie	3 + 2				1			
Sampson	39	3	2		2		4	1
Seal	30 + 7	12	2	1	2 + 1	1	1 + 3	
Tait	2 + 1							
Turley							3	
Van Dullemen	0 + 1		0 + 1					
Warburton	39		2		3		5	1
Warner	3 + 7				0 + 1		0 + 2	
West	1 + 1							
Wilson	1 + 8				0 + 1			
Woodman	46		2		5		3	

NORWICH CITY (DIV 1: 15th)

	P/FL App	Goals	FLC App	Goals	FAC App	Goals	Others App	Goals
Adams	30	4	2	1				
Bellamy	30 + 6	13	1		1			
Bradshaw	1		1					
Broughton	0 + 1							
Carey	11 + 3							
Coote	11 + 12	2						
Eadie	18 + 1	3	1					
Fenn	6 + 1	1						
Fleck	23 + 4	2	2		1			
Fleming	20 + 2	1	1		1			
Forbes	28 + 5	4						
Fuglestad	23 + 1	2			1			
Grant	33 + 2	3	1		1			
Gunn	4							
Jackson	39 + 2	3						
Kenton	7 + 4							
Llewellyn	10 + 5	4					0 + 1	
Marshall A	42		2				1	
Marshall L	2 + 2							
Milligan	20		1				1	
Mills	11 + 9						1	
Newman	10 + 5		1 + 1					
O'Neill	5 + 4	1	0 + 1		1			
Polston	7 + 5		2					
Roberts	29 + 2	5	2	2				
Russell	0 + 1							
Scott	22 + 2		1		1			
Segura	22 + 3		2		1			
Simpson	2 + 4							
Sutch	40	1	2		0 + 1			

NOTTINGHAM FOREST (DIV 1: 1st)

	P/FL App	Goals	FLC App	Goals	FAC App	Goals	Others App	Goals
Allen	1		2	1				
Armstrong	4 + 14		2 + 2	1	1			
Bart-Williams	30 + 3	4	3		1			
Beasant	41		3		1			
Bonalair	24 + 7	2	1		1			
Campbell	42	23	2		1			
Chettle	45	1	3		1			
Cooper	35	5	1		1			
Fettis			1					
Gemmill	43 + 1	2	3		1			

NOTTINGHAM FOREST cont.

	P/FL App	P/FL Goals	FLC App	FLC Goals	FAC App	FAC Goals	Others App	Others Goals
Guinan	1+ 1		1	1				
Harewood	1							
Hjelde	23+ 5	1	2	2	1			
Howe			1					
Johnson A	24+10	4	2+1					
Johnson D	5+ 1							
Lyttle	35		4		1			
Moore	2+ 8	1	0+2		1			
Pascolo	5		1					
Phillips			1+1					
Rogers	46	1	4		1			
Saunders	6+ 3	2	2+1	2				
Stone	27+ 2	2						
Thomas	13+ 7	3	2	1				
Van Hooijdonk	41+ 1	29	4	4	0+1	1		
Warner			0+1					
Woan	12+ 9	1	0+1					

NOTTS COUNTY (DIV 3: 1st)

	P/FL App	P/FL Goals	FLC App	FLC Goals	FAC App	FAC Goals	Others App	Others Goals
Baraclough	36+ 2	6	3+1	1	2		1	
Cunnington	3+ 6		1+2				1	
Derry	27+ 1	2	2+1		2+1	1		
Diuk	0+ 1		0+1				0+1	
Dudley	5+12	1	1+1	1	1+2			
Dyer	10							
Farrell	32+ 3	15	1		2	1		
Finnan	41+ 3	5	4		3	1		
Hendon	38		4	1	2+1			
Henshaw							0+1	
Hogg	4		1+1		1	1		
Hughes	12+ 3	2						
Jackson	4+11	1			0+1		1	
Jones	43+ 1	28	2+1		2+1			
Kiwomya	0+ 2						1	
Lormor	2+ 5							
Martindale	5+17	1	1+1		1+1		1	
Mitchell	0+ 1						1	
Otto	4		2					
Pearce	37+ 1	2	3		2+1		1	
Pollitt	2							
Poric	3+ 1							
Randall							0+1	
Redmile	32+ 2	3	4		3		1	
Richardson	25+ 5	2	2		1	1		
Robinson	30+10	3	2		2+1		1	
Robson	26+ 2	4	1		3		1	
Stevens			0+1					
Strodder	37+ 2	4	3		3			
Ward	44		4		3		1	
White	4+ 2	2	3	1				

OLDHAM ATHLETIC (DIV 2: 13th)

	P/FL App	P/FL Goals	FLC App	FLC Goals	FAC App	FAC Goals	Others App	Others Goals
Allott	10+12	2	0+1		2+2		1	
Barlow	31+ 1	12	2		3+1	1		
Boxall	18						1	
Clitheroe	1+ 2							
Duxbury	37+ 1	4	2		4		1	
Garnett	32+ 2	3	2		2		1	
Graham	34	4	1		3	1	1	
Grobbelaar	4							
Hodgson	22+ 6	4	0+2		3			
Holt	7+ 7	1			1			
Hotte	0+ 1							
Hughes	1+ 9		1		0+1		1	
Innes	2+ 2						1	
Ironside			1					
Jepson	9	4						
Kelly	26		1		4		1	
Kyratzoglou	0+ 1							

OLDHAM ATHLETIC cont.

	P/FL App	P/FL Goals	FLC App	FLC Goals	FAC App	FAC Goals	Others App	Others Goals
Littlejohn	5	3						
McCarthy	16+ 9	7	1		3	1	1	
McNiven D	2+ 6	1						
McNiven S	25+ 7	1	1+1		3+1		1	
Orlygsson	8+ 3		1					
Ormondroyd	0+ 1							
Pollitt	16							
Redmond	32+ 2		2		3			
Reid	44	5	2		4			
Richardson							0+1	
Rickers	35+ 5	4	1		4			
Ritchie	10+ 5	2	1	1	1+1			
Rush	11+ 5	1			0+3		0+1	
Salt	1+ 1						1	
Serrant	30		2		3	1		
Sinnott	11+ 2		1					
Starbuck	7+ 2	1						
Thompson	8							
Tipton	1+ 2						0+1	
Wright	10+ 2	2			1			

OXFORD UNITED (DIV 1: 12th)

	P/FL App	P/FL Goals	FLC App	FLC Goals	FAC App	FAC Goals	Others App	Others Goals
Aldridge	13+11	2	3+2	2				
Angel	9+13	1	2+2		0+1			
Banger	18+10	3	4+1	1				
Beauchamp	44	13	6	6	1			
Cook	9+11	2			0+1			
Davis	15	2						
Donaldson	6	2						
Folland	0+ 2							
Ford M	22	2	2		1			
Ford R	17+ 1	2	6					
Francis	15	7						
Gilchrist	35+ 4	2	5		1			
Gray	28+ 3	2	1		1			
Jackson	3		3					
Jemson	24	9	5	1	1			
Marsh	13+ 1		2					

OXFORD UNITED cont.

	P/FL App	P/FL Goals	FLC App	FLC Goals	FAC App	FAC Goals	Others App	Others Goals
Massey	14+ 3	1	0+1		1			
Murphy	15+14	2	0+3	1				
Powell	11+10	1	0+1		1			
Purse	27+ 1	4	6	2	1			
Remy	13+ 3		4		0+1			
Robinson	46		6	1	1			
Rose	0+ 1							
Smith	43+ 1	1	6		1			
Stevens	0+ 1							
Van Heusden	11		2					
Weatherstone	2+ 9	1						
Whelan	6+ 2		1					
Whitehead	32		1		1			
Wilsterman	15+ 9		1					
Wright	0+ 1							

PETERBOROUGH UNITED (DIV 3: 10th)

	P/FL App	P/FL Goals	FLC App	FLC Goals	FAC App	FAC Goals	Others App	Others Goals
Bodley	31	1	4		2		2	
Bullimore	8+ 7	1	0+3		0+1		1	
Carruthers	37+ 2	15	3+1	1	3	2	3	
Castle	34+ 3	3	4		2+1	2	2+1	1
Cleaver	4+10	2	0+2				0+2	
Cornforth	3+ 1							
Davies	4+ 2						1	
De Souza	8+16	3	1+1				1	1
Drury	24+ 7		1		1		4	
Edwards	46	2	4		3		4	
Etherington	2							
Farrell	40+ 2	6	4	1	3		4	1
Foran	3+ 1				1		1	
Gill	2							
Green	2+ 2	1						
Gregory	2+ 1	1					1	
Houghton	24+ 6	4	3		2		1	1
Inman	4	1						
Lewis	31+ 3		4		3		0+1	
Linton	25+ 5		2		2+1		2	
McMenamin	25+ 3		2		2		3	
Neal	2+ 2				0+1			
Payne	35+ 2	2	4		3		3	
Quinn	40+ 2	20	4	1	3	3	3+1	1
Rennie	18						4	
Roberts	2+ 1							
Rowe	3+ 3				0+1		0+2	
Shields	0+ 1							
Tyler	46		4		3		4	
Vickers	1							

PLYMOUTH ARGYLE (DIV 2: 22nd)

	P/FL App	P/FL Goals	FLC App	FLC Goals	FAC App	FAC Goals	Others App	Others Goals
Anthony	5		2					
Ashton			0+1					
Barlow	41+ 1	4			2		1	
Billy	41	1	1		2		1	
Beswetherick	0+ 2							
Clayton	0+ 1							
Collins	30+ 2	2	1				1	
Conlon	13	2						
Corazzin	38	17	1		2		1	
Currie	5+ 2							
Heathcote	36	4	2					
Hodges	9						1	
Illman	1+ 5		0+1		0+1			
Jean	16+20	4	1		2	1	0+1	
Littlejohn	27+ 4	6	2		2			
Logan	23+ 4	4	2	1	1		1	
Mauge	23+ 8	1	1		2	1		
O'Hagan	5+ 4				1		1	1
Phillips	3+ 7							
Rowbotham	23+ 2		2		0+1		1	

David Smith (Oxford United)

PLYMOUTH ARGYLE cont.

	P/FL App	Goals	FLC App	Goals	FAC App	Goals	Others App	Goals
Saunders	34+ 3	7			2		1	
Sheffield	46		2		2		1	
Starbuck	6+ 1				2			
Williams	39		2		2		1	
Wilson	7+ 4	1	1+1	1	1+1			
Woods	4+ 1							
Wotton	31+ 3	1	2		2		0+1	

PORTSMOUTH (DIV 1: 20th)

	P/FL App	Goals	FLC App	Goals	FAC App	Goals	Others App	Goals
Allen	4+10							
Aloisi	33+ 5	12	2		1			
Awford	36+ 3		1		2			
Carter	6+ 4				0+1			
Claridge	10	2						
Cook Aaron	1							
Cook Andy	1							
Durnin	23+11	10	1		1+1			
Enes	1+ 4							
Flahaven	26		2					
Foster	13+ 3	2			2	2		
Hall	22+ 7	5	1		2			
Harries	0+ 1							
Hillier	30		2	2	1			
Igoe	21+10	3	1		0+1			
Knight	20				2			
McLoughlin	34+ 3	4	2		2			
Perrett	15+ 1	1	1					
Pethick	43+ 1	2	1+1		2			
Robinson	15							
Russell	8		0+1	1	1			
Simpson F	17+ 2		1		1			
Simpson R	0+ 2							
Svensson	17+ 9	4	1	1	1+1			
Thomson	34+ 1	2	2		2			
Thorp	0+ 7		1+1	1				
Turner	12+ 4	1	0+1		1			
Vlachos	15							
Waterman	11+ 4		1		1			
Whitbread	38	1	2		1			

PORT VALE (DIV 1: 19th)

	P/FL App	Goals	FLC App	Goals	FAC App	Goals	Others App	Goals
Ainsworth	38+ 2	5			2			
Aspin	26		2		2			
Barnett	8+ 1	1						
Beesley	5							
Bogie	32+ 6	1	1		2			
Burns	0+ 1							
Carragher	26							
Corden	19+14	1	2		2	1		
Eyre	0+ 1							
Foyle	19+20	8	0+2		0+2			
Glover	21+ 4	1	1					
Griffiths	3							
Hill	25+ 2		2		2			
Jansson	22+11	5	1+1					
Koordes	9+ 1							
McCarthy	4		2					
Mahorn	0+ 1							
Mills	39+ 3	14	2	2	0+1			
Musselwhite	41		2		2			
Naylor	28+10	10	2		2			
Porter	28+13	1	0+1		2			
Snijders	22+ 2	2			2			
Stokes	5+ 3		1					
Talbot	42	6	2		2			
Tankard	39		2		2			
Van Heusden	5							

PRESTON NORTH END (DIV 2: 15th)

	P/FL App	Goals	FLC App	Goals	FAC App	Goals	Others App	Goals
Appleton	31+ 7	2	2+1		4	1	2	1
Ashcroft	37	14	4		3	2	2	
Atkinson	1+ 2							
Barrick	29+ 4	1	3+1	1	3		3	
Cartwright	24+12	2	3+1		0+1		3	1
Darby	6+ 6		1+1		2+1		0+1	
Davey	17+ 1	2					2	
Eyres	26+ 2	4			4	2	3	2
Gregan	33+ 2	2	3		4	1	3	
Holt	4+10		0+1		0+2		0+1	
Jackson	39+ 1	2	4		4		4	
Kidd	32+ 1	2	4		4		3	
Lormor	9+ 3	3			3		3	
Lucas	6				1		3	
Macken	20+ 9	6	2+2	2	2+1		0+3	
McKenna	4+ 1							
Moilanen	40		4		3		1	
Moyes	8+ 1				0+1	1		
Mullin	4+ 3						1	
Murdock	27		2		1+1		2	
Nogan	14+ 8	5	1+1		0+1		3	1
Parkinson	44+ 1	5	4		4	1	4	
Rankine	34+ 1	1	4		2		2	
Reeves	12+ 1	1	3+1	3				
Sissoko	4+ 3							
Sparrow	1							

QUEENS PARK RANGERS (DIV 1: 21st)

	P/FL App	Goals	FLC App	Goals	FAC App	Goals	Others App	Goals
Baraclough	8							
Bardsley	12							
Barker	20+ 3	3	2					
Brazier	8+ 3		0+1					
Brevett	20+ 3		2		2			
Bruce	1+ 4	1			0+1			
Dowie	9+ 2	1						
Gallen	19+ 8	3	1+1		0+2	1		
Graham			0+1					
Harper	36		2		1			
Heinola	0+10							
Jones	7	1						
Kennedy	8	2						
Kulcsar	11+ 1							
Maddix	23+ 2	1	1		1			
Mahoney-Johnson	0+ 1							
Morrow	31	1	2		1			
Murray	31+ 1	1	2	1	2			
Peacock	38+ 1	9	2	1	2			
Perry	6+ 2		2					
Quashie	30+ 3	3			2			
Ready	38+ 1	3			2			
Roberts	10				1			
Rose	13+ 3		2					
Rowland	7							
Ruddock	7							
Scully	7							
Sheron	36+ 4	11			2			
Sinclair	24+ 2	3	2		2			
Slade	3+19		1+1		0+2			
Spencer	22+ 1	5	1		2	1		
Yates	21+ 9				2			

READING (DIV 1: 24th)

	P/FL App	Goals	FLC App	Goals	FAC App	Goals	Others App	Goals
Asaba	31+ 1	8	7	3	3	1		
Bernal	34		6		5			
Bibbo	2				1			
Bodin	3+ 1		1		1			
Booty	24+ 1		4+1		5	1		
Bowen	11+ 3	1	0+1		5			

READING cont.

	P/FL App	Goals	FLC App	Goals	FAC App	Goals	Others App	Goals
Brayson	2+ 4	1						
Caskey	19+ 4		1+1		0+1			
Colgan	5							
Crawford	5+ 1							
Davies	17+ 1		1		3			
Fleck	3+ 2							
Glasgow	1+ 1							
Gray	7							
Hammond	18		2		4			
Hodges	20+ 4	6	5+1		4+1			
Holsgrove	1+ 1		0+1					
Houghton	20+ 5	1	5+1		2+2			
Howie	7							
Kelly	3							
Lambert	33+ 1	3	6	1	3			
Legg	10							
Lovell	8+ 7	1			2+1			
McIntyre	6							
McPherson	24		6	1				
Mautone	14		5					
Meaker	16+ 5	1	3	1	0+2			
Morley	17+ 6	5	2	1	5	3		
O'Neill	9	1						
Parkinson	36+ 1		5	1	5			
Primus	36	1	6		1			
Roach	0+ 8		1+4	1				
Robins	5							
Sandford	5							
Swales	26+ 5	1	6		5			
Thorp	0+ 3				0+1			
Wdowczyk	3+ 3		1+1					
Williams	25+ 4	6	4+2	2	1+1			

ROCHDALE (DIV 3: 18th)

	P/FL App	Goals	FLC App	Goals	FAC App	Goals	Others App	Goals
Atkinson	5+ 1							
Bailey	24+ 9		2				2	
Barlow	35+ 3		1		1			
Bayliss	23+ 6	2	1				2	
Bryson	12+ 3	1			1		2	
Bywater							1	
Carden	3+ 4							
Carter	7+ 4	2	1+1					
Edwards	27				1		1	
Farrell	40	4	2		1		2	
Fensome	42		2		1		2	
Gouck	36+ 2	5	2		1		1+1	
Hill	36+ 1	2	2		1			
Jones	17	2						
Key	19		2					
Lancashire	20+ 7	9					1	
Leonard	33	2	2		1		1	
Painter	45	17	2	1	1		2	
Pender	14		0+1				2	
Reed	10						2	1
Robson	0+ 7							
Russell	26+ 5	4	1	1	1		0+1	
Scott	1+ 2							
Smith	1+ 2		0+1					
Stuart	30+15	6	2		1		1+1	1

ROTHERHAM UNITED (DIV 3: 9th)

	P/FL App	Goals	FLC App	Goals	FAC App	Goals	Others App	Goals
Bass	13+ 5		1		0+1			
Berry	40+ 2	3	2		3	2		
Bos	6+10	4	1+1					
Clark	28		2		3			
Darby	3							
Dillon	14+ 2							
Druce	5+ 9		2		1	1	0+1	
Garner	37+ 3	3	1		4	3		

ROTHERHAM UNITED cont.

	P/FL App	P/FL Goals	FLC App	FLC Goals	FAC App	FAC Goals	Others App	Others Goals
Glover	36+ 1	17	1		4	1		
Goodwin	8+ 5	2	1+1		0+2		1	
Hayward	6+ 7	3			1+1		0+1	
Hudson	6+ 4				0+2	1	0+1	
Hurst	19+11		2		4			
Knill	38	3	2		3	1	1	
Martindale	7+ 1	2						
Mimms	43				4			
Monington	15	1					1	
Pettinger	3		2					
Poric	4							
Richardson	37+ 1	3	2	1	4	1	1	
Roscoe	43+ 2	7	2		4	2	1	
Scott	6+ 1				1		1	
Sedgwick	0+ 4		0+1					
Shuttleworth					0+1		1	
Taylor	10	3					1	
Thompson	32+ 7	3	1		3		1	
Warner	21				3			
White	26+ 1	12	2	1			1	

SCARBOROUGH (DIV 3: 6th)

	P/FL App	P/FL Goals	FLC App	FLC Goals	FAC App	FAC Goals	Others App	Others Goals
Atkin	26+ 8	1	1+1		1		2+1	
Bennett G	40+ 2	9	2	1	1		2	
Bennett T	24+10	2	1+1				2+1	
Brodie	43+ 1	10	2		1		2+1	
Brown	4	1						
Buxton	3				0+1			
Campbell	20+14	7			0+1		3	1
Conway	13	2						
Dobbin	1							
Elliott	15						2	
Heckingbottom	28+ 1						1	
Jackson	2							
Kay	40		2				3	
McElhatton	38+ 4	6	2		1		3	
Martin	17		2		1			
Mitchell	8+27	3	0+2		1		0+2	
Rhodes	11						1	
Robinson	28+ 8	4	1+1		1		1+2	
Rockett	32	2	1		1		3	2
Russell	0+ 2							
Snodin	33+ 2	1	1		1		1	
Sutherland	18+ 4	2	2		1		1+1	
Tate	3+21	1			0+1		1+1	
Van der Velden	5+ 3	1	2					
Williams	40+ 3	15	2		1		3	
Worrall	14+ 7	2	1+1				2	

SCUNTHORPE UNITED (DIV 3: 8th)

	P/FL App	P/FL Goals	FLC App	FLC Goals	FAC App	FAC Goals	Others App	Others Goals
Calvo-Garcia	39+ 5	6	4	3	4	1	2	1
Clarke	41		3		4		3	
D'Auria	37+ 4	10	4		4		3	
Evans	5		1					
Eyre	33+ 9	10	3		4		2+1	2
Featherstone	0+ 1							
Forrester	43+ 2	11	4	1	4	2	3	
Graves	0+ 3							
Harsley	11+ 4	1						
Hope	46	5	4		4		3	
Housham	17+ 7	1	3		2+1		1	1
Laws	9+ 5		1+1		0+2			
McAuley	30+ 5	1	3		2		1	
Marshall	12+ 9	1	0+1		1		1	
Murphy	1+ 2						1	
Neil	6+ 1		1					
Nottingham	1							
Ormondroyd	7+13				0+3		0+3	
Pemberton	3+ 3							

SCUNTHORPE UNITED cont.

	P/FL App	P/FL Goals	FLC App	FLC Goals	FAC App	FAC Goals	Others App	Others Goals
Phillips	2+ 1						1	
Regis	9	2						
Sertori	40+ 1	1	4		4		3	
Shakespeare	3+ 1		1+2		0+1		1	
Sheldon	0+ 1							
Stamp	4+ 6	1	0+1					
Stanton	0+ 1							
Walker	38+ 2	1	4		3		2	
Walsh	37+ 2	1	2		4		3	
Wilcox	30+ 1	2	2+1		4	2	3	
Woods	2							

SHEFFIELD UNITED (DIV 1: 6th)

	P/FL App	P/FL Goals	FLC App	FLC Goals	FAC App	FAC Goals	Others App	Others Goals
Barrett	5							
Beard	0+ 2		0+1		1+2			
Borbokis	36	2	5	2	6		1	1
Cullen	0+ 2							
Deane	24	11	4	2	1			
Dellas	5+ 4				0+2		0+1	
Derry	8+ 4							
Devlin	4+ 6	1					2	
Fjortoft	15+ 2	9	2+1	1	1+1	2		
Ford	20+ 3	1	8				2	
Hamilton	8	1					2	
Henry	1							
Holdsworth	40	2	5		8	1	2	
Hutchison	14+ 4		0+1		4	1		
Katchouro	6+10		3+1		1+6			
Kelly	19		1		4			
Lee	5							
McGrath	12		2					
Marcelo	12+ 9	6			5+1	1	1+1	1
Marker	43	2	4		8		2	
Morris	0+ 5				0+2		0+1	
Nilsen	18+ 4		1+1		5			
O'Connor	0+ 2							
Patterson	17+ 1	1	5					
Quinn	28	2	5		4+1		2	
Rush	4							
Sandford	15				6	1	2	
Saunders	23+ 1	10			6	2	2	
Scott	1+ 5		2	1				
Short	5		0+1		4			
Stuart	27+ 1	5			6		0+1	
Taylor	13+15	10	1+2		5+2		1	
Tiler	17	1	5					
Tracey	27		4		4		2	
Vonk	3							
Walker	0+ 1							
Ward	3+ 3	1						
White	0+ 1		1					
Whitehouse	17	3	5	3				
Wilder	7+ 1						1	
Woodhouse	4+ 5				1			

SHEFFIELD WEDNESDAY (PREM: 16th)

	P/FL App	P/FL Goals	FLC App	FLC Goals	FAC App	FAC Goals	Others App	Others Goals
Agogo	0+ 1							
Alexandersson	5+ 1				2	1		
Atherton	27	3	1		3			
Barrett	10							
Blondeau	5+ 1							
Booth	21+ 2	7			2			
Briscoe	3+ 4		1+1					
Carbone	28+ 5	9	1		2			
Clarke	2+ 1							
Clough	1		1					
Collins	8+11	5	2					
Di Canio	34+ 1	12	2	2	3			
Donaldson	1+ 4							

SHEFFIELD WEDNESDAY cont.

	P/FL App	P/FL Goals	FLC App	FLC Goals	FAC App	FAC Goals	Others App	Others Goals
Hinchcliffe	15	1						
Hirst	3+ 3							
Humphreys	2+ 5		0+1		0+3			
Hyde	14+ 8	1			1			
Magilton	13+ 8	1	2		1			
Mayrleb	0+ 3							
Newsome	25	2	1		3			
Nicol	4+ 3							
Nolan	27		2		3			
Oakes	0+ 4				0+2			
Pembridge	31+ 3	4	2		3			
Poric	0+ 4		0+1					
Pressman	36		2		3			
Quinn	0+ 1							
Rudi	19+ 3				3			
Sanetti	1+ 1	1						
Sedloski	3+ 1							
Stefanovic	19+ 1	2	1					
Thome	6							
Walker	38		2		3			
Whittingham	17+11	4	2		1			

SHREWSBURY TOWN (DIV 3: 13th)

	P/FL App	P/FL Goals	FLC App	FLC Goals	FAC App	FAC Goals	Others App	Others Goals
Berkley	28+ 8	3	0+1				1	
Blamey	9	1	1					
Brown	24+ 6	2	1+1				1	
Craven	1							
Currie	10+ 6	4	1	1	1			
Dempsey	8+ 4	1	1					
Dudley	3+ 1							
Edwards	34		2		0+1		1	
Evans	37+ 2	6	2		2		1	
Gall	11				2			
Gayle	23							
Germaine	1							
Griffiths	6							
Hanmer	39	1	1		2		1	
Herbert	23+ 1		2		2	1	1	
Jagielka	4+12	1	1+1					
Kerrigan	11+ 3	2						
Naylor	2		1					
Nwadike	1		0+1					
Overson	2							
Pountney	0+ 1							
Preece	25+ 2	1			2			
Scott	28+ 6	10	1		2		1	
Seabury	35+ 4	2	1+1		2			
Steele	37+ 1	13	2	3	1		1	
Taylor L	1				2			
Taylor M	17+ 1		2				1	
Tretton	14	1						
Walton	6	1	1					
Ward	3+ 3				0+1			
White	30+ 2	10			2		1	
Wilding	33+ 1	1			2		1	1
Williams	0+ 5							

SOUTHAMPTON (PREM: 12th)

	P/FL App	P/FL Goals	FLC App	FLC Goals	FAC App	FAC Goals	Others App	Others Goals
Basham	0+ 9							
Benali	32+ 1	1	2+1		1			
Beresford	10							
Bowen	1+ 2							
Charlton	2+ 1		1+1					
Davies	20+ 5	9	3+1	3	1			
Dodd	36		3		1			
Dryden	11+ 2		1					
Evans	6+ 4		2+1	1				
Gibbens	2							
Hirst	28	9	1		1			

	P/FL App Goals	FLC App Goals	FAC App Goals	Others App Goals
SOUTHAMPTON cont.				
Hughes	6 + 8		1	
Johansen	3 + 3	1 + 1		
Jones	38	4	1	
Le Tissier	25 + 1 11	3 3	1	
Lundekvam	31	4		
Maddison	5 + 1 1			
Magilton	5			
Monkou	30 + 2 1	3 1	1	
Neilson	3 + 5	2		
Oakley	32 + 1 1	4	1	
Ostenstad	21 + 8 11	1	0 + 1	
Palmer	26 3	3	1	
Richardson	25 + 3	4	1	
Robinson	0 + 1			
Slater	3 + 8	0 + 1		
Spedding	4 + 3	0 + 1		
Todd	9 + 1	1		
Van Gobbel	1 + 1			
Warner	0 + 1			
Williams	3 +17	1 + 2	0 + 1	
SOUTHEND UNITED (DIV 2: 24th)				
Aldridge	7 + 4 1			
Allen	5	1		
Beard	6 + 2			1
Beeston	5 + 1	3		
Boere	28 + 3 14	3	1 + 1	1
Byrne	9 + 1	3 1		
Clarke	42 + 3 5	4	2	1
Coleman	14			
Coulbault	30 + 4 4		2	1
Dublin	41 4	3	2	
Fitzpatrick	1 + 2			
Gridelet	31 + 6 2	2	2 1	
Hails	41 + 3	2 + 1	2	
Harris	26 + 1	3	2	
Henriksen			0 + 1	
Jobson	8 1			
Jones	34 + 5	4	2 1	0 + 1
Lewis	14 1	1 + 1	1 + 1	1
Maher	18 1			
Marsh	9 1	4 1		
N'Diaye	15 + 2 2		1	1
Nielsen	1 + 4			1
Nzamba	0 + 1			
Parris	1			
Perkins	3 + 2			1
Rammell	18 + 8 2	1 + 3	1 + 1	1
Roget	11	3		
Royce	37	4	2	1
Southall	9			
Stimson	17 + 3			1
Thomson	16 +17 6	2	2	0 + 1
Whyte	3 + 5 1			
Williams	6 1	1 + 1 2		
STOCKPORT COUNTY (DIV 1: 8th)				
Angell	45 18	4 3	2 2	
Armstrong	29 12	3 2	2 1	
Aunger	0 + 1			
Bennett	27 1	4	2	
Byrne	21 + 5 7		1 + 1	
Cavaco	0 + 2			
Connelly	45 2	4	2	
Cook	25 3		1	
Cooper	30 + 8 8	3 + 1 1	2	
Dinning	24 + 6 4	3 + 1 1	1 + 1	
Durkan	5 + 2 1	1 + 1		
Flynn	34 1	2 1	1	

	P/FL App Goals	FLC App Goals	FAC App Goals	Others App Goals
STOCKPORT COUNTY cont.				
Gannon	31 + 5 1	4	2	
Grant	9 + 7 3			
Gray	3	2		
Kalogeracos	0 + 2	1		
McGoldrick	2			
McIntosh	38 2	2	2	
Marsden	10	4		
Mutch	2 +18 2	1 + 2 2		
Nash	0 + 8			
Nixon	43	2	2	
Phillips	7 + 6			
Richardson	4 + 2			
Searle	27 + 4		2	
Travis	3 +10 2	0 + 1	0 + 1	
Wallwork	7			
Wilbraham	6 + 1 1			
Woodthorpe	29 + 3 1	4	1	
STOKE CITY (DIV 1: 23rd)				
Andrade	4 + 8 1	2		
Crowe	10 + 6 4	1 + 1		
Donaldson	2			
Forsyth	37 7	4 1	1	
Gabbiadini	2 + 6		1 1	
Griffin	23 1	4	1	
Heath	4 + 2			
Holsgrove	11 + 1 1			
Kavanagh	44 5	4 + 1 5		
Keen	37 + 3 1	5 1	1	
Lightbourne	9 + 4 2			
Macari	0 + 3			
MacKenzie	7 + 5	1 + 1		
McKinlay	3			
McMahon	7 +10	2 + 2		
McNally	3 + 1			
Muggleton	34	5	1	
Nyamah	9 + 1	1 + 1		
Pickering	42 1	5	1	
Schreuder		0 + 2		
Scully	7			
Sigurdsson	43 1	5	1	
Sobiech	3			
Southall	12			
Stewart	22 3	2	1	
Sturridge	0 + 1	0 + 1		
Taaffe	0 + 3			
Thorne	33 + 3 12	4 4	0 + 1	
Tiatto	11 + 4 1			
Tweed	35 + 3	5	1	
Wallace	36 + 3 3	5	1	
Whittle	15 + 5	0 + 4	1	
Woods	0 + 1			
Xausa	1			
SUNDERLAND (DIV 1: 3rd)				
Agnew	3	1		
Aiston	1 + 2			
Ball	29 + 2 3	2 + 1		3 1
Bracewell	0 + 1	2		
Bridges	6 + 3 1	2 1		
Byrne	4 + 4	1 + 1		
Clark	46 13	1	2	3
Craddock	31 + 1	3	2	3
Dichio	2 +11		1 + 2	
Gray	44 2	3	2	2
Hall	1 + 1			
Holloway	32		2	3
Johnston	38 + 2 11	2	2	3
Lumsdon	1			

	P/FL App Goals	FLC App Goals	FAC App Goals	Others App Goals
SUNDERLAND cont.				
Makin	23 + 2 1	3	1	1 + 1
Melville	10 1			
Mullin	1 + 5			
Ord	13 + 1			0 + 1
Perez	46	1	2	3
Phillips	42 + 1 29		2 4	3 2
Quinn	33 + 2 14		2 1	2 2
Rae	24 + 5 3	1 + 1 1	2	0 + 2
Russell	0 + 3	2 + 1		
Scott	8 3			
Smith	11 + 5 2	1 + 1 1	1	
Summerbee	22 + 3 3		2	3 1
Williams	35 + 1 2	3 1	1	3
Zoetebier	2			
SWANSEA CITY (DIV 3: 20th)				
Agnew	7			
Alsop	12 3			
Ampadu	16 + 2	2	0 + 1	
Appleby	33 + 2 3	1 + 1	1 1	
Barwood	1 + 2 1			
Bird	35 + 6 14	2	1	1
Bound	28			1 1
Brown	0 + 2			
Casey	2 + 4			1
Chapple	3 + 1			
Clode	7 + 1		1	1
Coates	42 + 2 7	2 1	1	0 + 1
Cusack	32		1	1
Edwards	32	2	1	
Freestone	43	2	1	
Harris	0 + 6	0 + 1		
Hartfield	22 2			1
Hills	7			
Howard	2 + 1			
Jenkins	14 + 7			1
Jones G	3 + 5	0 + 1		
Jones J	1			
Jones L	2			
Lacey	16 + 6 1	1		1
Mainwaring	2 + 1		0 + 1	
Molby	1			
Moreira	5	2		
Munroe	0 + 1			
Newhouse	3 + 5		1	
O'Gorman	11 +23 5	2		1
O'Leary	25 + 4		1	1
Phillips	0 + 6			
Price	31 + 3 3	2	1	
Puttnam	4	2		
Trevitt	1			
Walker	39 3	2	1	
Watkin	24 + 8 3		0 + 1	
SWINDON TOWN (DIV 1: 18th)				
Allison	16 3	2		
Borrows	40			
Bullock	26 + 5			
Casper	8 + 1 1			
Collins	22 + 4 1		1	
Cowe	8 + 9 2	0 + 1		
Cuervo	14 + 9	2		
Culverhouse	9 + 2		1	
Darras	12 + 2	2		
Davis	5 + 1			
Digby	38	1	1	
Drysdale	11 + 3	2	0 + 1	
Elliott	1 + 1			
Finney	17 + 6 4	1	0 + 1	

	P/FL App	P/FL Goals	FLC App	FLC Goals	FAC App	FAC Goals	Others App	Others Goals
SWINDON TOWN cont.								
Gooden	38+1	2	2		1			
Hay	30+6	14	1		1			
Howe	9+1							
Hulbert	0+1							
Kerslake	10							
Leitch	25+1	1	2	1				
McAreavey	0+1							
McDonald	30+3	1	2		1			
McMahon	0+1							
Meechan	0+1							
Mildenhall	4							
Ndah	14	2			1			
Onuora	6	1						
Pattimore	0+2							
Robinson	26+1	1	1		1			
Seagraves	5		2					
Smith	2+3							
Talia	2		1					
Taylor	28+4	2			1			
Thompson	10							
Walters	25+9	6	1+1		1	1		
Warner	2							
Watson	13+5				1			
TORQUAY UNITED (DIV 3: 5th)								
Barrow	0+2		0+1					
Bedeau	14+20	5	1+1		1+1		0+4	
Clayton	41	2	3		3	1	4	
Gibbs	40+1	7	4	1	3	1	3	1
Gittens	45	6	4		3		4	2
Gomm					0+1			
Gregg	19		4		1		1	
Gurney	44	9	4		3	1	3	
Hapgood	15+7	3	1+1		3		0+1	
Hill	31+6	7	4		3		1+1	
Jack	40	12	4	1	3		4	3
Leadbitter	21+5	1			0+2		4	
McCall	20+7	1	1+1				3	1
McFarlane	18+4	5	3	1			3	1
Mitchell	11+3	1	2				1	
Newell	0+1							
Oatway	2		1					
Partridge	4+1							
Roberts	13+1	6					1	
Robinson	46		4		3		3	
Thomas	5+16	1	0+1		2		1+3	
Tully	4+5				0+1		1	
Veysey	27				2		3	
Watson	46	1	4		3		4	
TOTTENHAM HOTSPUR (PREM: 14th)								
Allen	1+3							
Anderton	7+8							
Armstrong	13+6	5	2	1	0+1			
Baardsen	9				2+1			
Berti	17	3			2			
Brady	0+9				1+1			
Calderwood	21+5	4	1+1		1+1	1		
Campbell	34		3		3	1		
Carr	37+1		2		3			
Clemence	12+5		2		2	1		
Dominguez	8+10	2	2+1		1			
Edinburgh	13+3		2					
Fenn	0+4		1	1				
Ferdinand	19+2	5	1		2			
Fox	32	3	3	1	2			
Ginola	34	6	3	2	3	1		
Howells	14+6		1		0+1			
Iverson	8+5							

	P/FL App	P/FL Goals	FLC App	FLC Goals	FAC App	FAC Goals	Others App	Others Goals
TOTTENHAM HOTSPUR cont.								
Klinsmann	15	9			3			
Mabbutt	8+3		1					
Mahorn	2		0+1	1	0+1			
Nielsen	21+4	3	1					
Saib	3+6	1						
Scales	9+1		2					
Sinton	14+5		1		1			
Vega	22+3	3	2		3			
Walker	29		3		1			
Wilson	16				3			
TRANMERE ROVERS (DIV 1: 14th)								
Aldridge	7+7	5						
Branch	16+9	3	1+3		1			
Challinor	28+4	1	2		3			
Cook	9		4					
Coyne	16		5					
Frail	4+2							
Hill	13+1				2+1	1		
Irons	36+7	4	1+3		2			
Jones G	37+6	8	5	1	2+1	2		
Jones L	29+5	9	5	1				
Kelly	28+1	11	5	3	3			
Kubicki	12							
McGreal	42		5		3			
McIntyre	0+2							
Mahon	3+15	1	0+3		0+1			
Mellon	24+9	2			2+1			
Morgan	14+5		0+2		2			
Morrissey	27+10	2	5	1	1+1			
O'Brien	37+3	3	4+1	1	3			
Parkinson	8+10	1			2+1	1		
Simonsen	30				3			
Stevens	25	1	5					
Thompson	44	3	5		3			
Thorn	17		3		1			
WALSALL (DIV 2: 19th)								
Blake	16+7	1	1		0+2		1+2	1
Boli	41	12	6	2	4	4	6	6
Donowa	5+1		1					
Evans	43	1	6		4		6	
Eydelie	10+1						1	
Gadsby	0+1							
Hodge	35+4	8	5		3+1	2	5+1	
Keates	32+1	1	5+1		4		5	1
Keister	11+2		3		1			
Marsh	36		2		4		5	
Mountfield	26+1	1	6		2+1		1	
Peron	38	1	5		4		5	
Platt	12+8	1	1+1	1	0+1		1+3	
Porter	25+4	1	2+2		3	2	5	
Ricketts	6+18	1	0+1		1+1		3+1	1
Rogers	4		2					
Roper	18+3		0+2		1		4+1	
Ryder	11+2		1		1		3	
Skinner	10		3	1				
Tholot	13+1	4					1+1	1
Thomas	3+2		0+1				1	1
Viveash	42	3	6		4	1	4	
Walker	46		6		4		6	
Watson	23+4	7	5	4	4	3	3	1
Williams	0+1							
WATFORD (DIV 2: 1st)								
Andrews	0+2		0+2					
Bazeley	14+2	3	3					
Chamberlain	46		3		5			
Day			1				1	

	P/FL App	P/FL Goals	FLC App	FLC Goals	FAC App	FAC Goals	Others App	Others Goals
WATFORD cont.								
Easton	8+4		0+1		1		1	
Foley	2+6	1						
Gibbs	34+4	1	3		5			
Grieves							1	
Hazan	7+3							
Hyde	40	4	4	1	5			
Johnson	42	7	4		5			
Kennedy	34	11	4	1	5	1		
Lee	35+1	10	3		4		1	
Ljung							1	
Lowndes	1+3				1+1		1	
Melvang	4	1	1					
Millen	38		2		4			
Mooney	45	6	4		5			
Noel-Williams	27+11	7	3	1	4	3		
Page	41		4		4			
Palmer	32+9	2	2+1		3+1		1	
Pluck	1							
Robinson	14+8	2			1+1		1	
Rooney							1	
Rosenthal	24+1	8	3+1	1	2	2		
Slater	9+5		3					
Smith	0+1				0+1			
Talboys	0+2						1	
Thomas	8+8	3			1+3			
Ward							0+1	
WEST BROMWICH ALBION (DIV 1: 10th)								
Adamson	3							
Beesley	8							
Burgess	27	1	3					
Butler	31+3		2+1		1+1			
Carbon	16	1						
Carr	1+3							
Coldicott	7+15		1		0+1			
Crichton	2							
Dobson	6+5		0+2		2			
Evans	2+8	1			1+1			
Flynn	30+5	2	4		0+1			
Gilbert	0+4							
Hamilton	29+8	1	3+2		2			
Holmes	30		3		2			
Hughes	18+19	4	0+2		2			
Hunt	38	13	4	1	2			
Kilbane	42+1	4	5		2	1		
McDermott	13		2	1				
Mardon	18	1	2					
Miller	41		4		2			
Murphy	14+3	1	1		2			
Nicholson	16		2		2			
Nicol	9							
Peschisolido	6+2	3	3+1	3				
Potter	4+1							
Quailey	0+5							
Quinn	12+1	2						
Raven	8		4	1				
Smith	18+4		3					
Sneekes	37+5	3	5	1	2	2		
Spink			1					
Taylor	11+4	2	3	1				
Thomas	1+2							
Van Blerk	8							
WEST HAM UNITED (PREM: 8th)								
Abou	12+7	5	1+1	1	3+2			
Alves	0+4							
Berkovic	34+1	7	5		6	2		
Bishop	3		0+1	1				
Breacker	18+1		4		2+1			

WEST HAM UNITED cont.

Player	P/FL App	Goals	FLC App	Goals	FAC App	Goals	Others App	Goals
Dowie	7+5		2+1		0+1			
Ferdinand	35		5		6			
Forrest	13		3		4			
Hartson	32	15	5	6	5	3		
Hodges	0+2				0+3			
Hughes	2+3		1					
Impey	19		3		3			
Kitson	12+1	4	2		2	1		
Lama	12							
Lampard	27+4	5	5	4	6	1		
Lazaridis	27+1	2	1		6			
Lomas	33	2	4		5	1		
Mean	0+3							
Miklosko	13							
Moncur	17+3	1	1		2+1			
Moore	0+1							
Omoyinmi	1+4	2						
Pearce	30	1	3		6	1		
Potts	14+9		3+1		4+1			
Rieper	5	1						
Rowland	6+1		0+2					
Sinclair	14	7						
Terrier	0+1							
Unsworth	32	2	5		4			

WIGAN ATHLETIC (DIV 2: 11th)

Player	P/FL App	Goals	FLC App	Goals	FAC App	Goals	Others App	Goals
Barlow	9	3						
Bishop	7						1	
Black	0+1		0+1					
Bradshaw	27+1	1			1			
Branch	2+1							
Broughton	1+3							
Bruno	1							
Butler	17		1		1		1	
Carroll	29		1		2		2	
Diaz	1+1							
Fitzhenry	1+2						1	
Green	37+1	1	2		3		2	
Greenall	39	4	2		3		3	
Johnson	18+2	2	2		2			
Jones	28+5	9	1		3	1	3	4
Kilford	29+1	10	1+1		3		1+1	
Lancashire	0+1		0+1					
Lee	41+2	5	2	1	3	2	3	
Lowe	42+1	16	2		2+1	1	3	1
McGibbon	32+3		2		3		1	
Martinez	26+7	1	1		2	1	2+1	
Morgan	13	1			1		3	
Mustoe							0+1	
Newman	8							
O'Connell	17	5	2		1			
Rogers	32+6		2		1		2	
Saville	0+5		0+1					
Sharp	34+4		1+1		1+1		2	
Smeets	10+13	3	1				3	
Warne	3+22	2					0+2	
Whitworth	1+3							
Woods	1							

WIMBLEDON (PREM: 15th)

Player	P/FL App	Goals	FLC App	Goals	FAC App	Goals	Others App	Goals
Ardley	31+3	2			5	1		
Blackwell	35				4			
Castledine	3+3		3	2	1+2			
Clarke	1+13		2+1	1	0+4			
Cort	16+6	4	1+1	2	4+1			
Cunningham	32		3		3			
Earle	20+2	3	1		3			
Ekoku	11+5	4	1+1		0+1			
Euell	14+5	4	3	3	2	1		

WIMBLEDON cont.

Player	P/FL App	Goals	FLC App	Goals	FAC App	Goals	Others App	Goals
Fear	5+3	2	1		2			
Francis	0+2							
Gayle	21+9	2	2+1	1	3+1	1		
Heald			2					
Holdsworth	4+1		0+1					
Hughes C	13+4	1	2		2			
Hughes M	29	4			4	2		
Jones	22+2		1+1		3+1	1		
Jupp	3		1		2			
Kennedy	4							
Kimble	23+2		0+1		3			
Leaburn	15+1	4						
McAllister	4+3		3					
Perry	35		3		5			
Reeves			0+1					
Roberts	12	1						
Solbakken	4+2	1			1+1			
Sullivan	38		1		5			
Thatcher	23+3		3		3			

WOLVERHAMPTON WANDERERS (DIV 1: 9th)

Player	P/FL App	Goals	FLC App	Goals	FAC App	Goals	Others App	Goals
Atkins	30+4	2	5		4+1			
Bull	24+7	7	5	2	1+2			
Claridge	4+1				1			
Coleman	3+1							
Corica	0+1							
Crowe	0+2							
Curle	40	1	2		7	1		
Daley	0+2				0+1			
Diaz	2							
Emblen	6+1							
Ferguson	22+4		5	1	2	1		
Foley	1+4		0+2					
Freedman	25+4	10			5+1	2		
Froggatt	31+2	2	3		3			
Gilkes	3							
Goodman	29+1	8	2+1	1	6	1		
Keane	34+4	11	3+1		1+2			
Kubicki	12		4					
Muscat	22+2	3			5			
Naylor	14+2		1		4	1		
Osborn	23+1	2			3			
Paatelainen	10+13		4+1	1	4+1	4		
Richards	13				7	1		
Robinson	27+5	3	4		7	1		
San Juan	4		2+1	1				
Sedgley	18+1		2		6			
Segers	11				2			
Simpson	23+5	4			2+2			
Slater	4+2				0+1			
Smith	11		5					
Stowell	35		5		5			
Westwood	3+1	1	1+1					
Williams	20		2		2+2			
Wright J	0+4							
Wright S	3							

WREXHAM (DIV 2: 7th)

Player	P/FL App	Goals	FLC App	Goals	FAC App	Goals	Others App	Goals
Basham	4+1							
Brace	8		2					
Brammer	29+4	4	1				1	
Carey	43	1	2		3		1	
Cartwright	4							
Chalk	15+11	1	0+1		1+2			
Connolly	31+4	7	2	1	4	5	1	
Cross	2							
Hardy	34				4		1	
Humes	22+2				1			
Jones	12+2	1	2		1+1			

WREXHAM cont.

Player	P/FL App	Goals	FLC App	Goals	FAC App	Goals	Others App	Goals
Kelly	5+5	1						
McGregor	41+1	2	2		3		1	
Marriott	42		2		4		1	
Owen	36+4	7			4		1	
Phillips	14+6	1	2		2		0+2	
Ridler	18+2				4		1	
Roberts	29+5	8			3+1	1	0+1	
Russell	11+5		1		2			
Skinner	16+9	1	2				0+1	
Spink	33+3	6	2	1	1+1		1	
Wainwright	7+4	3			1		1	
Ward	35+2	6	2		4		1	
Watkin	0+3	1	0+1					
Williams	3							
Wilson	12+1	4						

WYCOMBE WANDERERS (DIV 2: 14th)

Player	P/FL App	Goals	FLC App	Goals	FAC App	Goals	Others App	Goals
Baird	0+2							
Beeton	15+5				1+1			
Bodin	5							
Brown	40	3	1+1		1		2	
Carroll	35+4	1	2		1		2	
Cornforth	18+6	5	2		2	2	0+1	
Cousins	25+4				2		1	
Forsyth	25		2				1	
Harkin	13+22	2	1+1	1	1		2	1
Kavanagh	43+2	1	2		1+1		2	
Kerslake	9+1						1	
McCarthy	28+3	1	2		1		1	
McGavin	35+2	2	1+1		2		2	
Mohan	33				2		1	
Parkin	1							
Patton	0+1							
Read	14+14	4	2	1	1+1			
Ryan	40	3	1	1	2		2	
Scott	28+1	11	1	1	2		0+1	
Simpson	10+11		2		0+2		1	
Stallard	43	17	1+1		2		2	1
Taylor	45		2		2		2	
Wraight	1						0+2	

YORK CITY (DIV 2: 16th)

Player	P/FL App	Goals	FLC App	Goals	FAC App	Goals	Others App	Goals
Alderson	0+1						0+1	
Atkinson	3+2				0+1		0+1	
Barras	38	6	4	1	2			
Bull	18+9	1	3+1	1	1+1			
Bushell	40	2	4	1	2		1	
Campbell	1		1					
Cresswell	18+8	4	0+1		1+1		1	
Davis	2							
Gabbiadini	5+2	1						
Greening	5+15	2	0+1				1	
Hall	31+1		4		1		1	
Himsworth	9+6				1+1			
Jones	23							
Jordan	6+10				0+1		1	
McMillan	30		4					
Murty	32+2	1	2	1	2		1	
Pouton	37+4	5	3+1		2	1	1	
Reed	21+1	2	2		2		1	
Rennison	1							
Rowe	38+3	11	3	1	2	3	1	1
Rush	1+2							
Samways	29		4		1			
Stephenson	34+1	5	3+1		2			
Thompson	12	2						
Tinkler	43+1	4	4		2		1	
Tolson	10+6	3	2+1					
Tutill	2		1					
Warrington	17							

PFA AWARDS 1998

Players' Player of the Year
DENNIS BERGKAMP

Young Player of the Year
MICHAEL OWEN

Special Merit Award
STEVE OGRIZOVIC

DIVISIONAL AWARDS

FA Carling Premiership

Nigel Martyn	Leeds United
Gary Neville	Manchester United
Graeme Le Saux	Chelsea
Gary Pallister	Manchester United
Colin Hendry	Blackburn Rovers
David Beckham	Manchester United
Ryan Giggs	Manchester United
Nicky Butt	Manchester United
David Batty	Newcastle United
Michael Owen	Liverpool
Dennis Bergkamp	Arsenal

Nationwide League Division 1

Alan Miller	West Bromich Albion
Kieron Dyer	Ipswich Town
Mauricio Taricco	Ipswich Town
Nigel Pearson	Middlesbrough
Colin Cooper	Nottingham Forest
Lee Clark	Sunderland
Georgiou Kinkladze	Manchester City
Robbie Keane	Wolverhampton Wanderers
John Robinson	Charlton Athletic
Pierre Van Hooijdonk	Nottingham Forest
Paul Merson	Middlesbrough

Nationwide League Division 2

Alec Chamberlain	Watford
Gary Parkinson	Preston North End
Peter Kennedy	Watford
Shaun Taylor	Bristol City
Chris Coleman	Fulham
Kevin Donovan	Grimsby Town
John Hodge	Walsall
Paul Bracewell	Fulham
Paul Groves	Grimsby Town
Roger Boli	Walsall
Shaun Goater	Bristol City

Nationwide League Division 3

Darren Ward	Notts County
Ian Hendon	Notts County
Dennis Pearce	Notts County
Gary Strodder	Notts County
Dean Walling	Lincoln City
David Farrell	Peterborough United
Scott Houghton	Peterborough United
Jon Cullen	Hartlepool United
Martin Ling	Leyton Orient
Jimmy Quinn	Peterborough United
Rodney Jack	Torquay United